MAIL ORDER
BUSINESS
DIRECTORY

34th Edition

BARRY T. KLEIN

Editor

TODD PUBLICATIONS
Boca Raton, Florida

MAIL ORDER BUSINESS DIRECTORY

34th Edition

Copyright © 2015

Todd Publications
1388 Sabal Palm Dr.
Boca Raton, FL 33432

(561) 910-0440
E-mail: toddpub@yahoo.com

ISBN 978-0-873400-343

Table of Contents

Preface

The *Mail Order Business Directory*, for 60 years, known to thousands as the primary source for mail order companies, lists and describes more than 5,500 mail order catalogs. The book is designed for consumers, businesses, professionals, librarians, researchers, and others interested in locating mail order companies and their catalogs. An invaluable aid for finding products for your home, business, or organization.

In this all-new 34th edition, we have continued research in locating new companies and updating information on companies listed in the previous edition. There are many new catalogs included in this edition and hundreds of changes to previously listed catalogs; and numerous catalogs have been deleted because they are no longer available.

Despite a recent slowing in the U.S. economy over the past few years, consumers, who account for two-thirds of all domestic spending, and businesses continue to buy, and most catalogers have prospered. In 2014, sales from print catalog purchases will surpass $300 billion and e-commerce, online catalogs will surpass $400 billion. Rather than being harmed by soaring cyber retail growth, sales in the print catalog industry have been growing steadily and it is estimated that by the end of this year sales will increase to more than $350 billion.

This volume provides complete information on catalogs distributed in the U.S. including address, toll-free telephone & fax numbers, e-mail and website addresses, contact name, frequency, circulation and sales range for each. Companies are arranged under more than 50 major product categories. The information contained herein has been thoroughly researched by questionnaire, phone and with the use of websites to make it as current and accurate as possible.

We would appreciate hearing from companies about any needed changes to their listings.

BARRY KLEIN, EDITOR

MAIL ORDER BUSINESS DIRECTORY

AMERICAN LIVESTOCK & PET SUPPLY   (800) 356-0700
613 Atlas Ave. • Madison, WI 53714
E-Mail: mary.bohne@walcointl.com
Website: www.americanlivestock.com
Fax Ordering: (800) 309-8947
Contact Name: Mary Bohne, Owner
Catalogs: Free. Frequency: Annual
Circulation: 100K. Sales: $1-3MM
Products: Horse Catalog & General Livestock Catalog;
horse, cattle & pet supplies; livestock products

ANIMAL MEDIC, INC.   (800) 767-5611
P.O. Box 575 • Manchester, PA 17345
E-Mail: sandyg@animalmedic.com
Website: www.animalmedic.com
Fax Ordering: (717) 266-2594
International Ordering: (717) 266-5611
Contact Name: Barry Noll, Executive V.P.
Catalog: Free. Pages: 64. Frequency: Semiannual
Circulation: 50K. Sales: $1-3MM
Products: Animal medic products; health & pet products,
farm & home supplies

COUNTRY MANUFACTURING   (800) 335-1880
P.O. Box 104 • Fredericktown, OH 43019
E-Mail: info@countrymfg.com
Website: www.countrymfg.com
Fax Ordering: (740) 694-5088
International Ordering: (740) 694-9926
Contact Name: Joe Chattin, President
Catalog: Free. Pages: 24. Frequency: Quarterly
Circulation: 50K. Sales: $1-3MM
Products: Horse stall systems, tractor & ATV accessories;
modular dog kennel systems

FARMTEK   (800) 327-6835
1440 Field of Dreams Way • Dyersville, IA 52040
E-Mail: sales@farmtek.com
Website: www.farmtek.com
Fax Ordering: (800) 457-8887
International Ordering: (563) 875-2288
Customer Service: (800) 245-9881
Contact Names: Barry Goldsher, President
Catalog: Free. Pages: 300. Frequency: Quarterly
Circulation: 10K. Sales: $20-50MM
Products: Agricultural supplies; greenhouses, poly buildings;
poultry, hog, dairy & livestock equipment; building supplies

HOEGGER GOAT SUPPLY   (800) 221-4628
160 Providence Rd. • Fayetteville, GA 30215
E-Mail: info@hoeggergoatsupply.com
Website: www.hoeggergoatsupply.com
Fax Ordering: (770) 461-7334
International Ordering: (770) 461-6926
Customer Service: (770) 461-5398
Contact Names: Anne Lauer, President
Catalog: Free. Frequency: Annual
Circulation: 100K. Sales: $3-5MM
Products: Dairy goat supplies

HORSE HEALTH USA   (800) 321-0235
2780 Richville Dr. SE • Massillon, OH 44646
E-Mail: info@pbhorsehealth.com
Website: www.horsehealthusa.com
Fax Ordering: (330) 830-2762
International Ordering: (330) 492-3000
Catalog: Free. Frequency: Quarterly
Circulation: 200K. Sales: $5-10MM
Products: Equine health products & livestock supplies

JEFFERS CATALOG   (800) 533-3377
P.O. Box 100 • Dothan, AL 36302
E-Mail: customerservice@jefferspet.com
Website: www.jefferspet.com
Fax Ordering: (334) 793-5179
International Ordering: (334) 793-6257
Contact Names: Dr. Keith Jeffers, President
Catalog: Free. Frequency: Quarterly
Circulation: 100K. Sales: $10-20MM
Products: Discount pet supplies

JRG SUPPLY ANIMAL HEALTH   (800) 354-7433
1357 3rd Ave. NW • Fort Dodge, IA 50501
E-Mail: info@jrgsupply.com
Website: www.jrgsupply.com
Fax Ordering: (515) 838-2442
International Ordering: (515) 838-2414
Contact Name: Roger Gustafson, Owners
Catalog: Free. Pages: 24. Frequency: Semiannual
Circulation: 25M. Sales: $500M
Products: Animal health supplies, pet food & supplies
& equipment; equine supplies, footwear, clothing

KV VET SUPPLY COMPANY   (800) 423-8211
3190 N Rd. • David City, NE 68632
E-Mail: kvvet@kvvet.com
Website: www.kvvet.com
Fax Ordering: (800) 269-0093
International Fax Ordering: (402) 367-6214
International Ordering: (402) 367-6047
Contact Name: Dr. Raymond Metzner, President
Catalogs: Free. Pages: 180. Frequency: Annual
Circulation: 100K. Sales: $10-20MM
Products: Wholesale prices on vet, pet, equine &
livestock equipment & supplies

KEN'S HATCHERY & FISH FARMS, INC.   (877) 536-3474
P.O. Box 449 • Alapaha, GA 31622
E-Mail: info@kens-fishfarm.com
Website: www.kens-fishfarm.com
Fax Ordering: (229) 532-7220
International Ordering: (229) 532-6135
Contact Name: Ken Holyoak, President
Catalog: Free. Frequency: Annual
Circulation: 10K. Sales: $1-3MM
Products: Fish farming supplies

MURRAY McMURRAY HATCHERY   (800) 456-3280
P.O. Box 458 • Webster City, IA 50595
E-Mail: info@mcmurrayhatchery.com
Website: www.mcmurrayhatchery.com
Fax Ordering: (515) 832-2213
International Ordering: (515) 832-3280
Contact Name: Mike Lubbers, President
Catalog: Free. Frequency: Annual
Circulation: 10K. Sales: $5-10MM
Products: Chickens & poultry supplies

MODERN FARM/CODY MERCANTILE   (800) 443-4934
205 N. Stephanie, Suite D
Henderson, NV 89074
E-Mail: customerservice@codymercantile.com
Website: www.codymercantile.com
Fax Ordering: (888) 486-9130
Contact Name: Paul Clymer, President
Catalog: Free. Frequency: Monthly
Circulation: 250K. Sales: $5-10MM
Products: Horse stalls, barn doors, feeders,
waterers, etc.

NASCO AGRICULTURAL SCIENCES   (800) 558-9595
P.O. Box 901 • Fort Atkinson, WI 53538
E-Mail: custserv@enasco.com
Website: www.enasco.com
Fax Ordering: (920) 563-8296
International Ordering: (920) 563-2446
Contact Names: Richard Ciurczak, President
Catalog: Free. Frequency: Annual
Circulation: 200K. Sales: $10-20MM
Products: Farm & ranch supplies & equipment

NATIONAL BRIDAL SHOP, INC.   (800) 251-3474
P.O. Box 2458 • Lewisburg, TN 37091
E-Mail: nbs@nationalbridal.com
Website: www.nationalbridal.com
Fax Ordering: (931) 359-8551
International Ordering: (931) 359-3210
Catalog: Free. Pages: 155. Frequency: Annual
Circulation: 50K. Sales: $3-5MM
Products: Horse & stable equipment & supplies

PET SUPPLIES DELIVERED CATALOG   (800) 367-4444
FIRST PLACE EQUINE CATALOG
CSR Co., Inc.
11143 Mockingham Dr. • Omaha, NE 68137
E-Mail: customerservice@omahavaccine.com
Website: www.omahavaccine.com
Fax Ordering: (800) 242-9447; (402) 731-9829
International Ordering: (402) 731-9600
Contact Name: Scott Remington, President
Catalog: Free. Frequency: Annual
Circulation: 1MM. Sales: $20-50MM
Products: Kennel & pet supplies for all animals

POULTRY & GAMEBREEDERS   (912) 236-0651
G.Q.F. Manufacturing Co.
P.O. Box 1552 • Savannah, GA 31402
E-Mail: info@gqfmfg.com
Website: www.gqfmfg.com
Fax Ordering: (912) 234-9978
Contact Name: Richard McGhee, President
Catalog: Free. Pages: 24. Frequency: Semiannual
Circulation: 100K. Sales: $10-20MM
Products: Incubators, feeders, waterers, medicines & supplies

STROMBERG'S CATALOG   (800) 720-1134
P.O. Box 400 • Pine River, MN 56474
E-Mail: sales@strombergschickens.com
Website: www.strombergschickens.com
Fax Ordering: (218) 587-4230
International Ordering: (218) 587-2222
Contact Name: Loy Stromberg, President
Catalog: Free. Frequency: Annual
Circulation: 75K. Sales: $3-5MM
Products: Chicken & poultry equipment

U.S. FARMER   (800) 845-2281
P.O. Box 73 • LaGrange, KY 40031
E-Mail: sales@usfarmer.com
Website: www.usfarmer.com
Fax Ordering: (502) 225-4451
International Ordering: (502) 225-4450
Catalog: Free. Frequency: Semiannual
Circulation: 50K. Sales: $5-10MM
Products: Farm equipment: tractors, attachments,
cars & trucks, harvesting, hay equipment, livestock &
handling, mowers & cutters, parts & accessories,
planting & seeding.

VALLEY VET SUPPLY CATALOG   (800) 419-9524
1118 Pony Express Hwy. • Marysville, KS 66508   (800) 835-2978
E-Mail: service@valleyvet.com
Website: www.valleyvet.com
Fax Ordering: (800) 446-5597
International Ordering: (785) 562-5106
Contact Name: Arnold Nagely, President
Catalog: Free. Frequency: 10x per year
Circulation: 50K. Sales: $3-5MM
Products: Veterinarian equipment & supplies

VET-VAX CATALOG   (800) 369-8297
P.O. Box 400 • Tonganoxie, KS 66086
E-Mail: orders@vetvax.com
Website: www.vetvax.com
Fax Ordering: (620) 325-3098
International Ordering: (913) 845-3760
Contact Name: Bud Moomau, President
Catalog: Free. Frequency: Semiannual
Circulation: 50K. Sales: $3-5MM
Products: Pet supplies for dogs, cats & horses;
vaccines, medications, supplements & grooming suplies
for pets & livestock; pet toys & training equipment

YOUR HORSE STALL COMPANY   (800) 648-3415
Woodstar Products, Inc.
1824 Hobbs Dr. • Delavan, WI 53115
E-Mail: info@wdstar.com
Website: www.wdstar.com
Fax Ordering: (262) 728-1813
International Ordering: (262) 728-8460
Contact Name: Gary Starck, President
Catalog: Free. Frequency: Annual
Circulation: 50K. Sales: $3-5MM
Products: Horse stalls, barn related accessories;
doors, feeders, waterers

AMERICAN HISTORICAL GUILD   (800) 544-1947
17 Firelight, Suite 10 • Dix Hills, NY 11746
E-Mail: ahguild@aol.com
Website: www.historicalautographs.com
Fax Ordering: (631) 499-8744
International Ordering: (631) 493-0303
Contact Name: Howard Zerwitz, President
Catalog: $2. Frequency: Bimonthly
Circulation: 50K. Sales: $500K
Products: Historic autographs, letters,
documents & vintage newspapers

AMERICAN JUDAICA CATALOG   (650) 343-9578
Historicana
1200 Edgehill Dr. • Burlingame, CA 94010
E-Mail: ungar@historicana.com
Website: www.historicana.com
Fax Ordering: (650) 579-6014
Contact Name: Irvin D. Ungar, President
Catalog: Free. Frequency: Annual
Circulation: 50K. Sales: $500K -1MM
Products: Rare books, manuscripts, autographs
& literary art. Established 1987.

ANTIQUE AUTOMOBILE LITERATURE   (315) 432-8282
6710 Brooklawn Pkwy. • Syracuse, NY 13211
E-Mail: info@autolit.com
Website: www.autolit.com
Fax Ordering: (315) 432-8256
Contact Name: Walter Miller, President
Catalog: Free. Frequency: Semiannual
Circulation: 50K. Sales: $500K
Products: Auto showroom items, repair manuals,
parts books & original automobile & truck sales
brochures

ANTIQUE COLLECTORS CLUB   (800) 252-5231
91 Market St. • Wappinger Falls, NY 12590
E-Mail: info@antiquecc.com
Website: www.antiquecc.com
Fax Ordering: (512) 869-2093
International Ordering: (512) 863-8318
Catalog: Free. Frequency: Annual
Circulation: 50K. Sales: $500K
Products: Books about architecture,
antiques & gardening

ANTIQUE QUILT SOURCE   (717) 492-9876
3064 Bricker Rd.. • Manheim, PA 17545
E-Mail: strongg@paonline.com
Website: www.antiquequiltsource.com
Fax Ordering: (717) 492-0285
Contact Name: Glenda Strong, President
Catalog: $8. Frequency: Bimonthly
Circulation:15K. Sales: $500K
Products: Antique American quilts from PA quilt
country, circa 1850-1940, including Amish &
Mennonite

ANTIQUES & COLLECTIBLES   (360) 694-2462
BOOKSHOP CATALOG
Twin Peaks Press
P.O. Box 129 • Vancouver, WA 98666
E-Mail: twinpeak@pacifier.com
Website: www.pacifier.com/~twinpeak
Fax Ordering: (360) 696-3210
Contact Names: Helen Hecker, President
Catalog: Free. Frequency: Bimonthly
Circulation: 100K. Sales: $500K
Products: Books & videos available from small to
mid-size publishers/producers on antiques & collectibles

ARCHIVAL QUALITY MATERIALS   (800) 628-1912
University Products
517 Main St. • Holyoke, MA 01040
E-Mail: info@universityproducts.com
Website: www.universityproducts.com
Fax Ordering: (800) 532-9281
Contact Name: John D. Magoon, President
Catalog: $2. Frequency: Annual
Circulation: 50K. Sales: $10-20MM
Products: Archival material for preservation,
conservation & restoration of collectibles

ARCHIVALWARE CATALOG   (800) 442-7576
Archival Co.
517 Main St. • Holyoke, MA 01040
E-Mail: custserv@archivalsuppliers.com
Website: www.archivalsuppliers.com
Fax Ordering: (800) 532-9281
International Ordering: (413) 532-3372
Contact Name: John Magoon, President
Catalog: Free. Frequency: Annual
Circulation: 250K. Sales: $3-5MM
Products: Materials for the preservation &
storage of photos & collectibles; devices for
serious collectors, hobbyists and scrapbookers

ART DISPLAY ESSENTIALS CATALOG   (800) 862-9869
P.O. Box U • Blairstown, NJ 07825
E-Mail: info@artdisplay.com
Website: www.artessentials.com
Fax Ordering: (908) 362-5246
International Ordering: (908) 496-4951
Contact Name: William Stender, President
Catalog: $2. Frequency: Monthly
Circulation: 100K. Sales: $3-5MM
Products: Display essentials, from plate stands
to holders for your collectibles

B&J COMPANY   (800) 722-3996
P.O. Box 67 • Georgetown, TX 78627
E-Mail: info@janhagara.com
Website: www.janhagara.com
Fax Ordering: (512) 869-2093
International Ordering: (512) 863-8318
Contact Name: Bill Hagara, President
Catalog: $5. Frequency: Annual
Circulation: 20K. Sales: $500K
Products: Jan Hagara collectible dolls, plates,
figurines, prints & miniatures

BARBIE COLLECTIBLES   (800) 491-7514
    (888) 201-7843
Spiegel
840 Fairway Pl. • Middleton, WI 53562
E-Mail: info@babyshoe.com
Website: www.babyshoe.com
Fax Ordering: (608) 836-0761
Contact Name: Jill Barad, CFO
Catalog: Free. Frequency: Quarterly
Circulation: 10MM. Sales: $100-500MM
Products: Barbie doll collectibles

BARKER ANIMATION ART GALLERIES   (800) 995-2357
1188 Highland Ave. • Cheshire, CT 06410
E-Mail: fun@barkeranimation.com
Website: www.barkeranimation.com
Fax Ordering: (203) 699-1188
International Ordering: (860) 232-8666
Catalog: Free. Frequency: Annual
Circulation:100K. Sales: $500K
Products: Art collectibles, including comic strip art,
movie & fine art posters, press books from major studios

BASEBALL DIRECT   (888) 244-8837
P.O. Box 7563 • Charlottesville, VA 22906   (800) 558-6273
E-Mail: baseball@cstone.net
Website: www.baseballdirect.com
Fax Ordering: (434) 974-4986
Catalog: $2. Frequency: Annual
Circulation: 10K. Sales: $1-3MM
Products: Baseball videos, CDs, DVDs, audiotapes,
calendars, books and other nostalgic collectibles

BEATLEFEST   (800) 232-8537
Mark Lapidos Productions
15 Charles St. • Westwood, NJ 07675
E-Mail: mark@beatlefest.com
Website: www.beatlefest.com
Fax Ordering: (201) 666-8687
International Ordering: (201) 666-5450
Contact Name: Mark Lapidos, President
Catalog: Free. Frequency: 3x per year
Circulation: 100K. Sales: $500K - $1MM
Products: Beatles videos, books, shirts,
posters & memorabilia

BETTY'S ATTIC   (800) 294-4068
Johnson Smith Catalog Company
P.O. Box 25600 • Bradenton, FL 34206
E-Mail: custservba@jsis.com
Website: www.bettysattic.com
Fax Ordering: (800) 551-4406
International Ordering: (941) 747-5566
Contact Name: Ralph Hoenie, President
Catalog: Free. Frequency: Monthly
Circulation: 100K. Sales: $500K - $1MM
Products: Collectibles and nostalgic items from the
1920s to the 1970s, including apparel & accessories,
books and calendars, toys and games, dollsm home
decor, videos and music

BIG-BANG CANNONS   (800) 987-2264
Conestoga Company
P.O. Box 405 • Bethlehem, PA 18016
E-Mail: sales@bigcannons.com
Website: www.bigbangcannons.com
Fax Ordering: (610) 433-8406
Contact Name: David J. Spinosa, President
Catalog: Free. Frequency: Semiannual
Circulation: 150K. Sales: $1-3MM
Products: Cannons made of cast iron &
sheet metal

BOEHM GALLERY PORCELAIN   (800) 257-9417
25 Princess Diana Dr. • Trenton, NJ 08638
E-Mail: info@boehmporcelain.com
Website: www.boehmporcelain.com
Fax Ordering: (609) 392-1437
International Ordering: (609) 392-2207
Contact Name: Helen Boehm, President
Catalog: Free. Frequency: Semiannual
Circulation: 25K. Sales: $10-20MM
Products: Porcelain, plates, sculpture &
paintings

BRADFORD EXCHANGE   (800) 323-5577
9333 N. Milwaukee Ave. • Niles, IL 60714
E-Mail: fun@collectiblestoday.com
Website: www.collectiblestoday.com
Fax Ordering: (847) 966-3121
International Ordering: (847) 966-2770
Contact Name: Richard Tinberg, President
Catalog: $4.50. Frequency: Annual
Circulation: 25K. Sales: $10-20MM
Products: Collectible plates

CAROUSEL SHOPPER   (800) 266-5767
Zon International Publishing
P.O. Box 6459 • Santa Fe, NM 87502
Fax Ordering: (505) 995-0103
Catalog: $2. Frequency: Annual
Circulation: 10K. Sales: $500K
Products: Antique carousel figures & books

CHEVROLET OFFICIAL   (858) 558-2500
LICENSED PRODUCTS
4365 Executive Dr. • San Diego, CA 92121
Contact Name: Katina Parker, Manager
Catalog: Free. Frequency: Semiannual
Circulation: 100K. Sales: $3-5MM
Products: Chevrolet brand merchandise,
collectibles, accessories, gifts

CINEMA CITY CATALOG   (231) 739-8303
P.O. Box 1012 • Muskegon, MI 49443
E-Mail: info@cinema-city.com
Website: www.cinema-city.com
Fax Ordering: (231) 733-7234
Contact Name: James Valk, President
Catalog: Online only. Sales: $500M
Products: Movie posters & memorabilia

COCA COLA COLLECTORS CATALOG   (800) 438-2653
P.O. Box 1734 • Atlanta, GA 30301
E-Mail: info@cocacola.com
Website: www.cocacola.com
Fax Ordering: (800) 332-2320
International Ordering: (404) 676-2121
Catalog: Free. Frequency: Monthly
Circulation: 1MM. Sales: $5-10MM
Products: Coca-cola collectible items; Coca-Cola
memorabilia, lifestyle products for the home and
licensed Coca-Cola brand apparel

COLLECTIBLE DOLL COMPANY   (800) 566-6646
4661 Sequim Dungeness Way
Sequim, WA 98381
E-Mail: jean@jeannordquistdolls.com
Website: www.jeannordquistdolls.com
Fax Ordering: (360) 683-4201
International Ordering: (360) 683-4202
Contact Name: Jean Nordquist, President
Catalog: Free. Frequency: Annual
Circulation: 100K. Sales: $500K - $1MM
Products: Dolls, molds & supplies

COLLECTING MAGAZINE   (800) 996-3977
Odyssey Publications
510 S. Corona Mall #A • Corona, CA 91719
E-Mail: odysgroup@aol.com
Website: www.autographcollector.com
Fax Ordering: (909) 371-7139
International Ordering: (909) 734-9636
Contact Name: Darrell Talbert, President
Catalog: $5. Frequency: Monthly
Circulation: 50K. Sales: $1-3MM
Products: Celebrity memorabilia

COLLECTOR BOOKS   (800) 626-5420
P.O. Box 3009 • Paducah, KY 42002
E-Mail: info@collectorbooks.com
Website: www.collectorbooks.com
Fax Ordering: (270) 898-8890
International Ordering: (270) 898-6211
Contact Name: Bill Schroeder, Jr., President
Catalog: Free. Frequency: Semiannual
Circulation: 100K. Sales: $1-3MM
Products: Books for every kind of collector

COLLECTOR'S ARMOURY (800) 494-2211
P.O. Box 59 • Alexandria, VA 22313
E-Mail: info@collectorsarmoury.com
Website: www.collectorsarmoury.com
Fax Ordering: (703) 683-5486
International Ordering: (703) 684-6111
Contact Name: Thomas Nelson, President
Catalog: $4. Frequency: Semiannual
Circulation: 50K. Sales: $3-5MM
Products: Historic collectibles

COLLECTOR'S PAPERWEIGHTS (800) 538-0766
L.H. Selman
123 Locust St. • Santa Cruz, CA 95060
E-Mail: info@paperweight.com
Website: www.paperweight.com
Fax Ordering: (831) 427-0111
International Ordering: (831) 427-1177
Contact Name: Larry Selman, President
Catalog: Free. Frequency: Monthly
Circulation: 50K. Sales: $1-3MM
Products: Antique & modern paperweights
for collectors

CREATIVE IRISH GIFTS (800) 453-6696
8157 Bavaria Rd. • Streetsboro, OH 44241 (800) 843-4538
E-Mail: gifts@shopirish.com
Website: www.shopirish.com
Fax Ordering: (877) 213-3660
International Ordering: (831) 427-1177
Contact Name: Diane O'Connor, President
Catalog: Free. Frequency: Quarterly
Circulation: 1MM. Sales: $10-20MM
Products: Irish gifts & collectibles

CUMBERLAND GENERAL STORE (800) 334-4640
1 Hwy. 68 • Crossville, TN 38555
E-Mail: generalstore@worldnet.ett.net
Website: www.cumberlandgeneral.com
Fax Ordering: (931) 456-1211
International Ordering: (931) 484-8481
Contact Name: Ann Ebert, President
Catalog: $4. Frequency: Annual
Circulation: 150K. Sales: $1-3M
Products: Antique, reproduction & turn
of the century artifacts

DESPERATE ENTERPRISES (800) 732-4859
P.O. Box 604 • Sharon Center, OH 44274
E-Mail: share@desperate.com
Website: www.desperate.com
Fax Ordering: (330) 239-0600
International Ordering: (330) 239-0500
Contact Name: Dan Hutchings, President
Catalog: Free. Frequency: Semiannual
Circulation: 100K. Sales: $5-10MM
Products: Licensed collectibles; poster advertising
reproductions, nostalgic tin signs, license plates &
metal detectors

DISNEY CATALOG (800) 328-0612
Disney Direct Marketing
11200 W. 93rd St. • Shawnee Mission, KS 66201
E-Mail: info@disneystore.com
Website: www.disneystore.com
Fax Ordering: (913) 752-1095
International Ordering: (913) 752-1000
Contact Name: Russ Gillam, President
Catalog: Free. Frequency: 20x per year
Circulation: 250K. Sales: $25-50MM
Products: Doll house building materials &
model building materials

DOLLHOUSES, SUPPLIES (800) 365-5468
& MINIATURES CATALOGUE
Dollhouse factory
P.O. Box 456 • Lebanon, NJ 08833
E-Mail: info@dollhousefactory.com
Website: www.dollhousefactory.com
Fax Ordering: (908) 236-7899
International Ordering: (908) 236-6404
Contact Name: Robert V. Dankanics, President
Catalog: $5. Frequency: 3x per year
Circulation: 10K. Sales: $500K
Products: Dollhouses & related miniatures

DOLLSVILLE DOLLS (800) 225-3655
& BEARSVILLE BEARS
292 N. Palm Canyon Dr.
Palm Springs, CA 92262
E-Mail: emailelf@dollsville.com
Website: www.dollsville.com
Fax Ordering: (760) 322-1691
International Ordering: (760) 325-2241
Contact Name: John McBride, President
Catalog: Free. Frequency: Quarterly
Circulation: 100K. Sales: $500K
Products: Dolls & teddy bears

ELECTION IDEAS CAMPAIGN GUIDE (800) 323-5656
Ideas Co. • P.O. Box 946 • Naperville, IL 60566
E-Mail: inquire@electionideas.com
Website: www.electionideas.com
Fax Ordering: (630) 357-7538
International Ordering: (630) 357-7522
Contact Name: Barbara Cherep, President
Catalog: Free. Frequency: Annual
Circulation: 100K. Sales: $1-3MM
Products: Custom imprinted campaign materials;
posters, bumper stickers, pins, matchbooks

EXIMIOUS OF LONDON (800) 221-9464
201 Northfield Rd. • Northfield, IL 60093
E-Mail: info@eximious.com
Website: www.eximious.com
Fax Ordering: (847) 446-6297
International Ordering: (847) 446-8171
Contact Name: Jeffrey H. Parnell, President
Catalog: Free. Frequency: 6x per year
Circulation: 250K. Sales: $5-10MM
Products: Imported luxury gifts & collectibles;
leather goods & home decor

EXOTO TIFOSI CATALOG (800) 872-2088
5440 Atlantis Ct. • Moorpark, CA 93021
E-Mail: exoto@aol.com
Website: www.exoto.com
Fax Ordering: (805) 530-3840
International Ordering: (805) 530-3830
Contact Name: Tony Keusseyan, President
Catalog: $15. Frequency: Bimonthly
Circulation: 25K. Sales: $5-10MM
Products: Automotive collectibles; racing
collectibles for Ford Motor Corporation

FANTAGRAPHICS BOOKS (800) 657-1100
7563 Lake City Way NE • Seattle, WA 98115
E-Mail: info@fantagraphics.com
Website: www.fantagraphics.com
Fax Ordering: (206) 524-2104
International Ordering: (206) 527-5314
Contact Name: Gary Groth, President
Catalog: Free. Frequency: Semiannual
Circulation: 100K. Sales: $500K
Products: Comic books, comic art & related merchandise

FLAGS BY CHRIS REID (800) 782-1510
Chris Reid Company
1080 Springfield Rd. • Union, NJ 07083
Fax Ordering: (908) 686-0305
International Ordering: (908) 687-2212
Contact Name: Alan R. Siegel, President
Catalog: Free. Frequency: 24x per year
Circulation: 10K. Sales: $500K - $1MM
Products: Flags, poles & accessories

FORD MOTOR COMPANY COLLECTION (800) 444-4503
P.O. Box 19787 • Birmingham, AL 35219
E-Mail: help@fordcollection.com
Website: www.fordcollection.com
Fax Ordering: (800) 283-1256
Contact Name: Donald O. Wheeler, President
Catalog: Free. Frequency: Annual
Circulation: 500K. Sales: $5-10MM
Products: Ford Motor Company collectible
items from clothing to gifts

LARRY FRITSCH CARDS (715) 344-8687
P.O. Box 863 • Stevens Point, WI 54481
E-Mail: larry@fritschcards.com
Website: www.fritschcards.com
Fax Ordering: (715) 344-1778
Contact Name: Larry Fritsch, President
Catalog: $3.95. Pages: 82.
Frequency: Semiannual
Circulation: 50K. Sales: $3-5MM
Products: Baseball memorabilia,
cards & supplies

GEARY'S CATALOG (800) 243-2797
Geary's of Beverly Hills
351 N. Beverly Dr.
Beverly Hills, CA 90210
E-Mail: sales@gearys.com
Website: www.gearys.com
Fax Ordering: (310) 858-7555
International Ordering: (310) 273-4741
Contact Name: Darrell S. Ross, President
Catalog: Free. Frequency: Bimonthly
Circulation: 2MM. Sales: $10-20MM
Products: Fine jewelry, tableware &
giftware for the home

GIFT WORLD (800) 544-8848
2324 Liberty St. • Hamilton, NJ 08629
E-Mail: wally@giftworldnj.com
Website: www.giftworldnj.com
Fax Ordering: (609) 586-0703
International Ordering: (609) 586-1200
Contact Name: Wally Kopec, President
Catalog: Free. Frequency: Bimonthly
Circulation: 3MM. Sales: $10-20MM
Products: Specialty gifts from Lenox,
Swarovski crystal, Hummels, David Winter,
et al

GIMBEL & SONS COUNTRY STORE (888) 633-1463
14/16 Commercial St.
Boothbay Harbor, ME 04538
Fax Ordering: (207) 633-5128
International Ordering: (207) 633-5088
Contact Name: Elisabeth Gimbel Mayre, President
Catalog: Free. Frequency: Quarterly
Circulation: 1MM. Sales: $3-5MM
Products: Figurines, collectibles & dolls

GREATFUL DEAD CATALOG (800) 225-3323
Greatful Dead Mercantile Company
P.O. Box 2139 • Novato, CA 94948
E-Mail: webmaster@dead.net
Website: www.dead.net
Fax Ordering: (415) 884-0585
International Ordering: (415) 884-5500
Contact Name: Elena Chieffo, Manager
Catalog: Free. Frequency: 3x per year
Circulation: 100M. Sales: $500M
Products: Official Greatful Dead merchandise,
music, gifts & clothing

HAAG METEORITES (520) 882-8804
P.O. Box 27527 • Tucson, AZ 85726
E-Mail: rhaag6@comcast.net
Website: www.meteoriteman.com
Fax Ordering: (520) 743-7225
Catalog: $5. Frequency: Annual
Circulation: 15K. Sales: $500K
Products: Meteorites & accessories

HAKE'S AMERICANA & COLLECTIBLES (717) 848-1333
P.O. Box 1444 • York, PA 17405
E-Mail: auction@hakes.com
Website: www.hakes.com
Fax Ordering: (717) 852-0344
Contact Name: Ted Hake, President
Catalog: $30. Pages: 240.
Frequency: Quarterly
Circulation: 25K. Sales: $1-3M

HERITAGE COLLECTORS' SOCIETY, INC. (215) 345-7955
P.O. Box 2131 • Doylestown, PA 18901
E-Mail: sales@heritageCS
Website: www.heritagecs.com
Catalog: Free. Frequency: Monthly
Circulation: 25K. Sales: $150K
Products: Historical documents &
autographs

MILITARY WAREHOUSE (888) 558-7761
P.O. Box 261 • Cambridge, MN 55008
E-Mail: john@militarywarehouse.net
Website: www.militarywarehouse.net
Fax Ordering: (763) 689-6897
International Ordering: (763) 689-1146
Contact Name: John W. Krueger, President
Catalog: Free. Pages: 14.
Frequency: Monthly
Circulation: 25K. Sales: $500K - $1MM
Products: Military collectibles & firearms

NAVY ARMS COMPANY (800) 669-NAVY
689 Bergen Blvd. • Ridgefield, NJ 07657
Fax Ordering: (201) 945-6859
International Ordering: (201) 945-8024
Contact Name: Val Forgett, President
Catalog: $2. Frequency: Annual
Circulation: 50K. Sales: $5-10MM
Products: Historical guns, replica fire arms
& swords

NORTHLAND POSTER COLLECTIVE (800) 627-3082
1613 E. Lake St. • Minneapolis, MN 55407
E-Mail: info@northlandposter.com
Website: www.northlandposter.com
Fax Ordering: (612) 297-2411
International Ordering: (612) 297-2920
Contact Name: Gary Ness, President

Catalog: Free. Frequency: Quarterly
Circulation: 100K. Sales: $500K
Products: Posters, t-shirts, bumper stickers, buttons & other goods celebrating history & grass roots culture

OLD TELEPHONES BY PHONECO (608) 582-4124
19813 E. Mill Rd. • Galesville, WI 54630
E-Mail: info@phonecoinc.com
Website: www.phonecoinc.com
Fax Ordering: (608) 582-4593
Contact Name: Mary Knappen, President
Catalog: $2. Frequency: Annual
Circulation: 50K. Sales: $1-3MM
Products: Telephones of all kinds & parts; repair catalog

PACIFIC TRADING CARDS (425) 774-8473
18424 Hwy. 99 • Lynwood, WA 98037
Fax Ordering: (425) 775-0774
Contact Name: Michael Cramer, President
Catalog: Free. Frequency: Quarterly
Circulation: 50K. Sales: $500K
Products: Baseball collections & trading cards

PANTHER PRIMITIVES (800) 487-2684
P.O. Box 32055 • Normantown, WV 25267
E-Mail: info@pantherprimitives.com
Website: www.pantherprimitives.com
Fax Ordering: (304) 462-7755
International Ordering: (304) 462-7718
Catalog: $2. Frequency: Annual
Circulation: 25K. Sales: $1-3MM
Products: Historical reproduction tents, teepees, cast iron & other historical camping gear

PARADISE GALLERIES (800) 673-6557
P.O. Box 57086 • Irvine, CA 92619
E-Mail: cs@paradisegalleries.com
Website: www.paradisegalleries.com
Fax Ordering: (949) 743-8974
International Ordering: (858) 793-4050
Catalog: Free. Frequency: Annual
Circulation: 25K. Sales: $500K - 1MM
Products: Collectible dolls

PENTREX RAILROAD CATALOG (800) 950-9333
Pentrex Media Group LLC
2652 E. Walnut St. • Pasadena, CA 91107
E-Mail: pentrex@pentrex.com
Website: www.pentrex.com
Fax Ordering: (626) 793-3797
International Ordering: (626) 793-3400
Contact Name: Michael Clayton, President
Catalog: Free. Frequency: Semiannual
Circulation: 50K. Sales: $500K
Products: Railroad videos & books

PINCH OF THE PAST (912) 232-5563
109 W. Broughton St.
Savannah, GA 31401
E-Mail: info@pinchofthepast.com
Website: www.pinchofthepast.com
Fax Ordering: (912) 232-5563
Contact Name: Noreene Parker, President
Catalog: Online; print, $5 (on demand)
Circulation: 1MM. Sales: $500K - $1MM
Products: Reproduction iron works, building hardware, door hardware, architectural antiques

BUD PLANT'S INCREDIBLE CATALOG (800) 242-6642
Bud Plant Comic Art
13393 Grass Valley Ave.
Grass Valley, CA 95945
E-Mail: cs@budplant.com
Website: www.budplant.com
Fax Ordering: (530) 273-0915
International Ordering: (530) 273-2166
Contact Name: Bud Plant, President
Catalog: $3. Frequency: Bimonthly
Circulation: 50K. Sales: $3-5MM
Products: Books, prints, graphic novels, related to comic books & comic strips, illustration, animation & art history

PRESTONS - SHIPS & SEA (800) 836-1165
Main St. Wharf • Greenport, NY 11944
Fax Ordering: (631) 477-8541
Contact Name: George Rowsom, President
Catalog: Free. Frequency: Annual
Circulation: 5MM. Sales: $10-20MM
Products: Decorative nautical items

PROFILES IN HISTORY (800) 942-8856
345 N. Maple Dr.
Beverly Hills, CA 90210
E-Mail: info@profilesinhistory.com
Website: www.profilesinhistory.com
Fax Ordering: (310) 859-3842
International Ordering: (310) 859-7701
Contact Name: Joseph Maddalena, President
Catalog: $30. Frequency: Quarterly
Circulation: 10K. Sales: $500K -$1MM
Products: Autographs, letters & collectible documents

PUPPETS ON THE PIER (800) 443-4463
39 Pier • San Francisco, CA 94133
E-Mail: info@puppetdreams.com
Website: www.puppetdreams.com
Fax Ordering: (415) 379-9544
Contact Name: Phillip Dicicco, President
Catalog: Free. Frequency: Annual
Circulation: 100K. Sales: $1-3MM
Products: Handmade puppets & marionettes

RADIO SPIRITS (800) 833-4248
P.O. Box 3107
Wallingford, CT 06492
E-Mail: info@radiospirits.com
Website: www.radiospirits.com
Fax Ordering: (203) 797-0819
International Ordering: (203) 265-8044
Contact Name: Michael Rophone, President
Catalog: Free. Pages: 32. Frequency: Monthly
Circulation: 100K. Sales: $1-3MM
Products: Timeless radio classics; oldtime radio shows on CD and TV shows on DVD & videocassette

RAVEN MAPS & IMAGES (800) 237-0798
P.O. Box 850 • Meford, OR 97501
E-Mail: sales@ravenmaps.com
Website: www.ravenmaps.com
Fax Ordering: (541) 773-6834
International Ordering: (541) 773-1436
Contact Name: Michael Beard, President
Catalog: Free. Frequency: Annual
Circulation: 200K. Sales: $500K - $1MM
Products: Shaded relief wall maps

RAWCLIFF & PARTHA PEWTER   (800) 243-6123
155 Public St. • Providence, RI 02903
Fax Ordering: (888) 729-2543
International Ordering: (401) 331-1645
Contact Name: Peter Brown, President
Catalog: Free. Frequency: Bimonthly
Circulation: 2MM. Sales: $10-20MM
Products: Fantasy items (figurines)

RESTORED CLASSIC COLLECTION   (800) 843-1320
Chicago Old Telephone
327 B Carthage St. • Sanford, NC 27330
E-Mail: marsh@interpath.com
Website: www.chicagooldtelephone.com
Fax Ordering: (919) 774-7666
International Ordering: (919) 774-6625
Contact Name: Richard R. Marsh, President
Catalog: Free. Frequency: Annual
Circulation: 25K. Sales: $500K
Products: Unique items for the home

RICK'S MOVIE GRAPHICS   (800) 252-0425
P.O. Box 23709 • Gainesville, FL 32602
E-Mail: sales@ricksmovie.com
Website: www.ricksmovie.com
Fax Ordering: (352) 373-2589
International Ordering: (352) 373-7202
Contact Name: Richard A. Stokes, President
Catalog: $3. Frequency: Quarterly
Circulation: 50K. Sales: $1-3MM
Products: Authentic movie advertising posters

RINALDI NAUTICAL ANTIQUES   (207) 967-3218
P.O. Box 765 • Kennebunkport, ME 04046
Fax Ordering: (207) 967-2918
Contact Name: John Rinaldi, President
Catalog: $5. Frequency: Annual
Circulation: 25K. Sales: $500K
Products: Nautical antiques, naval items, ship
models, instruments, carvings, marine paintings

ROCK N' ROLL MAGAZINES   (201) 641-4727
& COLLECTIBLES CATALOG
24 Orchard St. • Ridgefield Park, NJ 07660
E-Mail: henkellange@aol.com
Fax Ordering: (201) 641-7212
Contact Name: Dave Henkel, Owner
Catalog: Free. Frequency: Annual
Circulation: 10K. Sales: $250K
Products: Rockn'roll magazines &
collectibles

ROYAL MINIATURES   (800) 782-6464
14675 Titus St. • Panorama City, CA 91402
E-Mail: ryalmini@earthlink.net
Website: www.royalmini.com
Fax Ordering: (818) 781-6264
Customer Service: (818) 781-5994
Catalog: Free. Frequency: Semiannual
Circulation: 50K. Sales: $500K
Products: Dollhouse miniatures

ROSS - SIMONS   (800) 344-6011
P.O. Box 20990 • Cranston, RI 02920
E-Mail: info@ross-simons.com
Website: www.ross-simons.com
Fax Ordering: (800) 896-9191
Customer Service: (800) 521-7677
Contact Name: Karen Sharp Bishop, President
Catalog: Free. Frequency: Monthly
Circulation: 2MM. Sales: $20-50MM
Products: Fine jewelry & tableware collectibles

SADIGH GALLERY ANCIENT ART   (800) 426-2007
303 Fifth Ave. • New York, NY 10016
Fax Ordering: (212) 545-7612
International Ordering: (212) 725-7537
Contact Name: Michael Sadigh, President
Catalog: Free. Frequency: 7x per year
Circulation: 150K. Sales: $500K - $1MM
Products: Ancient artifacts, jewelry, coins
& collectibles

SAN FRANCISCO MUSIC BOX COMPANY   (800) 227-2190
P.O. Box 7817 • San Francisco, CA 94120
Fax Ordering: (925) 927-2810
International Ordering: (925) 939-4800
Contact Name: Dave Blessing, President
Catalog: Free. Frequency: 10x per year
Circulation: 2MM. Sales: $10-20MM
Products: Music boxes

H.J. SAUNDERS/U.S. MILITARY INSIGNIA   (800) 442-3133
5025 Tamiami Trail E • Naples, FL 34113
E-Mail: insignia@saundersinsignia.com
Website: www.saundersinnsignia.com
Fax Ordering: (239) 774-3323
International Ordering: (239) 775-2100
Contact Name: H.J. Saunders, President
Catalog: Free. Frequency: Weekly
Circulation: 60K. Sales: $500K - $1MM
Products: Insignias from 1940 to present

SCHIFFER BOOKS ANTIQUES &   (610) 593-1777
COLLECTIBLES, LIFESTYLE &
MILITARY HISTORY
Schiffer Publishing Ltd.
4990 Lower Valley Rd. • Atglen, PA 19310
E-Mail: info@schifferbooks.com
Website: www.schifferbooks.com
Fax Ordering: (610) 593-2002
Contact Name: Peter B. Schiffer, President
Catalog: Free. Pages: 16.
Frequency: Semiannual
Circulation: 250K. Sales: $1-3MM
Products: Reference books for collectors,
dealers & designers

SCHRADER'S RAIROAD GIFT CATALOG   (800) 842-4828
Schrader's Enterprises
230 S. Abbe Rd. • Fairview, MI 48621
E-Mail: info@railroadcatalog.com
Website: www.railroadcatalog.com
Fax Ordering: (989) 848-2240
Catalog: $2. Frequency: Annual
Circulation: 25K. Sales: $500K
Products: Unique items for the home

HUGH SHULL CATALOG   (803) 996-3660
P.O. Box 761 • Camden, SC 29020
E-Mail: marsh@interpath.com
Website: www.chicagooldtelephone.com
Fax Ordering: (803) 996-4885
Contact Name: Hugh Shull, President
Catalog: Free. Frequency: Annual
Circulation: 25K. Sales: $500K
Products: Confederate & obsolete currency,
and all old paper money, pre 1935

ALBERT S. SMYTH COMPANY   (800) 638-3333
29 Greenmeadow Dr. • Timonium, MD 21093
E-Mail: smyth@albertsmyth.com
Website: www.albertsmyth.com
Fax Ordering: (410) 252-2355
International Ordering: (410) 252-6666

Contact Name: Thomas Smyth, Manager
Catalog: Free. Frequency: Bimonthly
Circulation: 250K. Sales: $3-5MM
Products: Jewelry, tabletop, crystal, giftware

SOURCE FOR EVERYTHING JEWISH   (800) 426-2567
Hamakor Judaica
P.O. Box 48836 • Niles, IL 60714
E-Mail: service@jewishsource.com
Website: www.jewishsource.com
Fax Ordering: (847) 966-4033
Contact Name: Herschel Strauss, President
Catalog: Free. Frequency: 7x per year
Circulation: 100K. Sales: $1-3M
Products: Jewish items & gifts for home &
friends

SOVIETSKI COLLECTION   (800) 442-0002
P.O. Box 81347 • San Diego, CA 92138
E-Mail: sales@sovietski.com
Website: www.sovietski.com
Fax Ordering: (619) 294-2500
International Ordering: (619) 294-2000
Contact Name: Mitch Siegler, President
Catalog: Free. Frequency: Quarterly
Circulation: 100K. Sales: $1-3MM
Products: Gifts & collectibles from Russia &
Eastern Europe, including antiques & vintage
artifacts

STANDARD DOLL COMPANY   (800) 543-6557
P.O. Box 4125 • East Hampton, NY 11937
Fax Ordering: (631) 329-1062
Customer Service: (631) 329-5393
Contact Name: Paul Henfield, President
Catalog: $3. Frequency: Annual
Circulation: 250K. Sales: $3-5MM
Products: Dolls, accessories & repro antiques

STEINLAND GIFTS & COLLECTIBLES   (847) 428-3150
14 N 679 Rt. 25 • East Dundee, IL 60118
E-Mail: steinland@aol.com
Website: www.steinland.com
Fax Ordering: (847) 428-3170
Contact Name: Tony Steffen, President
Catalog: $1. Pages: 14. Frequency: Quarterly
Circulation: 50K. Sales: $500K
Products: Collectible steins

TESSERACT-EARLY
SCIENTIFIC INSTRUMENTS   (914) 478-2594
P.O. Box 151
Hastings-on-Hudson, NY 10706
E-Mail: coffeen@aol.com
Website: www.etesseract.com
Fax Ordering: (914) 478-5473
Contact Name: Dr. David Coffeen, President
Catalog: Free. Frequency: Quarterly
Circulation: 50K. Sales: $500K
Products: Antique scientific instruments

800-TREKKER-COM   (800) 873-5537
Brainstorms Internet Marketing
1230 Spruce St. • Reading, PA 19602
E-Mail: custservice@800-trekker.com
Website: www.800-trekker.com
Fax Ordering: (800) 329-8735
International Ordering: (610) 374-6000
Contact Name: David Blaise, President
Catalog: $3.50. Frequency: Bimonthly
Circulation: 25M. Sales: $1-3MM
Products: Science fiction collectibles

TYROL INTERNATIONAL   (800) 241-5404
House of Tyrol
66 E. Kytle St. • Cleveland, GA 30528
E-Mail: info@tyrolinternational.com
Website: www.tyrolinternational.com
Fax Ordering: (706) 865-5115
International Ordering: (706) 865-7794
Contact Name: Bernd Nagy, President
Catalog: Free. Frequency: 22x per year
Circulation: 2MM. Sales: $5-10MM
Products: Gifts & collectibles including, beer
steins, dolls, nutcrackers, decorative accessories

FREDERICK J. TYSON   (239) 414-4543
16576 Wellington Lakes Cir.
Fort Myers, FL 33908
E-Mail: racetrack@erinet.com
Fax Ordering: (239) 415-4547
Catalog: Free. Frequency: Semiannual
Circulation: 25K. Sales: $1-3MM
Products: Custom-made display models &
replicas; collectibles, miniatures & training aids.

VICTORY GLASS CATALOG   (515) 987-5765
3260 Ute Ave. • Waukee, IA 50263
E-Mail: info@victoryglass.com
Website: www.victoryglass.com
Fax Ordering: (515) 987-5762
Contact Name: Stephen Loots, President
Catalog: Free. Frequency: Annual
Circulation: 25K. Sales: $1-3MM
Products: Antique parts for jukeboxes

VINTAGE NEWSPAPERS   (800) 235-1919
P.O. Box 48621 • Los Angeles, CA 90048
Fax Ordering: (310) 935-3079
International Ordering: (310) 552-3176
Contact Name: Selwyn Landsberg, President
Catalog: Free. Frequency: Annual
Circulation: 50K. Sales: $500K
Products: Vintage newspapers 1850 to the
present & leather bound newspapers for your
date of birth

WEE-LINE CATALOG   (888) 933-6576
2380 Henry St. • Muskegon, MI 49441
E-Mail: weeline@aol.com
Website: www.weeline.com
Fax Ordering: (231) 759-3165
International Ordering: (231) 755-4069
Contact Name: Linda Olson, President
Catalog: Free. Frequency: Annual
Circulation: 25K. Sales: $1-3MM
Products: Dolls, doll clothing & accessories

HAROLD B. WEITZ & COMPANY   (800) 245-4807
6315 Forbes Ave. • Pittsburgh, PA 15217
E-Mail: info@weitzcoins.com
Website: www.weitzcoins.com
Fax Ordering: (412) 521-1750
International Ordering: (412) 521-1773
Contact Name: Harold Weitz, President
Catalog: Free. Frequency: 3x per year
Circulation: 25K. Sales: $500K - $1MM
Products: Collectibles, mostly coins

WILL GORGES CIVIL WAR CATALOG   (252) 636-3039
Antiques • 3910 US Hwy. 70 E
New Bern, NC 28560
E-Mail: rebel@civilwarantiques.com
Website: www.civilwareshop.com
Fax Ordering: (252) 637-1862

Contact Name: Will Gorges, President
Catalog: Online. **Sales:** $500M to $1MM
Products: Authentic Civil War memorabilia, firearms, gold & silver coins, quilts

WONDERLAND CATALOG   (800) 966-3655
Dollmaster's • 2148 Renard Ct.
Annapolis, MD 21401
E-Mail: info@dollmasters.com
Website: www.dollmasters.com
Fax Ordering: (410) 224-2515
International Ordering: (410) 224-4386
Contact Name: Florence Theriault, President
Catalog: Free. **Frequency:** Semiannual
Circulation: 250K. **Sales:** $5-10MM
Products: Doll-related items including clothing & books

WORLD PRODUCTS CATALOG   (805) 552-9597
Scan-Am Enterprises
11824 Trapani Ct. • Moorpark, CA 93021
Fax Ordering: (805) 552-9597
Contact Name: Finn Skeisvoll, President
Catalog: Free. **Frequency:** Annual
Circulation: 100K. **Sales:** $1-3MM
Products: Gifts & collectibles; home decor/table top, housewares; personal care, travel & children's items

WORLDWIDE COLLECTIBLES & GIFTS   (800) 644-2442
2 Lakeside Ave. • Berwyn, PA 19312
E-Mail: info@wwcag.com
Website: www.wwcag.com.com
Fax Ordering: (610) 889-9549
Contact Name: Frank Cusumano, President
Catalog: Free. **Frequency:** Annual
Circulation: 25K. **Sales:** $500K
Products: Collectibles & gifts from around the world

WORLDWIDE TREASURE BUREAU   (800) 437-0222
P.O. Box 5012 • Visalia, CA 93278
E-Mail: atb@worldwidetreasure.com
Website: www.worldwidetreasure.com
Fax Ordering: (559) 651-3498
International Ordering: (559) 651-3400
Contact Name: Samuel Cox, President
Catalog: Free. **Frequency:** Bimonthly
Circulation: 100K. **Sales:** $3-5MM
Products: Genuine ancient coins & artifacts; collectible U.S. & world coins, stamps & currency; historical documents & collectibles

YESTERYEAR TOYS & BOOKS   (800) 481-1353
Alexandria Bay, NY 13607
E-Mail: info@yesteryeartoys.com
Website: www.yesteryeartoys.com
Fax Ordering: (613) 475-3748
Catalog: $6.95. **Frequency:** Annual
Circulation: 25K. **Sales:** $500K
Products: Working model steam engines, accessories & parts; available in kits or assembled

A.R.T. STUDIO CLAY CO. (877) 278-2529
9320 Michigan Ave. • Sturtevant, WI 53177
E-Mail: orderdesk@artclay.com
Website: www.artclay.com
Fax Ordering: (262) 884-4343
International Ordering: (262) 884-4278
Contact Name: Chuck Trott, President
Catalog: $5. Frequency: Annual
Circulation: 50K. Sales: $1-3MM
Products: Ceramic, pottery supplies &
equipment; videos

AVL LOOMS (800) 626-9615
3851 Morrow Lane, #9 • Chico, CA 95928
E-Mail: info@avlusa.com
Website: www.avlusa.com
Fax Ordering: (530) 893-1372
International Ordering: (530) 893-4915
Contact Name: Peter Strauss, President
Catalog: Free. Frequency: Semiannual
Circulation: 50K. Sales: $3-5MM
Products: Handweaving floor looms and
weaving equipment

AIM KILN MANUFACTURING CO. (800) 246-5456
2516 Business Pkwy. Unit #E
Minden, NV 89423
E-Mail: aimkilns@yahoo.com
Website: www.aimkilns.com
Fax Ordering: (775) 267-2002
International Ordering: (775) 267-2607
Contact Name: John Degenfelder, President
Catalog: Free. Frequency: Annual
Circulation: 500K. Sales: $3-5MM
Products: Manufactures electric & gas fired kilns
for porcelain, ceramics; lampworking, glass fusing

AIRBRUSH BIBLE CATALOG (800) 232-7247
Bear Air Express
20 Hampden Dr. #2R • S. Easton, MA 02375
E-Mail: bearbrush5@aol.com
Website: www.bearair.com
Fax Ordering: (508) 230-5891
Tech Support: (888) 232-7227
Contact Name: Steve Angers, President
Catalog: Free. Frequency: Semiannual
Circulation: 100K. Sales: $5-10MM
Products: Complete assortment of airbrushes

ALLEN'S BASKETWORKS (800) 284-7333
P.O. Box 3217 • Palm Springs, CA 92263
E-Mail: basketry@teleport.com
Website: www.allensbasketworks.com
Fax Ordering: (760) 323-5181
International Ordering: (760) 320-4487
Contact Name: Allen Keeney, President
Catalog: Free. Frequency: Annual
Circulation: 10K. Sales: $250-500K
Products: Basketry materials for the basket
maker

AMERICAN FRAME HANDBOOK (800) 537-0944
American Frame Corporation (888) 628-3833
400 Tomahawk Dr. • Maumee, OH 43537
E-Mail: customer.service@americanframe.com
Website: www.americanframe.com
International Ordering: (419) 893-5595
Contact Name: Laura Jajko, President
Catalog: Free. Frequency: Semiannual
Circulation: 50K. Sales: $500K - $1MM
Products: Antique metal & wood frames,
mat board, and framing tools & accessories

AMERICAN HOME STENCILS (800) 742-4520
10816 W. Janesville Rd.
Hales Corners, WI 53130
E-Mail: service@americanhomestencils.com
Website: www.americanhomestencils.com
Fax Ordering: (800) 742-4520
International Ordering: (414) 425-5381
Contact Name: Ann Kooping, President
Catalog: Free. Frequency: Annual
Circulation: 10K. Sales: $500K
Products: Lasercut stencils for the home crafter;
extensive quilt design collection

ANIMAZING GALLERY ANIMATION ART (800) 303-4848
54 Greene St. • New York, NY 10013
E-Mail: info@animazing.com
Website: www.animazing.com
Fax Ordering: (212) 226-7428
International Ordering: (212) 226-7374
Contact Name: Heidi Leigh & Nick Leone, Owners
Catalog: Free. Frequency: Semiannual
Circulation: 100K. Sales: $500K
Products: Animation art, illustration art and fine art

ANNIE'S ATTIC NEEDLCRAFT CATALOG (800) 582-6643
1 Annie Lane • Big Sandy, TX 75755
E-Mail: info@anniesattic.com
Website: www.anniesattic.com
Fax Ordering: (800) 882-6643
International Ordering: (903) 636-4303
Contact Name: John Robinson, President
Catalog: $2. Frequency: Quarterly
Circulation: 100K. Sales: $5-10MM
Products: Patterns & supplies for crochet,
cross-stitch, knitting, plastic canvas, and other
needlecrafts

ANTINA'S DOLL SUPPLIES (800) 257-9450
P.O. Box 2130 • Estacada, OR 97023
E-Mail: info@dollsupply.com
Website: www.dollsupply.com
Fax Ordering: (503) 630-1905
Customer Service: (503) 630-1900
Contact Name: Tallina C. George, President
Catalog: Free. Frequency: Semiannual
Circulation: 50K. Sales: $5-10MM
Products: Doll supplies & accessories

ART & ARTIFAT CATALOG (800) 231-6766
5581 Hudson Industrial Pkwy.
Hudson, OH 44236
E-Mail: shop@artandartifact.com
Website: www.artandartifact.com
Fax Ordering: (800) 950-9569
Customer Service: (800) 950-9540
Catalog: Free. Frequency: Annual
Circulation: 10M. Sales: $500M
Products: Art, home decor, clothing &
collectible gifts

ART DIRECTION BOOK COMPANY (203) 353-1441
456 Glenbrook Rd. • Stamford, CT 06906
Fax Ordering: (203) 353-1371
Contact Name: Don Barron, President
Catalog: Free. Frequency: Semiannual
Circulation: 10K. Sales: $250-500K
Products: Books for graphic designers
& art directors

ART MATERIALS SERVICE (888) 522-5526
625 Joyce Kilmer Ave.
New Brunswick, NJ 08901

E-Mail: sales@artmaterialsservice.com
Website: www.artmaterialsservice.com
Fax Ordering: (732) 545-9166
International Ordering: (732) 545-8888
Contact Name: Joseph Eichert, President
Catalog: Free. Frequency: Annual
Circulation: 50K. Sales: $5-10MM
Products: Art materials hardware equipment

ART OF THE ANCIENT WORLD   (212) 355-2034
Royal-Athena Galleries
153 E. 57th St. • New York, NY 10022
E-Mail: ancientart@aol.com
Website: www.royalathena.com
Fax Ordering: (212) 688-0412
Contact Name: Jerome M. Eisenberg, PhD, President
Catalog: $5. Frequency: Annual
Circulation: 100K. Sales: $100-500MM
Products: Greek, Roman & Egyptian antiquities

ART SUPPLY WAREHOUSE   (800) 995-6778
6104 Maddry Oaks Ct. • Raleigh, NC 27616
E-Mail: info@aswexpress.com
Website: www.aswexpress.com
Fax Ordering: (919) 878-5075
International Ordering: (919) 878-5077
Catalog: Free. Frequency: Semiannual
Circulation: 100K. Sales: $5-10MM
Products: Art supplies & materials: acrylics, airbrush,
artist accessories, brushes, canvas, paper & boards,
easels & studio furniture; framing & matting; oil colors,
pastels; printmaking supplies; sculpture & modeling;
sketching & drawing; tools & equipment; watercolors

ARTINACLICK CATALOG   (888) 799-7888
450 Applejack Rd.
Manchester Center, VT 05255
E-Mail: custserv@artinaclick.com
Website: www.artinaclick.com
Fax Ordering: (802) 362-3286
International Ordering: (860) 749-2281
Catalog: Online. Sales: $3-5MM
Products: Art prints & posters, custom framing &
mounting services; oil paintings, fine art prints,
giclees & photography

ARTISAN/SANTA FE CATALOG   (800) 331-6375
2601 Cerrillos Rd. • Santa Fe, NM 87505
E-Mail: artsupply@artisan-santafe.com
Website: www.artisan-santafe.com
Fax Ordering: (505) 954-4180
International Ordering: (505) 954-4179
Contact Name: Ron Whitmore, President
Catalog: Free. Frequency: Annual
Circulation: 75K. Sales: $3-5MM
Products: Arts supplies & materials

ARTIST'S CLUB   (800) 845-6507
Crafts Americana Group
13118 NE 4th St. • Vancouver, WA 98684
E-Mail: info@artistsclub.com
Website: www.artistsclub.com
Fax Ordering: (360) 260-8877
International Ordering: (360) 260-8900
Customer Service: (800) 574-6454
Contact Name: Robert L. Petkun, President
Catalog: Free. Frequency: Semiannual
Circulation: 100K. Sales: $1-3MM
Products: Artist's tools & supplies; books,
packets, videos

ATKINSON'S COUNTRY HOUSE   (810) 280-6987
2775 Riniel Rd. • Lennon, MI 48449
E-Mail: sandy@sandyatkinson.com
Website: www.sandyatkinson.com
International Ordering: (810) 208-5148
Contact Name: Sandy Atkinson, President
Catalog: Free. Pages: 34-color. Frequency: Annual
Circulation: 25K. Sales: $100-250K
Products: Basket weaving supplies

AVIATION ART/MILICH FINE ARTS   (800) 443-3665
Milich Arts International, Inc.
10465 W. Center Ave. • Lakewood, CO 80226
E-Mail: art@milichj-arts.com
Website: www.milich-arts.com
Fax Ordering: (303) 980-1042
International Ordering: (303) 986-8547
Contact Name: Joe Milich, President
Catalog: Free. Frequency: Annual
Circulation: 25K. Sales: $250-500K
Products: Aviation art prints & paintings

AXNER POTTERY SUPPLY CATALOG   (800) 843-7057
Laguna Clay Co.
490 Kane Ct. • Oviedo, FL 32762
E-Mail: sales@axner.com
Website: www.axner.com
Fax Ordering: (407) 365-5573
International Ordering: (407) 365-2600
Contact Name: Howard Axner, President
Catalog: Free. Frequency: Semiannual
Circulation: 50K. Sales: $500K - $1MM
Products: Pottery & ceramic supplies, tools &
safety products; wheels and accessories; kilns &
accessories; glaze and glaze related equipment;
clay bodies & clay work equipment; books & videos

BADGE-A-MINIT   (800) 223-4103
345 N. Lewis Ave. • La Salle, IL 61301
E-Mail: info@badgeaminit.com
Website: www.badgeaminit.com
Fax Ordering: (815) 883-9696
International Ordering: (815) 883-8822
Contact Name: Cindy Kurkowski, President
Catalog: Free. Frequency: Semiannual
Circulation: 100K. Sales: $5-10MM
Products: Do-it-yourselves button-making
machines, accessories, computer software
and ideas

BADGER AIR-BRUSH COMPANY   (800) 247-2787
9128 Belmont Ave. • Franklin Park, IL 60131
E-Mail: customerservice@badgerairbrush.com
Website: www.badgerairbrush.com
Fax Ordering: (800) 572-23437(847) 671-4352
International Ordering: (847) 678-3104
Contact Name: Kenneth Schlotfeldt, President
Catalog: Free. Frequency: Annual
Circulation: 100K. Sales: $5-10MM
Products: Air brushes & air-brush related
accessories for artists, crafters & hobbyists

ELINOR PEACE BAILEY   (360) 892-6657
2001 SE 132bd Ct. • Vancouver, WA 98683
E-Mail: elinor@epbdolls.com
Website: www.epbdolls.com
Fax Ordering: (360) 892-6457
Contact Name: Elinor Peace Bailey, President
Catalog: Free. Frequency: Annual
Circulation: 50K. Sales: $100-250K
Products: Cloth doll patterns, books and tools

BALLOON TWISTING (800) 648-6221
T. Myers Magic, Inc.
6513 Thomas Springs Rd. • Austin, TX 78736
E-Mail: orders@tmyers.com
Website: www.tmyers.com
Fax Ordering: (512) 288-7694
International Ordering: (512) 288-7925
Contact Name: Tom Myers, President
Catalog: Free. Frequency: Annual
Circulation: 50K. Sales: $500K - $1MM
Products: Balloon twisting, face painters, jugglers,
magician's & clown's supplies

J.N. BARTFIELD GALLERIES (866) JNBARTS
30 W. 57th St. • New York, NY 100194482
E-Mail: galleryinfo@bartfield.com
Website: www.bartfield.com
Fax Ordering: (212) 541-4860
International Ordering: (212) 245-8890
Contact Name: Michael Frost, Contact
Catalog: Free. Frequency: Annual
Circulation: 50K. Sales: $3-5MM
Products: American Western & Sporting art,
19th century to present paintings & books

THE BASKET MAKER'S CATALOG (800) 447-7008
GH Productions, Inc.
P.O. Box 621 • Scottsville, KY 42164
E-Mail: mail@basketmakerscatalog.com
Website: www.basketmakerscatalog.com
Fax Ordering: (270) 237-5137
International Ordering: (270) 237-4821
Catalog: Free. Frequency: Annual
Circulation: 100K. Sales: $1-3MM
Products: Basket making & chair seating
supplies; basket kits, books, tools

BASKETVILLE CATALOG (800) 258-4553
Main St. • Putney, VT 05346
E-Mail: sales@basketville.com
Website: www.basketville.com
Fax Ordering: (802) 387-5235
International Ordering: (802) 387-5509
Contact Name: Greg Wilson, President
Catalog: Online. Sales: $5-10MM
Products: Baskets & woven products for
major retailers

THE BEAD WAREHOUSE (301) 565-0487
2740 Garfield Ave. • Silver Spring, MD 20910
E-mail: beadware@erols.com
Website: www.thebeadwarehouse.com
Fax Ordering: (301) 565-0489
International Ordering: (301) 565-0487
Contact: Marvin Schwab, Owner
Catalog: Free. Pages: 64. Frequency: Annual
Circulation: 100K. Sales: $1-3MM
Products: Fine gems, jewelry, beads, findings
& supplies

BEADBOX CATALOG (800) 232-3269
Artgems, Inc.
4860 E. Baseline Rd. #101 • Mesa, AZ 85206
E-Mail: hbudwig@artgemsinc.com
Website: www.artgemsinc.com
Fax Ordering: (480) 967-8555
International Ordering: (480) 545-6009
Contact Name: Herbert Budwig, President
Catalog: Free. Frequency: Semiannual
Circulation: 150K. Sales: $3-5MM
Products: Beads, craft products & supplies

S.A. BENDHEIM COMPANY (800) 221-7379
61 Willet St. • Passaic, NJ 07055
E-Mail: sales@bendheim.com
Website: www.bendheim.com
Fax Ordering: (973) 471-1640
International Ordering: (973) 471-1733
Contact Name: Robert Jayson, President
Catalog: Free. Frequency: Annual
Circulation: 100M. Sales: $3-5MM
Products: Architectural glass; wall systems;
art glass; restoration glass; cabinet glass;
needlework kits, cross stitch, latch hook

BINDER'S ART SUPPLIES & FRAMES (888) 472-6866
3330 Piedmont Rd. #18 • Atlanta, GA 30305
E-Mail: sales@bindersart.com
Website: www.bindersart.com
Fax Ordering: (404) 760-1979
International Ordering: (404) 237-6331
Contact Name: Moe Krinsky, President
Catalog: Free. Frequency: Quarterly
Circulation: 100K. Sales: $1-3MM
Products: Artist, graphic & computer graphic
supplies & parts

BOLEK'S CRAFT SUPPLIES (800) 743-2723
P.O. Box 465 • Dover, OH 44622
E-Mail: boleks@tusco.net
Website: www.bolekscrafts.com
Fax Ordering: (800) 649-3735; (330) 343-8009
International Ordering: (330) 364-8878
Contact Name: Richard Bolek, President
Catalog: Free. Frequency: Semiannual
Circulation: 100K. Sales: $3-5MM
Products: Craft supplies

BUTTERICK COMPANY (800) 782-0323
P.O. Box 3755 • Manhattan, KS 66505
E-Mail: orders@butterick.com
Website: www.butterick.com
International Ordering: (785) 776-4041
Customer Service: (800) 766-3619
Contact Name: Jay Stein, President
Catalog: Free. Frequency: Quarterly
Circulation: 150M. Sales: $5-10MM
Products: Seasonal patterns

CR's BEAR & DOLL SUPPLY CATALOG (877) 277-2782
CR's Crafts • P.O. Box 8 • Leland, IA 50453
E-Mail: info@crscraft.com
Website: www.crscraft.com
Fax Ordering: (641) 567-3652
International Ordering: (641) 567-3071
Contact Name: Clarice Brown, President
Catalog: $4. Frequency: Annual
Circulation: 5K. Sales: $500K
Products: Supplies to create bears & dolls from
mohair & designer porcelain to fun & fur and
vinyl doll kits, designer clothing and accessories

CANE & BASKET SUPPLY CO. (800) 468-3966
1283 S. Cochran Ave.
Los Angeles, CA 90019
E-Mail: info@canenbasket.com
Website: www.canebasket.com
Fax Ordering: (323) 939-7237
International Ordering: (323) 939-9644
Contact Name: William Fimpler, President
Catalog: Free. Frequency: Annual
Circulation: 100K. Sales: $250-500K
Products: Cane, bamboo and basketry supplies

CANER'S SOURCEBOOK   (800) 544-3373
The Caning Shop
926 Gilman St. • Berkeley, CA 94710
E-Mail: jim@caning.com
Website: www.caning.com
Fax Ordering: (510) 527-7718
International Ordering: (510) 527-5010
Contact Name: Jim Widess, President
Catalog: Free. Frequency: Annual
Circulation: 50K. Sales: $500K to $1MM
Products: Gourd crafting, chair caning & basketry supplies, tools, how-to-books

CERAMIC SUPPLY, INC.   (800) 723-7264
7 Route 46 West • Lodi, NJ 07644
E-Mail: orders@7ceramic.com
Website: www.7ceramic.com
Fax Ordering: (973) 340-0089
International Ordering: (973) 340-3005
Contact Name: Miriam Vogelman, President
Catalog: Free. Frequency: Annual
Circulation: 10K. Sales: $1-3MM
Products: Ceramic and pottery supplies & equipment

DAN CHASE TAXIDERMY SUPPLY CO.   (800) 535-8220
13599 Blackwater Rd. • Baker, LA 70714
E-Mail: info@danchase.com
Website: www.danchase.com
Fax Ordering: (225) 261-5526
International Ordering: (225) 261-3795
Contact Name: Dan Chase, President
Catalog: Free. Frequency: Semiannual
Circulation: 50K. Sales: $5-10MM
Products: Taxidermy supplies, videos

CLOTILDE   (800) 772-2891
P.O. Box 7500 • Big Sandy, TX 75755
E-Mail: craft-ndl@clotilde.com
Website: www.clotilde.com
Fax Ordering: (800) 863-3109
Customer Service: (800) 545-4002
Contact Name: Nancy Laman, President
Catalog: Free. Frequency: Semiannual
Circulation: 100K. Sales: $500K - $1MM
Products: Quilting patterns & notions; fabric; sewing patterns & notions; books & supplies

COLOR CONNECTION   (800) 999-7013
Sue Viders
9739 Tall Grass Cir. • Lone Tree, CO 80124
E-Mail: sueviders@comcast.net
Website: www.sueviders.com
Fax Ordering: (303) 799-1220
International Ordering: (303) 799-1220
Contact Name: Sue Viders, Marketing
Catalog: Free. Frequency: Quarterly
Circulation: 25K. Sales: $1-3MM
Products: Marketing products for visual artists; books, tapes & seminars

COLORADO MOULDING COMPANY   (800) 332-9013
2606 S. Raritan Cir. • Englewood, CO 80110
E-Mail: info@coloradomouldingcompany.com
Website: www.coloradomouldingcompany.com
Fax Ordering: (303) 934-2228
Customer Service: (303) 922-1919
Contact Name: Verlys Crokett, President
Catalog: Free. Frequency: Annual
Circulation: 25K. Sales: $5-10MM
Products: Mouldings, mat boards, liners, frames, mounting supplies & framing equipment

CONNECTICUT CANE & REED CO.   (800) 227-8498
P.O. Box 762 • Manchester, CT 06045
E-Mail: sales@chairseatweaving.com
Website: www.chairseatweaving.com
Fax Ordering: (860) 649-2221
International Ordering: (860) 646-6586
Contact Name: K.C. Parkinson, President
Catalog: Free. Frequency: Annual
Circulation: 100K. Sales: $500K to $1MM
Products: Chair seating & basketry supplies; Nantucket basketry accessories, wicker repair

COTTURA CATALOG   (800) 348-6608
2900 Rowena Ave. • Los Angeles, CA 90039
E-Mail: info@cottura.com
Website: www.cottura.com
Fax Ordering: (323) 662-4149
International Ordering: (323) 662-2112
Contact Names: Jim Zimmerman, President
Catalog: Free. Frequency: Quarterly
Circulation: 150K. Sales: $5-10MM
Products: Ceramic & glass art imports

CRAFT WHOLESALERS CATALOG   (800) 777-1442
77 Cypress St. SW • Reynoldsburg, OH 43068
E-Mail: info@craftcatalog.com
Website: www.craftcatalog.com
Fax Ordering: (740) 964-6212
International Ordering: (740) 964-6210
Contact Name: Farley Piper, President
Catalog: Free. Frequency: Quarterly
Circulation: 200K. Sales: $5-10MM
Products: Scrapbook, painting & craft supplies

CRAFTBOOKS CATALOG   (800) 858-8515
Chester Book Co.
8075 215th St. West • Lakeville, MN 55044
E-Mail: craftbooks@finneyco.com
Website: www.chesterbookco.com
Fax Ordering: (800) 330-6232; (952) 469-1968
International Ordering: (952) 469-6699
Contact Name: Lois Nadel, President
Catalog: Free. Frequency: Quarterly
Circulation: 150K. Sales: $500K to $1MM
Products: Books on arts, crafts & tools for professional craft artists, collectors & educators

CRAFTY NEEDLE   (800) 345-3332
P.O. Box 916010 • Longwood, FL 32791
E-Mail: shop@craftyneedle.com
Website: www.craftyneedle.com
Fax Ordering: (321) 206-3143
Customer Service: (321) 214-4379
Contact Name: Judy Rosenbaum, President
Catalog: Free. Frequency: Quarterly
Circulation: 100K. Sales: $500K to $1MM
Products: Needlework kits, cross stitch, latch hook; Jewish designs specialty

CRAZY CROW TRADING POST   (800) 786-6210
P.O. Box 847 • Pottsboro, TX 75076
E-Mail: orders@crazycrow.com
Website: www.crazycrow.com
Fax Ordering: (903) 786-9059
International Ordering: (903) 786-2287
Contact Name: J. Rex Reddick, President
Catalog: $5. Frequency: Annual
Circulation: 10K. Sales: $1-3MM
Products: Native American Indian arts & crafts' supplies; craft kits; books, videos, recordings

DELPHI GLASS   (800) 248-2048
3380 East Jolly Rd. • Lansing, MI 48910
E-mail: sales@delphiglass.com
Website: www.delphiglass.com
Fax Ordering: (800) 748-0374; (517) 394-5364
International Ordering: (517) 394-4631
Catalog: Free. Frequency: Semiannual
Circulation: 100K. Sales: $3-5MM
Products: Stained glass supplies, mosaics,
fusing, flameworking, jewelry

DICK BLICK ART MATERIALS   (800) 828-4548
Dick Blick Company
P.O. Box 1267 • Galesburg, IL 61402
E-Mail: info@dickblick.com
Website: www.dickblick.com
Fax Ordering: (800) 621-8293; (309) 343-5785
International Ordering: (309) 343-6181
Customer Service: (800) 723-2787
Product Information: (800) 933-2542
Contact Name: Bob Buchsbaum, President
Catalog: Free. Frequency: 3x per year
Circulation: 2MM. Sales: $50-100MM
Products: Fine artist & craft materials

DISCOUNT POTTERY   (781) 449-7687
BOOKS/TOOLS/VIDEOS
The Potters Shop
31 Thorpe Rd. • Needham Hts., MA 02494
E-Mail: pottersshop@aol.com
Website: www.thepottersshop.blogspot.com
Fax Ordering: (781) 449-9098
Contact Name: Steven Branfman, President
Catalog: Free. Frequency: Annual
Circulation: 25K. Sales: $500K
Products: Books & videos on pottey & ceramics

DISCOUNT SCHOOL SUPPLY   (800) 627-2829
P.O. Box 6013 • Carol Stream, IL 60197
E-mail: nco@discountschoolsupply.com
Website: www.discountschoolsupply.com
Fax Ordering: (800) 879-3753
International Ordering: (831) 333-5588
Catalog: Free. Pages: 290. Frequency: Semiannual
Circulation: 150K. Sales: $5-10MM
Products: Developmentally appropriate products for
young children in the classroom or child care setting

DIXIE ART SUPPLIES   (800) 783-2612
AIRBRUSH CATALOG
5005 Bloomfield St.
New Orleans, LA 70121
E-Mail: artdixie@aol.com
Website: www.dixieart.com
Fax Ordering: (504) 831-5738
International Ordering: (504) 833-2612
Contact Name: Keith Marshall, President
Catalog: Free. Frequency: Annual
Circulation: 100K. Sales: $5-10MM
Products: Discount fine art supplies

DOLLMAKER SUPPLIES   (732) 899-0804
Mimi's Books
3000 Nancy Dr. • Mt. Pleasant, NJ 08742
E-Mail: mimi@mimidolls.com
Website: www.mimidolls.com
Fax Ordering: (732) 714-9306
Contact Name: Gloria Winer, President
Catalog: Free. Frequency: Semiannual
Circulation: 25K. Sales: $250K
Products: Dollmaking books, tools & patterns

DOVE BRUSHES CATALOG   (800) 334-3683
Dove Brush Manufacturing, Inc.
1849 Oakmont Ave. • Tarpon Springs, FL 34689
E-Mail: mrdove23@aol.com
Website: www.dovebrushes.com
Fax Ordering: (727) 934-1142
International Ordering: (727) 934-5283
Contact Name: George N. Dovellos, President
Catalog: Free. Frequency: Annual
Circulation: 50K. Sales: $1-3MM
Products: Artist's brushes & tools; craft equipment

DRESSLER STENCIL COMPANY   (888) 656-4515
259 SW 41st St. • Renton, WA 98055
E-Mail: customerservice@dresslerstencils.com
Website: www.dresslerstencils.com
Fax Ordering: (425) 656-4381
International Ordering: (425) 656-4515
Contact Name: David Dressler, President
Catalog: Free, 2 vols. Frequency: Quarterly
Circulation: 50M. Sales: $1-3MM
Products: Laser cut stencils for home decoration
with detailed instructions, paint kits and brushes

EAGLE FEATHER'S CRAFTS   (801) 393-3991
& ARTS & CRAFTS SUPPLIES
Eagle Feather Trading Post
168 W. 12th St. • Ogden, UT 84404
E-Mail: sales@eaglefeathertradingpost.com
Website: www.eaglefeathertradingpost.com
Fax Ordering: (801) 393-4647
International Ordering: (801) 393-3991
Contact Name: Monte Smith, President
Catalog: $5. Frequency: Semiannual
Circulation: 50K. Sales: $500M
Products: Specializes in beads, beading & craft
supplies, and authentic Native American arts &
crafts; Indian motif mugs.

EASTERN ART GLASS CATALOG   (800) 872-3458
176-180 5th Ave. • Hawthorne, NJ 07506
E-Mail: customerservice@etchworld.com
Website: www.etchworld.com
Fax Ordering: (973) 427-8823
International Ordering: (973) 423-4002
Catalog: Free. Frequency: Annual
Circulation: 100K. Sales: $1-3MM
Products: Glass & mirror etching &
decorating supplies

EHRMAN TAPESTRY   (888) 826-8600
207 S. Cross St. #104
Chestertown, MD 21620
E-Mail: ehrman@toad.net
Website: www.ehrmantapestry.com
Fax Ordering: (410) 810-3034
International Ordering: (410) 810-3032
Contact Name: Marjorie Adams, President
Catalog: Free. Frequency: Annual
Circulation: 50K. Sales: $1-3MM
Products: Needlepoint kits from Britain

EMPEROR CLOCK, LLC   (800) 642-0011
340 Industrial park Dr. • Amherst, VA 24521
E-Mail: service@emperorclock.com
Website: www.emperorclock.com
Fax Ordering: (434) 946-1420
Catalog: Free. Frequency: Quarterly
Circulation: 250K. Sales: $5-10MM
Products: Clock and furniture kits, mechanical &
quartz movements, clock plans, assembled clocks

FACTORY DIRECT CRAFT SUPPLY　　　(800) 252-5223
315 Conover Dr. • Franklin, OH 45005
E-Mail: INFO@factorydirectcraft.com
Website: www.factorydirectcraft.com
Fax Ordering: (937) 743-5500
International Ordering: (937) 743-5855
Contact Name: Shari Kirker, President
Catalog: $5. Frequency: Annual
Circulation: 50K. Sales: $3-5MM
Products: Lace, hats, flowers, wood &
doll supplies, ribbon, paint & books

FLAX ART & DESIGN CATALOG　　　(415) 552-2355
1699 Market St. • San Francisco, CA 94103
E-Mail: orders@flaxart.com
Website: www.flaxart.com
International Ordering: (415) 552-2355
Contact Name: Philip Flax, President
Catalog: Free. Frequency: Monthly
Circulation: 150K. Sales: $10-20MM
Products: Art supplies, crafts; hobby kits;
albums, journals, gifts

FLORIDA CLAY ART COMPANY　　　(800) 211-7713
1645 Hangar Rd. • Sanford, FL 32773
E-Mail: orders@flclay.com
Website: www.flclay.com
Fax Ordering: (407) 330-5058
International Ordering: (407) 330-1116
Contact Name: Carol Taglie, President
Catalog: Free. Frequency: Annual
Circulation: 25K. Sales: $500K
Products: Pottery & ceramic supplies &
equipment; wheels, kilns, tile making

1451 MUSEUM EDITIONS CATALOG　　　(949) 798-3413
17802 Skypark Cir. • Irvine, CA 92614
E-Mail: nschuth@1451.com
Website: www.1451.com
Fax Ordering: (949) 261-1329
International Ordering: (949) 798-3413
Contact Name: Nancy Schuth, Contact
Catalog: $35. Frequency: Annual
Circulation: 10K. Sales: $500K to $1MM
Products: Prints & bronze reproductions from
the Vatican Library collection and other museums

FRANKEN FRAMES CATALOG　　　(800) 322-5899
609 W. Walnut St. • Johnson City, TN 37604
E-Mail: franken@usit.net
Website: www.frankenframes.com
Fax Ordering: (423) 926-5123
International Ordering: (423) 926-8853
Contact Name: Roger Chase, President
Catalog: Free. Frequency: Annual
Circulation: 25K. Sales: $500K to $1MM
Products: Custom frames, custom mats,
framing hardware, full service framing

FRANK'S CANE & RUSH SUPPLY　　　(714) 847-0707
7252 Hell Ave. • Huntington Beach, CA 92647
E-Mail: mfrank@franksupply.com
Website: www.franksupply.com
Fax Ordering: (714) 843-5645
Contact Name: Michael Frank, President
Catalog: Free. Frequency: Semiannual
Circulation: 100K. Sales: $250-500K
Products: Chair caning & seat weaving supplies,
wicker repair & upholstery supplies, basketry &
fibre arts supplies, wood parts & wood furniture kits,
raffia & hat making supplies, bambook & rattan poles,
videos & instruction books

A.I. FRIEDMAN CATALOG　　　(800) 204-6352
4 W. 18th St. • New York, NY 10011
E-Mail: customerservice@aifriedman.com
Website: www.aifriedman.com
Fax Ordering: (800) 204-6380; (212) 929-7320
Customer Service: (212) 337-8600
International Ordering: (212) 243-9000
Contact Name: James White, President
Catalog: Free. Frequency: Annual
Circulation: 100K. Sales: $20-50M
Products: Graphic art supplies & tools

FRIGHT CATALOG　　　(508) 970-4575
100 Barber Ave. Unit F
Worcester, MA 01606
Website: www.frightcatalog.com
E-mail: service@frightcatalog.com
International Ordering: (508) 852-8800
Catalog: $2. Frequency: Annual
Circulation: 150K. Sales: $1-3MM
Products: Halloween decorations, props,
costumes, masks, accessories

GETTY IMAGES　　　(800) 462-4379
122 S. Michigan Ave. #900
Chicago, IL 60603
E-Mail: sales@gettyimages.com
Website: www.gettyimages.com
International Ordering: (312) 344-4500
Catalog: Free. Frequency: Semiannual
Circulation: 100K. Sales: $10-20MM
Products: Original illustrations, photography;
photo objects & backgrounds on CD-ROMs;
royalty-free images

GS DIRECT GRAPHIC SUPPLIES　　　(800) 234-3729
6490 Carlson Dr. • Eden Prairie, MN 55346
E-Mail: info@gsdirect.net
Website: www.gsdirect.com
Fax Ordering: (952) 942-0216
International Ordering: (952) 942-6115
Contact Name: Charles Ehlers, President
Catalog: Free. Pages: 60. Frequency: Quarterly
Circulation: 150K. Sales: $3-5MM
Products: Graphic supplies; drafting & drawing
supplies & equipment; furniture, table & chairs;
design software & books

GLASS CRAFTERS STAINED GLASS　　　(800) 422-4552
398 Interstate Court • Sarasota, FL 34240
E-Mail: info@glasscrafters.com
Website: www.glasscrafters.com
Fax Ordering: (941) 379-8827
International Ordering: (941) 379-8333
Contact Name: J. Rohrer, President
Catalog: Free. Pages: 96. Frequency: Quarterly
Circulation: 100K. Sales: $1-3MM
Products: Stained glass suppliers & equipment

GLIMAKRA LOOMS 'N YARNS　　　(866) 890-7314
Glimakra-USA, LLC
50 Hall Lane • Clancy, MT 59634
E-Mail: joanne@glimakrausa.com
Website: www.glimakrausa.com
Fax Ordering: (406) 442-4892
International Ordering: (406) 442-0354
Contact Name: Joanne Hall, Contact
Catalog: Free. Frequency: Semiannual
Circulation: 100K. Sales: $1-3MM
Products: Swedish weaving equipment;
specialty books for textile industry

GRAPHIK DIMENSIONS, LTD. (800) 221-0262
2103 Brentwood St. • High Point, NC 27263
E-Mail: business@graphikdimensions.com
Website: www.pictureframes.com
Fax Ordering: (336) 887-3773
International Ordering: (336) 887-3700
Customer Service: (800) 332-8884
Contact Name: Steve Feinsod, President
Catalog: Free. Frequency: Monthly
Circulation: 1MM. Sales: $10-20MM
Products: Metal, custom & ready-made picture
frames; matting; framing kits & accessories

GREAT NORTHERN WEAVING (800) 370-7235
451 E. D Ave. • Kalamazoo, MI 49009
E-Mail: gnwemma@aol.com
Website: www.greatnorthernweaving.com
Fax Ordering: (269) 341-9525
International Ordering: (269) 341-9525
Contact Name: Emma Schering, President
Catalog: $2.50. Frequency: Annual
Circulation: 50M. Sales: $500M
Products: Rug weaving supplies; yarns, looms;
weaving equipment & books

GRIFFIN MANUFACTURING COMPANY (800) 344-6445
P.O. Box 10 • Webster, NY 14580
E-Mail: sales@grifhold.com
Website: www.grifhold.com
Fax Ordering: (585) 265-2621
International Ordering: (585) 265-1991
Contact Name: Theresa Papia, President
Catalog: Free. Frequency: Annual
Circulation: 75K. Sales: $500K - $1MM
Products: Artist hand tools, specialty tools,
knives & blades

H.O.M.E., INC. / EMMAUS (207) 469-7961
P.O. Box 10 • Orland, ME 04472
E-Mail: info@homecoop.net
Website: www.homecoop.net
Fax Ordering: (207) 469-1023
Contact Name: Lucy Poulin, President
Catalog: Free. Frequency: Annual
Circulation: 10K. Sales: $250K
Products: Craft cooperative offering local
Native American crafts; handcrafted gifts &
Christmas wreaths from Maine

HARD-TO-FIND NEEDLWORK BOOKS (617) 969-0942
96 Roundwood Rd. • Newton, MA 02464
E-Mail: hardtofind@needleworkbooks.com
Website: www.needleworkbooks.com
Fax Ordering: (617) 969-0942
Contact Name: Betty Feinstein, President
Catalog: $1. Frequency: Monthly
Circulation: 5K. Sales: $250K
Products: Needlework & rare books

HARRISVILLE DESIGNS- (800) 338-9415
LOOM & YARN CATALOG
P.O. Box 806 • Harrisville, NH 03450
E-Mail: info@harrisville.com
Website: www.harrisville.com
Fax Ordering: (603) 827-3335
International Ordering: (603) 827-3333
Contact Name: John Colony, III, President
Catalog: Free. Frequency: Semiannual
Circulation: 100K. Sales: $1-3MM
Products: Products for weaving and knitting
enthusiasts; pattens, yarns, looms, accessories,
educational toys

HEARTHSIDE QUILTS (800) 451-3533
P.O. Box 610 • Hinesburg, VT 05461
E-Mail: hearthsidequilts@att.net
Website: www.hearthsidequilts.com
Fax Ordering: (802) 482-7803
International Ordering: (802) 482-7800
Contact Name: George Wachob, President
Catalog: $2. Pages: 32-color. Frequency: Annual
Circulation: 50K. Sales: $500K to $1MM
Products: Quilt kits, fabrics & quilting frames;
quilt pictures

HERITAGE HOUSE GALLERIES (800) 890-9028
530 NE 43rd St. • Oakland Park, FL 33334
E-Mail: rosanne33314@aol.com
Website: www.heritagehouse.com
International Ordering: (954) 564-9255
Contact Name: Bonnie Barrett, President
Catalog: Free. Frequency: Monthly
Circulation: 100K. Sales: $500K-1MM
Products: Handpainted recreations of masterpiece
oil paintings ranging from $250 to $2500

HERRSCHNERS QUALITY CRAFTS (800) 441-0838
2800 Hoovers Rd. • Stevens Point, WI 54492
E-Mail: customerservice@herrschners.com
Website: www.herrschners.com
Fax Ordering: (715) 341-2250
Customer Service: (800) 713-1239
Contact Name: Ted Hesemann, President
Catalog: Free. Frequency: Quarterly
Circulation: 1MM. Sales: $20-50MM
Products: Needlework, embroidery, crochet &
rughooking; paper crafts & scrapbooking; quilting

HISTORICAL ART PRINTS CATALOG (203) 262-6680
P.O. Box 660 • Southbury, CT 06488-0660
E-Mail: haprints@aol.com
Website: www.historicalartprints.com
Fax Ordering: (203) 262-6979
Contact Name: Don Troiani, President
Catalog: Free. Pages: 22. Frequency: Quarterly
Circulation: 100K. Sales: $500K to $1MM
Products: Limited edition historical art prints;
books & sculpture

HOME SEW SEWING & CRAFT SUPPLIES (800) 344-4739
P.O. Box 4099 • Bethlehem, PA 18018
E-Mail: customerservice@homesew.com
Website: www.homesew.com
Fax Ordering: (610) 867-9717
International Ordering: (610) 867-3833
Contact Name: Edward Perusse, President
Catalog: Free. Frequency: Semiannual
Circulation: 200K. Sales: $1-3MM
Products: Sewing and craft supplies

HUDSON GLASS CO., INC. (800) 431-2964
219 N. Division St. • Peekskill, NY 10566 (800) 444-2748
E-Mail: sales@hudsonglass.com
Website: www.hudsonglass.com
Fax Ordering: (800) 999-3294; (914) 737-4447
International Ordering: (914) 737-2124
Contact Name: Herb Lewis, President
Catalog: Free. Frequency: Quarterly
Circulation: 25K. Sales: $1-3MM
Products: Stained glass tools, patterns &
supplies, bent & convex glass, starter kits; books

INDIAN HANDICRAFTS (800) 504-2723
Southwest Indian Foundation
100 West Coal Ave. • Gallup, NM 87301

E-Mail: swif@cia-g.com
Website: www.southwestindian.com.com
Fax Ordering: (505) 863-2760
International Ordering: (505) 863-4037
Customer Service: (877) 788-9962
Contact Name: William McCarthy, CEO
Catalog: Free. Frequency: Semiannual
Circulation: 200K. Sales: $500K - $1MM
Products: Indian crafts, jewelry, clothing, mugs, toys & books

INDUSTRIAL ARTS SUPPLY CATALOG   **(888) 919-0899**
5724 W. 36th St. • Minneapolis, MN 55416
Fax Ordering: (952) 920-2947
International Ordering: (952) 920-7393
Contact Name: Leslie Raymond, President
Catalog: Free. Frequency: Annual
Circulation: 50K. Sales: $1-3MM
Products: Industrial art supplies

CLOCKPARTS   **(888) 827-2387**
Innovations Specialties, Inc.
11869 Teale St. • Culver City, CA 90230
E-Mail: orders@clockparts.com
Website: www.clockparts.com
Fax Ordering: (310) 482-3480
International Ordering: (310) 398-8116
Contact Name: Mike Brosman, VP
Catalog: Free. Frequency: Annual
Circulation: 100K. Sales: $5-10MM
Products: Clock parts; clock kits & plans; wood products; grandfather clock accessories

JERRY'S CATALOG   **(800) 827-8478**
Jerry's Artarama
P.O. Box 58638J • Raleigh, NC 27658
E-Mail: info@jerryscatalog.com
Website: www.jerrysartarama.com
Fax Ordering: (919) 873-9565
International Ordering: (919) 878-6782
Contact Name: Ira Alan, President
Catalog: Free. Frequency: Semiannual
Circulation: 1MM. Sales: $10-20MM
Products: Discount art materials, picture frames, prints, brushes, canvas, studio furniture; books & videos; light boxes, projectors, easels & drawing tables

KARGES FINE ART CATALOG   **(800) 833-9185**
P.O. Box D-1 • Carmel, CA 93921
E-Mail: kargesfinart@kargesfineart.com
Website: www.kargesfineart.com
Fax Ordering: (831) 625-9649
International Ordering: (831) 625-4266
Contact Name: Thomas Myers, President
Catalog: Free. Frequency: Annual
Circulation: 100K. Sales: $500K - $1MM
Products: Early California & American paintings

KAYE WOOD CATALOG   **(800) 248-5293**
P.O. Box 456 • West Branch, MI 48661
E-Mail: lori@kayewood.com
Website: www.kayewood.com
Fax Ordering: (989) 345-3049
International Ordering: (989) 345-3028
Contact Names: Kaye Wood, President
Catalog: Free. Frequency: Annual
Circulation: 25K. Sales: $500K
Products: Books & videos on strip-quilting techniques, and strip-piecing tools & patterns

KEEPSAKE QUILTING   **(800) 865-9458**
Sabanek Associates
P.O. Box 1618 • Center Harbor, NH 03226
E-Mail: customerservice@keepsakequilting.com
Website: www.keepsakequilting.com
Fax Ordering: (603) 253-8346
International Ordering: (603) 253-8731
Contact Name: Judy Sprague Sabanek, President
Catalog: Free. Frequency: Semiannual
Circulation: 100K. Sales: $500K to $1MM
Products: Fabrics, tools & notions, patterns, Keppsake quick kits; books for quilting

KIDSART CATALOG   **(530) 926-5076**
P.O. Box 274 • Mt. Shasta, CA 96067
Website: www.kidsart.com
E-mail: service@kidsart.com
Fax Ordering: (530) 926-0851
Catalog: Free. Frequency: Quarterly
Circulation: 150K. Sales: $3-5MM
Products: Art teaching supplies; art gifts; children's drawing painting lessons

KLOCKIT CATALOG   **(800) 556-2548**
P.O. Box 636 • Lake Geneva, WI 53147
E-Mail: klockit@klockit.com
Website: www.klockit.com
Fax Ordering: (262) 248-9899
Tech Support: (800) 556-6474
Contact Name: Fred Koermer, President
Catalog: Free. Frequency: Quarterly
Circulation: 250K. Sales: $5-10MM
Products: Clock kits & supplies, clock movements, music movements and boxes

KLUTZ DIRECT   **(800) 737-4123**
450 Lambert Ave. • Palo Alto, CA 94306
E-Mail: thefolks@klutz.com
Website: www.klutz.com
Fax Ordering: (650) 857-9110
International Ordering: (650) 424-0739
Catalog: Free. Frequency: Quarterly
Products: Kids crafts supplies, gifts, art & drawing, games & puzzles, science & building

KOKOVOKO BREEDING FARM   **(800) 804-5541**
RR 3 Box 134 • Corinth, KY 41010
E-Mail: kokovoko@kih.net
Website: www.kokoweb.com
Fax Ordering: (859) 234-5707
International Ordering: (859) 234-5707
Contact Name: Leslie Benensee, President
Catalog: Free. Frequency: Annual
Circulation: 50K. Sales: $10-20MM
Products: Wool, spinning & weaving equipment & supplies

LACE HEAVEN   **(800) 478-5645**
2524 Dauphin Island Pkwy.
Mobile, AL 36605
E-Mail: laceheaven@comcast.net
Website: www.laceheaven.com
Fax Ordering: (251) 450-0489
International Ordering: (251) 478-5644
Contact Name: Patricia Puckett, President
Catalog: Free. Frequency: Semiannual
Circulation: 50K. Sales: $250-500K
Products: Appliques, buttons, fabrics, lace trims, ribbons, books

LACIS (510) 843-7178
3163 Adeline St. • Berkeley, CA 94703
E-Mail: staff@lacis.com
Website: www.lacis.com
Fax Ordering: (510) 843-5018
Contact Name: Jules Kliot, President
Catalog: Free. Frequency: Annual
Circulation: 10K. Sales: $500K
Products: Books, tools and materials for the
textile arts; manufactures specialized lace making
tools; publishes over 130 books relating to
needlework & costume; antique lace & textiles

LAGUNA CLAY PRODUCT CATALOG (800) 452-4862
& REFERENCE GUIDE
14400 Lomitas Ave.
City of Industry, CA 91746
E-Mail: info@lagunaclay.com
Website: www.lagunaclay.com
Fax Ordering: (626) 333-7694
International Ordering: (626) 330-0631
Contact Name: Jonathan Brooks, President
Catalog: Free. Frequency: Annual
Circulation: 100K. Sales: $50-100MM
Products: Clays, glazes, potter's wheels,
Laguna kickwheels, kilns, banding wheels

THE LAMP SHOP (603) 224-1603
P.O. Box 3606 • Concord, NH 03302
E-Mail: info@lampshop.com
Website: www.lampshop.com
Fax Ordering: (603) 224-6677
International Ordering: (603) 224-1603
Contact Name: Scott O. Kenyon, President
Catalog: Free. Frequency: Weekly
Circulation: 25K. Sales: $1-3MM
Products: Lampshade crafting supplies; lamps,
frames, wire, fabric, tools, parts; books; custom
lampshades and production lampshades

BETTY LAMPEN KNITTING BOOKS (415) 346-4673
2930 Jackson St. • San Francisco, CA 94115
E-Mail: orders@bettylampenknitbooks.com
Website: www.bettylampenknitbooks.com
Fax Ordering: (415) 674-1114
Contact Name: Betty Lampen, President
Catalog: Free. Frequency: Monthly
Circulation: 5K. Sales: $250K
Products: Books on knitting & crafts: dolls,
animals, hats, teddy bears

LION BRAND YARN (800) 258-9276
135 Kero Rd. • Carlstadt, NJ 07072
E-Mail: info@lionbrand.com
Website: www.lionbrand.com
Customer Service: (800) 661-7551
Technical Support: (800) 705-8636
Catalog: Free. Frequency: Semiannual
Circulation: 150K. Sales: $1-3MM
Products: Knitting yarn

LOOSE ENDS (503) 390-2348
2065 Madrona Ave. SE • Salem, OR 97302 (503) 390-7457
E-Mail: info@looseends.com
Website: www.looseends.com
Fax Ordering: (503) 390-4724
Contact Name: Art & Sandi Reinke, Owners
Catalog: Free. Frequency: Semiannual
Circulation: 50K. Sales: $1-3MM
Products: Handmade papers, gifts, interior
design and decorations, bamboo furniture

MAPLEWOOD CRAFTS (800) 899-0134
Humboldt Industries
1 Maplewood Dr.
West Hazleton, PA 18201
E-Mail: humboldt@ccomm.com
Fax Ordering: (570) 384-2500
International Ordering: (570) 384-5555
Contact Name: Melanie Rosenzweig, Marketing
Catalog: Free. Frequency: Bimonthly
Circulation: 250K. Sales: $10-25MM
Products: Crafts from bead kits to needlepoint

MARTINGALE & CO. CATALOGS (800) 426-3126
20205 144th Ave. NE
Woodinville, WA 98072
E-Mail: info@martingale-pub.com
Website: www.patchwork.com
Fax Ordering: (425) 486-7596
International Ordering: (425) 483-3313
Contact Name: Dan Martin, President
Catalog: Free. Frequency: Semiannual
Circulation: 100K. Sales: $10-20MM
Products: Craft & hobby books; knitting &
crochet; quilting; fiber arts

MARY MAXIM (800) 962-9504
P.O. Box 5019 • Port Huron, MI 48061
E-Mail: info@marymaxim.com
Website: www.marymaxim.com
Fax Ordering: (810) 987-5056
International Ordering: (810) 987-2000
Contact Name: Robert L. McManaman, Marketing
Catalog: Free. Frequency: Quarterly
Circulation: 250K. Sales: $10-20MM
Products: Needlework, crafts and latch hook rug;
knit & crochet; Christmas kits, fashion kits, decorator
Afghans; yarn crafts & accessories

MEININGER FINE ART SUPPLIES (800) 950-2787
499 Broadway • Denver, CO 80203
E-Mail: orders2@meininger.com
Website: www.meininger.com
Fax Ordering: (303) 871-8676
International Ordering: (303) 698-3838
Contact Name: Henry R. Meininger, Owner
Catalog: Free. Frequency: Annual
Circulation: 100K. Sales: $5-10MM
Products: Discount art supplies & materials

MICRO-MARK (800) 225-1066
340 Snyder Ave.
Berkeley Heights, NJ 07922
E-Mail: info@micromark.com
Website: www.micromark.com
Fax Ordering: (908) 665-9383
International Ordering: (908) 464-2984
Catalog: Free. Frequency: Monthly
Circulation: 100K. Sales: $1-3MM
Products: Crafts; hobby, professional and
educational model building; jewelry making;
gourd carving; dollhouse miniatures; home
machine shop

MIMI'S DOLLMAKER'S PARADISE (732) 899-0804
P.O. Box 662 • Point Pleasant, NJ 08742
E-Mail: mimi@mimidolls.com
Website: www.mimidolls.com
Catalog: Free. Frequency: Quarterly.
Circulation: 25K. Sales: $250-500K
Products: Dollmaking books & patterns

R.C. MOORE ARTS & CRAFTS   (888) 226-6673
1581 Niagara Falls Blvd.
Amherst, NY 14228
E-Mail: sales@acmoore.com
Website: www.acmoore.com
International Ordering: (716) 834-2290
Catalog: Free. Frequency: Annual
Circulation: 150K. Sales: $10-50MM
Products: Arts, crafts & floral merchandise

MOUNTAIN LOOM COMPANY   (800) 238-0296
P.O. Box 509 • Vader, WA 98593
E-Mail: custserv@mtnloom.com
Website: www.mtnloom.com
Fax Ordering: (360) 295-3287
International Ordering: (360) 295-3856
Contact Name: Joyce Anderson, President
Catalog: Free. Frequency: Annual
Circulation: 100K. Sales: $1-3MM
Products: Weaving looms for hand weaver
hobbyists and professionals; supplies and
accessories, books and bags

MY SENTIMENTS EXACTLY   (719) 260-6001
633 Elkton Dr.
Colorado Springs, CO 80907
E-Mail: orders@sentiments.com
Website: www.sentiments.com
Fax Ordering: (719) 522-0797
Contact Name: Amy L. Kennedy, President
Catalog: $4. Frequency: Semiannual
Circulation: 10K. Sales: $500K to $1MM
Products: Rubber stamps

NANCY'S NOTIONS   (800) 833-0690
P.O. Box 683 • Beaver Dam, WI 53916
Website: www.nancysnotions.com
E-mail: custserv@nancysnotions.com
Fax Ordering: (800) 255-8119; (920) 887-2133
International Ordering: (920) 887-0391
Customer Service: (800) 245-5116
Catalog: Free. Frequency: Semiannual
Circulation: 150K. Sales: $5-10MM
Products: Sewing & quilting supplies;
fabrics & patterns; embroidery designs

NASCO ARTS & CRAFTS CATALOG   (800) 558-9595
P.O. Box 901 • Fort Atkinson, WI 53538
E-Mail: custserv@enasco.com
Website: www.enasco.com
Fax Ordering: (920) 563-8296
International Ordering: (920) 563-2446
Contact Names: Richard Ciurczak, President
Catalog: Free. Frequency: Annual
Circulation: 200K. Sales: $10-20MM
Products: Kindergarten-to-college selection
of arts & crafts supplies

NATIONAL ARTCRAFT COMPANY   (888) 937-2723
300 Campus Dr. • Aurora, OH 44202
E-Mail: sales@nationalartcraft.com
Website: www.nationalartcraft.com
Fax Ordering: (800) 292-4916; (330) 562-3507
International Ordering: (330) 562-3500
Contact Name: Jon Berrie, President
Catalog: Free. Frequency: Semiannual
Circulation: 100K. Sales: $5-10MM
Products: Ceramic supplies; craft, hobby &
art supplies; wholesale resource for specialized
craft, dollmaking, art & hobby components
supplies and gifts

NAZ-DAR COMPANY CATALOG   (800) 736-7636
1087 N. Branch St. • Chicago, IL 60622
Fax Ordering: (312) 943-8215
International Ordering: (312) 943-8338
Contact Name: Jim Walsh, President
Catalog: Free. Frequency: Annual
Circulation: 200K. Sales: $10-20MM
Products: Fine arts printing supplies, banners,
binder covers, posters & textiles

NEEDLECRAFT SHOP CATALOG   (800) 259-4000
23 Old Pecan Rd. • Big Sandy, TX 75755
E-Mail: info@needlecraftshop.com
Website: www.needlecraftshop.com
Fax Ordering: (903) 636-4088
International Ordering: (903) 636-4011
Contact Name: Ange VanArman, Contact
Catalog: Free. Frequency: Quarterly
Circulation: 2MM. Sales: $5-10MM
Products: Plastic canvas and crochet
pattern tools and books

NEW ENGLAND BASKET CO.   (800) 524-4484
P.O. Box 1335 • N. Falmouth, MA 02556
E-Mail: sales@nebasketco.com
Website: www.nebasketco.com
Fax Ordering: (508) 295-4884
International Ordering: (508) 295-8298
Contact Name: Rick Spearin, President
Catalog: Free. Frequency: Annual
Circulation: 100K. Sales: $1-3MM
Products: Baskets & basketmaking supplies

NEW YORK CENTRAL ART SUPPLY   (800) 950-6111
62 Third Ave. • New York, NY 10003
E-Mail: info@nycentralart.com
Website: www.nycentralart.com
Fax Ordering: (212) 475-2513
International Ordering: (212) 473-7705
Contact Name: Steve Steinberg, President
Catalog: Free. Frequency: Semiannual
Circulation: 25K. Sales: $5-10MM
Products: Art & drafting materials

NORDIC NEEDLE   (800) 433-4321
1314 Gateway Dr. SW • Fargo, ND 58103
E-Mail: info@nordicneedle.com
Website: www.nordicneedle.com
Fax Ordering: (701) 235-0952
International Ordering: (701) 235-5231
Contact Name: Susan Meir, President
Catalog: Free. Frequency: Annual
Circulation: 100K. Sales: $1-3MM
Products: Needlework, cross stitch;
needlwrok supplies, kits & patterns; books

NORTH CAROLINA BASKET WORKS   (800) 338-4972
Suzanne Moore's NC Basket Works
P.O. Box 744 • Vass, NC 28394
E-Mail: suzanne@ncbasketworks.com
Website: www.ncbasketworks.com
Fax Ordering: (910) 245-3243
International Ordering: (910) 245-3049
Contact Name: Suzanne Moore, Owner
Catalog: Free. Frequency: Annual
Circulation: 150K. Sales: $500K
Products: Basketweaving supplies &
chair caning supplies

NORTHEASTERN SCALE MODELS   (800) 840-0028
609 Entler Ave. #3 • Chico, CA 95928
E-Mail: info@nesm.com

Website: www.nesm.com
Fax Ordering: (530) 896-0831
International Ordering: (530) 896-0801
Contact Name: Jean Oriol, President
Catalog: Free. Frequency: Annual
Circulation: 25K. Sales: $5-10MM
Products: Doll house building materials
& model building materials

NOVASPACE GALLERY CATALOG (800) 727-6682
P.O. Box 37197 • Tucson, AZ 85705
E-Mail: staff@novaspace.com
Website: www.novaspace.com
Fax Ordering: (520) 292-9852
International Ordering: (520) 888-2424
Contact Name: Kim Poor, President
Catalog: Free. Frequency: Annual
Circulation: 25K. Sales: $1-3MM
Products: Space art gallery, including paintings,
prints, posters & cards

ORIENTAL TRADING CO. CATALOGS (800) 875-8480
P.O. Box 2308 • Omaha, NE 68103 (800) 348-6483
E-Mail: info@orientaltrading.com In Canada (800) 228-8818
Website: www.orientaltrading.com
Fax Ordering: (800) 327-8904; (402) 596-2364
International Ordering: (402) 331-6800
Catalog: Free. Frequency: Quarterly
Circulation: 3MM. Sales: $50-100MM
Products: Collection of art, studio & aurbursh supplies

OSCE ROBERTS (800) 828-5449
412 37th St. • Birmingham, AL 35201
E-Mail: info@osceroberts.com
Website: www.osceroberts.com
Fax Ordering: (205) 595-8643
International Ordering: (205) 591-6284
Catalog: Free. Frequency: Annual
Circulation: 200K. Sales: $1-3MM
Products: Stamps and stamp supplies

PAM EAST CATALOG (678) 566-0447
4950 Streamside Dr.
Johns Creek, GA 30022
Alpharetta, GA 30022
E-Mail: sales@pameast.net
Website: www.pameast.net
Contact: Pam East, CEO
Catalog: Free. Frequency: Annual
Circulation: 50K. Sales: $250-500K
Products: Art clay silver and glass enamel bead
making tools & supplies

PAM TAILOR SUPPLY (617) 265-8500
625 Adams St. • Dorchester, MA 02122
E-Mail: info@kellycrafts.com
Website: www.kellycrafts.com
Fax Ordering: (617) 265-4540
Catalog: $2; 1st copy free. Frequency: Quarterly
Circulation: 50K. Sales: $500K
Products: Tailoring threads & supplies

PANTHER PRIMITIVES (800) 487-2684
P.O. Box 32 • Normantown, WV 25267
E-Mail: info@pantherprimitives.com
Website: www.pantherprimitives.com
Fax Ordering: (304) 462-7755
International Ordering: (304) 462-7718
Catalog: $2. Frequency: Annual
Circulation: 10K. Sales: $500K - $1MM
Products: Native American historical reproduction
tents & supplies, teepees, camping gear

PAPER WISHES (800) 227-9595
Hot Off the Press, Inc. (888) 300-3406
1250 NW Third Ave. • Canby, OR 97013
E-Mail: info@hotp.com
Website: www.paperwishes.com
Fax Ordering: (503) 266-8749
International Ordering: (503) 266-9102
Customer Service: (800) 753-7422
Catalog: Free. Frequency: Semiannual
Circulation: 100K. Sales: $1-3MM
Products: Craft ideas and instruction books;
kids scrapbooking, floral design, bridal crafts,
scrapbooking, and artsy collage

PEACOCK ALLEY NEEDLEPOINT (877) 550-9898
410 Ada Dr. • Ada, MI 49301
E-Mail: peacockalleynp@me.com
Website: www.peacockalleyneedlepoint.com
International Ordering: (616) 682-9854
Catalog: Free. Frequency: Annual
Circulation: 50K. Sales: $500MK
Products: Needlework kits & canvases

PETERBORO BASKET COMPANY (800) 553-3919
P.O. Box 120 • Peterborough, NH 03458
E-mail: info@peterborobasket.com
Website: www.peterborobasket.com
Fax Ordering: (603) 924-9261
International Ordering: (603) 924-3861
Catalog: Online newsletter. Sales: $5-10MM
Product: Handmade baskets made in the U.S.
including, picnic, waste, bread, laundry, etc.

H.H. PERKINS COMPANY (800) 462-6660
222 Universal Drive So.
North Haven, CT 06473
E-Mail: info@hhperkins.com
Website: www.hhperkins.com
Fax Ordering: (203) 787-1161
International Ordering: (203) 787-1123
Contact Name: Ray DeFrancesco, President
Catalog: Free. Frequency: Semiannual
Circulation: 150K. Sales: $1-3MM
Products: Caning, macrame; basketry kits &
supplies; seat & basket weaving supplies,
repair and furniture restorations

PLASTICWORKING CATALOG (800) 922-0977
Abbeon Call, Inc.
123 Gray Ave. • Santa Barbara, CA 93101
E-Mail: info@abbeon1.com
Website: www.abbeon1.com
Fax Ordering: (805) 966-7659
International Ordering: (805) 966-0810
Contact Name: Alice Wertheim, President
Catalog: Free. Frequency: Annual
Circulation: 150K. Sales: $5-10MM
Products: Plasticworking supplies & equipment

THE POTTERS SHOP (781) 449-7687
31 Thorpe Rd. • Needham, MA 02494
E-Mail: pottersshop@aol.com
Fax Ordering: (781) 449-9098
Catalog: Free. Frequency: Semiannual
Circulation: 50K. Sales: $500K
Products: Discount pottery books, videos & tools

PRAIRIE EDGE TRADING CO. (800) 541-2388
P.O. Box 8303 • Rapid City, SD 57709
E-Mail: prairie@rapidnet.com
Website: www.prairieedge.com
Fax Ordering: (605) 341-6415

International Ordering: (605) 342-3086
Contact Name: Ray Hillenbrand, President
Catalog: Free. Frequency: Annual
Circulation: 25K. Sales: $3-5MM
Products: Plains Indian art & artifacts; jewelry,
pottery, beads, craft supplies; books, tapes,
CDs & DVDs, videos.

PRIMA BEAD CATALOG   (800) 366-2218
P.O. Box 2918 • Largo, FL 33779
E-Mail: customerservice@primabead.com
Website: www.primabead.com
Fax Ordering: (800) 366-6121
International Ordering: (727) 536-1492
Contact Name: Michael Cousin, President
Catalog: Free. Frequency: Semiannual
Circulation: 500K. Sales: $5-10MM
Products: Jewelry-making supplies &
accessories, including beads, and kits

QUILTING BOOKS UNLIMITED   (800) 347-3261
13772 Cottage Dr. • Grand Haven, MI 49417
E-Mail: qbu@qbu.com
Website: www.qbu.com
International Ordering: (616) 842-3304
Contact Names: Betty Roberts, Owner
Catalog: Free. Frequency: Annual
Circulation: 25K. Sales: $250-500K
Products: Books on quilting & fiber arts,
such as stitchery & lacemaking

RGWS CATALOG   (800) 765-1272
Rio Grande Weavers Supply
216 B Pueblo Norte • Taos, NM 87571
E-Mail: weaving@weavingsouthwest.net
Website: www.weavingsouthwest.com
Fax Ordering: (575) 758-5839
International Ordering: (575) 758-0433
Contact Name: Rachel Brown, President
Catalog: Free. Frequency: Quarterly
Circulation: 10K. Sales: $500K
Products: Weaving and spinning equipment
& accessories; hand-dyed yarns for knitters &
weavers

RAINBOW ART GLASS   (800) 526-2356
1761 State Rt. 34 South
Farmingdale, NJ 07727
E-Mail: service@rainbowartglass.com
Website: www.rainbowartglass.com
Fax Ordering: (732) 681-4984
International Ordering: (732) 681-6003
Contact Name: Charles M. Longo, President
Catalog: Free. Frequency: Annual
Circulation: 50K. Sales: $3-5MM
Products: Stained glass kits

REX ART SUPPLIES   (800) 739-2782
3160 SW 22nd St. • Miami, FL 33145
E-Mail: info@rainbowartglass.com
Website: www.rainbowartglass.com
Fax Ordering: (305) 445-1412
International Ordering: (305) 445-1413
Catalog: Free. Frequency: Annual
Circulation: 50K. Sales: $3-5MM
Products: Graphic art supplies

ROWE POTTERY WORKS   (608) 423-3363
404 England St. • Cambridge, WI 53523
Fax Ordering: (608) 423-4273
Contact Name: James Rowe, President
Catalog: Free. Frequency: 3x per year

Circulation: 100K. Sales: $3-5MM
Products: Handmade salt-glaze stoneware,
redware pottery & wrought iron

ROYALWOOD BASKET WEAVING   (800) 526-1630
SEAT WEAVING SUPPLIES
Royalwood, Ltd.
517 Woodville Rd. • Mansfield, OH 44907
E-Mail: orders@royalwoodorders.com
Website: www.royalwoodltd.com
Fax Ordering: (888) 526-1618; (419) 526-1618
International Ordering: (419) 526-1630
International Fax Ordering: (419) 526-1618
Contact Name: Kathy Halter, President
Catalog: Free. Pages: 46. Frequency: Annual
Circulation: 25K. Sales: $500K
Products: Basketweaving and chair caning
supplies; threads, beads

RYNNE CHINA COMPANY   (800) 468-1987
222 W. Eight Mile Rd. • Hazel Park, MI 48030
E-Mail: info@rynnechina.com
Website: www.rynnechina.com
Fax Ordering: (248) 542-0047
International Ordering: (248) 542-9400
Contact Name: Cathy Damaska, President
Catalog: Free. Frequency: Annual
Circulation: 250K. Sales: $3-5MM
Products: White procelain and art supplies

S&S BEST OF THE BEST   (800) 243-9232
S&S Worldwide   (800) 288-9941
75 Mill St. • Colchester, CT 06415   (800) 937-3482
E-Mail: service@ssww.com
Website: www.ssww.com
Fax Ordering: (800) 566-6678; (860) 537-2866
International Ordering: (860) 537-2325
Contact Name: Stephen Schwartz, President
Catalog: Free. Frequency: Quarterly
Circulation: 500K. Sales: $20-50MM
Products: Kid tested arts & crafts supplies &
accessories, games & activities, novelties, &
personalized gift items

SAX ARTS & CRAFTS   (800) 558-6696
School Specialty, Inc.   (888) 388-3224
W6316 Design Dr. • Greenville, WI 54942
P.O. Box 8105 • Mansfield, OH 44901
E-Mail: orders@schoolspecialty.com
Website: www.saxfcs.com
Fax Ordering: (888) 388-6344; (419) 589-1600
International Ordering: (419) 589-1425
Contact Name: Greg Cessna, President
Catalog: Free. Frequency: Semiannual
Circulation: 250K. Sales: $20-50MM
Products: Arts & crafts supplies & equipment

SCHACHT SPINDLE COMPANY   (303) 442-3212
6101 Ben Pl. • Boulder, CO 80301
E-Mail: info@schachtspindle.com
Website: www.schachtspindle.com
Fax Ordering: (303) 447-9273
International Ordering: (303) 442-3212
Contact Name: Barry Schacht, President
Catalog: Free. Frequency: Annual
Circulation: 100K. Sales: $1-3MM
Products: Weaving and spinning equipment;
tools for handweavers and handspinners

SCHIFFER ARTS & CRAFTS CATALOG   (610) 593-1777
4880 Lower Valley Rd. • Atglen, PA 19310
E-Mail: info@schifferbooks.com

Website: www.schifferbooks.com
Fax Ordering: (610) 593-2002
Contact Name: Peter B. Schiffer, President
Catalog: Free. Pages: 32. Frequency: Quarterly
Circulation: 200K. Sales: $5-10MM
Products: Books on arts & crafts; wood carving, wood turning, model building & painting; textiles & materials; weaving & rugs; jewelry making & design; home & garden; sculpture & metalwork

SCHWARZ GALLERY CATALOG (215) 563-4887
1806 Chestnut St. • Philadelphia, PA 19103
E-Mail: mail@schwarzgallery.com
Website: www.schwarzgallery.com
Fax Ordering: (215) 561-5621
Contact Names: Robert Schwarz, President
Catalog: Free. Frequency: Semiannual
Circulation: 25K. Sales: $1-3MM
Products: Fine paintings, antique furniture & silver items

SCULPTURE HOUSE (609) 466-2986
P.O. Box 69 • Skillman, NJ 08558
E-Mail: customercare@sculpturehouse.com
Website: www.sculpturehouse.com
Fax Ordering: (888) 529-1980
Contact Name: Bruner F. Barrie, President
Catalog: Free. Frequency: Annual
Circulation: 100K. Sales: $1-3MM
Products: Sculpturing tools and materials; ceramic clays, mold making & casting, stone carving & stones, wood carving; modeling materials, tools & stands; books

SERRV HANDCRAFTS (800) 723-3712
P.O. Box 365 • New Windsor, MD 21776   (800) 422-5915
E-Mail: orders@serrv.org   (800) 423-0071
Website: www.serrv.org
Fax Ordering: (888) 294-6376; (410) 635-8774
International Ordering: (608) 255-0440; (410) 635-8750
Contact Name: Robert S. Chase, President
Catalog: Free. Frequency: Annual
Circulation: 50K. Sales: $3-5MM
Products: Handcrafted gifts & imported clothing

SHIPWRECK BEADS.COM (800) 950-4232
8560 Commerce Place Dr. NE
Lacey, WA 98516
Website: www.shipwreckbeads.com
E-mail: annac@shipwreckbeads.com
Catalog: Online
Products: Beads, beading needles, tools & accessories

SIEVERS LOOMS (920) 847-2264
P.O. Box 100 • Washington Island, WI 54246
Fax Ordering: (920) 847-2676
Contact Name: Ann Young, President
Catalog: $2. Frequency: Annual
Circulation: 100K. Sales: $1-3MM
Products: Looms, weaving accessories, low-cost plans to build your own looms, loom benches, and accessories

DANIEL SMITH CATALOG (800) 426-6740
4150 1st Ave. S • Seattle, WA 98124
E-Mail: sales@danielsmith.com
Website: www.danielsmith.com
Fax Ordering: (800) 238-4065; (206) 224-0404
International Ordering: (206) 812-5877
Contact Name: Daniel Smith, President
Catalog: Free. Frequency: Annual

Circulation: 250K. Sales: $10-20MM
Products: Graphics & art supplies; watercolor, acrylic & oil paints; brushes; pastels; drawing supplies; printmaking supplies & accessories

SOUTHWEST DECORATIVES (800) 530-8995
5711 Carmel Ave. NE
Albuquerque, NM 87113
E-Mail: swd@swdecoratives.com
Website: www.swdecoratives.com
Fax Ordering: (505) 821-6556
International Ordering: (505) 821-7400
Contact Names: Mary-Jo McCarthy, President
Catalog: Free. Frequency: Annual
Circulation: 50K. Sales: $1-3MM
Products: Quilting, applique, clothing & craft patterns and kits, all with a Southwest theme

SPACESHOTS - IMAGES & IMAGINATIONS (800) 272-2779
26943 Ruether Ave. • Santa Clarita, CA 91351
E-Mail: contact@spaceshots.com
Website: www.spaceshots.com
Fax Ordering: (661) 299-5586
International Ordering: (661) 299-5594
Contact Name: Laura Lancaster, President
Catalog: Free. Frequency: Annual
Circulation: 100K. Sales: $500M to $1MM
Products: Astronomy, NASA & satellite imagery posters; postcards, puzzles & other related space products

STANDARD CERAMIC SUPPLY CO. (412) 276-6333
P.O. Box 16240 • Pittsburgh, PA 15242
E-Mail: info@standardceramic.com
Website: www.standardceramic.com
Fax Ordering: (412) 276-7124
Contact Name: James Turnbull, President
Catalog: Free. Frequency: Annual
Circulation: 10K. Sales: $1-3MM
Products: Supplies & tools for potters

STEEBAR CORP. (800) 236-7300
P.O. Box 607 • Peapack, NJ 07977
E-Mail: sales@steebar.com
Website: www.steebar.com
Fax Ordering: (908) 204-0099
International Ordering: (908) 204-0095
Contact Name: Greg Smith, President
Catalog: Free. Frequency: Annual
Circulation: 150K. Sales: $1-5MM
Products: Clock kits; do-it-yourself clockmaking supplies, scroll saw, fretwork, woodworking plans & patterns, yard decorations, penmaking & turning suppliescomponents

STENCIL EASE (800) 334-1776
P.O. Box 1127 • Old Saybrook, CT 06475
E-Mail: info@stencilease.com
Website: www.stencilease.com
Fax Ordering: (860) 395-0166
International Ordering: (860) 305-0150
Contact Name: Brian Greenho, President
Catalog: Free. Frequency: Semiannual
Circulation: 100K. Sales: $3-5MM
Products: Stencils, home decorating stencils, paints, stencil brushes

SUDBERRY HOUSE (860) 739-6951
323 Boston Post Rd. #3   (860) 388-9045
Old Saybrook, CT 06475
E-Mail: sales@sudberry.com
Website: www.sudberry.com
Fax Ordering: (860) 739-9267

Contact Names: David & Judit Beers, Owners
Catalog: $2.50. Frequency: Annual
Circulation: 50K. Sales: $1-3MM
Products: Wood products and accessories
for displaying needlework

SUNBRAND CATALOG   (800) 241-6800
Dunlap Sunbrand International   (800) 626-9200
P.O. Box 751 • Hopkinsville, KY 42241
E-Mail: info@sunbrand.com
Website: www.sunbrand.com
Fax Ordering: (800) 228-7550; (270) 885-6210
International Ordering: (270) 886-1390
Catalog: Free. Frequency: Annual
Circulation: 50K. Sales: $20-50MM
Products: Reconditioned sewing, cutting and
finishing equipment; sewing machine parts, supplies
accessories, and equipment for manufacturers

SUNSHINE DISCOUNT CRAFTS   (800) 729-2878
P.O. Box 516 • Safety Harbor, FL 34695
E-Mail: info@sunshinecrafts.com
Website: www.sunshinecrafts.com
Fax Ordering: (727) 531-2739
International Ordering: (727) 538-2878
Contact Name: Cathy Damaska, President
Catalogs: $5 ea.Pages: 160.
Frequency: Annual, with bi-weekly newsletter
Circulation: 200K. Sales: $5-10MM
Products: 14,000 brand name discount craft supplies

SUNSHINE GLASSWORKS   (800) 828-7159
111 Industrial Pkwy. • Buffalo, NY 14227
E-Mail: info39@sunshineglass.com
Website: www.sunshineglass.com
Fax Ordering: (716) 668-2932
International Ordering: (716) 668-2918
Contact Name: Scott G. Emslie, President
Catalog: $5. Frequency: Quarterly
Circulation: 25K. Sales: $1-3MM
Products: Stained glass materials for the
professional and hobbyist

TC MOULDING CATALOG   (800) 735-3025
1880 Oakcrest Ave. • St. Paul, MN 55113
E-Mail: sales@tcmoulding.com
Website: www.tcmoulding.com
Fax Ordering: (800) 735-0860; (651) 636-8153
International Ordering: (651) 636-6646
Contact Name: Tom Swanson, President
Catalog: Free. Frequency: Semiannual
Circulation: 10K. Sales: $1-3MM
Products: Moulding, hardware & other
graphic supplies

TARA MATERIALS CATALOG   (800) 241-8129
P.O. Box 646 • Lawrenceville, GA 30046
E-Mail: info@taramaterials.com
Website: www.taramaterials.com
Fax Ordering: (800) 882-8272; (770) 963-1044
International Ordering: (770) 963-5256
Contact Name: Michael Benator, President
Catalog: Free. Frequency: Annual
Circulation: 200K. Sales: $10-20MM
Products: Artists' canvas, brushes & materials;
'picture frames

TEN PLUS, INC. CATALOG   (888) 944-8899
13620 Excelsior Dr.
Santa Fe Springs, CA 90670
E-Mail: tenplusframes@msn.com
Website: www.tenplusframes.com

Fax Ordering: (562) 404-9700
Contact Name: Gene Liao, President
International Ordering: (562) 404-0088
Catalog: Free. Frequency: Semiannual
Circulation: 100K. Sales: $3-5MM
Products: Picture frames & mouldings

TESTRITE VISUAL CATALOGS   (888) 873-2735
216 S. Newman St. • Hackensack, NJ 07601
E-Mail: info@testrite.com
Website: www.testrite.com
Fax Ordering: (201) 543-2195
International Ordering: (201) 543-0240
Contact Name: Laurence Ruben, President
Catalog: Free. Frequency: Annual
Circulation: 100K. Sales: $10-20MM
Products: Visual display accessories for the
exhiibitor, point-of-purchase, sign, store fixture,
visual merchandise; graphic display hardware;
easels & presentation products

TEXAS ART SUPPLY CATALOG   (800) 888-9278
2001 Montrose Blvd. • Houston, TX 77006
E-Mail: customerservice@texasart.com
Website: www.texasart.com
Fax Ordering: (713) 526-4062
International Ordering: (713) 526-5221
Contact Name: John Gilbreath, President
Catalog: Free. Frequency: Annual
Circulation: 100K. Sales: $10-20MM
Products: Art & craft supplies; books &
videos; kid's art supplies; gift ideas

TRAILSIDE GALLERIES CATALOG   (800) 777-6086
P.O. Box 1149 • Jackson, WY 83001
7330 Scottsdale Mall • Scottsdale, AZ 85251
E-Mail: info@trailsidegalleies.com
Website: www.trailsidegalleies.com
Fax Ordering: (307) 733-0369; (480) 946-9025
International Ordering: (307) 733-3186; (480) 945-7751
Contact Name: Thomas Myers, President
Catalog: Free. Frequency: Annual
Circulation: 100K. Sales: $1-3MM
Products: Fine Western art; landscape art;
Southwestern art

TURNCRAFT CLOCKS   (800) 544-1711
Meisel Hardware Specialties   (800) 441-9870
P.O. Box 70 • Mound, MN 55364
E-Mail: office@meiselwoodhobby.com
Website: www.meiselwoodhobby.com
Fax Ordering: (952) 471-8579
International Ordering: (952) 471-8550
Technical Support: (952) 746-2379
Contact Name: Eric Meisel, President
Catalog: Free. Frequency: Semiannual
Circulation: 100K. Sales: $5-10MM
Products: Wood clock plans, kits, movements
and hardware

TRIDENT INDUSTRIAL PRODUCTS   (800) 327-1830
5401 NW 102nd Ave., #101
Sunrise, FL 33351
E-Mail: tridnt8555@aol.com
Website: www.tridentfabrics.com
Fax Ordering: (954) 726-3713
International Ordering: (954) 726-0270
Catalog: Free. Frequency: Annual
Circulation: 150K. Sales: $1-3MM
Products: Recreational, industrial and
marine fabrics

UNICORN BOOKS & CRAFTS   (800) 289-9276
1338 Ross St. • Petaluma, CA 94954
E-Mail: info@unicornbooks.com
Website: www.unicornbooks.com
Fax Ordering: (707) 762-0335
International Ordering: (707) 762-3362
Catalog: Free. Frequency: Annual
Circulation: 100K. Sales: $1-3MM
Products: Needlework and textile craft books;
textile winding equipment; KA bamboo needles
& notions

UNITED ART GLASS   (800) 323-9670
2200 Ogden Ave. #300 • Lisle, IL 60532
E-Mail: unitedartglass@sbcglobal.net
Website: www.unitedartglass.com
Fax Ordering: (630) 852-7940
International Ordering: (630) 852-3344
Contact Name: Ed Pawlski, President
Catalog: Free. Frequency: Annual
Circulation: 100K. Sales: $1-3MM
Products: Stained glass supplies

UNIVERSAL ART IMAGES   (800) 326-1367
P.O. Box 698 • Osprey, FL 34229
E-Mail: ucslide@aol.com
Website: www.universalcolorslide.com
Fax Ordering: (800) 487-0250
International Fax Ordering: (941) 966-4069
International Ordering: (941) 966-3632
Contact Name: Marjorie Crawford, President
Catalogs: Free. Pages: 146. Frequency: Annual
Circulation: 150K. Sales: $1-3MM
Products: Digital images, resources for the visual arts

UTRECHT ART SUPPLIES   (800) 223-9132
6 Corporate Dr. • Cranbury, NJ 08512
E-mail: customerservice@utrecht.com
Website: www.utrechtart.com
Fax Ordering: (800) 382-1979; (609) 409-8002
International Ordering: (609) 409-8001
Customer Service: (800) 223-9132
Contact Name: Jim Peters, President
Catalog: Free. Frequency: Semiannual
Circulation: 100K. Sales: $1-3MM
Products: Art supplies, oil & acrylic colors,
canvas, pads, etc.

VI REED & CANE, INC.   (800) 852-0025
8522 Lakeview Bay Rd. • Rogers, AR 72756
E-Mail: INFO@basketweaving.com
Website: www.basketweaving.com
Fax Ordering: (561) 828-5968
International Ordering: (479) 789-2639
Contact Name: Linda Hebert, President
Catalog: Free. Frequency: Annual
Circulation: 200K. Sales: $1-3MM
Products: Basketweaving supplies & kits;
patterns, instructional videos, webbing, reed,
custom t-shirts

VOSE GALLERIES LLC   (866) 862-4871
238 Newbury St. • Boston, MA 02116
E-Mail: info@voseartgalleries.com
Website: www.voseartgalleries.com
Fax Ordering: (617) 247-8673
International Ordering: (617) 536-6176
Contact Name: Robert C. Vose III, President
Catalog: Free. Frequency: Quarterly
Circulation: 50K. Sales: $500K to $1MM
Products: 18th to 20th century art

WAKEDA TRADING POST   (209) 848-0500
P.O. Box 2114 • Oakdale, CA 95361
E-Mail: info@wakeda.com
Website: www.wakeda.com
Contact Name: Cliff C. Paulsen, President
Catalog: Free. Frequency: Monthly
Circulation: 100K. Sales: $250-500K
Products: Native American craft supplies, beads,
feathers, clothing, botanicals, how-to books, videos,
recordings

WARNER-CRIVELLARO STAINED GLASS   (800) 523-4242
795 Roble Rd., Suite A
Allentown, PA 18103
E-Mail: info@warner-criv.com
Website: www.warner-criv.com
Fax Ordering: (610) 264-1010
International Ordering: (610) 264-1100
Contact Name: Marianne Warner, President
Catalog: Free. Frequency: Annual
Circulation: 100K. Sales: $1-3MM
Products: Stained glass supplies

WEAVER LEATHER   (800) 932-8371
P.O. Box 68 • Mt. Hope, OH 44660
E-Mail: info@weaverleather.com
Website: www.leathersupply.com
Fax Ordering: (330) 674-0330
International Ordering: (330) 674-1782
Contact Name: Paul Weaver, President
Catalog: Free. Frequency: Semiannual
Circulation: 100K. Sales: $10-20MM
Products: Wholesale leather, leatherworking &
saddlery supplies; machinery, parts and tools

MARTIN F. WEBER COMPANY   (215) 677-5600
2727 Southampton Rd.
Philadelphia, PA 19154
E-Mail: info@weberart.com
Website: www.weberart.com
Fax Ordering: (215) 677-3336
Contact Name: Michael Gorak, President
Catalog: Free. Frequency: Annual
Circulation: 200K. Sales: $5-10MM
Products: Fine art supplies & accessories

WHITTEMORE-DURGIN CATALOG OF   (800) 262-1790
STAINED GLASS CRAFT SUPPLIES
Whittemore-Durgin Glass Company
825 Market St. • Rockland, MA 02370
E-Mail: info@whittemoredurgin.com
Website: www.whittemoredurgin.com
Fax Ordering: (800) 786-3457; (781) 871-5597
International Ordering: (781) 871-1743
Contact Name: James H. Hepburn, President
Catalog: $3. Frequency: Annual
Circulation: 50K. Sales: $5-10MM
Products: Stained glass supplies; art &
architectural glass

WILD WINGS COLLECTION CATALOG   (800) 445-4833
2101 South Hwy. 61 • Lake City, MN 55041
E-Mail: info@wildwings.com
Website: www.wildwings.com
Fax Ordering: (651) 345-2981
Contact Name: Jennifer White, Contact
Catalog: Free. Frequency: Quarterly
Circulation: 2MM. Sales: $5-10MM
Products: Nature art prints, sculpture,
home furnishings & apparel

WILDLIFE LITHOGRAPHS   (800) 523-1443
1625 Capital Ave. • Madison, WI 53705
E-Mail: wildlife@wildlifelitho.com
Website: www.wildlifelitho.com
Fax Ordering: (608) 233-9422
International Ordering: (608) 233-8650
Contact Name: Richard W. King, President
Catalog: Free. Frequency: Bimonthly
Circulation: 100K. Sales: $500K - $1MM
Products: Wildlife posters & prints

WIMPOLE STREET CREATIONS   (800) 765-0504
P.O. Box 540585
North Salt Lake City, UT 84054
E-Mail: friends@wimpolestreet.com
Website: www.wimpolestreet.com
Fax Ordering: (801) 298-1333
Contact Name: Jean Brown, President
Catalog: Free. Frequency: Bimonthly
Circulation: 100K. Sales: $500K - $1MM
Products: Crafts, crochet & dyed lace, dolls,
pattern books; gifts; home decor; baby items

WINN DEVON FINE ART COLLECTION   (800) 663-1166
6311 Westminster Hwy. #110
Richmond, BC V7C 4V4
E-Mail: sales@encoreartgroup.com
Website: www.winndevon.com
Fax Ordering: (888) 744-8275; (604) 276-4552
International Ordering: (604) 276-4551
Contact Name: Jackie Pederson, President
Catalog: $60. Frequency: Semiannual
Circulation: 1.5M. Sales: $1-3MM
Products: Limited edition prints & fine
art posters

WISCONSIN POTTERY   (800) 669-5196
1082 Park Ave. • Columbus, WI 53925
E-Mail: wispothuntley@ameritech.net
Website: www.wisconsinpottery.com
Fax Ordering: (920) 623-3702
International Ordering: (920) 623-3406
Contact Name: Debra Huntley, President
Catalog: Free. Frequency: Annual
Circulation: 50K. Sales: $500K
Products: Redware pottery

WORDEN SYSTEM   (800) 541-1103
H.L. Worden Company
P.O. Box 519 • Granger, WA 98932
E-Mail: info@wordensystem.com
Website: www.wordensystem.com
Fax Ordering: (509) 854-2021
International Ordering: (509) 854-1557
Contact Name: Howard Worden, President
Catalog: $1. Frequency: Annual
Circulation: 75K. Sales: $500K
Products: Patterns and kits for stained
glass lampshades

WORLDS OF WONDER CATALOG   (703) 847-4251
P.O. Box 814 • McLean, VA 22101
E-Mail: info@wow-art.com
Website: www.wow-art.com
Fax Ordering: (703) 790-9519
Contact Name: Jane Frank, Owner
Catalog: Online. Print (on demand), $15.
Pages: 40. Circulation: 5K. Sales: $500K
Products: Contemporary illustrative & cover art
in fantasy, science fiction & horror; 3-D artwork

WOVEN STITCH-INDIAN   (505) 491-6009
DESIGN NEEDLEWORK
1828 Corte Del Ranchero
Alamagordo, NM 88310
E-Mail: mikemosier@zianet.com
Website: www.zianet.com
Contact Name: Mike Mosier, President
Catalog: Online. Sales: $250-500K
Products: Indian designs in crochet,
needlepoint, latch hook kits and patterns

YARN BARN OF KANSAS, INC.   (800) 468-0035
VICTORIAN VIDEO   (800) 848-0284
930 Massachusetts • Lawrence, KS 66044
E-Mail: yarnbarn@sunflower.com
Website: www.yarnbarn-ks.com
Fax Ordering: (785) 842-0794
International Ordering: (785) 842-4333
Catalog: Free. Frequency: Semiannual
Circulation: 50K. Sales: $500K - $1MM
Products: Knitting supplies & crocheting yarns
for weaving, spinning, and dying; howInstructional
videos in various fiber & related arts

ADDCO INDUSTRIES CATALOG   **(800) 621-8916**
1596 Linville Falls Hwy. • Linville, NC 28646
E-Mail: info@addco.net
Website: www.addco.net
Fax Ordering: (828) 733-1562
Contact Name: Edmond De Marcellus, President
Catalog: Free. Frequency: Annual
Circulation: 25K. Sales: $3-5MM
Products: OEM production parts, service parts,
and performance anti-sway bars & associated parts;
after market high-performance anti-sway bar kits for
cars, trucks, vans, SUVs & RVs

ADSIT COMPANY CATALOG   **(800) 521-7656**
12440 S. Old Rd. • Muncie, IN 47302
E-Mail: info@adsitco.com
Website: www.adsitco.com .
Fax Ordering: (765) 286-4184
International Ordering: (765) 282-1593
Catalog: $9. Frequency: Annual
Circulation: 50K. Sales: $3-5MM
Products: New & used parts & accessories
for Mercedes Benz

ADVANCE ADAPTERS BUYER'S GUIDE   **(800) 350-2223**
P.O. Box 247 • Paso Robles, CA 93447
E-Mail: sales@advanceadapters.com
Website: www.advanceadapters.com
Fax Ordering: (805) 238-4201
International Ordering: (805) 238-7000
Contact Name: Mike Partridge, President
Catalog: Free. Frequency: 36x per year
Circulation: 100K. Sales: $5-10MM
Products: Engine & transmission conversion
adapters, advance adapters, parts & accessories;
transmissionn & transfer case components for 4WD

AEROSTICH RIDERWEARHOUSE   **(800) 222-1994**
8 S. 18th Ave. West • Duluth, MN 55806
E-Mail: sales@aerostich.com
Website: www.aerostich.com
Fax Ordering: (218) 720-3610
International Ordering: (218) 722-1927
Contact Name: Andrew Goldfine, President
Catalog: Free. Frequency: Weekly
Circulation: 250M. Sales: $3-5MM
Products: Motorcycle riders clothing

AIRTECH   **(760) 598-3366**
2530 Fortune Way • Vista, CA 92083
E-Mail: tech@airtech-streamlining.com
Website: www.airtech-streamlining.com
Fax Ordering: (760) 598-3336
Contact Name: Kent Riches, President
Catalog: $Free. Frequency: Annual
Circulation: 50K. Sales: $1-3M
Products: Motorcycle replacement parts

ALTO PRODUCTS CORP.   **(251) 368-7777**
One Alto Way • Atmore, AL 36502
E-Mail: sales@altousa.com
Website: www.altousa.com
Fax Ordering: (251) 368-7774
Catalog: Free. Frequency: Annual
Circulation: 50K. Sales: $20-50M
Products: Clutch plates & automatic
transmission parts

AMERICAN INTERNATIONAL PACIFIC   **(800) 336-6500**
1040 Avenida Acaso   **Canada** **(888) 922-3006**
Camarillo, CA 93012
E-Mail: anthonyp@aius.net
Website: www.aius.net
Fax Ordering: (805) 388-7950
International Ordering: (805) 388-6800
Contact Name: Robert Ponticelli, President
Catalog: Free. Frequency: Semiannual
Circulation: 50K. Sales: $50-100M
Products: Auto stereo installation kits &
automotive accessories

AMERICAN VAN EQUIPMENT   **(800) 526-4743**
149 Lehigh Ave. • Lakewood, NJ 08701
E-Mail: info@americanvan.com
Website: www.americanvan.com
Fax Ordering: (800) 833-8266
International Ordering: (732) 905-5900
Contact Name: Chuck Richter, President
Catalog: Free. Frequency: 9x per year
Circulation: 10K. Sales: $10-20MM
Products: Equipment for your van from racks
& storage to security

AMSOIL FACTORY DIRECT CATALOG   **(800) 777-8491**
14600 Cornwall Lane • Chester, VA 23836   **(888) 826-1166**
E-Mail: greid@amsoil.com
Website: www.synthoils.com
Fax Ordering: (323) 313-1531
International Ordering: (919) 269-3331
Contact Name: Patricia Reid, President
Catalog: Free. Frequency: Semiannual
Circulation: 400K. Sales: $10-20MM
Products: Synthetic motor oils and automotive,
RV & marine performance products

ANTIQUE AUTOMOBILE LITERATURE   **(315) 432-8282**
6710 Brooklawn Pkwy. • Syracuse, NY 13211
E-Mail: info@autolit.com
Website: www.autolit.com
Fax Ordering: (315) 432-8256
Contact Name: Walter Miller, President
Catalog: Free. Frequency: Semiannual
Circulation: 50K. Sales: $500K - $1M
Products: Auto showroom items, repair manuals,
parts books & original automobile & truck sales
brochures

ANTIQUE CYCLE SUPPLY   **(888) 636-8208**
P.O. Box 600 • Rockford, MI 49341
E-Mail: getparts@antiquecyclesupply.com
Website: www.antiquecyclesupply.com
Fax Ordering: (616) 636-8669
International Ordering: (616) 636-4028
Catalog: Free. Pages: 200+. Frequency: Annual
Circulation: 100K. Sales: $10-20MM
Products: Motorcycle parts, accessories, tools
& literature

AUSTIN HEALY CATALOG   **(800) 667-7872**
Moss Motors Ltd.
440 Rutherford St. • Goleta, CA 93117
E-Mail: order@mossmotors.com
Website: www.mossmotors.com
Fax Ordering: (805) 692-2525
International Ordering: (805) 681-3400
Contact Name: Glen Adamser, President
Catalog: Free. Frequency: Quarterly
Circulation: 250K. Sales: $20-50M
Products: British sports car parts &
performance car parts

AUTO BODY TOOLMART (800) 382-1200
2545 Millennium Dr., Unit B • Elgin, IL 60124
E-Mail: info@abtm.com
Website: www.abtm.com
Fax Ordering: (847) 462-9247
Catalog: Free. Frequency: Quarterly
Circulation: 200K. Sales: $10-20M
Products: Automotive equipment, tools & supplies

AUTO CUSTOM CARPETS (800) 352-8216
1429 Noble St. • Anniston, AL 36201
E-Mail: info@accmats.com
Website: www.accmats.com
Fax Ordering: (256) 236-7375
International Ordering: (256) 236-1118
Contact Name: Jeff Mosses, President
Catalog: Online. Sales: $20-50M
Products: Custom automotive carpet & floor
mats for cars & trucks

AUTO-MAT COMPANY (800) 645-7258
69 Hazel St. • Hicksville, NY 11801
E-Mail: info@autointeriors.biz
Website: www.autointeriors.biz
Fax Ordering: (516) 931-8438
International Ordering: (516) 938-8438
Contact Name: Timothy Browner, President
Catalog: Free. Frequency: Annual
Circulation: 50K. Sales: $5-10M
Products: Auto interior restoration products
& accessories

AUTO RESTORATION CAR PARTS (800) 888-5072
Mill Supply, Inc.
P.O. Box 28400 • Cleveland, OH 44128
E-Mail: info@millsupply.com
Website: www.millsupply.com
Fax Ordering: (216) 518-2700
International Ordering: (216) 518-5072
Contact Name: John Shega, Marketing
Catalog: Free. Frequency: Annual
Circulation: 100K. Sales: $10-20MM
Products: Auto & truck/SUV/Van restoration
& replacement parts & supplies

AUTOATLANTA PORSCHE CATALOG (800) 792-4944
Automobile Atlanta
505 S. Marietta Pkwy. SE • Marietta, GA 30060
E-Mail: autdatl@autoatlanta.com
Website: www.autoatlanta.com
Fax Ordering: (770) 424-6833
International Ordering: (770) 427-2844
Contact Name: George Hussey, President
Catalog: $5. Frequency: Quarterly
Circulation: 200M. Sales: $1-3MM
Products: Porsche parts & accessories

AUTOMOTION CATALOG (888) 787-3626
Performance Products
7733 Hayvenhurst Ave. • Van Nuys, CA 91406
E-Mail: ppe_sales@ecklers.net
Website: www.automotion.com
Fax Ordering: (800) 752-6196; (818) 787-2396
International Ordering: (818) 787-7500
Contact Name: Ron Rowen, President
Catalog: Free. Frequency: Annual
Circulation: 500K. Sales: $20-50MM
Products: Porsche parts & accessories

AUTOMOTIVE AIRFILTERS (800) 858-3333
K&N Engineering, Inc.
P.O. Box 1329 • Riverside, CA 92502
E-Mail: info@knfilters.com
Website: www.knfilters.com
Customer Service: (951) 826-4000
Contact Name: Nate Shelton, President
Catalog: Free. Frequency: Annual
Circulation: 150K. Sales: $50-100M
Products: High performance air filters, oil filters,
& air intakes; exhaust systems

AUTOSPORT CATALOG (800) 953-0814
P.O. Box 9036 • Charlottesville, VA 22906
E-Mail: sales@autosportcatalog.com
Website: www.autosportcatalog.com
Fax Ordering: (434) 973-2368
Customer Service: (800) 788-4495
Catalog: Free. Frequency: Semiannual
Circulation: 250K. Sales: $50-100M
Products: Automotive Outfitters; car care & wax,
car covers; clothing & personal; electronics &
navigation; seat covers, tire gauges & inflators

BAER BRAKE SYSTEMS (602) 233-1411
3108 W. Thomas Rd. • Phoenix, AZ 85017
E-Mail: brakes@baer.com
Website: www.baer.com
Fax Ordering: (602) 352-8445
Catalog: Free. Frequency: Annual
Circulation: 50K. Sales: $10-20MM
Products: Baer Claw System brakes

BARS PRODUCTS CATALOG (800) 622-1170
P.O. Box 187 • Holly, MI 48442 (800) 521-7475
E-Mail: mail@barsproducts.com
Website: www.barsproducts.com
Fax Ordering: (248) 634-1505
Catalog: Free. Frequency: Annual
Circulation: 50K. Sales: $10-20MM
Products: Rislone engine treatment, power
steering products; transmission products;
cooling system products; fuel injector cleaner,
ring seal, winter start & upgrade

BAVARIAN AUTOSPORT (800) 535-2002
275 Constitution Ave.
Portsmouth, NH 03801
E-Mail: info@bavauto.com
Website: www.bavauto.com
Fax Ordering: (603) 427-6116
International Ordering: (603) 427-2002
Contact Name: Dave Wason, President
Catalog: Free. Frequency: Quarterly
Circulation: 10K. Sales: $20-50MM
Products: BMW parts & accessories

BELL AUTOMOTIVE PRODUCTS (800) 342-6227
18940 N. Pima Rd. #200
Scottsdale, AZ 85255
E-Mail: info@bellautomotive.com
Website: www.bellautomotive.com
Contact Name: John Schenken, President
Catalog: Free. Frequency: Annual
Circulation: 50K. Sales: $20-50MM
Products: Automotive & truck accessories
& convenience products

ANDY BERNBAUM AUTO PARTS (800) 457-1250
315 Franklin St. • Newton, MA 02458
E-Mail: info@oldmoparts.com
Website: www.oldmoparts.com
Fax Ordering: (617) 244-1164
Customer Service: (617) 244-1118
Contact Name: Andrew F. Bernbaum, President

Catalog: Free. Frequency: Annual
Circulation: 25K. Sales: $500K - $1MM
Products: New parts for old Chrysler product cars

BOB'S AUTOMOBILIA (805) 434-2963
P.O. Box 2119 • Atascadero, CA 93423
E-Mail: bobs@bobsautomobolia.net
Website: www.bobsbuick.com
Fax Ordering: (805) 434-2626
Contact Name: Robert Carrubba, President
Catalog: Free. Frequency: Annual
Circulation: 10K. Sales: $500K
Products: Parts & accessories for 1920-1957 Buicks

BOB'S BMW CATALOG (800) 269-2627
10720 Guilford Rd. • Jessup, MD 20794
E-Mail: sales@bobsbmw.com
Website: www.bobsbmw.com
Fax Ordering: (301) 776-2338
Customer Service: (301) 497-8949
Catalog: Free. Frequency: Annual
Circulation: 100K. Sales: $3-5MM
Products: BMW motorcyles, parts & accessories

BORLA PERFORMANCE'S CATALOG (877) 462-6752
701 Arcturus Ave. • Oxnard, CA 93033
E-Mail: sales@borla.com
Website: www.borla.com
Fax Ordering: (805) 986-8940
International Ordering: (805) 986-8600
Contact Name: Alex Borla, President
Catalog: $4. Frequency: Annual
Circulation: 25K. Sales: $20-50MM
Products: Race winning exhaust systems

BRILLIANT SOLUTION CATALOG (800) 854-8073
Meguiar's, Inc.
17991 Mitchell S. • Irvine, CA 92614
E-Mail: espert@meguiars.com
Website: www.meguiars.com
Fax Ordering: (949) 752-6659
International Ordering: (949) 752-8000
Customer Service: (800) 347-5700
Contact Name: Barry Meguiar, President
Catalog: Free. Frequency: Annual
Circulation: 50K. Sales: $10-20MM
Products: Cleaners, polishes, waxes &
paint correction systems

JIM BUTLER PERFORMANCE CATALOG (866) 762-7527
2336 Hwy. 43 So. • Leoma, TN 38468
E-Mail: info@butlerperformace.net
Website: www.butlerperformance.net
Fax Ordering: (931) 766-1245
International Ordering: (931) 762-4596
Contact Name: David Butler, President
Catalog: Free. Frequency: Quarterly
Circulation: 50K. Sales: $3-5M
Products: Pontiac high performance parts
& supplies and complete engines

C&P 1955-57 CHEVY CARS & TRUCKS (800) 235-2475
C&P Automotive
P.O. Box 348 • Kulpsville, PA19443
E-Mail: sales@cpchevy.com
Website: www.cpchevy.com
Fax Ordering: (610) 584-9509
International Ordering: (610) 584-9105
Catalog: $5. Frequency: Annual
Circulation: 10K. Sales: $3-5M
Products: Two separate catalogs: Cars & Trucks.
Restoration supplies for 55-57 Chevrolet cars & trucks

CALIFORNIA MUSTANG CATALOGS (800) 775-0101
109400 San Jose Ave.
City of Industry, CA 91748
E-Mail: csmustang@cal-mustang.com
Website: www.cal-mustang.com
Fax Ordering: (909) 598-5611
International Ordering: (909) 598-3383
Catalog: Free. Frequency: Annual
Circulation: 100K. Sales: $5-10M
Products: California Mustang Parts & Accessories;
1965-73, 1979-93; 1994-current

CAPITAL CYCLE CORPORATION (800) 642-5100
P.O. Box 798 • Ashburn, VA 20146
E-Mail: sales@capitalcycle.com
Website: www.capitalcycle.com
Fax Ordering: (703) 421-7868
International Ordering: (703) 421-7861
Contact Name: Batiste DeLuka, President
Catalog: Free. Frequency: Annual
Circulation: 75K. Sales: $1-3MM
Products: BMW motorcycle OEM original &
aftermarket parts & accessories

CAR-FRESHENER CORPORATION (800) 545-5454
P.O. Box 719 • Watertown, NY 13601
E-Mail: info@little-trees.com
Website: www.little-trees.com
Fax Ordering: (315) 788-9589; 788-7467
International Ordering: (315) 785-5505
Customer Service: (315) 788-6250
Contact Name: Richard Flechtner, President
Catalog: Free. Frequency: Semiannual
Circulation: 150K. Sales: $10-20MM
Products: Air fresheners & car care products

CAR RACKS DIRECT (800) 722-5734
Outdoor Sports Center
80 Danbury Rd. • Wilton, CT 06897
E-Mail: info@carracksdirect.com
Website: www.carracksdirect.com
Fax Ordering: (203) 761-0812
International Ordering: (203) 762-8324
Contact Name: Jack Maxwell, President
Catalog: Free. Frequency: Annual
Circulation: 50K. Sales: $1-3MM
Products: Multipurpose roof racks, ski racks,
bike racks & rear mount systems

DENNIS CARPENTER CATALOGS (800) 476-9653
4140 Concord Pkwy. So. • Concord, NC 28027
E-Mail: info@dennis-carpenter.com
Website: www.dennis-carpenter.com
Fax Ordering: (704) 786-8180
International Ordering: (704) 786-8139
Contact Name: Dennis Carpenter, President
Catalog: Free. Frequency: Annual
Circulation: 25K. Sales: $5-10MM
Products: Automotive parts & accessories for
specific makes & models of Ford cars & trucks;
Cushman scooters; & 1939-64 Ford Tractors

CENTERLINE ALFA ROMEO PRODUCTS (888) 750-2532
1220 Commerce Ct. • Lafayette, CO 80026
E-Mail: info@centerlinealfa.com
Website: www.centerlinealfa.com
Fax Ordering: (303) 447-0257
International Ordering: (303) 447-0239
Contact Name: Ron Rowen, President
Catalog: Free. Frequency: Semiannual
Circulation: 10K. Sales: $1-3MM
Products: Alfa Romeo parts & accessories

CHEVS OF THE 40s   (800) 999-CHEV
1605 NE 112th St. • Vancouver, WA 98686
E-Mail: info@customclassictrucks.com
Website: www.customclassictrucks.com
Fax Ordering: (800) 888-2438; (360) 816-0215
International Ordering: (360) 816-0211
Contact Name: Ron Wade, President
Catalog: Free. Frequency: Annual
Circulation: 50K. Sales: $3-5MM
Products: Suppliers of 1937-1954 Chevy
car & truck parts

CHEVY TRUCK PARTS CATALOG   (800) 741-1678
1 Chevy Duty Dr. • Kansas City, MO 64150
E-Mail: customerservice@classicparts.com
Website: www.classicparts.com
Fax Ordering: (816) 741-5255
International Ordering: (816) 741-8029
Contact Name: Mark Jansen, President
Catalog: Free. Frequency: Annual
Circulation: 25K. Sales: $3-5MM
Products: Chevy truck parts & supplies

CLARK'S CORVAIR PARTS   (888) 267-8247
400 Mohawk Trail
Shelburne Falls, MA 01370
E-Mail: clarks@corvair.com
Website: www.corvair.com
Fax Ordering: (888) 625-8498; (413) 625-8498
International Ordering: (413) 625-9776
Contact Name: Calvin M. Clark, Jr., President
Catalog: $6. Frequency: Annual
Circulation: 10K. Sales: $3-5MM
Products: Corvair engines & parts

CLASSIC MOTORBOOKS   (800) 826-6600
Motorbooks • P.O. Box 1 • Osceola, WI 54020
E-Mail: customerservice@motorbooks.com
Website: www.motorbooks.com
Fax Ordering: (715) 294-4448
International Ordering: (715) 294-3345
Contact Name: Tim Parker, President
Catalog: Free. Frequency: Semiannual
Circulation: 100K. Sales: $3-5MM
Products: Automotive books, shop manuals
& restoration books

CLASSIC MUSTANG CATALOG   (800) 243-2742
24-A Robert Porter Rd.
Southington, CT 06489
E-Mail: mustangrestoration@yahoo.com
Website: www.cmustang.com
Fax Ordering: (860) 276-9986
International Ordering: (860) 276-9704
Contact Name: David Scranton, President
Catalog: $3. Frequency: Annual
Circulation: 10K. Sales: $3-5MM
Products: Mustang parts & accessories, 1965-2003

OBSOLETE CLASSIC AUTO PARTS   (800) 706-8801
8701 South Interstate 35   (800) 654-3247
Oklahoma City, OK 73149
E-Mail: mustang@classicautopartsgroup.com
Website: www.classicautopartsgroup.com
Fax Ordering: (405) 634-6815
International Ordering: (405) 631-3933
Contact Name: Rex Beagley, President
Catalog: Free. Frequency: Annual
Circulation: 10K. Sales: $3-5MM
Products: Mustang parts & accessories
for Classic Ford Mustang, 1964-1973

CLASSIC THUNDERBIRD ILLUS. PARTS   (800) 374-0914
CASCO • 795 High St.
Coshocton, OH 43812
E-Mail: casco@classictbird.com
Website: www.classictbird.com
Fax Ordering: (740) 622-5151
International Ordering: (740) 622-9700/8561
Catalog: $10. Pages: 72. Frequency: Annual
Circulation: 10K. Sales: $3-5MM
Products: Parts & accessories for classic
Ford Thunderbirds, 1955-1957

COMPETITION ACCESSORIES   (800) 543-4709
345 W. Leffel Lane • Springfield, OH 45506   (800) 543-8208
E-Mail: sales@compacc.com
Website: www.compacc.com
Fax Ordering: (937) 323-9793
International Ordering: (937) 323-0513
Customer Service: (800) 543-6321
Contact Name: Dan Conetta, President
Catalog: Free. Frequency: 9x per year
Circulation: 10K. Sales: $5-10MM
Products: Motorcycle parts & accessories

COVERCRAFT INDUSTRIES   (800) 444-9653
100 Enterprise Blvd. • Pauls Valley, OK 73075
E-Mail: sales@covercraft.com
Website: www.covercraft.com
Fax Ordering: (405) 238-9601
International Ordering: (405) 238-9651
Catalog: Free. Frequency: Semiannual
Circulation: 100K. Sales: $5-10MM
Products: Custom patterned vehicle covers

CORVETTE AMERICA   (800) 458-3475
Auto Accessories of America
100 Classic Car Dr. • Reedsville, PA 17084
E-Mail: info@corvetteamerica.com
Website: www.corvetteamerica.com
Fax Ordering: (717) 667-3174
International Ordering: (717) 667-3004
Contact Name: Peggy LeKander, President
Catalog: Free. Frequency: Annual
Circulation: 200K. Sales: $10-20MM
Products: Corvette parts & accessories, interiors,
fiberglass. Two catalogs: Vintage, 1953-82; 1984-09.

CUSTOM ACCESSORIES   (800) 962-6676
6440 W. Howard St. • Niles, IL 60714
E-Mail: info@causa.com
Website: www.causa.com
Fax Ordering: (847) 966-9650
International Ordering: (847) 966-6900
Contact Name: Ken Matthew, President
Catalog: Free. Frequency: Annual
Circulation: 10K. Sales: $20-50MM
Products: Automotive accessories including car
& wheel covers, mirrors, license frames

DANCHUK MANUFACTURING   (800) 648-9554
3201 S. Standard Ave.
Santa Ana, CA 92705
E-Mail: custserv@danchuk.com
Website: www.danchuk.com
Fax Ordering: (714) 850-1957
International Ordering: (714) 751-1957
Contact Name: Art Danchuk, President
Catalog: Free. Frequency: Annual
Circulation: 30K. Sales: $5-10MM
Products: 1955-57 Chevy restoration parts
& accessories

GLOBAL ACCESSORIES CATALOG   (800) 327-3362
(800) 950-9502
Covercraft Industries, Inc.
P.O. Box 4656 • Logan, UT 84323
E-Mail: customer_questions@global-accessories.com
Website: www.global-accessories.com
Catalog: Free. Frequency: Annual
Circulation: 50K. Sales: $20-50MM
Products: Automotive accessories & convenience
products: Dashmat, Wolf & LeBra brands

DEFLECTA-SHIELD ACCESSORIES   (800) 247-2440
(888) 586-6049
Lund International, Inc.   (800) 782-5448
4325 Hamilton Mill Rd. • Buford, GA 30518
E-Mail: info@lundinternational.com
Website: www.lundinternational.com
Contact Name: Dennis Vollmershausen, President
Catalog: Free. Frequency: Annual
Circulation: 50K. Sales: $20-50MM
Products: Automotive accessories including hood
guards, louvers, fiberglass steps; truck, van,
SUV/CUV accessories

DELTA CONSOLIDATED INDUSTRIES   (800) 643-0084
P.O. Box 1846 • Jonesboro, AR 72403
E-Mail: info@deltastorage.com
Website: www.deltastorage.com
Fax Ordering: (870) 935-4994
Contact Name: Thomas R. Joyce, President
Catalog: Free. Frequency: Annual
Circulation: 25K. Sales: $50-100MM
Products: Truck storage containers, tanks & chests

DESERT RAT OFF-ROAD CATALOG   (800) 528-3402
(866) 444-5337
Desert Rat Truck Center
3705 Palo Verde Rd. • Tucson, AZ 85713
E-Mail: info@desertrat.com
Website: www.desertrat.com
Fax Ordering: (520) 750-1918
International Ordering: (520) 790-9550
Contact Name: Mike Furrier, President
Catalog: Free. Frequency: Semiannual
Circulation: 200K. Sales: $5-10MM
Products: Accessories, tires & wheels for
pickups & 4WD

DISCOUNT VOLVO PARTS   (510) 524-7200
RPR Co., Inc.
599 San Pablo Ave. • Albany, CA 94706
E-Mail: rusty@rprusa.com
Website: www.rprusa.com
Fax Ordering: (510) 524-7409
Catalog: Free. Frequency: Weekly
Circulation: 10K. Sales: $500K - $1MM
Products: Volvo parts & accessories

DOMI RACER DISTRIBUTORS, INC.   (877) 451-0354
VINTAGE CATALOG
P.O. Box 30439 • Cincinnati, OH 45230
E-Mail: domiracer@fuse.net
Website: www.domiracer.com
Fax Ordering: (513) 871-6684
International Ordering: (513) 871-1678
Catalog: Free. Frequency: Annual
Circulation: 50K. Sales: $1-3MM
Products: Vintage British & European
motorcycle parts & accessories

GREG DONAHUE CATALOG   (352) 344-4329
Collector Car Restorations
12900 S. Betty Point • Floral City, FL 34436
E-Mail: info@gregdonahue.com
Website: www.gregdonahue.com

Fax Ordering: (352) 344-0015
Contact Name: Greg Donahue, President
Catalog: $8. Pages: 198. Frequency: Annual
Circulation: 15K. Sales: $500K
Products: Automotive parts & accessories;
specializes in reproduction & NOS Galaxie
parts, from 1963-64

DRIVE RIGHT CATALOG   (800) 678-3669
Davis Instruments Corp.
3465 Diablo Ave. • Hayward, CA 94545
E-Mail: sales@davisnet.com
Website: www.davisnet.com
Fax Ordering: (510) 670-0589
International Ordering: (510) 732-9229
Technical Support: (510) 732-7814
Contact Name: Bob Selig, President
Catalog: Free. Frequency: Annual
Circulation: 150K. Sales: $10-20MM
Products: Vehicle monitor which tracks speed,
acceleration, deceleration & distance for a
comprehensive driving record

JAMES DUFF ENTERPRISES CATALOGS   (865) 938-6696
3231 NW Park Dr. • Knoxville, TN 37921
E-Mail: info@jamesduff.com
Website: www.jamesduff.com
Fax Ordering: (865) 938-6746
Contact Name: James M. Duff, President
Catalogs: $5 & $3. Frequency: Annual
Circulation: 100K. Sales: $5-10MM
Products: Catalogs of accessories & parts for
classic early Ford Bronco, 1966-77; and
Bronco II & Ranger

EAGLE EQUIPMENT - AUTOMOTIVE   (800) 336-2776
SHOP SPECIALISTS
4810 Clover Rd. • Greensboro, NC 27405
E-Mail: info@eagleequip.com
Website: www.eagleequip.com
Fax Ordering: (800) 590-9814
Contact Name: Marc DelChercolo, Marketing
Catalog: Free. Frequency: Annual
Circulation: 100K. Sales: $5-10MM
Products: Automotive shop equipment
specializing in above ground lifts

EASTWOOD CO. AUTOMOTIVE TOOLS   (800) 345-1178
& SUPPLIES FOR AUTO REPAIR &   (800) 343-9353
RESTORATION
263 Shoemaker Rd. • Pottstown, PA 19464
E-Mail: tedg@eastwood.com
Website: www.eastwood.com
Fax Ordering: (610) 644-0560
International Ordering: (610) 640-1450
Technical Support: (866) 759-2131
Contact Name: Curt Strohacker, President
Catalog: Free. Frequency: Monthly
Circulation: 250K. Sales: $20-50MM
Products: Specialty auto restoration tools
& supplies; diecast collectibles

ECKLER'S 1953-2001 CORVETTE   (800) 327-4868
PARTS & ACCESSORIES   (800) 284-3906
Eckler Industries, LLC
5200 S. Washington Ave. • Titusville, FL 32780
E-Mail: sales@ecklers.com
Website: www.ecklers.com
Fax Ordering: (321) 383-2059; 385-2102
International Ordering: (321) 269-9651
Customer Service: (877) 748-4555
Contact Name: Gary Mills, President

Catalog: Free. Frequency: Annual
Circulation: 50K. Sales: $20-50MM
Products: After-market supplier of parts
& accessories for Corvettes

EGGE MACHINE COMPANY   (800) 866-3443
11707 Slauson Ave.
Santa Fe Springs, CA 90670
E-Mail: info@egge.com
Website: www.egge.com
Fax Ordering: (562) 693-1635
International Ordering: (562) 945-3419
Contact Name: Ernie Silvers, CEO
Catalog: Free. Frequency: Annual
Circulation: 10K. Sales: $3-5MM
Products: Automotive parts for older cars, all
makes & models, specializing in American cars

EURO-TIRE CATALOG   (800) 631-0080
500 US Hwy. 46 • Fairfield, NJ 07004
E-Mail: eurotire@att.net
Website: www.eurotire.com
Fax Ordering: (973) 575-6800
International Ordering: (973) 575-0080
Contact Name: William Bloomfield, President
Catalog: Free. Frequency: Semiannual
Circulation: 50K. Sales: $3-5MM
Products: European auto tires & wheels

EXOTO TIFOSI CATALOG   (800) 872-2088
5440 Atlantis Ct. • Moorpark, CA 93021
E-Mail: exoto@aol.com
Website: www.exoto.com
Fax Ordering: (805) 530-3840
International Ordering: (805) 530-3830
Contact Name: Tony Keusseyan, President
Catalog: Free. Frequency: Quarterly
Circulation: 100K. Sales: $5-10MM
Products: Automotive collectibles; racing
collectibles for Ford Motor Corporation

FILLING STATION CATALOG   (800) 841-6622
990 S. Second St. • Lebanon, OR 97355
E-Mail: info@fillingstation.com
Website: www.fillingstation.com
Fax Ordering: (541) 258-6968
Tech Support: (541) 258-2114
Contact Name: Jim Egge, President
Catalog: $7. Frequency: Annual
Circulation: 10K. Sales: $3-5MM
Products: Chevrolet & GMC reproduction parts.

FOLEY-BELSAW LOCKSMITHS   (800) 821-3452
6300 Equitable Rd. • Kansas City, MO 64120
E-Mail: foley@foley-belsaw.com
Website: www.foley-belsaw.com
Fax Ordering: (816) 483-5010
International Ordering: (816) 483-4200
Contact Name: George Doetzl, President
Catalog: Free. Frequency: Quarterly
Circulation: 100K. Sales: $20-50MM
Products: Small engine parts, tools & accessories
for lawnmowers, chainsaws & trimmers

FORD MOTOR COMPANY COLLECTION (888) 380-6663
80 Tech Row • Madison Heights, MI 48071
E-Mail: help@fordcollection.com
Website: www.fordcollection.com
Fax Ordering: (888) 262-9930; (248) 816-5748
International Ordering: (248) 458-5313
Contact Name: Donald O. Wheeler, President
Catalog: Free. Frequency: Annual

Circulation: 200K. Sales: $5-10MM
Products: Ford Motor Company collectible
items from clothing to gifts

FORD PARTS SPECIALISTS   (800) 221-0172
Joblot Automotive, Inc.
98-11 211th St. • Queens Village, NY 11429
E-Mail: joblot@joblotauto.com
Website: www.joblotauto.com
Fax Ordering: (718) 468-8686
International Ordering: (718) 468-8585
Contact Name: Robert Schaeffer, President
Catalog: $2. Frequency: Annual
Circulation: 25K. Sales: $10-20MM
Products: Ford auto parts & supplies

FREEDOM DESIGN CATALOG   (800) 296-8850
Electrodyne, Inc.
4750 Eisenhower Ave. • Alexandria, VA 22304
E-Mail: info@freedomdesign.com
Website: www.freedomdesign.com
Fax Ordering: (703) 823-0842
International Ordering: (703) 823-0202
Contact Name: Chester Vincentz, President
Catalog: $3. Frequency: Semiannual
Circulation: 50K. Sales: $5-10MM
Products: Auto styling, road wheels & accessories
for Porsch, BMW, Mercedes, Volkswagon & Audi

GALAXY TIRE & WHEEL CATALOG   (800) 343-3276
GPX International Tire Corp.
730 Eastern Ave. • Malden, MA 02148
E-Mail: info@gpxtire.com
Website: www.galaxytire.com
Fax Ordering: (781) 322-2147
International Ordering: (781) 321-3910
Contact Name: David Gans, President
Catalog: Free. Frequency: Annual
Circulation: 50K. Sales: $20-50MM
Products: Architectural & industrial tires:
Pneumatic tires, solid tires, radion wheels

GASLIGHT AUTO PARTS   (800) 242-6491
P.O. Box 291 • Urbana, OH 43078
E-mail: gaslight@ctcn.net
Website: www.gaslightauto.com
Fax Ordering: (937) 652-2147
International Ordering: (937) 652-2145
Contact Name: Robert McConnell, President
Catalog: Free. Pages: 194. Frequency: Annual
Circulation: 25K. Sales: $1-3MM
Products: Ford parts for 1909-1948 models

GO-KART WORLD   (770) 253-5374
369-A Temple Ave. • Newman, GA 30263
E-Mail: sales@gokarts.net
Website: www.gokarts.net
Catalog: Free. Frequency: Annual
Circulation: 75K. Sales: $5-10MM
Products: GO Kart tores, wheels, kits & parts;
minibikes, engines, trailer kits & scooters

GOLD EAGLE COMPANY   (800) 621-1251
4400 S. Kildare Ave. • Chicago, IL 60632   (800) 367-3245
E-mail: marketing@goldeagle.com
Website: www.goldeagle.com
Fax Ordering: (773) 376-5749
International Ordering: (773) 376-4400
Contact Name: Richard Hirsch, President
Catalog: Free. Frequency: Annual
Circulation: 150K. Sales: $20-50MM
Products: Power steering, transmission & brake fluids

GOLDEN STATE PICKUP PARTS (800) 235-5717
3493 Arrowhead Dr. • Carson City, NV 89706
E-Mail: info@gspp.com
Website: www.gspp.com
Fax Ordering: (888) 732-2495; (775) 886-7007
International Ordering: (775) 886-7000
Contact Name: Dennis Van Alphen, Production
Catalog: $10. Frequency: Annual
Circulation: 10K. Sales: $3-5MM
Products: Parts for 1947-1987 Chevy
& GMC trucks

MANUAL GOMEZ & ASSOCIATES (800) 325-5646
2013 SW 1st St. • Miami, FL 33135
E-Mail: usamgomez@aol.com
Fax Ordering: (305) 642-7912
International Ordering: (305) 642-0311
Contact Name: Manual Gomez, President
Catalog: Free. Frequency: 8x per year
Circulation: 40K. Sales: $3-5MM
Products: Auto parts & supplies; motor
equipment

HARMON'S CHEVROLET (800) 851-2433
RESTORATION PARTS (888) 439-3522
P.O. Box 100 • Geneva, IN 46740
E-Mail: harmons@harmons.com
Website: www.harmons.com
Fax Ordering: (260) 368-9396
International Ordering: (260) 368-7221
Tech Support: (260) 368-7221
Catalog: $5. Frequency: Annual
Circulation: 50K. Sales: $3-5MM
Products: Weatherstripping, interiors, emblems,
chrome, lenses, sheet metal, fuel tanks owner's
manuals, seat covers

HEIDTS CATALOG (800) 841-8188
Hot Rod Shop
111 Kerry Ln. • Wauconda, IL 60084
E-Mail: sales@heidts.com
Website: www.heidts.com
Fax Ordering: (847) 487-0156
International Ordering: (847) 487-0150
Contact Name: Gary Heidts, President
Catalog: Free. Frequency: Annual
Circulation: 100K. Sales: $3-5MM
Products: Hot rod & Muscle Car parts
& accessories

HEMMING'S CATALOG (800) 227-4373
Hemmings Motor News
P.O. Box 100 • Bennington, VT 05201
E-Mail: info@hemmings.com
Website: www.hemmings.com
Fax Ordering: (802) 447-9631
International Ordering: (802) 442-3101
Contact Name: Terry Ehrich, President
Catalog: Free. Frequency: Semiannual
Circulation: 150K. Sales: $1-3MM
Products: Automotive books, automobilia,
calendars

HIGHLAND GROUP INDUSTRIES (800) 234-6992
Cequent Consumer Products
31200 Solon Rd. • Solon, OH 44139
E-Mail: info@highlandusa.com
Website: www.highlandusa.com
Fax Ordering: (440) 498-1038
International Ordering: (440) 498-4742
Contact Name: Craig Manchen, President
Catalog: Free. Frequency: Annual

Circulation: 100K. Sales: $20-50MM
Products: Accessories for light trucks, sport
utility vehicles, recreation vehicles, passenger
cars & trailers, including car & truck splash
guards, louvers, car top carriers, ski racks,
travel accessories, interior protection

HOPKINS MANUFACTURING CORP. (800) 524-1458
P.O. Box 1157 • Emporia, KS 66801   (800) 279-3212
E-Mail: info@hopkinsmfg.com
Website: www.hopkinsmfg.com
Fax Ordering: (800) 411-0799
International Ordering: (620) 342-7320
Tech Support: (800) 835-0129
Contact Name: Brad Kraft, President
Catalog: Free. Frequency: Semiannual
Circulation: 50K. Sales: $50-100MM
Products: Automotive aftermarket products;
juice booster cables, trailer wiring systems,
ice scrapers, snowbrushes & squeegees

IPD PARTS & ACCESSORIES FOR VOLVOS (800) 444-6473
Import Parts Distributing
11744 NE Ainsworth Cir. • Portland, OR 97220
E-Mail: sales@ipdusa.com
Website: www.ipdusa.com
Fax Ordering: (503) 257-7596
International Ordering: (503) 257-7500
Contact Name: Richard Gordon, President
Catalog: Free. Frequency: Semiannual
Circulation: 75K. Sales: $5-10MM
Products: Parts & accessories for Volvos

IMPCO MACHINE TOOLS CATALOG (517) 484-9411
3417 W. ST. Joseph St. • Lansing, MI 48917
E-Mail: info@impco.com
Website: www.impco.com
Fax Ordering: (517) 484-0502
International Ordering: (517) 484-9411
Contact Name: Ron Rowen, President
Catalog: Free. Frequency: Semiannual
Circulation: 200K. Sales: $20-50MM
Products: Worldstar & worldflex machines for
microfinishing technology used in engine
manufacturing

INDUSTRIAL INFORMATION (800) 762-3361
RESOURCES CATALOG
2277 Plaza Dr. #300 • Sugar Land, TX 77479
Fax Ordering: (713) 266-9306
International Ordering: (713) 783-5147
Contact Name: Edward Lewis, President
Catalog: Free. Frequency: Annual
Circulation: 200K. Sales: $3-5MM
Products: Reports & directories about the
global industrial industry

INTERNATIONAL AUTO PARTS (800) 726-1199
P.O. Box 9036 • Charlottesville, VA 22906
E-Mail: info@international-auto.com
Website: www.international-auto.com
Fax Ordering: (434) 973-2368
International Ordering: (434) 974-7118
Contact Name: Paul Opiela, President
Catalog: Free. Frequency: Quarterly
Circulation: 100K. Sales: $10-20MM
Products: Car care products; auto & travel
accessories for Alfa Romeos, Fiats and Lancias

INTERNATIONAL AUTO PARTS (800) 726-0555
P.O. Box 9036 • Charlottesville, VA 22906
E-Mail: sales@international-auto.com

Website: www.international-auto.com
Fax Ordering: (434) 973-2368
International Ordering: (434) 973-0555
Tech Support: (800) 788-2095
Customer Service: (800) 726-4305
Contact Name: Paul Opiela, President
Catalog: Free. Frequency: 3x per year
Circulation: 500K. Sales: $50-100MM
Products: Porsche racing parts & accessories

JACOBS ELECTRONICS CATALOG   (800) 627-8800
Prestolite Performance
10601 Memphis Ave. #12
Cleveland, OH 44144
E-Mail: info@jacobselectronics.com
Website: www.jacobselectronics.com
Fax Ordering: (915) 687-5951
International Ordering: (216) 688-8300
Contact Name: Christopher A. Jacobs, President
Catalog: Free. Frequency: Monthly
Circulation: 10K. Sales: $20-50MM
Products: High performance ignition systems
for street, coils, plug wires; ACCEL Silver
Tip spark plugs' lightweight battery cables

JAGUAR ACCESSORIES   (800) 832-5839
1815 Maplelawn Dr. • Troy, MI 48084
E-Mail: info@accessories.jaguar.com
Website: www.accessories.jaguar.com
Fax Ordering: (248) 643-9261
International Ordering: (248) 643-7894
Contact Name: Robert Elder, President
Catalog: Free. Frequency: Quarterly
Circulation: 100K. Sales: $10-20MM
Products: Accessories for Jaguars

JARDINE PERFORMANCE PRODUCTS   (800) 347-8664
1180 Railroad St. • Corona, CA 92882
E-Mail: jpinfo@jardineproducts.com
Website: www.jardineproducts.com
Fax Ordering: (909) 371-1623
International Ordering: (951) 371-1623
Contact Name: Rick May, President
Catalog: $4. Frequency: Annual
Circulation: 50K. Sales: $10-20MM
Products: Motorcycle exhaust systems,
grips, footpegs, backrests, racks, etc.

JEFF'S BRONCO GRAVEYARD   (248) 437-5060
7843 Lochlin Dr. • Brighton, MI 48116
E-Mail: jeff@broncograveyard.com
Website: www.broncograveyard.com
Fax Ordering: (248) 437-9354
Contact Name: Jeff Trapp, President
Catalog: Free. Frequency: Quarterly
Circulation: 15K. Sales: $3-5MM
Products: Bronco parts & accessories
for models 1964-1996

K&N HIGH PERFORMANCE AIRFILTERS   (800) 858-3333
P.O. Box 1329 • Riverside, CA 92502
E-Mail: tech@knfilter.com
Website: www.knfilter.com
International Ordering: (951) 826-4000
Contact Name: Nate Shelton, President
Catalog: $3. Frequency: Semiannual
Circulation: 50K. Sales: $20-50MM
Products: Air filters for motorcycles,
autos & off road vehicles

KAMINARI AERODYNAMICS CATALOG   (800) 289-5488
10865 Kalama River Ave.
Fountain Valley, CA 92708
E-Mail: info@kaminari.com
Website: www.kaminari.com
Fax Ordering: (775) 965-6834
International Ordering: (775) 351-2240
Contact Name: Erik Cutter, President
Catalog: $4. Frequency: Annual
Circulation: 15M. Sales: $3-5MM
Products: Auto & truck restoration parts & supplies

KANTER AUTO PRODUCTS   (800) 526-1096
76 Monroe St. • Boonton, NJ 07005
E-Mail: sales1@kanter.com
Website: www.kanter.com
Fax Ordering: (973) 334-5423
International Ordering: (973) 334-9575
Contact Name: Naoimi Becker, Marketing
Catalog: Free. Frequency: Semiannual
Circulation: 100K. Sales: $5-10MM
Products: Front end kits, engine parts,
interior/exterior trim. exhaust, leather,
fuel & water pumps, domestic auto parts

KENT-MOORE AUTOMOTIVE   (800) 345-2233
SPX Corp.
13515 Ballanyne Corporate Pl.
Charlotte, NC 28277
E-Mail: info@spx.com
Website: www.spx.com
International Ordering: (704) 752-4400
Catalog: Free. Frequency: Annual
Circulation: 50K. Sales: $10-20MM
Products: Special service tools for
transportation industry

KEYSTONE AUTOMOTIVE INDUSTRIES   (800) 822-1478
700 E. Bonita Ave. • Pomona, CA 91767   (800) 772-5557
E-Mail: info@keystone-auto.com
Website: www.keystone-auto.com
Fax Ordering: (909) 624-9136
International Ordering: (909) 624-8041
Catalog: Free. Frequency: Annual
Circulation: 100K. Sales: $50-100MM
Products: Collision replacement parts &
accessories; specialty parts for trucks, cars,
vans & sport utility vehicles

DENNIS KIRK CATALOG   (800) 328-9280
955 S. Field Ave. • Rush City, MN 55069   (800) 969-7501
E-Mail: info@denniskirk.com
Website: www.denniskirk.com
Fax Ordering: (320) 358-4019
International Ordering: (320) 358-4791
Contact Name: P.A. Humphries, President
Catalog: Free. Frequency: Annual
Circulation: 150K. Sales: $5-10MM
Products: Motorcycle, snowmobile, ATV,
dirt bike, harley davidson parts & accessories

KIWI INDIAN MOTORCYCLE PARTS   (800) 601-5494
17399 Sage St. • Riverside, CA 92504
E-Mail: info@kiwiindian.com
Website: www.kiwi-indian.com
Fax Ordering: (909) 780-7722
International Ordering: (909) 780-5400
Contact Name: Mike "Kiwi" Tomas, President
Catalog: Free. Frequency: Annual
Circulation: 25K. Sales: $10-20MM
Products: Kiwi Indian motorcycles, engines,
supplies & accessories; apparel; books & DVDs

KORMAN AUTOWORKS CATALOG   (336) 275-1494
2629 Randleman Rd. • Greensboro, NC 27406
E-Mail: sales@kormanautoworks.com
Website: www.kormanautoworks.com
Fax Ordering: (800) FAST-BMW; (336) 274-8003
Contact Name: Ray Korman, President
Catalog: Free. Frequency: Annual
Circulation: 10K. Sales: $5-10MM
Products: High performance BMW parts
& accessories

LANG'S OLD CAR (MODEL T FORD) PARTS   (800) 872-7871
202 School St. • Winchendon, MA 01475
E-Mail: sales@modeltford.com
Website: www.modeltford.com
Fax Ordering: (978) 297-2126
International Ordering: (978) 297-1919
Contact Name: James Lang, President
Catalog: Free. Frequency: Annual
Circulation: 10K. Sales: $3-5MM
Products: Model T Ford parts.

LISLE CORPORATION CATALOG   (712) 542-5101
P.O. Box 89 • Clarinda, IA 51632
E-Mail: info@lislecorp.com
Website: www.lislecorp.com
Fax Ordering: (712) 542-6591
Contact Name: John Lisle, President
Catalog: Free. Pages: 66. Frequency: Annual
Circulation: 100K. Sales: $20-50MM
Products: Automotive specialty tools & products;
OEM products; grinders

LMC TRUCK PARTS & ACCESSORIES   (800) 562-8782
15450 W. 108th St. • Lenexa, KS 66219
E-Mail: info@lmctruck.com
Website: www.lmctruck.com
Fax Ordering: (800) 541-8525; (913) 599-0323
International Ordering: (913) 541-0684
Catalog: Free. Frequency: Semiannual
Circulation: 100K. Sales: $10-20MM
Products: Chevy GMC Ford & Dodge truck parts

LONG ISLAND CORVETTE SUPPLY   (800) 466-6367
1445 S. Strongs Rd. • Copiague, NY 11726
E-Mail: info@licorvette.com
Website: www.licorvette.com
Fax Ordering: (631) 225-5030
International Ordering: (631) 225-3000
Catalog: Free. Frequency: Semiannual
Circulation: 50K. Sales: $3-5MM
Products: Auto parts & accessories for
specific makes & models, specializing in
1963-67 Corvettes

LOU FUSZ TOYOTA CATALOG   (800) 325-9581
10725 Manchester Rd. • Kirkwood, MO 63122   (800) 551-0114
E-Mail: info@toyota.fusz.com
Website: www.toyota.fusz.com
Fax Ordering: (314) 966-2353
International Ordering: (314) 966-5404
Contact Name: Stephen Koon, President
Catalog: Free. Frequency: Annual
Circulation: 100K. Sales: $20-50MM
Products: Toyota parts & accessories

MAC'S ANTIQUE AUTO PARTS   (800) 777-0948
6150 Donner • Lockport, NY 14094   (800) 828-1051
E-Mail: customerservice@macsauto.com
Website: www.macsautoparts.com
Fax Ordering: (716) 210-1370
International Ordering: (716) 210-1340

Contact Name: Robert McIntosh, President
Catalog: Free. Frequency: Annual
Circulation: 30K. Sales: $5-10MM
Products: 1909-1972 Ford, Mercury & Edsel parts,
including Model T, A, and early V8 trucks

MAIER MANUFACTURING   (800) 336-2437
416 Crown Point Cir.
Grass Valley, CA 95945
E-Mail: maier@telis.org
Website: www.maier-mfg.com
Fax Ordering: (530) 272-4306
International Ordering: (530) 272-9036
Contact Name: Charles Maier, President
Catalog: $3. Frequency: Semiannual
Circulation: 25K. Sales: $5-10MM
Products: Manufacturers motorcycle body parts

MAKE WAVES INSTRUMENT CORP.   (800) 445-1391
4444 Broadway • Buffalo, NY 14043
E-Mail: makewaves@c1mail.com
Website: www.makewavesinstrumentcorp.com
Fax Ordering: (716) 681-3412
International Ordering: (716) 681-7524
Contact Name: John Patterson, President
Catalog: Free. Frequency: Annual
Circulation: 10K. Sales: $3-5MM
Products: Tachometers, interior, exterior & wheel
accessories, gauges, engine gaskets, valve covers,
horns, etc.

MALM'S CAR WAXES &   (914) 764-5775
POLISHING MATERIALS
Malm Chemical Corporation
P.O. Box 300 • Pound Ridge, NY 10576
E-Mail: custserv1@malms.com
Website: www.malms.com
Fax Ordering: (914) 764-5785
Contact Name: Jay Kolinsky, President
Catalog: Free. Frequency: Semiannual
Circulation: 150K. Sales: $20-50MM
Products: Special car waxes & polishes
for car buffs

MAN-A-FRE CATALOG   (877) 626-2373
1775 N. Surveyor Ave.
Simi Valley, CA 93063
E-Mail: sales@man-a-free.com
Website: www.man-a-fre.com
Fax Ordering: (805) 578-8762
Customer/Tech Support: (805) 578-8712
Contact Name: Al Colebank, President
Catalog: Free. Frequency: Annual
Circulation: 25K. Sales: $3-5M
Products: Toyota Land Cruiser parts & accessories

MANUFACTURERS' SUPPLY CATALOG   (800) 826-8563
P.O. Box 208 • Medford, WI 54425
E-Mail: sales@mfgsupply.com
Website: www.mfgsupply.com
Fax Ordering: (800) 294-4144
Contact Name: Bill Hall, President
Catalog: Free. Frequency: Annual
Circulation: 50K. Sales: $5-10MM
Products: Parts for snowmobiles, go-karts
& mini-bikes; small engines, chain saws

MAS RACING PRODUCTS CATALOG   (651) 644-6811
2288 University Ave. W • St. Paul, MN 55114
E-Mail: forums@hotrodders.com
Website: www.hotrodders.com
Fax Ordering: (651) 644-1635

Contact Name: Richard Kohn, President
Catalog: Free. Frequency: Annual
Circulation: 25K. **Sales:** $3-5MM
Products: Auto racing parts & accessories

MID AMERICA MOTORWORKS (800) 588-2844
P.O. Box 1368 • Effingham, IL 62401 (866) 350-4543
E-Mail: mail@mamotorworks.com
Website: www.mamotorworks.com
Fax Ordering: (217) 347-2952
International Ordering: (217) 540-4200
Contact Name: Michael Yager, President
Catalog: Free. Frequency: 6x per year
Circulation: 10K. **Sales:** $5-10MM
Products: Corvette Catalog & Air-Cooled
VW Catalog; parts & accessories

M.E. MILLER TIRE CATALOG (800) 621-1955
17386 State Hwy. 2 • Wauseon, OH 43567
E-Mail: memiller@bright.net
Website: www.millertire.com
Fax Ordering: (419) 335-9881
International Ordering: (419) 335-7010
Contact Name: M.E. Miller, President
Catalog: Free. Frequency: Annual
Circulation: 50K. **Sales:** $10-20M
Products: Tractor tires

MOSS MOTORS CATALOGS (800) 642-8295
440 Rutherford St. • Goleta, CA 93117 (888) 234-1104
E-Mail: grimesc@mossmotors.com (800) 667-7872
Website: www.mossmotors.com (800) 895-2471
Websites: www.miatamania.com
Fax Ordering: (805) 692-2525
International Ordering: (805) 681-3400
Customer Service: (800) 689-9313
Tech Support: (805) 681-3411
Contact Name: Robert Goldman, V.P.
Catalog: Free. **Pages:** 114. Frequency: Semiannual
Circulation: 200K. **Sales:** $20-50MM
Products: Catalogs for Mazda Miata, Triumph,
MG, MGB, Jaguar, Austin-Healey, Hummer H2,
BMW Mini parts & accessories; British classic
auto parts; apparel & accessories, brakes, engine,
exterior, interior.

MOTORACE CATALOG (800) 628-4040
P.O. Box 861 • Wilbraham, MA 01095
E-Mail: motorace@motorace.com
Website: www.motorace.com
Fax Ordering: (413) 731-8999
International Ordering: (413) 734-6211
Contact Name: S.L. Smeed, President
Catalog: Free. Frequency: Annual
Circulation: 15K. **Sales:** $5-10MM
Products: Motorcycle accessories specializing
in protective gear; studded motorcycle tires,
specialized lubricants, exhaust systems,
luggage & Pivot Works bearing kits

MOTORAD OF AMERICA CATALOG (800) 328-7828
6292 Walmore Rd. • Niagara Falls, NY 14304
E-Mail: info@motoradusa.com
Website: www.motoradusa.com
Fax Ordering: (716) 731-6436
International Ordering: (716) 731-6442
Contact Name: Joseph Fishman, President
Catalog: Free. Frequency: Annual
Circulation: 50M. **Sales:** $1-3MM
Products: Auto & truck thermostats & power
elements, fan switches, gaskets, radiator, switches,
seals & gaskets, oil filler, fuel & radiator caps

MOTORCARS INTERNATIONAL (866) 970-6800
2701 E. Sunshine St.
Springfield, MO 65804
E-Mail: info@motorcars-intl.com
Website: www.motorcars-intl.com
Fax Ordering: (417) 831-9995
International Ordering: (417) 831-9999
Contact Name: Randy McCall, Sales Contact
Catalog: Free. Frequency: Annual
Circulation: 50K. **Sales:** $3-5MM
Products: Motoring accessories & clothing

MUSTANG MOTORCYCLE PRODUCTS (800) 243-1392
P.O. Box 29 • Terryville, CT 06786
E-Mail: info@mustangseats.com
Website: www.mustangseats.com
Fax Ordering: (800) 243-1399; (860) 585-0407
International Ordering: (860) 582-9633
Contact Name: Al Simmons, President
Catalog: $3. Frequency: Annual
Circulation: 250K. **Sales:** $10-20MM
Products: Seats for Mustang, Harley-Davidson,
Honda, Yamaha, Victory, Kawasaki & Suzuki
motorcycles

MUSTANGS & MORE CATALOG (800) 356-6573
2065 Sperry Ave. • Ventura, CA 93003
E-Mail: sales@mustangs-more.com
Website: www.mustangs-more.com
Fax Ordering: (805) 642-6468
International Ordering: (805) 642-0887
Contact Name: Sue Smith, Owner
Catalog: Free. Frequency: Annual
Circulation: 25K. **Sales:** $3-5MM
Products: Mustang (1965-73, Falcon
& Fairlane auto parts & accessories

MUSTANGS UNLIMITED CATALOGS (888) 398-9898
440 Adams St. • Manchester, CT 06042 (888) 229-2929
2505 Newpoint Pkwy. (800) 243-7278
Lawrenceville, GA 30043
E-Mail: info@mustangsunlimited.com
Website: www.mustangsunlimited.com
Fax Ordering: CT (860) 649-1260
Fax Ordering: GA (770) 446-3055
International Ordering: CT (860) 647-1965
International Ordering: GA (770) 446-1965
Website: www.mustangsunlimited.com
Catalog: $4.95. Frequency: Annual
Circulation: 20K. **Sales:** $10-20M
Products: Mustang Catalog (1965-73) restoration
& performance parts & accessories; Shelby Catalog
(1965-70) with restoration parts & accessories

NATIONAL TIRE & WHEEL CATALOG (800) 847-3287
5 Garden Ct. • Wheeling, WV 26003
E-Mail: info@ntwonline.com
Website: www.ntwonline.com
Fax Ordering: (304) 233-2286
International Ordering: (304) 233-7917
Customer Service: (800) 391-1113
Contact Name: Greg Eaton, President
Catalog: Free. Frequency: Bimonthly
Circulation: 100K. **Sales:** $20-50MM
Products: National & international tires,
wheels & accessories

NEWARK AUTO PRODUCTS (800) 275-4695
23 Centerway • East Orange, NJ 07017
E-Mail: info@newark-auto.com
Website: www.newark-auto.com
Fax Ordering: (973) 677-9335

International Ordering: (973) 677-9935
Contact Name: Alexander Seaman, President
Catalog: Free. Frequency: Annual
Circulation: 50K. Sales: $5-10MM
Products: Auto & truck carpets, rubber mats, vacuum cleaners, security items, fans & fender covers

NIEHAUS CYCLE SALES, INC. (800) 373-6565
718 Old Rt. 66 North • Litchfield, IL 62056
E-Mail: info@niehauscycle.com
Website: www.niehauscycle.com
Fax Ordering: (217) 324-6563
International Ordering: (217) 324-6565
Contact Name: Brad Niehaus, President
Catalog: Free. Frequency: Semiannual
Circulation: 100K. Sales: $5-10MM
Products: Apparel & accessories for Honda & Yamaha motorcycles & ATVs

NORTHERN AUTO PARTS (800) 831-0884
801 Lewis Blvd. • Sioux City, IA 51105
E-Mail: info@northernautoparts.com
Website: www.northernautoparts.com
Fax Ordering: (712) 258-0088
International Ordering: (712) 258-4131
Catalog: Free. Frequency: Semiannual
Circulation: 200K. Sales: $10-20MM
Products: Auto parts & accessories; engine kits

OHIO LIGHT TRUCK PARTS COMPANY (800) 333-3536
7643 Fort Laurens Rd. NW
Strasburg, OH 44680
E-Mail: optronics@ohiolighttruckparts.com
Website: www.ohiolighttruckparts.com
Fax Ordering: (330) 364-3616
International Ordering: (330) 878-6587
Contact Name: Bruce Goeder, President
Catalog: Free. Frequency: Annual
Circulation: 25K. Sales: $10-20MM
Products: Steel truck body parts & supplies

OPTRONICS CATALOG (800) 364-5483
401 S. 41st St. • East Muskogee, OK 74403
E-Mail: sales@optronicsinc.com
Website: www.optronicsinc.com
Fax Ordering: (918) 683-9517
International Ordering: (918) 478-2443
Contact Name: Duncan M. Payne, President
Catalog: Free. Frequency: Annual
Circulation: 10K. Sales: $10-20MM
Products: Fog/driving light kits, spotlights, truck & trailer lighting, reflectors, worklights

PERFORMANCE PRODUCTS (800) 775-7603
7733 Hayvenhurst Ave. • Van Nuys, CA 91406 (800) 423-3173
E-Mail: ppe_sales@ecklers.net (888) 787-3626
Website: www.performanceproducts.com
Fax Ordering: (800) 752-6196; (818) 787-2396
International Ordering: (818) 787-2396
Contact Name: Ron Rowen, President
Catalog: Free. Frequency: Semiannual
Circulation: 250K. Sales: $20-50MM
Products: Performance parts, accessories; seat covers, roof/ski/bike racks, emergency items, and safety products for Jeeps, Fords, Chevys & Toyotas; restoration & enhancement products for Porsches; catalogs for Porsche, Mercedes & Toyotas

PERFORMANCE SUSPENSION (800) 247-2288
TECHNOLOGY (877) 226-4101
P.O. Box 396 • Montville, NJ 07045
E-Mail: info@p-s-t.com

Website: www.p-s-t.com
Fax Ordering: (973) 299-6377
International Ordering: (973) 299-8019
Contact Name: Naomi Becker, President
Catalog: Free. Frequency: Annual
Circulation: 250K. Sales: $20-50MM
Products: The muscle car & truck performance specialists

PIERCE SALES (800) 658-6301
549 US Hwy. 287 S • Henrietta, TX 76365
E-Mail: sales@piercesales.com
Website: www.piercesales.com
Fax Ordering: (940) 538-4382
International Ordering: (940) 538-5643
Contact Name: Jeff Pierce, President
Catalog: Free. Frequency: Annual
Circulation: 250M. Sales: $10-20MM
Products: Manufacturers of winches and towing equipment; remote systems; hydaulics; farm & ranch equipment; electrical-lights, motors, sirens; chain hoists

PINGEL ENTERPRISES, INC. (888) 474-6435
2072 11th Ave. • Adams, WI 53910
E-Mail: info@pingelonline.com
Website: www.pingelonline.com
Fax Ordering: (608) 339-9164
Tech Support: (608) 339-7999
Catalog: Free. Frequency: Annual
Circulation: 50K. Sales: $3-5MM
Products: Motorcycle supplies & accessories

QC SUPPLY (800) 433-6340
P.O. Box 581 • Schuyler, NE 68661
E-Mail: qcsupply@qcsupply.com
Website: www.qcsupply.com
Fax Ordering: (402) 352-8825
International Ordering: (402) 352-3167
Catalog: Free. Frequency: Annual
Circulation: 100K. Sales: $10-20M
Products: Automotive equipment & supplies; household, office products; greenhouse & garden products; lighting products

QUADRATEC CATALOG (800) 745-2348
1028 Saunders Lane
West Chester, PA 19380
E-Mail: customerservice@quadratec.com
internationalorder@quadratec.com
Website: www.quadratec.com
Fax Ordering: (610) 701-2402
International Ordering: (610) 701-3336
Customer Service: (800) 745-6037
Catalog: Free. Frequency: Semiannual
Circulation: 100K. Sales: $5-10M
Products: Jeep parts, accessories, soft tops, lift kits

RK SPORT CATALOG (800) 214-8030
26900 Jefferson Ave. • Murrieta, CA 92562
E-Mail: customersupport@rksport.com
Website: www.rksport.com
Fax Ordering: (951) 894-7920
International Ordering: (951) 894-7883
Contact Name: R.K. Smith, President
Catalog: Free. Frequency: Semiannual
Circulation: 150K. Sales: $10-20MM
Products: Enhancements, parts & accessories

RACER WALSH COMPANY (800) 334-0151
1849 Foster Dr. • Jacksonville, FL 32216

E-Mail: info@racerwalsh.com
Website: www.racerwalsh.com
International Ordering: (904) 721-2289
Contact Name: Eddie Miller, President
Catalog: Free. Frequency: Annual
Circulation: 25K. Sales: $3-5MM
Products: Ford auto parts & accessories

REGITAR USA CATALOG   (334) 244-1885
2575 Container Dr. • Montgomery, AL 36109
E-Mail: info@regitar.com
Website: www.regitar.com
Fax Ordering: (334) 244-1901
Contact Name: Yu-Tueng Tsai, President
Catalog: Free. Frequency: Annual
Circulation: 10K. Sales: $3-5MM
Products: Auto electronic parts, power tools,
ignition modular, ignition modular coils, voltage
regulators, distributor caps, etc.

RESTORATION SPECIALTIES & SUPPLY   (814) 467-9842
P.O. Box 328 • Windber, PA 15963
E-Mail: info@restorationspecialties.com
Website: www.restorationspecialties.com
Fax Ordering: (814) 467-5323
Contact Name: David A. Mihalko, President
Catalog: $3.50. Frequency: Annual
Circulation: 50K. Sales: $1-3MM
Products: Antique car parts & accessories;
supplier of hard-to-find restoration parts

RUBBER PARTS FOR CLASSIC CARS   (800) 878-2237
Metro Moulded Parts   (866) 586-7516
P.O. Box 48130 • Minneapolis, MN 55448
E-Mail: metrosales@metrommp.com
Website: www.metrommp.com
Fax Ordering: (877) 399-2562; (763) 757-2803
Contact Name: Douglas Hajicek, President
Catalog: $3. Frequency: Annual
Circulation: 25M. Sales: $5-10MM
Products: Rubber parts & weatherstripping
for classic cars & trucks, 1929-1975

SCOGGIN-DICKEY CATALOG   (800) 456-0211
5901 Spur 327 • Lubbock, TX 79424
E-Mail: info@sdpc2000.com
Website: www.sdpc2000.com
Fax Ordering: (806) 798-4086
International Ordering: (806) 798-4108
Catalog: Free. Frequency: Semiannual
Circulation: 100K. Sales: $20-50MM
Products: GM performance parts; automotive
racing & performance parts

SEARS AUTOMOTIVE ACCESSORIES   (800) 349-4358
333 Beverly Rd. • Hoffman Estates, IL 60179
E-Mail: info@sears.com
Website: www.sears.com
Catalog: Free. Frequency: Quarterly
Circulation: 500K. Sales: $50-100MM
Products: Accessories for trucks, cars,
vans & sport utility vehicles

SECURITY CHAIN COMPANY   (800) 547-6806
P.O. Box 949 • Clackamas, OK 97015
E-Mail: contactscc@scc-chain.com
Website: www.scc-chain.com
Fax Ordering: (800) 468-4430; (503) 656-4836
International Ordering: (503) 656-5400
Contact Name: Brian McCourt, President
Catalog: Free. Frequency: Annual
Circulation: 50K. Sales: $10-20MM

Products: Cable, tire & hardware chains,
Load & tow straps & other winter traction
products

SNAP-ON TOOLS CORPORATION   (262) 656-5200
P.O. Box 1410 • Kenosha, WI 53141
E-Mail: sales@snapon.com
Website: www.snapon.com
Fax Ordering: (262) 656-5577
International Ordering: (262) 656-5200
Customer Service: (877) 762-7664
Contact Name: Robert Cornog, President
Catalog: Free. Frequency: Annual
Circulation: 50K. Sales: $20-50MM
Products: Auto accessories for cars, trucks,
vans & RVs

SPECIFIC CRUISE SYSTEMS/FRIGETTE   (800) 433-1740
P.O. Box 40550 • Fort Worth, TX 76140   (800) 433-9280
E-Mail: info@scsfrigette.com
Website: www.scsfrigette.com
Fax Ordering: (817) 293-8014
International Ordering: (817) 293-5313
Contact Name: Brad Hickman, President
Catalog: Free. Frequency: Annual
Circulation: 100K. Sales: $50-100MM
Products: Auto security systems, electronic
cruise controls, auto air conditioners & parts

STATE OF NINE CATALOG   (877) 449-7222
1 Chestnut St. #222 • Nashua, NH 03060
E-Mail: customerservice@stateofnine.com
Website: www.stateofnine.com
Fax Ordering: (617) 917-1601
International Ordering: (617) 917-1601
Catalog: Free. Frequency: Annual
Circulation: 100K. Sales: $10-20MM
Products: Saab performance parts & accessories

STILLEN SUPER TRUCKS & SPORTS CARS   (866) 250-5542
3176 Airway Ave. • Costa Mesa, CA 92626
E-Mail: sales@stillen.com
Website: www.stillen.com
Fax Ordering: (714) 540-5784
International Ordering: (714) 540-5566
Customer Service:(800) 891-1058
Catalog: Free. Frequency: Annual
Circulation: 100K. Sales: $20-50MM
Products: Manufacturer & multi-line
warehouse distributor

STINGER CATALOG   (800) 477-2267
AAMP of America
13160 56th Court • Clearwater, FL 33760
E-Mail: stinger@aampofamerica.com
Website: www.aampofamerica.com
Fax Ordering: (727) 573-9326
International Ordering: (727) 572-9255
Contact Name: Micah Ansley, President
Catalog: Free. Frequency: Annual
Circulation: 25K. Sales: $5-10MM
Products: High performance car audio
accessories

STOCK DRIVE PRODUCTS CATALOGS   (800) 819-8900
Sterling Instruments
2101 Jericho Tpke., Box 5416
New Hyde Park, NY 11040
E-Mail: support@sdp-si.com
Website: www.sdp-si.com
Fax Ordering: (516) 326-8827
International Ordering: (516) 326-3300

Contact Name: Herb Arum, Marketing Manager
Catalog: Free. **Frequency:** Annual
Circulation: 100K. **Sales:** $20-50MM
Products: Auto engines & machine components

STODDARD IMPORTED CAR PARTS (800) 342-1414
38845 Mentor Ave. • Willoughby, OH 44094
E-Mail: pdlcesare@stoddard.com
Website: www.stoddard.com
Fax Ordering: (440) 946-9410
International Ordering: (440) 951-1040
Contact Name: Fritz Hinterberger, President
Catalog: Free. **Frequency:** Annual
Circulation: 25K. **Sales:** $5-10MM
Products: Porsche repair & restoration parts
& accessories

STOUDT AUTO SALES (800) 523-8485
1350 Carbon St. • Reading, PA 19601 (800) 482-3033
E-Mail: info@sevenwaves.com
Website: www.sevenwaves.com
Fax Ordering: (610) 372-7283
International Ordering: (610) 374-4856
Contact Name: J.K. Stoudt, President
Catalog: Free. **Frequency:** Annual
Circulation: 25K. **Sales:** $5-10MM
Products: Motorcycle, snowmobile, ATV,
dirt bike, harley davidson parts & accessories

STYLIN TRUCKS CATALOG (800) 586-9713
7820 E. Pleasant Valley Rd.
Independence, OH 44131
E-Mail: info@stylintrucks.com
Website: www.stylintrucks.com
Fax Ordering: (800) 883-1855; (216) 643-6610
International Ordering: (216) 643-6600
Customer Service: (888) 780-0358
Contact Name: John Milos, President
Catalog: Free. **Frequency:** Monthly
Circulation: 100K. **Sales:** $10-20MM
Products: Truck & SUV accessories, sport truck
& sport compact after market accessories

SUMMIT RACING EQUIPMENT (800) 230-3030
P.O. Box 909 • Akron, OH 44398
E-Mail: sales@summitracing.com
Website: www.summitracing.com
Fax Ordering: (330) 630-5333
International Ordering: (330) 630-3030
Customer Service: (800) 517-1035
Catalog: Free. **Frequency:** Semiannual
Circulation: 100K. **Sales:** $20-50M
Products: Auto & truck racing equipment
& parts

TOMCO, INC. CATALOG (800) 325-9972
7208A Weil Ave. • St. Louis, MO 63132
E-Mail: info@tomco-inc.com
Website: www.tomco-inc.com
Fax Ordering: (314) 567-1732
International Ordering: (314) 567-4520
Contact Name: Robert Killion, President
Catalog: Free. **Frequency:** Annual
Circulation: 75K. **Sales:** $10-20M
Products: Fuel & emission control parts

TOOLS OF THE TRADE (800) 782-4356
Helm, Inc.
14310 Hamilton Ave.
Highland Park, MI 48203
E-Mail: info@helminc.com

Website: www.helminc.com
Fax Ordering: (313) 865-5927
International Ordering: (313) 865-5000
Catalog: Free. **Frequency:** Semiannual
Circulation: 50K. **Sales:** $10-20MM
Products: Autocare instructor guides, service
manuals, videotapes and reference books

TRANSPORTATION COLLECTIBLES (800) 345-1178
Eastwood Company (800) 343-9353
263 Shoemaker Rd.
Pottstown, PA 19464
E-Mail: sales@eastwoodco.com
Website: www.eastwoodco.com
Fax Ordering: (610) 644-0560
Tech Support: (866) 759-2131
Contact Name: Curt Strohacker, President
Catalog: Free. **Frequency:** Monthly
Circulation: 150K. **Sales:** $20-50MM
Products: Specialty auto repair & restoration
tools & supplies; diecast collectibles; paints &
coatings; rust prevention products

UNITED SPEEDOMETER SERVICE (800) 877-4798
3746 Comer Ave. • Riverside, CA 92507
E-Mail: uslmail@earthlink.net
Website: www.speedometershop.com
Fax Ordering: (909) 684-0146
International Ordering: (909) 684-0292
Contact Name: John Young, Marketing
Catalog: Free. **Frequency:** Annual
Circulation: 50K. **Sales:** $10-20MM
Products: Speedometers, temperature gauges,
clocks, tachometers, cruise control, & accessories
for autos

VIRGINIA CLASSIC MUSTANG, INC. (540) 896-2695
P.O. Box 487 • Broadway, VA 22815
E-Mail: info@vamustang.com
Website: www.vamustang.com
Fax Ordering: (540) 896-9310
Contact Name: Bob Halterman, President
Catalog: Free. **Frequency:** Semiannual
Circulation: 25K. **Sales:** $5-10MM
Products: Restoration parts & accessories
for Mustangs GRI-73

WHAT'S NEW FOR HOME & AUTO (800) 525-8624
Progressive Energy Corporation
650 Corte Raquel • San Marcos, CA 92069
E-Mail: pkilleen@pec.win.net
Fax Ordering: (760) 727-0947
International Ordering: (760) 727-2906
Contact Name: Patrick Killeen, President
Catalog: Free. **Frequency:** Semiannual
Circulation: 100K. **Sales:** $3-5MM
Products: Auto accessories & home security

J.C. WHITNEY CATALOGS (800) 529-4486
1104 S. Wabash Ave. • Chicago, IL 60605 (866) 529-5530
E-Mail: info@jcwhitney.com
Website: www.jcwhitney.com
Fax Ordering: (312) 431-5625
International Ordering: (312) 431-6000
Contact Name: Thomas M. West, President
Catalog: Free. **Frequency:** Monthly
Circulation: 50K. **Sales:** $5-10MM
Products: Jeep & Wrangler Catalog; Truck Catalog;
Classic Volkswagen; Motorcycle Catalog; RV &
Camping catalogAuto parts, accessories & tools

WHOLESALE CAR CARE PRODUCTS   (800) 633-8245
P.O. Box 450023 • Sunrise, CA 33345
E-Mail: info@wholesalecarcare.com
Website: www.wholesalecarcare.com
Fax Ordering: (954) 749-3564
International Ordering: (954) 749-1342
Contact Name: Richard Block, President
Catalog: Free. Frequency: Annual
Circulation: 100K. Sales: $5-10MM
Products: Orbital polishers & detailing products

WOLF AUTOMOTIVE PRODUCTS   (888) 765-1711
Truck Specialties, Inc.
P.O. Box 819 • Lorena, TX 76655
E-Mail: info@truckspecialties.com
Website: www.truckspecialties.com.com
Fax Ordering: (254) 230-9736
International Ordering: (254) 230-4615
Contact Name: Micah Ansley, President
Catalog: $20. Frequency: Annual
Circulation: 100K. Sales: $20-50MM
Products: Truck accessories

YEAR ONE CATALOG   (800) 932-7663
P.O. Box 521 • Braselton, GA 30085
E-Mail: info@yearone.com
Website: www.yearone.com
Fax Ordering: (800) 680-6806; (706) 654-5355
International Ordering: (706) 658-2140
Contact Name: Kevin King, President
Catalog: Free. Frequency: Annual
Circulation: 150K. Sales: $3-5MM
Products: New & reproduction restoration
parts for older model cars

ZYGMUNT MOTORS CATALOG   (215) 348-3121
70 Green St. • Doylestown, PA 18901
E-Mail: cmuzy@aol.com
Website: www.bimmerparts.com
Fax Ordering: (215) 348-2005
Tech Support: (215) 688-1350
Contact Name: Chris Muzy, President
Catalog: Online. Sales: $1-3MM
Products: BMW parts & accessories

ASA CATALOG   (800) 272-2359
Aviation Supplies & Academics, Inc.
7005 132nd Pl. SE • Newcastle, WA 98059
E-Mail: sales@asa2fly.com
Website: www.asa2fly.com
Fax Ordering: (425) 235-0128
International Ordering: (425) 235-1500
Contact Name: Joe Finelli, President
Catalog: Free. Frequency: Semiannual
Circulation: 100K. Sales: $1-3MM
Products: Aviation training books & pilot
supplies

AERONAUTICAL &   (800) 423-2708
MILITARY AVIATION BOOKS
Aviation Book Company
7201 Perimeter Rd. S • Seattle, WA 98108
E-Mail: sales@aviationbook.com
Website: www.aviationbook.com
Fax Ordering: (206) 763-3428
International Ordering: (206) 767-5232
Contact Name: Nancy Griffith, President
Catalog: Free. Frequency: Semiannual
Circulation: 100K. Sales: $500K to $1MM
Products: Aviation books, pilot supplies & gifts

AIRCRAFT FREEBIE   (785) 625-6346
RANS Co. • 4600 Hwy. 183 Alt.
Hays, KS 67601
E-mail: rans@rans.com
Website: www.rans.com
Fax Ordering: (785) 625-2795
Contact Names: Randy Schlitter, President
Catalog: Free. Frequency: Bimonthly
Circulation: 25K. Sales: $1-3MM
Products: Sport aircraft kitplanes & aircraft
parts; bicycles

AIRCRAFT SPRUCE & SPECIALTY CO.   (877) 477-7823
P.O. Box 4000 • Corona, CA 92878
E-Mail: info@aircraftspruce.com
Website: www.aircraftspruce.com
Fax Ordering: (800) 329-3020; (951) 372-0555
International Ordering: (951) 372-9555
Contact Name: James Irwin, President
Catalog: Free. Frequency: Annual
Circulation: 100K. Sales: $10-20MM
Products: Aircraft parts & supplies for certified
& homebuilt aircraft

AIRCRAFT TOOL SUPPLY CO. CATALOG   (800) 248-0638
P.O. Box 370 • Oscoda, MI 48750
E-Mail: sales@aircraft-tool.com
Website: www.aircraft-tool.com
Fax Ordering: (989) 739-1448
International Ordering: (989) 739-1447
Catalog: Free. Frequency: Annual
Circulation: 75K. Sales: $5-10MM
Products: Specialty aircraft tools including
riveting equipment and repair & maintenance
tools; inspoection equipment; sheet metal tools

AIRLINERS CATALOG   (800) 875-6711
Airliners Publications
6355 NW 36 St. #600 • Miami, FL 33166
E-Mail: vito@airliners.tv
Website: www.airlinersonline.com
International Ordering: (786) 264-6692
Contact Name: NVito La Forgia, Publisher
Catalog: Free. Frequency: Annual
Circulation: 100K. Sales: $3-5MM
Products: Airline merchandise

AMERICAN AVIONICS CATALOG   (800) 518-5858
7023 Perimeter Rd. S. • Seattle, WA 98108
E-Mail: sales@americanavionics.com
Website: www.americanavionics.com
Fax Ordering: (206) 763-2036
International Ordering: (206) 763-8530
Catalog: Free. Frequency: Annual
Circulation: 100K. Sales: $5-10MM
Products: GPS technology, overhauled &
surplus avionics equipment; aircraft parts

AVIATION BOOK COMPANY   (800) 423-2708
7201 Perimeter Rd. S., Suite C
Seattle, WA 98108
E-Mail: sales@aviationbook.com
Website: www.aviationbook.com
Fax Ordering: (206) 763-3428
International Ordering: (206) 767-5232
Contact Name: N. Griffith, President
Catalog: Free. Frequency: Annual
Circulation: 150K. Sales: $500K to $1MM
Products: Books & gifts for aviation enthusiasts

AVIATION CATALOG   (800) 535-9544
Ashgate Publishing
2252 Ridge Rd. • Brookfield, VT 05036
E-Mail: info@ashgate.com
Website: www.ashgate.com
Fax Ordering: (802) 276-3837
International Ordering: (802) 276-3162
Contact Name: Richard Slappey, President
Catalog: Free. Frequency: Annual
Circulation: 100K. Sales: $3-5MM
Products: Specialized books, focusing on
aviation

CGS AVIATION INFORMATION PACK   (251) 957-4295
9090 Louis Tillman Dr. • Grand Bay, AL 36541
E-Mail: sales@cgsaviation
Website: www.cgsaviation.com
Contact Name: Charles Slusarczyk, President
Catalog: Free. Frequency: Annual
Circulation: 50K. Sales: $5-10MM
Products: Ultra-light & light aircraft used for
recreation & utility; the CGS Hawk II Arrow;
t-shirts & hats

CHIEF AIRCRAFT, INC. CATALOG   (800) 447-3408
Grants Pass Airport
1301 Brookside Blvd.
Grants Pass, OR 97526
E-Mail: aircraft@chiefaircraft.com
Website: www.chiefaircraft.com
Fax Ordering: (541) 479-4431
International Ordering: (541) 476-6605
Catalog: Free. Frequency: Quarterly
Circulation: 100K. Sales: $5-10MM
Products: Electronic aviation equipment &
accessories; aircraft parts for privately owned
planes

FLIGHT COMPUTING CATALOG   (800) 824-5946
Tailwinds • 45 San Clemente Dr.
Corte Madera, CA 94925
E-Mail: service@tailwinds.com
Website: www.tailwinds.com
Fax Ordering: (415) 927-0199
International Ordering: (415) 927-4242
Contact Name: Nancy Palozola, President
Catalog: Free. Frequency: Quarterly
Circulation: 10K. Sales: $3-5MM
Products: Gifts for flying & flight enthusiasts

FLIGHT SUITS CATALOG   (800) 748-6693
Gibson & Barnes
1900 Weld Blvd. #140 • El Cajon, CA 92020
E-Mail: info@gibson-barnes.com
Website: www.gibson-barnes.com
Fax Ordering: (800) 748-6694; (619) 440-4618
International Ordering: (619) 440-2700
Catalog: Free. Frequency: Annual
Circulation: 10K. Sales: $3-5MM
Products: Flightsuits, uniforms, leather jackets
& flying helmets for aviation

MARV GOLDEN DISCOUNT SALES   (800) 348-0014
8690 Aero Dr. #102 • San Diego, CA 92123
E-Mail: sales@marvgolden.com
Website: www.marvgolden.com
Fax Ordering: (858) 569-4508
International Ordering: (858) 569-5220
Contact Name: Marv Golden, President
Catalog: Free. Frequency: Annual
Circulation: 25K. Sales: $1-3MM
Products: Pilot supplies & equipment; aircraft
manuals, supplies, apparel, avionics; books, CDs,
DVDs; flight bags, computers, guides, jackets,
simulators; GPS systems; gifts for pilots; headsets

HORIZON INSTRUMENTS   (800) 541-8128
600 S. Jefferson St., Suite C
Placentia, CA 92870
E-Mail: sales@horizoninstruments.com
Website: www.horizoninstruments.com
Fax Ordering: (714) 524-5937
International Ordering: (714) 524-1919
Contact Name: Ron Jacobs, President
Catalog: Free. Frequency: Annual
Circulation: 50K. Sales: $3-5MM
Products: Aircraft & aero activities, offering
avionics & communications equipment, specializing
in compact high visibility engine instruments

LEADING EDGE AIR FOILS   (800) 532-3462
P.O. Box 231 • Lyons, WI 53148
E-Mail: info@leadingedge-airfoils.com
Website: www.leadingedge-airfoils.com
Fax Ordering: (262) 763-1920
International Ordering: (262) 763-4087
Contact Name: Bill Read, President
Catalog: Free. Frequency: Semiannual
Circulation: 50K. Sales: $3-5MM
Products: Ultralight & aero activities, offering
aircraft kits - fixed wing powered, specializes
in one & two place open-cockpit biplane

MOUNTAIN HIGH EQUIPMENT & SUPPLY   (800) 468-8185
625 S.E. Salmon Ave. #2
Redmond, OR 97756
E-Mail: sales@mhoxygen.com
Website: www.mhoxygen.com
Fax Ordering: (541) 923-4141
International Ordering: (541) 923-4100
Catalog: Free. Frequency: Annual
Circulation: 50K. Sales: $3-5MM
Products: Custom carry on & built in
oxygen systems

MY PILOTS STORE   (877) 314-7575
7432 E. Tierra Buena Ln. #105
Scottsdale, AZ 85260
E-Mail: service@mypilotstore.com
Website: www.mypilotstore.com
Fax Ordering: (480) 556-0500
Contact Name: Raymond V. Malpocher, President

Catalog: Free. Frequency: Annual
Circulation: 50K. Sales: $20-50MM
Products: Pilot's headset; Aircraft supplies;
flight bags, flight computers, flight simulators;
apparel; books & magazines

POLY-FIBER   (800) 362-3490
P.O. Box 3129 • Riverside, CA 92519
E-Mail: info@polyfiber.com
Website: www.polyfiber.com
Fax Ordering: (951) 684-0518
International Ordering: (951) 684-4280
Catalog: Free. Frequency: Annual
Circulation: 25K. Sales: $1-3MM
Products: Aircraft coatings, fabric
covering & painting

PRECISION AERODYNAMICS   (423) 949-9499
P.O. Box 1596 • Dunlap, TN 37327
E-Mail: information@precision.aero
Website: www.precision.aero
Fax Ordering: (423) 370-1213
International Ordering: (423) 949-9499
Contact Name: Paul Farsai, President
Catalog: Free. Frequency: Quarterly
Circulation: 1MM. Sales: $5-10MM
Products: Aircraft & aero activities offering
aircraft recovery systems & paragear,
specializing in skydiving equipment

RANS AIRCRAFT   (785) 625-6346
RANS, Inc. • 4600 Hwy. 183 Alt.
Hays, KS 67601
E-Mail: rans@rans.com
Website: www.rans.com
Fax Ordering: (785) 625-2795
Catalog: Free. Frequency: Annual
Circulation: 25K. Sales: $5-10MM
Products: Aircraft kits: fixed wing powered,
two-place low-wing & one & two-place high
wing aircraft

ROBINSON HELICOPTER COMPANY   (310) 539-0508
2901 Airport Dr. • Torrance, CA 90505
E-Mail: thane@robinsonheli.com
Website: www.robinsonheli.com
Fax Ordering: (310) 539-5198
Catalog: Free. Frequency: Annual
Circulation: 10K. Sales: $5-10MM
Products: Aircraft kits: helicopters & gyroplanes,
specializing in one-place helicopter

SCHWEIZER AIRCRAFT COMPANY   (607) 739-3821
Elmira/Corning Regional Airport
1250 Schweizer Rd. • Horseheads, NY 14845
E-Mail: murphy.kayla@sacusa.com
Website: www.sacusa.com
Fax Ordering: (607) 796-2488
Customer Support: (607) 378-6019
Contact Name: Paul Schweizer, President
Catalog: Free. Frequency: Annual
Circulation: 25K. Sales: $100-500MM
Products: Gliders, glider equipment & supplies;
helicopters

SIG MANUFACTURING CO.   (800) 247-5008
P.O. Box 520 • Montezuma, IA 50171
E-Mail: mail@sigmfg.com
Website: www.sigmfg.com
Fax Ordering: (641) 623-3922
International Ordering: (641) 623-5154
Contact Name: Dave Arenat, President

Catalog: Free. Frequency: Annual
Circulation: 25K. Sales: $10-20MM
Products: Model kits for airplanes

SPORTY'S CATALOGS   (800) 776-7897
Sportsman's Market, Inc.
Cleremont Co. Sport's Airport
2001 Sporty's Dr. • Batavia, OH 45103
E-Mail: info@sportys.com
Website: www.sportys.com
Fax Ordering: (800) 543-8633; (513) 735-9200
Customer Service: (513) 735-9000
Contact Name: Hal Shevers, President
Catalog: Free. Frequency: Quarterly
Circulation: 20MM. Sales: $20-50MM
Products: Pilot Shop Catalog & Wright Bros.
Collection Catalog, Flight Center Catalog.
Aviation supplies; aviation gifts & memorabilia

STRONG ENTERPRISES   (800) 344-6319
11236 Satellite Blvd. • Orlando, FL 32837
E-Mail: sales@strongparachutes.com
Website: www.strongparachutes.com
Fax Ordering: (407) 850-6978
International Ordering: (407) 859-9317
Contact Name: Ted Strong, President
Catalog: Free. Frequency: Annual
Circulation: 50K. Sales: $5-10MM
Products: Parachute design & development;
skydiving equipment; tandem parachutes;
aerial delivery systems; specializing in
emergency safety chutes for pilots; military
parachutes.

VELOCITY AIRCRAFT   (772) 589-1860
200 W. Airport Dr. • Sebastian, FL 32958
E-Mail: info@velocityaircraft.com
Website: www.velocityaircraft.com
Fax Ordering: (772) 589-1893
Catalog: Free. Frequency: Annual
Circulation: 10K. Sales: $10-20MM
Products: Aircraft kits: fixed wing powered,
specializing in four-place canard pusher-type
airplane

WAG/AERO CATALOG   (800) 558-6868
1216 North Rd. • Lyons, WI 53148
E-Mail: wagaero-sales@wagaero.com
Website: www.wagaero.com
Fax Ordering: (262) 763-7595
International Ordering: (262) 763-9586
Contact Name: Mary Myers, President
Catalog: Free. Frequency: Quarterly
Circulation: 250K. Sales: $5-10MM
Products: Aircraft parts, supplies & aviation
accessories

WICK'S AIRCRAFT SUPPLY CATALOG   (800) 221-9425
410 Pine St. • Highland, IL 62249
E-Mail: info@wicksaircraft.com
Website: www.wicksaircraft.com
Fax Ordering: (888) 440-5727; (618) 654-6253
International Ordering: (618) 654-7447
Contact Name: Jerome Hediger, President
Catalog: Free. Frequency: Annual
Circulation: 25K. Sales: $5-10MM
Products: Wood & hardware for aircrafts

ZENITH AVIATION   (540) 361-7700
1321 Lafayette Blvd. #102
Fredericksburg, VA 22401
E-Mail: info@zenithaviation.com
Website: www.zenithaviation.com
Fax Ordering: (540) 361-7800
Catalog: Free. Frequency: Annual
Circulation: 50M. Sales: $20-50MM
Products: Aircraft parts & supplies;

ZENITH PRESS   (800) 826-6600
P.O. Box 1 • Osceola, WI 54020
E-Mail: customerservice@mbipublishing.com
Website: www.zenithpress.com
Fax Ordering: (715) 294-4448
International Ordering: (715) 294-3345
Contact Name: Tim Parker, President
Catalog: $3.95. Frequency: Annual
Circulation: 20K. Sales: $3-5MM
Products: Aviation books & videos

AMERICAN COUNTRY CATALOG   (800) 998-7077
Gazebo of New York
306 E. 61st St. • New York, NY 10021
E-Mail: reply@thegazebo.com
Website: www.thegazebo.com
Fax Ordering: (212) 754-0571
International Ordering: (212) 832-7077
Contact Name: Robert LoMonaco, President
Catalog: $6. Frequency: Annual
Circulation: 100M. Sales: $500M to $1MM
Products: Handmade quilts, pillows, rag &
braided rugs, collectible ornaments

ANDERSON ULTIMATE BED   (800) 851-9213
Anderson Manufacturing Co.
5300 13th St. • Menominee, MI 49858
E-Mail: ultimatebed@cyberzn.com
Website: www.ultimatebed.com
Fax Ordering: (906) 863-8715
International Ordering: (906) 863-8223
Contact Name: Robert F. Anderson, President
Catalog: Free. Frequency: Annual
Circulation: 250M. Sales: $5-10MM
Products: Bedroom organizers for the home

BED RIZER   (800) 513-1987
A-1 Manufacturing
726 Federal St. • Davenport, IA 52803
E-Mail: info@bedrizer.com
Website: www.bedrizer.com
Fax Ordering: (563) 324-7416
International Ordering: (563) 324-6629
Contact Name: Betty Roggenkamp, President
Catalog: Free. Frequency: Annual
Circulation: 50M. Sales: $1-3MM
Products: Bed skirts & legs

BLAIR SHOPPE HOME PRODUCTS   (800) 458-2000
Blair Corp. • 220 Hickory St.
Warren, PA 16366
E-Mail: blair@blair.com
Website: www.blair.com
Fax Ordering: (814) 726-6466
International Ordering: (814) 723-3600
Contact Name: Blair T. Smoulder, President
Catalog: Free. Frequency: 6x per year
Circulation: 15-20MM. Sales: $50-100MM
Products: Area rugs, bedding, bed & bath
accessories, window treatments, kitchen utensils,
appliances, flatwear & cookware; exercise
equipment; furniture

BLOWING ROCK CRAFTS   (800) 816-9996
Goodwin Weavers
P.O. Box 408 • Blowing Rock, NC 28605
Fax Ordering: (828) 295-7886
International Ordering: (828) 295-3577
Contact Name: David H. Harman, President
Catalog: Free. Frequency: Annual
Circulation: 50M. Sales: $1-3MM
Products: Bedspreads, table cloths, drapery
fabrics, and blankets

BRASS BEDS DIRECT   (800) 242-1330
4866 W. Jefferson Blvd.
Los Angeles, CA 90016
Fax Ordering: (323) 737-1977
International Ordering: (323) 737-6865
Contact Name: G. Kalsa, President
Catalog: Free. Frequency: Annual
Circulation: 25M. Sales: $500M to $1MM
Products: Solid brass beds

BRYLANE HOME CATALOG   (800) 528-5150
P.O. Box 8384 • Indianapolis, IN 46283
E-Mail: bhcustserv@brylane.com
Website: www.brylanehome.com
Fax Ordering: (972) 285-7677
Customer Service: (800) 677-0339
Catalog: Free. Frequency: Annual
Circulation: 100M. Sales: $1-3MM
Products: Bathroom, bedding & linen products,
home accents; bath & towels; window treatments,
slipcovers; kitchenware

CARTER CANOPIES
(800) 538-4071
P.O. Box 808 • Troutman, NC 28116
E-Mail: jcarter@abts.net
Website: www.cartercanopies.com
Fax Ordering: (704) 528-6437
International Ordering: (704) 528-4071
Contact Name: Elsie Carter, President
Catalog: Free. Frequency: 36x per year
Circulation: 15M. Sales: $500M
Products: Bed canopies, bedding &
window treatments

CHAMBERS CATALOG   (800) 334-9790
Williams-Sonoma • P.O. Box 7841
San Francisco, CA 94120
Fax Ordering: (702) 363-2657
International Ordering: (415) 421-7900
Customer Service: (800) 334-1254
Contact Name: Cathy Halligan, Marketing Manager
Catalog: Free. Frequency: Bimonthly
Circulation: 5MM. Sales: $100-500MM
Products: Gifts for the bed and bath

COLDWATER CREEK HOME CATALOG   (800) 262-0040
1 Coldwater Creek Dr. • Sandpoint, ID 83864   (800) 510-2808
E-Mail: info@coldwatercreek.com
Website: www.coldwatercreek.com
Fax Ordering: (208) 263-1582
International Ordering: (208) 263-2266
Contact Name: Dennis Pence, President
Catalog: Free. Frequency: Bimonthly
Circulation: 25MM. Sales: $50-100MM
Products: Bedding, decorative accessories,
clothing & gifts

COMING HOME CATALOG   (800) 356-4444
Lands' End, Inc.   (800) 963-4816
Lands End Lane • Dodgeville, WI 53595
E-Mail: sales@landsend.com
Website: www.landsend.com
Fax Ordering: (800) 332-0103; (608) 935-4260
International Ordering: (608) 935-9341
Contact Name: Michael J. Smith, President
Catalog: Free. Frequency: Monthly
Circulation: 100MM. Sales: $500MM to $1B
Products: Linens, bed & bath

THE COMPANY STORE CATALOG   (800) 285-3696
Hanover Direct   (800) 323-8000
500 Company Store Rd. • LaCross, WI 54601
E-Mail: info@thecompanystore.com
Website: www.thecompanystore.com
Fax Ordering: (201) 272-3177
International Ordering: (201) 863-7300
Contact Name: Jeff Potts, President
Catalog: Free. Frequency: Annual
Circulation: 10MM. Sales: $250-500MM
Products: Bedding, bath products, comforters,
home accessories

CUDDLEDOWN OF MAINE (800) 323-6793
312 Canco Rd. • Portland, ME 04103
E-Mail: service@cuddledown.com
Website: www.cuddledown.com
Fax Ordering: (207) 761-1948
International Ordering: (207) 761-1855
Contact Name: Chris Bradley, President
Catalog: Free. Frequency: Monthly
Circulation: 250M. Sales: $3-5MM
Products: Down comforters & quilts

ELDRIDGE TEXTILE COMPANY (212) 576-2991
17 E. 37th St. • New York, NY 10016
E-Mail: info@eldridgetextile.com
Website: www.eldridgetextile.com
Fax Ordering: (212) 576-2994
Contact Name: Warren Leber, President
Catalog: Online. Sales: $500M to $1MM
Products: Bed & bath linens, window treatments,
bedspreads, duvet covers

ELECTROEASE PRODUCTS (800) 528-3974
907 N. Hollywood Way • Burbank, CA 91505
E-Mail: electroease@hotmail.com
Website: www.electroease.com
Fax Ordering: (818) 953-7421
International Ordering: (818) 953-7419
Contact Name: Chuck Liau, President
Catalog: Online. Sales: $1-3MM
Products: Electric adjustable beds, electric
lift-chairs, stair-lifts & scooters

ESSENTIAL ALTERNATIVES (800) 640-8834
22 Center St. • Rutland, VT 05701
E-Mail: info@rutlandherald.com/essentialalternatives/
Website: www.rutlandherald.com/essentialalternatives/
Fax Ordering: (802) 773-8834
International Ordering: (802) 773-8834
Contact Name: Carol Macleod, President
Catalog: $1. Frequency: Semiannual
Circulation: 25MM. Sales: $3-5MM
Products: Futon mattresses, bed frames & bedding

FEATHERED FRIENDS (206) 292-6292
1119 Mercer St. • Seattle, WA 98109
E-Mail: customerservice@featheredfriends.com
Website: www.featheredfriends.com
Fax Ordering: (206) 292-6403
Contact Name: Peter Hickner, President
Catalog: Free. Frequency: Annual
Circulation: 75M. Sales: $1-3MM
Products: Down bedding, accessories,
down sleeping bags and down jackets

FRONTGATE (800) 626-6488
5566 West Chester Rd.
West Chester, OH 45069
E-Mail: info@frontgate.com
Website: www.frontgate.com
Fax Ordering: (800) 436-2105
International Ordering: (513) 603-1444 Fax 603-1492
Customer Service: (800) 537-8484
Contact Name: Pete McAdams, Contact
Catalog: Free. Frequency: Quarterly
Circulation: 200M. Sales: $5-10MM
Products: Kitchen, bath, and home office
accessories; electronics and outdoor furniture

HARDWARE, BATH & MORE (800) 760-3278
20830 Coolidge Hwy.
Oak Park, MI 48237
E-Mail: magazone@hbm.com

Website: www.h.b.m.com
Fax Ordering: (248) 546-2328
International Ordering: (248) 398-7560
Contact Name: Gerald Isarz, President
Catalog: Free. Frequency: Annual
Circulation: 100M. Sales: $5-10MM
Products: Hardware, furnishings &
accessories for the bath

JANICE'S (800) 526-4237
30 Arbor St. South • Hartford, CT 06106
E-Mail: info@janices.com
Website: www.janices.com
Fax Ordering: (860) 523-4178
International Ordering: (860) 523-4479
Contact Name: Janice, President
Catalog: Free. Frequency: Annual
Circulation: 100K. Sales: $1-5MM
Products: Organic cotton sheets, pillows &
blankets; organic cotton masks & gloves; water
purifiers; organic cotton socks & slippers, hats &
gloves; organic cotton lingerie & clothing; personal
care products; organic cleaning & household
products

K&R INTERIORS, INC. (800) 444-2128
736 W. 300 S. • Salt Lake City, UT 84104
E-Mail: info@krbedspreads.com
Website: www.krbedspreads.com
Fax Ordering: (800) 898-7480
International Ordering: (801) 364-2128
Contact Name: Kathy Rowberny, President
Catalog: Free. Frequency: Semiannual
Circulation: 100M. Sales: $500M to $1MM
Products: Line of bedspreads, coverlets,
comforters, chenille & cotton sets

LEONARDS (888) 336-8585
600 Taunton Ave. • Seekonk, MA 02771
E-Mail: sales@leonardsdirect.com
Website: www.leonardsdirect.com
Fax Ordering: (508) 336-4884
International Ordering: (508) 336-8585
Contact Name: Jeffrey B. Jenkins, President
Catalog: Free. Frequency: Annual
Circulation: 100M. Sales: $3-5MM
Products: Antique beds

LINENSOURCE CATALOG (800) 434-9812
P.O. Box 31151 • Tampa, FL 33631 (800) 431-2620
E-Mail: info@linensource.com
Website: www.linensource.com
Fax Ordering: (813) 882-4605
International Ordering: (813) 885-9378
Customer Service: (800) 466-8447
Contact Name: Robert Franzblau, President
Catalog: Free. Pages: 88. Frequency: Semiannual
Circulation: 1MM. Sales: $100-500MM
Products: Bed linens & bath items

LISA VICTORIA BRASS BEDS (888) 296-2966
17106 S. Crater Rd.
Petersburg, VA 23805
E-Mail: sales@lisavictoria.com
Website: www.lisavictoria.com
Fax Ordering: (804) 796-3875
International Ordering: (804) 862-1491
Contact Name: Mary Hurt, President
Catalog: $4. Frequency: Annual
Circulation: 50M. Sales: $500M
Products: Brass beds

MURPHY BED CO., INC. (800) 845-2337
42 Central Ave. • Farmingdale, NY 11735
E-Mail: sales@murphybedcompany.com
Website: www.murphybedcompany.com
Fax Ordering: (631) 420-4337
International Ordering: (631) 420-4330
Contact Name: Clark Murphy, President
Catalog: Free. Frequency: Bimonthly
Circulation: 15M. Sales: $3-5MM
Products: Folding wall beds, wall units,
associated cabinetry

QUILTALOG (800) 828-8218
Old Country Store
P.O. Box 419 • Intercourse, PA 17534
E-Mail: sales@murphybedcompany.com
Website: www.murphybedcompany.com
Fax Ordering: (717) 768-3433
International Ordering: (717) 768-7171
Contact Name: Merle Good, President
Catalog: $2. Frequency: Semiannual
Circulation: 25M. Sales: $3-5MM
Products: handmade quilts

SEVENTH AVENUE CATALOG (800) 356-9090
1112 7th Ave. • Monroe, WI 53566
E-Mail: sales@seventhavenue.com
Website: www.seventhavenue.com
Fax Ordering: (608) 328-8457
International Ordering: (608) 324-7777
Contact Name: Gary Schwager, President
Catalog: Free. Frequency: 8x per year
Circulation: 250M. Sales: $100-250MM
Products: Bedding & accessories, home
furnishings, clothing, jewelry, gifts

SCHWEITZER LINEN (800) 554-6367
457 Columbus Ave. • New York, NY 10024
E-Mail: sales@schweitzer-linen.com
Website: www.schweitzer-linen.com
Fax Ordering: (212) 737-6328
International Ordering: (212) 799-9629
Contact Name: Robert Schweitzer, President
Catalog: Free. Frequency: Annual
Circulation: 25M. Sales: $500M
Products: Fine bedding & linens

SHERLE WAGNER INTERNATIONAL (888) 992-4637
60 E. 57th St. • New York, NY 10022
E-Mail: info@sherlewagner.com
Website: www.sherlewagner.com
Fax Ordering: (212) 207-8010
International Ordering: (212) 758-3300
Contact Name: Vincent Jeffrey, President
Catalog: $10. Frequency: Annual
Circulation: 50M. Sales: $3-5MM
Products: Bathroom fixtures, sinks, hardware;
lighting, furniture, linens, wall coverings, textiles

TOUCH OF CLASS CATALOG (800) 457-7456
709 W. 12th St. • Huntingburg, IN 47542
E-Mail: sales@touchofclasscatalog.com
Website: www.touchofclasscatalog.com
Fax Ordering: (812) 683-5921
International Ordering: (812) 683-3707
Contact Name: Frederick Bell, President
Catalog: Free. Frequency: Monthly
Circulation: 10MM. Sales: $50-100MM
Products: Home decor including bedding,
bath, wall decor, lamps, home accents, kids

VICTORIAN HEART (888) 334-3099
P.O. Box 6280 • Branson, MO 65615
E-Mail: vhc@tri-lakes.net
Website: www.victorianheart.com
Fax Ordering: (877) 775-3833; (417) 335-3833
International Ordering: (417) 334-3099
Contact Name: Ken Kline, President
Catalog: Free. Frequency: Quarterly
Circulation: 200M. Sales: $5-10MM
Products: Wholesale imported quilts,
pillows, shams, throws & linens

WAKE UP FRANKIE (866) 925-3872
1701 Quincy Ave. #14 • Naperville, IL 60540
E-Mail: customerservice@wakeupfrankie.com
Website: www.wakeupfrankie.com
Fax Ordering: (630) 420-2202
International Ordering: (630) 420-2332
Catalog: Free. Frequency: Semiannual
Circulation: 100K. Sales: $10-20MM
Products: Crib bedding

B & B HONEY FARM   (800) 342-4811
Rt. 2, Box 245 • Houston, MN 55943
E-Mail: bbhoney@acegroup.cc
Website: www.bbhoneyfarms.com
Fax Ordering: (507) 896-4134
International Ordering: (507) 896-3955
Contact Names: Robin Bernacchi, President
Catalog: $2. Frequency: Annual
Circulation: 10K. Sales: $1-3MM
Products: Beekeeping supplies & equipment;
candle making supplies

BEEKEEPER & CANDLEMAKING SUPPLIES   (800) 289-7668
A.I. Root Co.
623 W. Liberty St. • Medina, OH 44256
E-Mail: corporate@airoot.com
Website: www.rootcandles.com
Fax Ordering: (330) 725-5624
International Ordering: (330) 725-6677
Contact Names: John A. Root, President
Catalog: Free. Frequency: Annual
Circulation: 50K. Sales: $20-50MM
Products: Beekeeper and candle making supplies

BETTERBEE   (800) 632-3379
8 Meader Rd. • Greenwich, NY 12834
E-Mail: betterbee@betterbee.com
Website: www.betterbee.com
Fax Ordering: (518) 692-9802
Contact Name: Robert A. Stevens, President
Catalog: Free. Frequency: Annual
Circulation: 50K. Sales: $1-3MM
Products: Honey & candles, beekeeping &
candle making supplies; soap making supplies

BRUSHY MOUNTAIN BEE FARM   (800) 233-7929
610 Bethany Church Rd.
Moravian Falls, NC 28654
E-Mail: info@brushymountainbeefarm.com
Website: www.brushymountainbeefarm.com
Fax Ordering: (336) 921-2681
International Ordering: (336) 921-3640
Contact Names: Stephen Forrest, President
Catalog: Free. Frequency: Annual
Circulation: 75K. Sales: $1-3MM
Products: Beekeeping supplies & equipment;
candle making supplies; soap and skin care
supplies; mead and wine supplies; videos,
books; protective clothing

CANDLECHEM COMPANY   (508) 586-1880
56 Intervale St. • Brockton, MA 02302
E-Mail: info@candlechem.com
Website: www.candlechem.com
Fax Ordering: (508) 586-1784
International Ordering: (508) 586-1880
Catalog: Online. Sales: $500M to $1MM
Products: Candle making supplies

THE CANDLE FACTORY   (800) 292-3616
301 Grandview Pkwy. • Traverse City, MI 49684
E-Mail: info@candles.net
Website: www.candles.net
Catalog: Online. Sales: $1-5MM
Products: Candles, gifts & accessories.

GLORYBEE MAIL ORDER   (800) 456-7923
GloryBee Foods, Inc.
P.O. Box 2744 • Eugene, OR 97402
E-Mail: info@glorybeefoods.com
Website: www.glorybeefoods.com
Fax Ordering: (541) 689-9692

International Ordering: (541) 762-7173
Contact Name: Richard Turanski, President
Catalog: Free. Frequency: Annual
Circulation: 50K. Sales: $5-10MM
Products: Candlemaking, beekeeping &
soapmaking supplies; nutritional supplements,
aromatherapy supplies, honey

WALTER T. KELLEY COMPANY   (800) 233-2899
807 W. Main St. • Clarkson, KY 42726
E-Mail: kelleybees@kynet.net
Website: www.kelleybees.com
Fax Ordering: (270) 242-4801
International Ordering: (270) 242-2012
Contact Names: Sarah Manion, President
Catalog: Free. Frequency: Annual
Circulation: 50K. Sales: $10-20MM
Products: Beekeeping supplies & equipment

MANN LAKE, LTD.   (800) 880-7694
501 S. 1st St. • Hackensack, MN 56452
E-Mail: beekeeper@mannlakeltd.com
Website: www.mannlakeltd.com
Fax Ordering: (218) 675-6156
Contact Name: Cathy Damaska, President
Catalog: Free. Frequency: Annual
Circulation: 500K. Sales: $1-3MM
Products: Honey wax and candle-flex molds
and candle luster spray, plaster, soap

POURETTE CANDLE &   (800) 888-9425
SOAP MAKING SUPPLIES
1418 NW 53rd St. • Seattle, WA 98107
E-Mail: sales@pourette.com
Website: www.pourette.com
Fax Ordering: (206) 789-3640
International Ordering: (206) 789-3188
Contact Name: Mike Kovacs, President
Catalog: $3. Frequency: Annual
Circulation: 10K. Sales: $3-5MM
Products: Candle and soap making supplies

QUALLA ARTS & CRAFTS MUTUAL   (828) 497-3103
645 Tsali Blvd. • Cherokee, NC 28719
E-Mail: info@quallaartsandcrafts.org
Website: www.quallaartsandcrafts.org
Fax Ordering: (828) 497-4841
International Ordering: (828) 497-3103
Contact Name: Jackie Bradley, President
Catalog: $3. Frequency: Annual
Circulation: 10K. Sales: $1-3MM
Products: Candle & soap making supplies

THE SOAP SALOON   (916) 334-4894
1805 Tribute Rd. #G • Sacramento, CA 95838
E-Mail: sales@soapsaloon.com
Website: www.soapsaloon.com
Fax Ordering: (916) 921-9464
Contact Name: Jack Schade, President
Catalog: Online. Sales: $500K to $1MM
Products: Custom made soap molds;
soap and candlemaking supplies; oils

SUNFEATHER NATURAL SOAP CO.   (315) 265-3648
1551 State Hwy. 72 • Potsdam, NY 13676
E-Mail: sales@sunfeather.com
Website: www.sunfeather.com
Fax Ordering: (315) 265-2902
Contact Name: Sandy Maine, President
Catalog: $2. Frequency: Annual
Circulation: 250M. Sales: $1-3MM
Products: Soap and soap making suppliesm & equipment

AIRE CATALOG   **(800) 247-3432**
P.O. Box 186 • Meridian, ID 83680
E-Mail: info@aire.com
Website: www.aire.com
Fax Ordering: (800) 701-2473; (208) 884-2089
International Ordering: (208) 888-1772
Catalog: Free. Frequency: Annual
Circulation: 100K. Sales: $3-5MM
Products: Whitewater rafts, catarafts &
inflatable kayaks

ARMCHAIR SAILOR BOOKS & CHARTS   **(800) 292-4278**
543 Thames St. • Newport, RI 02840
E-Mail: sales@bluewaterweb.com
Website: www.bluewaterweb.com
Fax Ordering: (401) 847-1219
International Ordering: (401) 847-4252
Contact Name: Susan Dye, President
Catalog: Free. Frequency: Annual
Circulation:75K. Sales: $1-3MM
Products: Marine books, videos, games,
charts & software

BARR MARINE PRODUCTS CATALOG   **(866) 255-9265**
100 Douglas Way
Natural Bridge Station, VA 24579
E-Mail: sales@barmarine.net
Website: www.barmarine.net
Fax Ordering: (540) 291-4185
International Ordering: (540) 291-4180
Contact Name: Michael Gibbs, Marketing
Catalog: Free. Frequency: Annual
Circulation: 100K. Sales: $5-10MM
Products: Marine exhaust parts & accessories

BART'S WATERSPORTS CATALOG   **(800) 348-5016**
Bart's Water Sports
P.O. Box 294 • North Webster, IN 46555
E-Mail: info@bartswatersports.com
Website: www.bartswatersports.com
Fax Ordering: (574) 834-4246
International Ordering: (574) 834-7666
Contact Name: Mike Wilson, Marketing
Catalog: Free. Frequency: Qaurterly
Circulation: 1MM. Sales: $10-20MM
Products: Personal watercraft & boating
accessories; clothing

BAY PATTERN WORKS CATALOG   **(419) 499-4602**
Bay Manufacturing; Div. of HEMCO Corp.
P.O. Box 1250 • Milan, OH 44846
E-Mail: baymfg@accnorwalkcom
Website: www.baymfg.com
Fax Ordering: (419) 499-4603
Contact Name: M.J. McGuire, President
Catalog: Free. Frequency: Annual
Circulation: 50K. Sales: $5-10MM
Products: Outboard motor extension kits

BECKMANN BOATSHOP   **(401) 294-1030**
P.O. Box 26 • Slocum, RI 02877
E-Mail: boatshop@netsense.net
Website: www.steamboating.net
Fax Ordering: (401) 783-1859
Contact Name: Walter Beckmann, President
Catalog: $20. Frequency: Quarterly
Circulation: 10K. Sales: $3-5MM
Products: Antique & classic launches &
tugboats, steam & electric

BECKSON MARINE CATALOG   **(203) 333-1412**
165 Holland Ave. • Bridgeport, CT 06605
E-Mail: info@beckson.com
Website: www.beckson.com
Fax Ordering: (203) 384-6954
Contact Name: Frank S. Beckerer, Jr., President
Catalog: Free. Frequency: Semiannual
Circulation: 100K. Sales: $10-20MM
Products: Marine pumps & equipment &
accessories for OEM and aftermarket;
hatches & ports

BENNETT MARINE VIDEO   **(800) 733-8862**
2321 Abbot Kinney Blvd. • Venice, CA 90291
E-Mail: sales@bennettmarine.com
Website: www.bennettmarine.com
Fax Ordering: (310) 827-8074
International Ordering: (310) 827-8064
Catalog: Free. Frequency: Semiannual
Circulation: 100K. Sales: $1-3MM
Products: Instructional videos on boating,
cruising, sailing, fishing, diving and water sports

BLUEWATER BOOKS & CHARTS   **(800) 942-2583**
1811 Cordova Rd. • Ft.Lauderdale, FL 33316
E-Mail: sales@bluewaterweb.com
Website: www.bluewaterweb.com
Fax Ordering: (401) 847-1219
International Ordering: (954) 763-6533
Contact Name: Melanie Neal, Contact
Catalog: Free. Frequency: Annual
Circulation: 75K. Sales: $3-5MM
Products: Marine books, videos, games,
charts & software

BOATING EQUIPMENT REPORTS   **(800) 937-2628**
BoatUS • 880 S. Pickett St.
Alexandria, VA 22304
E-Mail: customercare@westmarine.com
Website: www.boatus-store.com
Fax Ordering: (703) 461-2847
International Ordering: (703) 823-9550
Contact Name: Nancy Michelman, President
Catalog: Free. Frequency: Semiannual
Circulation: 100K. Sales: $20-50MM
Products: Boating equipment & supplies

BOATLIFE CATALOG   **(800) 382-9706**
4060 Bridge View Dr.
N. Charleston, SC 29405
E-Mail: boatlife@boatlife.com
Website: www.boatlife.com
Fax Ordering: (843) 566-1275
International Ordering: (843) 566-1225
Contact Name: Grace L. Schmidt, President
Catalog: Free. Frequency: Annual
Circulation: 50K. Sales: $3-5MM
Products: Marine sealant compunds, finishes,
waxes & cleaners

C. CUSHIONS CATALOG   **(800) 531-1014**
206 Hwy. 35 South • Rockport, TX 78382
E-Mail: ccushions@sbcglobal.net
Website: www.ccushions.com
Fax Ordering: (361) 729-1260
International Ordering: (361) 729-1244
Contact Name: Bill Coxwell, President
Catalog: Free. Frequency: Annual
Circulation:100K. Sales: $3-5MM
Products: Boat cushions

THE CARLISLE & FINCH COMPANY   (513) 681-6080
4562 W. Mitchell Ave. • Cincinnati, OH 45232
E-Mail: searchlight@msn.com
Website: www.carlislefinch.com
Fax Ordering: (513) 681-6226
International Ordering: (618) 258-3549
Contact Name: Chrissy Banks, Sales
Catalog: Free. Frequency: Annual
Circulation: 25K. Sales: $3-5MM
Products: Marine lights; searchlight technology

CASCADE OUTFITTERS CATALOG   (800) 223-7238
604 E. 45th St. • Boise, ID 83714
E-Mail: mail@cascadeoutfitter.com
Website: www.cascadeoutfitters.com
Fax Ordering: (208) 322-5016
International Ordering: (208) 322-4411
Contact Name: Jack Nelson, President
Catalog: Free. Frequency: Annual
Circulation: 75K. Sales: $1-3MM
Products: Rafts, kayaks & boating accessories

CAVINESS WOODWORKING, INC.   (800) 626-5195
200 N. Aycock Ave. • Calhoun City, MS 38916
E-Mail: sales@cavinesspaddles.com
Website: www.cavinesspaddles.com
Fax Ordering: (662) 628-8580
International Ordering: (662) 628-5195
Contact Name: Don Caviness, President
Catalog: Free. Frequency: Annual
Circulation:100K. Sales: $10-20MM
Products: Paddles & oars

CELESTAIRE CATALOG   (800) 727-9785
4609 E. Kellogg Dr. • Wichita, KS 67218   (888) 628-4428
E-Mail: info@celestaire.com
Website: www.celestaire.com
Fax Ordering: (316) 686-8926
International Ordering: (316) 686-9785
Contact Name: K.L. Gebhart, President
Catalog: Free. Frequency: Annual
Circulation: 75K. Sales: $5-10MM
Products: Navigation equipment, sextants,
weather equipment & astronomy equipment

CLARK CRAFT BOAT KIT & PLANS &   (716) 873-2640
CLARK CRAFT SUPPLY CATALOGS
16-99 Aqua Lane • Tonawanda, NY 14150
E-Mail: info@clarkcraft.com
Website: www.clarkcraft.com
Fax Ordering: (716) 873-2651
Catalog: $5 - Boat Kit & Plans;
Free - Supply Catalog; Frequency: Annual
Circulation: 25K. Sales: $5-10MM
Products: Boat kits, plans, patterns &
materials; boat supplies

CLASSIC AIRBOATERS CATALOG   (800) 247-2628
300 N. Wilson Ave. • Cocoa, FL 32922
E-Mail: info@airboats.com
Website: www.airboats.com
Fax Ordering: (321) 632-6043
International Ordering: (321) 632-1722
Contact Name: W. Bishop Jordan, President
Catalog: $3. Frequency: Annual
Circulation: 25K. Sales: $5-10MM
Products: Airboats & accessories

COBRA KAYAKS CATALOG   (310) 327-9216
Aquatx Distribution Corp.
P.O. Box 3134 • Gardena, CA 90247
E-Mail: info@cobrakayaks.com

Website: www.cobrakayaks.com
Fax Ordering: (310) 327-8952
Contact Name: Wes Ogle, VP
Catalog: Free. Frequency: Annual
Circulation: 50K. Sales: $5-10MM
Products: 12 sit-on-top kayaks, paddles
& accessories

DEFENDER MARINE BUYER'S GUIDE   (800) 628-8225
Defender Industries
42 Great Neck Rd. • Waterford, CT 06385
E-Mail: info@defender.com
Website: www.defender.com
Fax Ordering: (800) 654-1616
International Ordering: (860) 701-3400
Contact Name: Stephan Lance, President
Catalog: Free. Frequency: Annual
Circulation: 100K. Sales: $20-50MM
Products: Boating, marine & watersports
equipment, accessories & supplies; marine
electronics, inflatable boats, outboard motors

DWYER ALUMINUM MAST COMPANY   (203) 484-0419
2 Commerce Dr. • North Branford, CT 06471
E-Mail: sail@dwyermast.com
Website: www.dwyermast.com
Fax Ordering: (203) 484-2014
Contact Name: Robert Dwyer, President
Catalog: Free. Frequency: Semiannual
Circulation: 50K. Sales: $5-10MM
Products: Masts, boats & hardware for sailboats

EASY RIDER CANOE & KAYAK CO.   (425) 228-3633
P.O. Box 88108 • Seattle, WA 98138
E-Mail: info@easyriderkayaks.com
Website: www.easyriderkayaks.com
Fax Ordering: (425) 277-8778
Catalog: $10 - 4 catalogs. Frequency: Annual.
Circulation: 5K. Sales: $500K
Products: Catalogs: Kayaks, Canoes,
Multi-Use Rowing Craft, Specialty Paddlecraft

EDSON INTERNATIONAL CATALOG   (508) 995-9711
146 Duchaine Blvd. • New Bedford, MA 02745
E-Mail: info@edsonintl.com
Website: www.edsonmarine.com
Fax Ordering: (508) 995-5021
Contact Name: William M. Keene, President
Catalog: Free. Frequency: Annual
Circulation: 100K. Sales: $10-20MM
Products: Boat parts & hardware

EL CAPITAN SPORTS CENTER   (800) 627-6457
1590 NW 27th Ave. • Miami, FL 33125
E-Mail: info@elcapitan.com
Website: www.elcapitan.com
Fax Ordering: (305) 633-3812
International Ordering: (305) 635-7500
Contact Name: Xavier Coto, President
Catalog: Free. Frequency: 3x per year
Circulation: 150K. Sales: $10-20MM
Products: Marine accessories & supplies;
fishing accessories; diving equipment; electronics;
electrical accessories; trailer equipment; engine
system; books, charts & video; apparel, eyeware
& footwear; coolers

FOLBOT CORPORATION   (800) 528-9592
4209 Pace St. • Charleston, SC 29405   (800) 533-5099
E-Mail: info@folbot.com
Website: www.folbot.com
Fax Ordering: (843) 744-7783

International Ordering: (843) 744-3483
Contact Name: Philip W. Cotton, President
Catalog: Free. Frequency: Annual
Circulation: 75K. Sales: $5-10MM
Products: Folding boats

FOLLANSBEE DOCK SYSTEMS   (800) 223-3444
P.O. Box 610 • Follansbee, WV 26037
E-Mail: info@follansbeedocks.com
Website: www.follansbeedocks.com
Fax Ordering: (304) 527-4507
International Ordering: (304) 527-4500
Contact Name: Doran Wickham, Sales
Catalog: Free. Frequency: Annual
Circulation: 150K. Sales: $20-50MM
Products: Boat docks, wood dock hardware,
flotation drums, swim float kits & dock
accessories

FORESPAR PRODUCTS CORP.   (949) 858-8820
22322 Gilberto
Rancho Santa Margarita, CA 92688
E-Mail: sales@forespar.com
Website: www.forespar.com
Fax Ordering: (949) 858-0505
Catalog: Free. Frequency: Annual
Circulation: 50K. Sales: $5-10MM
Products: Sailing equipment & accessories

FREEPORT MARINE SUPPLY COMPANY   (800) 645-2565
47 W. Merrick Rd. • Freeport, NY 11520
E-Mail: info@freeportmarine.com
Website: www.freeportmarine.com
Fax Ordering: (516) 379-2909
International Ordering: (516) 379-2610
Catalog: Free. Frequency: Annual
Circulation: 150M. Sales: $5-10MM
Products: Boating & marine supplies & equipment

FOUR CORNERS MARINE   (800) 426-7637
360 S. Camino Del Rio • Durango, CO 81301
E-Mail: sales@riversports.com
Website: www.riversports.com
Fax Ordering: (970) 247-7819
International Ordering: (970) 247-2330
Contact Name: Nancy Wiley, President
Catalog: Free. Frequency: Annual
Circulation: 75M. Sales: $500M to $1MM
Products: Supplies & accessories for
canoeing, kayaking & rafting

GRAFFRIG CATALOG   (847) 548-5900
Livorsi Marine
10 Graffrig Dr. • Grayslake, IL 60030
E-Mail: sales@livorsi.com
Website: www.livorsi.com
Fax Ordering: (847) 548-5903
Contact Name: Mike Livorsi, President
Catalog: Free. Pages: 120. Frequency: Annual
Circulation: 75M. Sales: $500M to $1MM
Products: Waterproof/anti-fog gauges,
controls & accessories for your boat

GOUGEON BROTHERS CATALOG   (989) 684-7286
P.O. Box 908 • Bay City, MI 48707
E-Mail: webmaster@gougeonbrothers.com
Website: www.gougeonbrothers.com
Fax Ordering: (989) 684-1374
Contact Name: Meade Gougeon, President
Catalog: Free. Frequency: Annual
Circulation: 50M. Sales: $5-10MM
Products: Supplies for boat repairs

HAMILTON MARINE CATALOG   (800) 639-2715
P.O. Box 227 • Searsport, ME 04974
E-Mail: mail@hamiltonmarine.com
Website: www.hamiltonmarine.com
Fax Ordering: (800) 548-6352
International Ordering: (207) 548-2985
Contact Name: Wayne Hamilton, President
Catalog: Free. Frequency: Annual
Circulation: 50M. Sales: $5-10MM
Products: Marine hardware, fasteners & supplies

HOBIE CAT COMPANY CATALOG   (760) 758-9100
4925 Oceanside Blvd.
Oceanside, CA 92056
E-Mail: info@hobiecatcom
Website: www.hobiecat.com
Fax Ordering: (760) 758-1841
Contact Name: Matt Miller, Marketing
Catalog: Free. Frequency: Annual
Circulation: 50M. Sales: $10-20MM
Products: Hobie Cat fishing boats

ITT JABSCO PRODUCTS   (949) 609-5106
20 Icon • Foothill Ranch, CA 92610
E-Mail: sales@jabsco.com
Website: www.jabsco.com
Fax Ordering: (949) 853-1254
Contact Name: Lawrence K. Dart, President
Catalog: Free. Frequency: Annual
Circulation: 150M. Sales: $20-50MM
Products: Marine pumps & water systems

INTERNATIONAL MARINE BOATING BOOKS   (800) 262-4729
P.O. Box 220 • Camden, ME 04843
E-Mail: info@books.mcgraw-hill.com
Website: www.books.mcgraw-hill.com
Fax Ordering: (207) 236-6314
International Ordering: (207) 236-4837
Catalog: Free. Frequency: Annual
Circulation: 50M. Sales: $1-3MM
Products: Nautical books, videos & software

JSI - THE SAILING SOURCE   (800) 234-3220
3000 Gandy Blvd. N
St. Petersburg, FL 33702
E-Mail: mail@jsisail.com
Website: www.jsisail.com
Fax Ordering: (727) 577-3220
International Ordering: (727) 576-1306
Contact Name: Larry B. French, President
Catalog: Free. Frequency: 7x per year
Circulation: 250M. Sales: $5-10MM
Products: Sailing hardware & gear; Sobstad sails,
spars, rigging, cushions & canvas

JASON/EQUINE CATALOG   (800) 255-6366
Bausch & Lomb/Bushnell
9200 Cody St. • Overland Park, KS 66214
Fax Ordering: (913) 752-3550
International Ordering: (913) 752-3400
Contact Name: James F. Huntington, President
Catalog: Free. Frequency: Annual
Circulation: 100M. Sales: $10-20MM
Products: Binoculars, magnifiers &
weather instruments

KRISTI'S CATALOG   (800) 334-6541
Overton's
111 Red Banks Rd. • Greenville, NC 27858
E-Mail: info@overtonsonline.com
Website: www.overtonsonline.com
Fax Ordering: (252) 355-2923

Contact Name: Parker Overton, President
Catalog: Free. Frequency: 6x per year
Circulation: 10MM. Sales: $50-100MM
Products: Marine accessories, watersports equipment, swimwear & other related apparel

LANDFALL NAVIGATION (800) 941-2219
151 Harvard Ave. • Stamford, CT 06902
E-Mail: info@landfallnavigation.com
Website: www.landfallnavigation.com
Fax Ordering: (203) 487-0776
International Ordering: (203) 487-0775
Catalog: Free. Frequency: Semiannual
Circulation: 100M. Sales: $5-10MM
Products: Marine safety products & nautical charts

LAUGHING LOON CANOES & KAYAKS (413) 773-5375
833 N. Colrain Rd. • Greenfield, MA 01301
E-Mail: laughing_loon@shaysnet.com
Website: www.laughingloon.com
Fax Ordering: (413) 772-3771
Catalog: $5. Frequency: Annual
Circulation: 10M. Sales: $500M to $1MM
Products: Custom canoes & kayaks

MARINE ASSOCIATES CATALOG (715) 386-5144
1651 Hanley Rd. • Hudson, WI 54016
Fax Ordering: (715) 386-5357
Contact Name: Mark Johnston, President
Catalog: Free. Frequency: Annual
Circulation: 50M. Sales: $3-5MM
Products: Marine hardware

MARINE PRODUCTS CATALOG (301) 373-2372
43985 Commerce Ave.
Hollywood, MD 20636
E-Mail: sales@ssicustomplastics.com
Website: www.ssicustomplastics.com
Fax Ordering: (301) 373-2734
Catalog: Free. Pages: 30. Frequency: Annual
Circulation: 100M. Sales: $5-10MM
Products: Boating accessories & fish coolers

NANTAHALA OUTDOOR CENTER (800) 367-3521
13077 Hwy. 19 W • Bryson City, NC 28713
E-Mail: storecatalog@noc.com
Website: www.noc.com
Fax Ordering: (828) 488-2498
International Ordering: (828) 488-2175
Contact Name: Larry Pitt, President
Catalog: Free. Frequency: Annual
Circulation: 75M. Sales: $5-10MM
Products: Kayaks, canoes, paddles, paddle jackets, booties & racks

NAUTICAL BOATIQUE CATALOG (800) 327-6457
1590 NW 27th Ave. • Miami, FL 33125
E-Mail: sales@nauticalboatique.com
Website: www.nauticalboatique.com
Fax Ordering: (305) 633-6586
International Ordering: (305) 871-3040
Contact Name: Martha Bolanos, President
Catalog: Free. Frequency: Annual
Circulation:75M. Sales: $500M to $1MM
Products: Clothing & shoes for boating

NEWFOUND WOODWORKS (603) 744-6872
67 Danforth Brook Rd. • Bristol, NH 03222
E-Mail: sales@newfound.com
Website: www.newfound.com
Fax Ordering: (618) 258-3084

International Ordering: (618) 258-3549
Contact Name: Michael Vermouth, President
Catalog: $5. Frequency: Semiannual
Circulation: 5M. Sales: $500M
Products: Cedar strip canoes, kayaks & rowing boat kits

NICHOLS NET & TWINE COMPANY (800) 878-6387
2200 State Rt. 111 • Granite City, IL 62040
Fax Ordering: (618) 797-0212
International Ordering: (618) 797-0211
Contact Name: John Rogenski, President
Catalog: Free. Frequency: Annual
Circulation: 15M. Sales: $500M
Products: Nylon netting, twines & rope

NORTHWEST OUTDOOR CENTER (800) 683-0637
2100 Westlake Ave. N • Seattle, WA 98109
E-Mail: mail@nwoc.com
Website: www.nwoc.com
Fax Ordering: (206) 282-0690
International Ordering: (206) 281-9694
Contact Name: Herbie Meyer, President
Catalog: Free. Frequency: Annual
Circulation: 50M. Sales: $500M to $1MM
Products: Sea kayaking & whitewater paddling gear & kayaks; clothing, westsuits, booties, gloves; books & videos

NORTHWEST RIVER SUPPLIES (800) 635-5202
2009 S. Main St. • Moscow, ID 83843
Fax Ordering: (208) 883-4787
International Ordering: (208) 882-2383
Contact Name: Bill Parks, President
Catalog: Free. Frequency: 3x per year
Circulation: 300M. Sales: $5-10MM
Products: Inflatable rafts, kayaks, canoes & accessores, including high quality paddles

OSCO MOTORS CORPORATION (215) 855-8268
P.O. Box 136 • Souderton, PA 18964
Fax Ordering: (215) 855-5976
Contact Name: Thomas R. Cooper, President
Catalog: Free. Frequency: Annual
Circulation: 25M. Sales: $1-3MM
Products: Marine engine exhaust systems

OVERTON'S DISCOUNT BOATING ACCESSORIES (800) 334-6541
P.O. Box 8228 • Greenville, NC 27835
E-Mail: custserv@overtons.com
Website: www.overtons.com
Fax Ordering: (252) 355-2923
International Ordering: (252) 355-7600
Contact Name: Parker Overton, President
Catalog: Free. Frequency: Bimonthly
Circulation: 6MM. Sales: $50-100MM
Products: Marine accessories, watersports equipment, swimwear & other related apparel

PHOENIX POKE BOATS (800) 354-0190
P.O. Box 100 • Berea, KY 40403
E-Mail: pokeboats@pokeboat.com
Website: www.pokeboat.com
Fax Ordering: (859) 986-3277
International Ordering: (859) 986-2336
Contact Name: Peggy Wilson, President
Catalog: Free. Frequency: Bimonthly
Circulation: 500M. Sales: $1-3MM
Products: Small lightweight boats, canoes, kayaks, duck boats

PIRAGIS BOUNDARY WATERS CATALOG   (800) 223-6565
Piragis Northwoods Company
105 N. Central Ave. • Ely, MN 55731
E-Mail: info@piragis.com
Website: www.boundarywaterscatalog.com
Fax Ordering: (218) 365-6220
International Ordering: (218) 365-6745
Contact Name: Steve Piragis, President
Catalog: Free. Frequency: Semiannual
Circulation: 500M. Sales: $1-3MM
Products: Canoing, kayaking, accessories, adventure travel, gifts, clothing, books

POMPANETTE CATALOG   (954) 525-6367
1515 SE 16th St. • Ft. Lauderdale, FL 33316
E-Mail: sales@flaghouse.com
Website: www.flaghouse.com
Fax Ordering: (954) 525-4025
Contact Name: Mary Hubener, President
Catalog: Free. Frequency: Annual
Circulation: 50M. Sales: $500M to $1MM
Products: Marine accessories

PORTA-BOTE CATALOG   (800) 227-8882
1074 Independence Ave.
Mountain View, CA 94043
E-Mail: info@portaboat.com
Website: www.porta-bote.com
Fax Ordering: (650) 961-3800
International Ordering: (650) 961-5334
Contact Name: Sandy Kaye, President
Catalog: Free. Frequency: Annual
Circulation: 100M. Sales: $5-10MM
Products: Portable, folding & inflatable boats

PROFESSIONAL RIVER OUTFITTERS   (800) 648-3236
P.O. Box 635 • Flagstaff, AZ 86002
E-Mail: sales@proriver.com
Website: www.proriver.com
Fax Ordering: (928) 213-0936
International Ordering: (928) 779-1512
Catalog: Free. Frequency: Weekly
Circulation: 150M. Sales: $500M to $1MM
Products: Rafting equipment

PYRAMID TECHNOLOGY, LLC CATALOG   (203) 238-0550
48 Elm St. • Meriden, CT 06450
E-Mail: info@pyramid.com
Website: www.pyramid.com
Fax Ordering: (203) 634-1696
Contact Name: John Augustyn, President
Catalog: Free. Frequency: Annual
Circulation: 10M. Sales: $10-20MM
Products: Marine lights & accessories

RANGER BOAT CATALOG   (870) 453-2222
P.O. Box 179 • Flippin, AR 72634
Fax Ordering: (870) 453-7398
Contact Name: Randy Hopper, President
Catalog: Free. Frequency: Annual
Circulation: 200M. Sales: $10-20MM
Products: Power boats

RARITAN ENGINEERING COMPANY   (856) 825-4900
P.O. Box 1157 • Millville, NJ 08332
E-Mail: info@raritaneng.com
Website: www.raritaneng.com
Fax Ordering: (856) 825-4409
Contact Name: Arthur J. Britnell, Jr., President
Catalog: Free. Frequency: Annual
Circulation: 20M. Sales: $5-10MM
Products: Boat sanitation & water systems

E.S. RITCHIE & SONS CATALOG   (781) 826-5131
243 Oak St. • Pembroke, MA 02359
E-Mail: info@ritchienavigation.com
Website: www.ritchienavigation.com
Fax Ordering: (781) 826-7336
Contact Name: Paul Sherman, President
Catalog: Free. Frequency: Annual
Circulation: 150M. Sales: $20-50MM
Products: Marine instruments

ROLOFF ANCHORS CATALOG   (920) 766-3501
Roloff Manufacturing Corporation
400 Gortrude St. • Kaukauna, WI 54130
E-Mail: sales@roloffmfg.com
Website: www.roloffmfg.com
Fax Ordering: (920) 766-3896
Contact Name: Robert J. Roloff, President
Catalog: $5. Frequency: Annual
Circulation: 15M. Sales: $1-3MM
Products: Boat anchors, dock & pier hardware

ROSS MARINE IDEAS CATALOG   (800) 327-8929
2756 N. Dixie Hwy. • Ft. Lauderdale, FL 33334
E-Mail: unameit@aol.com
International Ordering: (954) 561-4200
Contact Name: Joan S. Rossheim, President
Catalog: Free. Frequency: Annual
Circulation: 25M. Sales: $500M
Products: Personalized boat products

ROTOCAST PLASTIC PRODUCTS   (800) 537-8888
5061 S. National Dr. • Knoxville, TN 37914
E-Mail: tennessee@rotonics.com
Website: www.rotonics.com
Fax Ordering: (865) 524-0170
International Ordering: (865) 522-9902
Catalog: Free. Frequency: Annual
Circulation: 100M. Sales: $3-5MM
Products: Canoe, kayak & pantoon boat kits

SAILRITE CATALOG   (800) 348-2769
305 W. Van Buren St.
Columbia City, IN 46725
E-Mail: sailrite@sailrite.com
Website: www.sailrite.com
Fax Ordering: (618) 258-3084
International Ordering: (618) 258-3549
Contact Name: Jim Grant, President
Catalog: Free. Frequency: Annual
Circulation: 50M. Sales: $1-3MM
Products: Supplies & instructions for sailmaking & canvas work, sewing machines; kits for sails, covers, awnings & dodgers

SEA EAGLE CATALOG   (800) 944-7496
19 N. Columbia St.
Port Jefferson, NY 11776
E-Mail: staff@seaeagle.com
Website: www.seaeagle.com
Fax Ordering: (631) 473-7308
International Ordering: (631) 473-7398
Contact Name: Cecil C. Hoge, Jr., President
Catalog: Free. Frequency: 5x per year
Circulation: 100M. Sales: $3-5MM
Products: Sea eagle inflatable boats, floats, accessories & fishing lures

SEVYLOR USA CATALOG   (800) 821-4645
6651 E. 26th St. • Los Angeles, CA 90040
E-Mail: sales@sevylor.com
Website: www.sevylor.com
Fax Ordering: (323) 726—0481

International Ordering: (323) 727-6013
Contact Name: Conny Klimenko, President
Catalog: Free. Frequency: Annual
Circulation: 35M. Sales: $10-20MM
Products: Inflatable boats

SKIPPER MARINE ELECTRONICS   (800) 621-2378
1511 Riedel Dr. • Mundelein, IL 60062
Fax Ordering: (847) 566-5211
International Ordering: (847) 566-1800
Contact Name: Donna Shifers, President
Catalog: Free. Frequency: Annual
Circulation: 100M. Sales: $5-10MM
Products: Marine electronics

SPRING CREEK CANOE ACCESSORIES   (800) 937-8881
8873 Spring St. • Mountain Iron, MN 55768
E-Mail: newberg@canoegear.com
Website: www.canoegear.com
Fax Ordering: (218) 735-8018
International Ordering: (218) 735-8719
Contact Name: Vy Newberg, President
Catalog: Free. Frequency: Annual
Circulation: 15M. Sales: $500M TO $1MM
Products: Canoe & kayak accessories

SPRINT/ROTHAMMER CATALOG   (800) 235-2156
720 Aerovista Dr. • San Luis Obispo, CA 93401
E-Mail: info@sprintaquatics.com
Website: www.sprintaquatics.com
Fax Ordering: (805) 541-5339
International Ordering: (805) 541-5330
Contact Name: Dianne Rothhammer, President
Catalog: Free. Frequency: Annual
Circulation: 125M. Sales: $500M $1MM
Products: Aquatic & therapy products

STEARNS, INC.   (800) 697-5801
P.O. Box 1498 • St. Cloud, MN 56302
E-Mail: stearns@stearnsnet.com
Website: www.stearnsinc.com
Fax Ordering: (320) 252-4425
International Ordering: (320) 252-1642
Contact Name: David G. Cook, President
Catalog: Free. Frequency: Annual
Circulation: 100M. Sales: $5-10MM
Products: Flotation devices & foul weather gear

TEMPO PRODUCTS COMPANY   (440) 248-1450
6200 Cochran Rd. • Cleveland, OH 44139
E-Mail: sales@tempoproducts.com
Website: www.tempoproducts.com
Fax Ordering: (440) 349-4241
Contact Name: Ronald Eureka, President
Catalog: $1. Frequency: Annual
Circulation: 10M. Sales: $10-20MM
Products: Tanks for boats

VETUS CATALOG   (800) 468-3887
7251 National Dr. • Hanover, MD 21076
E-Mail: info@vetus.com
Website: www.vetus.com
Fax Ordering: (410) 712-0985
International Ordering: (410) 712-0985
Contact Name: Leo J. Van Hemert, President
Catalog: Free. Frequency: Semiannual
Circulation: 50M. Sales: $5-10MM
Products: Marine accessories, flexible tanks,
exhaust systems, decorative lights, engines, etc.

WATERMASTER RAFTS CATALOG   (800) 239-7238
P.O. Box 5043 • Missoula, MT 59806

E-Mail: info@kickboat.com
Website: www.kickboat.com
Fax Ordering: (406) 251-3338
International Ordering: (406) 251-3337
Contact Name: Kevin McCarthy, President
Catalog: Free. Frequency: Annual
Circulation: 10M. Sales: $500M
Products: Rafts & raft supplies

WEEMS & PLATH CATALOG   (800) 638-0428
214 Eastern Ave. • Annapolis, MD 21403
E-Mail: trogdon@weems-plath.com
Website: www.weems-plath.com
Fax Ordering: (410) 268-8713
International Ordering: (410) 263-6700
Contact Name: Peter Trogdon, President
Catalog: Free. Frequency: Annual
Circulation: 100M. Sales: $3-5MM
Products: Nautical instruments

WEL-NO-NAH CANOES CATALOG   (507) 454-5430
P.O. Box 247 • Winona, MN 55987
Fax Ordering: (507) 454-5448
Contact Name: Mike Cichanowski, President
Catalog: Free. Frequency: Annual
Circulation: 50M. Sales: $3-5MM
Products: Canoes

WEST MARINE CATALOG   (800) 262-8464
P.O. Box 50070 • Watsonville, CA 95076
E-Mail: sales@westmarine.com
Website: www.westmarine.com
Fax Ordering: (831) 761-4421, 761-4020
International Ordering: (831) 761-4800
Special Orders: (888) 888-3221
Contact Name: John Edmondson, President
Catalog: $10. Frequency: Annual
Circulation: 50K. Sales: $20-50MM
Products: Boat supplies & accessories

WILDWASSER SPORT USA, INC.   (303) 444-2336
Wildwasser Sport USA
P.O. Box 4617 • Boulder, CO 80306
E-Mail: info@wildnet.com
Website: www.wildwasser.net.com
Fax Ordering: (303) 444-2375
Catalog: Free. Pages: 50. Frequency: Semiannual
Circulation: 50M. Sales: $3-5MM
Products: Kayaks & accessories

WIND IN THE RIGGING   (800) 236-7444
125 E. Main St. • Port Washington, WI 53074
E-Mail: wind@execpc.com
Website: www.windintherigging.com
Fax Ordering: (262) 284-0067
International Ordering: (262) 284-3494
Contact Name: William F. Schanen, III, President
Catalog: Free. Frequency: Monthly
Circulation: 150M. Sales: $1-3MM
Products: Boating gear, nautical clothing,
accessories, gifts, books

WYOMING RIVER RAIDERS CATALOG   (800) 247-6068
300 N. Salt Creek • Casper, WY 82605
E-Mail: info@riverraiders.com
Website: www.riverraiders.com
Fax Ordering: (307) 234-0154
International Ordering: (307) 235-8624
Contact Name: Gary Wren, President
Catalog: Free. Frequency: Annual
Circulation: 150M. Sales: $5-10MM
Products: Kayaks, canoes, inflatable rafts; accessories

ACS PUBLICATIONS   (866) 953-8458
Starcrafts Publishing
334 Calef Hwy. • Epping, NH 03042
E-Mail: sales@astrocom.com
Website: www.astrocom.com
Fax Ordering: (603) 734-4311
International Ordering: (603) 734-4300
Catalog: Free. Frequency: Quarterly
Circulation: 100K. Sales: $500M - $1MM
Products: Titles on astrology, holistic health,
metaphysics & related subjects

AEGIS PUBLISHING GROUP, LTD.   (866) 464-3202
Hoovers, D&B Company   (866) 307-3812
796 Aquidneck Ave. • Middletown, RI 02842
E-Mail: aegis@aegisbooks.com
Website: www.aegisbooks.com
Fax Ordering: (401) 849-4231
International Ordering: (401) 849-4200
Contact Names: Robert Mastin, Publisher
Catalog: Free. Frequency: Semiannual
Circulation: 50K. Sales: $500K - $1MM
Products: Telecom books for small businesses,
teleworkers, telecom managers & end users

AERONAUTICAL & MILITARY   (800) 423-2708
AVIATION BOOKS
Aviation Book Company
7201 Perimeter Rd. S • Seattle, WA 98108
E-Mail: sales@aviationbook.com
Website: www.aviationbook.com
Fax Ordering: (206) 763-3428
International Ordering: (206) 767-5232
Contact Name: Nancy Griffith, President
Catalog: Free. Frequency: Semiannual
Circulation: 200K. Sales: $500K to $1MM
Products: Aviation books, pilot supplies & gifts

ALLWORTH PRESS CATALOG   (800) 491-2808
Allworth Communications
10 E. 23rd St. #510 • New York, NY 10010
E-Mail: pub@allworth.com
Website: www.allworth.com
Fax Ordering: (212) 777-8261
International Ordering: (212) 777-8395
Contact Name: Tad Crawford, President
Catalog: Free. Frequency: Annual
Circulation: 50K. Sales: $1-3MM
Products: Business & self-help information
books for artists, designers, photographers,
writers, film & performing artists

AMACON BOOKS IN PRINT   (800) 714-6395
American Management Association
1601 Broadway • New York, NY 10019
E-Mail: pubs_cust_serv@amanet.org
Website: www.amanet.org
Fax Ordering: (212) 903-8083
International Ordering: (212) 586-8100
Contact Name: Irene Majuk, Marketing
Catalog: Free. Frequency: Annual
Circulation: 100K. Sales: $5-10MM
Products: Professional books on management,
marketing & public relations

AMERICAN SOCIETY OF   (800) 843-2763
MECHANICAL ENGINEERS
P.O. Box 2300 • Fairfield, NJ 07007
E-Mail: infocentral@asme.org
Website: www.asme.org
Fax Ordering: (973) 882-1717
International Ordering: (973) 882-1170

Contact Name: Jeff Howitt, Marketing
Catalog: Free. Frequency: Annual
Circulation: 150K. Sales: $3-5MM
Products: Technical publications for
mechanical engineers

AQUA QUEST PUBLICATIONS   (800) 933-8989
P.O. Box 700 • Locust Valley, NY 11560
E-Mail: info@aquaquest.com
Website: www.aquaquest.com
Fax Ordering: (516) 759-4519
International Ordering: (516) 759-0476
Catalog: Free. Frequency: Semiannual
Circulation: 150K. Sales: $1-3MM
Products: Scuba diving books & books
related to the underwater world

ARE PRESS CATALOG   (800) 723-1112
215 67th St. • Virginia Beach, VA 23451   (800) 333-4499
12 Perrine Rd. • Monmouth Junction, NJ 08852
E-Mail: customerservice@edgarcayce.org
Website: www.arebookstore.com
Fax Ordering: (757) 329-6687
International Ordering: (757) 428-3588
Contact Name: Melinda Ball, Marketing Manager
Catalog: Free. Frequency: Monthly
Circulation: 150K. Sales: $3-5MM
Products: Educational videos, software, CD-ROMs,
books and posters; Edgar Cayce & related books &
tapes for personal transformation & spiritual
development

ARTSCROLL CATALOG   (800) 637-6724
Mesorah Publications, Ltd.
222 44th St. • Brooklyn, NY 11232
E-Mail: orders@artscroll.com
Website: www.artscroll.com
Fax Ordering: (718) 680-1875
International Ordering: (718) 921-9000
Contact Name: Meir Zlotowitz, President
Catalog: Free. Frequency: Annual
Circulation: 50M. Sales: $5-10MM
Products: Jewish books

ASHGATE CATALOGS   (800) 535-9544
Ashgate Publishing Company
101 Cherry St., Suite 420
Burlington, VT 05401
E-Mail: info@ashgate.com
Website: www.ashgate.com
Fax Ordering: (802) 276-3837
International Ordering: (802) 276-3162
Contact Name: Richard Slappey, President
Catalog: Free. Frequency: Annual
Circulation: 200K. Sales: $5-10MM
Products: *Catalogs*: Aviation; Business & Economics;
History; Geography; Law & Legal Studies; Library &
Information management; Literary Studies; Medieval
Studies; Music; Philosophy; Politics & International
Relations; Religion & Theology; Renaissance Studies;
Social Policy & Social Work; Sociology, Ethnic &
Gender Studies; Training; Variorum.

ASPEN PUBLISHERS CATALOG   (800) 638-8437
7201 McKinley Cir. • Frederick, MD 21704 legal (800) 447-1717
E-Mail: customerservice@aspenpubl.com
Website: www.aspenpublishers.com
Fax Ordering: (301) 644-3550
International Ordering: (301) 644-3599
Customer Service: (800) 234-1660
Catalog: Free. Frequency: Semiannual
Circulation: 200K. Sales: $5-10MM

Products: Books, manuals, texts, journal newsletters, electronic products and on-line services for those involved in law, business, health care & education

AUDIO EDITIONS-BOOKS ON CASSETTES (800) 231-4261
Audio Partners
131 E. Placer St. • Auburn, CA 95603
E-Mail: info@audioeditions.com
Website: www.audioeditions.com
Fax Ordering: (800) 882-1840
International Ordering: (530) 888-7801
Contact Name: Grady Hesters, President
Catalog: Free. Frequency: Monthly
Circulation: 1MM. Sales: $5-10MM
Products: Audio books on cassettes & CD

AUDIO-FORUM CATALOG (800) 243-1234
One Orchard Park Rd. • Madison, CT 06443
E-Mail: info@audioforum.com
Website: www.audioforum.com
Fax Ordering: (888) 453-4329; (203) 245-0769
International Ordering: (203) 245-0195
Contact Name: Jeffrey Norton, President
Catalog: Free. Frequency: Quarterly
Circulation: 250K. Sales: $5-10MM
Products: Audio self-instructional language courses

AUDIOBOOKSTAND (800) 854-7859
P.O. Box 481 • Grand Haven, MI 49417
E-Mail: help@audiobookstand.com
Website: www.audiobookstand.com
Website: www.brillianceaudio.com
Fax Ordering: (616) 846-0630
International Ordering: (616) 846-5256
Customer Service: (800) 854-7859
Contact Name: Michael Snodgrass, President
Catalog: Online. Frequency: Monthly
Circulation: 200K. Sales: $5-10MM
Products: Audio books.

AUTOMOBILE QUARTERLY CATALOG (866) 838-2886
800 E. Eighth St. • New Albany, IN 47150
E-Mail: info@autoquarterly.org
Website: www.autoquarterly.org
Fax Ordering: (812) 948-2816
International Ordering: (812) 948-2886
Contact Name: Stephen J. Esser
Catalog: Free. Frequency: Quarterly
Circulation: 150K. Sales: $1-3MM
Products: Automobile books & posters

BAKER PUBLISHING GROUP (800) 877-2665
6030 E. Fulton Rd. • Ada, MI 49301
E-Mail: info@bakerpublishinggroup.com
Website: www.bakerpublishinggroup.com
Fax Ordering: (800) 398-3111; (616) 676-9185
International Ordering: (616) 676-9573
Catalog: Free. Frequency: Annual
Circulation: 500K. Sales: $20-50MM
Products: Paperback original & reprint
Christian-related books

BARNES & NOBLE DIRECT (800) 843-2665
1 Pond Rd. • Rockleigh, NJ 07647
E-Mail: sales@barnesandnoble.com
Website: www.barnesandnoble.com
Fax Ordering: (201) 784-4213
International Ordering: (201) 767-6600
Contact Name: Len Riggio, President
Catalog: Free. Frequency: 13x per year
Circulation: 20MM. Sales: $20-50MM
Products: Books, audiotapes, CDs, videotapes

BEACON HILL PRESS CATALOG (800) 877-0700
Nazarene Publishing House
P.O. Box 419527
Kansas City, MO 64109
E-Mail: info@nph.com
Website: www.nph.com
Fax Ordering: (816) 753-4071
International Ordering: (816) 931-1900
Catalog: Free. Frequency: Quarterly
Circulation: 250K. Sales: $5-10MM
Products: Christian books; bible studies & commentaries; spiritual growth & formation; ministry resources; homeschool resources

BELLEROPHON BOOKS (800) 253-9943
P.O. Box 21307 • Santa Barbara, CA 93121
E-Mail: sales@bellerophonbooks.com
Website: www.bellerophonbooks.com
Fax Ordering: (805) 965-8286
International Ordering: (805) 965-7034
Contact Name: Harry Knill, President
Catalog: Free. Frequency: Annual
Circulation: 150K. Sales: $5-10MM
Products: Coloring books & art books
for children

BENNETT-WALLS CATALOG (800) 624-1739
P.O. Drawer 1 • Rotan, TX 79546
E-Mail: ovie@prodigy.net
Fax Ordering: (915) 735-3693
International Ordering: (915) 735-3186
Contact Name: Len Riggio, President
Catalog: Free. Frequency: Semiannual
Circulation: 100K. Sales: $500K - $1MM
Products: Historical books; genealogy

BETHANY HOUSE PUBLISHERS (800) 877-2665
Baker Publishing Group
6030 E. Fulton Rd. • Ada, MI 49301
E-Mail: info@bethanyhouse.com
Website: www.bethanyhouse.com
Fax Ordering: (800) 398-3111; (616) 676-9573
International Ordering: (616) 676-9185
Contact Name: Gary Johnson, President
Catalog: Free. Frequency: 3x per year
Circulation: 1MM. Sales: $10-20MM
Products: Self-help, fiction, family titles,
Christian fiction books

BLACKSTONE AUDIOBOOKS (800) 729-2665
P.O. Box 969 • Ashland, OR 97520
E-Mail: catalog@blackstoneaudio.com
Website: www.blackstoneaudio.com
Fax Ordering: (541) 482-9294
International Ordering: (541) 482-9239
Contact Name: Craig W. Black, President
Catalog: Free. Frequency: Annual
Circulation: 250K. Sales: $5-10MM
Products: Audio books: fiction, history, biography, mystery, humor, art, business, politics, children's, economics, philosophy & religion

BOOKCASSETTE SALES CATALOG (800) 854-7859
(800) 648-2312
Brilliance Audio, Inc.
1704 Eaton Dr. • Grand Haven, MI 49417
E-Mail: customerservice@brillianceaudio.com
Website: www.brillinaceaudio.com
Fax Ordering: (616) 846-0630
International Ordering: (616) 846-5256
Catalog: Free. Frequency: Monthly
Circulation: 300K. Sales: $10-20MM
Products: Fiction & nonfiction audiobooks

BOOKS FOR YOUR BUSINESS   **(631) 754-0500**
Forum Publishing
383 E. Main St. • Centerport, NY 11721
E-Mail: forumpublishing@aol.com
Website: www.bizbooks.org
Fax Ordering: (631) 754-0630
Contact Name: martin Stevens, President
Catalog: Free. Frequency: 24x per year
Circulation: 200K. Sales: $5-10MM
Products: Books & directories to help start or
expand your business; books on how to create
cartoons; salesman's & chain store guides;
mail order; money & finance; trade magazines;
real estate; internet; franchising

BOOKS OF WONDER NEWS   **(800) 835-4315**
18 W. 18th St. • New York, NY 10011
E-Mail: info@booksofwonder.com
Website: www.booksofwonder.com
Fax Ordering: (212) 989-1203
International Ordering: (212) 989-3475
Contact Name: Peter Glassman, President
Catalog: Free. Frequency: Bimonthly
Circulation: 50K. Sales: $5-10MM
Products: Children's books

BOOKS ON TAPE CATALOG   **(800) 733-3000**
LIVING LANGUAGE CATALOG   **(800) 924-1396**
LISTENING LIBRARY CATALOG
LARGE PRINT CATALOG
Random House, Inc.
400 hahn Rd. • Westminster, MD 21157
E-Mail: sales@booksontape.com
Website: www.booksontape.com
Fax Ordering: (800) 940-7046
Catalog: Free. Frequency: Semiannual
Circulation: 250K. Sales: $20-50MM
Products: Great books on tape; large type books;

BOOKS WITH IMPACT CATALOG   **(800) 246-7228**
Impact Publishers
P.O. Box 6016 • Atascadero, CA 93423
12 Perrine Rd. • Monmouth Junction, NJ 08852
E-Mail: info@impactublishers.com
Website: www.impactpublshers.com
International Ordering: (805) 466-5917
Contact Name: Melinda Ball, Marketing Manager
Catalog: Free. Frequency: Monthly
Circulation: 150K. Sales: $5-10MM
Products: Resources for individuals & professionals
in professional psychology & self-improvement books;
addiction/recovery; anger/aggression; divorce/separation;
relationships, stress management, assertiveness;
child custody.

BOOKSHOP CATALOG   **(360) 694-2462**
Twin Peaks Press
P.O. Box 8 • Vancouver, WA 98666
E-Mail: twinpeak@pacifier.com
Website: www.twinpeakspress.com
Fax Ordering: (360) 696-3210
Contact Names: Helen Hecker, President
Catalog: Free. Frequency: Bimonthly
Circulation: 100K. Sales: $500K - $1MM
Products: Books, DVDs, videos & software
about writing, publishing, promoting & marketing
books; books for authorsself-publishing

BOYS TOWN PRESS CATALOG   **(800) 282-6657**
14100 Crawford St. • Boys Town, NE 68010
E-Mail: btpress@boystown.org
Website: www.boystown.org

Fax Ordering: (402) 498-1310
International Ordering: (402) 498-1320
Contact Name: Barbara Lonnborg, Marketing
Catalog: Free. Frequency: Quarterly
Circulation: 300K. Sales: $1-3MM
Products: Books & videos for professionals,
educators & parents working with youth

BROOKES PUBLISHING CO. CATALOG   **(800) 638-3775**
P.O. Box 10624 • Baltimore, MD 21285
E-Mail: custserv@brookespublishing.com
Website: www.brookespublishing.com
Fax Ordering: (410) 337-8539
International Ordering: (410) 337-9580
Catalog: Free. Frequency: Annual
Circulation: 50K. Sales: $500K to $1MM
Products: Books & videos on special education,
developmental disabilities, rehabilitation, audiology,
therapeutic services, mental health, behavior

CWLA CATALOG OF PUBLICATIONS **(800) 407-6273**
Child Welfare League of America
2427 Bond St. • University Park, IL 60484
E-Mail: order@cwla.org
Website: www.cwla.org
Fax Ordering: (708) 534-7803
International Ordering: (202) 638-2952
Contact Name: Harry Knill, President
Catalog: Free. Frequency: Semiannual
Circulation: 250K. Sales: $1-3MM
Products: Child welfare related books & services

CARROLL PUBLISHING   **(800) 336-4240**
4701 Sangamore Rd., Suite S-155
Bethesda, MD 20816
E-Mail: info@carrollpub.com
Website: www.carrollpub.com
Fax Ordering: (301) 263-9801
International Ordering: (301) 263-9800
Customer Service: (866) 921-4007
Catalog: Free. Frequency: Semiannual.
Circulation: 100K. Sales: $3-5MM
Products: Government directories, charts
& programs

CHANNING BETE COMPANY   **(800) 477-4776**
One Community Pl. • So. Deerfield, MA 01373
E-Mail: custserv@channing-bete.com
Website: www.channing-bete.com
Fax Ordering: (800) 499-6464; (413) 665-7117
International Ordering: (413) 263-5685
Catalog: Free. Frequency: 4x per year
Circulation: 1MM. Sales: $10-20MM
Products: Books, audiotapes, CDs, videotapes on
health care, human services, public health & safety

CHERRY LANE MUSIC CATALOG   **(212) 561-3000**
Cherry Lane Music Publishing Co., Inc.
6 E. 32nd St. • New York, NY 10016
E-Mail: info@cherrylane.com
Website: www.cherrylane.com
Fax Ordering: (212) 251-0804
Contact Name: Ida Gurwicz, President
Catalog: Free. Frequency: Semiannual
Circulation: 100K. Sales: $5-10MM
Products: Music songbooks

CHINA BOOKS & PERIODICALS   **(800) 818-2017**
360 Swift Ave., Suite 48
So. San Francisco, CA 94080
E-Mail: info@chinabooks.com
Website: www.chinabooks.com

Fax Ordering: (650) 872-7808
International Ordering: (650) 872-7076
Contact Name: Chris Noyes, President
Catalog: Free. Frequency: Semiannual
Circulation: 100K. Sales: $1-3MM
Products: Books from and about China

CHINABERRY & ISABELLA CATALOG   (800) 776-2242
2780 Via Orange Way
Spring Valley, CA 91978
E-Mail: customerservice@chinaberrybooks.com
Website: www.chinaberrybooks.com
Fax Ordering: (619) 670-5203
International Ordering: (619) 670-5200
Customer Service: (888) 481-6744
Contact Name: Gary Demaine, President
Catalog: Free. Frequency: Annual
Circulation: 100K. Sales: $5-10MM
Products: Books for children

CHIPS BOOKS CATALOG   (979) 263-5685
10777 Mazoch Rd. • Weimar, TX 78962
E-Mail: ordept@chipsbooks.com
Website: www.chipsbooks.com
Fax Ordering: (979) 263-5683
Contact Name: Harry Noe, President
Catalog: Free. Frequency: Monthly
Circulation: 200K. Sales: $1-3MM
Products: Books & videotapes relating to agriculture,
architecture, cosmetic science & technology,
environmental science, and foodservice, culinary
& hospitality industry

CLASSIC MOTORBOOKS   (800) 826-6600
Motorbooks-Quayside Publishing Group
P.O. Box 1 • Osceola, WI 54020
E-Mail: customerservice@motorbooks.com
Website: www.motorbooks.com
Fax Ordering: (715) 294-4448
International Ordering: (715) 294-3345
Contact Name: Tim Parker, President
Catalog: Free. Frequency: Semiannual
Circulation: 100K. Sales: $3-5MM
Products: Automotive books, shop
manuals & restoration books

CLOSE UP PUBLISHING CATALOG   (800) 765-3131
Close Up Foundation Press
44 Canal Center Plaza • Alexandria, VA 22314
E-Mail: cup@closeup.org
Website: www.closeup.org
Fax Ordering: (703) 706-3564
International Ordering: (703) 706-3560
Contact Name: Steve Janger, President
Catalog: Free. Frequency: Semiannual
Circulation: 150K. Sales: $1-3MM
Products: Books, simulations & videotapes
dealing with current issues

COBBLESTONE PUBLISHING   (800) 821-0115
Div. of Carus Publishing Co.
30 Grove St., Suite C
Peterborough, NH 03458
E-Mail: customerservice@caruspub.com
Website: www.cobblestonepub.com
Fax Ordering: (603) 924-7380
International Ordering: (603) 924-7209
Contact Name: Jack Olbrych, President
Catalog: Free. Frequency: Semiannual
Circulation: 25K. Sales: $500K - $1MM
Products: Children's magazines & teacher
resources for grades K-10

COLUMBIA BOOKS, INC.   (888) 265-0600
8120 Woodmont Ave. #110
Bethesda, MD 20814
E-Mail: info@columbiabooks.com
Website: www.columbiabooks.com
Fax Ordering: (202) 464-1775
International Ordering: (202) 464-1662
Catalog: Free. Frequency: Semiannual.
Circulation: 100K. Sales: $5-10MM
Products: Directories of associations,
corporations, lobbying firms, foundations,
political action committees, special interest
advocates, and Washington, DC-area
businesses

COMMUNITY ASSOCIATIONS   (888) 224-4321
INSTITUTE PRESS
225 Reinekers Lane, #300
Alexandria, VA 22314
E-Mail: caidirect@caionline.org
Website: www.caisecure.net
Fax Ordering: (703) 684-1581
International Ordering: (703) 548-8600
Catalog: Online. Sales: $1-3MM
Products: Books, periodicals, videos, e-news service
resources available for community associations

COMPASSION BOOKS   (800) 970-4220
7036 State Hwy. 80 South
Burnsville, NC 28714
E-Mail: orders@compassionbooks.com
Website: www.compassionbooks.com
Fax Ordering: (828) 675-9687
International Ordering: (828) 675-5909
Contact Name: Donna O'Toole, President
Catalog: Free. Frequency: Semiannual
Circulation: 50K. Sales: $500K
Products: Books that help children &
adults through periods of loss & grief

CONSTRUCTION BOOK EXPRESS   (800) 253-0541
P.O. Box 5196 • Janesville, WI 53547
E-Mail: info@constructionbook.com
Website: www.constructionbook.com
Fax Ordering: (800) 647-7233; (608) 743-8037
International Ordering: (608) 743-8031
Contact Name: Scott Forde, President
Catalog: Free. Frequency: Semiannual
Circulation: 150K. Sales: $1-3MM
Products: Construction books, manuals,
audio & videotapes, CD-ROMs & software
covering building codes & contractor's guides

CONSTRUCTION REFERENCE   (800) 829-8123
Craftsman Book Company
6058 Corte Del Cedro • Carlsbad, CA 92011
E-Mail: info@craftsman-book.com
Website: www.craftsman-book.com
Fax Ordering: (760) 438-0398
International Ordering: (760) 438-7828
Contact Name: Gary Moselle, President
Catalog: Free. Frequency: 3x per year
Circulation: 300K. Sales: $1-3M
Products: Professional construction books

CONSUMER INFORMATION CATALOG   (888) 878-3256
Federal Citizen Information Center
Pueblo, CO 81009
E-Mail: catalog.pueblo@gsa.gov
Website: www.pueblo.gsa.gov
Fax Ordering: (719) 948-9724
International Ordering: (719) 948-3334

Contact Name: Teresa Nasif, Director
Catalog: Free. Frequency: Quarterly
Circulation: 25MM. Sales: Non-profit
Products: Listing of over 200 free & low cost
federal consumer publications

CORWIN PRESS CATALOGS   (800) 233-9936
2455 Teller Rd.
Thousand Oaks, CA 91320
E-Mail: info@corwinpress.com
Website: www.corwinpress.com
Fax Ordering: (800) 417-2466; (805) 499-5323
International Ordering: (805) 499-9734
Catalog: Free. Frequency: Annual.
Circulation: 400K. Sales: $10-20M
Products: Educational publisher dedicated
to providing solutions for PreK-12 educators;
New Titles Catalog; Subject Catalogs;
Course Adoption Catalogs

CQ PRESS   (800) 638-1710
Congressional Quarterly Press   (866) 427-7737
2300 N St., NW #800
Washington, DC 20037
Washington, DC 20037
E-Mail: customerservice@cqpress.com
Website: www.cqpress.com
Fax Ordering: (800) 380-3810; (202) 729-1807
International Ordering: (202) 729-1900
Catalog: Free. Frequency: Annual.
Circulation: 150K. Sales: $5-10MM
Products: U.S. Government Congressional staff
directories; political science texts; contact information
for the federal government; directory of decision-
makers & staff

CRISP LEARNING CANADA CATALOG   (800) 446-4797
60 Briarwood Ave.
Mississauga, ON L5G 3N6
E-Mail: info@crisplearning.com
Website: www.crisplearning.com
Fax Ordering: (866) 722-1822; (905) 278-2801
International Ordering: (905) 274-5678
Contact Names: Mike Crisp, President
Catalog: Free. Frequency: Semiannual.
Circulation: 100K. Sales: $5-10MM
Products: Books, videos, audios, CD-ROMs,
and online courses; 50-minute Series Books;
Group Training Video Series; Self-Study Video
& Audio Series; Self-Study Audio Book Series;
CD-ROM Series; Online Learning Series.

CYPRESS HOUSE CATALOG   (800) 773-7782
155 Cypress St. • Fort Bragg, CA 95437
E-Mail: books@cypresshouse.com
Website: www.cypresshouse.com
Fax Ordering: (707) 964-7531
International Ordering: (707) 964-9520
Contact Name: Cynthia Frank, President
Catalog: Free. Frequency: Semiannual
Circulation: 100K. Sales: $3-5MM
Products: Books on health & healing, art,
history, poetry, fiction, children's book, reference

DAEDALUS BOOKS & MUSIC   (800) 395-2665
P.O. Box 6000 • Columbia, MD 21045
E-Mail: custserv@daedalusbooks.com
Website: www.daedalusbooks.com
Fax Ordering: (800) 866-5578; (410) 309-2707
International Ordering: (410) 309-2705
Customer Service: (800) 944-8879; (410) 309-2706
Contact Name: Helaine Harris, President

Catalog: Free. Frequency: 7x per year
Circulation: 4MM. Sales: $10-20MM
Products: Remainder books at bargain prices

DAVIES PUBLISHING   (877) 792-0005
32 S. Raymond Ave. • Pasadena, CA 91105
E-Mail: daviescorp@aol.com
Website: www.daviespublishing.com
Fax Ordering: (626) 792-5308
International Ordering: (626) 792-3046
Contact Name: Michael Davies, President
Catalog: Free. Frequency: Monthly
Circulation: 100K. Sales: $500K - $1MM
Products: Medical books; reviews for professionals
takin AROMS exam; audio & videotapes, CD-ROMs

DELTA PRESS CATALOG   (800) 852-4445
DELTA FORCE CATALOG
215 S. Washington Ave.
El Dorado, AR 71730
E-Mail: customerservice@deltapress.com
Website: www.deltapress.com
Fax Ordering: (870) 862-9671
International Ordering: (870) 862-3811
Contact Name: Billy Blann, President
Catalog: $6. Frequency: Quarterly
Circulation: 100K. Sales: $3-5MM
Products: Gun related books

DOWN EAST ENTERPRISE BOOKS   (800) 685-7962
P.O. Box 679 • Camden, ME 04843
E-Mail: support@downeast.com
Website: www.secure.downeast.com
Fax Ordering: (207) 594-7215
International Ordering: (207) 594-9544
Contact Names: Bob Fernald, President
Catalog: Free. Frequency: Annual
Circulation: 100K. Sales: $500K
Products: Maine/New England based books

EDEN PRESS   (800) 338-8484
P.O. Box 8410 • Fountain Valley, CA 92728
E-Mail: edenpressinc@hotmail.com
Website: www.edenpress.com
Fax Ordering: (714) 636-1682
International Ordering: (714) 636-4623
Contact Names: Barry Reid, President
Catalog: Free. Frequency: Semiannual
Circulation: 150K. Sales: $500K
Products: Books on privacy, prosperity
& business opportunities

ELSEVIER BOOK CATALOGS   (800) 545-2522
3251 Riverport Ln.
Maryland Hts., MO 63043
E-Mail: bookcustomerservice-usa@elsevier.com
Websites: www.elsevier.com; www.books.elsevier.com
   www.elsevierhealth.com
Fax Ordering: (800) 535-9935 (314) 447-8030
International Ordering: (800) 460-3110;
   (314) 447-8010
Catalog: Free. Frequency: Quarterly
Circulation: 500K. Sales: $100-500MM
Products: Science, technology, health &
business books

ENSLOW PUBLISHERS, INC.   (800) 398-2504
P.O. Box 398 • Berkeley Hts., NJ 07922
E-Mail: customerservice@enslow.com
Website: www.enslow.com
Fax Ordering: (908) 771-0925
International Ordering: (908) 771-9400

Catalog: Free. Frequency: Semiannual
Circulation: 150K. Sales: $5-10MM
Products: K-12 nonfiction library books

LAWRENCE ERLBAUM ASSOCIATES (800) 926-6579
Taylor & Francis Group   (800) 354-1420
325 Chestnut St. #800
Philadelphia, PA 19106
E-Mail: cserve@routledge-ny.com
Website: www.leaonline.com
Fax Ordering: (215) 625-2940
International Ordering: (215) 625-8900
Catalog: Free. Pages: 46. Frequency: Annual
Circulation: 100K. Sales: $5-10MM
Products: Library books on education, psychology,
health & counseling, human factors, management

FACTS ON FILE, FERGUSON (800) 322-8755
CHELSEA HOUSE   (800) 306-9941
Infobase Publishing
132 W. 31st St., 17th Fl.
New York, NY 10001
E-Mail: custserv@factsonfile.com
Website: www.factsonfile.com
Fax Ordering: (800) 306-9942; (800) 678-3633
Catalog: Free. Frequency: Semiannual
Circulation: 500K. Sales: $50-100MM
Products: Reference books on U.S. history,
world history, language & literature, science &
technology, social issues, military, multicultural,
career & vocational guidance

FORECAST INTERNATIONAL CATALOGS (800) 451-4975
22 Commerce Rd. • Newtown, CT 06470
E-Mail: info@forecast1.com
Website: www.forecastinternational.com
Fax Ordering: (203) 426-0223
International Ordering: (203) 426-0800
Contact Name: Ed Nebinger, President
Catalog: Free. Frequency: Annual
Circulation: 100K. Sales: $5-10MM
Products: Directories, bulletins, CD-ROMs
& other services forecasting the aerospace,
government and industry; defense-related-
military; transportation; energy industries

FREE SPIRIT PUBLISHING (800) 735-7323
217 Fifth Ave. North, #200
Minneapolis, MN 55401
E-Mail: info@freespirit.com
Website: www.freespirit.com
Fax Ordering: (866) 419-5199; (612) 337-5050
International Ordering: (612) 338-2068
Customer Service: (866) 703-7322
Catalog: Free. Frequency: Semiannual
Circulation: 150K. Sales: $500K to $1MM
Products: Books for children, parents & teachers
about learning to cope with life in general

THE GALE GROUP (800) 347-4253
27500 Drake Rd.   (800) 877-4253
Farmington Hills, MI 48331
E-Mail: galeord@gale.com
Website: www.gale.com
Fax Ordering: (800) 414-5043; (248) 699-8035
International Ordering: (248) 699-4253
Contact Names: Timothy J. Smith, President
Catalog: Free. Frequency: Semiannual
Circulation: 2MM. Sales: $250-500MM
Products: Reference books & directories,
including the Taft Catalog

GAMBLER'S BOOK SHOP CATALOG (800) 522-1777
630 S. 11th St. • Las Vegas, NV 89101
E-Mail: gambler@wizard.com
Website: www.gamblersbook.com
Fax Ordering: (702) 382-7594
International Ordering: (702) 382-7555
Contact Name: Edna Luckman, President
Catalog: Free. Frequency: Annual
Circulation: 75K. Sales: $1-3MM
Products: Books, software & videos
on the subject of gambling

GENEALOGICAL PUBLISHING COMPANY (800) 296-6687
3600 Clipper Mill Rd. #260   (800) 599-9561
Baltimore, MD 21211
E-Mail: INFO@genealogical.com
Website: www.genealogical.com
Fax Ordering: (410) 752-8492
International Ordering: (410) 837-8271
Contact Name: Barry Chodak, President
Catalog: Free. Frequency: Monthly
Circulation: 200K. Sales: $3-5MM
Products: How-to, reference books,
CD-ROMs on genealogy & local history

GLOBE PEQUOT PRESS CATALOG (888) 249-7586
P.O. Box 480 • Guilford, CT 06437
E-Mail: info@globepequot.com
Website: www.globepequot.com
Fax Ordering: (800) 820-2329
International Ordering: (860) 395-0440
Contact Name: Linda Kennedy, President
Catalog: Free. Frequency: Semiannual
Circulation: 250K. Sales: $10-20MM
Products: Travel, outdoor/recreation,
language books

GREAT CHEFS TELEVISION (800) 321-1499
GCI • P.O. Box 56757
New Orleans, LA 70156
E-Mail: info@greatchefs.com
Website: www.greatchefs.com
Fax Ordering: (504) 581-1188
International Ordering: (504) 581-5000
Contact Names: John Shoup, President
Catalog: Free. Frequency: Semiannual
Circulation: 100K. Sales: $500K to $1MM
Products: Cookbooks, cooking & music videos

GREY HOUSE PUBLISHING (800) 562-2139
P.O. Box 56 • Amenia, NY 12501
E-Mail: books@greyhouse.com
Website: www.greyhouse.com
Fax Ordering: (518) 789-0556
International Ordering: (518) 789-8700
Contact Names: Richard Gottlieb, President
Catalog: Free. Frequency: Semiannual
Circulation: 250K. Sales: $20-50MM
Products: Reference directories in business,
health & education

GRYPHON HOUSE EARLY CHILDHOOD (800) 638-0928
10726 Tucker St. • Beltsville, MD 20705
E-Mail: info@ghbooks.com
Website: www.gryphonhouse.com
Fax Ordering: (877) 638-7576; (301) 595-0051
International Ordering: (301) 595-9500
Contact Name: Larry Rood, President
Catalog: Free. Frequency: Quarterly
Circulation: 100K. Sales: $500K
Products: Activities & resource books for
teachers & parents of young children

H.W. WILSON COMPANY (800) 367-6770
950 University Ave. • Bronx, NY 10452
E-Mail: custserv@hwwilson.com
Website: www.hwwilson.com
Fax Ordering: (800) 590-1617; (718) 590-1617
International Ordering: (718) 588-8400
Contact Names: Regina Williams, Manager
Catalog: Free. Frequency: Annual
Circulation: 150K. Sales: $10-20MM
Products: Library reference books

EDWARD R. HAMILTON, BOOKSELLER (800) 677-3483
Falls Village, CT 06031
E-Mail: comments@erhbooks.com
Website: www.erhbooks.com
Contact Names: Edward Hamilton, President
Catalog: Free. Frequency: Quarterly
Circulation: 100K. Sales: $500K
Products: Books on history, politics, religion,
travel, sports, wildlife & pets, gardening, art &
architecture, cookbooks, computers & children's
books; audiotapes

HARPER AUDIO/CAEDMON CATALOG (800) 242-7737
HarperCollins Publishers
10 E. 53rd St. • New York, NY 10022
E-Mail: orders@harpercollins.com
Website: www.harpercollins.com
Fax Ordering: (212) 207-7552
International Ordering: (212) 207-7000
Contact Name: George Craig, President
Catalog: Free. Frequency: Annual
Circulation: 500K. Sales: $20-50M
Products: Books on tape for adults & children

THE HAWORTH PRESS, INC. (800) 429-6784
Taylor & Francis Group (800) 634-7064
6000 Broken Sound Pkwy. #300
Boca Raton, FL33487
E-Mail: orders@taylorandfrancis.com
Website: www.taylorandfrancis.com
Fax Ordering: (800) 895-0582; (561) 241-7856
International Ordering: (561) 994-0555
Contact Names: Kathy Miner, Customer Service
Catalog: Free. Frequency: Semiannual
Circulation: 100K. Sales: $10-20MM
Products: Books and journals in marketing,
advertising and business

HERITAGE BOOKS, INC. (800) 876-6103
100 Railroad Ave. #104
Westminster, MD 21157
E-Mail: info@heritagebooks.com
Website: www.heritagebooks.com
Fax Ordering: (410) 558-6574
International Ordering: (410) 876-6101
Catalog: Free. Frequency: Semiannual
Circulation: 150K. Sales: $5-10M
Products: Books, CDs & maps in history
& genealogy

HIGHLIGHTS FOR CHILDREN (800) 255-9517
P.O. Box 269 • Columbus, OH 43216
E-Mail: info@highlights.com
Website: www.highlights.com
Fax Ordering: (614) 487-2700
International Ordering: (614) 486-0631
Customer Service: (800) 962-3661
Contact Name: Elmer C. Meider, Jr., President
Catalog: Free. Frequency: Semiannual
Circulation: 200K. Sales: $20-50MM
Products: Children's books, games, puzzles

HOME BUILDER BOOKSTORE CATALOG (800) 368-5242
1201 15th St., NW
Washington, DC 20005
E-Mail: info@nahb.com
Website: www.nahb.com
Fax Ordering: (202) 266-8400
International Ordering: (202) 266-8200
Contact Names: Charlotte McKenny, President
Catalog: Free. Frequency: Semiannual
Circulation: 50K. Sales: $500K to $1MM
Products: Professional books for the
residential builder, remodeler or developer

HOME ECONOMICS CATALOG (800) 468-4227
Cambridge Educational
12 Perrine Rd.
Monmouth Junction, NJ 08852
E-Mail: sales@cambridgeeducational.com
Website: www.cambridgeeducational.com
Fax Ordering: (800) 329-6687
Contact Names: Steve Jones, President
Catalog: Free. Frequency: Monthly
Circulation: 1MM. Sales: $5-10MM
Products: Home economics books, videos,
software, CD-ROMs & posters

INDIANA UNIVERSITY PRESS CATALOG (800) 842-6796
601 N. Morton St. • Bloomington, IN 47404
E-Mail: sales@iupress.indiana.edu
Website: www.iupress.indiana.edu
Fax Ordering: (812) 855-8507
International Ordering: (812) 855-8817
Catalog: Free. Frequency: Semiannual
Circulation: 50K. Sales: $5-10MM
Products: Scholarly books & journals in history,
music, philosophy, Native American, African-
American studies, paleontology, philanthropy

INFOAMERICA (800) 326-7419
SJT Enterprises, Inc.
29307 Clemens Rd.
Westlake, OH 44145
E-Mail: info@sjtent.com
Websites: www.legalkits.com; www.sjtent.com
Fax Ordering: (440) 617-0987
International Ordering: (440) 617-1100
Contact Names: Timothy J. Smith, President
Catalog: Free. Frequency: Semiannual
Circulation: 100K. Sales: $500K to $1MM
Products: Business and legal kits

INFORMATION USA, INC. (800) 955-7693
12079 Nebel St.• Rockville, MD 20852
E-Mail: customerservice@lesko.com
Website: www.myamericanbenefitsplan.com
Fax Ordering: (301) 770-1253
Contact Names: Matthew Lesko, President
Catalog: Free. Frequency: Semiannual.
Circulation: 100K. Sales: $500K to $1MM
Products: Books on free Government programs
available to consumers & entrepreneurs

INTERNATIONAL BIBLE SOCIETY (800) 524-1588
P.O. Box 35700
Colorado Springs, CO 80935
E-Mail: biblicadirectservice@biblica.com
Website: www.ibsdirect.com
Fax Ordering: (719) 867-2870
International Ordering: (719) 867-2700
Catalog: Free. Frequency: Semiannual
Circulation: 100K. Sales: $5-10MM
Products: Bibles, religious booklets

INTERNATIONAL WEALTH SUCCESS   (800) 323-0548
P.O. Box 186 • Merrick, NY 11566
E-Mail: admin@iwsmoney.com
Website: www.iwsmoney.com
Fax Ordering: (516) 766-5919
International Ordering: (516) 766-5850
Contact Names: Tyler Hicks, President
Catalog: Free. Frequency: Bimonthly
Circulation: 50K. Sales: $250K
Products: Self-help books for the small
businessman & opportunity seekers; real
estate & home-based business opportunities

JOURNAL OF IRISH FAMILIES   (816) 454-2410
Irish Genealogical Foundation
P.O. Box 7575 • Kansas City, MO 64116
E-Mail: mike@irishroots.com
Website: www.irishroots.com
Contact Names: Michael O'Laughlin, President
Catalog: Free. Frequency: Quarterly
Circulation: 25K. Sales: $250-500K
Products: Irish genealogical & historical
publications

ISLAND PRESS CATALOG   (800) 828-1302
1718 Connecticut Ave., NW #300
Washington, DC 20009
E-Mail: info@islandpress.org
Website: www.islandpress.org
Fax Ordering: (800) 621-2736; (202) 234-1328
International Ordering: (202) 232-7933
Contact Names: Charles Savitt, President
Catalog: Free. Frequency: Semiannual
Circulation: 50K. Sales: $3-5MM
Products: Conservation & environmental books

JANE'S CATALOG   (800) 824-0768
Jane's Information Group
110 N. Royal St. #200 • Alexandria, VA 22314
E-Mail: customer.servicesus@janes.com
Website: www.janes.com
Fax Ordering: (800) 836-0297; (703) 836-0297
International Ordering: (703) 683-3700
Contact Names: Joseph J. Bria, President
Catalog: Free. Frequency: Semiannual
Circulation: 100K. Sales: $10-20MM
Products: Directories, books & magazines
on aerospace, aviation & the military

JESSICA'S BISCUIT CATALOG   (800) 878-4264
82-84 Needham St. • Newton, MA 02461
E-Mail: customerservice@ecookbooks.com
Website: www.ecookbooks.com
Fax Ordering: (617) 244-3376
International Ordering: (617) 965-0530
Contact Names: David Strymish, President
Catalog: Free. Frequency: 7x per year
Circulation: 2MM. Sales: $3-5MM
Products: Cookbooks

JOSSEY-BASS, INC.   (800) 956-7739
John Wiley & Sons   (800) 225-5945
989 Market St.
San Francisco, CA 94103
E-Mail: sales@wiley.com
Website: www.wiley.com
Fax Ordering: (800) 605-2665; (415) 433-0499
International Ordering: (415) 433-1740
Catalog: Free. Frequency: Semiannual.
Circulation: 100K. Sales: $5-10MM
Products: Books on innovations in leadership
in business

KRAUSE PUBLICATIONS   (800) 258-0929
700 E. State St. • Iola, WI 54990
E-Mail: zielkec@krausebooks.com
Website: www.krausebooks.com
Fax Ordering: (715) 445-4087
International Ordering: (715) 445-2214
Contact Name: Corinne Zielke
Catalog: Free. Frequency: Semiannual
Circulation: 100K. Sales: $1-3MM
Products: Hobby & collectible books: antiques,
toys, model railroads, comics, records, coins &
paper money, stamps, sports collectibles,
automotive, firearms; crafts, sewing, quilting,
outdoor activities, cookbooks, videos

LAWYER'S DIARY & MANUAL   (800) 444-4041
Skinder - Strauss Associates
P.O. Box 50 • Newark, NJ 07101
E-Mail: mail@lawdiary.com
Website: www.lawdiary.com
Fax Ordering: (973) 242-1905
International Ordering: (973) 642-4436
Contact Name: Edward C. Denne, President
Catalog: Free. Frequency: Semiannual
Circulation: 350K. Sales: $10-20MM
Products: Directories, calendars & planners
for lawyers

LEADERSHIP DIRECTORIES   (212) 627-4140
104 Fifth Ave. • New York, NY 10011   (202) 347-7757
1001 G St. #200 E • Washington, DC 20001
E-Mail: info@leadershipdirectories.com
Website: www.leadershipdirectories.com
Fax Ordering: (212) 645-0931; (202) 628-3430
Contact Name: David Hurvitz, President
Catalog: Free. Frequency: Quarterly
Circulation: 100K. Sales: $3-5MM
Products: Business, government & professional
organization directories

LISTENING LIBRARY/RANDOM HOUSE   (800) 726-0600
1745 Broadway • New York, NY 10019
E-Mail: contact@randomhouse.com
Website: www.randomhouse.com
Fax Ordering: (212) 572-6066
International Ordering: (410) 848-1900
Contact Name: Tim Ditlow, Publisher
Catalog: Free. Frequency: Annual
Circulation: 250K. Sales: $5-10MM
Products: Audio books

LLEWELLYN WORLDWIDE   (800) 843-6666
2143 Woodale Dr. • Woodbury, MN 55125
E-Mail: customerservice@llewellyn.com
Website: www.llewellyn.com
Fax Ordering: (651) 291-1908
International Ordering: (651) 291-1970
Catalog: Free. Frequency: Semiannual
Circulation: 200K. Sales: $5-10M
Products: New Age books in health & wellness,
self-help, astrology, tarot & divination, shamanism

MANUFACTURERS' NEWS, INC.   (888) 752-5200
1633 Central St. • Evanston, IL 60201
E-Mail: info@manufacturersnews.com
Website: www.mninfo.com
Fax Ordering: (847) 332-1100
International Ordering: (847) 864-7000
Customer Service: (847) 864-7590
Catalog: Free. Frequency: Semiannual
Circulation: 200K. Sales: $5-10MM
Products: Manufacturers directories, CD-ROMs

McFARLAND & CO. PUBLISHERS   (800) 253-2187
P.O. Box 611 • Jefferson, NC 28640
E-Mail: info@mcfarlandpub.com
Website: www.mcfarlandpub.com
Fax Ordering: (336) 246-4403
International Ordering: (336) 246-4460
Contact Name: Robert Franklin, President
Catalog: Free. Frequency: Annual
Circulation: 300K. Sales: $3-5MM
Products: Reference & scholarly works,
including history, women's studies &
performing arts books

MEADOWBROOK PRESS   (800) 338-2232
5451 Smetana Dr. Blvd.
Minnetonka, MN 55343
E-Mail: info@meadowbrookpress.com
Website: www.meadowbrookpress.com
Fax Ordering: (952) 930-1940
Contact Name: Bruce Lansky, President
Catalog: Free. Frequency: Annual
Circulation: 100K. Sales: $3-5MM
Products: Books on parenting, kids,
baby names & humor

METAMORPHOUS PRESS   (503) 228-4972
P.O. Box 10616 • Portland, OR 97296
E-Mail: customerservice@metamodels.com
Website: www.metamodels.com
Fax Ordering: (503) 223-9117
International Ordering: (503) 228-4972
Contact Name: David Balding, President
Catalog: Free. Frequency: Weekly
Circulation: 100K. Sales: $1-3MM
Products: Self-help books on psychology,
business, education & fitness, hypnosis

METROPOLITAN MUSEUM OF ART   (800) 468-7386
66-26 Metropolitan Ave.
Middle Village, NY 11381
E-Mail: customer.service@metmuseum.org
Website: www.store.metmuseum.org
Fax Ordering: (718) 628-5485 or 366-5375
International Ordering: (718) 731-1498
Catalog: Free. Frequency: Semiannual
Circulation: 100K. Sales: $3-5MM
Products: Museum prints, slides & gifts;
art books, jewelry, stationery & toys

MILITARY BOOKS CATALOG   (480) 488-1377
Pieces of History
P.O. Box 4470 • Cave Creek, AZ 85327
E-Mail: sandy@piecesofhistory.com
Website: www.piecesofhistory.com
Fax Ordering: (480) 488-1316
Contact Names: Lowell Jackson, President
Catalog: Free. Frequency: Quarterly
Circulation: 100K. Sales: $1-3MM
Products: Military books & videos;
USA & worldwide medals, gifts

MOTORBOOKS/ZENITH PRESS   (800) 826-6600
P.O. Box 1 • Osceola, WI 54020
E-Mail: customerservice@motorbooks.com
Website: www.mbipublishing.com
Fax Ordering: (715) 294-4448
International Ordering: (715) 294-3345
Contact Name: Tim Parker, President
Catalog: Free. Frequency: Annual
Circulation: 50K. Sales: $3-5MM
Products: Military history; aviation
& history books & DVDs, calendars

MOUNTAIN PRESS PUBLISHING CO.   (800) 234-5308
P.O. Box 2399 • Missoula, MT 59806
E-Mail: info@mtnpress.com
Website: www.mountain-press.com
Fax Ordering: (406) 728-1635
International Ordering: (406) 728-1900
Contact Names: John Rimel, President
Catalog: Free. Frequency: Quarterly
Circulation: 100K. Sales: $1-3MM
Products: Books on natural history & geology,
western history & western Americana

MUSIC BOOKS PLUS   (800) 265-8481
Norris-Whitney Communications
4600 Witmer Industrial Estates #6
Niagara Falls, NY 14305
E-Mail: order@nor.com
Website: www.musicbooksplus.com
Fax Ordering: (888) 665-1307; (716) 297-0975
International Ordering: (905) 641-0552
Contact Name: Jim Norris, President
Catalog: Free. Frequency: Annual
Circulation: 100K. Sales: $500K to $1MM
Products: Books, videos, audiocassettes,
DVDs, CD-ROMs & software

NCFR CATALOG OF RESOURCES   (888) 781-9331
National Council on Family Relations
3989 Central Ave. NE #550
Minneapolis, MN 55421
E-Mail: info@ncfr.com
Website: www.ncfr.com
Fax Ordering: (763) 781-9348
International Ordering: (763) 781-9331
Contact Name: Diane Cushman, Exec. Director
Catalog: Free. Frequency: Annual
Circulation: 25K. Sales: $500K
Products: NCFR teaching materials & resources

NATIONAL FIRE PROTECTION   (800) 344-3555
ASSOCIATION CATALOG
1 Batterymarch Park • Quincy, MA 02169
E-Mail: info@nfpa.org
Website: www.nfpa.org
Fax Ordering: (617) 770-0700
International Ordering: (617) 777-3000
Contact Name: George Miller, President
Catalog: Free. Frequency: 5x per year
Circulation: 100K. Sales: $5-10MM
Products: Books on fire prevention, protection
training materials, books, manuals & tapes

NATIVE AMERICAN COLLECTION   (800) 948-3161
Cherokee Publications
P.O. Box 430 • Cherokee, NC 28719
E-Mail: info@cherokeepublications.net
Website: www.cherokeepublications.net
Fax Ordering: (828) 488-6934
International Ordering: (828) 488-8856
Catalog: $1. Frequency: 2x per year
Circulation: 150K. Sales: $500K
Products: Native Americans; herbal remedies/
health, spiritual/shamanism, cooking/food,
craft & design, gift/specialty items

NATIVE VOICES CATALOG   (800) 695-2241
The Book Publishing Co.
P.O. Box 180 • Summertown, TN 38483
E-Mail: info@nativevoices.com
Website: www.nativevoices.com
Fax Ordering: (931) 964-2291
International Ordering: (931) 964-2241

Contact Names: Cynthia Holzapfel, President
Catalog: Free. **Frequency:** Semiannual
Circulation: 250K. **Sales:** $500K
Products: Native American books, videos & music;
as well as craft items, scents, food & cookbooks

NATUREGRAPH PUBLISHERS   (800) 390-5353
P.O. Box 1047 • Happy Camp, CA 96039
E-Mail: nature@sisqtel.net
Website: www.naturegraph.com
Fax Ordering: (530) 493-5240
International Ordering: (530) 493-5353
Contact Name: Barbara Brown, Owner
Catalog: Free. **Pages:** 20. **Frequency:** Annual
Circulation: 100K. **Sales:** $250-500K
Products: Native American nature books

JOHN NEAL, BOOKSELLER CATALOG   (800) 369-9598
Letter Arts Book Club
1833 Spring Garden St. • Greensboro, NC 27403
E-Mail: info@johnnealbooks.com
Website: www.johnnealbooks.com
Fax Ordering: (336) 272-9015
International Ordering: (336) 272-6139
Contact Names: John Neal, President
Catalog: Free. **Frequency:** Annual
Circulation: 50K. **Sales:** $250-500K
Products: Books, tools & materials
for calligraphy & bookbinding

NOLO PRESS   (800) 992-6656
950 Parker St. • Berkeley, CA 94710   (800) 728-3555
E-Mail: info@nolo.com
Website: www.nolo.com
Fax Ordering: (800) 645-0895
International Ordering: (510) 549-4660
Contact Name: Linda Hanger, President
Catalog: Free. **Frequency:** Semiannual
Circulation: 500K. **Sales:** $5-10MM
Products: Self-help legal books & software

OMNIGRAPHICS, INC.   (800) 234-1340
P.O. Box 625 • Holmes, PA 19043
E-Mail: info@omnigraphics.com
Website: www.omnigraphics.com
Fax Ordering: (800) 875-1340; (610) 532-9001
International Ordering: (610) 461-3548
Catalog: Free. **Frequency:** Semiannual.
Circulation: 250K. **Sales:** $10-20MM
Products: Business directories;
health reference series

OSBORNE/McGRAW-HILL CATALOG   (800) 227-0900
2100 Powell St., 10th Fl.
Emeryville, CA 94608
E-Mail: info@osborne.com
Website: www.mhprofessional.com
Fax Ordering: (609) 426-7917
International Ordering: (609) 426-5793
Customer Service: (877) 833-5524
Contact Name: Larry Levitsky, President
Catalog: Free. **Frequency:** Annual
Circulation: 300K. **Sales:** $10-20MM
Products: Computer books

PALADIN PRESS CATALOG   (800) 392-2400
7077 Winchester Cir. • Boulder, CO 80301   (800) 466-6868
E-Mail: service@paladin-press.com
Website: www.paladin-press.com
Fax Ordering: (303) 442-8741
International Ordering: (303) 443-7250
Contact Names: Peter C. Lund, President

Catalog: Free. **Frequency:** Bimonthly
Circulation: 200K. **Sales:** $3-5MM
Products: Books & videos on fighting & self-defense

PARA PUBLISHING BOOKS   (800) 727-2782
P.O. Box 8206 • Santa Barbara, CA 93118
E-Mail: info@parapublishing.com
Website: www.parapublishing.com
Fax Ordering: (805) 968-1379
International Ordering: (805) 968-7277
Contact Name: Dan Poynter, President
Catalog: Free. **Frequency:** Semiannual
Circulation: 50K. **Sales:** $500K
Products: Books on book promotion

PELICAN PUBLISHING CATALOGS   (800) 843-1724
1000 Burmaster St. • Gretna, LA 70053   (888) 573-5426
E-Mail: sales@pelicanpub.com
Website: www.pelicanpub.com
Fax Ordering: (504) 368-1195
International Ordering: (504) 368-1175
Contact Name: Milburn Calhoun, President
Catalog: Free. **Frequency:** Semiannual
Circulation: 200K. **Sales:** $3-5MM
Products: Books & audiocassettes;
children's books

PENFIELD PRESS BOOKS   (800) 728-9998
215 Brown St. • Iowa City, IA 52245
E-Mail: penfield@penfieldbooks.com
Website: www.penfield-press.com
Fax Ordering: (319) 351-6846
International Ordering: (319) 337-9998
Catalog: Free. **Frequency:** Annual
Circulation: 100K. **Sales:** $500K - $1MM
Products: Cookbooks & recipes featuring
ethnic cooking & culture books

PETERSON'S/NELNET CO. CATALOG   (800) 338-3282
Princeton Pike Corporate Center
2000 Lenox Dr. • Lawrenceville, NJ 08648
E-Mail: support@petersons.com
Website: www.petersons.com
Fax Ordering: (609) 896-4531
International Ordering: (609) 896-1800
Contact Names: Richard J. Harrington, President
Catalog: Free. **Frequency:** Semiannual
Circulation: 500K. **Sales:** $25-50MM
Products: Books on education and test prep
resources, including career planning, financial aid,
secondary school, college & graduate school guides.

PFEIFFER PUBLISHING   (800) 274-4434
John Wiley & Sons
350 Sansome St. • San Francisco, CA 94104
E-Mail: sales@pfeiffer.com
Website: www.pfeiffer.com
Catalog: Free. **Frequency:** Semiannual
Circulation: 100K. **Sales:** $1-3MM
Products: Training solutions for human
resource development professionals

PIERIAN PRESS BOOKS   (800) 648-2435
P3196 Maple Dr. • Ypsilanti, MI 48197
E-Mail: mew_42strat@yahoo.com
Website: www.pierianpress.com
Fax Ordering: (734) 434-6409
International Ordering: (734) 434-4074
Contact Name: C. Edward Wall, President
Catalog: Free. **Frequency:** Annual
Circulation: 100K. **Sales:** $3-5MM
Products: Library reference materials

BUD'S ART BOOKS CATALOG   (800) 242-6642
BUD'S INCORRIGIBLE CATALOG
Bud Plant Commic Art
P.O. Box 1689 • Grass Valley, CA 95945
E-Mail: info@budsartbooks.com
Website: www.budsartbooks.com
Fax Ordering: (530) 273-0915
International Ordering: (530) 273-2166
Contact Name: Bud Plant, President
Catalog: $5. Frequency: 6x per year
Circulation: 50K. Sales: $1-5MM
Products: Books, prints, graphic novels, etc.
related to comic books and comic strips,
illustration, animation, and art history

PRINCETON UNIVERSITY PRESS   (800) 777-4726
41 William St. • Princeton, NJ 08540
E-Mail: orders@press.princeton.edu
Website: www.press.princeton.edu
Local Phone: (609) 258-4900
Fax Ordering: (609) 258-6305
International Ordering: (609) 883-1759
Contact Name: Peter Dougherty, Director
Catalog: Free. Frequency: Semiannual
Circulation: 100K. Sales: $5-10MM
Products: Library reference materials

THE AYN RAND INSTITUTE   (800) 729-6149
2121 Alton Pkwy. #250 • Irvine, CA 92606
E-Mail: inquiries@secondrenaissance.com
Website: www.rationalmind.com
Fax Ordering: (949) 222-6558
International Ordering: (949) 222-6550
Contact Name: Kate Sherwood, Admin. Coord.
Catalog: Free. Frequency: Semiannual
Circulation: 100K. Sales: $500K to $1MM
Products: Books & audiotapes on Ayn Rand
and individual rights

READER'S DIGEST   (800) 234-9000
BOOKS, VIDEOS & MUSIC   (800) 310-2181
Reader's Digest Rd.
Pleasantville, NY 10570
E-Mail: info@rd.com
Website: www.rd.com
Fax Ordering: (914) 244-7599
International Ordering: (914) 238-1000
Customer Service: (800) 304-2807
Contact Name: Thomas O. Ryder, President
Catalog: Free. Frequency: Quarterly
Circulation: 250K. Sales: $20-50MM
Products: Select editions, reading series,
do-it-yourself books, home improvement,
cooking, health, gardening, children's books,
recorded music collections

RECORDED BOOKS, LLC   (800) 638-1304
270 Skipjack Rd.
Prince Frederick, MD 20678
E-Mail: info@recordedbooks.com
Website: www.recordedbooks.com
Fax Ordering: (410) 535-5499
International Ordering: (410) 535-5590
Contact Name: Andrea Jung, President
Catalog: Free. Frequency: Quarterly
Circulation: 150K. Sales: $500K - $1MM
Products: Books on tape for adults, children
& young adults; self-improvement audiobooks

REFERENCE SERVICE PRESS   (916) 939-9620
5000 Windplay Dr., #4
El Dorado Hills, CA 95762

E-Mail: findaid@aol.com
Website: www.rspfunding.com
Fax Ordering: (916) 939-9626
Contact Names: Gail Schachter, President
Catalog: Free. Frequency: Annual
Circulation: 50K. Sales: $250-500K
Products: Financial aid directories

RESOURCE PUBLICATIONS   (888) 273-7782
160 E. Virginia St. • San Jose, CA 95112
E-Mail: info@rpinet.com
Website: www.rpinet.com
Fax Ordering: (408) 287-8748
International Ordering: (408) 286-8505
Contact Name: William Burns, President
Catalog: Free. Frequency: Quarterly
Circulation: 150K. Sales: $1-3MM
Products: Religious books; software &
educational books

RIP OFF PRESS CATALOG   (530) 885-8183
P.O. Box 4686 • Auburn, CA 95604
E-Mail: mail@ripoffpress.com
Website: www.ripoffpress.com
Fax Ordering: (530) 885-8219
Contact Name: Frederic Todd, President
Catalog: $1. Frequency: Annual
Circulation: 20K. Sales: $250K
Products: Adult & underground comics,
books & related items

RIZZOLI/UNIVERSE INT'L PUBNS.   (800) 733-3000
300 Park Ave. So. • New York, NY 10010
E-Mail: info@rizzoliusa.com
Website: www.rizzoliusa.com
Fax Ordering: (212) 387-3535
International Ordering: (212) 387-3400
Contact Names: William Gworkin,, Marketing
Catalog: $2. Frequency: Semiannual
Circulation: 50K. Sales: $5-10MM
Products: Books on art, architecture &
photography; interior decorating

ROUTLEDGE BOOKS   (800) 634-7064
Taylor & Francis Group   Canada (800) 665-1148
7625 Empire Dr. • Florence, KY 41042
E-Mail: orders@taylorandfrancis.com
Website: www.routledge-ny.com
Fax Ordering: (800) 248-4724
Catalog: Free. Frequency: Semiannual
Circulation: 500K. Sales: $10-20MM
Products: Encyclopedias, reference books,
textbooks & publications on education

RTS UNLIMITED, INC.   (303) 403-1840
P.O. Box 150412 • Lakewood, CO 80215
E-Mail: rtsunlimited@earthlink.net
Website: www.rtsunlimited.com
Fax Ordering: (303) 403-1837
International Ordering: (303) 459-3366
Contact Name: Tim Collins, President
Catalog: $5. Frequency: Semiannual
Circulation: 25K. Sales: $1-3MM
Products: Comic books

SME CATALOG   (800) 733-4763
Society of Manufacturing Engineers
One SME Dr. • Dearborn, MI 48121
E-Mail: info@sme.org
Website: www.sme.org
Fax Ordering: (313) 425-3400
International Ordering: (313) 425-3000

Catalog: Free. Frequency: 5x per year
Circulation: 100K. Sales: $1-3MM
Products: Books, videos & software
from the Society

THE SCARECROW PRESS (800) 462-6420
4501 Forbes Blvd. #200
Lanham, MD 20706
E-Mail: custserv@rowman.com
Website: www.scarecrowpress.com
Fax Ordering: (800) 338-4550; (717) 794-3803
International Ordering: (717) 794-3800
Contact Name: James E. Lyons, President
Catalog: Free. Frequency: Annual
Circulation: 100K. Sales: $3-5MM
Products: Reference & scholarly books

SCHIFFER BOOKS (610) 593-1777
Schiffer Publishing Ltd.
4880 Lower Valley Rd. • Atglen, PA 19310
E-Mail: info@schifferbooks.com
Website: www.schifferbooks.com
Fax Ordering: (610) 593-2002
Contact Name: Peter B. Schiffer, President
Catalogs: Free. Frequency: Semiannual
Circulation: 250K. Sales: $3-5MM
Products: Catalogs for Lifestyle-Spirit; Antiques,
Collectibles & The Arts; Military & Aviation History;
Arts & Crafts

SCHOLAR'S BOOKSHELF CATALOGS (609) 395-6933
110 Melrich Rd. • Cranbury, NJ 08512
E-Mail: books@scholarsbookshelf.com
Website: www.scholarsbookshelf.com
Fax Ordering: (609) 395-0755
Contact Name: Abbot Friedland, President
Catalog: Free. Frequency: Monthly
Circulation: 1MM. Sales: $5-10MM
Products: Books & videos; catalogs for
History, Military, Fine Arts, Literature, Religion.

SELF-COUNSEL PRESS (877) 877-6490
1704 N. State St.   Canada (800) 663-3007
Bellingham, WA 98225
E-Mail: sales@self-counsel.com
Website: www.self-counsel.com
Fax Ordering: (360) 676-4549
International Ordering: (360) 676-4530
Canadian Orders: (604) 986-3366 Fax 986-3947
Catalog: Free. Frequency: Semiannual
Circulation: 100K. Sales: $500K to $1MM
Products: Reference books on starting a
business, law, real estate, publicity, sales &
marketing, human resources, writing, law, etc.

SIERRA SOLAR FLARE CATALOG (888) 667-6527
Sierra Solar Systems
563 C Idaho Maryland Rd.
Grass Valley, CA 95945
E-Mail: solarjon@sierrasolar.com
Website: www.sierrasolar.com
Fax Ordering: (530) 273-1760
International Ordering: (530) 273-6754
Contact Name: Jonathan Hill, President
Catalog: Free. Pages: 68. Frequency: Semiannual
Circulation: 100K. Sales: $1-3MM
Products: Solar related books & videos;
energy production, solar water pumping,
inverters, solar oven, solar hot water;
solar gadgets & gismos

SOCIAL STUDIES CATALOG (800) 468-4227
Cambridge Educational (800) 257-5126
200 American Metro Blvd. #124
Hamilton, NJ 08852
E-Mail: custserv@films.com
Website: www.cambridge.films.com
Fax Ordering: (800) 329-6687
Contact Name: Steve Jones, President
Catalog: Free. Frequency: Monthly
Circulation: 1MM. Sales: $5-10MM
Products: Social studies books, videos
& audiotapes

SOUNDPRINT'S (800) 228-7839
Trudy Corporation
353 Main Ave. • Norwalk, CT 06851
E-Mail: soundprints@soundprints.com
Website: www.soundprints.com
Fax Ordering: (203) 846-1776
International Ordering: (203) 846-2274
Contact Name: William Burnham, President
Catalog: Free. Frequency: Semiannual
Circulation: 100K. Sales: $500K to $1M
Products: Children's storybooks, audiocassettes
and toys focused on nature & the environment

SOUNDS TRUE, INC. (800) 333-9185
413 S. Arthur Ave. • Louisville, KY 80027
E-Mail: customerservice@soundstrue.com
Website: www.shop.soundstrue.com
International Ordering: (303) 665-3151
Contact Name: Tami Simon, Owner
Catalog: Free. Frequency: Semiannual
Circulation: 150K. Sales: $1-3MM
Products: Audio courses, books, videos,
& music for personal & spiritual transformation

STERLING PUBLISHING BOOKS (800) 367-9692
387 Park Ave. So. • New York, NY 10016
E-Mail: custservice@sterlingpublishing.com
Website: www.sterlingpublishing.com
Fax Ordering: (212) 213-2495
International Ordering: (212) 532-7160
Contact Name: Lincoln Boehm, President
Catalog: Free. Frequency: Semiannual
Circulation: 300K. Sales: $3-5M
Products: Trade books & videos: Do-it-yourself books;
arts & crafts books; home decorating, woodworking,
gardening, photography, science & nature,
children's books & New Age books

STOREY COMMUNICATIONS (800) 441-5700
Storey Publishing, LLC
210 Mass Moca Way
North Adams, MA 01247
E-Mail: sales@storey.com
Website: www.storey.com
Fax Ordering: (800) 865-3429; (413) 346-2199
International Ordering: (413) 346-2100
Customer Service: (800) 827-7444
Contact Name: Pam Art, President
Catalog: Free. Frequency: Semiannual
Circulation: 250K. Sales: $10-20MM
Products: Books, gifts & calendars on gardening,
health & beauty, equine/pets, herbs, cooking,
crafts, building & animals

STRAND BOOK STORE (800) 366-3664
828 Broadway • New York, NY 10003
E-Mail: strand@strandbooks.com
Website: www.strandbooks.com
Fax Ordering: (212) 473-2591

International Ordering: (212) 473-1452
Contact Name: Fred Bass, President
Catalog: Free. Frequency: Monthly
Circulation: 200K. Sales: $1-3MM
Products: Books in all fields; bargain
remainders

SURVIVAL SELECTIONS (800) 323-0037
Calibre Press
200 Green St. #200
San Francisco, CA 94111
E-Mail: orders@calibrepress.com
Website: www.thecalibreshop.com
Fax Ordering: (866) 225-4273; (214) 545-3061
International Ordering: (214) 5445-3060
Catalog: Free. Frequency: Monthly
Circulation: 200K. Sales: $500K to $1MM
Products: Police books; Law enforcement
books, videos, seminars & clothing

GIFTED EDUCATION CATALOG (800) 998-2208
Prufrock Press
P.O. Box 8813 • Waco, TX 76714
E-Mail: gbates@prufrock.com
Website: www.prufrock.com
Fax Ordering: (800) 240-0333; (214) 756-3339
International Ordering: (254) 756-3337
Contact Name: Dr. Marvin Gold, President
Catalog: Free. Frequency: Annual
Circulation: 100K. Sales: $500K
Products: Books, magazines & research
journals supporting gifted & talented education

TIME-LIFE CATALOG (800) 621-7026
P.O. Box 4002011 • Des Moines, IA 50340
E-Mail: info@timelife.com
Website: www.timelife.com
Fax Ordering: (703) 838-7225
International Ordering: (703) 838-7000
Contact Name: Steve Janes, President
Catalog: Free. Frequency: Quarterly
Circulation: 1MM. Sales: $10-20MM
Products: Books, music & DVDs on home
improvement, historical, cooking, hobby &
geographical series titles

TRUTH SEEKER CO. CATALOG (760) 489-5211
239 S. Juniper St.
Escondido, CA 92025
E-Mail: info@truthseeker.com
Website: www.truthseeker.com
Fax Ordering: (760) 489-5311
International Ordering: (760) 489-5211
Contact Name: Bonnie Lange, President
Catalog: Free. Frequency: Semiannual
Circulation: 25K. Sales: $250-500K
Products: Books, videos & other items
specializing in freethought philosophy;
ancient mysteries, UFOs & extraterrestrials,
new science, conspiracies, etc.

TWIN PALMS PUBLISHERS (800) 797-0680
TWELVETREES PRESS
54.5 E. San Francisco St.
Santa Fe, NM 87501
E-Mail: twinpalmsp@twinpalms.com
Website: www.twinpalms.com
Fax Ordering: (505) 988-7011
International Ordering: (505) 988-5717
Catalog: Free. Frequency: Semiannual
Circulation: 100K. Sales: $500K to $1MM
Products: Photography & art books

UN PUBLICATIONS CATALOG (800) 253-9646
2 United Nations Plaza • Rm. DC2-853
New York, NY 10017
E-Mail: publications@un.org
Website: www.unp.un.org
Fax Ordering: (212) 963-8302
International Ordering: (212) 963-3489
Contact Name: Susanna Johnston, President
Catalog: Free. Frequency: Annual
Circulation: 50K. Sales: $1-3MM
Products: Books & manuals published
by the United Nations

U.S. PHARMACOPEIA CATALOG (800) 822-8772
12601 Twinbrook Pkwy. (800) 227-8772
Rockville, MD 20852
E-Mail: custserv@usp.org
Website: www.usp.org
Fax Ordering: (301) 816-8148
International Ordering: (301) 881-0666
Contact Name: Jerome Halpern, President
Catalog: Free. Frequency: 5x per year
Circulation: 150K. Sales: $3-5MM
Products: Drug information in print &
electronic formats

UPSTART BOOKS (800) 448-4887
Upstart Promotions (800) 558-2110
P.O. Box 5207 • Janesville, WI 53547
E-Mail: custsvc@upstartpromotion.com
Website: www.highsmith.com
Fax Ordering: (800) 448-5828
International Ordering: (920) 563-0571
Contact Name: Duncan Highsmith, President
Catalog: Free. Frequency: Semiannual
Circulation: 50K. Sales: $500K to 1MM
Products: Books on creative ideas for library
and classroom (grades PK-12) learning

VEGETARIAN & HEALTH CATALOG (800) 695-2241
The mail Order Catalog
P.O. Box 180 • Summertown, TN 38483
E-Mail: askus@healthy-eating.com
Website: www.healthy-eating.com
Fax Ordering: (931) 964-2291
International Ordering: (931) 964-2241
Contact Names: Cynthia Holzapfel, President
Catalog: Free. Frequency: 5x per year
Circulation: 250K. Sales: $500K - $1MM
Products: Quick-cooking meat substitutes
& soyfoods, vegetarian products & books

VINTAGE NEWSPAPERS (800) 235-1919
P.O. Box 48621 • Los Angeles, CA 90048
E-Mail: customerservice@newspaperarchive.com
Website: www.newspaperarchive.com
Fax Ordering: (310) 935-3079
International Ordering: (310) 552-3176
Contact Name: Selwyn Landsberg, President
Catalog: Free. Frequency: Annual
Circulation: 50K. Sales: $500K
Products: Vintage newspapers 1850 to the
present & leather bound newspapers for
your date of birth

WESSEL & LIEBERMAN BOOKSELLERS (888) 383-3631
208 First Ave. South • Seattle, WA 98104
E-Mail: orders@wlbooks.com
Website: www.wlbooks.com
Fax Ordering: (206) 682-2391
International Ordering: (206) 682-3545
Catalog: Free. Frequency: Semiannual

Circulation: 150K. **Sales:** $3-5M
Products: New, used, rare, and out-of-print books and related material

WILDERNESS PRESS (800) 443-7227
1345 8th St. • Berkeley, CA 94710
E-Mail: mail@wildernesspress.com
Website: www.wildernesspress.com
Fax Ordering: (510) 558-1696
International Ordering: (510) 558-1666
Contact Name: Caroline Winnette, President
Catalog: Free. **Frequency:** Semiannual
Circulation: 50K. **Sales:** $1-3MM
Products: Outdoor books & maps of western U.S.

WILSHIRE BOOK CO. (818) 700-1522
9731 Variel Ave. • Chatsworth, CA 91311
E-Mail: mpowers@mpowers.com
Website: www.mpowers.com
Fax Ordering: (818) 700-1527
Contact Name: Melvin Powers, President
Catalog: Free. **Frequency:** Quarterly
Circulation: 100K. **Sales:** $3-5MM
Products: Self-improvement books

WOODBINE HOUSE (800) 843-7323
6510 Bells Mill Rd. • Bethesda, MD 20817
E-Mail: info@woodbinehouse.com
Website: www.woodbinehouse.com
International Ordering: (301) 897-3570
Catalog: Free. **Frequency:** Semiannual
Circulation: 100K. **Sales:** $500K - $1MM
Products: Books on disabilities for adults & children

WOODLAND BOOKS (800) 777-2665
515 South 700 East (800) 277-3243
Salt Lake City, UT 84102
E-Mail: info@woodlandpublishing.com
Website: www.woodlandpublishing.com
Fax Ordering: (801) 615-2305
Contact Name: Trent Tenney, President
Catalog: Free. **Frequency:** Semiannual
Circulation: 50K. **Sales:** $3-5MM
Products: Natural health titles covering herbs, nutrition & dietary supplements

WORLD ALMANAC BOOKS (800) 322-8755
Infobase Publishing (800) 223-2336
132 West 31st St. • New York, NY 10001
E-Mail: custserv@factsonfile.com
Website: www.worldalmanac.com
Fax Ordering: (800) 943-9831; (917) 339-0325
International Ordering: (646) 312-6800
Catalog: Free. **Frequency:** Annual
Circulation: 250K. **Sales:** $10-20M
Products: Books & software for the whole language/ethnicity classroom from World Almanac

WORLD BOOK STORE (800) 967-5325
233 N. Michigan Ave. #2000 (800) 975-3250
E-Mail: info@worldbook.com
Website: www.worldbook.com
Fax Ordering: (312) 729-5600
Catalog: Free. **Frequency:** Quarterly
Circulation: 2MM. **Sales:** $10-50MM
Products: Encyclopedias, dictionaries & learning resources; books on early learning, science & nature, social studies & geography, world languages

WRITTEN HERITAGE (800) 301-8009
P.O. Box 1390 • Folsom, LA 70437
E-Mail: info@writtenheritage.com
Website: www.writtenheritage.com
Fax Ordering: (985) 796-9236
International Ordering: (985) 796-5433
Contact Name: Jack Heriard, President
Catalog: Free. **Pages:** 64
Frequency: Semiannual
Circulation: 100K. **Sales:** $250-500K
Products: Books, videos, DVDs on American Indians, past & present; Indian clothing patterns.

WRITERS DIGEST BOOKS (800) 289-0963
F & W Publications
1507 Dana Ave. • Cincinnati, OH 45207
E-Mail: writersdig@fwpubs.com
Website: www.writersdigest.com
Fax Ordering: (513) 294-4448
International Ordering: (513) 294-3345
Contact Name: Stephen J. Kent, President
Catalog: Free. **Frequency:** Semiannual
Circulation: 300K. **Sales:** $20-50MM
Products: Books on writing, crafts, fine arts, woodworking, genealogy

ZEPHYS PRESS CATALOG (800) 888-4741
Chicago Review Press
814 N. Franklin St. • Chicago, IL 60610
E-Mail: info@zephyrpress.com
Website: www.zephyrpress.com
Fax Ordering: (312) 337-5985
International Ordering: (312) 337-0747
Contact Name: Jerome Pohlen, Sr. Editor
Catalog: Free. **Frequency:** Semiannual
Circulation: 100K. **Sales:** $5-10MM
Products: Books specializing in innovative teaching methods

AD-LIB ADVERTISING, INC.   (800) 622-3542
109 White Oak Lane • Old Bridge, NJ 08857
E-Mail: info@adlibadvertising.com
Website: www.adlibadvertising.com
Fax Ordering: (732) 679-9511
International Ordering: (732) 679-9226
Contact Name: Edmond Cogland, President
Catalog: Free. Frequency: Monthly
Circulation: 150K. Sales: $3-5MM
Products: Promotional products: business
accessories, electronics, food gifts, golf
accessories, office supplies

ADCAPITOL   (704) 283-2147
1400 Goldmine Rd. • Monroe, NC 28110
E-Mail: sales@adcapitol.com
Website: www.adcapitol.com
Fax Ordering: (800) 309-4778
International Ordering: (704) 283-2147
Contact Name: Lance Dunn, President
Catalog: Free. Frequency: Quarterly
Circulation: 200K. Sales: $10-20MM
Products: Premium and incentive products

ADSOURCES   (866) 394-0000
MS 689 • Glen Cove, NY 11542
E-Mail: info@adsources.com
Website: www.adsources.com
Fax Ordering: (866) 394-8101; (516) 656-0668
International Ordering: (516) 656-5600
Catalog: Free. Frequency: Semiannual
Circulation: 200K. Sales: $5-10M
Products: Promotional products: business
gifts; 500, 000 ideas & promotional solutions

ADVERITISNG SPECIALTIES   (800) 943-9494
& BUSINESS GIFTS
Promotion Plus, Inc.
4104 Vachell Lane
San Luis Obispo, CA 93401
E-Mail: wluffee@promoplus.com
Website: www.promoplus.com
Fax Ordering: (805) 541-4795
International Ordering: (805) 541-5730
Contact Name: Bill Luffee, President
Catalog: Free. Frequency: Annual
Circulation: 100K. Sales: $3-5MM
Products: Premium and incentive gifts;
graphic design, printing & fulfillment

AMACON BOOKS IN PRINT   (800) 714-6395
American Management Association
1601 Broadway • New York, NY 10019
E-Mail: pubs_cust_serv@amanet.org
Website: www.amanet.org
Fax Ordering: (212) 903-8083; (518) 891-0368
International Ordering: (212) 586-8100
Customer Service: (800) 714-6395
Catalog: Free. Frequency: Annual
Circulation: 100K. Sales: $3-5MM
Products: Professional books

AMERICAN TAPE MEASURES, INC.   (773) 327-6667
4001 N. Ravenswood #604
Chicago, IL 60613
E-Mail: kurt@americantapemeasures.com
Website: www.americantapemeasures.com
Fax Ordering: (773) 327-6318
International Ordering: (773) 327-6667
Contact Name: Kurt Pusczan
Catalog: Free. Frequency: Annual
Circulation: 100K. Sales: $3-5MM

Products: Custon Tyvek tape measures
for advertising, clothing, uniform & sewing
industries, medical & health industries; scales.

AMERICAN TROPHIES   (925) 754-7878
516 W. 3rd St. • Antioch, CA 94509
E-Mail: mandj@netvista.net
Website: www.americantrophies.com
Fax Ordering: (925) 778-8970
Catalog: Free. Frequency: Annual
Circulation: 100K. Sales: $3-5MM
Products: Promotional products;
yrophies for business; awards & engraving

AMERICAN TROPHY   (401) 438-3060
250 Taunton Ave.
East Providence, RI 02914
E-Mail: amtrophy@rcn.com
Website: www.americantrophy.com
Fax Ordering: (401) 435-5626
Contact Name: Kristen Ann Gossler, Contact
Catalog: Free. Frequency: Annual
Circulation: 150K. Sales: $3-5MM
Products: Trophies for business &
recreational areas

AMSTERDAM PRINTING   (800) 203-9917
166 Wallins Corner Rd.
Amsterdam, NY 12010
E-Mail: customerservice@amsterdamprinting.com
Website: www.amsterdamprinting.com
Fax Ordering: (518) 843-5204
Catalog: Free. Frequency: Annual
Circulation: 100K. Sales: $3-5MM
Products: Promotional & Moticational
products; printing; office products

ARTLITE PENS & GIFTS   (800) 327-7367
2531 Piedmont Rd. NE • Atlanta, GA 30324
E-Mail: pens@artlite.net
Website: www.artlitepens.com
Fax Ordering: (404) 875-2623
International Ordering: (404) 875-7271
Contact Name: Steve Light, President
Catalog: Free. Frequency: Annual
Circulation: 25K. Sales: $1-3MM
Products: Office supplies, writing instruments,
pens, travelware, briefcases, gifts

AVIVA DESIGN   (866) 603-3360
1537 Terry Lynn Lane • Concord, CA 94521
E-Mail: sales@avivadesign.com
Website: www.avivadesign.com
Fax Ordering: (866) 338-9494
International Ordering: (925) 946-1566
Catalog: Online. Sales: $5-10MM
Products: Promotional merchandise; office
supplies; food gifts; embroidery & silkscreen
imprinting for corporate apparel

AWARD COMPANY OF AMERICA   (800) 633-2021
3200 Rice Mine Rd. • Tuscaloosa, AL 35406
E-Mail: sales@awardcompany.com
Website: www.awardcompany.com
Fax Ordering: (800) 900-1683; (205) 345-0958
International Ordering: (205) 349-2990
Customer Service: (800) 633-5953
Contact Name: Julie Gresham, Account Executive
Catalog: Free. Frequency: Quarterly
Circulation: 250K. Sales: $5-10MM
Products: Recognition & promotional products;
awards, plaques, and imprinted ribbons & specialties

AWARDS.COM (800) 429-2737
1040 Holland Dr. • Boca Raton, FL 33487
E-Mail: info@awards.com
Website: www.awards.com
Fax Ordering: (561) 998-7716
Catalog: Online. Sales: $5-10MM
Products: Awards, trophies, medals, plaques,
corporate gifts, logo apparel, promotional
products, textiles, candy & food baskets

BALDWIN COOKE CATALOG (800) 762-5000
P.O. Box 312 • Gloversville, NY 12078
E-Mail: cs@baldwincooke.com
Website: www.baldwincooke.com
Fax Ordering: (888) 870-2966
Catalog: Free. Frequency: Annual
Circulation: 1MM. Sales: $20-50MM
Products: Corporate pocket calendar
& custom day planners

BAUDVILLE CATALOG (800) 728-0888
5380 52nd St. SE • Grand Rapids, MI 49512
E-Mail: service@baudville.com
Website: www.baudville.com
Fax Ordering: (616) 698-0554
International Ordering: (616) 698-0889
Catalog: Free. Frequency: Annual
Circulation: 200K. Sales: $10-20M
Products: Corporate gifts; employee
recognition awards & ideas

BELL COMPANY (800) 828-3564
106 Morrow Ave. • Trussville, AL 35173
E-Mail: info@bellcoinc.com
Website: www.bellcoinc.com
Fax Ordering: (205) 655-2138
International Ordering: (205) 655-2135
Contact Name: Neil Bell, President
Catalog: Free. Frequency: Annual
Circulation: 150K. Sales: $10-30MM
Products: Engraving machines & supplies;
cast bronze and aluminum plaques;
personalized badges, signs & desk
nameplates

BERMAN LEATHERCRAFT (617) 426-0870
229 A St. • Boston, MA 02210
E-Mail: info@bermanleather.com
Fax Ordering: (617) 357-8564
Contact Name: Robert S. Berman, President
Catalog: $3, & Online. Frequency: Semiannual.
Circulation: 15K. Sales: $1-3MM
Products: Leather promotional and business
products; leathercraft tools & supplies

BEST IMPRESSIONS CATALOG (800) 635-2378
345 N. Lewis Ave. • Oglesby, IL 61348
E-Mail: service@bestimpressions.com
Website: www.bestimpressions.com
Fax Ordering: (815) 883-8346
International Ordering: (815) 883-3532
Contact Name: Shelly Greening, Marketing
Catalog: Free. Frequency: Semiannual
Circulation: 200M. Sales: $10-20MM
Products: Promotional products & custom
imprinted items; advertising sepcialties for
promotions, incentives and gift giving

BLOOMNGDALE'S CORP. SERVICES (800) 472-0788
P.O. Box 8215 • Mason, OH 45040
E-Mail: info@bloomingdales.com
Website: www.bloomingdales.com

Fax Ordering: (212) 705-3254
International Ordering: (212) 705-3556
Catalog: Free. Frequency: Annual
Circulation: 20MM. Sales: $50-100MM
Products: Gift ideas for corporate gift giving

BOOKS FOR YOUR BUSINESS (631) 754-0500
Forum Publishing Company
383 E. Main St. • Centerport, NY 11721
E-Mail: forumpublishing@aol.com
Website: www.bizbooks.org
Fax Ordering: (631) 754-0630
Contact Name: Martin Stevens, President
Catalog: Free. Frequency: Monthly
Circulation: 250K. Sales: $3-5MM
Products: Books & directories to help
start or expand your business

BRASSCO ENGRAVING SUPPLY (800) 447-7712
405 Tarpan Trail • Celina, TX 75009
E-Mail: brassco@flash.net
Fax Ordering: (972) 385-3299
International Ordering: (972) 385-1534
Contact Name: John Strange, President
Catalog: Free. Frequency: Annual
Circulation: 100K. Sales: $500M
Products: Plaques, awards, trophies,
nameplates

BULLETLINE CATALOG (800) 920-9223
E-Mail: info@bulletline.com
Website: www.bulletline.com
Contact Name: Herb Stone, President
Catalog: Online. Sales: $5-10MM
Products: Business promotional products

BUSINESS GIFT CATALOG (800) 323-2676
The Popcorn Factory
13970 W. Laurel Dr.
Lake Forest, IL 60045
E-Mail: info@thepopcornfactory.com
Website: www.thepopcornfactory.com
Fax Ordering: (888) 333-4595
Customer Service: (888) 238-8107
Catalog: Free. Frequency: Annual
Circulation: 100K. Sales: $5-10MM
Products: Corporate gifts

CAMBRIDGE EDUCATIONAL (800) 468-4227
200 American Metro Blvd., Suite 124 (800) 257-5126
Hamilton, NJ 08619
E-Mail: custserv@films.com
Website: www.cambridge.films.com
Fax Ordering: (800) 329-6687; (609) 671-0266
Contact Name: Melinda Ball, Marketing Mgr.
Catalog: Free. Frequency:
Circulation: 150K. Sales: $10-20MM
Products: Business videos, software,
CD-ROMs, books and posters

CENTURY BUSINESS SOLUTIONS (800) 767-0777
P.O. Box 2393 • Brea, CA 92822
E-Mail: info@centurybusinesssolutions.com
Website: www.centurybusinesssolutions.com
Fax Ordering: (800) 786-7939
International Ordering: (714) 441-4550
Contact Name: Bill Martin, Marketing
Catalog: Free. Frequency: Monthly
Circulation: 3MM. Sales: $10-20MM
Products: Office & photo archival supplies
including CD & media storage; binders &
accessories; planners & address books

CHECKS IN THE MAIL (800) 733-4443
2435 Goodwin Lane
New Braunfels, TX 78135
E-Mail: info@citm.com
Website: www.citm.com
Fax Ordering: (800) 822-0005; 800-2432
Fax Internet Ordering: (800) 800-2432
Catalog: Free. Frequency: Annual
Product: Personal & business checks,
address labels, photo products

CMS - Consolidated Mailing Service (800) 303-8117
P.O. Box 495 • St. James, NY 11780
E-Mail: info@educationallists.com
Website: www.educationallists.com
Fax Ordering: (631) 584-4355
International Ordering: (631) 584-7283
Contact Name: Mark Bradbard, President
Catalog: Free. Frequency: Annual
Product: Mailing Lists: schools, colleges,
libraries and hospitals

CORPORATE IMAGE (800) 624-2348
Promotional Products Company
1700 W. Sam Houston Pkwy. N
Houston, TX 77043
E-Mail: sales@promotionalproductsco.com
Website: www.promotionalproductsco.com
Fax Ordering: (713) 465-8932
International Ordering: (713) 465-1254
Catalog: Free. Frequency: Annual
Circulation: 100K. Sales: $5-10MM
Products: Promotional products for corporations

CR MANUFACTURING CO. (877) 789-5844
10240 Deerpark Rd. • Waverly, NE 68462
E-Mail: info@crmfg.com
Website: www.crmfg.com
Fax Ordering: (402) 786-2096
International Ordering: (402) 786-2000
Contact Name: Fred Guttormson, President
Catalog: Free. Frequency: Annual
Circulation: 25K. Sales: $10-20MM
Products: Promotional products and specialty
items; foodservice restaurant & bar supplies

CRESTLINE COMPANY (800) 221-7797
P.O. Box 2027 • Lewiston, ME 04241
E-Mail: crestlinehelp@crestline.com
Website: www.crestline.com
Fax Ordering: (800) 242-8290
Customer Service: (866) 488-4975
Contact Name: Robert Schulz, Marketing Mgr.
Catalog: Free. Frequency: 24x per year
Circulation: 100K. Sales: $5-10 MM
Products: Custom imprinted and embroidered
promotional products for advertising, trade shows
& conventions, incentives, branding, corporate
apparel, personalized promos & more.

CROWN AWARDS (800) 227-1557
9 Skyline Dr. • Hawthorne, NY 10532
E-Mail: custserv@crownawards.com
Website: www.crownawards.com
Fax Ordering: (914) 347-7008
Customer Service: (800) 765-2003
Catalog: Free. Frequency: Quarterly
Circulation: 350M. Sales: $20-50MM
Products: Trophies, medals, plaques, ribbons
& certificates, pins, sculptures; corporate awards,
promotional products.

CUSTOM-PRINTED PROMOTIONAL ITEMS (800) 397-7923
Larry Fox & Co.
P.O. Box 729 • Valley Stream, NY 11582
E-Mail: ellen@larryfox.com
Website: www.larryfox.com
Fax Ordering: (516) 791-1022
International Ordering: (516) 791-7929
Contact Name: Larry Fox, President
Catalog: Free. Frequency: Semiannual
Circulation: 25K. Sales: $500K to $1MM
Products: Promotional gifts & imprinted products
for businesses, organizations & schools

DINN BROTHERS TROPHIES (800) 628-9657
221 Interstate Dr.
West Springfield, MA 01089
E-Mail: sales@dinntrophy.com
Website: www.dinntrophy.com
Fax Ordering: (800) 876-7497; (413) 733-4949
International Ordering: (413) 750-3466
Customer Service: (800) 628-3466
Contact Name: Mike Dinn, Marketing Manager
Catalog: Free. Frequency: Monthly
Circulation: 500K. Sales: $5-10MM
Products: Trophies and plaques

DIRECT PROMOTIONS (800) 444-7706
23935 Ventura Blvd. • Calabasas, CA 91302
E-Mail: sales@directpromotions.net
Website: www.directpromotions.net
Fax Ordering: (818) 591-2071
International Ordering: (818) 591-9010
Contact Name: Randy Perry, President
Catalog: Free. Frequency: Annual
Circulation: 100K. Sales: $1-3MM
Products: Promotional products and
business gifts

DISMAR CORPORATION (800) 347-6271
4415 Marlton Pike • Pennsauken, NJ 08109
E-Mail: info@dismar.com
Website: www.dismar.com
Fax Ordering: (856) 488-1664
International Ordering: (856) 488-0100
Contact Name: Stanley Silverman, President
Catalog: Free. Frequency: Bimonthly
Circulation: 75M. Sales: $5-10MM
Products: Signs and displays for retailers;
promotional products

HUGO DUNHILL MAILING LISTS, INC. (800) 611-0557
542 Main St. 4th Fl • New Rochelle, NY 10801
E-Mail: info@hdml.com
Website: www.hdml.com
Fax Ordering: (212) 213-9245
International Ordering: (212) 213-9300
Contact Name: Hugo Dunhill, President
Catalog: Free. Frequency: Annual
Circulation: 100K. Sales: $5-10MM
Products: Mailing lists

EASTERN EMBLEM MFG. CORP. (800) 344-5112
P.O. Box 828 • Union City, NJ 07087
E-Mail: info@easternemblem.com
Website: www.easternemblem.com
Fax Ordering: (201) 867-7248
International Ordering: (201) 867-3159
Contact Name: S. Lefkowitz, President
Catalog: Free. Frequency: Annual
Circulation: 50K. Sales: $1-3MM
Products: Emblems and insignia for advertising

ELCO MFG. ADVERTISING GIFTS (516) 767-3577
26 Ivy Way • Port Washington, NY 11050
E-Mail: sales@elcomfg.com
Website: www.elcomfg.com
Fax Ordering: (516) 767-3567; (212) 255-4331
International Ordering: (516) 767-3577;
 (212) 255-4300
Contact Name: Stan Weintraub, President
Catalog: Free. Frequency: Quarterly
Circulation: 100K. Sales: $3-5MM
Products: Leather goods and stationery
specialties, premiums, promotional products,
custom imprinted giveaways

EMED COMPANY (800) 442-3633
P.O. Box 369 • Buffalo, NY 14240 (866) 222-4743
E-Mail: customerservice@emedco.com
Website: www.emedco.com
Fax Ordering: (800) 344-2578; (716) 626-1630
International Ordering: (716) 626-1616
Contact Name: Paul Steinwachs, President
Catalog: Free. Frequency: Annual
Circulation: 100M. Sales: $1-3MM
Products: Engraved signs, frames & graphic
 communication products

EXECUTIVE GALLERY (800) 848-2618
3090 Scioto Darby Executive Ct.
Hilliard, OH 43026
E-Mail: eg@executivegallery.com
Website: www.executivegallery.com
Fax Ordering: (614) 457-8755
International Ordering: (614) 457-9600
Contact Name: Al Lach, Owner
Catalog: Online. Sales: $3-5MM
Products: Personalized gifts for business

FACEMAKERS, INC. (815) 273-3944
140 Fifth St. • Savanna, IL 61074
E-Mail: facemakers@aol.com
Website: www.facemakersincorporated.com
Fax Ordering: (815) 273-3966
Contact Name: Alan St. George, President
Catalog: $15 print; Online. Frequency: Monthly
Circulation: 5K. Sales: $1-3MM
Products: Corporate & school mascots,
costumes, animal & character costumes;
reproduction of logos or artwork

FOR COUNSEL CATALOG (800) 637-0098
10965 SW Commerce Cir., Suite E
Wilsonville, OR 97070
E-Mail: forcounsel@forcounsel.com
Website: www.forcounsel.com
Fax Ordering: (503) 682-9430
International Ordering: (503) 682-8070
Contact Name: Art Kroos, President
Catalog: Free. Frequency: 5x per year
Circulation: 200K. Sales: $1-3MM
Products: Products & gifts for lawyers

4IMPRINT (877) 446-7746
101 Commerce St. • Oshkosh, WI 54901
E-Mail: 4care@4imprint.com
Website: www.4imprint.com
Fax Ordering: (800) 355-5043
International Ordering: (920) 236-7272
Customer Service: (888) 298-8190
Contact Name: Richard Nelson, President
Catalog: Free. Frequency: Quarterly
Circulation: 1MM. Sales: $50-100MM
Products: Imprinted promotional products

FRIDAY CASUALS (800) 638-7070
10722 Hanna St. • Beltsville, MD 20705
E-Mail: sales@fridaycasuals.com
Website: www.fridaycasuals.com
Fax Ordering: (301) 937-2916
International Ordering: (301) 937-4843
Contact Name: Gerry Flaig, President
Catalog: Free. Frequency: Quarterly
Circulation: 250K. Sales: $5-10MM
Products: Fundraising promotions; custom
embroidered and screen-printed image wear:
apparel embroidered or screen-printed with
your company logo

HARRIS INFOSOURCE (800) 888-5900
2057 E. Aurora Rd.
Twinsburg, OH 44087
E-Mail: info@harrisinfo.com
Website: www.harrisinfo.com;
Fax Ordering: (707) 887-9650
International Ordering: (707) 887-1587
Contact Name: Dennis Abrahams, President
Catalog: Free. Frequency: Semiannual
Circulation: 150K. Sales: $10-20MM
Products: Manufacturers' lists; web-based
marketing online database

HEWIG - MARVIC (201) 568-1939
2 Bradford Ct. • Tenafly, NJ 07670
E-Mail: hwgmarvic@aol.com
Fax Ordering: (201) 568-0625
International Ordering: (201) 568-1939
Contact Name: David Obedian, President
Catalog: Free. Frequency: Semiannual
Circulation: 75K. Sales: $3-5MM
Products: Imprinting on gifts & giveaways
for business advertising

HODGES BADGE CO., INC. (800) 556-2440
P.O. Box 1290 • Portsmouth, RI 02871
E-Mail: info@hodgesbadge.com
Website: www.hodgesbadge.com
Fax Ordering: (800) 292-7377; (401) 682-2329
International Ordering: (401) 682-2000
Catalog: Free. Frequency: Annual
Circulation: 100K. Sales: $5-10MM
Products: Promotional products ; badges,
award ribbons, medals, rosettes, sashes

ILLINI (800) 935-5472
450 E. Bunker Ct.
Vernon Hills, IL 60061
E-Mail: info@illini.com
Website: www.illini.com
Fax Ordering: (847) 549-0352
Contact Name: Neil Fine, President
Catalog: Free. Frequency: Annual
Circulation: 100K. Sales: $5-10MM
Products: Promotional products

INFOAMERICA (800) 326-7419
SJT Enterprises, Inc.
29307 Clemens Rd. • Westlake, OH 44145
E-Mail: info@sjtent.com
Website: www.sjtent.com/legalkits
Fax Ordering: (440) 617-0987
International Ordering: (440) 617-1100
Contact Names: Timothy J. Smith, President
Catalog: Free. Frequency: Semiannual
Circulation: 100K. Sales: $1-3MM
Products: Business and legal kits; magnets,
stickers, awards

INFO USA   (866) 752-3755
5711 S. 86th Cir. • Omaha, NE 68127
E-Mail: brokerhelp@infousa.com
Website: www.infousa.com
Fax Ordering: (402) 331-1505
International Ordering: (402) 593-4500
Contact Name: Vinod Gupta, CEO
Catalog: Free. Frequency: Quarterly
Circulation: 200K. Sales: $10-20MM
Products: Business and consumer sales
leads and mailing lists

JOSSEY-BASS, INC.   (800) 956-7739
350 Sansome St.
San Francisco, CA 94104
E-Mail: sales@josseybass.com.com
Website: www.josseybass.com
Fax Ordering: (800) 605-2665
International Ordering: (415) 433-0499
Catalog: Free. Frequency: Semiannual.
Circulation: 100K. Sales: $1-3MM
Products: Books on innovations in
leadership in business

MAGNA VISUAL, INC.   (800) 843-3399
9400 Watson Rd. • St. Louis, MO 63126
E-Mail: magna@magnavisual.com
Website: www.magnavisual.com
Fax Ordering: (314) 843-0000
International Ordering: (314) 843-9000
Contact Name: William Cady, President
Catalog: Free. Frequency: Annual
Circulation: 100K. Sales: $5-10MM
Products: Magnetic visual communication
systems; magnetic custom planning board
kits

MAIL ADVERTISING SUPPLY CATALOG   (800) 841-7301
1450 S. West Ave. • Waukesha, WI 53189
E-Mail: sales@lauterbachgroup.com
Website: www.lauterbachgroup.com
Fax Ordering: (800) 784-2591
International Fax Ordering: (262) 549-3614
International Ordering: (262) 549-1730
Contact Name: H.W. Lauterbach, President
Catalog: Online. Sales: $10-20MM
Products: Labels & paper products for the
mailing industry; decals, magnets

MARQUIS AWARDS & SPECIALTIES   (800) 327-2446
108 N. Bent St. • Powell, WY 82435
E-Mail: marquisawards@bresnan.net
Website: www.rushawards.com
Fax Ordering: (307) 754-9577
International Ordering: (307) 754-2272
Contact Name: John Collins, President
Catalog: Free. Frequency: Monthly
Circulation: 150K. Sales: $1-3MM
Products: Corporate awards; sportswear;
promotional products & gifts for business

MCH - MAILINGS CLEARING HOUSE   (800) 776-6373
P.O. Box 295 • Sweet Springs, MO 65351
E-Mail: sales@mailings.com
Website: www.mailings.com
Fax Ordering: (660) 335-4157
International Ordering: (660) 335-6373
Contact Name: John F. Hood, President
Catalog: Free. Frequency: Annual
Circulation: 100K. Sales: $1-3MM
Products: Library mailing lists

MERCHANDISING SOLUTIONS   (800) 394-1632
M.F. Blouin • 710 Main St.
Rollinsford, NH 03869
E-Mail: info@mfblouin.com
Website: www.mfblouin.com
Fax Ordering: (603) 742-9539
International Ordering: (603) 742-0104
Contact Name: John Dubois, President
Catalog: Free. Frequency: Monthly
Circulation: 200K. Sales: $5-10MM
Products: Merchandising fixtures,
dispensers, letter boards

MONARCH ACCOUNTING SUPPLIES   (800) 828-6718
Marcus Co., Inc.
750 Main St. • Holyoke, MA 01040
E-Mail: sales@monarchtaxforms.com
Website: www.monarchtaxforms.com
Fax Ordering: (413) 536-3477
International Ordering: (413) 536-3444
Catalog: Free. Frequency: Annual
Circulation: 100K. Sales: $3-5MM
Products: Packaging products & office supplies

MYLLYMAKI & CO, INC.   (800) 767-1969
P.O. Box 2069 • Mill Valley CA 94942
E-Mail: info@liststhatwork.com
Website: www.liststhatwork.com
Fax Ordering: (415) 459-7333
International Ordering: (415) 459-7400
Contact Name: Jan Myllymaki, President
Catalog: Free. Frequency: Semiannual
Circulation: 250K. Sales: $1-3MM
Products: Mailing lists

MYRON BUSINESS GIFTS   (800) 526-9766
205 Maywood Ave. • Maywood, NJ 07607   (877) 803-3358
E-Mail: sales@myron.com
Website: www.myron.com
Fax Ordering: (800) 753-7173; (201) 843-8390
International Ordering: (201) 843-6464
Contact Name: Mike Adler, President
Catalog: Free. Frequency: Annual
Circulation: 1MM. Sales: $100-200MM
Products: Promotional products; calendars &
planners; personalized business gifts; office
supplies & executive gifts

NATIONAL CUSTOM INSIGNIA   (800) 781-8806
8875 Hidden River Pkwy., Suite 300
Tampa, FL 33637
E-Mail: info@labelpins.com
Website: www.labelpins.com
Fax Ordering: (800) 649-3893; (727) 781-8506
International Ordering: (727) 843-6464
Contact Name: Mike Adler, President
Catalog: Free. Frequency: Annual
Circulation: 1MM. Sales: $100-200MM
Products: Custom lapel pins and emblematic
jewelry; promotional products

ODDSON PROMOTIONS   (888) 827-2249
6195 Ridgeview Ct., Suite D
Reno, NV 89509
E-Mail: info@oddsonpromotions.com
Website: www.oddsonpromotions.com
Catalog: Free. Frequency: Annual
Circulation: 200K. Sales: $10-20MM
Products: Conducts and insures contest
promotions for business including sports &
retail events; games & marketing campaigns

PARKWAY BUSINESS PROMOTIONS (800) 562-1735
1725 Roe Crest Dr.
North Mankato, MN 56002
Fax Ordering: (651) 426-9292
International Ordering: (651) 633-8122
Catalog: Free. Frequency: Semiannual
Circulation: 250K. Sales: $1-3MM
Products: Business promotional products
and gifts

PED-LINE (800) 377-2020
Montco Advertising Specialties
131 E. 10th Ave.
Conshohocken, PA 19428
E-Mail: sales@pedlineusa.com
Website: www.pedlineusa.com
Fax Ordering: (610) 825-1884
International Ordering: (610) 825-2929
Contact Name: Michael J. Lorah, President
Catalog: Free; online. Frequency: Semiannual
Circulation: 50K. Sales: $1-3MM
Products: Advertising & promotional
products:buttons, magnets, posters,
t-shirts; lapel pins, calendars

PIN GALLERY BY S.G.G. (800) 896-9219
P.O. Box 64784 • St. Paul, MN 55164
E-Mail: sales@pingallery.com
Website: www.pingallery.com
Fax Ordering: (800) 352-9501
Customer Service: (800) 221-7708
Catalog: Free. Frequency: Semiannual
Circulation: 50K. Sales: $1-3MM
Products: Over 1,000 exclusive stock pin designs:
motivational, achievement, employee recognition,
customer care, safety, service awards, training;
also, motivational prints, mugs, desk accessories,
candles & keytags, buttons & appliques

POSITIVE IMPRESSIONS (800) 895-5505
IDEA SHOWCASE
150 Clearbrook Rd. • Elmsford, NY 10523
E-Mail: sales@positiveimpressions.com
Website: www.positiveimpressions.com
Fax Ordering: (914) 591-4194
International Ordering: (914) 591-4123
Contact Name: J. Doyle, Contact
Catalog: Free. Frequency: Annual
Circulation: 50K. Sales: $1-3MM
Products: Personalized incentives & awards;
promotional products & gift ideas

PROMOPEDDLER.COM (800) 455-1350
16004 SW Tualatin-Sherwood Rd. #711
Sherwood, OR 97140
E-Mail: sales@promopeddler.com
Website: www.promopeddler.com
Fax Ordering: (415) 598-2660
Catalog: Online. Sales: $5-10MM
Products: Custom promotional products
& corporate gifts

QUALATEX CATALOGS (800) 331-6865
Pioneer Balloon Company
5000 E. 29th St. N. • Wichita, KS 67220
E-Mail: johannep@pioneerballoon.com
Website: www.qualatex.com
International Ordering: (316) 685-2266
Catalog: Free. Frequency: Semiannual
Circulation: 200K. Sales: $5-10MM
Products: Promotional latex & microfoil
balloons for balloon distributors

R&M RETAIL MERCHANDISING (800) 231-9600
Russell & Miller
P.O. Box 2152 • Santa Fe Springs, CA 90670
E-Mail: sales@russellandmiller.net
Website: www.russellandmiller.com
Fax Ordering: (800) 527-2488
International Ordering: (562) 946-6900
  Fax (562) 906-4606
Contact Name: Julie Janbarne, Marketing
Catalog: Free. Frequency: Semiannual
Circulation: 100K. Sales: $20—50MM
Products: Point-of-sale products & supplies
for retailers

REBECHINI STUDIOS (800) 229-6050
680 Fargo Ave. • Elk Grove Village, IL 60007
E-Mail: info@rsi-design.com
Website: www.rsi-design.com
Fax Ordering: (847) 437-0324
International Ordering: (847) 437-9030
Contact Name: F. Rebechini, President
Catalog: Free. Frequency: Annual
Circulation: 75K. Sales: $1-3MM
Products: Awards, plaques, figurines,
memorials

SALES GUIDES (800) 352-9899
4937 Otter Lake Rd. • St. Paul, MN 55110
International Ordering: (651) 426-6006
Contact Name: Cindy Penth, Marketing
Catalog: Free. Frequency: Semiannual
Circulation: 50K. Sales: $1-3MM
Products: Promotional items and gifts

SETON IDENTIFICATION PRODUCTS (800) 243-6624
Seton Name Plate Corporation (800) 571-2596
P.O. Box 819 • Branford, CT 06405
E-Mail: seton_mailroom@seton.com
Website: www.seton.com
Fax Ordering: (800) 345-7819
International Ordering: (203) 488-8059
Contact Name: Richard L. Fisk, President
Catalog: Free. Frequency: Semiannual
Circulation: 200K. Sales: $10-20MM
Products: Products for safety and regulation;
signs, labels, tags and identification products

SHAMROCK LEATHERS (800) 728-5184
9722 320th St. • St. Joseph, MN 56374
E-Mail: shleathers@aol.com
Website: www.shamrockleathers.com
Fax Ordering: (320) 363-7441
Contact Name: Edward Brophy, President
Catalog: Free. Frequency: Semiannual
Circulation: 50K. Sales: $1-3MM
Products: Corporate awards programs;
leather awards; leather shooting products
& trophies

SIEGEL DISPLAY PRODUCTS (800) 626-0322
300 Sixth Ave. North, Suite 200
 Minneapolis, MN 55440
E-Mail: customerservice@siegeldisplay.com
Website: www.siegeldisplay.com
Fax Ordering: (800) 230-5598; (610) 825-1884
International Ordering: (610) 825-2929
Contact Name: Edward Siegel, President
Catalog: Free. Frequency: Semiannual
Circulation: 100K. Sales: $10-20MM
Products: Displays for books, novelties,
and trade show displays; magazine racks;
retail displays; sign holders

STAR CASE - E&B GIFTWEAR (914) 964-5200
4 Executive Plaza • Yonkers, NY 10701
E-Mail: corporate@ebgift.com
Website: www.ebgift.com
Fax Ordering: (914) 964-3068
Contact Name: Jason Ross, President
Catalog: Free. Frequency: Annual
Circulation: 100K. Sales: $10-20MM
Products: Fitness products; premiums &
incentives for businesses; marketing programs;
travel accessories; retail merchandising ; gift products

SUCCESS BUILDER (800) 762-5000
Baldwin Cooke Co. (800) 231-2332
P.O. Box 312 • Gloversville, NY 12078
E-Mail: sales@baldwincooke.com
Website: www.baldwincooke.com
Fax Ordering: (888) 870-2966; (847) 948-7654
International Ordering: (847) 236-9400
Contact Name: Karen Weinberg, Buyer
Catalog: Free. Frequency: Quarterly
Circulation: 500M. Sales: $20-50MM
Products: Promotional products; motivational
awards & gifts; pocket/wall/desk planners;
executive gifts; forms & stationery; labels; diaries

SUCCESSFULL EVENTS (800) 896-9221
P.O. Box 190 • Hagaman, NY 12086
E-Mail: customerservice@successfuleventsonline.com
Website: www.successfuleventsonline.com
Fax Ordering: (800) 352-9501; (518) 770-7026
Customer Service: (800) 628-8447
Contact Name: Elizabeth Clark, Catalog Manager
Catalog: Free. Frequency: Semiannual
Circulation: 100K. Sales: $5-10MM
Products: Custom imprinted products for
meetings, conventions, and tradeshows

SUCCESSORIES (800) 535-2773
1040 Holland Dr. • Boca Raton, FL 33487
E-Mail: contactus@successories.com
Website: www.successories.com
Fax Ordering: (800) 932-9673; (561) 998-7716
Contact Name: Gary Rovansek, President
Catalog: Free. Frequency: Monthly
Circulation: 400K. Sales: $20-50MM
Products: Executive & motivational gifts
& awards

TAYLOR & FRANCIS GROUP (800) 634-7064
7625 Empire Dr. • Florence, KY 41042
E-Mail: orders@taylorandfrancis.com
Website: www.taylorandfrancis.com
Fax Ordering: (800) 248-4724; (561) 241-7856
International Ordering: (561) 994-0555
Catalog: Free. Frequency: Semiannual
Circulation: 150K Sales: $10-20MM
Products: Books and journals in marketing,
advertising & business

TRAINER'S WAREHOUSE (800) 299-3770
89 Washington Ave. • Natick, MA 01760
E-Mail: info@trainerswarehouse.com
Website: www.trainerswarehouse.com
Fax Ordering: (508) 651-2674
Contact Name: Sue Doctoroff Landay, President
Catalog: Free. Frequency: Semiannual
Circulation:200K. Sales: $3-5MM
Products: Hard-to-find & innovative products
for trainers, educators & presenters

TROPHYLAND USA, INC. (800) 327-5820
7001 W. 20th Ave. • Hialeah, FL 33014
E-Mail: info@trophyland.com
Website: www.trophyland.com
Fax Ordering: (305) 823-4836
International Ordering: (305) 823-4830
Contact Name: Paul Fields, President
Catalog: Free. Frequency: Semiannual
Circulation:50K. Sales: $1-3MM
Products: Trophies, plaques, medals

UNION PEN COMPANY (800) 846-6600
70 Riverdale Ave. • Greenwich, CT 06831
E-Mail: upinfo@unionpen.com
Website: www.unionpen.com
Fax Ordering: (800) 688-4877
International Ordering: (203) 531-4240
Contact Name: Morton Tenny, President
Catalog: Free. Frequency: Bimonthly
Circulation: 2MM. Sales: $10-20MM
Products: Imprinted promotional products

UPBEAT (800) 325-3047
4350 Duncan Ave. • St. Louis, MO 63110
E-Mail: custservice@upbeatinc.com
Website: www.upbeatinc.com
Fax Ordering: (314) 535-4419
International Ordering: (314) 535-5005
Contact Name: Pamela Hutchins, President
Catalog: Free. Frequency: Bimonthly
Circulation: 2MM. Sales: $3-5MM
Products: Business furniture, benches,
message centers, picnic tables & receptacles

VNU BUSINESS MEDIA (800) 223-2194
Edith Roman List Brokerage & Management
P.O. Box 1556 • Pearl River, NY 10965
E-Mail: julius.single@edithroman.com
Website: www.edithroman.com
Fax Ordering: (845) 620-9035
International Ordering: (845) 620-9000
Customer Service: (845) 731-2731
Contact Name: Greg Grdodian, Sr. VP
Catalog: Free. Frequency: Monthly
Circulation: 200M. Sales: $500M to $1MM
Products: Mailing lists; business databases,
e-mail lists, subscriber lists

WESTERN WEB PRINTING (800) 843-6805
P.O. Box 5184 • Sioux Falls, SD 57117
E-Mail: sales@westernwebprinting.com
Website: www.westernwebprinting.com
Fax Ordering: (605) 339-1523
International Ordering: (605) 339-2383
Contact Names: Rick Donaldson & Ken Reiste
Catalog: Free. Frequency: Annual
Circulation: 100M. Sales: $1-3MM
Products: Printed products

WILSON TROPHY COMPANY (800) 721-5050
P.O. Box 482-Osterville, MA 02655
E-Mail: sales@wilsontrophy.com
Website: www.wilsontrophy.com
Fax Ordering: (508) 420-5498
Contact Names: Chris Wilson, President
Catalog: Free. Frequency: Annual
Circulation: 100M. Sales: $3-5MM
Products: Corporate awards and trophies

ACTION AIR PARACHUTES — (800) SKYDIVE / (888) 772-28466
24390 Aviation Ave. • Davis, CA 95616
E-Mail: sales@actionair.com
Website: www.actionair.com
Fax Ordering: (530) 753-8572
International Ordering: (530) 753-2651
Contact Name: Ray Ferrell, President
Catalog: Free. Frequency: Annual
Circulation: 25K. Sales: $1-3MM
Products: Parachuting gear

AERO STORE CORPORATION — (800) 237-6759
120 N. Charlotte St. • Pottstown, PA 19464
E-Mail: aerostore@aerostore.com
Website: www.aerostore.com
Fax Ordering: (610) 327-8445
International Ordering: (610) 327-8555
Contact Name: Marco Castanon, President
Catalog: Free. Frequency: Annual
Circulation: 10K. Sales: $1-3MM
Products: Parachuting equipment &
accessories

AMERICAN TAILGATER — (888) 844-4263
855 N. Skokie Hwy., Suite J
Lake Bluff, IL 60044
E-Mail: sales@americantailgater.com
Website: www.americantailgater.com
Fax Ordering: (847) 235-2093
Customer Service: (888) 215-1490
Contact Name: Lula Lincoln, President
Catalog: Free. Frequency: 5x per year
Circulation: 250K. Sales: $5-10MM
Products: Camping equipment, tailgating
or outdoor picnicing equipment

THE BACKPACKER — (800) 414-4685
7656 Jefferson Hwy.
Baton Rouge, LA 70809
E-Mail: info@backpackerbr.com
Website: www.backpackerbr.com
International Ordering: (225) 925-2667
Catalog: Online. Sales: $20-50MM
Products: Wilderness clothing & equipment;
outdoor gear

EDDIE BAUER CATALOG — (800) 625-7935 / (800) 426-8020
P.O. Box 7001 • Groveport, OH 43125
E-Mail: info@eddiebauer.com
Website: www.eddiebauer.com
Contact Name: Richard Fersch, President
Catalog: Free. Frequency: Monthly
Circulation: 10MM. Sales: $100-200MM
Products: Outdoor clothing & equipment;
casual clothing & accessories

L.L. BEAN CATALOG — (800) 221-4221 / (800) 341-4341 / (800) 441-5713
Freeport, ME 04033
E-Mail: info@llbean.com
Website: www.llbean.com — Corporate Sales (800) 832-1889
Fax Ordering: (207) 552-3080 — TTY Service (800) 545-0090
Corporate Sales Fax: (800) 243-4994
International Ordering: (207) 552-6878
Fax (207) 552-1080
Customer Service: (800) 341-4341;
(207) 552-6879
Contact Name: Leon Gorman, President
Catalog: Free. Frequency: Quarterly
Circulation: 25MM. Sales: $200-500MM
Products: Casual women's & men's clothing
& accessories; outdoor gear

BEVAL SADDLERY — (800) 524-0136
10 Lackawanna Ave. • Gladstone, NJ 07934
E-Mail: sales@beval.com
Website: www.beval.com
Fax Ordering: (908) 234-1952
International Ordering: (908) 234-2828
Catalog: Free. Frequency: Annual
Circulation:100K. Sales: $3-5MM
Products: Horseback riding equipment
& apparel; sporting clothes; books & gifts

BIG SKY LEATHERWORKS — (800) 488-0938
5243 Hwy. 312 E • Billings, MT 59105
E-Mail: questions@bigskyleatherworks.com
Website: www.bigskyleatherworks.com
Fax Ordering: (406) 373-5937
Contact Name: Beverly Huffman, President
Catalog: Free. Frequency: Semiannual
Circulation: 50K. Sales: $500K
Products: Leather supplies for horses

BILOW CATALOG — (800) 872-3353
Libertyville Saddle Shop
306 Peterson Rd. • Libertyville, IL 60048
E-Mail: info@saddleshop.com
Website: www.saddleshop.com
Fax Ordering: (800) 346-3353; (847) 680-2491
International Ordering: (847) 362-0580
Customer Service: (866) 847-4945
Contact Name: Jack L. Martin, President
Catalog: Free. Frequency: Quarterly
Circulation: 50K. Sales: $1-3MM
Products: Horseback riding apparel, saddles,
equipment & gifts

BLACK DIAMOND EQUIPMENT, LTD. — (801) 278-5533
2084 East 3900 South
Salt Lake City, UT 84125
E-Mail: bdmo@bdel.com
Website: www.bdel.com
Fax Ordering: (801) 278-5544
Contact Name: Peter Metcalf, President
Catalog: Free. Frequency: Semiannual
Circulation: 50K. Sales: $1-3MM
Products: Rock climbing, mountaineering
& backcountry skiing equipment

BOY SCOUTS OF AMERICA CATALOG — (800) 323-0732 / (800) 323-0736
National Supply Group
P.O. Box 7143 • Charlotte, NC 28241
E-Mail: customerservice@scoutstuff.org
Website: www.scoutstuff.org
Fax Ordering: (972) 580-2255
International Ordering: (972) 580-2440
Contact Name: Michael Ashline, Director
Catalog: Free. Frequency: Annual
Circulation: 100K. Sales: $5-10MM
Products: Camping equipment & uniforms

BRIGADE QUARTERMASTERS, LTD. — (800) 338-4327
P.O. Box 100001 • Kennesaw, GA 30152
E-Mail: customerservice@brigadeqm.com
Website: www.brigadeqm.com; www.actiongear.com
Fax Ordering: (770) 426-7726; (800) 892-2999
International Ordering: (770) 428-1234
Customer Service: (800) 228-7344
Contact Name: Raymond E. Bagley, President
Catalog: Free. Pages: 266. Frequency: Semiannual
Circulation: 200K. Sales: $10-50MM
Products: Army/navy clothes, action gear &
survival equipment

CMC RESCUE EQUIPMENT (800) 235-5741
P.O. Box 6870 • Santa Barbara, CA 93160
E-Mail: customerservice@cmcrescue.com
Website: www.cmcrescue.com
Fax Ordering: (800) 823-8951; (805) 235-8951
International Ordering: (805) 562-9120
Contact Name: James Frank, President
Catalog: Free. Frequency: Annual
Circulation: 100K. Sales: $10-20MM
Products: Rescue equipment

CAMPING WORLD (800) 626-5944
P.O. Box 90018 • Bowling Green, KY 42102 (888) 626-7576
E-Mail: info@campingworld.com
Website: www.campingworld.com
Fax Ordering: (270) 796-8991
International Ordering: (270) 781-2718
Customer Service: (800) 416-7757
Technical Support: (866) 838-5304
Contact Name: Tad Donnelly, President
Catalog: Free. Frequency: Bimonthly
Circulation: 1MM. Sales: $50-100MM
Products: Camping accessories for RV owners

CAMPMOR CATALOG (888) 226-7667
P.O. Box 997-A • Paramus, NJ 07653
E-Mail: info@campmor.com
Website: www.campmor.com
Fax Ordering: (800) 230-2153
International Ordering: (201) 825-8300
Customer Service: (800) 525-4784
Contact Name: Morton Jarashow, President
Catalog: Free. Frequency: 5x per year
Circulation: 100K. Sales: $20-50MM
Products: Outdoor equipment for camping,
climbing, biking & water sports; rugged
clothing & outerwear

CHICK'S HARNESS & SUPPLY CATALOG (800) 444-2441
P.O. Box 59 • Harrington, DE 19952
E-Mail: saddles@chicksaddlert.com
Website: www.chicksaddlery.com
Fax Ordering: (302) 398-3920
International Ordering: (302) 398-4630
Contact Name: Frank Chick, President
Catalog: Free. Frequency: Bimonthly
Circulation: 150K. Sales: $3-5MM
Products: English & Western saddlery,
tack horse supplies, riding apparel & gifts

CHOICE BRANDS EQUESTRIAN (800) 214-4295
Choice brands Equestrian Products Corp. 800-526-6310
254 N. Cedar St. • Hazleton, PA 18201
E-Mail: ride@choicebrandseq.com
Website: www.choicebrandseq.com
Fax Ordering: (570) 579-0033
International Ordering: (570) 579-0026
Catalog: $5. Frequency: Annual
Circulation: 50M. Sales: $5-10MM
Products: English & women's riding
equipment & apparel

CLOUD 9 SOARING CENTER CATALOG (801) 576-6460
12665 Minuteman Dr. • Draper, UT 84020
E-Mail: info@paragliders.com
Website: www.paragliders.com
Fax Ordering: (801) 576-6482
Contact Name: Steve Mayer, President
Catalog: Free. Frequency: Semiannual
Circulation: 15K. Sales: $500K - $1MM
Products: Hang & paragliding instruction
& equipment

COUNTRY MANUFACTURING (800) 335-1880
P.O. Box 104
Fredericktown, OH 43019
E-Mail: info@countrymfg.com
Website: www.countrymfg.com
Fax Ordering: (740) 694-5088
International Ordering: (740) 694-9926
Contact Name: Joe Chattin, President
Catalog: Free. Frequency: Monthly
Circulation: 50K. Sales: $3-5MM
Products: Horse stalls, stall systems &
equipment; dog kennels

COUNTRY SUPPLY CATALOG (800) 637-6721
P.O. Box 369 • Louisiana, MO 63353
E-Mail: customercare@horse.com
Website: www.horse.com
Fax Ordering: (888) 262-3655;
  (641) 684-7668
International Ordering: (641) 682-8161
Contact Name: Scott Mooney, President
Catalog: Free. Frequency: 8x per year
Circulation: 2MM. Sales: $10-20MM
Products: Horse equipment & riding supplies

CRAZY CREEK PRODUCTS (800) 331-0304
P.O. Box 1050 • Red Lodge, MT 59068
E-Mail: chairs@crazycreek.com
Website: www.crazycreek.com
Fax Ordering: (406) 446-1411
International Ordering: (406) 446-3446
Contact Name: Rob Hart, President
Catalog: Free. Frequency: Annual
Circulation: 100K. Sales: $3-5MM
Products: Portable lightweight chairs for
canoeing, kayaking, sailing, rafting, camping,
backpacking, hiking, fishing, hunting, beach

CRITTER MOUNTAIN WEAR (800) 686-9327
Alien Air Force, Inc.
P.O. Box 975 • Crested Butte, CO 81224
E-Mail: domsinfo@crestedbutte.net
Website: www.crittermountainwear.com
International Ordering: (970) 349-9327
Contact Name: Richard Kocurek, Jr., President
Catalog: Free. Frequency: Annual
Circulation: 25K. Sales: $3-5MM
Products: Outerwear for mountaineering

DOM'S OUTDOOR OUTFITTERS (800) 447-9629
1870 First St. • Livermore, CA 94550
E-Mail: domsinfo@domsoutdoor.com
Website: www.domsoutdoor.com
Fax Ordering: (925) 447-0195
International Ordering: (925) 447-9629
Contact Name: Dom Saccullo, President
Catalog: Free. Frequency: Quarterly
Circulation: 100K. Sales: $3-5MM
Products: Camping equipment, footwear
& clothing

EQUINE PERSONALIZED PRODUCTS (800) 431-5257
625 West Summer St. #100
Hartford, WI 53027
E-Mail: info@pphorse.com
Website: www.pphorse.com
Fax Ordering: (262) 673-6707
International Ordering: (262) 673-6300
Catalog: Free. Frequency: Annual
Circulation: 50M. Sales: $500M to $1MM
Products: Apparel for horse & rider

C.C.FILSON COMPANY (800) 624-0201
P.O. Box 34020 • Seattle, WA 98124
E-Mail: service@filson.com
Website: www.filson.com
Fax Ordering: (206) 624-4539
International Ordering: (206) 624-4437
Contact Name: Steve Matson, President
Catalog: Free. Frequency: Semiannual
Circulation:200K. Sales: $10-20MM
Products: Rugged outdoor clothing including
garments, headwear, shoes & luggage

FORT WESTERN OUTPOST (866) 843-3678
903 Central Ave.
Nebraska City, NE 68410
E-Mail: help@fortwestern.com
Website: www.fortwestern.com
Fax Ordering: (866) 329-3678; (402) 873-3914
International Ordering: (402) 873-7395
Contact Name: C.S. Wohlfarth, VP
Catalog: Free. Frequency: Semiannual
Circulation: 25K. Sales: $5-10MM
Products: Accessories & clothing for the
horse & rider

FOX OUTDOOR PRODUCTS CATALOG (800) 523-4332
2040 N. 15th Ave. • Melrose Park, IL 60160
E-Mail: info@foxoutdoor.com
Website: www.foxoutdoor.com
Fax Ordering: (708) 338-9210
International Ordering: (708) 338-9200
Contact Name: D.J. Fox, President
Catalog: Free. Frequency: Annual
Circulation: 150K. Sales: $10-20MM
Products: Army/Navy military & outdoor wear;
backpacks, gear bags, tool bags, travel bags;
clothing, cookware, army surplus; sundries &
novelties; assault gear, survival accessories;
books & videos

FOX RIDGE OUTFITTERS CATALOG (800) 243-4570
P.O. Box 1700 • Rochester, NH 03866
E-Mail: info@foxridgeoutfitters.com
Website: www.foxridgeoutfitters.com
Fax Ordering: (800) 343-4570
International Ordering: (603) 335-3883
Contact Name: Robert Gustafson, President
Catalog: Free. Frequency: Semiannual
Circulation: 200K. Sales: $5-10MM
Products: Outdoor items for sportsmen &
women; camping, hiking, outdoor survival gear;
clothing; cutlery; fishing products; gifts &
jewelry; books

GEMPLER'S CATALOG (800) 382-8473
P.O. Box 44993 • Madison, WI 53744
E-Mail: customerservice@gemplers.com
Website: www.gemplers.com
International Ordering: (608) 662-3301
Customer Service: (800) 332-6744
Tech Support: (800) 874-4755
Catalog: Free. Frequency: Semiannual
Circulation: 200K. Sales: $10-20MM
Products: Outdoor equipment; workwear,
footwear, safety equipment, tires & supplies;
ATV, tractor & vehicle supplies; shop &
maintenance supplies

GIRL SCOUTS OF THE USA (800) 478-7248
420 Fifth Ave. • New York, NY 10018
E-Mail: info@girlscouts.org
Website: www.girlscouts.org

Fax Ordering: (212) 852-6509
International Ordering: (212) 852-8000
Customer Service: (800) 223-0624
Contact Name: Connie Matsui, President
Catalog: Free. Frequency: Annual
Circulation: 1MM. Sales: $20-50MM
Products: Uniforms, accessories & outdoor
equipment

DON GLEASON'S CAMPING SUPPLY (800) 257-0019
9 Pearl St. • Northampton, MA 01060
E-Mail: contact_us@gleasoncamping.com
Website: www.gleasoncamping.com
Fax Ordering: (413) 586-8770
International Ordering: (413) 584-4895
Contact Name: John Gleason, President
Catalog: Free. Frequency: Weekly
Circulation: 150K. Sales: $3-5MM
Products: Camping equipment & supplies;
outdoor clothing & footwear

I. GOLDBERG ARMY & NAVY CATALOG (215) 925-9393
1300 Chestnut St. • Philadelphia, PA 19107
E-Mail: feedback@igoco.com
Website: www.igoco.com
Fax Ordering: (215) 925-2955
Contact Name: Charles Goldberg, President
Catalog: Online & print. Frequency: Annual
Circulation:50K. Sales: $3-5MM
Products: Wholesale camping & outdoor
clothing & equipment

HORSE & PET SUPPLY CATALOG (800) 356-0700
American Livestock & Pet Supply, Inc.
613 Atlas Ave. • Madison, WI 53714
E-Mail: mary.bohne@walcointl.com
Website: www.americanlivestock.com
Fax Ordering: (800) 309-8947
Contact Name: Mary Bohne, Contact
Catalog: Free. Frequency: Quarterly
Circulation: 100K. Sales: $5-10MM
Products: Horse & pet related products

HORSE HEALTH USA (800) 321-0235
2780 Richville Dr. SE • Massillon, OH 44646
E-Mail: info@horsehealthusa.com
Website: www.horsehealthusa.com
Fax Ordering: (330) 830-2762
International Ordering: (330) 834-3000
Contact Name: J. Daniel Mattews, President
Catalog: Free. Frequency: Semiannual
Circulation: 100K. Sales: $5-10MM
Products: Horse health products, supplements,
tack & supplies

HORSE LOVER'S GIFT GUIDE (800) 767-1452
Equestrian Enterprise, Inc.
204 Mayflower Dr. • Woodstock, GA 30188
E-Mail: info@horseloversgifts.com
Website: www.horseloversgifts.com
Fax Ordering: (800) 309-0199; (770) 591-0199
International Ordering: (770) 591-3806
Contact Name: Ana Maria Collantes, President
Catalog: Free. Frequency: Semiannual
Circulation: 100K. Sales: $20-50MM
Products: Gifts & clothing for the horse lover

MAJOR SURPLUS & SURVIVAL CATALOG (800) 441-8855
435 W. Alondra Blvd. • Gardena, CA 90248
E-Mail: sales@majorsurplus.com
Website: www.majorsurplus.com
Fax Ordering: (310) 324-6909

International Ordering: (310) 324-8855
Contact Name: Steve Akison, President
Catalog: Free. Frequency: Quarterly
Circulation: 100K. Sales: $3-5MM
Products: Military surplus, outdoor &
camping supplies, survival products

MARMOT MOUNTAIN (888) 357-3262
2321 Circadian Way
Santa Rosa, CA 95407
E-Mail: info@marmot.com
Website: www.marmot.com
Fax Ordering: (707) 544-1344
International Ordering: (707) 544-4590
Contact Name: Steve Crisafulli, President
Catalog: Free. Frequency: Semiannual
Circulation: 150K. Sales: $10-20MM
Products: Pullovers, parkas, jackets,
mountain climbing suits, windpants & shirts,
bags & accessories for the outdoorsman

MILLER HARNESS COMPANY (800) 553-7655
P.O. Box 406 • Westford, MA 01460 (800) 784-5831
E-Mail: customerservice@millerharness.com
Website: www.millerharness.com
Contact Name: Michael Berg, President
Catalog: Free. Frequency: Quarterly
Circulation: 50K. Sales: $10-20MM
Products: Equestrian equipment & clothing

DAVID MORGAN CATALOG (800) 324-4934
11812 N. Creek Pkwy. N #103
Bothell, WA 98011
E-Mail: catalog@davidmorgan.com
Website: www.davidmorgan.com
Fax Ordering: (800) 364-3961
International Fax Ordering: (425) 486-0224
International Ordering: (425) 485-2132
Contact Name: David Morgan, President
Catalog: Free. Frequency: Semiannual
Circulation: 150K. Sales: $3-5MM
Products: Rugged outdoor clothing including
garments, headwear, shoes & luggage

MOUNTAIN GEAR CATALOG (800) 829-2009
6021 E. Mansfield
Spokane Valley, WA 99212
E-Mail: info@mountaingear.com
Website: www.mountaingear.com
Fax Ordering: (509) 340-1170
International Ordering: (509) 340-1165
Catalog: Free. Frequency: Annual
Circulation: 50K. Sales: $3-5MM
Products: Outdoor clothing & gear for
mountain sports, including skiing, climbers,
paddlers, cyclists, hikers, runners, etc.

MOUNTAINEERS BOOKS (800) 553-4453
1001 SW Klickitat Way #201
Seattle, WA 98134
E-Mail: mbooks@mountaineersbooks.org
Website: www.mountaineersbooks.org
Fax Ordering: (206) 223-6306
International Ordering: (206) 223-6303
Catalog: Free. Frequency: Semiannual
Circulation: 100K. Sales: $1-3MM
Products: How-tos & guidebooks on hiking,
climbing, paddling, cycling, backpacking, skiing.

NATIONAL PARACHUTE INDUSTRIES (888) 708-9585
P.O. Box 245 • Palenville, NY 12463
E-Mail: onelastchance@nationalparachute.com

Website: www.nationalparachute.com
Fax Ordering: (908) 782-5638
International Ordering: (908) 782-1646
Contact Name: Larry Krueger, President
Catalog: Free. Frequency: Annual
Circulation: 25K. Sales: $1-3MM
Products: Parachuting equipment & supplies

NEW ENGLAND CAMP / DISCOUNTER (888) 909-8809
New England Camp & Recreation Supply
P.O. Box 7087 • Dallas, TX 75209
E-Mail: feednec@sportsupplygroup.com
Website: www.sportsupplygroup.com
Fax Ordering: (888) 909-5899
Catalog: Free. Frequency: Annual
Circulation: 50K. Sales: $1-3MM
Products: Full line of camp & recreational
equipment

NRS CATALOG (877) 677-4327
2009 S. Main St. • Moscow, ID 83843
E-Mail: service@nrsweb.com
Website: www.nrsweb.com
Fax Ordering: (877) 567-7329; (208) 883-4787
International Ordering: (208) 882-6704
Catalog: Free. Frequency: Semiannual
Circulation: 150K. Sales: $10-20MM
Products: Camping equipment & apparel;
kayaks & accessories; rafting equipment;
rood racks; books & videos

ORTHO-FLEX CATALOG (501) 375-7822
Ortho-Flex Saddleworks Co.
P.O. Box 3320 • Little Rock, AR 72203
E-Mail: saddles@ortho-flex.com
Website: www.ortho-flex.com
Fax Ordering: (501) 372-1445
Contact Name: Acie Johnson, President
Catalog: Free. Frequency: Quarterly
Circulation: 100K. Sales: $3-5MM
Products: Saddles, tack & accessories

OUTDOOR FUN STORE CO. (877) 386-1700
8551 Ronda Dr. • Canton, MI 48187
E-Mail: info@outdoorfunstore.com
Website: www.outdoorfunstore.com
Fax Ordering: (847) 679-8644
International Ordering: (847) 679-5905
Catalog: Free. Frequency: Semiannual
Circulation: 100K. Sales: $5-10MM
Products: Swingsets, playsets, playground
equipment

PARA-GEAR EQUIPMENT CATALOG (800) 323-0437
3839 W. Oakton St. • Skokie, IL 60076
E-Mail: info@para-gear.com
Website: www.para-gear.com
Fax Ordering: (847) 679-8644
International Ordering: (847) 679-5905
Contact Name: Lowell Bachman, President
Catalog: $5. Pages: 312. Frequency: Annual
Circulation: 25K. Sales: $1-3MM
Products: Parachuting equipment & supplies

PARACHUTES FOR PILOTS (800) 344-6319
Strong Enterprises
11236 Satellite Blvd. • Orlando, FL 32837
E-Mail: sales@strongparachutes.com
Website: www.strongparachutes.com
Fax Ordering: (407) 850-6978
International Ordering: (407) 859-9317
Contact Name: Edward Strong, President

Catalog: Free. Frequency: Annual
Circulation: 25K. **Sales:** $5-10MM
Products: Parachuting equipment; pilot
emergency parachutes; tandem systems;
sport parachutes; military systems

PATAGONIA, INC. CATALOG (800) 336-9090
P.O. Box 32050 • Reno, NV 89523 (800) 638-6464
E-Mail: sales@patagonia.com
Website: www.patagonia.com
Fax Ordering: (800) 543-5522; (775) 747-6159
International Ordering: (775) 747-1992
Contact Name: Yvon Chounard, President
Catalog: Free. Frequency: Bimonthly
Circulation: 500K. **Sales:** $100-250MM
Products: Outdoor apparel for men & women

PIGEON MOUNTAIN INDUSTRIES (888) 764-1437
P.O. Box 803 • Lafayette, GA 30728
E-Mail: info@pmirope.com
Website: www.pmirope.com
Fax Ordering: (800) 952-3747; (706) 764-1531
International Ordering: (706) 764-1437
Customer Service: (800) 282-7673
Contact Name: Steve Hudson, President
Catalog: Free. Frequency: 8x per year
Circulation: 50K. **Sales:** $5-10MM
Products: Life safety ropes, fall protection gear,
rockclimbing protective gear & devices

RECREONICS BUYERS GUIDE (800) 428-3254
4200 Schmitt Ave. • Louisville, KY 40213
E-Mail: Info@recreonics.com
Website: www.recreonics.com
Fax Ordering: (800) 428-0133; (502) 458-9777
International Ordering: (502) 456-5706
Catalog: Free. Frequency: Semiannual
Circulation: 150K. **Sales:** $5-10MM
Products: Swimming pool equipment
& supplies

RU OUTSIDE CATALOG (800) 279-7123
Neoprene Distributors International, Inc.
11859 Lakeshore North • Auburn, CA 95602
E-Mail: rachel@ruoutside.com
Website: www.ruoutside.com
Fax Ordering: (800) 704-8909; (208) 354-3450
International Ordering: (208) 354-3455
Catalog: Free. Frequency: Semiannual
Circulation: 200K. **Sales:** $10-20MM
Products: Snowmobile clothing, snowboots,
accessories

RICHMOOR CORPORATION CATALOG (800) 423-3170
P.O. Box 8092 • Van Nuys, CA 91409
E-Mail: mail@richmoor.com
Website: www.richmoor.com
Fax Ordering: (916) 624-1604
Contact Name: Debbie Nichols, President
Catalog: Free. Frequency: Annual
Circulation: 100K. **Sales:** $5-10MM
Products: Freeze-dried camping food

ROCKY MOUNTAIN CONNECTION (800) 679-3600
Fun Wear Brands
P.O. Box 2800 • Estes Park, CO 80517
E-Mail: orders@rmconnection.com
Website: www.rmconnection.com
Fax Ordering: (970) 814-4900; 586-3302
International Ordering: (970) 586-3361/2114
Contact Name: E.J. Petrocine, President
Catalog: $2. Frequency: Quarterly

Circulation: 100K. **Sales:** $10-20MM
Products: Outdoor, rugged & technical
clothing & equipment

ROYAL ROBBINS COMPANY (800) 587-9044
1524 Princeton Ave. • Modesto, CA 95350
E-Mail: rrmail@royalrobbins.com
Website: www.royalrobbins.com
Fax Ordering: (209) 522-5511
International Ordering: (209) 529-6913
Contact Name: Dan Costa, President
Catalog: Free. Frequency: Semiannual
Circulation: 50K. **Sales:** $10-20MM
Products: Rugged outdoor clothing for men
& women; hiking clothes

SAHALIE CATALOG (800) 458-4438
3188 NW Aloclek Dr. • Hillsboro, OR 97124
E-Mail: info@sahalie.com
Website: www.sahalie.com
Fax Ordering: (800) 821-1282
Customer Service: (877) 718-7902
Contact Name: Becky Jewett, President
Catalog: Free. Frequency: Monthly
Circulation: 2MM. **Sales:** $10-20MM
Products: Men's and women's outdoor
clothing; gear & gadgets; Army surplus &
genuine military products

SEATTLE MANUFACTURING CORP. (800) 426-6251
6930 Salashan Pkwy. • Ferndale, WA 98248
E-Mail: smc@smcgear.net
Website: www.smcgear.net
Fax Ordering: (360) 366-5723
International Ordering: (360) 366-5534
Contact Name: Kathy Hughes, President
Catalog: Free. Frequency: Weekly
Circulation: 75K. **Sales:** $5-10MM
Products: Technical climbing equipment

SEIRUS INNOVATION CATALOG (800) 447-3787
13975 Danielson St. • Poway, CA 92064
Website: www.seirus.com
Fax Ordering: (858) 513-7878
International Ordering: (858) 513-1212
Contact Name: Michael Carey, President
Catalog: $5. Frequency: Annual
Circulation: 50K. **Sales:** $5-10MM
Products: Gloves & outdoor accessories
for sports

SIERRA TRADING POST (800) 713-4534
5025 Campstool Rd.
Cheyenne, WY 82007
E-Mail: customerservice@sierratradingpost.com
Website: www.sierratradingpost.com
Fax Ordering: (800) 378-8946; (307) 775-8301
International Ordering: (307) 775-8050
Contact Name: Keith Richardson, President
Catalog: Free. Frequency: Semiannual
Circulation: 150K. **Sales:** $10-20MM
Products: Outdoor & casual clothes, footwear,
home decor; outdoor sports gear

SPORTSMAN'S GUIDE CATALOGS (800) 888-3006
P.O. Box 239 • South St. Paul, MN 55075 (800) 882-2962
E-Mail: custserv@sportsmansguide.com
Website: www.sportsmansguide.com
Fax Ordering: (651) 450-6130
International Ordering: (651) 451-3030
Customer Service: (888) 844-0667
Contact Name: Gregory Binkley, President

Catalog: Free. Frequency: Monthly
Circulation: 50MM. Sales: $500MM to $1B
Products: Outdoor apparel, fishing & camping
equipment; ammo & shooting supplies; military
surplus; hunting supplies

STAFFORD'S CATALOG   (800) 826-0948
P.O. Box 2055 • Thomasville, GA 31799
E-Mail: staffcat@rose.net
Website: www.stafford-catalog.com
Fax Ordering: (229) 226-1287
International Ordering: (229) 749-7600
Contact Name: G. Walter Stafford, President
Catalog: Free. Frequency: Annual
Circulation: 100K. Sales: $1-3MM
Products: Outdoor apparel, hunting clothes;
gifts; luggage & accessories; books

SURVIVAL CENTER CATALOG   (800) 321-2900
P.O. Box 234 • McKenna, WA 98558
E-Mail: info@survivalcenter.com
Website: www.survivalcenter.com
Fax Ordering: (360) 458-6868
International Ordering: (360) 458-6778
Contact Name: Todd Webber, President
Catalog: $2. Pages: 56. Frequency: Semiannual
Circulation: 25K. Sales: $1-3MM
Products: Outdoor apparel, hunting
accessories, fishing & camping equipment

THE TERRITORY AHEAD CATALOG   (800) 882-4323
419 State St. • Santa Barbara, CA 93101
E-Mail: info@territoryahead.com
Website: www.territoryahead.com
Fax Ordering: (800) 232-9882
International Ordering: (805) 962-5558
Customer Service: (800) 686-8212
Contact Name: Bruce Willard, President
Catalog: Free. Frequency: Monthly
Circulation: 2MM. Sales: $20-50MM
Products: Outdoor clothing & accessories
for men & women

THOUSAND MILE OUTDOOR WEAR   (800) 786-7577
7330 Opportunity Rd., Ste. D
San Diego, CA 92111
E-Mail: customerservice@thousandmile.com
Website: www.thousandmile.com
Fax Ordering: (858) 503-0195
Contact Name: Jennifer Miller, President
Catalog: Online. Sales: $5-10MM
Products: Sports apparel, outdoor clothing,
active wear & accessories for men & women

TILLEY ENDURABLES   (800) 363-8737
3176 Abbott Rd., Bldg. A
Orchard Park, NY 14127
E-Mail: info@tilley.com
Website: www.tilley.com
International Ordering: (416) 444-4465
Contact Name: Stephanie Kubiszyn, President
Catalog: Free. Frequency: Annual
Circulation: 200K. Sales: $20-50MM
Products: Hats & travel clothing &
accessories; bags & belts

U.S. CAVALRY CATALOGS   (800) 777-7172
2855 Centennial Ave. • Radcliff, KY 40160
E-Mail: info@uscav.com
Website: www.uscav.com
Fax Ordering: (270) 352-0266
International Ordering: (270) 351-1164
Contact Name: Randy Acton, President
Catalog: Free. Frequency: Semiannual
Circulation: 100K. Sales: $20-50MM
Products: Law & Military Catalogs: Army/
Navy surplus & military related equipment;
law enforcement & homeland security
equipment; outdoor adventure equipment

WEAVER LEATHER CATALOG   (800) 932-8371
P.O. Box 68 • Mount Hope, OH 44660
E-Mail: info@weaverleather.com
Website: www.leathersupply.com
Fax Ordering: (330) 674-0330
International Ordering: (330) 674-1782
Contact Name: Paul Weaver, President
Catalog: Free. Frequency: Semiannual
Circulation: 200M. Sales: $10-20MM
Products: Equine products; leather &
leatherworking/saddlery supplies, parts
& tools; Pet products; machinery & hardware
for use by leatherworkers, crafters &
manufacturers

AMERICAN BRONZING COMPANY (800) 423-5678
1313 Alum Creek Dr. • Columbus, OH 43209
E-Mail: bronzinfo@bronshoe.com
Website: www.abcbronze.com
Fax Ordering: (614) 252-4602
International Ordering: (614) 252-7388
Contact Name: Robert Kaynes, Jr., President
Catalog: Free. Frequency: Annual
Circulation: 100K. Sales: $5-10MM
Products: Baby shoe bronzing

AMERICAN GIRL (800) 360-1861
Pleasant Company
P.O. Box 620497 • Middleton, WI 53562
E-Mail: info@americangirl.com
Website: www.americangirl.com
Fax Ordering: (608) 836-0761
International Ordering: (608) 836-4848
Customer Service: (800) 845-0005
Contact Name: Ellen Brothers, President
Catalog: Free. Frequency: 8x per year
Circulation: 25MM. Sales: $50-100MM
Products: Dolls & clothing for girls 8 and up;
gifts, books

HANNA ANDERSSON (800) 222-0544
1010 NW Flanders • Portland, OR 97209
E-Mail: fc@hannaandersson.com
Website: www.hannaandersson.com
Fax Ordering: (503) 222-0544
International Ordering: (503) 242-0920
Contact Name: Phil Iosca, President
Catalog: Free. Frequency: Quarterly
Circulation: 10MM. Sales: $50-100MM
Products: Children's & baby clothing & toys

AVENT CATALOG (800) 542-8368
Philips • 475 Supreme Dr.
Bensenville, IL 60106
E-Mail: inquiry@aventamerica.com
Website: www.aventamerica.com
Fax Ordering: (630) 350-0400
International Ordering: (630) 350-2600
Catalog: Free. Frequency: Annual
Circulation: 100K. Sales: $5-10MM
Products: Breastfeeding systems for babies

BABY BUNZ & COMPANY (800) 676-4559
P.O. Box 113 • Lynden, WA 98264
E-Mail: info@babybunz.com
Website: www.babybunz.com
Fax Ordering: (360) 354-1203
International Ordering: (360) 354-1320
Contact Name: Carynia Van Buren, President
Catalog: Free. Frequency: Annual
Circulation: 100K. Sales: $5-10MM
Products: Diaper covers, cloth diapers &
diapering supplies; feeding, blankets & bedding,
bathtime; wooden toys, parenting books,
organic baby clothing & toys

BABY CARRIAGE CATALOG (800) 228-8946
4007 N. Nashville Ave. • Chicago, IL 60634
E-Mail: ababyc1955@aol.com
Website: www.abcarriage.tripod.com
Fax Ordering: (773) 237-4521
International Ordering: (773) 237-4300
Contact Name: Seymour Krause, Owner
Catalog: Free. Frequency: Quarterly
Circulation: 150K. Sales: $20-50MM
Products: Twin, triplets & quad strollers, parts
& repair for all strollers, cribs & all baby furniture

BABY CATALOG OF AMERICA (800) 752-9736
78 Washington Ave. • West Haven, CT 06516
E-Mail: info@babycatalog.com
Website: www.babycatalog.com
Fax Ordering: (203) 933-1147
International Ordering: (203) 931-7760
Catalog: Free. Frequency: Semiannual
Circulation: 100K. Sales: $10-50MM
Products: Discounted baby products, from car
seats & strollers to toys, bedding & furniture

BABY GO-TO-SLEEP PRODUCTS (800) 537-7748
Audio-Therapy Innovations
P.O. Box 550 • Colorado Springs, CO 80901
E-Mail: sandman@audiotherapy.com
Website: www.babygotosleep.com
Fax Ordering: (800) 863-3395
International Ordering: (719) 473-0100
Contact Name: Terry Woodford, President
Catalog: Free. Frequency: Monthly
Circulation: 10MM. Sales: $20-50MM
Products: Music therapy recordings designed
to help baby stop crying & help children sleep
all night

BABY JOGGER COMPANY (800) 241-1848
8575 Magellan Pkwy. #1000
Richmond, VA 23227
E-Mail: customerservice@babyjogger.com
Website: www.babyjogger.com
Fax Ordering: (804) 262-6277
International Ordering: (509) 457-0925
Contact Name: Mary Baechler, President
Catalog: Free. Frequency: 4x per year
Circulation: 150K. Sales: $10-20MM
Products: Strollers

BABY WORKS CATALOG (800) 422-2910
2431 NW Thurman St. #A
Portland, OR 97210
E-Mail: customerservice@babyworks.com
Website: www.babyworks.com
Fax Ordering: (503) 645-4913
International Ordering: (503) 224-4696
Contact Name: Paula DeVore, President
Catalog: Free. Frequency: Annual
Circulation: 50K. Sales: $20-50MM
Products: Eco-friendly diapers, diaper systems
& accessories; baby clothes, nursing items

BELLEROPHON BOOKS (800) 253-9943
P.O. Box 21307 • Santa Barbara, CA 93121
E-Mail: sales@bellerophon.com
Website: www.bellerophonbooks.com
Fax Ordering: (805) 965-8286
International Ordering: (805) 965-7034
Contact Name: Harry Knill, President
Catalog: Free. Frequency: Annual
Circulation: 150K. Sales: $3-5MM
Products: Coloring books & art books for children

BOOKS OF WONDER NEWS (800) 835-4315
16 W. 18th St. • New York, NY 10011
E-Mail: info@booksofwonder.com
Website: www.booksofwonder.com
Fax Ordering: (212) 989-1203
International Ordering: (212) 989-3270
Customer Service: (800) 207-6968
Contact Name: Peter Glassman, President
Catalog: Free. Frequency: Semiannual
Circulation: 25K. Sales: $1-3MM
Products: Children's books

BURT'S BEES CATALOG   (800) 849-7112
8221 Brownleigh Dr. #A
Raleigh, NC 27612
E-Mail: info@burtsbees.com
Website: www.burtsbees.com
Fax Ordering: (800) 429-7487
International Ordering: (919) 998-5200
Contact Name: Roxanne Quimby, President
Catalog: Free. Frequency: Annual
Circulation: 50K. Sales: $1-3MM
Products: Baby products & accessories

COMPANYKIDS   (800) 356-9367
The Company Store   (800) 323-8000
500 Company Store Rd.
La Crosse, WI 54601
E-Mail: info@companykids.com
Website: www.thecompanystore.com
Fax Ordering: (800) 238-0271
Catalog: Free. Frequency: Quarterly
Circulation: 100K. Sales: $20-50MM
Products: Clothing & furniture for kids

C•W•D (CHILDREN'S WEAR DIGEST)   (800) 242-5437
3607 Mayland Court
Richmond, VA 23233
E-Mail: info@cwdkids.com
Website: www.cwdkids.com
Fax Ordering: (800) 863-3395
International Ordering: (276) 670-2192
Contact Name: James W. Klaus, President
Catalog: Free. Frequency: Monthly
Circulation: 5MM. Sales: $20-50MM
Products: Brand name children's clothing,
ages 0-12

CHILDWORKS/CHILDSPLAY CATALOG   (800) 962-1141
Guidance Channel
P.O. Box 1246 • Wilkes-Barre, PA 18703
E-Mail: info@childswork.com
Website: www.childswork.com
Fax Ordering: (800) 262-1886
Contact Name: Dr. Lawrence Shapiro, President
Catalog: Free. Frequency: Quarterly
Circulation: 100K. Sales: $1-3MM
Products: Books, games & playtime activities
for childhood development

CHOCK CATALOG CORP.   (800) 222-0020
3011 Avenue J • Brooklyn, NY 11210
E-Mail: questions@chockcatalog.com
Website: www.chockcatalog.com
Fax Ordering: (212) 941-6787
International Ordering: (718) 252-4340
Contact Name: Ann Zell, President
Catalog: Free. Frequency: Annual
Circulation: 25K. Sales: $500K to $1MM
Products: Name brand children's clothing

EARTHBEAT! MUSIC FOR LITTLE PEOPLE   (800) 409-2457
P.O. Box 1460 • Redway, CA 95560
E-Mail: customerservice@mflp.com
Website: www.mflp.com
Fax Ordering: (707) 923-3241
International Ordering: (707) 923-3991
Contact Name: Sharon Sherman, President
Catalog: Free. Frequency: Annual
Circulation: 100K. Sales: $5-10MM
Products: Educational & multicultural
recordings for children & families

EDDIE BAUER CATALOG   (800) 426-8020
P.O. Box 7001 • Groveport, OH 43125
E-Mail: info@eddiebauerfriends.com
Website: www.eddiebauer.com
Customer Service: (888) 838-1920
Contact Name: Richard Fersch, President
Catalog: Free. Frequency: Monthly
Circulation: 20MM. Sales: $50-100MM
Products: Quality bedding for babies

FISHER-PRICE CATALOG   (800) 747-8697
636 Girard Ave. • East Aurora, NY 14052   (800) 432-5437
E-Mail: info@fisher-price.com
Website: www.fisher-price.com
Fax Ordering: (716) 687-3636
International Ordering: (716) 687-3000
Contact Name: Byron Davis, President
Catalog: Free. Frequency: 5x per year
Circulation: 5MM. Sales: $50-100MM
Products: Toys & layette items

FLAP HAPPY CATALOG   (800) 234-3527
2330 Michigan Ave.
Santa Monica, CA 90404
E-Mail: custserv@flaphappy.com
Website: www.flaphappy.com
Fax Ordering: (310) 829-1485
International Ordering: (310) 453-3527
Contact Name: Laurie Snyder, President
Catalog: Free. Frequency: Semiannual
Circulation: 50K. Sales: $20-50MM
Products: Protective hats for infants & toddlers;
swimwewar & playwear

GARNET HILL CATALOG   (800) 622-6216
231 Main St. • Franconia, NH 03580   (800) 870-3513
E-Mail: info@garnethill.com
Website: www.garnethill.com
Fax Ordering: (888) 842-9696; (603) 869-4647
International Ordering: (603) 882-6394
Contact Name: Brian Gowen, President
Catalog: Free. Frequency: Semiannual
Circulation: 10MM. Sales: $50-100MM
Products: Quality natural fiber baby clothing
& linens; maternity clothes

GENTLE WIND CATALOG   (888) 386-7664
P.O. Box 3103 • Albany, NY 12203
E-Mail: hello@gentlewind.com
Website: www.gentlewind.com
Fax Ordering: (518) 436-0391
International Ordering: (518) 482-9023
Contact Name: Jill Person, President
Catalog: Free. Frequency: Annual
Circulation: 25K. Sales: $1-3MM
Products: Children's audiotapes; songs
& stories for children

GRACO CHILDREN'S PRODUCTS   (800) 345-4109
P150 Oaklands Blvd. • Exton, PA 19341   (800) 837-4044
E-Mail: info@gracobaby.com   Canada (800) 667-8184
Website: www.gracobaby.com
Catalog: Free. Frequency: Quarterly
Circulation: 1MM. Sales: $20-50MM
Products: Swings, strollers, walkers,
high chairs, play yards

HEARTHSONG CATALOG   (800) 325-2502
P.O. Box 1050 • Madison, VA 22727
E-Mail: info@hearthsong.com
Website: www.hearthsong.com

Fax Ordering: (800) 638-5102
Customer Service: (800) 533-4397
Contact Name: Barbara Kane, Owner
Catalog: Free. Frequency: Semiannual
Circulation: 1MM. Sales: $10-20MM
Products: Children's gifts, clothing & toys

HIGHLIGHTS FOR CHILDREN　　(800) 255-9517
P.O. Box 269 • Columbus, OH 43216
E-Mail: info@highlightkids.com
Website: www.highlightkids.com
Fax Ordering: (614) 487-2700
International Ordering: (614) 486-0631
Contact Name: Elmer C. Meider, Jr., President
Catalog: Free. Frequency: Semiannual
Circulation: 5MM. Sales: $20-50M
Products: Children's books, games, puzzles
& activitity kits

IMAGINE THE CHALLENGE　　(888) 777-1641
61 Clark Rd. • Battle Creek, MI 49037
E-Mail: customercare@imaginetoys.com
Website: www.imaginetoys.com
Fax Ordering: (269) 968-4260
Catalog: Free. Frequency: Annual
Circulation: 100K. Sales: $5-10MM
Products: Affordable, creative & pretend play,
art & music, science & discovery, games &
puzzles, active play & learning toys for chilren

J.C. PENNY CATALOGS　　(800) 222-6161
P.O. Box 10001 • Dallas, TX 75301　　(800) 322-1189
E-Mail: info@jcpenny.com
Website: www.jcpenny.com
Fax Ordering: (425) 869-4647
International Ordering: (425) 882-6394
Customer Service: (800) 709-5777
Contact Name: Richard Fersch, President
Catalogs: Free. Frequency: Annual
Circulation: 5MM. Sales: $20-50MM
Products: Baby Book (baby clothes,
furniture & accessories); Maternity
Collection (maternity wear & baby
items such as cribs, bedding & accessories) ;
Pennies From Heaven (baby bedding)

KATIE'S KISSES CATALOG　　(888) 881-0404
P.O. Box 22784 • Bullhead City, AZ 86439
E-Mail: joyce@katieskisses.com
Website: www.katieskisses.com
International Ordering: (928) 219-5084
Catalog: Free. Frequency: Annual
Circulation: 100K. Sales: $25-50MM
Products: Cloth diapers; nursing, maternity,
underwear & nursing pads, diaper covers
& other accessories

KID'S CATALOG　　(800) 356-4444
Lands' End　　(800) 963-4816
1 Lands End Ln. • Dodgeville, WI 53595
E-Mail: landsend@landsend.com
Website: www.landsend.com
Fax Ordering: (608) 935-4260
International Ordering: (608) 935-4013
Contact Name: David Dyer, President
Catalog: Free. Frequency: Quarterly
Circulation: 10MM. Sales: $100-200MM
Products: Kid's clothing & accessories

KIDSPORT CATALOG　　(800) 833-1729
821 Eubanks Dr. #A • Vacaville, CA 95688　　(888) 554-8326
E-Mail: info@kidsportathletic.com

Website: www.kidsportathletic.com
Fax Ordering: (707) 447-4817
International Ordering: (707) 447-8326
Catalog: Free. Frequency: Quarterly
Circulation: 500K. Sales: $10-20MM
Products: Outdoor apparel for children

L.L. BEAN KIDS CATALOG　　(800) 552-5437
L.L. Bean • Freeport, ME 04033　　(800) 441-5713
E-Mail: info@llbean.com
Website: www.llbean.com
Fax Ordering: (207) 552-3080
Contact Name: Leon Gorman, President
Catalog: Free. Frequency: Bimonthly
Circulation: 2MM. Sales: $20-50MM
Products: Outdoor gear for kids

LEAPS AND BOUNDS!　　(800) 477-2189
P.O. Box 517 • Lake Bluff, IL 60044
E-Mail: info@leapsandbounds.com
Website: www.leapsandbounds.com
Fax Ordering: (847) 615-2162
Customer Service: (888) 203-2265
Contact Name: Karen Scott
Catalog: Free. Frequency: Quarterly
Circulation: 200K. Sales: $5-10MM
Products: Children's indoor and outdoor
products, including play kitchens, art activities,
educational toys, bedroom furniture, health &
safety products, video games, etc.

LANDS' END CATALOGS　　(800) 345-3696
1 Lands End Lane • Dodgeville, WI 53595　　(800) 356-4444
E-Mail: info@landsend.com
Website: www.landsend.com
Fax Ordering: (800) 332-0103
International Ordering: (608) 935-4013
Contact Name: Michael Atkin, Marketing
Catalog: Free. Frequency: 13x per year
Circulation: 20MM. Sales: $500MM to $1B
Products: Coming Home Catalog: Bedding,
diaper bags, kid's clothing, layette items;
Kids Catalog: Clothing; School Catalog:
Uniforms & school spiritwear

LEAPFROG　　(866) 334-5327
6401 Hollis St. #100 • Emeryville, CA 94608
E-Mail: info@leapfrog.com
Website: www.leapfrog.com
International Ordering: (510) 596-3333
Catalog: Free. Frequency: Quarterly
Circulation: 200K. Sales: $1-3MM
Products: Educational toys games for
pre-school to middle school children

LILLY'S KIDS　　(800) 285-5555
Lillian Vernon Corporation　　(800) 901-9402
2600 International Pkwy.
Virginia Beach, VA 23452
E-Mail: custom@lillianvernon.com
Website: www.lillianvernon.com
Fax Ordering: (800) 852-2365
International Ordering: (757) 463-7451
Contact Name: Howard Goldberg, President
Catalog: Free. Frequency: Quarterly
Circulation: 25MM. Sales: $50-100MM
Products: Gifts & toys for kids

LITTLE TIKES CATALOG　　(800) 321-0183
P.O. Box 2277 • Hudson, OH 44236　　(800) 748-2204
E-Mail: info@littletikes.com　　(866) 806-9061
Website: www.littletikes.com

Fax Ordering: (330) 650-3130
International Ordering: (330) 650-3000
Contact Name: Gary Kleinjan, President
Catalog: Free. Frequency: Annual
Circulation: 150K. Sales: $20-50MM
Products: Toys, games & furniture for infants

MATTEL PRODUCTS CATALOG   (800) 524-8697
333 Continental Blvd.
El Segundo, CA 90245
E-Mail: info@mattel.com
Website: www.mattel.com
International Ordering: (310) 252-2000
Contact Name: Byron Davis, President
Catalog: Free. Frequency: Quarterly
Circulation: 10MM. Sales: $100-500MM
Products: Toys & other items for children

MOTHERWEAR CATALOG   (800) 633-0303
Motherwear International   (800) 950-2500
320 Riverside Dr. • Florence, MA 01062
E-Mail: customerservice@motherwear.com
Website: www.motherwear.com
Fax Ordering: (413) 532-4058
Contact Name: Jody Wright, President
Catalog: Free. Frequency: Semiannual
Circulation: 1MM. Sales: $5-10MM
Products: Fashions designed specifically
for discreet breastfeeding

MUSIC FOR LITTLE PEOPLE   (800) 409-2457
P.O. Box 1460 • Redway, CA 95560   (877) 286-4701
E-Mail: customerservice@mflp.com
Website: www.musicforlittlepeople.com
Fax Ordering: (707) 869-4647
International Ordering: (707) 882-6394
Contact Name: Sharon Sherman, President
Catalog: Free. Frequency: Semiannual
Circulation: 500M. Sales: $1-3MM
Products: Children's audio & video tapes,
games, toys & musical instruments

MY TWIN DOLL WORKSHOP   (800) 469-8946
3231 S. Platte River Dr.
Englewood, CO 80110
E-Mail: info@mytwin.com
Website: www.mytwin.com
Fax Ordering: (303) 789-4399
Catalog: Free. Frequency: Quarterly
Circulation: 100K. Sales: $500K to $1MM
Products: Dolls created to look like children

NATURAL BABY CATALOG   (800) 388-2229
Kids Stuff   (800) 922-7397
7090 Whipple Ave. NW
North Canton, OH 44720
E-Mail: info@kidsstuff.com
Website: www.kidsstuff.com
Fax Ordering: (330) 244-9518
International Ordering: (330) 649-5700
Contact Name: William Miller, President
Catalog: Free. Frequency: Annual
Circulation: 100K. Sales: $10-20MM
Products: Bedding, baby & children's
clothing, diapers & bath items

ONE STEP AHEAD   (800) 274-8440
P.O. Box 517 • Lake Bluff, IL 60044
E-Mail: questions@onestepahead.com
Website: www.onestepahead.com
Fax Ordering: (847) 615-2162

Customer Service: (800) 950-5120
Catalog: Free. Frequency: Quarterly
Circulation: 200K. Sales: $10-20MM
Products: Products for kids 0-3, including apparel, nursery, safety,
nursing & feeding, playtime, bath, health, outdoor fun, etc.

PARENTING CONCEPTS CATALOG   (800) 727-3683
25060 Hancock Ave. #103-124
Murrieta, CA 92562
E-Mail: info@parentingconcepts.com
Website: www.parentingconcepts.com
Fax Ordering: (951) 461-7424
International Ordering: (951) 461-7424
Contact Name: Tracy Urban, President
Catalog: Free. Frequency: Annual
Circulation: 50M. Sales: $500M
Products: Baby slings, breastfeeding
& lactation needs; nursery goods; toys;

PARENTING & FAMILY LIFE CATALOG   (800) 257-5126
Cambridge Educational Films
1160 E. Bryan Ave.
Salt lake City, UT 84105
E-Mail: custserv@films.com
Website: www.cambridgefilms.com
Fax Ordering: (800) 329-6687
International Ordering: (801) 550-4271
Catalog: Free. Frequency: Monthly
Circulation: 2MM. Sales: $20-50MM
Products: Child care; culinaryt arts, life skills,
parenting & child development; Newborn care,
baby-sitting, pregnancy & drug-free healthy
living books & videos; educational videos,
software, CD-ROMs, books and posters

PATAGONIA KIDS   (800) 638-6464
P.O. Box 32050 • Reno, NV 89533
E-Mail: customer_service@patagonia.com
Website: www.patagonia.com
Fax Ordering: (800) 543-5522; (775) 747-6159
International Ordering: (775) 747-1887/1992
Contact Name: Michael Crook, President
Catalog: Free. Frequency: Quarterly
Circulation: 1MM. Sales: $5-10MM
Products: Functional outdoor clothing for
children ages 0-14

PERFECTLY SAFE CATALOG   (800) 837-5437
Kids Stuff
7090 Whipple Ave. NW
North Canton, OH 44720
E-Mail: psafe@cannet.com
Website: www.kidsstuff.com
Fax Ordering: (330) 244-9518
International Ordering: (330) 649-5700
Contact Name: William Miller, President
Catalog: Free. Frequency: Annual
Circulation: 100K. Sales: $10-20MM
Products: Safety products for the nursery,
kitchen, bathroom, toys, windows & doors

POSH TOTS   (866) 767-4868
5500 Cox Rd. • Glenn Allen, VA 23060
E-Mail: customerservice@poshtots.com
Website: www.poshtots.com
Fax Ordering: (804) 935-0844
Catalog: Free. Frequency: Annual
Circulation: 75K. Sales: $3-5MM
Products: Baby furniture, children's
furnishings, bedding for baby & child

POTTERY BARN KIDS & TEEB (800) 430-7373
(800) 993-4923
P.O. Box 379909 • Las Vegas, NV 89137
E-Mail: info@potterybarnkids.com
Website: www.potterybarnkids.com
Fax Ordering: (702) 363-2541
Customer Service: (866) 395-8597
Catalog: Free. Pages: 120. Frequency: Quarterly
Circulation: 10MM. Sales: $50-100MM
Products: Children's furniture, bed & bath
products

PRINCE LIONHEART CATALOG (800) 544-1132
2421 S. Westgate Rd.
Santa Maria, CA 93455
E-Mail: customerservice@princelionheart.com
Website: www.princelionheart.com
Fax Ordering: (805) 922-9442
International Ordering: (805) 922-2250
Catalog: Free. Frequency: Annual
Circulation: 50K. Sales: $1-3MM
Products: Baby care products

RUNABOUT CATALOG (800) 832-2376
Berg Design
18770 SW Rigert Rd. • Aloha, OR 97007
E-Mail: runabout@teleport.com
Website: www.runabouts.net
Fax Ordering: (503) 591-9435
International Ordering: (503) 649-7922
Contact Name: Roger Berg, President
Catalog: Free. Frequency: Annual
Circulation: 100K. Sales: $3-5MM
Products: Big wheeled strollers for
walking & jogging

SENSATIONAL BEGINNINGS (800) 444-2147
987 Stewart Rd. • Monroe, MI 48162
E-Mail: customerservice@sb-kids.com
Website: www.sb-kids.com
Fax Ordering: (734) 242-8278
International Ordering: (734) 242-2147
Customer Service: (800) 444-6058
Contact Name: Debra Shah, President
Catalog: Free. Frequency: Quarterly
Circulation: 250K. Sales: $3-5MM
Products: Toys and tools that celebrate
the wonders of childhood, including
playhouses, dollhouses, toy train sets

SOUNDPRINT'S (800) 228-7839
Trudy Corporation
353 Main Ave. • Norwalk, CT 06851
E-Mail: soundprints@soundprints.com
Website: www.soundprints.com
Fax Ordering: (203) 846-1776
International Ordering: (203) 846-2274
Contact Name: William Burnham, President
Catalog: Free. Frequency: Semiannual
Circulation: 100K. Sales: $1-3MM
Products: Children's storybooks, audiocassettes
and toys focused on nature & the environment

TALBOT'S KIDS CATALOG (800) 543-7123
(800) 825-2687
One Talbot's Dr. • Hingham, MA 02043
E-Mail: customerservice@talbots.com
Website: www.talbots.com
Fax Ordering: (781) 741-4369
International Ordering: (781) 740-8888
Contact Name: Arnold Zetcher, President
Catalog: Free. Frequency: Quarterly
Circulation: 5MM. Sales: $50-100MM
Products: Infants, toddlers & children's clothing

THE WOODEN SOLDIER (800) 375-6002
P.O. Box 800 • North Conway, NH 03860
E-Mail: customerservice@woodensoldier.com
Website: www.woodensoldierltd.com
Fax Ordering: (603) 356-3530
International Ordering: (603) 356-7041
Customer Service: (800) 375-6003
Contact Names: David Mennella, President
Catalog: Free. Frequency: Semiannual
Circulation: 500K. Sales: $5-10MM
Products: Infants & children's special
occasion clothing

WORLD BOOK'S (800) 967-5325
ADVENTURES FOR CHILDREN (800) 975-3250
233 N. Miochigan Ave. #2000
Chicago, IL 60601
E-Mail: info@truthseeker.com
Website: www.worldbook.com
Fax Ordering: (312) 729-5600
International Ordering: (312) 729-5800
Contact Name: John Denson, Marketing
Catalog: Free. Frequency: 5x per year
Circulation: 1MM. Sales: $5-10MM
Products: Books, toys, crafts, kits &
other fun learning kid stuff

A1A SPORTSWEAR   (800) 447-6111
910 Jimmy Ann Dr.
Daytona Beach, FL 32117
Fax Ordering: (386) 274-1141
International Ordering: (386) 274-1777
Contact Name: Ron Frederick, President
Catalog: Free. Frequency: Semiannual
Circulation:125M. Sales: $3-5MM
Products: Fashionable sportswear

AB LAMBDIN   (800) 554-9231
U.S. Hwy. 19 N • Americus, GA 31710
E-Mail: info@talkshop.com
Website: www.talkshop.com
Fax Ordering: (800) 221-9231
International Ordering: (770) 849-9444
Contact Name: Karen Sharp Bishop, President
Catalog: Free. Frequency: Monthly
Circulation:10MM. Sales: $10-20MM
Products: Swim & resort apparel

ABRACADABRA MATERNITY SHOP   (800) 854-1213
17965 SW Rigert Rd. • Aloha, OR 97007
E-Mail: customerservice@momshop.com
Website: www.momshop.com
Fax Ordering: (503) 345-9238
Contact Name: Rex Stevens, Marketing
Catalog: Free. Frequency: Annual
Circulation: 50M. Sales: $1-3MM
Products: Maternity clothing & accessories,
nursing clothing & accessories

ACTIVE GIRLS (AMOGIRLS) MAILORDER   (800) 590-4997
1360 E. Locust St. • Ontario, CA 91761   (800) 588-3911
E-Mail: info@amogirls.com;
   info@activemailorder.com
Website: www.amogirls.com;
   www.activemailorder.com
Fax Ordering: (909) 930-3884
International Ordering: (909) 673-7780
Catalog: Free. Pages: 40. Frequency: Monthly
Circulation:1MM. Sales: $5-10MM
Products: Activewear & accessories for girls

ALGY TEAM COLLECTION   (800) 458-2549
440 NE First Ave. • Hallandale, FL 33009
E-Mail: algy@algyteam.com
Website: www.algyteam.com
Fax Ordering: (888) 928-2282
International Fax Ordering: (954) 454-7370
International Ordering: (954) 457-8100
Contact Name: Laurie Godbout, President
Catalog: Free. Frequency: Semiannual
Circulation: 50M. Sales: $5-10MM
Products: Costumes, marching band uniforms

ALLOY   (888) 552-5569
730 E. Church St. • Martinsville, VA 24112   (888) 452-5569
E-Mail: catalog@alloy.com
Website: www.alloy.com
Fax Ordering: (888) 312-5569
Catalog: Free. Frequency: Semiannual
Circulation: 200M. Sales: $5-10MM
Products: Clothing & accessories for teen girls

AMAZON DRY GOODS CATALOG   (800) 798-7979
411 Brady St. • Davenport, IA 52801
E-Mail: info@amazondrygoods.com
Website: www.amazondrygoods.com
Fax Ordering: (563) 322-4003
International Ordering: (563) 322-6800
Contact Name: J. Burgess, President

Catalog: $7. Frequency: Annual
Circulation: 100M. Sales: $1-3MM
Products: Clothing, corsets, fans, hats,
parasols, snoods, toiletries, books, toys,
household accessories

AMY LEE BRIDAL CATALOG   (713) 532-7070
3905 Braxton Dr. • Houston, TX 77063
E-Mail: chris@amyleebridal.com
Website: www.amyleebridal.com
Fax Ordering: (713) 532-9486
Catalog: Free. Frequency: 3x per year
Circulation: 250M. Sales: $1-3MM
Products: Bridal apparel

ARES SPORTSWEAR   (800) 439-8614
3650 Parkway Lane • Hilliard, OH 43026
E-Mail: info@areswear.com
Website: www.cheerlouder.com
Fax Ordering: (614) 527-3794
International Ordering: (614) 767-1950
Contact Name: Mike Leibrand &
   MikeCampbell, Owners
Catalog: Free. Frequency: Semiannual
Circulation: 100M. Sales: $5-10MM
Products: Custom uniforms, warmups,
sweats, bags, tees; screen printing,
embroidery & tackle twill

HANNA ANDERSSON   800) 222-0544
1010 NW Flanders • Portland, OR 97209
E-Mail: fc@hannaandersson.com
Website: www.hannaandersson.com
Fax Ordering: (503) 222-0544
International Ordering: (503) 242-0920
Contact Name: Phil Iosca, President
Catalog: Free. Frequency: Quarterly
Circulation: 12MM. Sales: $50-100MM
Products: Children's & baby clothing & toys

ANGELICA'S IMAGE APPAREL   (800) 222-3112
700 Rosedale • St. Louis, MO 63112
E-Mail: info@angelica-corp.com
Website: www.angelica-corp.com
Fax Ordering: (314) 889-1143
International Ordering: (314) 889-1111
Contact Name: Larry Newman, President
Catalog: Free. Frequency: 3x per year
Circulation: 600M. Sales: $10-20MM
Products: Healthcare, foodservice &
lodging uniforms

ANTHONY RICHARDS CATALOG   (877) 268-9594
Amerimark Direct
6864 Engle Rd. • Cleveland, OH 44130
E-Mail: info@amerimark.com
Website: www.amerimark.com
Fax Ordering: (440) 234-8925
International Ordering: (440) 325-2000
Contact Name: Gary Giesler, President
Catalog: Free. Frequency: Monthly
Circulation: 12MM. Sales: $20-50MM
Products: High styled fashions for the
mature woman

ANTHROPOLOGIE CATALOG   (800) 309-2500
1700 Sansom St. • Philadelphia, PA 19103
E-Mail: info@anthropologie.com
Website: www.anthropologie.com
Catalog: Free. Pages: 100. Frequency: Annual
Circulation: 12MM. Sales: $20-50MM
Products: Fashion, jewelry, children's clothes

APPLESEED'S CATALOG   (800) 767-6666
30 Tozer Rd. • Beverly, MA 01915
E-Mail: info@appleseeds.com
Website: www.appleseeds.com
Fax Ordering: (800) 755-7557
International Ordering: (978) 922-2040
Contact Name: Brenda Koskinen, President
Catalog: Free. Frequency: 6x per year
Circulation:6MM. Sales: $50-100MM
Products: Women's clothing & accessories

ARCTIC SHEEPSKIN CATALOG   (800) 428-9276
565 County Rd. T #WB
Hammond, WI 54015
E-Mail: arctic@win.bright.net
Fax Ordering: (715) 796-2295
International Ordering: (715) 796-2292
Contact Name: Joe Bacon, President
Catalog: $2. Frequency: Quarterly
Circulation: 25M. Sales: $3-5MM
Products: Sheepskin clothing & accessories

ASHRO LIFESTYLE   (866) 274-7646
2748 Wisconsin Ave.
Downers Grove, IL 60515
E-Mail: sales@ashro.com
Website: www.ashro.com
Fax Ordering: (630) 852-3133
International Ordering: (630) 515-8811 ext. 244
Catalog: Free. Pages: 64 pp.
Frequency: Quarterly
Circulation: 250M. Sales: $5-10MM
Products: Women's clothing & accessories

ATHLETA   (888) 322-5515
1622 Corporate Cr. • Petaluma, CA 94954
E-Mail: sales@athleta.com
Website: www.athleta.com
Fax Ordering: (888) 806-4499
Catalog: Free. Pages: 52. Frequency: Quarterly
Circulation: 250M. Sales: $5-10MM
Products: Women's athletic, workout, fitness apparel

AVENTURA CLOTHING   (800) 921-1655
c/o Sportif USA
1415 Greg St., Suite 101 • Sparks, NV 89431
E-Mail: customerservice@aventuraclothing.com
Website: www.aventuraclothing.com
Fax Ordering: (800) 776-3291; (775) 353-3400
International Ordering: (775-359-6400
Catalog: Free. Frequency: Quarterly
Circulation: 100M. Sales: $5-10MM
Products: Sports & outdoor clothing

AVIREX AVIATOR'S CLUB   (800) 354-5514
3300 47th Ave.
Long Island City, NY 11101
E-Mail: sales@avirex.com
Website: www.avirex.com
Fax Ordering: (718) 482-1881
International Ordering: (718) 482-1860
Contact Name: Jeff Clyman, President
Catalog: $1. Frequency: Annual
Circulation: 100M. Sales: $5-10MM
Products: Aviation apparel & accessories

AVIVA DESIGN   (925) 946-1566
14 Pleasant Ct. • Walnut Creek, CA 94597
E-Mail: sales@avivadesign.com
Website: www.avivadesign.com
Fax Ordering: (888) 701-1088
International Ordering: (925) 946-1566
Catalog: $1. Frequency: Annual
Circulation: 150M. Sales: $5-10MM
Products: Men & women's apparel iems
& promotional products

AWESOME IMPRESSIONS   (800) 367-2374
Catalog Sales Companies
599 Canal St. • Lawrence, MA 01840
E-Mail: info@cheapaprons.com
Website: www.cheapaprons.com
Fax Ordering: (978) 689-2483
International Ordering: (978) 975-1330
Contact Name: Sherry Aldrich, President
Catalog: Free. Frequency: 4x per year
Circulation: 60MM. Sales: $1-3MM
Products: Custom printed & monogrammed
apparel

BACHRACH   (800) 222-4722
One Bachrach Ct. • Decatur, IL 62526
E-Mail: info@bachrach.com
Website: www.bachrach.com
Fax Ordering: (217) 875-0030
International Ordering: (217) 875-1020
Catalog: Free. Frequency: 4x per year
Circulation: 100M. Sales: $5-10MM
Products: Menswear

BANANA REPUBLIC   (888) 277-8953
5900 N. Meadows Dr.
Grove City, OH 43123
E-Mail: info@gapinc.com
Website: www.bananarepublic.com
Fax Ordering: (888) 906-2465
Contact Name: Jean Jackson, President
Catalog: Free. Frequency: Semiannual
Circulation: 500M. Sales: $50-100MM
Products: Men & women's casual clothes,
suits & home products

JOS. A BANK CLOTHIERS CATALOG   (800) 285-2265
P.O. Box 1000 • Hampstead, MD 21074
E-Mail: info@josbank.com
Website: www.josbank.com
Fax Ordering: (888) 329-5222; (410) 239-5911
International Ordering: (410) 239-4911
Customer Service: (800) 999-7472
Contact Name: Frank Tworecke, President
Catalog: Free. Frequency: 16x per year
Circulation: 10MM. Sales: $50-100MM
Products: Men's clothing & furnishings

BARELY NOTHINGS LINGERIE   (805) 489-5592
1514 Grand Ave. • Grover Beach, CA 93433
E-Mail: lingerie@barelynothings.com
Website: www.barelynothings.com
Fax Ordering: (805) 489-5987
Contact Name: Sandi Spinelli, President
Catalog: Free. Frequency: 6x per year
Circulation: 300M. Sales: $1-3MM
Products: Dress size 4 to 26 lingerie and more

BARRIE PACE   (800) 441-6011
P.O. Box 4400
Forrester Center, WV 25438
E-Mail: orders@barriepace.com
Website: www.barriepace.com
Fax Ordering: (800) 525-5562
Contact Name: Beth McCall, President
Catalog: Free. Pages: 72. Frequency: Semiannual
Circulation: 1MM. Sales: $5-10MM
Products: Women's businesswear

BATES LEATHERS CATALOG (562) 426-8668
1663 E. 28th St. • Signal Hill, CA 90755
E-Mail: info@batesleathers.com
Website: www.batesleathers.com
Fax Ordering: (562) 426-4001
Contact Name: Lance Grindle, President
Catalog: $5. Frequency: Annual
Circulation: 50M. Sales: $1-3MM
Products: Leather clothing accessories
including hats & gloves

EDDIE BAUER CATALOG (800) 625-7935
P.O. Box 183012 (800) 426-8020
Columbus, OH 43218-3012
E-Mail: customerservice@csceddiebauer.com
Website: www.eddiebauer.com
Fax Ordering: (800) 414-6110; (614) 497-1617
International Ordering: (506) 638-6914
Catalog: Free. Pages: 148 pp.
Frequency: Semiannual
Circulation:10MM. Sales: $20-50MM
Products: Outdoor & casual clothing &
accessories for both men & women

BAUM'S DANCEWEAR (800) 832-6246
106 S. 11th St. • Philadelphia, PA 19107
E-Mail: info@baumsdancewear.com
Website: www.baumsdancewear.com
Fax Ordering: (215) 592-4194
International Ordering: (215) 923-2244
Contact Name: Peter Cohen, President
Catalog: Free. Frequency: Semiannual
Circulation: 50M. Sales: $1-3MM
Products: Dance & theatrical costume
apparel

L.L. BEAN (800) 221-4221
Freeport, ME 04033 (800) 341-4341
E-Mail: info@llbean.com (800) 441-5713
Website: www.llbean.com
Fax Ordering: (207) 552-3080
Corporate Sales: (800) 832-1889
Corporate Sales Fax: (800) 243-4994
International Ordering: (207) 552-6878
  Fax (207) 552-4080
TTY Ordering: (800) 545-0090
Customer Service: (800) 341-4341; (207) 552-6879
Contact Name: Leon Gorman, President
Catalog: Free. Pages: 220. Frequency: Quarterly
Circulation: 50MM. Sales: $100-500MM
Products: Casual women's and men's clothing &
accessories; outdoor gear

BEAU TIES OF VERMONT (800) 488-8437
69 Industrial Ave. • Middlebury, VT 05753
E-Mail: info@jeanparee.com
Website: www.beauties.com
Fax Ordering: (802) 388-7808
International Ordering: (802) 388-0108
Contact Name: Bill Kenerson, President
Catalog: Free. Frequency: 7x per year
Circulation: 50M. Sales: $1-3MM
Products: Wigs for men & women

BEAUTIFUL FULL COLOR (281) 933-9678
WEDDING GOWN CATALOG
P.C. Mary's Bridals
P.O. Box 1588 • Stafford, TX 77497
Fax Ordering: (281) 933-2295
Catalog: $2. Frequency: Semiannual
Circulation: 10M. Sales: $500M to 1MM
Products: Bridals, informals, headpieces

BEAUTY TRENDS (800) 777-7772
P.O. Box 9323 • Hialeah, FL 33014
E-Mail: 4service@beautytrends.com
Website: www.beautytrends.com
Fax Ordering: (305) 823-0626
International Ordering: (305) 823-0600
Customer Service: (800) 268-7210
Contact Name: Chris Proir, Marketing
Catalog: Free. Frequency: Semiannual
Circulation: 150M. Sales: $1-3MM
Products: Wigs and hair add ons

BEDFORD FAIR LIFESTYLES (800) 964-1000
421 Landmark Dr. • Wilmington, NC 28410
E-Mail: info@bedfordfair.com
Website: www.bedfordfair.com
Fax Ordering: (520) 790-1332
Contact Name: Steven Lightman, President
Catalog: Free. Frequency: Quarterly
Circulation:250M. Sales: $5-10MM
Products: Casual & sophisticated women's
clothing

BEMIDJI WOOLEN MILLS (888) 751-5166
301 Irvine Ave. NW • Bemidji, MN 56601
E-Mail: info@bemidjiwoolenmills.com
Website: www.bemidjiwoolenmills.com
Fax Ordering: (218) 751-4659
International Ordering: (218) 751-5166
Contact Name: Bill Batchelder, President
Catalog: Free. Frequency: Annual
Circulation: 100M. Sales: $1-3MM
Products: Hats, gloves & blankets;
woolen garments

BENCONE UNIFORMS CATALOG (800) 326-3261
940 Chatham Rd.
Winston-Salem, NC 27104
E-Mail: info@bencone.com
Website: www.bencone.com
Fax Ordering: (336) 722-1960
International Ordering: (336) 722-1270
Contact Name: Sanders Mosley, President
Catalog: $5. Frequency: 6x per year
Circulation: 750M. Sales: $1-3M
Products: Medical uniforms & accessories

BERGAMOT CATALOG (800) 922-6733
820 E. Wisconsin St. • Delavan, WI 53115
Fax Ordering: (262) 728-3750
International Ordering: (262) 728-5572
Contact Name: Wayne Smith, President
Catalog: Free. Frequency: Annual
Circulation: 100M. Sales: $10-20MM
Products: Custom designed belt buckles,
money clips

BERGDORF GOODMAN CATALOG (800) 967-3788
Neiman Marcus Group
745 Fifth Ave. • New York, NY 10019
Fax Ordering: (972) 556-6805
International Ordering: (212) 753-7300
Contact Name: Dawn Mello, President
Catalog: $7. Frequency: 13x per year
Circulation: 2MM. Sales: $10-20MM
Products: Women's clothing & accessories

BERLIN GLOVE COMPANY (800) 236-3367
150 W. Franklin St. • Berlin, WI 54923
E-Mail: berlingloveco@vbe.com
Website: www.berlingloveco.com
Fax Ordering: (920) 361-5055

International Ordering: (920) 361-5050
Contact Name: John Scherer, President
Catalog: $2. Frequency: Annual
Circulation: 25M. Sales: $1-3MM
Products: Deerskin gloves, coats, handbags, moccasins & accessories

BEVERLY HILLS FASHIONS (800) 995-0785
289 S. Robertson Blvd.
Beverly Hills, CA 90211
Fax Ordering: (562) 886-9723
International Ordering: (310) 273-7193
Contact Name: C.F. Allen, President
Catalog: Free. Frequency: 6x per year
Circulation: 25MM. Sales: $5-10MM
Products: Evening wear & lingerie

BIG DOGS SPORTSWEAR (800) 642-3647
121 Gray Ave. • Santa Barbara, CA 93101
E-Mail: info@bigdogs.com
Website: www.bigdogs.com
Fax Ordering: (805) 963-8048
International Ordering: (805) 963-8727
Contact Name: Andy Feshback, President
Catalog: Free. Frequency: Annual
Circulation: 100M. Sales: $3-5MM
Products: Apparel; shoes, swimwear, toys, watches

BIOBOTTOMS (800) 766-1254
Mia Bambini
P.O. Box 6009 • Petaluma, CA 94955
E-Mail: sales@miabambini.com
Website: www.miabambini.com
Fax Ordering: (707) 778-0619
International Ordering: (707) 769-2846
Contact Name: Jonathan Rosenberg, President
Catalog: Free. Frequency: 4x per year
Circulation: 400M. Sales: $5-10MM
Products: Apparel for the entire family

BLAIR CATALOG (800) 458-2000
220 Hickory St. • Warren, PA 16366
E-Mail: info@blair.com
Website: www.blair.com
Fax Ordering: (814) 726-6466
Customer Service: (800) 458-6057
Catalog: Free. Frequency: Quarterly
Circulation: 1MM. Sales: $5-10MM
Products: Women's clothing & accessories

BLOOMINGDALE'S BY MAIL (800) 777-0000
P.O. Box 8262 • Mason, OH 45040
E-Mail: sales@bloomingdales.com
Website: www.bloomingdales.com
Fax Ordering: (800) 596-2116
Customer Service: (800) 472-0788
Corporate Gift Service: (800) 283-3730
TDD Ordering: (800) 838-2892
Contact Name: Phil Blanco, President
Catalog: Free. Pages: 76.
Frequency: 10x per year
Circulation: 50MM. Sales: $50-100MM
Products: Women's clothing, accessories; gifts & items for your home

BLUE RIVER TRADING COMPANY (888) 761-1197
1500 NE 62nd St. • Ft. Lauderdale, FL 33334
Fax Ordering: (954) 772-3143
International Ordering: (954) 776-6766
Contact Name: Robyn Roberts, President
Catalog: Free. Frequency: 10x per year

Circulation: 250M. Sales: $1-3MM
Products: Southwestern apparel & furnishings

BOSTON PROPER (800) 243-4300
P.O. Box 3048 • Boca Raton, FL 33487
E-Mail: info@bostonproper.com
Website: www.bostonproper.com
Fax Ordering: (561) 241-6621
Customer Service: (800) 411-4080
Contact Name: Michael Tiernan, President
Catalog: Free. Pages: 76. Frequency: Monthly
Circulation: 20MM. Sales: $20-50MM
Products: Upscale women's apparel; accessories & gifts

BRAT CATALOG (800) 598-5264
Bowe Industries
8836 77th Ave. • Glendale, NY 11385
E-Mail: bratgirl@bratcatalog.com
Website: www.bratcatalog.com
Fax Ordering: (718) 441-8624
International Ordering: (718) 441-6464
Contact Name: Dan Barasch, President
Catalog: Free. Frequency: 4x per year
Circulation: 2MM. Sales: $3-5MM
Products: Clothing, accessories & room decor for teen girls

BRIGADE•QM (800) 338-4327
P.O. Box 100001 • Kennesaw, GA 30156
E-Mail: customerservice@brigaeqm.com
Website: www.actiongear.com
Fax Ordering: (800) 892-2999
Customer Service: (800) 228-7344
Catalog: Free. Frequency: Quarterly
Circulation: 150M. Sales: $3-5MM
Products: Adventure clothing, foot, head & handwear; rain gear; logo apparel

BRODER BROTHERS COMPANY (800) 521-0850
45555 Port St. • Plymouth, MI 48170
Fax Ordering: (734) 454-8971
International Ordering: (734) 454-4800
Contact Name: Harold Broder, President
Catalog: Free. Frequency: Quarterly
Circulation: 500M. Sales: $50-100MM
Products: Printable sportswear

BROOKS BROTHERS CATALOG (800) 274-1816
346 Madison Ave. • New York, NY 10017
E-Mail: sales@brooksbrothers.com
Website: www.brooksbrothers.com
Fax Ordering: (212) 309-7372
International Ordering: (212) 682-8800
Contact Name: Claudio Del Vecchio, President
Catalog: Free. Frequency: 5x per year
Circulation: 500M. Sales: $10-20MM
Products: Men's clothing & accessories

BROWNSTONE STUDIO CATALOG (800) 221-2468
421 Landmark Dr. • Wilmington, NC 28410 (800) 964-1956
Fax Ordering: (212) 953-6830
Contact Name: Kenneth Grossman, President
Catalog: Free. Frequency: 4x per year
Circulation: 3MM. Sales: $10-20MM
Products: High quality women's clothing; suits, eveningwear

BULLOCK & JONES CATALOG (800) 227-3050
P.O. Box 884510 • San Francisco, CA 94188
E-Mail: info@bullockandjones.com
Website: www.bullockandjones.com

Fax Ordering: (800) 922-9920
Customer Service: (800) 358-5832
Contact Name: Sidney Goodwill, President
Catalog: Free. Pages: 32-48. Frequency: Quarterly
Circulation: 250M. Sales: $20-50MM
Products: Men's apparel & accessories

C&D JARNAGIN COMPANY   (662) 287-4977
P.O. Box 1860 • Corinth, MS 38834
E-Mail: sales@jarnaginco.com
Website: www.jarnaginco.com
Fax Ordering: (662) 287-6033
Contact Name: Carolyn Jarnagin, President
Catalog: Online only. Sales: $1-3MM
Products: 18th & 19th century military
uniforms & equipment

CABLE CAR CLOTHIERS   (415) 397-4740
Robert Kirk, Ltd.
200 Bush St. • San Francisco, CA 94104
E-Mail: charles@cablecarclothiers.com
Website: www.cablecarclothiers.com
Fax Ordering: (415) 616-8998
Contact Name: Charles Pivnick, President
Catalog: Free. Frequency: Semiannual
Circulation: 200M. Sales: $1-3MM
Products: Men's & women's clothing
& accessories

CALIFORNIA MUSCLE   (800) 888-4718
11718 Montana Ave., Suite 7
Los Angeles, CA 90049
Fax Ordering: (310) 826-3980
International Ordering: (310) 826-7171
Catalog: $4. Frequency: Semiannual
Circulation: 100M. Sales: $1-3MM
Products: Form-fitting styles for the body
conscious

CALIFORNIA STYLE   (800) 477-7722
5823 Newton Dr. • Carlsbad, CA 92008
E-Mail: sales@castyle.com
Website: www.castyle.com
Fax Ordering: (760) 438-4701
International Ordering: (760) 918-3700
Contact Name: Ann Hjemboe, President
Catalog: Free. Frequency: 15x per year
Circulation: 2MM. Sales: $20-50MM
Products: Leisure wear

CALYCO CROSSING &   (800) 627-0412
TRIPLE R WESTERN WEAR
407 Main St. • Laurel, MD 20707
E-Mail: calycocrossing@calyco.com
Website: www.calyco.com
Fax Ordering: (301) 498-2262
International Ordering: (301) 498-2111
Contact Name: Carol McAdams, President
Catalog: Free. Frequency: 21x per year
Circulation: 10M. Sales: $500M
Products: Square dance & country Western
apparel

CAPEZIO CATALOG   (800) 533-1887
1650 Broadway • New York, NY 10019
Fax Ordering: (212) 262-1747
International Ordering: (212) 586-5140
Contact Name: Gayle Miller, President
Catalog: $1. Frequency: Annual
Circulation: 100M. Sales: $1-3MM
Products: Complete line of dance &
exercise wear

CARABELLA CORP. CATALOG   (800) 227-2235
17662 Armstrong Ave. • Irvine, CA 92614
E-Mail: carabella@earthlink.net
Website: www.carabella.com
Fax Ordering: (949) 263-2323
International Ordering: (949) 263-2300
Contact Name: Houshang Jalili, President
Catalog: Free. Frequency: 10x per year
Circulation: 8MM. Sales: $5-10MM
Products: Junior, missy & contemporary
women's swimwear, sportswear & eveningwear;
men's & children's swimwear

CARROLL & COMPANY   (800) 238-9400
425 N. Canon Dr. • Beverly Hills, CA 90210
Fax Ordering: (310) 273-7974
International Ordering: (310) 273-9060
Contact Name: John Carroll, President
Catalog: Free. Frequency: 3x per year
Circulation: 50M. Sales: $5-10MM
Products: Men's clothing, sportswear,
furnishings & accessories

CAROLINA GLOVE COMPANY   (800) 438-6888
P.O. Box 820 • Newton, NC 28658
E-Mail: sales@carolinaglove.com
Website: www.carolinaglove.com
Fax Ordering: (828) 464-1710
International Ordering: (828) 464-1132
Contact Name: Becky Biesel, President
Catalog: Free. Frequency: 10x per year
Circulation: 100M. Sales: $1-3MM
Products: Leisure & work gloves

CARUSHKA BODYWEAR   (800) 247-5113
7716 Kester Ave. • Van Nuys, CA 91405
Fax Ordering: (818) 988-8419
International Ordering: (818) 904-0574
Contact Name: Carushka Jarecka, President
Catalog: $5. Frequency: Monthly
Circulation: 5M. Sales: $5-10MM
Products: Women's exercise clothing
& sportswear

CATALOG SALES COMPANIES   (800) 367-2374
599 Canal St. • Lawrence, MA 01840
E-Mail: info@cheapaprons.com
Website: www.cheapaprons.com
Fax Ordering: (978) 689-2483
International Ordering: (978) 689-0694
Contact Name: Rick Kurman, President
Catalog: Free. Frequency: Semiannual
Circulation: 100M. Sales: $3-5MM
Products: Aprons, chef attire, t-shirts,
hats & jackets

CATTLE KATE CATALOG   (800) 332-5283
205 Ellen St. • Boise, ID 83714
E-Mail: cattlekate@misp.com
Website: www.cattlekate.com
Fax Ordering: (208) 375-3827
International Ordering: (208) 337-5283
Contact Name: Kathy Bressler, President
Catalog: Free. Frequency: 5x per year
Circulation: 150M. Sales: $500M to $1MM
Products: Old fashion Western Clothing and
designer Western wear.

CHADWICK'S OF BOSTON   (800) 525-6650
P.O. Box 1600 • Taunton, MA 02780   (800) 677-0340
E-Mail: chadwicks@brylane.com
Website: www.chadwicks.com

Fax Ordering: (800) 448-5767; (508) 583—2071
International Ordering: (508) 583-8110
Customer Service: (800) 525-4420
Contact Name: Kevin Doyle, President
Catalog: Free. Pages: 156. Frequency: Quarterly
Circulation: 4MM. Sales: $100-500MM
Products: Women's wear & accessories

CHAMPAGNE FORMALS (888) 245-5538
Bill Levkoff
1385 Broadway • New York, NY 10018
E-Mail: sales@champagneformals.com
Website: www.champagneformals.com
Fax Ordering: (212) 764-4253
International Ordering: (212) 221-0085
Contact Name: John Levkoff, President
Catalog: Free. Frequency: Semiannual
Circulation: 500M. Sales: $5-10MM
Products: Women's evening wear;
bridesmaid apparel

THE CHAPIN COMPANY (866) 888-8682
15522 Holdridge Dr. • Wayzata, MN 55391
E-Mail: info@chapincompany.com
Website: www.chapincompany.com
Fax Ordering: (952) 473-4384
International Ordering: (952) 473-4383
Catalog: Free. Frequency: Semiannual
Circulation: 100M. Sales: $10-20MM
Products: Sporting clothes for boating

CHEF REVIVIAL USA (800) 352-2433
22 Industrial Rd. • Lodi, NJ 07644
E-Mail: Info@chefrevival.com
Website: www.chefrevival.com
Fax Ordering: (973) 916-6680
Contact Name: Bill Rosenblum, President
Catalog: Free. Frequency: 24x per year
Circulation: 100M. Sales: $5-10MM
Products: Chef jackets, tunics, pants, hats,
aprons & accessories; footwear, cutlery

CHEFWEAR CATALOG (800) 568-2433
3111 N. Knox Ave. • Chicago, IL 60641
E-Mail: info@chefwear.com
Website: www.chefwear.com
Fax Ordering: (773) 427-8665
International Ordering: (773) 427-6700
Contact Name: Rochelle Huppin, President
Catalog: Free. Frequency: 3x per year
Circulation: 250M. Sales: $5-10MM
Products: Clothing & accessories for chefs
& home gourmets

CHOCK CATALOG (800) 222-0020
74 Orchard St. • New York, NY 10002
E-Mail: chock1@juno.com
Website: www.chockcatalog.com
Fax Ordering: (212) 473-6273
International Ordering: (212) 282-1929
Contact Name: Ann Zell, President
Catalog: Free. Frequency: Annual
Circulation: 100M. Sales: $1-3MM
Products: Brand name clothing

CLARK'S REGISTER (877) 243-9060
21 South Park • San Francisco, CA 94107
E-Mail: customerservice@clarksregister.com
Website: www.clarksregister.com
Fax Ordering: (415) 512-0315
Customer Service: (877) 243-9011
Catalog: Free. Pages: 40. Frequency: Semiannual

Circulation: 100M. Sales: $5-10MM
Products: Men's apparel & accessories

CLOTHES THAT WORK (800) 543-2040
Van Dyne Crotty
P.O. Box 422 • Dayton, OH 45401
E-Mail: info@vandynecrotty.com
Website: www.vandynecrotty.com
Fax Ordering: (800) 233-6329
International Ordering: (937) 236-1506
Contact Name: Daniel Crotty, President
Catalog: Free. Frequency: Annual
Circulation: 500M. Sales: $20-50MM
Products: Work clothes & uniforms

COACH LEATHERWARE (888) 262-6224
One Coach Way • Jacksonville, FL 32218
E-Mail: Info@coach.com
Website: www.coach.com
Fax Ordering: (800) 553-1422
Customer Service: (800) 444-3611
Contact Name: Lew Frankfort, President
Catalog: Free. Frequency: Annual
Circulation: 250M. Sales: $20-50MM
Products: Men's & women's accessories,
including, leather purses, belts, handags,
portfolios, wallets, travel items, gifts

COLDWATER CREEK SPIRIT CATALOG (800) 968-0980
751 W. Hanley Ave. • Coeur D'Alene, ID 83815
E-Mail: info@coldwatercreek.com
Website: www.coldwatercreek.com
Fax Ordering: (800) 262-0080
International Ordering: (208) 263-2266
TDD Ordering: (800) 305-7975
Contact Name: Dennis Pence, President
Catalog: Free. Pages: 76. Frequency: Quarterly
Circulation: 4MM. Sales: $25-50MM
Products: Women's apparel & accessories

COLDWATER CREEK HOME CATALOG (800) 262-0040
1 Coldwater Creek Dr. • Sandpoint, ID 83864 (800) 510-2808
E-Mail: Info@coldwatercreek.com (800) 968-0980
Website: www.coldwatercreek.com
Fax Ordering: (208) 263-1582
International Ordering: (208) 263-2266
Contact Name: Dennis Pence, President
Catalog: Free. Frequency: Bimonthly
Circulation: 40MM. Sales: $50-100MM
Products: Women's apparel & accessories,
home furnishings, decorative accessories & gifts

COMPANY STORE CATALOG (800) 289-8508
500 Company Store Rd. • La Crosse, WI 54601 (800) 285-3696
E-Mail: sales@thecompanystore.com
Website: www.thecompanystore.com
Fax Ordering: (608) 791-5776
Contact Name: Frank Keery, President
Catalog: Free. Frequency: Semiannual
Circulation: 2MM. Sales: $20-50MM
Products: Men's, women's & children clothing
for winter; down pillows & comforters, bedding
& feather products

COOLIBAR (800) 926-6509
2401 Edgewood Ave. So.
Minneapolis, MN 55426
E-Mail: service@coolibar.com
Website: www.coolibar.com
Fax Ordering: (952) 922-1455
Contact Name: Carol Schuler, PR
Catalog: Free. Frequency: Quarterly

Circulation: 150M. **Sales:** $3-5MM
Products: Sun protection apparel

CARLA CORSINI   (800) 229-1234
62 Spark St. • Brockton, MA 02302
E-Mail: carlawigs@aol.com
Website: www.alcasosp.com/carla-corsini
Fax Ordering: (508) 843-1674
International Ordering: (508) 843-2501
Contact Name: B. Paul Auer, President
Catalog: Free. Frequency: 8x per year
Circulation: 150M. **Sales:** $500M to $1MM
Products: Wigs & fashion accessories

CREATIVE LEATHER CONCEPTS   (800) 746-7532
Harbor Towne Office Complex
P.O. Box 368 • Grand Island, NY 14072
E-Mail: info@clcleather.com
Website: www.clcleather.net
Fax Ordering: (888) 674-0631
International Ordering: (716) 773-6300
Contact Name: Karen Widman
Catalog: Free. Frequency: Quarterly
Circulation: 150K. **Sales:** $5-10MM
Products: Leather accessories, including
wallets, briefcases, portfolios, purses

J. CREW CATALOG   (800) 932-0043
1 Ivy Crescent • Lynchburg, VA 24513   (800) 562-0258
E-Mail: info@jcrew.com
Website: www.jcrew.com
Fax Ordering: (434) 385-5750
Contact Name: Charles Silver Marketing
Catalog: Free. Frequency: Monthly
Circulation: 6MM. **Sales:** $100-500MM
Products: Sport clothes for the whole family

DAILY PLANET   (800) 733-7747
180 Varick St. • New York, NY 10014
Fax Ordering: (212) 807-7252
Contact Name: Sydney Sherman, President
Catalog: Free. Frequency: 5x per year
Circulation:500M. **Sales:** $3-5MM
Products: Clothing & gifts from around
the world

DANCE DISTRIBUTORS   (800) 333-2623
50 S. Cameron St. • Harrisburg, PA 17101
E-Mail: info@dancedistributors.com
Website: www.dancedistributors.com
Catalog: Free. Frequency: Quarterly
Circulation: 1MM. **Sales:** $10-20MM
Products: Dance apparel

DELIA'S   (800) 335-4269
P.O. Box 6143 • Westerville, OH 43086
E-Mail: info@delias.com
Website: www.delias.com
Fax Ordering: (800) 335-4265
International Ordering: (614) 212-5953
Catalog: Free. Pages: 48-72.
Frequency: Quarterly
Circulation: 1MM. **Sales:** $10-20MM
Products: Women's clothing & accessories

DeSANTIS HOLSTER & LEATHER GOODS   (800) 424-1236
431 Bayview Ave. • Amityville, NY 11701
E-Mail: info@desantisholster.com
Website: www.desantisholster.com
Fax Ordering: (631) 841-6320
International Ordering: (631) 841-6300
Contact Name: Eugene DeSantis, President

Catalog: $5. Frequency: Annual
Circulation: 75M. **Sales:** $1-3MM
Products: Holsters & accessories for police
& security officers

DESMOND'S FORMAL WEAR   (800) 369-4889
P.O. Box 1447 • LaCrosse, WI 54602
E-Mail: sales@desmonds.com
Website: www.desmonds.com
Fax Ordering: (608) 781-5125
International Ordering: (608) 784-4824
Contact Name: John Desmond, Jr., President
Catalog: Free. Frequency: Annual
Circulation:100M. **Sales:** $20-50MM
Products: Men's & women's formal wear

DOCKERS CATALOG   (800) 362-5377
Levi Strauss Company
1155 Battery St. • San Francisco, CA 94111
E-Mail: info@levistrauss.com
Website: www.levistrauss.com
Fax Ordering: (415) 501-3939
International Ordering: (415) 544-6000
Contact Name: Phil Marineau, President
Catalog: Free. Frequency: Semiannual
Circulation:100M. **Sales:** $5-10MM
Products: Khaki pants & shorts for men & women

DOUBLE EXPOSURE FASHION COMPANY   (800) 582-6282
69 Main St. • Vincentown, NJ 08088
E-Mail: info@dblexp.com
Website: www.dblexp.com
Fax Ordering: (609) 859-3974
International Ordering: (609) 859-3397
Contact Name: Warren Eichhorn, President
Catalog: Free. Frequency: Annual
Circulation:50M. **Sales:** $500M
Products: Imprinted apparel, totes, etc.

DRAPER'S & DAMON'S   (800) 843-1174
P.O. Box 57088 • Irvine, CA 95619
E-Mail: info@drapers.com
Website: www.drapers.com
Fax Ordering: (949) 784-3332
International Ordering: (949) 784-3000
Contact Name: Brad Farmer, President
Catalog: Free. Frequency: 14x per year
Circulation:20M. **Sales:** $50-100MM
Products: Classic style fashions for women

DRESS BARN CATALOG   (800) 684-4253
30 Dunnigan Dr. • Suffern, NY 10901
E-Mail: info@dressbarn.com
Website: www.dressbarn.com
Fax Ordering: (800) 686-6495
International Ordering: (845) 369-4500
Catalog: Free. Frequency: Semiannual
Circulation:100M. **Sales:** $10-20MM
Products: Women's clothing

DRYSDALES CATALOG   (800) 444-6481
1555 N. 107th E Ave. • Tulsa, OK 74116
E-Mail: sales@drysdales.com
Website: www.drysdales.com
Fax Ordering: (918) 832-8900
International Ordering: (918) 836-9600
Customer Service: (800) 608-9800
Contact Name: Chris Schwier, President
Catalog: Free. Frequency: Quarterly
Circulation: 1MM. **Sales:** $10-20MM
Products: Fashion & traditional western
clothing; gifts & accessories

EARLY WINTERS   (800) 458-4438
Norm Thompson Outfitters   (877) 718-7902
P.O. Box 4333 • Portland, OR 97208
E-Mail: info@earlywinters.com
Website: www.earlywinters.com
Fax Ordering: (800) 821-1282
Customer Service: (800) 821-1286
Contact Name: Becky Jewett, President
Catalog: Free. Frequency: Monthly
Circulation: 5MM. Sales: $10-20MM
Products: Men's and women's outdoor
apparel & gear

EASTBAY CATALOG   (800) 826-2205
111 S. 1st Ave. • Wausau, WI 54401
E-Mail: info@eastbay.com
Website: www.eastbay.com
Fax Ordering: (715) 261-9550
Customer Service: (715) 845-5538
Contact Name: Richard A. Johnson, President
Catalog: Free. Frequency: Monthly
Circulation: 60MM. Sales: $100-500MM
Products: Men's and women's sportswear,
shoes, bags, protective gear, imprinted products

EISNER BROTHERS CATALOG   (800) 426-7700
75 Essex St. • New York, NY 10002
E-Mail: info@eisnerbros.com
Website: www.eisnerbros.com
Fax Ordering: (212) 475-6824
International Ordering: (212) 475-6868
Contact Name: Charles Eisner, President
Catalog: Free. Frequency: Semiannual
Circulation:50M. Sales: $5-10MM
Products: Licensed printed casual wear: caps,
jackets, outerwear, uniforms, totebags, towels

ELITE SPORTSWEAR, LP   (800) 345-4087
P.O. Box 16400 • Reading, PA 19612
E-Mail: custumerservice@gkelite.com
Website: www.gk-elitesportswear.com
Fax Ordering: (610) 921-0208
International Ordering: (610) 921-1469
Contact Name: Sallie Weaver, President
Catalog: Free. Frequency: Quarterly
Circulation: 2MM. Sales: $50-100MM
Products: GK gymnastics apparel, warmup
suits, skating wear; cheerleader briefs;
special order team apparel

ESPRIT CATALOG   (800) 437-7748
900 Minnesota St.
San Francisco, CA 94107
E-Mail: info@esprit.com
Website: www.esprit.com
Fax Ordering: (415) 550-3505
International Ordering: (415) 648-6900
Contact Name: Jay Margolis, President
Catalog: Free. Frequency: 4x per year
Circulation: 4MM. Sales: $50-100MM
Products: Women's clothing & accessories

FABULOUS FURS CATALOG   (800) 848-4650
601 Madison Ave. • Covington, KY 41011
E-Mail: info@fabulousfurs.com
Website: www.fabulousfurs.com
Fax Ordering: (859) 291-9687
International Ordering: (859) 291-3300
Contact Name: Donna Salyers, President
Catalog: Free. Frequency: 3x per year
Circulation: 300M. Sales: $1-3MM
Products: Fake furs

FARIBAULT WOOLEN MILLS CATALOG   (800) 448-9665
P.O. Box 369 • Faribault, MN 55021
E-Mail: info@faribowool.com
Website: www.faribowool.com
Fax Ordering: (507) 332-2936
International Ordering: (507) 334-6444
Contact Name: Warren Malkerson, President
Catalog: Free. Frequency: Semiannual
Circulation: 200M. Sales: $10-20MM
Products: Wool robes, blankets & scarves

C.C.FILSON COMPANY   (800) 624-0201
P.O. Box 34020 • Seattle, WA 98124
E-Mail: service@filson.com
Website: www.filson.com
Fax Ordering: (206) 624-4539
International Ordering: (206) 624-4437
Contact Name: Steve Matson, President
Catalog: Free. Frequency: Semiannual
Circulation:500M. Sales: $10-20MM
Products: Rugged outdoor clothing including
garments, headwear, shoes & luggage

FITIGUES CATALOG   (800) 235-9005
1535 N. Dayton St. • Chicago, IL 60622
E-Mail: sales@fitigues.com
Website: www.fitigues.com
Fax Ordering: (312) 255-8868
International Ordering: (312) 255-8866
Contact Name: Steven Rosenstein, President
Catalog: Free. Frequency: 5x per year
Circulation: 2MM. Sales: $10-20MM
Products: Clothing for men, women & children

FITNESS STUFF CATALOG   (877) 937-8833
4141 D3 State St.
Santa Barbara, CA 93110
E-Mail: info@fitness-stuff.com
Website: www.fitness-stuff.com
Fax Ordering: (805) 884-0724
Contact Name: Carol Woody, President
Catalog: Free. Frequency: Quarterly
Circulation: 50M. Sales: $500M
Products: Exercise wear, sportswear &
exercise equipment

FLIRT FASHIONS OF FLORIDA   (800) 323-5478
151 Center St.
Cape Canaveral, FL 32920
E-Mail: sales@flirtcatalog.com
Website: www.flirtcatalog.com
Fax Ordering: (321) 783-1729
International Ordering: (321) 783-3714
Contact Name: Ronald Alan Abeles, President
Catalog: $2. Frequency: 5x per year
Circulation: 1MM. Sales: $10-20MM
Products: Women's apparel & lingerie,
club clothes

FOX OUTDOOR PRODUCTS CATALOG   (800) 523-4332
1600 Foster St. • Evanston, IL 60201
E-Mail: info@foxoutdoor.com
Website: www.foxoutdoor.com
Fax Ordering: (847) 869-1569
International Ordering: (847) 869-1400
Contact Name: D.J. Fox, President
Catalog: Free. Frequency: Annual
Circulation: 150M. Sales: $5-10MM
Products: Military & outdoor wear,
clothing, cookware, army surplus

FRANKLIN COVEY CO. (800) 441-6600
2200 West Parkway Blvd.
Salt Lake City, UT 84119
E-Mail: sales@franklincovey.com
Website: www.franklincovey.com
Stores: (800) 360-8118
Catalog: Free. Pages: 24
Frequency: Quarterly
Circulation: 1MM. Sales: $3-5MM
Products: Business & professional bags;
totes & binders

FREDERICK'S OF HOLLYWOOD (800) 323-9525
P.O. Box 2949 • Phoenix, AZ 85062 (800) 323-2181
E-Mail: sales@fredericks.com
Website: www.fredericks.com
Fax Ordering: (602) 760-2181
International Ordering: (323) 466-5151
Contact Name: Linda Lore, President
Catalog: Free. Frequency: Annual
Circulation: 50MM. Sales: $100-500MM
Products: Women's lingerie

FRENCH CREEK SHEEP & WOOL CO. (800) 977-4337
RR 1 • Elverson, PA 19520
E-Mail: info@frenchcreeksw.com
Website: www.frenchcreeksw.com
Fax Ordering: (610) 286-0324
International Ordering: (610) 286-5700
Contact Name: Jean Flaxenburg, President
Catalog: $3. Frequency: Semiannual
Circulation: 10M. Sales: $3-5MM
Products: Men's & women's sheepskin
& wool clothing

FRIDAY CASUALS CATALOG (800) 638-7070
10722 Hanna St. • Beltsville, MD 20705
E-Mail: info@fridaycasuals.com
Website: www.fridaycasuals.com
Fax Ordering: (301) 937-2916
International Ordering: (301) 937-4843
Contact Name: Gerald Flaig, President
Catalog: Free. Frequency: Quarterly
Circulation: 200M. Sales: $5-10MM
Products: Relaxed dress code wear;
golf shirts, sweatshirts, sweaters,
denim shirts, wind shirts, jackets

GARNET HILL CATALOG (800) 622-6216
231 Main St. • Franconia, NH 03580
E-Mail: info@garnethill.com
Website: www.garnethill.com
Fax Ordering: (603) 823-7034
International Ordering: (603) 823-5545
Contact Name: Brian Gowen, President
Catalog: Free. Frequency: 7x per year
Circulation: 16MM. Sales: $50-100MM
Products: Quality natural fabric baby
clothing & linens, maternity clothes

GOTKEYS LOUNGEWEAR (888) 248-9924
300 Bedford St. • Manchester, NH 03101
E-Mail: gotkeys@aol.com
Website: www.gotkeysunlimited.com
Fax Ordering: (603) 624-7388
International Ordering: (603) 624-6859
Catalog: Free. Frequency: Semiannual
Circulation: 250M. Sales: $5-10MM
Products: Men's boxers, pants & shirts;
loungewear

HABAND COMPANY CATALOG (201) 651-1000
110 Bauer Dr. • Oakland, NJ 07436
E-Mail: service@haband.net
Website: www.haband.com
Fax Ordering: (201) 405-7777
Contact Name: Duke Habernickel, President
Catalog: Free. Frequency: Semiannual
Circulation: 200M. Sales: $5-10MM
Products: Men's & women's clothing

HANKS CLOTHING (866) 444-2657
99 Lester Ave. • Johnson City, NY 13790
E-Mail: service@hanksclothing.com
Website: www.hanksclothing.com
Fax Ordering: (607) 729-4989
International Ordering: (607) 729-8688
Catalog: Free. Frequency: Quarterly
Circulation: 200M. Sales: $5-10MM
Products: Men's & women's clothing,
footwear & home furnishings

HAROLD'S CATALOG (800) 676-5373
P.O. Box 2970 • Norman, OK 73070
E-Mail: info@harolds.com
Website: www.harolds.com
Fax Ordering: (405) 366-2588
International Ordering: (405) 329-4045
Contact Name: Cynde Stewart, Production Mgr.
Catalog: Free. Frequency: Annual
Circulation:250M. Sales: $10-20MM
Products: Casual apparel & accessories
for men & women; upscale retail clothing

HARTFORD YORK (800) 936-5646
P.O. Box 337 • French Camp, CA 95231
Website: www.hartfordyork.com
E-Mail: hartford@hartfordyork.com
Fax Ordering: (800) 564-6291
Contact Name: Steve Singer, President
Catalog: Free. Frequency: Semiannual
Circulation:200K. Sales: $5-10MM
Products: Hats & accessories

HARVARD COOP INSIGNIA CATALOG (800) 368-1882
Harvard Cooperative Society
1400 Massachusetts Ave.
Cambridge, MA 02138
Fax Ordering: (800) 242-1882
International Ordering: (617) 499-2000
Contact Name: J. Murphy, President
Catalog: Free. Frequency: Annual
Circulation:250M. Sales: $10-20MM
Products: Harvard & M.I.T. products,
private label men's wear

HUGG SWIMWEAR & ACCESSORIES (800) 255-7946
44 1/2 Butler Ave. • Ambler, PA 19002
E-Mail: support@sportssection.com
Website: www.sportssection.com
Fax Ordering: (888) 646-1280
Contact Name: William Hugg, Jr., President
Catalog: Free. Frequency: 3x per year
Circulation: 10M. Sales: $500M
Products: Fitness & swimwear apparel

INTERNATIONAL MALE (800) 414-1114
Brawn of California
741 "F" St. • San Diego, CA 92101
E-Mail: service@internationalmale.com
Website: www.internationalmale.com
Fax Ordering: (717) 633-3214

International Ordering: (717) 633-3413
Contact Name: Don Wilson, President
Catalog: $2. Frequency: Quarterly
Circulation:100M. Sales: $10-20MM
Products: Workout & fitness apparel for men

ISABELLA BIRD CATALOG (888) 472-2473
419 State St. • Santa Barbara, CA 93101
E-Mail: sales@isabellabird.com
Website: www.isabellabird.com
Fax Ordering: (800) 232-9882
International Ordering: (805) 962-5558
Catalog: Free. Frequency: Semiannual
Circulation: 200M. Sales: $3-5MM
Products: Women's upscale apparel &
accessories

JJ HAT CENTER CATALOG (800) 622-1911
310 Fifth Ave. • New York, NY 10001
Fax Ordering: (212) 971-0406
International Ordering: (212) 239-4368
Contact Name: Ira O'Toole, President
Catalog: Free. Frequency: Annual
Circulation: 100M. Sales: $500M
Products: Hats & caps

JANICE'S NATURAL (800) 526-4237
COMFORT COLLECTION
Janice Corp. • 109 US Hwy. 46
Budd lake, NJ 07828
E-Mail: info@janices.com
Website: www.janices.com
Fax Ordering: (973) 691-5459
International Ordering: (973) 691-2979
Contact Name: Janice Swack, President
Catalog: Free. Frequency: Weekly
Circulation: 250M. Sales: $3-5MM
Products: Natural products, mainly
cotton, from socks to mattresses

JASCO UNIFORM CO. (800) 222-4445
P.O. Box 6810 • Vernon Hills, IL 60061
E-Mail: info@jascouniform.com
Website: www.jascouniform.com
Fax Ordering: (800) 323-2329
Catalog: Free. Frequency: Semiannual
Circulation: 100M. Sales: $500M to $1MM
Products: Uniforms; nursing scrubs

JAZZERTOGS CATALOG (800) 348-4748
1050 Joshua Way • Vista, CA 92083
E-Mail: jazzine@jazzercise.com
Website: www.jazzercise.com
Fax Ordering: (760) 602-7180
International Ordering: (760) 598-3837
Contact Name: Judi Sheppard Missett, President
Catalog: Free. Frequency: 10x per year
Circulation: 1.5MM. Sales: $3-5MM
Products: Aerobic, dance-fitness apparel;
accessories & fitness products

JEAN PAREE WIGS (800) 422-9447
4041 S 700 E #2
So. Salt Lake City, UT 84111
E-Mail: info@jeanparee.com
Website: www.jeanparee.com
Fax Ordering: (801) 261-2047
International Ordering: (801) 328-9756
Contact Name: Gloria Van Woerkom, President
Catalog: Free. Frequency: 5x per year
Circulation: 50M. Sales: $1-3MM
Products: Wigs for men & women

JESSICA LONDON CATALOG (800) 784-1667
P.O. Box 1600 • Taunton, MA 02780
E-Mail: sales@jesicalondon.com
Website: www.jesicalondon.com
Fax Ordering: (800) 448-5767
Customer Service: (800) 819-0813
International Ordering: (212) 613-9500
Contact Name: Claudio Del Vecchio, President
Catalog: Free. Pages: 100
Frequency: Quarterly
Circulation: 1MM. Sales: $10-20MM
Products: Clothing for plus size women

J.JILL THE CATALOG (800) 642-9989
P.O. Box 2006 • Tilton, NH 03276   (800) 498-9960
E-Mail: catalogservice@jjill.com
Website: www.jjill.com
Fax Ordering: (603) 266-2802
International Ordering: (603) 266-2600
Customer Service: (800) 343-5700; (800) 329-9713
Contact Name: Greg Karr, President
Catalog: Free. Frequency: Semiannual
Circulation: 200K. Sales: $5-10MM
Products: Women's fashions and accessories

JUNONIA CATALOG (877) 647-4300
2950 Lexington Ave. • St. Paul, MN 55121
E-Mail: customerservice@junonia.com
Website: www.junonia.com
Fax Ordering: (977) 647-4300
International Ordering: (651) 365-1830
Contact Name: Ann Kelly, President
Catalog: Free. Frequency: 3 per year
Circulation:150M. Sales: $10-20MM
Products: Activewear in sizes 14 and up

JUST MY SIZE CATALOG (800) 522-9567
P.O. Box 748 • Rural Hall, NC 27045
Fax Ordering: (800) 545-5613
Contact Name: Sherry Aldrich, President
Catalog: Free. Frequency: 4x per year
Circulation: 150M. Sales: $1-3MM
Products: Lingerie, hosiery & casual wear

KALE UNIFORM COMPANY (800) 873-5417
555 W. Roosevelt Rd. • Chicago, IL 60607
Fax Ordering: (312) 563-0080
International Ordering: (312) 226-4534
Contact Name: Dick Benchley, President
Catalog: Free. Frequency: Annual
Circulation: 250M. Sales: $3-5MM
Products: Work clothes & uniforms

KAST-A-WAY SWIMWEAR (800) 543-2763
9356 Cincinnati Columbus Rd.
Cincinnati, OH 45241
E-Mail: sales@kastawayswimwear.com
Website: www.kastawayswimwear.com
Fax Ordering: (513) 777-1062
International Ordering: (513) 777-7967
Contact Name: Patti Kast, President
Catalog: Free. Frequency: Semiannual
Circulation: 175M. Sales: $5-10MM
Products: Competition swimwear & accessories,
aquatic fitness videos, training equipment & books

GLORIA KAY UNIFORM (800) 242-7454
4040 N. 128th St. • Brookfield, WI 53005
E-Mail: info@gloriakay.com
Website: www.gloriakay.com
Fax Ordering: (262) 790-0077
International Ordering: (262) 790-0099

Contact Name: Leo Weinshel, President
Catalog: Free. Frequency: Quarterly
Circulation: 200M. Sales: $1-3MM
Products: Uniforms, aprons, formal wear, chef apparel

KINGSIZE FOR MEN CATALOG (800) 806-4152
P.O. Box 4408 • Taunton, MA 02780
E-Mail: kscustserv@brylane.com
Website: www.kingsizedirect.com
Fax Ordering: (800) 682-8109
International Ordering: (212) 613-9500
Customer Service: (800) 677-0249
Contact Name: Sheila Garelik, President
Catalog: Free. Frequency: 5x per year
Circulation: 1MM. Sales: $20-50MM
Products: Stylish sportswear, business & dress wear, activewear, outerwear, sleepwear, underwear, shoes & accessories in big & tall sizes

KINGSIZE CORPORATION (800) 846-1600
2300 SE Ave. • Indianapolis, IN 46201
E-Mail: info@kingsizemen.com
Website: www.kingsizemen.com
Fax Ordering: (800) 944-5045
International Ordering: (317) 266-3747
Contact Name: Kenneth Lubar, Marketing
Catalog: Free. Frequency: 4x per year
Circulation: 500M. Sales: $10-20MM
Products: Clothing for big & tall men

KOALA MEN'S SWIMWEAR (800) 238-2941
P.O. Box 5519 • Sherman Oaks, CA 91413
E-Mail: sales@koalaswim.com
Website: www.koalaswim.com
Fax Ordering: (818) 780-5170
International Ordering: (818) 727-7620
Contact Name: Michael D. Young, President
Catalog: $2. Frequency: 3x per year
Circulation: 1MM. Sales: $3-5MM
Products: Swimwear for men

LADY GRACE STORES CATALOG (800) 922-0504
P.O. Box 128 • Malden, MA 02148
E-Mail: info@ladygrace.com
Website: www.ladygrace.com
Fax Ordering: (781) 321-8476
International Ordering: (781) 322-1721
Contact Name: Steven Barsen, President
Catalog: Free. Frequency: 8x per year
Circulation: 1MM. Sales: $5-10MM
Products: Intimate apparel

LANDS' END CATALOGS (800) 356-4444
Lands End Lane • Dodgeville, WI 53595 (800) 963-4816
E-Mail: corpsales@landsend.com
Website: www.landsend.com
Fax Ordering: (800) 332-0103; (608) 935-4260
International Ordering: (608) 935-9341
Contact Name: Michael J. Smith, President
Catalog: Free. Frequency: Monthly
Circulation: 200MM. Sales: $500MM to $1B
Products: Men's, women's & children's clothing, school uniforms, home furnishings, linenes, travel

LANE BRYANT CATALOG (800) 677-0216
Brylane • 463 7th Ave.
New York, NY 10018
E-Mail: lbcustserv@brylane.com
Website: www.brylane.com
Fax Ordering: (800) 387-8290

Contact Name: Sheila Garelik, President
Catalog: Free. Frequency: 5x per year
Circulation: 2MM. Sales: $10-20MM
Products: Women's clothing, shoes, intimate apparel; women's plus sizes

LEATHER MASTERS CATALOG (800) 417-2636
969 Park Ave. • San Jose, CA 95126
E-Mail: orders@leathermasters.com
Website: www.leathermasters.com
Fax Ordering: (408) 293-7685
International Ordering: (408) 293-7660
Contact Name: Dave Carranza, President
Catalog: Free. Frequency: Annual
Circulation: 100M. Sales: $1-3MM
Products: Custom leather, cleaning & alterations

LERNER CATALOG (800) 677-0248
Brylane • 35 United Dr.
W. Bridgewater, MA 02379
E-Mail: lecustserv@brylane.com
Website: www.brylane.com
Fax Ordering: (800) 288-0448
Catalog: Free. Frequency: 5x per year
Circulation: 500M. Sales: $10-20MM
Products: Women's clothing & accessories

LIFESTYLES DIRECT (800) TAN-0440
P.O. Box 152929 • Tampa, FL 33684
E-Mail: customerservice@lifestylesdirect.com
Website: www.lifestylesdirect.com
Fax Ordering: (813) 882-4321
International Ordering: (941) 906-9172
Customer Service: (813) 882-4320
Contact Name: Gary Giesler, President
Catalog: Free. Frequency: Annual
Circulation: 50MM. Sales: $50-100MM
Products: Swimwear & accessories for both women & men

LIMITED TOO CATAZINE (866) 458-3866
P.O. Box 551527 • Dallas, TX 75355
E-Mail: orders@limitedtoo.com
Website: www.limitedtoo.com
Fax Ordering: (614) 479-3619
Catalog: Free. Frequency: Semiannual
Circulation: 500M. Sales: $10-20MM
Products: Apparel, shoes & accessories for girls age 7-14

LINGERIE PLACE CATALOG (877) 268-9594
Amerimark Direct
6864 Engle Rd. • Cleveland, OH 44130
E-Mail: orders@amerimark.com
Website: www.amerimark.com
Fax Ordering: (440) 234-8925
International Ordering: (440) 826-1900
Contact Name: Gary Giesler, President
Catalog: Free. Frequency: Annual
Circulation: 50MM. Sales: $50-100MM
Products: High fashion lingerie for the mature woman

LITTLE'S GOOD GLOVES (888) 967-8548
301 Shangri Lane • Sedona, AZ 86336
E-Mail: sales@fortunoff.com
Website: www.fortunoff.com
Fax Ordering: (928) 203-9764
International Ordering: (928) 203-9769
Contact Name: Mark Dzierson, President
Catalog: Free. Frequency: Annual

Circulation: 250M. Sales: $500M
Products: Gloves & accessories

PEGGY LUTZ PLUS   (800) 498-3294
7650 Bell Rd. • Windsor, CA 95492
E-Mail: peg@peglutz.com
Website: www.plus-size.com
Fax Ordering: (707) 837-1899
International Ordering: (707) 837-1897
Contact Name: Peggy Lutz, President
Catalog: $5. Frequency: Semiannual
Circulation: 100M. Sales: $500M to $1MM
Products: Clothing for plus & supersize women,
sizes 14, 16 & up, petite, medium & all. Career
wear, sruise wear, evening clothes.

MAKING IT BIG CATALOG   (877) 644-1995
501 Aaron St. • Cotati, CA 94931
E-Mail: mib@bigwomen.com
Website: www.makingitbigonline.com
Fax Ordering: (707) 795-4874
International Ordering: (707) 795-1995
Contact Name: Cynthia Riggs, President
Catalog: $2. Frequency: Weekly
Circulation: 5M. Sales: $500M to $1MM
Products: Natural fiber clothing for large
& super-sized women

MALE POWER CATALOG   (800) 447-4720
Comme-Ci Comme-Ca
94 4th Ave. • Bay Shore, NY 11706
E-Mail: info@teensyweensy.com
Website: www.teensyweensy.com
Fax Ordering: (631) 666-8155
International Ordering: (631) 666-8423
Contact Name: Sam Baker, President
Catalog: $5. Frequency: Annual
Circulation: 50M. Sales: $1-3MM
Products: Swimwear & underwear for
young men; club wear for women

J. MARCO   (800) 948-3100
4939 Panther Pkwy.• Seville, OH 44273
E-Mail: sales@jmarco.com
Website: www.jmarco.com
Fax Ordering: (330) 769-2212
Catalog: Free. Pages: 68. Frequency: Quarterly
Circulation: 1MM. Sales: $10-20MM
Products: Women's clothing & accessories

MARKETPLACE: HANDWORK OF INDIA   (800) 726-8905
1455 Ashland Ave. • Evanston, IL 60201
E-Mail: info@marketplaceindia.com
Website: www.marketplaceindia.com
Fax Ordering: (847) 328-4061
International Ordering: (847) 328-4011
Contact Name: Pushpika Freitas, President
Catalog: Free. Frequency: Semiannual
Circulation: 500M. Sales: $1-3MM
Products: Women's fashions of India

MARMOT MOUNTAIN   (800) 882-2490
2321 Circadian Way • Santa Rosa, CA 95407
E-Mail: info@marmot.com
Website: www.marmot.com
Fax Ordering: (707) 544-1344
International Ordering: (707) 544-4590
Contact Name: Steve Crisafulll, President
Catalog: Free. Pages: 82. Frequency: Semiannual
Circulation: 250M. Sales: $10-20MM
Products: Pullovers, parkas, jackets, mountain climbing suits,
windpants & shirts, bags & accessories for the outdoorsman

BILLY MARTIN'S   (310) 289-5000
8605 W. Sunset Blvd. • Los Angeles, CA 90069
E-Mail: info@billymartin.com
Website: www.billymartin.com
Fax Ordering: (904) 641-0977
Contact Name: Daryle Scott, President
Catalog: Online. Sales: $5-10MM
Products: Upscale country-western apparel

MENSHATS.COM   (800) 357-4287
Div. of STARK & LEGUM, INC.
739 Granby St. • Norfolk, VA 235210
E-Mail: slcatsls@inflonline.net
Website: www.menshats.com
Fax Ordering: (757) 626-3912
Customer Service: (800) 645-3570
Catalog: Free. Pages: 32. Frequency: Quarterly
Circulation: 500M. Sales: $3-5MM
Products: Men's hats

METROSTYLE   (800) 288-4000
P.O. Box 4400 • Taunton, MA 02780   (800) 416-9471
E-Mail: sales@metrostyle.com
Website: www.metrostyle.com
Fax Ordering: (800) 288-0448
Customer Service: (800) 288-7004
Catalog: Free. Pages: 84. Frequency: Quarterly
Circulation: 250M. Sales: $10-50MM
Products: Women's apparel & accessories

MONTEREY BAY CLOTHING CO.   (800) 569-4740
5857 Owens Ave. • Carlsbad, CA 92008
E-Mail: sales@shopthebay.com
Website: www.shopthebay.com
Fax Ordering: (800) 964-1975
Customer Service: (800) 308-0358
International Ordering: (425) 485-2132
Catalog: Free. Pages: 64. Frequency: Quarterly
Circulation: 1MM. Sales: $20-50MM
Products: Women's fashions

JACQUES MORET BODYWEAR   (800) 441-1999
1350 Broadway • New York, NY 10018
Fax Ordering: (212) 354-1052
International Ordering: (212) 967-4664
Contact Name: Joseph Harary, President
Catalog: Free. Frequency: 4x per year
Circulation: 400M. Sales: $5-10MM
Products: Bodywear for men, women & children

DAVID MORGAN CATALOG   (800) 324-4934
11812 N. Creek Pkwy. N., Suite 103
Bothell, WA 98011
E-Mail: catalog@davidmorgan.com
Website: www.davidmorgan.com
Fax Ordering: (800) 364-3961
International Fax Ordering: (425) 486-0224
International Ordering: (425) 485-2132
Contact Name: David Morgan, President
Catalog: Free. Pages: 128
Frequency: Semiannual
Circulation: 250M. Sales: $1-3MM
Products: Rugged outdoor clothing including
garments, headwear, shoes & luggage

JIM MORRIS ENVIRONMENTAL T-SHIRT CO.   (800) 788-5411
P.O. Box 18270 • Boulder, CO 80308
E-Mail: morris@indra.com
Website: www.jimmorris.com
Fax Ordering: (972) 401-6827
International Ordering: (972) 969-3100
Contact Name: Jim Morris, President

Catalog: Free. Frequency: 40x per year
Circulation: 50MM. Sales: $50-100MM
Products: Printed designs on t-shirts,
sweatshirts, hats & totebags

MOTHERWEAR CATALOG   (800) 633-0303
320 Riverside Dr. • Florence, MA 01062
E-Mail: info@motherwear.com
Website: www.motherwear.com
Fax Ordering: (413) 586-2712
Contact Name: Jody Wright, President
Catalog: Free. Frequency: 3x per year
Circulation: 1MM. Sales: $5-10MM
Products: Stylish, comfortable fashions designed
specifically for discreet breastfeeding

NATIONAL WHOLESALE COMPANY   (800) 433-0580
400 National Blvd. • Lexington, NC 27294
E-Mail: customerservice@shopnational.com
Website: www.shopnational.com
Fax Ordering: (336) 249-9326
International Ordering: (336) 248-5904
Contact Name: Edward C. Smith, Sr., President
Catalog: Free. Frequency: Annual
Circulation: 3MM. Sales: $20-50MM
Products: Apparel, loungewear, intimate
apparel, hosiery, footwear, accessorie

NEIMAN MARCUS   (800) 825-8000
P.O. Box 650589 • Dallas, TX 75265
E-Mail: sales@neiumanmarcus.com
Website: www.neimanmarcus.com
International Ordering: (972) 556-6021
TDD Ordering: (800) 533-1312
Catalog: Free. Frequency: Quarterly
Circulation: 2MM. Sales: $25-50MM
Products: Gifts, paper & paper products,
albums, journals, pens

NEWPORT NEWS   (800) 688-2830
Spiegel Group
5100 City Line Rd. • Hampton, VA 23630
E-Mail: service@csc.newport-news.com
Website: www.newport-news.com
Fax Ordering: (800) 765-2866
Customer Service: (800) 828-2672
Contact Name: George Ittner, President
Catalog: Free. Pages: 60. Frequency: Monthly
Circulation: 5MM. Sales: $50-100MM
Products: Women's clothing & accessories; dress
& casual wear, outerwear & footwear, lingerie

NIEMAN MARCUS DIRECT   (800) 621-0851
111 Customer Way • Irving, TX 75039
E-Mail: orders@niemanmarcus.com
Website: www.niemanmarcus.com
Fax Ordering: (972) 401-6827
International Ordering: (972) 969-3100
Contact Name: Karen Katz, President
Catalog: Free. Frequency: 40x per year
Circulation: 10MM. Sales: $50-100MM
Products: Clothing, accessories, household
items, home furnishings, gifts, food

NORDSTROM, INC.   (800) 285-5800
P.O. Box 91018 • Seattle, WA 98111
E-Mail: contact@nordstrom.com
Website: www.nordstrom.com
Fax Ordering: (800) 285-7288; (206) 215-7288
International Ordering: (206) 215-7100
TDD Ordering: (800) 285-7344
Contact Name: Dan Nordstrom, President

Catalog: Free. Pages: 60. Frequency: Monthly
Circulation: 50MM. Sales: $100-500MM
Products: Clothing, accessories, footwear

NORTH COUNTRY CATALOG   (800) 262-0040
Coldwater Creek
P.O. Box 2069 • Sandpoint, ID 83864
E-Mail: info@coldwatercreek.com
Website: www.coldwatercreek.com
Fax Ordering: (208) 263-1582
International Ordering: (208) 263-2266
Contact Name: Tony Savlino, President
Catalog: Free. Frequency: Bimonthly
Circulation: 500K. Sales: $10-20MM
Products: Nature related gifts & apparel

NORTHSTYLE CATALOG   (800) 336-5666
Northwoods Trail
P.O. Box 6529 • Chelmsford, MA 01824
E-Mail: sales@northstyle.com
Website: www.northstyle.com
Fax Ordering: (800) 986-5666
Catalog: Free. Pages: 56. Frequency: 6x/year
Circulation: 1MM. Sales: $5-10MM
Products: Apparel, jewelry, cabinware,
gifts & homegoods

NORTHWEST EXPRESS CATALOG   (800) 727-7243
Bear Creek Corporation
P.O. Box 1548 • Medford, OR 97501
E-Mail: sales@northwestexpress.com
Website: www.northwestexpress.com
Fax Ordering: (800) 648-6640
International Ordering: (541) 776-2121
Contact Name: Bill Williams, President
Catalog: Free. Frequency: 5x per year
Circulation: 50K. Sales: $10-20MM
Products: Clothing & accessories; housewares
& fine foods from the Pacific Northwest

OFFICIAL U.S. OLYMPIC   (800) 843-8326
TRAINING CENTERS
U.S. Olympic Committee
1 Olympic Plaza • Colorado Springs, CO 80935
E-Mail: usoc@businessoutsourcing.com
Website: www.usoc.org
Fax Ordering: (719) 579-9007
Catalog: Free. Frequency: Annual
Circulation: 250K. Sales: $3-5MM
Products: Sports clothing & gifts

OLD PUEBLO TRADERS   (800) 362-8400
Arizona Mail Order Company   (800) 362-8410
3740 E. 34th St. • Tucson, AZ 85713
E-Mail: customerservice@oldpueblotraders.com
Website: www.oldpueblotraders.com
Fax Ordering: (800) 964-1975; (520) 790-5648
International Ordering: (520) 745-4500
Contact Name: Steven Lightman, President
Catalog: Free. Frequency: 7x per year
Circulation: 2MM. Sales: $50-100MM
Products: Women's apparel, intimate wear,
shoes, jewelry & swimwear; fashion acessories

ON SITE'S GREAT WORKPLACE   (800) 800-4966
On Site Companies
11760 Justen Cir. • Maple Grove, MN 55369
Fax Ordering: (763) 493-4274
International Ordering: (763) 428-2666
Catalog: Free. Frequency: Quarterly
Circulation: 250K. Sales: $10-20MM
Products: Protective clothing for the workplacce

ONE HANES PLACE   (800) 300-2600
P.O. Box 748 • Rural Hall, NC 27098   (800) 671-1674
E-Mail: sales@ohpcatalog.com
Website: www.ohpcatalog.com
Fax Ordering: (800) 545-5613
International Ordering: (336) 744-1170
Customer Service: (800) 671-5056
Catalog: Free. Frequency: Semiannual
Circulation: 250M. Sales: $3-5MM
Products: Brand name undergarments,
lingerie & hosiery at discount prices

THE ORVIS COMPANY   (888) 235-9763
1711 Blue Hills Dr. • Roanoke, VA 24012
E-Mail: sales@orvis.com
Website: www.orvis.com
Fax Ordering: (540) 343-7053
International Ordering: (540) 345-4606
Catalog: Free. Frequency: Quarterly
Circulation: 200M. Sales: $10-20MM
Products: Men's & women's apparel;
outdoor clothing: hunting & fishing equipment
& accessories; gifts & home furnishings

PARADISE ON A HANGER   (800) 921-3050
4389 F Rd. • Crawford, CO 81415
E-Mail: sales@carolinaglove.com
Website: www.carolinaglove.com
Fax Ordering: (970) 921-3055
International Ordering: (970) 921-3050
Contact Name: Steve Duffy, President
Catalog: Free. Frequency: 5x per year
Circulation:150M. Sales: $1-3MM
Products: Hawaiian shirts & dresses;
aloha wear & related gifts for the whole
family

PATAGONIA CATALOG   (800) 336-9090
Patagonia, Inc.   (800) 638-6464
P.O. Box 32050 • Reno, NV 89523
E-Mail: sales@patagonia.com
Website: www.patagonia.com
Fax Ordering: (800) 543-5522; (775) 747-6159
International Ordering: (775) 747-1992
Contact Name: Yvon Chounard, President
Catalog: Free. Frequency: Bimonthly
Circulation: 500M. Sales: $100-250MM
Products: Outdoor apparel for men & women

PAUL FREDRICK MENSTYLE   (800) 247-1417
223 W. Poplar St. • Fleetwood, PA 19522
E-Mail: info@jeanparee.com
Website: www.jeanparee.com
Fax Ordering: (610) 944-6452
International Ordering: (610) 944-6120
Contact Name: Paul Sacher, President
Catalog: $1. Frequency: 6x per year
Circulation: 50M. Sales: $5-10MM
Products: Men's dress shirts &
accessories

PAUL STUART CATALOG   (866) 278-8278
Madison Ave. @ 45th St.
New York, NY 10017
E-Mail: paulstuart@paulstuart.com
Website: www.paulstuart.com
International Ordering: (212) 682-0320
Contact Name: Clifford Grodd, President
Catalog: Free. Frequency: Semiannual
Circulation: 150M. Sales: $20-50MM
Products: Men's & women's clothing
& accessories

J.C. PENNY CATALOGS   (800) 222-6161
P.O. Box 10001 • Dallas, TX 75301
E-Mail: orders@jcpenny.com
Website: www.jcpenny.com
Fax Ordering: (972) 591-9322
International Ordering: (972) 431-1000
Contact Name: James Osterreicher, President
Catalog: Free. Frequency: Annual to semiannual
Circulation: 50MM. Sales: $100-500MM
Products: Various catalogs; general merchandise

PERUVIAN CONNECTION   (800) 255-6429
RR 1 Box 990 • Tonganoxie, KS 66086
E-Mail: info@peruvianconnection.com
Website: www.peruvianconnection.com
Fax Ordering: (913) 845-2460
Contact Name: Annie Hurlbut, President
Catalog: $5. Frequency: 3x per year
Circulation: 3MM. Sales: $5-10MM
Products: Wigs for men & women

PLUS WOMAN CATALOG   (800) 628-5525
FSA • 85 Laurel Haven Rd.
Fairview, NC 28730
E-Mail: info@pluswoman.com
Website: www.pluwoman.com
Fax Ordering: (828) 628-2610
International Ordering: (828) 628-3562
Catalog: Free. Frequency: Semiannual
Circulation:100M. Sales: $1-3MM
Products: Large & supersized clothing
for women size 22 and up

QUEENSBORO SHIRT COMPANY   (800) 847-4478
1400 Marstellar St. • Wilmington, NC 28401
E-Mail: custserv@queensboro.com
Website: www.queensboro.com
Fax Ordering: (910) 251-7771
International Ordering: (910) 251-1251
Contact Name: Bob Cronin, Marketing
Catalog: Free. Frequency: Monthly
Circulation: 10M. Sales: $3-5MM
Products: Custom embroidery logos on polos,
woven shirts, sweatshirts, t-shirts & accessories

REPP BY MAIL BIG & TALL   (800) 690-7377
555 Turnpike St. • Canton, MA 02021
E-Mail: info@reppbigandtall.com
Website: www.reppbigandtall.com
Fax Ordering: (801) 261-2047
International Ordering: (801) 328-9756
Contact Name: Robby Yarbrough, President
Catalog: Free. Frequency: Monthly
Circulation: 150M. Sales: $5-10MM
Products: Men's big & tall size clothing

RITCHIESWIMWEAR   (800) 220-7946
15712 SW 41st St., #7 • Davie, FL 33331
E-Mail: ritchie@ritchieswimwear.com
Website: www.ritchieswimwear.com
Fax Ordering: (954) 659-8955 or 8954
International Ordering: (954) 659-8880
Customer Service: (954) 659-8570
Catalog: $5. Frequency: Quarterly
Circulation: 250M. Sales: $10-20MM
Products: Swimsuits & bikinis for women, kids & men

ROAMAN'S   (800) 436-0800
P.O. Box 4405 • Taunton, MA 02780
E-Mail: sales@roamans.com
Website: www.roamans.com
Fax Ordering: (800) 274-3102

Customer Service: (800) 274-7240
TDD Ordering: (800) 274-0260
Catalog: Free. Frequency: Monthly
Circulation: 250M. Sales: $5-10MM
Products: Women's clothing & accessories

ROCHESTER BIG & TALL CATALOG　　(800) 282-8200
700 Mission St. • San Francisco, CA 94103
Fax Ordering: (415) 227-0727
International Ordering: (415) 982-6455
Contact Name: Robert L. Sockolov, President
Catalog: Free. Frequency: 3x per year
Circulation: 500M. Sales: $3-5MM
Products: High end apparel for big & tall men

ROCKY MOUNTAIN CONNECTION　　(800) 679-3600
Fun Wear Brands
P.O. Box 2800 • Estes Park, CO 80517
E-Mail: info@rmconnection.com
Website: www.rmconnection.com
Fax Ordering: (800) 814-4900; (970) 586-3302
International Ordering: (970) 586-3361
Contact Name: E.J. Petrocine, President
Catalog: Free. Frequency: Quarterly
Circulation: 150K. Sales: $5-10MM
Products: Outdoor, rugged & technical
clothing & equipment

ROYAL ROBBINS COMPANY　　(800) 587-9044
1524 Princeton Ave. • Modesto, CA 95350
E-Mail: info@royalrobbins.com
Website: www.royalrobbins.com
Fax Ordering: (209) 522-5511
International Ordering: (209) 529-6913
Contact Name: Dan Costa, President
Catalog: Free. Frequency: Semiannual
Circulation: 50M. Sales: $10-20MM
Products: Rugged outdoor clothing for
men & women; hiking clothes

S&S UNIFORMS CORPORATION　　(800) 210-5295
200 William St. • Port Chester, NY 10573
E-Mail: info@sandhuniforms.com
Website: www.sandhuniforms.com
Fax Ordering: (914) 937-0741
Contact Name: Glen Ross, President
Catalog: Free. Frequency: 5x per year
Circulation: 50MM. Sales: $20-50MM
Products: Uniforms

SAKS FIFTH AVE. CATALOGS　　(800) 345-3454
750 Lakeshore Pkwy.
Birmingham, AL 35211
E-Mail: orders@saksfifthavenue.com
Website: www.saksfifthavenue.com
Fax Ordering: (865) 981-6325
International Ordering: (205) 940-4000
Contact Name: James Coggin, President
Catalog: Free. Frequency: 26x per year
Circulation: 10MM. Sales: $50-100MM
Products: Numerous catalogs: Upscale women's
apparel & home decor; men's apparel; salon;
shoes & accessories

DONNA SALYERS' FABULOUS~FURS　　(800) 848-4650
25 W. Robbins St. • Covington, KY 41011
E-Mail: custserv@fabulousfurs.com
Website: www.fabulousfurs.com
Fax Ordering: (859) 291-9687
Catalog: Free. Pages: 56. Frequency: Semiannual
Circulation: 100M. Sales: $5-10MM
Products: Luxurious alternative to animal fur

SCOTCH HOUSE SWEATERS　　(800) 700-8396
FROM SCOTLAND
Scotch House Scotish Imports, Ltd.
P.O. Box 1825 • Carmel, CA 93921
E-Mail: scotchhouse@aol.com
Fax Ordering: (831) 624-0595
International Ordering: (831) 624-0595
Contact Name: Gerald Blackstock, President
Catalog: $2.50. Frequency: Annual
Circulation: 10M. Sales: $500M
Products: Scotish cashmeres, woolens &
unique gifts from the British Isles; books

SCOTTISH LION IMPORT SHOP　　(800) 355-7268
P.o. Box 1700 • North Conway, NH 03860
E-Mail: info@scottishlion.com
Website: www.scottishlion.com
Fax Ordering: (603) 356-9032
International Ordering: (603) 356-6383
Contact Name: Judith Hurley, President
Catalog: Free. Frequency: Quarterly
Circulation:15M. Sales: $3-5MM
Products: Scottish imported clothing & gifts

SEARS SHOP AT HOME CATALOGS　　(800) 679-5656
333 Beverly Rd. • Hoffman Estates, IL 60179
E-Mail: info@sears.com
Website: www.sears.com
Fax Ordering: (800) 944-5045
Customer Relations: (800) 762-3048
Catalog: Free. Frequency: Varies
Circulation: 50MM. Sales: $100-500MM
Products: Clothing catalogs include: Woman's
View; Big & Tall; WorkWear; Smart Choice

SHEPLER'S CATALOG　　(800) 835-4004
6501 W. Kellogg • Wichita, KS 67209
E-Mail: info@sheplers.com
Website: www.sheplers.com
Fax Ordering: (316) 946-3632
International Ordering: (316) 946-3838
Contact Name: Louis Cohen, President
Catalog: Free. Frequency: Quarterly
Circulation:100M. Sales: $10-20MM
Products: Western wear

SHORT SIZES CATALOG　　(800) 272-9000
6051 Mayfield Rd. • Cleveland, OH 44124
E-Mail: ssi@shortsizeinc.com
Website: www.shortsizeinc.com
Fax Ordering: (440) 605-1065
International Ordering: (440) 605-1000
Contact Name: Robert Stern, President
Catalog: Free. Frequency: 4x per year
Circulation: 100M. Sales: $1-3MM
Products: Apparel for men under 5'8" tall

SIERRA TRADING POST　　(800) 713-4534
5025 Campstool Rd. • Cheyenne, WY 82007
E-Mail: customerservice@sierratradingpost.com
Website: www.sierratradingpost.com
Fax Ordering: (800) 378-8946
International Ordering: (440) 605-1000
Catalog: Free. Frequency: Quarterly
Circulation: 150M. Sales: $5-10MM
Products: Men & Women's apparel; outdoor
gear & outerwear; shoes & boots, home decor

SILHOUETTES CATALOG　　(800) 704-3322
Hanover Direct • Hanover, PA 17333
E-Mail: info@silhouettes.com

Website: www.silhouettes.com
Fax Ordering: (201) 392-5009
International Ordering: (201) 863-7300
Contact Name: Tom Shull, President
Catalog: Free. Pages: 60. Frequency: Quarterly
Circulation: 2MM. Sales: $100-500MM
Products: Fashion for large-size women

BEN SILVER COLLECTION   **(800) 221-4671**
Ben Silver Corporation
149 King St. • Charleston, SC 29401
E-Mail: bensilver@bensilver.com
Website: www.bensilver.com
Fax Ordering: (843) 723-1543
International Ordering: (843) 577-4556
Contact Name: Sue Prenner, President
Catalog: $5. Frequency: Annual
Circulation: 100M. Sales: $5-10MM
Products: Silk neckties, crested blazer
buttons, fine men's & women's furnishings

SIMPLY SOUTHWEST BY MAIL   **(800) 447-6177**
1501 12th St. NW
Albuquerque, NM 87104
E-Mail: info@simply-southwest.com
Website: www.simply-southwest.com
Fax Ordering: (505) 242-9188
International Ordering: (505) 242-7633
Contact Name: Robert Jackson, President
Catalog: Free. Frequency: 6x per year
Circulation: 5MM. Sales: $5-10MM
Products: Unique apparel, accessories,
furnishings, jewelry & gifts with a southwest flair

ALAN SLOANE & COMPANY   **(800) 252-6266**
80 Kean St. • West Babylon, NY 11704
Fax Ordering: (631) 643-1015
International Ordering: (631) 643-2260
Contact Name: Alan Sloane, Chairman
Catalog: Free. Frequency: Annual
Circulation: 100M. Sales: $500M to $1MM
Products: Men's & women's clothing accessories

SMART SAVER CATALOG   **(800) 772-8371**
210 S. 5th St. • St. Charles, IL 60174
Fax Ordering: (630) 584-2406
International Ordering: (630) 584-0600
Contact Name: Stan & Diane Grushkin, Owners
Catalog: Free. Frequency: 8x per year
Circulation: 250M. Sales: $1-3MM
Products: Traditional intimate apparel

SOFT SURROUNDINGS   **(800) 749-7638**
8920 Pershall Rd. • Hazelwood, MO 63042
E-Mail: info@softsurroundings.com
Website: www.softsurroundings.com
Fax Ordering: (314) 521-5780
International Ordering: (314) 262-4949
Customer Service: (800) 240-7076; (888) 414-7638
Catalog: Free. Pages: 88. Frequency: Quarterly
Circulation: 150M. Sales: $5-10MM
Products: Women's fashions, accessories,
makeup, home furnishings, bed & bath, etc.

SOLAR TAN THRU SWIM SUITS   **(800) TAN-0440**
Lifestyles Direct, Inc.
P.O. Box 152929 • Tampa, FL 33684
E-Mail: info@lifestylesdirect.com
Website: www.lifestylesdirect.com
Fax Ordering: (813) 882-4321
International Ordering: (813) 882-4320

Catalog: Free. Pages: 54. Frequency: Annual
Circulation: 500M. Sales: $1-3MM
Products: Shear swimwear, opaque to the
human eye, will tan through

SOUTHWEST INDIAN FOUNDATION   **(505) 863-4037**
P.O. Box 86 • Gallup, NM 87302
E-Mail: info@southwestindian.com
Website: www.southwestindian.com
Fax Ordering: (505) 863-2760
Customer Service: (877) 788-9962
Contact: Bill McCarthy, Executive Director
Catalog: Free. Pages: 100. Frequency: Semiannual
Circulation: 25M. Sales: $500M
Products: Indian fashions & accessories, and
jewelry, hand-made by Indians of the Southwest

SPECTOR'S HAIRGOODS FOR MEN   **(412) 673-3259**
SPECTOR'S WIGS FOR WOMEN
Beauty by Spector
1 Spector Pl. • McKeesport, PA 15134
Fax Ordering: (412) 678-3978
Contact Name: Myer Spector, President
Catalog: Free. Frequency: Annual
Circulation: 100M. Sales: $1-3MM
Products: Hairpieces and toupees for
men and wigs for women

SPORTHILL CATALOG   **(800) 622-8444**
725 McKinley St. • Eugene, OR 97402
E-Mail: info@sporthill.com
Website: www.sporthill.com
Fax Ordering: (541) 343-7261
International Ordering: (541) 345-9623
Catalog: Free. Frequency: Annual
Circulation: 100M. Sales: $5-10MM
Products: Running, skiing & adventure apparel

SPORTIF USA   **(800) 921-1655**
Aventura Clothing & Waterfronts Clothing   **(888) 260-7676**
1415 Greg St., Suite 101 • Sparks, NV 89431
E-Mail: customerservice@sportif.com
Website: www.sportif.com
Fax Ordering: (800) 776-3291; (775) 353-3400
International Ordering: (775-359-6400)
Catalog: Free. Frequency: Quarterly
Circulation: 100M. Sales: $5-10MM
Products: Sports & outdoor clothing

SPORTS SECTION CATALOG   **(800) 625-3200**
9300 Corbin Ave. • Northridge, CA 91324
E-Mail: support@sportssection.com
Website: www.sportssection.com
Fax Ordering: (818) 998-7100
International Ordering: (818) 998-6200
Contact Name: Arri Gubner, President
Catalog: Free. Frequency: Quarterly
Circulation: 1MM. Sales: $5-10MM
Products: Sports apparel

STAFFORD'S CATALOG   **(800) 826-0948**
P.O. Box 2055 • Thomasville, GA 31799
Website: www.stafford-catalog.com
E-Mail: staffcat@rose.net
Fax Ordering: (229) 226-1287
International Ordering: (229) 226-4306
Contact Name: G. Walter Stafford, President
Catalog: Free. Frequency: Annual
Circulation: 100M. Sales: $1-3MM
Products: Outdoor apparel, hunting clothes;
gifts, luggage & accessories

SUNUP SUNDOWN CATALOG   (800) 926-8081
P.O. Box 11899 • Fort Lauderdale, FL 33339
Fax Ordering: (954) 564-1515
International Ordering: (954) 238-3289
Contact Name: Thomas Farley, President
Catalog: $3.50. Frequency: Quarterly
Circulation: 500M. Sales: $500M to $1MM
Products: Men's & women's exotic swimwear &
other beachwear including wrap skirts & dresses

TAFFORD MANUFACTURING CATALOG   (800) 283-0065
P.O. Box 1001 • Montgomeryville, PA 18936
Fax Ordering: (215) 643-4922
International Ordering: (215) 643-9666
Contact Name: Jennifer Olson, Marketing
Catalog: Free. Frequency: Quarterly
Circulation: 100M. Sales: $5-10MM
Products: Uniforms, shoes & acessories
for medical professionals

TALBOTS CATALOG   (800) 825-2687
One Talbot's Dr. • Hingham, MA 02043
E-Mail: sales@talbots.com
Website: www.talbots.com
Fax Ordering: (781) 741-4369
International Ordering: (781) 749-7600
Contact Name: Arnold Zetcher, President
Catalog: Free. Frequency: 26x per year
Circulation: 60MM. Sales: $50-100MM
Products: Women's, missy kids, petites,
intimates & accessories

TALL CLASSICS CATALOG   (866) 825-5382
Tall Etc.
468 E. Colorado Blvd.
Pasadena, CA 91101
E-Mail: catalog@talletc.com
Website: www.tallclassics.com
Fax Ordering: (626) 431-2819
Contact Name: DeAnn Warner, President
Catalog: Free. Frequency: Semiannual
Circulation:400M. Sales: $1-3MM
Products: Clothing for women over 5'10" tall,
proportioned to fit the taller woman

TEAM ADVANTAGE CATALOG   (800) 336-8326
6150 Nancy Ridge Dr.
San Diego, CA 92121
Fax Ordering: (800) 832-6619
International Ordering: (858) 455-0558
Contact Name: Philip Zimmerman, President
Catalog: Free. Frequency: Quarterly
Circulation: 100M. Sales: $1-3MM
Products: Team suits & imprinted athletic wear

THE TERRITORY AHEAD   (800) 882-4323
419 State St. • Santa Barbara, CA 93101
E-Mail: info@territoryahead.com
Website: www.territoryahead.com
Fax Ordering: (800) 232-9882
International Ordering: (805) 962-5558
Contact Name: Bruce Willard, President
Catalog: Free. Pages: 76. Frequency: Monthly
Circulation:2MM. Sales: $20-50MM
Products: Outdoor clothing & accessories
for men & women

TERRY PRECISION CYCLING   (800) 289-8379
1657 E. Park Rd. • Macedon, NY 14502
E-Mail: talktours@terrybicycles.com
Website: www.terrybicycles.com
Fax Ordering: (315) 986-2104

International Ordering: (315) 986-2103
Contact Name: Gregory Terry, President
Catalog: Free. Frequency: 10x per year
Circulation: 1.5MM. Sales: $5-10MM
Products: Bicycling apparel & accessories

THAI SILKS CATALOG   (800) 722-7455
252 State St. • Los Altos, CA 94022   In CA(800) 221-7455
E-Mail: silks@thaisilks.com
Website: www.thaisilks.com
Fax Ordering: (650) 948-3426
International Ordering: (650) 948-8611
Catalog: Free. Frequency: Quarterly
Circulation: 60M. Sales: $3-5MM
Products: Exotic silks & lingerie

THOMAS BROTHERS CO   (888) 889-7200
1717 N. Beckley Ave. • Dallas, TX 75203
E-Mail: info@thomasbrothersco.com
Website: www.desantiscollection.com
Fax Ordering: (888) 388-7321
Catalog: Free. Frequency: Quarterly
Circulation: 150K. Sales: $25-50MM
Products: Men's & women's apparel &
accessories

NORM THOMPSON CATALOG   (800) 547-1160
P.O. Box 3999 • Portland, OR 97208
E-Mail: webrep@normthompson.com
Website: www.normthompson.com
Fax Ordering: (800) 821-1282; (503) 614-4599
International Ordering: (503) 614-4600
Customer Service: (800) 821-1287
Contact Name: Becky Jewett, President
Catalog: Free. Pages: 84. Frequency: Monthly
Circulation: 25MM. Sales: $100-500MM
Products: Clothing for men & women;
footwear, travel, gifts & home; food & floral

THOUSAND MILE   (800) 786-7577
2002 S. Coast Hwy. • Oceanside, CA 92054
E-Mail: info@thousandmile.com
Website: www.thousandmile.com
Fax Ordering: (760) 721-4340
International Ordering: (760) 721-4343
Contact Name: Jennifer Miller, President
Catalog: Free. Frequency: 6x per year
Circulation: 5M. Sales: $500M
Products: Sports apparel, outdoor clothing,
active wear & accessories for men & women

TILLEY ENDURABLES   (800) 363-8737
300 Langner Rd. • West Seneca, NY 14224
E-Mail: info@thousandmile.com
Website: www.thousandmile.com
Fax Ordering: (760) 721-4340
International Ordering: (760) 721-4343
Contact Name: Stephanie Kubiszyn, President
Catalog: Free. Frequency: Annual
Circulation: 200M. Sales: $500M
Products: Travel & adventure clothing

TITLE NINE SPORTS   (800) 609-0092
6201 Doyle St. • Emeryville, CA 94608
E-Mail: info@title9sports.com
Website: www.title9sports.com
Fax Ordering: (510) 655-9191
Customer Service: (800) 342-4448
Catalog: Free. Frequency: Semiannual
Circulation: 10MM. Sales: $10-20MM
Products: Sportswear and workout fashions
& accessories for women

THE TOG SHOP (800) 342-6789
30 Tozer Rd. • Beverly, MA 01915
E-Mail: info@togshop.com
Website: www.togshop.com
Fax Ordering: (800) 755-7557
Customer Service: (800) 262-8888
Contact Name: Carl Tott, President
Catalog: Free. Frequency: 6x per year
Circulation: 10MM. Sales: $20-50MM
Products: Clothing, shoes & accessories
for women

TOMORROW'S WORLD (800) 229-7571
9665 1st View St. • Norfolk, VA 23503
E-Mail: comments@tomorrowsworld.com
Website: www.tomorrowsworld.com
Fax Ordering: (757) 480-3148
International Ordering: (757) 480-8500
Contact Name: Cheryl Hahn, President
Catalog: $2. Frequency: Monthly
Circulation:250M. Sales: $5-10MM
Products: Natural fashions, organic cotton,
hemp, wool & flax

TRAVELSMITH (800) 950-1600
60 Leveroni Court • Novato, CA 94949
E-Mail: info@travelsmith.com
Website: www.travelsmith.com
Fax Ordering: (800) 950-1656
International Ordering: (415) 884-1350
   Fax (415) 884-1351
Catalog: Free. Frequency: Quarterly
Circulation: 250M. Sales: $3-5MM
Products: Travel clothing and accessories
for both men & women

TUTTLE GOLF COLLECTION (800) 882-7511
P.O. Box 888 • Wallingford, CT 06492
E-Mail: info@tuttlegolf.com
Website: www.tuttlegolf.com
Fax Ordering: (203) 949-4288
International Ordering: (203) 949-4290
Catalog: Free. Frequency: 5x per year
Circulation: 150M. Sales: $3-5MM
Products: Sportswear for men & women

TUXEDOS CATALOG (800) 289-2889
Chilbert & Company
101 4th Ave. • Coraopolis, PA 15108
E-Mail: info@chilbert.com
Website: www.chilbert.com
Fax Ordering: (316) 946-3632
International Ordering: (316) 946-3838
Contact Name: Guy Tucci, President
Catalog: Free. Frequency: Annual
Circulation: 50M. Sales: $1-3MM
Products: Tuxedos & accessories

TWC - THE WIG COMPANY (800) 456-1788
P.O. Box 12950 • Pittsburgh, PA 15241
E-Mail: custserv@twcwigs.com
Website: www.twcwigs.com
Fax Ordering: (412) 257-8181
International Ordering: (412) 221-4790
Contact Name: Vince DeCarlucci, President
Catalog: Free. Frequency: 24x per year
Circulation: 300M. Sales: $10-20MM
Products: Ladies wigs and hairpieces
of synthetic hair fiber

TWO POTATO CATALOG (800) 358-2828
14331 Chambers Rd. • Tustin, CA 92780
E-Mail: twopotato@worldnet.att.net
Fax Ordering: (714) 544-4916
International Ordering: (714) 544-9360
Catalog: Free. Frequency: Semiannual
Circulation: 250M. Sales: $3-5MM
Products: Women's clothing in cottons
& rayons, size XS to 3X

UA SCRUBS (UNIFORM ADVANTAGE) (888) 433-5522
3350 Enterprise Ave. #180 • Weston, FL 33331 (800) 283-8708
E-Mail: info@uascrubs.com
Website: www.uniformadvantage.com
Fax Ordering: (954) 626-2112
Catalog: Free. Pages: 64.
Frequency: Quarterly
Circulation: 500M. Sales: $5-10MM
Products: Medical scrubs, nursing uniforms,
and nurses shoes

UBER CATALOG (507) 451-1990
Uber Tanning & Uber Glove Co.
308 Adams Ave. • Owatonna, MN 55060
E-Mail: nvutdc@deskmedia.com
Website: www.uberglove.com
Fax Ordering: (507) 444-0727
Contact Name: Harry A. Uber, President
Catalog: Free. Pages: 22.
Frequency: Quarterly
Circulation: 50M. Sales: $500M
Products: Deerskin clothing & accessories

UJENA SWIMWEAR (800) 227-8318
101 1st St. • Los Altos, CA 94022
E-Mail: ujena.bob@cwixmail.com
Website: www.ujena.com
Fax Ordering: (650) 948-3653
International Ordering: (650) 917-6945
Contact Name: Bob Anderson, President
Catalog: $3. Frequency: Quarterly
Circulation: 200M. Sales: $5-10MM
Products: Swimwear

UNDER THE CANOPY (888) 226-6799
12926 Hyland Cr. • Boca Raton, FL 33428
E-Mail: info@underthecanopy.com
Website: www.underthecanopy.com
Fax Ordering: (561) 487-3266
Contact Name: Marci Zaroff, President
Catalog: Free. Frequency:
Circulation: 100M Sales: $500M
Product: EcoFashions for women, men &
children, as well as natural bed & bath ware,
giftware, footwear & accessories; all made
from natural and recycled fabrics, including
organic cotton/wool/silk/linen, hemp, tencel,
eco-fleece, and low impact dyes.

UNDERGEAR CATALOG (800) 853-8555
Hanover Direct • Hanover, PA 17333
E-Mail: service@undergear.com
Website: www.undergear.com
Fax Ordering: (800) 757-9997; (717) 633-3214
International Ordering: (717) 633-3413
Contact Name: Tom Shull, President
Catalog: Free. Frequency: Quarterly
Circulation: 1MM. Sales: $10-50MM
Products: Men's activewear, workout wear
& fashion underwear

UA SCRUBS UNIFORM ADVANTAGE　　　(888) 433-5522
3350 Enterprise Ave. #180
Weston, FL 33331
E-Mail: info@uascrubs.com
Website: www.uascrubs.com
Fax Ordering: (954) 626-2112
Catalog: Free. Frequency: Semiannual
Circulation: 150M. Sales: $10-20MM
Products: Medical scrubs, shoes & accessories

VENUS SWIMWEAR　　　(800) 366-7946
11711 Marco Beach Dr.
Jacksonville, FL 32224
E-Mail: info@venusswimwear.com
Website: www.venusswimwear.com
Fax Ordering: (904) 641-0977
International Ordering: (904) 645-6000
Contact Name: Daryle Scott, President
Catalog: $5. Frequency: 3x per year
Circulation: 1MM. Sales: $20-50MM
Products: Swimwear

VETERINARY APPAREL COMPANY　　　(800) 922-1456
847 Main St. • Battle Creek, MI 49015
E-Mail: info@veterinaryapparel.com
Website: www.veterinaryapparel.com
Fax Ordering: (616) 963-0341
Catalog: Free. Frequency: Annual
Circulation: 250M. Sales: $10-20MM
Products: Clothing for veterinarians

VICTORIA'S SECRET DIRECT　　　(800) 888-8200
P.O. Box 16589 • Columbus, OH 43216
E-Mail: info@victoriassecret.com
Website: www.victoriassecret.com
Fax Ordering: (614) 337-5555
Customer Service: (800) 411-5116
Catalog: Free. Frequency: Annual
Circulation: 10MM. Sales: $50-100MM
Products: Lingerie, pajamas, clothing,
accessories, footwear & beauty products

WASSERMAN UNIFORMS　　　(800) 8848-3576
1160 W. Broad St. • Columbus, OH 43222
E-Mail: wasuniform@aol.com
Website: www.wassermanuniform.com
Fax Ordering: (614) 279-8888
International Ordering: (614) 279-7000
Contact Name: Harvey Wasserman, President
Catalog: Free. Frequency: Annual
Circulation: 100M. Sales: $3-5MM
Products: Uniforms

WATERFRONTS CLOTHING　　　(800) 260-7676
c/o Sportif USA
1415 Greg St., Suite 101 • Sparks, NV 89431
E-Mail: customerservice@waterfrontsclothing.com
Website: www.waterfrontsclothing.com
Fax Ordering: (800) 776-3291; (775) 353-3400
International Ordering: (775-359-6400
Catalog: Free. Frequency: Quarterly
Circulation: 100M. Sales: $5-10MM
Products: Sports & outdoor clothing

WEARGUARD CORPORATION　　　(800) 388-3300
141 Longwater Dr. • Norwell, MA 02061　　(800) 870-6539
E-Mail: info@wearguard.com
Website: www.wearguard.com
Fax Ordering: (800) 436-3132; (781) 871-6239
International Ordering: (781) 871-4100
Contact Name: George MacNaughton, President
Catalog: Free. Pages: 68. Frequency: Monthly

Circulation: 35MM. Sales: $100-500MM
Products: Work clothes, uniforms & accessories

WESTPRO CATALOG　　　(800) 533-3885
2294 Mountain Vista Ln.
Provo, UT 84066
E-Mail: info@westpro.net
Website: www.westpro.net
Fax Ordering: (801) 373-8778
International Ordering: (801) 373-2525
Contact Name: Steve Clement, President
Catalog: Free. Frequency: 4x per year
Circulation: 100M. Sales: $1-3MM
Products: Custom sportswear, embroidered
& screen printed clothing & blank hats

WIG AMERICA CO.　　　(800) 338-7600
270 Oyster Point Blvd.
So. San Francisco, CA 94080
E-Mail: sales@wigamerica.com
Website: www.wigamerica.com
Fax Ordering: (650) 266-6860
International Ordering: (650) 266-6862
Customer Service: (800) 268-7210
Contact Name: Donald Lee, Marketing
Catalog: Free. Frequency: Annual
Circulation: 5M. Sales: $1-3MM
Products: Wigs & hairpieces

WILD WOMEN ENTERPRISES　　　(401) 949-0049
2 Douglas Pike • Smithfield, RI 02917
E-Mail: women@wildwomen-ent.com
Website: www.wildwomen-ent.com
Contact Name: Linda Hogan, President
Catalog: Free. Frequency: Annual
Circulation: 50M. Sales: $500M
Products: Feminist women's apparel;
music & books

WILLOW RIDGE CATALOG　　　(800) 388-8555
421 Landmark Dr. • Wilmington, NC 28410
E-Mail: info@willowridgecatalog.com
Website: www.willowridgecatalog.com
Fax Ordering: (520) 790-1332
Contact Name: Steven Lightman, President
Catalog: Free. Frequency: 5x per year
Circulation: 1MM. Sales: $10-20MM
Products: Women's apparel

WINDSOR COLLECTIONS CATALOG　　　(877) 268-9594
Amerimark Direct
6864 Engle Rd. • Cleveland, OH 44130
E-Mail: info@amerimark.com
Website: www.amerimark.com
Fax Ordering: (440) 826-1267
International Ordering: (440) 826-1900
Contact Name: Gary Giesler, President
Catalog: Free. Frequency: Quarterly
Circulation: 25MM. Sales: $20-50MM
Products: High styled fashions for the
mature woman

WINTER SILKS CATALOG　　　(800) 648-7455
White Pine Company
11711 Marco Beach Dr.
Jacksonville, FL 32224
E-Mail: mailbox@wintersilks.com
Website: www.wintersilks.com
Fax Ordering: (800) 648-0411
International Ordering: (608) 280-9000
Contact Name: Chris Vig, President
Catalog: Free. Frequency: Monthly

CLOTHING & ACCESSORIES

Circulation: 24MM. Sales: $5-10MM
Products: Silk ready-to-wear apparel, intimate wear

WOMENSWEAR   (800) 458-2000
Blair Corporation
220 Hickory St. • Warren, PA 16366
E-Mail: blair@blair.com
Website: www.blair.com
Fax Ordering: (814) 726-6208
International Ordering: (814) 723-3600
Contact Name: John E. Zawacki, President
Catalog: Free. Frequency: 9x per year
Circulation: 10MM. Sales: $100-500MM
Products: A full range of women's apparel, including lingerie, footwear & accessories

WORKERS CHOICE CATALOG   (800) 342-5437
Dickies • P.O. Box 2507
Fort Worth, TX 76113
E-Mail: sales@dickies.com
Website: www.dickies.com
Fax Ordering: (800) 336-8643
International Ordering: (817) 336-7201
Catalog: Free. Frequency: Quarterly
Circulation: 150K. Sales: $1-3MM
Products: Authentic American workwear professional quality dickies

WORLD WIDE AQUATICS   (800) 726-1530
10500 University Center Dr.
Tampa, FL 33612
Fax Ordering: (813) 972-0905
International Ordering: (813) 972-0818
Contact Name: Mark Levine, President
Catalog: Free. Frequency: Bimonthly
Circulation: 250M. Sales: $5-10MM
Products: Swimwear & accessories

WORTH & WORTH CATALOG   (800) 428-7467
101 W. 55th St. • New York, NY 10019
E-Mail: info@hotshop.com
Website: www.hatshop.com
Fax Ordering: (212) 867-5693
International Ordering: (212) 265-2887
Contact Name: Harold Rosenholtz, President
Catalog: Free. Frequency: Annual
Circulation: 50K. Sales: $500K
Products: Fine hats, caps & assorted accessories

YALE SPORTSWEAR CATALOG   (800) 922-9253
1500 Industrial Park Rd.
Frederecksburg, MD 21632
E-Mail: info@yalesports.com
Website: www.yalesports.com
Fax Ordering: (410) 754-5555
International Ordering: (410) 754-5500
Contact Name: Charlie Nemphos, President
Catalog: $5. Frequency: Annual
Circulation: 50K. Sales: $5-10MM
Products: Sportswear

PAULA YOUNG CATALOG   (800) 343-9695
Specialty Catalog Corp.
P.O. Box 483 • Brockton, MA 02375
E-Mail: custserv@scdirect.com
Website: www.paulayoung.com
Fax Ordering: (508) 238-1965
International Ordering: (508) 238-0199
Customer Service: (800) 472-4017
Contact Name: Stephen O'Hara, President
Catalog: Free. Frequency: Monthly
Circulation: 5MM. Sales: $20-50MM
Products: Wigs & wig accessories

ZEN HOME STITCHERY   (949) 631-5389
120 E. 18th St.
Costa Mesa, CA 92627
E-Mail: zhs@ix.netcom.com
Fax Ordering: (949) 631-8891
Contact Name: Carol L. Mudd, President
Catalog: Free. Frequency: Annual
Circulation: 10K. Sales: $500K
Products: Custom-made meditation clothing & accessories

ABACUS   (800) 451-4319
5130 Patterson SE • Grand Rapids, MI 49512
E-Mail: sales@abacuspub.com
Website: www.abacuspub.com
Fax Ordering: (616) 698-0325
Customer Service: (616) 698-0330
Contact Names: Arnie Lee, President
Catalog: Free. Frequency: Semiannual
Products: Computer books & software

ACADEMIC SUPERSTORE   (800) 817-2347
2101 E. St. Elmo Rd. #360 • Austin, TX 78744
E-Mail: contact@academicsuperstore.com
Website: www.academicsuperstore.com
Fax Ordering: (866) 947-4525
International Ordering: (512) 450-1199
Catalog: Free. Frequency: Semiannual.
Circulation: 20 0K. Sales: $10-20MM
Products: Academic software for students,
teachers & schools

ACCU-TIME SYSTEMS   (800) 355-4648
420 Somers Rd. • Ellington, CT 06029
E-Mail: sales@accu-tme.com
Website: www.accu-time.com
Fax Ordering: (860) 872-1511
International Ordering: (860) 870-5000
Contact Names: Chris Broders, President
Catalog: Online. Sales: $10-20MM
Products: Time and data collection terminals

ACMA COMPUTERS   (800) 786-6888
1505 Reliance Way • Fremont, CA 94539   (800) 578-1888
E-Mail: sales@acma.com
Website: www.acma.com
Fax Ordering: (510) 257-6801
International Orders: (510) 257-6800
Customer Service: (800) 786-8998
Contact Names: Allen Lee, President
Products: High performance storage &
server solutions; computers, computer
accessories, software

THE ACP COMPUTER HOTLINE   (800) 366-3227
Advanced Computer Products, Inc.
3621 W. Warner Ave. • Santa Ana, CA 92704
Fax Ordering: (714) 558-9423
Customer Service: (714) 558-8822
Contact Names: David Freeman, President
Catalog: Free. Frequency: Annual
Circulation: 100K. Sales: $5-10MM
Products: A full line of brand name computers,
laptops, diskettes, hard & floppy disk drives,
motherboards, add-on cards, keyboards,
monitors, modems, power devices, cables,
cartridges, components, printers, scanners,
templates, other accessories and supplies.

ACTION INSTRUMENTS COMPANY   (703) 443-0000
Eurotherm Controls, Inc.
741-F Miller Dr. • Leesburg, VA 20175
E-Mail: actionsales@eurotherm.com
Website: www.actionio.com
Fax Ordering: (703) 669-1300
Catalog: Free. Sales: $20-50MM
Products: Industrial micro computers,
software, peripherals and accessories

ADDONICS TECHNOLOGIES   (408) 573-8580
1918 Junction Ave. • San Jose, CA 95131
E-Mail: sales@addonics.com
Website: www.addonics.com

Fax Ordering: (408) 573-8588
General Information: (408) 573-8580
Technical Support: (408) 453-6212
Contact Name: May Lee, President
Catalog: Free. Sales: $1-3MM
Products: Hard drives; flash memory;
host controller / adapter; optical storage;
IO converter; accessories

ADOBE SYSTEMS   (800) 833-6687
345 Park Ave. • San Jose, CA 95110
E-Mail: sales@adobe.com
Website: www.adobe.com
Fax Ordering: (408) 537-6000
International Orders: (408) 536-6000
Catalog: Free. Frequency: Semiannual
Credit cards: All. Sales: $50-100MM
Products: Software for desktop publishing
& graphic design - PageMaker Plug-Ins;
Adobe Flash Player; Photoshop Plugins;
Acrobat Plug-Ins; Adobe Reader; Adobe
Fetch Plug-Ins; Adobe Illustrator Plug-Ins;
Tools & Utilities; Images.

ADTRAN NETWORKING PRODUCTS   (800) 923-8726
Alliance Datacom   (888) 872-5619
10455 Markison Rd. • Dallas, TX 75238
E-Mail: info@adtran.com
Website: www.adtran.com
Fax Ordering: (214) 341-3811
Customer Service: (214) 550-6201
Catalog: Free. Frequency: Annual.
Circulation: 50K. Sales: $10-20MM
Product: Transmission networking products

AESP, INC. NETWORKING CATALOG   (800) 446-2377
16295 NW 13th Ave., Suite A
Miami, FL 33169
E-Mail: sales@aesp.com
Website: www.aesp.com
Fax Ordering: (305) 949-4483
International Ordering: (305) 944-7710
Contact Names: Slav Stein, President & CEO
Catalog: Free. Frequency: Semiannual.
Circulation: 75K. Sales: $5-10MM
Products: Advanced electronics support products;
computer networks & network products

AGIO DESIGNS, INC.   (800) 688-2446
21195 NW Evergreen Pkwy.
Hillsboro, OR 97123
E-Mail: info@agiodesigns.com
Website: www.agiodesigns.com
Fax Ordering: (503) 629-8545
Customer Service: (503) 242-1342
Contact Name: Bert Good, President
Catalog: Free. Frequency: Semiannual.
Circulation: 50K. Sales: $10-20MM
Products: Macintosh furniture and accessories.

ALLDATA, LLC   (800) 697-2533
9412 Big Horn Blvd. • Elk Grove, CA 95758   (800) 684-1250
E-Mail: sales@alldata.com
Website: www.alldata.com
Fax Ordering: (916) 684- 5225
Customer Service: (800) 859-3282
General Information: (916) 684-5200
Contact Names: Brett Easley, President
Catalog: Free. Frequency: Semiannual.
Circulation: 25K. Sales: $10-20MM
Products: Automotive professionals'
software and online services.

ALTEX ELECTRONICS   (800) 531-5369
11342 IH 35 N • San Antonio, TX 78233
E-Mail: sales@altex.com
Website: www.altex.com
Fax Ordering: (210) 637-3264
Customer Service: (210) 655-8882
Catalog: Free. Frequency: Semiannual
Circulation: 50K. Sales: $5-10MM
Products: Computer hardware, software,
accessories & supplies

AMERICAL MICRO PRODUCTS, INC.   (800) 288-8025
7750 Gloria Ave. • Van Nuys, CA 91406
E-Mail: amp.support@vend4less.com
Website: www.americal.com
Fax Orders: (818) 994-6900
International Orders: (818) 909-4900
Contact Name: Fred Chadorchi, President
Catalog: Free. Frequency: Annual
Circulation: 100K. Sales: $5-10MM
Products: Wholesale PC supplies, including
diskettes, data cartridges & tape, storage
systems, printer ribbons, modems, and mice.

AMERICAN CHEMICAL SOCIETY SOFTWARE (800) 227-5558
1155 16th St., NW • Washington, DC 20036
E-Mail: help@acs.com
Website: www.acs.com
Fax Ordering: (202) 872-4615
International Ordering: (202) 872-4600 Fax 872-4615
Contact Name: William Fuccolosky, Contact
Catalog: Free. Frequency: Annual
Circulation: 50K. Sales: $1-5MM
Products: Scientific software for PC and
Mac computers

AMERICAN COMPUTER SUPPLY   (800) 527-0832
Great North American
2828 Forest Lane, #2071
Dallas, TX 75234-7517
E-mail: cpinto@gnamerican.com
Fax Ordering: (972) 481-6214
International Ordering: (972) 241-3388
Customer Service: (972) 481-6100
Contact Names: Joseph J. Salatino, President
Catalog: Free. Frequency: Semiannual
Circulation: 200K. Sales: $10-20MM
Products: Computer supplies & accessories.
Data communications products: modems, cables,
switches, connectors; laser printer supplies;
ribbons and accessories; paper supplies and
accessories; printer accessories; diskettes and
accessories; magnetic tape and accessories;
PC accessories; power conditioning and protection;
PC workstations and furniture; and software.

AMERICAN MICROSYSTEMS   (800) 648-4452
2190 Regal Parkway • Euless, TX 76040
E-Mail: sales@barcodepower.com
Website: www.barcodepower.com
Fax Ordering: (817) 571-6176
International Ordering: (817) 571-9015
Technical Support: (877) 842-3990
Catalog: Free. Frequency: Annual
Circulation: 200K. Sales: $10-50MM
Products: Barcode scanners, readers
& laser scanners

AMERICAN POWER CONVERSION   (800) 800-4272
132 Fairgrounds Rd. • W. Kingston, RI 02892   (877) 272-2722
E-Mail: sales@apcc.com
Website: www.apcc.com

Fax Ordering: (401) 789-3710
Customer Service: (401) 789-5735
Technical Support: (800) 555-2725
Contact Name: Rodger Dowdell, Jr., President
Catalog: Free. Frequency: Annual
Circulation: 100K. Sales: $5-10MM
Products: Power protection products;
power sources, network shutdown software
and interface kits

ANDERSON INVESTORS' SOFTWARE   (800) 286-4106
130 S. Bemiston Ave. #101
Clayton, MO 63105
E-Mail: sales@investorsoftware.com
Website: www.investorsoftware.com
Fax Ordering: (314) 918-0980
International Ordering: (314) 918-0990
Contact Name: Chris Anderson, President
Circulation: 150K. Sales: $3-5MM
Products: Financial Software to simplify
investors' finances and teach investors
about the market; real estate software

ANTHROEAR   (800) 325-3841
Anthro Corporation
10450 SW Manhasset Dr.
Tualatin, OR 97062
E-Mail: anthroear@anthro.com
Website: www.anthro.com
Fax Ordering: (800) 325-0045
International Ordering: (503) 691-2556
Contact Name: Shoaib Tareen, President
Catalog: Free. Frequency: Semiannual
Circulation: 100K. Sales: $3-5MM
Products: Technology furniture and computer
workstations

APS TECHNOLOGIES   (800) 374-5688
22985 NW Evergreen Pkwy.
Hillsboro, OR 97124
E-Mail: sales@lacie.com
Website: www.lacie.com
Fax Ordering: (503) 844-4508
Customer Service: (503) 844-4500
Catalog: Free. Frequency: Annual
Circulation: 50K. Sales: $25-50MM
Products: Systems, drives, & accessories

AREY JONES-EDUCATIONAL SOLUTIONS   (800) 998-9199
8693-A La Mesa Blvd. • La Mesa, CA 91941
E-Mail: marketing@areyjones.com
Website: www.areyjones.com
Fax Ordering: (800) 403-8828
Catalog: Free. Frequency: Annual
Products: Computer hardware, educational
software, network integration services

ARROW ELECTRONICS   (800) 833-3557
50 Marcus Dr. • Melville, NY 11747
E-Mail: sales@arrow.com
Website: www.arrow.com
Fax Ordering: (631) 851-2468
International Ordering: (631) 847-2000
Customer Service: (877) 237-8621
Catalog: Free. Frequency: Semiannual.
Circulation: 200K. Sales: $25-50MM
Products: AT&T, Altos, Intel, NCR & Wyse
computer systems; Acer & Texas Instruments
laptop systems; AT&T and Intel/Banyan local
area networks; drives & controllers; computer
enhancements; terminals, monitors, printers,
modems; cables & media.

ARTWORX SOFTWARE CO., INC. (800) 828-6573
6017 Pine Ridge Rd. #280 • Naples, FL 34119
E-Mail: orders@artworx.com
Website: www.artworx.com
Fax Ordering: (239) 455-5178
Technical Support: (239) 455-2348
Contact Name: Arthur Walsh, President
Catalog: Free. Frequency: 3x/year
Products: Entertainment/educational software,
accessories. For IBM compaitbles.

ATTACHMATE CORPORATION (800) 426-6283
1500 Dexter Ave. N. • Seattle, WA 98109 (800) 872-2829
E-Mail: salesrecept@attachmate.com
Website: www.attachmate.com
Fax Ordering: (206) 217-7515
International Ordering: (206) 217-7100
Contact Name: Joy Miller, Contact
Products: PC-mainframe connectivity
hardware (adapters & cables) & software
(for Windows, DOS, Graphics).

B&R INDUSTRIAL AUTOMATION CORP. (800) 752-2637
1250 Northmeadow Pkwy. S-130
Roswell, GA 30076-3861
E-Mail: office@br-automation.com
Website: www.br-automation.com
Fax Ordering: (770) 772-0243
Customer Service: (770) 772-0400
Contact Names: Marc Ostertag, President
Circulation: 100K. Sales: $5-10MM
Products: Programmable controllers, industrial
computers, automation software and support

BAUDVILLE CATALOG (800) 728-0888
5380 52nd St., SE
Grand Rapids, MI 49512
E-Mail: service@baudville.com
Website: www.baudville.com
Fax Ordering: (616) 698-0554
Customer Service: (616) 698-0888
Contact Name: Debra Sikanas, President
Catalog: Free. Frequency: Quarterly
Circulation: 1MM. Sales: $5-10MM
Products: Computer software & accessories
for entertainment, productivity and education.
Includes CD-ROM clip art collection; and
software for font collection, and laser award
maker for education,

BAY AREA LABELS (408) 432-1980
1980 Lundy Ave. • San Jose, CA 95131
E-Mail: sales@bal.com
Website: www.bayarealabels.com
Fax Ordering: (408) 434-6407
International Ordering: (408) 432-1980
Catalog: Free. Frequency: Quarterly
Circulation: 25K. Sales: $5-10MM
Contact Name: Oliver Flach, President
Products: Product identification components;
computer supplies & products

BETA ELECTRONICS (800) 546-2382
4480 Summit Ridge Dr.
Columbus, OH 43220
E-Mail: sales@betalaser.com
Website: www.betalaser.com
Fax Ordering: (888) 329-2382; (614) 538-8209
Customer Service: (614) 538-8207
Contact Names: Ming Liou, President
Catalog: Free. Frequency: Semiannual
Circulation: 150K. Sales: $5-10MM

Products: Laser screenwriter; power point
presenter; laser pointers; and mini laptop
computers for presentations

BIBLE RESEARCH SYSTEMS (800) 423-1228
1771 Wells Branch Pkwy. #110B-322
Austin, TX 78728
E-Mail: bible@brs-inc.com
Website: www.brs-inc.com/bible
Fax Ordering: (512) 251-4401
International Ordering: (512) 251-7541
Contact Name: Kent Ochel, President
Catalog: Free. Frequency: Semiannual
Circulation: 25K. Sales: $1-3MM
Products: Bible study software

BIOS UPGRADES (800) 800-2467
Unicore Software
1538 Turnpike St. • N. Andover, MA 01845
E-Mail: sales@biosagentplus.com
Website: www.biosagentplus.com
Fax Ordering: (978) 683-1630
International Ordering: (978) 686-6468
Technical Support: (978) 686-2204 Fax 725-6777
Catalogs: Online. Sales: $3-5MM
Products: The latest enhancements to keep
your PC up-to-date with the latest technology.

BLACK BOX CORPORATION (724) 746-5500
1000 Park Dr. • Lawrence, PA 15055
E-Mail: info@blackbox.com
Website: www.blackbox.com
Fax Ordering: (800) 321-0746
International Fax Ordering: (724) 746-0746
Contact Names: Fred Young, President
Catalogs: Free. Frequency: Semiannual
Circulation: 5MM. Sales: $50-100 MM
Products: Data communication devices &
accessories that allow computers to communicate,
including modems, protocol converters, switches,
cable, and local area network products.

BOXLIGHT CORPORATION (360) 464-2119
P.O. Box 2609 • Belfair, WA 98528
E-Mail: sales@boxlight.com
Website: www.boxlight.com
Fax Ordering: (360) 282-6141
Contact Names: Herb Myers, President
Catalog: Free. Frequency: Semiannual
Products: Computer projection panels,
all-in-one projectors, overhead projectors
and presentation tools.

BRETFORD, INC. CATALOG (800) 521-9614
11000 Seymour Ave.
Franklin Park, IL 60131
E-Mail: sales@bretford.com
Website: www.bretford.com
Fax Ordering: (800) 343-1779; (847) 678-0852
International Ordering: (847) 678-2545
Contact Name: Edward Petrick, President
Catalog: Free. Frequency: Annual
Circulation: 1MM. Sales: $20-50MM
Products: Computer furniture projection screens;
AV & Notebook carts; workstations, seating &
shelving; projection screens; carrels; book trucks

BROOKE BUSINESS FORMS & SUPPLIES (800) 228-0202
50 Hwy. 9, Suite 303 • Morganville, NJ 07751
E-Mail: info@brookebusiness.com
Website: www.brookebusiness.com
Fax Ordering: (732) 617-7553

Contact Name: Neil Rosen, President
Customer Service: (732) 617-7550
Catalog: Free. Frequency: Annual.
Products: Computer business forms & supplies;
magnetic tape, hard disk cartridges, printer
ribbons, etc.

BSI - GSA CATALOG (800) 872-4547
Broadax Systems, Inc,
17539 E. Rowland St.
City of Industry, CA 91731
E-Mail: info@bsicomputer.com
Website: www.bsicomputer.com
Fax Ordering: (626) 964-2665
Customer Service: (626) 964-2600
Contact Names: David Chen, President
Catalog: Free. Frequency: Annual
Circulation: 100K. Sales: $5-10MM
Products: Specializes in notebooks, laptops,
CPUs, Power System, Floppy Disk Drives

BUSINESS RESOURCE SOFTWARE, INC. (800) 423-1228
1779 Wells Branch Pkwy. #110B-322
Austin, TX 78728
E-Mail: brs@brs-inc.com
Website: www.brs-inc.com
Fax Ordering: (512) 251-4401
Technical Support: (512) 251-7541
Contact Name: Kent Ochel, President
Catalog: Free. Frequency: Semiannual.
Circulation: 25K. Sales: $1-3MM
Products: Marketing & business planning
software

CABLES TO GO (800) 826-7904
3599 Kettering Blvd. • Moraine, OH 45439 (800) 506-9607
E-Mail: order@cablestogo.com
Website: www.cablestogo.com
Fax Ordering: (800) 331-2841; (937) 496-2666
International Ordering: (937) 224-8646
Catalog: Free. Frequency: Semiannual
Circulation: 100K. Sales: $5-10MM
Products: Networking computer equipment;
computer cables, audio video cables, DVI cables,
USB cables

CABLEXPRESS (800) 913-9465
CXTEC • P.O. Box 479 • Syracuse, NY 13221
E-Mail: info@cablexpress.com
Website: www.cablexpress.com
Fax Ordering: (315) 455-1800
International Ordering: (315) 476-3000
Contact Names: Michael Lorenz, President
Catalog: Free. Frequency: Annual
Circulation: 3MM. Sales: $50-100 MM
Products: Computer networking equipment,
including cables, accessories & connectivity
products for users of IBM & compatible computer
systems.

CALIFORNIA DIGITAL, INC. (888) 546-8948
46832 Lakeview Blvd. • Fremont, CA 94538
E-Mail: sales@californiadigital.com
Website: www.californiadigital.com
Fax Ordering: (510) 651-8844
International Ordering: (408) 905-7144
Technical Support: (510) 580-5055
Contact Names: Terry Reiter, President
Catalog: Free. Frequency: Semiannual
Circulation: 250K. Sales: $10-20MM
Products: Laser systems; medical electronics;
computers, boards, memory modules, hard drives,

controllers, CD/ROM's, optical disk drives,
floppy disk drives, tape drives, scanners,
video adapters, printers & accessories,
magnetic media, monitors, terminals,
modems, power conditioners & supplies,
cables, and software.

CAMBRIDGE SOFT PRODUCTS (800) 315-7300
100 CambridgePark Dr.
Cambridge, MA 02140
E-Mail: info@cambridgesoft.com
Website: www.cambridgesoft.com
Fax Ordering: (617) 588-9190
International Ordering: (617) 588-9100
Catalog: Free. Frequency: Annual
Circulation: 100K. Sales: $3-5MM
Products: Chemistry information & teaching
tools on CD-ROMs and computer software

CDW (800) 781-4CDW
Computer Discount Warehouse (800) 255-6227
300 N. Milwaukee Ave. • Vernon Hills, IL 60061 (800) 774-4239
E-Mail: sales@cdw.com (800) 849-4239
Website: www.cdw.com (800) 838-4239
Fax Ordering: (847) 465-6800 (800) 592-4239
International Ordering: (847) 465-6000 (800) 547-5444
Customer Service: (800) 750-4239; (847) 465-6550
Contact Name: Greg Zeman, President
Catalog: Free. Pages: 100. Frequency: Irregular
Circulation: 1MM. Sales: $100-250MM
Products: Name brand computer hardware,
peripherals, software and accessories at
discount prices. Includes desktops, laptops,
terminals, printers, monitors, plotters, digitizers
& scanners, networking accessories; tape and
hard drives; system boards; power protectors;
software, modems, etc.

CHAMPS SOFTWARE, INC. (352) 795-2362
1255 N. Vantage Point Dr.
Crystal River, FL 34429
E-Mail: mmelfi@champsinc.com
Website: www.champsinc.com
Fax Ordering: (352) 795-9100
Contact Names: Bryan K. Gay, Sales
Catalog: Free. Frequency: Quarterly
Circulation: 150K. Sales: $5-10MM
Products: CHAMPS/2 - computerized
maintenance management systems software

CHEMSW, INC. (800) 536-0404
4771 Mangles Blvd. • Fairfield, CA 94534
E-Mail: info@chemsw.com
Website: www.chemsw.com
Fax Ordering: (707) 864-2815
International Ordering: (707) 864-0845
Contact Name: Brian Stafford, President
Catalog: Free. Frequency: Annual
Circulation: 100K. Sales: $10-25MM
Products: PC Windows-based chemistry
and laboratory software chemical inventory
management; asset management software
for laboratories providing inventory &
laboratory solutions

CLUB MAC (800) 217-9153
2555 West 190th St. • Torrance, CA 90504 (800) 258-2621
E-Mail: sales@clubmac.com
Website: www.clubmac.com
Fax Ordering: (949) 768-9354
International Ordering: (310) 354-5600
Customer Service: (800) 217-9153

Tech Support: (800) 217-9153
Contact Name: Michael McNeill, President
Catalog: Free. Frequency: Quarterly
Circulation: 250K. Sales: $20-50MM
Products: Apple authorized catalog reseller offering Apple Macintosh systems, Apple PowerBooks; Apple system accessories; memory, storage, CD-ROMs, CD recordables & media; accelerator cards; monitors; printers/accessories; scanners; networking/ modems, software, and more.

COMPONENTS & COMPUTER PRODUCTS   (800) 831-4242
Jameco Electronics
1355 Shoreway Rd. • Belmont, CA 94002
E-Mail: sales@jameco.com
Website: www.jameco.com
Fax Ordering: (800) 237-6948
International Ordering: (650) 592-8097 Fax 592-2503
Customer Service: (800) 536-4316
Technical Support: (800) 831-4242
Contact Names: Dennis Farrey, President
Catalog: Free. Frequency: Quarterly
Circulation: 100K. Sales: $20-50MM
Products: Computers, accessories, software & supplies

COMPUSA CATALOG   (800) 266-7872
P.O. Box 440309 • Miami, FL 33144
E-Mail: sales@compusa.com
Website: www.compusa.com
Catalog: Free. Frequency: Semiannual
Circulation: 200K. Sales: $100-250MM
Products: PCs & Peripherals; Electronics; Component Upgrades; Accessories; Gaming

COMPUTER DYNAMICS SALES   (864) 627-8800
7640 Pelham Rd.
Greenville, SC 29615-5789
E-Mail: cdisales@gefanug.com
Website: www.cdynamics.com
Fax Ordering: (864) 675-0106
Contact Name: Earl Foster, President
Catalog: Free. Frequency: Annual
Circulation: 100K. Sales: $20-50MM
Products: Industrial rack mount computers & monitors; military, marine & custom built computer systems; PC compatible single board computers for OEM applications; flat panel display systems including both monitors and computers for the OEM & individual end-user.

COMPUTER FRIENDS, INC.   (800) 547-3303
14250 NW Science Park Dr.
Portland, OR 97229
E-Mail: cfi@cfriends.com
Website: www.cfriends.com
Fax Ordering: (503) 643-5379
International Ordering: (503) 626-2291
Technical Support: (503) 620-4433
Contact Name: Jimmie Mogila, President
Catalog: Free. Frequency: Annual
Circulation: 200K. Sales: $3-5MM
Products: Printer support products, cartridges, recycling systems, jet, laser, dot matrix

COMPUTER FURNITURE DIRECT   (800) 555-6126
11619 Beach Blvd. • Jacksonville, FL 32246
E-Mail: help@cf-direct.com
Website: www.cf-direct.com
Fax Ordering: (904) 565-1123

International Ordering: (904) 565-1163
Catalog: Free. Frequency: Semiannual
Circulation: 150K. Sales: $1-3MM
Products: Computer furniture

COMPUTER GATE INTERNATIONAL   (888) 437-0895
2995 Gordon Ave. • Santa Clara, CA 95051
E-Mail: sales@computergate.com
Website: www.computergate.com
Fax Ordering: (408) 730-0735
Customer Service: (408) 730-0673
Contact Names: Richard NG, Contact
Catalog: $6.95. Frequency: Semiannual
Circulation: 50K. Sales: $5-10MM
Products: PC components & accessories; computer hardware & supplies

COMPUTER GEAR CATALOG   (800) 373-6353
19510 144th Ave NE, Suite E-5
Woodinville, WA 98072
E-Mail: service@computergear.com
Website: www.computergear.com
Fax Ordering: (425) 883-4218
International Ordering: (425) 883-9052
Catalog: Free. Frequency: Semiannual
Circulation: 10K. Sales: $1-3MM
Products: Fun computer gifts; t-shirts, desktop toys, gadgets & gizmos

COMPUTER RESET   (214) 348-6484
9525 Skillman St. • Dallas, TX 75243
E-Mail: sales@c-reset.com
Website: www.c-reset.com
Fax Ordering: (214) 343-3150
Contact Name: Monique Byron, President
Catalog: Free. Frequency: Semiannual
Circulation: 50K. Sales: $1-3MM
Products: Reseller of used, demo, & refurbished computers & computer equipment

COMPUTER SUPPLIES UNLIMITED   (800) 841-1117
1370 Tully Rd., #502 • San Jose, CA 95122
E-Mail: info@computersuppliesultd.com
Website: www.computersuppliesultd.com
Fax Ordering: (408) 998-4004
International Ordering: (408) 998-8101
Contact Name: Cynthia E. Yandow
Catalog: Free. Frequency: Annual
Circulation: 100K. Sales: $3-5MM
Products: Name brand computers, monitors & video boards, printers & supplies, ribbons & supplies, laser printer accessories, modems, monitors & accessories, mass storage products, boards, scanners & mice, power protection products, cleaning supplies, workstations & furniture.

CONCENTRIC SYSTEMS, INC.   (800) 573-6146
4300 82nd St., Unit 1
Sacramento, CA 95826
E-Mail: info@concentric-systems.com
Website: www.concentric-systems.com
Fax Ordering: (916) 273-4807
International Ordering: (770) 576-2700
Contact Name: Brett Berto, President
Products: Computer desktops, notebooks, servers, and accessories

CORPORATE EXPRESS   (888) 238-6329
Staples Advantage
1 Environmental Way
Broomfield, CO 80021
E-Mail: sales@cexp.com

Website: www.cexp.com
Fax Ordering: (888) 664-3311
International Ordering: (303) 664-2000
Contact Names: Richard Young, President
Catalog: Free. Frequency: Annual
Circulation: 1MM. Sales: $100-200MM
Products: Computer graphic imaging, media storage
and computer furniture & accessories. Brand name
computer supplies, accessories - diskettes,
magnetic media, data cartridges, ribbons;
laser printer & ink jet supplies; paper and
labels; power protection equipment; & furniture.

CORPORATE SYSTEMS CENTER (408) 330-5538
2695 Walsh Ave. • Santa Clara, CA 95051
E-Mail: sales@corpsys.com
Website: www.corpsys.com
Fax Ordering: (408) 969-2655
Contact Name: Martin Bodo, President
Catalog: Free. Frequency: Monthly
Circulation: 50K. Sales: $5-10MM
Products: Surplus hard drives, disk arrays,
disk drives, duplication systems, CD-ROMs
and accessories.

COSMIC PATTERNS SOFTWARE (800) 779-2559
6212 NW 43rd St., Suite B
Gainesville, FL 32653
E-Mail: kepler@astrosoftware.com
Website: www.astrosoftware.com
Fax Ordering: (352) 374-8826
Technical Support: (352) 373-1504
Contact Names: David Cochrane, President
Catalog: Free. Frequency: Annual
Circulation: 5M. Sales: $500M
Products: Astrology software for IBM
compatib;e computers, astrology chart
services, & astrology
education/

CREATIVE PRODUCT CATALOG (800) 998-1000
Creativer Labs, Inc.
1901 McCarthy Blvd. • Milpitas, CA 95035
E-Mail: sales@creative.com
Website: www.creative.com
Fax Ordering: (408) 428-6611
Catalog: Free. Frequency: Annual.
Circulation: 50K. Sales: $5-10MM
Products: Digital entertainment products
for your PC and the Internet; computerr
hardware and components for sound
production on PCs and for video and
CD-ROM production, and DVD.

CYBERGUYS (800) 892-1010
11321 White Rock Rd.
Rancho Cordova, CA 95742
E-Mail: info@cyberguys.com
Website: www.cyberguys.com
Fax Ordering: (916) 858-1009
Customer Service: (800) 892-0164
Contact Names: Jay Springer, President
Catalog: Free. Frequency: Monthly
Circulation: 1MM. Sales: $20-50MM
Products: Computer parts & accessories

CYBER RESEARCH, INC. (800) 341-2525
25 Business Park Dr., Unit E
Branford, CT 06405
E-Mail: sales@cyberresearch.com
Website: www.cyberresearch.com
Fax Ordering: (203) 483-9024

International Ordering: (203) 483-8815
Contact Names: Robert Molloy, President
Catalog: Free. Frequency: Quarterly
Circulation: 50K. Sales: $10-20MM
Products: Desktop and rackmount PC systems,
displays, monitors, workstations, PC accessories,
motherboards, and engineering software.

DALCO ELECTRONICS (800) 445-5342
425 S. Pioneer Blvd.
Springboro, OH 45066
E-Mail: sales@dalco.com
Website: www.dalco.com
Fax Ordering: (513) 743-9251
Customer Service: (513) 743-8042
Contact Names: David & Dale Ditmer
Catalog: Free. Frequency: Semiannual
Circulation: 25K. Sales: $10-20MM
Products: Computer systems and hardware;
motherboards, memory, CPUs, all types of
computer cables, hard drives, COROM drives,
adapter cards, networking hardware.

DAMARK (800) 729-9000
Damark International, Inc.
7101 Winnetka Ave. N.
Minneapolis, MN 55428
E-Mail: support@damark.com
Website: www.damark.com
Fax Ordering: (763) 531-0180
Customer Service: (763) 531-0066
Contact Name: Mark Cohen, President
Catalog: Free. Frequency: Quarterly
Circulation: 5MM. Sales: $100-200MM
Products: Computer systems, drives &
storage, modems and networking, monitors
and video, printers & peripherals, furniture,
accessories, supplies, and software.

DATACAL DIRECT (800) 223-0123
1345 N. Mondel Dr. • Gilbert, AZ 85233
E-Mail: info@datacal.com
Website: www.datacal.com
Fax Ordering: (480) 545-8090
International Ordering: (480) 813-3100
Contact Name: Jim Lunt, President
Catalog: Free. Frequency: Semiannual
Circulation: 25K. Sales: $1-3MM
Products: Computer training videos, CD's,
and software, hardware and accessories,
keyboard protective covers for standard
keyboards and laptop computers, keyboard
templates and keytop overlays.

DAVKA CORPORATION (800) 621-8227
2750 W. Pratt Blvd. • Chicago, IL 60645
E-Mail: sales@davka.com
Website: www.davka.com
Fax Ordering: (773) 583-5456
Customer Service: (773) 583-2333
Technical Support: (773) 583-5510
Catalog: Free. Frequency: Annual.
Circulation: 150K. Sales: $3-5MM
Products: Judaic software & gift catalog,
with over 100 titles to its credit in the areas
of Jewish history, Hebrew language, customs,
traditions and other related areas.

DCS TECHNOLOGIES CORP. (800) 827-3271
6501 Route 123 • Franklin, OH 45005
E-Mail: info@dcs-tech.com
Website: www.dcs-tech.com

Fax Ordering: (937) 743-4056
Technical Service: (937) 743-4060
Catalog: Free. Frequency: Semiannual
Circulation: 50K. Sales: $5-10MM
Products: Laser printer services & supplies

DELL COMPUTER CORP.   (800) 901-3355
P.O. Box 224588 • Dallas, TX 75222   (800) 757-8434
E-Mail: sales@dell.com   (800) 509-3355
Website: www.dell.com   (800) 545-1587
Fax Ordering: (800) 727-8320
Customer Service: (800) WWW-DELL
Technical Support: (800) 624-9896
Contacts: Michael S. Dell, CEO;
   Lee Walker, President
Catalog: Free. Frequency: Monthly
Circulation: 25MM. Sales: $250-500MM
Products: Computer systems built to order.
Manufacturer-direct prices and responsive
service and support. Computer systems:
Notebook, laptop and desktop systems.
Hard disk drives, monitors, modems & mice.
Workstations. Networking: Interface cards
and operating systems. Printers: Dot matrix
& laser printers; software & peripheral products.

DELUXE BUSINESS & COMPUTER FORMS   (800) 328-0304
P.O. Box 1186 • Lancaster, CA 93584   Canada (800) 826-3714
E-Mail: sales@deluxeforms.com
Website: www.deluxforms.com
Fax Ordering: (800) 336-1112; (800) 447-1407
Contact Names: Gene Bidon, President
Catalog: Free. Frequency: Semiannual
Circulation: 2MM. Sales: $50-100MM
Products: Computer checks, forms & supplies
compatible with a variety of software; laser printer
forms and supplies; Print-a-Form Software to
help you automate your accounting.

DEMCO BUSINESS CATALOG   (800) 279-1586
P.O. Box 7488 • Madison, WI 53707
E-Mail: order@demco.com
Website: www.demco.com
Fax Ordering: (800) 245-1329; (608) 241-1799
International Ordering: (608) 241-1201
Customer Service: (800) 962-4463
Contact Name: Ed Muir, President
Catalog: Free. Frequency: Annual.
Circulation: 5MM. Sales: $100-200MM
Products: Office supplies & equipment; library
supplies; computer paper, diskettes, cartridges,
cleaning supplies; furniture & workstations.

DIRECTORY OF COMPUTER SOFTWARE   (800) 553-6847
National Technical Information Service
5285 Port Royal Rd. • Springfield, VA 22161
E-Mail: orders@ntis.gov
Website: www.ntis.gov
Fax Ordering: (703) 321-8547
International Ordering: (703) 487-4650
Catalog: $62. Frequency: Annual.
Circulation: 2K. Sales: $150K
Products: Describes 1,600 federal software
packages, applications and tools, compiled in
cooperation with hundreds of U.S. Government
agencies.

DIRECTRON.COM   (713) 773-9898
10402 Harwin Dr. • Houston, TX 77036
E-Mail: general_sales@directron.com
Website: www.directron.com
Fax Ordering: (713) 773-9393

Customer Service: (713) 773-3636 ext.1500
Catalog: Online. Sales: $10-20MM
Products: CPU computer parts, PC power
supply; cables & adapters, cases & fans,
hard drives, software, hardware, accessories

THE DRAWING BOARD   (800) 527-9530
101 E. Ninth St. • Waynesboro, PA 17268
E-Mail: sales@thedrawing-board.com
Website: www.thedrawing-board.com
Fax Ordering: (800) 253-1838; (800) 822-0256
Customer Service: (800) 562-5468
Contact Name: Lee Bracken, President
Catalog: Free. Frequency: 8x per year
Circulation: 500K. Sales: $10-20MM
Products: Computer checks & forms, and
software compatible forms; diskettes & supplies,
disk storage accessories, data cartridges,
magnetic tape, printer ribbons, paper & labels,
forms, stationery, laser printer products, power
line conditioners & vacuums, dust covers and
copy holders.

ECOST.COM   (877) 888-2678
500 N. Central Expressway, Suite 500
Plano, TX 75074
E-Mail: sales@ecost.com
Website: www.ecost.com
International Orders: (310) 658-5000
Catalog: Free. Sales: $20-50MM
Circulation: 100K. Sales: $3-5MM
Products: Computers & electronics
for home & business

EDIMAX COMPUTER COMPANY   (408) 496-1105
3350 Scott Blvd., Bldg. 15
Santa Clara, CA 95054
E-Mail: sales@edimax.com
Website: www.edimax.com
Fax Ordering: (408) 980-1530
Contact Names: Danny Hwang, President
Catalog: Free. Frequency: Quarterly
Circulation: 150K. Sales: $3-5MM
Products: PC networking products

EDUCATIONAL RESOURCES   (800) 544-3472
1550 Executive Dr. • Elgin, IL 60123   (800) 860-7004
E-Mail: sales@edresources.com
Website: www.edresources.com
Fax Ordering: (800) 610-5005
Customer Service: (800) 624-2926
Catalog: Free. Frequency: Quarterly
Circulation: 150K. Sales: $5-10MM
Products: Educational technology, hardware,
accessories, and supplemental products for K-12

ELECTRONIC SPECIALISTS   (800) 225-4876
75 Middlesex Ave. • Natick, MA 01760
E-Mail: esp@elect-spec.com
Website: www.elect-spec.com
Fax Ordering: (508) 653-0268
Customer Service: (508) 655-1532
Contact Names: F.J. Stifter, President
Catalog: Free. Frequency: Annual
Circulation: 10K. Sales: $1-3MM
Products: Computer protection products

FOCUS ELECTRONICS & COMPUTERS   (800) 223-3411
Focus Electronics, Inc.
4509 13th Ave. • Brooklyn, NY 11219
E-Mail: sales@focususa.com
Website: www.focususa.com

Fax Ordering: (718) 438-4263
Customer Service: (718) 436-4646
Contact Names: Ann Singer, President
Circulation: 250K. Sales: $5-10MM
Products: Computers & office equipment

FONT & FUNCTION CATALOG (408) 536-6000
Adobe Systems, Inc.
345 Park Ave. • San Jose, CA 95110
E-Mail: sales@adobe.com
Website: www.adobe.com
Fax Ordering: (408) 537-6000
Technical Support: (800) 833-6687
Catalog: Free. Frequency: Semiannual
Circulation: 500K. Sales: $50-100MM
Products: Software for desktop publishing
& graphic design as well as articles on type.

FUJITSU AMERICA, INC. (800) 831-3183
125 E. Arques Ave. • Sunnyvale, CA 94085 (800) FUJITSU
E-Mail: solutions@us.fujitsu.com
Website: www.shopfujitso.com
Fax Ordering: (408) 764-5060
International Ordering: (408) 746-6000
Catalog: Online. Sales: $10-50MM
Products: Computer hardware for PCs

GAMMATECH CORP. (800) 995-8946
48303 Fremont Blvd. • Fremont, CA 94538
E-Mail: sales@gammatechusa.com
Website: www.gammatechusa.com
Fax Ordering: (510) 492-0820
Technical Support: (510) 492-0828 Fax 492-0832
Contact Names: Bill Liu, President
Catalog: Free. Frequency: Quarterly
Circulation: 50K. Sales: $10-20MM
Products: Computer notebooks & laptops

GATEWAY, INC. (800) 846-2000
7565 Irvine Center Dr. • Irvine, CA 92618 (800) GATEWAY
P.O. Box 6137 • Temple, TX 76503
E-Mail: sales@gateway.com
Website: www.gateway.com
Fax Ordering: (605) 232-2023
International Ordering: (605) 232-2000
Contact Names: Theodore Waitt, President
Catalog: Free.Frequency: Quarterly
Circulation: 2MM. Sales: $100-500MM
Products: Desktop, notebook & netbook PCs;
display monitors; accessories

GCC PRINTERS USA (800) 422-7777
209 Burlington Rd. • Bedford, MA 01730
E-Mail: sales@gccprinters.com
Website: www.gccprinters.com
Fax Ordering: (800) 442-2329 or (781) 275-1115
International Ordering: (781) 275-5800
Contact Name: Kevin Curran, President
Catalog: Free. Frequency: Monthly
Circulation: 100K. Sales: $25-50MM
Products: Macintosh peripherals; laser printers

GERBER SCIENTIFIC PRODUCTS (800) 222-7446
83 Gerber Rd. • So. Windsor, CT 06074
E-Mail: sales@gspinc.com
Website: www.gspinc.com
Fax Ordering: (860) 648-8595
International Ordering: (860) 643-1551
Customer Service: (800) 828-5406
Contact Names: Elaine Pullen, President
Catalog: Free. Frequency: Quarterly
Circulation: 1MM. Sales: $50-100MM

Products: Computer-based systems, equipment,
software & supplies that generate high-quality
mass-customized products

GLOBAL COMPUTER SUPPLIES (800) 446-9662
11 Harbor Park Dr.
Port Washington, NY 11050
E-Mail: sales@globalcomputer.com
Website: www.globalcomputer.com
Fax Ordering: (800) 882-5740; (800) 562-6622
Customer Service: (800) 262-6622
Contact Name: Robert Leeds, President
Catalog: Free. Frequency: Semiannual
Circulation: 5MM. Sales: $50-100MM
Products: Hardware - mice, disk drives, scanners,
keyboards, etc. Supplies - disks, ribbons &cartridges,
paper, furniture-workstations, accessories, supplies,
modems, printers and accessories; laser printers
and accessories; tools, peripherals, cables and
switches; cleaning kits & accessories; productivity
boosters and aids; power protection equipment.
Software - spreadsheets, desktop publishing,
CAD/CAM, communications, utilities, word
processing, tutorials, training tapes.

GRANITE DIGITAL (888) 819-2190
SCSI Solution Company
3101 Whipple Rd. • Union City, CA 94587
E-Mail: info@granitedigital.com
Website: www.granitedigital.com
Fax Ordering. (510) 471-6267
Technical Support: (510) 471-6442
Products: Computer accessories - SATA &
USB products, FireWire storage systems &
SCSI peripherals; DV & AV storage solutions

GRAYARC COMPUTER FORMS CATALOG (800) 243-5250
101 E. Ninth St. • Waynesboro, PA 17268
E-Mail: customerservice@grayarc.com
Website: www.grayarc.com
Fax Ordering: (800) 292-4729
Customer Service: (800) 527-9530
Catalog: Free. Frequency: Semiannual.
Products: Computer supplies, forms &
paper goods.

HARMONY COMPUTERS (800) 441-1144
1801 Flatbush Ave. • Brooklyn, NY 11210 (877) 427-6669
E-Mail: info@shopharmony.com
Website: www.shopharmony.com
Fax Ordering: (718) 692-4535
Customer Service: (718) 692-2828
Contact Name: Stan Frost, Manager
Catalog: Free. Frequency: Annual
Circulation: 50K. Sales: $10-20MM
Products: All major brands of computers &
peripherals, including printers, monitors, video
cards, modems, laptops, supplies, etc. Also,
golf equipment, automotive GPS, radar detectors;
marine.outdoor products

HEATHKIT EDUCATIONAL SYSTEMS (800) 253-0570
2024 Hawthorne Ave. • St. Joseph, MI 49085
E-Mail: info@heathkit.com
Website: www.heathkit.com
Fax Ordering: (269) 925-2898
International Ordering: (269) 925-6000
Contact Names: William Johnson, President
Catalog: Free. Frequency: Quarterly
Circulation: 1MM. Sales: $10-25 MM
Products: Computers and accessories for kit-
building enthusiasts; and software for them.

HI-VAL CATALOG   (949) 707-4800
4 Marconi • Irvine, CA 92618
E-Mail: webmaster@hival.com
Website: www.hival.com
Fax Ordering: (949) 855-3550
Technical Support: (949) 707-4888
Catalog: Free. Frequency: Annual.
Circulation: 25K. Sales: $1-3MM
Products: CD Rewritable drives, CD-ROM drives,
Floppy rives, I/O products, decoder cards, DVD
drives, modems, media accessories, mice, sound cards

HICE & ASSOCIATES   (513) 779-7977
8586 Monticello Dr.
West Chester, OH 45069
Fax Ordering: (513) 779-7977
Catalog: Free. Frequency: Annual
Circulation: 50K. Sales: $500K
Products: Software packaging, including disk
and CD holders and cases; labels

HP DIRECT COMPUTER USERS CATALOG   (800) 538-8787
Hewlett-Packard Co.   (800) 752-0900
3000 Hanover St. • Palo Alto, CA 94304   (888) 999-4747
E-Mail: sales@hp.com   (800) 888-9909
Website: www.hp.com   (877) 801-5657
Fax Ordering: (650) 857-5518   (888) 280-4069
Contact Names: Martin Neil, President
Catalog: Free. Frequency: Semiannual
Circulation: 1MM. Sales: $100-200MM
Products: HP home & home office computers,
supplies and accessories: printers & accessories;
LANs & cables; disks & tapes; Vectra PC accessories;
terminals; data communications & power conditioners;
networking software & accessories; and furniture/
workstations.

HIGHSMITH CO. CATALOGS   (800) 558-2110
W5527 Hwy. 106 • Fort Atkinson, WI 53538
E-Mail: service@highsmith.com
Website: www.highsmith.com
Fax Ordering: (800) 835-2329
Customer Service: (800) 558-3899
Contact Names: Duncan Highsmith, President
Catalog: Free. Frequency: Semiannual.
Circulation: 500K. Sales: $20-50MM
Products: Multimedia hardware & software,
desktop publishing software and supplies,
administrative software, library automation
software, personal computing furniture, paper,
ribbons, diskettes and storage, printer stands,
monitor and keyboard accessories, maintenance
and security supplies, data switches and cables.

HOOLEON CORPORATION   (800) 937-1337
P.O. Box 589 • Melrose, NM 88124
E-Mail: sales@hooleon.com
Website: www.hooleon.com
Fax Ordering: (575) 253-4299
Customer Service: (575) 253-4503
Contact Name: Joan Crozier, President
Catalog: Free. Frequency: Quarterly
Circulation: 100K. Sales: $5-10M
Products: Computer keyboard enhancements, c
ustom key imprinting services; keyboards and
macro devices; do-it-yourself key applications;
custom label imprinting services and label kits; l
ock-outs, key wipes, keyboard protectors, templates.

IBM LOTUS SOFTWARE   (800) 426-4968
One Rogers St. • Cambridge, MA 02142   (888) 746-7426
E-Mail: sales@ibm.com/lotus
Website: www.ibm.com/lotus.com
Fax Ordering: (800) 314-1092
Customer Service: (877) 426-6006; (617) 577-8500
Catalog: Free. Frequency: Quarterly.
Circulation: 500K. Sales: $100-250MM
Products: IBM Lotus software for communications,
desktop publishing, education, graphics, home/
business applications, producivity, utilities, and
word processing programs.

IBM PC DIRECT SOURCEBOOK   (877) 999-7115
3039 Cornwallis Rd., Bldg. 203
Research Triangle Park, NC 27709
E-Mail: sales@ibm.com
Website: www.ibm.com
Fax Ordering: (800) 242-6329
Technical Support: (800) 772-2227
Catalog: Free. Frequency: Quarterly.
Circulation: 250K. Sales: Over $100MM
Products: IBM PC consumable supplies,
peripherals, & accessories to IBM system users.

IBM, TRAINING SOLUTIONS   (800) 426-4968
1133 Westchester Ave.
White Plains, NY 10604
E-Mail: info@ibm.com
Website: www.ibm.com
Fax Ordering: (800) 426-4329
Contact Names: Timothy F. Hamill, Marketing
Catalog: Free. Frequency: Monthly
Circulation: 25K. Sales: $5-10MM
Products: Technology course catalogs - 4 books

IMAGE SOLUTIONS   (973) 560-0404
23911 Garnier St. • Torrance, CA 90505
E-Mail: info@imagesolutions.com
Website: www.imagesolutions.com
International Orders: (973) 560-0404
Technical Support: (973) 576-9100
Contact Name: Jinsoo Kim, President
Catalog: Free. Frequency: Semiannual
Circulation: 75K. Sales: $1-5MM
Products: Computer hardware equipment &
supplies for Macintosh computers and software

INDUS INTERNATIONAL   (800) 843-9377
340 S. Oak St. • West Salem, WI 54669
E-Mail: inausmis@aol.com
Website: www.indususa.com
Fax Ordering: (608) 786-0786
International Ordering: (608) 786-0300
Contact Names: Ameen Ayoob, President
Catalog: Free. Frequency: Monthly
Circulation: 200K. Sales: $10-20MM
Products: Optical disk systems, micrographic
readers and printers

INDUSTRIAL COMPUTER MASTER SOURCEBOOK   (888) 294-4558
Kontron America
14118 Stowe Dr. • Poway, CA 92064
E-Mail: sales@kontron.com
Website: www.kontron.com
Fax Ordering: (858) 677-0898
Customer Service: (888) 311-4690
Contact Names: Chuck Philyaw, President
Catalog: Free. Frequency: Annual
Circulation: 1MM. Sales: $50-100MM
Products: Manufacturer & designer of industrial
computers, interface cards, and rack accessories
for IBM PC/XT/AT compatible computers. Includes
computer systems, I/O, networking & software.

INFOSOURCE, INC. (800) 393-4636
1300 City View Center Canada (800) 253-2995
Oviedo, FL 32765
E-Mail: isisale@howtomaster.com
Website: www.infosourcelearning.com
Fax Ordering: (407) 796-5190
International Ordering: (407) 677-0300
Contact Name: Thomas Warmer, President
Catalog: Free. Frequency: Annual
Circulation: 1MM. Sales: $5-10MM
Product: Self-pacing training software for PCs

INSIGHT COMPUTERS (800) 467-4448
6820 S. Harl Ave. • Tempe, AZ 85283
E-Mail: jdixon@insight.com
Website: www.insight.com
Fax Ordering: (480) 760-7940
Customer Service: (800) 467-4448
Contact Name: John-Scott Dixon, VP Marketing
Products: Variety of PC equipment, hardware
and software; business and productivity software;
computer accessories & supplies; photo equipment
and supplies.

INTERACTI CD-ROM, INC. (800) 479-1323
350 S. Lake Ave. #112 • Pasadena, CA 91101
E-Mail: contact-interact@interactcd.com
Website: www.interactcd.com
Fax Ordering: (626) 683-5639
Customer Service: (626) 578-7282
Contact Name: Dave Sparks, President
Catalog: Free. Frequency: Quarterly
Circulation: 1MM. Sales: $50-100MM
Products: Wide variety of CD-ROM games
and other software for the PC & Mac

J & R COMPUTER WORLD (800) 806-1115
23 Park Row • New York, NY 10002 (800) 221-3191
E-Mail: sales@jandr.com
Website: www.jandr.com
Fax Ordering: (800) 232-4432; (212) 238-9175
Customer Service: (800) 426-6027
International Orders: (718) 340-0406
Catalog: Free. Frequency: Quarterly
Circulation: 10MM. Sales: $50-100MM
Products: Computers and accessories of all kinds

JAMECO ELECTRONICS (800) 831-4242
1355 Shoreway Rd. • Belmont, CA 94002
E-Mail: sales@jameco.com
Website: www.jameco.com
Fax Ordering: (800) 237-6948; (650) 592-2503
International Ordering: (650) 592-8097
Corporate/Educational Sales: (800) 794-9100
Customer Service: (800) 536-4316
Technical Support: (800) 831-4242
Contact Name: Dennis Farrey, President
Catalog: Free. Frequency: Quarterly
Circulation: 1MM. Sales: $3-5MM
Products: Computers, computer peripherals
and supplies

JDR COMPUTER PRODUCTS (800) 538-5000
1723 Rogers Ave. Unit O
San Jose, CA 95112
E-Mail: sales@jdr.com
Website: www.jdr.com
Fax Ordering: (800) 538-5005; (408) 416-0906
Customer Service: (800) 538-5001
Technical support: (800) 538-5002
International Orders: (408) 392-0100
Bulletin Board: (408) 559-0253

Contact Name: Jeffrey D. Rose, President
Catalog: Free. Frequency: Quarterly
Circulation: 1MM. Sales: $10-25MM
Products: Computer systems-PCs, portables &
accessories; cables & connectors; storage-disk drives,
interface cards; integrated circuits; communications-
modems & networking products; display platforms-
monitors & display cards; system basics-motherboards,
cases and power supplies; Input/Output-keyboards,
mice, printers and accessores, and scanners;
developer's world-board level products & plug-in
peripherals. Software designed for Windows, general,
disk & memory utility programs; operating environments,
productivity, and communications.

KEITHLEY INSTRUMENTS (800) 348-0033
28775 Aurora Rd. • Cleveland, OH 44139 (800) 552-1115
E-Mail: INFO@keithley.com
Website: www.keithley.com
Fax Ordering: (440) 498-2895; 248-6168
International Ordering: (440) 248-0400
Contact Names: Dick Heaton, President
Catalog: Free. Frequency: Annual
Circulation: 1MM. Sales: $20-50MM
Products: Data acquisition & control systems
series 500 hardware, software & accessories.
Includes entry level data acquisition systems,
portable monitoring systems, sophisticated
measurement & control systems; a full spectrum
of software for novice to expert use for IBM
PC/XT/AT, PS/2 and MicroChannel computers.

KEYDATA INTERNATIONAL (800) 486-4800
201 Circle Dr. N., Suite 101
Piscataway, NJ 08854
E-Mail: info@keydata-pc.com
Website: www.keydata-pc.com
Fax Ordering: (732) 868-6356
International Ordering: (732) 868-0588
Contact Name: Eric Miao, Manager
Catalog: Free. Frequency: Quarterly
Circulation: 50K. Sales: $10-20MM
Products: Notebooks & accessories

KONTRON AMERICA (888) 294-4558
14118 Stowe Dr. • Poway, CA 92064
E-Mail: sales@us.kontron.com
Website: www.us.kontron.com
Fax Ordering: (858) 677-0898
Customer Service: (800) 480-0044
Catalog: Free. Frequency: Semiannual.
Circulation: 50K. Sales: $20-50MM
Products: Computer-on-Modules,
Advanced TCA / Advanced MC, MicroTCA,
Motherboards, Slot Boards, I/O products
& solutions, etc.

LASER LABEL TECHNOLOGIES (800) 882-4050
LLT Bar Code & Label
4560 Darrow Rd. • Stowe, OH 44224
E-Mail: sales@lltproducts.com
Website: www.lltproducts.com
Fax Ordering: (800) 395-4721
Customer Service: (312) 243-9826
Contact Names: Denis Corrado, President
Catalog: Free. Frequency: Bimonthly
Circulation: 50M. Sales: $10-20MM
Products: National distributor of bar code
systems, thermal printing supplies, laser &
impact supplies, and point of sale systems.
Includes labels, and mobile computers and
printers. Save up to 50% off list prices.

LEXMARK INTERNATIONAL   (800) 539-6275
740 New Circle Rd. NW
Lexington, KY 40550
E-Mail: sales@lexmark.com
Website: www.lexmark.com
International Ordering: (859) 232-2000
Contact Name: Paul Rooke, Marketing
Catalog: Online. Sales: $4.5B
Product: Computer printers; ink & toner;
printer supplies

LIBRARY COMPUTER SOFTWARE   (631) 424-7777
Right On Programs
778 New York Ave. • Huntington, NY 11743
E-Mail: rightonsoft@aol.com
Website: www.rightonprograms.com
Fax Ordering: (631) 424-7207
Contact Name: Barbara Feinstein, President
Catalog: Free. Frequency: Semiannual
Circulation: 150K. Sales: $3-5MM
Products: Computer software for librarians

LINKSYS BY CISCO   (800) 546-5797
120 Theory Dr. • Irvine, CA 92617
E-Mail: sales@linksys.com
Website: www.shoplinksys.com
Fax Ordering: (949) 823-3007
Customer Service: (877) 959-7467
Technical Support: (800) 326-7114
Contact Name: Victor Tsao, President
Catalog: Free. Frequency: Quarterly
Circulation: 100K. Sales: $50-100MM
Products: Computer networking products

THE LIQUID ATE HER   (541) 431-0592
MCS Investments, Inc.
P.O. Box 23333 • Eugene, OR 97402
E-Mail: sales@theliquidateher.com
Website: www.theliquidateher.com
Fax Ordering: (541) 349-8694
Customer Service: (541) 431-0592
Contact Names: Mark LaPalme, President
Catalog: Free. Frequency: Annual
Circulation: 50K. Sales: $1-3MM
Products: Software for architectural, landscape,
and interior design as well as model railroad
design, organizational planning and education.
Programs for Apple II & IIgs, Macintosh, and
IBM & compatible computers.

LOGIC COMPUTER PRODUCTS   (800) 423-3197
P.O. Box 4069 • Valley Village, CA 91617
E-Mail: sales@logiccp.com
Website: www.logiccp.com
Fax Ordering: (818) 487-1818
Contact Name: Paula Abbott
Catalog: Free. Frequency: Annual
Circulation: 150K. Sales: $3-5MM
Products: Computer hardware, accessories
& peripherals; software; word processing
ribbons & supplies; printer supplies; cartridges,
tape, diskettes

MACMALL   (800) 622-6255
2555 West 190th St. • Torrance, CA 90504
E-Mail: sales@macmall.com
Website: www.macmall.com
Intenational Ordering: (310) 366-6900
Technical Support: (800) 760-0300
Contact Name: Peter Godfrey, President
Catalog: Free. Frequency: Quarterly
Circulation: 1MM. Sales: $100-250MM

Products: Authorized reseller of Apple &
Macintosh hardware, software, supplies &
accessories; furniture, data communications
devices. iPod & iPhone accessories; disk drives,
monitors, modems, printers, scanners, input
devices, power line protectors, cables.

MAIL ADVERTISING SUPPLY CO., INC.   (800) 558-2126
Lauterbach Group   (800) 841-7301
W222 N5710 Miller Wat • Sussex, WI 53089
E-Mail: info@lauterbachgroup.com
Website: www.lauterbachgroup.com
Fax Ordering: (800) 784-2591; (262) 820-1806
International Ordering: (262) 820-8130
Contact Names: H.W. Lauterbach, President
Catalog: Free. Frequency: Annual
Circulation: 50K. Sales: $1-3MM
Products: Inkjet/laser labels, tags & toners;
continuous pressure-sensitive, laser cards,
laser foil, laser card "business booster products",
thermal transfer products, EDP labels.

MEI/MICRO CENTER   (800) 634-3478
4119 Leap Rd. • Hilliard, OH 43026
E-Mail: sales@mei-microcenter.com
Website: www.mei-microcenter.com
Fax Ordering: (614) 486-6417
International Ordering: (614) 481-4417
Contact Name: Scott Voelker, President
Catalog: Free. Frequency: Semiannual.
Circulation: 2MM. Sales: $50-100MM
Products: Computers & computer parts;
electronics; diskettes & accessories, data
cartridges, paper & labels, printer ribbons
& stands, cleaning kits, laser toner cartridges,
surge protectors, monitor screens.
Multimedia kits & CD-ROMs, books.

MELISSA DATA CORP.   (800) 635-4772
22381 Avenita Empressa
Rancho Santa Marguerita, CA 92688
E-Mail: info@melissadata.com
Website: www.melissadata.com
Fax Ordering: (949) 589-5211
Technical Support: (949) 858-3000
Contact Names: Ray Melissa, President
Catalog: Free. Frequency: Quarterly.
Credit cards: All. Sales: $5-10 MM
Products: Mailing software; data
enhancement services

MICRO EXPRESS   (800) 989-9900
8 Hammond Dr. #105 • Irvine, CA 92618
E-Mail: info@microexpress.net
Website: www.microexpress.net
Fax Ordering: (949) 269-3070
Customer Service: (949) 460-9911
Contact Name: Art Afshar, President
Catalog: Free brochures as they become available
Products: Desktop & laptop computer systems.
Best known for its Regal series of lunch-box-style
transportables and laptops; printers and software.

MICRO SOLUTIONS, INC.   (800) 585-5389
P.O. Box 1001 • South Hill, VA 23970
E-Mail: sales@microsolutionsinc.com
Website: www.microsolutionsinc.com
Fax Ordering: (866) 813-3516
International Ordering: (434) 447-6121
Contact Names: Janice Currin, President
Catalog: Free. Sales: $10-20MM
Products: Corporate, Government & Educational

computers, as well as individual end-users.
Desktops, notebooks, servers, storage servers,
small form factor PCs

MICROBIZ CORPORATION (800) 937-2289
17075 Newhope St., Suite A
Fountain Valley, CA 92808
E-Mail: sales@microbiz.com
Website: www.microbiz.com
Catalog: Free. Frequency: Semiannual
Circulation: 50K. Sales: $3-5MM
Products: Point-of-Sale software, systems &
hardware, including demo kits, pole displays,
scanners, keyboards, printers and more.

MICROLINK ENTERPRISE, INC. (800) 829-3688
20955 Pathfinder Rd., Suite 100
Diamond Bar, CA 91746
E-Mail: erin.ellery@microlinkenterprise.com
Website: www.microlinkenterprise.com
Fax Ordering: (562) 205-1886
International Ordering: (562) 205-1888
Catalog: Free. Frequency: Annual.
Circulation: 100K Sales: $5-10MM
Products: Hardware & software products;
high quality computers and servers for
all business and education applications,
specializing in network security solutions;
Intel wireless and wired LAN connectivity,
and application development services.

MICRON TECHNOLOGY (208) 368-4000
P.O. Box 6 • Boise, ID 83687
E-Mail: sales@micron.com
Website: www.microN.com
Fax Ordering: (208) 368-4435

International Orders: (208) 368-4000
Catalog: Free. Frequency: Quarterly
Circulation: 1MM. Sales: $50-100MM
Products: Memory, storage, and imaging
semiconductor products; computer systems;
desktops, notebooks, servers, software and
services; office equipment & supplies

MICROREF SYSTEMS, INC. (847) 579-1456
1808 Rosemary Rd.
Highland Park, IL 60035
E-Mail: info@microref.com
Website: www.microref.com
Fax Ordering: (847) 579-1458
International Ordering: (847) 579-1456
Catalog: Free. Frequency: Semiannual
Circulation: 100K. Sales: $3-5MM
Products: Speech recognition, dictation
and medical notes software

MICROTECH SYSTEMS (800) 223-3693
2 Davis Dr. • Belmont, CA 94002
E-Mail: sales@microtech.com
Website: www.microtech.com
Fax Ordering: (650) 596-1915
Customer Support: (650) 596-1900
Products: High quality disc conversion,
CD/DVD duplication & publishing software
and hardware

MICROMATH RESEARCH (800) 942-6284
9202 Litzsinger Rd. • St. Louis, MO 63144
E-Mail: sales@micromath.com
Website: www.micromath.com
Fax Ordering: (800) 942-6284

Customer Service: (800) 942-6284
Contact Name: W. Robin Kemker, Contact
Catalog: Free. Frequency: Annual
Products: Pre-packaged software used by
scientists & engineers tp model, simulate,
analyze, fit & graph experimental data.
Scientific software (i.e., Chemist for Windows,
MicroMath Scientist for Windows V2.01 and
PKAnalyst for Windows): plotting, non-linear
curve fitting, scientific graphics, PC engineering
package, numeric computation

MOBILITY ELECTRONICS (800) 311-3274
iGo, Inc. (888) 205-0093
17800 N. Perimeter Dr.
Scottsdale, AZ 85255
E-Mail: websales@igo.com
Website: www.igo.com
Fax Ordering: (480) 596-0349
International Ordering: (480) 596-0061
Catalog: Free. Frequency: Quarterly.
Circulation: 100K. Sales: $25-50MM
Products: Universal chargers for laptops &
mobile devices such as mobile phones,
bluetooth headsets, smartphones, portable
gaming devices, digital cameras; accessories

MYERS POWER PRODUCTS (800) 526-5088
2000 Highland Ave. • Bethlehem, PA 18020
E-Mail: info@myerspowerproducts.com
Website: www.myerspowerproducts.com
Fax Ordering: (610) 868-8686
Customer Service: (610) 868-3500
Contact Names: Mike Vaughn, Marketing Manager
Catalog: Free. Frequency: Annual
Circulation: 25K. Sales: $3-5MM
Products: Power protection equipment

NATIONAL BUSINESS FURNITURE (800) 558-1010
P.O. Box 514052 • Milwaukee, WI 53203
E-Mail: sales@nationalbusinessfurniture.com
Website: www.nationalbusinessfurniture.com
Fax Ordering: (800) 329-9349
Customer Service: (800) 626-6060
Contact Names: George Mosher, President
Catalog: Free. Frequency: Monthly
Circulation: 15MM. Sales: $50-100MM
Product: Wholesale computer furniture.

NATIONAL INSTRUMENTS (800) 433-3488
11500 N. Mopac Expwy. • Austin, TX 78759 (888) 280-7645
E-Mail: sales@ni.com
Website: www.ni.com
Fax Ordering: (512) 683-8411
Customer Service: (800) 531-5066; (512) 683-0100
Contact Names: Jim Truchard, President
Catalog: Free. Frequency: Annual
Circulation: 200K. Sales: $100-250MM
Products: Instrumentation solutions for engineers
and scientists. Application tutorials & specifications
for hundreds of the leading hardware and software
products. PC, PS/2, Macintosh, and workstations;
interface boards and cables; signal conditioning
and accessories; software libraries for BASIC,
FORTRAN, C, and Pascal LabVIEW, LabWindows,
Measure application software.

NCR DIRECT (800) 543-8130
2651 Satellite Blvd. • Duluth, GA 30096 (800) 225-5627
E-Mail: sales@ncr.com
Website: www.ncr.com
Fax Ordering: (937) 439-8572

International Ordering: (937) 445-1936
Customer Service: (937) 439-8200
Contact Name: Dan Enneking, President
Catalog: Free. Frequency: Semiannual
Circulation: 2MM. Sales: $50-100MM
Products: Computer supplies and accessories.
Paper, ribbons, cartridges, tapes, keyboards,
monitors/glare filters, workstations, and more

NEBS COMPUTER FORMS & SOFTWARE   (800) 225-9550
New England Business Service   Canada   (800) 461-7572
500 Main St. • Groton, MA 01470   (888) 823-6327
E-Mail: sales@nebs.com
Website: www.nebs.com
Fax Ordering: (866) 449-3794; (800) 234-4324
Canada Fax Ordering: (705) 526-2764
Customer Service: (800) 225-9540
Contact Names: Richard Riley, President
Catalog: Free. Frequency: Quarterly
Circulation: 4MM. Sales: $50-100MM
Guarantee: Unconditional guarantee
Products: Stocks over 1,500 computer related
forms & supplies; & about 1,000 software packages.

NEC SOLUTIONS   (800) 284-4484
NEC Technologies, Inc.
1414 Massachusetts Ave.
Foxborough, MA 01719
E-Mail: info@necdisplay.com
Website: www.necdisplay.com
Fax Ordering: (508) 264-8831
Catalog: Free. Frequency: Quarterly
Circulation: 150K. Sales: $10-50MM
Products: Computer equipment including
hardware and software solutions

NETWORKING SOLUTIONS   (580) 243-1559
Innovative Technology, Ltd.
P.O. Box 726 • Elk City, OK 73648
E-Mail: info@itlnet.net
Website: www.itlnet.net
Fax Ordering: (580) 243-2810
Catalog: Free. Frequency: Quarterly
Circulation: 100K. Sales: $10-20MM
Products: Networking equipment, software,
accessories and supplies

NETWORKS NOW   (800) 913-9467
CABLExpress Corporation
P.O. Box 4799 • Syracuse, NY 13221
E-Mail: info@cablexpress.com
Website: www.cablexpress.com
Fax Ordering: 315) 455-1800
International Ordering: (315) 476-3000
Contact Names: William G. Pomeroy, President
Catalog: Free. Frequency: Semiannual
Circulation: 200K. Sales: $100-200MM
Products: Computer related cables & connectors;
networking hardware, testing equipment,
mainframe data center products, data
communications equipment, & wiring systems.

THE NEWMAN GROUP   (734) 426-3200
7400 Newman Blvd. • Dexter, MI 48130
E-Mail: sales@newman.com
Website: www.newman.com
Fax Ordering: (734) 426-0777
Contact Names: Allan Newman, President
Catalog: Free. Frequency: Monthly
Circulation: 200K. Sales: $10-20MM
Products: DEC/Compaq products. Computer systems;
hardware & supplies; terminals, printers, disks & tapes.

NOTHINGBUTSOFTWARE.COM   (800) 755-4619
SpaceBound, Inc.
280 Opportunity Way • LaGrange, OH 44050
E-Mail: pm@msbcd.com
Website: www.nothingbutsoftware.com
Fax Ordering: (440) 355-8009
International Ordering: (440) 355-8008
Contact Names: Anthony Saliba, President
Catalog: Free. Frequency: Monthly
Circulation: 200K. Sales: $5-10MM
Products: Software for the family & business

OCEAN INTERFACE COMPANY   (909) 595-1212
20545 Paseo Del Prado • Walnut, CA 91789
E-mail: ocean@oceanusa.com
Website: www.oceanusa.com
Fax Ordering: (909) 595-9683
Contact Names: Chuck Mei Fan, President
Catalog: Free. Frequency: Semiannual
Circulation: 25K. Sales: $3-5MM
Products: Computer systems, notebooks,
monitors, networking, peripherals, & storage.

OFFICE DEPOT COMPUTER SUPPLIES   (800) 463-3768
6600 N. Military Trail • Boca Raton, FL 33496   (888) GO-DEPOT
E-Mail: sales@officedepot.com
Website: www.officedepot.com
Fax Ordering: (800) 685-5010
Customer Service: (888) 263-3423
Tech Support: (800) 269-6888
Catalog: Free. Frequency: Semiannual
Circulation: 50MM. Sales: $250-500MM
Products: Computer supplies & accessories:
word & data processing paper, laser paper,
labels, printer ribbons, mouse pads & cleaner,
diskettes, keyboard, data cartridges, software,
cables and switches, and workstations.

O'REILLY & ASSOCIATES   (800) 998-9938
1005 Gravenstein Hwy. N.
Sebastopol, CA 95472
E-Mail: catalog@oreilly.com
Website: www.oreilly.com
Fax Ordering: (707) 829-0104
International Ordering: (707) 827-7000
Contact Name: Tim O'Reilly, President
Catalog: Free. Frequency: Semiannual
Circulation: 50K. Sales: $1-3MM
Products: Books, manuals and software

OSBORNE/McGRAW-HILL CATALOG   (800) 227-0900
160 Spear St. #700 • San Francisco, CA 94105
E-Mail: info@mhprofessional.com
Website: www.mhprofessional.com
Fax Ordering: (609) 308-4484; 426-7917
International Ordering: (609) 426-5793
Customer Service: (877) 833-5524
Contact Name: Steve Chapman, Publisher
Catalog: Free. Frequency: Annual
Circulation: 500K. Sales: $10-20MM
Products: Academic, consumer & professional
computer books

PACIFIC COMPUTER SUPPLY   (800) 521-7688
922 San Leandro Ave.
Mountain View, CA 94043
E-Mail: customerservice@pacificcs.com
Website: www.pacificcs.com
Fax Ordering: (800) 367-7271
Contact Name: John B. Sanchez, President
Catalog: Free. Frequency: Semiannual
Circulation: 100K. Sales: $5-10MM

Products: Nationwide authorized reseller of computer & office products. Computer hardware, peripherals, printer supplies & accessories.

PAPER DIRECT (800) 272-7377
1005 E. Woodmen Rd.
Colorado Springs, CO 80935
E-Mail: customerservice@paperdirect.com
Website: www.paperdirect.com
Fax Ordering: (800) 443-2973; (719) 534-1741
International Orders: (719) 534-1741
Contact Names: Ted Struhl, President
Catalog: Free. Frequency: Semiannual
Circulation: 150K. Sales: $10-25MM
Products: Paper for all laser printer copiers & desktop publishing needs.

PATTERSON OFFICE SUPPLIES (800) 637-1140
P.O. Box 9009 • Champaign, IL 61826
E-Mail: sales@pattersonofficesupplies.com
Website: www.pattersonofficesupplies.com
Fax Ordering: (800) 843-3676; (217) 351-5413
Customer Service: (800) 475-5036
Contact Names: Smith DeVoe, President
Catalog: Free. Frequency: Semiannual
Circulation: 250K. Sales: $10-25MM
Products: Practice management software for medical, dental & veterinarians; computer-aided design and ceramic tooth restoration system; hospital patient monitoring systems; computer plotter paper; receipt pads; business & computer forms and stationery, including labels.

PATTON ELECTRONICS CO. CATALOG (301) 975-1000
7622 Rickenbacker Dr.
Gaithersburg, MD 20879
E-Mail: sales@patton.com
Website: www.patton.com
Fax Ordering: (301) 869-9293
Support Services: (301) 975-1007
Contact Names: Burton Patton, President
Catalog: Free. Frequency: Semiannual.
Circulation: 150K. Sales: $5-10 MM
Products: Short range modems, data line surge protectors, interface convertors, peripheral sharing productss, adapters, data switches (manual & automatic), cables and accessories,

PC AMERICA (800) 722-6374
P.O. Box 1546 • Pearl River, NY 10965
E-Mail: sales@pcamerica.com
Website: www.pcamerica.com
Fax Ordering: (845) 920-0880
International Ordering: (845) 920-0800
Customer Service: (845) 920-0888
Catalog: Free. Frequency: Semiannual
Circulation: 100K. Sales: $10-20MM
Products: PC hardware, software & accessories. PC is the national distributor of The General Store, the leading point of sale software product and its complementary hardware peripherals.

PC AVIATOR FLIGHT SIMULATION (800) 664-0033
P.O. Box 15907 • Surfside Beach, SC 29575
E-Mail: info@pcaviatornetwork.com
Website: www.pcaviatornetwork.com
Fax Ordering: (843) 716-1619
International Orders: (843) 716-1616
Technical Support: (843) 716-1616
Catalog: Free. Frequency: Semiannual
Circulation: 100K. Sales: $10-20MM
Products: Flight simulation products & accessories

PC CONNECTION/MAC CONNECTION
(888) 800-0323
(888) 213-0607
(800) 998-0009
(800) 800-1111
(800) 800-5555
(800) 986-4420
Rt. 101A, 730 Milford Rd.
Merrimack, NH 03054
E-Mail: salespricing@pcconnection.com
Website: www.pcconnection.com
www.macconnection.com
Fax Ordering: (603) 446-7791
International Orders: (603) 355-6005
Customer Service: (800) 213-0259
Technical Support: (800) 213-0447
Contact Name: Patricia Gallup, President
Catalog: Free. Frequency: Monthly
Circulation: 3MM. Sales: $100-200MM
Products: PC/IBM compatible hardware, software, accessories and supplies. Software: business, graphics & design, educational & recreational, networks & communications, utilities & programming; hardware & accessories for the IBM compatible.

PC MALL/MAC MALL
(800) 555-6255
(800) 328-2790
(800) 552-8883
(800) 560-6800
2555 W. 190th St. • Torrance, CA 90504
E-Mail: sales@pcmall.com; sales@macmall.com
Website: www.pcmall.com; www.macmall.com
Fax Ordering: (310) 225-4000
PC Mall Government Sales: (800) 323-2704
PC Mall Education Sales: (800) 328-2793
International Ordering: (310) 225-2600
Customer Service: (877) 233-9124
Technical Support: (800) 760-0300 (MAC); (800) 727-7579 (PC)
Contact Name: Dan DeVries, President
Catalog: Free. Pages: 76. Frequency: Biweekly
Circulation: 3MM. Sales: $100-200MM
Products: The largest authorized full line of PC and Apple Macintosh mail order superstore. Over 2,500 products - hardware and software for the PC and Mac.

PC MALL GOV (800) 625-5468
7421 Gateway Ct. • Manassas, VA 20109
E-Mail: sales@pcmallgov.com
Website: www.pcmallgov.com
Fax Ordering: (703) 378-4464
Tech Support: (800) 727-7579
Catalog: Free. Frequency: Semiannual
Circulation: 200K. Sales: $5-10MM
Products: Computer systems & accessories for business, education, government institutions, and professional consumers

PC POWER & COOLING (800) 722-6555
OCZ Technology Group Co.
5995 Avenida Encinas • Carlsbad, CA 92008
E-Mail: sales@pcpow.com
Website: www.pcpowercooling.com
International E-Mail: intsales@pcpow.com
Tech Support E-Mail: support@pcpow.com
Fax Ordering: (760) 931-6988
Tech Support: (760) 931-5700
Catalog: Free. Frequency: Semiannual
Circulation: 100K. Sales: $5-10MM
Contact Name: Denise Kaplan, Marketing Manager
Products: Computer cooling systems & accessories

PCNAMETAG
(877) 626-3824
(800) 233-9767
124 Horizon Dr. • Verona, WI 53593
E-Mail: sales@pcnametag.com
Website: www.pcnametag.com
Fax Ordering: (800) 233-9787; (608) 845-1860
International Ordering: (608) 845-1850
Tech Support: (800) 369-8622
Contact Names: Nick Topitzes, President
Catalog: Free. Frequency: Semiannual

Circulation: 50M. Sales: $1-3MM
Products: PC/Nametag & Nametent (sign &
lamination service) - software for the meeting
planner. Also computer supplies and specialty
products for those who produce trade shows,
coventions & seminars

PKWARE, INC.	(888) 4PK-WARE
648 N. Plankinton #220
Milwaukee, WI 53203
E-Mail: sales@pkware.com
Website: www.pkware.com
Fax Ordering: (414) 289-9789
International Ordering: (414) 289-9788
Contact Name: Phil Katz, President
Catalog: Free. Frequency: Annual.
Circulation: 100K. Sales: $5-10MM
Products: Data secutiry & file compression/
extraction software & related products

PM COMPANY	(800) 327-4359
9220 Glades Dr. • Fairfield, OH 45011
E-Mail: generalinquiries@pmcompany.com
Website: www.pmcompany.com
Fax Ordering: (800) 577-7695; (513) 825-2877
International Ordering: (513) 825-7626
Contact Name: Don O'Neill, President
Catalog: Free. Frequency: Annual
Circulation: 150K. Sales: $5-10MM
Products: Facsimile products; laser printer supplies;
replacement toner cartridge products; overhead
transparencies; financial equipment supplies;
mailing & shipping supplies, business machine
supplies. Recycled laser toner cartridges.

POLYWELL COMPUTERS	(800) 999-1278
1461 San Mateo Ave.	(800) 900-5836
So. San Francisco, CA 94080
E-Mail: sales@polywell.com
Website: www.polywell.com
Fax Ordering: (650) 583-1974
International Sales: (650) 583-7222 Fax 583-1974
Customer Service: (800) 676-6618
Tech Support: (800) 300-7659; (650) 871-3920
Contact Name: Chin Lo, President
Catalog: Free. Frequency: Quarterly
Circulation: 100K. Sales: $10-20MM
Products: IBM personal computers compatible
386, 486. Custom made PCs, Polyservers,
workstations, UNIX servers & woprkstations;
notebooks, SAN storage/networking.

POWERFUL PRESENTATIONS CATALOG	(800) 424-1011
Visual Horizons
180 Metro Park • Rochester, NY 14623
E-Mail: cs@visualhorizons.com
Website: www.visualhorizons.com
Fax Ordering: (800) 424-5411; (585) 424-5313
International Ordering: (585) 424-5300
Contact Name: Stan Feingold, President
Catalog: Free. Frequency: Monthly
Circulation: 250K. Sales: $5-10MM
Products: Media storage. Diskette & CD storage

PRECISION DATA PRODUCTS	(800) 968-0888
P.O. Box 8367 • Grand Rapids, MI 49518	(800) 968-2468
E-Mail: sales@precision.com
Website: www.precision.com
Fax Ordering: (616) 698-9047
Customer Service: (616) 698-2242
Contact Name: Kevin Andrea, General Manager
Catalog: Free. Frequency: Quarterly

Circulation: 100K. Sales: $5-10MM
Products: Batteries, cables & switches,
cleaning products, data cartridges, diskettes
& accessories, dust covers, laser printer
supplies, paper & labels, power protection
products, printer ribbons, printwheels, tape
& accessories. Brand name products.

THE PRINTER WORKS	(800) 225-6116
3481 Arden Rd. • Hayward, CA 94545
8547 154th Ave. NE
Redmond, WA 98052 (Sales Office)
E-Mail: info@printerworks.com
Website: www.printerworks.com
Fax Ordering: (510) 786-0589
International Ordering: (510) 670-2700
Technical Support: (800) 235-6116
Contact Name: Stephen Roberts, President
Catalog: Free. Frequency: Annual
Circulation: 100K. Sales: $5-10MM
Products: HP laserjet printers & accessories;
HP parts & fusers; laserjet repair kits

PROGRAMMER'S PARADISE	(800) 445-7899
1157 Shrewsbury Ave.	(800) 599-4388
Shrewsbury, NJ 07702
E-Mail: sales@pparadise.com
Website: www.pparadise.com
Fax Ordering: (732) 389-2263
International Ordering: (732) 389-8950
Customer Service: (732) 460-9310
Contact Names: Stephen Watson, President
Catalog: Free. Frequency: Quarterly
Circulation: 2MM. Sales: $10-20MM
Products: Software development tools:
hardware and software...all types and brands
of software programming tools — over 2,500
of the more popular (e.g. Microsoft, Ashton Tate)
to the most obscure.

PROSTAR	(800) 576-6776
ProStar Computers
837 S. Lawson St.
City of Industry, CA 91748
E-Mail: sales@pro-star.com
Website: www.pro-star.com
Fax Ordering: (626) 854-3438
International Orders: (626) 854-3428
Tech Support: (888) 576-4742
Catalog: Free. Frequency: Annual.
Circulation: 100K. Sales: $3-5MM
Products: Notebook computers & accessories

PROTECT KEYBOARD COVERS	(800) 669-7739
P.O. Box 1002 • Centerville, UT 84014
E-Mail: protectcov@aol.com
Website: www.protectcovers.com
Fax Ordering: (801) 295-7786
International Ordering: (801) 295-7739
Contact Names: Gil Workman, President
Catalog: Free. Frequency: Annual.
Circulation: 150K. Sales: $3-5MM
Products: Laptop & keyboard covers

PROVANTAGE	(800) 336-1166
7249 Whipple Ave. NW
North Canton, OH 44720
E-Mail: sales@provantage.com
Website: www.provantage.com
Fax Ordering: (330) 494-5260
International Orders: (330) 494-8715
Contact Names: Michael Coralik, President

Catalog: Free. Frequency: Quarterly
Circulation: 50K. Sales: $10-20MM
Product: Discount PC hardware, software,
and programmer's development tools

PUBLISHING PERFECTION (800) 782-5974
21155 Watertown Rd. • Waukesha, WI 53186
E-Mail: web@publishingperfection.com
Website: www.publishingperfection.com
Fax Ordering: (262) 717-0745
Customer Service: (262) 717-0600
Catalog: Free. Frequency: Annual.
Circulation: 200K. Sales: $5-10MM
Products: Desktop publishing software
and hardware; graphic design software

PURCHASE POINT (866) 659-7926
Enpointe Technologies, Inc. (800) 800-4214
18701 S. Figueroa St. • Gardena, CA 90248 (888) 888-8223
E-Mail: sales@enpointe.com
Website: www.enpointe.com
Fax Ordering: (310) 338-4855
Customer Service: (310) 337-5200
Contact Names: Bob Din, President
Catalog: Free. Frequency: Annual
Circulation: 100K. Sales: $5-10MM
Products: Supplies I.T. products & services to
medium & large enterprises, educational institutions,
government agencies & non-profits nationwide

QUALSTAR CORPORATION (888) 583-7744
3990-B Heritage Oak Ct.
Simi Valley, CA 93063
E-Mail: sales@qualstar.com
Website: www.qualstar.com
Fax Ordering: (805) 583-7749
International Ordering: (805) 583-7744
Contact Name: Bob Covey, VP Marketing
Catalog: Free. Frequency: Annual.
Circulation: 150K. Sales: $5-10MM
Products: Tape drives and tape drive software
for backup, data interchange, and storage
management; archival storage & disaster
protection.

QUEUE, INC. (800) 232-2224
1 Controls Dr. • Shelton, CT 06484
E-Mail: jdk@queueinc.com
Website: www.queueinc.com
Fax Ordering: (800) 775-2729;
Contact Name: Monica Kantrowitz, President
Catalog: Free. Frequency: Semiannual.
Circulation: 200K. Sales: $5-10MM
Products: Educational software for the Mac
& PC computers. Offers over 2,000 educational
programs from more than one hundred publishers.
They have two catalogs, Kindergarten-Grade 8
and High School/College.

QUILL CORP. - COMPUTERS, PRINTERS (800) 789-0605
& BUSINESS MACHINES CATALOG (800) 789-1331
P.O. Box 94080 • Palatine, IL 60094 (800) 789-8955
E-Mail: sales@quillcorp.com
Website: www.quillcorp.com
Fax Ordering: (800) 789-6630
Contact Names: Jack Miller, President
Catalog: Free. Frequency: Semiannual.
Circulation: 2MM. Sales: $50-100MM
Products: A major mail order office supplies
company with an extensive line of microcomputer
and word processing supplies. They have some
software, cables, disks, printers, printer ribbons,

printwheels, power supplies, surge suppressors,
computer furniture, forms, letterheads, labels,
and other accessories; also laser & inkjet paper
& supplies. The software includes word processing,
financial, and office operating software by Leading Edge,
Peachtree, Sidekick, Rolodex, & FlashCalc.

RADIO SHACK CATALOG (800) 843-7422
300 RadioShack Cir.
Fort Worth, TX 76102
E-Mail: commsales@radioshack.com
Website: www.radioshack.com
Fax Ordering: (800) 291-6515; (817) 415-3240
International Ordering: (817) 415-3700
Contact Name: Bernard Appel, President
Catalog: Free. Frequency: Annual
Circulation: 1MM. Sales: $100-200MM
Products: Personal computer & consumer
electronics, software, and accessories.

RAPIDFORMS (800) 257-8354
P.O. Box 1186 • Lancaster, CA 93584
E-Mail: service@rapidforms.com
Website: www.rapidforms.com
Fax Ordering: (800) 451-8113
Customer Service: (800) 257-5287
Catalog: Free. Frequency: Semiannual
Circulation: 2MM. Sales: $5-10 Million
Products: Software compatible business
forms, tags, labels. A complete line of continuous
computer forms including a compatibility index for
numerous software programs.

REAL ESTATE SOFTWARE CATALOG (800) 526-5588
Z-Law Software
P.O. Box 40602 • Providence, RI 02940
E-Mail: catalog@z-law.com
Website: www.z-law.com
Fax Ordering: (401) 421-5334
International Ordering: (401) 331-3002
Contact Name: Gary Sherman, President
Catalog: Free. Frequency: Annual.
Circulation: 10K. Sales: $500K- $1MM
Products: PC and MAC software for realtors,
investors, developers, property managers,
and anyone involved in real estate.

RECYCLED SOFTWARE, INC. (760) 534-5338
3764 Serenity Trail
Palm Springs, CA 92262
E-Mail: webstore@recycledsoftware.com
Website: www.recycledsoftware.com1
Contact Name: Diane M. Hathaway, President
Catalog: Free. Frequency: Semiannual
Circulation: 100K. Sales: $250-500K
Products: Recycled software for Windows
and DOS systems on disk and CD-ROM

RELIABLE HOME OFFICE (800) 735-4000
Reliable Corporation
1501 E. Woodfield Rd.
Schaumburg, IL 60173
E-Mail: sales@reliable.com
Website: www.reliable.com
Fax Ordering: (847) 413-8250
Customer Service: (800) 359-5000
Contact Names: Rick L. Black, President
Catalog: Free. Frequency: Quarterly
Circulation: 500K. Sales: $50-100MM
Products: Complete line of computer and
word processing supplies, office products,
furniture, and equipment.

RMS TECHNOLOGY, INC. (800) 533-3211
P.O. Box 249 • Molalla, OR 97038
E-Mail: info@rmstek.com
Website: www.rmstek.com
Fax Ordering: (503) 829-6568
International Ordering: (503) 829-6167
Product Support: (503) 829-6166
Contact Name: Neal Christman, President
Catalog: Free. Frequency: Weekly
Circulation: 100K. Sales: $1-3MM
Products: Flight planning computer software
and moving map software

ROCKWARE, INC. (800) 775-6745
2221 East St. #1 • Golden, CO 80401
E-Mail: sales@rockware.com
Website: www.rockware.com
Fax Ordering: (303) 278-4099
International Ordering: (303) 278-3534
Contact Names: Dean Jacobsen, President
Catalog: Free. Frequency: Annual
Circulation: 150K. Sales: $1-3MM
Products: Software products for earth science

ROSE ELECTRONICS (800) 333-9343
10707 Stancliff Rd. • Houston, TX 77099
E-Mail: sales@rose.com
Website: www.rose.com
Fax Ordering: (281) 933-0044
Customer Service: (281) 933-7673
Contact Names: David Rahvar, President
Catalog: Free. Frequency: Quarterly
Circulation: 100K. Sales: $10-20MM
Products: Data communication equipment
& computer peripheral sharing devices,
including: networking switches & software,
automatic switches, code activated switches,
laser printer sharing cards, DATA PBX switches,
protocol converters, buffers and converters,
manual switches, cables and accessories.

RPMS (800) 776-7435
11771 W. 112th St.
Overland Park, KS 66210
E-Mail: info@rpms.com
Website: www.rpms.com
Fax Ordering: (800) 337-7056; (913) 338-2279
International Ordering: (913) 338—0266
Contact Names: Bob Williams, President
Circulation: 75K. Sales: $1-3MM
Product: Profit management system software

SAGER NOTEBOOKS (800) 669-1624
18005 Cortney Ct.
City of Industry, CA 91748
E-Mail: sales@sagernotebook.com
Website: www.sagernotebook.com
Fax Ordering: (626) 964-2381
Tech Support: (800) 741-2219; (626) 964-4849
Customer Service: (626) 964-8682
Contact Name: Brian Liaw, Buyer
Catalog: Free. Frequency: Annual
Circulation: 50K. Sales: $10-20MM
Products: Computer equipment & supplies

HENRY SCHEIN MEDICAL GROUP (800) 772-4346
135 Duryea Rd. • Melville, NY 11747   (800) 972-2611
E-Mail: medsls@henryschein.com
Website: www.henryschein.com
Fax Ordering: 800) 329-9109
Customer Support: (631) 843-5500
Technical Support: (800) 356-5788

Contact: James Breslawski, President
Catalog: Free. Frequency: Annual
Circulation: 100K. Sales: $20-50MM
Products: Healthcare software

SCHOLASTIC SOFTWARE (800) 724-6527
Scholastic, Inc.   (800) 541-5513
524 Broadway • New York, NY 10012
E-Mail: sales@scholastic.com
Website: www.scholastic.com
Fax Ordering: (212) 965-7250
International Ordering: (212) 965-7349
Contact Names: Scott Bowker, Sales Director
Catalog: Free. Frequency: Annual
Circulation: 350K. Sales: $100-250MM
Products: Educational software for teachers
and schools

SENECA DATA, INC. (800) 227-3432
7401 Round Pond Rd.
N. Syracuse, NY 13212
E-Mail: sales@senecadata.com
Website: www.senecadata.com
Fax Ordering: (315) 433-0945
International Ordering: (315) 433-1160
Catalog: Online. Sales: $10-20MM
Products: Business computer systems -
custom computer manufacturer. Nexlink brand
of custom built desktops, notebooks, servers,
and storage devices for business, government,
education, healthcare

SHAREWARE SPECTACULAR (800) 243-1515
Star-Byte, Inc.   (800) 944-4237
611 Jeffers Cir. • Exton, PA 19341
E-Mail: sales@mediasupply.com
Website: www.mediasupply.com
Fax Ordering: (610) 884-4500
Catalog: Free. Frequency: Semiannual
Circulation: 100K. Sales: $3-5MM
Products: CD duplication; CD/DVD
replication; software and CD-ROMs

SHECOM COMPUTERS (800) 366-4433
3181 E. Miraloma Ave. • Anaheim, CA 92806
E-Mail: customerservice@shecom.com
Website: www.shecom.com
Fax Ordering: (714) 990-3964
International Ordering: (714) 990-9300
Customer Service: (714) 692-7070
Tech Support: (800) 352-2929; (714) 990-3551
Catalog: Free. Frequency: Annual
Circulation: 50K. Sales: $10-20MM
Products: Computer equipment & accessories;
hardware, computers & memory products

SMX CATALOG (800) 366-2491
Micro Digital, Inc.
2900 Bristol St. #G204
Costa Mesa, CA 92626
E-Mail: sales@smxrtos.com
Website: www.smxrtos.com
Fax Ordering: (714) 432-0490
International Ordering: (714) 437-7333
Contact Name: Ralph Moore, President
Catalog: Free. Frequency: Semiannual
Products: Provides hardware & software
design services to OEM's

SOCIAL STUDIES SCHOOL SERVICE (800) 421-4246
10200 Jefferson Blvd. • Culver City, CA 90232
E-Mail: access@socialstudies.com

Website: www.socialstudies.com
Fax Ordering: (800) 944-5432; (310) 839-2249
International Ordering: (310) 839-2436
Catalog: Free. Frequency: Semiannual
Circulation: 150K. Sales: $3-5MM
Products: Educational software

SOFTDISK PUBLISHING   (800) 831-2694
P.O. Box 1240 • Shreveport, LA 71163
E-Mail: info@softdisk.com
Website: www.softdisk.com
Fax Ordering: (318) 221-8870
Customer Service: (318) 221-8718
Contact Names: Arnold Lincove, President
Catalog: Free. Frequency: Semiannual
Circulation: 100K. Sales: $3-5MM
Products: Download software by publishers

SOFTMART   (800) 328-1319
450 Acorn Lane • Downingtown, PA 19335
E-mail: customerservice@softmart.com
Website: www.softmart.com
Fax Ordering: (800) 423-0612; (610) 518-4057
International Ordering: (610) 518-4166
Contact Names: Dean Picciotti, President
Catalog: Free. Frequency: Quarterly
Circulation: 100K. Sales: $3-5MM
Products: Computer hardware & packaged
software.

SOFTWARE EXPRESS   (800) 527-7638
EDUCATORS CATALOG
4128-A South Blvd. • Charlotte, NC 28209
E-Mail: nicepeople@swexpress.com
Website: www.swexpress.com
Fax Ordering: (704) 529-1010
Customer Service: (704) 522-7638
Catalog: Free. Frequency: Semiannual
Circulation: 100K. Sales: $3-5MM
Products: Educational software for teachers
and students

SOFTWARE SPECTRUM   (800) 882-9506
Insight Enterprises, Inc.   (800) 888-4880
6820 S. Harl Ave. • Tempe, AZ 85283   (800) 624-0503
E-Mail: sales@insight.com   (800) 787-1166
Website: www.insight.com   (800) 467-4448
Fax Ordering: (800) 677-4008
Contact Names: Mark McGrath, President
Catalog: Free. Frequency: Semiannual
Circulation: 250K. Sales: $3-4BB
Products: Software reseller; Microsoft
& Macintosh software from 3,700 publishers

SPRINGER SOFTWARE & CD-ROM's   (800) 777-4643
Springer New York, LLC
233 Spring St. • New York, NY 10013
P.O. Box 2485 • Secaucus, NJ 07094
E-Mail: service-ny@springer.com
Website: www.springer.com
Fax Ordering: (212) 460-1575 (201) 348-4505
International Ordering: (212) 460-1500
Contact Name: Richard Sabol, Marketing
Catalog: Free. Frequency: Semiannual.
Circulation: 5MM. Sales: $500+MM
Products: Software and CD-ROM's;
electronic media

STANLEY SUPPLY & SERVICES   (800) 225-5370
335 Willow St. • North Andover, MA 01845
E-Mail: service@stanleysupplyservices.com
Website: www.stanleysupplyservices.com

Fax Ordering: (800) 743-8141
International Ordering: (978) 682-9844
Customer Service: (888) 887-9473
Technical Support: (888) 866-5487
Catalog: Free. Frequency: Semiannual
Circulation: 200K. Sales: $50-100MM
Products: Products for test, assembly and
repair of electronic equipment, tool kits and
cases. Static protection/contamination control
products/adhesives/gloves/cleaners

STAPLES TECHNOLOGY DIRECT   (800) 828-9949
500 Staples Dr. • Framingham, MA 01702   (800) STAPLES
E-Mail: sales@staples.com   (800) 378-2753
Website: www.staples.com
Fax Ordering: (800) 333-3199
International Ordering: (508) 253-5000
Contact Names: Jack Bingleman, President;
Catalog: Free. Frequency: Monthly
Circulation: 2MM. Sales: $100-500MM
Products: Computers, software, supplies
& accessories.

SUNSHINE UNLIMITED   (785) 227-3880
P.O. Box 71 • Lindsborg, KS 67456
E-Mail: cpeterjr@aol.com
Website: www.sunshine-unlimited.com
Fax Ordering: (785) 227-3880
Contact Name: Chester Peterson, Jr., President
Catalog: Free. Frequency: Annual
Circulation: 50K. Sales: $500K
Products: Computer spreadsheet
template programs

TAPE RESOURCES   (800) 827-3462
5265 Providence Rd., Suite 403
Virginia Beach, VA 23464
E-Mail: sales@taperesources.com
Website: www.taperesources.com
Fax Ordering: (757) 464-4112
International Ordering: (757) 460-4111
Catalog: Free. Frequency: Annual
Circulation: 100K. Sales: $5-10MM
Products: Tape & removable media; blank
mini DV tapes; mini DV tapes; USB/Flash
Memory Cards; DVD discs; CD-R discs;
cleaning cassettes; storage media; hardware;
USB/Flash memory; software; audio; accessories

TECHNOLAND SYSTEMS   (800) 292-4500
1050 Stewart Dr. • Sunnyvale, CA 94086
E-Mail: sales@ibase-usa.com
Website: www.ibase-usa.com
Fax Ordering: (408) 992-0808
Customer Support: (408) 992-0888
Contact Name: Susan Wei, Marketing Manager
Catalog: Free. Frequency: Annual
Circulation: 25K. Sales: $500K - $1MM
Products: IPC ready solutions for digital
signage, gaming; medical automation,
infotainment; computer parts, supplies
& accessories

TERRAPIN SOFTWARE   (800) 774-5646
955 Massachusetts Ave. #365
Cambridge, MA 02138
E-Mail: info@terrapinlogo.com
Website: www.terrapinlogo.com
Fax Ordering: (800) 776-4610; (508) 487-1252
International Ordering: (508) 487-4141
Catalog: Free. Frequency: Annual
Circulation: 100K. Sales: $50-100MM

Products: Logo computer language and Logo-related products that encourages students to create and explore.

THEOS RESOURCE DIRECTORY (800) 600-5660
Theos Software Corp.
1280 Boulevard Way, #206
Walnut Creek, CA 94595
E-Mail: sales@theos-software.com
Website: www.theos-software.com
Fax Ordering: (925) 935-1177
Customer Service: (925) 935-1118
Contact Names: Jack Dyer, President
Catalog: Free. Frequency: Annual
Circulation: 100K. Sales: $10-25MM
Products: Business software; multiuse operating systems, communications software & development languages

3COM (800) 876-3266
350 Campus Dr. • Marlborough, MA 01752
E-Mail: john_vincenzo@3com.com
Website: www.3com.com
Fax Ordering: (508) 323-1111
International Ordering: (508) 323-5000
Contact Name: Ron Sege, President & COO
Catalog: Free. Frequency: Monthly.
Circulation: 150K. Sales: $100-200MM
Product: Platforms & IP phones; LAN switches (modular & stackable/Edge); routers; security productrs; wireless switches

TIGER DIRECT CATALOG (800) 800-8300
7795 W. Flagler St., Suite 35
Miami, FL 33144
E-Mail: info@tigerdirect.com
Website: www.tigerdirect.com
Fax Ordering: (305) 228-3400; 415-2202
International Ordering: (305) 415-2201
Customer Service: (800) 888-6111
Contact Names: Carl Florentino, President
Catalog: Free. Frequency: Monthly.
Circulation: 2MM. Sales: $100-200MM
Products: Computers, Software, Accessories & Supplies; Laptops, Hard Drives, Fonts, Virus Protection, Power Protectors, Desktop Page Scanners, Laserwriters and Printers, Scanners, Furniture, and other Peripherals

TOSHIBA ACCESSORIES CATALOG (800) TOSHIBA
9740 Irvine Blvd. • Irvine, CA 92618 (800) 316-0920
E-Mail: sales@toshibadirect.com
Website: www.toshibadirect.com
Fax Ordering: (800) 950-4373
International Ordering: (949) 583-3000
Customer Service: (800) 618-4444
Tech Support: (800) 457-7777; (949) 859-4273
Catalog: Free. Frequency: Quarterly.
Circulation: 2MM. Sales: $100-200MM
Products: Toshiba brand computer systems; laptops, notebooks & accessories, electronics & projectors

TRIUS, INC. CATALOG (978) 794-9377
P.O. Box 249 • N. Andover, MA 01845
E-Mail: info@triusinc.com
Website: www.triusinc.com
Fax Ordering: (978) 688-6312
Catalog: Free. Frequency: Semiannual
Circulation: 50K. Sales: $10-20MM
Products: GIS and mapping technology solutions

TRUE DATA PRODUCTS (800) 635-0300
775 Quaker Highway • Uxbridge, MA 01569
E-Mail: sales@truedataproducts.com
Website: www.truedataproducts.com
Fax Ordering: (508) 278-6748
International Ordering: (508) 278-6555
Contact Name: Mark Rachwal, President
Catalog: Free. Frequency: Quarterly
Circulation: 50K. Sales: $5-10MM
Products: Refurbished laptop and notebook computers and accessories

UMAX TECHNOLOGIES (214) 739-7033
Techville, Inc.
11343 N. Central Expwy.
Dallas, TX 75243
E-Mail: sales@umax.com
Website: www.umax.com
Fax Ordering: (214) 739-7042
Technical Support: (214) 739-1915
Catalog: Free. Frequency: Semiannual
Circulation: 100K. Sales: $50-100MM
Products: Flatbed scanners

UNICOM - PREMISE WIRING (800) 346-6668
908 Canada Ct. • City of Industry, CA 91748
E-Mail: info@unicomlink.com
Website: www.unicomlink.com
Fax Ordering: (626) 964-7880
International Ordering: (626) 964-7873
Contact Names: Jeffrey Lo, President
Catalog: Free. Frequency: Semiannual
Circulation: 100K. Sales: $10-20MM
Products: Voice and data networking products

VIEWSONIC (800) 881-8781
381 Brea Canyon Rd. • Walnut, CA 91789 (800) 888-8583
E-Mail: salesinfo@viewsonic.com
Website: www.viewsonic.com
Fax Ordering: (909) 468-1202
International Ordering: (424) 233-2530
Customer Support: (800) 688-6688
Catalog: Free. Frequency: Semiannual
Circulation: 50K. Sales: $5-10MM
Products: LCD TVs, monitors & projectors; digital photo frames

VILLAGE SOFTWARE, INC. (617) 695-9332
76 Summer St. • Boston, MA 02110
E-Mail: requests@villagesoft.com
Website: www.villagesoft.com
Fax Ordering: (617) 695-1935
Customer Service: (617) 695-9332
Contact Names: Ford Cavallari, President
Catalog: Free. Frequency: Quarterly
Circulation: 1MM. Sales: $5-10MM
Products: Business and financial software solutions with templates which work with Lotus SmartSuite, Microsoft Office & Corel's Office Suite.

VISIBLE COMPUTER SUPPLY CORP. (800) 323-0628
R.R. Donnelley (877) 526-3894
1750 Wallace Ave. • St. Charles, IL 60174
E-Mail: sales@visibletax.com
Website: www.visibletax.com
Fax Ordering: (800) 233-2016
Customer Service: (630) 377-2586
Catalog: Free. Frequency: Semiannual
Circulation: 2MM. Sales: $20-50MM
Products: Computer forms, paper, disks and disk storage, monitor screen filters,

cables, outlet strips, and maintenance supplies & equipment. Also workstations & printer stands. Special offers on new products, bonuses with minimum orders, and quantity discounts available.

VIZIFLEX SEELS, INC. (800) 627-7752
221 Gracie Pl. • Hackensack, NJ 07601
E-Mail: info@viziflex.com
Website: www.viziflex.com
Fax Ordering: (201) 487-3266
Contact Name: Michael Glicksman, President
Catalog: Free. Frequency: Quarterly
Circulation: 100K. Sales: $3-5MM
Products: Computer protection products: Viziflex Seels, Carpal Eez, diskette wallets, mouse pads, anti-static mats, and anti-static wipes; keyboard covers, dust covers, cleaning products

WESTCON NETWORK CATALOG (800) 527-9516
520 White Plains Rd. • Tarrytown, NY 10591
E-Mail: sales@westcon.com
Website: www.westcon.com
Tech Support: (914) 829-7000
Catalog: Free. Frequency: Annual.
Circulation: 50K. Sales: $50-100MM
Products: Computer network systems, including peripherals, interfaces, software

WRITER'S COMPUTER STORE (866) 229-7483
2040 Westywood Blvd.
Los Angeles, CA 90025
E-Mail: presales@writersstore.com
Website: www.writersstore.com
Fax Ordering: (800) 486-4006; (310) 441-0944
International Ordering: (310) 441-5151
Catalog: Free. Frequency: Semiannual
Circulation: 150K. Sales: $3-5MM
Products: Software and books for writers

XEROX OFFICE SUPPLIES CATALOG (800) 822-2200
Xerox Corp. Marketing Center (800) 599-2198
300 N. Route 303 • Blauvelt, NY 10913 (800) 835-6100
Fax Ordering: (800) 338-7020
Customer Service: (800) 275-9376
Catalog: Free. Frequency: Quarterly
Circulation: 250K. Sales: $50-100MM
Products: Laser printer supplies; paper, labels, computer forms; transparencies; diskettes, ribbons and printwheels; software.

ZEPHYR CATALOG (800) 966-3270
8 E. Greenway Plaza, Suite 1414
Houston, TX 77046
E-Mail: mail@zephyrcorp.com
Website: www.zephyrcorp.com
Fax Ordering: (713) 623-0091
International Ordering: (713) 623-0089
Catalog: Free. Frequency: Semiannual
Circulation: 500K. Sales: $10-20MM
Products: Terminal Emulation Software & Host Integration. Software for IBM and compatibles. Over 140 programs for home & office, school and personal use (games, puzzles). Astronomy software, New Age software, and office software

ZONES, INC. (PCZONE & MACZONE) (800) 408-9663
Multiple Zones International (800) 258-8088
1102 15th St. SW #702 • Renton, WA 98001
E-Mail: sales@zones.com
Websites: www.zones.com;
  www.maczone.com; www.pczone.com
MacZone Sales: (800) 454-3686; (800) 248-0800
Education Sales: (800) 750-4923
Government Sales: (800) 372-9663
Fax Ordering: (800) 417-1993
International Ordering: (425) 430-3000 Fax 430-3600
Customer Support: (800) 248-9948
Technical Support: (800) 248-0800
Contact Names: Bill Chillalji, President
Catalog: Free. Frequency: Monthly
Circulation: 1MM. Sales: $50-100MM
Products: Computer hardware, software, accessories, and peripherals, including desktops, notebooks, handhelds/PDAs, laser printers, and LCD monitors. Software and peripheral hardware for the MAC and IBM-PC and compatibles. Over 2,000 brand name products of hardare and software for business and entertainment. Software: accounting & finance, spreadsheets, databases, presentation graphics, integrated software, management software, personal info managers, word processing, illustration & drawing, graphing & charting, fonts & cartridges, multimedia, entertainment, education, music, and programming; also games, windows, fonts, networking & connectivity, utilities. Also modems, monitors, scanners and drives.

ABILITATIONS-SCHOOL SPECIALTY   (800) 850-8603
P.O. Box 1579 • Appleton, WI 54912   (888) 388-3224
E-Mail: customercare@schoolspecialty.com
Website: www.schoolspecialty.com
Fax Ordering: (888) 388-6344; (419) 589-1600
International Ordering: (419) 589-1425
Catalog: Free. Frequency: Annual
Circulation: 150K. Sales: $5-10MM
Products: Therapeutic equipment for children
with physical challenges, including the areas of
speech pathology, special education, physical
& occupational therapy; general school supplies
and equipment

ALTIMATE MEDICAL CATALOG   (800) 342-8968
P.O. Box 180 • Morton, MN 56270
E-Mail: info@easystand.com
Website: www.easystand.com
Fax Ordering: (877) 342-8968; (507) 697-6900
International Ordering: (507) 697-6393
Contact Name: Alan Tholkes, President
Catalog: Free. Frequency: Quarterly
Circulation: 150K. Sales: $3-5MM
Products: Standing equipment for mobility
impaired children & adults; rehab equipment

AMERICAN HEALTH SERVICE MAGNETICS   (800) 635-7070
13822 W. Boulton Blvd. • Mettawa, IL 60045   (800) 422-4733
E-Mail: bill@americanhealthservice.com
Website: www.americanhealthservice.com
Fax Ordering: (847) 680-4440
International Ordering: (847) 680-3050
Contact Name: William Lapletra, President
Catalog: Free. Frequency: Quarterly
Circulation: 150K. Sales: $1-3MM
Products: Magnetic therapy products

AMERICAN PRINTING   (800) 223-1839
HOUSE FOR THE BLIND
P.O. Box 6085 • Louisville, KY 40206
E-Mail: info@aph.org
Website: www.aph.org
Fax Ordering: (502) 899-2274
International Ordering: (502) 895-2405
Contact Name: Tuck Tinsley, III, President
Catalog: Free. Frequency: Annual
Circulation: 25K. Sales: $20-50MM
Products: Products & services for people
who are visually impaired

AMIGO PRODUCT SELECTION GUIDE   (800) 248-9130
Amigo Mobility International, Inc.   (800) 692-6446
6693 Dixie Hwy. • Bridgeport, MI 48722
E-Mail: info@myamigo.com
Website: www.myamigo.com
Fax Ordering: (800) 334-7274; (989) 777-8184
International Ordering: (989) 777-0910
Contact Name: Allan R. Thieme, President
Catalog: Free. Frequency: Semiannual
Circulation: 150K. Sales: $10-20MM
Products: Power mobility scooters;
car/van lifts; travel scooters

ARCOLA VEHICLES   (800) 272-6521
FOR THE HANDICAPPED
Arcola Sales & Service Corp.
51 Kero Rd. • Carlstadt, NJ 07072
E-Mail: info@arcolasales.com
Website: www.arcolasales.com
Fax Ordering: (201) 507-5372
International Ordering: (201) 507-8500
Contact Name: Andrew Rolfe, President

Catalog: Free. Frequency: Annual
Circulation: 100K. Sales: $10-20MM
Products: Vehicles for the handicapped

AT SURGICAL COMPANY   (800) 225-2023
115 Clemente St. • Holyoke, MA 01040
E-Mail: info@atsurgical.com
Website: www.atsurgical.com
Fax Ordering: (413) 532-0826
International Ordering: (413) 532-4551
Contact Name: Eugene Kirejczyk, President
Catalog: Free. Frequency: Semiannual
Circulation: 25K. Sales: $5-10MM
Products: Orthopedics, back & knee braces,
healthcare products

BAILEY MANUFACTURING COMPANY   (800) 321-8372
P.O. Box 130 • Lodi, OH 44254
E-Mail: info@baileymfg.com
Website: www.baileymfg.com
Fax Ordering: (800) 224-5390; (330) 948-4439
International Ordering: (330) 948-1080
Contact Name: Larry Strimple, President
Catalog: Free. Frequency: Quarterly
Circulation: 200K. Sales: $5-10MM
Products: Rehabilitation equipment

BEST PRICED PRODUCTS   (800 824-2939
P.O. Box 1174 • White Plains, NY 10602
E-Mail: info@best-priced-products.com
Website: www.best-priced-products.com
Fax Ordering: (800) 356-8587; (914) 345-0300
International Ordering: (914) 345-3800
Catalog: Free. Frequency: 8x per year
Circulation: 150K. Sales: $5-10MM
Products: Products for physical therapy,
occupational therapy, and athletic training

BEST 25 CATALOG RESOURCES   (608) 824-0402
FOR MAKING LIFE EASIER
9042 Aspen Grove Ln. • Madison, WI 53717
E-Mail: help@meetinglifeschallenges.com
Website: www.meetinglifeschallenges.com
Fax Ordering: (608) 824-0403
Contact Name: Shelley P. Schwarz, President
Catalog: Online. Sales: $250-500K
Products: Web page providing information to
help people locate useful & hard-to-find adaptive
devices to make daily living tasks easier for the
aging, and those with chronic illness or disability

BRAUN CORPORATION   (800) 843-5438
P.O. Box 310 • Winamac, IN 46996
E-Mail: info@braunability.com
Website: www.braunability.com
Fax Ordering: (219) 946-4670
International Ordering: (219) 946-6157
Contact Name: Ralph Braun, Founder & CEO
Catalog: Free. Frequency: Annual
Circulation: 100K. Sales: $100-200MM
Products: Wheelchair carrier lifts; transit
vehicles & wheelchair ramps

BROOKES PUBLISHING COMPANY   (800) 638-3775
P.O. Box 10624 • Baltimore, MD 21285
E-Mail: custserv@brookespublishing.com
Website: www.brookespublishing.com
Fax Ordering: (410) 337-8539
International Ordering: (410) 337-9580
Catalog: Free. Frequency: Annual
Circulation: 50K. Sales: $500K to $1MM
Products: Books & videos, guidebooks, curricula

& tools based on the best research in disabilities, special education & child development

BRUNO INDEPENDENT LIVING AIDS   (800) 882-8183
P.O. Box 84 • Oconomowoc, WI 53066
E-Mail: info@bruno.com
Website: www.bruno.com
Fax Ordering: (262) 953-5501
International Ordering: (262) 567-4990
Contact Name: Michael Bruno, President
Catalog: Free. Frequency: Annual
Circulation: 125K. Sales: $10-20MM
Products: Scooter-lifts, wheelchair lifters; stair lifts, vehicle lifts

CAROLYN'S LOW VISION PRODUCTS   (800) 648-2266
3938 S. Tamiami Trail • Sarasota, FL 34231
E-Mail: support@carolynscatalog.com
Website: www.carolynscatalog.com
Fax Ordering: (941) 739-5503
International Ordering: (941) 373-9100
Contact Name: Samuel B. Sheldon, President
Catalog: Free. Frequency: Annual
Circulation: 25K. Sales: $250-500K
Products: Low vision products for the visually impaired person

CLOSING THE GAP   (507) 248-3294
P.O. Box 68 • Henderson, MN 56044
E-Mail: info@closingthegap.com
Website: www.closingthegap.com
Fax Ordering: (507) 248-3810
Contact Name: Budd & Dolores Hagen, Owners
Catalog: Free. Frequency: Annual
Circulation: 25K. Sales: $250-500K
Products: Listing of about 300 suppliers of computer hardware & software designed for use by people with disabilities

COMMUNICATION AIDS   (414) 351-0311
FOR CHILDREN & ADULTS
Crestwood Communication Aids, Inc.
6589 N. Crestwood Dr.
Milwaukee, WI 53209
E-Mail: crestcomm@aol.com
Website: www.communicationaids.com
Fax Ordering: (414) 446-9255
Contact Name: Ruth Leff, President
Catalog: Free. Frequency: Annual
Circulation: 50K. Sales: $500K to $1MM
Products: Communication aids for children & adults with disabilities; light & high tech aids '& switches, adapted & voice-activated toys

COMMUNITY PLAYTHINGS   (800) 777-4244
P.O. Box 2 • Ulster Park, NY 12487
E-Mail: sales@communityplaythings.com
Website: www.communityplaythings.com
Fax Ordering: (800) 336-5948; (845) 658-8065
International Ordering: (845) 658-7720
Contact Name: Samuel B. Sheldon, President
Catalog: Free. Frequency: Annual
Circulation: 250K. Sales: $3-5MM
Products: Equipment & classroom furniture for children with handicaps

COMPLETE LEARNING   (800) 562-2139
DISABILITIES DIRECTORY
Grey House Publishing
P.O. Box 56 • Amenia, NY 12501
E-Mail: books@greyhouse.com
Website: www.greyhouse.com

Fax Ordering: (518) 789-0556
International Ordering: (518) 789-8700
Contact Name: Richard Gottlieb, President
Books: $150. Frequency: Annuals
Circulation: Varies. Sales: $1-3MM
Products: Books providing products & services, organizations & facilities available for the disabled: People With Pediatric Disorders; People With Rare Disorders; People With Chronic Illness; People With Disabilities; People With Learning Disabilities; People With Mental Illness.

DISABILITY BOOKSHOP CATALOG   (360) 694-2462
Twin Peaks Press
P.O. Box 129 • Vancouver, WA 98666
E-Mail: twinpeak@twinpeakspress.com
Website: www.twinpeakspress.com
Fax Ordering: (360) 696-3210
Contact Names: Helen Hecker, President
Catalog: Free. Frequency: Bimonthly
Circulation: 200K. Sales: $500M to $1MM
Products: Books & videos relating to disability, medical, health, travel, home business & computers available from small to mid-size publishers & producers

DISCOUNT RAMPS CATALOG   (888) 651-3431
760 S. Indiana Ave.
West Bend, WI 53095
E-Mail: info@discountramps.com
Website: www.discountramps.com
Fax Ordering: (262) 306-8035
International Ordering: (262) 338-3431
Catalog: Free. Frequency: Semiannual
Circulation: 50K. Sales: $10-20MM
Products: Wheelchair ramps, lifts/carriers; tie downs & accessories

DRIVE-MASTER CO., INC.   (973) 808-9709
37 Daniel Rd. West • Fairfield, NJ 07004
E-Mail: sales@drivemaster.net
Website: www.drive-master.com
Fax Ordering: (973) 808-9713
Contact Name: Peter Ruprecht, President
Catalog: Free. Frequency: Annual
Circulation: 100K. Sales: $10-20MM
Products: Adaptive devices for physically disabled persons to drive; handicapped lifts-lowered floor mini vans-hand controls

ELECTRIC MOBILITY CORPORATION   (800) 662-4548
591 Mantua Blvd. • Sewell, NJ 08080
E-Mail: reward@electricmobility.com
Website: www.rascalscooters.com
Fax Ordering: (856) 468-2075
International Ordering: (856) 468-1000
Contact Name: Michael Flowers, President
Catalog: Free. Frequency: Quarterly
Circulation: 50K. Sales: $50-100MM
Products: Electric mobility vehicles

ELECTROPEDIC PRODUCTS   (858) 560-6446
8252 Clairemont Mesa Blvd.
San Diego, CA 92111
E-Mail: info@electropedic.com
Website: www.electropedic.com
Contact Name: Chuck Liau, President
Catalog: Free. Frequency: Annual
Circulation: 50K. Sales: $3-5MM
Products: Elecropedic adjustable beds; electric lift-chair, stair-lifts & scooters

FLAGHOUSE REHAB CATALOG   (800) 793-7900
601 Flaghouse Dr.
Hasbrouck Hts., NJ 07604
E-Mail: info@flaghouse.com
Website: www.flaghouse.com
Fax Ordering: (800) 793-7922; (201) 288-7887
International Ordering: (201) 288-7600
Contact Name: George Carmel, President
Catalog: Free. Frequency: Bimonthly
Circulation: 2MM. Sales: $20-50MM
Products: Rehabilitation products

GOLD VIOLIN   (877) 648-8400
P.O. Box 126 • Jessup, PA 18434
E-Mail: connie@goldviolin.com
Website: www.goldviolin.com
Fax Ordering: (434) 923-3279
International Ordering: (434) 923-3277
Contact Name: Connie Hallquist, Founder
Catalog: Free. Frequency: Semiannual
Circulation: 200K. Sales: $5-10MM
Products: Products for independent living

GRESHAM DRIVING AIDS   (800) 521-8930
3080 Wixom Rd. • Wixom, MI 48393
E-Mail: gpersons@handiramp.com
Website: www.greshamdrivingaids.com
Fax Ordering: (248) 624-6358
International Ordering: (248) 624-1533
Contact Name: Gerald Gresham, President
Catalog: Free. Frequency: Annual
Circulation: 50K. Sales: $3-5MM
Products: Driving aids, handicap equipment

**GUIDE TO TOYS FOR
THE VISUALLY IMPAIRED**   (800) 232-5463
American Foundation for the Blind
2 Penn Plaza #1102 • New York, NY 10121
E-Mail: afbinfo@afb.net
Website: www.afb.org
Fax Ordering: (212) 502-7777
International Ordering: (212) 502-7600
Contact Name: Michael Sylvie, President
Catalog: Free. Frequency: Annual
Circulation: 100K. Sales: $3-5MM
Products: Creative & educational toys & games
for children who are blind or visually impaired

HANDI-RAMP CATALOG   (800) 876-7267
510 North Ave. • Libertyville, IL 60048
E-Mail: info@handiramp.com
Website: www.handiramp.com
Fax Ordering: (847) 816-7689
International Ordering: (847) 680-7700
Contact Name: Thomas Disch, President
Catalog: Free. Frequency: Annual
Circulation: 25K. Sales: $5-10MM
Products: Ramps for personal or business needs

HARRIS COMMUNICATIONS   (800) 825-6758
15155 Technology Dr.
Eden Prairie, MN 55344
E-Mail: mail@harriscomm.com
Website: www.harriscomm.com
Fax Ordering: (866) 384-3147; (952) 906-1099
International Ordering: (952) 906-1180
Contact Name: Robert Harris, President
Catalog: Free. Frequency: Annual
Circulation: 200K. Sales: $10-20MM
Products: Products for deaf & hard of hearing people;
books, videos, telecommunications & assistive devices

HUMANIZED SOLUTIONS   (800) 722-3393
HumanWare
P.O. Box 800 • Champlain, NY 12919
E-Mail: us.info@humanware.com
Website: www.humanware.com
Fax Ordering: (888) 871-4828
Contact Name: Jim Halliday, President
Catalog: Free. Frequency: Annual
Circulation: 50K. Sales: $5-10MM
Products: Devices for the learning disabled,
blind & visually impaired

ILA COMPREHENSIVE CATALOG   (800) 537-2118
Independent Living Aids, LLC
P.O. Box 9022 • Hicksville, NY 11802
E-Mail: can-do@independentliving.com
Website: www.independentliving.com
Fax Ordering: (516) 937-3906
International Ordering: (516) 937-1848
Contact Name: Marvin Sandler, President
Catalog: Free. Frequency: Annual
Circulation: 200K. Sales: $5-10MM
Products: Low vision & hearing products

INCLINATOR COMPANY OF AMERICA   (800) 343-9007
P.O. Box 1557 • Harrisburg, PA 17105
E-Mail: sales@inclinator.com
Website: www.inclinator.com
Fax Ordering: (717) 939-8075
International Ordering: (717) 939-8420
Contact Name: Stephen Nock, President
Catalog: Free. Frequency: Annual
Circulation: 100K. Sales: $5-10MM
Products: Stair lifts & home elevators

LARK OF AMERICA CATALOG   (800) 824-1068
EZ-International, Inc.
P.O. Box 1647 • Brookfield, WI 53045
E-Mail: info@ez-international.com
Website: www.ez-international.com
Fax Ordering: (262) 790-5204
International Ordering: (262) 790-5200
Contact Name: Ann LaMarche, President
Catalog: Free. Frequency: Annual
Circulation: 150K. Sales: $20-50MM
Products: Electric motorized 3+4 wheel
convenience/mobility scooters; pediatric
rehab products

**NATIONAL LIBRARY SERVICES FOR
THE BLIND & PHYSICALLY HANDICAPPED**   (800) 424-8567
1291 Taylor St. NW • Washington, DC 20542
E-Mail: nls@loc.gov
Website: www.loc.gov/nls
Fax Ordering: (202) 707-0712
International Ordering: (202) 707-5100
Contact Name: Frank Cylke, Director
Catalog: Free. Frequency: Annual
Circulation: 250K. Sales: Government service
Products: National library service providing braille
& recorded books & magazines on free loan to
anyone who cannot read standard print because
of permanent or temporary visual or physical
disabilities

LIGHTHOUSE INTERNATIONAL CATALOG   (800) 829-0500
111 E. 59th St. • New York, NY 10022
E-Mail: info@lighthouse.org
Website: www.lighthouse.org
Fax Ordering: (212) 821-9702
International Ordering: (212) 821-9384

Catalog: Free. Frequency: Annual
Circulation: 50K. Sales: $1-3MM
Products: Items for the visually impaired

LLOYDS HEARING AID CATALOG (800) 323-4212
4435 Manchester Dr. • Rockford, IL 61109
E-Mail: hearingaids@lloydhearingaid.com
Website: www.lloydhearingaid.com
Fax Ordering: (815) 964-8378
International Ordering: (815) 964-4191
Contact Name: Andrew Palmquist, President
Catalog: Free. Frequency: Annual
Circulation: 100K. Sales: $1-3MM
Products: Hearing aids & accessories

M&M HEALTH CARE APPAREL COMPANY (718) 871-8188
1541 60th St. • Brooklyn, NY 11219
E-Mail: info@fashionease.com
Website: www.fashionease.com
Fax Ordering: (718) 436-2067
Contact Name: Abraham Klein, President
Catalog: Free. Frequency: Semiannual
Circulation: 100K. Sales: $3-5MM
Products: Specialized adaptive clothing with
easy closures for disabled adults

MAXI AIDS CATALOG (800) 522-6294
42 Executive Blvd.
Farmingdale, NY 11735
E-Mail: sales@maxiaids.com
Website: www.maxiaids.com
Fax Ordering: (631) 752-0689
International Ordering: (631) 752-0521
Catalog: Free. Frequency: Annual
Circulation: 25K. Sales: $250-500M
Products: Aids, appliances & home health
care products for the disabled, physically
challenged, and mature adult

MOBILITY PLUS CATALOG (800) 323-4212
P.O. Box 1645 • Rockford, IL 61110
E-Mail: info@hearingaids.com
Website: www.lloydhearingaids.com
Fax Ordering: (815) 964-8378
Catalog: Free. Frequency: Annual
Circulation: 100K. Sales: $1-3MM
Products: Wheelchairs, walkers, scooters
& other supplies for the disabled

NATIONAL ASSOCIATION OF THE DEAF (301) 587-1788
814 Thayer Ave.
Silver Spring, MD 20910
E-Mail: nadinfo@nad.org
Website: www.nad.org
Fax Ordering: (301) 587-1791
Contact Name: Libby Pollard, President
Catalog: Free. Frequency: Weekly
Circulation: 100K. Sales: $500K - $1MM
Products: Deafness materials, books,
videotapes & gift items

NEW VISION STORE (215) 629-2990
919 Walnut St. • Philadelphia, PA 19107
E-Mail: sales@thenewvisionstore.com
Website: www.thenewvisionstore.com
Contact Name: Bill Ankenbrant, President
Catalog: Free. Frequency: Annual
Circulation: 25M. Sales: $250M
Products: Items for visually impaired persons

OPTP HEALTH CARE CATALOG (800) 367-7393
P.O. Box 47009 • Minneapolis, MN 55447 (888) 819-0121
E-Mail: customerservice@optp.com
Website: www.optp.com
Fax Ordering: (763) 553-9355
International Ordering: (763) 553-0452
Contact Name: Shari Schroeder, President
Catalog: Free. Frequency: Monthly
Circulation: 25K. Sales: $500K to $1MM
Products: Orthopedic physical therapy products

PARENT MAGIC, INC. (800) 442-4453
800 Roosevelt Rd. #B-309
Glen Ellyn, IL 60137
E-Mail: custcare@parentmagic.com
Website: www.parentmagic.com
Fax Ordering: (800) 635-8301; (630) 469-4571
International Ordering: (630) 469-0484
Contact Name: Thomas W. Phelan, President
Catalog: Free. Frequency: Semiannual
Circulation: 100K. Sales: $1-3MM
Products: Books, videos, audiocassettes on the
subject of parenting & Attention Deficit Disorder

POWER ACCESS CORPORATION (800) 344-0088
P.O. Box 1050 • New Hartford, CT 06057
E-Mail: salesint@power-access.com
Website: www.power-access.com
Fax Ordering: (860) 693-0641
International Ordering: (860) 693-0751
Contact Name: Nils Sellman, President
Catalog: Free. Frequency: Annual
Circulation: 25K. Sales: $1-3MM
Products: Automatic door openers for the disabled

PRESTON PRODUCTS (800) 631-7277
FOR PHYSICAL THERAPY
J.A. Preston Corporation
744 W. Michigan Ave. • Jackson, MI 49201
Fax Ordering: (517) 789-3299
International Ordering: (517) 787-1600
Catalog: Free. Frequency: Annual
Circulation: 25K. Sales: $250-500K
Products: Physical therapy & rehabilitation
machines & equipment for the injured and/or
disabled

PROFESSIONAL FIT CLOTHING (800) 422-2348
831 N. Lake St. #1 • Burbank, CA 91502
E-Mail: admin@professionalfit.com
Website: www.professionalfit.com
Fax Ordering: (818) 563-1834
International Ordering: (818) 563-1975
Contact Name: Tom Pirruccello, President
Catalog: Free. Frequency: Annual
Circulation: 25K. Sales: $3-5MM
Products: Adaptable clothing for
people with developental disabilities

PSYCHOLOGICAL ASSESSMENT (800) 627-7271
& INTERVENTION CATALOG
Pearson Education, Inc.
P.O. Box 599700 • San Antonio, TX 78259
E-Mail: info@psychcorp.com
Website: www.psychcorp.pearsonaassessments.com
Fax Ordering: (800) 232-1223
International Ordering: (210) 299-1061
Contact Name: Ronald H. Weintraub, President
Catalog: Free. Frequency: Annual
Circulation: 200K. Sales: $5-10MM
Products: Psychological assessments &
intervention behavioral healthcare products

RESEARCH PRESS   (800) 519-2707
P.O. Box 9177 • Champaign, IL 61826
E-Mail: info@researchpress.com
Website: www.researchpress.com
Fax Ordering: (217) 352-1221
International Ordering: (217) 352-3273
Contact Name: Ann Wendel, President
Catalog: Free. Frequency: Annual
Circulation: 100K. Sales: $3-5MM
Products: Books & videos on counseling,
therapy, psychology, education, parent
training & developmental disabilities

SPRI MEDICAL & REHAB   (800) 345-3456
PRODUCTS CORPORATION
642 Anthony Trail • Northbrook, IL 60062
Fax Ordering: (847) 272-0420
International Ordering: (847) 272-7211
Contact Name: John Vuckovich, President
Catalog: Free. Frequency: Semiannual
Circulation: 25K. Sales: $3-5MM
Products: Physical therapy products,
shower wheelchairs

SENSORY AIDS RESOURCE GUIDE   (800) 888-7400
VISION RESOURCES
Science Products
P.O. Box 888 • Southeastern, PA 19399
Fax Ordering: (610) 296-0488
International Ordering: (610) 296-2111
Contact Name: Lee Benham, President
Catalog: Free. Frequency: Annual
Circulation: 100K. Sales: $5-10MM
Products: Magnifiers, large-print books,
calculators, technical aids, low-vision aids,
toys & games; technical aids for the visually
impaired, health aids & employment aids

SPECIAL CLOTHES CATALOGS   (508) 430-2410
P.O. Box 333 • Harwich, MA 02645
E-Mail: specialclo@aol.com
Website: www.special-clothes.com
Fax Ordering: (508) 430-2410
Contact Name: Judith Sweeney, President
Catalog: Free. Frequency: Annual
Circulation: 25K. Sales: $500K
Products: Adaptable clothing for children
& adults with developental disabilities

THYSSENKRUPP ACCESS CATALOG   (800) 925-3100
P.O. Box 1061 • Yonkers, NY 10703   (800) 829-9760
E-Mail: info@tkaccess.com   (800) 924-5438
Website: www.tkaccess.com
Fax Ordering: (914) 423-4243
International Ordering: (914) 423-4200
Contact Name: Michael Mahoney, President
Catalog: Free. Frequency: Semiannual
Circulation: 250K. Sales: $20-50MM
Products: Stair lifts, wheelchair lifts &
elevators; Aids for people with handicaps

TUMBLEFORMS CATALOG   (800) 323-5547
Patterson Medical - Sammons Preston
P.O. Box 5071 • Bolingbrook, IL 60440
E-Mail: customersupport@patterson-medical.com
Website: www.sammonspreston.com
Fax Ordering: (800) 547-4333; (630) 378-6010
International Ordering: (630) 378-6000
Customer Support: (800) 343-9742
Contact Name: Ed Donnelly, President
Catalog: Free. Frequency: Semiannual
Circulation: 50K. Sales: $10-20MM
Products: Rehabilitation/home health
products for the disabled child

YOUR GUIDE TO BETTER HEARING AIDS   (800) 799-4327
Better Hearing
202 E. 2nd St. • Brookport, Il 62910
Fax Ordering: (618) 564-2612
International Ordering: (618) 564-2558
Contact Name: David Rhodes, President
Catalog: Free. Frequency: Annual
Circulation: 50K. Sales: $1-3MM
Products: Hearing aids, supplies & repairs

AAVIM CATALOG (800) 228-4689
American Assn for Vocational
Instructional Materials
220 Smithsonia Rd. • Winterville, GA 30683
E-Mail: sales@aavim.com
Website: www.aavim.com
Fax Ordering: (706) 742-7005
International Ordering: (706) 742-5355
Contact Names: Karen Seabaugh, President
Catalog: Free. Frequency: Quarterly
Circulation: 150K. Sales: $1-3MM
Products: Developer, producer and distributor
of instructional materials for vocational education
(agriscience, technology and life science)
including publications, CD-ROM, videos and
computer software.

ACADEMIC SUPERSTORE (800) 817-2347
2101 E. St. Elmo Rd. #360 • Austin, TX 78744 (800) 220-9305
E-Mail: contact@academicsuperstore.com
Website: www.academicsuperstore.com
Fax Ordering: (866) 947-4525
International Ordering: (512) 450-1199
Catalog: Free. Frequency: Quarterly
Circulation: 250K. Sales: $5-10MM
Products: Software, computer products,
electronics, teacher products, learning &
games, music & audio, A/V equipment,
bags & backpacks, books, videos & DVDs.

ACHIEVEMENT PRODUCTS FOR CHILDREN (800) 373-4699
P.O. Box 6013 • Carol Stream, IL 60197
E-Mail: info@specialkidszone.com
Website: www.specialkidszone.com
Fax Ordering: (800) 766-4303
Catalog: Free. Frequency: Quarterly
Circulation: 150K. Sales: $5-10MM
Products: Acievement products, top quality
therapy, sensory integration, adapted toys,
positioning aids

AFRICAN AMERICAN IMAGES (800) 552-1991
P.O. Box 1799 • Sauk Village, IL 60412
E-Mail: aa@africanamericanimages.com
Website: www.africanamericanimages.com
Fax Ordering: (708) 672-0466
International Ordering: (708) 672-4909
Contact Names: Jawanza Kunjufu, President
Catalog: Free. Frequency: Semiannual
Circulation: 25K. Sales: $500K to 1MM
Products: Educational material (including books)
of interest to African Americans.

AGING RESOURCES (800) 327-4269
Attainment Company
P.O. Box 930160 • Verona, WI 53593
E-Mail: info@attainmentcompany.com
Website: www.attainmentcompany.com
Fax Ordering: (800) 942-3865; (608) 845-8040
International Ordering: (608) 845-7880
Catalog: Free. Frequency: Annual
Products: Aging Resource Products: Mental
Fitness Program; Whole Brain Workouts;
Thinking Cards; Sharpen Your Senses Cards;
Dementia Caregivers' Training package;
Mind Your Mind

AIMS EDUCATION FOUNDATION (888) 733-2467
P.O. Box 8120 • Fresno, CA 93747
E-Mail: aimsed@aimsedu.org
Website: www.aimsedu.org
Fax Ordering: (559) 255-6396

International Ordering: (559) 255-4094
Catalog: Free. Frequency: Annual
Circulation: 50K. Sales: $500K
Products: Books, AIMS magazine, workshops,
science lab supplies; data organizers & charts;
multimedia resources

AMACO PRODUCTS CATALOG (800) 374-1600
6060 GuionRd. • Indianapolis, IN 46254
E-Mail: salessupport@amaco.com
Website: www.amaco.com
Fax Ordering: (317) 248-9300 or 822-7093
International Ordering: (317) 374-1600 ext. 1359
International Fax Ordering: (317) 244-6871
Catalog: Free. Frequency: Semiannual
Circulation: 100K. Sales: $5-10MM
Products: Supplies for pottery, education
& crafts; ceramics & pottery making tools,
wheels & supplies.

AMERICAN EDUCATIONAL PRODUCTS (800) 289-9299
P.O. Box 2121 • Fort Collins, CO 80522
E-Mail: sales@hubbardscientific.com
Website: www.hubbardscientific.com
Fax Ordering: (970) 484-1198
International Ordering: (970) 484-7445
Contact Name: Cliff Thygesen, President
Catalogs: Free. Frequency: Annual
Circulation: 200K. Sales: $5-10MM
Products: Scott Resources; Hubbard Scientific;
National Teaching Aids; Ginsberg Scientific.
Math and science teaching products

ANATOMICAL CHART CO. (800) 621-7500
Wolters Kluwer Health
E-Mail: service@anatomical.com
Website: www.anatomical.com
Fax Ordering: (301) 223-2400
Customer Service: (800) 621-7500
Catalog: Free. Frequency: Semiannual
Circulation: 100K. Sales: $10-20MM
Products: Anatomical charts & training aids;
educational products for medicine, health,
nutrition, childbirth & science-related topics

ANDERSON'S PROM & PARTY (800) 328-9640
4875 White Bear Pkwy.
White Bear Lake, MN 55110
E-Mail: sales@andersonsprom.com
Website: www.andersonsprom.com
Fax Ordering: (651) 426-0275
Contact Names: Angie Holmstrom, President
Catalog: Free. Frequency: Annual
Circulation: 150K. Sales: $10-20MM
Products: Prom catalog provides decorations
& supplies; Homecoming Catalog services the
needs of high schools; also catalogs for the
needs of elementary and middle schools,
cheeleaders, pep squads and booster clubs.

ANNENBERG MEDIA (800) 532-7637
P.O. Box 55742 • Indianapolis, IN 46205
E-Mail: annenbergmedia@fpdirect.com
Website: www.learning.org
Fax Ordering: (317) 579-0402
International Ordering: (317) 558-4834
Catalog: Free. Frequency: Annual
Circulation: 100K. Sales: $1-3MM
Products: Videos, CD-ROMs and online
learning programs for the arts, education,
foreign languages, literature and language
arts, math, science and history.

AUDIO-FORUM (800) 243-1234
Jeffrey Norton Publishers, Inc.
One Orchard Park Rd.
Madison, CT 06443
E-Mail: info@audioforum.com
Website: www.audioforum.com
Fax Ordering: (888) 453-4329; (203) 245- 0769
International Ordering: (203) 245-0195
Contact Name: Jeffrey Norton, President
Catalog: Free. Frequency: Quarterly
Circulation: 250K. Sales: $3-5MM
Products: Self-teaching audio & video language
courses; personal development and educational
audiovisual materials In the U.S. Includes a large
selection of of courses & related cultural materials
for Native American languages. Audio & video
programs for children & young adults. Stories,
lullabies, self-help for children, & American Indian
tales.

BALE CO. ACHIEVEMENT AWARDS (800) 822-5350
222 Public St. • Providence, RI 02940
E-Mail: info@bale.com
Website: www.bale.com
Fax Ordering: (401) 831-5500
International Ordering: (401) 331-1666
Contact Name: Jane Byrne, President
Catalog: Free. Frequency: Annual
Circulation: 100K. Sales: $1-3MM
Products: Award medals, pins, plaques,
trophies, school jewelry, and class rings

BOYS TOWN PRESS CATALOG (800) 282-6657
14100 Crawford St.
Boys Town, NE 68010
E-Mail: btpress@boystown.org
Website: www.boystown.org
Fax Ordering: (402) 498-1310
International Ordering: (402) 498-1300
Contact Name: Barbara Lonnborg, Marketing
Catalog: Free. Frequency: Monthly
Circulation: 150K. Sales: $3-5MM
Products: Books & videos for professionals,
educators & parents working with youth

CALLOWAY HOUSE (800) 233-0290
451 Richardson Dr.
Lancaster, PA 17603
E-Mail: service@callowayhouse.com
Website: www.callowayhouse.com
Fax Ordering: (717) 299-6754
International Ordering: (717) 299-5703
Catalog: Free. Frequency: Semiannual
Circulation: 150K. Sales: $5-10MM
Products: Educational classroom supplies
& materials

CAMBRIDGE EDUCATIONAL CATALOGS (800) 468-4227
Films Media Group (800) 257-5126
200 American Metro Blvd. #124
Hamilton, NJ 08619
E-Mail: custserv@films.com
Website: www.cambridge.films.com
Fax Ordering: (800) 329-6687; (609) 671-0266
International Ordering: (609) 419-8000
Contact Names: Melinda Ball, Marketing Manager
Catalog: Free. Frequency: Monthly
Circulation: 1MM. Sales: $10-20MM
Products: Educational videos, software,
CD-ROMs, books and posters physical
education & health videos; vocational books,

CAMBRIDGE UNIVERSITY JOURNALS (212) 924-3900
Cambridge University Press
21 Ave. of the Americas
New York, NY 10013
E-Mail: info@cup.org
Website: www.cambridge.org
Fax Ordering: (212) 691-3239
International Ordering: (212) 924-3900
Catalog: Free. Frequency: Semiannual.
Circulation: 50K. Sales: $10-20MM
Products: Academic and educational journals
that focus on the acquisition, advancement,
conservation & dissemination of knowledge
in all subjects. Also bibles.

CAROLINA BIOLOGICAL SUPPLY CO. (800) 334-5551
P.O. Box 6010 • Burlington, NC 27215
E-Mail: customer_service@carolina.com
Website: www.carolina.com
Fax Ordering: (800) 222-7112; (336) 538-6330
International Ordering: (336) 584-0381
Contact Names: Larry Gross, President
Catalog: Free. Frequency: Annual
Circulation: 100K. Sales: $20-50MM
Products: Instructional materials & services
for teaching in biology, biotechnology, chemistry,
health, physics & mathematics

CENTER ENTERPRISES (800) 542-2214
P.O. Box 331361
West Hartford, CT 06133
E-Mail: ceinc@netcom.com
Website: www.ceinc.com
Fax Ordering: (800) 373-2923
Catalog: Free. Frequency: Annual.
Circulation: 100K. Sales: $1-3MM
Products: Rubber stamps & accessories
with an educational focus on instructional
resource materials, for preschool &
kindergarten through grade 12.

CHENG & TSUI COMPANY (800) 554-1963
25 West St. • Boston, MA 02111
E-Mail: orders@cheng-tsui.com
Website: www.cheng-tsui.com
Fax Ordering: (617) 426-3669; 556-8964
International Ordering: (617) 988-2400
Catalog: Free. Frequency: Semiannual
Circulation: 50K. Sales: $1-3MM
Products: Software, books, films on
Asian languages and cultures

THE CONOVER COMPANY (800) 933-1933
Div. of Oakwood Solutions, LLC
4 Brookwood Ct. • Appleton, WI 54914
E-Mail: sales@conovercompany.com
Website: www.conovercompany.com
Fax Ordering: (800) 933-1943; (920) 231-4809
International Ordering: (920) 231-4667
Contact Name: Terry Schmitz, President
Catalog: Free. Frequency: Semiannual
Circulation: 100K. Sales: $5-10MM
Products: Software for emotional intelligence
assessment, skill enhancement materials,
anger management and conflict resolution.
Programs include: The Success Profiler;
The Anger Management program; Emotional
Intelligence Profiler; Substance Abuse
Prevention Program; Conflict Resolution
Program; MECA (technology education,
career exploration); Functional Literacy System.

CONSTRUCTIVE PLAYTHINGS (800) 448-1412
13201 Arrington Rd. • Grandview, MO 64030
E-Mail: custservice@cptoys.com
Website: www.cptoys.com
Fax Ordering: (816) 761-9295
Catalog: Free. Frequency: Annual.
Circulation: 100K. Sales: $5-10MM
Products: Early childhood educational toys,
 equipment, books, records, tapes, art supplies,
 and teaching aids.

CORWIN PRESS CATALOGS (800) 233-9936
2455 Teller Rd. • Thousand Oaks, CA 91320
E-Mail: info@corwinpress.com
Website: www.corwinpress.com
Fax Ordering: (800) 417-2166; (805) 499-5323
International Ordering: (805) 499-9734
Catalog: Free. Online. Frequency: Annual
Circulation: 50K. Sales: $3-5MM
Products: Educational publisher dedicated
 to providing solutions for preK-12 educators.

CREATION ENGINE, INC. (800) 431-8713
348 E. Middlefield Rd.
Mountain View, CA 94043
E-Mail: info@creationengine.com
Website: www.creationengine.com
Fax Ordering: (650) 934-3234
International Ordering: (650) 934-0176
Catalog: Free. Frequency: Semiannual
Circulation: 50K. Sales: $1-3MM
Products: Software & hardware to the
K-12 and higher education markets

CREATIVE TEACHING PRESS (800) 287-8879
P.O. Box 2723
Huntington Beach, CA 93727
E-Mail: info@creativeteaching.com
Website: www.creativeteaching.com
Fax Ordering: (800) 229-9929;
 (714) 895-6547
International Ordering: (714) 895-5047
Contact Names: Jim Connelly, President
Catalog: Free. Frequency: Semiannual
Circulation: 150K. Sales: $5-10MM
Products: Non-electronic educational
games for grades PreK-12 covering math,
language, arts, science, geography, and
bible-based activities.

THE CRITICAL THINKING CO. (800) 458-4849
P.O. Box 1610 • Seaside, CA 93955
E-Mail: info@criticalthinking.com
Website: www.criticalthinking.com
Fax Ordering: (831) 393-3277
International Ordering: (831) 393-3288
Catalog: Free. Frequency: Monthly
Circulation: 100K Sales: $3-5MM
Products: PreK-12 educational books
& software

CURRICULUM ASSOCIATES (800) 225-0248
153 Rangeway Rd.
North Billerica, MA 01862
E-Mail: cainfo@curriculumassociates.com
Website: www.cuirriculumassociates.com
Fax Ordering: (800) 366-1158; (978) 667-5706
International Ordering: (978) 667-8000
Contact Names: Frank Ferguson, President
Catalog: Free. Frequency: Semiannual
Circulation: 250K. Sales: $1-3MM
Products: Educational instructional materials

DISCOUNT SCHOOL SUPPLY (800) 627-2829
P.O. Box 6013 • Carol Stream, IL 60197
E-Mail: customerservice@discountschoolsupply.com
Website: www.discountschoolsupply.com
Fax Ordering: (800) 879-3753
International Ordering: (831) 333-5588
Catalog: Free. Frequency: Semiannual
Circulation: 250K. Sales: $10-50MM
Products: Discount school supplies

DISCOVERY STORE CHANNEL CATALOG (800) 627-9399
P.O. Box 877 • Florence, KY 41022   (800) 889-9950
E-Mail: customer_care@discovery.com
Website: www.discovery.com
Fax Ordering: (859) 342-0633
Customer Service: (800) 889-9950
Catalog: Free. Frequency: Semiannual
Circulation: 200K. Sales: $10-20MM
Products: Gifts from shows on the Discovery
Channel, including: videos, DVDs, books,
telescopes, optics, toys and games, health
and home products.

EARLY ADVANTAGE (888) 248-0480
P.O. Box 4063 • Monroe, CT 06468   In Canada (888) 806-8165
E-Mail: customerservice@early-advantage.com
Website: www.early-advantage.com
Fax Ordering: (800) 301-9268
International Ordering: (203) 261-4426
Customer Service: (888) 999-4670
Catalog: Free. Frequency: Semiannual
Circulation: 150K. Sales: $5-10MM
Products: Learning programs for young
children, including the Early Advantage
family of programs, such as MUZZY,
BBC Language Course for Children.

EDUCATIONAL RESOURCES (800) 624-2926
1550 Executive Dr. • Elgin, IL 60123   (800) 860-7004
E-Mail: custserv@edresources.com
Website: www.edresources.com
Fax Ordering: (800) 610-5005;
 (847) 888-8499
Customer Service: (708) 888-8300
Contact Name: John Crowley, President
Catalog: Free. Frequency: Semiannual
Circulation: 300K. Sales: $10-25MM
Products: Educational software for the
daily education of children. Teacher tools,
accessories, laser disks, and supplies.

EME CORP. SCIENCE CATALOG (800) 848-2050
P.O. Box 1949 • Stuart, FL 34995
E-Mail: emecorp@aol.com
Website: www.emescience.com
Fax Ordering: (772) 219-2209
International Ordering: (772) 219-2206
Contact Name: Thomas McMahon, President
Catalog: Free. Frequency: Annual
Circulation: 100K. Sales: $1-3MM
Products: Science and math software

EMPAK PUBLISHING COMPANY (800) 477-4554
P.O. Box 8596 • Chicago, IL 60680
Fax Ordering: (312) 642-9657
International Ordering: (312) 642-3434
Contact Name: Richard Green, President
Catalog: Free. Frequency: Annual
Circulation: 50K. Sales: $500K to $1MM
Products: Books, games & products
focusing on historical figures in African-
American history

ENCYCLOPEDIA BRITANNICA   (800) 323-1229
310 S. Michigan Ave. • Chicago, IL 60604   (800) 621-3900
E-Mail: sales@britannica.com   Canada (800) 465-9439
Website: www.britannica.com
Fax Ordering: (312) 347-2104
International Ordering: (312) 347-7159
Contact Name: Shantha Uddin, President
Catalogs: Free. Frequency: Semiannual.
Circulation: 150K. Sales: $5-10M
Products: CD-ROMs, DVDs & video-discs,
films and textbooks

ENSLOW PUBLISHERS, INC.   (800) 398-2504
P.O. Box 398 • Berkeley Hts., NJ 07922
E-Mail: customerservice@enslow.com
Website: www.enslow.com
Fax Ordering: (908) 771-0925
International Ordering: (908) 771-9400
Catalog: Free. Frequency: Semiannual
Circulation: 150K. Sales: $5-10M
Products: K-12 nonfiction library books

ENVIRONMENTAL MEDIA CORP.   (843) 474-0147
P.O. Box 99 • Beaufort, SC 29901
E-Mail: bpendergraft@envmedia.com
Website: www.envmedia.com
Fax Ordering: (843) 986-9093
Contact Name: Bill Pendergraft, President
Catalog: Free. Frequency: Quarterly
Circulation: 25K. Sales: $250-500K
Products: Media to support environmental
education for the classroom & community

ENVIRONMENTS, INC.   (800) 342-4453
P.O. Box 1348 • Beaufort, SC 29901
E-Mail: environments@eichild.com
Website: www.eichild.com
Fax Ordering: (800) 343-2987
International Ordering: (843) 846-8155
  Fax (843) 846-2999
Contact Name: Beecher Hoogenboom, President
Catalogs: Free. Frequency: Annual
Circulation: 100K. Sales: $10-20MM
Products: Products for early childhood development

ETA/CUISENAIRE   (800) 445-5985
500 Greenview Ct. • Vernon Hills, IL 60061
E-Mail: info@etacuisenaire.com
Website: www.etacuisenaire.com
Fax Ordering: (800) 382-9326; (847) 816-5066
Fax Customer Service: (800) 875-9643
International Ordering: (847) 816-5050
Catalog: Free. Frequency: Semiannual
Circulation: 100K. Sales: $3-5MM
Products: 8,000 manipulative based educational
& supplemental materials for pre-K and K-12 that
enrich teaching and engage students in math,
reading/language, arts & science

FISHER SCIENCE EDUCATION   (800) 955-1177
Fisher Scientific International
4500 Turnberry Dr. • Hanover Park, IL 60133
E-Mail: sales@fishersci.com
Website: www.fishersci.com
Fax Ordering: (800) 955-0740; (800) 926-1166
International Ordering: (630) 655-4410
Customer Service: (800) 766-7000
Contact Name: Josh Leichtung, Marketing
Catalog: Free. Frequency: Annual
Circulation: 150K. Sales: $5-10MM
Products: Science suppliers for teachers

FLINN SCIENTIFIC CATALOGS   (800) 452-1261
P.O. Box 219 • Batavia, IL 60510
E-Mail: flinn@flinnsci.com
Website: www.flinnsci.com
Fax Ordering: (866) 452-1436
Contact Name: L.C. Flinn, President
Catalog: Free. Frequency: Annual
Circulation: 100K. Sales: $10-20MM
Products: Flinn Scientific Chemical &
Biological Catalog; Flinn Science Catalog;
resources for the chemistry teacher; chemistry
supplies & laboratory equipment; chemistry
workshops.

FREE SPIRIT PUBLISHING   (800) 735-7323
217 Fifth Ave. North, Suite 200
Minneapolis, MN 55401-1299
E-Mail: info@freespirit.com
Website: www.freespirit.com
Fax Ordering: (612) 337-5050
International Ordering: (612) 338-2068
Customer Service: (866) 703-7322
Catalog: Free. Frequency: Semiannual
Circulation: 150K. Sales: $500K to $1MM
Products: Books for children, parents &
teachers about learning to cope with life
in general

FREY SCIENTIFIC   (800) 225-3739
School Specialty Frey Scientific
P.O. Box 3000 • Nashua, NH 03061
E-Mail: customercare.frey@schoolspecialty.com
Website: www.freyscientific.com
Fax Ordering: (877) 256-3739
Contact Name: Garrett Reid, President
Catalog: Free. Frequency: Semiannual
Circulation: 100K. Sales: $3-5MM
Products: Frey Scientific provides you with
creative solutions in science by offering
innovative products & services for education.

FRIENDSHIP HOUSE EDUCATION   (800) 791-9876
29355 Ranney Pkwy.
Westlake, OH 44145
E-Mail: info@friendshiphouse.com
Website: www.friendshiphouse.com
Fax Ordering: (440) 871-0858
International Ordering: (440) 871-8040
Contact Name: Mike Bennett, President
Catalog: Free. Frequency: Semiannual
Circulation: 50K. Sales: $1-3MM
Products: Musical gifts, awards & teaching aids;
classroom decorations, reproducibles, teachers'
helpers, multimedia

FTC PUBLISHING   (888) 237-6740
P.O. Box 1361 • Bloomington, IL 61702
E-Mail: ftc@ftcpublishing.com
Website: www.ftcpublishing.com
Fax Ordering: (309) 663-5025
Catalogs: Free. Frequency: Annual
Circulation 100K. Sales: $1-3MM
Products: Software & books for education;
multimedia resources for the classroom

FOOTHILLS ADULT EDUCATION   (800) 300-4781
355 Goshen Rd. • Litchfield, CT 06759
E-Mail: info@educationconnection.org
Website: www.educationconnection.org
Fax Ordering: (860) 567-3381
International Ordering: (860) 567-0863

Contact Name: Danuta Thibodeau, PhD
Catalog: Free. Frequency: Annual
Circulation 100K. Sales: $1-3MM
Products: Educational materials, adult education

FUN & FUNCTION (800) 221-6329
P.O. Box 11 • Merion Station, PA 19066
E-Mail: sales@funandfunction.com
Website: www.funandfunction.com
Fax Ordering: (866) 343-6863
Catalog: Free. Frequency: Semiannual
Circulation 100K. Sales: $1-3MM
Products: Creative therapy toys; resources
for therapeutic play & education

GUIDANCE ASSOCIATES (800) 431-1242
31 Pine View Rd. • Mt. Kisco, NY 10549
E-Mail: sales@guidanceassociates.com
Website: www.guidanceassociates.com
Fax Ordering: (914) 666-5319
International Ordering: (914) 666-4100
Contact Name: William Goodman, President
Catalogs: Free. Frequency: Annual
Circulation 500K. Sales: $5-10MM
Products: School DVD & video catalog
lists over 1,500 DVDs & videos for K-12
education schools & business ; also,
audiovisual materials for schools, colleges
and corporations

HAWKHILL SCIENCE (800) 422-4295
125 E. Gilman St. • Madison, WI 53703
E-Mail: customerservice@hawkhill.com
Website: www.hawkhill.com
Fax Ordering: (608) 251-3924
International Ordering: (608) 251-3934
Contact Name: Bill Stonebarger, President
Catalog: Free. Frequency: Semiannual
Circulation: 50K. Sales: $500K to $1MM
Products: 150+ science videos, CD-ROMs
and DVDs to teach science & civic literacy

HEARLIHY & CO. (866) 622-1003
P.O. Box 1747 • Pittsburg, KS 66762
E-Mail: hearlihy@hearlihy.com
Website: www.hearlihy.com
Fax Ordering: (800) 443-2260
International Ordering: (620) 231-2424
Contact Names: Patrick Hearlihy, President
Catalog: Free. Frequency: Quarterly
Circulation: 50K. Sales: $5-10MM
Products: Industrial technology educational
materials, videos and software. Life Education,
Technology Education, and Drafting catalogs

HEATHKIT EDUCATIONAL SYSTEMS (800) 253-0570
2024 Hawthorne Ave. • St. Joseph, MI 49085
E-Mail: info@heathkit.com
Website: www.heathkit.com
Fax Ordering: (269) 925-2898
International Ordering: (269) 925-6000
Contact Names: William Johnson, President
Catalog: Free. Frequency: Quarterly
Circulation: 2MM. Sales: $10-25MM
Products: Classroom & home electronics courses

HOMEROOM CATALOG (800) 222-8270
P.O. Box 388 • Centerbrook, CT 06409
E-Mail: customerservice@homeroomdirect.com
Website: www.homeroomcatalog.com
Fax Ordering: (860) 767-4381
Contact Name: Thomas Romano, President

Catalog: Free. Frequency: 8x per year
Circulation: 3MM. Sales: $3-5MM
Products: Gifts for the teaching profession,
primarily for teachers in K-8

INTELLITOOLS, INC. (800) 899-6687
Cambium Learning Technologies (800) 547-6747
4185 Salazar Way • Frederick, CO 80504
E-Mail: info@intellitools.com
Website: www.intellitools.com
Fax Ordering: (888) 819-7767; (781) 276-0650
International Ordering: (781) 276-0600
Contact Name: Arjan Khalsa, President
Catalog: Free. Frequency: Annual
Circulation: 100K. Sales: $5-10MM
Products: Research-based cuirriculum
software in reading and math

KIDS ART TEACHING SUPPLIES CATALOG (530) 926-5076
P.O. Box 274 • Mount Shasta, CA 96067
E-Mail: info@kidsart.com
Website: www.kidsart.com
Fax Ordering: (530) 926-0851
Contact Name: Kim Solga, President
Catalog: Free. Frequency: Semiannual
Circulation: 50K. Sales: $500K - $1MM
Products: Kid's art teaching supplies;
art books & kits

JONTI-CRAFT, INC. (800) 543-4149
P.O. Box 30 • Wabasso, MN 56293
E-Mail: sales@jonti-craft.com
Website: www.jonti-craft.com
Fax Ordering: (507) 342-5617
International Ordering: (507) 342-5169
Catalog: Free. Frequency: Annual
Circulation: 150K. Sales: $5-10MM
Products: Early learning furniture

KIDSAFETY OF AMERICA CATALOG (800) 524-1156
66251 Schaefer Ave., Suite B
Chino, CA 91710
E-Mail: feedback@kidsafetystore.com
Website: www.kidsafetystore.com
Fax Ordering: (909) 902-1343
International Ordering: (909) 902-1340
Contact Name: Peter D. Osilaja, President
Catalog: Free. Frequency: Semiannual
Circulation: 100K. Sales: $1-3MM
Products: Child health, safety education
media for children, families & caregivers,
including books, videos, posters, CD-ROM,
stickers, and more

KNOWLEDGE UNLIMITED (800) 356-2303
P.O. Box 52 • Madison, WI 53701
E-Mail: csis@newscurrents.com
Website: www.thekustore.com
Fax Ordering: (800) 618-1570; (608) 442-1525
International Ordering: (608) 661-5666
Contact Names: Judith Laitman, President
Catalog: Free. Frequency: Semiannual
Circulation: 200K. Sales: $3-5MM
Products: Instructional materials for the educator:
posters, videos, teaching kits & current events
programs suitable for grades 3 and up

LAKESHORE LEARNING MATERIALS (800) 778-4456
2695 E. Dominguez St. • Carson, CA 90895 (800) 421-5354
E-Mail: lakeshore.lakeshorelearning.com
Website: www.lakeshorelearning.com
Fax Ordering: (800) 537-5403; (310) 638-6871

International Ordering: (310) 537-8600
Customer Service: (800) 428-4414
Contact Name: Michael Kaplan, President
Catalog: Free. Frequency: Annual
Products: Early learning materials for preschools,
day care programs, headstart programs, public
& private schools

LEARNING ANNEX (800) 872-6639
443 Park Ave. So. #501
New York, NY 10016
E-Mail: feedback@learningannex.com
Website: www.learningannex.com
Fax Ordering: (212) 290-2430
International Ordering: (212) 371-0280
Contact Name: Bill Zanker, President
Catalog: Free. Frequency: Semiannual
Circulation: 250K. Sales: $5-10MM
Products: Educational classes & materials

MAP & GLOBE CATALOG (800) 327-7992
First State Map & Globe Co.
3301 Lancaster Ave.
Wilmington, DE 19805
Fax Ordering: (302) 576-8900
International Ordering: (302) 998-6009
Catalog: Free. Frequency: Annual
Circulation: 100K. Sales: $1-3MM
Products: Maps and globes

MASTER TEACHER (800) 669-9633
P.O. Box 1207 • Manhattan, KS 66505
E-Mail: info@masterteacher.com
Website: www.masterteacher.com
Fax Ordering: (785) 669-1132
International Ordering: (785) 539-0555
Catalog: Free. Frequency: Semiannual
Circulation: 100K. Sales: $500K to $1MM
Products: Educational & teaching material,
including videos, posters, books, etc.

McGRUFF SPECIAL PRODUCTS (888) 776-7763
1 Prospect St. • Amsterdam, NY 12010
E-Mail: mcgruff@spocentral.com
Website: www.mcgruffspo.com
Fax Ordering: (800) 995-5121
International Ordering: (518) 842-4388
Catalog: Free. Frequency: Semiannual
Circulation: 150K. Sales: $500K to $1MM
Products: Crime prevention education materials
with the official McGruff mascot. Stickers,
key chains, safety-rul rulers, coloring books,
posters, brochures and booklets.

MEDIA BASICS VIDEO (800) 542-2505
705 Boston Post Rd. • Guilford, CT 06437
E-Mail: info@mediabasicsvideo.com
Website: www.mediabasicsvideo.com
Fax Ordering: (203) 458-2505
Contact Name: Matt Lehman, Manager
Catalog: Free. Frequency: Quarterly
Circulation: 100K. Sales: $500K to $1MM
Products: Educational videos for schools
and libraries

MINDWARE (800) 999-0398
2100 County Rd. C W
Roseville, MN 55113
E-Mail: info@mindwareonline.com
Website: www.mindwareonline.com
Fax Ordering: (888) 299-9273

Customer Service: (800) 274-6123
Catalog: Free. Frequency: Semiannual
Circulation: 75K. Sales: $500K to $1MM
Products: Early learning, reading material;
brainy toys, puzzles and games for children

MMI CORPORATION (410) 366-1222
P.O. Box 19907 • Baltimore, MD 21211
E-Mail: mail@mmicorporation@com
Website: www.mmicorporation.com
Fax Ordering: (410) 366-6311
Contact Name: Ralph C. Levy, President
Catalog: Free. Frequency: Semiannual
Circulation: 100K. Sales: $5-10MM
Products: Educational materials & equipment
for astronomy & geology

MUGGINS MATH SERIES (800) 962-8849
4860 Burnt Mountain Rd.
Ellijay, GA 30540
E-Mail: muggins@mugginsmath.com
Website: www.mugginsmath.com
Fax Ordering: (706) 635-7611
International Ordering: (706) 635-7612
Contact Name: Alan Schuler, President
Catalog: Free. Frequency: Annual
Circulation: 150K. Sales: $5-10MM
Products: Math educational boardgames

NASCO ONLINE CATALOGS (800) 558-9595
901 Janesville Ave. • Ft. Atkinson, WI 53538
E-Mail: custserv@enasco.com
Website: www.enasco.com
Fax Ordering: (920) 563-8296
International Ordering: (920) 563-2446
Contact Names: Richard Ciurczak, President
Catalog: Free. Frequency: Annual
Circulation: 500K. Sales: $20-50MM
Products: Distributes the following catalogs:
Agricultural Sciences; Anatomical & Nursing
Educational Materials; Early Learning Essentials;
Arts & Crafts; Dissection Materials & Select
Living Organisms; Elementary Math & Science
Materials; Math; Family & Consumer Sciences;
Farm & Ranch; Fitness Fundamentals; Geometry
& Algebra; Hands-On Health Catalog; Health Care
Educational Materials; Nutrition Teaching Aids;
Physical Education; Laboratory Sampling Products;
Science; School Age, Senior Activities; Special
Education Learning Essentials; To-Sew.

NATIONAL ARCHIVES PUBLICATIONS (800) 234-8861
700 Pennsylvania Ave., NW (866) 272-6272
Washington, DC 20408
E-Mail: info@archives.gov/publications
Website: www.archives.gov/publications
Fax Ordering: (202) 501-7170
International Ordering: (202) 357-5332
Catalog: Free. Frequency: Annual
Circulation: 150K. Sales: $5-10MM
Products: Aids for genealogical research

NATIONAL GEOGRAPHIC CATALOG (888) 225-5647
777 S. State Rd. 7 • Margate, FL 33068 (800) 962-1643
E-Mail: info@nationalgeographic.com (888) 915-3276
Website: www.nationalgeographic.com
Fax Ordering: (888) 242-0531
Catalog: Free. Frequency: Semiannual
Circulation: 250K. Sales: $5-10MM
Products: Nature and geography multimedia,
including books, maps, videos, DVDs, posters

NATIONAL SCHOOL PRODUCTS (800) 627-9393
1523 Old Niles Ferry Rd.
Maryville, TN 37804
E-Mail: customerservice@nationalschoolproducts.com
Website: www.nationalschoolproducts.com
Fax Ordering: (865) 983-9355
International Ordering: (865) 984-3960
Contact Name: John Nowell, President
Catalog: Free. Frequency: Semiannual
Circulation: 300K. Sales: $5-10MM
Products: Educational computer software
& school supplies

NATURE WATCH (800) 228-5816
5312 Derry Ave. • Agoura Hills, CA 91301
E-Mail: info@nature-watch.com
Website: www.nature-watch.com
Fax Ordering: (800) 228-5814
Catalog: Free. Frequency: Annual
Circulation: 100K. Sales: $3-5MM
Products: Educational products & craft
activity kits designed for teaching
children about nature

G. NEIL CATALOG (800) 999-9111
P.O. Box 450939 • Sunrise, FL 33345 (877) 968-7471
E-Mail: tcs@gneil.com
Website: www.gneil.com
Fax Ordering: (954) 514-1011
Catalog: Free. Frequency: Semiannual
Circulation: 100K. Sales: $500K - $1MM
Products: Human Resources; tools to manage
& motivate people; personnel software; training
games & tools; motivational gifts for employees;
greeting cards

NEW YORK OPEN CENTER (212) 219-2527
22 E. 30th St. • New York, NY 10016
E-Mail: info@opencenter.org
Website: www.opencenter.org
Fax Ordering: (212) 226-4056
Catalog: Free. Frequency: Semiannual
Circulation: 100K. Sales: $250-500K
Products: Holistic programs and classes,
videos, books and cassettes

NUTRITION ACTION HEALTHLETTER (202) 332-9110
Center for Science in the Public Interest
1875 Connecticut Ave., NW #300
Washington, DC 20009
E-Mail: cspi@cspinet.org
Website: www.cspinet.org
Fax Ordering: (202) 265-4954
Catalog: Free. Frequency: Monthly
Product: Latest research & practical advice
on nutrition, diet & related health issues,
as well as the politics of nutrition. Includes
recipes, books, and educational material.

OMEGA INSTITUTE CATALOG (800) 944-1001
Omega Institute for Holistic Studies (877) 944-2002
150 Lake Dr. • Rhinebeck, NY 12572
E-Mail: info@eomega.org
Website: www.eomega.org
Fax Ordering: (845) 266-3769
Customer Service: (845) 266-4444
Catalog: Free. Frequency: Annual
Circulation: 100K. Sales: $500K - $1MM
Product: Educational workshops & retreats;
wellness vacations

OMNI RESOURCES CATALOG (800) 742-2677
P.O. Box 2096 • Burlington, NC 27216
E-Mail: inquiries@omnimap.com
Website: www.omnimap.com
Fax Ordering: (336) 227-3748
International Ordering: (336) 227-8300
Contact Name: Rod Anderson, Marketing
Catalog: Free. Frequency: Semiannual
Circulation: 50K. Sales: $1-3MM
Products: Maps, globes, nature gifts
& school science supplies

PERFECTION LEARNING CATALOGS (800) 831-4190
P.O. Box 500 • Logan, IA 51546
E-Mail: orders@perfectionlearning.com
Website: www.perfectionlearning.com
Fax Ordering: (800) 543-2745
International Ordering: (712) 644-2831
Contact Name: Clint Keay, President
Catalogs: Free. Frequency: Semiannual
Circulation: 250K. Sales: $5-10MM
Products: Catalogs include: Elelemntary,
Middle School, High School, Intervention
& Instruction, K-8 Literacy; 6-12 Language
Arts & Social Studies. Contain software &
books

PHILLIP ROY, INC. CATALOG (800) 255-9085
P.O. Box 130 • Largo, FL 33785
E-Mail: info@philliproy.com
Website: www.philliproy.com
Fax Ordering: (877) 595-2685; (727) 595-2685
International Ordering: (727) 593-2700
Catalogs: Free. Frequency: Semiannual
Circulation: 100K. Sales: $1-3MM
Products: Character education & life skill
programs; early learning school programs

PRO-ED, INC. CATALOG (800) 897-3202
8700 Shoal Creek Blvd.
Austin, TX 78757
E-Mail: info@jalmarpress.com
Website: www.proedinc.com
Fax Ordering: (800) 397-7633; (512) 451-8542
International Ordering: (512) 451-3246
Contact Name: Bradley Winch, President
Catalog: Free. Frequency: Annual
Circulation: 150K. Sales: $5-10MM
Products: Activity-driven books for helping
teachers, counselors & parents guide students,
K-12 in developing skills; speech, language &
hearing products; special education &
rehabilitation; psychology & counseling;
occupational & physical therapy

QUEUE, INC. (800) 232-2224
1 Controls Dr. • Shelton, CT 06484
E-Mail: jjdk@qworkbooks.com
Website: www.qworkbooks.com
Fax Ordering: (800) 775-2729
Contact Name: Monica Kantrowitz, President
Catalog: Free. Frequency: Semiannual.
Circulation: 200K. Sales: $5-10MM
Products: Educational software for the
Mac & PC computers. Offers over 2,000
educational programs from more than one
hundred publishers. They have two catalogs,
Kindergarten-Grade 8 & High School/College.

REALY GOOD STUFF   (800) 366-1920
448 Pepper St. • Monroe, CT 06468
E-Mail: writeus@reallygoodstuff.com
Website: www.reallygoodstuff.com
Fax Ordering: (203) 268-1796
International Ordering: (203) 261-1920
Customer Support: (877) 867-1920
Catalog: Free. Frequency: Semiannual
Circulation: 100K. Sales: $5-10MM
Products: Fun and creative teaching
tools for the classroom

RESOURCES & SERVICES/   (800) 336-5191
TECHNOLOGY-USING EDUCATORS
International Society
for Technology in Education (ISTE)
480 Charnelton St. • Eugene, OR 97401
E-Mail: iste@iste.org
Website: www.iste.org
Fax Ordering: (541) 302-3778
International Ordering: (541) 302-3777
Catalog: Free. Frequency: Semiannual
Circulation: 100K. Sales: 1-3MM
Products: Resources and support material for
teachers who use computers in the classroom

RESOURCES FOR THE GIFTED   (800) 642-2822
Kolbe Corporation
3421 N. 44th St. • Phoenix, AZ 85018
E-Mail: info@kolbe.com
Website: www.kolbe.com
Fax Ordering: (602) 952-2706
International Ordering: (602) 840-9770
Contact Name: David Kolbe, President
Catalog: Free. Frequency: Annual
Circulation: 100K. Sales: $3-5MM
Products: Educational materials for the gifted

ROUTLEDGE CATALOGS   (800) 634-7064
Taylor & Francis Group
10650 Toebben Dr.
Independence, KY 41051
E-Mail: info@routledge-ny.com
Website: www.routledge-ny.com
Fax Ordering: (800) 248-4724
Catalog: Free. Frequency: Semiannual
Circulation: 500K. Sales: $50-100MM
Products: Encyclopedias, reference books,
textbooks & publications on education

SARGENT-WELCH   (800) 727-4368
P.O. Box 4130 • Buffalo, NY 14217   (800) 950-1079
E-Mail: customerservice@sargantwelch.com
Website: www.sargantwelch.com
Fax Ordering: (800) 676-2540
Catalog: Free. Frequency: Semiannual
Circulation: 200K. Sales: $5-10MM
Products: Science education equipment,
supplies & lab furniture

SCHOLAR'S BOOKSHELF   (609) 395-6933
110 Melrich Rd. • Cranbury, NJ 08512
E-Mail: books@scholarsbookshelf.com
Website: www.scholarsbookshelf.com
Fax Ordering: (609) 395-0755
Contact Name: Abbot Friedland, President
Catalog: Free. Frequency: Monthly
Circulation: 1MM. Sales: $5-10MM
Products: Books & videos on the subjects
of the military, history, fine arts, literature,
philosophy, religion, music

SCHOLASTIC CATALOGS   (800) 724-6527
557 Broadway • New York, NY 10012
E-Mail: info@scholastic.com
Website: www.scholastic.com
International Ordering: (212) 343-6100
Contact Name: Peter Bergen, President
Catalog: Free. Frequency: Monthly
Circulation: 500K. Sales: $50-100MM
Products: Educational materials & services;
teaching resources; school software; children's
books

SCHOOL SPECIALTY   (888) 388-3224
P.O. Box 1579 • Appleton, WI 54912   (800) 248-9171
E-Mail: customercare@schoolspecialty.com   (877) 698-1988
Website: www.schoolspecialty.com
Fax Ordering: (888) 388-6344; (419) 589-1600
International Ordering: (419) 589-1425
Contact Name: Joe Renzy, Marketing Manager
Catalog: Free. Frequency: Annual
Circulation: 250K. Sales: $20-50MM
Products: School supplies, teaching aids,
early childhood materials; classroom resources,
electronic education, educational computer
software, accessories, supplies and furniture.

SCHOOL SPECIALTY INTERVENTION   (800) 435-7728
Educators Publishing Service   (800) 225-5750
P.O. Box 9031 • Cambridge, MA 02139
E-Mail: feedback.intervention@schoolspecialty.com
Website: www.intervention.schoolspecialty.com
Fax Ordering: (888) 440-2665
Catalog: Free. Frequency: Quarterly
Products: Books, kits and supplies for
K-12 schools. Specializes in language
arts materials that support academic
standards and build basic skills.

SCHOOLMASTERS SCIENCE & SAFETY   (800) 521-2832
School-Tech, Inc.
P.O. Box 1941 • Ann Arbor, MI 48108
E-Mail: science@school-tech.com
Website: www.schoolmasters.com
Fax Ordering: (800) 654-4321
International Ordering: (734) 761-5135
Contact Name: Donald Canham, President
Catalog: Free. Frequency: Annual
Circulation: 200K. Sales: $5-10MM
Products: Two separate catalogs; cience
equipment & teaching aids, safety equipment
& videos

SCIENCE FIRST CATALOG   (800) 875-3214
86475 Gene Lasserre Blvd.
Yulee, FL 32097
E-Mail: info@sciencefirst.com
Website: www.sciencefirst.com
Fax Ordering: (800) 799-8115;
  (904) 225-2228
International Ordering: (904) 225-5558
Contact Name: Betty A. Phillips, President
Catalog: Free. Frequency: Annual
Circulation: 100K. Sales: $3-5MM
Products: 100 hands-on labs for learning &
experimenting with physical science; astronomy
and earth science models and materials.

SCIENCE KIT & BOREAL LABORATORIES   (800) 828-7777
BWR Scientifics
P.O. Box 5003 • Tonawanda, NY 14150
E-Mail: customerservice@sciencekit.com

Website: www.scienncekit.com
Fax Ordering: (800) 828-3299; (716) 874-9572
International Ordering: (716) 874-6020
Contact Name: Tom Rosenecker, Marketing
Catalogs: Free. Frequency: Annual
Circulation: 100K. Sales: $20-50MM
Products: 3 Catalogs: K-6, Middle-High School,
Teacher Developed, Classroom Tested. Science
kits & components for educational institutions

SCIENCE SOURCE CATALOGS   (800) 833-9033
Div. of Photo Researchers
60 E. 56th St. • New York, NY 10022
E-Mail: info@photoresearchers.com
Website: www.sciencesource.com
Fax Ordering: (212) 355-0731
International Ordering: (212) 758-3420
Contact Name: Anita Duncan, Sales
Catalogs: Free. Frequency: Annual
Circulation: 50K. Sales: $5-10MM
Products: Science & technology education
materials

SLOSSON EDUCATIONAL PUBLICATIONS   (888) 756-7766
P.O. Box 544 • East Aurora, NY 14052
E-Mail: info@slosson.com
Website: www.slosson.com
Fax Ordering: (716) 655-3840
International Ordering: (716) 652-0930
Contact Names: Steve Slosson, President
Catalog: Free. Frequency: Semiannual
Circulation: 150K. Sales: $3-5MM
Products: Books & materials on educational testing,
school screening, achievement, speech-language,
aptitude, developmental abilities, test preparations

SUMMIT LEARNING   (800) 777-8817
P.O. Box 755 • Fort Atkinson, WI 53538
E-Mail: custserv@summitlearning.com
Website: www.summitlearning.com
Fax Ordering: (800) 317-2194
Catalog: Free. Frequency: Semiannual
Circulation: 100K. Sales: $3-5 MM
Products: Educational materials for teachers
and parents in grades K-9

SUNBURST TECHNOLOGY   (800) 321-7511
1550 Executive Dr. • Elgin, IL 60121   (800) 431-1934
E-Mail: service@sunburst.com
Website: www.sunburst.com
Fax Ordering: (888) 800-3028
Contact Name: Conall Ryan, President
Catalog: Free. Frequency: Monthly
Circulation: 1MM. Sales: $5-10MM
Products: Health & guidance education
software, videos and posters

THE SYCAMORE TREE   (800) 779-6750
Sycamore Academu   (888) 334-6711
2179 Meyer Pl. • Costa Mesa, CA 92627
E-Mail: info@sycamoretree.com
Website: www.sycamoretree.com
Fax Ordering: (714) 668-1344
Customer Service: (714) 668-1338
Contact Name: William B. Gogel, Director
Catalog: Free. Frequency: Semiannual
Circulation: 50K. Sales: $1-3M
Products: Provides home-school education
services to K-12 worldwide. Contains more than
3,000 items to supplement home-school curriculums.

TEACHER'S MEDIA COMPANY   (800) 262-8837
Cerebellum Corp.   (866) 386-0253
1661 Tennessee St., Suite 3D
San Francisco, CA 94107
E-Mail: customerservice@cerebellum.com
Website: www.teachersvideo.com
Fax Ordering: (805) 426-8136
Catalog: Free. Frequency: Annual
Circulation: 150K. Sales: $5-10MM
Products: Educational DVDs & videos
on all popular curriculum topics; also,
posters and software

THE TEACHING COMPANY   (800) 832-2412
4840 Westfield Blvd. #500
Chantilly, VA 20151
E-Mail: custserv@teach12.com
Website: www.teach12.com
Fax Ordering: (703) 378-3819
Catalog: Free. Frequency: Semiannual
Circulation: 100K. Sales: $1-3MM
Products: Video series of non-credit
courses in more than 100 disciplines

THINKING ALLOWED PRODUCTIONS   (800) 999-4415
5966 Zinn Dr. • Oakland, CA 94611
E-Mail: info@thinkingallowed.com
Website: www.thinkingallowed.com
Fax Ordering: (510) 339-8004
International Ordering: (510) 339-1588
Contact Name: Arthur Bloch, President
Catalog: Free. Frequency: Annual
Circulation: 50K. Sales: $250-500K
Products: Educational DVDs & videos

TRANSPARENT LANGUAGE, INC.   (800) 567-9619
12 Murphy Dr. • Nashua, NH 03062   (888) 245-1829
E-Mail: info@transparent.com
Website: www.transparent.com
Fax Ordering: (603) 262-6476
International Ordering: (603) 262-6300
Catalog: Free. Frequency: Semiannual
Circulation: 200K. Sales: $1-3MM
Products: Language-learning diskettes
and CD-ROMs for Windows and Mac

TROLL CARNIVAL BOOK CLUBS   (800) 654-3037
P.O. Box 3730 • Jefferson City, MO 65102 (800) 724-6527
E-Mail: info@trollcarnival.com
Website: www.trollcarnival.com
Fax Ordering: (800) 979-8765
Catalog: Free. Frequency: Annual
Circulation: 100K. Sales: $10-20MM
Products: Educational videos & books;
book clubs

URSA MAJOR CATALOG   (800) 798-4327
Div. of On Time Publications
900 S. Deere Rd. • Macomb, IL 61455
E-Mail: info@ontimecolor.com
Website: www.ontimecolor.com
Fax Ordering: (309) 836-4149
International Ordering: (309) 368-6664
Contact Name: Bill Hermann, President
Catalog: Free. Frequency: Semiannual
Circulation: 50K. Sales: $1-3MM
Products: Astronomy education material,
including star maps, world and USA maps

US GAMES CATALOG (800) 327-0484
Sports Supply Group
P.O. Box 7726 • Dallas, TX 75209
E-Mail: feedusgames@sportssupplygroup.com
Website: www.usgames.com
Fax Ordering: (800) 899-0149
Catalog: Free. Frequency: Annual
Circulation: 100K. Sales: $5-10MM
Products: Sports & fitness products;
game tables & board games.

VIDEO LEARNING LIBRARY, LLC (800) 383-8811
15838 North 62nd St. • Scottsdale, AZ 85254
E-Mail: info@videolearning.com
Website: www.videolearning.com
Fax Ordering: (480) 596-9973
International Ordering: (480) 596-9970
Catalog: $29.95. Frequency: Annual
Circulation: 5K. Sales: $1-3MM
Products: Lists & describes about
13,000 special interest videos.

VISUAL EDUCATION (800) 243-7070
P.O. Box 1666 • Springfield, OH 45501
E-Mail: sales@vis-ed.com
Website: www.vis-ed.com
Fax Ordering: (937) 324-5967
International Ordering: (937) 328-2854
Catalog: Free. Frequency: Annual
Circulation: 100K. Sales: $3-5MM
Products: Study card sets for high school
and college, including: subjects of: math,
language, science, bible studies, business,
medical, computers, and SAT Prep.

WARD'S NATURAL SCIENCE CATALOGS (800) 962-2660
P.O. Box 92912 • Rochester, NY 14692
E-Mail: customer_service@wardsci.com
Website: www.wardsci.com
Fax Ordering: (585) 334-6174; (585) 321-9105
International Ordering: (585) 359-2502
Contact Name: Gerry Christian, President
Catalog: Free to qualified educational institutions.
Frequency: Annual. Circulation: 100K.
Sales: $10-20M
Products: Science educational materials
for middle school through college

WILKEN-ANDERSON COMPANY (800) 847-2222
4525 W. Division St. • Chicago, IL 60651
E-Mail: info@waco-lab-supply.com
Website: www.waco-lab-supply.com
Fax Ordering: (773) 384-6260
International Ordering: (773) 384-4433
Contact Name: Bruce Wilkens, President
Catalog: Free. Frequency: Semiannual
Circulation: 150K. Sales: $5-10MM
Products: Laboratory equipment, supplies,
and chemicals

WINCRAFT, INC. CATALOG (800) 533-8100
P.O. Box 888 • Winona, MN 55987
E-Mail: contact@wincraft.com
Website: www.wincraft.com
Fax Ordering: (507) 453-0690
International Ordering: (507) 454-5510
Contact Name: John Kilen, President
Catalog: Free. Frequency: Annual
Circulation: 250K. Sales: $20-50MM
Products: Professional sports' official
licensed products, as well as major college teams

WORLD ALMANAC BOOKS (800) 322-8755
Infobase Publishing
132 W. 31st St. • New York, NY 10001
E-Mail: custserv@factsonfile.com
Website: www.worldalmanac.com
Fax Ordering: (917) 339-0325
Contact Names: Ben Jacobs, Coreena Schultz
Catalog: Free. Frequency: Annual
Circulation: 200K. Sales: $10-20MM
Products: Books & software for the whole
language/ethnicity classroom from World Almanac

WOLVERINE SPORTS (800) 521-2832
School-Tech, Inc.
P.O. Box 1941 • Ann Arbor, MI 48106
E-Mail: info@wolverinesports.com
Website: www.wolverinesports.com
Fax Ordering: (800) 654-4321; (734) 761-8711
International Ordering: (734) 761-5072
Contact Name: Don Canham, President
Catalog: Free. Frequency: Semiannual
Circulation: 200K. Sales: $5-10MM
Products: Sports equipment for physical
education classes; educational & sports
videos and CD-ROMs; science equipment.

ZEPHYR PRESS CATALOG (800) 232-2187
814 N. Franklin St. • Chicago, IL 60611
E-Mail: info@zephyrpress.com
Website: www.zephyrpress.com
Fax Ordering: (312) 337-5985
International Ordering: (312) 337-1651
Contact Name: Joe Tanner, President
Catalog: Free. Frequency: Semiannual
Circulation: 100K. Sales: $1-3MM
Products: Books specializing in innovative
teaching methods

ACCU-TECH CORP. CABLE (800) 221-4767
200 Hembree Park Dr. • Roswell, GA 30076 (888) 222-8832
E-Mail: sales@accu-tech.com (800) 740-2240
Website: www.accu-tech.com
Fax Ordering: (770) 740-2260
International Ordering: (770) 740-2240
Contact Name: Ed Ellis, President
Catalog: Free. Frequency: Annual
Circulation: 100K. Sales: $50-100MM
Products: Connectivity products; fiber optic
products, networking products, tools & test
equipment, electrical wire and cables.

AMPROBE TEST TOOLS (877) 267-7623
3270 Executive Way • Miramar, FL 33025
E-Mail: info@amprobe.com
Website: www.amprobe.com
Fax Ordering: (954) 499-5452; 499-5512
International Ordering: (954) 499-5531; 499-5454
Contact Name: Bill Mulvihill & Bill McDonough
Catalog: Free. Frequency: Annual
Circulation: 200K. Sales: $20-50MM
Products: Advanced testing products;
electrical equipment; test & service tools

AEMC INSTRUMENTS (800) 343-1391
Chauvin Arnoux, Inc.
200 Foxborough Blvd.
Foxborough, MA 02035
E-Mail: sales@aemc.com
Website: www.aemc.com
Fax Ordering: (508) 698-2118
International Ordering: (508) 698-2115
Contact Name: David Peters, President
Catalog: Free. Frequency: Annual
Circulation: 100K. Sales: $5-10MM
Products: Electrical testing & measurement
equipment

AGT BATTERY SUPPLY (800) 340-3900
7D Great Meadow Ln. • E. Hanover, NJ 07936
Website: www.batterysupplier.com
E-Mail: info@batterysupplier.com
Fax Ordering: (973) 781-1102
International Ordering: (973) 781-1100
Catalog: Free. Frequency: Annual
Circulation: 150K. Sales: $5-10MM
Products: Batteries & accessories

AFTER TOUCH - NEW MUSIC DISCOVERIES (800) 882-4262
Creative Musicians Coalition
P.O. Box 6205 • Peoria, IL 61601
E-Mail: aimcmc@aol.com
Website: www.aimcmc.com
Fax Ordering: (309) 685-4879
International Ordering: (309) 685-4843
Contact Name: Ronald Wallace, President
Catalog: Free. Frequency: Annual
Circulation: 25K. Sales: $1-3MM
Products: Music CDs & videos from
independent artists

ALFA ELECTRONICS (800) 526-2532
24 Rosewood Ct.
Princeton Junction, NJ 08550
E-Mail: sales@alfaelectronics.com
Website: www.alfaelectronics.com
Fax Ordering: (609) 897-0206
International Ordering: (609) 897-0168
Contact Name: Wennie Kao, President
Catalog: Free. Frequency: Semiannual
Circulation: 50K. Sales: $3-5MM

Products: Electronic test equipment, digital
meters, oscilloscopes, power supplies

ALL ELECTRONICS CORP. (888) 826-5432
14928 Oxnard St. • Van Nuys, CA 91411
E-Mail: allcorp@allcorp.com
Website: www.allelectronics.com
Fax Ordering: (818) 781-2653
International Ordering: (818) 904-0524
Customer Service: (800) 344-5555
Contact Names: Allen Kantner, President
Catalog: Free. Frequency: Quarterly
Circulation: 50K. Sales: $5-10MM
Products: Electronics & electromechanical
parts & supplies

ALL PRO SOUND (800) 925-5776
806 Beverly Pkwy. • Pensacola, FL 32505
E-Mail: catalog@allprosound.com
Website: www.allprosound.com
Fax Ordering: (850) 432-0844
International Ordering: (850) 432-5780
Catalog: Free. Frequency: Semiannual
Circulation: 200K. Sales: $20-50MM
Products: Audio, video, lighting systems

ALLIED ELECTRONICS (800) 433-5700
7410 Pebble Dr. • Fort Worth, TX 76118 (866) 433-5722
E-Mail: sales@alliedelec.com
Website: www.alliedelec.com
Fax Ordering: (817) 595-6444
International Ordering: (817) 595-3500
Contact Name: David Yaniko, President
Catalog: Free. Frequency: Annual
Circulation: 200K. Sales: $5-10MM
Products: Electronic componenets

ALLTRONICS (408) 778-3868
P.O. Box 808 • San Martin, CA 95046
E-Mail: ejohnson@alltronics.com
Website: www.alltronics.com
Fax Ordering: (408) 778-2558
Contact Name: Sam Goode, President
Catalog: Free. Frequency: Annual.
Circulation: 100K. Sales: $5-10MM
Products: Consumer electronics, electronic
components and kits

AMAZING ELECTRONIC DEVICES (800) 221-1705
Information Unlimited
P.O. Box 716 • Amherst, NH 03031
E-Mail: info@amazing1.com
Website: www.amazing1.com
Fax Ordering: (603) 672-5406
International Ordering: (603) 673-6493
Contact Name: Robert Alannini, President
Catalog: $2.99. Frequency: Semiannual
Circulation: 100K. Sales: $5-10MM
Products: Electronic products and kits, science
projects, lasers, tesla coils, high voltage
devices, home/personal protection devices.

AMERICAN INNOVATIONS (845) 371-0000
383 West Route 59 • Spring Valley, NY 10977
E-Mail: info@spysite.com
Website: www.spysite.com
Fax Ordering: (845) 371-3885
Catalog: Free. Frequency: Annual
Circulation: 100K. Sales: $5-10MM
Products: Surveillance, motion/remote cameras,
listening/recording devices, privacy protection
devices, weapon/metal detectors, optical products

AMERICAN MICROSYSTEMS, LTD. (800) 648-4452
2190 Regal Pkwy. • Euless, TX 76040 (800) 206-2123
E-Mail: sales@barcodepower.com
Website: www.barcodepower.com
Fax Ordering: (817) 685-6232
International Ordering: (817) 571-9015
Contact Name: Robert Alannini, President
Catalog: Free. Frequency: Annual
Circulation: 75K. Sales: $10-50MM
Products: Bar code readers & laser scanners

ANTIQUE ELECTRONIC SUPPLY (480) 820-5411
6221 S. Maple Ave. • Tempe, AZ 85283
E-Mail: info@tubesandmore.com
Website: www.tubesandmore.com
Fax Ordering: (800) 706-6789; (480) 820-4643
Contact Names: Noreen Cravener, President
Catalog: Free. Frequency: Annual
Circulation: 50K. Sales: $5-10MM
Products: Vacuum tubes and related
electronic components

APOLLO/BOONE (800) 777-3750
PRESENTATION PRODUCTS (800) 359-1230
ACCO Brands, Inc.
300 Yower Pkwy. • Lincolnshire.IL 60069
Fax Ordering: (800) 247-1317; 628-5723
   (847) 918-7740
International Ordering: (847) 918-8405
Tech Support: (800) 476-8226
Contact Name: Harry G. Charlston, President
Catalog: Free. Frequency: Quarterly
Circulation: 150K. Sales: $50-100MM
Products: Audio visual for presentations,
furniture lamps

APX TECHNOLOGIES, INC. (516) 433-1313
264 Duffy Ave. • Hicksville, NY 11801
E-Mail: apx@apxonline.com
Website: www.apxonline.com
Fax Ordering: (516) 433-1457
Contact Name: Y. Ofek, President
Catalog: Free. Frequency: Annual.
Circulation: 50K. Sales: $3-5MM
Products: Electrical components,
power supplies, transformers

ARCO ELECTRIC PRODUCTS (800) 428-4370
2325 E. Michigan Rd. • Shelbyville, IN 46176
E-Mail: Info@arco-electric.com
Website: www.arco-electric.com
Fax Ordering: (317) 398-2655
International Ordering: (317) 398-9713
Contact Name: Hal Pike, President
Catalog: Free. Frequency: Annual.
Circulation: 50K. Sales: $10-50MM
Products: Motors, generators, capacitors

ARROW ELECTRONICS ONLINE CATALOG (877) 237-8621
50 Marcus Dr. • Melville,, NY 11747 (800) 833-3557
E-Mail: sales@arrow.com
Website: www.arrow.com
International Ordering: (631) 847-2000
Contact Name: Robert Schiesel, Marketing
Catalog: Online. Sales: $20-50MM
Products: Electronic components &
computer products

ARROW TECHNOLOGIES, LLC (303) 694-4390
7348 S. Alton Way Unit 9D
Centennial, CO 80112
E-Mail: sales@arrowtechnologiesllc.com

Website: www.arrowtechnologiesllc.com
Fax Ordering: (303) 221-2123
International Ordering: (303) 694-4390
Contact Name: Jackie Millard, President
Catalog: Free. Frequency: Annual
Circulation: 100K. Sales: $50-100MM
Products: Cable descramblers, cable
accessories, speakers, portable
electronics, audio video furniture

ASI HOME (800) 263-8608
566 Route 390 • Tafton, PA 18464
E-Mail: sales@asihome.com
Website: www.asihome.com
Fax Ordering: (866) 542-0470
Contact Name: Richard Scholl, President
Catalog: Free. Frequency: Annual
Circulation: 50K. Sales: $3-5MM
Products: Home automation products,
including home theaters, telephones
& Intercoms, home security products,
heating & cooling, driveway sensors,
X-10 compatible switches & modules;
tools, books & videos

ATLANTA CABLE SALES (800) 241-9881
495 Horiizon Dr. #200
Suwanee, GA 30024
E-Mail: atlcable@atlantacable.com
Website: www.atlantacable.com
Fax Ordering: (678) 775-0209
International Ordering: (678) 775-0208
Contact Name: D. Merenda, President
Catalog: Free. Frequency: Annual
Circulation: 50K. Sales: $5-10MM
Products: Telecommunications &
audio/video components

AUDIO ACCESSORIES, INC. (603) 446-3335
P.O. Box 360 • Marlow, NH 03456
E-Mail: audioacc@patchbays.com
Website: www.patchbays.com
Fax Ordering: (603) 446-7543
Contact Name: Marion Hall, President
Catalog: Free. Frequency: Annual
Circulation: 100K. Sales: $5-10MM
Products: Audio wired panels, audio &
video jacks and panels

AUDIO ADVISOR (800) 942-0220
3427 Kraft Ave. SE
Grand Rapids, MI 49512
E-Mail: orders@audioadvisor.com
Website: www.audioadvisor.com
Fax Ordering: (616) 254-8875
International Ordering: (616) 254-8871
Customer Service: (800) 451-5445
Contact Name: Beth Thomas, Service Rep.
Catalog: Free. Frequency: Semiannual
Circulation: 100K. Sales: $10-20MM
Products: High end audio products

AUDIO CONCEPTS, INC. (608) 784-4570
901 S. 4th St. • La Crosse, WI 54601
E-Mail: sales@audioc.com
Website: www.audioc.com
Fax Ordering: (678) 775-0209
International Ordering: (608) 784-6367
Contact Name: Michael Dzurko, President
Catalog: Free. Frequency: Annual
Circulation: 100K. Sales: $3-5MM
Products: Audio and home theater speakers

AUDIOLAB ELECTRONICS, INC. (800) 624-1903
10620 Industrial Ave. #100
Roseville, CA 95841
E-Mail: info@audiolabelectronics.com
Website: www.audiolabelectronics.com
Fax Ordering: (916) 784-1425
International Ordering: (916) 784-0200
Contact Name: Robert Stofan, President
Catalog: Free. Frequency: Annual
Circulation: 100K. Sales: $3-5MM
Products: Formatted audio discs

AUDIOVOX CORPORATION (800) 645-7750
150 Marcus Blvd. • Hauppauge, NY 11788
E-Mail: sales@audiovox.com
Website: www.audiovox.com
Fax Ordering: (631) 231-2968
Customer Service: (800) 645-229-1235; 645-4994
International Ordering: (631) 231-7750
Contact Name: John J. Shalam, President
Catalog: Free. Frequency: Annual
Circulation: 200K. Sales: $50-100MM
Products: Audio/home security, car radios/
stereos, personal/portable home stereo &
theater systems, speakers, amplifiers, pocket
PC's, wireless/cordless telephones, remote
starters & car security systems, two-way radios.

AUER PRECISION COMPANY (480) 834-4637
1050 W. Birchwood Ave. • Mesa, AZ 85210
E-Mail: sales@auerprecision.com
Website: www.auerprecision.com
Fax Ordering: (480) 964-8237
Contact Name: Peggy Heins, Marketing
Catalog: Free. Frequency: Annual
Circulation: 100K. Sales: $20-50MM
Products: Electronics, automotive, aerospace,
medical, semiconductor, optoelectronics,
commercial and consumer products.

BARKSDALE CONTROL PRODUCTS (800) 835-1060
3211 Fruitland Ave. • Los Angeles, CA 90058
E-Mail: sales@barksdale.com
Website: www.barksdale.com
Fax Ordering: (323) 589-3463
International Ordering: (323) 589-6181
Contact Name: Margie Mueller, Marketing
Catalog: Free. Frequency: Annual
Circulation: 100K. Sales: $20-50MM
Products: Valves, switches & transducers

BATTERY NETWORK (800) 797-9750
955 Borra Pl. • Escondido, CA 92029
E-Mail: sales@batterynetwork.com
Website: www.batterynetwork.com
Fax Ordering: (888) 858-6828
Contact Name: Steve Rade, President
Catalog: Free. Frequency: Annual
Circulation: 50K. Sales: $1-3MM
Products: Batteries and accessories
for radios, laptop computers, cellular
phones, camcorders, etc.

BATTERY PROS, INC. (800) 451-7171
P.O. Box 54 • Horseshoe Beach, FL 32648
E-Mail: sales@batteryprosinc.com
Website: www.batteryprosinc.com
Fax Ordering: (352) 498-2482
International Ordering: (352) 498-2477
Contact Name: E.F. Sherry, President
Catalog: Free. Frequency: Semiannual.
Circulation: 100K. Sales: $10-50MM

Products: OEM battery design & supply;
battery assemblies; name brand batteries
and cells.

BOSE CORPORATION (800) 999-2673
The Mountain • Framingham, MA 01701 (800) 242-9008
E-Mail: bose@bose.com
Website: www.bose.com
Fax Ordering: (508) 766-7543
International Ordering: (508) 766-1099
Tech Support: (877) 210-3782
Catalog: Free. Frequency: Annual
Circulation: 150K. Sales: $100-200MM
Products: Headsets, radios, stereos,
speakers and accessories

BROOKE DISTRIBUTORS, INC. (800) 275-8792
16250 NW 52nd Ave. • Miami, FL 33014
E-Mail: sales@brooke.com
Website: www.brooke.com
Fax Ordering: (305) 620-3988
Contact Name: David Rutter, President
International Ordering: (305) 624-9752
Catalog: Free. Frequency: Annual
Circulation: 100M. Sales: $10-50MM
Products: Consumer electronics, computers

C & H SURPLUS (800) 325-9465
805 Highland Ave. • Duarte, CA 91010
E-Mail: candhsurplus@yahoo.com
Website: www.candhsales.com
Fax Ordering: (626) 796-4875
International Ordering: (626) 256-7907
Contact Name: Carl Izbicki, President
Catalog: Free. Frequency: Annual
Circulation: 100K. Sales: $1-3MM
Products: Electronics surplus components
to developers, hobbyists and consumers

C & S SALES (800) 292-7711
150 Carpenter Ave. • Wheeling, IL 60090
E-Mail: sales@cs-sales.com
Website: www.cs-sales.com
Fax Ordering: (847) 541-9904
International Ordering: (847) 541-0710
Contact Name: Jim Cecchin, Marketing
Catalog: Free. Frequency: Semiannual
Circulation: 100K. Sales: $1-3MM
Products: Science, electronics, educational
products, toys & test equipment & tools

CABLESCAN, INC. (800) 898-5783
3022 Inland Empire Blvd.
Ontario, CA 91764
E-Mail: sales@cablescan.com
Website: www.cablescan.com
Fax Ordering: (909) 483-2463
International Ordering: (909) 483-2436
Contact Name: Ken Rockwell, Marketing
Catalog: Free. Frequency: Annual
Circulation: 50K. Sales: $3-5MM
Products: Electronic instruments;
assembly and conntinuity testers;
cables and back planes

CAM AUDIO CATALOG (800) 527-3458
Missionary Tape & Equipment Supply
2210 Executive Dr. • Garland, TX 75041
E-Mail: sales@camaudio.com
Website: www.camaudio.com
Fax Ordering: (972) 271-1555
International Ordering: (972) 271-2800

Contact Name: Dean Harrison, President
Catalog: Free. Frequency: Annual
Circulation: 200K. Sales: $5-10MM
Products: Audio, video & compact disc
equipment & supplies

CAMBRIDGE SOUND WORKS (800) 367-4434
120 Water St. • North Andover, MA 01845
E-Mail: sales@cambridgesoundworks.com
Website: www.cambridgesoundworks.com
Fax Ordering: (978) 794-2903
International Ordering: (978) 623-4400
Contact Name: Thomas DeVesto, President
Catalog: Free. Frequency: Semiannual
Circulation: 100K. Sales: $5-10MM
Products: Sound equipment for your
home & office

CCI SOLUTIONS (800) 426-8664
P.O. Box 481 • Olympia, WA 98507 (800) 562-6006
E-Mail: info@ccisolutions.com
Website: www.ccisolutions.com
Fax Ordering: (800) 399-8273;
 (360) 754-1566
International Ordering: (360) 943-5378
Catalog: Free. Frequency: Semiannual
Circulation: 100K. Sales: $10-20MM
Products: High performance accoustics,
sound, video & lighting systems

CEF INDUSTRIES (800) 888-6419
320 S. Church St. • Addison, IL 60101
E-Mail: sales@cefind.com
Website: www.cefind.com
Fax Ordering: (630) 628-1386
International Ordering: (630) 628-2593
Contact Name: Andy Dimitriou, Marketing
Catalog: Free. Frequency: Semiannual
Circulation: 100K. Sales: $1-3MM
Products: Electronic equipment &
machinery

CHEMART COMPANY (800) 521-5001
15 New England Way
Lincoln, RI 02865
E-Mail: sales@chemart.com
Website: www.chemart.com
Fax Ordering: (401) 333-1634
International Ordering: (401) 333-9200
Contact Name: S. Clegg, Marketing
Catalog: Free. Frequency: Annual
Circulation: 100K. Sales: $10-20MM
Products: Precision etched parts for
electronic and industrial applications;
Christmas ornaments, collectibles,
memorabilia

COLE-PARMER INSTRUMENT CO. (800) 323-4340
625 E. Bunker Ct. • Vernon Hills, IL 60061
E-Mail: info@coleparmer.com
Website: www.coleparmer.com
Fax Ordering: (847) 247-2929
International Ordering: (847) 549-7600
Contact Name: Andy Dimitriou, Marketing
Catalog: Free. Frequency: Annual
Circulation: 100K. Sales: $5-10MM
Products: Alarms, controllers, thermometers,
thermocouples and other instruments for use
in temperature applications; industrial safety
products; tubing pump systems; products for
sampling, field testing and lab anaylsis.

COLORADO FUTURESCIENCE (719) 634-0185
2405 Eagle View Dr.
Colorado Springs, CO 80909
E-Mail: je@scitechmail.com
Website: www.futurescience.com
Fax Ordering: (719) 633-3438
Contact Name: Jerry Emanuelson, President
Catalog: Free. Frequency: Annual.
Circulation: 100K. Sales: $1-3MM
Products: Superconductors; kits for
making superconductors

COMMUNICATIONS ELECTRONICS (800) 872-7226
P.O. Box 1045 • Ann Arbor, MI 48106
E-Mail: cei@usascan.com
Website: www.usascan.com
Fax Ordering: (734) 663-8888
International Ordering: (734) 996-8888
Tech Support: (800) 297-1023
Contact Name: Ken Ascher, President
Catalog: Free. Frequency: Quarterly
Circulation: 200K. Sales: $3-5 MM
Products: Electronic shortwave radios,
scanners, CB radios, phones

CONSOLIDATED ELECTRONICS (800) 543-3568
P.O. Box 20070 • Dayton, OH 45420
E-Mail: scoy@celtron.com
Website: www.celtron.com
Fax Ordering: (937) 252-4066
International Ordering: (937) 252-5662
Contact Name: Steve Coy, President
Catalog: Free. Frequency: Annual
Circulation: 50K. Sales: $3-5MM
Products: Electronic parts & equipment

CONSUMERTRONICS (505) 321-1034
P.O. Box 23097, Albuquerque, NM 87192
E-Mail: wizguru@tsc-global.com
Website: www.consumertronics.net
Fax Ordering: (505) 275-5637
Contact Name: John J. Williams, President
Catalog: $3. Frequency: Annual
Circulation: 50K. Sales: $1-3MM
Products: How-to manuals, make-it-yourself
electronic kits, books & other publications

CONTACT KIT CATALOG (800) 451-8423
Zap Supply
P.O. Box 837 • Spring, TX 77383
Fax Ordering: (281) 292-0088
International Ordering: (281) 292-0077
Contact Name: Rob Bailey, Marketing
Catalog: Free. Frequency: Quarterly
Circulation: 50K. Sales: $1-3MM
Products: Motor control equipment
replacement parts, contact kits, timers,
relays, starters, switches, elevators, lifts
and hoists

CONTINENTAL ELECTRONICS CORP. (800) 733-5011
4212 S. Buckner Blvd. • Dallas, TX 75227
E-Mail: sales@contelec.com
Website: www.contelec.com
Fax Ordering: (214) 381-3250
International Ordering: (214) 381-7161
Customer Service: (214) 388-5800
Contact Name: Robert McDonald, President
Catalog: Free. Frequency: Annual
Circulation: 150K. Sales: $10-20MM
Products: Broadcast transmitters

CONTROLLED POWER CO. (800) 521-4792
1955 Stephenson Hwy. • Troy, MI 48083
E-Mail: info@controlledpwr.com
Website: www.controlledpwr.com
Fax Ordering: (248) 528-0411
International Ordering: (248) 528-3700
Contact Name: Henry Tazzia, President
Catalog: Free. Frequency: Annual
Circulation: 150K. Sales: $10-20MM
Products: Power protection products;
emergency lighting systems; power
purification systems; shielded K-rated
isolation transformers and rectifers for
industrial, automation, medical, &
telecommunications.

COPPER ELECTRONICS (800) 626-6343
3315 Gilmore Industrial Blvd.
Louisville, KY 40213
E-Mail: corpsales@copper.com
Website: www.copper.com
Fax Ordering: (502) 968-0449
International Ordering: (502) 968-8500
Catalog: Free. Frequency: Semiannual
Circulation: 250K. Sales: $5-10MM
Products: Computers, consumer electronics
&communciations equipment

CRESTWOOD COMMUNICATION AIDS (414) 351-0311
P.O. Box 090107 • Milwaukee, WI 53209
E-Mail: crestcomm@aol.com
Website: www.communicationaids.com
Fax Ordering: (414) 446-9255
Contact Name: Ruth B. Leff, President
Catalog: Free. Frequency: Semiannual.
Circulation: 50K. Sales: $1-3MM
Products: Communication aids for children
& adults, including communication boards,
devices, picture cards, and adaptive toys
to help people.

CRUTCHFIELD (800) 955-9009
1 Crutchfield Park • Charlottesville, VA 22911 (888) 955-6000
E-Mail: corpsales@crutchfield.com
Website: www.crutchfield.com
Fax Ordering: (434) 817-1010
International Ordering: (434) 817-1000
Customer Service: (888) 809-5145
Contact Name: William Crutchfield, Owner
Catalog: Free. Frequency: Quarterly
Circulation: 3MM. Sales: $100-200MM
Products: Audio and video components,
home theaters, car stereos, telephones,
pagers and digital satellite systems

CSI/SPECO (800) 645-5516
200 New Highway • Amityville, NY 11701
E-Mail: info@csi-speco.com
Website: www.csi-speco.com
Fax Ordering: (631) 957-9142
Contact Name: L.W. Keller
Catalog: Free. Frequency: Annual
Circulation: 100K. Sales: $5-10MM
Products: Residential & commercial
audio & video security products

CURRENTS CATALOG (877) 272-2722
American Power Conversion (877) 800-4272
132 Fairgrounds Rd.
West Kingston, RI 02892
E-Mail: sales@apcc.com
Website: www.apcc.com

Fax Ordering: (401) 788-2787
International Ordering: (401) 789-5735
Technical Support: (800) 555-2725
Contact Name: Roger Dowdell, President
Catalog: Free. Frequency: Quarterly
Circulation: 200K. Sales: $100-500MM
Products: Surge protectors, battery backups
for computers

DA-LITE SCREEN COMPANY (800) 622-3737
P.O. Box 137 • Warsaw, IN 46581
E-Mail: info@da-lite.com
Website: www.da-lite.com
Fax Ordering: (877) 325-4832; (574) 267-7804
International Ordering: (574) 267-8101
Contact Name: Richard Lundin, President
Catalog: Free. Frequency: Annual
Circulation: 200K. Sales: $250-500MM
Products: Front and rear projection screens,
monitor mounts, audio visual and monitor
carts and stands, overhead projectors.

DATA DISPLAY PRODUCTS (800) 421-6815
445 S. Douglas St. • El Segundo, CA 90245
E-Mail: atoniolo@ddp-leds.com
Website: www.ddp-leds.com
Fax Ordering: (214) 640-7639
International Ordering: (310) 640-0442
Contact Name: Anthony Toniolo, Manager
Catalog: Free. Frequency: Annual
Circulation: 100K. Sales: $5-10MM
Products: LED's, lights, sockets & supplies

DIELECTRIC COMMUNICATIONS (800) 341-9678
SPX Dielectric Corp. (877) 247-3797
P.O. Box 949 • Raymond, ME 04071
E-Mail: sales@dielectric.com
Website: www.dielectric.com
Fax Ordering: (207) 655-8173
International Ordering: (207) 655-8100
Contact Name: Lewis Kling, President
Catalog: Free. Frequency: Annual.
Circulation: 100K. Sales: $5-10MM
Products: Antenna systems

DURANT (800) 386-1911
Eaton Corporation
1111 Superior Ave. • Cleveland, OH 44114
E-Mail: sales@eaton.com
Website: www.eaton.com
Fax Ordering: (800) 822-0256
International Ordering: (216) 523-4400
Contact Name: Feroze Motafram, President
Catalog: Free. Frequency: Annual.
Circulation: 50K. Sales: $5-10MM
Products: Industrial controls & display

DYNACORP (815) 229-3190
5173 26th Ave. • Rockford, IL 61109
E-Mail: sales@autogard.com
Website: www.autogard.com
Fax Ordering: (815) 229-4615
Catalog: Free. Frequency: Annual.
Circulation: 100K. Sales: $5-10MM
Products: Power transmission products

EAGLE OPTICS (800) 289-1132
2120 Greenview Dr. • Middleton, WI 53562
E-Mail: information@eagleoptics.com
Website: www.eagleoptics.com
Fax Ordering: (608) 836-4416
Catalog: Free. Frequency: Annual.

Circulation: 100K. **Sales**: $5-10MM
Products: Binoculars, spotting scopes, and tripods

ECOST.COM (877) 888-2678
500 N. Central Expressway #500
Plano, TX 75074
E-Mail: sales@ecost.com
Website: www.ecost.com
International Ordering: (310) 658-5000
Catalog: Free. Frequency: Annual.
Circulation: 150K. **Sales**: $20-50MM
Products: Computers & electronics for home & business

ECHOLAB (978) 715-1020
267 Boston Rd. #11 • Billerica, MA 01862
E-Mail: sales@echolab.com
Website: www.echolab.com
Fax Ordering: (978) 262-0179
Customer Service: (978) 715-1030
Contact Name: Ken Swanton, President
Catalog: Free. Frequency: Semiannual.
Circulation: 100K. **Sales**: $5-10MM
Products: Digital & analog video switchers

EDIROL CORPORATION (800) 380-2580
425 Sequoia Dr. • Bellingham, WA 98226
E-Mail: sales@rolandsystemsgroup.com
Website: www.rolandsystemsgroup.com
Fax Ordering: (800) 634-8202; (360) 594-4271
International Ordering: (360) 594-4273
Technical Support: (888) 233-4765; (360) 594-4276
Contact Name: James Foude, Manager
Catalog: Free. Frequency: Annual
Circulation: 100K. **Sales**: $5-10MM
Products: Field recording, video converters; integrated & compatible audio/video software & hardware tools

ELAN HOME SYSTEMS (859) 269-7760
1300 E. New Circle Rd. #150
Lexington, KY 40505
E-Mail: elan@elanhomesystems.com
Website: www.elanhomesystems.com
Fax Ordering: (859) 269-7972
Catalog: Free. Frequency: Annual
Circulation: 50K. **Sales**: $5-10MM
Products: Products for multi-room audio/video systems, integrating stereos, televisions and telephones

ELECTRONIC DEVICES, INC. (EDI) (800) 678-0828
21 Gray Oaks Ave. • Yonkers, NY 10710
E-Mail: sales@edidiodes.com
Website: www.edidiodes.com
Fax Ordering: (914) 965-5531
International Ordering: (914) 965-4400
Contact Name: Donald Bedell, Manager
Catalog: Free. Frequency: Annual
Circulation: 100K. **Sales**: $5-10MM
Products: HV diodes, bridges, rectifiers & packs

ELECTRONIC WHOLESALE DISTRIBUTORS (305) 594-3928
6971 NW 51st St. • Miami, FL 33166
Fax Ordering: (305) 594-0969
Contact Name: Jorge Maderos, President
Catalog: $1. Frequency: Semiannual
Circulation: 50K. **Sales**: $5-10MM
Products: Video equipment: recorders, cameras, tape, TV, etc.

ELECTRONIX CORPORATION (800) 223-3205
1 Herald Sq. • Fairborn, OH 45324
E-Mail: sales@electronix.com
Website: www.electronix.com
Fax Ordering: (937) 878-1972
International Ordering: (937) 878-1828
Contact Name: David W. Kushner, President
Catalog: Free. Frequency: Quarterly.
Circulation: 50K. **Sales**: $3-5MM
Products: Replacement parts for consumer electronics & computer accessories

ENABLE MART (888) 640-1999
4210 E. 4th Plain Blvd.
Vancouver, WA 98661
E-Mail: sales@enablemart.com
Website: www.enablemart.com
Fax Ordering: (866) 487-0410; (360) 695-4133
International Ordering: (360) 695-4155
Contact Name: Sara Durkacht, PR & Media
Catalog: Free. Frequency: Semiannual.
Circulation: 100K. **Sales**: $5-10MM
Products: Assistive technology devices for vision, hearing, mobility, communication, learning, keyboards & mice, environmental control, ergonomics, etc.

ETS-LINDGREN (512) 531-6400
1301 Arrow Point Dr.
Cedar Park, TX 78613
E-Mail: info@ets-lindgren.com
Website: www.ets-lindgren.com
Fax Ordering: (512) 531-6500
Contact Name: Dave Baron, Manager
Catalog: Free. Frequency: Annual
Circulation: 25K. **Sales**: $3-5MM
Products: EMC, wireless or RF microwave testing equipment; non-ionizing radiation test equipment

FALCON FINE WIRE (800) 874-7230
2401 Discovery Blvd.
Rockwall, TX 75032
E-Mail: falconwire@aol.com
Website: www.falconfinewire.com
Fax Ordering: (214) 271-9667
International Ordering: (214) 771-3441
Contact Name: William Lecount, President
Catalog: Free. Frequency: Annual
Products: Wiring & cabling products

FINGERHUT ELECTRONICS (800) 603-7052
6250 Ridgewood Rd.
St. Cloud, MN 56303
E-Mail: sales@fingerhut.com
Website: www.fingerhut.com
Fax Ordering: (952) 936-5412
International Ordering: (952) 932-3100
Customer Service: (800) 208-2500
Contact Name: Theodore Deikel, President
Catalog: Free. Frequency: Monthly
Circulation: 5MM. **Sales**: $100-200MM
Products: Consumer electronics & general merchandise

FLUKE ELECTRONICS (800) 903-5853
P.O. Box 9090 • Everett, WA 98206
E-Mail: sales@fluke.com
Website: www.fluke.com
Fax Ordering: (425) 446-5116
International Ordering: (425) 347-6100
Contact Name: Tom Gross, President

Catalog: Free. Frequency: Annual
Circulation: 2MM. Sales: $50-100MM
Products: Electronic test & measurement
equipment & software

FMA DIRECT (800) 343-2934
5713 Industry Lane #50
Frederick, MD 21704
E-Mail: sales@fmadirect.com
Website: www.fmadirect.com
Fax Ordering: (301) 668-7619
Technical Support: (301) 668-4280
Contact Name: Jamie Marks, Manager
Catalog: Free. Frequency: Annual
Circulation: 25K. Sales: $5-10MM
Products: Radio control switches,
batteries, and receivers

FOCUS CAMERA (800) 221-0828
4509 13th Ave. • Brooklyn, NY 11219
E-Mail: info@focuscamera.com
Website: www.focuscamera.com
Fax Ordering: (718) 437-8895
International Ordering: (718) 437-8810
Customer Service: (888) 901-4438;
  (718) 437-8899
Catalog: Free. Frequency: Monthly
Circulation: 50K. Sales: $20-50MM
Products: Cameras, video, telescopes,
and binoculars

GC & WALDOM ELECTRONICS (800) 435-2931
1801 Morgan St. • Rockford, IL 61102
E-Mail: sales@gcelectronics.com; waldom.com
Website: www.gcelectronics.com; waldom.com
Fax Ordering: (800) 527-3436; (815) 968-9029
International Ordering: (815) 968-9661
Contact Name: Scott Campbell, President
Catalog: Free. Frequency: Annual
Circulation: 50K. Sales: $20-50MM
Products: Electronic hookup accessories
for audio, video, telephones & computers

GENEVA GROUP (800) 358-5600
7109 31st Ave. N.
Minneapolis, MN 55427
E-Mail: sales@thegenevainc.com
Website: www.thegenevainc.com
Fax Ordering: (763) 546-0933
International Ordering: (763) 546-8652
Contact Name: Ed Griffin, President
Catalog: Free. Frequency: Quarterly
Circulation: 200K. Sales: $10-20MM
Products: Audio/video compact disc
accessories

GOURMET ELECTRONICS LTD. (800) 648-5260
1805 Junction Ave. • San Jose, CA 95131
E-Mail: sales@gourmetelectronics.com
Website: www.gourmetelectronics.com
Fax Ordering: (408) 467-1860
International Ordering: (408) 467-1100
Contact Name: Tom Gross, President
Catalog: Free. Frequency: Annual
Circulation: 50K. Sales: $5-10MM
Products: Electronic componenets,
hardware, and custom cable assembly

HARDY INSTRUMENTS (800) 821-5831
3860 Calle Fortunada • San Diego, CA 92123
E-Mail: sales@hardyinstruments.com
Website: www.hardyinstruments.com

Fax Ordering: (858) 278-6700
International Ordering: (858) 278-2900
Contact Name: Robert Murphy, President
Catalog: Free. Frequency: Annual
Circulation: 50K. Sales: $10-50MM
Products: Weighing systems; manufacturers
of load cell weigh modules, weight indicators
and transmitters; loop tension controllers

HARWIL CORPORATION (800) 562-2447
541 Kinetic Dr. • Oxnard, CA 93030
E-Mail: sales@harwil.com
Website: www.harwil.com
Fax Ordering: (805) 988-6804
International Ordering: (805) 988-6800
Contact Name: H.D. Hutchinson, President
Catalog: Free. Frequency: Annual
Circulation: 1MM. Sales: $10-50MM
Products: Fluid flow & liquid level switches,
liquid level pump up/down controllers &
pump emergency shutdown controllers;
pool & spa switches

HEADSETS.COM (800) 432-3738
One Daniel Burnham Ct. #400C (800) 450-7686
San Francisco, CA 94109 (800) 752-6876
E-Mail: customer_service@headsets.com
Website: www.headsets.com
Fax Ordering: (800) 457-0467
Contact Name: Mike Faith, President
Catalog: Free. Frequency: Semiannual
Circulation: 50K. Sales: $10-50MM
Products: Wireless, corded & cellular headsets;
computer headsets; conference phones

HEARTLAND AMERICA (800) 229-2901
8085 Century Blvd. • Chaska, MN 55318
E-Mail: sales@heartlandamerica.com
Website: www.heartlandamerica.com
Fax Ordering: (800) 943-4096
Contact Name: Mark Platt, President
Catalog: Free. Frequency: Monthly
Circulation: 2MM. Sales: $20-50MM
Products: Phones, electronics &
audio/video products

HEFFERNAN AUDIO VISUAL CATALOG (800) 752-1392
Heffernan Supply Company
435 Isom Rd. #210
San Antonio, TX 78216
E-Mail: sales@heffernanav.com
Website: www.heffernanav.com
Fax Ordering: (210) 732-5906
International Ordering: (210) 732-4333
Contact Name: Paul Heffernan, President
Catalog: Free. Frequency: Annual
Circulation: 25K. Sales: $5-10MM
Products: Blank audio/video discs;
audio-video equipment

HENSHAW'S ELECTRONIC SUPPLY (888) 445-3434
7622 Wornall Rd. • Kansas City, MO 64114
E-Mail: sales@henshaws.com
Website: www.henshaws.com
Fax Ordering: (888) 363-4626; (816) 363-4466
International Ordering: (816) 444-3434
Contact Name: Joe & Steve Henshaw
Catalog: Free. Frequency: Annual
Circulation: 200K. Sales: $10-50MM
Products: Consumer communication equipment;
CB antennas; car stereos; car alarms & remote
starters

HERBACH & RADEMAN CO.   (800) 848-8001
16 Roland Ave. • Mount Laurel, NJ 08054
E-Mail: sales@herbach.com
Website: www.herbach.com
Fax Ordering: (856) 802-0465
Tech Support: (856) 802-0422
Contact Name: Frank Lobascio, President
Catalog: Free. Frequency: Quarterly
Circulation: 250K. Sales: $5-10MM
Products: Electro-mechanical devices:
adapters, audio/visual equipment, batteries,
cable/cords/wires, breadboards/workstations,
computer components, heating/cooling devices,
laser devices, magnets/magnetic devicxes, optics,
power supplies, relays, test equipment, tools,
kits-educational & robotics, security equipment.

HMC ELECTRONICS   (800) 482-4440
33 Springdale Ave. • Canton, MA 02021
E-Mail: sales@hmcelectronics.com
Website: www.hmcelectronics.com
Fax Ordering: (781) 821-4133
International Ordering: (781) 821-1870
Catalog: Free. Frequency: Semiannual
Circulation: 100K. Sales: $5-10MM
Products: Products for electronic assembly
& repair: adhesives & sealants, cleaning
chemicals, hand & power tools, test
equipment, tool kits & cases

HOMETECH SOLUTIONS   (888) 257-4406
10600 S. De Anza Blvd.
Cupertino, CA 95014
E-Mail: info@hometech.com
Website: www.hometech.com
Fax Ordering: (408) 257-4389
International Ordering: (408) 257-4406
Catalog: Free. Frequency: Quarterly
Circulation: 100K. Sales: $5-10MM
Products: Remote control of lights &
appliances; structured wiring systems;
whole house audio and automated
lighting control; security systems

HOSFELT ELECTRONICS, INC.   (888) 264-6464
P.O. Box 4369 • Steubenville, OH 43952
E-Mail: sales@hosfelt.com
Website: www.hosfelt.com
Fax Ordering: (800) 524-5414
International Ordering: (740) 264-6464
Catalog: Free. Frequency: Annual
Circulation: 100K. Sales: $5-10MM
Products: Electronic components, tools,
kits; adapters, audio/video cables,
batteries, bridge rectifiers, 3M products.

IGO CORPORATION   (888) 205-0093
17800 N. Perimeter Dr. • Scottsdale, AZ 85255   (888) 205-0064
E-Mail: support@igo.com
Website: www.igo.com
Fax Ordering: (775) 746-6156
International Ordering: (480) 596-0061
Technical Support: (800) 342-5446
Catalog: Free. Frequency: Semiannual
Circulation: 100K. Sales: $10-20MM
Products: Electronics & accessories

IKEGAMI ELECTRONICS   (800) 368-9171
37 Brook Ave. • Maywood, NJ 07607
2631 Manhattan Beach Blvd.
Redondo Beach, CA 90278
E-Mail: sales@ikegami.com

Website: www.ikegami.com
Fax Ordering: (201) 569-1626; (310) 536-9550
International Ordering: (201) 368-9171; (310) 297-1900
Catalog: Free. Frequency: Monthly
Circulation: 100K. Sales: $3-5MM
Products: Video cameras

INSTRUMENT & DATA PRODUCTS GUIDE   (800) 874-7123
Technology Rental & Services
P.O. Box 619260 • DFW Airport, TX 75261
E-Mail: trs@trs-rentalco.com
Website: www.trs-rentalco.com
Fax Ordering: (800) 645-5360; (972) 456-4002
International Ordering: (972) 456-4000
Catalog: Free. Frequency: Annual
Circulation: 150K. Sales: $5-10MM
Products: Electronic test, measurement
& computer equipment

INTERNET PHONE T6   (815) 547-3885
1890 Chrysler Dr. • Belvidere, IL 61008
E-Mail: sales@t6b.com
Website: www.t6b.com
Fax Ordering: (815) 547-8897
Tech Support: (815) 544-1990
Contact Name: Mark Stitch, President
Catalog: Free. Frequency: Semiannual
Circulation: 200K. Sales: $5-10MM
Products: Internet phones, two-way pagers,
radio accessories

INTERPOWER CORP. SHORTFORM   (800) 662-2290
P.O. Box 115 • Oskaloosa, IA 52577
E-Mail: info@interpower.com
Website: www.interpower.com
Fax Ordering: (608) 741-4140
International Ordering: (608) 752-8181
Catalog: Free. Frequency: Semiannual
Circulation: 100K. Sales: $5-10MM
Products: Power systems components
for electrical & electronic equipment

JDS TECHNOLOGIES   (800) 983-5537
12200 Thatcher Ct. • Poway, CA 92064
E-Mail: onlinejds@aol.com
Website: www.jdstechnologies.com
Fax Ordering: (858) 486-8789
International Ordering: (858) 486-8787
Contact Name: Jeff Stein, President
Catalog: Free. Frequency: Semiannual
Circulation: 100K. Sales: $5-10MM
Products: Home automation & environmental
control systems, software & accessories;
remote control systems & accessories

KEITHLEY INSTRUMENTS, INC.   (800) 552-1115
28775 Aurora Rd. • Cleveland, OH 44139
E-Mail: info@keithley.com
Website: www.keithley.com
Fax Ordering: (440) 248-6168
International Ordering: (440) 248-0400
Contact Name: Ellen Modock, Manager
Catalog: Free. Frequency: Annual.
Circulation: 150K. Sales: $50-100MM
Products: Electronic instruments, plug-in
boards; software for production test,
process monitoring & research

KELVIN ELECTRONICS   (800) 535-8469
280 Adams Blvd. • Farmingdale, NY 11735
E-Mail: kelvin@kelvin.com
Website: www.kelvin.com

Fax Ordering: (800) 756-1025; (631) 756-1763
International Ordering: (631) 756-1750
Contact Name: Avi Hada, President
Catalog: Free. Frequency: Annual
Circulation: 100K. Sales: $5-10MM
Products: Educational electronics, robotics & test equipment; books, build your own technology labs & systems

KEPCO POWER SUPPLIES CATALOG (718) 461-7000
131-38 Sanford Ave. • Flushing, NY 11352
E-Mail: hq@kepcopower.com
Website: www.kepcopower.com
Fax Ordering: (718) 767-1102
Contact Name: Saul Kugforberg, Manager
Catalog: Free. Frequency: Annual
Circulation: 100K. Sales: $1-3MM
Products: Regulated DC power supplies

LANEL, INC. (800) 645-8030
504 Cherry Lane • Floral Park, NY 11001
E-Mail: lanelinc@aol.com
Website: www.beautytech.com
Fax Ordering: (516) 352-0465
International Ordering: (516) 437-5119
Contact Name: Isadore Epstein, President
Catalog: Free. Frequency: 3x per year
Circulation: 150K. Sales: $5-10MM
Products: Nail Dryer TV Station; manicure & pedicure dryers for nail salons

LECTROSONICS (800) 821-1121
P.O. Box 15900 • Rio Rancho, NM 87174
E-Mail: sales@lectrosonics.com
Website: www.lectrosonics.com
Fax Ordering: (505) 892-6243
International Ordering: (505) 892-4501
Contact Name: John Arasim, President
Catalog: Free. Frequency: Semiannual.
Circulation: 75K. Sales: $1-3MM
Products: Audio processing equipment; DSP matrix mixers; Wireless mic systems, audio signal processing

LINE ELECTRIC PRODUCTS (800) 331-1137
P.O. Box 127 • So. Glastonbury, CT 06073
E-Mail: info@lineelectric.com
Website: www.lineelectric.com
Fax Ordering: (860) 659-3576
International Ordering: (860) 659-3573
Contact Name: Bill Harris, President
Catalog: Free. Frequency: Annual
Circulation: 100K. Sales: $3-5MM
Products: Relays, audible devices, solenoids and actuators; accessories, relay headers and enclosures

LITTLITE, LLC. (810) 231-9373
P.O. Box 430 • Hamburg, MI 48139
E-Mail: sales@littlite.com
Website: www.littlite.com
Fax Ordering: (810) 231-1631
Contact Name: Donn Deniston, Manager
Catalog: Free. Frequency: Annual
Circulation: 100K. Sales: $5-10MM
Products: Flexible task lamps

LONG'S ELECTRONICS CATALOG (800) 633-3410
2630 5th Ave. So. • Irondale, AL 35210
E-Mail: info@longselectronics.com
Website: www.longselectronics.com
Fax Ordering: (800) 633-2530; (205) 956-6772

International Ordering: (205) 956-6767
Customer Service: (800) 566-4748
Contact Name: James N. Long, President
Catalog: Free. Frequency: Quarterly
Circulation: 1MM. Sales: $50-100MM
Products: Audio & visual products

LYNXMOTION, INC. (866) 512-1024
P.O. Box 818 • Pekin, IL 61555
E-Mail: sales@lynxmotion.com
Website: www.lynxmotion.com
Fax Ordering: (309) 353-2775
International Ordering: (309) 382-1816
Tech Support: (309) 353-2777
Contact Name: Jim Frye, President
Catalog: Free. Frequency: Semiannual
Circulation: 50K. Sales: $1-3MM
Products: Educational robotics & accessories; robot kits & books

MCM ELECTRONICS CATALOG (800) 543-4330
405 S. Pioneer Blvd. • Springboro, OH 45459 (888) 235-4692
E-Mail: talk@mcmelectronics.com
Website: www.mcmelectronics.com
Fax Ordering: (800) 765-6960
International Ordering: (937) 434-0031
Contact Name: Andrew Verey, President
Catalog: Free. Frequency: Semiannual
Circulation: 150K. Sales: $5-10MM
Products: Audio/video parts & accessories, computer hardware, security products

MAGELLANS (800) 962-4943
110 W. Sola St. • Santa Barbara, CA 93101 (888) 962-5631
E-Mail: sales@magellans.com
Website: www.magellans.com
Fax Ordering: (800) 962-4940; (805) 568-5406
International Ordering: (805) 568-5400
Contact Name: John McManus, President
Catalog: Free. Frequency: Quarterly
Circulation: 150K. Sales: $10-20MM
Products: Travel supplies & accessories, including flashlights, binoculars; electrical supplies

MENDELSON ELECTRONICS (800) 344-4465
340 E. First St. • Dayton, OH 45402 (800) 422-3525
E-Mail: meci@meci.com
Website: www.meci.com
Fax Ordering: (800) 344-6324
International Ordering: (937) 461-3525
  Fax (937) 461-3391
Contact Name: Howard Pinski, Manager
Catalog: Free. Frequency: Semiannual
Circulation: 100K. Sales: $5-10MM
Products: Surplus electronic and hobbiest items; fusers, transformers, power cords, cables, wires, relays and various other electronic supplies

MEREDITH INSTRUMENTS - (623) 934-9387
SOURCE FOR LASERS
P9880 W. Peoria Ave. • Peoria, AZ 85345
E-Mail: info@mi-lasers.com
Website: www.mi-lasers.com
Fax Ordering: (623) 934-9482
International Ordering: (440) 934-9387
Contact Name: Dennis Meredith, President
Catalog: Free. Frequency: Semiannual
Circulation: 50K. Sales: $5-10MM
Products: Laser kits, laser tubes, laser power supplies, laser optics, laser books

MILTRONICS MANUFACTURING SERVICES (800) 828-9089
95 Krif Rd. • Keene, NH 03431
E-Mail: sales@miltronics.com
Website: www.miltronics.com
Fax Ordering: (603) 352-4444
International Ordering: (603) 352-3333
Technical Support: (603) 355-6677
Catalog: Free. Frequency: Semiannual
Circulation: 100K. Sales: $5-10MM
Products: Alert products, receiver
accessories & optional sensor/transmitters

MOUSER ELECTRONICS (800) 346-6873
1000 N. Main St. • Mansfield, TX 76063
E-Mail: sales@mouser.com
Website: www.mouser.com
Fax Ordering: (817) 804-3899
International Ordering: (817) 804-3888
Contact Name: Glen Smith, President
Catalog: Free. Frequency: Quarterly
Circulation: 150K. Sales: $50-100MM
Products: Electronic componenet distributors,
including semiconductors, optoelectronics,
interconnects, diodes & rectifiers, transistors,
passives, tools and supplies.

MULTI-MEDIA CABLE & ACCESSORIES (888) 999-4283
HAVE, Inc.
350 Power Ave. • Hudson, NY 12534
E-Mail: have@haveinc.com
Website: www.haveinc.com
Fax Ordering: (518) 828-2008
International Ordering: (518) 828-2000
Contact Name: Nancy Gordon, President
Catalog: Free. Frequency: Annual
Circulation: 100K. Sales: $5-10MM
Products: Audio, video data cable,
cable accessories, tape supplies,
CD & CD-ROM supplies & services.

NDT INTERNATIONAL (610) 793-1700
711 S. Creek Rd.
West Chester, PA 19382
E-Mail: info@ndtint.com
Website: www.ndtint.com
Fax Ordering: (610) 793-1702
Contact Name: David Kailer, Manager
Catalog: Free. Frequency: Monthly
Circulation: 50K. Sales: $5-10MM
Products: Ultrasonic thickness gauges,
flaw detectors & accessories; testing
equipment & supplies

NTE ELECTRONICS (973) 748-5089
44 Farrand St. • Bloomfield, NJ 07003
E-Mail: general@nteinc.com
Website: www.nteinc.com
Fax Ordering: (973) 748-6224
Contact Name: W. Horstmann, V.P.
Catalog: Free. Frequency: Annual
Circulation: 100K. Sales: $10-20MM
Products: Electronic components; hookup
lines, fusers, capacitors, power cords, cables,
wires, transformers & other electronic supplies

NEWARK ELECTRONICS (800) 463-9275
P.O. Box 94151 • Palatine, IL 60094
E-Mail: info@newark.com
Website: www.newark.com
Fax Ordering: (888) 551-4801; (773) 907-5890
International Ordering: (773) 784-5100
Contact Name: Karen Fisher, Manager

Catalog: Free. Frequency: Annual
Circulation: 250K. Sales: $10-25MM
Products: Electronic component parts
& accessories

NIGHTINGALE-CONANT CORP. (800) 323-5552
6245 W. Howard St. • Niles, IL 60714 (800) 557-1660
E-Mail: info@nightingale.com
Website: www.nightingale.com
Fax Ordering: (847) 647-7145
International Ordering: (847) 647-0300
Customer Service: (800) 560-6081
Contact Name: Victor Conant, President
Catalog: Free. Frequency: 6x per year
Circulation: 150K. Sales: $50-100MM
Products: Audio-video equipment &
accessories

NOREN PRODUCTS, INC. (866) 936-6736
1010 O'Brien Dr. • Menlo Park, CA 94025
E-Mail: sales@norenproducts.com
Website: www.norenproducts.com
Fax Ordering: (650) 324-1348
International Ordering: (650) 322-9500
Contact Name: Rich Knight, Manager
Catalog: Free. Frequency: Annual
Circulation: 100K. Sales: $10-20MM
Products: Thermal products; electronic
enclosure cooling products; heat pipes,
thermal pins

PANASONIC CORP. (800) 211-7262
1 Panasonic Way • Secaucus, NJ 07094
E-Mail: sales@panasonic.com
Website: www.panasonic.com
Contact Name: Richard Kraft, President
Catalog: Free. Frequency: Semiannual
Circulation: 250K. Sales: $100-500MM
Products: Variety of consumer electronic
products, including audio/video systems,
computers, telephones & faxes, TV's,
cameras, VCR's & DVD's.

PARTS EXPRESS (800) 338-0531
725 Pleasant Valley Dr.
Springboro, OH 45066
E-Mail: sales@partsexpress.com
Website: www.partsexpress.com
Fax Ordering: (937) 743-1677
Catalog: Free. Frequency: Annual.
Circulation: 100K. Sales: $10-50MM
Products: Audio/video accessories:
connectors, speakers, wire/cable

PASTERNACK ENTERPRISES (866) 727-8376
P.O. Box 16759 • Irvine, CA 92623
E-Mail: sales@pasternack.com
Website: www.pasternack.com
Fax Ordering: (949) 261-7451
International Ordering: (949) 261-1920
Catalog: Free. Frequency: Annual.
Circulation: 100K. Sales: $5-10MM
Products: Fiber optic products; coaxial
connectors, adapters, and cables

PHONECO, INC. (608) 582-4124
P.O. Box 70 • Galesville, WI 54630
E-Mail: sales@phonecoinc.com
Website: www.phonecoinc.com
Fax Ordering: (608) 582-4593
Contact Name: Ron & Mary Knappen, Owners
Catalog: Free. Frequency: Annual.

Circulation: 50K. **Sales:** $3-5MM
Products: Wood telephones, art deco &
candlestick phones, quality reproductions
& parts

PINNACLE MICRO (800) 392-6962
3400 W. Warner Ave., #E
Santa Ana, CA 92704
E-Mail: sales@pinnaclemicro.com
Website: www.pinnaclemicro.com
Fax Ordering: (714) 662-6859
International Ordering: (714) 662-4959
Catalog: Free. Frequency: Semiannual
Circulation: 100K. **Sales:** $10-20MM
Products: Firewire & USB CD-RW Drives,
Flex DVD-RAM drives, Peak Jukeboxes,
Magneto Optical Drives, Optical Library
Systems, Recordable CD-Drives

PREMAX PRODUCTS (201) 750-4900
55 Walnut St. #201 • Norwood, NJ 07648
E-Mail: sales@premiermetal.com
Website: www.premiermetal.com
Fax Ordering: (201) 750-4937
Contact Name: Tony Bozza, Manager
Catalog: Free. Frequency: Annual
Circulation: 50K. **Sales:** $5-10MM
Products: Electronic enclosures &
accessories

PREMIER MEDIA SOLUTIONS, LLC (800) 426-8399
P.O. Box 785 • Patterson, LA 70392 (800) 347-5618
E-Mail: sales@premiermediaav.com
Website: www.premiermediaav.com
Fax Ordering: (985) 861-5164
International Ordering: (985) 365-5106
Catalog: Free. Frequency: Semiannual
Circulation: 100K. **Sales:** $10-50MM
Products: CD player/cassette recorder,
microphones, projectors, recorders,
duplicators & screens

PREMIUM PARTS ELECTRONICS (800) 645-2202
Russell Industries, Inc. • Conco Electronics
3375 Royal Ave. • Oceanside, NY 11572
E-Mail: sales@russellind.com
Website: www.russellind.com
Fax Ordering: (800) 645-2200; (516) 764-5747
International Ordering: (516) 536-5000
Contact Name: Adam Russell, President
Catalog: Free. Frequency: Annual
Circulation: 100K. **Sales:** $10-20MM
Products: Electronic replacement parts &
VCR assemblies; MRO products; passice
components products; wire & cable
management products; cable assemblies,
connectors.

PROFESSIONAL EQUIPMENT (800) 323-2000
Honeywell / Zellweger (800) 334-9291
GHC Specialty Brands, LLC
P.O. Box 5197 • Janesville, WI 53547
E-Mail: info@professionalequipment.com
Website: www.professionalequipment.com
Fax Ordering: (888) 776-3187; (608) 743-8039
International Ordering: (608) 743-8002
Catalog: Free. Frequency: Weekly
Circulation: 100K. **Sales:** $50-100MM
Product: Testing & inspection equipment;
detection and measurement instrumentation;
portable gas monitors

R-K ELECTRONICS, INC. (800) 543-4936
7405 Industrial Row Rd.
Mason, OH 45040
E-Mail: salesrke@rke.com
Website: www.rke.com
Fax Ordering: (513) 204-6061
International Ordering: (513) 204-6060
Contact Name: John L. Keller, President
Catalog: Free. Frequency: Annual
Circulation: 75K. **Sales:** $5-10MM
Products: Electronics products, including
relays. sockets, switches, control panels

RADIO SHACK PRODUCT CATALOG (800) 843-7422
200 Taylor St., Suite 600
Fort Worth, TX 76102
E-Mail: sales@radioshack.com
Website: www.radioshack.com
Fax Ordering: (817) 415-6880 or 6804
International Ordering: (817) 415-3700
Catalog: Free. Frequency: Semiannual
Circulation: 2MM. **Sales:** $250-500MM
Products: Electronic consumer products

RBE ELECTRONICS OF SD (800) 342-1912
714 Corporation St. • Aberdeen, SD 57401
E-Mail: info@rbeelectronics.com
Website: www.rbeelectronics.com
Fax Ordering: (605) 226-0710
International Ordering: (605) 226-2448
Contact Name: Roger Ernst, President
Catalog: Free. Frequency: Annual
Circulation: 100K. **Sales:** $10-25MM
Products: Electronic controls, sensors &
timers; alarm systems, engine controls &
accessories, temperature controls, testers
& accessories for engines/vehicles/trailers.

RELAY SPECIALTIES (800) 526-5376
17 Raritan Rd. • Oakland, NJ 07436
E-Mail: sales@relayspec.com
Website: www.relayspec.com
Fax Ordering: (201) 337-1862
International Ordering: (201) 337-1000
Contact Name: Barry Sauer, President
Catalog: Free. Frequency: Annual
Circulation: 50K. **Sales:** $10-20MM
Products: Electronic components

RENCO ELECTRONICS (800) 645-5828
595 International Place
Rockledge, FL 32955
E-Mail: sales@rencousa.com
Website: www.rencousa.com
Fax Ordering: (321) 637-1600
International Ordering: (321) 637-1000
Contact Name: John Rensing, President
Catalog: Free. Frequency: Annual
Circulation: 100K. **Sales:** $10-20MM
Products: Electronics equipment, including
transformers, surface mount, toroids,
chokes, coils and inductors

RWS WIRE & CABLE, INC. (800) 241-9465
2300 W. Park Place Blvd., #160
Stone Mountain, GA 30087
E-Mail: sales@rwswire.com
Website: www.rwswire.com
Fax Ordering: (770) 469-3556
International Ordering: (770) 469-3515
Contact Name: John Woods, President

Catalog: Free. Frequency: Annual
Circulation: 100K. Sales: $5-10MM
Products: Electronics & telecommunications
wire and cable products

ROBOTIKITSDIRECT CO. (310) 515-6800
17141 Kingsview Ave. • Carson, CA 90746
E-Mail: info@owirobot.com
Website: www.robotikitsdirect.com
Fax Ordering: (310) 515-0927
Catalog: Free. Frequency: Annual
Circulation: 150K. Sales: $5-10MM
Products: Robot kits for the classroom,
science educational centers, & science
clubs.

SAG HARBOR INDUSTRIES (800) 724-5952
1668 Sag Harbor Tpke.
Sag Harbor, NY 11963
E-Mail: info@sagharborind.com
Website: www.sagharborind.com
Fax Ordering: (631) 725-4234
International Ordering: (631) 725-0440
Catalog: Free. Frequency: Annual
Circulation: 100K. Sales: $10-20MM
Products: Manufactures electric
transformers and coils.

SCANNER WORLD, USA (800) 476-8050
17 Interstate Ave. • Albany, NY 12205
E-Mail: info@scannerworld.com
Website: www.scannerworld.com
Fax Ordering: (518) 465-2945
International Ordering: (518) 436-9606
Catalog: Free. Frequency: Annual.
Circulation: 150K. Sales: $10-50MM
Products: Radio scanners, antennas,
CB radios, rechargable batteries,
frequency books, accessories, power
supplies & cords, two-way radios

SCHNEIDER OPTICS (800) 228-1254
7701 Haskell Ave. • Van Nuys, CA 91406 (800) 645-7239
285 Oser Ave. • Hauppauge, NY 11788
E-Mail: century@schneideroptics.com
Website: www.schneideroptics.com
Fax Ordering: (818) 505-9865; (631) 761-5090
International Ordering: (818) 766-3715;
 (631) 761-5000
Contact Name: Bill Turner, VP
Catalog: Free. Frequency: Monthly
Circulation: 100K. Sales: $10-20MM
Products: Century Film & Video; filters, motion
picture & television camera lenses & lens
accessories; software

SEASTROM MANUFACTURING CO. (800) 634-2356
456 Seastrom St. • Twin Falls, ID 83301
E-Mail: info@seastrom-mfg.com
Website: www.seastrom-mfg.com
Fax Ordering: (208) 734-7222
International Ordering: (208) 737-4300
Catalog: Free. Frequency: Annual.
Circulation: 100K. Sales: $5-10MM
Products: Electrical & electronic hardware

SHAPE LLC (800) 367-5811
2105 Corporate Dr. Unit 101
Addison, IL 60101
E-Mail: sales@shapellc.com
Website: www.shapellc.com
Fax Ordering: (630) 620-0784

International Ordering: (630) 620-8394
Contact Name: Glen Olsen, Manager
Catalog: Free. Frequency: Annual
Circulation: 150K. Sales: $10-20MM
Products: Custom magnetic products;
linear transformers; ferroresonant transformers;
line conditioners; advances assemblies;
power conditioners

THE SHARPER IMAGE (877) 714-7444
1370 Broadway #1107
New York, NY 10018
E-Mail: info@sharperimage.com
Website: www.sharperimage.com
Fax Ordering: (212) 967-6008
International Ordering: (212) 967-6000
Catalog: Online. Sales: $10-50MM
Products: High quality consumer
electronics & unique gifts

SHORTRIDGE INSTRUMENTS, INC. (480) 991-6744
7855 E. Redfield Rd. • Scottsdale, AZ 85260
E-Mail: info@shortridge.com
Website: www.shortridge.com
Fax Ordering: (480) 443-1267
International Ordering: (480) 991-6744
Contact Name: Ernest R. Shortridge, President
Catalog: Free. Frequency: Annual
Circulation: 75K. Sales: $5-10MM
Products: Manufacturers of AirData
Multimeters & HydroData Multimeters

SIERRA VIDEO SYSTEMS (888) 886-8875
P.O. Box 2462 • Grass Valley, CA 95945
E-Mail: info@sierravideo.com
Website: www.sierravideo.com
Fax Ordering: (530) 478-1105
International Ordering: (530) 478-1000
Contact Name: Richard Zehm, President
Catalog: Free. Frequency: Annual
Circulation: 100K. Sales: $10-20MM
Products: Audio & video broadcast
equipment & supplies

SKYTEL COMMUNICATIONS (800) 395-5304
515 E. Amite St. • Jackson, MS 39201 (800) 552-6835
E-Mail: skyinfo@skytel.com
Website: www.skytel.com
Fax Ordering: (601) 944-3360
Customer Service: (800) 759-8737
Catalog: Free. Frequency: Semiannual
Circulation: 100K. Sales: $10-20MM
Products: Pager products & accessories

SKYVISION (800) 500-9275
1010 Frontier Dr. • Fergus Falls, MN 55637
E-Mail: skyinfo@skyvision.com
Website: www.skyvision.com
Fax Ordering: (218) 739-5231
Customer Service: (800) 644-5705; 500-9281
Catalog: Free. Frequency: Semiannual
Circulation: 100K. Sales: $10-20MM
Products: Dish network & DirecTV accessories;
home electronics & security products

SMARTHOME, INC. (800) 762-7846
16542 Nillikan Ave. • Irvine, CA 92606
E-Mail: catalog@smarthome.com
Website: www.smarthome.com
Fax Ordering: (800) 242-7329; (949) 221-9240
International Ordering: (949) 221-9200
Contact Name: Mike Scharnagl

Catalog: Free. Frequency: Quarterly
Circulation: 150K. Sales: $20-50MM
Products: Home automation & remote control
products, such as: lighting systems, security
systems, digital home wiring systems, smart
appliances, home automation controllers,
home networking, et al.

SPX POWER TEAM (800) 541-1418
5885 11th St. • Rockford, IL 61109
E-Mail: info@powerteam.com
Website: www.powerteam.com
Fax Ordering: (800) 288-7031
International Ordering: (815) 874-5556
Contact Name: Lannie Cocks, President
Catalog: Free. Frequency: Annual
Circulation: 150K. Sales: $20-50MM
Products: Hydraulic special service tools &
equipment for motor vehicle and industrial
markets. Products include pumps, cylinders,
valves, clamping components, and related
hydraulic accessories, and special tools
and equipment.

SPY OUTLET (716) 695-8660
2148 Niagara Falls Blvd.
Tonawanda, NY 14150
E-Mail: sales@spyoutlet.com
Website: www.spyoutlet.com
Fax Ordering: (716) 695-7380
Contact Name: R.J. Crowley, President
Catalog: Free. Frequency: Quarterly
Circulation: 50K. Sales: $5-10MM
Products: Spy cameras, vehicle tracking,
bug detectors, surveillance and security
equipment

STORE SMART EXPRESS CATALOG (800) 424-1011
VisualHorizons
180 Metro Park • Rochester, NY 14623
E-Mail: cs@storesmart.com
Website: www.storesmart.com
Fax Ordering: (585) 424-1064
International Ordering: (585) 424-5300
Contact Name: Reenie Feingold, Founder
Catalog: Free. Frequency: Weekly
Circulation: 200K. Sales: $3-5MM
Products: Diskettes & CD-ROMs;
laminating equipment

SUN EQUIPMENT CORPORATION (800) 870-1955
1352 S. Grove Ave., Suite A
Ontario, CA 01761
E-Mail: info@sunequipco.com
Website: www.sunequipco.com
Fax Ordering: (909) 947-8802
Contact Name: Richard H. Sun, President
International Ordering: (909) 947-8080
Catalog: Free. Frequency: Annual.
Circulation: 100K. Sales: $5-10MM
Products: Generators, frequency counters,
digital multimeters, soldering tools &
toolkits, production line testers, electronic
& electrical control labs, LCD & LED
modules, IC fabrication lab

SUPREME AUDIO (800) 445-7398
P.O. Box 550 • Marlborough, NH 03455
E-Mail: info@supremeaudio.com
Website: www.supremeaudio.com
Fax Ordering: (800) 346-4867; (603) 876-4001
International Ordering: (603) 876-3636

Catalog: Free. Frequency: Annual.
Circulation: 100K. Sales: $3-5MM
Products: Wireless microphones
and fitness sound systems

SURPLUSTRADERS ONLINE (514) 739-9328
P.O. Box 276 • Alburg, VT 05440
E-Mail: sales@surplustraders.net
Website: www.surplustraders.net
Fax Ordering: (450) 902-0495
International Ordering: (514) 739-8723
Catalog: Free. Frequency: Annual.
Circulation: Online. Sales: $5-10M
Products: Computer & surplus electronics

TATUNG COMPANY OF AMERICA (800) 827-2850
2850 El Presidio St. • Long Beach, CA 90810 (310) 637-2105
E-Mail: tus@tatungusa.com
Website: www.tatungusa.com
Fax Ordering: (310) 637-8484
Tech Support: (888) 4-TATUNG
Contact Name: Edward Chen, Manager
Catalog: Free brochures. Frequency: Periodic
Circulation: 250K. Sales: $100-500MM
Products: PC and TV monitors, consumer
and internet appliances

TEST EQUIPMENT DEPOT (800) 517-8431
Fotronic Corporation (800) 996-3837
99 Washington St. • Melrose, MA 02176
E-Mail: sales@fotronic.com;
  sales@testequipmentdepot.com
Website: www.fotronic.com;
  www.testequipmentdepot.com
Fax Ordering: (781) 665-0780
International Ordering: (781) 665-1400
Catalog: Online. Minimum Order: $20.
Products: Electronic test products &
equipment

TELEFLEX MEDICAL (800) 548-6600
P.O. Box 12600 (866) 246-6990
Research Triangle Park, NC 27709
E-Mail: sales@teleflexmedical.com
Website: www.teleflexmedical.com
Fax Ordering: (919) 361-3914
International Ordering: (919) 544-8000
Contact Name: Diane Fukuda, Manager
Catalog: Free. Frequency: Annual.
Circulation: 50K. Sales: $20-50MM
Products: Medical tubing, devices &
guidewires

TIGER DIRECT CATALOG (800) 888-4437
7795 W. Flagler St. #35 • Miami, FL 33144 (800) 800-8300
E-Mail: info@tigerdirect.com
Website: www.tigerdirect.com
Fax Ordering: (305) 415-2202
International Ordering: (305) 415-2201
Contact Name: Carl Fiorentino, President
Catalog: Free. Frequency: Semiannual
Circulation: 10MM. Sales: $100-500MM
Products: Computers & electronics; software,
accessories & supplies

TOLEETO FASTENERS INTERNATIONAL (800) 267-3569
1658 Precision Park Ln.
San Ysidro, CA 92173
E-Mail: sales@cord-lox.com
Website: www.cord-lox.com
Fax Ordering: (619) 662-1486
International Ordering: (619) 662-1355

Contact Name: Dave Davenport, President
Catalog: Free. Frequency: Triennial
Circulation: 50K. Sales: $5-10MM
Products: Electronic hook & loop fasteners, and cable wrap and ties

TRANSPO ELECTRONICS, INC.   (800) 877-3340
WAI Global
411 Eagleview Blvd. #100
Exton, PA 19341
E-Mail: info@waiglobal.com
Website: www.waiglobal.com
Fax Ordering: (800) 948-6121
International Ordering: (484) 875-6600
Contact Name: Frank Oropeza, President
Catalog: Free. Frequency: Annual.
Circulation: 100K. Sales: $20-50MM
Products: Rotating Electric; Electriucal System; alternator parts, starter parts, voltage regulators & rectifiers; replacement products for motor vehicles of all kinds

TRIARCH, INC.   (800) 848-0810
P.O. Box 98 • Ripon, WI 54971
E-Mail: triarch@centurytel.net
Website: www.triarchmicroslides.com
Fax Ordering: (888) 848-0810; (920) 748-3034
International Ordering: (920) 748-5125
Contact Name: Paul L. Conant, President
Catalog: Free. Frequency: Annual
Circulation: 50K. Sales: $5-10MM
Products: Microscope and microscope supplies at discount prices

TRUMETER COMPANY, INC.   (800) 537-2261
1020 NW 6th St.
Deerfield Beach, FL 33442
E-Mail: sales.usa@trumeter.com
Website: www.trumeter.com
Fax Ordering: (888) 276-5599; (954) 725-5599
International Ordering: (954) 725-6699
Contact Name: Derek Rawden-Lewis, President
Catalog: Free. Frequency: Annual
Circulation: 50K. Sales: $5-10MM
Products: Electronic, electro-mechanical and mechanical counters, counting, measuring & inspection instrumentation for length and distance measuring.

TUCKER ELECTRONICS   (877) 667-6044
1717 Reserve St. • Garland, TX 75042
E-Mail: customerservice@tucker.com
Website: www.tucker.com
Fax Ordering: (214) 348-0367
International Ordering: (214) 348-8800
Catalog: Free. Frequency: Semiannual
Circulation: 50K. Sales: $5-10MM
Products: New, refurbished, and used electronic test & measurement equipment

ULTIMA CASES   (800) 467-4561
Spencer Industries, Inc.
902 Buffaloville Rd. • Dale, IN 47523
E-Mail: smessmer@spencerindustries.com
Website: www.spencerindustries.com
Fax Ordering: (812) 937-4637
International Ordering: (812) 937-4561
Contact Name: Tom Messmer, President
Catalog: Free. Frequency: Annual
Circulation: 50K. Sales: $10-50MM
Products: Carrying cases for cameras, videos, and computers

UNIVERSAL RADIO   (800) 431-3939
6830 Americana Pkwy.
Reynoldsburg, OH 43068
E-Mail: catalog@universal-radio.com
Website: www.universal-radio.com
Fax Ordering: (614) 866-2339
International Ordering: (614) 866-4267
Catalog: Free. Frequency: Annual.
Circulation: 50K. Sales: $10-50MM
Products: Shortwave, amateur and CB communications equipment, antennas, power supplies, books and accessories.

U.V. PROCESS SUPPLY   (800) 621-1296
1229 W. Cortland St. • Chicago, IL 60614
E-Mail: info@uvps.com
Website: www.uvprocess.com
Fax Ordering: (800) 99FAXUV;
  (773) 880-6647
International Ordering: (773) 248-0099
Catalog: Free. Frequency: Annual
Circulation: 100K. Sales: $5-10MM
Products: Ultraviolet lamps; UV curing equipment; UV test equipment

VECTOR-VID   (800) 332-4336
Radwell International
111 Mt. Holly Bypass • Lumberton, NJ 08048
E-Mail: sales@piccenter.com
Website: www.piccenter.com
Fax Ordering: (800) 257-2869; (609) 288-9417
International Ordering: (609) 288-9393
Contact Name: Ronald L. Miller, President
Catalog: Free. Frequency: Annual
Products: Electronic test equipment

VICOR EXPRESS   (800) 735-6200
Vicor Corporation
25 Frontage Rd. • Andover, MA 01810
E-Mail: vicorexp@vicr.com
Website: www.vicr.com
Fax Ordering: (978) 475-6715
International Ordering: (978) 470-2900
Tech Support: (800) 927-9474; Fax (978) 749-3341
Contact Name: Mark Glazer, President
Catalog: Free. Frequency: Semiannual.
Circulation: 100K. Sales: $20-50MM
Products: State-of-the-art power conversion products

VIDEO & AUDIO SUPPLY CATALOG   (800) 522-2025
Markertek Video Supply
P.O. Box 397 • Saugerties, NY 12477
E-Mail: info@markertek.com
Website: www.markertek.com
Fax Ordering: (845) 246-1757
International Ordering: (845) 246-3036
Catalog: Free. Frequency: Annual
Circulation: 150K. Sales: $20-50MM
Products: Audio & video equipment & supplies

VIDEOTEK CATALOG   (800) 442-7747
Harris Corporation
1025 W. NASA Blvd. • Melbourne, FL 32919
E-Mail: webmaster@harris.com
Website: www.harris.com
Fax Ordering: (610) 327-9295
International Ordering: (321) 727-9207
Contact Name: Philip Steyaert, President
Catalog: Free. Frequency: Semiannual
Circulation: 100K. Sales: $50-100MM
Products: Broadcasting equipment & supplies

VINTEN/CAMERA DYNAMICS   (888) 284-6836
The Vitec Group - Camera Dynamics, Inc.
709 Executive Blvd.
Valley Cottage, NY 10989
E-Mail: info-cd-usa@vitecgroup.com
Website: www.vinten.com
Fax Ordering: (845) 268-9324
International Ordering: (845) 268-0100
Contact Name: Stephen Savitt, Manager
Catalog: Free. Frequency: Weekly
Circulation: 25K. Sales: $50-100MM
Products: TV camera support equipment,
including studio pedestals, tripod systems
& remote controlled robotic pan/tilt systems.

VISIONS OF VIDEO   (800) 719-2626
9030 Balboa • Northridge, CA 91325
E-Mail: video2@woldnet.att.net
Website: www.visionsofvideo.com
Fax Ordering: (800) 244-5121;
  (818) 891-1518
International Ordering: (818) 891-6161
Catalog: Free. Frequency: Annual
Circulation: 100K. Sales: $10-50MM
Products: Audio/visual equipment &
Motorola original batteries, replacement
parts and accessories

WORTHINGTON DISTRIBUTION   (800) 282-8864
PHC 1 Box 1748 • Tafton, PA 18451
E-Mail: catalog@worthingtondistribution.com
Website: www.worthingtondistribution.com
Fax Ordering: (866) 542-0470
International Ordering: (570) 451-4700
Tech Support: (800) 282-8864
Contact Name: Richard School, Jr., President
Catalog: Free. Frequency: Annual
Circulation: 100K. Sales: $10-50MM
Products: Home automation equipment;
power supplies, test equipment, relayes,
audio-video equipment, security equipment;
books and reference materials

ZIERICK MANUFACTURING CORP.   (800) 882-8020
131 Radio Circle • Mt. Kisco, NY 10549
E-Mail: zierick@zierick.com
Website: www.zierick.com
Fax Ordering: (914) 666-0216
International Ordering: (914) 666-2911
Contact Name: Gretchen Zierick, President
Catalog: Free. Frequency: Annual
Circulation: 100K. Sales: $10-50MM
Products: Electronic and electrical devices;
interconnection hardware and terminals

ACHOO! ALLERGY & AIR PRODUCTS (800) 339-7123
3411 Pierce Dr. • Atlanta, GA 30341
E-Mail: info@achooallergy.com
Website: www.achooallergy.com
Fax Ordering: (800) 237-9618
International Ordering: (770) 455-9999
Catalog: Free. Frequency: Annual
Circulation: 100K. Sales: $10-20MM
Products: Air purifiers, allergy armor, allergy
bedding, vacuum cleaners, dehumidifiers,
humidifiers, furnace filters, nasal irrigation,
asthma treatment, cleaning products, eco
products

ALTERNATE ENERGY (ALTE) STORE (877) 878-4060
43 Broad St., Suite A408
Hudson, MA 01749
E-Mail: info@altestore.com
Website: www.altestore.com
Fax Ordering: (978) 562-5854
International Ordering: (978) 562-5858
Catalog: Online. Sales: $10-20 MM
Products: Batteries, books & educational
videos, energy efficient products, portable
power products, solar energy products,
wind turbines.

ALTERNATIVE ENERGY TECHNOLOGIES (800) 874-2190
1057 N. Ellis Rd. #4 • Jacksonville, FL 32254
E-Mail: info@aetsolar.com
Website: www.aetsolar.com
Fax Ordering: (904) 781-1911
International Ordering: (904) 781-8305
Contact Names: Rich Squires, President
Catalog: Free. Frequency: Semiannual
Circulation: 100K. Sales: $3-5MM
Products: Solar energy systems & components
for water heating & solar electrical systems

BIO-SUN SYSTEMS, INC. (800) 847-8840
RR #2, Box 134A • Millerton, PA 16936
E-Mail: info@bio-sun.com
Website: www.bio-sun.com
Fax Ordering: (570) 537-6200
International Ordering: (570) 537-2200
Catalog: Free. Frequency: Quarterly
Circulation: 25K. Sales: $20-50 MM
Products: Waterless toilet systems

EARTHNWARE.COM (856) 467-5400
PTP Consulting, Inc.
531 Kings Hwy. • Swedesboro, NJ 08085
E-Mail: info@ehsprogress.com
Website: www.earthnware.com
Fax Ordering: (856) 467-9643
International Ordering: (856) 467-5400
Contact Name: Joseph DeMarco
Catalog: Free. Frequency: Semiannual
Circulation: 50K. Sales: $3-5MM
Products: Environmentally friendly
home products and gifts

ENERGY EFFICIENT ENVIRONMENTS (800) 336-3749
2119 Inverness Lane • Glenview, IL 60025
E-Mail: energy@mcs.com
International Ordering: (847) 475-3005
Catalog: Free. Frequency:Quarterly
Products: Efficient and earth-friendly
devices for energy, water and light use

GAIAM HARMONY (800) 869-3446
P.O. Box 3095 • Boulder, CO 80307   (877) 989-6321
E-Mail: customerservice@gaiam.com
Website: www.gaiam.com
Fax Ordering: (800) 456-1139
International Ordering: (800) 254-8464 (Canada)
Catalog: Free. Frequency: Quarterly
Circulation: 100K. Sales: $5-10MM
Products: Products for a more natural &
healthy way of life with respect for the
environment, including natural bedding,
household cleaners & pest control, air &
water filters, outdoor & home decor & lighting

GREENPEACE (800) 326-0959
702 H St., NW, Suite 300
Washington, DC 20001
E-Mail: info@wdc.greenpeace.org
Website: www.greenpeace.org
Fax Ordering: (202) 462-4517
International Ordering: (202) 462-1177
Catalog: Free. Frequency: Semiannual
Circulation: 100K. Sales: $3-5MM
Products: Environmentally and socially
responsible apparel, accessories and gifts

LEHMAN'S CATALOG (877) 438-5346
P.O. Box 270 • Kidron, OH 44636
E-Mail: info@lehmans.com
Website: www.lehmans.com
Fax Ordering: (888) 780-4975;
   (330) 857-5785
International Ordering: (330) 857-5785
Customer Service: (888) 438-5346
Catalog: Free. Frequency: Semiannual
Circulation: 100K. Sales: $5-10MM
Products: Products without electricity for simple,
self-sufficient living, including housewares,
appliances for non-electric homes, heating &
cooking stoves, cast iron kitchenware

McILVAINE COMPANY (847) 784-0012
191 Waukegan Rd., #208
Northfield, IL 60093
E-Mail: editor@mcilvainecompany.com
Website: www.mcilvainecompany.com
Fax Ordering: (847) 784-0061
Contact Name: Robert McIlvaine, President
Catalog: Free. Frequency: Monthly
Circulation: 100K. Sales: $5-10MM
Products: Pollution and contamination
control products. Environmental filters,
absorbers and supplies

PETA CATALOG (800) 483-4366
100 Pine Ave. • Holmes, PA 19043
E-Mail: support@petacatalog.org
Website: www.petacatalog.org
International Ordering: (610) 870-0194
Catalog: Free. Frequency: Semiannual
Circulation: 100K. Sales: $3-5MM
Products: Vegetarian cookbooks, animal
rights T-shirts, gifts, & cruelty-free cleaning
products

PLANET NATURAL CATALOG (800) 289-6656
1612 Gold Ave. • Bozeman, MT 59715
E-Mail: info@planetnatural.com
Website: www.planetnatural.com

Fax Ordering: (406) 587-0223
International Ordering: (406) 587-5891
Contact Name: Wayne Vinje, President
Catalog: Free. **Frequency:** Annual
Circulation: 50K. **Sales:** $500K - $1MM
Products: Natural, organic, & environmentally friendly products for the home, lawn & garden.

REAL GOODS SOLAR   (800) 919-2400
833 W. S. Boulder Rd. • Louisville, CO 80027   (800) 762-7325
E-Mail: service@realgoods.com
Website: www.realgoods.com
Fax Ordering: (800) 456-1139
Customer Service: (800) 347-0070
Catalog: Free. **Frequency:** Quarterly
Circulation: 100K. **Sales:** $5-10MM
Products: Environmental gifts & household goods; recycled paper; renewable energy products; air & water filters; CDs, videos & books

TERRA TECH   (800) 321-1037
2635 W. 7th Pl. • Eugene, OR 97402
E-Mail: customerservice@terratech.net
Website: www.terratech.net
Fax Ordering: (541) 687-2244; (800) 933-4569
International Ordering: (541) 345-0597
Catalog: Free. **Frequency:** Annual
Circulation: 75K. **Sales:** $500K - $1MM
Products: Reforestation equipment & supplies; tools for firefighters

WATER & AIR ESSENTIALS   (800) 964-4303
1850 N. Greenville Ave. #184
Richardson, TX 75081
E-Mail: info@ewater.com
Website: www.ewater.com
Technical Service: (866) 913-6296
Contact Name: Fred Van Liew, President
Catalog: Free. **Frequency:** Quarterly brochure
Circulation: 50K. **Sales:** $1-3MM
Products: Water filtration, reverse osmosis systems, shower filters, water revitalization, air purification, energy mugs, books

WATERWISE, INC.   (800) 874-9028
P.O. Box 494000 • Leesburg, FL 34749
E-Mail: sales@waterwise.com
Website: www.waterwise.com
Fax Ordering: (866) 329-8123
International Ordering: (541) 345-0597
Contact Name: Jack Barber, President
Catalog: Free. **Frequency:** Annual
Circulation: 100K. **Sales:** $3-5MM
Products: Water & air purification systems

ACOUSTIC SOUNDS   (800) 716-3553
P.O. Box 1905 • Salina, KS 67401   (888) 926-2564
E-Mail: info@acousticsounds.com
Website: www.acousticsounds.com
Fax Ordering: (785) 825-0156
International Ordering: (785) 825-8609
Contact Names: Chad Kassem, President
Catalog: Free. Frequency: Quarterly.
Circulation: 100M. Sales: $1-3MM
Products: LPs and CDs

ACTIVE PARENTING CATALOG   (800) 825-0060
1955 Vaughn Rd. NW, Suite 108   (800) 235-7755
Kennesaw, GA 30144-7808
E-Mail: cservice@activeparenting.com
Website: www.activeparenting.com
Fax Ordering: (770) 429-0334
International Ordering: (770) 429-0565
Contact Name: Michael H. Popkin, PhD, President
Catalog: Free. Frequency: 3x per year
Circulation: 300M. Sales: $1-3MM
Products: Video-based discussion programs
& resources for parent education, parent
involvement, loss education & self esteem
education

ADVENTURES IN CASSETTES   (800) 328-0108
Division of Metacom
5353 Nathan Lane N • Plymouth, MN 55442
E-Mail: aic4radio@aol.com
Fax Ordering: (763) 553-0424
International Ordering: (763) 557-7777
Contact Names: Sue Hamilton, Manager
Catalog: Free. Frequency: 5x per year
Circulation: 500M. Sales: $1-3MM
Products: Old time radio shows on cassette

ALDEN FILMS   (732) 462-3522
P.O. Box 449 • Clarksburg, NJ 08510
E-Mail: info@aldfilms.com
Website: www.aldenfilms.com
Fax Ordering: (732) 294-0330
Contact Name: Paul Weinberg, President
Catalog: Free. Frequency: Annual
Circulation: 10M. Sales: $200M
Products: Videos, CDs & DVDs on Israel
and Judaica

APPALSHOP   (606) 633-0108
91 Madison Ave.
Whitesburg, KY 41858
E-Mail: info@appalshop.org
Website: www.appalshop.org
Fax Ordering: (606) 633-1009
Catalog: Free. Frequency: Semiannual
Circulation: 60M. Sales: $1-3MM
Products: Education & training programs;
films, video, theater, music and spoken-word
recordings, radio, photography, and book

ART VIDEO PRODUCTIONS   (877) 227-8843
P.O. Box 92343 • Pasadena, CA 91109
E-Mail: support@artvideostore.com
Website: www.artvideostore.com
Fax Ordering: (626) 792-4547
International Ordering: (770) 206-7478
Customer Service: (626) 792-4545
Contact Name: Hal Reed, President
Catalog: Free. Frequency: Quarterly
Circulation: 50M. Sales: $250M
Products: Art instructional videotapes

BIBLE IN LIVING SOUND   (800) 634-0234
P.O. Box 234 • Nordland, WA 98358
E-Mail: info@@bibleinlivingsound.org
Website: www.bibleinlivingsound.org
Fax Ordering: (360) 385-1124
International Ordering: (360) 385-0234
Contact Names: Dean L. Sanders, President
Catalog: Free. Frequency: Semiannual
Circulation: 50M. Sales: $250-500M
Products: Audiocassettes of dramatization
of bible stories for children

BLACKSMITH CORPORATION   (800) 531-2663
P.O. Box 1752 • Chino Valley, AZ 86323
International Ordering: (520) 636-4456
Contact Names: Nancy Padua, President
Catalog: Free. Frequency: Bimonthly
Circulation: 10M. Sales: $250M
Products: Technical books and videos
on firearms, hunting, outdoor sports & history

BROADWAY-HOLLYWOOD RECORDINGS   (888) 627-3993
Original Cast Records
P.O. Box 496 • Georgetown, CT 06829
E-Mail: info@originalcastrecords.com
Website: www.originalcastrecords.com
Fax Ordering: (203) 544-8288
Contact Name: Bruce Yeko, President
Catalog: $2. Frequency: Annual
Products: Out-of-print and hard-to-find
LP's & CD's of broadway & film soundtracks

CANYON CINEMA   (415) 626-2255
145 Ninth St., Suite 260
San Francisco, CA 94103
E-Mail: films@canyoncinema.com
Website: www.canyoncinema.com
Fax Ordering: (415) 626-2255
Contact Name: Dominic Angerame, President
Catalog: $35. Frequency: Annual
Circulation: 25M. Sales: $250M
Products: 8mm & 16mm motion pictures,
VHS tapes of avant garde/experimental films

CAREERTRACK/FRED PRYOR SEMINARS   (800) 944-8503
9757 Metcalf Ave. • Overland Park, KS 66212
E-Mail: customerservice@pryor.com
Website: www.careertrack.com
Fax Ordering: (866) 750-5695; (913) 967-8849
Catalog: Free. Frequency: Quarterly
Circulation: 50M. Sales: $5-10MM
Products: Self-development and career
viideotapes, audiocassettes, books and
CD-ROMs; seminars

CATALOG OF USED COMPACT DISCS   (810) 695-3515
Audio House Compact Disc Club
8105 Hawkcrest Dr. • Grand Blanc, MI 48439
E-Mail: info@audiohousecd.com
Website: www.audiohousecd.com
Fax Ordering: (810) 694-7441
Contact Name: Terry Duffy, President
Catalog: Free. Frequency: Monthly
Circulation: 10M. Sales: $250-500M
Products: Used CD's to buy, sell or trade

CCC OF AMERICA   (800) 935-2222
P.O. Box 166349 • Irving, TX 75063   Canada (888) 236-2353
E-Mail: info@cccofamerica.com
Website: www.cccofamerica.com
Fax Ordering: (972) 929-3366

International Ordering: (972) 929-3360
Contact Name: Mario Skertchly, President
Catalog: Free. Frequency: Semiannual
Circulation: 500M. Sales: $5-10MM
Products: Family entertainment videos

CD WAREHOUSE (800) 641-9394
900 N. Broadway • Oklahoma City, OK 73102
E-Mail: customerservice@cdwarehouse.com
Website: www.cdwarehouse.com
Fax Ordering: (405) 949-2566
Catalog: Free. Frequency: Semiannual
Circulation: 100M. Sales: $5-10MM
Products: CD's new and used

CLASSES IN MEDIA ARTS (800) 262-8862
First Light Video Publishing
2321 Abbot Kinney Blvd.
Venice, CA 90291
E-Mail: info@firstlightvideo.com
Website: www.firstlightvideo.com
Fax Ordering: (310) 574-0886
International Ordering: (310) 577-8581
Contact Name: Michael Bennett, President
Catalog: Free. Frequency: Semiannual
Circulation: 100M. Sales: $1-3MM
Products: Technical training videos,
CD-ROMs, DVDs teaching students,
educators & professionals in the media arts

COLLAGE VIDEO (800) 819-7111
5390 Main St. NE • Minneapolis, MN 55421
E-Mail: collage@collagevideo.com
Website: www.collagevideo.com
Fax Ordering: (763) 571-5906
International Ordering: (763) 571-5840
Catalog: Free. Pages: 60. Frequency: Annual
Circulation: 150K. Sales: $5-10MM
Products: Exercise videos: DVDs & CDs

COMPLETE GUIDE TO (800) 383-8811
SPECIAL INTEREST VIDEOS
Video Learning Library
15838 North 62nd St. • Scottsdale, AZ 85254
E-Mail: info@videolearning.com
Website: www.videomarketplace.com
Fax Ordering: (480) 596-9973
International Ordering: (480) 596-9970
Contact Name: James Spencer, President
Catalog: $29.95. Frequency: Annual
Circulation: 25M. Sales: $1-3MM
Products: 15,000 in-stock how-to &
special interest videos

CREATIVE VIDEO PRODUCTS (800) 339-8158
P.O. Box 7032 • Endicott, NY 13761
E-Mail: sales@creativevideopro.com
Website: www.creativevideopro.com
Fax Ordering: (607) 754-0476
International Ordering: (607) 754-6767
Catalog: Free. Frequency: Semiannual
Circulation: 25M. Sales: $500M to 1MM
Products: Photography catalog offering
albums and photo mounts, specializes in
video cassette albums, special event video
sleeves, cameo frames, high gloss video
jackets, VHS & DVD leather signature.

CRITICS CHOICE VIDEO (800) 367-7765
P.O. Box 749 • Itasca, IL 60143
E-Mail: vcatalog@ccvideo.com
Website: www.ccvideo.com

Fax Ordering: (630) 775-3355
Contact Name: Herb Laney, President
Catalog: Free. Frequency: Quarterly
Circulation: 20MM. Sales: $20-50MM
Products: Catalog of over 40,000 videos
and 500 DVD's

DANCE VISION (800) 851-2813
8933 W. Sahara Ave.
Las Vegas, NV 89117
E-Mail: info@dancevision.com
Website: www.dancevision.com
Fax Ordering: (702) 256-4227
International Ordering: (702) 256-3830
Contact Name: Wayne Eng, President
Catalog: Free. Frequency: Annual
Circulation: 100M. Sales: $500M to 1MM
Products: Catalog of over 500 instruction
videos on a variety of ballroom/dance
Sport taught by world champions and
top professionals. Also, an array of CD's,
fashion, jewelry, and book.

DEEP HEALING/SOURCE (800) 528-2737
P.O. Box 803 • Nevada City, CA 95959
E-Mail: drmiller@drmiller.com
Website: www.drmiller.com
Fax Ordering: (800) 882-1840 *2; (530) 478-0160
International Ordering: (530) 478-1807
Contact Name: Emmett E. Miller, MD, President
Catalog: Free. Frequency: 3x per year
Circulation: 10M. Sales: $500M to 1MM
Products: Audiocassettes, CD & videotapes
by Dr. Miller designed for relaxation, stress
management, behavior changes, self-healing
and self-empowerment.

DIRECT CINEMA LIMITED (310) 636-8200
P.O. Box 10003 • Santa Monica, CA 90410
E-Mail: orders@directcinemalimited.com
Website: www.directcinemalimited.com
Fax Ordering: (310) 636-8228
Contact Name: Mitchell W. Block, President
Catalog: Free. Frequency: 10x per year
Circulation: 100M. Sales: $1-3MM
Products: Short films and documentaries for
use in your educational program, business,
or community group

EDUCATION 2000 INCORPORATED (800) 653-4567
P.O. Box 11118 • Fort Lauderdale, FL 33339
E-Mail: info@education2000I.com
Website: www.education2000I.com
Fax Ordering: (954) 565-8775
International Ordering: (954) 565-8888
Contact Name: Reto Lingenhag, President
Catalog: Free. Frequency: Weekly
Circulation: 20M. Sales: $1-3MM
Products: Special interest DVD's VHS,
cassettes, books and CD's

EFFECTIVE LEARNING SYSTEMS (800) 966-5683
3461 Bonita Bay Blvd. #212
Bonita Springs, FL 34134
E-Mail: administrator@efflearn.com
Website: www.efflearn.com
Fax Ordering: (239) 948-1664
International Ordering: (239) 948-1660
Contact Name: Robert Griswold, President
Catalog: Free. Frequency: Annual
Circulation: 10M. Sales: $500M to 1MM
Products: Self-help and relaxation audiocassettes

FACETS MULTIMEDIA (800) 331-6197
1517 W. Fulleton Ave. • Chicago, IL 60614
E-Mail: sales@forcets.org
Website: www.forcets.org
Fax Ordering: (773) 929-5437
International Ordering: (773) 281-9075
Contact Name: Milos Stehlik, President
Catalog: $4. Frequency: Quarterly
Circulation: 10M. Sales: $1-3MM
Products: Foreign, classic American,
documentary, and fine arts videos

FILM CLASSICS ON VIDEOCASSETTE (800) 514-2804
Cable Films & Video
P.O. Box 7171 • Kansas City, MO 64113
Fax Ordering: (913) 362-2804
Contact Name: Herb Miller, President
Catalog: Free. Frequency: Weekly
Circulation: 10M. Sales: $500M to 1MM
Products: 300 feature film classic videocassettes,
from silent era to 1950's in all genres

FILM MAKERS COOPERATIVE CATALOG (212) 267-5665
c/o The Clocktower Gallery
108 Leonard St., 13th Floor
New York, NY 10013
E-Mail: film6000@aol.com
Website: www.film-makerscoop.com
Fax Ordering: (212) 267-5666
Catalog: $20. Frequency: Annual
Circulation: 10M. Sales: $500M to $1MM
Products: More than 5,000 independent &
avante-garde films & videos

FILMS MEDIA GROUP (800) 468-4227
Cambridge Educational (800) 257-5126
P.O. Box 2053 • Princeton, NJ 08543
E-Mail: custserv@filmsmediagroup.com
Website: www.cambridgeeducational.com
Fax Ordering: (800) 329-6687; (609) 671-0266
International Ordering: (609) 419-8000
Contact Name: Melinda Ball, Manager
Catalog: Free. Frequency: Monthly
Circulation: 150M. Sales: $5-10MM
Products: ART, Business, Career, Family
& Consumer Science, Foreign Languages,
Health, Journalism & Media, Legal Studies,
Literature, Math & Computer Science, Science,
Teacher Education, etc. videos, software,
CD-ROMs, books and posters

FLOWER FILMS (800) 572-7618
10341 San Pablo Ave.
El Cerrito, CA 94530
E-Mail: blankfilm@aol.com
Website: www.lesblank.com
Fax Ordering: (510) 525-1204
International Ordering: (510) 525-0942
Contact Name: Les Blank, President
Catalog: Free. Frequency: Annual
Circulation: 10M. Sales: $500M to 1MM
Products: 16mm and video on real food,
roots music and people full of passion for
what they do . Founded in 1967.

FOLK LEGACY RECORDS (800) 836-0901
P.O. Box 1148 • Sharon, CT 06069
E-Mail: folklegacy@snet.net
Website: www.folklegacy.com
Fax Ordering: (860) 364-1050
International Ordering: (860) 364-5661
Contact Name: Charles A. Paton, President

Catalog: Free. Frequency: Annual
Circulation: 20M. Sales: $500M to 1MM
Products: Folk music CDs and cassettes

GATEWAYS TO A BETTER LIFE (800) 477-8908
Gateways Fulfillment
428 Bryant Circle • Ojai, CA 93023
E-Mail: gwgateways@msn.com
Fax Ordering: (805) 646-0980
International Ordering: (805) 646-0267
Contact Name: Mark Stein, President
Catalog: Free. Frequency: Semiannual
Circulation: 1.5MM. Sales: $3-5MM
Products: Self-improvement audiotapes

GENTLE WIND (888) 386-7664
P.O. Box 3103 • Albany, NY 12203
E-Mail: hello@gentlewind.com
Website: www.gentlewind.com
International Ordering: (518) 436-0391
Contact Name: Jill Person, President
Catalog: Free. Frequency: Annual
Circulation: 10M. Sales: $200M
Products: Children's audiocassettes

GRAPEVINE VIDEO (602) 973-3661
P.O. Box 46161 • Phoenix, AZ 85063
E-Mail: jbhardy@grapevinevideo.net
Website: www.grapevinevideo.com
Fax Ordering: (602) 973-2973
Contact Name: Jack Hardy, President
Catalog: Free. Frequency: Annual
Circulation: 10M. Sales: $250M
Products: Classic silent films & early
TV shows

CARL GURLEY COMPANY (919) 936-7333
P.O. Box 995 • Princeton, NC 27569
E-Mail: gurley@esn.net
Fax Ordering: (919) 936-2200
Contact Name: Carl R. Gurley, Manager
Catalog: $2. Frequency: Monthly
Circulation: 5M. Sales: $1-3MM
Products: Old original and rare records,
toy trains and antique toys

H&B RECORDING DIRECT (800) 222-6872
P.O. Box 309
Waterbury Center, VT 05677
E-Mail: staff@hbdirect.com
Website: www.hbdirect.com
Fax Ordering: (802) 244-4199
International Ordering: (802) 244-5290
Catalog: $14. Frequency: Annual
Circulation: 5M. Sales: $1-3MM
Products: Classical music CDs &
DVD video

HARTLEY FILM FOUNDATION (800) 937-1819
49 Richmondville Ave., Suite 204
Westport, CT 06880
E-Mail: customerservice@hartleyvideos.org
Website: www.hartleyvideos.org
Fax Ordering: (203) 227-6938
International Ordering: (203) 226-9500
Contact Name: Elda Hartley, President
Catalog: Free. Frequency: Annual
Circulation: 10M. Sales: $200M
Products: Educational video programs on
world religions, philosophy, meditiation,
alternative health, holistic health, aging,
reincarnation, death and dying, & new age.

INTERNATIONAL HISTORIC FILMS   (773) 927-2900
P.O. Box 5796 • Chicago, IL 60680
E-Mail: info@ihffilm.com
Website: www.ihffilm.com
Fax Ordering: (773) 927-9211
International Ordering: (773) 927-2900
Contact Name: Peter Bernotas, President
Catalog: $1. Frequency: Annual
Circulation: 100M. Sales: $3-5MM
Products: Videocassettes, DVD's, CD's
and books on military, political and social
history of the 20th Century

KIMBO EDUCATIONAL   (800) 631-2187
P.O. Box 477 • Long Branch, NJ 07740
E-Mail: info@kimboed.com
Website: www.kimboed.com
Fax Ordering: (732) 870-3340
International Ordering: (732) 229-4949
Contact Name: Gertrude Kimble, President
Catalog: Free. Frequency: Semiannual
Circulation: 400M. Sales: $1-3MM
Products: Children's CDs, cassettes and
videos for musical instructions & appreciation

KRAUSE PUBLICATIONS, INC.   (800) 258-0929
700 E. State St. • Iola, WI 54990
E-Mail: info@ @collect.com
Website: www.collect.com
Fax Ordering: (715) 445-4087
International Ordering: (715) 445-4612
Catalogs: Free. Frequency: Monthly
Circulation: 100M. Sales: $3-5MM
Products: Books, records & CDs

LASERDISCS, DVDS & ACCESSORIES   (800) 893-0390
Lasertown Videos Discs, Inc.
P.O. Box 406 • Kulpsville, PA 19443
E-Mail: info@lasertown.com
Website: www.lasertown.com
Fax Ordering: (610) 584-9509
International Ordering: (610) 584-0172
Catalog: Free. Frequency: Semiannual
Circulation: 50M. Sales: $500M to 1MM
Products: DVD's, laserdiscs & accessories

LYRICHORD DISCS, INC.   (212) 929-8234
P.O. Box 1977 • New York, NY 10011
E-Mail: info@lyrichord.com
Website: www.lyrichord.com
Fax Ordering: (212) 929-8245
Contact Name: Nick Fritsch, President
Catalog: Free. Frequency: Semiannual
Circulation: 10M. Sales: $250M
Products: Traditional world & early music

GENE MICHAEL PRODUCTIONS   (800) 955-0619
441 Post Rd. • Buchanan, MI 49107
E-Mail: info@gmpmusic.com
Website: www.gmpmusic.com
Fax Ordering: (269) 695-4005
International Ordering: (269) 695-4000
Contact Name: Gene Ort, President
Catalog: Free. Frequency: Annual
Circulation: 10M. Sales: $500M to 1MM
Products: CDs, cassettes and records

MILITARY VIDEO CATALOG   (480) 488-1377
A Pieces of History
P.O. Box 7590 • Cave Creek, AZ 85327
Fax Ordering: (480) 488-1316
Catalog: Free. Frequency: Annual

Circulation: 10M. Sales: $500M
Products: Military videos

WARREN MILLER ENTERTAINMENT   (800) 729-3456
2540 Frontier Ave. • Boulder, CO 80301
E-Mail: feedback@warrenmiller.com
Website: www.warrenmiller.com
Fax Ordering: (303) 442-3402
International Ordering: (303) 442-3430
Contact Name: Kurt Miller, President
Catalog: Free. Frequency: Annual
Circulation: 250M. Sales: $3-5MM
Products: Sports feature films; skiing, sailing

MONITOR RECORDINGS   (914) 664-2567
10 Fiske Pl. • Mount Vernon, NY 10550
Fax Ordering: (914) 667-2072
Contact Name: Michael Stillman, President
Catalog: Free. Frequency: 5x per year
Circulation: 5M. Sales: $1-3MM
Products: Worldwide popular CDs,
cassettes and records

MOVIECRAFT HOME VIDEO   (708) 460-9082
P.O. Box 438 • Orland Park, IL 60462
E-Mail: orders@moviecraft.com
Website: www.moviecraft.com
Fax Ordering: (708) 460-9099
Contact Name: Larry Urbanski, President
Catalog: $1. Frequency: Annual
Circulation: 10M. Sales: $250M
Products: Videocassettes on lost TV shows,
railroad nostalgia, antique & classic cars, etc.

MOVIES UNLIMITED   (800) 668-4344
3015 Darnell Rd. • Philadelphia, PA 19154
E-Mail: movies@moviesunlimited.com
Website: www.moviesunlimited.com
Fax Ordering: (215) 637-2350
International Ordering: (215) 637-4444
Contact Name: Jerry Frebowitz, President
Catalog: $12.95. Frequency: 8x per year
Circulation: 1.5MM. Sales: $10-20MM
Products: Catalog describes virtually every
video from early silent classics to today's
newest releases.

MULTICULTURAL MEDIA   (802) 223-1294
56 Browns Mill Rd. • Berlin, VT 05602
E-Mail: email@multiculturalmedia.com
Website: www.multiculturalmedia.com
Fax Ordering: (802) 229-1834
Contact Name: Stephen McArthur, President
Catalog: Free. Frequency: Semiannual
Circulation: 25M. Sales: $500M
Products: Traditional world music and dance
audiocassettes and videotapes, including the
Smithsonian Folkways video collection

MUSIC VIDEO DISTRIBUTORS   (800) 888-0486
MVD Entertainment Group
422 Business Center
H-840 N. Circle Dr. • Oaks, PA 19456
E-Mail: sales@musicvideodistributors.com
Website: www.musicvideodistributors.com
Fax Ordering: (610) 650-9102
International Ordering: (610) 650-8200
Catalog: Free. Frequency: Annual
Circulation: 10M. Sales: $500M to 1MM
Products: Music videos, DVDs, VHS,
laserdiscs; t-shirts

MUSICIAN'S WORKSHOP   (800) 543-6125
P.O. Box 161921 • Austin, TX 78716
E-Mail: folks@musicians-workshop.com
Website: www.musicians-workshop.com
Fax Ordering: (512) 327-6603
International Ordering: (512) 452-8348
Catalog: Free. Frequency: Weekly
Circulation: 100M. **Sales:** $500M to 1MM
Products: Music instruction videos, DVD's, CD's,
cassettes, books, accessories, electronics and
instruments

MYSTIC FIRE VIDEO   (800) 292-9001
19 Gregory Dr. • S. Burlington, VT 05403   (800) 862-8900 x541
E-Mail: ordering@mysticfire.com
Website: www.mysticfire.com
Fax Ordering: (802) 846-1850
Contact Name: Sheldon Rachlin, President
Catalog: Free. Frequency: Semiannual
Circulation: 10M. **Sales:** $500M
Products: Spiritual, psychological and
artistic audio and video tapes

NATIONAL FILM BOARD OF CANADA   (800) 542-2164
350 Fifth Ave. • New York, NY 10118
E-Mail: new york@nfb.ca
Website: www.nfb.ca
Fax Ordering: (212) 629-8502
International Ordering: (212) 629-8890
Contact Name: John Sirabella, President
Catalog: Free. Frequency: Semiannual
Circulation: 50M. **Sales:** $1-3MM
Products: Film documentaries, drama &
animation. Catalogs for home & school use.

NETFLIX, INC.   (866) 636-3076
100 Winchester Clr. • Los Gatos, CA 95032   (866) 519-1190
E-Mail: info@netflix.com
Website: www.netflix.com
Fax Ordering: (408) 540-3737
Catalog: Online. **Frequency:** Monthly
Circulation: 10M. **Sales:** $100-200MM
Products: Online DVD rental service with
over 100,000 DVD's by mail. Catalog.

NEW & UNIQUE VIDEOS   (800) 365-8433
Crystal Pyramid Productions
7323 Rondel Court • San Diego, CA 92119
E-Mail: cpp@newuniquevideos.com
Website: www.newunique.com
Fax Ordering: (619) 644-3001
International Ordering: (619) 644-3000
Contact Name: Mark Schulze, President
Catalog: Free. Frequency: Annual
Circulation: 10M. **Sales:** $1-3MM
Products: Special interest videos; bicycling

NOSTALGIA FAMILY VIDEO, INC.   (800) 784-3362
P.O. Box 606 • Baker City, OR 97814
Website: www.nostalgiafamilyvideo.com
Catalog: Online. Frequency: Annual
Circulation: 100M. **Sales:** $3-5MM
Products: Hard-to-find classic motion
pictures on video.

OGM PRODUCTION MUSIC   (800) 421-4163
6464 Sunset Blvd. • Hollywood, CA 90028
E-Mail: info@ogmmusic.com
Website: www.ogmmusic.com
Fax Ordering: (323) 461-1543
International Ordering: (323) 461-2701
Contact Name: Ole Georg, President

Catalog: Free. Frequency: Annual
Circulation: 10M. **Sales:** $500M to $1MM
Products: CD-quality sound for auditioning,
ordering and receiving electronically, music
selections from the OGM library. 6,000 tracks
available for Internet, CD-ROM, multimedia
and more.

PBS HOME VIDEO CATALOG   (800) 344-3337
Public Broadcasting Service
1320 Braddock Pl. • Alexandria, VA 22314
E-Mail: info@shoppbs.org
Website: www.shoppbs.org
Fax Ordering: (703) 739-5269
International Ordering: (703) 739-5000
Contact Name: Ervin S. Duggan, President
Catalog: Free. Frequency: Monthly
Circulation: 10MM. **Sales:** $20-50MM
Products: PBS videos & video collections,
DVD's, CD's and books

POLYLINE CORPORATION   (800) 701-7689
845 N. Church Ct. • Elmhurst, IL 60126   (800) 701-5865
E-Mail: sales@polylinecorp.com
Website: www.polylinecorp.com
Fax Ordering: (800) 816-3330
International Ordering: (847) 357-1259
Catalog: Free. Frequency: Semiannual
Products: Duplicating, packaging supplies
for audio video and CD's

PRECEPT MINISTRIES INTERNATIONAL   (800) 763-8280
P.O. Box 182218 • Chattanooga, TN 37422   (888) 678-5660
E-Mail: info@precept.org
Website: www.precept.org
Fax Ordering: (423) 894-2449
International Ordering: (423) 892-6814
Contact Name: Jack & Kay Arthur, President
Catalog: Free. Frequency: Semiannual
Circulation: 150M. **Sales:** $5-10MM
Products: Bible study materials & software;
Christian recordings

RADIO SPIRITS   (800) 833-4248
P.O. Box 3107 • Wallingford, CT 06492
E-Mail: info@radiospirits.com
Website: www.radiospirits.com
Fax Ordering: (203) 797-0819
International Ordering: (203) 265-8044
Contact Name: Michael Rophone, President
Catalog: Free. **Pages:** 32. **Frequency:** Monthly
Circulation: 100M. **Sales:** $1-3MM
Products: Timeless radio classics; oldtime
radio shows on CD and TV shows on DVD
& videocassette

RANDOM HOUSE   (800) 733-3000
1745 Broadway • New York, NY 10019
E-Mail: sales@randomhouse.com
Website: www.randomhouse.com
Fax Ordering: (212) 572-4961
International Ordering: (212) 782-9000
Customer Service: (800) 726-0600
Contact Name: Peter Olsonale, President
Catalog: Free. Frequency: Semiannual
Circulation: 200M. **Sales:** $10-50MM
Products: Records, cassettes & videotapes

RECORD ROUNDUP   (800) 443-4727
Roundup Records
1 Camp St. • Cambridge, MA 02140
Fax Ordering: (617) 868-8769

International Ordering: (617) 661-6308
Contact Name: Dennis MacDonald, President
Catalog: $2. Frequency: Annual
Circulation: 100M. Sales: $500M
Products: CDs, LPs and cassettes

RECORD-RAMA SOUND ARCHIVES   (412) 367-7330
1130 Perry Hwy. • Pittsburgh, PA 15237
E-Mail: recrama@record-rama.com
Website: www.record-rama.com
Fax Ordering: (412) 367-7388
Contact Name: Paul C. Mawhinney, President
Catalog: Free. Frequency: Weekly
Circulation: 100M. Sales: $1-3MM
Products: Database of more than 600,000
recordings

RIDE WITH ME AUDIO   (800) 752-3195
RWM Associates
P.O. Box 1324 • Bethesda, MD 20817
E-Mail: info@rwmaudio.com
Website: www.rwmaudio.com
Fax Ordering: (301) 299-7817
Contact Name: Bob Magee, President
Catalog: Online. Frequency: Annual
Circulation: 100M. Sales: $500M
Products: Travel audiotapes

ROOTS & RHYTHM   (888) 766-8766
P.O. Box 837 • El Cerrito, CA 94530
E-Mail: roots@toast.net
Website: www.rootsandrhythm.com
Fax Ordering: (510) 526-9001
International Ordering: (510) 526-8373
Contact Name: Patrick Noonan, President
Catalog: Free. Frequency: Bimonthly
Circulation: 100M. Sales: $500M-1MM
Products: Records, cassettes, CDs &
music related books, videos and magazines,
specializing in blues, R&B, rockabilly, country,
folk and world music.

SOUNDS TRUE, INC.   (800) 333-9185
413 S. Arthur Ave. • Louisville, CO 80027
E-Mail: info@soundstrue.com
Website: www.soundstrue.com
Fax Ordering: (303) 665-5292
International Ordering: (303) 665-3151
Contact Name: Tami Simon, President
Catalog: Free. Frequency: Bimonthly
Circulation: 1MM. Sales: $3-5MM
Products: Original spokenword, audio
programs, instruction, video, world music,
spirituality, health, psychology, meditation
and yoga.

STARSHIP INDUSTRIES   (703) 450-5780
605 Utterback Store Rd.
Great Falls, VA 22066
E-Mail: starship@starslaser.com
Website: www.starlaser.com
Fax Ordering: (360) 530-7345
Contact Name: Greg Streeter, President
Catalog: Online. Newsletter available.
Sales: $1-3MM
Products: Laser discs, DVD's,
equipment and accessories

SUBTECHNIQUE   (703) 212-0080
4950-C Eisenhower Ave.
Alexandria, VA 22304
E-Mail: info@subtechnique.com

Website: www.subtechnique.com
Fax Ordering: (703) 212-0085
Contact Name: James Thera, President
Catalog: Free. Frequency: Semiannual
Circulation: 50M. Sales: $10-20MM
Products: Video & machine vision cameras
and components, lighting, lensing, image
capture devices and parts inspection; video
inspection and duplication systems.

TEXAS MUSIC & VIDEO ONLINE CATALOG   (512) 474-2500
Waterloo Records & Video
600A N. Lamar Blvd. • Austin, TX 78703
E-Mail: info@waterloorecords.com
Website: www.waterloorecords.com
Fax Ordering: (512) 474-2522
Catalog: Online. Sales: $3-5MM
Products: Records, CDs, tapes and
videos & DVDs in all genres

V.I.E.W. VIDEO   (800) 843-9843
34 E. 23rd St. • New York, NY 10010
E-Mail: info@view.com
Website: www.view.com
Fax Ordering: (212) 979-0266
International Ordering: (212) 674-5550
Contact Name: Bob Karcy, President
Catalog: Free. Frequency: 3x per year
Circulation: 500M. Sales: $5-10MM
Products: Collectible, award-winning videos;
parenting, kids, health & fitness, documentaries,
rare films, performing arts, jazz & pop music,
dance, opera, sports, art, travel, etc.

VCI ENTERTAINMENT   (800) 331-4077
11333 East 60th Place • Tulsa, OK 74146
E-Mail: vci@vcientertainment.com
Website: www.vcientertainment.com
Fax Ordering: (918) 254-6117
International Ordering: (918) 254-6337
Contact Name: Don Blair, Sales Manager
Catalog: $3. Frequency: 10x per year
Circulation: 200M. Sales: $1-3MM
Products: Movie videos

VICTORIAN VIDEO PRODUCTIONS   (800) 848-0284
Yarn Barn
P.O. Box 334 • Lawrence, KS 66044
E-Mail: crafts@victorianvid.com
Website: www.victorianvid.com
Fax Ordering: (785) 842-0794
International Ordering: (785) 842-1675
Contact Name: Susan Bateman, President
Catalog: Free. Frequency: Semiannual
Circulation: 20M. Sales: $500M to 1MM
Products: Instructional videos on tyraditional
and contemporary handcraft techniques

VIDEO ARTISTS INTERNATIONAL   (800) 477-7146
109 Wheeler Ave. • Pleasantville, NY 10570
E-Mail: inquiries@vaimusic.com
Website: www.vaimusic.com
Fax Ordering: (914) 769-5407
International Ordering: (914) 769-3691
Contact Name: Ernest Gilbert, President
Catalog: Free. Frequency: Semiannual
Circulation: 30M. Sales: $500M to $1MM
Products: Audio CDs of instrumental, opera
& vocal concerts & recitals; VHS & DVD videos
of ballet, comedy, documentary, films, jazz,
conductors & orchestras, instrumental, opera
& highlights, and vocal concerts and recitals.

VIDEO PROJECT   (800) 475-2638
200 Estates Dr.
Ben Lomond, CA 95005
E-Mail: video@videoproject.net
Website: www.videoproject.net
Fax Ordering: (415) 821-7204
International Ordering: (415) 241-2514
Contact Name: Thomas M. Edinger, President
Catalog: Free. Frequency: Annual
Circulation: 30M. Sales: $500M
Products: Educational videos on the
environment, science, and social studies

VIDEO UNIVERSITY PRODUCT CATALOG   (845) 355-1400
Oak Tree Press
256 Guinea Hill Rd. • Slate Hill, NY 10973
E-Mail: video@videouniversity.com
Website: www.videouniversity.com
Fax Ordering: (845) 355-4807
Contact Name: Hal Landen, President
Catalog: Free. Frequency: Annual
Circulation: 100M. Sales: $250M
Products: Products for starting or expanding
home-based business producing corporate
videos; home study course, books, software

WALT DISNEY HOME VIDEO   (800) 723-4763
350 S. Buena Vista St.
Burbank, CA 91521
E-Mail: info@disney.com
Website: www.disney.com
Fax Ordering: (818) 560-1930
International Ordering: (818) 560-5000
Contact Name: Michael Johnson, President
Catalog: Free. Frequency: Quarterly
Circulation: 100M. Sales: $5-10MM
Products: Videocassettes & DVD's of
Disney movies

WHOLE TOON CATALOG   (800) 331-6197
Facets Video • 1517 Fullerton Ave.
Chicago, IL 60614
E-Mail: sales@facets.org
Website: www.facets.org
Fax Ordering: (773) 929-5437
International Ordering: (773) 281-9075
Catalog: Free. Frequency: 10x per year
Circulation: 25M. Sales: $1-3MM
Products: Pre-recorded video/audio & CDs;
blank media/tapes

WINDHAM HILL GROUP   (888) 649-4455
8750 Wilshire Blvd.
Beverly Hills, CA 90211
E-Mail: sales@windham.com
Website: www.windham.com
Fax Ordering: (310) 358-4803
International Ordering: (310) 358-4800
Contact Name: Steve Vining, President
Catalog: Free. Frequency: Bimonthly
Circulation: 100M. Sales: $1-3MM
Products: Pre-recorded video/audio
& CDs; blank media/tapes

WOMEN MAKE MOVIES   (212) 925-0606
462 Broadway, #500W
New York, NY 10013
E-Mail: info@wmm.com
Website: www.wmm.com
Fax Ordering: (212) 925-2052
Catalog: Free. Frequency: Annual
Circulation: 50M. Sales: $500M
Products: Women filmmakers and
their movies

WOODWORKER'S LIBRARY   (800) 345-4447
Linden Publishing
2006 S. Mary • Fresno, CA 93721
E-Mail: info@lindenpub.com
Website: www.lindenpub.com
Fax Ordering: (559) 233-6933
International Ordering: (559) 233-6633
Contact Name: Richard Sorsky, President
Catalog: Free. Frequency: Annual
Circulation: 50M. Sales: $500M to $1MM
Products: Discount books, plans, & videos
on all phases of woodworking

WORLD REPLICATION GROUP   (800) 334-2484
4600 Witmer Industrial Estates #2
Niagara Falls, NY 14305
E-Mail: bob@worldreplication.com
Website: www.worldreplication.com
Fax Ordering: (905) 433-1868
International Ordering: (716) 754-7401
Contact Name: Bob Stone, President
Catalog: $2. Frequency: 3x per year
Circulation: 30M. Sales: $500M
Products: Manufacturers and packagers
of custom CD's and cassettes

ZIPPORAH FILMS   (617) 576-3603
1 Richdale Ave. • Cambridge, MA 02140
E-Mail: info@zipporah.com
Website: www.zipporah.com
Fax Ordering: (617) 864-8006
Contact Name: Karen Konicek, President
Catalog: Free. Frequency: Annual
Circulation: 20M. Sales: $1-3MM
Products: Documentary films by
Frederick Wiseman

API OUTDOORS CATALOG (800) 228-4846
602 Kimbrough Dr. • Tallulah, LA 71282
E-Mail: customerservice@apioutdoors.com
Website: www.apioutdoors.com
Fax Ordering: (318) 574-4428
International Ordering: (318) 574-4903
Contact Name: Paul Meeks, President
Catalog: Free. Frequency: Annual
Circulation: 50M. Sales: $10-20MM
Products: Treestands, ladders & towers,
safety harnesses & accessories, ATV and
Hunting accessories

AMERICA'S FOREMOST SPORTING GOODS (800) 899-7810
Wolfe Publishing Company
2625 Steaman Rd., Suite A
Prescott, AZ 86301
E-Mail: wolfpub@riflemagazine.com
Website: www.riflemagazine.com
Fax Ordering: (928) 778-5124
International Ordering: (928) 445-7810
Contact Name: Mark Harris, President
Catalog: Free. Frequency: Semiannual
Circulation: 50K. Sales: $5-10MM
Products: *Handloader, Rifle* & *Successful Hunting*
magazines; Western wear; camouflage accessories;
hunting & shooting accessories & supplies - boots,
decoys, gloves, rifle hats, reloading products;
gun cleaning supplies; gunsmithing products;
GPS systems; optics - binoculars, scopes; wildlife,
military & reloading books; videos/DVDs/software

ANGLER'S SUPPLY HOUSE CATALOG (800) 326-6612
E. Hill Company
218 Market St. • So. Williamsport, PA 17702
E-Mail: info@anglersupplyhouse.com
Website: www.anglerssupplyhouse.com
Fax Ordering: (570) 323-9995
International Ordering: (570) 323-7564
Contact Name: Ken Rice, President
Catalog: Free. Frequency: Monthly
Circulation: 25K. Sales: $1-5MM
Products: Fishing supplies; rods, hooks,
rods & rod building, flies & lures, custom
rod quilts & dinnerware; books & videos

B-SQUARE COMPANY CATALOG (800) 433-2909
13386 International Parkway
Jacksonville, FL 32218
E-Mail: customercare.fsfa@baesystems.com
Website: www.b-square.com
Fax Ordering: (800) 588-0399
International Ordering: (904) 741-5400
Contact Name: Daniel Bechtel, President
Catalog: Free. Frequency: Semiannual
Circulation: 100K. Sales: $5-10MM
Products: Gun equipment & tools, shooting
accesories, scope mounts, bipods, and
gunsmithing tools

DAN BAILEY'S FLY SHOP (800) 356-4052
P.O. Box 1019 • Livingston, MT 59047
E-Mail: info@dan-bailey.com
Website: www.dan-bailey.com
Fax Ordering: (406) 222-8450
International Ordering: (406) 222-8450
Contact Name: John Bailey, President
Catalog: Free. Frequency: Quarterly
Circulation: 100M. Sales: $1-3MM
Products: Fly fishing & tying products;
videos & books; clothing, household gifts

BALLISTIC PRODUCT CATALOG (888) 273-5623
P.O. Box 293 • Hamel, MN 55340
E-Mail: info@ballisticproducts.com
Website: www.ballisticproducts.com
Fax Ordering: (763) 494-9236
International Ordering: (763) 494-9237
Contact Name: Ken Hall, President
Catalog: Free. Frequency: Semiannual
Circulation: 150M. Sales: $10-20MM
Products: Shotguns & hunting accessories;
novelty items

BASS PRO SHOPS CATALOG (800) 227-7776
2011 S. Campbell Ave.
Springfield, MO 65807
E-Mail: info@basspro.com
Website: www.basspro.com
Fax Ordering: (800) 566-4600
International Ordering: (417) 891-5373
Contact Name: John L. Morris, President
Catalog: Free. Pages: 724. Frequency: Monthly
Circulation: 2MM. Sales: $20-50MM
Products: Fishing & outdoor sporting goods;
electronics, clothing, shoes & boots, gifts,
hobbies & golf

L.L. BEAN CATALOG (800) 441-5713
Freeport, ME 04033 (800) 341-4341
E-Mail: info@llbean.com (800) 221-4221
Website: www.llbean.com
Fax Ordering: (207) 552-3080; 552-4080
Corporate Sales Fax: (800) 243-4994
International Ordering: (207) 552-3028
Contact Name: Leon Gorman, President
Catalog: Free. Frequency: Quarterly
Circulation: 50MM. Sales: $100-500MM
Products: Hunting & fishing gear, clothing
& accessories

BERETTA USA CATALOG (800) 237-3882
17601 Beretta Dr. • Accokeek, MD 20607 (800) 929-2901
E-Mail: estore@berettausa.com
Website: www.berettausa.com
Fax Ordering: (301) 283-0435
International Ordering: (301) 283-2191
Contact Name: Steve Parsick, President
Catalog: $5.96. Frequency: Annual
Circulation: 50K. Sales: $1-3MM
Products: Firearms, shooting gear,
hunting bags, clothing, hunting accessories
& knives

BIANCHI INTERNATIONAL CATALOG (800) 347-1200
3120 E. Mission Blvd. • Ontario, CA 91761
E-Mail: info@ballisticproducts.com
Website: www.bianchi-intl.com
Fax Ordering: (800) 366-1669; (909) 676-6777
International Ordering: (909) 923-7300
Contact Name: Gary French, President
Catalog: $5. Frequency: Annual
Circulation: 50K. Sales: $5-10MM
Products: Law enforcement products:
holsters, duty gear & accessories

BOB'S GUN SHOP CATALOG (501) 767-1970
P.O. Box 200 • Royal, AR 71968
E-Mail: gunparts@hsnp.com
Website: www.gun-parts.com
Fax Ordering: (501) 767-2750
International Ordering: (501) 767-1970
Minimum Order: $10.

Contact Name: Bob Brown, Sr., President
Catalog: Online. **Sales:** $500K
Products: Gun parts, firing pins & magazines

BROWNELLS CATALOG   (800) 741-0015
Brownells, Inc.
200 S. Front St. • Montezuma, IA 50171
E-Mail: info@brownells.com
Website: www.brownells.com
Fax Ordering: (641) 623-3068; 623-3896
International Ordering: (641) 623-5401
Contact Name: F.R. Brownell, President
Catalog: $5. Frequency: Annual
Circulation: 50K. Sales: $3-5MM
Products: Gunsmithing tools, supplies &
custom accessories; shooting accessories,
optics & mounting, rifle, shotgun & handgun
parts; gun cleaning & chemicals

BURRIS COMPANY CATALOG   (970) 356-1670
331 E. 8th St. • Greeley, CO 80631
E-Mail: customerservice@burrisoptics.com
Website: www.burrisoptics.com
Fax Ordering: (970) 356-8702
Contact Name: W.W. Ames, President
Catalog: Free. Frequency: Annual
Circulation: 100K. Sales: $10-20MM
Products: Gun sights; telescopic scopes,
mounts; binoculars

CABELA'S, INC.   (800) 237-4444
One Cabela Dr. • Sidney, NE 69160   (800) 431-2904
E-Mail: info@cabelas.com
Website: www.cabelas.com
Fax Ordering: (800) 496-6329; (308) 254-2200
International Ordering: (308) 234-5555
Contact Name: Dennis Highby, President & CEO
Catalog: Free. Pages: 616. Frequency: Semiannual
Circulation: 500K. Sales: $10-20MM
Products: Hunting, fishing, archery &
bowhunting equipment & supplies; clothing
& outdoor (camping) gear & supplies; gifts
& home furnishings

CAPT. HARRY'S FISHING SUPPLY   (800) 327-4088
100 NE 11th St. • Miami, FL 33132
E-Mail: info@captharry.com
Website: www.captharry.com
Fax Ordering: (305) 374-3713
International Ordering: (305) 374-4661
Contact Name: Harry Vernon, President
Catalog: Free. Frequency: Annual
Circulation: 100M. Sales: $1-3MM
Products: Saltwater fishing equipment,
supplies & gear

LEN CODELLA'S VINTAGE TACKLE   (352) 637-5454
Len Codella's Sporting Collectibles
2201 S. Carnegie Dr. • Inverness, FL 34450
E-Mail: len@codella.com
Website: www.codella.com
Fax Ordering: (352) 637-5420
Contact Name: Len Codella, President
Catalog: Free. Frequency: Weekly
Circulation: 20M. Sales: $500M to $1MM
Products: Bamboo fly rods; buy, sell &
trade quality fly rods & related items

CORBIN MANUFACTURING & SUPPLY   (541) 826-5211
P.O. Box 2659 • White City, OR 97503
E-Mail: sales@corbins.com
Website: www.corbins.com

Fax Ordering: (541) 826-8669
International Ordering: (541) 826-5211
Contact Name: D.R. Corbin, President
Catalog: $9.50. Pages: 8. Frequency: Quarterly
Circulation: 100K. Sales: $5-10MM
Products: Bullet making tools & supplies

CRAZY CREEK PRODUCTS   (800) 331-0304
P.O. Box 1050 • Red Lodge, MT 59068
E-Mail: chairs@crazycreek.com
Website: www.crazycreek.com
Fax Ordering: (406) 446-1411
International Ordering: (406) 446-3446
Contact Name: Rob Hart, President
Catalog: Free. Frequency: Annual
Circulation: 100M. Sales: $3-5MM
Products: Portable lightweight chairs
for canoeing, kayaking, sailing, rafting,
camping, backpacking, hiking, fishing,
hunting, beach, etc.

DAY ONE CAMOUFLAGE   (800) 347-2979
3300 S. Knox Ct. • Englewood, CO 80110
E-Mail: garydayonecamo@aol.com
Website: www.dayonecamouflage.com
Fax Ordering: (303) 761-3135
International Ordering: (303) 761-2070
Contact Name: Gary Christofferson, President
Catalog: Free. Frequency: Annual
Circulation: 50K. Sales: $1-3MM
Products: Camouflage clothing; parkas, vests
& shirts designed for the serious hunter; pants,
bibs & gaitors; head, hand & foot gear; packs
& accessories

DEER SHACK CATALOG   (800) 443-3337
Outdoor Images Unlimited Corp.
7155 Hwy. B • Belgium, WI 53004
E-Mail: info@deershack.com
Website: www.deershack.com
Fax Ordering: (920) 994-4099
International Ordering: (920) 994-9818
Contact Name: Joseph M. O'Connell, President
Catalog: $2. Frequency: Annual
Circulation: 500M. Sales: $1-3MM
Products: Deer related & hunting products;
gifts & gear for the sportsman

DILLON PRECISION PRODUCTS   (800) 223-4570
8009 E. Dillons Way • Scottsdale, AZ 85260
E-Mail: info@dillonprecision.com
Website: www.dillonprecision.com
Fax Ordering: (480) 998-2786
International Ordering: (480) 948-8009
Customer Service: (800) 762-3845
Contact Name: John Keefe, Marketing
Catalog: Free. Frequency: Monthly
Circulation: 2MM. Sales: $10-20MM
Products: Shotgun reloading components;
hunting supplies

DIXIE GUN WORKS CATALOG   (800) 238-6785
P.O. Box 130 • Union City, TN 38281
E-Mail: info@dixiegunworks.com
Website: www.dixiegunworks.com
Fax Ordering: (731) 885-0440
International Ordering: (731) 885-0700
Contact Name: J. Lee Fry, President
Catalog: Free. Frequency: Semiannual
Circulation: 75K. Sales: $5-10MM
Products: Antique firearms, accessories
& shooting supplies

EPPINGER MANUFACTURING   (888) 771-8277
6340 Schaefer Rd.
Dearborn, MI 48126
E-Mail: info@eppinger.net
Website: www.eppinger.net
Fax Ordering: (313) 582-0110
International Ordering: (313) 582-3205
Contact Name: Karen Eppinger, President
Catalog: $3. Frequency: Quarterly
Circulation: 25K. Sales: $10-20MM
Products: Freshwater fishing lures

THE FISH NET COMPANY CATALOG   (800) 256-5256
P.O. Box 462 • Jonesville, LA 71343
E-Mail: sales@fishnetco.com
Website: www.fishnetco.com
Fax Ordering: (318) 339-7198
International Ordering: (318) 339-9655
Catalog: Free. Frequency: Semiannual
Circulation: 50K. Sales: $5-10MM
Products: Custom nets, sports nets,
commercial fishing nets & supplies;
batting cages

FISHING HOT SPOTS CATALOG   (800) ALL-MAPS
2389 Air Park Rd.
Rhinelander, WI 54501
E-Mail: sales@fishinghotspots.com
Website: www.fishinghotspots.com
Fax Ordering: (715) 365-5575
International Ordering: (715) 365-5555
Contact Name: Mike Michalak, President
Catalog: Free. Frequency: Semiannual
Circulation: 100M. Sales: $500M
Products: Fishing publications & maps

THE FLY SHOP CATALOG   (800) 669-3474
4140 Churn Creek Rd.
Redding, CA 96002
E-Mail: eric@theflyshop.com
Website: www.theflyshop.com
Fax Ordering: (530) 222-3572
International Ordering: (530) 222-3555
Catalog: Free. Frequency: Semiannual
Circulation: 250K. Sales: $1-3MM
Products: Fly fishing equipment,
supplies & vacation packages

GUN VIDEO CATALOG   (800) 942-8273
Lenny Magill Productions
4585 Murphy Canyon Rd.
San Diego, CA 92123
E-Mail: info@gunvideo.com
Website: www.gunvideo.com
Fax Ordering: (858) 569-0505
International Ordering: (858) 569-4000
Contact Name: Lenny Magill, President
Catalog: Free. Frequency: Bimonthly
Circulation: 400K. Sales: $1-3MM
Products: Gun videos

GUNBOOKSALES.COM   (858) 569-4000
Mike Stegan
19030 N. 14th St. • Phoenix, AZ 85024
E-Mail: contact@gunbooksales.com
Website: www.gunbooksales.com
Fax Ordering: (858) 569-0505
International Ordering: (858) 569-4000
Contact Name: Mike Stegan, Owner
Catalog: Online. Sales: $250K
Products: Gun books

HAGEN'S CATALOG   (800) 541-4586
3150 W. Havens St. • Mitchell, SD 57301
E-Mail: hagensfish@hagensfish.com
Website: www.hagensfish.com
Fax Ordering: (605) 996-8946
International Ordering: (605) 996-1891
Contact Name: Kevin Hagen, President
Catalog: Free. Frequency: Annual
Circulation: 100K. Sales: $5-10MM
Products: Assortment of fishing tackle
components

HAPPY JACK CATALOG   (800) 326-5225
P.O. Box 475 • Snow Hill, NC 28580
E-Mail: happyjack@happyjackinc.com
Website: www.happyjackinc.com
Fax Ordering: (252) 747-4111
International Ordering: (252) 747-2911
Contact Name: Ashe B. Exum, President
Catalog: Free. Frequency: 6x per year
Circulation: 250K. Sales: $1-5MM
Products: Hunters' sportswear, gifts &
accessories; health care products for dogs

HERTER'S CATALOG   (800) 654-3825
P.O. Box 24626 • Burnsville, MN 55337
Fax Ordering: (952) 894-0083
International Ordering: (952) 882-1904
Contact Name: Don Kotula, President
Catalog: Free. Frequency: 6x per year
Circulation: 1MM. Sales: $5-10MM
Products: Hunting supplies & equipment;
outdoor equipment

HOOK & HACKLE COMPANY CATALOG   (800) 552-8342
607 Ann St. Rear • Homestead, PA 15120
E-Mail: ron@hookhack.com
Website: www.hookhack.com
Fax Ordering: (412) 476-8639
International Ordering: (412) 476-8620
Contact Name: Robert Ellsworth, President
Catalog: Free. Frequency: Annual
Circulation: 50K. Sales: $1-3MM
Products: Fly fishing supplies & equipment
at discounted prices

HUMMINBIRD CATALOG   (800) 633-1468
Techsonic Industries
678 Humminbird Lane
Eufaula, AL 36027
E-Mail: info@humminbird.com
Website: www.humminbird.com
Fax Ordering: (334) 687-1165
International Ordering: (334) 687-6613
Contact Name: Charles Scott, President
Catalog: Free. Frequency: Annual
Circulation: 100M. Sales: $50-100MM
Products: Electronic fish finders, UHF
radios, GPS

HUNTERS ANGLING SUPPLIES CATALOG   (800) 331-8558
Stone River Outfitters
132 Bedford Center Rd. • Bedford, NH 03110
E-Mail: sales@stoneriveroutfitters.com
Website: www.huntersangling.com
Fax Ordering: (603) 472-3105
International Ordering: (603) 472-3191
Contact Name: Nick Wilder, President
Catalog: $3. Frequency: Annual
Circulation: 25K. Sales: $500M to $1MM
Products: Fly fishing, fly tying supplies & equipment

JANN'S NETCRAFT CATALOG   (800) 346-6590
3350 Briarfielld Blvd. • Maumee, OH 43537
E-Mail: info@jannsnetcraft.com
Website: www.jannsnetcraft.com
Fax Ordering: (419) 868-8338
International Ordering: (419) 868-8288
Contact Name: Dave Jann, President
Catalog: $2. Frequency: Annual
Circulation: 50M. Sales: $3-5MM
Products: Luremaking, rod building,
netmaking & flytying materials

JANTZ SUPPLY   (800) 351-8900
address unknown
E-Mail: info@jantzsupply.com
Website: www.jantzsupply.com
International Ordering: (580) 369-2316
Catalog: $5. Frequency: Annual
Circulation: 50M. Sales: $3-5MM
Products: Knife making supplies, leather
craft tools, finishing supplies, engraving
tools, abrasives.

JENSON FISHING TACKLE COMPANY   (800) 594-7688
3601 W. Parmer Lane • Austin, TX 78727
Fax Ordering: (512) 836-2169
International Ordering: (512) 836-1788
Contact Name: James Yett, President
Catalog: Free. Frequency: Annual
Circulation: 25M. Sales: $500M to $1MM
Products: Fishing lures, tackle & accessories

K&K FLYFISHERS CATALOG   (800) 795-8118
8643 Grant St. • Overland Park, KS 66212
E-Mail: sales@kkflyfisher.com
Website: www.kkflyfisher.com
Fax Ordering: (913) 341-1252
International Ordering: (913) 341-8118
Contact Name: Kevin Kurz, President
Catalog: Free. Frequency: Semiannual
Circulation: 50M. Sales: $500M to $1MM
Products: Rods & reels, waders & boots,
tools, bags, vises; videos, schools, travel
packages

KAUFMAN'S STREAMBORN CATALOG   (800) 442-4359
P.O. Box 23032 • Portland, OR 97281
E-Mail: kaufman@kman.com
Website: www.kman.com
Fax Ordering: (503) 684-7025
International Ordering: (503) 639-6400
Catalog: Free. Frequency: Annual
Circulation: 20M. Sales: $1-3MM
Products: Fly fishing & fly tying supplies,
equipment; schools & travel

LEE PRECISION CATALOG   (262) 673-3075
4275 Hwy. U • Hartford, WI 53027
E-Mail: info@leeprecision.com
Website: www.leeprecision.com
Fax Ordering: (262) 673-9273
Contact Name: John Lee, President
Catalog: $1. Frequency: Annual
Circulation: 100M. Sales: $1-3MM
Products: Reloaders, bullet molds,
casting & accessories

G. LOOMIS CATALOG   (800) 662-8818
1359 Down River Dr.
Woodland, WA 98674
E-Mail: loomis@gloomis.com

Website: www.gloomis.com
Fax Ordering: (360) 225-7169
International Ordering: (360) 225-6516
Contact Name: Toyo Shimano, President
Catalog: Free. Frequency: Annual
Circulation: 250M. Sales: $20-50MM
Products: Graphite fishing rods

LUHR JENSEN & SONS CATALOG   (800) 535-1711
P.O. Box 297 • Hood River, OR 97031
E-Mail: info@luhrjensen.com
Website: www.luhrjensen.com
Fax Ordering: (541) 386-4917
International Ordering: (541) 386-3811
Contact Name: Philip Jensen, President
Catalog: $3. Frequency: Annual
Circulation: 100M. Sales: $10-20MM
Products: Fishing lures, AC smoker

MARKSMAN PRODUCTS   (800) 227-2744
Beeman Precision Airguns
5454 Argosy Dr.
Huntington Beach, CA 92649
E-Mail: info@beeman.com
Website: www.beeman.com
Fax Ordering: (714) 890-4808
International Ordering: (714) 890-4800
Contact Name: Robert Eck, President
Catalog: Free. Frequency: Annual
Circulation: 100M. Sales: $3-5MM
Products: Sporting air rifles & pistols,
pellets, scopes & sights, traps, accessories,
cases & holsters

MARLIN FIREARMS CO. CATALOG   (800) 544-8892
P.O. Box 248 • North Haven, CT 06473
E-Mail: info@marlinfirearms.com
Website: www.marlinfirearms.com
Fax Ordering: (203) 234-7991
International Ordering: (203) 239-5621
Contact Name: Robert Behn, President
Catalog: Free. Frequency: Annual
Circulation: 500M. Sales: $20-50MM
Products: Sporting rifles

MEMPHIS NET & TWINE COMPANY   (800) 238-6380
SPORT NETS & EQUIPMENT   (888) 674-7638
P.O. Box 80331 • Memphis, TN 38108
E-Mail: fishinfo@memphisnet.net
Website: www.memphisnet.net
Fax Ordering: (901) 458-1601
International Ordering: (901) 458-2656
Contact Name: Albert Caruthers, President
Catalog: Free. Frequency: Semiannual
Circulation: 200K. Sales: $5-10MM
Products: Commercial fishing nets, rope
& twine

MEPPS FISHING GUIDE   (800) 237-9877
Sheldons', Inc.
626 Center St. • Antigo, WI 54409
E-Mail: shep@mepps.com
Website: www.mepps.com
Fax Ordering: (715) 623-3001
International Ordering: (715) 623-2382
Contact Name: J.M. Sheldon, President
Catalog: Free. Pages: 40. Frequency: Annual
Circulation: 350K. Sales: $5-10MM
Products: Fishing lures, Mepps spinners
& spoons

MIDWAY USA CATALOG (800) 243-3220
5875 W. Van Horn Tavern Rd.
Columbia, MO 65203
E-Mail: info@midwayusa.com
Website: www.midwayusa.com
Fax Ordering: (573) 446-1018
International Ordering: (573) 445-6363
Contact Name: Larry Potterfield, President
Catalog: Free. Frequency: Monthly
Circulation: 100K. Sales: $10-20MM
Products: Metallic cartridge reloading supplies,
shooting supplies, optics, ammunition

NITE-LITE COMPANY CATALOG (800) 648-5483
3801 Woodland Hts. Rd.
Little Rock, AR 72212
Fax Ordering: (501) 227-4892
International Ordering: (501) 227-9050
Contact Name: Tim Mariani, President
Catalog: Free. Frequency: Semiannual
Circulation: 100M. Sales: $5-10MM
Products: Hunting & dog supplies

KEN NOLAN CATALOG (800) 972-9280
16901 Millikan • Irvine, CA 92606
E-Mail: info@kennolan.com
Website: www.kennolan.com
Fax Ordering: (949) 863-1536
International Ordering: (949) 863-1531
Contact Name: Ken Nolan, President
Catalog: $2. Frequency: Annual
Circulation: 500M. Sales: $10-20MM
Products: Military products, law enforcement,
survival, emergency preparedness, BB &
pellet air guns

NUMRICH GUN PARTS CORPORATION (866) 686-7424
226 Williams Lane • West Hurley, NY 12491
E-Mail: info@gunpartscorp.com
Website: www.e-gunparts.com
Fax Ordering: (877) GUN-PART
Customer Service: (845) 679-4867
Contact Name: Gregory M. Jenks, President
Catalog: $12.95. Frequency: Weekly
Circulation: 100M. Sales: $5-10MM
Products: Gunparts & firearm accessories

ORVIS FISHING & HUNTING (800) 541-3541
The Orvis Company, Inc. (888) 235-9763
178 Conservation Way
Sunderland, VT 05250
E-Mail: customer_service@orvis.com
Website: www.orvis.com
Fax Ordering: (802) 362-3525; 362-0141
International Ordering: (802) 362-3622
Technical Support: (800) 778-4778
Contact Name: Leigh Perkins, CEO
Catalog: Free. Frequency: Monthly
Circulation: 25MM. Sales: $100-250MM
Products: Hunting & fishing equipment;
clothing, gifts

PACHMAYR CATALOG (800) 423-9704
Lyman Products Corporation
475 Smith St. • Middletown, CT 06457
E-Mail: info@pachmayr.com
Website: www.pachmayr.com
Fax Ordering: (860) 632-1699
International Ordering: (860) 632-2020
Catalog: Free. Frequency: Annual
Circulation: 300M. Sales: $5-10MM
Products: Hunting & fishing accessories

PRECISION RELOADING CATALOG (800) 223-0900
165 Crooked S Rd.
Stafford Springs, CT 06076
E-Mail: info@precisionreloading.com
Website: www.precisionreloading.com
Fax Ordering: (860) 684-6788
International Ordering: (860) 684-7979
Contact Name: Peter Maffei, President
Catalog: Free. Frequency: Annual
Circulation: 50M. Sales: $1-3MM
Products: Hunting & reloading components;
shooting supplies & clothing

A.G. RUSSELL KNIVES CATALOG (800) 255-9034
1920 N. 26th St. • Lowell, AR 72745
E-Mail: ag@agrussell.com
Website: www.agrussell.com
Fax Ordering: (479) 631-8493
Contact Name: Goldie Russell, President
Catalog: Free. Frequency: 5x per year
Circulation: 750M. Sales: $10-20MM
Products: Knives, hunting & collectibles

SHEPHERD HILLS CUTLERY (800) 727-4643
P.O. Box 909 • Lebanon, MO 65536 (888) 4CASE XX
E-Mail: info@shephills.com
Website: www.casexx.com
Fax Ordering: (417) 532-6044
International Ordering: (865) 453-5871
Catalog: Free. Frequency: Quarterly
Circulation: 200M. Sales: $3-10MM
Products: Case knife collectible dealer

SHOOTER'S BIBLE (800) 631-0722
Stoeger Industries
5 Mansard Ct. • Wayne, NJ 07470
Fax Ordering: (201) 440-2707
International Ordering: (201) 440-2700
Contact Name: Robert E. Weise, President
Catalog: $20. Frequency: Annual
Circulation: 250M. Sales: $1-3MM
Products: Firearms & accessories

SMOKY MOUNTAIN KNIFE WORKS (800) 251-9306
P.O. Box 4430 • Sevierville, TN 37864
E-Mail: info@eknifeworks.com
Website: www.eknifeworks.com
Fax Ordering: (865) 428-5991
International Ordering: (865) 453-5871
Contact Name: Kevin Pipes, President
Catalog: Free. Frequency: Quarterly
Circulation: 750M. Sales: $10-20MM
Products: Assorted knives & hunting equipment

SOUTHEASTERN OUTDOOR SUPPLIES (800) 368-5924
537 Old Quary Rd. • Bassett, VA 24055
Fax Ordering: (276) 638-7841
International Ordering: (276) 638-4698
Contact Name: John Hundley, President
Catalog: Free. Frequency: Annual
Circulation: 50M. Sales: $500M to $1MM
Products: Hunting supplies, archery &
sporting goods equipment

SPORTSMAN'S GUIDE CATALOGS (800) 888-3006
411 Farwell Ave. • So. St. Paul, MN 55075 (800) 882-2962
E-Mail: info@sportsmansguide.com
Website: www.sportsmansguide.com
Fax Ordering: (651) 450-6130
International Ordering: (651) 451-3030
Contact Name: Gregory Binkley, President

Catalog: Free. Frequency: 5x per year
Catalogs: Shooting Supplies catalog;
Christmas Gifts catalog; Military Surplus catalog;
Hunting Supplies Catalog.
Circulation: 50MM. Sales: $500MM to $1B
Products: Outdoor apparel, hunting accessories,
fishing & camping equipment

STAFFORDS CATALOG   (800) 826-0948
P.O. Box 2055 • Thomasville, GA 31799
E-Mail: guestbook@staffordcatalog.com
Website: www.staffordcatalog.com
Fax Ordering: (229) 228-1333
International Ordering: (229) 226-4306
Contact Name: G. Warren Stafford, President
Catalog: Free. Frequency: Annual
Circulation: 500M. Sales: $1-3MM
Products: Outdoor apparel, hunting clothes,
gifts, accessories

SURFCASTER CATALOG   (203) 610-6965
360 Sniffens Lane • Stratford, CT 06820
E-Mail: info@surffishing.com
Website: www.surffishing.com
Fax Ordering: (203) 610-6967
Contact Name: William Preinsberger, President
Catalog: Free. Frequency: Semiannual
Circulation: 150M. Sales: $1-3MM
Products: Fishing tackle equipment

TACKLE CATALOG   (800) 344-6331
The Original Mister Twister
P.O. Drawer 1152 • Minden, LA 71058
E-Mail: sales@mistertwister.com
Website: www.mistertwister.com
Fax Ordering: (318) 377-8862
International Ordering: (318) 8818
Catalog: Free. Frequency: Annual
Circulation: 250M. Sales: $1-3MM
Products: Fishing tackle equipment

TACKLE SHOP CATALOG   (800) 707-0208
P.O. Box 830369 • Richardson, TX 75083
Fax Ordering: (972) 690-4044
International Ordering: (972) 231-5982
Contact Name: William Barlow, President
Catalog: Free. Frequency: Annual
Circulation: 100M. Sales: $3-5MM
Products: Fly fishing materials

THOMPSON CENTER ARMS CATALOG   (603) 332-2333
P.O. Box 5002 • Rochester, NH 03866
Fax Ordering: (603) 332-5133
Contact Name: Robert W. Gustafson, President
Catalog: Free. Frequency: Annual
Circulation: 250M. Sales: $10-20MM
Products: Sporting firearms, handguns, rifles

TIDEWATER SPECIALTIES CATALOG   (800) 433-5277
P.O. Box 158 • Wye Mills, MD 21679
Fax Ordering: (410) 364-5215
International Ordering: (410) 745-5678
Contact Name: Don Blouch, President
Catalog: Free. Frequency: Semiannual
Circulation: 600M. Sales: $1-3MM
Products: Gifts & gear for hunters, dog owners
& golfers

WALTER CRAIG CATALOG   (800) 633-2564
Hwy. 22 W • Selma, AL 36702
E-Mail: pkeller@wyoming.com
Website: www.woolcamo.com
Fax Ordering: (334) 875-6627
International Ordering: (334) 875-7989
Contact Name: Ray Denmark, President
Catalog: Free. Frequency: 8x per year
Circulation: 25M. Sales: $20-50MM
Products: Firearms, accessories, hunting
equipment, optics, reloaders, archery,
black powder, guns, etc.

WARM & COLD WEATHER   (800) 334-5457
CLOTHING SYSTEMS CATALOG
Sleeping Indian Designs
P.O. Box 8517 • Jackson, WY 83002
E-Mail: pkeller@wyoming.com
Website: www.woolcamo.com
Fax Ordering: (307) 739-9804
International Ordering: (307) 739-9802
Contact Name: Ted Ranck, President
Catalog: Free. Frequency: Annual
Circulation: 50M. Sales: $1-3MM
Products: Accessories & camouflage
clothing for hunting

WESTBANK ANGLERS   (800) 922-3474
FLY FISHING CATALOG
P.O. Box 523 •Teton Village, WY 83025
E-Mail: custserv@westbank.com
Website: www.westbank.com
Fax Ordering: (307) 733-9382
International Ordering: (307) 733-6483
Contact Name: Baker Salsbury, President
Catalog: Free. Frequency: Annual
Circulation: 100M. Sales: $1-3MM
Products: Fishing tackle & accessories

WILDLIFE TREASURES   (888) 669-0956
16 S. 19th Ave. E. • Ely, MN 55731
E-Mail: info@wildlifetreasures.com
Website: www.wildlifetreasures.com
International Ordering: (218) 365-7799
Contact Name: Pat & Deb Kowal, President
Catalog: Free. Frequency: Annual
Circulation: 50K. Sales: $1-3MM
Products: Gifts for deer hunters, furry
animals, wildlife lovers; clothing

WING SUPPLY CATALOG   (800) 388-9464
Fauntleroy Supply
820 N. Main St. • Greenville, KY 42345
Fax Ordering: (270) 338-0057
International Ordering: (270) 338-5866
Contact Name: Lee Fauntleroy, President
Catalog: Free. Frequency: Annual
Circulation: 50MM. Sales: $1-3MM
Products: Camp clothing & hunting accessories

ALPINEAIRE FOODS
(800) 322-6325
(866) 322-6325
TyRy, Inc.
P.O. Box 1799 • Rocklin, CA 95677
E-Mail: info@aa-foods.com
Website: www.aa-foods.com
Fax Ordering: (916) 624-1604
International Ordering: (916) 624-6050
Contact Name: Greg Karr, President
Catalog: Free. Frequency: Bimonthly
Circulation: 25K. Sales: $1-3MM
Products: Freeze-dried, dehydrated &
ready-to-eat instant meals and foods for
camping, outdoor recreation and RV's

BROADBENT'S CATALOG
(800) 841-2202
257 Mary Blue Rd. • Kuttawa, KY 42055
E-Mail: order@broadbenthams.com
Website: www.broadbenthams.com
Fax Ordering: (270) 388-0613
International Ordering: (270) 235-5294
Contact Name: Ronny Drennan, President
Catalog: Free. Frequency: Annual
Circulation: 25K. Sales: $1-3MM
Products: Country hams & sausages;
sweets & treats; barbecue spices & sauces;
gifts and other country products

BIRKETT MILLS
(315) 536-3311
163 Main St. • Penn Yan, NY 14527
E-Mail: service@thebirkettmills.com
Website: www.thebirkettmills.com
Fax Ordering: (315) 536-6740
Contact Name: Jeffrey S. Gifford, President
Catalog: Free. Frequency: Semiannual
Circulation: 100K. Sales: $5-10MM
Products: Buckwheat products;
Stone-ground flours, & pancake mixes

BOB'S RED MILL NATURAL FOODS
(800) 349-2173
5000 SE International Way
Milwaukee, OR 97222
E-Mail: info@bobsredmill.com
Website: www.bobsredmill.com
Fax Ordering: (503) 653-1339
International Ordering: (503) 654-3215
Customer Service: (800) 349-2173
Contact Name: Bob Moore, President
Catalog: Free. Frequency: Annual
Circulation: 100K. Sales: $10-20MM
Products: Natural & organic whole grain foods

BOUDIN SOURDOUGH GIFTS
(800) 992-1849
Boudin Bakery Gift Catalogue
161 B Starlite • So. San Francisco, CA 94080
E-Mail: catalog@boudinbakery.com
Website: www.boudinbakery.com
Fax Ordering: (800) 992-1877
Catalog: Free. Frequency: Annual
Circulation: 500K. Sales: $5-10MM
Products: Breads & bakery items; gift baskets

BREAD ALONE
(800) 769-3328
Route 28 • Boiceville, NY 12412
E-Mail: info@breadalone.com
Website: www.breadalone.com
Fax Ordering: (845) 657-6228
International Ordering: (845) 657-3328
Contact Name: Daniel M. Leader, President
Catalog: Free. Frequency: Semiannual
Circulation: 50K. Sales: $5-10MM
Products: Organic & whole grain hearth loaf
& sourdough breads

THE CHILE SHOP
(505) 983-6080
109 E. Water St. • Santa Fe, NM 87501
E-Mail: info@thechileshop.com
Website: www.thechileshop.com
Fax Ordering: (505) 984-0737
Catalog: Free. Frequency: Annual
Circulation: 25K. Sales: $250M
Products: Southwest items, chile powders,
herbs; pottery, crystal

DEAN & DELUCA CATALOG
(800) 221-7714
4115 E. Harry • Wichita, KS 67218
E-Mail: customercare@deandeluca.com
Website: www.deandeluca.com
Fax Ordering: (800) 781-4050
International Ordering: (316) 821-3200
Contact Name: Dane Meller, President
Catalog: Free. Frequency: Quarterly
Circulation: 100K. Sales: $10-20MM
Products: Gourmet foods & gift baskets;
specialty foods, desserts, fine wines,
kitchenware, gifts

DELIGHTFUL DELIVERIES
(800) 777-1911
Los Angeles, CA
(800) 941-1334
E-Mail: service@delightfuldeliveries.com
Website: www.delightfuldeliveries.com
Fax Ordering: (310) 626-8473
Contact Name: Gina Ezratty, President
Catalog: Free. Frequency: Semiannual
Circulation: 100K. Sales: $500K
Products: Gourmet food and gift baskets;
flowers; balloons

DUCKTRAP RIVER OF MAINE
(800) 434-8727
57 Little River Dr. • Belfast, ME 04915
E-Mail: smoked@ducktrap.com
Website: www.ducktrap.com
Fax Ordering: (207) 338-6288
International Ordering: (207) 338-6280
Catalog: Free. Frequency: Semiannual
Circulation: 50K. Sales: $500K
Products: Naturally smoked seafood
direct from Maine

FIDDLER'S GREEN FARM
(800) 729-7935
P.O. Box 254 • Belfast, ME 04915
E-Mail: orders@fiddlersgreenfarm.com
Website: www.fiddlersgreenfarm.com
Fax Ordering: (207) 338-3872
Contact Name: Laine Alexander, President
Catalog: Free. Frequency: Annual
Circulation: 15K. Sales: $500K
Products: Organic baking mixes and cereals;
nuts, sweets, organic jams, syrup, coffee, tea,
organic flours and corn meal

FINE FOOD NOW
(800) 423-2942
P.O. Box 8011 • Charlottesville, VA 22906
(800) 350-9937
E-Mail: seycomail@pacbell.net
Website: www.finefoodnow.com
Fax Ordering: (434) 975-2326
Contact Name: Andrew Dunstan, President
Catalog: Free. Frequency: Semiannual
Circulation: 10K. Sales: $500K
Products: Hundreds of unique & hard-to-find
specialty foods

FRENCH MEADOW BAKERY
(877) 669-3278
1000 Apollo Rd. • Eagan, MN 55121
E-Mail: info@frenchmeadow.com
Website: www.frenchmeadow.com

Fax Ordering: (651) 454-3327
International Ordering: (651) 286-7861
Contact Name: Lynn R. Gorden, President
Catalog: Free. Frequency: Annual
Circulation: 10K. Sales: $3-5MM
Products: Certified organic breads, bagels,
rolls and pizza crusts

GOOSEBERRY PATCH　　　(800) 854-6673
P.O. Box 190 • Delaware, OH 43015
E-Mail: info@gooseberrypatch.com
Website: www.gooseberrypatch.com
Fax Ordering: (740) 363-7225
International Ordering: (740) 369-1554
Contact Names: JoAnn Martin & Vickie Hutchins
Catalog: Free. Frequency: Monthly
Circulation: 25K. Sales: $5-10MM
Products: Food gifts and enamelware;
kitchen pottery, cookbooks, ornaments

THE GREAT VALLEY MILLS　　　(800) 688-6455
1774 County Line Rd. • Barto, PA 19504
E-Mail: gym1710@ptd.net
Fax Ordering: (610) 754-6490
International Ordering: (610) 754-7800
Contact Name: Steve Kantoor, President
Catalog: Free. Frequency: Semiannual
Circulation: 25K. Sales: $1-3MM
Products: Homemade country foods, cheeses,
meats and desserts. Family farm grown and
produced foods

HARVEST CATALOG　　　(520) 622-5561
Native Seeds/SEARCH
526 N. 4th Ave. • Tucson, AZ 85705
E-Mail: info@nativeseeds.org
Website: www.nativeseeds.org
Fax Ordering: (520) 622-5591
International Ordering: (520) 622-5561
Contact Name: Mahiena Drees, President
Catalog: Free. Frequency: Annual
Circulation: 25K. Sales: $250-500K
Products: Native seeds; video/audio & CDs;
blank media/tapes

THE HONEYBAKED HAM CO.　　　(800) 892-4267
6145 Merger Dr. • Holland, OH 43528　　(800) 641-8290
E-Mail: hbexpert@hbfoodsinc.com
Website: www.honeybakedcatalog.com
Fax Ordering: (800) 867-3860; (419) 867-3860
Catalog: Free. Frequency: Quarterly
Circulation: 50K. Sales: $1-3MM
Products: Hams, turkeys, cheese, ribs,
and other foods

HOUSE OF WEBSTER CATALOG　　　(800) 369-4641
P.O. Box 1988 • Rogers, AR 72757
E-Mail: info@houseofwebster.com
Website: www.houseofwebster.com
Fax Ordering: (479) 636-2974
International Ordering: (479) 636-4640
Contact Name: Dale Webster, President
Catalog: Free. Frequency: Semiannual
Circulation: 1MM. Sales: $5-10MM
Products: Gift packs; mixes, preserves,
meats, cheeses, spreads, recipes;
gourmet food items

LUNDBERG FAMILY FARMS　　　(530) 882-4551
P.O. Box 369 • Richvale, CA 95974
E-Mail: info@lundberg.com
Website: www.lundberg.com

Fax Ordering: (530) 882-4500
Contact Name: Eldon Lundberg, President
Catalog: Free. Frequency: Semiannual
Circulation: 50K. Sales: $10-50MM
Products: Organic rice products

MORABITO'S BAKING COMPANY　　　(800) 525-7747
757 Kohn St. • Norristown, PA 19401
E-Mail: sales@morabito.com
Website: www.morabito.com
Fax Ordering: (610) 275-0358
International Ordering: (610) 275-5419
Contact Name: Michael A. Morabito, Jr., President
Catalog: Free. Frequency: Semiannual
Circulation: 50K. Sales: $3-5MM
Products: Manufacturer of Italian, Jewish,
Sourdough and Pita breads and rolls.

NASFT SPECIALTY FOODS CATALOG　　　(800) 627-3869
National Assn for the Specialty Food Trade
120 Wall St., 27th Floor • New York, NY 10005
E-Mail: info@specialtyfood.com
Website: www.specialtyfood.com
Fax Ordering: (212) 482-6459
International Ordering: (212) 482-6440
Contact Name: John Roberts, President
Catalog: $5. Frequency: Annual
Circulation: 50K. Sales: $1-3MM
Products: Specialty foods; seminars &
educational programs

RED COOPER CATALOG　　　(800) 876-4733
P.O. Box 3089 • Mission, TX 78573
E-Mail: sales@redcooper.com
Website: www.redcooper.com
Fax Ordering: (956) 205-7331
Customer Service: (800) 825-8531
Contact Name: Red Cooper, President
Catalog: Free. Frequency: Quarterly
Circulation: 150K. Sales: $1-3MM
Products: Fruit gift baskets; dried fruits;
smoked meats

WESTERN TRAILS　　　(406) 377-4284
313 W. Valentine • Glendive, MT 59330
E-Mail: info@westerntrailsfood.com
Website: www.westerntrailsfood.com
Fax Ordering: (406) 377-4284
Contact Name: Jean Clem, President
Catalog: Free. Frequency: Annual
Circulation: 25K. Sales: $1-3MM
Products: Hulless Barley grains, soups,
flours, cereals and barbecue sauces

WOLFERMAN'S CATALOG　　　(800) 798-6241
P.O. Box 9100 • Medford, OR 97501
E-Mail: wolf@wolfermans.com
Website: www.wolfermans.com
Fax Ordering: (800) 999-7548
Customer Service: (800) 999-0169
Contact Name: Margaret Hartnett, Marketing
Catalog: Free. Frequency: Monthly
Circulation: 2MM. Sales: $10-20MM
Products: English muffins & other gourmet
breads, scones, crompets, and desserts,
all available in gift baskets and towers.

ZINGERMAN'S MAIL ORDER CUPBOARD　　　(888) 636-8162
422 Detroit St. • Ann Arbor, MI 48104
E-Mail: service@zingermans.com
Website: www.zingermans.com
Fax Ordering: (734) 477-6988

International Ordering: (734) 769-1625
Contact Name: Mo Frechette, Marketing
Catalog: Free. Frequency: 3x per year
Circulation: 60K. Sales: $3-5MM
Products: Traditionally made foods and gifts:
sweet stuff, breads, cheese, olive oil & vinegar

CANDY, CHOCOLATE, NUTS, DESSERTS

AMERICANDY (502) 583-1776
1401 Lexington Rd. • Louisville, KY 40206
E-Mail: omar@americandy.com
Website: www.americandy.com
Fax Ordering: (502) 583-6627
Contact Name: Omar L. Tatum, President
Catalog: Free. Frequency: Quarterly
Circulation: 25K. Sales: $250-500K
Products: 50 state gourmet chocolates
representing America, tastefully packaged
in red, white and blue gift boxes.

ANDRE'S CONFISERIE SUISSE (800) 892-1234
5018 Main St. • Kansas City, MO 64112
E-Mail: customer_service@andreschocolates.com
Website: www.andreschocolates.com
Fax Ordering: (816) 561-2922
International Ordering: (816) 561-6484
Contact Name: Marcel Bollier, President
Catalog: Free. Frequency: Annual
Circulation: 25K. Sales: $1-3MM
Products: Swiss chocolate candies

APLETS & COTLETS (800) 888-5696
Liberty Orchards Co.
117 Mission Ave. • Cashmere, WA 98815
E-Mail: service@libertyorchards.com
Website: www.libertyorchards.com
Fax Ordering: (509) 782-4776
International Ordering: (509) 782-1000
Contact Name: Greg Taylor, President
Catalog: Free. Frequency: Semiannual
Circulation: 50K. Sales: $1-3MM
Products: Manufacturer of fruit & nut candy,
chocolates baked goods and gifts.

ART COCO CHOCOLATE COMPANY (877) 232-9901 2248
Gary Lane • Geneva, IL 60134
E-Mail: info@artcoco.com
Website: www.artcoco.com
Fax Ordering: (630) 232-2528
International Ordering: (630) 232-2500
Contact Name: Ken Wolf, President
Catalog: Free. Frequency: Annual
Circulation: 25K. Sales: $1-3MM
Products: Assortment of fine chocolates

ASTOR CHOCOLATE CATALOG (732) 901-1000
651 New Hampshire Ave.
Lakewood, NJ 08701
E-Mail: info@astorchocolate.com
Website: www.astorchocolate.com
Fax Ordering: (732) 901-1003
Contact Name: Erwin Grunhut, President
Catalog: Free. Frequency: Bimonthly
Circulation: 25K. Sales: $5-10MM
Products: Gourmet chocolates;
mints, truffles and gift boxes

BATES BROTHERS NUT FARM (800) 642-0348
15954 Woods Valley Rd.
Valley Center, CA 92082
E-Mail: info@batesnutfarm.biz
Website: www.batesnutfarm.biz
Fax Ordering: (760) 749-9499
International Ordering: (760) 749-333
Contact Names: Walter Bates, President
Catalog: Free. Frequency: Annual
Circulation: 50K. Sales: $1-3MM
Products: Nuts, candy, dried fruits

BEANS WITHOUT THE BANG (800) 648-4851
CRM Farms, Inc.
P.O. Box 237 • Gooding, ID 83330
E-Mail: fartless@fartless.com
Website: www.fartless.com
Fax Ordering: (208) 934-5969
International Ordering: (208) 934-4527
Catalog: Free. Frequency: Quarterly
Circulation: 10K. Sales: $500K
Products: Chili, pancake mix, popcorn,
bean dip and beans without the gas;
gift boxes

BELLOWS HOUSE BAKERY (800) 358-6302
P.O. Box 818 • Walpole, NH 03608
E-Mail: info@bellowshouse.com
Website: www.bellowshouse.com
Fax Ordering: (603) 445-1973
International Ordering: (603) 445-1974
Contact Name: Lois Ford, President
Catalog: Free. Frequency: Semiannual
Circulation: 25K. Sales: $500K - $1MM
Products: Cookies, brownies, shortbread,
fruit squares, whoopie pies, scones, gifts.

BISSINGER FRENCH CONFECTIONS (800) 325-8881
3983 Gratiot St. • St. Louis, MO 63110
E-Mail: orders@bissingers.com
Website: www.bissingers.com
Fax Ordering: (314) 534-2419
International Ordering: (314) 534-2401
Contact Name: M. Kolbrener, President
Catalog: Free. Frequency: Quarterly
Circulation: 1MM. Sales: $3-5MM
Products: French confections, including
gurmet chocolates; cakes, cookies, gourmet
candies, chocolate-covered fruit, and pies;
specializes in petit fours double-dipped in
chocolate with a choice of fillings.

BOWLBY'S INC. (800) 826-0492
P.O. Box 312 • Waupaca, WI 54981
E-Mail: sales@bowlbys.com
Website: www.bowlbys.com
Fax Ordering: (715) 258-2734
International Ordering: (715) 258-3711
Contact Name: Kostas Tsantir, President
Catalog: Free. Frequency: Quarterly
Circulation: 50M. Sales: $1-3MM
Products: Bowlby's Bits; nuts & gourmet
candies and caramel corn

BUCHANAN HOLLOW NUT FARM (800) 532-1500
6510 Minturn Rd. • Le Grand, CA 95333
E-Mail: bhnc@bhnc.com
Website: www.bhnc.com
Fax Ordering: (209) 389-4321
International Ordering: (209) 389-4594
Contact Names: Sharleen Robson, President
Catalog: Free. Frequency: Annual

Circulation: 100K. **Sales:** $1-3MM
Products: Almonds, pistachios; pastel
chocolate cherries, gift baskets

BYRD COOKIE COMPANY (800) 291-2973
P.O. Box 13086 • Savannah, GA 31416
E-Mail: custserv@byrdcookiecompany.com
Website: www.byrdcookiecompany.com
Fax Ordering: (912) 355-4431
International Ordering: (912) 355-1716
Contact Name: Amy Waddell, Marketing Manager
Catalog: Free. Frequency: 3x per year
Circulation: 25K. **Sales:** $5-10MM
Products: Gourmet cookies and cocktail snacks,
Keylime coolers, raspberry tarts, Benne wafers
and cinnamon & mint chip cookies; gift sets,
baskets & towers.

CAJUN PECAN HOUSE (800) 432-2586
14808 West Main • Cut Off, LA 70345
E-Mail: cajun@mobiletel.com
Website: www.cajunpecanhouse.com
Fax Ordering: (985) 632-7525
International Ordering: (985) 632-2337
Catalog: Free. Frequency: Annual
Circulation: 50K. **Sales:** $500K
Products: Pecans, pecan pies, fruitcakes
with pecans; pineapple & cherries

CATHERINE'S CHOCOLATE SHOP (800) 345-2462
260 Stockbridge Rd.
Great Barrington, MA 01230
E-Mail: info@catherineschocolates.net
Website: www.catherineschocolates.net
Fax Ordering: (413) 528-6052
International Ordering: (413) 528-2510
Contact Name: Kathleen Sinico, President
Catalog: Free. Frequency: 3x per year
Circulation: 25K. **Sales:** $250-500K
Products: Hand-dipped chocolates,
candles and gifts

CHERYL & COMPANY (800) 367-2714
GOURMET FOODS & GIFTS (800) 443-8124
646 McCorkle Blvd. • Westerville, OH 43082
E-Mail: sales@cherylandco.com
Website: www.cherylandco.com
Fax Ordering: (614) 891-8699
International Ordering: (614) 776-1529
Customer Service: (800) 367-2715
Catalog: Free. Frequency: Semiannual
Circulation: 50K. **Sales:** $250-500M
Products: Gift baskets and gifts featuring
cookies and candy

CHOCOLATE INN (516) 887-4445
7 Bixley Heath • Lynbrook, NY 11563
E-Mail: info@chocolateinn.com
Website: www.chocolateinn.com
Fax Ordering: (516) 887-1245
Contact Name: George Miller, President
Brochures: Free. Frequency: Annual
Catalog: 25K. **Sales:** $1-3MM
Products: Custom molded chocolates

CHUKAR CHERRY CO. (800) 624-9544
P.O. Box 510 • Prosser, WA 99350
E-Mail: sales@chukar.com
Website: www.chukar.com
Fax Ordering: (509) 786-2591
Catalog: Free. Frequency: Annual.
Circulation: 150K. **Sales:** $1-3MM

Products: Baskets, chocolate covered
cherries, dried fruit, preserves & sauces

COLLIN STREET BAKERY (800) 504-1896
401 W. 7th Ave. • Corsicana, TX 75110 (800) 292-7400
E-Mail: info@collinstreetbakery.com
Website: www.collinstreetbakery.com
Fax Ordering: (903) 872-6879
International Ordering: (903) 475-3589
Customer Service: (800) 267-4657
Contact Name: John Crawford, Marketing
Catalog: Free. Frequency: Semiannual
Circulation: 3MM. **Sales:** $20-50MM
Products: Fruitcake & Pecan Cakes;
cheesecakes, pecan pies, breads &
muffins, gift sets

COOKIE BOUQUETS (800) 233-2171
6665-H Huntley Rd. • Columbus, OH 43229
E-Mail: chips@cookiebouquets.com
Website: www.cookiebouquets.com
Fax Ordering: (614) 841-3950
International Ordering: (614) 888-2171
Contact Name: Dinene Clark, President
Catalog: Free. Frequency: Semiannual
Circulation: 50K. **Sales:** $1-5MM
Products: Floral-like bouquets of freshly
baked, colorfully wrapped chocolate chip
cookies for all occasions.

COOKIE GARDEN (800) 582-9191
362 Belnoris Dr. • Wood Dale, IL 60191
E-Mail: webmaster@cookiegarden.com
Website: www.cookiegarden.com
International Ordering: (630) 766-3040
Contact Name: David Anfuso, Owner
Catalog: Free. Frequency: Quarterly
Circulation: 50K. **Sales:** $1-3MM
Products: Cookies; fruit collections & baskets;
tote bags, flowers; baby & kid gifts; holiday gifts;
themed gifts.

COOKIES FOR YOU (800) 814-5334
117 S. Main St. • Minot. ND 58701
E-Mail: sales@cookiesforyou.com
Website: www.cookiesforyou.com
Fax Ordering: (701) 838-8874
International Ordering: (701) 839-4975
Catalog: Free. Frequency: Semiannual
Circulation: 25K. **Sales:** $250-500K
Products: Homemade cookie gifts,
gift baskets and tins

COUNTRY KITCHEN SWEETART (800) 497-3927
4621 Speedway Dr. • Fort Wayne, IN 46825
E-Mail: cntryktchn.aol.com
Website: www.countrykitchensa.com
Fax Ordering: (260) 483-4091
Customer Service: (260) 482-4835
Contact Name: Vi Whittington, President
Catalog: Free. Frequency: Annual
Circulation: 50K. **Sales:** $500K - $1MM
Products: Cake and candy supplies,
ideas and recipes

CRYER CREEK KITCHENS (800) 468-0088
401 West 7th Ave. • Corsicana, TX 75110
E-Mail: info@cryercreekkitchens.com
Website: www.cryercreekkitchens.com
Fax Ordering: (903) 654-6725
International Ordering: (903) 872-8411
Customer Service: (800) 353-7437

Contact Name: Norman E. Shaw, President
Catalog: Free. Frequency: Annual
Circulation: 50K. Sales: $500K - $1MM
Products: Handmade desserts: cookies,
nuts and brittle, cheesecakes, fruit and
pecan cakes

DAVID ALAN CHOCOLATIER (800) 428-2310
1700 N. Lebanon St. • Lebanon, IN 46052
E-Mail: david@davidalanchoc.com
Website: www.davidalanchoc.com
Fax Ordering: (765) 482-5660
International Ordering: (765) 482-7273
Contact Name: David Alan Honan, President
Catalog: Free. Frequency: Weekly
Circulation: 60K. Sales: $500M
Products: Swiss-style truffles; fruits & nuts

DeSOTO CONFECTIONARY & NUT CO. (800) 237-8689
Crickle Co. (800) 330-8351
5415 Opportunity Ct. • Hopkins, MN 55343
E-Mail: sales@crickle.com
Website: www.crickle.com
Fax Ordering: (952) 933-9942
International Ordering: (952) 933-9732
Contact Name: Harry Jones, Contact
Catalog: Free. Frequency: Annual
Circulation: 30K. Sales: $500M to 1MM
Products: Pecans, peanuts, popcorn,
and candies

DESSERTS BY DAVID GLASS (860) 769-5570
1280 Blue Hills Ave. • Bloomfield, CT 06002
E-Mail: david@davidglass.com
Website: www.davidglass.com
Fax Ordering: (860) 242-4408
International Ordering: (860) 769-5570
Contact Name: David Glass, President
Catalog: Free. Frequency: Annual
Circulation: 25K. Sales: $1-3MM
Products: Gourmet desserts, including
chocolate mousse & chocolate truffle cakes

eDIET SHOPPE (800) 325-5409
P.O. Box 1037 • Evanston, IL 60204
E-Mail: editshop@edietshop.com
Website: www.ediet-shop.com
Fax Ordering: (847) 679-5417
International Ordering: (847) 679-5409
Catalog: Free. Frequency: Annual
Circulation: 25K. Sales: $500K to 1MM
Products: Sugar-free candies & chocolate

DIVINE DELIGHTS (800) 443-2836
1250 Holm Rd. • Petaluma, CA 94954
E-Mail: info@divinedelights.com
Website: www.divinedelights.com
International Ordering: (707) 782-9826
Contact Name: Bill Fry, Owner
Catalog: Free. Frequency: Quarterly
Circulation: 60K. Sales: $500K - $1MM
Products: Petits fours; cookies, cakes
& tarts; chocolate confections; tea;
samplers & baskets

DUREY LIBBY EDIBLE NUTS (800) 332-6887
100 Industrial Rd. • Carlstadt, NJ 07072
E-Mail: info@dureylibby.com
Website: www.dureylibby.com
Fax Ordering: (201) 939-0386
International Ordering: (201) 939-2775
Contact Names: Reba Dicker, President

Catalog: Free. Frequency: Weekly
Circulation: 100K. Sales: $1-3MM
Products: Wholesale nuts & seeds,
dried fruit & candy

EARTHY DELIGHTS (800) 367-4709
1161 E. Clark Rd., #260
DeWitt, MI 48820
E-Mail: information@earthy.com
Website: www.earthy.com
Fax Ordering: (517) 668-1213
International Ordering: (517) 668-2402
Contact Name: Ed Baker, President
Catalog: Free. Frequency: Annual
Circulation: 150K. Sales: $5-10MM
Products: Gourmet specialty foods for
the professional chefs

EILENBERGER'S BAKERY (800) 788-2996
P.O. Box 710 • Palestine, TX 75802
E-Mail: customercare@eilenbergerbakery.com
Website: www.eilenbergerbakery.com
Fax Ordering: (903) 723-2889
International Ordering: (903) 729-2176
Contact Name: Sarah Pryor, Manager
Catalog: Free. Frequency: Quarterly
Circulation: 250K. Sales: $1-3MM
Products: Australian cake, fruit cakes,
Texas pecan cake, apricot angels,
pound cakes & candied coated pecans.

ELI'S CHEESECAKE COMPANY (800) 999-8300
6701 W. Forest Preserve Dr. (800) 354-2253
Chicago, IL 60634
E-Mail: sales@elicheesecake.com
Website: www.elicheesecake.com
Fax Ordering: (773) 205-3801
International Ordering: (773) 736-3417
Contact Name: Marc S. Schulman, President
Catalog: Free. Frequency: Annual
Circulation: 100K. Sales: $10-50MM
Products: Cheesecake, & other specialty desserts

ENSTROM CANDIES (800) 367-8766
P.O. Box 1088 • Grand Junction, CO 81502
E-Mail: toffee@enstrom.com
Website: www.enstrom.com
Fax Ordering: (970) 683-1011
International Ordering: (970) 242-1655
Contact Name: Doug Simons, President
Catalog: Free. Frequency: Annual
Circulation: 50K. Sales: $3-5MM
Products: Assorted candies; almond toffee;
gourmet chocolate; sugar free almond toffee,
toffee popcorn, nut assortment; gift items

ETHEL M. CHOCOLATES (800) 438-4356
P.O. Box 91030 • Allentown, PA 18109 (800) 471-0352
E-Mail: info@ethelschocolate.com
Website: www.ethelschocolate.com
Fax Ordering: (800) 392-2587
Media Inquiries: (702) 433-2595
Catalog: Free. Frequency: Quarterly
Circulation: 50K. Sales: $500K - $1MM
Products: Chocolates

FANNIE MAY CANDIES (800) 333-3629
8550 W. Bryn Mawr Ave. #550
Chicago, IL 60631
E-Mail: customerservice@fanniemay.com
Website: www.fanniemay.com
Fax Ordering: (888) 600-3629

International Ordering: (312) 243-2700
Contact Name: Ted Shepherd, President
Catalog: Free. Frequency: Annual
Circulation: 250K. Sales: $50-100MM
Products: Candy, chocolates, nuts, cookbooks

FAIRYTALE BROWNIES   (800) 324-7982
4610 E. Cotton Center Blvd. #100
Phoenix, AZ 85040
E-Mail: orders@brownies.com
Website: www.brownies.com
Fax Ordering: (602) 489-5122
International Ordering: (602) 489-5100
Customer Service: (800) 531-5209
Contact Name: Eileen Spitalny, President
Catalog: Free. Frequency: 5x per year
Circulation: 50K. Sales: $1-3MM
Products: Belgian chocolate brownies; nut-base brownies; sugar free brownies; coffee, cocoa & tea; specialty gift packages

FERIDIES PEANUT PATCH   (800) 544-0896
P.O. Box 186 • Courtland, VA 23837   (866) 732-6883
E-Mail: customerservice@feridies.com
Website: www.feridies.com
Fax Ordering: (757) 653-9530
International Ordering: (757) 653-2028
Contact Name: Judy Riddick, President
Catalog: Free. Frequency: 3x per year
Circulation: 100K. Sales: $1-3MM
Products: Gourmet Virginia peanuts & peanut candies; hams and gourmet foods; gift assortments & baskets

GOLDEN KERNEL PECAN COMPANY   (800) 845-2448
P.O. Box 613 • Cameron, SC 29030
E-Mail: info@goldenkernel.com
Website: www.goldenkernel.com
Fax Ordering: (803) 823-2080
International Ordering: (803) 823-2311
Contact Name: David K. Summers, Jr., President
Catalog: Free. Frequency: Annual
Circulation: 25K. Sales: $1-3MM
Products: Pecans, nuts, candies, fruit cakes, hams

GOODIVA CHOCOLATIER   (800) 946-3482
139 Mill Rock Rd. East
Old Saybrook, CT 06475
E-Mail: customerservice@godivachoc.com
Website: www.godiva.com
Fax Ordering: (860) 510-7331
International Ordering: (860) 510-7300
Contact Name: Thomas H. Fey, President
Catalog: Free. Frequency: Quarterly
Circulation: 3MM. Sales: $20-50MM
Products: Chocolates, Godiva special roast coffee, Godiva ice cream

GOURMET GIFT BASKETS.COM   (866) 842-1050
1050 Holt Ave. • Manchester, NH 03109
E-Mail: sales@gourmetgiftbaskets.com
Website: www.gourmetgiftbaskets.com
Fax Ordering: (603) 657-9083
International Ordering: (603) 606-5269
Customer Service: (888) 208-3098
Catalog: Free. Frequency: Semiannual
Circulation: 50K. Sales: $3-5MM
Products: Gourmet fruit cakes & dessert cakes made from fruits and

GRANDMA'S BAKE SHOPPE   (800) 228-4030
Beatrice Bakery Co.
201 S. 5th St. • Beatrice, NE 68310
E-Mail: rony@metzbaking.com
Website: www.grandmasbakeshoppe.com
Fax Ordering: (402) 223-4465
International Ordering: (402) 223-2358
Contact Name: Rebecca Brown, Sales Rep.
Catalog: Free. Frequency: Annual
Circulation: 50K. Sales: $3-5MM
Products: Gourmet fruit cakes & dessert cakes made from fruits and nuts, brandies, rum and bonded bourbon.

HAMMONS BLACK WALNUTS   (800) 872-6879
Hammons Product Co.   (888) 429-6887
P.O. Box 140 • Stockton, MO 65785
E-Mail: kernelinfo@black-walnuts.com
Website: www.hammonsproducts.com
Fax Ordering: (417) 276-5187
International Ordering: (417) 276-5181
Customer Service: (800) 872-6879
Contact Name: Susan Zartman, Manager
Catalog: Free. Frequency: Annual
Circulation: 50K. Sales: $10-20MM
Products: Black walnuts, cakes, cookies, fudges and candies

HARBOR CANDY SHOP   (800) 331-5856
248 MAIN ST.• Ogunnquit, ME 03907
E-Mail: info@harborcandy.com
Website: www.harborcandy.com
Fax Ordering: (207) 646-0599
International Ordering: (207) 646-8078
Contact Name: Jean Sotoripoulos, President
Catalog: Free. Frequency: Semiannual
Circulation: 10K. Sales: $500K to $1MM
Products: Candy, handmade chocolates from Maine

HARBOR SWEETS   (800) 243-2115
Palmer Cove • 85 Leavitt St.
Salem, MA 01970
E-Mail: info@harborsweets.com
Website: www.harborsweets.com
Fax Ordering: (207) 832-0806
International Ordering: (978) 745-7648
Customer Service: (800) 234-4860
Contact Name: Phyllis B. LeBlanc, Owner
Catalog: Free. Frequency: Semiannual
Circulation: 10K. Sales: $500M to $1MM
Products: Handmade chocolates

HARRY LONDON'S CANDIES   (800) 321-0444
P.O. Box 663 • Westerville, OH 43086   (800) 444-3629
E-Mail: customerservice@harrylondon.com
Website: www.harrylondon.com
Fax Ordering: (330) 499-6902
International Ordering: (330) 494-0833
Contact Name: Allison Waggoner, President
Brochure: Free. Frequency: Semiannual
Circulation: 50K. Sales: $25-50MM
Products: Gourmet chocolates and candies

HERSHEY'S GIFT CATALOG   (800) 454-7737
P.O. Box 801 • Hershey, PA 17033   (800) 233-2168
E-Mail: info@hersheygifts.com   (800) 468-1714
Website: www.hersheys.com
Fax Ordering: (717) 534-5995/7947
International Ordering: (717) 534-4900
Contact Name: Albe Kerkendall, Marketing

Catalog: Free. Frequency: Bimonthly
Circulation: 3MM. Sales: $10-50MM
Products: Chocolates & other related food gifts

HONEY OF A CATALOG   (800) 558-7745
Honey Acres
P.O. Box 46 • Ashippun, WI 53003
E-Mail: info@honeyacres.com
Website: www.honeyacres.com
Fax Ordering: (920) 474-4018
International Ordering: (920) 474-4411
Contact Name: Walter J. Diehnelt, President
Catalog: Free. Frequency: Annual
Circulation: 10M. Sales: $1-3MM
Products: Honey, gifts, honey candy &
honey mustard

HONEY OF A GIFT   (800) 225-7553
Queen Bee Gardens
1863 Lane 11.5 • Lovell, WY 82431
E-Mail: spitt@queenbeegardens.com
Website: www.queenbeegardens.com
Fax Ordering: (307) 548-6721
International Ordering: (307) 548-2543
Contact Name: Clarence Zeller, President
Catalog: Free. Frequency: Semiannual
Circulation: 10K. Sales: $500K
Products: Truffles, almond bark, honey moons,
English toffee, pralines and caramel kisses;
gift packs of pure Wyoming honey.

HUBBARD PEANUT COMPANY   (800) 889-7688
P.O. Box 94 • Sedley, VA 23878
E-Mail: hubs@hubspeanuts.com
Website: www.hubspeanuts.com
Fax Ordering: (757) 562-2741
Contact Name: Lynne H. Rabi, President
Catalog: Free. Frequency: Annual
Circulation: 50K. Sales: $1-3MM
Products: Peanuts from Virginia

LINDA'S DIET DELITES   (866) 833-0634
1049A Raritan Rd. • Clark, NJ 07066
E-Mail: candies@lindasdietdelites.com
Website: www.lindasdietdelites.com
International Ordering: (732) 382-1099
Catalog: Free. Frequency: Annual
Circulation: 25K. Sales: $3-5MM
Products: Low Carb, Low Calorie,
& Gluten Free cookies, muffins, pies,
chocolate truffles, donuts

KOEZE DIRECT   (800) 555-9688
2555 Burlingame Ave. SW
Grand Rapids, MI 49509
E-Mail: service@koezedirect.com
Website: www.koezedirect.com
Fax Ordering: (866) 817-0147; (616) 243-5430
International Ordering: (616) 245-5700
Customer Service: (800) 555-9688 ext. 2
Contact Name: Jeffrey S. Koeze, President
Catalog: Free. Frequency: Semiannual
Circulation: 150K. Sales: $5-10MM
Products: Colossal cashews, mixed nuts,
mixed nuts with Macadamias, pistachios,
chocolates, cream-nut peanut butter,
caramel corn, chocolate-dipped dried fruit

KOINONIA PARTNERS   (877) 738-1741
1324 Georgia Hwy. 49 S
Americus, GA 31709
E-Mail: products@koinoniapartners.com

Website: www.koinoniapartners.com
Fax Ordering: (229) 924-6504
International Ordering: (229) 924-0391
Contact Name: Sandra Thornburgh, Fulfillment
Catalog: Free. Frequency: Annual
Circulation: 50K. Sales: $1-3MM
Products: Pecans, chocolates, granola,
coffee, fruitcakes, peanuts, carob; books
& tapes

LAKE CHAMPLAIN CHOCOLATES   (800) 465-5909
750 Pine St. • Burlington, VT 05401   (800) 634-8105
E-Mail: info@lakechamplainchocolate.com
Website: www.lakechamplainchocolate.com
Fax Ordering: (802) 864-1806
International Ordering: (802) 864-1808
Contact Name: Jim Lampman, President
Catalog: Free. Frequency: Semiannual
Circulation: 50K. Sales: $5-10MM
Products: Gourmet chocolates

LAMMES CANDIES   (800) 252-1885
P.O. Box 1885 • Austin, TX 78767
E-Mail: info@lammes.com
Website: www.lammes.com
Fax Ordering: (512) 238-2019
International Ordering: (512) 310-2223
Contact Name: David Teich, President
Catalog: Free. Frequency: Semiannual
Circulation: 50K. Sales: $5-10MM
Products: Chocolates candies; taffies
& toffee; assorted chocolates

MALLEY'S CHOCOLATES   (800) 275-6255
13400 Brookpark Rd.
Cleveland, OH 44135
E-Mail: contact@malleys.com
Website: www.malleys.com
Fax Ordering: (216) 226-0643
International Ordering: (216) 226-8300
Contact Name: Adele Ryan Malley, President
Catalog: Free. Frequency: Annual
Circulation: 25K. Sales: $1-3MM
Products: Chocolates

MANHATTAN FRUITIER   (800) 841-5718
105 E. 29th St. • New York, NY 10016
E-Mail: info@manhattanfruitier.com
Website: www.manhattanfruitier.com
Fax Ordering: (212) 686-0479
International Ordering: (212) 686-0404
Catalog: Free. Frequency: Semiannual
Circulation: 100K. Sales: $3-5MM
Products: Fruit baskets, flowers, fine
food gifts

MARSHALL'S FUDGE   (800) 343-8343
Marshall's, Inc.
308 E. Central Ave.
Mackinaw City, MI 49701
E-Mail: info@marshallsfudge.com
Website: www.marshallsfudge.com
Fax Ordering: (231) 436-5107
International Ordering: (231) 436-5082
Contact Name: Joseph D. Scheerems, President
Catalog: Free. Frequency: Annual
Circulation: 25K. Sales: $500K - $1MM
Products: Fudge and homemade candies

MARY OF PUDDIN HILL   (800) 545-8889
P.O. Box 241 • Greenville, TX 75403
E-Mail: customerservice@puddinhill.com

Website: www.puddinhill.com
Fax Ordering: (903) 455-4522
International Ordering: (903) 455-2651
Contact Name: Ron Massey, President
Catalog: Free. Frequency: Quarterly
Circulation: 50K. Sales: $1-5MM
Products: Chocolates, cakes, candies,
gift packages

MATTHEWS 1812 HOUSE   (800) 662-1812
P.O. Box 15 • Cornwall Bridge, CT 06754
E-Mail: info@matthews1812house.com
Website: www.matthews1812house.com
Fax Ordering: (860) 672-1812
International Ordering: (860) 672-0149
Contact Name: Blaine Matthews, Manager
Catalog: Free. Frequency: Annual
Circulation: 50K. Sales: $500K to $1MM
Products: Cakes & tortes, chocolate explosion
brownies, candies, fruits, nuts, sauces & syrups

MISSOURI DANDY PANTRY   (800) 872-6879
414 North St. • Stockton, MO 65785
Fax Ordering: (417) 276-5187
International Ordering: (417) 485-2311
Contact Name: Donna Hammons, President
Catalog: Free. Frequency: Quarterly
Circulation: 150K. Sales: $1-3MM
Products: Black walnuts, cashews,
pecans, almonds, candy, gift packs

MORAVIAN SUGAR CRISP COMPANY   (888) 764-1402
Mrs. Hanes Moravian Cookie Crisps
4643 Friedberg Church Rd.
Clemmons, NC 27012
E-Mail: hanes@hanescookies.com
Fax Ordering: (888) 764-4072; (336) 764-8637
International Ordering: (336) 764-1402
Contact Name: Hanes Templin, President
Catalog: Free. Frequency: Semiannual
Circulation: 75K. Sales: $500K - $1MM
Products: Handmade, unique cookies
n six flavors; gift packs

MOTHER MYRICK'S CONFECTIONERY   (888) 669-7425
P.O. Box 1142 • Manchester Center, VT 05255
E-Mail: callmom@mothermyricks.com
Website: www.mothermyricks.com
Fax Ordering: (802) 362-6001
International Ordering: (802) 362-1560
Contact Name: Jacqueline Baker, President
Catalog: Free. Frequency: Quarterly
Circulation: 25K. Sales: $1-3MM
Products: Chocolates, cakes & cookies; gift baskets

MRS. BEASLEY'S FOOD   (800) 710-7742
16803 Central Ave. • Carson, CA 90746
E-Mail: general@mrsbeasleys.com
Website: www.mrsbeasleys.com
Fax Ordering: (800) 668-2148; (310) 668-2148
International Ordering: (310) 668-2105
Contact Name: Ken Harris, President
Catalog: Free. Frequency: Quarterly
Circulation: 1MM. Sales: $5-10MM
Products: Specialty gourmet desserts

MRS. FIELDS GOURMET GIFTS   (800) 266-5437
Mrs. Fields Gifts, Inc.
440 W. Lawndale Dr.
Salt Lake City, UT 84115
E-Mail: giftideas@mrsfields.com
Website: www.mrsfields.com

Fax Ordering: (801) 412-8899
International Ordering: (402) 223-2358
Contact Name: Barry Berccha, President
Catalog: Free. Pages: 8. Frequency: 6x per year
Circulation: 60K. Sales: $5-10MM
Products: Assorted cookies and gifts

MYER'S GOURMET POPCORN   (800) 684-1155
8025 W. US Hwy. 24 • Cascade, CO 80809
E-Mail: ppgpop@aol.com
Fax Ordering: (719) 684-2402
International Ordering: (719) 684-9174
Contact Name: Mike Myers, President
Catalog: Free. Frequency: Semiannual
Circulation: 35K. Sales: $500K - $1MM
Products: Gourmet popcorn in flavors

THE NUTHOUSE/THREE GEORGES   (800) 633-1306
558 S. Broad St. • Mobile, AL 36603
E-Mail: sales@threegeorges.com
Website: www.3georges.com
Fax Ordering: (334) 433-3364
International Ordering: (334) 433-1689
Contact Name: Scott Gonzalez, President
Catalog: Free. Frequency: Annual
Circulation: 100K. Sales: $1-3MM
Products: Pecans, nuts, chocolates,
candy, bakery goods, gift items

THE ORIGINAL YA-HOO! BAKING CO.   (888) 869-2466
5302 Texoma Pkwy. • Sherman, TX 75090
E-Mail: customerservice@yahoocake.com
Website: www.yahoocake.com
Fax Ordering: (903) 893-5036
International Ordering: (903) 893-8151
Contact Name: David A. Millican, Manager
Catalog: Free. Frequency: Annual
Circulation: 100K. Sales: $3-5MM
Products: Cakes, cookies, brownies,
teacakes, and specialty desserts

PARADIGM FOODWORKS   (800) 234-0250
5875 Lakeview Blvd. #100
Lake Oswego, OR 97035
E-Mail: info@paradigmfoodworks.com
Website: www.paradigmfoodworks.com
Fax Ordering: (503) 636-4886
International Ordering: (503) 595-4360
Contact Name: Lynne Barra, President
Catalog: Free. Frequency: Annual
Circulation: 25K. Sales: $3-5MM
Products: Specialty foods and chocolates

PEARL RIVER PASTRY & CHOCOLATES   (800) 632-2639
4 Dexter Plaza • Pearl River, NY 10965
E-Mail: info@prpastry.com
Website: www.prpastry.com
Fax Ordering: (845) 735-6434
International Ordering: (845) 735-5100
Catalog: Free. Frequency: Annual
Circulation: 150K. Sales: $5-10MM
Products: Chocolates and confections

PENN STREET BAKERY   (800) 842-2537
Savory Foods, Inc.   (800) 878-2583
900 Hynes, SW • Grand Rapids, MI 49507
E-Mail: sales@pennstreet.com
Website: www.pennstreetbakery.com
Fax Ordering: (616) 241-6332
International Ordering: (616) 241-2583
Contact Name: Dan Abraham, President
Catalog: Free. Frequency: Quarterly

Circulation: 250K. **Sales:** $5-10MM
Products: Gourmet gift baskets; Penn Street cakes, hand dipped chocolates and homemade cookies available in designer tins & gift baskets.

PERFECTLY SWEET (800) 815-0009
7292 NW 25th St. • Miami, FL 33122
E-Mail: orders@perfectlysweet.com
Website: www.perfectlysweet.com
Fax Ordering: (305) 477-5582
International Ordering: (305) 477-6700
Contact Name: David Taks, President
Catalog: Free. Frequency: Annual
Circulation: 100K. **Sales:** $1-3MM
Products: Sugar free and no sugar added products

THE POPCORN FACTORY (888) 216-0235
13970 W. Laurel Dr.
Lake Forest, IL 60045
E-Mail: service@thepopcornfactory.com
Website: www.thepopcornfactory.com
Fax Ordering: (888) 333-4595(847) 362-9680
International Ordering: (847) 362-0028
Catalog: Free. Frequency: Annual
Circulation: 150K. **Sales:** $5-10MM
Products: Popcorn in designed tins; gift packages

PRIESTER'S PECANS (800) 277-3226
280 Old Fort Rd. East
Fort Deposit, AL 36032
E-Mail: customerservice@priesters.com
Website: www.priesters.com
Fax Ordering: (334) 227-4294
International Ordering: (334) 227-8355
Contact Name: Ned Ellis, President
Catalog: Free. Frequency: Annual
Circulation: 100K. **Sales:** $1-3MM
Products: Shelled pecans and homemade candies with pecans

ROCKY MOUNTAIN CHOCOLATE FACTORY (800) 344-9630
265 Turner Dr. • Durango, CO 81301
E-Mail: info@rmcf.com
Website: www.rmcf.com
Fax Ordering: (970) 247-9593
International Ordering: (970) 259-0554
Customer Service: (888) 525-2462
Contact Name: Franklin Crail, President
Catalog: Free. Frequency: Semiannual
Circulation: 50K. **Sales:** $5-10MM
Products: Handmade chocolates gifts

ROWENA'S (800) 627-8699 (800) 980-CAKE
758 W. 22nd St. • Norfolk, VA 23517
E-Mail: info@rowenas.com
Website: www.rowenas.com
Fax Ordering: (757) 627-1505
International Ordering: (757) 627-8699
Contact Name: Cameron Foster, Manager
Catalog: Free. Frequency: 6x per year
Circulation: 400K. **Sales:** $1-5MM
Products: Gourmet pound cakes, jams, cooking sauces & baking mixes; fruit baskets

SENOR MURPHY CANDYMAKER (877) 988-4311
1904 Chamisa St. • Santa Fe, NM 87505
E-Mail: chocolate@senormurphy.com
Website: www.senormurphy.com
Fax Ordering: (505) 988-2050
International Ordering: (505) 988-4311

Contact Name: Elsie Thurman, President
Catalog: Free. Frequency: Annual
Circulation: 15K. **Sales:** $500K
Products: Handmade gourmet chocolates; sugar-free candies; specialty nuts, jellies & jams, gift baskets

STANDARD CANDY COMPANY (800) 226-4340
715 Massman Dr. • Nashville, TN 37210
E-Mail: jbarthel@standardcandy.com
Website: www.googoo.com
Fax Ordering: (615) 889-7775
International Ordering: (615) 889-6360
Contact Name: Robert Schneider, President
Catalog: Free. Frequency: Semiannual
Circulation: 100K. **Sales:** $50-100MM
Products: Goo Goo Clusters, Pecan Rolls, Coconut Waves, ABC Fruit Chomps

SUNNYLAND FARMS (800) 999-2488
P.O. Box 8200 • Albany, GA 31706
E-Mail: info@sunnylandfarms.com
Website: www.sunnylandfarms.com
Fax Ordering: (229) 317-4979
International Ordering: (912) 882-3085
Contact Name: Jane Wilson, Owner
Catalog: Free. Frequency: Semiannual
Circulation: 150K. **Sales:** $10-20MM
Products: Pecans, other nuts, pecan candies, chocolate candies, homemade cakes & cookies, dried fruits, citrus & other specialty food items.

SWEET TOOTH CANDIES (877) 581-5132
1020 Saratoga St. • Newport, KY 41071
E-Mail: info@sweettoothchocolates.com
Website: www.sweettoothchocolates.com
Fax Ordering: (859) 581-1979
International Ordering: (859) 581-4663
Contact Name: Robert Schneider, President
Catalog: Free. Frequency: Semiannual
Circulation: 10K. **Sales:** $500M to $1MM
Products: Chocolates and candies

TEUSCHER CHOCOLATES (800) 554-0924
OF SWITZERLAND (800) 554-0624
620 Fifth Ave. • New York, NY 10020
E-Mail: ny@teuscherchocolates.com
Website: www.teuscherchocolates.com
Fax Ordering: (212) 765-8134
International Ordering: (212) 246-4416
Contact Name: Bernard Bloom, President
Catalog: Free. Frequency: Semiannual
Circulation: 10K. **Sales:** $500M
Products: Chocolate truffles

TROPHY NUT COMPANY (800) 219-9005
P.O. Box 199 • Tipp City, OH 45371
E-Mail: bwilke@trophynut.com
Website: www.trophynut.com
Fax Ordering: (937) 669-5160
International Ordering: (937) 667-8478
Contact Name: Bob Wilke, VP Sales
Catalog: Free. Frequency: Semiannual
Circulation: 30K. **Sales:** $1-3MM
Products: Nut giftpacks

VELVET CREME POPCORN COMPANY (888) 551-6708
4710 Belinder Rd. (800) 552-6708
Shawnee Mission, KS 66205
E-Mail: customerservice@velvetcremepopcorn.com
Website: www.velvetcremepopcorn.com
Fax Ordering: (913) 236-9631

International Ordering: (913) 236-7742
Contact Name: Barbara Odle, President
Catalog: Free. Frequency: Semiannual
Circulation: 10K. **Sales**: $500M to $1MM
Products: Popcorn and snacks

YOUNG PECAN COMPANY   (800) 829-6864
1200 Pecan St. • Florence, SC 29501   (800) 729-8004
E-Mail: sales@youngpecan.com
Website: www.youngpecan.com
Fax Ordering: (843) 664-2344
International Ordering: (843) 662-8591
Contact Name: James Swink, President
Catalog: Free. Frequency: Semiannual
Circulation: 100K. **Sales**: $3-5MM
Products: Pecans and pecan products

ZAPP'S POTATO CHIPS   (800) HOT-CHIP
P.O. Box 1533 • Gramercy, LA 70052
E-Mail: sales@zapps.com
Website: www.zapps.com
Fax Ordering: (225) 869-9779
International Ordering: (225) 869-9777
Contact Name: Ron Zapp, President
Catalog: Free. Frequency: Semiannual
Circulation: 50K. **Sales**: $20-50MM
Products: Sweet potato chips, potato chips
and cheezers

CHEESE

CABOT CREAMERY   (888) 792-2268
1 Home Farm Way • Montpelier, VT 05602   (877) 229-4045
E-Mail: info@cabotcheese.com
Website: www.cabotcheese.com
Fax Ordering: (802) 563-2263
International Ordering: (802) 371-1248
Customer Service: (800) 639-3198
Contact Name: Richard Stammer, President
Catalog: Free. **Frequency**: Annual
Circulation: 100K. **Sales**: $20-50MM
Products: Cheddar cheese

CALEF'S COUNTRY STORE   (800) 462-2118
P.O. Box 57 • Barrington, NH 03825
E-Mail: info@calefs.com
Website: www.calefs.com
Fax Ordering: (603) 664-5857
International Ordering: (603) 664-2231
Contact Name: Clev & Lindy Horton, President
Catalog: Free. Frequency: Annual
Circulation: 10K. **Sales**: $1-3MM
Products: Cheeses, pretzel dips, jams
& jellies, maple syrup, candies, gift boxes

CHEESE BOX   (800) 345-6105
801 S. Wells St. • Lake Geneva, WI 53147
E-Mail: info@cheesebox.com
Website: www.cheesebox.com
Fax Ordering: (262) 248-6468
International Ordering: (262) 248-3440
Contact Name: Edward Schwinn, President
Catalog: Free. Frequency: Annual
Circulation: 25M. **Sales**: $500M
Products: Wisconsin cheese & sausage
gift boxes

DAKIN FARM-QUALITY FOODS   (800) 993-2546
5797 Route 7 • Ferrisburgh, VT 05456
E-Mail: customerservice@dakinfarm.com
Website: www.dakinfarm.com
Fax Ordering: (802) 425-2765
International Ordering: (802) 425-3971
Contact Name: Sam Cutting, IV, President
Catalog: Free. Frequency: Quarterly
Circulation: 100K. **Sales**: $5-10MM
Products: Smoked meats, cheeses &
maple syrup; gift baskets

EICHTEN'S CHEESE & BISON   (800) 657-6752
P.O. Box 216 • Center City, MN 55012
E-Mail: eichten@frontiernet.net
Website: www.specialtycheese.com
Fax Ordering: (651) 257-6286
International Ordering: (651) 257-1566
Contact Name: Ed Eichten, President
Catalog: Free. Frequency: Semiannual
Circulation: 10K. **Sales**: $3-5MM
Products: European-style cheeses &
American Bison meat

GIBBSVILLE CHEESE SALES   (920) 564-3242
W2663 CTY OO
Sheboygan Falls, WI 53085
E-Mail: sales@gibbsvillecheese.com
Website: www.gibbsvillecheese.com
Fax Ordering: (920) 564-6129
Contact Name: R. Van Tatenhove, President
Catalog: Online. Brochure: Free. **Sales**: $1-3MM
Products: Wisconsin cheese

GRAFTON VILLAGE CHEESE CO.   (800) 472-3866
P.O. Box 87 • Grafton, VT 05146
E-Mail: info@graftonvillagecheese.com
Website: www.graftonvillagecheese.com
Fax Ordering: (802) 843-2210
International Ordering: (802) 843-2221
Contact Name: Peter Mohn, VP
Catalog: Free. Frequency: Annual
Circulation: 15K. **Sales**: $3-5MM
Products: Vermont cheddars & Vermont
specialty products; bacon and ham

GRANVILLE COUNTRY STORE   (800) 356-3141
P.O. Box 141 • Granville, MA 01034
Fax Ordering: (413) 357-6376
International Ordering: (413) 357-8555
Contact Name: Tina & Tracy, Proprietors
Catalog: Free. Frequency: Annual
Circulation: 10K. **Sales**: $1-3MM
Products: Cellar-aged cheddar cheese

HARMAN'S CHEESE & COUNTRY STORE   (603) 823-8000
P.O. Box 624 • Sugar Hill, NH 03585
E-Mail: cheese@harmanscheese.com
Website: www.harmanscheese.com
Contact Name: Maxine Aldrich, President
Catalog: Free. Frequency: Semiannual
Circulation: 10K. **Sales**: $500K
Products: Aged cheddar cheese & cheese
spreads; jams and jellies; soldier beans;
maple products; pancake mixes; salad
dresings; and other gourmet condiments

HELUVA GOOD CHEESE   (800) 445-0269
P.O. Box 410 • Sodus, NY 14551
E-Mail: hgc1@heluvagood.com
Website: www.heluvagood.com

Fax Ordering: (315) 483-6971
International Ordering: (315) 483-9927
Customer Service: (888) 611-4341
Contact Name: Laurie McFaul-Frey, President
Catalog: Free. Frequency: Weekly
Circulation: 15K. Sales: $500M to $1MM
Products: Gift packages featuring cheese,
gourmet foods; specialty gifts made on request

HICKORY FARMS   (800) 222-GIFT
1505 Holland Rd. • Maumee, OH 43537   (800) 753-8558
E-Mail: sales@hickoryfarms.com
Website: www.hickoryfarms.com
Fax Ordering: (419) 893-8068 or 893-0164
International Ordering: (419) 893-7611
Contact Name: Robert Dyer, President
Catalogs: Hickory Farms, Ace Specialty Foods,
Almond Plaza, Mission Orchard, Pfaelzer
Brothers, Squire's Choice
Frequency: Semiannual.
Circulation: 3MM. Sales: $100-500MM
Products: Beef & Cheese, Fresh Fruit,
Dessert, Sweets & Nuts, Meat & Seafood

IDEAL CHEESE SHOP, LTD.   (800) 382-0109
942 First Ave. • New York, NY 10022
E-Mail: cheeseinfo@idealcheese.com
Website: www.idealcheese.com
Fax Ordering: (212) 223-1245
International Ordering: (212) 688-7579
Contact Name: Edward Edelman, President
Catalog: Free. Frequency: Weekly
Circulation: 15K. Sales: $500K to $1MM
Products: Gourmet cheeses

MAYTAG DAIRY FARMS   (800) 247-2458
2282 E. 8th St. N. • Newton, IA 50208
E-Mail: info@maytagdairyfarms.com
Website: www.maytagdairyfarms.com
Fax Ordering: (641) 792-1567
International Ordering: (641) 792-1133
Contact Name: James W. Stevens, President
Catalog: Free. Frequency: Semiannual
Circulation: 200K. Sales: $3-5MM
Products: Maytag blue cheese, white cheddar

NEW ENGLAND CHEESEMAKING SUPPLY   (413) 628-3808
P.O. Box 85 • Ashfield, MA 01330
E-Mail: info@cheesemaking.com
Website: www.cheesemaking.com
Fax Ordering: (413) 628-4061
Contact Name: Ricki Carroll, President
Catalog: Free. Frequency: Semiannual
Circulation: 25K. Sales: $500M to $1MM
Products: Supplies and equipment to make
cheese & other dairy related products at home.

RISING SUN FARMS   (800) 888-0795
5126 S. Pacific Hwy. • Phoenix, OR 97535
E-Mail: info@risingsunfarms.com
Website: www.risingsunfarms.com
Fax Ordering: (541) 535-8350
International Ordering: (541) 535-8331
Contact Name: Elizabeth & Richard Fujas, Owners
Catalog: Free. Frequency: Semiannual
Circulation: 25K. Sales: $3-5MM
Products: Natural/organic specialty foods:
cheese tortas, pesto sauces, vialgrettes
& marinade, recipes.

SHELBURNE FARMS   (802) 985-8686
1611 Harbor Rd. • Shelburne, VT 05482
E-Mail: sales@shelburnefarms.org
Website: www.shelburnefarms.org
Fax Ordering: (802) 985-8123
Contact Name: Kevin O'Donnell, President
Catalog: Free. Frequency: Semiannual
Circulation: 50K. Sales: $1-3MM
Products: Cheddar cheese

SONOMA CHEESE FACTORY   (800) 535-2855
2 Spain St. "On the Plaza"
Sonoma, CA 95476
E-Mail: retailstore@sonomacheesefactory.com
Website: www.sonomacheesefactory.com
Fax Ordering: (707) 935-8846
International Ordering: (707) 996-1931
Contact Name: David Viviani, President
Catalog: Free. Frequency: Annual
Circulation: 25K. Sales: $500K
Products: Sonoma Jack & Cheddar
Cheeses; gift packs

STATE OF MAINE CHEESE CO.   (800) 762-8895
461 Commercial St. • Rockport, ME 04856
E-Mail: info@cheese-me.com
Website: www.cheese-me.com
Fax Ordering: (207) 236-9591
International Ordering: (207) 236-8895
Contact Name: Cathy Morrill, President
Catalog: Free. Frequency: Annual
Circulation: 20K. Sales: $500K to $1MM
Products: Jack and cheddar cheese

SUGARBUSH FARM   (800) 281-1757
591 Sugarbush Farm Rd.
Woodstock, VT 05091
E-Mail: contact@sugarbushfarm.com
Website: www.sugarbushfarm.com
Fax Ordering: (802) 457-3269
International Ordering: (802) 457-1757
Contact Name: Elizabeth Luce, President
Catalog: Free. Frequency: 5x per year
Circulation: 75K. Sales: $1-5MM
Products: Cheese, Vermont maple syrup,
pancake mix, food gift boxes.

THE SWISS COLONY   (800) 544-9036
1112 7th Ave. • Monroe, WI 53566
E-Mail: info@swisscolony.com
Website: www.swisscolony.com
Fax Ordering: (608) 328-8457
International Ordering: (608) 328-8635
Customer Service: (608) 324-4603
Contact Name: John Baumann, President
Catalog: Free. Frequency: Annual
Circulation: 2MM. Sales: $10-20MM
Products: Cheese, meats, fruits & nuts,
pastries, and gift packs

VERMONT BUTTER & CHEESE CO.   (800) 884-6287
P.O. Box 95 • Websterville, VT 05678
E-Mail: info@vtbutterandcheeseco.com
Website: www.vtbutterandcheeseco.com
Fax Ordering: (802) 479-3674
International Ordering: (802) 479-9371
Contact Name: Allison Hooper, President
Catalog: Free. Frequency: Annual
Circulation: 25K. Sales: $10-20MM
Products: Cheese and dairy products

WSU CREAMERY   (800) 457-5442
Washington State University Creamery
P.O. Box 641122 • Pullman, WA 99164
E-Mail: info@wsu.edu/creamery
Website: www.wsu.edu/creamery
Fax Ordering: (800) 572-3289
International Ordering: (509) 335-4014
Contact Name: Elizabeth Luce, President
Catalog: Free. Frequency: Annual
Circulation: 25K. Sales: $1-3MM
Products: Natural cheeses

WISCONSIN CHEESEMAN   (800) 698-1721
P.O. Box 1 • Madison, WI 53701   (800) 698-1751
E-Mail: customerservice@wisconsincheeseman.com
Website: www.wisconsincheeseman.com
Fax Ordering: (800) 244-2161; (608) 244-2161
International Ordering: (608) 837-8600
Contact Name: Holly Cremer, President
Catalog: Free. Frequency: Annual
Circulation: 50K. Sales: $50-100MM
Products: Cheeses, sausage & meat gifts;
desserts and nuts; chocolate & candy gifts;
sugar-free gifts; gift baskets & boxes

COFFEE & TEA

BARNIE'S COFFEE & TEA CO.   (800) 284-1416
2126 W. Landstreet Rd. #300
Orlando, FL 32809
E-Mail: customerservice@barniescoffee.com
Website: www.barniescoffee.com
Fax Ordering: (407) 854-6636
Contact Name: Shannon Kidd, Manager
Catalog: Free. Frequency: Quarterly
Circulation: 100K. Sales: $1-5MM
Products: Coffee and tea

BARONET COFFEE   (800) 227-6638
P.O. Box 987 • Hartford, CT 06143
E-Mail: info@baronetcoffee.com
Website: www.baronetcoffee.com
Fax Ordering: (860) 524-9130
International Ordering: (860) 527-7253
Contact Name: Leon Goldsmith, President
Catalog: Free. Frequency: Annual
Circulation: 25K. Sales: $1-3MM
Products: Blends and flavored coffees
in both regular & decaf

BARROWS TEA COMPANY   (774) 488-8684
P.O. Box 40278 • New Bedford, MA 02744
E-Mail: madhatter@barrowstea.com
Website: www.barrowstea.com
Contact Name: Sam Barrows, President
Catalog: Free. Frequency: Annual
Circulation: 25K. Sales: $500K
Products: Barrows Teas; organic teas

BIGELOW TEA   (888) 244-3569
R.C. Bigelow, Inc.
201 Black Rock Tpk. • Fairfield, CT 06825
E-Mail: sugar@bigelowtea.com
Website: www.bigelowtea.com
Fax Ordering: (203) 334-5114
Catalog: Free. Frequency: Semiannual
Circulation: 50K. Sales: $50-100MM
Products: Line of tea assortments and loose tea

CAFE DU MONDE   (800) 772-2927
1039 Decatur St.
New Orleans, LA 70116
E-Mail: info@cafedumonde.com
Website: www.cafedumonde.com
Fax Ordering: (504) 587-0847
International Ordering: (504) 581-2914
Contact Name: Jay Roman, General Manager
Catalog: Free. Frequency: Semiannual
Circulation: 75K. Sales: $5-10MM
Products: Cafe Du Monde coffe & beignets

CAJUN CREOLE PRODUCTS   (800) 946-8688
5610 Daspit Rd. • New Iberia, LA 70563
E-Mail: info@cajuncreole.com
Website: www.cajuncreole.com
Fax Ordering: (337) 229-4814
International Ordering: (337) 229-8464
Contact Name: Joel Wallins, President
Catalog: Free. Frequency: Semiannual
Circulation: 50K. Sales: $3-5MM
Products: Specialty Cajun Creole coffee,
Cajun Creole hot nuts, and Cajun spices

CHARLESTON TEA PLANTATION   (800) 443-5987
6617 Maybank Hwy.
Wadmalaw Island, SC 29487
E-Mail: sugar@bigelowtea.com
Website: www.bigelowtea.com
Fax Ordering: (843) 559-3049
International Ordering: (843) 559-0383
Contact Name: Sarah Fleming McLester, President
Catalog: Free. Frequency: Annual
Circulation: 15K. Sales: $500K to $1MM
Products: American classic teas

EMPIRE COFFEE & TEA CO., INC.   (800) 262-5908
568 Ninth Ave. • New York, NY 10036
E-Mail: owners@empirecoffeetea.com
Website: www.empirecoffeetea.com
Fax Ordering: (212) 268-2960
International Ordering: (212) 268-1220
Contact Name: Paul Shaylin, President
Catalog: Free. Frequency: Semiannual
Circulation: 25K. Sales: $500K
Products: Gourmet coffee & specialty tea

ESPRESSO ZONE   (800) 345-8945
Exodus Trading Co.
1206 Lake Ave. • Ashtabula, OH 44004
E-Mail: support@espressozone.com
Website: www.espressozone.com
Fax Ordering: (440) 964-7440
International Ordering: (440) 964-7400
Contact Name: Paul Shaylin, President
Catalog: Free. Frequency: Semiannual
Circulation: 25K. Sales: $500K
Products: Gourmet coffee for the coffee
enthusiast

GEVALIA CATALOG   (800) 438-2542
P.O. Box 6276 • Dover, DE 19905
E-Mail: customer_service@gevalia.com
Website: www.gevalia.com
Fax Ordering: (302) 440-7279
Catalog: Free. Frequency: Semiannual
Circulation: 200K. Sales: $20-50MM
Products: Coffee and coffee accessories,
gift baskets, confectionaries, housewares.

GREEN MOUNTAIN COFFEE   (888) TRY-GMCR
33 Coffee Lane • Waterbury, VT 05676   (800) 545-2326
E-Mail: info@greenmountaincoffee.com
Website: www.greenmountaincoffee.com
Fax Ordering: (888) 438-4627
Contact Name: Rick Slade, Marketing Manager
Customer Service: (866) 639-2326
Catalog: Free. Frequency: Semiannual
Circulation: 100K. Sales: $10-50MM
Products: Coffee and gifts; specialty coffees, including flavored, organic and signature blends; gift baskets, specialty foods, & coffee-related items.

HARNEY & SONS FINE TEAS   (888) 427-6398
P.O. Box 665 • Salisbury, CT 06068
E-Mail: ht@harney.com
Website: www.harney.com
Fax Ordering: (518) 789-2100
Contact Name: Michael Harney, Manager
Catalog: Free. Frequency: Semiannual
Circulation: 25K. Sales: $3-5MM
Products: Gourmet tea supplies & tea foods

KOBOS COFFEE COMPANY   (800) 557-5226
2355 NW Vaughn St. • Portland, OR 97210
E-Mail: kobos@kobos.com
Website: www.kobos.com
Fax Ordering: (503) 796-9366
International Ordering: (503) 222-2302
Contact Names: David Kobos, President
Catalog: Free. Frequency: Annual
Circulation: 50M. Sales: $1-3MM
Products: Specialty coffee & tea; culinary herbs and spices; cookware

LUZIANE ICED TEA & COFFEE   (800) 692-7895
Reily Foods Company
640 Magazine St. • New Orleans, LA 70130
E-Mail: service@luzianne.com
Website: www.luzianne.com
Fax Ordering: (504) 539-5427; (800) 759-8477
International Ordering: (504) 524-6131
Customer Service: (9800) 535-1961
Contact Name: Bruce Bramen, Manager
Catalog: Free. Frequency: Annual
Circulation: 25K. Sales: $10-20MM
Products: Coffee and tea; brownie mix; sauces & seasonings

MARKET SPICE   (800) 735-7198
14690 NE 95th St.
Redmond, WA 98052
E-Mail: info@marketspice.com
Website: www.marketspice.com
Fax Ordering: (425) 881-5603
International Ordering: (425) 883-1220
Contact Name: Jim Samuel, President
Catalog: Free. Frequency: Annual
Circulation: 10K. Sales: $1-5MM
Products: Teas and spices including market spice tea

McNULTY'S TEA & COFFEE   (800) 356-5200
109 Christopher St. • New York, NY 10014
E-Mail: info@mcnultys.com
Website: www.mcnultys.com
International Ordering: (212) 242-5351
Contact Name: David Wong, President
Catalog: Free. Frequency: Annual
Circulation: 25K. Sales: $500K
Products: Coffee, tea and coffee makers

NEW MEXICO PINON COFFEE   (800) 572-0624
4431 Anaheim Ave. NE
Albuquerque, NM 87113
E-Mail: customercare@nmpinoncoffee.com
Website: www.nmpinoncoffee.com
Fax Ordering: (505) 237-8182
International Ordering: (505) 298-1964
Contact Name: James Franco, President
Catalog: Free. Frequency: Annual
Circulation: 25K. Sales: $1-3MM
Products: Coffee, herbal & sun tea, cocoa, coffee candy, chocolates, salsas, nuts & jams, seasoning & mixes, gift baskets.

NORTHWESTERN COFFEE MILLS   (800) 243-5283
Northwestern Tea & Spice Co.
30950 Nevers Rd. • Washburn, WI 54891
E-Mail: order@nwcoffeemills.com
Website: www.nwcoffeemills.com
Fax Ordering: (715) 373-0072
International Ordering: (715) 363-2109
Contact Name: Harry Demorest, President
Catalog: Free. Frequency: Annual
Circulation: 10K. Sales: $500K
Products: Coffee, tea, spices, seasonings and coffee filters

SPECIALTEAS, INC.   (888) 365-6983
500 Long Beach Blvd. • Stratford, CT 06615
E-Mail: service@specialteas.com
Website: www.specialteas.com
Fax Ordering: (203) 375-6820
International Ordering: (203) 375-2409
Catalog: Free. Frequency: Annual
Circulation: 25K. Sales: $500K
Products: Teas; flavored, scented, decaf, herbal & fruite blended; tea ware & preparation products.

PEERLESS COFFEE CO.   (800) 310-KONA
260 Oak St. • Oakland, CA 94607
E-Mail: tellme@peerlesscoffee.com
Website: www.peerlesscoffee.com
Fax Ordering: (510) 763-5026
International Ordering: (510) 763-1763
Contact Name: Sonia Vukasin, President
Catalog: Free. Frequency: Semiannual
Circulation: 50K. Sales: $1-5MM
Products: Coffee, tea, spices and gift baskets; books, coffee makers

PEET'S COFFEE & TEA   (800) 999-2132
P.O. Box 12509 • Berkeley, CA 94712
E-Mail: info@peets.com
Website: www.peets.com
Fax Ordering: (510) 704-0311
International Ordering: (510) 653-7876
Catalog: Free. Frequency: Annual
Circulation: 25K. Sales: $500K
Products: Specialty coffee and tea

SIGNATURE COFFEE COMPANY   (707) 923-2661
3455 Redwood Dr. • Redway, CA 95560
E-Mail: signature@asis.com
Fax Ordering: (707) 923-9166
Catalog: Free. Frequency: Annual
Circulation: 10K. Sales: $500K
Products: Organic coffees and teas

SIMPSON & VAIL   (800) 282-8327
P.O. Box 765 • Brookfield, CT 06804
E-Mail: info@svtea.com

Website: www.svtea.com
Fax Ordering: (203) 775-0462
International Ordering: (203) 775-0240
Contact Name: James F. Harron, Jr., President
Catalog: Free. Frequency: Annual
Circulation: 100K. Sales: $3-5MM
Products: Coffees, teas, brewing accessories,
gourmet foods, china and gifts

STASH TEA CATALOG   (800) 826-4218
P.O. Box 910 • Portland, OR 97207
E-Mail: stash@stashtea.com
Website: www.stashtea.com
Fax Ordering: (503) 684-4424
International Ordering: (503) 624-1911
Customer Service: (503) 684-9725; (800) 800-8327
Contact Name: Dorothy Arnold, Manager
Catalog: Free. Frequency: Quarterly
Circulation: 500K. Sales: $20-50MM
Products: Specialty teas, tea gifts, accessories
and baked goods

TEA IMPORTERS   (203) 226-3301
47 Riverside Ave. • Westport, CT 06880
E-Mail: teaimport@aol.com
Website: www.teaimporters.com
Fax Ordering: (203) 227-1629
Contact Name: J.H. Wertheim, President
Catalog: Free. Frequency: Monthly
Circulation: 25K. Sales: $1-5MM
Products: Teas from all producing countries

THANKSGIVING COFFEE CO.   (800) 648-6491
P.O. Box 1918 • Fort Bragg, CA 95437   (800) 462-1999
E-Mail: info@thanksgivingcoffee.com
Website: www.thanksgivingcoffee.com
Fax Ordering: (707) 964-0351
International Ordering: (707) 964-0118
Contact Name: Susan Coy, Contact
Catalog: Free. Frequency: Semiannual
Circulation: 25K. Sales: $5-10MM
Products: Organic and shade grown coffee

UPTON TEA IMPORTS   (800) 234-8327
34-A Hayden Rowe St.
Hopkinton, MA 01748
E-Mail: cservice@uptontea.com
Website: www.uptontea.com
Fax Ordering: (508) 435-9955
International Ordering: (508) 435-9922
Catalog: Free. Frequency: Semiannual
Circulation: 100K. Sales: $5-10MM
Products: Organic teas, sampler sets.

VISIONS ESPRESSO SERVICE   (800) 277-7277
2737 1st Avenue South • Seattle, WA 98134
E-Mail: info@visionsespresso.com
Website: www.visionsespresso.com
Fax Ordering: (206) 623-6710
International Ordering: (206) 623-6709
Contact Name: Dawn Loraas, President
Catalog: Free. Frequency: 10x per year
Circulation: 50M. Sales: $500M to $1MM
Products: Espresso machine parts,
cleaning supplies and accessories.

ETHNIC & REGIONAL FOODS

CREOLE DELICACIES COMPANY   (800) 523-6425
533 St. Ann St. • New Orleans, LA 70116
E-Mail: hubs@cookincajun.com
Website: www.cookincajun.com
Fax Ordering: (504) 523-4787
International Ordering: (504) 523-6425
Contact Name: Lysette Sutton, President
Catalog: Free. Frequency: Annual
Circulation: 20K. Sales: $500K
Products: Cajun & creole specialty sauces
& foods

CROCKETT FARMS   (800) 580-1900
P.O. Box 1150 • Harlingen, TX 78551
E-Mail: texasfruit@crockettfarms.com
Website: www.crockettfarms.com
Fax Ordering: (956) 412-6381
International Ordering: (956) 412-1747
Contact Name: Terry Crockett, President
Catalog: Free. Frequency: Semiannual
Circulation: 50K. Sales: $3-5MM
Products: Texas citrus or seasonal produce;
red rubies & oranges; jellies & dressings;
Texas meats & nuts

FERRARA FOODS & CONFECTIONS   (212) 226-6150
195 Grand St. • New York, NY 10013
E-Mail: info@ferraracafe.com
Website: www.ferraracafe.com
Fax Ordering: (212) 226-0667
Contact Name: Alfred Lepore, President
Catalog: Free. Frequency: Annual
Circulation: 100K. Sales: $10-20MM
Products: Italian gourmet foods, coffees,
cakes and syrups

GASPAR'S SAUSAGE COMPANY   (800) 542-2038
384 Faunce Corner Rd.
No. Dartmouth, MA 02747
E-Mail: gaspars@linguica.com
Website: www.linguica.com
Fax Ordering: (508) 998-2015
International Ordering: (508) 998-2012
Contact Name: Fernando Gaspar, President
Catalog: Free. Frequency: Annual
Circulation: 100K. Sales: $5-10MM
Products: Portuguese sausage

HOUSE OF SPICES   (718) 507-4900
127-40 Willets Point Blvd.
Flushing, NY 11368
E-Mail: customerservice@hosindia.com
Website: www.hosindia.com
Fax Ordering: (718) 507-4798
Contact Name: G.L. Soni, President
Catalog: Free. Frequency: Annual
Circulation: 10K. Sales: $5-10MM
Products: Indo erthnic foods, spices
and provisions

INDIAN HARVEST SPECIALTIFOODS   (800) 346-7032
P.O. Box 428 • Bemidji, MN 56619
E-Mail: customerservice@indianharvest.com
Website: www.indianharvest.com
Fax Ordering: (800) 752-8588; (218) 751-8519
Catalog: Free. Frequency: Annual
Circulation: 50K. Sales: $5-10MM
Products: Gourmet rice, grains & legumes

JYOTI CUISINE INDIA   (610) 522-2650
P.O. Box 516 • Berwyn, PA 19312
E-Mail: jyoti@jyotifoods.com
Website: www.jyotifoods.com
Fax Ordering: (610) 522-2652
Contact Name: Jyoti Gupta, President
Catalog: $1. Frequency: Quarterly
Circulation: 25K. Sales: $1-3MM
Products: Indian cuisine; spicy vegetarian
and ready-to-serve curries and sauces

KOSHER GIFT BOX   (866) 925-7747
P.O. Box 696 • Westport, CT 06880
E-Mail: info@koshergiftbox.com
Website: www.koshergiftbox.com
Fax Ordering: (203) 222-9542
International Ordering: (203) 222-0400
Contact Name: Jane Moritz, Owner
Catalog: Online. Sales: $1-3MM
Products: Kosher gourmet food gifts

KOSHER.COM   (866) 567-4379
P.O. Box 575 • Cedarhurst, NY 11516
E-Mail: customerservice@kosher.com
Website: www.kosher.com
Fax Ordering: (866) 456-8877
Catalog: Online. Sales: $1-3MM
Products: Kosher foods

LISBON SAUSAGE COMPANY   (800) 262-7257
433 S. 2nd St. • New Bedford, MA 02740
E-Mail: sausage@amarals.com
Website: www.amarals.com
Fax Ordering: (508) 994-0453
International Ordering: (508) 993-7645
Contact Name: Antonio Rodrigues, President
Catalog: Free. Frequency: Annual
Circulation: 50K. Sales: $3-5MM
Products: Portuguese sausage products
and other foods

LOU MALNATI'S PRIORITY PIZZA   (800) 568-8646
3685 Woodhead Dr. • Northbrook, IL 60062
E-Mail: heylou@loutogo.com
Website: www.loutogo.com
Fax Ordering: (847) 714-1035
International Ordering: (847) 714-1024
Contact Name: Lou Malnati, President
Catalog: Free. Frequency: Semiannual
Circulation: 50K. Sales: $500K
Products: Deep-dish pizza

PENDERY'S CATALOG   (800) 533-1870
1221 Manufacturing St. • Dallas, TX 75207
E-Mail: email@penderys.com
Website: www.penderys.com
Fax Ordering: (214) 761-1966
International Ordering: (214) 741-1870
Contact Name: Patrick Hagerty, President
Catalog: Free. Frequency: Quarterly
Circulation: 50K. Sales: $500K
Products: Mexican chiles and spices

POLANA   (888) 765-2621
3512 N. Kostner Ave. • Chicago, IL 60641
E-Mail: info@polana.com
Website: www.polana.com
Fax Ordering: (773) 545-6800
International Ordering: (773) 545-4900
Contact Name: Mario Malanicki, Manager
Catalog: Free. Frequency: Semiannual
Circulation: 50K. Sales: $500K - $1MM

Products: Polish sausage, bread, soups,
cakes, pierogies, stuffed cabbage, gift baskets

ROSSI PASTA   (800) 227-6774
P.O. Box 930 • Marietta, OH 45750
E-Mail: info@rossipasta.com
Website: www.rossipasta.com
Fax Ordering: (740) 373-5310
International Ordering: (740) 373-5155
Contact Name: John Rossi, President
Catalog: Free. Frequency: 8x per year
Circulation: 50K. Sales: $5-10MM
Products: Gourmet pasta and sauces;
gift boxe, baskets & sets

SCHALLER & WEBER   (800) 847-4115
22-35 46th St. • Astoria, NY 11105
E-Mail: info@schallerweber.com
Website: www.schallerweber.com
Fax Ordering: (718) 956-9157
International Ordering: (718) 721-5480
Contact Name: Ferdinand Schaller, President
Catalog: Free. Frequency: Annual
Circulation: 50K. Sales: $3-5MM
Products: German gourmet foods;
meat products

SULTAN'S DELIGHT   (800) 852-5046
Nuts About Nuts, Inc.
P.O. Box 090302 • Brooklyn, NY 11209
E-Mail: sales@sultansdelight.com
Website: www.sultansdelight.com
Fax Ordering: (718) 745-2563
International Ordering: (718) 745-2121
Contact Name: Joseph G. Sayour, President
Catalog: Free. Frequency: Semiannual
Circulation: 10K. Sales: $250-500K
Products: Mediterranean Middle Eastern foods

TODARO BROS. SPECIALTY FOODS   (877) 472-2767
555 Second Ave. • New York, NY 10016
E-Mail: eat@todarobros.com
Website: www.todarobros.com
Fax Ordering: (212) 689-1679
International Ordering: (212) 532-0633
Contact Name: Mary Todaro, President
Catalog: Free. Frequency: Annual
Circulation: 25K. Sales: $3-5MM
Products: Imported Italian gourmet foods
& gifts; olive oil, condiments & spices,
cured meats, olives, cheese, cakes & pies

FISH & SEAFOOD

BLUE CRAB BAY - TASTES   (800) 221-2722
OF CHESAPEAKE BAY
Bay Beyond
29368 Atlantic Dr. • Melfa, VA 23410
E-Mail: sales@bluecrabbay.com
Website: www.bluecrabbay.com
Fax Ordering: (757) 787-3430
International Ordering: (757) 787-3602
Contact Name: Pamela Barefoot, President
Catalog: Free. Frequency: Annual
Circulation: 50K. Sales: $1-3MM
Products: Specialty foods with flavor
of the Chesapeake Bay

BOSTON & MAINE FISH COMPANY   (800) 626-7866
27 Drydock Ave. • Boston, MA 02210
Fax Ordering: (781) 321-2565
International Ordering: (617) 723-4111
Contact Name: Larry Smith, President
Catalog: Free. Frequency: Annual
Circulation: 25K. Sales: $500K
Products: Lobsters and seafood

CAVIARTERIA   (800) 422-8427
502 Park Ave. • New York, NY 10022
E-Mail: info@caviarteria.com
Website: www.caviarteria.com
Fax Ordering: (718) 482-8985
International Ordering: (212) 759-7410
Contact Name: Bruce Sobol, President
Catalog: Free. Frequency: Quarterly
Circulation: 250M. Sales: $5-10MM
Products: Caspian and American caviars,
smoked Scottish salmon, caviar servers
and utensils, caviar cake

CLAMBAKES-TO-GO   (877) 792-7771
Clambake Celebrations
1223 Main St. • Chatham, MA 02633
E-Mail: clambake@capecod.net
Website: www.blambake-to-go.com
Fax Ordering: (402) 223-4465
International Ordering: (402) 223-2358
Contact Name: Jo-Van Tucker, President
Catalog: Free. Frequency: 3x per year
Circulation: 50M. Sales: $500M to $1MM
Products: New England lobster clambakes
in a steamer pot.

DUCKTRAP RIVER FISH FARM   (800) 828-3825
57 Little River Dr. • Belfast, ME 04915
E-Mail: smoked@ducktrap.com
Website: www.ducktrap.com
Fax Ordering: (207) 338-9020
International Ordering: (207) 338-9019
Contact Name: Eric Rector, Manager
Catalog: Free. Frequency: Annual
Circulation: 50M. Sales: $500M to $1MM
Products: Naturally smoked seafood
direct from Maine

GRAFFAM BROTHERS   (800) 535-5358
P.O. Box 340 • Rockport, ME 04856
E-Mail: graffams@mint.net
Website: www.lobsterstogo.com
Fax Ordering: (207) 236-2569
International Ordering: (207) 236-3396
Contact Name: james H. Graffam, President
Catalog: Free. Frequency: Annual
Circulation: 5M. Sales: $5-10MM
Products: Maine lobsters

HEGG & HEGG SMOKED SALMON   (800) 622-7775
801 Marine Dr. • Port Angeles, WA 98363
Fax Ordering: (360) 457-1205
International Ordering: (360) 457-3344
Contact Name: Tony Chapman, Manager
Catalog: Free. Frequency: Annual
Circulation: 25M. Sales: $1-3MM
Products: Smoked salmon

HORTON'S SMOKED SEAFOODS   (800) 346-6066
Horton's Downeast Foods
P.O. Box 430 • Waterboro, ME 04087
E-Mail: dhorton@hortons.com
Website: www.hortons.com

Fax Ordering: (207) 985-9407
International Ordering: (207) 247-6900
Contact Name: Jean Horton, President
Catalog: Free. Frequency: Annual
Circulation: 10M. Sales: $1-3MM
Products: Smoked salmon, trout, mussels;
scallops & shrimp; & smoked seafood pates

JOE'S GOES DIRECT   (800) 780-CRAB
11 Washington Ave.
Miami Beach, FL 33139
E-Mail: info@joesstonecrab.com
Website: www.joesstonecrab.com
Fax Ordering: (305) 534-2108
International Ordering: (305) 673-9035
Contact Name: Stephen Sawitz, President
Catalog: Free. Frequency: Annual
Circulation: 20M. Sales: $1-3MM
Products: Stone crabs, key lime pie,
cream spinach clam chowder

JOSEPHSON'S SMOKEHOUSE & DOCK   (800) 772-3474
106 Marine Dr. • Astoria, OR 97103
E-Mail: sales@josephsons.com
Website: www.josephsons.com
Fax Ordering: (503) 325-4075
International Ordering: (503) 325-2190
Contact Name: Michael Josephson, President
Catalog: Free. Frequency: Quarterly
Circulation: 10M. Sales: $500M to $1MM
Products: Specialty smoked seafood

LEGAL SEAFOODS   (800) 343-5804
33 Everett St. • Allston, MA 02134
E-Mail: sales@legalseafoods.com
Website: www.legalseafoods.com
Fax Ordering: (617) 254-5809
International Ordering: (617) 254-7000
Contact Name: Roger Berkowitz, President
Catalog: Free. Frequency: Annual
Circulation: 5M. Sales: $1-3MM
Products: Maine lobsters, New England
clambakes and other seafood specialties

LOUISIANA FISH FRY PRODUCTS   (800) 356-2905
5215 Plank Rd. • Baton Rouge, LA 70805
E-Mail: info@tonyseafood.com
Website: www.tonyseafood.com
Fax Ordering: (225) 355-5451
International Ordering: (225) 357-9669
Contact Name: Cliff Pizzolato, President
Catalog: Free. Frequency: Annual
Circulation: 25M. Sales: $10-20MM
Products: Seafood

NELSON SEATREATS   (800) 262-0069
Nelson Crab
P.O. Box 520 • Tokeland, WA 98590
E-Mail: seatreats@nelsoncrab.com
Website: www.nelsoncrabonline.com
Fax Ordering: (360) 267-2921
International Ordering: (360) 267-2911
Contact Name: Chris B. Nelson, President
Catalog: Free. Frequency: Weekly
Circulation: 10M. Sales: $5-10MM
Products: Smoked canned specialties,
including salmon, shrimp, tuna, sturgeon,
and crabmeat.

PETROSSIAN   (800) 828-9241
419 W. 13th St. • New York, NY 10014
E-Mail: customersupport@petrossian.com

FOOD & BEVERAGE

187

Website: www.petrossian.com
Fax Ordering: (212) 337-0822
International Ordering: (212) 337-0808
Contact Name: Adam Borden, Marketing Manager
Catalog: Free. Frequency: Annual
Circulation: 50M. Sales: $20-50MM
Products: Finest caviar & serving pieces,
smoked fish, chocolates and gift ideas

ROMANOFF CAVIAR   **(800) 654-7264**
24 Sunderland Rd. • Tenafly, NJ 07670
Fax Ordering: (614) 848-8330
International Ordering: (201) 784-3344
Contact Name: Helen G. Hessol, President
Catalog: Free. Frequency: Semiannual
Circulation: 25M. Sales: $10-20MM
Products: Caviar, Scottish salmon, fish
delicacies and other specialties

SALMOLUX   **(253) 874-2026**
34100 9th Ave. S.
Federal Way, WA 98003
E-Mail: seafood@salmolux.com
Fax Ordering: (253) 874-4042
Contact Name: George Kuetgens, President
Catalog: Free. Frequency: Weekly
Circulation: 25M. Sales: $10-20MM
Products: Smoked salmon, rainbow trout,
halibut, whitefish, gourmet seafood butters
and spreads

SEA BEAR   **(800) 645-3474**
605 30th St. • Anacortes, WA 98221
E-Mail: info@seabear.com
Website: www.seabear.com
Fax Ordering: (360) 293-4097
International Ordering: (360) 293-4661
Contact Name: Michael Mondello, President
Catalog: Free. Frequency: 5x per year
Circulation: 1MM. Sales: $5-10MM
Products: Smoked wild salmon & other
seafood

TAKU STORE CATALOG   **(800) 582-5122**
Taku Store, Smokeries & Fishery
550 S. Franklin St. • Juneau, AK 99801
E-Mail: mailorder@takustore.com
Website: www.takustore.com
Fax Ordering: (907) 463-5209
International Ordering: (907) 463-3474
Contact Name: Sendro Lane, President
Catalog: Free. Frequency: Annual
Circulation: 150K. Sales: $10-20MM
Products: Alaskan smoked salmon

TSAR NICOULAI CAVIAR   **(800) 952-2842**
60 Dorman Ave. • San Francisco, CA 94124
E-Mail: concierge@tsarnicoulai.com
Website: www.tsarnicoulai.com
Fax Ordering: (415) 543-5172
International Ordering: (415) 543-3007
Contact Name: Mats Engstrom, President
Catalog: Free. Frequency: Monthly
Circulation: 25M. Sales: $1-5MM
Products: Imported caviars, beluga,
osetra and smoked fish

WAR EAGLE MILL CATALOG   **(866) 492-7324**
11045 War Eagle Rd. • Rogers, AR 72756
E-Mail: info@wareaglemill.com
Website: www.wareaglemill.com
Fax Ordering: (479) 789-5100

International Ordering: (479) 789-5343
Contact Name: Cliff Pizzolato, President
Catalog: Free. Frequency: Annual
Circulation: 25K. Sales: $1-3MM
Products: Gourmet whole grain & fish mixes;
organic flours & meals; salsas & sauces;
kitchenware & graniteware; jellies, honey
& cookbooks

WEATHERVANE SEAFOODS   **(800) 914-1774**
31 Badgers Island West • Kittery, ME 03904
E-Mail: info@weathervaneseafoods.com
Website: www.weathervaneseafoods.com
Fax Ordering: (207) 338-9718
International Ordering: (207) 439-0335
Catalog: Free. Frequency: Annual
Circulation: 20K. Sales: $1-5MM
Products: Seafood - lobsters, scallops, clams

JAMS, JELLIES, HONEY & SYRUP

AMERICAN SPOON FOODS   **(888) 735-6700**
P.O. Box 566 • Petoskey, MI 49770
E-Mail: information@spoon.com
Website: www.spoon.com
Fax Ordering: (800) 647-2512; (231) 347-2512
International Ordering: (231) 347-9030
Customer Service: (800) 222-5886
Contact Name: Justin Rashid, President
Catalog: Free. Frequency: Semiannual
Circulation: 250K. Sales: $5-10MM
Products: Fruit preserves, condiments,
sauces, dried fruit, nuts, dates, mushrooms,
and gift packs.

APPLESOURCE   **(800) 588-3854**
1716 Apples Rd. • Chapin, IL 62628
E-Mail: vorbeck@csj.net
Website: www.applesource.com
Fax Ordering: (217) 245-7844
International Ordering: (217) 245-7589
Contact Name: Jill Vorbeck, Contact
Catalog: Free. Frequency: Annual
Circulation: 25K. Sales: $500K
Products: Fresh specialty apples in season;
fruit butters and spreads; apple peeler, corer
& slicer; apple cookbook.

BETH'S FARM KITCHEN   **(800) 331-5267**
P.O. Box 113 • Stuyvesant Falls, NY 12174
E-Mail: bfk@bethsfarmkitchen.com
Website: www.bethsfarmkitchen.com
Fax Ordering: (518) 799-2042
International Ordering: (518) 799-3414
Contact Name: Beth Linskey, President
Catalog: Free. Frequency: Annual
Circulation: 5M. Sales: $250M
Products: Jams, chutneys and pickled
products; recipes, gifts

BUTTERNUT MOUNTAIN FARM   **(800) 828-2376**
37 Industrial Park Dr. • Morrisville, VT 05661
E-Mail: steens@buttermountainfarm.com
Website: www.buttermountainfarm.com
Fax Ordering: (802) 888-5909
International Ordering: (802) 888-3491
Contact Name: David Marvin, President
Catalog: Free. Frequency: Annual
Circulation: 25K. Sales: $1-3MM
Products: Vermont maple syrup & sugar products

C.S. STEEN'S SYRUP MILL   (800) 725-1654
P.O. Box 339 • Abbeville, LA 70510
E-Mail: steens@steensyrup.com
Website: www.steensyrup.com
Fax Ordering: (337) 893-2478
International Ordering: (337) 893-1654
Contact Name: Charley Steen, General Mgr.
Catalog: Free. Frequency: Annual
Circulation: 25K. Sales: $3-5MM
Products: Pure cane syrup

TONY CHACHERE'S   (800) 551-9066
CAJUN COUNTRY CATALOG
P.O. Box 1639 • Opelousas, LA 70571
E-Mail: creole@cajunspice.com
Website: www.tonychachere.com
Fax Ordering: (337) 948-6854
International Ordering: (337) 948-4691
Contact Name: Donald Chachere, Jr., President
Catalog: Free. Frequency: Semiannual
Circulation: 100K. Sales: $10-20MM
Products: Cajun-style seasonings, rice
dinner mixes, cookbooks and gift packages

CHAMPLAIN VALLEY APIARIES   (800) 841-7334
P.O. Box 127 • Middlebury, VT 05753
E-Mail: info@champlainvalleyhoney.com
Website: www.champlianvalleyhoney.com
Fax Ordering: (802) 388-1653
International Ordering: (802) 388-7724
Contact Name: Stanley Liscow, President
Catalog: Free. Frequency: Annual
Circulation: 25K. Sales: $1-3MM
Products: Honeys

CLEARBROOK FARMS   (800) 222-9966
3015 E. Kemper Rd.
Sharonville, OH 45241
E-Mail: mailorders@clearbrookfarms.com
Website: www.clearbrookfarms.com
Fax Ordering: (513) 771-8381
International Ordering: (513) 771-2000
Contact Name: Stanley Liscow, President
Catalog: Free. Frequency: Annual
Circulation: 25K. Sales: $1-5MM
Products: Fruit preserves, spreads,
dessert sauces, fruit tarts

COLD HOLLOW CIDER MILL   (800) 327-7537
P.O. Box 420 • Waterbury Center, VT 05677
E-Mail: micheller@coldhollow.com
Website: www.coldhollow.com
Fax Ordering: (802) 244-7212
International Ordering: (802) 244-8771
Contact Name: Michelle Rutledge, Mail Order
Catalog: Free. Frequency: Semiannual
Circulation: 50K. Sales: $1-5MM
Products: Maple products, cheddar cheese,
apple cider, apple products, jams, jellies,
mustards, and gift packages.

FISCHER & WIESER SPECIALTY FOODS   (800) 880-8526
411 S. Lincoln St.
Fredericksburg, TX 78624
E-Mail: info@jelly.com
Website: www.jelly.com
Fax Ordering: (830) 997-0455
Contact Name: Mark Wieser, President
Catalog: Free. Frequency: Semiannual
Circulation: 50K. Sales: $500K
Products: Jams, jellies and mustards

GIFT & GOURMET SHOP BY MAIL   (800) 356-5880
The Goodjam Company
20211 Vashon Hwy. SW
Vashon, WA 98070
E-Mail: info@vashoncountrystore.com
Website: www.goodjam.com; or,
  www.vashoncountrystore.com
Fax Ordering: (206) 463-3679
International Ordering: (206) 463-9659
Contact Name: Peter Shepherd, President
Catalog: Free. Frequency: 3x per year
Circulation: 50M. Sales: $1-3MM
Products: Maury Island Farm preserves,
fruits and berries; fancy chocolates;
smoked salmon; gourmet gifts.

GREEN MOUNTAIN SUGAR HOUSE   (800) 643-9338
Rte. 100N, Box 820 • Ludlow, VT 05149
E-Mail: info@gmsh.com
Website: www.gmsh.com
Fax Ordering: (802) 228-2298
International Ordering: (802) 228-7521
Contact Name: Ann H. Rose, President
Catalog: Free. Frequency: Annual
Circulation: 25K. Sales: $500K - $1MM
Products: Maple syrup & products, cheddar
cheese, VT bacon jams; gift packages

HERSHEY'S MAUNA LOA   (800) 832-9993
The Hershey Company   (866) 972-6879
601 22nd St. • San Francisco, CA 94107
E-Mail: maunaloa@worldpantry.com
Website: www.maunaloa.com
Fax Ordering: (415) 401-0087
International Ordering: (415) 401-0080
Catalog: Free. Frequency: Semiannual
Circulation: 50K. Sales: $3-5MM
Products: Specialty foods including
Macadamia nuts, Kona coffee, fruits
and exotic flowers from Hawaii.

HILLSIDE ORCHARD FARMS   (800) 262-9429
105 Mitchum Cir. • Tiger, GA 30576   (866) 782-4995
E-Mail: orders@hillsideorchard.com
Website: www.hillsideorchard.com
Fax Ordering: (706) 782-7848
International Ordering: (706) 782-4995
Contact Name: Robert D. Mitcham, President
Catalog: Free. Frequency: Annual
Circulation: 25K. Sales: $500K to $1MM
Products: Southern gourmet jellies, meat
sauces, rice mixes and dressings

KNOTT'S BERRY FARM FOODS   (866) 828-5502
1 Strawberry Lane • Orrville, OH 44667
E-Mail: info@knottsberryfarmfoods.com
Website: www.knottsberryfarmfoods.com
Catalog: Free. Frequency: Annual
Circulation: 1MM. Sales: $5-10MM
Products: Jams, jellies, preserves, cheese,
salad dressings, candy and baked goods

KOZLOWSKI FARMS/   (800) 473-2767
SONOMA COUNTY CLASSICS
5566 Gravenstein Hwy. 116
Forestville, CA 95436
E-Mail: koz@kozlowskifarms.com
Website: www.kozlowskifarms.com
Fax Ordering: (707) 887-9650
International Ordering: (707) 887-1587
Contact Name: Carol Kozlowski-Every, President
Catalog: Free. Frequency: Annual

Circulation: 100K. Sales: $500K to $1MM
Products: Specialty foods from the Russian
River Valley. Sauces - fruit syrup-n-sauces,
fudge sauce, marinades & dipping sauces;
gift baskets.

MAPLE GROVE FARMS OF VERMONT (800) 525-2540
1052 Portland St. • St. Johnsbury, VT 05819
E-Mail: mailorder@maplegrove.com
Website: www.maplegrove.com
Fax Ordering: (802) 748-0839
International Ordering: (802) 748-5141
Contact Name: Dave Wenner, President
Catalog: Free. Frequency: Semiannual
Circulation: 100K. Sales: $20-50MM
Products: Maple syrup, pancake & waffle mix;
maple candy & cookies; preserves & spreads;
sugar free products; gift baskets

MOONLITE GOOD & GIFT CATALOG (800) 322-8989
Moonlite Bar-B-Q Inn
2840 W. Parrish Ave.
Owensboro, KY 42301
E-Mail: pbosley@moonlite.com
Website: www.moonlite.com
Fax Ordering: (270) 684-8105
International Ordering: (270) 684-8143
Contact Name: Pat Bosley, Marketing Manager
Catalog: Free. Frequency: Annual
Circulation: 50K. Sales: $5-10MM
Products: Barbequed meats & sauces
in the Kentucky tradition

THE NUNS NEW SKETE (518) 677-3810
343 Ash Grove Rd.
Cambridge, NY 12816
E-Mail: nuns@newskete.com
Website: www.newskete.com
Fax Ordering: (518) 677-3001
Contact Names: Brother Elias, President
Catalog: Free. Frequency: Semiannual
Circulation: 5K. Sales: $250K
Products: Cheesecakes, fruitcakes,
biscotti, muffins & cookies

OREGON FANCY FOOD GROUP (800) 426-3086
1471 Railroad Blvd. #L6
Eugene, OR 97404
E-Mail: the best@ofpc.com
Fax Ordering: (541) 685-1683
International Ordering: (541) 685-1681
Contact Name: Paul Gahlar, President
Catalog: Free. Frequency: Quarterly
Circulation: 10K. Sales: $500K to $1MM
Products: Tarts, marmalade, jams, syrups,
candies, cranberry products, fudges

PURELY AMERICAN FOODS (800) 359-7873
5991 Industrial Park Rd. • Athens, OH 45701
E-Mail: customerservice@purelyamerican.com
Website: www.purelyamerican.com
Fax Ordering: (740) 592-4610
International Ordering: (740) 592-3800
Contact Name: Rod Millar, President
Catalog: Free. Frequency: Annual
Circulation: 50K. Sales: $3-5MM
Products: American mixes; slow cooker
gourmet; gourmet Virginia peanuts; pasta
salad, bean soups and bakery mixes

RENT MOTHER NATURE (800) 232-4048
P.O. Box 380193 • Cambridge, MA 02238
E-Mail: info@rentmothernature.com
Website: www.rentmothernature.com
Fax Ordering: (800) 296-9443; (617) 296-9443
International Ordering: (617) 868-5162
Customer Service: (800) 296-9445
Contact Name: Richard Hill, President
Catalog: Free. Frequency: Annual
Circulation: 25K. Sales: $500K
Products: New England gift baskets:
maple syrup, honey, pancakes

SALSA EXPRESS (800) 437-2572
P.O. Box 1157 • Fredericksburg, TX 78624
E-Mail: sales@salsaexpress.com
Website: www.salsaexpress.com
Fax Ordering: (830) 990-9481
International Ordering: (830) 997-1498
Contact Name: Harry Goodwin, President
Catalog: Free. Frequency: Annual
Circulation: 50K. Sales: $1-3MM
Products: Southwest spicy foods

SALT LICK GENERAL STORE (888) 725-8542
Salt Lick BBQ
18300 FM 1826 • Driftwood, TX 78619
E-Mail: saltlick@saltlickbbq.com
Website: www.saltlickbbq.com
Fax Ordering: (512) 858-2038
International Ordering: (512) 894-3117
Contact Name: Susan J. Goff, President
Catalog: Free. Frequency: Annual
Circulation: 50K. Sales: $5-10MM
Products: Barbeque meats, sauces;
merchandise

SANTA FE SCHOOL OF COOKING (800) 982-4688
116 W. San Francisco St.
Santa Fe, NM 87501
E-Mail: cookin@santafeschoolofcooking.com
Website: www.santafeschoolofcooking.com
Fax Ordering: (505) 983-7540
International Ordering: (505) 983-4511
Contact Name: Susan Curtis, President
Catalog: Free. Frequency: Annual
Circulation: 75K. Sales: $500K
Products: Southwestern foods & ingredients

SARABETH'S KITCHEN (800) 773-7378
1161 E. 156 St. • Bronx, NY 10474
E-Mail: info@sarabeth.com
Website: www.sarabeth.com
Fax Ordering: (718) 589-8412
International Ordering: (718) 589-2900
Contact Name: William J. Levine, President
Catalog: Free. Frequency: Quarterly
Circulation: 25K. Sales: $250-500K
Products: Fruit preserves, cakes, cookies,
soup and granola

SMITHFIELD COLLECTION (800) 628-2242
P.O. Box 250 • Portsmouth, VA 23705
E-Mail: info@smithfieldcollection.com
Website: www.smithfieldcollection.com
Fax Ordering: (757) 673-7005
Contact Name: Peter Pruden, President
Catalog: Free. Frequency: Semiannual
Circulation: 100K. Sales: $5-10MM
Products: Smoked meats, Smithfield hams,
country hams, smoked turkey & pheasants,
cheesecakes, soups and stews.

SMUCKERS CATALOG   (800) 742-6729
J.M. Smucker Company
P.O. Box 197 • Orrville, OH 44667
E-Mail: sales@smuckers.com
Website: www.smuckers.com
Fax Ordering: (330) 684-6410
Customer Service: (800) 258-1928
Catalog: Free. Pages: 30. Frequency: Semiannual
Circulation: 100K. Sales: $20-50MM
Products: Jams, jellies, peanut butter,
gourmet products

A TASTE OF THE SOUTH   (888) 828-2783
P.O. Box 210236 • Columbia, SC 29210
E-Mail: info@atasteofthesouth.com
Website: www.atasteofthesouth.com
Fax Ordering: (803) 798-7387
International Ordering: (803) 772-0940
Catalog: Free. Pages: 16. Frequency: Semiannual
Circulation: 100K. Sales: $3-5MM
Products: Southern pecans; gift baskets

TRIFLES   (800) 456-7019
Neiman Marcus Direct
5950 Cowell Blvd. • Irving, TX 75039
Website: www.neimanmarcus.com
Fax Ordering: (972) 969-3192
International Ordering: (972) 969-3100
Contact Name: Bernie Feiwus, President
Catalog: Free. Frequency: Annual
Circulation: 100K. Sales: $5-10MM
Products: California fruit, baked goods,
ice cream

VERMONT HARVEST SPECIALTY FOODS   (800) 338-5354
1799 Mountain Rd. • Stowe, VT 05672
E-Mail: info@vtharvest.com
Website: www.vtharvest.com
Fax Ordering: (802) 253-7139
International Ordering: (802) 253-7138
Contact Name: Patty Foltz, President
Catalog: Free. Frequency: Annual
Circulation: 25K. Sales: $500K
Products: Vermont harvest conserves,
jams & jellies, mustards, chutney

VERMONT MAPLE OUTLET   (800) 858-3121
3929 Vermont, Rt. 15
Jeffersonville, VT 05464
E-Mail: info@vermontmapleoutlet.com
Website: www.vermontmapleoutlet.com
Fax Ordering: (802) 644-5038
International Ordering: (802) 644-5482
Contact Name: Mr. Marsh, Owner
Catalog: Free. Frequency: Annual
Circulation: 15K. Sales: $250-500M
Products: Vermont maple products &
specialty foods

VIRGINIA TRADITIONS   (800) 222-4267
S. Wallace Edwards & Sons
P.O. Box 25 • Surry, VA 23883
E-Mail: info@virginiatraditions.com
Website: www.virginiatraditions.com
Fax Ordering: (757) 294-5378
International Ordering: (757) 294-3121
Customer Service: (800) 290-9213
Contact Name: Jim Padgitt, Manager
Catalog: Free. Frequency: 5x per year
Circulation: 250K. Sales: $5-10MM
Products: Authentic Southern smoked meats,
seafood, snacks, and dessert specialties

WILLLABAY: CRANNIE CONDIMENTS   (360) 665-6585
Oysterville Sea Farms
P.O. Box 6 • Oysterville, WA 98641
E-Mail: info@willabay.com
Website: www.willabay.com
Fax Ordering: (360) 665-3425
International Ordering: (360) 665-6585
Catalog: Free. Frequency: Annual
Circulation: 50K. Sales: $1-5MM
Products: Condiments: jams, sauces,
dried fruits and baking mixes, naturegrains,
cereal, spices

FRUITS & VEGETABLES

ALBRITTON FRUIT COMPANY   (800) 237-3682
5430 Proctor Rd. • Sarasota, FL 34233
E-Mail: info@albrittonfruit.com
Website: www.albrittonfruit.com
Fax Ordering: (941) 924-1462
International Ordering: (941) 923-2573
Contact Name: John Albritton, President
Catalog: Free. Frequency: Annual
Circulation: 150K. Sales: $1-3MM
Products: Citrus, fresh squeezed orange &
grapefruit juice, candy & marmalades; fruit
gift baskets

APRICOT FARM   (800) 233-4413
420 Lucy Brown Ln.
San Juan Bautista, CA 95045
E-Mail: sales@apricot-farm.com
Website: www.apricot-farm.com
Fax Ordering: (831) 637-3949
International Ordering: (831) 623-4711
Contact Name: Thomas E. Dotta, President
Catalog: Free. Frequency: Semiannual
Circulation: 50K. Sales: $1-5MM
Products: California dried fruits,
nuts and mixes

BOUQUET OF FRUITS   (800) 243-7848
2668 N. Fordham • Fresno, CA 93727
E-Mail: service@bofmail.com
Website: www.bouquetoffruits.com
Fax Ordering: (559) 346-0210
International Ordering: (559) 346-0210
Customer Service: (888) 903-7848
Contact Name: Stephen Paul, President
Catalog: Free. Frequency: Annual
Circulation: 100K. Sales: $1-3MM
Products: California tree-ripened
fresh fruit and nuts

CHUKAR CHERRY COMPANY   (800) 624-9544
P.O. Box 510 • Prosser, WA 99350
E-Mail: sales@chukar.com
Website: www.chukar.com
Fax Ordering: (509) 786-2591
International Ordering: (509) 786-2055
Contact Name: Pamela Auld, President
Catalog: Free. Frequency: Monthly
Circulation: 250K. Sales: $500K to $1MM
Products: All natural dried cherries; dried
berries & apples; fruit & nut mixes; chocolate
covered dried berries; roasted nuts; espresso
beans; pure fruit jams; dessert toppings,
BBQ sauces, pie fillings

CUSHMAN'S FRUIT CO.   (800) 776-7575
P.O. Box 15005 • West Palm Beach, FL 33406   (877) 233-7000
E-Mail: info@honeybell.com   (800) 222-9696
Website: www.honeybell.com
Fax Ordering: (800) 776-4329; (561) 968-7263
International Ordering: (561) 965-3535
Contact Name: Allen Cushman, President
Catalog: Free. Frequency: Monthly
Circulation: 500K. Sales: $5-10MM
Products: Citrus gifts including Cushman
Honeybells, a rare hybrid of a Fancy Tangerine
and Duncan Grapefruit; Indian River naval
oranges, ruby red grapefruit & other citrus gifts.

DAVIDSON OF DUNDEE   (800) 654-0647
28421 US Hwy. 27 N • Dundee, FL 33838   (800) 294-2266
E-Mail: sales@davidsonofdundee.com
Website: www.davidsonofdundee.com
Fax Ordering: (863) 439-5049
International Ordering: (863) 439-2284; 439-1698
Contact Name: Glen Davidson, President
Catalog: Free. Frequency: Annual
Circulation: 50K. Sales: $3-5MM
Products: Citrus fruit gift baskets; oranges
& grapefruits; citrus candies, nuts, marmalades,
jellies, butters; chocolate gifts

DIAMOND ORGANICS   (888) 674-2642
1272 Hwy. 1 • Moss Landing, CA 95039
E-Mail: info@diamondorganics.com
Website: www.diamondorganics.com
Fax Ordering: (888) 888-6777
International Ordering: (831) 763-9677
Contact Name: Jasch Hamilton, President
Catalog: Free. Frequency: Semiannual
Circulation: 150K. Sales: $1-3MM
Products: Organic lettuces, fresh herbs,
specialty greens and sprouts; gift baskets

DIXIE DINER/HARVEST DIRECT   (800) 233-3668
Dixie USA
P.O. Box 1969 • Tomball, TX 77377
E-Mail: info@dixiediner.com
Website: www.dixiediner.com
Fax Ordering: (800) 688-2507
International Ordering: (281) 516-3535
Contact Name: Brenda K. Oswalt, President
Catalog: Free. Frequency: Monthly
Circulation: 25K. Sales: $3-5MM
Products: Lentils, soups, salads & chillies

DRIFTWOOD FRUIT COMPANY   (877) 593-4643
P.O. Box 3502 • Vero Beach, FL 32964
E-Mail: tomrhodes@driftwoodfruit.com
Website: www.driftwoodfruit.com
Fax Ordering: (772) 770-1520
Contact Name: Thomas Rhodes, President
Catalog: Free. Frequency: Annual
Circulation: 25K. Sales: $1-3MM
Products: Indian River oranges & grapefruits

FRANK LEWIS ALAMO FRUITS   (800) 477-4773
100 N. Tower Rd. • Alamo, TX 78516
Fax Ordering: (956) 787-1428
International Ordering: (956) 787-5971
Contact Name: Richard Hamilton, Manager
Catalog: Free. Frequency: Annual
Circulation: 50K. Sales: $1-5MM
Products: Fruits, smoked meats,
candies and honey

THE FRUIT COMPANY   (800) 387-3100
2900 Van Horn Dr.
Hood River, OR 97031
E-Mail: info@thefruitcompany.com
Website: www.thefruitcompany.com
Fax Ordering: (541) 387-3104
International Ordering: (541) 387-3100
Contact Name: Thomas Rhodes, President
Catalog: Free. Frequency: Annual
Circulation: 25K. Sales: $1-3MM
Products: Fruit baskets & boxes;
desserts & confections

GOLDEN GEM GROWERS   (800) 323-3201
P.O. Drawer 9 • Umatilla, FL 32784
Fax Ordering: (352) 669-1993
International Ordering: (352) 669-2101
Contact Name: Jack Nelson, President
Catalog: Free. Frequency: Annual
Circulation: 20K. Sales: $1-3MM
Products: Gift fruit

HALE GROVES   (800) 289-4253
Hale Indian River Groves   (800) 356-7264
P.O. Box 691237, Vero Beach, FL 32969   (800) 678-1154
E-Mail: customercare@halegroves.com
Website: www.halegroves.com
Fax Ordering: (877) 329-4253; (772) 589-8889
International Ordering: (772) 589-4334
Customer Service: (800) 562-4502
Contact Name: Steven Hale, President
Catalog: Free. Frequency: Annual
Circulation: 100K. Sales: $10-50MM
Products: Honeybells, oranges, ruby red
grapefruits & citrus fruit baskets, avocado,
tangelos, jams & jellies; gourmet food gifts

HAPPY VALLEY RANCH   (913) 849-3103
16577 W. 327th St. • Paola, KS 66071
E-Mail: info@happyvalleyranch.com
Website: www.happyvalleyranch.com
Fax Ordering: (913) 849-3104
Contact Name: Ray Stagg, President
Catalog: Free. Frequency: Annual
Circulation: 40K. Sales: $500M to $1MM
Products: Cider and fruit presses and
accessories

HYATT FRUIT COMPANY   (866) 991-8889
P.O. Box 639 • Vero Beach, FL 32961
E-Mail: service@hyattfruitco.com
Website: www.hyattfruitco.com
Fax Ordering: (772) 567-0973
International Ordering: (772) 567-3766
Contact Name: Thomas R. Jones, President
Catalog: Free. Frequency: Semiannual
Circulation: 50K. Sales: $3-5MM
Products: Indian River citrus; gift boxes
and baskets; vine ripe tomatoes, vidalia
onions, steaks, smoked meats & citrus candy

INDIAN RIVER FRUIT CO.   (800) 343-7848
P.O. Box 6188 • Vero Beach, FL 32961
E-Mail: sharon@indianriverfruits.com
Website: www.indianriverfruits.com
Catalog: Free. Frequency: Annual
Circulation: 25K. Sales: $3-5MM
Products: Florida oranges & grapefruits;
honeybells; fruit gift boxes

MELISSA'S/WORLD VARIETY PRODUCE   (800) 588-0151
P.O. Box 21127 • Los Angeles, CA 90021
E-Mail: hotline@melissas.com
Website: www.melissas.com
Fax Ordering: (323) 588-9774
International Ordering: (323) 588-0151
Contact Name: Joe Hernandez, President
Catalog: Free. Frequency: Annual
Circulation: 25K. Sales: $500K to $1MM
Products: Specialty produce, both fresh &
dried; dried exotic fruits, nuts and gourmet
produce, organic produce

NATURAL FOOD DISTRIBUTORS   (800) 860-0006
3040 Hill Ave. • Toledo, OH 43607
Fax Ordering: (419) 531-6887
International Ordering: (419) 537-1713
Contact Name: Frank Dietrich, President
Catalog: Free. Frequency: Quarterly
Circulation: 50K. Sales: $1-3MM
Products: Dried fruits, grains, nuts,
beans and seeds

NUNES FARMS   (800) 255-2641
P.O. Box 311 • Newman, CA 95360
E-Mail: info@nunesfarms.com
Website: www.nunesfarms.com
Fax Ordering: (209) 862-1038
International Ordering: (209) 862-3033
Contact Name: Maureen Nunes, President
Catalog: Free. Frequency: Annual
Circulation: 10K. Sales: $500K to $1MM
Products: Fruits and nut candies; snacks,
almonds

ORANGE BLOSSOM GROVES   (800) 362-4381
P.O. Box 5515 • Salem, OR 97304
E-Mail: orchardcrestfarms@msn.com
Website: www.orchardcrestfarms.com
Fax Ordering: (503) 363-3850
International Ordering: (503) 362-4381
Contact Name: Wayne & Myrna Simmons
Catalog: Free. Frequency: Annual
Circulation: 10K. Sales: $500K to $1MM
Products: Dried fruit, snacks, nuts, mixes;
preserves, whole-fruit syrups

POINSETTIA GROVES   (800) 327-8624
P.O. Box 1388 • Vero Beach, FL 32961
E-Mail: customer.service@poinsettiagroves.com
Website: www.poinsettiagroves.com
Fax Ordering: (772) 562-3629
International Ordering: (772) 562-3356
Contact Name: Jeb Hudson, President
Catalog: Free. Frequency: Bimonthly
Circulation: 100M. Sales: $10-50MM
Products: Indian River oranges &
grapefruits; gift fruit baskets & boxes

PREMIUM FRUIT   (877) 792-5866
77704 Flora Rd. Suite C3
Palm Desert, CA 92211
E-Mail: orders@premiumfruit.com
Website: www.premiumfruit.com
Fax Ordering: (760) 360-7881
International Ordering: (760) 360-9559
Catalog: Free. Frequency: Quarterly
Circulation: 50K. Sales: $1-3MM
Products: Fruit packages

RED COOPER   (800) 876-4733
P.O. Box 3089 • Mission, TX 78573
E-Mail: customercare@redcooper.com
Website: www.redcooper.com
Fax Ordering: (956) 787-1428, 205-7331
International Ordering: (956) 787-9971
Customer Service: (800) 825-8531
Contact Name: Richard Hamilton, Manager
Catalog: Free. Frequency: Annual
Circulation: 150K. Sales: $3-5MM
Products: Texas grapefruit; other fruits,
nuts, candies

SHIELD'S DATE GARDENS   (800) 414-2555
80-225 U.S. Hwy. 111 • Indio, CA 92201
E-Mail: shieldate@aol.com
Website: www.shieldsdates.com
Fax Ordering: (760) 342-3288
International Ordering: (760) 347-0996
Contact Name: Dick Wilson, President
Catalog: Free. Frequency: Annual
Circulation: 50K. Sales: $500K to $1MM
Products: Dried fruit, gift packages

SULLIVAN-VICTORY GROVES   (800) 672-6431
P.O. Box 10 • Cocoa, FL 32923
E-Mail: sullivanvictory@worldnet.att.net
Website: www.sullivancitrus.com
Fax Ordering: (800) 886-0917; (321) 639-4069
International Ordering: (321) 632-0550
Customer Service: (866) 676-4311
Contact Name: Frank E. Sullivan, Owner
Catalog: Free. Frequency: Quarterly
Circulation: 250K. Sales: $3-5MM
Products: Florida's Indian River oranges
& grapefruits, tangerines; honeybells;
gift fruit, jams & jellies

SWEET ONION EXPRESS   (877) 664-6674
P.O. Box 3119 • Mission, TX 78573
 E-Mail: sales@sweetonionexpress.com
Website: www.sweetonionexpress.com
Catalog: Free. Frequency: Semiannual
Circulation: 50K. Sales: $500K to $1MM
Products: Fresh produce; pears, naval oranges,
clementines, apples, farmhouse tomatoes,
grapefruits, lemons & limes, vinatge grapes

WOOD PRAIRIE FARM   (800) 829-9765
49 Kinney Rd. • Bridgewater, ME 04735
E-Mail: orders@woodprairie.com
Website: www.woodprairie.com
Fax Ordering: (800) 300-6494
International Ordering: (207) 425-7741
Contact Name: Jim Gerritsen, President
Catalog: Free. Frequency: Semiannual
Circulation: 50K. Sales: $500K
Products: Organic potato samplers,
vegetable seed; certified seed potatoes;
aged cheeses; grain & flours; cooking
supplies; organic gardening gift baskets

GOURMET & GIFT BASKETS

1-877-SPIRITS.COM, INC.   (877) 774-7487
99 Powerhouse Rd., Suite 200
Roslyn Heights, NY 11577
E-Mail: info@877spirits.com
Website: www.1-877spirits.com

Fax Ordering: (516) 626-4164
International Orders: (516) 626-4150
Contact Name: Avi Ishofsky, Contact
Catalog: Free. Frequency: Annual
Circulation: 1MM. Sales: $5-10MM
Products: Worldwide gift delivery service
of champagnes, fine wines, spirits, cigars,
caviar and gourmet gift baskets.

BLAND FARMS
(800) 843-2542
(800) 440-9543
1126 Raymond Bland Rd.
Glennville, GA 30427
E-Mail: sandra@blandfarms.com
Website: www.blandfarms.com
Fax Ordering: (912) 654-3532
International Ordering: (912) 654-2726
Contact Name: Sandra Bland, President
Catalog: Free. Frequency: Semiannual
Circulation: 50K. Sales: $1-3MM
Products: Vidalia onion selections,
jellies and jams, confections, pecans,
and baked goods

BLUE DIAMOND GROWERS
(800) 987-2329
1701 C St. • Sacramento, CA 95811
E-Mail: customerservice@bdgrowers.com
Website: www.bluediamond.com
Fax Ordering: (916) 329-3331
International Ordering: (916) 46-8438
Contact Name: Walt Payne, President
Catalog: Free. Frequency: Semiannual
Circulation: 100K. Sales: $3-5MM
Products: Almonds; Gourmet foods
and nut gifts

CLUBS OF AMERICA
(800) 258-2872
426 Scotland Rd. • Lakemoor, IL 60050
E-Mail: greatclubs@aol.com
Website: www.greatclubs.com
Fax Ordering: (815) 363-4677
International Ordering: (815) 363-4000
Customer Service: (800) 800-9122
Contact Name: Douglas M. Doretti, President
Catalog: Free. Frequency: Annual
Circulation: 100K. Sales: $10-20MM
Products: Gift of the month clubs: beer,
wine, flowers, cigars, pizza, coffee, &
chocolates

CONNOISSEUR COLLECTION
(800) 554-0001
Big Apple Florist
228 E. 45th St. • New York, NY 10017
E-Mail: comments@bigappleflorist.com
Website: www.bigappleflorist.com
Fax Ordering: (212) 687-5939
International Ordering: (212) 687-3434
Catalog: Free. Frequency: Quarterly
Circulation: 50K. Sales: $500K to $1MM
Products: Gift cards & baskets

CORTI BROTHERS
(800) 509-3663
5810 Folsom Blvd.
Sacramento, CA 95819
E-Mail: cortibros@sbcglobal.net
Website: www.cortibros.biz
Fax Ordering: (916) 736-3807
International Ordering: (916) 736-3800
Contact Name: Darrell Corti, President
Catalog: Free. Frequency: Quarterly
Circulation: 25K. Sales: $5-10MM
Products: Fine wine & gourmet foods

EDEN BASKETS
(800) 969-3336
38 E. Ridgewood Ave. #344
Ridgewood, NJ 07450
E-Mail: info@edenbaskets.com
Website: www.edenbaskets.com
Fax Ordering: (201) 210-8415
International Ordering: (201) 963-0120
Contact Name: Teresa Gerunger, President
Catalog: Free. Frequency: Annual
Circulation: 100K. Sales: $500K - $1MM
Products: Food, fruit and gourmet gift baskets,
holiday gifts, Easter baskets, kosher baskets

FARM BASKET
(800) 432-1107
2008 Langhorne Rd.
Lynchburg, VA 24501
E-Mail: customercare@thefarmbasket.com
Website: www.thefarmbasket.com
Fax Ordering: (434) 847-8622
International Ordering: (434) 528-1107
Contact Name: Perkins Flippin, President
Catalog: Free. Frequency: Annual
Circulation: 25K. Sales: $1-3MM
Products: Personalized gift baskets;
gourmet food shop; apples

FIGI'S GIFTS IN GOOD TASTE
FIGI'S SUGAR FREE
(800) 422-3444
3200 S. Maple Ave.
Marshfield, WI 54404
E-Mail: info@figis.com
Website: www.figis.com
Fax Ordering: (715) 384-1129
International Ordering: (715) 387-6311
Contact Name: Mike Lindquist, VP Marketing
Catalog: Free. Frequency: Bimonthly
Circulation: 50K. Sales: $1-3MM
Products: Fancy food and gifts;
sugar-free food products

GALLERY OF GIFTS BY CHALET SUZANNE
(800) 433-6011
Chalet Suzanne Foods
3800 Chalet Suzanne Dr.
Lake Wales, FL 33859
E-Mail: info@chaletsuzanne.com
Website: www.chaletsuzanne.com
Fax Ordering: (863) 676-1814
International Ordering: (863) 676-6011
Contact Name: Vita Hinshaw, President
Catalog: Free. Frequency: Annual
Circulation: 50M. Sales: $1-3MM
Products: Gourmet soups and sauces

GETHSEMANI FARMS CATALOG
(800) 549-0912
3642 Monks Rd. • Trappist, KY 40051
E-Mail: info@gethsemanifarms.org
Website: www.gethsemanifarms.org
Fax Ordering: (502) 549-4124
International Ordering: (502) 549-3117
Customer Service: (800) 549-1619
Contact Name: Timothy Kelly, President
Catalog: Free. Frequency: Annual
Circulation: 200K. Sales: $5-10MM
Products: Bourbon fruitcakes & fudge,
Trappist cheese & Gethsemani gifts

GIFT & BASKET EXPRESSIONS
(800) 351-3331
Bensenville, IL 60007
E-Mail: customerservice@giftandbasket.com
Website: www.giftandbasket.com
Fax Ordering: (630) 594-1805
Contact Name: Sally Hansen, President

Catalog: Free. **Frequency:** Semiannual
Circulation: 150K. **Sales:** $3-5MM
Products: Gift baskets of gourmet and
specialty foods, and home baskets
including baby, get well, birthday, etc.

GIFTBASKET.COM   (800) 785-0955
P.O. Box 139 • Mt. Aukum, CA 95656
E-Mail: customercare@giftbasket.com
Website: www.giftbasket.com
Fax Ordering: (530) 620-1127
Contact Name: Randy Dirth, President
Catalog: Online. Sales: $500K - $1MM
Products: Gourmet gift baskets of all kinds
for all occasions & holidays

GOURMETGIFTBASKETS.COM   (866) 842-1050
1050 Holt Ave. • Manchester, NH 03109
E-Mail: sales@gourmetgiftbaskets.com
Website: www.gourmetgiftbaskets.com
Fax Ordering: (603) 657-9083
International Ordering: (603) 606-5269
Customer Service: (888) 208-3098
Catalog: Free. Frequency: Annual
Circulation: 150K. Sales: $5-10MM
Products: Gourmet gift baskets of all kinds

GOURMET GIFTMAIL   (800) GIFTMAIL
P.O. Box 805 • Nashua, NH 03060
E-Mail: randy@gourmetgiftmail.com
Website: www.gourmetgiftmail.com
Fax Ordering: (603) 471-1969
Contact Name: Randy Dirth, President
Catalog: Free. Frequency: Annual
Circulation: 100K. Sales: $1-3MM
Products: Gourmet foods, gift baskets,
candy

HARRY AND DAVID GOURMET GIFTS   (800) 345-5655
Bear Creek Corporation   (877) 322-1200
2500 S. Pacific Hwy. • Medford, OR 97501
E-Mail: info@harryanddavid.com
Website: www.harryanddavid.com
Fax Ordering: (800) 648-6640
International Ordering: (541) 773-1267
Contact Name: Bill Williams, President
Catalog: Free. Frequency: 8x per year
Circulation: 100K. Sales: $5-10MM
Products: Gifts, gift baskets, gourmet
foods, corporate gifts, fruits

HOLIDAY FOODS CATALOG   (800) 877-7434
2050 McKinley St. • Hollywood, FL 33020
E-Mail: info@holidayfoods.com
Website: www.holidayfoods.com
Fax Ordering: (954) 921-5425
International Ordering: (954) 921-7786
Catalog: Free. Frequency: Annual
Circulation: 150K. Sales: $1-3MM
Products: Quiche Lorraine with
seafood or mushrooms

HORCHOW CATALOG   (800) 456-7000
Neiman Marcus Direct
5950 Colwell Blvd. • Irving, TX 75039
E-Mail: info@horchow.com
Website: www.horchow.com
Fax Ordering: (972) 969-3192
International Ordering: (972) 969-3100
Contact Name: Sharon Jester Turney, President
Catalog: $5.50. Frequency: 15x per year
Circulation: 25MM. Sales: $50-100MM

Products: Gourmet foods, home decor,
antiques & collectibles, desktop & stationery,
bedding & bath, garden products.

KITCHEN KETTLE VILLAGE   (800) 717-6198
P.O. Box 380 • Intercourse, PA 17534   (800) 732-8261
E-Mail: info@kitchenkettle.com
Website: www.kitchenkettle.com
Fax Ordering: (717) 768-3614
International Ordering: (717) 768-8261
Contact Name: Michael K. Burnley, President
Catalog: Free. Frequency: Semiannual
Circulation: 100K. Sales: $3-5MM
Products: Old fashioned relishes, dressings,
jams, jellies and gift baskets

OAKVILLE GROCERY   (800) 973-6324
P.O. Box 86 • Oakville, CA 94562
E-Mail: grady.harrison@oakvillegrocery.com
Website: www.oakvillegrocery.com
Fax Ordering: (800) 736-6602; (707) 944-1844
International Ordering: (707) 944-8802
Contact Name: Steve Carlin, President
Catalog: Free. Frequency: Annual
Circulation: 200K. Sales: $3-5MM
Products: Specialty products, gift baskets

PECANS PLAIN & FANCY   (800) 999-2488
Sunnyland Farms
P.O. Box 8200 • Albany, GA 31706
E-Mail: ilweb@sfi-wfc.com
Website: www.nutsandcandies.com
Fax Ordering: (229) 317-4979
Contact Name: Jane Wilson, President
Catalog: Free. Frequency: 3x per year
Circulation: 150K. Sales: $20-50MM
Products: Specialty nuts and fruits

SECHLER'S PICKLES   (800) 332-5461
5686 SR 1 • St. Joe, IN 46785
E-Mail: info@gourmetpickles.com
Website: www.gourmetpickles.com
Fax Ordering: (260) 337-5771
International Ordering: (260) 337-5461
Contact Name: David Sechler, President
Catalog: Free. Frequency: Semiannual
Circulation: 150K. Sales: $5-10MM
Products: Gourmet pickles

STEW LEONARD'S GIFT BY MAIL   (800) 729-7839
100 Westport Ave. • Norwalk, CT 06851
E-Mail: info@stewleonards.com
Website: www.stewleonards.com
Fax Ordering: (203) 750-6178
International Ordering: (203) 847-7214
Contact Name: Stew Leonard, Jr., President
Catalog: Free. Frequency: Annual
Circulation: 2MM. Sales: $100-500MM
Products: Dairy products, cheeses & desserts

WILLIAM POLL GOURMET FOODS   (800) 993-7655
1051 Lexington Ave. • New York, NY 10021
E-Mail: wpollny@aol.com
Website: www.williampoll.com
Fax Ordering: (212) 288-2844
International Ordering: (212) 288-0501
Contact Name: Stanley Poll, President
Catalog: Free. Frequency: Annual
Circulation: 25K. Sales: $3-5MM
Products: Gourmet specialty foods: smoked
salmon, fresh caviar, soups and desserts,
prepared dinners.

THOMAS GOURMET FOODS

(800) 867-2823

P.O. Box 8822 • Greensboro, NC 27419
E-Mail: customerservice1@thomassauce.com
Website: www.thomassauce.com
Fax Ordering: (336) 299-7852
International Ordering: (336) 299-6263
Catalog: Free. Frequency: Semiannual
Circulation: 50K. Sales: $1-3MM
Products: Sauces

ZABAR'S CATALOG

(800) 697-6301
(212) 496-1234

2245 Broadway • New York, NY 10024
E-Mail: zabarscatalog@zabars.com
Website: www.zabars.com
Fax Ordering: (212) 496-0392
International Ordering: (800) 697-6301;
  (212) 496-1234
Contact Name: Saul Zabar, President
Catalog: Free. Frequency: Semiannual
Circulation: 500K. Sales: $10-25MM
Products: Gourmet foods; kosher foods;
cookware and housewares

HEALTH FOODS

DIXIE DINER CLUB SOYFOODS

(800) 233-3668

Dixie USA • P.O. Box 1969
Tomball, TX 77377
E-Mail: info@dixieusa.com
Website: www.dixiediner.com
Fax Ordering: (800) 688-2507; (281) 516-3070
International Ordering: (713) 516-3535
Contact Name: Brenda K. Oswalt, President
Catalog: Online. Sales: $1-3MM
Products: Soy food products & meat substitutes

EDIET SHOP

(800) 325-5409

P.O. Box 1037 • Evanston, IL 60204
E-Mail: edietshop@edietshop.com
Website: www.edietshop.com
Fax Ordering: (847) 679-5417
International Ordering: (847) 679-5409
Contact Name: Steven Bernard, President
Catalog: Free. Frequency: Semiannual
Circulation: 50K. Sales: $3-5MM
Products: Gourmet dietetic foods and
candy; books

JAFFE BROTHERS

(877) 975-2333

28560 Lilac Rd. • Valley Center, CA 92082
E-Mail: jaffebros@att.net
Website: www.organicfruitsandnuts.com
Fax Ordering: (760) 749-1282
International Ordering: (760) 749-1133
Contact Name: Allen Jaffe, President
Catalog: Free. Frequency: Annual
Circulation: 30K. Sales: $1-3MM
Products: Organic, untreated natural foods;
dried fruit & nuts

LUMEN FOODS

(800) 256-2253

409 Scott St. • Lake Charles, LA 70601
E-Mail: support@soybean.com
Website: www.soybean.com
Fax Ordering: (337) 436-1769
International Ordering: (337) 436-6748
Contact Name: Cathryn E. Caton, President
Catalog: Free. Frequency: Annual
Circulation: 50K. Sales: $500M to $1M
Products: Meats & dairy replacement products

LUNDBERG FAMILY FARMS

(530) 882-4551

P.O. Box 369 • Richvale, CA 95974
E-Mail: info@lundberg.com
Website: www.lundberg.com
Fax Ordering: (530) 882-4500
International Ordering: (530) 882-4551
Contact Name: Eldon Lundberg, President
Catalog: Free. Frequency: Semiannual
Circulation: 50K. Sales: $10-50MM
Products: Organic rice products; syrup,
flour, cereal, pasta

MAIL ORDER CATALOG
FOR HEALTHY EATING

(800) 695-2241
(800) 835-2867

P.O. Box 180 • Summertown, TN 38483
E-Mail: catalog@usit.net
Website: www.healthy-eating.com
Fax Ordering: (931) 964-2291
International Ordering: (931) 964-2241
Contact Name: Cynthia Holzapfel, President
Catalog: Free. Frequency: Weekly
Circulation: 250K. Sales: $500K to $1MM
Products: Vegetarian products and other
meat substitutes; soyfoods; gift baskets;
sampler packs; yoga supplies; cooking
appliances; personal care & household
products; vegetarian pet food

NATURAL LIFESTYLE MARKET

(800) 752-2775

16 Lookout Dr. • Asheville, NC 28804
E-Mail: order@natural-lifestyle.com
Website: www.natural-lifestyle.com
Fax Ordering: (866) 752-2775; (828) 253-75357
International Ordering: (828) 254-9606
Contact Names: Tom & Debi Athos, Owners
Catalog: Free. Frequency: Semiannual
Circulation: 75K. Sales: $250-500K
Products: Organic foods; health, beauty,
home products; kitchenware; earthcare gifts
and books.

NATURAL RESOURCES

(800) 747-0390

6680 Harvard Dr.
Sebastopol, CA 95472
E-Mail: info@natres.com
Website: www.natres.com
Fax Ordering: (337) 436-1769
International Ordering: (337) 436-6748
Contact Name: Deborah Adams, President
Catalog: Online. Sales: $250-500K
Products: Herbal teas; natural foods; vitamins
& supplements; personal care products; natural
pet supplies.

HERBS, SPICES & SAUCES

ANNIE'S NATURALS

(800) 288-1089

564 Gateway Dr. • Napa, CA 94558
E-Mail: sales@annienaturals.com
Website: www.annienaturals.com
Fax Ordering: (707) 259-0219
International Ordering: (707) 254-3700
Contact Name: Aimee Sands, Contact
Catalog: Free. Frequency: Quarterly
Circulation: 100K. Sales: $5-10MM
Products: Condiments; flavored olive oils;
naturla & organic salad dressing; marinades

ATLANTIC SPICE COMPANY   (800) 316-7965
2 Shore Rd. • North Truro, MA 02652
E-Mail: orders@atlanticspice.com
Website: www.atlanticspice.com
Fax Ordering: (508) 487-2550
International Ordering: (508) 487-6100
Contact Name: Mark Irving, President
Catalog: Free. Frequency: Semiannual
Circulation: 50K. Sales: $3-5MM
Products: Ingredients for potpourri &
spices, teas, and herbs

ATTAR HERBS & SPICES   (800) 541-6900
P.O. Box 245 • New Ipswich, NH 03071
E-Mail: richard@attarherbs.com
Website: www.attarherbs.com
Fax Ordering: (603) 878-4231
International Ordering: (603) 878-1780
Contact Name: Dick Martin, President
Catalog: Free. Frequency: Annual
Circulation: 50K. Sales: $3-5MM
Products: Herbs and spices

BEAVERTON FOODS   (800) 223-8076
P.O. Box 687 • Beaverton, OR 97075
E-Mail: info@beavertonfoods.com
Website: www.beavertonfoods.com
Fax Ordering: (503) 644-9204
International Ordering: (503) 646-8138
Contact Name: Gene Biggi, President
Catalog: Free. Frequency: Annual
Circulation: 100K. Sales: $10-20MM
Products: Mustards, gourmet sauces;
garlics; horseradish

FRONTIER NATURAL PRODUCTS CO-OP   (800) 669-3275
P.O. Box 299 • Norway, IA 52318
E-Mail: customercare@frontiercoop.com
Website: www.frontiercoop.com
Fax Ordering: (800) 717-4372
Catalog: Free. Frequency: Annual
Circulation: 50K. Sales: $5-10MM
Products: Frontier herbs, spices, foods
& teas; organic coffee, essential oils, herbal
extracts, body care & aromatherapy products

GARDEN MEDICINALS & CULINARIES   (540) 872-8351
P.O. Box 460 • Mineral, VA 23117
E-Mail: info@gardenmedicinals.com
Website: www.gardenmedicinals.com
Fax Ordering: (540) 894-9481
Contact Name: Jeff McCormack, President
Catalog: Online. Sales: $1-5MM
Products: A variety of herb seed, roots, &
specialty garlics; extracts and supplies &
equipment for herb growers and herbalists.

GEL SPICE COMPANY   (800) 922-0230
48 Hook Rd. • Bayonne, NJ 07002
E-Mail: sales@gelspice.com
Website: www.gelspice.com
Fax Ordering: (201) 339-0024
International Ordering: (201) 339-0700
Contact Name: J. Dean Sedinger, President
Catalog: Free. Frequency: Annual
Circulation: 25K. Sales: $500K - $1MM
Products: Spices, bakery, seed & specialty
items; garlic products for garden and kitchen

GOLD PURE FOOD PRODUCTS CO.   (516) 483-5600
1 Brooklyn Rd. • Hempstead, NY 11550

E-Mail: generalcomments@goldshorseradish.com
Website: www.goldshorseradish.com
Fax Ordering: (516) 483-5798
Contact Name: Herbert Gold, President
Catalog: Free. Frequency: Annual
Circulation: 50K. Sales: $5-10MM
Products: Kosher condiments, sauces &
specialty soups

HERB PRODUCTS COMPANY   (800) 877-3104
                                              (888) 339-HERB
11664 Tuxford St. • Sun Valley, CA 91352
E-Mail: info@herbproducts.com
Website: www.herbproducts.com
Fax Ordering: (818) 767-6285
International Ordering: (818) 767-6134
Contact Name: Geneva "Betty" DuVal, President
Catalog: Free. Frequency: Annual
Circulation: 50K. Sales: $1-3MM
Products: Herbs and herb products

LE JARDIN DU GOURMET   (800) 659-1446
P.O. Box 75
St. Johnsbury Center, VT 05863
E-Mail: orderdesk@artisticgardens.com
Website: www.artisticgardens.com
Fax Ordering: (802) 748-1446
International Ordering: (802) 748-1446
Contact Names: Paul Taylor, President
Catalog: Free. Frequency: Annual
Circulation: 50K. Sales: $500KM
Products: Herbs, vegetables, flower
seeds, plants; books

MAGIC SEASONINGS MAIL ORDER   (800) 457-2857
Magic Seasoning Blends
P.O. Box 23342 • New Orleans, LA 70183
E-Mail: info@chefpaul.com
Website: www.chefpaul.com
Fax Ordering: (504) 731-3576
International Ordering: (504) 731-3590
Contact Names: Paul Prudhomme, Owner
Catalog: Free. Frequency: Annual
Circulation: 200K. Sales: $3-5MM
Products: Seasonings, cookbooks, gift packs,
smoked meats; cookware and recipes

MAURICE'S GOURMET BARBEQUE   (800) 628-7423
P.O. Box 6847 • West Columbia, SC 29171
E-Mail: mail@mauricesbbq.com
Website: www.mauricesbbq.com
Fax Ordering: (803) 791-8707
International Ordering: (803) 791-5887
Contact Names: Maurice Bessinger, President
Catalog: Free. Frequency: Annual
Circulation: 50K. Sales: $3-5MM
Products: Gourmet barbeque sauces & ribs

NEW ORLEANS SCHOOL OF COOKING   (800) 237-4841
LOUISIANA GENERAL STORE
524 St. Louis St. • New Orleans, LA 70130
E-Mail: alison@nosoc.com
Website: www.neworleansschoolofcooking.com
Fax Ordering: (504) 596-2150
International Ordering: (504) 525-2665
Contact Names: Alison Blondeau, Sales
Catalog: Free. Frequency: Annual
Circulation: 100K. Sales: $1-3MM
Products: Gift baskets, cookbooks, mixes,
hot sauces, pralines, seasonings, snacks,
coffee/desserts, marinades & sauces,
kitchenware, CD's

OLDE WESTPORT SPICE & TRADING CO. (800) 537-6470
P.O. Box 12525 • Shawnee Mission, KS 66282
E-Mail: orders@oldewestportspice.com
Website: www.oldewestportspice.com
Fax Ordering: (913) 894-7878
International Ordering: (913) 649-1993
Contact Names: Ann Peterson, President
Catalog: Free. Frequency: Semiannual
Circulation: 75K. Sales: $1-3MM
Products: Spice blends & seasonings;
soups; bulk spices; cookbooks

ORIENTAL HERB COMPANY (800) 635-4372
3202 Northwest Hwy. • Cary, IL 60013
E-Mail: sales@orientalherb.com
Website: www.orientalherb.com
Fax Ordering: (847) 639-7199
International Ordering: (847) 639-7191
Contact Names: Dean Chambers, President
Catalog: Free. Frequency: Annual
Circulation: 10K. Sales: $250-500K
Products: Chinese herbal first aid products
including linaments and assorted teas;
herbal liquors, equine herbal formulas.

PECOS VALLEY SPICE COMPANY (800) 473-8226
2655 Pan American NE, Suite F
Albuquerque, NM 87107
Fax Ordering: (505) 243-8296
International Ordering: (505) 248-1727
Contact Names: Gordon McMeen, President
Catalog: Free. Frequency: Quarterly
Circulation: 50K. Sales: $1-3MM
Products: Spices for southwest cooking

PENDERY'S (800) 533-1870
1221 Manufacturing St. • Dallas, TX 75207
E-Mail: email@penderys.com
Website: www.penderys.com
Fax Ordering: (214) 761-1966
International Ordering: (214) 741-1870
Contact Names: Pat Haggerty, President
Catalog: Free. Frequency: Semiannual
Circulation: 50K. Sales: $5-10MM
Products: Chile pepers; spices & seasonings;
sauces & salsa; gourmet food; Mexican &
Southwest cooking; books; apparel & textiles;
housewares; home & garden; seasonal &
Holiday gifts

PENN HERB COMPANY (800) 523-9971
10601 Decatur Rd.
Philadelphia, PA 19154
E-Mail: orders@pennherb.com
Website: www.pennherb.com
Fax Ordering: (215) 632-7945
International Ordering: (215) 632-6100
Contact Names: Ron Betz, President
Catalog: Free. Frequency: Semiannual
Circulation: 100K. Sales: $5-10MM
Products: Medicinal herbs and natural
remedies including rare essential oils,
herbal extracts, homeopathic preparations
nd gensing.

PENZEY'S SPICES (800) 741-7787
12201 W. Capitol Dr.
Wauwatosa, WI 53150
E-Mail: sales@penzeys.com
Website: www.penzeys.com
Fax Ordering: (414) 760-7317
Catalog: Free. Frequency: Bimonthly

Circulation: 250K. Sales: $5-10MM
Products: Herbs, spices and seasonings;
gift boxes

PRAIRIE HERB, INC. (800) 447-2867
P.O. BOX 3375 • Gillette, WY 82717
E-Mail: phc@vcn.com
Website: www.gourmetvinegar.com
Fax Ordering: (307) 686-2253
International Ordering: (307) 686-1784
Contact Names: Cecilia M. Stanford, President
Catalog: Free. Frequency: Semiannual
Circulation: 50M. Sales: $500M
Products: Gourmet wine vinegars; gift baskets

PURE SPICE (866) 258-9517
E-Mail: info@purespice.com
Website: www.purespice.com
Contact Names: Brian M. Benko, President
Catalog: Free. Frequency: Semiannual
Circulation: 50K. Sales: $3-5MM
Products: 350 gourmet herbs & spices

SAN FRANCISCO HERB (800) 227-2830
& NATURAL FOOD CO.
47444 Kato Rd. • Freemont, CA 94538
E-Mail: info@herbspicetea.com
Website: www.herbspicetea.com
Fax Ordering: (510) 770-9021
International Ordering: (510) 770-1215
Contact Names: Barry Meltzer, President
Catalog: Free. Frequency: Annual
Circulation: 50K. Sales: $5-10MM
Products: Over 1,000 different medicinal
botanicals, culinary herbs & spices;
essential oils; fragrance oils; tea blends

SAN FRANCISCO HERB COMPANY (800) 227-4530
250 14th St. • San Francisco, CA 94103
E-Mail: info@sfherb.com
Website: www.sfherb.com
Fax Ordering: (415) 861-4440
International Ordering: (415) 861-7174
Contact Names: Neil Hanscomb, President
Catalog: Free. Frequency: Semiannual
Circulation: 100K. Sales: $1-3MM
Products: Culinary herbs, spices, teas,
extracts, botanicals for health, potpourri
ingredients, and essential oils.

SOUTHERN FLAVORING COMPANY (800) 765-8565
P.O. Drawer 341 • Bedford, VA 24523
E-Mail: john@southernflavoring.com
Website: www.southernflavoring.com
Fax Ordering: (800) 440-7694; (540) 586-8568
International Ordering: (540) 586-8565
Contact Names: John P. Messler, President
Catalog: Free. Frequency: 5x per year
Circulation: 100K. Sales: $5-10MM
Products: Seasonings, flavorings, cheesecake,
candles, candy, novelties, greeting cards

SOUTHWEST SPECIALTY FOODS, INC. (800) 536-3131
700 N. Bullard Ave. • Goodyear, AZ 85338
E-Mail: info@asskickin.com
Website: www.asskickin.com
Fax Ordering: (623) 931-9931
International Ordering: (623) 935-4700
Catalog: Free. Frequency: Annual
Circulation: 50K. Sales: $1-3MM
Products: Seasonings, salsas, condiments &
spices, snacks, hot sauces; gift baskets; apparel

SPECIALTY SAUCES   (800) 728-2371
638 Anthony Trail • Northbrook, IL 60062
E-Mail: sauces@specialtysauces.com
Website: www.specialtysauces.com
Fax Ordering: (847) 498-5551
International Ordering: (847) 509-8200
Contact Names: Ellen Robinson, President
Catalog: Free. Frequency: Semiannual
Circulation: 50K. Sales: $1-3MM
Products: Gourmet barbecue, salsa &
pasta sauces

SPICES, ETC.   (800) 827-6373
P.O. Box 2088 • Savannah, GA 31402
E-Mail: spices@spicesetc.com
Website: www.spicesetc.com
Fax Ordering: (800) 827-0145
Contact Names: Wes Wyse, Fulfillment
Catalog: Free. Frequency: Quarterly
Circulation: 1MM. Sales: $3-5MM
Products: Packaged herbs & spices,
pepper & peppermills, spice blends,
specialty seasonings, dried vegetables,
natural flavorings, gourmet dried mushrooms,
teas, sauces, salsas & snacks; baskets,
crates & racks; grinders & books

TABASCO COUNTRY STORE   (800) 634-9599
McIlhenny Co.
Hwy. 329 • Avery Island, LA 70513
E-Mail: info@countrystore.tabasco.com
Website: www.countrystore.tabasco.com.com
Fax Ordering: (337) 369-8326
International Ordering: (337) 365-8173
Contact Names: Edward Simmons, President
Catalog: Free. Frequency: Annual
Circulation: 100K. Sales: $10-20MM
Products: Pepper sauces, tabasco sauce

THOMAS GOURMET FOODS   (800) 867-2823
P.O. Box 8822 • Greensboro, NC 27419
E-Mail: order1@thomassauce.com
Website: www.thomassauce.com
Fax Ordering: (336) 299-7852
International Ordering: (336) 299-6263
Contact Names: Dwight C. Thomas, President
Catalog: Free. Frequency: Semiannual
Circulation: 30K. Sales: $500K
Products: Herbs, spices and teas

USEFUL GUIDE TO HERBAL HEALTH CARE   (800) 544-4225
Health Center for Better Living
1414 Rosemary Lane • Naples, FL 34103
E-Mail: customer.support@hcbl.com
Website: www.hcbl.com
Fax Ordering: (941) 643-6335
International Ordering: (941) 643-6563
Catalog: Free. Frequency: Quarterly
Circulation: 50M. Sales: $1-5MM
Products: Variety of herbs for health care

VANILLA, SAFFRON IMPORTS   (415) 648-8990
949 Valencia St. • San Francisco, CA 94110
E-Mail: saffron@saffron.com
Website: www.saffron.com
Fax Ordering: (415) 648-2240
International Ordering: (415) 648-8990
Contact Names: Juan San Mames, President
Catalog: Free. Frequency: Monthly
Circulation: 100K. Sales: $500K to 1MM
Products: Vanilla extract and vanilla beans,
saffron and wild muffins

J.R. WATKINS NATURALS   (800) 928-5467
150 Liberty St. • Winona, MN 55987
E-Mail: info@watkinsonline.com
Website: www.watkinsonline.com
Fax Ordering: (507) 452-6723
International Ordering: (507) 457-3300
Contact Names: Mark Jacobs, President
Catalog: Free. Frequency: Annual
Circulation: 50K. Sales: $10-20MM
Products: Organic spices & extracts;
home remedies; home, health and
personal care products

WHO WANTS TO BE A MUSTARDAIRE   (800) 438-6878
Mount Horeb Mustard Museum
P.O. Box 468 • Mount Horeb, WI 53572
E-Mail: curator@mustardmuseum.com
Website: www.mustardmuseum.com
Fax Ordering: (608) 437-4018
International Ordering: (608) 437-3986
Contact Names: Michael Carr, President
Catalog: Free. Frequency: Annual
Circulation: 100M. Sales: $500K - $1MM
Products: Mustard & gourmet sauces; souvenirs

MEAT & POULTRY

AIDELL'S SAUSAGE CO.   (800) 546-5795
1625 Alvarado St. • San Leandro, CA 94577   (877) 243-3557
E-Mail: info@aidells.com
Website: www.aidells.com
Fax Ordering: (510) 614-2846
International Ordering: (510) 614-5450
Contact Names: Ernie Gabiati, President
Catalog: Free. Frequency: Annual
Circulation: 50K. Sales: $5-10MM
Products: Sausages of all kinds

ALLEN BROTHERS   (800) 957-0111
3737 S. Halsted St. • Chicago, IL 60609
E-Mail: info@allenbrothers.com
Website: www.allenbrothers.com
Fax Ordering: (800) 890-9146
International Ordering: (773) 890-5100
Customer Service: (800) 548-7777
Catalog: Free. Frequency: Annual
Circulation: 50K. Sales: $5-10MM
Products: Suppliers of meat and steaks
to restaurants

AMANA MEAT SHOP & SMOKEHOUSE   (800) 373-6328
P.O. Box 158 • Amana, IA 52203
E-Mail: info@amanameatshop.com
Website: www.amanameatshop.com
Fax Ordering: (319) 622-6245
International Ordering: (319) 622-7580
Contact Names: Greg Hergert, President
Catalog: Free. Frequency: Annual
Circulation: 100K. Sales: $5-10MM
Products: Smoked meats, fresh meats,
hams and bacon

AMERICAN BISON WORLD   (888) 854-4449
Sayers Brook Bison Ranch   (888) 472-9377
11820 Sayersbrook Rd. • Potosi, MO 63664
E-Mail: infos@sayersbrook.com
Website: www.sayersbrook.com
Fax Ordering: (573) 438-2948
International Ordering: (573) 438-4449
Contact Names: H.M. Sayers, President

Catalog: Free. Frequency: Bimonthly
Circulation: 250K. Sales: $5-10MM
Products: Bison food products

BROADBENT'S B&B FOOD PRODUCTS (800) 841-2202
257 Mary Blue Rd. • Kuttawa, KY 42055
E-Mail: ORDER@broadbenthams.com
Website: www.broadbenthams.com
Fax Ordering: (270) 388-0613
International Ordering: (270) 235-5294
Contact Names: Ronny Drennan, President
Catalog: Free. Frequency: Annual
Circulation: 50K. Sales: $5-10MM
Products: Country hams, hickory smoked
bacon and sausage

BROKEN ARROW RANCH (800) 962-4263
3296 Junction Hwy. • Ingram, TX 78025
E-Mail: sales@brokenarrowranch.com
Website: www.brokenarrowranch.com
Fax Ordering: (510) 770-9021
International Ordering: (510) 770-1215
Contact Names: Mike Hughes, President
Catalog: Free. Frequency: Annual
Circulation: 50K. Sales: $1-3MM
Products: Free-range venison, antelope,
& wild boar meat from Central & South Texas

BURGERS' SMOKEHOUSE (800) 624-5426
Burgers' Ozark Country Cured Hams (800) 345-5185
32819 Hwy. 87 South • California, MO 65018
E-Mail: service@smokehouse.com
Website: www.smokehouse.com
Fax Ordering: (573) 796-3137
International Ordering: (573) 796-3134
Contact Names: Keith Fletcher, Marketing
Catalog: Free. Frequency: Quarterly
Circulation: 50K. Sales: $5-10MM
Products: Cured & smoked meats & poultry

CALLAWAY GARDENS COUNTRY STORE (800) 280-7524
P.O. Box 2000 • Pine Mountain, GA 31822
E-Mail: sales@callawaygardens.com
Website: www.callawaygardens.com
Fax Ordering: (706) 663-5068
International Ordering: (706) 663-2281
Contact Names: George P. Fischer, President
Catalog: Free. Frequency: Annual
Circulation: 50K. Sales: $1-3MM
Products: Hams, bacon & muscadine products

GODSHALL'S QUALITY MEATS (800) 932-8377
675 Mill Rd. • Telford, PA 18969 (888) 463-7425E-
Mail: info@godshalls.com
Website: www.godshalls.com
Fax Ordering: (215) 274-6103
International Ordering: (215) 256-8867
Contact Names: R.M. Trider, President
Catalog: Free. Frequency: Semiannual
Circulation: 50K. Sales: $5-10MM
Products: Smoked meats; turkey bacon;
gift baskets

EARLY'S HONEY STAND (800) 523-2015
P.O. Box 908 • Spring Hill, TN 37174
Fax Ordering: (615) 302-1121
International Ordering: (615) 302-2802
Contact Names: Jean Cathey, President
Catalog: Free. Frequency: Semiannual
Circulation: 150K. Sales: $1-3MM
Products: Country sausage, boiled ham,
Canadian bacon; mixes, jams, jellies.

FOUR OAKS FARM (800) 858-5006
P.O. Box 987 • Lexington, SC 29071
E-Mail: fouraks@fouroaksfarm.com
Website: www.fouroaksfarm.com
Fax Ordering: (803) 951-0843
International Ordering: (803) 356-3194
Contact Names: Donald Mathias, President
Catalog: Free. Frequency: Semiannual
Circulation: 25K. Sales: $1-3MM
Products: Smoked meats, condiments,
jams; gift boxes

GOLDEN TROPHY STEAKS (800) 835-6607
3548 N. Kostner Ave. • Chicago, IL 60641
E-Mail: info@giftsteaksonline.com
Website: www.giftsteaksonline.com
Fax Ordering: (800) 835-6601
International Ordering: (847) 302-3300
Contact Names: Butch Pfagizer, President
Catalog: Free. Frequency: Quarterly
Circulation: 75K. Sales: $5-10MM
Products: Gourmet meats & food products

HARRINGTON'S OF VERMONT (802) 434-4444
210 E. Main St. • Richmond, VT 05477
E-Mail: info@harringtonham.com
Website: www.harringtonham.com
Fax Ordering: (802) 434-3166
International Ordering: (802) 434-4444
Customer Service: (802) 434-3415
Contact Names: Peter Klingenberg, President
Catalog: Free. Frequency: 9x per year
Circulation: 1MM. Sales: $20-50MM
Products: Corncob smoked meats & fine foods

HOME BISTRO (800) 628-5588
P.O. Box 275 • Wittenburg, WI 54499 (800) 749-1170
E-Mail: customerservice@homebistro.com
Website: www.homebistro.com
Customer Service: (800) 343-5588
Contact Names: Chef Noche, Executive Chef
Catalog: Free. Frequency: Semiannual
Circulation: 50K. Sales: $5-10MM
Products: Chef prepared meals delivered
to your door

THE HONEY BAKED HAM CO. (800) 367-2426
P.O. Box 370 • Carrollton, GA 30117 (800) 343-4267
E-Mail: info@honeybaked.com
Website: www.honeybaked.com;
    www.hbhship.com
Fax Ordering: (800) 728-4426; (770) 214-1045
International Ordering: (770) 836-5900
Contact Names: Kim Hunter, President
Catalog: Free. Frequency: Semiannual
Circulation: 500K. Sales: $25-50MM
Products: Hams, turkey, BBQ ribs, desserts,
gift baskets

JACKSON HOLE BUFFALO MEAT CO. (800) 543-6328
P.O. Box 1770 • Jackson, WY 83001
E-Mail: info@jhbuffalomeat.com
Website: www.jhbuffalomeat.com
Fax Ordering: (307) 733-7244
International Ordering: (307) 733-4159
Contact Names: Dan Marino, Owner
Catalog: Free. Frequency: Semiannual
Circulation: 50K. Sales: $5-10MM
Products: Gift packs of smoked meats & trout,
bison steaks, salami; buffalo & elk gift packs

JAMISON FARM   (800) 237-5262
171 Jamison Lane • Latrobe, PA 15650
E-Mail: john@jamisonfarm.com
Website: www.jamisonfarm.com
Fax Ordering: (724) 837-2287
International Ordering: (724) 834-7424
Contact Names: John Jamison, President
Catalog: Free. Frequency: Semiannual
Circulation: 50K. Sales: $5-10MM
Products: Natural farm raised lamb & products

KANSAS CITY STEAK COMPANY   (800) 524-1844
100 Osage Ave. • Kansas City, KS 66105
E-Mail: info@herbspicetea.com
Website: www.kasnascitysteak.com
Fax Ordering: (800) 331-8707
International Ordering: (913) 371-1107
Contact Names: Edward Scavuzzo, President
Catalog: Free. Frequency: Quarterly
Circulation: 75K. Sales: $5-10MM
Products: Steaks; roasts; pork & poultry;
seafood; seasonings

KLEMENT'S SAUSAGE CO., INC.   (800) 553-6368
207 E. Lincoln Ave. • Milwaukee, WI 53207
E-Mail: info@klements.com
Website: www.klements.com
Fax Ordering: (414) 744-2438
International Ordering: (414) 744-2330
Contact Names: Don F. Klement, President
Catalog: Free. Frequency: Annual
Circulation: 100K. Sales: $20-50MM
Products: Sausage & cheese gift boxes

LOVELESS HAMS & JAMS CATALOG   (800) 889-2432
8400 Hwy. 100 • Nashville, TN 37221
E-Mail: loveless@lovelesscafe.com
Website: www.lovelesscafe.com
Fax Ordering: (615) 770-9021
International Ordering: (615) 646-0067
Contact Names: George McCabe, President
Catalog: Free. Frequency: Semiannual
Circulation: 100K. Sales: $5-10MM
Products: Smoked country hams, bacon,
sausage; homemade preserves; gift packages

MAHOGANY SMOKED MEATS   (888) 624-6426
P.O. Box 1387 • Bishop, CA 93515
E-Mail: info@smokedmeats.com
Website: www.smokedmeats.com
Fax Ordering: (760) 773-8761
International Ordering: (760) 873-5311
Contact Names: Joann Murdy, President
Catalog: Free. Frequency: Quarterly
Circulation: 50K. Sales: $1-3MM
Products: Smoked meats

MILLER'S COUNTRY HAMS   (800) 622-0606
7110 HWY. 190 • Dresden, TN 38225
Fax Ordering: (731) 364-5338
International Ordering: (731) 364-3940
Catalog: Free. Frequency: Annual
Circulation: 50K. Sales: $3-5MM
Products: Hams and turkeys

NEBRASKA'S FAMOUS STEAKS   (888) 463-8823
P.O. Box 198 • Hastings, NE 68902
E-Mail: info@famoussteaks.com
Website: www.famoussteaks.com
Fax Ordering: (402) 463-6715
International Ordering: (402) 463-8823
Contact Names: Barry Meltzer, President

Catalog: Free. Frequency: Annual
Circulation: 50K. Sales: $5-10MM
Products: Steaks, chops, smoked turkeys,
ham, meat & cheese pies, seafood, desserts

NEW BRAUNFELS SMOKEHOUSE   (800) 537-6932
P.O. Box 311159 • New Braunfels, TX 78131
E-Mail: Info@nbsmokehouse.com
Website: www.smokehouse.com
Fax Ordering: (800) 284-5330
International Ordering: (830) 303-5905
Contact Names: Dudley Snyder, President
Catalog: Free. Frequency: Quarterly
Circulation: 100K. Sales: $20-50MM
Products: Hickory-smoked meats from Texas

NODINE'S SMOKEHOUSE   (800) 222-2059
65 Fowler Ave. • Torrington, CT 06790
E-Mail: nodines@snet.net
Website: www.nodinesmokehouse.com
Fax Ordering: (860) 496-9787
International Ordering: (860) 489-3213
Contact Names: Ron Nodine, President
Catalog: Free. Frequency: Annual
Circulation: 20K. Sales: $5-10MM
Products: Smoked meats, poultry, cheese, fish

NORTH COUNTRY SMOKEHOUSE   (800) 258-4304
P.O. Box 1415 • Claremont, NH 03743
E-Mail: info@ncsmokehouse.com
Website: www.ncsmokehouse.com
Fax Ordering: (603) 543-3016
International Ordering: (603) 542-8323
Contact Names: Michael Satzow, President
Catalog: Free. Frequency: Annual
Circulation: 25K. Sales: $5-10MM
Products: Smoked hams & chops, chicken
& duck, bacons, cheeses, turkeys, sausages,
gift packages

NUESKE APPLEWOOD   (800) 392-2266
SMOKED SPECIALTY MEATS
Nueske Hillcrest Farm Meats
RR 2, P.O. Box D • Wittenberg, WI 54499
E-Mail: info@nueske.com
Website: www.nueske.com
Fax Ordering: (800) 962-2266
Customer Service: (800) 720-1153
Contact Names: Robert D. Nueske, President
Catalog: Free. Frequency: 5x per year
Circulation: 250K. Sales: $20-50MM
Products: Applewood smoked specialty
meats and poultry

OAKWOOD GAME FARM   (800) 328-6647
P.O. Box 274 • Princeton, MN 55371
E-Mail: info@oakwoodgamefarm.com
Website: www.oakwoodgamefarm.com
Fax Ordering: (763) 389-2077
International Ordering: (763) 389-2031
Contact Names: Jim Meyer, President
Catalog: Free. Frequency: Annual
Circulation: 10K. Sales: $500K to $1MM
Products: Fesh & smoked game birds
including wild turkey; adult game birds;
quail, pheasant, partridge, & mallard ducks.

OMAHA STEAKS   (800) 228-9055
P.O. Box 3300 • Omaha, NE 68103   (800) 960-8400
E-Mail: custserv@omahasteaks.com   (888) 959-9464
Website: www.omahasteaks.com
Fax Ordering: (877) 329-6328; (402) 597-8222

International Ordering: (402) 597-3000
Customer Service: (800) 228-9872
Contact Names: Todd Simon, Sr. VP
Catalog: Free. Frequency: 3x per year
Circulation: 250K. Sales: $20-50MM
Products: Gourmet steaks, soups, meats,
seafood and poultry; desserts & specialty
items; gourmet frozen & prepared meals;
a variety of easy-to-fix complete meals
from A La Zing.

OSCAR'S HICKORY HOUSE (800) 627-3431
Oscar's Adirondack Mountain Smokehouse
22 Raymond Lane • Warrensburg, NY 12885
E-Mail: oscar@capital.net
Website: www.oscarssmokedmeats.com
Fax Ordering: (518) 623-3982
International Ordering: (518) 623-3431
Contact Names: Ron Nodine, President
Catalog: Free. Frequency: Annual
Circulation: 25K. Sales: $5-10MM
Products: Hickory smoked meats; bacon,
chicken, pork, sausage, poultry, cheeses;
syrup

OZARK MOUNTAIN SMOKE HOUSE (800) 643-3437
P.O. Box 37 • Farmington, AR 72730
E-Mail: nodines@snet.net
Website: www.ozarkmountainsmokehouse.com
Fax Ordering: (497) 267-2620
Contact Names: Tom Bourdeaux, Owner
Catalog: Free. Frequency: Annual
Circulation: 10K. Sales: $500K to $1MM
Products: Smoked meats; poultry, sausage
& cheese, fish

RALPH'S PACKING COMPANY (800) 522-3979
P.O. Box 249 • Perkins, OK 74059
E-Mail: sales@ralphspacking.com
Website: www.ralphspacking.com
Fax Ordering: (405) 547-2364
International Ordering: (405) 547-2464
Contact Names: Gary Crane, President
Catalog: Free. Frequency: Quarterly
Circulation: 50K. Sales: $10-20MM
Products: Fresh & smoked meat;
sugar-cured hams and bacon

RANCH HOUSE MESQUITE (800) 749-6329
SMOKED MEATS
P.O. Box 977 • Menard, TX 76859
E-Mail: sales@brisket.net
Website: www.brisket.net
Fax Ordering: (888) 917-6328
International Ordering: (915) 396-2101
Contact Names: Max Stabel, President
Catalog: Free. Frequency: 10x per year
Circulation: 100K. Sales: $10-20MM
Products: Mesquite smoked meats

ROY L. HOFFMAN & SONS (800) 356-3193
13225 Cearfoss Pike
Hagerstown, MD 21740
E-Mail: dluhouse@hoffmanmeats.com
Website: www.hoffmanmeats.com
Fax Ordering: (301) 733-5549
International Ordering: (301) 739-2332
Contact Names: Don Hoffman, President
Catalog: Free. Frequency: Annual
Circulation: 25K. Sales: $5-10MM
Products: Country smoked ham, bacon
and sausage

SMITHFIELD HAMS (800) 926-8448
P.O. Box 250 • Portsmouth, VA 23705
E-Mail: info@smithfieldhams.com
Website: www.smithfieldhams.com
Fax Ordering: (757) 673-7004
Contact Names: Alexa Ricketts, Manager
Catalog: Free. Frequency: Annual
Circulation: 50K. Sales: $5-10MM
Products: Smithfield hams, country hams,
BBQ sauces and meats, smoked turkey,
cakes & confections; gourmet gift baskets;
cookbooks and other items.

SMOKING & MEAT CURING (888) 490-8525
SUPPLY & EQUIPMENT CATALOG
SausageMaker
1500 Clinton St., Bldg. 123 • Buffalo, NY 14206
E-Mail: customerservice@sausagemaker.com
Website: www.sausagemaker.com
Fax Ordering: (716) 824-6465
International Ordering: (716) 824-6510
Customer Service: (716) 824-5814
Contact Names: Wes Smyzynski, President
Catalog: Free. Frequency: Semiannual
Circulation: 10K. Sales: $5-10MM
Products: Sausage making equipment
& supplies

STOCK YARDS CHICAGO (800) 621-3687
P.O. Box 12450 • Chicago, IL 60612 (877) 785-9273
E-Mail: customerservice@stockyards.com
Website: www.stockyards.com
Fax Ordering: (312) 733-1746
International Ordering: (312) 733-6050
Contact Names: Doug Atkinson, President
Catalog: Free. Frequency: Quarterly
Circulation: 150K. Sales: $50-100MM
Products: USDA prime and choice beef;
gourmet foods and seafood; lamb & pork;
appetizers & desserts.

SUGARDALE FOODS (800) 860-4267
3768 Progress St. NE • Canton, OH 44705 (800) 860-6777
E-Mail: retail@sugardalefoods.com
Website: www.sugardalefoods.com
Fax Ordering: (800) 860-1522
International Ordering: (330) 456-8810
Contact Names: Joe Pellegrene, President
Catalog: Free. Frequency: 3x per year
Circulation: 100K. Sales: $5-10MM
Products: Smoked & processed meats to the
retail industry; seafood, cheese, preserves,
cakes & candy

THE SWISS COLONY/TENDER FILET (800) 228-1214
1112 7th Ave. • Monroe, WI 53566
E-Mail: sales@swisscolony.com
Website: www.swisscolony.com
Fax Ordering: (608) 328-8457
International Ordering: (608) 328-8635;
324-4603
Contact Names: Raymond Kubly, President
Catalog: Free. Frequency: Quarterly
Circulation: 250K. Sales: $100-200MM
Products: Steaks, smoked meats,
seafood, desserts

USINGER'S FAMOUS SAUSAGE (800) 558-9998
Fred Usinger, Inc.
1030 N. Old World Third St.
Milwaukee, WI 53203
E-Mail: usinger@etecps.com

Website: www.usinger.com
Fax Ordering: (414) 291-5277
International Ordering: (414) 276-9100
Contact Names: Fritz Usinger, President
Catalog: Free. Frequency: Annual
Circulation: 150K. Sales: $20-50MM
Products: German sausages, ham, angus
beef steaks, Wisconsin cheeses, gift packs

WINES & LIQUOR

BEER & WINE HOBBY   (800) 523-5423
155 New Boston St. • Woburn, MA 01801
E-Mail: info@beer-wine.com
Website: www.beer-wine.com
Fax Ordering: (781) 933-1359
International Ordering: (781) 933-8818
Contact Name: Fernando Gaspar, President
Catalog: Free. Frequency: Semiannual
Circulation: 75K. Sales: $1-3MM
Products: Beer and wine making supplies

GEERLINGS & WADE   (800) 782-9463
2545 Napa Valley Corp. Dr., Suite C   (866) 409-9463
Napa, CA 94558
E-Mail: info@geerwade.com
Website: www.geerwade.com
Fax Ordering: (800) 435-1329
Contact Name: David Pearce, President
Catalog: Free. Frequency: Semiannual
Circulation: 100K. Sales: $10-20MM
Products: Wine and wine accessories

GREAT AMERICAN BEER & WINE CLUBS   (800) 879-2747
Clubs of America   (800) 258-2872
426 Scotland Rd. • Lakemoor, IL 60050
E-Mail: greatclubs@aol.com
Website: www.greatclubs.com
Fax Ordering: (815) 363-4677
International Ordering: (815) 363-4000
Customer Service: (800) 800-9122
Contact Name: Douglas M. Doretti, President
Catalog: Free. Frequency: 3x per year
Circulation: 500K. Sales: $5-10MM
Products: Mail order microbrewed beer
and wine of the month clubs; each month
you'll receive a 12-pack of four different
types of handcrafted microbrewed beer
in 12 once bottles per month; each month
you'll receive two different bottles of rare wine.

GUIDE TO GOOD HOSTING & GIFTS   (800) 723-8372
Beverage Media Group
116 John St., 23rd Fl. • New York, NY 10038
E-Mail: info@bevmedia.com
Website: www.bevnetwork.com
Fax Ordering: (212) 571-4443
International Ordering: (212) 571-3232
Contact Name: William Slone, President
Catalog: Free. Frequency: Annual
Circulation: 10K. Sales: $3-5MM
Products: Wines & liquor

HENNESSEY'S WINES & SPIRITS   (888) 300-2900
545 2nd St. • San Francisco, CA 94107
E-Mail: orders@gourmetwines.com
Website: www.gourmetwines.com
Fax Ordering: (415) 777-9004
International Ordering: (415) 348-1432

Contact Name: Les Hennessy, President
Catalog: Free. Frequency: Semiannual
Circulation: 20K. Sales: $1-3MM
Products: Wines and cigars; chesses,
specialty foods and gift baskets; wine club

INTERNATIONAL WINE ACCESSORIES   (800) 527-4072
9600 Bell Rd. • Windsor, CA 95492
E-Mail: customerservice@iwawine.com
Website: www.iwawine.com
Contact Name: Robert Crenstein, President
Catalog: Free. Frequency: Monthly
Circulation: 50K. Sales: $5-10MM
Products: Wine cellar kits, including stemware,
corkscrews, racking; home decor; entertainment
& barware; books, media & education; gifts

LIQUOR.COM   (800) 774-7483
4205 W. Irving Park Rd.
Chicago, IL 60641
E-Mail: info@liquor.com
Website: www.liquor.com
Fax Ordering: (800) 232-9529
International Ordering: (773) 427-8622
Catalog: Free. Frequency: Annual
Circulation: 25K. Sales: $1-3MM
Products: Champagnes, beers, spirits, gifts

MARTINIWARE   (563) 505-0738
E-Mail: sales@martiniware.com
Website: www.martiniware.com
International Ordering: (563) 505-0738
Catalog: Free. Frequency: Semiannual
Circulation: 100K. Sales: $1-3MM
Products: Martini glasses, shakers, clothing,
gourmet olives & garnishes

MORRELL & COMPANY   (800) 969-4637
One Rockefeller Plaza
New York, NY 10020
E-Mail: customerservice@winesbymorrell.com
Website: www.winesbymorrell.com
Fax Ordering: (212) 223-1846
International Ordering: (212) 688-9370
Contact Name: Roberta Morrell, President
Catalog: Free. Frequency: Semiannual
Circulation: 250K. Sales: $10-20MM
Products: Fine wines and spirits

SECRET CELLAR WINE CLUB   (763) 670-5043
11071 Sprucewood Lane N.
Champlin, MN 55316
E-Mail: deb@secretcellarwineclub.com
Website: www.secretcellarwineclub.com
Catalog: Free. Frequency: Semiannual
Circulation: 200M. Sales: $500Kto $1MM
Products: Monthly shipments of two bottles
of California wine; also Champagne,
international wines, gourmet coffees and teas.

SHERRY LEHMANN WINE & SPIRITS   (212) 838-7500
505 Park Ave. • New York, NY 10022
E-Mail: inquiries@sherry-lehmann.com
Website: www.sherry-lehmann.com
Fax Ordering: (212) 838-9285
International Ordering: (212) 838-7500
Contact Name: Sara Weinberg, Manager
Catalog: Free. Frequency: Semiannual
Circulation: 250M. Sales: $10-50MM
Products: Fine wines and liquor; specialty foods;
gift baskets; chees & chocolates

WINDSOR VINEYARDS   (800) 333-9987
9600 Bell Rd. • Windsor, CA 95492   (800) 289-9463
E-Mail: webmaster@windsorvineyards.com
Website: www.windsorvineyards.com
Fax Ordering: (707) 836-5900
International Ordering: (707) 836-5000
Catalog: Free. Frequency: Quarterly
Circulation: 10K. Sales: $10-20MM
Products: Manufacturers and distributors
of premium wines; gift baskets, wine-food,
picnic items, wine-related products

WINE CELLAR INNOVATIONS   (800) 229-9813
4575 Eastern Ave. • Cincinnati, OH 45226
E-Mail: orders@winecellarinnovations.com
Website: www.winecellarinnovations.com
Fax Ordering: (513) 979-5280
International Ordering: (513) 321-3733
Catalog: Free. Frequency: Semiannual
Circulation: 100K. Sales: $3-5MM
Products: Custom wine cellars & wine racks

WINE COUNTRY GIFT BASKETS   (800) 394-0394
P.O. Box 5530 • Fullerton, CA 92838
E-Mail: orders@winecountrygiftbaskets.com
Website: www.winecountrygiftbaskets.com
Fax Ordering: (714) 525-0746
Customer Service: (800) 324-2793
Contact Name: Tim Dean, President
Catalog: Free. Pages: 26.
Frequency: Semiannual
Circulation: 100K. Sales: $3-5MM
Products: Wine gift baskets, gourmet food
gift baskets

WINE ENTHUSIAST   (800) 356-8466
P.O. Box 39 • Pleasantville, NY 10570
E-Mail: custserv@wineenthusiast.com
Website: www.wineenthusiast.com
Fax Ordering: (800) 833-8466
Customer Service: (800) 648-6058
Catalog: Free. Frequency: Semiannual
Circulation: 250K. Sales: $10-50MM
Products: Wine accessories, wine gifts,
wine cellars, wine racks, wine glasses

WINE EXPRESS   (800) 962-8463
P.O. Box 459 • Pleasantville, NY 10570
E-Mail: custserv@wineexpress.com
Website: www.wineexpress.com
Fax Ordering: (800) 200-9463
Contact Name: Josh Farrell, Wine Director
Catalog: $4. Frequency: Semiannual
Circulation: 100K. Sales: $5-10MM
Products: Fine wines

A.M. LEONARD   (800) 543-8955
P.O. Box 816 • Piqua, OH 45356
E-Mail: info@amleo.com
Website: www.amleo.com
Fax Ordering: (800) 433-0633; (937) 773-9959
International Ordering: (937) 773-2694
Contact Name: Gregory Stephens, President
Catalog: Free. Frequency: Quarterly
Circulation: 100K. Sales: $3-5MM
Products: Lawn and garden supplies:
hand tools, power equipment, work apparel

ABBEY GARDEN CACTUS   (562) 905-3520
P.O. Box 2249 • La Habra, CA 90632
Fax Ordering: (562) 905-3522
Contact Name: Lem & Pat Higgs, Owners
Catalog: $2 refundable. Frequency: Annual
Circulation: 10M. Pages: 56. Sales: $250M
Products: 1700+ species of cactus & succulents

ADAMS COUNTY NURSERY   (717) 677-8105
P.O. Box 108 • Aspers, PA 17304
E-Mail: acn@cvn.net
Website: www.acnursery.com
Fax Ordering: (717) 677-4124
International Ordering: (717) 677-8105
Contact Name: John Baugher, President
Catalog: Free. Frequency: Annual
Circulation: 50K. Sales: $1-3MM
Products: Fruit trees

AITKEN'S SALMON CREEK GARDEN   (360) 573-4472
608 NW 119th St. • Vancouver, WA 98685
E-Mail: aitken@flowerfantasy.net
Website: www.flowerfantasy.net
Fax Ordering: (360) 576-7012
International Ordering: (360) 573-4472
Contact Name: Terry & Barbara Aitken, Owners
Catalog: Print (free) & Online. Frequency: Annual
Circulation: 10K. Sales: $100-500K
Products: Irises and orchids

ALL SEASONS HOMESTEAD HELPERS   (800) 649-9147
P.O. Box 99 • Jeffersonville, VT 05464
E-Mail: info@homesteadhelpers.com
Website: www.homesteadhelpers.com
Fax Ordering: (802) 644-5112
Catalog: Free. Frequency: Semiannual
Circulation: 25K. Sales: $250-500K
Products: Garden supplies; tools &
power equipment

ALLEN, STERLING & LOTHROP   (207) 781-4142
191 US Rt. 1 • Falmouth, ME 04105
E-Mail: sales@allensterlinglothrop.com
Website: www.allensterlinglothrop.com
Fax Ordering: (207) 781-4143
Contact Names: Ashley & Shaw Brannigan
Catalog: $1 for print; Online Frequency: Annual
Circulation: 5K. Sales: $250-500K
Products: Vegetable, flower & herb seeds;
gardening supplies

ALOHA TROPICALS   (760) 631-2880
P.O. Box 6042 • Oceanside, CA 92054
E-Mail: alohatrop@aol.com
Website: www.alohatropicals.com
Fax Ordering: (760) 631-2880
Contact Name: Andy & Sally Zuckowich, Owners
Catalog: $4. Frequency: Annual
Circulation: 25K. Sales: $500K to 1MM
Products: Exotic tropical plants

ALPEN GARDENS   (503) 662-3951
12010 NE Flett Rd. • Gaston, OR 07119
E-Mail: info@alpengardens.com
Website: www.alpengardens.com
Fax Ordering: (503) 662-4952
Contact Names: J.D. & Cydney Stables
Catalog: Free print; Online Frequency: Annual
Circulation: 50K. Sales: $500K to $1MM
Products: Dahlias tubers

AMADOR FLOWER FARM   (209) 245-6660
2201 Shenandoah School Rd.
Plymouth, CA 95669
E-Mail: sales@amadorflowerfarm.com
Website: www.amadorflowerfarm.com
Fax Ordering: (209) 245-6648
Contact Name: Jeanne Denver, President
Catalog: $1. Frequency: Weekly
Circulation: 20K. Sales: $500K to $1MM
Products: Daylilies, unusual perennials
and grapes; gardening items

AMBERGATE GARDENS   (877) 211-9769
8730 County Rd. 43 • Chaska, MN 55318
E-Mail: mjhamber@aol.com
Website: www.ambergategardens.com
Fax Ordering: (952) 443-2248
International Ordering: (952) 443-2248
Contact Name: Michael Heger, President
Catalog: $3. Frequency: Annual
Circulation: 10K. Sales: $500K to $1MM
Products: Perennial flowers; gardening
books & tools

AMERICAN ARBORIST SUPPLIES   (800) 441-8381
882 S. Matlack St.
West Chester, PA 19382
E-Mail: info@arborist.com
Website: www.arborist.com
Fax Ordering: (888) 441-8382
International Ordering: (610) 296-4126
Contact Name: Richard W. Miller, President
Catalog: Free. Frequency: Semiannual
Circulation: 100K. Sales: $1-5MM
Products: Supplies for arborists: tools &
equipment; books on aboriculture

AMERICAN DAYLILY & PERENNIALS   (800) 770-2777
P.O. Box 210 • Grain Valley, MO 64029
E-Mail: catalog@americandaylily.com
Website: www.americandaylily.com
Fax Ordering: (816) 443-2849
International Ordering: (816) 224-2852
Contact Name: Jo Roberson, Marketing
Catalog: Free. Frequency: Annual
Minimum order: $35. Minimum quantity: 3
Circulation: 25K. Sales: $1-3MM
Products: Perennials: daylilies, lantanas,
cannas, cleomes; grasses, shrubs, trees;
growing guides

AMERICAN FORESTS   (800) 320-8733
HISTORIC TREE NURSERY
8701 Old Kings Rd.
Jacksonville, FL 32219
E-Mail: customerservice@historictrees.org
Website: www.historictrees.org
Fax Ordering: (904) 768-4630
Catalog: Free. Frequency: Annual
Circulation: 25K. Sales: $500M to $1MM
Products: Christmas trees; Preserve trees; Cypress
trees; Willow trees; Fiber Optic trees; Bonsai trees

AMSI MINIATURE LANDSCAPING (800) 227-2760
P.O. Box 750638 • Petaluma, CA 94975
E-Mail: amsistuff@comcast.net
Website: www.amsi.miniature.net
Fax Ordering: (707) 763-6061
International Ordering: (707) 763-6000
Contact Name: Mary Costello, Marketing
Catalog: Free. Frequency: Weekly
Circulation: 20K. Sales: $500K
Products: Miniature landscaping

ANTIQUE ROSE EMPORIUM (800) 441-0002
9300 Lueckemeyer Rd.
Brenham, TX 77833
E-Mail: roses@weareroses.com
Website: www.antiqueroseemporium.com
Fax Ordering: (979) 836-0928
International Ordering: (979) 836-9051
Contact Name: Alison Duckworth, Marketing
Catalog: Free. Frequency: Annual
Circulation: 50K. Sales: $1-3MM
Products: Antique and old garden roses

ANTONELLI BROTHERS (888) 423-4664
BEGONIA GARDENS
407 Hecker Pass Rd.
Watsonville, CA 95076
E-Mail: skippant@cruzio.com
Website: www.antonellibegonias.com
Fax Ordering: (831) 475-7066
International Ordering: (831) 724-6367
Catalog: Free. Frequency: Semiannual
Circulation: 25K. Sales: $500K to $1MM
Products: Tuberous begonias; dahlias,
gladiolas, lilies, etc.

AQUATIC ECO-SYSTEMS (877) 347-4788
2395 Apopka Blvd. #100
Apopka, FL 32703
E-Mail: info@aquaticeco.com
Website: www.aquaticeco.com
Fax Ordering: (407) 886-6787
International Ordering: (407) 886-3939
Tech Support: (407) 598-1401
Contact Name: A.J. Amatuzio, President
Catalog: $5. Frequency: Annual
Circulation: 100K. Sales: $5-10MM
Products: Aquatic research & education,
books & videos; water garden; aquarium;
aquaculture; pond, lake, fish farming;
hydroponics & aquaponics

ARBICO ORGANICS (800) 827-2847
Arbico Environmentals
P.O. Box 8910 • Tucson, AZ 885738
E-Mail: info@arbico.com
Website: www.arbico.com
Fax Ordering: (520) 825-2038
International Ordering: (520) 825-9785
Contact Name: Rick Frey, President
Catalog: Free. Frequency: Annual
Circulation: 100K. Sales: $5-10MM
Products: Gardening supplies, pet products,
fertilizers; insect & pest control products;
natural household products.

AUDUBON WORKSHOP (513) 354-1485
5200 Schenley Pl. • Lawrenceburg, IN 47025
E-Mail: info@audubonworkshop.com
Website: www.audubonworkshop.com
Fax Ordering: (513) 354-1487
Customer Service: (513) 354-1486

Catalog: Free. Frequency: Semiannual
Circulation: 150K. Sales: $500K to $1MM
Products: Bird feeders, bird food, bird houses,
bird baths; ponds & water plants; nature
friendly gardens, perennials, tools & accessories

B&D LILIES (360) 765-4341
P.O. Box 2007 • Port Townsend, WA 98368
E-Mail: lilygarden@bdlilies.com
Website: www.bdlilies.com
Fax Ordering: (360) 765-4074
Contact Name: Bob & Dianna Gibson, Owners
Catalog: Free. Frequency: Semiannual
Circulation: 100K. Sales: $250K to $500K
Products: Lily bulbs

BAMBOO SOURCERY (707) 823-5866
666 Wagnon Rd. • Sebastopol, CA 95472
E-Mail: info@bamboosourcery.com
Website: www.bamboosourcery.com
Fax Ordering: (707) 829-8106
Contact Name: Jennifer York, President
Catalog: $3 print or Online. Frequency: Annual
Circulation: 25K. Sales: $250K to $500K
Products: 300 species of bamboo plants;
garden accessoires; books; fencing

BAMERT SEED COMPANY (800) 262-9892
1897 CR 1018 • Muleshoe, TX 79347
E-Mail: natives@bamertseed.com
Website: www.bamertseed.com
Fax Ordering: (806) 221-5619
International Ordering: (806) 221-5614
Contact Name: Nick Bamert, President
Catalog: Free. Frequency: Annual
Circulation: 100K. Sales: $1-3MM
Products: 40 species of native grass seeds;
legumes, and forbs for prairie restoration,
wildlife habitat, wildlife food plots, reclamation
and conservation reserve programs

BANANA TREE (610) 253-9589
715 Northampton St. • Easton, PA 18042
E-Mail: faban@banana-tree.com
Website: www.banana-tree.com
Fax Ordering: (610) 253-4864
Contact Name: Fred Saleet, President
Catalog: $2. Frequency: Annual
Circulation: 250M. Sales: $500K
Products: Tropical seeds and bulbs;
vegetable seeds, herbal seeds; cactus
& succulents

BEATY FERTILIZER CO. (800) 845-2325
P.O. Box 2516 • Cleveland, TN 37320
E-Mail: info@millsmix.com
Website: www.millsmix.com
Fax Ordering: (423) 472-5492
Catalog: Free. Frequency: Annual
Circulation: 50K. Sales: $1-3MM
Products: Mills Magic Rose Mix; garden
supplies, tools & power equipment;
irrigation supplies & equipment; fertilizer,
weed & pest control products.

BLOSSOM FLOWER SHOP (800) 544-4401
980 McLean Ave. • Yonkers, NY 10704 (888) 425-0019
275 Mamaroneck Ave.
White Plains, NY 10605
E-Mail: sales@blossomflower.com
Website: www.blossomflower.com
Fax Ordering: (914) 237-3213

International Ordering: (914) 237-2511; 304-5374
Catalog: Free. Frequency: Monthly
Circulation: 100K. Sales: $500K to $1MM
Products: Flowers, plants, fruit & gourmet
gift baskets

BLUESTONE PERENNIALS   (800) 852-5243
7211 Middle Ridge Rd. • Madison, OH 44057
E-Mail: service@bluestoneperennials.com
Website: www.bluestoneperennials.com
Fax Ordering: (440) 428-7198
Contact Name: William Boonstra, President
Catalog: Free. Frequency: Semiannual
Circulation: 25K. Sales: $500K
Products: Perennials, grasses, mums,
herbs, ornamental shrubs, and bulbs

BOUNTIFUL GARDENS   (707) 459-6410
18001 Shafer Ranch Rd. • Willits, CA 95490
E-Mail: bountiful@sonic.net
Website: www.bountifulgardens.org
Fax Ordering: (707) 459-1925
Contact Name: Bill Bruneau, President
Catalog: Free. Frequency: Annual
Circulation: 50K. Sales: $500K
Products: Vegetable, herbs and flower seeds;
green manure crops and grains; gardening
books, tools and organic supplies

BRAMEN COMPANY   (800) 234-7765
45 Mason St. • Salem, MA 01970
E-Mail: info@bramen.com
Website: www.bramen.com
Fax Ordering: (978) 745-7425
International Ordering: (978) 745-7765
Contact Name: Robert Strom, President
Catalog: Free. Frequency: Semiannual
Circulation: 25K. Sales: $500K to $1MM
Products: Greenhouse equipment

BRENT & BECKY'S BULBS   (877) 661-2852
7900 Daffodil Lane • Gloucester, VA 23061
E-Mail: info@brentandbeckysbulbs.com
Website: www.brentandbeckysbulbs.com
Fax Ordering: (804) 693-9436
International Ordering: (804) 693-3966
Contact Names: Brent & Becky Heath, Owners
Catalog: Free. Frequency: Semiannual
Circulation: 500M. Sales: $3-5MM
Products: Flowers, bulbs and accessories

BRUSSEL'S BONSAI NURSERY   (800) 582-2593
8125 Center Hill Rd. • Olive Branch, MS 38654
E-Mail: shirley@brusselsbonsai.com
Website: www.brusselsbonsai.com
Fax Ordering: (662) 895-4157
Contact Name: Brussel Martin, Owner
Catalog: Free. Frequency: Annual
Circulation: 50K. Sales: $1-5MM
Products: Bonsai plants, pottery, and
accessories

BURGESS SEED & PLANT CO.   (309) 662-7761
905 Four Seasons Rd. • Bloomington, IL 61701
E-Mail: customerservice@eburgess.com
Website: www.eburgess.com
Fax Ordering: (309) 663-6691
Contact Name: Richard Owen, President
Catalog: Free. Frequency: 3x per year
Circulation: 50K. Sales: $5-10MM
Products: Vegetable seeds, bulbs, perennial
and ornamentals plants

BURPEE GARDEN CATALOG   (800) 888-1447
W. Atlee Burpee & Co.
300 Park Ave. • Warminster, PA 18974
E-Mail: custserv@burpee.com
Website: www.burpee.com
Fax Ordering: (800) 487-5530
International Ordering: (215) 674-4900
Customer Service: (800) 333-5808
Contact Name: Don Zeidler, Manager
Catalog: Free. Frequency: Annual
Circulation: 2MM. Sales: $20-50MM
Products: Flower bulbs, seeds and trees;
vegetables, flowers & herbs; annuals &
perennials; garden gear

BURRELL'S BETTER SEEDS   (866) 254-7333
D.V. Burrell Seed Growers Co.
P.O. Box 150 • Rocky Ford, CO 81067
E-Mail: burrellseeds@centurytel.net
Website: www.burrellseeds.us
Fax Ordering: (719) 254-3319
International Ordering: (719) 254-3318
Contact Names: William & Richard Burrell
Catalog: Free. Pages: 104. Frequency: Annual
Circulation: 25K. Sales: $3-5MM
Products: Vegetable, flowers, herbs seeds;
garden tools, supplies & accessories

BUSSE GARDENS   (800) 544-3192
17160 245th Ave. • Big Lake, MN 55309
E-Mail: customer.service@bussegardens.com
Website: www.bussegardens.com
Fax Ordering: (763) 263-1013
International Ordering: (763) 263-3403
Contact Name: Aine Busse, President
Catalog: $3. Pages: 72. Frequency: Annual
Circulation: 25K. Sales: $3-5MM
Products: Perennials

C&O NURSERY COMPANY   (800) 232-2636
P.O. Box 116 • Wenatchee, WA 98807
E-Mail: tree@c-onursery.com
Website: www.c-onursery.com
Fax Ordering: (509) 662-4519
International Ordering: (509) 662-7164
Contact Name: Jack Snyder, President
Catalog: Free. Frequency: Monthly
Circulation: 25K. Sales: $3-5MM
Products: Greenhouses, sunrooms,
solariums, atriums; accessories

CALYX FLOWERS   (800) 800-7788
Calyx & Corolla, Inc.
6655 Shelburne Rd.
Shelburne, VT 05482
E-Mail: info@calyxflowers.com
Website: www.calyxflowers.com
Fax Ordering: (802) 985-1304
International Ordering: (802) 497-6789
Contact Name: Ruth Owades, President
Catalog: Free. Frequency: Monthly
Circulation: 50K. Sales: $1-3MM
Products: Flowers

CARINO NURSERIES   (800) 223-7075
P.O. Box 538 • Indiana, PA 15701
E-Mail: info@carinonurseries.com
Website: www.carinonurseries.com
Fax Ordering: (724) 463-3050
International Ordering: (724) 463-3350
Contact Name: James & Laura Carino, President
Catalog: Free. Frequency: Semiannual

Circulation: 50M. Sales: $500M to $1MM
Products: Christmas trees; Evergreen &
deciduous seedlings suitable for Christmas
trees; ornamentals and timber for landscaping

CARNIVOROUS PLANTS & SUPPLIES — (585) 394-7397
Peter Paul's Nursery
2661 State Rt. 21 • Canandaigua, NY 14424
Fax Ordering: (585) 394-4122
Contact Name: Jay Miller, President
Catalog: Free. Frequency: Monthly
Circulation: 20K. Sales: $250-500K
Products: Carnivorous plants, seeds, supplies

CAROLINA EXOTIC GARDENS — (252) 758-2600
2237 Sunny Side Rd. • Greenville, NC 27834
E-Mail: cegnursery@aol.com
Website: www.carnivorousplant.info
Fax Ordering: (252) 757-2601
Contact Name: D.R. Minton, President
Catalog: Free. Frequency: Weekly
Circulation: 100M. Sales: $500M
Products: Carnivorous plants & seeds;
venus flytraps; book

CARTER & HOLMES ORCHIDS — (803) 276-0579
629 Mendenhall Rd. • Newberry, SC 29108
E-Mail: orchids@carterandholmes.com
Website: www.carterandholmes.com
Fax Ordering: (803) 276-0588
Contact Name: Mac Holmes, President
Catalog: $2.50. Online. Frequency: Annual.
Circulation: 25K. Sales: $1-3MM
Products: Orchids, seedlings; houseplants;
supplies; gift items; books

CASCADE FORESTRY NURSERY — (800) 596-9437
21995 Fillmore Rd. • Cascade, IA 52033
E-Mail: cascade@netins.net
Website: www.wildflower.org
Fax Ordering: (563) 852-5004
International Ordering: (563) 852-3042
Contact Name: Leo H. Frueh, President
Catalog: Free. Frequency: Semiannual
Circulation: 50K. Sales: $1-3MM
Products: Nut trees, other trees, conifers,
tree planting, timber consulting

CATALOG OF BENEFICIALS — (800) 248-2847
Rincon-Vitova Insectaries
P.O. Box 1555 • Ventura, CA 93002
E-Mail: bugnet@rinconvitova.com
\Website: www.rinconvitova.com
Fax Ordering: (805) 643-6267
International Ordering: (805) 643-5407
Contact Name: Ron Whitehurst, Advisor
Catalog: Free. Frequency: Annual
Circulation: 25K. Sales: $1-3MM
Products: Bio-control insect & pest control,
and IPM supplies

CHAMBLEE'S ROSE NURSERY — (800) 256-7673
10926 US Hwy. 69 N. • Tyler, TX 75706
E-Mail: roses@chambleeroses.com
Website: www.chambleeroses.com
Fax Ordering: (903) 882-3597
International Ordering: (903) 882-5153
Catalog: Free. Frequency: Semiannual
Circulation: 20K. Sales: $500K
Products: Over 300 varieties of antique &
modern garden roses, ground cover and
miniature roses

CHARLEY'S GREENHOUSE SUPPLY — (800) 322-4707
17979 State Rt. 536
Mount Vernon, WA 98273
E-Mail: cgh@charleysgreenhouse.com
Website: www.charleysgreenhouse.com
Fax Ordering: (800) 233-3078; (360) 392-5225
International Ordering: (360) 392-7101
Contact Names: Charles & Carol Yaw, Owners
Catalog: Free. Frequency: Quarterly
Circulation: 200K. Sales: $3-5MM
Products: Greenhouses and greenhouse
materials and supplies; plant lights, misting
systems; books

CLYDE ROBIN SEED COMPANY — (800) 647-6475
P.O. Box 411 • Santa Clara, UT 84765
E-Mail: sales@clyderobin.com
Website: www.clyderobin.com
Fax Ordering: (435) 216-5414
Customer Service: (510) 315-6720
Contact Name: Steve Atwood, Contact
Catalog: Free. Frequency: Annual
Circulation: 100K. Sales: $1-3MM
Products: Wildflower seeds, regional mixes
& blends; shrubs and trees; garden supplies

COLORBLENDS — (888) 847-8637
Schipper & Co. USA
747 Barnum Ave. • Bridgeport, CT 06608
E-Mail: info@colorblends.com
Website: www.colorblends.com
Fax Ordering: (203) 338-0744
International Ordering: (203) 338-0776
Contact Name: Tim Schipper, President
Catalog: Free. Frequency: Annual
Circulation: 100K. Sales: $1-3MM
Products: Wholesale flowerbulbs; Tulip &
Daffadil bulbs; Spring flowering bulbs from
The Netherlands; Tulips for Fall planting

COMSTOCK, FERRE & CO. — (800) 733-3773
263 Main St. • Wethersfield, CT 06109
E-Mail: info@comstockferre.com
Website: www.comstockferre.com
Fax Ordering: (860) 571-6595
International Ordering: (860) 571-6590
Contact Name: Pierre Bennerup, President
Catalog: Free. Frequency: Annual
Circulation: 50K. Sales: $1-3MM
Products: Vegetable, flower and herb seeds

THE COOK'S GARDEN — (800) 457-9703
P.O. Box 535 • Londonderry, VT 05148
E-Mail: info@cooksgarden.com
Website: www.cooksgarden.com
Fax Ordering: (800) 457-9705
Contact Names: Shepherd & Ellen Ogden, Owners
Catalog: Free. Frequency: Annual
Circulation: 50K. Sales: $500K to $1MM
Products: Vegetable & herb seeds & plants;
cottage flowers; supplies for the garden

COOLEY'S GARDENS — (800) 225-5391
P.O. Box 126 • Silverton, OR 97381
E-Mail: office@cooleysgardens.com
Website: www.cooleysgardens.com
Fax Ordering: (503) 873-5812
International Ordering: (503) 873-5463
Contact Name: Richard Ernst, President
Catalog: Free. Frequency: Annual
Circulation: 50K. Sales: $1-3MM
Products: 300+ varieties of bearded Iris

CROPKING (800) 321-5656
134 West Dr. • Lodi, OH 44254
E-Mail: cropking@cropking.com
Website: www.cropking.com
Fax Ordering: (330) 302-4204
International Ordering: (330) 302-4203
Contact Name: Paul Brentlinger, President
Catalog: Online. Sales: $3-5MM
Products: Greenhouses and supplies and
equipment for hydroponic growers; books
& videos

DABNEY HERBS (502) 893-5198
P.O. Box 22061 • Louisville, KY 40252
E-Mail: info@dabneyherbs.com
Website: www.dabneyherbs.com
Fax Ordering: (502) 893-5198
Contact Names: Davy Dabney, Owner
Catalog: Free. Frequency: Semiannual
Circulation: 50K. Sales: $500M
Products: Herbs, geraniums, perennials &
wildflowers; potpouri supplies and essential
oils; books and related gardening products

DAKOTA INDUSTRIES - (800) 237-7785
TREE & TURF EQUIPMENT
6945 Indiana Court #400
Arvanda, CO 80007
E-Mail: sales@protreeturf.com
Website: www.protreeturf.com
Fax Ordering: (303) 421-4142
International Ordering: (303) 422-7608
Contact Name: Rick Veenstra, President
Catalog: Free. Frequency: Annual
Circulation: 50K. Sales: $1-3MM
Products: Professional tree & turf spray
equipment; parts & accessories

DAVID AUSTIN'S ROSES (800) 328-8893
15059 Hwy. 64 W. • Tyler, TX 75704
E-Mail: us@davidaustinroses.com
Website: www.davidaustinroses.com
Fax Ordering: (903) 526-1900
International Ordering: (903) 526-1800
Contact Name: David Austin, President
Catalog: Free. Frequency: Annual
Circulation: 50K. Sales: $1-3MM
Products: Over 200 varieties of roses

DAVIDSON GREENHOUSE & NURSERY (877) 723-6834
3147 E. Ladoga Rd. • Crawfordsville, IN 47933
E-Mail: vicki@davidsongreenhouse.com
Website: www.davidsongreenhouse.com
Fax Ordering: (800) 276-3691
International Ordering: (765) 364-0556
Catalog: Free. Frequency: Semianual
Circulation: 25K. Sales: $1-3MM
Products: Basket plants, begonias, succulents,
fertilizer, geraniums, herbs, outdoor plants, pest
control products

DAYLILY DISCOUNTERS (800) 329-5459
Pinecliffe Gardens
6745 Foster Rd. • Philpot, KY 42366
E-Mail: daylily@pinecliffegardens.com
Website: www.daylily-discounters.com
Fax Ordering: (270) 281-4160
International Ordering: (270) 281-9791
Contact Name: Tom Allin, President
Catalog: Free. Frequency: Annual
Circulation: 50K. Sales: $1-3MM
Products: Daylilies and hostas; garden books

DAYLILY WORLD (407) 416-9119
1301 Gilberts Creek Rd.
Lawrenceburg, KY 40342
E-Mail: hybridizer@aol.com
Website: www.daylilyworld.com
Contact Name: David Kirchhoff, President
Catalog: Free. Frequency: Annual
Minimum Order: $100
Circulation: 25K. Sales: $500K to $1MM
Products: Variety of daylilies

DBS HIGHLIGHTS (570) 226-3239
Dorothy Biddle Service
348 Greeley Lake Rd. • Greeley, PA 18425
E-Mail: info@dorothybiddle.com
Website: www.dorothybiddle.com
Fax Ordering: (570) 226-0349
Contact Name: Lynn J. Dodson, President
Catalog: Free. Frequency: Annual
Circulation: 40M. Sales: $500M to $1MM
Products: Wholesale florist supplies &
garden accessories

DEEPROCK MANUFACTURING (800) 333-7762
P.O. Box 1 • Opelika, AL 36803 (800) 633-8798
E-Mail: info@deeprock.com
Website: www.deeprock.com
Fax Ordering: (334) 749-5601
International Ordering: (334) 749-3377
Contact Name: Mike Beasley, President
Catalog: Free. Frequency: Annual
Circulation: 25K. Sales: $10-20MM
Products: Drilling equipment, commercial
drilling rigs; lawn cultivators, tillers, trimmers,
seeders and accessories

DeGIORGI SEED COMPANY (800) 858-2580
6011 N St. • Omaha, NE 68117
E-Mail: lisadechant@degiorgiseed.com
Website: www.degiorgiseed.com
Fax Ordering: (402) 731-8475
International Ordering: (402) 731-3901
Contact Name: Linda Dechant, President
Catalog: Free. Frequency: Annual
Circulation: 20K. Sales: $500K - 1MM
Products: Seeds for herbs, grasses,
perennials, vegetables and wildflowers

DeGRANDCHAMP'S BLUEBERRY FARM (888) 483-7431
76241 14th Ave. • South Haven, MI 49090
E-Mail: info@degrandchamps.com
Website: www.degrandchamps.com
Fax Ordering: (269) 637-2531
International Ordering: (269) 637-3915
Contact Name: Joseph DeGrandchamp, President
Catalog: Free. Frequency: Semiannual
Circulation: 50K. Sales: $10-20MM
Products: Blueberries

DOORNBOSCH BROS. (800) 684-4526
P.O. Box 129 • Osceola, IN 46561
E-Mail: sales@doornboschbros.com
Website: www.doornboschbros.com
Contact Name: Susan Vandervlugt, Manager
Catalog: Free. Frequency: Semiannual
Circulation: 25K. Sales: $1-3MM
Products: Flower bulbs and perennials

DOYLE'S THORNLESS BLACKBERRY, INC. (812) 254-2654
1600 Bedford Rd. • Washington, IN 47501
E-Mail: tomdoyle@fruitsandberries.com
Website: www.fruitsandberries.com

Fax Ordering: (812) 254-2655
International Fax Ordering: (812) 254-2654
Contact Name: Joe Perrotto, President
Catalog: Free. Frequency: 8x per year
Circulation: 50K. Sales: $1-3MM
Products: Annuals, perennials, exotic plants
& flowers, flowerr, vegetable & wildflower seeds;
fruit trees & berries; garden supplies, tools &
power equipment; ground covers, shrubs,
trres & vines; herbs & vegetables; fertilizer,
weed & pest control products

DR POWER EQUIPMENT   (800) 687-6575
Country Home Products
P.O. Box 25 • Vergennes, VT 05491
E-Mail: info@countryhomeproducts.com
Website: www.countryhomeproducts.com
Fax Ordering: (802) 877-1213 (U.S.)
International Fax Ordering: (802) 877-1216
Contact Name: Joe Perrotto, President
Catalog: Free. Frequency: 8x per year
Circulation: 100K. Sales: $10-20MM
Products: Property care tools and equipment
including outdoor power equipment, attachments
and accessories.

DRAMM PRODUCTS   (800) 258-0848
Dramm Corporation
P.O. Box 1960 • Manitowoc, WI 54221
E-Mail: information@dramm.com
Website: www.dramm.com
Fax Ordering: (920) 684-4499
International Ordering: (920) 684-0227
Contact Name: Kurt Dramm, President
Catalog: Free. Frequency: Annual
Circulation: 50K. Sales: $1-3MM
Products: Professional watering tools;
integrated plant health; organic & susta
inable fertilizer

DRIP IRRIGATION CATALOG   (800) 692-4100
Hydromatic Irrigation
P.O. Box 3965 • Lubbock, TX 79452
E-Mail: info@submatic.com
Website: www.submatic.com
Fax Ordering: (806) 745-8010
International Ordering: (806) 799-0700
Contact Name: Curry Blackwell, President
Catalog: Free. Frequency: Semiannual
Circulation: 20K. Sales: $5-10MM
Products: Drip irrigation products &
sprinklers, including kits, poly flex hose,
fittings, emitters & accessories; jets,
mini-sprinklers & micro tubing, stakes,
regulators & filters, injectors & timers,
and specialty items

DRIPWORKS   (800) 522-3747
190 Sanhedrin Cir. • Willits, CA 95490
E-Mail: sales@dripworksusa.com
Website: www.dripworksusa.com
Fax Ordering: (707) 459-9645
International Ordering: (707) 459-6323
Contact Name: Leon & Jerry Springer, Owners
Catalog: Free. Pages: 60. Frequency: Annual
Circulation: 100K. Sales: $5-10MM
Products: Drip irrigation & micro irrigation
systems and products, including drippers &
sprayers, filters, regulators; Everliner pond
liners.

DUTCH GARDENS, INC.   (877) 527-7575
1021 N. Second St. • Chillicothe, IL 61523
E-Mail: info@dutchgardens.com
Website: www.dutchgardens.com
Fax Ordering: (309) 274-2810
International Ordering: (309) 274-2820
Customer Servcie: (800) 950-4470
Catalog: Free. Frequency: Annual
Circulation: 150K. Sales: $5-10MM
Products: Specialty bulbs; perennials;
lillles; roses; gladiolas; begonias; dahlias;
cannas; fruits & berries; shrubs & vines

ePONDS.COM   (866) 620-6088
P.O. Box 5564 • Saginaw, MI 48603
E-Mail: info@eponds.com
Website: www.eponds.com
Fax Ordering: (989) 921-4666
Catalog: Free. Frequency: Semiannual
Circulation: 100K. Sales: $3-5MM
Products: Pond supplies & water gardening

EDIBLE LANDSCAPING   (800) 524-4156
361 Spirit Ridge Lane • Afton, VA 22920
E-Mail: janet@ediblelandscaping.com
Website: www.ediblelandscaping.com
Fax Ordering: (434) 361-1916
International Ordering: (434) 361-9134
Contact Name: Michael McConkey, President
Catalog: $2.00. Frequency: Monthly
Circulation: 50K. Sales: $500M to $1MM
Products: Low maintenance plants for your
garden or yard

EDMUNDS' ROSES   (888) 481-7673
335 S. High St. • Randolph, WI 53965
E-Mail: info@edmundsroses.com
Website: www.edmundsroses.com
Fax Ordering: (503) 682-1275
International Ordering: (503) 682-1476
Contact Names: Philip & Kathy Edmunds, Owners
Catalog: Free. Frequency: Annual
Circulation: 50K. Sales: $500K
Products: Hybrid tea roses, floribunda roses,
grandiflora and climbing roses; miniature roses,
climbing roses

EPIES BY PAT   (714) 524-0994
247 Wilson Ave.
Placentia, CA 92870
E-Mail: epies@roadrunner.com
Website: www.epies.net
Fax Ordering: (714) 682-1275
International Ordering: (714) 524-0994
Contact Names: Pat, President
Catalog: Free. Frequency: Semiannual
Circulation: 25K. Sales: $100-500K
Products: Over 2000 Epiphyllum plants
& 600 Daylily plants.

ERICKSON BIRDHOUSES   (800) 382-2473
1140 Elizabeth Ave., Suite 1
Lancaster, PA 17601
E-Mail: erickson@paonline.com
Website: www.bird-houses.com
Fax Ordering: (717) 397-2266
Contact Name: Eric Berman, Owner
Catalog: Free. Frequency: Weekly
Circulation: 50K. Sales: $500K - 1MM
Products: Birdhouses

ERNST CONSERVATION SEEDS (800) 873-3321
9006 Mercer Pike • Meadville, PA 16335
E-Mail: sales@ernstseed.com
Website: www.ernstseed.com
Fax Ordering: (814) 336-5191
International Ordering: (814) 336-2404
Contact Names: Calvin & Robin Ernst, Owners
Catalog: Free. Frequency: Annual
Circulation: 20K. Sales: $1-3MM
Products: Seeds and plants

ESCORT LIGHTING (800) 856-7948
51 N. Elm St. • Wernersville, PA 19565
E-Mail: info@escortlighting.com
Website: www.escortlighting.com
Fax Ordering: (610) 670-5170
International Ordering: (610) 670-2517
Contact Names: Mike Hartman, President
Catalog: Free. Frequency: Annual
Circulation: 50K. Sales: $1-3MM
Products: Garden lighting fixtures

EVERYTHING FOR THE LILYPOOL (863) 293-7151
Slocum Water Gardens
3914 S. Florida Ave. • Lakeland, FL 33813
E-Mail: sales@slocumwatergardens.com
Website: www.slocumwatergardens.com
Fax Ordering: (800) 322-1896
Contact Names: Peter Slocum, President
Catalog: Free. Frequency: Annual
Circulation: 10K. Sales: $500M
Products: Garden pool products; water
lilies, lotus, aquatics, pumps, filters, pools,
liners and books on water gardening.

FARMER SEED & NURSERY (507) 334-1623
818 NW 4th St. • Faribault, MN 55021
E-Mail: customerservice@farmerseed.com
Website: www.farmerseed.com
Fax Ordering: (507) 334-8214
Contact Name: Don Prodohl, President
Catalog: Free. Frequency: Annual
Circulation: 75K. Sales: $3-5MM
Products: Vegetable & flower seeds;
fruits & nuts, herbs, plants, daylilies,
roses, trees & bulbs

FEDCO SEEDS (207) 873-7333
P.O. Box 520 • Waterville, ME 04903
E-Mail: sales@fedcoseeds.com
Website: www.fedcoseeds.com
Fax Ordering: (207) 873-8317
Contact Name: Joanna Linden, President
Catalog: $1. Frequency: Quarterly
Circulation: 25K. Sales: $1-3MM
Products: Garden seeds, bulbs, fruit
& nut trees, seed potatoes; books &
accessories

FERTRELL COMPANY (800) 347-1566
601 N. Second St. • Bainbridge, PA 17502
E-Mail: info@fertrell.com
Website: www.fertrell.com
Fax Ordering: (717) 367-9319
International Ordering: (717) 367-1566
Contact Name: Dave Mattocks, Marketing
Catalog: Free. Frequency: Annual
Circulation: 20K. Sales: $10-20MM
Products: Organic fertilizers; animal
nutrition products

FIELDSTONE GARDENS (207) 923-3836
55 Quaker Lane • Vassalboro, ME 04989
E-Mail: sales@fieldstonegardens.com
Website: www.fieldstonegardens.com
Fax Ordering: (207) 923-3836
Contact Name: Steven Jones, President
Catalog: $2.50. Frequency: Annual
Circulation: 25K. Sales: $1-3MM
Products: Perennial plants, rock &
garden plants

FLICKINGERS' NURSERY (800) 368-7381
P.O. Box 245 • Sagamore, PA 16250
E-Mail: info@flicknursery.com
Website: www.flicknursery.com
Fax Ordering: (724) 783-6528
International Ordering: (724) 783-6528
Contact Names: Richard & Thomas Flickinger
Catalog: Free. Frequency: Annual
Circulation: 50K. Sales: $1-3MM
Products: Evergreen seedlings for Christmas
trees, ornamentals & reforestation, wildlife
cover and erosion control; lanscaping.

FLORENTINE CRAFTSMEN (800) 971-7600
46-24 28th St. • Long Island City, NY 11101
E-Mail: info@florentinecraftsmen.com
Website: www.florentinecraftsmen.com
Fax Ordering: (718) 937-9858
International Ordering: (718) 937-7632
Contact Names: Graham Brown, President
Catalog: $5 print. Online. Frequency: Annual
Circulation: 10K. Sales: $1-3MM
Products: Handcrafted garden furniture,
ornaments, planters, fountains, & statuaries;
bird baths, gazebos/trellis, sundials

FLORIAN RATCHET-CUT PRUNING TOOLS (800) 275-3618
157 Water St. • Southington, CT 06489
E-Mail: sales@florianratchetcut.com
Website: www.florianratchetcut.com
Fax Ordering: (860) 628-6036
International Ordering: (860) 628-9643
Contact Names: Nat Florian, President
Catalog: Free. Frequency: Semiannual
Circulation: 100K. Sales: $3-5MM
Products: Gardening tools, equipment &
accessories; bird feeders, organic pest
control products; landscape maintenance
equipment; gardening gifts; books & software

FORESTFARM (541) 846-7269
990 Tetherow Rd. • Williams, OR 97544
E-Mail: plants@forestfarm.com
Website: www.forestfarm.com
Fax Ordering: (541) 846-6963
Contact Name: Ray Prag, President
Catalog: $4. Frequency: Semiannual
Circulation: 50K. Sales: $1-3MM
Products: Plants from around the world

FOREST KEELING NURSERY (800) 356-2401
P.O. Box 135 • Elsberry, MO 63343
E-Mail: info@fknursery.com
Website: www.fknursery.com
Fax Ordering: (573) 898-5803
International Ordering: (573) 898-5571
Contact Name: Wayne Lovelace, President
Catalog: Free. Frequency: Semiannual
Circulation: 50K. Sales: $5-10MM
Products: Nursery stock, seedlings & small trees

FORK & SPADE (800) 829-5919
1313 Scenic Dr. • Modesto, CA 95355
E-Mail: patrick@forkandspade.com
Website: www.forkandspade.com
Fax Ordering: (209) 523-1615
Catalog: Free. Frequency: Annual
Circulation: 25K. Sales: $500K
Products: Bulbs; fruit trres & berries;
garden supplies, tools & power equipment;
bird feeders; garden decor; gifts & decorative
accessories; roses.

GARDENS ALIVE (513) 354-1482
5100 Schenley Pl.
Lawrenceburg, IN 47025
E-Mail: info@gardensalive.com
Website: www.gardensalive.com
Fax Ordering: (513) 354-1484
Contact Name: Niles Kinerk, President
Catalog: Free. Frequency: Monthly
Circulation: 150K. Sales: $5-10MM
Products: Natural lawn & garden products,
including insect & pest control products &
fertilizers; vegetable & flower gardening;
backyard birding; organic pet care; tools
& accessories

GARDEN CATALOG GUIDE (410) 540-9830
Mailorder Gardening Association
5836 Rockburn Woods Way
Elkridge, MO 21075
E-Mail: consumer@mailordergardening.com
Website: www.mailordergardening.com
Fax Ordering: (410) 540-9827
Contact Name: Camille Cimino, Exec.Director
Catalog: Free. Frequency: Annual
Circulation: 10K. Sales: $500K
Products: Lists companies that sell
environmentally responsible gardening
products

GARDEN CITY SEEDS (509) 964-7016
P.O. Box 307 • Thorp, WA 98946
E-Mail: seeds@montana.com
Website: www.gardencityseeds.com
Fax Ordering: (800) 964-9210
Contact Name: Greg Lutousky, President
Catalog: Free. Frequency: Annual
Circulation: 50K. Sales: $1-3MM
Products: Vegetable, herb and flowers seeds

GARDEN TOOLS BY LEE VALLEY (800) 871-8158
Lee Valley Tools
P.O. Box 6782 • Ogdensburg, NY 13669
E-Mail: customerservice@leevalley.com
Website: www.leevalley.com
Fax Ordering: (800) 513-7885
International Ordering: (613) 596-0350
Contact Name: Leonard Lee, President
Catalog: $5. Frequency: Monthly
Circulation: 50K. Sales: $1-3MM
Products: Gardening & woodworking
hand tools & accessories

GARDENER'S CATALOG (800) 733-4146
Kinsman Co.
P.O. Box 428 • Pipersville, PA 18947
E-Mail: info@kinsmangarden.com
Website: www.kinsmangarden.com
Fax Ordering: (215) 766-5624
Contact Names: Graham Kinsman, President
Catalog: Free. Frequency: Semiannual

Circulation: 400M. Sales: $5-10MM
Products: Garden supplies and accessories

GARDENER'S SUPPLY CO. (888) 833-1412
America's Gardening Resource
128 Intervale Rd. • Burlington, VT 05401
E-Mail: info@gardeners.com
Website: www.gardeners.com
Fax Ordering: (800) 551-6712; (802) 660-3501
International Ordering: (802) 660-3500
Contact Name: Jim Felnson, President
Catalog: Free. Frequency: Weekly
Circulation: 10MM. Sales: $20-50MM
Products: Garden tools & supplies; seeds
& plants; greenhouses, fertilizers, furniture,
organic pest controls, natural home & health
products; Vermont made products.

GARDENING WITH KIDS (800) 538-7476
National Gardening Association
1100 Dorsett St. • South Burlington, VT 05403
E-Mail: mk@kidsgardening.com
Website: www.kidsgardening.com
Fax Ordering: (802) 863-5962
International Ordering: (802) 863-5251
Contact Name: Mitchel Kurver, Marketing
Catalog: Free. Frequency: Semiannual
Circulation: 150K. Sales: $1-3MM
Products: Children gardening books &
products

GARY'S PERENNIALS (800) 898-6653
1122 E. Welsh Rd. • Ambler, PA 19002
E-Mail: roots@garysperennials.com
Website: www.garysperennials.com
Fax Ordering: (215) 628-0216
International Ordering: (215) 628-4070
Contact Name: Gary & Andrea Steinberg, Owners
Catalog: Free. Frequency: Semiannual
Circulation: 30K. Sales: $1-3MM
Products: Wholesale fieldgrown perennials

GILBERT H. WILD & SON (888) 449-4537
3044 State Hwy. 37 • Sarcoxie, MO 64862
E-Mail: customer service@gilberthwild.com
Website: www.gilberthwild.com
Fax Ordering: (888) 548-6831; (417) 548-6831
International Ordering: (417) 548-3514
Contact Name: Greg Jones, President
Catalog: $3. Frequency: Annual
Circulation: 10K. Sales: $1-3MM
Products: Daylilies, peonies and iris;
hostas, bare root plants

GIRARD NURSERIES (440) 466-2881
P.O. Box 428 • Geneva, OH 44041
E-Mail: girardnurseries@suite224.net
Website: www.girardnurseries.com
Fax Ordering: (440) 466-3999
Contact Name: Pete Girard, Jr., President
Catalog: Free. Frequency: Annual
Circulation: 25K. Sales: $1-3MM
Products:Plants, conifers and flowers

GLASSHOUSE WORKS (800) 837-2142
Church St. • Stewart, OH 45778
E-Mail: plants@glasshouseworks.com
Website: www.glasshouseworks.com
Fax Ordering: (740) 662-2120
International Ordering: (740) 662-2142
Contact Name: Thomas Winn, President
Catalog: $2. Frequency: Semiannual

Circulation: 20K. Sales: $1-3MM
Products: Plants, garden art and supplies

GOLDEN STATE BULB GROWERS　　(831) 728-0500
1260 Hwy. 1 • Moss Landing, CA 95039
E-Mail: vicki@davidsongreenhouse.com
Website: www.davidsongreenhouse.com
Fax Ordering: (831) 761-1282
International Ordering: (831) 728-0500
Catalog: Free. Frequency: Annual
Circulation: 15K. Sales: $1-3MM
Products: Annuals, bulbs, perennials,
flower, vegetable & wildflower seeds

GOOD SCENTS　　(800) 723-6834
Davidson Greenhouse & Nursery
3147 E. Lagoda Rd. • Crawfordsville, IN 47933
E-Mail: vicki@davidsongreenhouse.com
Website: www.davidsongreenhouse.com
Fax Ordering: (800) 276-3691
International Ordering: (765) 364-0556
Contact Name: Mark Davidson, President
Catalog: Free. Frequency: Annual
Circulation: 15M. Sales: $3-5MM
Products: Scented geraniums, begonias,
impatiens; houseplants, herbs

GOODWIN CREEK GARDENS　　(800) 846-7359
P.O. Box 83 • Williams, OR 97544
E-Mail: info@goodwincreekgardens.com
Website: www.goodwincreekgardens.com
Fax Ordering: (541) 846-7357
Contact Name: James Becker, President
Catalog: Free. Frequency: Weekly
Circulation: 25M. Sales: $500M to $1MM
Products: Herb plants and seeds; fragrent
bath essentials; home & garden gifts & books

GOOSEN INDUSTRIES　　(800) 228-6542
925 W. Court St. • Beatrice, NE 68310
Fax Ordering: (402) 223-2245
International Ordering: (402) 228-4226
Contact Name: Louis Goossen, President
Catalog: Free. Frequency: Annual
Circulation: 5M. Sales: $5-10MM
Products: Mulching machines,
clippers/shredders

GOURMET GARDENER　　(888) 404-4769
12287 117th Drive • Live Oak, FL 32060
E-Mail: information@gourmetgardener.com
Website: www.gourmetgardener.com
Fax Ordering: (407) 650-2691
Contact Name: Barbara Barker, President
Catalog: $2. Frequency: Annual
Circulation: 10K. Sales: $1-3MM
Products: Gourmet vegetable, herb &
edible flower seeds

GREAT GARDENS　　(800) 828-5500
Garden Way Manufacturing Co.
29 102nd St. • Troy, NY 12180
E-Mail: info@gardenway.com
Website: www.gardenway.com
Fax Ordering: (518) 391-7332
International Ordering: (518) 391-7000
Contact Name: Jairo Estrada, President
Catalog: Free. Frequency: Quarterly
Circulation: 150M. Sales: $10-20MM
Products: Outdoor power & garden equipment

GREAT PLAINS MANUFACTURING　　(800) 654-2630
P.O. Box 5060 • Salina, KS 67402
Fax Ordering: (785) 822-5600
International Ordering: (785) 823-3276
Contact Name: John Quinley, Manager
Catalog: Free. Frequency: Annual
Circulation: 50M. Sales: $5-10MM
Products: Landscaping equipment &
farm machinery

THE GREATEST GIFT　　(866) 259-0728
Langenbach　　(800) 362-1991
644 Enterprise Ave. • Galesburg, IL 61401
E-Mail: dhughes@thegrteatestgift.com
Website: www.thegreatestgift.com
Fax Ordering: (800) 362-4490
International Ordering: (309) 344-4820
Contact Name: Robert Wallace, President
Catalog: Free. Frequency: Quarterly
Circulation: 5MM. Sales: $3-5MM
Products: Garden equipment, supplies,
tools, and decorative products

GREENHOUSE SUPPLIES　　(204) 327-5540
Northern Greenhouse Sales
P.O. Box 42 • Nech, ND 58265
E-Mail: info@northerngreenhousesales.com
Website: www.northerngreenhousesales.com
Fax Ordering: (204) 327-5527
Contact Name: Bob & Margaret Davis, Owners
Catalog: Free. Frequency: Monthly
Circulation: 20K. Sales: $1-3MM
Products: Greenhouse plastic; pond liners
and shelter covers

GREENHOUSES & HORTICULTURAL　　(800) 531-4769
SUPPLY CATALOG
Gothic Arch Greenhouses
P.O. Box 1564 • Mobile, AL 36633
E-Mail: gothic@yellowhammer.com
Website: www.gothicarchgreenhouses.com
Fax Ordering: (251) 432-7972
International Ordering: (251) 432-7259
Contact Name: Paul Sierke, Jr., President
Catalog: Free. Frequency: Quarterly
Circulation: 15K. Sales: $1-3MM
Products: Greenhouses & horticultural
equipment & supplies; greenhouse kits,
school & hobby greenhouses.

GREENLEAF NURSERY COMPANY　　(800) 331-2982
28406 Highway 82 • Park Hill, OK 74451
E-Mail: info@glnsy.com
Website: www.glnsy.com
Fax Ordering: (918) 457-5550
International Ordering: (918) 457-5172
Contact Name: Jim Zangger, President
Catalog: Free. Frequency: Annual
Circulation: 100K. Sales: $10-20MM
Products: Shrubs, flowers, trees, plants

GREER GARDENS　　(800) 548-0111
1280 Goodpasture Island Rd.
Eugene, OR 97401
E-Mail: orders@greengardens.com
Website: www.greengardens.com
Fax Ordering: (541) 686-0910
International Ordering: (541) 686-8266
Contact Name: Harold Greer, President
Catalog: Free. Frequency: Semiannual
Circulation: 25M. Sales: $1-3MM
Products: Trees and shrubs

GRO'N SELL, INC. (215) 822-1276
320 Lower State Rd. • Chalfont, PA 18914
E-Mail: growers@grower-supply.com
Website: www.grower-supply.com
Fax Ordering: (215) 997-1770
Contact Name: Dave Eastburn, Owner
Catalog: Free. Frequency: Annual
Circulation: 50K. Sales: $1-3MM
Products: Perennials, annuals & specialty crops

GROWER'S SUPPLY COMPANY (734) 426-5852
P.O. Box 219 • Dexter, MI 48130
E-Mail: growers@grower-supply.com
Website: www.grower-supply.com
Fax Ordering: (734) 426-5750
Contact Name: Donna Draper, President
Catalog: Free. Frequency: Annual
Circulation: 50K. Sales: $5-10MM
Products: Indoor gardening products

GURNEY'S SEED & NURSERY CO. (513) 354-1491
P.O. Box 4178 • Greendale, IN 47025
E-Mail: sales@gurneys.com
Website: www.gurneys.com
Fax Ordering: (513) 354-1493
Catalog: Free. Frequency: Semiannual
Circulation: 25M. Sales: $500M to $1MM
Products: Perennials; flowers, vegetable &
wildflower seeds; fruit trees & berries; ground
covers, shrubs, trees, vines; herbs & vegetables;
fertilizer, weed & pest control products;
ornamental grasses & plants; roses

HARRIS SEEDS (800) 544-7938
P.O. Box 24966 • Rochester, NY 14624
E-Mail: gardeners@harrisseeds.com
Website: www.harrisseeds.com
Fax Ordering: (877) 892-9197; (716) 295-3608
International Ordering: (716) 295-3600
Contact Name: Richard Chamberlin, President
Catalog: Free. Frequency: Annual
Circulation: 500K. Sales: $1-3MM
Products: Herbs, vegetable & flower seeds;
annuals, plants & bulbs; greenhouses & indoor
gardening supplies; fruit trees & berries; fertilizer,
weed & pest control products; magazines & books

HARTMANN'S PLANT COMPANY (269) 253-4281
P.O. Box 100 • Lacota, MI 49063
E-Mail: info@hartmannsplantcompany.com
Website: www.hartmannsplantcompany.com
Fax Ordering: (269) 253-4457
Contact Name: Daniel P. Hartmann President
Catalog: Free. Frequency: Semiannual
Circulation: 50K. Sales: $1-3MM
Products: Fruit plants; specialty plants;
equipment & supplies; books & CDs

THE HARVEST HELPER (800) 897-3525
7 Olympic Dr. • Danbury, CT 06810
E-Mail: theharvesthelper@snet.net
Website: www.theharvesthelper.com
Fax Ordering: (203) 794-0757
Catalog: Free. Frequency: Semiannual
Circulation: 25K. Sales: $500K to $1MM
Products: Garden supplies, tools & power
equipment; magazines & books

HAWAII'S FLOWERS (800) 367-5155
Island Tropicals
P.O. Box 1989 • Keaau, HI 96749
E-Mail: hawaii@interpac.net

Website: www.islandtropicals.com
Fax Ordering: (808) 966-7684
International Ordering: (808) 961-0606
Contact Name: Mike Goldstein President
Catalog: Free. Frequency: Monthly
Circulation: 50K. Sales: $1-3MM
Products: Hawaiian flowers; eco-gifts;
Kona coffee

HEIRLOOM ROSES (503) 538-1576
24062 NE Riverside Dr.
St. Paul, OR 97137
E-Mail: info@heirloomroses.com
Website: www.heirloomroses.com
Fax Ordering: (503) 538-5902
Contact Name: John & Louise Clements, Owners
Catalog: $5. Frequency: Annual
Circulation: 25K. Sales: $5-10MM
Products: Garden roses, landscape,
ground cover

HENRY FIELD'S SEED & NURSERY CO. (513) 354-1494
P.O. Box 397 • Aurora, IN 47001
E-Mail: info@henryfields.com
Website: www.henryfields.com
Fax Ordering: (513) 354-1496
Customer service: (513) 354-1495
Contact Name: Chris Fetters, Manager
Catalog: Free. Frequency: Semiannual
Circulation: 100K. Sales: $10-20MM
Products: Vegetable seeds & plants; flower
& grass seeds; perennials & roses; fruit &
nut trees; flower bulbs; nursery stock; yard
& garden supplies

HERONSWOOD NURSERY, LTD (360) 297-4172
7530 NE 288th St. • Kingston, WA 98346
E-Mail: info@heronswood.com
Website: www.heronswood.com
Fax Ordering: (360) 297-8321
International Ordering: (616) 253-4281
Contact Name: Paul Sierke, Jr., President
Catalog: $5. Frequency: Annual
Circulation: 10M. Sales: $1-3MM
Products: Plants

HIDA TOOL & HARDWARE CO. (800) 443-5512
1333 San Pablo Ave. • Berkeley, CA 94702
E-Mail: hidatool@hidatool.com
Website: www.hidatool.com
Fax Ordering: (510) 524-3423
International Ordering: (510) 524-3700
Catalog: $2. Frequency: Annual
Circulation: 50K. Sales: $10-20MM
Products: Japanese gardening and bonsai
tools; woodworking tools, kitchen knives &
garden tools.

HIGH COUNTRY GARDENS (800) 925-9387
Santa Fe Greenhouses
2902 Rufina St. • Santa Fe, NM 87505
E-Mail: plants@highcountrygardens.com
Website: www.highcountrygardens.com
Fax Ordering: (800) 925-0097
International Ordering: (505) 473-2700
Contact Name: David & Ava Salmon, Owners
Catalog: Free. Frequency: 10x per year
Circulation: 100K. Sales: $1-3MM
Products: Plants & flowers for the garden;
flower, vegetable & wildflower seeds; fertilizer,
weed & pest control products; garden supplies,
tools & equipment

HIGHLAND SUCCULENTS
(740) 256-1428
1446 Bear Run Rd. • Gallipolis, OH 45631
E-Mail: hsinfo@zoomnet.net
Website: www.highlandsucculents.com
Fax Ordering: (800) 925-0097
International Ordering: (740) 256-1428
Catalog: Online. Sales: $100-300K
Minimum Order: $30.
Products: Over 2,000 rare & endangered
succulent plants: Pachypodium, Adenium,
Crassulaceae, Echeveria, et al.

HOBBS FARM
(207) 763-4606
979 Barnestown Rd. • Hope, ME 04847
E-Mail: plants@hobbsfarm.com
Website: www.hobbsfarm.com
Fax Ordering: (207) 763-3428
International Ordering: (207) 763-4606
Catalog: Print & Online. Sales: $500K
Products: Specialty geraniums

HOME & GARDEN
(304) 267-2673
Berkely House Direct
809 Virginia Ave. • Martinsburg, WV 25401
Fax Ordering: (304) 267-2673
Contact Names: Helen Holmes, Marketing
Catalog: Free. Frequency: Quarterly
Circulation: 100K. Sales: $1-3MM
Products: Furniture & gifts for home &
garden; gadgets

HOOPHOUSE
(800) 760-5192
1358 Route 28 • So. Yarmouth, MA 02664
E-Mail: hoophouse@cape.com
Website: www.hoophouse.com
Fax Ordering: (508) 760-5244
International Ordering: (508) 760-5191
Contact Name: M.H. Pleau, President
Catalog: Free. Frequency: Annual
Circulation: 20K. Sales: $3-5MM
Products: Greenhouse kits

HORTICULTURAL SUPPLY CATALOG
(800) 531-GROW
Gothic Arts Greenhouses
P.O. Box 1564 • Mobile, AL 36633
E-Mail: info@healthylight.com
Website: www.healthylight.com
Fax Ordering: (203) 921-2427
International Ordering: (203) 708-8937
Contact Names: Nicholas & Michelle Harmon
Catalog: Free. Frequency: Semiannual
Circulation: 25K. Sales: $1-3MM
Products: Trees and shrubs

HOUSE OF WESLEY
(309) 663-9551
1704 Morrissey Dr.
Bloomington, IL 61704
E-Mail: info@directgardening.com
Website: www.directgardening.com
Fax Ordering: (309) 663-6691
Contact Name: Richard Owen President
Catalog: Free. Frequency: Annual
Circulation: 50M. Sales: $3-5MM
Products: Nursery stock

INDIANA BERRY & PLANT CO.
(800) 295-2226
5218 W 500 S • Huntington, IN 47542
E-Mail: berryinfo@inberry.com
Website: www.inberry.com
Fax Ordering: (812) 683-2004
International Ordering: (812) 683-3055
Contact Name: James Erwin President
Catalog: Free. Frequency: 3x per year
Circulation: 50M. Sales: $1-3MM
Products: Fruit & vegetable plants; produce

INDOOR GARDENING SUPPLIES
(800) 823-5740
P.O. Box 527 • Dexter, MI 48130
E-Mail: igs@indoorgardensupplies.com
Website: www.indoorgardensupplies.com
Fax Ordering: (866) 823-4978
Contact Name: Tina Havro, Marketing
Catalog: Free. Frequency: Annual
Circulation: 100K. Sales: $5-10MM
Products: Indoor gardening equipment
& supplies

IRISH EYES WITH A HINT OF GARLIC
(877) 733-3001
P.O. Box 307 • Thorp, WA 98946
E-Mail: potatoes@irish-eyes.com
Website: www.irish-eyes.com
Fax Ordering: (800) 964-9210
International Ordering: (509) 964-7000
Contact Name: Greg A. Lutoivsky, President
Catalog: Free. Frequency: Annual
Circulation: 50M. Sales: $1-3MM
Products: Seed potatoes, garlic and shallots

ISON'S NURSERY & VINEYARDS
(800) 733-0324
P.O. Box 190 • Brooks, GA 30205
E-Mail: isons@aol.com
Website: www.isons.com
Fax Ordering: (770) 599-1727
International Ordering: (770) 599-6970
Contact Name: Janet McCurie President
Catalog: Free. Frequency: Annual
Circulation: 50M. Sales: $1-3MM
Products: Fruit trees, grapes, muscadines,
nuts

JACKSON & PERKINS
(800) 292-4769
2 Floral Ave. • Hodges, SC 29653
E-Mail: service@jacksonandperkins.com
Website: www.jacksonandperkins.com
Fax Ordering: (800) 242-0329
Catalog: Free. Frequency: Annual
Circulation: 100K. Sales: $10-20MM
Products: Roses, bulbs, perennials, gifts

JANCO GREENHOUSES
(800) 323-6933
Bright Tower Manufacturing Co., Inc.
138 Cathedral St. • Elkton, MD 21921
E-Mail: info@jancoinc.com
Website: www.jancoinc.com
Fax Ordering: (410) 392-7876
International Ordering: (410) 392-7875
Contact Name: Benjamin J. Hendrickson, Sr., President
Catalog: Free. Frequency: Annual
Circulation: 100K. Sales: $5-10MM
Products: Greenhouses, sunrooms, solariums,
atriums; accessories

JOHNNY'S SELECTED SEEDS
(877) 564-6697
955 Benton Ave. • Winslow, ME 04901
E-Mail: homegarden@johnnyseeds.com
Website: www.johnnyseeds.com
Fax Ordering: (800) 738-6314
International Ordering: (207) 861-3900
Contact Name: Robert L. Johnston, Jr., President
Catalog: Free. Frequency: Annual
Circulation: 250K. Sales: $3-5MM
Products: Vegetable, herb and flower seeds;
gardening tools, organic seeds & supplies;
supplies & accessories; and books

JUNG SEEDS & PLANTS (800) 247-5864
(800) 297-3123
J.W. Jung Seed Co.
335 S. High St. • Randolph, WI 53957
E-Mail: info@jungseed.com
Website: www.jungseed.com
Fax Ordering: (800) 692-5864
International Ordering: (920) 326-3121
Contact Name: Richard Zondag, President
Catalog: Free. Frequency: Semiannual
Circulation: 2MM. Sales: $10-20MM
Products: Seeds, plants, shrubs, trees;
gardening supplies

JUST FRUITS & EXOTICS (850) 926-5644
30 St. Frances St.
Crawfordsville, FL 32327
E-Mail: justfruits@hotmail.com
Website: www.justfruitsandexotics.com
Fax Ordering: (850) 926-9885
International Ordering: (850) 926-5644
Contact Name: Ted & Brandy Cowley, Owners
Catalog: Free. Frequency: Annual
Circulation: 10K. Sales: $1-3MM
Products: Fruits, ornamentals, plants

KLEHM'S SONG SPARROW (800) 553-3715
Song Sparrow Perennial Farm
13101 E. Rye Rd. • Avalon, WI 53505
E-Mail: info@sonsparrow.com
Website: www.songsparrow.com
Fax Ordering: (608) 883-2257
Catalog: Free. Frequency: Semiannual
Circulation: 50K. Sales: $1-3MM
Products: Perennials, ground covers,
shrubs, trees, vines; magaznes & books;
ornamental grasses & plants.

LANGENBACH FINE GARDEN TOOLS (800) 362-1991
137 Stillwater Station Rd.
Newton, NJ 07860
Fax Ordering: (800) 362-4490
International Ordering: (973) 383-6811
Contact Names: Paul Langenbach, President
Catalog: Free. Frequency: Semiannual
Circulation: 2MM. Sales: $10-20MM
Products: Garden tools

LAWYER NURSERY (800) 551-9875
6625 Montana Hwy. 200
Plains, MT 59859
E-Mail: trees@lawyernursery.com
Website: www.lawyernursery.com
Fax Ordering: (406) 826-5700
International Ordering: (406) 826-3881
Contact Name: John N. Lawyer, President
Catalog: Free. Frequency: Quarterly
Circulation: 200K. Sales: $3-5MM
Products: Nursery stock; wholesale
trees & shrubs

LEISURE WOODS (888) 442-9326
P.O. Box 248 • Genoa, IL 60135
E-Mail: info@leisure-woods.com
Website: www.leisure-woods.com
Fax Ordering: (815) 784-2499
International Ordering: (815) 784-2497
Contact Name: Charles Scordato, Jr., President
Catalog: Free. Frequency: 9x per year
Circulation: 10K. Sales: $1-3MM
Products: Custom cedar gazebo kits

LIBERTY SEED COMPANY (800) 541-6022
461 Robinson Dr. SE
New Philadelphia, OH 44663
E-Mail: vicki@davidsongreenhouse.com
Website: www.davidsongreenhouse.com
Fax Ordering: (330) 364-6415
International Ordering: (330) 364-1661
Contact Names: William & Tracy Watson
Catalog: Free. Frequency: Annual
Circulation: 25K. Sales: $3-5MM
Products: Scented geraniums, begonias,
impatiens; houseplants, herbs

LILYPONS WATER GARDENS (800) 999-5459
P.O. Box 10 • Buckeystown, MD 21717
E-Mail: info@lilypons.com
Website: www.lilypons.com
Fax Ordering: (800) 879-5459; (301) 874-2959
International Ordering: (301) 874-5503
Contact Name: Margaret Koogle, President
Catalog: Free. Frequency: 5x per year
Circulation: 100K. Sales: $3-5MM
Products: Water gardens with water lilies,
pond liners, pumps, filters, fish

LOGEE'S GREENHOUSES (888) 330-8038
141 N St. • Danielson, CT 06239
E-Mail: info@logees.com
Website: www.logees.com
Fax Ordering: (860) 774-9932
International Ordering: (860) 774-8038
Contact Name: Byron E. Martin, President
Catalog: Free. Frequency: 5x per year
Circulation: 200K. Sales: $1-3MM
Products: Plants & herbs

LOWE'S HOME IMPROVEMENT (800) 445-6937
P.O. Box 1111 • No. Wilkesboro, NC 28656
E-Mail: info@lowes.com
Website: www.lowes.com
Fax Ordering: (845) 382-6093
International Ordering: (845) 382-6000
Customer Service: (800) 890-5932
Contact Name: Robert Tillman, President
Catalog: Free. Frequency: Annual
Circulation: 100K. Sales: $10-20MM
Products: Gardening & home improvement
supplies

MacKENZIE NURSERY SUPPLY (800) 777-5030
3891 Shepard Rd. • Perry, OH 44081
E-Mail: info@mnsinc.com
Website: www.mnsinc.com
Fax Ordering: (440) 259-3004
International Ordering: (440) 259-3517
Catalog: Free. Frequency: Semiannual
Circulation: 25K. Sales: $500K to $1MM
Products: Aquatic plants & water gardens;
garden supplies, tools & power equipment;
gifts & decorative accessories; greenhouses
& indoor gardening supplies; irrigation
supplies & equipment; magaznes & books

MARYLAND AQUATIC NURSERIES (877) 736-1807
3427 N. Furnace Rd.
Jarrettsville, MD 21084
E-Mail: info@marylandaquatic.com
Website: www.marylandaquatic.com
Fax Ordering: (410) 692-2837
International Ordering: (410) 557-7615
Contact Name: Richard Schuck, President

Catalog: Free. Frequency: Annual
Circulation: 10K. **Sales:** $1—3MM
Products: Aquatic plants and water
gardening products

MANTIS   (800) 366-6268
1028 Street Rd.
Southampton, PA 18966
E-Mail: info@mantisgardentools.com
Website: www.mantisgardentools.com
Fax Ordering: (215) 357-1071
International Ordering: (215) 355-9700
Contact Name: Robert Bell, Manager
Catalog: Free. Frequency: Annual
Circulation: 100M. **Sales:** $10-20MM
Products: Gardening equipment

MELLINGER'S   (800) 321-7444
2310 WS Range Rd.
North Lima, OH 44452
E-Mail: mellgarden@aol.com
Website: www.mellingers.com
Fax Ordering: (330) 549-3716
International Ordering: (330) 549-9861
Contact Name: Philip Steiner, President
Catalog: Free. Frequency: Annual
Circulation: 500M. **Sales:** $10-20MM
Products: Seeds for vegetables and trees;
plants, bulbs, shrubs; gardening supplies,
greenhouses

MICHIGAN BULB COMPANY   (513) 354-1497
P.O. Box 4180 • Lawrenceburg, IN 47025
E-Mail: customerservice@michiganbulb.com
Website: www.michiganbulb.com
Fax Ordering: (513) 354-1499
Customer Service: (513) 354-1498
Contact Name: Robert Ostertag, Jr., President
Catalog: Free. Frequency: 5x per year
Circulation: 10MM. **Sales:** $20-50MM
Products: Roses, perennials, bulbs, tress,
shrubs, vines, vegetables, fruits, herbs,
houseplants, gardens, ground cover,
hedges and accessories

J.E. MILLER NURSERIES   (800) 836-9630
5060 West Lake Rd.
Canandaigua, NY 14424
E-Mail: jmiller@millernurseries.com
Website: www.millernurseries.com
Fax Ordering: (716) 396-2154
International Ordering: (716) 396-2647
Contact Name: John Miller, President
Catalog: Free. Frequency: Quarterly
Circulation: 1MM. **Sales:** $5-10MM
Products: Gardening supplies, fruit trees,
shade trees, roses

MISTLETOE-CARTER SEEDS   (800) 872-7711
780 N. Glen Annie Rd. • Goleta, CA 93117
E-Mail: purchasing@mcseeds.com
Website: www.mcseeds.com
Fax Ordering: (805) 968-2242
International Ordering: (805) 968-4818
Contact Name: Tom Frick, President
Catalog: Free. Frequency: Annual
Circulation: 100K. **Sales:** $3-5MM
Products: Seeds for trees, shrubs, palms,
pines, eucalytpus, ornamental grasses,
tropicals, wildflowers; herbs

MUDDY BOOTS MERCANTILE   (828) 628-4922
3 Chestnut Mountain Ridge
Asheville, NC 28803
E-Mail: info@landscapeusa.com
Website: www.landscapeusa.com
Fax Ordering: (828) 628-4854
Catalog: Free. Frequency: Semiannual
Circulation: 10K. **Sales:** $250-500K
Products: Gifts & decorative accessories;
greenhouses & indoor gardening supplies;
ground covers, shrubs, trees, vines; herbs
& vegetables; irrigation supplies & equipment;
fertilizer, weed & pest control products;
magaznes & books; ornamental grasses
& plants; roses

MUSSER FORESTS   (800) 643-8319
P.O. Box 340 • Indiana, PA 15701
E-Mail: sales@musserforests.com
Website: www.musser forests.com
Fax Ordering: (716) 396-2154
International Ordering: (716) 396-2647
Contact Name: Fred A. Musser, Jr., President
Catalog: Free. Frequency: Semiannual
Circulation: 500K. **Sales:** $5-10MM
Products: Evergreen & hardwood seedlings
& transplants; ornamental shrubs &groundcover

NATIONAL GARDENING ASSOCIATION   (802) 863-5251
1100 Dorset St. • So. Burlington, VT 05403
E-Mail: info@garden.org
Website: www.garden.org
Fax Ordering: (802) 864-6889
Catalog: Free. Frequency: Semiannual
Circulation: 50K. **Sales:** $500M to $1MM
Products: Flower, vegetable & wildflower
seeds; gifts & decorative accessories;
greenhouses & indoor gardening supplies;
ground covers, shrubs, trees, vines; herbs
& vegetables; irrigation supplies & equipment;
fertilizer, weed & pest control products;
magaznes & books

NATIVE SEEDS/SEARCH   (520) 622-5561
526 N. 4th Ave. • Tucson, AZ 85705
E-Mail: info@nativeseeds.org
Website: www.nativeseeds.org
Fax Ordering: (520) 622-5591
Contact Name: Bryn Jones, Director
Catalog: $1. Frequency: Quarterly
Circulation: 25K. **Sales:** $250M
Products: Seeds of crops grown by
Native Americans

THE NATURAL GARDENER   (512) 288-6113
8648 Old Bee Caves Rd. • Austin, TX 78735
E-Mail: sales@naturalgardeneraustin.com
Website: www.naturalgardeneraustin.com
Fax Ordering: (512) 288-6114
Contact Name: John Dromgoole, President
Catalog: Online. **Sales:** $3-5MM
Products: Specialty garden products, tools,
organic fertilizer, natural pest control products

NATURE HILLS NURSERY, INC.   (888) 864-7663
3334 North 88th Plaza • Omaha, NE 68134
E-Mail: info@naturehills.com
Website: www.naturehills.com
Fax Ordering: (866) 550-9556
International Ordering: (402) 934-8116
Catalog: Free. Frequency: Quarterly

Circulation: 100K. Sales: $1-3MM
Products: Trees, plants, bulbs, seeds;
fruit trees, shrubs & hedges

NEW ENGLAND WILD FLOWER (508) 877-7630
SEED & BOOK CATALOG
New England Wild Flower Society
180 Hemenway Rd. • Framingham, MA 01701
E-Mail: newfs@newfs.org
Website: www.newfs.org
Fax Ordering: (508) 877-3658
Contact Name: Malinda Dress, President
Catalog: $1. Frequency: Quarterly
Circulation: 25K. Sales: $250M
Products: 200 varieties of wild flower
seeds and fern spores

NICHE GARDENS (919) 967-0078
1111 Dawson Rd. • Chapel Hill, NC 27516
E-Mail: mail@nichegardens.com
Website: www.nichegardens.com
Fax Ordering: (919) 967-4026
Contact Name: Kim Hawks, President
Catalog: $3. Frequency: Annual
Circulation: 50K. Sales: $500M to $1MM
Products: Southeastern wildflowers &
native plants, perennials, ornamental
grasses, herbs and shrubs

NICHOLS GARDEN NURSERY (866) 408-4851
1190 Old Salem Rd. NE • Albany, OR 97321 (800) 422-3985
E-Mail: nichols@nicholsgardennursery.com
Website: www.nicholsgardennursery.com
Fax Ordering: (800) 231-5306
International Ordering: (541) 928-9280
Contact Name: Rose Marie Nichols McGee, President
Catalog: Free. Pages: 76. Frequency: Annual
Circulation: 150M. Sales: $500M to $1MM
Products: Herb seeds and plants

NITRON INDUSTRIES (800) 835-0123
5703 Hewitt • Johnson, AR 72741
E-Mail: ffinger@nitron.com
Website: www.nitron.com
Fax Ordering: (501) 587-0177
International Ordering: (501) 587-1777
Contact Name: Frank J. Finger, President
Catalog: Free. Frequency: Annual
Circulation: 25M. Sales: $1-3MM
Products: Natural fertilizers, soil conditioners,
and organic pest control products

NOR'EAST MINIATURE ROSES (800) 426-6845
P.O. Box 307 • Rowley, MA 01969
E-Mail: nemr@noreast-miniroses.com
Website: www.noreast-miniroses.com
Fax Ordering: (978) 948-5487
International Ordering: (978) 948-7964
Contact Name: John Saville, President
Catalog: Free. Frequency: Annual
Circulation: 100M. Sales: $500M to $1MM
Products: 100+ varieties of miniature rose plants

NOURSE FARMS (413) 665-2658
41 River Rd. • So. Deerfield, MA 01373
E-Mail: info@noursefarms.com
Website: www.noursefarms.com
Fax Ordering: (413) 665-7888
Contact Name: Tim Nourse, President
Catalog: Free. Frequency: Annual
Circulation: 75M. Sales: $1-3MM
Products: Fruit & vegetable plants

OAKES DAYLILIES (800) 532-9545
P.O. Box 268 • Corryton, TN 37721
E-Mail: info@oakesdaylilies.com
Website: www.oakesdaylilies.com
Fax Ordering: (865) 688-8186
International Ordering: (865) 687-3770
Contact Names: Stewart & Kenneth Oakes
Catalog: Free. Frequency: Annual
Circulation: 75M. Sales: $500M to $1MM
Products: Hybrid daylilies

OFE INTERNATIONAL (305) 253-7080
12100 SW 129th Ct. • Miami, FL 33186
E-Mail: sales@ofe-intl.com
Website: www.ofe-intl.com
Fax Ordering: (305) 251-8245
Contact Name: Carlos Cahiz, President
Catalog: $3. Frequency: 3x per year
Circulation: 10M. Sales: $1-3MM
Products: Orchid growing supplies

ORCHIDS BY HAUSERMANN (630) 543-6855
2N 134 Addison Rd. • Villa Park, IL 60181
E-Mail: orchidorders@orchidsbyhausermann.com
Website: www.orchidsbyhausermann.com
Fax Ordering: (630) 543-9842
International Ordering: (630) 543-6855
Contact Name: Gene Hausermann, President
Catalog: $1. Frequency: Annual
Circulation: 30K. Sales: $1-3MM
Products: Orchid plants and accessories

PARADISE WATER GARDENS (800) 955-0161
14 May St. • Whitman, MA 02382
E-Mail: contact@paradisewatergardens.com
Website: www.paradisewatergardens.com
Fax Ordering: (800) 966-4591; (781) 447-4591
International Ordering: (781) 447-4711
Contact Name: Paul Stetson, Sr., President
Catalog: Free. Frequency: Annual
Circulation: 50K. Sales: $1-3MM
Products: Aquatic plants including water
lilies and lotus; fiberglass pools and liners

PARK SEED COMPANY (800) 845-3369
1 Parkton Ave. • Greenwood, SC 29647 (800) 213-0076
E-Mail: info@parkseed.com
Website: www.parkseed.com
Fax Ordering: (800) 275-9941; (864) 275-9941
International Ordering: (864) 223-8555
Contact Name: Leonard Park, President
Catalog: Free. Frequency: Semiannual
Circulation: 5MM. Sales: $10-20MM
Products: Seeds, bulbs & plants; garden
supplies, books

PEACEFUL VALLEY FARM SUPPLY (888) 784-1722
P.O. Box 2209 • Grass Valley, CA 95945
E-Mail: contact@groworganic.com
Website: www.groworganic.com
Fax Ordering: (530) 272-4794
International Ordering: (530) 272-4769
Contact Name: Eric Boudier, President
Catalog: Free. Frequency: Weekly
Circulation: 150M. Sales: $3-5MM
Products: Organic gardening tools
and supplies

PERENNIAL CATALOG (800) 553-3715
Klehm's Song Sparrow Perennial Farm
13101 E. Rye Rd. • Avalon, WI 53505
E-Mail: info@songsparrow.com

Website: www.songsparrow.com
Fax Ordering: (608) 883-2257
International Ordering: (608) 883-2221
Contact Name: Roy Klehm, President
Catalog: Free. Frequency: Annual
Circulation: 50M. Sales: $1-3MM
Products: Perennials, shrubs, trees

PERENNIAL WISHBOOK   (262) 639-2040
Milaeger's Gardens
4838 Douglas Ave. • Racine, WI 53402
Fax Ordering: (262) 639-1855
Contact Name: Kevin Milaeger, President
Catalog: Free. Frequency: Semiannual
Circulation: 250M. Sales: $1-3MM
Products: Perennials

PHELPS FARM ORCHIDS, INC.   (877) 537-1595
15808 Timberwood Dr. • Tampa, FL 33625
E-Mail: orchidspf@tampabay.rr.com
Website: www.phelpsfarm.com
Fax Ordering: (813) 961-8427
International Ordering: (813) 961-8427
Catalog: Online. Sales: $100-500K
Products: Orchids

PIKE'S PEAK NURSERIES   (800) 787-6730
Rt. 422 Hwy., Box 8289
Penn Run, PA 15765
E-Mail: pikespeak@stargate.net
Fax Ordering: (724) 463-0775
International Ordering: (724) 463-7747
Contact Name: David K. Smith, Marketing
Catalog: Free. Frequency: Annual
Circulation: 25M. Sales: $500M to $1MM
Products: Evergreen seedlings &
transplants, native wood plant material

PINETREE GARDEN SEEDS   (207) 926-3400
P.O. Box 300 • New Gloucester, ME 04260
E-Mail: superseeds@superseeds.com
Website: www.superseeds.com
Fax Ordering: (888) 527-3337
Contact Name: Richard Meiners, President
Catalog: Free. Frequency: Annual
Circulation: 250K. Sales: $1-3MM
Products: Flower, herb, houseplant &
vegetable seeds; gardening tools and
supplies; books

PLANET NATURAL   (800) 289-6656
Spark Boy Enterprises
1612 Gold Ave. • Bozeman, MT 59715
E-Mail: info@planetnatural.com
Website: www.planetnatural.com
Fax Ordering: (406) 587-0223
International Ordering: (406) 587-5891
Contact Name: Eric Vinje, President
Catalog: Free. Frequency: Annual
Circulation: 150K. Sales: $500K - $1MM
Products: Organic gardening supplies,
fertilizers, composting equipment, and
beneficial insects; health household products

PLANTFIELDS   (800) 541-5185
Piedmont Plant Company
P.O. Box 424 • Albany, GA 31702
E-Mail: info@plantfields.com
Website: www.plantfields.com
Fax Ordering: (229) 432-2888
International Ordering: (229) 883-7029
Contact Name: William I. Parker, President

Catalog: Free. Frequency: Annual
Circulation: 250K. Sales: $500M
Products: Herbs, perennials, Spring bulbs,
vegetable transplants; tools and gifts

PLOW & HEARTH   (800) 627-1712
   (800) 494-7544
P.O. Box 6000 • Madison, VA 22727
E-Mail: info@plowhearth.com
Website: www.plowhearth.com
Fax Ordering: (800) 843-2509
International Ordering: (540) 948-2272
Contact Name: Peter Rice, President
Catalog: Free. Frequency: Quarterly
Circulation: 100M. Sales: $50-100MM
Products: Products for home & hearth;
outdoor living; yard & garden; footwear
& apparel

THE POND GUY, INC.   (888) 766-3520
6135 King Rd. • Marine City, MI 48039
E-Mail: jblake@thepondguy.com
Website: www.thepondguy.com
Fax Ordering: (810) 765-8600
Catalog: Free. Frequency: Semiannual
Circulation: 25K. Sales: $500M to $1MM
Products: Aquatic plants & water gardens;
garden supplies, tools & power equipment;
gifts & decorative accessories; irrigation
supplies & equipment; magaznes & books

PRAIRIE NURSERY   (800) 476-9453
P.O. Box 306 • Westfield, WI 53964
E-Mail: cs@prairienursery.com
Website: www.prairienursery.com
Fax Ordering: (608) 296-2741
International Ordering: (608) 296-3679
Contact Name: Neil Diboll, President
Catalog: Free. Frequency: Weekly
Circulation: 100K. Sales: $1-3MM
Products: Seeds for wildflowers & grasses

RAINTREE NURSERY   (360) 496-6400
391 Butts Rd. • Morton, WA 98356
E-Mail: info@raintreenursery.com
Website: www.raintreenursery.com
Fax Ordering: (888) 770-8358
Contact Name: Sam Benowitz, President
Catalog: Free. Frequency: Semiannual
Circulation: 200M. Sales: $1-3MM
Products: Fruit, nut and berry plants;
bamboo plants

RAT-X   (800) 662-5021
300 N. Elizabeth St.
Chicago, IL 60607
E-Mail: sales@bird-x.com
Website: www.bird-x.com
Fax Ordering: (312) 226-2480
International Ordering: (312) 226-2473
Contact Name: Ron Schwarcz, President
Catalog: Free. Frequency: Annual
Circulation: 100K. Sales: $5-10MM
Products: Bird control products

RIO GRANDE CACTI   (505) 835-0687
2188 NM Hwy. 1 • Socorro, NM 87801
E-Mail: riogrande@hotmail.com
Website: www.riogrande-cacti.com
International Ordering: (505) 835-0687
Catalog: Online. Sales: $100K
Products: Southwestern cacti and indoor
succulents

RIVERBEND NURSERY   (800) 638-3362
1295 Mt. Elbert Rd. NW • Riner, VA 24149
E-Mail: info@riverbendnursery.com
Website: www.riverbendnursery.com
Fax Ordering: (540) 763-2022
International Ordering: (540) 763-3362
Contact Name: Jim Snyder, President
Catalog: Free. Frequency: Annual
Circulation: 250K. Sales: $3-5MM
Products: Perennials & ornamental grasses
to the trade; wholesale groundcovers

ROCK-IT CREATIONS   (866) 2-ROCK-IT
P.O. Box T • Council, ID 83612
E-Mail: info@rockitcreations.com
Website: www.rockitcreations.com
Fax Ordering: (208) 253-4558
International Ordering: (208) 253-4557
Catalog: $1. Frequency: Quarterly
Circulation: 125K. Sales: $1-3MM
Products: Garden stones; gift of engraved
stones, gift items

ROHRER SEEDS   (717) 299-2571
P.L. Rohrer & Brothers
P.O. Box 250 • Smoketown, PA 17576
E-Mail: info@rohrerseeds.com
Website: www.rohrerseeds.com
Fax Ordering: (800) 468-4944
Contact Name: Earl W. Rohrer, President
Catalog: $2. Frequency: Annual
Circulation: 20K. Sales: $500M to $1MM
Products: Garden, farm, turf & wildlife seeds

ROSLYN NURSERY   (631) 643-9347
211 Burrs Lane • Dix Hills, NY 11746
E-Mail: roslyn@roslynnursery.com
Website: www.roslynnursery.com
Fax Ordering: (631) 427-0894
Contact Name: Philip Waldman, President
Catalog: Free. Frequency: Annual
Circulation: 50K. Sales: $1-3MM
Products: Outdoor plants including trees,
shrubs, conifers and perennials

S&S SEEDS, INC.   (800) 423-8112
P.O. Box 1275 • Carpinteria, CA 93014
E-Mail: paul@ssseeds.com
Website: www.ssseeds.com
Fax Ordering: (805) 684-2798
International Ordering: (805) 684-0436
Contact Name: Paul J. Albright, Jr., President
Catalog: Free. Frequency: Annual
Circulation: 50M. Sales: $5-10MM
Products: California native seeds:
grass seed, turf & pasture mixes,
wildflowers and cover crops

SCHREINERS IRIS GARDENS   (800) 525-2367
3625 Quinaby Rd. NE • Salem, OR 97303
E-Mail: info@schreinersgardens.com
Website: www.shreinersgardens.com
Fax Ordering: (503) 393-5590
International Ordering: (503) 393-3232
Contact Name: David Shreiner, President
Catalog: Free. Frequency: Annual
Circulation: 50K. Sales: $1-3MM
Products: Irises

SEED SAVERS EXCHANGE   (563) 382-5990
3076 N. Winn Rd. • Decorah, IA 52101
E-Mail: tara@seedsavers.org

Website: www.seedsavers.org
Fax Ordering: (563) 382-5872
Contact Name: David Shreiner, President
Catalog: Free. Frequency: Annual
Circulation: 50K. Sales: $1-3MM
Products: Heirloom seeds, plants;
gardening books and gifts

SEEDS FOR THE WORLD   (800) 349-1071
Vermont Bean Seed Company
334 W. Stroud St. • Randolph, WI 53956
E-Mail: info@vermontbean.com
Website: www.vermontbean.com
Fax Ordering: (888) 500-7333
Contact Name: John Burke, III, President
Catalog: Free. Frequency: Annual
Circulation: 500M. Sales: $3-5MM
Products: Bean, herb, vegetable, green
and flower seeds

SEEDS OF CHANGE   (888) 762-7333
P.O. Box 15700 • Santa Fe, NM 87592
E-Mail: gardener@seedsofchange.com
Website: www.seedsofchange.com
Fax Ordering: (505) 438-7052
Contact Name: Stephen Badger, President
Catalog: Free. Frequency: Annual
Circulation: 50M. Sales: $500M to $1MM
Products: Organic seeds; fruit trees, cover
crops, organic produce; garden tools, books
and gifts

SEEDWAY COMMERCIAL VEGETABLE SEED   (800) 952-7333
ORGANIC GROWER VEGETABLE SEED
1225 Zeager Rd. • Elizabethtown, PA 17022
E-Mail: info@seedway.com
Website: www.seedway.com
Fax Ordering: (800) 645-2574
Contact Name: Donald Wertmann, President
Catalog: Free. Frequency: Annual
Circulation: 50K. Sales: $3-5MM
Products: Commercial vegetable seeds

SELECT SEEDS ANTIQUE FLOWERS   (800) 653-3304
180 Stickney Hill Rd. • Union, CT 06076
E-Mail: info@selectseeds.com
Website: www.selectseeds.com
Fax Ordering: (860) 684-9224
International Ordering: (860) 684-9310
Contact Name: Marilyn Barlow, President
Catalog: Free. Frequency: Annual
Circulation: 50K. Sales: $500K
Products: Unique, high-quality seeds
and plants

SHADY OAKS NURSERY   (800) 504-8006
P.O. Box 708 • Waseca, MN 56093
E-Mail: shadyoaks@shadyoaks.com
Website: www.shadyoaks.com
Fax Ordering: (507) 883-2257
International Ordering: (507) 883-2221
Contact Name: Gordon J. Oslund, President
Catalog: Free. Frequency: Annual
Circulation: 200K. Sales: $3-5MM
Products: Perennial plants, hostas

SHEPHERD'S GARDEN SEEDS   (800) 5003-9624
30 Irene St. • Torrington, CT 06790
E-Mail: garden@shepherdseeds.com
Website: www.shepherdseeds.com
Fax Ordering: (860) 482-0532
International Ordering: (860) 482-3638

Contact Name: Lorraine Calder, President
Catalog: Free. Frequency: Annual
Circulation: 250K. Sales: $5-10MM
Products: Herb and vegetable seeds;
kitchen supplies; seed starting supplies

R.H. SHUMWAY SEEDS   (800) 342-9461
334 W. Shoud St. • Randolph, WI 53956
E-Mail: info@rhshumway.com
Website: www.rhshumway.com
Fax Ordering: (888) 437-2733
Catalog: Free. Frequency: Annual
Circulation: 500K. Sales: $10-20MM
Products: Seeds & bulbs for vegetables,
small fruit, herbs & flowers; garden supplies

SMITH & HAWKEN   (800) 776-3336
P.O. Box 431 • Milwaukee, WI 53201   (800) 940-1170
E-Mail: sales@smithandhawken.com
Website: www.smithandhawkin.com
Fax Ordering: (859) 727-1166
Contact Name: David McCreight, President
Catalog: Free. Frequency: Monthly
Circulation: 100K. Sales: $1-3MM
Products: Portable greenhouse; indoor
gardening supplies and accessories,
plants, furniture, clothing.

SONG SPARROW PERENNIAL FARM   (800) 553-3715
13101 E. Rye Rd. • Avalon, WI 53505
E-Mail: info@songsparrow.com
Website: www.beavercreeknursery.com
Fax Ordering: (608) 883-2257
Contact Name: Roy G. Klehm, President
Catalog: Free. Frequency: Annual
Circulation: 25K. Sales: $500K
Products: Perennials, including peonies,
callis, Siberian iris and companion plants

SOUTHERN EXPOSURE SEED EXCHANGE   (540) 894-9480
P.O. Box 460 • Mineral, VA 23117
E-Mail: gardens@southernexposure.com
Website: www.southernexposure.com
Fax Ordering: (540) 894-9481
Contact Name: J.H. McCormack, President
Catalog: $2. Frequency: Annual
Circulation: 50K. Sales: $500M
Products: Over 500 varieties of vegetable, flower
and herb seeds; heirloom flower bulbs, seed
potatoes; books, supplies & gardening information

SPALDING LABORATORIES   (800) 845-2847
760 Printz Rd. • Arroyo Grande, CA 93420 (888) 562-5696
E-Mail: sales@spalding-labs.com
Website: www.spalding-labs.com
Fax Ordering: (805) 489-0336
Contact Name: Pat Spalding, President
Catalog: Free. Frequency: Semiannual
Circulation: 50K. Sales: $1-3MM
Products: Pesticide free fly-flea control
products and fly-flea predators

SPRAY-N-GROW GARDENING   (800) 323-2363
20 Hwy. 35 South • Rockport, TX 78382
E-Mail: info@spray-n-growgardening.com
Website: www.spray-n-growgardening.com
Fax Ordering: (361) 790-9313
Catalog: Free. Frequency: Semiannual
Circulation: 50K. Sales: $1-3MM
Products: Garden supplies, tools & power
equipment; greenhouses & indoor gardening
supplies; fertilizer, weed & pest control products;

SPRING HILL NURSERIES   (513) 354-1509
P.O. Box 330 • Harrison, OH 45030
E-Mail: info@springhillnursery.com
Website: www.springhillnursery.com
Fax Ordering: (513) 354-1510
Catalog: Free. Frequency: Semiannual
Circulation: 100M. Sales: $10-20MM
Products: Perennials, flowering shrubs,
roses & ground cover, bulbs & houseplants

STARK BROS. NURSERIES   (800) 775-6415
& ORCHARDS CO., INC.
P.O. Box 1800 • Louisiana, MO 63343
E-Mail: info@starkbros.com
Website: www.starkbros.com
Fax Ordering: (573) 754-3701
Catalog: Free. Frequency: Semiannual
Circulation: 50M. Sales: $1-3MM
Products: Fruit trees & berries; ground
covers, shrubs, trees, vines; ornamental
grasses & plants; roses

STEVENS AGRI SUPPLY   (800) 333-9143
RR 1 Box 32B • Coushatta, LA 71019
E-Mail: stevenstractor@juno.com
Website: www.stevenstractor.com
Fax Ordering: (318) 932-9800
International Ordering: (318) 932-5118
Catalog: Free. Frequency: Annual
Circulation: 50M. Sales: $1-5MM
Products: Tractor parts & equipment,
ATV implements & accessories

STOCK SEED FARMS   (800) 759-1520
28008 Mill Rd. • Murdock, NE 68407
E-Mail: prairie@stockseed.com
Website: www.stockseed.com
Fax Ordering: (402) 867-2442
International Ordering: (402) 867-3771
Contact Name: David Stock, President
Catalog: Free. Frequency: Annual
Circulation: 50M. Sales: $1-3MM
Products: Seeds for wildflowers, prairiegrasses
and buffalograsses; mixtures

STOKES TROPICALS   (800) 624-9706
P.O. Box 9868 • New Iberia, LA 70562
E-Mail: info@stokestropicals.com
Website: www.stokestropicals.com
Fax Ordering: (337) 365-6991
International Ordering: (337) 365-6998
Contact Name: Glenn M. Stokes, President
Catalog: Free. Frequency: Annual
Circulation: 50M. Sales: $1-3MM
Products: Over 600 tropical plants; planting
mix and fertilizer; books on tropical plants

SUDBURY LAWN & GARDEN PRODUCTS   (602) 285-1660
Security Products
301 W. Osborn Rd. • Phoenix, AZ 85013
Fax Ordering: (602) 285-1803
Contact Name: Rick Pontz, President
Catalog: Free. Frequency: Annual
Circulation: 50M. Sales: $500M to $1MM
Products: Interior landscape fertilizers &
products; composting products

STUEWE & SONS, INC.   (800) 553-5331
2290 SE Kiger Island Dr.
Corvallis, OR 97333
E-Mail: info@stuewe.com
Website: www.stuewe.com

Fax Ordering: (541) 754-6617
International Ordering: (541) 757-7798
Contact Name: Eric & Sally Stuewe, Owners
Catalog: Free. Frequency: Annual
Circulation: 10M. Sales: $500M
Products: Tree seedling containers

SUN PORCH STRUCTURES (800) 221-2550
495 Post Rd. E • Westport, CT 06880
E-Mail: info@sunporch.com
Website: www.sunporch.com
Fax Ordering: (203) 454-0020
International Ordering: (203) 454-0040
Contact Name: Dean Adams, Marketing
Catalog: Free. Frequency: Quarterly
Circulation: 250M. Sales: $5-10MM
Products: Sunporch & patio structures;
greenhouse & sunroom kits

SUNCAST CORP. HOSE REELS/PRODUCTS (800) 444-3310
701 N. Kirk Rd. • Batavia, IL 60510
E-Mail: sales@suncast.com
Website: www.suncast.com
Fax Ordering: (630) 879-6112
International Ordering: (630) 879-2050-2473
Catalog: Free. Frequency: Annual
Circulation: 100M. Sales: $5-10MM
Products: Hose reels and lawn edging supplies
for lawn & garden watering, spreading & snow
handling

SUNGLO SOLAR GREENHOUSES (800) 647-0606
2626 15th Ave. W • Seattle, WA 98119
Fax Ordering: (206) 284-8945
International Ordering: (206) 283-9495
Contact Name: Joe Pattalardo, President
Catalog: Free. Frequency: Annual
Circulation: 100M. Sales: $1-5MM
Products: Greenhouses and solariums

SUNSHINE FARM & GARDENS (304) 497-2208
HC67 Box 539B • Renick, WV 24966
E-Mail: barry@sunfarm.com
Website: www.sunfarm.com
Contact Name: Barry Glick, President
Catalog: Free. Frequency: Annual
Circulation: 100M. Sales: $500M to $1MM
Products: Plants, perennials

SURPLUS CENTER (800) 488-34007
Burden Sales Company
P.O. Box 82209 • Lincoln, NE 68501
Fax Ordering: (402) 474-5198
International Ordering: (402) 474-4055
Contact Name: David Burden, President
Catalog: Free. Frequency: Annual
Circulation: 400M. Sales: $5-10MM
Products: New and surplus industrial goods,
hardware

SWAN ISLAND DAHLIAS (800) 410-6540
P.O. Box 700 • Canby, OR 97013
E-Mail: info@dahlias.com
Website: www.dahlias.com
Fax Ordering: (503) 266-8768
International Ordering: (503) 266-7711
Contact Name: Nicholas Gitts, President
Catalog: Free. Frequency: Annual
Circulation: 40M. Sales: $500M
Products: Dahlias

SYCAMORE CREEK (518) 398-6393
P.O. Box 16 • Ancram, NY 12502
E-Mail: sycamorecreek@taconic.net
Website: www.sycamorecreek.com
Fax Ordering: (518) 398-7697
Contact Name: Carol Smillie, President
Catalog: $1. Frequency: Annual
Circulation: 10K. Sales: $500K to $1MM
Products: Handcrafted garden furnishings:
trillises, ornaments, arbors, hardware, books

TEAS NURSERY COMPANY (800) 446-7723
P.O. Box 1603 • Bellaire, TX 77402
E-Mail: catalog@teasnursery.com
Website: www.teasnursery.com
Fax Ordering: (713) 295-5170
International Ordering: (713) 664-4400
Contact Names: Tom & Dian Teas
Catalog: Free. Frequency: Annual
Circulation: 25K. Sales: $1-3MM
Products: Tropical plants, orchids, hibiscus,
plumerias, tillandsias; growing supplies & books

TERRITORIAL SEED COMPANY (541) 942-9547
P.O. Box 158
Cottage Grove, OR 97424
E-Mail: tertrl@territorial-seed.com
Website: www.territorialseed.com
Fax Ordering: (888) 657-3131
Contact Name: Tom Johns, President
Catalog: Free. Frequency: Semiannual
Circulation: 200K. Sales: $1-3MM
Products: Vegetable, flower and herb seeds;
plants, tools, organic gardening supplies

TEXAS GREENHOUSE COMPANY (800) 227-5447
812 E. Northside Dr.
Fort Worth, TX 76102
E-Mail: tgci@airmail.net.com
Website: www.texas greenhouse.com
Fax Ordering: (817) 334-0818
International Ordering: (817) 335-5447
Contact Name: Kathy Carlile, President
Catalog: Free. Frequency: Weekly
Circulation: 25K. Sales: $1-3MM
Products: Greenhouse kits and accessories

THOMPSON & MORGAN SEED CATALOG (800) 274-7333
Thompson & Morgan Seedmen, Inc.
220 Faraday Ave. • Jackson, NJ 08527
E-Mail: tmince@tmseeds.com
Website: www.tmseeds.com
Fax Ordering: (888) 466-4769; (732) 363-9356
International Ordering: (732) 363-2225
Catalog: Free. Frequency: Semiannual
Circulation: 100K. Sales: $3-5MM
Products: Seeds for annuals & perennials;
flower, vegetable & wildflower seeds;
magazines & books

TIMBER PRESS CATALOG (800) 327-5680
133 SW 2nd Ave. • Portland, OR 97204
E-Mail: mail@timberpress.com
Website: www.timberpress.com
Fax Ordering: (503) 227-3070
International Ordering: (503) 227-2878
Contact Name: Robert B. Conklin, President
Catalog: Free. Frequency: Annual
Circulation: 25K. Sales: $3-5MM
Products: Books on gardening & horticulture

TINARI GREENHOUSES   (215) 947-0144
African Violet Specialists
2283 Valley Rd.
Huntingdon Valley, PA 19006
E-Mail: info@tinarigreenhouses.com
Website: www.tinarigreenhouses.com
Fax Ordering: (215) 947-2163
International Ordering: (215) 947-0144
Contact Name: Frank A. Tinari President
Catalog: Free. Frequency: Weekly
Circulation: 150K. Sales: $500M to $1MM
Products: African violets and supplies

TRICKL-EEZ COMPANY   (800) 874-2553
4266 Hollywood Rd.
St. Joseph, MI 49085
E-Mail: trickle2@parrett.net
Website: www.trickle-eez.com
Fax Ordering: (616) 429-6669
International Ordering: (616) 429-8200
Contact Name: John & Sandra Nye, Owners
Catalog: Free. Frequency: Annual
Circulation: 10K. Sales: $1-3MM
Products: Agricultural and garden
irrigation systems and supplies

TULIPS.COM   (866) 488-5477
P.O. Box 1248 • Mt. Vernon, WA 98273
E-Mail: Info@tulips.com
Website: www.tulips.com
Fax Ordering: (360) 424-3113
Catalog: Online. Sales: $3-5MM
Products: Seeds for annuals, bulbs &
exotic plants & flower; gifts & decorative
accessories; ornamental grasses & plants

TURF, TREE & ORNAMENTAL   (800) 648-7626
Growth Products, Ltd.
P.O. Box 1252 • White Plains, NY 10602
E-Mail: info@growthproducts.com
Website: www.growthproducts.com
Fax Ordering: (914) 428-2780
International Ordering: (914) 428-1316
Contact Name: Nicole Campbell, Manager
Catalog: Free. Frequency: Monthly
Circulation: 25K. Sales: $1-3MM
Products: Natural organics for lawns, trees,
gardens; liquid fertilizers, micronutrients,
microbial inoculant, root stimulator, biological
fungicide, pH adjuster, slow release nitrogen,
soil conditioner. horticultural & greenhouse
products.

TURNER GREENHOUSES   (800) 672-4770
P.O. Box 1260 • Goldsboro, NC 27533
E-Mail: info@turnergreenhouses.com
Website: www.turner greenhouses.com
Fax Ordering: (919) 734-6167
International Ordering: (919) 734-8345
Contact Name: G. Smithwick, President
Catalog: Free. Frequency: Weekly
Circulation: 25M. Sales: $1-3MM
Products: Pre-fabricated hobby
greenhouses, supplies and accessories

URBAN FARMER STORE   (800) 753-3747
2833 Vicente St.
San Francisco, CA 94116
E-Mail: info@urbanfarmerstore.com
Website: www.urbanfarmerstore.com
Fax Ordering: (415) 661-7826
International Ordering: (415) 661-2204

Contact Name: Jeff Parker, Marketing
Catalog: Free. Frequency: Annual
Circulation: 25K. Sales: $1-3MM
Products: Sprinklers, drip irrigation
supplies, ponds & fountains, outdoor
lighting. Call or go online for your free
copy of "Drip Irrigation handbook."

VAN BOURGONDIEN   (800) 622-9997
P.O. Box 2000 • Virginia Beach, VA 23450
E-Mail: blooms@dutchbulbs.com
Website: www.dutchbulbs.com
Fax Ordering: (800) 327-4268
   (732) 363-9356
Customer Service: (800) 622-9959
Catalog: Free. Frequency: Semiannual
Circulation: 50K. Sales: $1-3MM
Products: Seeds for bulbs & perennials;
exotic plants & flowers; ground covers,
shrubs, trees & vines; ornamental grasses
& plants

VAN DYCK'S FLOWER FARM   (800) 248-2852
P.O. Box 430 • Brightwaters, NY 11718
Fax Ordering: (631) 669-3518
Contact Name: Jan Van Dyke, President
Catalog: Free. Frequency: Annual
Circulation: 100K. Sales: $1-3MM
Products: Dutch flower bulbs

VAN WELL NURSERY   (800) 572-1553
P.O. Box 1339 • Wenatchee, WA 98807
E-Mail: info@vanwell.net.com
Website: www.vanwell.net.com
Fax Ordering: (509) 883-2257
International Ordering: (509) 886-8189
Contact Name: Peter Van Well, President
Catalog: $1. Frequency: Annual
Circulation: 50K. Sales: $1-3MM
Products: Fruit trees

VANS PINES NURSERY   (800) 888-7337
14731 Baldwin St. • West Olive, MI 49460
E-Mail: gvanslooten@egl.net
Fax Ordering: (616) 399-1652
International Ordering: (616) 399-1620
Contact Name: gary Van Slooten, President
Catalog: Free. Frequency: Annual
Circulation: 25K. Sales: $1-3MM
Products: Evergreen seedlings & transplants

VIXEN HILL GAZEBOS   (800) 423-2766
Vixen Hill • Elverson, PA 19520
E-Mail: info@vixenhill.com
Website: www.vixenhill.com
Fax Ordering: (610) 286-2099
International Ordering: (610) 286-0909
Contact Name: Christopher Peeples, President
Catalog: Free. Frequency: Annual
Circulation: 10K. Sales: $3-5MM
Products: Western red cedar gazebos,
pavillions, porch systems

WALKER MOWERS   (800) 279-8537
Walker Manufacturing Co.
5925 E. Harmony Rd.
Fort Collins, CO 80528
E-Mail: info@walkermowers.com
Website: www.walkermowers.com
Fax Ordering: (970) 221-5619
International Ordering: (970) 221-5614
Contact Name: Bob Walker, President

Catalog: Free. Frequency: Annual
Circulation: 100K. **Sales:** $20-50MM
Products: Riding lawn mowers

WALT NICKE'S GARDENTALK (800) 822-4114
36 McLeod Lane • Topsfield, MA 01983
E-Mail: info@gardentalk.com
Website: www.gardentalk.com
Fax Ordering: (978) 887-9853
International Ordering: (978) 887-3388
Contact Name: Katrina Nicke, President
Catalog: $1. Frequency: Quarterly
Circulation: 10K. **Sales:** $500K - $1MM
Products: Gardening tools

WATER VISIONS (800) 205-2425
Vann Ness Water Gardens
2460 N. Euclid Ave. • Upland, CA 91784
E-Mail: vnwg@vnwg.com
Website: www.vnwg.com
Fax Ordering: (909) 949-7217
International Ordering: (909) 982-2425
Contact Name: William Uber, President
Catalog: Free. Frequency: Annual
Circulation: 10K. **Sales:** $250M
Products: Aquatic plants and related filters,
pumps, waterlilies, aquatic products, pond
specialists

WATERFORD GARDENS (201) 327-0721
74 E. Allendale Rd. • Saddle River, NJ 07458
E-Mail: splash@waterfordgardens.com
Website: www.waterfordgardens.com
Fax Ordering: (201) 327-0684
Contact Name: John Meeks, President
Catalog: $5. Frequency: Annual
Circulation: 25K. **Sales:** $1-3MM
Products: Waterlilies, lotus and other aquatic
plants; pools, fish, filters, supplies; books
on water gardening.

WAYSIDE GARDENS (800) 213-0379
1 Garden Lane • Hodges, SC 29695
E-Mail: info@waysidecs.com
Website: www.waysidegardens.com
Fax Ordering: (800) 817-1124
Catalog: Free. Frequency: Semiannual
Circulation: 150K. **Sales:** $1-3MM
Products: Perennials, bulbs, trees &
shrubs; fruit trees, tropical plants,
roses; gifts & garden art

WELL-SWEEP HERB FARM (908) 852-5390
205 Mt. Bethel Rd. • Port Murray, NJ 07865
E-Mail: info@wellsweep.com
Website: www.wellsweep.com
Fax Ordering: (908) 852-1649
Contact Names: Louise & David Hyde
Catalog: $2. Frequency: Annual
Circulation: 10K. **Sales:** $500M
Products: Herbs, perennials & rare
plants, seeds, dried flowers; books

WHAT'S IN A NAME? (800) 253-5766
Seed Research of Oregon
27630 Llewellyn Rd. • Corvallis, OR 97333
E-Mail: info@sroseed.com
Website: www.sroseed.com
Fax Ordering: (541) 758-5305
International Ordering: (541) 757-2663
Contact Name: Mike Robinson, President
Catalog: Free. Frequency: 40x per year

Circulation: 50K. **Sales:** $1-3MM
Products: Bluegrass, perennial, turfseed mixes and blends

WHITE FLOWER FARM (800) 503-9624
P.O. Box 50 • Litchfield, CT 06759
E-Mail: custserv@whiteflowerfarm.com
Website: www.whiteflowerfarm.com
Fax Ordering: (860) 496-1418
International Ordering: (860) 496-9624
Contact Name: Lorraine Calder, President
Catalog: Free. Frequency: 3x per year
Circulation: 100K. **Sales:** $5-10MM
Products: Perennials, annuals, bulbs,
roses, shrubs, gardener's gifts

WILDSEED FARMS
REFERENCE GUIDE & SEED CATALOG (800) 848-0078
P.O. Box 3000 • Fredericksburg, TX 78624
E-Mail: orders1@wildseedfarms.com
Website: www.wildseedfarms.com
Fax Ordering: (830) 990-8090
International Ordering: (830) 990-8080
Contact Name: David Shreiner, President
Catalog: Free. Frequency: Annual
Circulation: 150K. **Sales:** $5-10MM
Products: Wildflower seeds, herbs &
wildlife foods

WILLHITE SEED (800) 828-1840
P.O. Box 23 • Poolville, TX 76487
E-Mail: info@willhiteseed.com
Website: www.willhiteseed.com
Fax Ordering: (817) 599-5843
International Ordering: (817) 599-8656
Contact Name: Robyn Coffey, President
Catalog: Free. Frequency: Annual
Circulation: 100K. **Sales:** $1-3MM
Products: 500 seed varieties & accessories

WOMANNSWORK (800) 639-2709
412 E. 55th St. • New York, NY 10022
E-Mail: info@womanswork.com
Website: www.womanswork.com
Fax Ordering: (212) 753-1010
International Ordering: (212) 753-1086
Contact Name: Dorian Winslow, President
Catalog: Free. Frequency: Semiannual
Circulation: 100M. **Sales:** $500M
Products: Work and gardening gloves,
garden tools and accessories

WOODEN SHOE BULB CO. (800) 711-2006
33814 S. Meridian Rd.
Woodburn, OR 97071
E-Mail: iverson@molala.net
Website: www.woodenshoe.com
Fax Ordering: (503) 634-2710
Catalog: Free. Frequency: Semiannual
Circulation: 25K. **Sales:** $500K to $1MM
Products: Seeds for bulbs & perennials

WOODPRAIRIE FARM (800) 829-9765
49 Kinney Rd. • Bridgewater, ME 04735
E-Mail: orders@woodprairie.com
Website: www.woodprairie.com
Fax Ordering: (800) 300-6494
International Ordering: (207) 425-7741
Catalog: Free. Frequency: Semiannual
Circulation: 100K. **Sales:** $5-10MM
Products: Organic seeds; specialty potatoes;
gardening tools & supplies

WORM'S WAY   **(800) 274-9676**
7850 N. State Rd. 37
Bloomington, IN 47404
E-Mail: info@wormsway.com
Website: www.wormsway.com
Fax Ordering: (800) 316-1264
International Ordering: (812) 876-6450
Contact Name: Martin Heydt, President
Catalog: Free. Frequency: Weekly
Circulation: 500K. Sales: $10-20MM
Products: Hydroponic and organic
gardening supplies

CANADA

DOMINION SEED HOUSE   **(800) 784-3037**
P.O. Box 2500
Georgetown, ON L7G 5L6 Canada
E-Mail: mail@dominion-seed-house.com
Website: www.dominion-seed-house.com
Fax Ordering: (800) 282-5746
International Ordering: (905) 873-3037
Contact Name: Martin Heydt, President
Catalog: Free. Frequency: Weekly
Circulation: 800M. Sales: $10-20MM
Products: Bulbs, annuals, vegetables,
herbs, mushrooms, perennials, berries -
fruit trees; trees, shrubs, roses, gardening

AMAZON DRYGOODS CATALOGS (800) 798-7979
411 Brady St. • Davenport, IA 52801
E-Mail: info@amazondrygoods.com
Website: www.amazondrygoods.com
Fax Ordering: (563) 322-4003
International Ordering: (563) 322-6800
Contact Name: Janet Burgess, President
Catalog: General, $4; Shoe, $5; Pattern, $7;
  Window Treatment, $3. Frequency: Semiannual
Circulation: 250K. Sales: $5-10MM
Products: Clothing, shoes, reproduction clothing
& household accessories; toiletries; books; toys

AMERICAN GIRL CATALOG (800) 845-0005
P.O. Box 620497 • Middleton, WI 53562 (800) 360-1861
E-Mail: info@americangirl.com
Website: www.americangirl.com
Fax Ordering: (608) 836-0761
International Ordering: (608) 831-5210
Contact Name: Ellen Brothers, President
Catalog: Free. Frequency: 8x per year
Circulation: 50MM. Sales: $100-500MM
Products: Children's dolls, gifts, books
& clothing

EDDIE BAUER CATALOG (800) 426-8020
P.O. Box 7001 • Groveport, OH 43125 (888) 838-1920
E-Mail: info@eddiebauer.com
Website: www.eddiebauer.com
Contact Name: Richard Fersch, President
Catalog: Free. Frequency: 20x per year
Circulation: 10MM. Sales: $100-200MM
Products: General merchandise; casual
clothing, home furnishings, bed & bath

BLOOMINGDALE'S BY MAIL (800) 777-0000
P.O. Box 8215 • Mason, OH 45040 (866) 593-2540
E-Mail: sales@bloomingdales.com
Website: www.bloomingdales.com
Fax Ordering: (800) 596-2116
Customer Service: (800) 472-0788; (866) 593-3927
Corporate Gift Service: (800) 283-3730
Furniture Delivery: (800) 323-7857
TDD Ordering: (800) 838-2892
Contact Name: Phil Blanco, President
Catalog: Free. Pages: 76. Frequency: 10x per year
Circulation: 50MM. Sales: $50-100MM
Products: Clothing, accessories; furniture
& mattresses; gifts & items for your home

BLUE BOOK CATALOG (800) 621-2626
Bennett Brothers, Inc.
30 E. Adams St. • Chicago, IL 60603
E-Mail: bluebook@bennettbrothers.com
Website: www.bennettbrothers.com
Fax Ordering: (312) 285-0504
International Ordering: (312) 621-1620
Customer Service: (800) 868-9132
Contact Name: Gail K. Bennett, President
Catalog: Free. Frequency: Annual
Circulation: 2MM. Sales: $20-50MM
Products: General department store catalog

BROOKSTONE COLLECTIONS (800) 926-7000
One Innovation Way • Merrimack, NH 03054 (866) 576-7337
E-Mail: customerservice@brookstone.com
Website: www.brookstone.com
Fax Ordering: (573) 581-7113
International Ordering: (866) 576-7337
Customer Service: (800) 846-3000
Contact Name: Michael Anthony, President
Catalog: Free. Frequency: Bimonthly

Circulation: 24MM. Sales: $50-100MM
Products: Hard-to-find tools, household
products, garden accessories

THE COMPANY STORE CATALOG (800) 289-8508
500 Company Store Rd. • La Crosse, WI 54601 (800) 285-3696
E-Mail: sales@thecompanystore.com
Website: www.thecompanystore.com
Fax Ordering: (608) 791-5776
Customer Service: (800) 323-8000
Contact Name: Frank Keery, President
Catalog: Free. Frequency: Semiannual
Circulation: 2MM. Sales: $20-50MM
Products: Men's, women's & children clothing;
down pillows & comforters, bedding & feather
products

CONCORD ENTERPRISES (800) 960-0896
2957 E. 46 St. • Los Angeles, CA 90058
E-Mail: sales@dollaritem.com
Website: www.dollaritem.com
Fax Ordering: (323) 588-8080
International Ordering: (323) 588-8888
Catalog: Free. Pages: 200. Frequency: Semiannual
Circulation: 200K. Sales: $10-20MM
Products: Wholesale products, gifts, apparel
& merchandise

FREDERICK'S OF HOLLYWOOD (800) 323-9525
6608 Hollywood Blvd. • Hollywood, CA 90028
E-Mail: sales@fredericks.com
Website: www.fredericks.com
Fax Ordering: (323) 962-9935
International Ordering: (323) 466-5151
Consumer Relations: (602) 760-2111
Contact Name: Linda Lore, President
Catalog: Free. Frequency: Annual
Circulation: 50MM. Sales: $50-100MM
Products: Women's lingerie

HAMMACHER SCHLEMMER (800) 543-3366
147 E. 57th St. • New York, NY 10022
E-Mail: customerservice@hammacher.com
Website: www.hammacher.com
Fax Ordering: (800) 440-4020; (513) 860-3396
Customer Service: (800) 233-4800; (800) 321-1484
Technical Questions: (800) 227-3528
International Ordering: (513) 860-3397
Contact Name: Fred Berns, Marketing Manager
Catalog: Free. Pages: 96. Frequency: Quarterly
Circulation: 5MM. Sales: $50-100MM
Products: Gifts, home & outdoor living,
home care, electronics, sports & leisure,
personal care items, apparel, travel, collectibles,
children's and baby clothing & items

HEARTLAND AMERICA (800) 229-2901
8085 Century Blvd. • Chaska, MN 55318
E-Mail: sales@heartlandamerica.com
Website: www.heartlandamerica.com
Fax Ordering: (800) 943-4096
Contact Name: Mark Platt, President
Catalog: Free. Pages: 40. Frequency: Quarterly
Circulation: 10MM. Sales: $20-50 MM
Products: Gifts & collectibles; phones,
electronics & audio/video products; fashion,
household, auto & hardware

HORCHOW COLLECTION (800) 456-7000
Neiman Marcus Direct
P.O. Box 620048 • Dallas, TX 75262
E-Mail: sales@horchow.com

Website: www.horchow.com
Fax Ordering: (972) 401-6414
International Ordering: (972) 401-6300
Contact Name: Jessica Weiland, Manager
Catalog: $2. Frequency: Annual
Circulation: 5MM. Sales: $50-100MM
Products: Apparel, home furnishings, lighting, shoes & handbags, jewelry & accessories, beauty & fragrance, bed & bath, entertainment, gifts & collectibles.

LANDS' END CATALOG (800) 356-4444
1 Lands' End Lane • Dodgeville, WI 53595 (800) 963-4816
E-Mail: landsend@landsend.com
Website: www.landsend.com
Fax Ordering: (800) 332-0103; (608) 935-4000
International Ordering: (608) 935-6170
TTY Ordering: (800) 541-3459
Contact Name: Michael J. Smith, President
Catalog: Free. Pages: 84. Frequency: 13x per year
Circulation: 20MM. Sales: $500MM to $1B
Products: Men's, women's & children's clothing, home furnishings, linenes, travel

MACY'S (800) 456-2297
Advertex Communications, Inc.
151 West 34th St. • New York, NY 10001
E-Mail: sales@macysjobs.com
Website: www.macysjobs.com
Catalog: Free. Pages: 84. Frequency: Monthly
Circulation: 25MM. Sales: $500MM to $1B
Products: Clothing, accessories, footwear, home furnishings, housewares, jewelry

MILES KIMBALL CATALOG (800) 546-2255
250 City Center • Oshkosh, WI 54906
E-Mail: csr@mileskimball.com
Website: www.mileskimball.com
Fax Ordering: (920) 231-6942; (800) 863-3395
International Ordering: (920) 270-7401
Customer Service: (800) 255-4500
Catalog: Free. Frequency: Monthly
Circulation: 50MM. Sales: $100-500MM
Products: General merchandise; kitchen, home, desktop & office, outdoor, apparel & personal care, travel & auto, leisure, kids, gifts & collectibles

NEIMAN MARCUS DIRECT (888) 888-4757
111 Customer Way • Irving, TX 75039
E-Mail: orders@neimanmarcus.com
Website: www.neimanmarcus.com
Fax Ordering: (972) 401-6827
International Ordering: (972) 969-3100
Contact Name: Karen Katz, President
Catalog: Free. Frequency: 40x per year
Circulation: 50MM. Sales: $100-250MM
Products: Clothing, accessories, household items, home furnishings, gifts, food

NORDSTROM DIRECT (800) 285-5800
1700 Seventh Ave., #300 • Seattle, WA 98101 (888) 282-6060
E-Mail: contactcustinersrvc@nordstrom.com
Website: www.nordstrom.com
Fax Ordering: (206) 215-7737
International Ordering: (319) 846-4140
Canada Ordering: (877) 794-5304
Contact Name: Dan Nordstrom, President
Catalog: Free. Frequency: Quarterly
Circulation: 50MM. Sales: $250-500MM
Products: Clothing, accessories, footwear

NORTHSTYLE (800) 336-5666
P.O. Box 6529 • Chelmsford, MA 01824
E-Mail: HELP@northstyle.com
Website: www.northstyle.com
Fax Ordering: (800) 866-3235
International Ordering: (978) 256-4100
Contact Name: Jonathan Fleischman, President
Catalog: Free. Frequency: Semiannual
Circulation: 100M. Sales: $20-50MM
Products: Apparel, jewelry, cabinware, gifts, home decor, kitchen & bath, yard & garden

ORVIS GIFTS & CLOTHING (800) 541-3541
The Orvis Company (888) 235-9763
1711 Blue Hills Dr. • Roanoke, VA 24012
E-Mail: customer_service@orvis.com
Website: www.orvis.com
Fax Ordering: (802) 362-3525
International Ordering: (540) 345-4606
Contact Name: Perk Perkins, President
Catalog: Free. Frequency: 16x per year
Circulation: 25MM. Sales: $100-250MM
Products: Clothing; gifts; electronics; hunting & fishing equipment; home furnishings; luggage

J.C. PENNY CATALOGS (800) 222-6161
P.O. Box 10001 • Dallas, TX 75301 (800) 322-1189
E-Mail: orders@jcpenny.com
Website: www.jcpenny.com
Fax Ordering: (972) 591-9322
International Ordering: (972) 431-1000
Contact Name: James Osterreicher, President
Catalog: Free. Frequency: Annual
Circulation: 50MM. Sales: $100-500MM
Products: Various catalogs; general merchandise

J. PETERMAN COMPANY (888) 647-2555
1001 Primrose Ct. • Lexington, KY 40511
E-Mail: orders@jpeterman.com
Website: www.jpeterman.com
Fax Ordering: (859) 254-0869
International Ordering: (859) 254-5444
Contact Name: Arnie Cohen, President
Catalog: Free. Frequency: 5x per year
Circulation: 15-20MM. Sales: $50-100MM
Products: Romantic, hard-to-find unique & nostolgic items from around the world; from clothing & household goods & furnishings to fine art & collectibles

S&S WORLDWIDE (800) 243-9232
75 Mill St. • Colchester, CT 06415 (800) 937-3482
E-Mail: cservice@ssww.com (800) 288-9941
Website: www.ssww.com
Fax Ordering: (860) 537-2866; (800) 566-6678
International Ordering: (860) 537-3451
Contact Name: Stephen Schwartz, President
Catalog: Free. Frequency: Weekly
Circulation: 5MM. Sales: $20-50MM
Products: General merchandise: arts & crafts supplies; educational supplies; games, party novelties; sports & recreation

SAKS FIFTH AVENUE (877) 551-7257
700 Hickory Lane • Aberdeen, MD 21001
E-Mail: orders@saksfifthavenue.com
Website: www.saksfifthavenue.com
Fax Ordering: (601) 968-5281
Contact Name: Steve Sadove, CEO
Catalog: Free. Frequency: 26x per year
Circulation: 10MM. Sales: $50-100MM
Products: Upscale women's apparel & home decor

SEARS CATALOGS
(800) 948-8800
(800) 349-4358

P.O. Box 40 • Hanover, PA 17331
E-Mail: sales@sears.com
Website: www.sears.com
Fax Ordering: (800) 757-9997
International Ordering: (717) 633-3333
Catalog: Free. Frequency: Annual
Circulation: 10MM. Sales: $200-500MM
Products: Appliances, housewares,
kitchen & bath

SERVICE MERCHANDISE CATALOG
(800) 832-4481

1801 Clint Moore Rd. #108
Boca Raton, FL 33487
E-Mail: rz@servicemerchandise.com
Website: www.servicemerchandise.com
Fax Ordering: (561) 999-9817
International Ordering: (561) 999-9815
Contact Name: Gary Witkin, President
Catalog: Free. Frequency: Monthly
Circulation: 5MM. Sales: $20-50MM
Products: Jewelry, gifts, outdoor living

SEVENTH AVENUE CATALOG
(800) 356-9090

1112 7th Ave • Monroe, WI 53566
E-Mail: info@seventhavenue.com
Website: www.seventhavenue.com
Fax Ordering: (608) 328-5578
International Ordering: (608) 324-7000
Customer Service: (608) 324-4637
Contact Name: Gary Schwager, President
Catalog: Free. Frequency: 8x per year
Circulation: 4MM. Sales: $100-500MM
Products: General merchandise: Furniture,
home decor, bed & bath, clothing, jewelry,
electronics, fitness, apparel & accessories,
outdoor, gifts, collectibles

SGT GRIT MARINE SPECIALTIES
(866) 776-2607

7100 SW 4th St. • Oklahoma City, OK 73179
E-Mail: contact@grunt.com
Website: www.grunt.com
Fax Ordering: (866) 776-2610; (405) 602-5470
International Ordering: (405) 602-5490
Catalog: Free. Frequency: Semiannual
Circulation: 250K. Sales: $10-20MM
Products: U.S. Marine Corps merchandise:
books, swwords, stickers, patches, flags, clothing

SHOPPERS ADVANTAGE
(800) 516-4848

Trilegiant, Inc.
100 Connecticut Ave. • Norwalk, CT 06850
E-Mail: kbuonagura@trilegiant.com
Website: www.trilegiant.com
Fax Ordering: (203) 365-5227
International Ordering: (203) 956-1000
Contact Name: Matt Lipman, President
Catalog: Free. Frequency: 8x per year
Circulation: 4MM. Sales: $50-100MM
Products: General merchandise

SIERRA TRADING POST
(800) 713-4534

5025 Campstool Rd. • Cheyenne, WY 82007
E-Mail: customerservice@sierratradingpost.com
Website: www.sierratradingpost.com
Fax Ordering: (800) 378-8946; (307) 775-8301
International Ordering: (307) 775-8050
Contact Name: Keith Richardson, President
Catalog: Free. Frequency: Semiannual
Circulation: 500M. Sales: $20-50MM
Products: Outdoor & casual clothes, footwear,
home decor, outdoor sports gear and more

SPIEGEL CATALOGS
(800) 345-4500

Easy Style Dr. • Hampton, VA 23670
E-Mail: sales@spiegel.com
Website: www.spiegel.com
Customer Service: (800) 222-5680
Contact Name: George Ittner, President
Catalog: Free. Frequency: 24x per year
Circulation: 10MM. Sales: $500MM to $1B
Products: General merchandise: clothing,
shoes & accessories, jewelry, electronics,
home furnishings & accessories, giftware;
swim & travel

SUNDANCE CATALOG
(800) 422-2770

3865 West 2400 South
Salt Lake City, UT 84120
E-Mail: service@sundance.net
Website: www.sundancecatalog.com
Fax Ordering: (800) 843-9445
International Ordering: (801) 973-2711
Contact Name: Jessica Bassin, Contact
Catalog: Free. Frequency: 7x per year
Circulation: 1MM. Sales: $10-20MM
Products: Home & garden decor, furniture,
men's & women's apparel, jewelry, accessories,
footwear with a flavor of the American West
and native cultures of the world.

VALU DISPLAY CATALOG
(888) 421-4241

P.O. Box 2288 • Whittler, CA 90610
E-Mail: sales@valudisplay.com
Website: www.valudisplay.com
Fax Ordering: (888) 567-6259
Catalog: Free. Frequency: Quarterly
Circulation: 250M. Sales: $5-10MM
Products: General detail display products:
bags, banners & flags, business forms,
computer software & supplies, decorative
products, display products, gift wrapping
supplies, hangers & accessories, labels,
promotional products, store supplies

LILLIAN VERNON CATALOGS
(800) 545-5426
(800) 901-9402

Lillian Vernon Corporation
100 Lillian Vernon Dr.
Virginia Beach, VA 23479-0002
E-Mail: custserv@lillianvernon.com
Website: www.lillianvernon.com
Fax Ordering: (800) 852-2365; (914) 949-2685
International Ordering: (914) 949-1979
TDD Ordering: (800) 285-5536
Customer Service: (800) 505-2250
Contact Name: Howard Goldberg, President
Catalog: Free. Pages: 56. Frequency: Monthly
Circulation: 50MM. Sales: $100-500MM
Products: Gifts; household, kitchen, toys &
games, decorative, gardening, holiday &
seasonal merchandise; infant & children's gifts,
kidswear & accessories, educational products

VISTA CATALOG
(214) 333-2111

B&F System
3920 S. Walton Walker Blvd.
Dallas, TX 75236
E-Mail: sales@bnfusa.com
Website: www.bnfusa.com
Fax Ordering: (214) 333-2137
International Ordering: (214) 333-2137
Contact Name: Bill Meyer, President
Catalog: Free. Frequency: Semiannual
Circulation: 5MM. Sales: $20-50MM
Products: General wholesalemerchandise

VOICE OF THE MOUNTAINS (802) 362-4667
Vermont Country Store (802) 362-8460
P.O. Box 6993 • Rutland, VT 05702
E-Mail: sales@vermontcountrystore.com
Website: www.vermontcountrystore.com
Fax Ordering: (802) 362-0285
Contact Name: Lyman Orton, President
Catalog: Free. Frequency: 13x per year
Circulation: 15MM. Sales: $20-50MM
Products: Apparel, personal care products,
food, country home products, Kitchen gadgets,
rubber boots, work gloves, rugs, socks &
underwear, jams

A.W. ENTERPRISES (800) 334-4884
6543 S. Laramie Ave.
Bedford Park, IL 60638
E-Mail: info@caseguys.net
Website: www.awenterprises.com
Fax Ordering: (708) 458-9023
International Ordering: (708) 458-8989
Contact Name: Edward Otrusina, President
Catalog: Free. Frequency: Annual
Circulation: 100K. Sales: $3-5MM
Products: Cell phone cases, two-way radio
cases & accessories; musical instrument
cases; custom cases

ABBEY PRESS (800) 962-4760
One Hill Dr. • St. Meinrad, IN 47577
E-Mail: customerservice@abbeypress.com
Website: www.abbeypress.com
Fax Ordering: (518) 352-7678
Customer Service: (888) 374-4226
Contact Name: Vickie Sandtford, Buyer
Catalog: Free. Frequency: Annual
Circulation: 50K. Sales: $1-3MM
Products: Gifts of faith, holidays & occasions;
personalized Christian gifts; Christmas gifts

THE ADDED TOUCH (888) 238-6824
P.O. Box 4 • Niagara Falls, NY 14304
E-Mail: customerservice@addedtouch.ca
Website: www.addedtouch.com
Fax Ordering: (888) 232-4040; (905) 338-1486
International Ordering: (905) 338-6767
Catalog: Free. Frequency: Semiannual
Circulation: 1MM. Sales: $10-50MM
Products: General gifts: auto & travel,
books, candles, clothing, gift baskets,
entertainment, sports & hobbies, pet
stuff, wine accessories

ADIRONDACK MUSEUM STORE (518) 352-7311
Rt. 28N & 30 • Blue Mt. Lake, NY 12812
E-Mail: info@adkmuseum.org
Website: www.adkmuseum.org
Fax Ordering: (518) 352-7653
Contact Name: Vickie Sandtford, Buyer
Catalog: Free. Frequency: Annual
Circulation: 50K. Sales: $500M to $1MM
Products: Gifts; games & toys; jewelry; pillows &
rugs; posters & photos; books & maps; clothing

AIRLINE INTERNATIONAL, INC. (800) 592-1234
8701 Montana Ave. • El Paso, TX 79925
E-Mail: orders@airlineintl.com
Website: www.airlineintl.com
Fax Ordering: (915) 778-1533
International Ordering: (915) 778-1234
Catalog: Free. Frequency: Semiannual
Circulation: 150M. Sales: $3-5MM
Products: Luggage, pens, gifts, jewelry,
games & puzzles< travel accessories

ALBERENE ROYAL MAIL (800) 843-9078
P.O. Box 902 • Harrisville, NH 03450
E-Mail: info@alberene.com
Website: www.alberene.com
Fax Ordering: (603) 827-5513
International Ordering: (603) 827-5514
Catalog: Free. Frequency: Annual
Circulation: 250K. Sales: $10-50MM
Products: Artwork, books, CDs, DVDs,
clothing, jewelry, food & tea, nautical, pets,
sports, tableware & crystal, clocks,

AMERICA! (800) 927-8277
30 S. Quaker Lane
Alexandria, VA 22314
E-Mail: service@america-store.com
Website: www.america-store.stores.yahoo.net
Fax Ordering: (703) 212-8969
International Ordering: (703) 836-1491
Contact Name: Jane Crawford, President
Catalog: Free. Frequency: Quarterly
Circulation:100K. Sales: $1-3MM
Products: Political clothing, patriotic gifts,
flags

AMERICAN FLAG & GIFT CATALOG (800) 448-3524
1101 Highland Way, Suite B
Grover Beach, CA 93433
E-Mail: sales@anyflag.com
Website: www.anyflag.com
Fax Ordering: (805) 473-0126
International Ordering: (805) 473-0395
Contact Name: Bridgett Solley, President
Catalog: Free. Frequency: Annual
Circulation: 25K. Sales: $1-3MM
Products: Decorative & sports flags; world,
state & custom flags; flagpoles & hardware;
advertising flags; gifts with flags

LINDA ANDERSON (800) 621-3411
310 S. Campbell Ave.
Springfield, MO 65806
E-Mail: info@lindaanderson.com
Website: www.lindaanderson.com
Fax Ordering: (417) 862-5002
Catalog: Online. Sales: $1-3MM
Products: Gifts; jewelry, furniture,
clothing & accessories; arts & crafts

ANTIQUE FIREBACK REPLICAS (800) 233-9945
Country Iron Foundry
180 Franklin St.
Framingham, MA 01702
E-Mail: info@firebacks.com
Website: www.firebacks.com
Fax Ordering: (508) 879-3735
International Ordering: (239) 434-7207
Catalog: Free. Frequency: Semiannual
Circulation: 100K. Sales: $3-5MM
Products: Firebacks for fireplaces

ARCHIE McPHEE & CO. (425) 349-3009
P.O. Box 30852 • Seattle, WA 98113
E-Mail: mcphee@mcphee.com
Website: www.mcphee.com
Fax Ordering: (425) 349-5188
Catalog: Free. Frequency: Semiannual
Circulation: 200K. Sales: $5-10MM
Products: Toys, gifts and novelties

ARCHITECTURAL BRONZE (800) 339-6581
& ALUMINUM CORP.
655 Deerfield Rd., Suite 100
Deerfield, IL 60015
E-Mail: sales@architecturalbronze.com
Website: www.architecturalbronze.com
Fax Ordering: (847) 266-7301
Contact Names: Kenneth Cooper, President
Catalog: Free. Frequency: Annual
Circulation: 200K. Sales: $5-10MM
Products: Manufactureres of cast bronze &
aluminum plaques, engravings, awards, medals,
medallions, etc.

ARIZONA HIGHWAYS GIFT CATALOG (800) 543-5432
2039 W. Lewis Ave. • Phoenix, AZ 85009
E-Mail: arizonahighwaysproducts@
emailcustomerservice.com
Website: www.arizonahighways.com
Fax Ordering: (602) 254-4505; (480) 393-5725
International Ordering: (602) 712-2018
Contact Name: Win Holden, President
Catalog: Free. Frequency: Annual
Circulation: 1MM. Sales: $5-10MM
Products: Southwestern theme gifts,
decorative items, books

ART INSTITUTE OF CHICAGO (888) 301-9612
MUSEUM SHOP
111 S. Michigan Ave. • Chicago, IL 60603
E-Mail: info@artinstituteshop.org
Website: www.artinstituteshop.org
Fax Ordering: (423) 867-8495
International Ordering: (312) 443-3583
Contact Name: James Wood, President
Catalog: Free. Frequency: Annual
Circulation: 250K. Sales: $10-20MM
Products: Museum gifts, apparel & accessories,
books, jewelry, wall art, stationery

ASPREY (800) 883-2777
725 Fifth Ave. • New York, NY 10022
E-Mail: info@asprey.com
Website: www.asprey.com
Fax Ordering: (212) 826-3746
International Ordering: (212) 688-1811
Contact Name: Philip Warner, President
Catalog: Free. Frequency: Annual
Circulation: 150K. Sales: $20-50MM
Products: High quality gifts, jewelry,
china, glass, executive gifts

AUSTRALIAN CATALOGUE COMPANY (800) 808-0938
146 Riverview Park Rd. • Jackson, GA 30233
E-Mail: sales@aussiecatalog.com
Website: www.aussiecatalog.com
Fax Ordering: (770) 775-6655
International Ordering: (404) 762-1204
Contact Name: Terri Steel, President
Catalog: Free. Frequency: 16x per year
Circulation: 350K. Sales: $5-10MM
Products: Australian foods, music, books,
videos, t-shirts

BABYSHOE.COM (800) 543-8566
306 Hebron St. • Hendersonville, NC 28739
E-Mail: info@babyshoe.com
Website: www.babyshoe.com
Fax Ordering: (828) 697-5815
International Ordering: (828) 697-5811
Contact Name: Michael Schwartz, President
Catalog: Free. Frequency: Annual
Circulation: 50K. Sales: $500K
Products: Personalized baby gifts,
including baby shoes and blankets

BARRONS CATALOG (800) 762-7145
P.O. Box 994 • Novi, MI 48376 (800) 538-6340
E-Mail: barronssdw@aol.com
Website: www.barronscatalog.com
Fax Ordering: (248) 344-4342
International Ordering: (248) 348-7050
Contact Name: Thomas Heslops, President
Catalog: Free. Frequency: 8x per year
Circulation: 100M. Sales: $3-5MM
Products: Gifts, fine dinnerware & home decor

BASEBALL GIFTS (877) 209-7318
National Baseball Hall of Fame
25 Main St. • Cooperstown, NY 13326
E-Mail: info@baseballhall.org
Website: www.shop.baseballhall.org
Fax Ordering: (607) 547-2044
International Ordering: (607) 547-7200
Contact Name: Barbara L. Shinn, Marketing
Catalog: Free. Frequency: 3x per year
Circulation: 150K. Sales: $1-3MM
Products: Baseball collectibles, memorabilia
& gifts, clothing and accessories

BETTY'S ATTIC (800) 294-4068
Johnson Smith Catalog Company
P.O. Box 25600 • Bradenton, FL 34206
E-Mail: custservba@jsis.com
Website: www.bettysattic.com
Fax Ordering: (800) 551-4406
International Ordering: (941) 747-5566
Customer Service: (800) 558-6961; (800) 303-9928
Contact Name: Ralph Hoenie, President
Catalog: Free. Frequency: Weekly
Circulation: 250M. Sales: $500M to $1MM
Products: Collectibles and nostalgic items from
the 1920s to the 1970s, including apparel &
accessories, books and calendars, toys &
games, dollism home decor, videos and music

BITS & PIECES CATALOG (866) 503-6395
P.O. Box 4150 • Lawrenceburg, IN 47025
E-Mail: customerservice@bitsandpieces.com
Website: www.bitsandpieces.com
Fax Ordering: (513) 354-1290
Catalog: Free. Frequency: Semiannual
Circulation: 250K. Sales: $3-5MM
Products: Puzzles, gifts, and kids games

THE BREWERY SHOP (800) 765-6288
Matt Brewing Co.
811 Edward St. • Utica, NY 13502
E-Mail: leighd@saranac.com
Website: www.schultzanddooleyonline.com
Fax Ordering: (315) 732-4296
International Ordering: (315) 732-0762
Contact Name: Nicholas Matt, President
Catalog: Free. Frequency: Semiannual
Circulation: 100K. Sales: $1-3MM
Products: Collector steins & brewery-related items

BRIDGE BUILDING IMAGES (800) 325-6263
P.O. Box 1048 • Burlington, VT 05402
E-Mail: bbi@bridgebuilding.com
Website: www.bridgebuilding.com
Fax Ordering: (802) 865-2434
International Ordering: (802) 864-8346
Catalog: Free. Frequency: Quarterly
Circulation: 200K. Sales: $1-3MM
Products: Religious cards & gifts

BUDSHOP.COM (800) 742-5283
Anheiser-Busch (800) 342-5BUD
20 Constitution Blvd. S • Shelton, CT 06484
E-Mail: sales@budshop.com
Website: www.budshop.com
Fax Ordering: (314) 577-2900
International Ordering: (314) 577-4283
Contact Name: Tim Schoen, Manager
Catalog: Online. Sales: $100-200MM
Products: Gifts for home bar; personalized
coolers; , steins, sporting goods, clothing,
commemorative collectibles, beer signs, glassware

BUNNIES BY THE BAY   (877) 467-7248
P.O. Box 1630 • Anacortes, WA 98221
E-Mail: customerservice@bunniesbythebay.com
Website: www.bunniesbythebay.com
Fax Ordering: (360) 293-4729
International Ordering: (360) 293-8037
Catalog: Free. Frequency: Semiannual
Circulation: 50K. Sales: $1-3MM
Products: Stuffed animals (bunnies)
and gifts for babies to adults

CALLAWAY GARDENS CATALOG   (800) 225-5292
P.O. Box 2000 • Pine Mountain, GA 31822
E-Mail: info@callawayonline.com
Website: www.callawayonline.com
Fax Ordering: (706) 663-6812
International Ordering: (706) 663-2281
Contact Name: Kathy Tilley, Marketing Director
Catalog: Free. Frequency: Annual
Circulation: 100K. Sales: $20-50MM
Products: Food, home decor, bath & beauty,
jewelry, videos & CDs, books, toys, plants,
outdoors.

CARROT-TOP'S FLAG & BANNER   (800) 628-3524
Carrot-Top Industries, Inc.
328 Elizabeth Brandy Rd, #820
Hillsborough, NC 27278
E-Mail: service@carrot-top.com
Website: www.carrot-top.com
Fax Ordering: (919) 732-5526
International Ordering: (919) 732-6200
Contact Name: Dwight A. Morris, President
Catalog: Free. Frequency: Bimonthly
Circulation: 1MM. Sales: $3-5MM
Products: Flags, banners, ribbons,
flagpoles, display cases, signage

HARRIET CARTER GIFTS   (800) 377-7878
425 Stump Rd. • North Wales, PA 19454
E-Mail: customerservice@harrietcarter.com
Website: www.harrietcarter.com
Fax Ordering: (215) 361-5344
International Ordering: (215) 361-5122
Customer Service: (800) 230-3833
Contact Name: Ronald P. Lassin, President
Catalog: Free. Frequency: Semiannual
Circulation: 1MM. Sales: $50-100MM
Products: Gifts & novelties; bed & bath,
home decor, collectibles, health & beauty,
apparel, jewelry, law/garden/outddors, sports,
auto acessories, books, videos & games.

CASUAL LIVING   (800) 843-1881
P.O. Box 31273 • Tampa, FL 33631
E-Mail: info@casualivingusa.com
Website: www.casualivingusa.com
Fax Ordering: (813) 882-4605
International Ordering: (813) 884-6955
Customer Service: (800) 466-9440
Contact Name: Robert Franzblau, President
Catalog: Free. Pages: 72. Frequency: Bimonthly
Circulation: 1MM. Sales: $5-10MM
Products: Gifts & home furnishings for casual living

CELESTIAL PRODUCTS CATALOG   (800) 235-3783
P.O. Box 801 • Middleburg, VA 20118
E-Mail: customerservice@celestialproducts.com
Website: www.celestialproducts.com
Fax Ordering: (540) 338-4042
International Ordering: (540) 338-4040
Catalog: Free. Frequency: Annual
Circulation: 50K. Sales: $500K to $1MM
Products: Gifts, reference materials,
moon calendars, calendars, books,
posters, charts & note cards designed
to stimulate understanding of our universe

CHEVYMALL   (858) 558-2550
625 Second St. #210 • Petaluma, CA94952
E-Mail: info@chevymall.com
Website: www.chevymall.com
Fax Ordering: (707) 766-8400
International Ordering: (707) 766-6391
Catalog: Free. Frequency: Semiannual
Circulation: 500K. Sales: $5-10MM
Products: Official Chevrolet licensed
merchandise; accessories, gifts

CHIASSO   (877) 244-2776
1440 N. Dayton St., #307 • Chicago, IL 60622   (888) 642-8595
E-Mail: info@chiasso.com
Website: www.chiasso.com
Fax Ordering: (312) 447-3827
International Ordering: (616) 957-1717
Customer Service: (800) 654-3570
Catalog: Free. Frequency: Quarterly
Circulation: 100K. Sales: $1-3MM
Products: Contemporary & modern furniture;
gifts and novelties. housewares, accessories
for the home

CLASSIC TOY SOLDIERS   (970) 225-9782
2818 McKeag Dr. • Fort Collins, CO 80526
E-Mail: orders@clasictoysoldiers.com
Website: www.classictoysoldiers.com
Fax Ordering: (913) 451-2946
Contact Name: David Payne, President
Catalog: $3. Frequency: Quarterly
Circulation: 15K. Sales: $500MK
Products: Manufacturer & distributor
of classic toy soldiers

CLEVELAND MUSEUM OF ART   (216) 707-2333
11150 E. Boulevard • Cleveland, OH 44106
E-Mail: info@clevelandart.org
Website: www.clevelandart.org
Fax Ordering: (216) 421-1736
Contact Name: Emily Rosen, Production Manager
Catalog: Free. Frequency: Annual
Circulation: 50K. Sales: $500K to $1MM
Products: Art repros and museum gifts

COCA-COLA CATALOG   (800) 438-2653
P.O. Box 1734 • Atlanta, GA 30301
E-Mail: info@cocacola.com
Website: www.cocacola.com
Fax Ordering: (800) 332-2320
Catalog: Free. Frequency: Monthly
Circulation: 3MM. Sales: $50-100MM
Products: Coca-Cola memorabilia, lifestyle
products for the home & licensed Coca-Cola
brand apparel

COLORFUL IMAGES   (800) 458-7999
P.O. Box 35022
Colorado Springs, CO 80935
E-Mail: info@colorfulimages.com
Website: www.colorfulimages.com
Fax Ordering: (800) 458-6999
Customer Service: (800) 272-9209
Catalog: Free. Frequency: Annual
Circulation: 1MM. Sales: $5-10MM
Products: Gifts; personalized address labels

CONRAD'S COLLEGE GIFTS   (888) 443-8678
316 W. Lane Ave. • Columbus, OH 43201
E-Mail: osu@conrads.com
Website: www.conrads.com
Fax Ordering: (877) 232-9678; (614) 291-3106
International Ordering: (614) 297-0497
Contact Names: Jack & Rob Cohen, Owners
Catalog: Free. Frequency: Quarterly
Circulation: 50K. Sales: $1-3MM
Products: Ohio State University Buckeye gifts

CRAZY CROW TRADING POST   (800) 786-6210
P.O. Box 847 • Pottsboro, TX 75076
E-Mail: orders@crazycrow.com
Website: www.crazycrow.com
Fax Ordering: (903) 786-9059
International Ordering: (903) 786-2287
Contact Name: J. Rex Reddick, President
Catalog: $5. Frequency: Annual
Circulation: 10K. Sales: $1-3MM
Products: American Indian arts & crafts'
supplies; craft books, camp supplies,
Indian craft kits; Indian knives, blankets,
clothing, flutes, furs & hides

CURRENT CATALOG   (800) 848-2848
Order Processing Center
Colorado Springs, CO 80941
E-Mail: info@currentcatalog.com
Website: www.currentcatalog.com
Fax Ordering: (719) 531-2122
Customer Service: (877) 665-4458
Catalog: Free. Frequency: Bimonthly
Circulation: 150K. Sales: $3-5MM
Products: Personalized greeting cards,
address books, address labels,
ornaments and T-shirts

DELIGHTFUL-DELIVERIES   (800) 777-1911
2127 Westwood Blvd. #200   (800) 941-1334
Los Angeles, CA 90025
E-Mail: service@delightfuldeliveries.com
Website: www.delightfuldeliveries.com
Fax Ordering: (310) 626-8473
International Ordering: (310) 770-7319
Contact Name: Eric Lituchy, President
Catalog: Free. Frequency: Quarterly
Circulation: 200K. Sales: $3-5MM
Products: Gift baskets & food baskets;
gourmet gift baskets

DISNEY CATALOG   (800) 328-0612
Disney Direct Marketing
11200 W. 93rd St.
Shawnee Mission, KS 66201
E-Mail: info@disneystore.com
Website: www.disneystore.com
Fax Ordering: (913) 752-1095
International Ordering: (913) 752-1000
Contact Name: Russ Gillam, President
Catalog: Free. Frequency: 20x per year
Circulation: 1MM. Sales: $50-100MM
Products: Disney character gifts and films

EPHEMERA   (541) 535-4195
P.O. Box 490 • Phoenix, OR 97535
E-Mail: ephemera@mind.net
Website: www.ephemera-inc.com
Fax Ordering: (541) 535—5016
International Ordering: (541) 535-4195
Contact Names: Ed Polish & Jeff Errick, Owners
Catalog: $4. Frequency: Annual

Circulation: 10K. Sales: $1-3MM
Products: Novelty buttons, magnets, and stickers

EXCLUSIVELY WEDDINGS   (800) 759-7666
Pace Communications
2305 Soabar St. • Greensboro, NC 27406
E-Mail: service@exclusivelyweddings.com
Website: www.exclusivelyweddings.com
Fax Ordering: (336) 275-4165
International Ordering: (336) 378—6065
Contact Name: Sher Silver, President
Catalog: Free. Frequency: Annual
Circulation: 100K. Sales: $3-5MM
Products: Wedding planners, albums, favors
& gifts for the attendants and parents

EXOTIC SILKS   (800) 845-7455
1959 Leghorn St.
Mountain View, CA 94043
E-Mail: silks@exoticsilks.com
Website: www.exoticsilks.com
Fax Ordering: (650) 965-0712
International Ordering: (650) 965-7760
Contact Name: Deanne Morgan Shute, President
Catalog: Free. Frequency: Semiannual
Circulation: 50K. Sales: $10-20MM
Products: Silk & cotton fabric, brocades,
silk chiffon, satin silks, velvets

EXPRESSIONS CATALOG   (800) 388-2699
P.O. Box 6529 • Chelmsford, MA 01824
E-Mail: help@expressionscatalog.com
Website: www.expressionscatalog.com
Fax Ordering: (800) 866-3235
International Ordering: (508) 359-7702
Contact Name: Sue Knowles, President
Catalog: Free. Frequency: Bimonthly
Circulation: 250K. Sales: $10-30MM
Products: Gifts and decorative accessories

FEMAIL CREATIONS   (800) 996-9223
E-Mail: customerservice@femailcreations.com
Website: www.femailcreations.com
Contact Name: Lisa Hammond, President
Catalog: Free. Frequency: Semiannual
Circulation: 100K. Sales: $3-5MM
Products: Gifts to celebrate & inspire women

MICHAEL C. FINA   (800) 289-3462
545 Fifth Ave. • New York, NY 10017
E-Mail: info@mcfina.com
Website: www.michaelcfina.com
Fax Ordering: (718) 937-7193
International Ordering: (212) 922-0303
Contact Name: George Fina, President
Catalog: Free. Frequency: Semiannual
Circulation: 1MM. Sales: $20-50MM
Products: Jewelry-wedding rings; tableware &
flatwear, silver, bath accessories, home decor,
giftware

FINGERHUT CATALOG   (800) 233-3588
6250 Ridgewood Rd. • St. Cloud, MN 56303   (800) 603-7052
E-Mail: customerservice@fingerhut.com
Website: www.fingerhut.com
Fax Ordering: (320) 654-3920
International Ordering: (952) 932-3100
Customer Service: (800) 208-2500
Contact Name: William Lansing, President
Catalog: Free. Frequency: Monthly
Circulation: 5MM. Sales: $10-20MM
Products: General gift merchandise including

apparel, appliances, electronics, bed & bath, garage & patio, health & beauty, home furnishings, jewelry, toys, video games, kitchen, sporting goods, luggage

FLAG FABLES
(800) 257-1025
1458 Riverdale St. #4
West Springfield, MA 01089
E-Mail: staff@flagfables.com
Website: www.flagfables.com
Fax Ordering: (800) 214-4773
International Ordering: (413) 747-0525
Contact Name: Wendy Diamond, President
Catalog: $2. Frequency: Bimonthly
Circulation: 150M. Sales: $500M to $1MM
Products: Decorative flags

FLAGS UNLIMITED
(800) 648-3993
4238 29th St. • Kentwood, MI 49512
E-Mail: custserv@flags-unlimited.com
Website: www.flags-unlimited.com
Fax Ordering: (616) 243-2969
International Ordering: (616) 243-2600
Contact Name: Tim Mohney, President
Catalog: Free. Frequency: Annual
Circulation: 25K. Sales: $500M to $1MM
Products: Custom flags & banners

THE FORD COLLECTION
(888) 380-6663
800 Tech Row • Madison Heights, MI 48071
E-Mail: help@fordcollection.com
Website: www.fordcollection.com
Fax Ordering: (800) 283-1256; (248) 816-5748
International Ordering: (248) 458-5313
Contact Name: Donald O. Wheeler, President
Catalog: Free. Frequency: Annual
Circulation: 250K. Sales: $5-10MM
Products: Ford Motor Company collectible items from clothing to gifts

FOREVER & ALWAYS COMPANY
(800) 404-4025
1014 Rabbit Ear Pass • Victor, NY 14564
E-Mail: custsvc@foreverandalways.com
Website: www.foreverandalways.com
Fax Ordering: (888) 254-7822
Catalog: Free. Frequency: Monthly
Circulation: 50K. Sales: $500K - $1MM
Products: Wedding favors, bridal accessories, bridal party gifts and decorative accessories

FORGET ME KNOT GIFTS
(800) 878-4438
P.O. Box 361 • Edgewater, NJ 07020
E-Mail: emailsales@forgetmeknot.com
Website: www.forgetmeknot.com
Fax Ordering: (206) 339-7114
International Ordering: (201) 224-3400
Contact Name: Sharon L. Mitzman, President
Catalog: Free. Frequency: Monthly
Circulation: 1MM. Sales: $10-50MM
Products: Gift baskets & edible gifts

FORTUNOFF CATALOG
(800) 937-4376
(800) 367-8866
P.O. Box 1550 • Westbury, NY 11590
E-Mail: sales@fortunoff.com
Website: www.fortunoff.com
Fax Ordering: (516) 873-6984
International Ordering: (516) 542-0027
Contact Name: Alan Fortunoff, President
Catalog: $2. Frequency: Monthly
Circulation: 2MM. Sales: $50-100MM
Products: Jewelry, tableware & giftware ; bed & bath, baby & bridal registry

4H SOURCE BOOK
(301) 961-2934
National 4H Council
7100 Connecticut Ave.
Chevy Chase, MD 20815
E-Mail: 4hstuff@fourhcouncil.edu
Website: www.4-hmall.org
Fax Ordering: (301) 961-2937
Contact Name: Ed Gershon, Manager
Catalog: Free. Frequency: Annual
Circulation: 250K. Sales: $3-5MM
Products: 4-H items, gifts & educational material

FRIGHT CATALOG
(508) 970-4575
P.O. Box 60210 • Worcester, MA 01606
E-Mail: service@frightcatalog.com
Website: www.4-frightcatalog
Catalog: Free. Frequency: Annual
Circulation: 150K. Sales: $1-3MM
Products: Halloween decorations, props, costumes, masks

FRONTGATE
(800) 263-9850
5566 West Chester Rd.
West Chester, OH 45069
E-Mail: info@frontgate.com
Website: www.frontgate.com
Fax Ordering: (800) 436-2105; (513) 603-1492
International Ordering: (513) 603-1434
Customer Service: (800) 626-6488
Contact Name: Paul Tarvin. President
Catalog: Free. Frequency: Quarterly
Circulation: 1MM. Sales: $20-50MM
Products: Gifts & novelties; holiday decor, indoor & outdoor decor & furniture; bed & bath, pet products, entertainment & electronics, kitchen gourmet, home care

GADGETUNIVERSE
(800) 429-0039
(800) 429-1139
P.O. Box 4808 • Chatsworth, CA 91311
E-Mail: help@gadgetuniverse.com
Website: www.gadgetuniverse.com
Fax Ordering: (888) 867-4988
Customer Service: (800) 478-4703
Catalog: Free. Frequency: Quarterly
Circulation: 500K. Sales: $5-10MM
Products: Gifts & novelties of all kinds; electronics, toys, health & Fitness, home, car, outdoor, clocks & watches

GEARY'S CATALOG
(800) 243-2797
(800) 793-6670
Geary's of Beverly Hills
351 N. Beverly Dr.
Beverly Hills, CA 90210
E-Mail: sales@gearys.com
Website: www.gearys.com
Fax Ordering: (310) 858-7555
International Ordering: (310) 273-4741
Contact Name: Darrell S. Ross, President
Catalog: Free. Frequency: Bimonthly
Circulation: 5MM. Sales: $10-20MM
Products: Fine jewelry, tableware & giftware for the home

THE GLASS GALLERY
(800) 538-0766
L.H. Selman Ltd.
410 S. Michigan Ave. #207
Chicago, IL 60605
E-Mail: info@theglassgallery.com
Website: www.theglassgallery.com
Fax Ordering: (831) 427-0111
International Ordering: (831) 427-1177

Contact Name: Larry Selman, President
Catalog: Free. Frequency: Semiannual
Circulation: 100K. Sales: $5-10MM
Products: Glass paperweights; contemporary
glass; jewelry, museum quality art & giftware

GOLDEN FLEECE DESIGNS   (800) 468-7245
441 S. Victory Blvd. • Burbank, CA 91502
E-Mail: goldenfleecedesign@sbcglobal.net
Fax Ordering: (818) 566-7100
International Ordering: (818) 848-7724
Contact Name: Simeon Argyropoulos, President
Catalog: Free. Frequency: Annual
Circulation: 50K. Sales: $1-3MM
Products: Giftware, apparel, marine equipment

GOOSEBERRY PATCH   (800) 854-6673
P.O. Box 190 • Delaware, OH 43015
E-Mail: info@gooseberrypatch.com
Website: www.gooseberrypatch.com
Fax Ordering: (740) 363-7225
Wholesale Ordering: (877) 854-7400
  Fax (740) 362-5655
International Ordering: (740) 369-1554
Customer Service: (877) 854-7403
Contact Name: Vickie & Jo Ann, Contacts
Catalog: Free. Frequency: Semiannual
Circulation: 100K. Sales: $5-10MM
Products: Cookbooks, calendars,
night lights, quilts & throws, kitchen gifts,
organizers & planners

GORHAM FLAG CENTER   (800) 345-2999
376 Main St. • Gorham, ME 04038
E-Mail: flaginfo@gorhamflag.com
Website: www.gorhamflag.com
Fax Ordering: (207) 839-3952
International Ordering: (207) 839-4675
Contact Name: Paul Auclair, President
Catalog: Free. Frequency: Annual
Circulation: 50K. Sales: $500K - $1MM
Products: U.S. flags; residential flags & poles;
military flags; historical flags

GRACELAND GIFTS   (888) 822-3584
P.O. Box 16508 • Memphis, TN 38186
E-Mail: merchandise@elvis.com
Website: www.shopelvis.com
Fax Ordering: (901) 344-3131
International Ordering: (901) 332-3322
Contact Name: Jack Soden, President
Catalog: Free. Frequency: Semiannual
Circulation: 150K. Sales: $10-20MM
Products: Elvis-related gift products

GRAPHIQUE DE FRANCE   (800) 444-1464
9 State St. • Woburn, MA 01801
E-Mail: consumersupport@graphiquedefrance.com
Website: www.graphiquedefrance.com
Fax Ordering: (800) 288-4331; (781) 935-5145
International Ordering: (781) 935-3405
Catalog: Free. Frequency: Annual
Circulation: 100K. Sales: $1-5MM
Products: Gifts and stationery

HAMPSHIRE PEWTER COMPANY   (800) 639-7704
P.O. Box 1570 • Wolfeboro, NH 03894
E-Mail: gifts@hampshirepewter.com
Website: www.hampshirepewter.com
Fax Ordering: (603) 569-4524
International Ordering: (603) 569-4944
Contact Name: Robert Steele, President

Catalog: Free. Frequency: Annual
Circulation: 50K. Sales: $500M to $1MM
Products: Pewter gifts, lamps, ornaments,
tableware, and collectibles

HARD HAT   (270) 926-7000
422 Frederica St. • Owensboro, KY 42301
E-Mail: sales@hardhatusa.com
Website: www.hardhatusa.com
Fax Ordering: (270) 683-1234
Contact Name: Dan Clark, President
Catalog: Free. Frequency: Annual
Circulation: 250K. Sales: $5-10MM
Products: Knives & flashlights

HARMONY CATALOG   (800) 869-3446
Gaiam, Inc.   Canada (800) 254-8464
P.O. Box 3095 • Boulder, CO 80307
E-Mail: customerservice@gaiam.com
Website: www.gaiam.com
Fax Ordering: (800) 456-1139
International Ordering: (516) 542-0027
Customer Service: (877) 989-6321
Catalog: Free. Frequency: Quarterly
Circulation: 100K. Sales: $3-5MM
Products: Cooking equipment and gifts;
yoga & fitness, health foods, books & media,
outdoor, home & garden, solar energy,
natural household cleaners, home furnishings
and accessories.

HARRY & DAVID CATALOG   (800) 547-3033
P.O. Box 172 • Medford, OR 97501   (877) 322-1200
E-Mail: sales@harryanddavid.com
Website: www.harryanddavid.com
Fax Ordering: (800) 456-1139
Customer Service: (800) 345-5655
Catalog: Free. Pages: 70. Frequency: Quarterly
Circulation: 200K. Sales: $5-10MM
Products: Gourmet gift baskets & boxes;
fruits & nuts, cheeses, chocolates, baked items

HEARTLAND AMERICA   (800) 229-2901
8085 Century Blvd. • Chaska, MN 55318
E-Mail: sales@heartlandamerica.com
Website: www.heartlandamerica.com
Fax Ordering: (800) 943-4096
Contact Name: Mark Platt, President
Catalog: Free. Pages: 40. Frequency: Quarterly
Circulation: 10MM. Sales: $20-50 MM
Products: Gifts & collectibles; phones, electronics
& audio/video products; fashion, household, auto
& hardware

HEIRLOOM EUROPEAN TAPESTRIES   (800) 699-6836
P.O. Box 136 • Berkeley, CA 94705
E-Mail: heirloom@tapestries-inc.com
Website: www.tapestries-inc.com
Fax Ordering: (510) 527-2022
International Ordering: (510) 527-2003
Contact Name: James Waite, President
Catalog: $30. Frequency: Annual
Circulation: 25K. Sales: $5-10MM
Products: Museum tapestry reproductions

HERRINGTON CATALOG   (800) 622-5221
3 Symmes Dr. • Londonderry, NH 03053   (866) 558-7487
E-Mail: customerservice@herringtoncatalog.com
Website: www.herringtoncatalog.com
Fax Ordering: (603) 437-3492
International Ordering: (603) 437-1600
Customer Service: (800) 903-2878

Contact Name: Lee Herrington, President
Catalog: Free. Pages: 60. Frequency: Bimonthly
Circulation: 3MM. Sales: $10-20MM
Products: Gifts; apparel, sports & health,
travel, tools & gadgets, electronics, golf,
photography, footwear, housewares,
bed and bath, and executive accessories.

HISTORIC NEWSPAPER ARCHIVES (800) 221-3221
1582 Hart St. • Rahway, NJ 07065
E-Mail: orders@historicnewspapers.com
Website: www.historicnewspapers.com
Fax Ordering: (732) 381-2699
International Ordering: (732) 381-2332
Contact Name: Peter Heydon, President
Catalog: Free. Frequency: Quarterly
Circulation: 100K. Sales: $1-3MM
Products: Original newspapers for gifts

HODGES BADGE COMPANY (800) 556-2440
P.O. Box 1290 • Portsmouth, RI 02871
E-Mail: info@hodgesbadge.com
Website: www.hodgesbadge.com
Fax Ordering: (800) 292-7377; (401) 682-2329
International Ordering: (401) 682-2000
Contact Name: Rick Hodges, President
Catalog: Free. Frequency: Quarterly
Circulation: 100K. Sales: $3-5MM
Products: Corporte, sports & school awards,
ribbons, medals and buttons

HONORS MILITARY (888) 223-1159
Hoover's Manufacturing Co.
P.O. Box 547 • Peru, IL 61354
E-Mail: info@hmchonors.com
Website: www.hmchonors.com
Fax Ordering: (888) 333-1499;
  (815) 223-1499
Contact Name: David R. Hoover, President
Catalog: Free. Frequency: Quarterly
Circulation: 100K. Sales: $1-3MM
Products: Military designs, hat pins,
medals, ball caps, buckles & patches

HORCHOW COLLECTION (800) 456-7000
Neiman Marcus Direct
P.O. Box 620048 • Dallas, TX 75262
E-Mail: sales@horchow.com
Website: www.horchow.com
Fax Ordering: (972) 401-6414
International Ordering: (972) 401-6300
Contact Name: Jessica Weiland, Manager
Catalog: $2. Frequency: Annual
Circulation: 5MM. Sales: $50-100MM
Products: Apparel, home furnishings,
lighting, shoes & handbags, jewelry &
accessories, beauty & fragrance, bed & bath,
entertainment, gifts & collectibles.

HORSE LOVER'S GIFT GUIDE (800) 767-1452
204 Mayflower Dr.
Woodstock, GA 30188
E-Mail: info@horseloversgifts.com
Website: www.horseloversgifts.com
Fax Ordering: (800) 309-0199; (770) 591-0199
International Ordering: (770) 591-3806
Contact Name: Ana Maria Collantes, President
Catalog: Free. Frequency: Semiannual
Circulation: 100K. Sales: $5-10MM
Products: Horselover's gifts, including jewelry,
t-shirts, calendars, stationery, calendars, clocks,
sweaters, sweatshirts, et al.

HOUSE OF WEBSTER CATALOG (800) 369-4641
P.O. Box 1988 • Rogers, AR 72757
E-Mail: info@houseofwebster.com
Website: www.houseofwebster.com
Fax Ordering: (479) 636-2974
International Ordering: (479) 636-4640
Contact Name: Dale Webster, President
Catalog: Free. Frequency: Semiannual
Circulation: 1MM. Sales: $5-10MM
Products: Gift packs; mixes, preserves,
meats, cheeses, spreads, recipes;
gourmet food items

HUMANE TROPHIES (888) 515-2327
Diane Shapiro Soft Sculpture
37 Beebarn Rd. • Guilford, VT 05301
E-Mail: info@pophouse.com
Website: www.humanetrophies.com
Fax Ordering: (802) 254-6059
International Ordering: (802) 254-8431
Contact Names: Diane & Howard Shapiro, Owners
Catalog: Free. Frequency: Annual
Circulation: 50K. Sales: $1-3MM
Products: Animal trophies; rugs, tuffets,
sewing kits; wall decor & rustic cabing
finishings; soft sculpture of functional
and/or decorative animals

IMPROVEMENTS CATALOG (800) 634-9484
5566 West Chester Rd.
West Chester, OH 45069
E-Mail: sales@improvementscatalog.com
Website: www.improvementscatalog.com
Fax Ordering: (800) 757-9997
International Ordering: (216) 831-6191
Catalog: Free. Frequency: Quarterly
Circulation: 500K. Sales: $10-20MM
Products: Home improvement gifts; outdoor
furniture and gardening accessories; garage
maintenance; storage products to get organized;
pet products; health & safety aids; seasonal
decorations; solar lighting.

JOHNSON SMITH COMPANY (941) 747-5566
P.O. Box 25500 • Bradenton, FL 34206
E-Mail: info@johnsonsmith.com
Website: www.johnsonsmith.com
Fax Ordering: (941) 746-7962
International Ordering: (941) 747-5566
Catalog: Free. Frequency: Quarterly
Circulation: 50M. Sales: $50-100M
Products: A series of nine catalogs of
novelties, gifts & collectibles, including china,
crystal & silver; children's gifts

KEYPOINT COMPANY (800) 521-5004
1320 Chemical St., Suite B • Dallas, TX 75207
E-Mail: sales@keypointcompany.com
Website: www.keypointcompany.com
Fax Ordering: (972) 343-1192
International Ordering: (214) 630-3544
Catalog: Free. Frequency: Semiannual
Circulation: 2MM. Sales: $10-20MM
Products: Themed photo frames & photo
albums; nostalgia gift items; handcrafted
ornaments, sculptures, frames, etc. for
Christmas; home accessories.

KIPP BROTHERS CATALOG (800) 428-1153
9760 Mayflower Park Dr. • Carmel, IN 46032
E-Mail: sales@kipptoys.com
Website: www.kipptoys.com

Fax Ordering: (800) 832-5477; (317) 704-8138
International Ordering: (317) 704-8120
Contact Name: Bob Glenn, President
Catalog: Free. Frequency: Annual
Circulation: 100K. Sales: $10-20MM
Products: Giftware & novelties; stuffed toys,
games, religious, electronics, sports, candy,
jewelry/accessories, headwear, stationery

KNIGHT'S EDGE   (800) 516-EDGE
5696 N. Northwest Hwy. • Chicago, IL 60646
E-Mail: sales@knightsedge.com
Website: www.knightsedge.com
Fax Ordering: (773) 775-3339
International Ordering: (773) 775-3888
Catalog: Free. Frequency: Annual
Circulation: 100K. Sales: $1-3MM
Products: Swords, armor, medieval weapons,
jewelry & home decor

KRONBERG'S FLAGS   (800) 344-3524
7106 Mapleridge St. • Houston, TX 77081
E-Mail: office@kronbergsflagsandflagpoles.com
Website: www.kronbergsflagsandflagpoles.com
Fax Ordering: (713) 661-7022
International Ordering: (713) 661-9222
Contact Name: Ron Kronberg, President
Catalog: Free. Frequency: Semiannual
Circulation: 70K. Sales: $1-3MM
Products: Flags, banners & flag poles

KRUENPEEPER CREEK GIFTS   (800) 391-1521
P.O. Box 1069 • Reynoldsburg, OH 43068
E-Mail: info@kpcreek.com
Website: www.kpcreek.com
Fax Ordering: (800) 955-5915; (740) 964-6212
International Ordering: (740) 964-6210
Catalog: Free. Frequency: Annual
Circulation: 200K. Sales: $5-10MM
Products: Country gifts, candles, lamps
& lights, wall hangings, garden style gifts,
glassware/ceramic gifts, books, decorative
box sets

LANE'S GIFTS & COLLECTIBLES   (800) 421-8697
720 Realtor Ave. • Texarkana, AR 71854
E-Mail: info@lanescollectibles.com
Website: www.lanescollectibles.com
Fax Ordering: (870) 773-2126
International Ordering: (870) 773-2123
Catalog: Free. Frequency: Annual
Circulation: 1MM. Sales: $5-10MM
Products: Gifts, toys, dolls, figurines,
handbags, costume jewelry, tableware,
candles

LEATHER UNLIMITED CORPORATION   (920) 994-9464
7155 County Hwy. B • Belgium, WI 53004
E-Mail: leather@execpc.com
Fax Ordering: (920) 994-4099
Contact Name: Joseph M. O'Connell, President
Catalog: $2. Frequency: Quarterly
Circulation: 250M. Sales: $1-3MM
Products: Leathr hides, leather goods,
cycle accessories, belts, buckles, kits, lace,
feathers, black powder, Indianlore

LIBERTY FLAG & SPECIALTY   (800) 274-7001
P.O. Box 398 • Reedsburg, WI 53959
E-Mail: liberty@liberty-flag.com
Website: www.liberty-flag.com
Fax Ordering: (608) 524-8238

International Ordering: (608) 524-2834
Contact Name: Dave Gonzales, President
Catalog: Free. Frequency: Annual
Circulation: 50K. Sales: $1-3MM
Products: Flags, banners, drapes, buntings,
flagpoles & Christmas decorations

LIGHTHOUSE DEPOT   (800) 758-1444
P.O. Box 427 • East Machias, ME 04090
E-Mail: support@lighthousedepot.com
Website: www.lighthousedepot.com
International Ordering: (207) 259-2121
Customer Service: (800) 519-5743
Contact Name: Don Devine, Contact
Catalog: Free. Frequency: Semiannual
Circulation: 100K. Sales: $1-3MM
Products: Lighthouse gifts; nautical products

MAG INSTRUMENT, INC.   (909) 947-1006
P.O. Box 50600 • Ontario, CA 91761
E-Mail: info@maglite.com
Website: www.maglite.com
Fax Ordering: (909) 947-3116
Contact Name: Anthony Maglica, President
Catalog: Free. Frequency: Annual
Circulation: 250K. Sales: $10-50MM
Products: Mag lite flashlights

MAGNETS-PERPETUAL ENERGY SOURCE   (877) 856-3042
AZ Industries, Inc.
P.O. Box 539 • Ash Flat, AR 72513
E-Mail: azind@centurytel.net
Website: www.azind.com
Fax Ordering: (870) 856-3590
International Ordering: (870) 856-3041
Catalog: Free. Frequency: Semiannual
Circulation: 100K. Sales: $3-5MM
Products: Permanent magnets, magnetic tools
& instruments, magnet assemblies

MANDY'S HOUSE OF GIFTS   (501) 225-2838
6 White Aspen Ct. • Little Rock, AR 72212
E-Mail: mandys3hp@aol.com
Website: www.mandyshouseofgifts.com
Fax Ordering: (501) 219-9611
International Ordering: (501) 225-2838
Contact Name: Asha Sahita, President
Catalog: Free. Frequency: Semiannual
Circulation: 100M. Sales: $250-500M
Products: Gift bags, wine bottle bags,
ladies hand bags, Christmas ornaments,
star lanterns, candleholders, picture frames.

MATHEWS WIRE GIFTWARE CATALOG   (800) 826-9650
654 W. Morrison St. • Frankfort, IN 46041
E-Mail: mwire@mathewswire.com
Website: www.mathewswire.com
Fax Ordering: (800) 600-8269; (765) 659-1059
International Ordering: (765) 659-3542
Contact Name: Martin Mathews, President
Catalog: Free to businesses.
Frequency: Semiannual
Circulation: 100K. Sales: $3-5MM
Products: Wholesale country giftware &
accessories; candle accessories

MIT MUSEUM SHOP   (617) 253-4462
265 Massachusetts Ave.
Cambridge, MA 02139
E-Mail: mitshop@mit.edu
Fax Ordering: (617) 258-6563
Contact Name: Kathleen Thurston, President

Catalog: Free. Frequency: Annual
Circulation: 150M. **Sales**: $500M to $1MM
Products: Educational toys & games, books,
t-shirts

METROPOLITAN MUSEUM OF ART   (800) 468-7386
Special Services Office
66-26 Metropolitan Ave.
Middle Village, NY 11381
E-Mail: customer.service@metmuseum.org
Website: www.metmuseum.org/store
Fax Ordering: (718) 628-5485 or 366-5375
International Ordering: (212) 731-1498
Customer Service: (800) 662-3397
Catalog: $1. Frequency: Semiannual
Circulation: 150K. **Sales**: $3-5 MM
Products: Museum prints, art books,
jewelry, stationery, toys, slides and gifts

METROPOLITAN OPERA SHOP   (212) 501-3482
70 Lincoln Center Plaza
New York, NY 10023
Fax Ordering: (212) 870-7695
International Ordering: (212) 501-3482
Catalog: Free. Frequency: Annual
Circulation: 50K. **Sales**: $1-3MM
Products: Opera and music related gifts;
audo, video, books, child items

MONTICELLO CATALOG   (800) 243-1743
Thomas Jefferson Memorial Foundation
P.O. Box 318 • Charlottesville, VA 22902
E-Mail: catalog@monticello.org
Website: www.monticellocatalog.org
Fax Ordering: (434) 984-7730
Catalog: Free. Frequency: Semiannual
Customer Service: (800) 243-0743
Circulation: 50K. **Sales**: $1-3MM
Products: Gifts selected to reflect
Thomas Jefferson's taste; home decor,
outdoor & garden, books

MUSEUM PRODUCTS COMPANY   (800) 395-5400
84 Route 27 • Mystic, CT 06355
E-Mail: contact@museumproducts.net
Website: www.museumproducts.net
Fax Ordering: (860) 572-9589
International Ordering: (860) 536-6433
Contact Name: John Bannister, President
Catalog: Free. Frequency: Annual
Circulation: 50K. **Sales**: $500M to $1MM
Products: Luggage, wallets, business cases,
pens, travel items

MUSEUM REPLICAS LIMITED   (800) 883-8838
Atlanta Cutlery   (800) 241-3664
2147 Gees Mill Rd. • Conyers, GA 30013
E-Mail: musrep@mindspring.com
Website: www.museumreplicas.com
Fax Ordering: (770) 388-0246
International Ordering: (770) 922-7500
Contact Name: Hank Reinhart, President
Catalog: Free. Frequency: Annual
Circulation: 100K. **Sales**: $3-5MM
Products: Museum replicas: period clothing,
jewelry, sculptures, edged weapons

MUSEUM OF FINE ARTS, BOSTON   (617) 369-3575
Bookstore & Giftshop   (508) 894-2863
465 Huntington Ave. • Boston, MA 02115   (617) 267-9300
E-Mail: customerservice@mfa.org
Website: www.mfa.org/shop

Fax Ordering: (508) 588-9678
International Ordering: (508) 894-2863
Contact Name: Kelly Worrelling, Marketing
Catalog: $2. Frequency: Quarterly
Circulation: 5MM. **Sales**: $20-50MM
Products: Art reproductions, gifts, jewelry
& posters

MUSEUM SHOP CATALOG   (888) 301-9612
Art Institute of Chicago
111 S. Michigan Ave. • Chicago, IL 60603
E-Mail: artinstituteshop@artic.edu
Website: www.artinstituteshop.org
Fax Ordering: (423) 867-8495
Contact Name: James Wood, President
Catalog: Free. Frequency: Annual
Circulation: 100K. **Sales**: $1-3MM
Products: Museum gifts, accessories,
stationery

NASHVILLE WRAPS   (800) 547-9727
242 Molly Walton Dr.
Hendersonville, TN 37075
E-Mail: info@nashvillewraps.com
Website: www.nashvillewraps.com
Fax Ordering: (800) 646-0046
International Ordering: (615) 338-3200
Catalog: Free. Frequency: Annual
Minimum Order: $25.
Circulation: 150K. **Sales**: $5-10MM
Products: Custom printing packaging;
wholesale packaging supplies

NATIONAL GEOGRAPHIC   (888) 225-5647
HOLIDAY GIFT CATALOG
National Geographic Society
P.O. Box 6916 • Hanover, PA 17331
E-Mail: ngs@keystoneinternet.com
Website: www.nationalgeographic.com
Fax Ordering: (888) 242-0548
International Ordering: (801) 783-2144
Contact Name: John M. Fahey, Jr., President
Catalog: Free. Frequency: Annual
Circulation: 100M. **Sales**: $3-5MM
Products: More than 250 gift ideas, from
clothing, furniture, toys, videos, software,
books, maps & globes, electronics, jewelry

NATIONAL LATEX PRODUCTS   (800) 537-6723
246 E. 4th St. • Ashland, OH 44805
E-Mail: sales@natlatex.com
Website: www.natlatex.com
Fax Ordering: (419) 289-7118
International Ordering: (419) 289-3300
Contact Name: H. Gill, President
Catalog: Free. Frequency: Annual
Circulation: 200K. **Sales**: $5-10MM
Products: Rubber toy balloons & plastic
playballs; bath toys; toy trains & vehicles;
party supplies

NATURE BY DESIGN OF VERMONT   (888) 552-3747
P.O. Box 499 • Barton, VT 05822
E-Mail: sales@naturebydesign.com
Website: www.naturebydesign.com
Fax Ordering: (802) 754-2626
International Ordering: (802) 754-6400
Contact Name: Peter R. LeBlanc, President
Catalog: Free. Frequency: Annual
Circulation: 150K. **Sales**: $500M
Products: Christmas wreaths, centerpieces,
trees, swags and garlands; gift packs

NATURE GIFTS CATALOG   (800) 822-9919
National Wildlife Federation
11100 Wildlife Center Dr.
Reston, VA 20190
E-Mail: info@nwf.org
Website: www.nwf.org
Fax Ordering: (540) 722-5399
Contact Name: Mark Van Patten, President
Catalog: Free. Frequency: Quarterly
Circulation: 5MM. Sales: $5-10MM
Products: Nature-related and educational gifts,
including holiday cards, calendars, home
accessories, and apparel with a wildlife theme

NEDOBECK GRAPHICS   (800) 642-9953
811 N. Highland Ave. • Deland, FL 32720
E-Mail: nedobeckorders@gmail.com
Website: www.alphabetbooks.com
Fax Ordering: (414) 276-0835
International Ordering: (386) 738-3041
Contact Name: Don Nedobeck, President
Catalog: $3. Frequency: Annual
Circulation: 10K. Sales: $500K
Products: Prints, books, cards & calendars
with original design; shirts

NOAH'S ANIMALS CATALOG   (800) 368-6624
17150 Newhope St.
Fountain Valley, CA 92708
E-Mail: noahsanimals@sbcglobal.net
Website: www.noahsanimals.com
Fax Ordering: (714) 641-7496
International Ordering: (714) 641-8651
Contact Name: J. Swenson, President
Catalog: Free. Frequency: Annual
Circulation: 50K. Sales: $500M
Products: Wildlife & pet related gift items

NORDIC SHOP CATALOG   (507) 285-9143
111 S. Broadway, Skyway Level
Rochester, MN 55904
E-Mail: info@thenordicshop.net
Website: www.thenordicshop.net
Fax Ordering: (507) 285-5573
International Ordering: (507) 285-9143
Catalog: Free. Frequency: 3x per year
Circulation:50K. Sales: $500M to $1MM
Products: Scandinavian gifts: apparel, glassware,
jewelry, dinnerware, flatware, linens, candles

NORTH COUNTRY CATALOG   (800) 262-0040
Coldwater Creek   (800) 510-2808
751 W. Hanley Ave.   (800) 787-9196
Coeur d'Alene, ID 83815
E-Mail: customerservice@thecreek.com
Website: www.coldwatercreek.com
Fax Ordering: (800) 262-0080; (208) 263-1582
International Ordering: (208) 263-2266
Contact Name: Tony Savlino, President
Catalog: Free. Frequency: Quarterly
Circulation:500K. Sales: $10-20MM
Products: Nature related gifts & apparel

OF SHIPS & SEAS   (800) 836-1165
S.T. Preston & Sons
P.O. Box 2115 • Greenport, NY 11944
E-Mail: sales@prestons.com
Website: www.prestons.com
Fax Ordering: (631) 477-8541
International Ordering: (631) 477-1990
Contact Name: George Rowsom, President

Catalog: Free. Frequency: Quarterly
Circulation: 250K. Sales: $3-5MM
Products: Nautical gifts & furniture,
framed prints, clothing, ship models,
videos

OLD GLORY DISTRIBUTING   (800) 892-3323
90 Knothe Rd. • Westbrook, CT 06498
E-Mail: customerservice@oldglory.com
Website: www.oldglory.com
Fax Ordering: (860) 399-7786
International Ordering: (860) 399-1213
Contact Name: Glenn Morelli, President
Catalog: Free. Frequency: Quarterly
Circulation: 2MM. Sales: $5-10MM
Products: Rock-n-roll merchandise, t-shirts,
hats, videos, memoribilia & collectibles

OLD WEST SHOP   (800) 455-4011
P.O. Box 5232 • Vienna, WV 26105
E-Mail: oldwestshop@aol.com
Website: www.oldwestshop.com
Fax Ordering: (304) 295-3143
International Ordering: (304) 295-3161
Catalog: $10. Frequency: Semiannual
Minimum Order: $20
Circulation:50M. Sales: $500M
Products: Western posters, prints,
books, badges

ORIENTAL TRADING CO., INC.   (800) 228-2269
P.O. Box 2308 • Omaha, NE 68103   (800) 875-8480
E-Mail: info@orientaltrading.com   (800) 526-9300
Website: www.orientaltrading.com
Fax Ordering: (800) 327-8904
International Fax Ordering: (402) 596-2364
International Ordering: (402) 331-6800
TDD Ordering: (800) 833-7352
Customer Service: (800) 228-0475; 228-7450
Contact Name: Terry Watanabe-Gerdes, President
Catalogs: Free. Frequency: 8/year
Circulation: 20MM. Sales: $50-75MM
Products: Costumes & accessories; crafts &
activities; novelties; novelty jewelry; party supplies;
small toys & games; stationery; home decor & gifts.
Halloween & Business Editions.

ORION TELESCOPES & BINOCULARS   (800) 447-1001
89 Hangar Way • Watsonville, CA 95076
E-Mail: info@telescope.com
Website: www.telescope.com
Fax Ordering: (831) 763-7017
International Ordering: (831) 763-7000
Customer Service: (800) 676-1343;
   (831) 763-7024
Catalog: Free. Frequency: Semiannual
Circulation:1MM. Sales: $20-50MM
Products: Telescopes & binoculars

ORNAMENTS 2 REMEMBER   (800) 330-3382
28170 SW Boberg Rd. #1
Wilsonville, OR 97070
E-Mail: info@ornaments2remember.com
Website: www.ornaments2remember.com
Fax Ordering: (866) 582-3958
International Ordering: (831) 763-7017
Contact Name: Treasa Robinson, President
Catalog: Free. Frequency: Semiannual
Circulation:100K, Sales: $500K
Products: Christmas tree ornaments &
decorations

OSBORNE COINAGE COMPANY (800) 488-2646
2851 Massachusetts Ave.
Cincinnati, OH 45225
E-Mail: sales@osbornecoin.com
Website: www.osbornecoinage.com
Fax Ordering: (513) 681-5604
International Ordering: (513) 681-5424
Contact Name: Ted Schuh, Sales Manager
Catalog: Free. Frequency: Semiannual
Circulation:200K. Sales: $3-5MM
Products: Custom coins; awards & gifts;
commemorative coins; promotional products;
key tags, tokens & medallions; casino products

OUR DESIGNS (800) 382-5252
1212 W. Fourth Plain Blvd.
Vancouver, WA 98660
E-Mail: sales@ourdesigns.com
Website: www.ourdesigns.com
Fax Ordering: (800) 347-3367; (360) 567-1766
International Ordering: (360) 567-2530
Catalog: Free. Frequency: Semiannual
Circulation:100K. Sales: $1-3MM
Products: Gifts for EMT's, firefighters,
paramedics and the police

PACIFIC SPIRIT'S NEW AGE COLLECTION (503) 357-1566
1334 Pacific Ave. • Forest Grove, OR 97116
E-Mail: info@pacificspiritcatalog.com
Website: www.pacificspiritcatalog.com
Fax Ordering: (503) 357-1669
Catalog: Free. Frequency: Quarterly
Circulation:100K. Sales: $1-3MM
Products: Spiritual books, videos, art,
new age jewelry & other items

PACIFIC SPORTSWEAR & EMBLEM CO. (800) 872-8778
6160 Fairmount Ave. • San Diego, CA 92120
E-Mail: hatman@pacsport.com
Website: www.pacsport.com
Fax Ordering: (619) 281-6687
International Ordering: (619) 281-6688
Contact Name: Rich Soergel, President
Catalog: Free. Frequency: Monthly
Circulation: 100K. Sales: $3-5MM
Products: Headwear, embroidered
patches & pins, keychains & label pins

PARTY KITS EQUESTRIAN GIFTS (800) 993-3729
KY Derby Party Supplies
8007 Vinecrest Ave. #9
Louisville, KY 40222
E-Mail: info@partykits.com
Website: www.derbygifts.com
Fax Ordering: (502) 425-5230
International Ordering: (502) 425-2126
Contact Name: Becky Biesel, President
Catalog: Free. Frequency: Semiannual
Circulation:50M. Sales: $1-3MM
Products: Equestrian party supplies,
gifts & Kentucky foods for horse lovers

PEACE FROGS CATALOG (800) 447-3223
P.O. Box 137 • White Marsh, VA 23183
E-Mail: mail.order@peacefrogs.com
Website: www.peacefrogs.com
Fax Ordering: (804) 695-1714
International Ordering: (804) 695-1314
Contact Name: Catesby Jones, President
Catalog: Free. Frequency: Quarterly
Circulation:100K. Sales: $1-3MM
Products: Clothing, toys, computer accessories, gifts

J.C. PENNEY BIG GIFT BOOK (800) 222-6161
P.O. Box 10001 • Dallas, TX 75301
E-Mail: info@jcpenney.com
Website: www.jcpenney.com
Fax Ordering: (972) 591-9322
International Ordering: (972) 431-1000
Customer Service: (800) 322-1189 or 709-5777
Catalog: $5. Frequency: Annual
Circulation: 2MM. Sales: $50-100MM
Products: Toys, gifts, apparel

PERSONAL CREATIONS (800) 326-6626
19W661 101st St. • Lemont, IL 60439 (888) 527-1404
E-Mail: sales@personalcreations.com
Website: www.personalcreations.com
Fax Ordering: (630) 655-3299
International Ordering: (630) 655-3200
Customer Service: (866) 834-7695
Contact Name: John Semmelhack, President
Catalog: Free. Frequency: Quarterly
Circulation: 3MM. Sales: $10-20MM
Products: Personalized gifts, toys,
ornaments and clothing

PERSONALIZED PRODUCTS (909) 867-4494
2443 Hunsaker Dr.
Running Springs, CA 92382
Fax Ordering: (909) 867-3258
Contact Name: Stan Pearlman, Marketing
Catalog: Free. Frequency: Annual
Circulation: 100K. Sales: $1-3MM
Products: Apparel, bed & bath, costume
jewelry, housewares, collectibles, audio
& video tapes, giftware

PLOW & HEARTH (800) 627-1712
P.O. Box 6000 • Madison, VA 22727 (800) 494-7544
E-Mail: info@plowhearth.com
Website: www.plowhearth.com
Fax Ordering: (800) 843-2509
Customer Service: (800) 866-6072
Catalog: Free. Frequency: Quarterly
Circulation: 150K. Sales: $5-10MM
Products: Products for country living,
including furniture, yard & garden, footwear
& apparel, holiday gifts and novelties.

PORT CANVAS COMPANY (800) 333-6788
P.O. Box H • Kennebunkport, ME 04046
E-Mail: quality@portcanvas.com
Website: www.portcanvas.com
Fax Ordering: (207) 985-9768
International Ordering: (207) 985-9767
Contact Name: Margot L. Thompson, President
Catalog: Free. Frequency: Quarterly
Circulation: 100K. Sales: $1-3MM
Products: Products & gifts for the legal profession

POSH PAPERS (401) 331-9873
73 Terrace Ave. • Providence, RI 02915
E-Mail: info@poshpapersonline.com
Website: www.poshpapersonline.com
Fax Ordering: (401) 331-2229
Contact Name: Judi Boren, President
Catalog: $1. Frequency: Semiannual
Circulation: 50K. Sales: $500K
Products: Personalized handcrafted
notecards, gift boxed & decorated

PREFERRED LIVING (800) 776-7897
Sportsman's Market
2001 Sporty's Dr. • Batavia, OH 45103

E-Mail: info@sportys.com
Website: www.sportys.com
Fax Ordering: (800) 543-8633
International Ordering: (513) 735-9200
Customer Service: (513) 735-9000
Contact Name: Hal Shevers, President
Catalog: Free. Frequency: Quarterly
Circulation: 10MM. Sales: $20-50MM
Products: Home items & gifts; gardening,
workshop products, outdoor & recreation
& decoration; auto/marine

PROFLOWERS (800) 315-4754
5005 Wateridge Vista Dr. (800) 580-2913
San Diego, CA 92121
E-Mail: wecare@customercare.proflowers.com
Website: www.proflowers.com
Catalog: Free. Frequency: Periodically
Circulation: 150K. Sales: $10-20MM
Products: Fresh flowers, plants &
gourmet gifts

THE PYRAMID COLLECTION (800) 333-4220
Catalogue Ventures
P.O. Box 3333 • Chelmsford, MA 01824
E-Mail: help@pyramidcollection.com
Website: www.pyramidcollection.com
Fax Ordering: (800) 866-3235
International Ordering: (978) 256-4100
Contact Name: Robert L. Webb, Marketing
Catalog: Free. Frequency: Semiannual
Circulation: 1MM. Sales: $10-25MM
Products: Ethnic and spirituall gifts, jewelry,
apparel, t-shirts & sweats, books & collectibles

REDENVELOPE (877) 733-3683
P.O. Box 600040 • San Diego, CA 92160 (877) 473-3249
E-Mail: sales@redenvelope.com
Website: www.redenvelope.com
International Ordering: (619) 528-4888
Catalog: Free. Frequency: Semiannual
Circulation: 150K. Sales: $3-5MM
Products: Gifts & promotional items

REWARDS CATALOG (800) 292-0195
9722 Great Hills Trail #300
Austin, TX 78759
E-Mail: info@shoprewards.com
Website: www.shoprewards.com
Fax Ordering: (512) 502-9153
International Ordering: (512) 502-9799
Contact Name: Russ Stromberg, President
Catalog: Free. Frequency: Annual
Circulation: 50K. Sales: $1-3MM
Products: Contemporary & Western
belt buckles, belts, money clips & key
rings, jewelry

RHODE ISLAND NOVELTY (800) 528-5599
5 Industrial Rd. • Cumberland, RI 02864
E-Mail: info@rinovelty.com
Website: www.rinovelty.com
Fax Ordering: (800) 448-1775; (401) 335-3313
International Ordering: (401) 335-3300
Corporate Sales: (800) 435-3456
Catalog: Free. Frequency: Semiannual
Circulation: 100K. Sales: $3-5MM
Products: Novelties, jokes, party supplies,
toys

ROCKY MOUNTAIN SHEEPSKIN (800) 428-7216
1008C Blossom Hill Rd.
San Jose, CA 95123
E-Mail: rocky@rmsheepskin.com
Website: www.rmsheepskin.com
Fax Ordering: (408) 266-6535
International Ordering: (408) 266-2110
Contact Name: James Peterson, President
Catalog: Free. Frequency: Annual
Circulation: 50K. Sales: $3-5MM
Products: Sheepskin seatcovers, rugs &
slippers; Ugg boots & sheepskin accessories

A.G. RUSSELL KNIVES (800) 255-9034
2900 S. 26th St. • Rogers, AR 72758
E-Mail: ag@agrussell.com
Website: www.agrussell.com
Fax Ordering: (479) 631-8493
International Sales: (479) 631-0130
Contact Name: A.G. Russell, President
Catalog: Free. Frequency: 5x per year
Circulation: 500K. Sales: $10-20MM
Products: Knives & collectibles

S.Q.P. (800) 648-4789
1985 Swarthmore Ave.
Lakewood, NJ 08701
E-Mail: info@sqpinc.com
Website: www.sqpinc.com
Fax Ordering: (732) 363-8828
International Ordering: (732) 905-3344
Contact Name: Sal Quartuccio, President
Catalog: Free. Frequency: Semiannual
Circulation: 150K. Sales: $250-500MK
Products: Fantasy and science fiction
magazines, books, gifts, t-shirts

S&S WORLDWIDE (800) 288-9941
P.O. Box 513 • Colchester, CT 06415
E-Mail: info@ssww.com
Website: www.ssww.com
Fax Ordering: (800) 566-6678
International Ordering: (860) 537-3451
Contact Name: Charlie McCormack, President
Catalog: Free. Frequency: Semiannual
Circulation: 250K. Sales: $5-10MM
Products: Arts & crafts supplies, craft kits,
educational supplies, games, party items,
novelties, sports & recreation products, gifts

SALLY DISTRIBUTORS (800) 472-5597
4100 Quebec Ave. N.
Minneapolis, MN 55427
E-Mail: info@sallydist.com
Website: www.sallydist.com
Fax Ordering: (800) 575-1453
International Ordering: (763) 533-7100
Contact Name: Bruce Kane, President
Catalog: Free. Frequency: Quarterly
Circulation: 150K. Sales: $3-5MM
Products: Toys, games, party favors,
decorations, balloons, candy & fashion

SAVE THE CHILDREN GIFT CATALOG (800) 728-3843
Save the Children Federation
54 Wilton Rd. • Westport, CT 06880
E-Mail: info@savethechildren.org
Website: www.savethechildren.org
Fax Ordering: (203) 221-3784
International Ordering: (203) 221-4000

Contact Name: Charlie McCormack, President
Catalog: Free. Frequency: Semiannual
Circulation: 150K. Sales: $1-3MM
Products: Jewelry, art objects, & handmade gifts

SCENES OF WEST VIRGINIA (877) 987-2363
1709-11 St. Marys Ave.
Parkersburg, WV 26101
E-Mail: info@scenesofwv.com
Website: www.scenesofwv.com
Fax Ordering: (304) 428-1169
International Ordering: (304) 428-0772
Contact Name: J. Easton, President
Catalog: Free. Frequency: Bimonthly
Circulation: 50K. Sales: $500K
Products: Gifts from West Virginia

NAT SCHWARTZ & COMPANY (800) 526-1440
524 Bloomfield Ave. • Verona, NJ 07044
E-Mail: schwartzandcompany@gmail.com
Website: www.natschwartz.com
Fax Ordering: (973) 571-2165
Contact Name: Rose Schwartz, President
Catalog: Free. Frequency: Bimonthly
Circulation: 200K. Sales: $1-3MM
Products: Fine tableware; china, silverware
and gifts

SHARPER GRAPHICS CARD & PRINTS (800) 727-6006
125 Kemp Lane • Easton, MD 21601
E-Mail: sales@sharpergraphics.com
Website: www.sharpergraphics.com
Fax Ordering: (410) 820-9396
International Ordering: (410) 820-7272
Contact Name: Robert A. Porter, Jr., President
Catalog: Free. Frequency: Quarterly
Circulation: 100K. Sales: $500M to $1MM
Products: Lighthouse, waterfowl &
Native American notecards & prints

SHINDIGZ (800) 314-8736
One Party Pl. • South Whitley, IN 46787
E-Mail: csr@shindigz.com
Website: www.shindigz.com
Contact Name: Wendy Moyle, Owner
Catalog: Free. Frequency: Semiannual
Circulation: 150K. Sales: $500K
Products: 36,000 party products, including
banners, favors, tableware, balloons, invitations,
wall decals, etc.

SIGNALS CATALOG (800) 669-9696
P.O. Box 2599 • Hudson, OH 44236
E-Mail: sales@signals.com
Website: www.signals.com
Fax Ordering: (800) 950-9569
Customer Service: (800) 669-5225
Catalog: Free. Frequency: Semiannual
Circulation: 100K. Sales: $10-20MM
Products: Apparel & accessories; books,
videos, audios; children's products; Gifts
and collectibles

SIMPLY NORTHWEST (800) 214-2686
11808 E. Sprague Ave.
Spokane, WA 99206
E-Mail: snw@simplynorthwest.com
Website: www.simplynorthwest.com
Contact Name: Sharon Osborn, President
Catalog: Free. Frequency: Semiannual
Circulation: 50K. Sales: $1-3MM
Products: Chocolates, candies, children's gifts,

gift baskets and other Washington
State products benefiting at-risk
children and families

SKYMALL (800) 759-6255
Skymall, Inc.
1520 E. Pima St. • Phoenix, AZ 85034
E-Mail: info@skymall.com
Website: www.skymall.com
Fax Ordering: (602) 254-6075
International Ordering: (602) 254-9777
Contact Name: Robert Worsley
Catalog: Free. Frequency: Quarterly
Circulation: 10MM. Sales: $20-50MM
Products: Airline catalog gifts; apparel,
electronics, automotive, bath accessories,
computer supplies, furniture, appliances,
telephones

SMITHSONIAN CATALOG (800) 322-0344
Smithsonian Institution
3900 F Stonecroft Blvd. • Shantilly, VA 20150
E-Mail: customerserv@catalog.si.edu
Website: www.smithsonianstore.com
Fax Ordering: (703) 605-5094
International Ordering: (703) 605-5000
Catalog: Free. Frequency: 5x per year
Circulation: 150K. Sales: $5-10MM
Products: Gifts, reproductions, jewelry, toys,
home furnishings, home office, clothing &
accessories, decorative

SOLUTIONS CATALOG (800) 342-9988
P.O. Box 6878 • Portland, OR 97228
E-Mail: solutions@solutions.com
Website: www.solution.com
Fax Ordering: (800) 821-1282
Business Gift Services: (800) 722-7471
Catalog: Free. Frequency: Quarterly
Circulation: 250K. Sales: $10-20MM
Products: Gifts & novelties; home organizers,
cleaners, kitchen, travel, pets, garden;
unique gift ideas

SORMANI CALENDARS (800) 321-9327
P.O. Box 6059 • Chelsea, MA 02150
E-Mail: info@sormanicalendars.com
Website: www.sormanicalendars.com
Fax Ordering: (617) 387-6379
International Ordering: (627) 387-7300
Contact Name: Judith Jenkins, President
Catalog: Free. Frequency: 3x per year
Circulation: 250K. Sales: $1-3MM
Products: Calendars of all kinds

STATUE.COM (877) 675-2634
100 N. Main St. • Edwardsville, IL 62025
E-Mail: gloria@statue.com
Website: www.statue.com
Fax Ordering: (618) 692-6775
International Ordering: (618) 692-1121
Catalog: Online. Sales: $1-3MM
Products: Sculptures, bird baths, bird feeders
& houses, clocks & time pieces, contemporary
art deco & art nouveau, dragons, fountains,
garden accessories, wall decor, weathervanes

STEUBEN GLASS CATALOG (800) 424-4240
667 Madison Ave. • New York, NY 10022
E-Mail: info@steubenglass.com
Website: www.steuben.com
Fax Ordering: (212) 371-5798

International Ordering: (212) 752-1441
Contact Name: Marie McKee, President
Catalog: Free. Frequency: Annual
Circulation: 1MM. Sales: $20-50MM
Products: Functional & sculptural crystal gifts;
ornamental designs, candleholders, vases,
stemware & barware

STONE FOREST (888) 682-2987
P.O. Box 2840 • Santa Fe, NM 87504
E-Mail: info@stoneforest.com
Website: www.stoneforest.com
Fax Ordering: (505) 982-2712
International Ordering: (505) 986-8883
Contact Name: Michael Zimber, President
Catalog: Free. Frequency: Annual
Circulation: 100K. Sales: $3-5MM
Products: Hard carved granite: kitchen & bath;
garden collection; fountains, stone sinks,
Japanese lanterns, birdbaths and spheres

STUMPS CATALOG (800) 348-5084
Stump Printing Co.
P.O. Box 305 • South Whitley, IN 46787
E-Mail: csr@stumpsparty.com
Website: www.stumpsparty.com
Fax Ordering: (260) 723-6976
International Ordering: (260) 723-5171
Contact Name: Shep Moyle, President
Catalog: Free. Frequency: Annual
Circulation:50K. Sales: $1-3MM
Products: Prom & party supplies,
display items

SUCCESSORIES CATALOG (800) 535-2773
1040 Holland Dr. • Boca Raton, FL 33487
E-Mail: sales@successories.com
Website: www.successories.com
Fax Ordering: (561) 998-7716
Contact Name: Gary Rovansek, President
Catalog: Free. Frequency: Monthly
Circulation: 500K. Sales: $20-50MM
Products: Executive gifts; desktop motivation
products; awards & recognition products;
promotional products

SUNLINE PRODUCTS (800) 677-0071
1454 E. Summitry Cir.
Katy, TX 77449
E-Mail: info@sunlineproducts.com
Website: www.sunlineproducts.com
Fax Ordering: (281) 398-6650
International Ordering: (281) 398-6655
Catalog: Free. Frequency: Quarterly
Circulation: 150K. Sales: $1-3MM
Products: T-shirts with screen printing;
promotional & sepciality items; patches
& custome stitching

TAYLOR GIFTS (800) 829-1133
600 Cedar Hollow Rd.
Paoli, PA 19301
E-Mail: info@taylorgifts.com
Website: www.taylorgifts.com
Fax Ordering: (610) 725-1144
International Ordering: (610) 725-1122
Contact Name: B. Loyall Taylor, Jr., President
Catalog: Free. Frequency: 5x per year
Circulation: 10MM. Sales: $25-50MM
Products: Gifts, housewares & novelties,
home decor, outdoor living, kitchen

TENDER HEART TREASURES (800) 443-1367
P.O. Box 2310 • Omaha, NE 68103
E-Mail: customerservice@tenderheart.com
Website: www.tenderheart.com
Fax Ordering: (402) 593-1316
International Ordering: (402) 593-1313
Contact Name: Pamela Watanabe, President
Catalog: Free. Frequency: 8x per year
Circulation: 10MM. Sales: $10-20MM
Products: Country home and gifts

TEXAS BASKET COMPANY (800) 657-2200
P.O. Box 1110 • Jacksonville, TX 75766
E-Mail: sales@texasbasket.com
Website: www.texasbasket.com
Fax Ordering: (903) 586-0988
International Ordering: (903) 586-8014
Contact Names: Martin Swanson, President
Catalog: Free. Frequency: Annual
Circulation: 100K. Sales: $3-5MM
Minimum Order: $100.
Products: Manufacturer of fruit & vegetable
baskets, wooden display racks, crates,
novelty baskets, custom baskets, treated
nursery baskets, brick veneer, specialty items

THINGS REMEMBERED CATALOG (800) 274-7367
5500 Avion Park Dr. • Highland Hts., OH 44143
E-Mail: sales@thingsremembered.com
Website: www.thingsremembered.com
Fax Ordering: (440) 473-2018
International Ordering: (440) 473-2000
Customer Service: (866) 902-4438
Contact Name: Michael J. Lorah, President
Catalog: Free. Frequency: 3x per year
Circulation: 2MM. Sales: $20-50MM
Products: Personalized recognition &
incentive gifts

THINGS YOU NEVER KNEW EXISTED (800) 843-0762
Johnson Smith Co. Catalogs   Espanol (800) 655-4177
P.O. Box 25600 • Bradenton, FL 34206
E-Mail: info@johnsonsmith.com
Website: www.thingsyouneverknew.com
Fax Ordering: (800) 551-4406; (941) 746-7962
International Ordering: (941) 747-5566 Fax 746-7896
Customer Service: (800) 826-8125
Catalog: $2.95. Frequency: Monthly
Circulation: 200K. Sales: $20-50MM
Products: Gifts, hobbies, novelties,
funmakers, jokes, gadgetry, electronics

NORM THOMPSON CATALOG (800) 547-1160
P.O. Box 126 • Jessup, PA 18434
E-Mail: info@normthompson.com
Website: www.normthompson.com
Fax Ordering: (800) 821-1282
Customer Service: (877) 718-7899
Catalog: Free. Frequency: Monthly
Circulation: 500K. Sales: $10-20MM
Products: Clothing, shoes & handbags,
accessories, food, gift novelties

UNO ALLA VOLTA (ONE AT A TIME) (800) 625-1866
242 Branford Rd. • North Branford, CT 06471
E-Mail: custserv @unoallavolta.com
Website: www.unoallavolta.com
Fax Ordering: (800) 296-8039
Contact Name: Terri S. Alpert, Founder & CEO
Catalog: Free. Frequency: Quarterly
Products: Artisan gifts, including glassware
cutlery items, earthenware, pewter, combs

THE VERMONT COUNTRY STORE   (802) 362-8460
P.O. Box 6993 • Rutland, VT 05702
E-Mail: customerservice@vermontcountrystore.com
Website: www.vermontcountrystore.com
Fax Ordering: (802) 362-0285
Contact Name: Larry Shaw, Marketing
Catalog: Free. Frequency: Quarterly
Circulation: 150K. Sales: $5-10MM
Products: Clothing, accessories, apothecary,
food & candy, footwear, home accessories,
household, kitchen, sleepwear, toys, games
& crafts

VERMONT LIFE CATALOG   (800) 455-3399
Vermont Life Magazine
6 Baldwin St. • Montpelier, VT 05602
E-Mail: products@vtlife.com
Website: www.vermontlifecatalog.com
Fax Ordering: (802) 828-3366
International Ordering: (802) 828-3241
Contact Name: Andrew Jackson, Buyer
Catalog: Free. Frequency: Annual
Circulation: 250M. Sales: $500M to $1MM
Products: Vermont life books, calendars,
videos, gifts, foods, housewares, children's
toys & games

VICTORY CORPS - FLAGS, FLOATS   (800) 328-6120
6801 Shingle Creek Pkwy. • New Hope, MN 55427
E-Mail: cs@victorycorps.com
Website: www.victorycorps.com
Fax Ordering: (763) 561-8523
International Ordering: (763) 561-5600
Contact Name: Dennis Flaherty, President
Catalog: Free. Frequency: Quarterly
Circulation: 50K. Sales: $500K - $1MM
Products: Flags, banners, poles, parade floats,
signs, trade show displays & accessories

WALTER DRAKE CATALOG   (877) 925-8373
(800) 525-9291
P.O. Box 3680 • Oshkosh, WI 54903
E-Mail: help@wdrake.com
Website: www.wdrake.com
Fax Ordering: (888) 252-8462; (719) 596-3853
International Ordering: (719) 638-2595
Customer Service: (800) 858-4979
Contact Name: John Medved, President
Catalog: Free. Frequency: Quarterly
Circulation: 2MM. Sales: $20-50MM
Products: Gifts, household gadgetry,
kitchenware, organizers, home & garden,
personal care, labels, stationery &
greeting cards

WARNER BROTHERS STUDIO STORES   (866) 373-4389
1935 Buena Vista • Burbank, CA 91504
E-Mail: customerservice@wbshop.com
Website: www.wbshop.com
Fax Ordering: (800) 676-3299
International Ordering: (818) 954-5674
Contact Name: George Jones, President
Catalog: Free. Frequency: Semiannual
Circulation: 3MM. Sales: $20-50MM
Products: Warner Brothers merchandise

GEORGE WATTS & SON   (888) 607-9575
(800) 747-9288
761 N. Jefferson St. • Milwaukee, WI 53202
E-Mail: info@georgewatts.com
Website: www.georgewatts.com
Fax Ordering: (414) 276-2777
International Ordering: (414) 291-5120
Contact Name: Sue Thome, President

Catalog: Free. Frequency: Annual
Circulation: 200K. Sales: $5-10MM
Products: Tabletop, dinnerware, gifts

WHALES & FRIENDS   (800) 234-1022
P.O. Box 388 • Centerbrook, CT 006409
E-Mail: customerservice@whalesdirect.com
Website: www.whalesdirect.com
Fax Ordering: (860) 767-4381
International Ordering: (860) 767-4200
Customer Service: (800) 234-1024
Contact Names: Caroll & Thomas Romano
Catalog: Free. Pages: 48. Frequency: Quarterly
Circulation: 2MM. Sales: $5-10MM
Products: Nature-oriented catalog offering
marine, bird and mammal products; apparel,
footwear, home decor, jewelry, animal toys,
books

WHAT ON EARTH   (800) 945-2552
Universal Screen Arts
2451 E. Enterprise Pkwy.
Twinsburg, OH 44087
E-Mail: sales@whatonearthcatalog.com
Website: www.whatonearthcatalog.com
Fax Ordering: (800) 950-9569
International Ordering: (216) 425-4600
Contact Name: Jared Florian, President
Catalog: Free. Frequency: Quarterly
Circulation: 250K. Sales: $10-20MM
Products: Gifts from t-shirts to home decor

WILLIAMS-SONOMA   (877) 812-6235
110 7th Ave. • New York, NY 10011
E-Mail: sales@williams-sonoma.com
Website: www.williams-sonoma.com
Fax Ordering: (702) 363-2541
International Ordering: (405) 717-6131
Contact Name: Chuck Williams, President
Catalog: Free. Frequency: Semiannual
Circulation: 5MM. Sales: $100-200M
Products: Cookware, bakeware, dinnerware,
food; gifts & novelties

WINDY CITY NOVELTIES, INC.   (800) 442-9722
300 N. Lakeview Park
Vernon Hills, IL 60061
E-Mail: sales@wcnovelties.com
Website: www.windycitynovelties.com
Fax Ordering: (847) 680-9250
International Ordering: (847) 403-0000
Catalog: Free. Pages: 146.
Frequency: Semiannual
Circulation: 250K. Sales: $5-10MM
Products: Party supplies, glow products & novelties

WINE COUNTRY GIFT BASKETS   (800) 394-0394
(888) 394-0394
4225 N. Palm St. • Fullerton, CA 92835
E-Mail: orders@winecountrygiftbaskets.com
Website: www.winecountrygiftbaskets.com
Fax Ordering: (714) 525-0746
Customer Service: (800) 324—2793
Contact Name: Tim Dean, President
Catalog: Free. Frequency: Quarterly
Circulation: 150K. Sales: $5-10M
Products: Handcrafted holiday gift baskets;
wine gift baskets

WINTERTHUR   (800) 448-3883
Winterthur Museum, Garden & Library
Rte. 52 • Winterthur, DE 19735
E-Mail: museumstore@winterthur.org

Website: www.winterthur.org
Fax Ordering: (302) 888-4644
International Ordering: (302) 888-4822
Contact Name: Dwight P. Lanmon, President
Catalog: Free. Frequency: Quarterly
Circulation: 250K. Sales: $5-10MM
Products: Museum gifts, reproductions,
home accessories, jewelry, Christmas
ornaments

WIRELESS CATALOG   (800) 669-9999
5581 Hudson Industrial Pkwy.
Hudson, OH 44236
E-Mail: sales@thewirelesscatalog.com
Website: www.thewirelesscatalog.com
Fax Ordering: (800) 950-9569
Customer Service: (800) 687-9250
Contact Name: Donna Avery, President
Catalog: Free. Frequency: Semiannual
Circulation: 250K. Sales: $5-10MM
Products: Gifts: Apparel, books, DVDs,
audiocassettes; jewelry; home & garden;
personalizeed gifts; children's gifts

WORLD OF PRODUCTS CATALOG   (843) 345-5569
Wollitz Online Enterprises - Home 'n Gifts
137 Netherfield Dr. • Summerville, SC 29445
Catalog: Free. Frequency: Annual
Circulation: 100K. Sales: $5-10MM
Products: Gifts/collectibles; home
decor/tabletop; personal care & travel;
children's items

FRANK LLOYD WRIGHT   (877) 848-3559
PRESERVATION TRUST
Catalog Sales Dept.
931 Chicago Ave. • Oak Park, IL 60304
E-Mail: info@shopwright.com
Website: www.shopwright.com
Fax Ordering: (708) 848-2327
International Ordering: (708) 848-9518
Catalog: Free. Frequency: Annual
Circulation: 150K. Sales: $1-3MM
Products: Collector's gifts inspired by
Frank Lloyd Wright and books covering
his life and works

AARP PHARMACY SERVICES CATALOG   (800) 456-2277
AARP Pharmacy Services
P.O. Box 40011 • Roanoke, VA 24022
E-Mail: info@aarppharmacy.com
Website: www.aarppharmacy.com
Fax Ordering: (800) 456-7631; (703) 684-0246
International Ordering: (703) 684-0244
Contact Name: Brian S. Frid, President
Catalog: Free. Frequency: Quarterly
Circulation: 1MM. Sales: $10-20MM
Products: Prescription drugs, health & beauty
aids; vitamins & supplements; home aids

ACTIVEFOREVER.COM   (800) 377-8033
10799 N. 90th ST. • Scottsdale, AZ 85260
E-Mail: customerservice@activeforever.com
Website: www.activeforever.com
Fax Ordering: (602) 296-0297
International Ordering: (480) 767-6800
Catalog: Online. Sales: $5-10MM
Products: Daily living aids. Medical supplies
catalogs: Fitness/Physical Therapy Catalog;
Movement Disorders Solutions Catalog;
Caregiver Education Catalog; Low Vision/
Hearing Loss Catalog; Athletic Training &
Sports Therapy Catalog; Healthcare
Innovations Catalog.

AIR PURIFIERS DIRECT 2U   (800) 773-4971
Direct2U, Inc.
2210 Brindlewood Dr. • Plainfield, IL 60586
E-Mail: contactus@airpurifiersdirect2u.com
Website: www.airpurifiersdirect2u.com
Fax Ordering: (847) 966-3068
International Ordering: (847) 966-2952
Contact Name: Kenneth J. Kaugman, President
Catalog: Free. Frequency: Semiannual
Circulation: 100K. Sales: $10-20MM
Products: Alergy & asthma products,
preventive equipment, environmental

ALLERGY ASTHMA TECHNOLOGY LTD.   (800) 621-5545
8224 Lehigh Ave. • Morton Grove, IL 60053
E-Mail: info@allergyasthmatech.com
Website: www.allergyasthmatech.com
Fax Ordering: (847) 966-3068
International Ordering: (847) 966-2952
Contact Name: Kenneth J. Kaugman, President
Catalog: Free. Frequency: Semiannual
Circulation: 100K. Sales: $5-10MM
Products: Alergy & asthma products, preventive
equipment, environmental products

ALLERGY BUYERS CLUB   (888) 236-7231
486 Totten Pond Rd. • Waltham, MA 02451
Website: www.allergybuyersclub.com
E-Mail: info@allergybuyersclub.com
Fax Ordering: (781) 890-3560
International Ordering: (781) 419-5500
Catalogs: Free. Frequency: Annual
Circulation: 100K. Sales: $1-3MM
Products: Allergy products & supplies

ALLERGY SUFFERER'S SURVIVAL GUIDE   (800) 339-7123
3411 Pierce Dr. • Atlanta, GA 30341
Website: www.achooallergy.com
E-Mail: info@achooallergy.com
Fax Ordering: (800) 237-9618
International Ordering: (770) 455-9999
Catalog: Free. Frequency: Annual
Circulation: 100K. Sales: $10-20MM
Products: Air purifiers, allergy armor, ,

allergy bedding, vacuum cleaners,
dehumidifiers, humidifiers, furnace filters,
nasal irrigation, asthma treatment,
cleaning products, eco products

ALTERNATIVE HEALTH PUBLISHER   (800) 824-6396
Lotis Press
P.O. Box 325 • Twin Lakes, WI 53181
Website: www.lotuspress.com
E-Mail: info@lotuspress.com
Fax Ordering: (262) 889-2461
International Ordering: (262) 889-8561
Contact Name: Santosh Krinsky, President
Catalog: Free. Frequency: Semiannual
Circulation: 25K. Sales: $1-3MM
Products: Books on alternative health & wellness,
including herbalism, reiki, philosophy & spirituality

ALTERNATIVE SOURCE CATALOG   (800) 274-8366
954 Lexington Ave. • New York, NY 10021
Fax Ordering: (718) 282-1708
Catalog: $2. Frequency: Annual
Circulation: 100M. Sales: $500M
Products: Aromatherapy candles &
natural body products

AMERICAN DIABETES WHOLESALE (ADM)   (877) 241-9002
1501 NW 34th Pl. • Pompano Beach, FL 33069
Website: www.americandiabeteswholesale.com
E-Mail: cs@americandiabeteswholesale.com
Fax Ordering: (866) 995-4820
Catalog: Online. Sales: $10-20MM
Products: Diabetic supplies. Glucose monitor kits;
testing accessories; diabetic food; blood pressure
monitors; insulin; needles/syringes; insulin pumps
& supplies.

AMERICAN HEALTH FOOD   (800) 858-2143
875 W. Roger Rd. • Tucson, AZ 85705
E-Mail: support@amerhealth.com
Website: www.amerhealth.com
Fax Ordering: (800) 352-0569
International Ordering: (510) 888-8324
Contact Name: Homer Cionch, President
Catalog: Free. Frequency: Semiannual
Circulation: 50K. Sales: $1-3MM
Products: Natural vitamins & supplements

AMERICAN HEALTH SERVICE MAGNETICS   (800) 635-7070
14092 W. Lambs Ln. • Libertyville, IL 60048
E-Mail: bill@americanhealthservice.com
Website: www.powersleeper.com
Fax Ordering: (847) 680-4440
International Ordering: (847) 573-8750
Contact Name: William Lapietra President
Catalog: Free. Frequency: Quarterly
Circulation: 150K. Sales: $1-3MM
Products: Magnetic therapy products

AMERICAN NUTRITION   (800) 454-3724
Bellaire St. • Thornton, CO 80229
E-Mail: info@americannutrition.com
Website: www.americannutrition.com
Fax Ordering: (303) 814-0187
Catalog: Free. Frequency: Semiannual
Circulation: 1MM. Sales: $10-20MM
Products: Brand vitamins, herbs & supplements

AMERICAN SPORTS NETWORK   (626) 292-2222
P.O. Box 6100 • Rosemead, CA 91770
E-Mail: info@fitnessamerica.com
Website: www.fitnessamerica.com

Fax Ordering: (626) 292-2221
Contact Name: Louis Zwick, President
Catalog: Free. Frequency: Bimonthly
Circulation: 25K. Sales: $5-10MM
Products: Sport, fitness, health &
bodybuilding videos

AMES WALKER CATALOG (877) 525-7224
P.O. Box 1027 • Asheboro, NC 27204
E-Mail: customerservice@ameswalker.com
Website: www.ameswalker.com
Fax Ordering: (336) 629-0632
Catalog: Free. Frequency: Bimonthly
Circulation: 25K. Sales: $5-10MM
Products: Support hosiery for men & women
for diabetics, arthritics, maternity, etc.; diabetic
socks and shoes; foot & nail care accessories;
supports, braces.

APOTHECARY (802) 362-8460
P.O. Box 1108
Manchester Center, VT 05255
E-Mail: customerservice@vermontcountrystore.com
Website: www.vermontcountrystore.com
Fax Ordering: (802) 362-0285
Customer Service: (802) 362-8499
Contact Name: Lymon Ortman, President
Catalog: Free. Frequency: Semiannual
Circulation: 25K. Sales: $500K
Products: Personal care products; skin care,
fragrances, vitamins, etc.

APOTHECARY PRODUCTS (800) 328-2742
11750 12th Ave. S. • Burnsville, MN 55337
Fax Ordering: (952) 890-0418
International Ordering: (952) 890-1940
Contact Name: John Creel, President
Catalog: Free. Frequency: 3x per year
Circulation: 100M. Sales: $20-50MM
Products: Pharmaceutical products

APRIL VICTORIA (734) 428-7011
231 E. Main St. • Manchester, MI 48158
Fax Ordering: (734) 428-7955
Catalog: $2. Frequency: Quarterly
Circulation: 50K. Sales: $500K
Products: Bath products, soaps, potpourris

ARMSTRONG MEDICAL INDUSTRIES (800) 323-4220
575 Knightsbridge Pkwy. #700
Lincolnshire, IL 60069
E-Mail: info@armstrongmedical.com
Website: www.armstrongmedical.com
Fax Ordering: (847) 913-0138
International Ordering: (847) 913-0101
Contact Name: Warren G. Armstrong, President
Catalog: $2. Frequency: Annual
Circulation: 100K. Sales: $5-10MM
Products: Medical teaching and training aids;
medical carts and equipment, anatomical models;
and equipment for hospitals, EMS, anesthesia,
and education

AROMA THERAPEUTIX (800) 308-6284
Cinegraph Communications
P.O. Box 2908 • Seal Beach, CA 90740
Fax Ordering: (714) 894-9814
International Ordering: (714) 891-7779
Contact Name: Glen Wolfe, President
Catalog: Free. Frequency: Bimonthly
Circulation: 600K. Sales: $1-3MM
Products: Aromatherapy guide, oils and diffusers

ARTISTIC VIDEO (888) 982-4244
87 Tyler Ave. • Sound Beach, NY 11789
E-Mail: bobklein@villagenet.com
Website: www.artisticvideos.com
Fax Ordering: (631) 744-5993
International Ordering: (631) 744-5999
Contact Name: Bob Klein, President
Catalog: Free. Frequency: Semiannual
Circulation: 25K. Sales: $500K
Products: Health & fitness & martial arts videos

ATLANTIC FITNESS PRODUCTS (800) 445-1855
P.O. Box 300 • Linthicum, MD 21090
E-Mail: atlantic@atlantic-fitness.com
Website: www.atlantic-fitness.com
Fax Ordering: (410) 859-3907
International Ordering: (410) 859-3538
Contact Name: Faye Miller, President
Catalog: Free. Frequency: Semiannual
Circulation: 100K. Sales: $3-5MM
Products: Equipment for weightlifting
& fitness

ATLANTIC SPICE COMPANY (800) 316-7965
P.O. Box 205 • North Truro, MA 02652
E-Mail: atlantic2@capecod.net
Website: www.atlanticspice.com
Fax Ordering: (508) 487-2550
International Ordering: (508) 487-6100
Contact Name: Mark Irving, President
Catalog: Free. Frequency: Semiannual
Circulation: 25K. Sales: $1-3MM
Products: Ingredients for potpourri &
spices, teas, herbs

ATLANTIC TAN DISTRIBUTORS (800) 831-7649
5251 Z-Max Boulevard (800) 647-8870
Harrisburg, NC 28075
E-Mail: info@atlantictan.com
Website: www.atlantictan.com
Fax Ordering: (704) 455-7846
International Ordering: (704) 455-7840
Contact Name: Aubrey Hampton, President
Catalog: Free. Frequency: Semiannual
Circulation: 50K. Sales: $5-10MM
Products: Tanning beds, body wraps,
tanning lamps, tan products & accessories

ALEXANDRA AVERY (800) 669-1863
PURELY NATURAL BODY CARE
4717 SE Belmont St.
Portland, OR 97215
E-Mail: avery@hawaii.rr.com
Fax Ordering: (503) 234-7272
Contact Name: Alexandra Avery, President
Catalog: Free. Frequency: 10x per year
Circulation: 20K. Sales: $500K
Products: Natural & cruelty free aromatherapy
products for face & body care

AUBREY ORGANICS (800) 282-7394
4419 N. Manhattan Ave.
Tampa, FL 33614
E-Mail: info@aubreyorganics.com
Website: www.aubreyorganics.com
Fax Ordering: (813) 876-8166
International Ordering: (813) 877-4186
Contact Name: Aubrey Hampton, President
Catalog: Free. Frequency: Quarterly
Circulation: 100K. Sales: $10-20MM
Products: Certified organic hair, skin &
body care products

BACKSAVER CORPORATION   (800) 251-2225
53 Jeffrey Ave. • Holliston, MA 01746
E-Mail: info@backsaver.com
Website: www.backsavercorp.com
Fax Ordering: (800) 443-9609; (508) 429-8698
International Ordering: (508) 429-5940
Contact Name: Samuel B. Sheldon, President
Catalog: Free. Frequency: 8x per year
Circulation: 2.5MM. Sales: $5-10MM
Products: Ergonomic furniture & accessories;
recliners; office furniture; products for back pains

BARE ESCENTUALS   (866) 214-4076
P.O. Box 600 • San Francisco, CA 94104
E-Mail: info@bareescentuals.com
Website: www.bareescentuals.com
Fax Ordering: (415) 489-5994
Contact Name: Leslie A. Blodgett, CEO
Catalog: Free. Frequency: Semiannual
Circulation: 250K. Sales: $5-10MM
Products: BareMinerals makeup

BARTH VITAMIN CATALOG   (800) 645-2328
3890 Park Central Blvd. N.
Pompano Beach, FL 33064
Fax Ordering: (954) 978-9097
International Ordering: (954) 978—3055
Contact Name: Dennis Schoen, President
Catalog: Free. Frequency: Monthly
Circulation: 100K. Sales: $10-20MM
Products: Vitamins, minerals, food supplements,
herbal & homeopathic remedies, health & beauty
aids, health equipment & supplies

BEAUTIFUL TIMES   (800) 223-1216
The Vitamin Shoppe
4700 W. Side Ave.
North Bergen, NJ 07047
E-Mail: info@vitaminshoppe.com
Website: www.vitaminshoppe.com
Fax Ordering: (800) 852-7153; (201) 866-9513
International Ordering: (201) 866-7711
Contact Name: Jeff Howard, President
Catalog: Free. Frequency: Quarterly
Circulation: 100K. Sales: $1-3MM
Products: Vitamins & supplements; herbal
& homeopathic; sports nutrition products;
personal care products; family beauty,
health concerns; books

BEAUTY BOUTIQUE   (800) 497-7463
AmeriMark Direct   (877) 268-9594
6836 Engle Rd. • Cleveland, OH 44130
E-Mail: info@amerimark.com
Website: www.amerimark.com
Fax Ordering: (440) 826-1267
International Ordering: (440) 826-2000
Contact Name: Gary Geisler, President
Catalog: Free. Frequency: Monthly
Circulation: 500K. Sales: $50-100MM
Products: Cosmetic & beauty products;
discounted fragrences; general merchandise

BEAUTYTRENDS   (800) 777-7772
P.O. Box 9323 • Hialeah, FL 33014
E-Mail: 4service@beautytrends.com
Website: www.beautytrends.com
Fax Ordering: (305) 828-1271
Customer Service: (800) 820-0135
Catalog: Free. Pages: 48. Frequency: Quarterly
Circulation: 150K. Sales: $5-10MM
Products: Fashion hair, cosmetics, accessories

BECK-LEE, INC.   (800) 235-2852
P.O. Box 528 • Stratford, CT 06615
E-Mail: info@becklee.com
Website: www.becklee.com
Fax Ordering: (800) 525-4568
Catalog: Free. Frequency: Semiannual
Circulation: 100K. Sales: $10-20M
Products: Medical supplies; cardiology
& ecg machines & supplies

BEEHIVE BOTANICALS   (800) 233-4483
16297 W. Nursery Rd.
Hayward, WI 54843
E-Mail: beehive@win.bright.net
Website: www.beehive-botanicals.com
Fax Ordering: (715) 634-3523
International Ordering: (715) 634-4274
Contact Name: Linda Graham, President
Catalog: Free. Frequency: 3x per year
Circulation: 50K. Sales: $1-3MM
Products: Skin care, hair care, oral care
& health supplements

BODYJAZ   (866) 503-7235
P.O. Box 2148 • Eugene, OR 97402
E-Mail: info@bodyjaz.com
Website: www.thebodyjaz.com
Fax Ordering: (541) 868-8758
International Ordering: (541) 868-1575
Catalog: Free. Frequency: Semiannual
Circulation: 100K. Sales: $1-5MM
Products: Massage equipment, comfort &
natural pain relief products; massage videos
& relaxation music

BODY SHOP   (800) 263-9746
5036 One World Way
Wake Forest, NC 27587
E-Mail: vnewman@bodyshop.com
Website: www.thebodyshop.com
Fax Ordering: (719) 579-9007; (919) 554-4361
International Ordering: (919) 933-9281; 554-4900
Contact Name: Virginia Newman, Marketing
Catalog: Free. Frequency: Bimonthly
Circulation: 1MM. Sales: $10-20MM
Products: Skin & hair care products

CAROL BOND HEALTH FOODS   (800) 833-8282
P.O. Box 47 • Liberty, TX 77575
E-Mail: sherry@carolbond.com
Website: www.carolbond.com
Fax Ordering: (936) 336-6226
International Ordering: (936) 336-9001
Contact Name: Carol Bond, President
Catalog: Free. Frequency: Semiannual
Circulation: 100K. Sales: $500K
Products: Vitamin supplements; health foods;
herbs, beauty care products; diet products;
digestive aids

BOSS RETAIL CATALOG   (800) 666-8870
Bob O'Leary Sports Science
P.O. Box 79 • Scranton, PA 18504
E-Mail: info@bossonline.net
Website: www.bossonline.net
Fax Ordering: (570) 342-1368
International Ordering: (570) 342-4984
Contact Name: Bob O'Leary, President
Catalog: Free. Frequency: Annual
Circulation: 25K. Sales: $1-3MM
Products: Wholesale distributor of sports
nutrition & fitness accessories

BOTANIC CHOICE   (800) 644-8327
Indiana Botanic Gardens
3401 W. 37th Ave. • Hobart, IN 46342
E-Mail: info@botanichealth.com
Website: www.botanichealth.com
Fax Ordering: (219) 947-4148
International Ordering: (219) 947-4040
Customer Service: (800) 514-1068
Contact Name: Tim Leland, President
Catalog: Free. Frequency: Monthly
Circulation: 250K. Sales: $10-20MM
Products: Herbs & vitamins; herbal health
& beauty products; teas & natural cosmetics

BRONSON LABORATORIES   (800) 235-3200
Website: www.bronsonvitamins.com
E-Mail: help@bronsonvitamins.com
Fax Ordering: (800) 596-4242
International Ordering:
Catalog: Free. Frequency: Quarterly
Circulation: 100K. Sales: $10-20MM
Products: Vitamins & minerals; anti-aging
products; energy boosters; products for
diabetic support; eye health products;
skin & body products; specialty products;
sleep aids

CARE & COMFORT   (800) 645-2328
865 Merrick Ave. • Westbury, NY 11590
Fax Ordering: (410) 859-3907
International Ordering: (410) 859-3538
Contact Name: Ron Sanchez, President
Catalog: Free. Frequency: Monthly
Circulation: 100K. Sales: $3-5MM
Products: Home healthcare & exercise
equipment

CASWELL-MASSEY CATALOGUE   (800) 326-0500
P.O. Box 6161 • Edison, NJ 08837
E-Mail: info@caswellmasseyltd.com
Website: www.caswellmassey.com
Fax Ordering: (732) 225-2385
International Ordering: (732) 225-2181
Contact Name: Barbara Rogers, Marketing
Catalog: Free. Frequency: 5x per year
Circulation: 2.5MM. Sales: $10-20MM
Products: Fragrances, toiletries, grooming
& personal care products

CHINESE HERBS CATALOG   (800) 258-6878
East Earth Trade Winds
P.O. Box 493151 • Redding, CA 96049
E-Mail: sales@eastearthtrade.com
Website: www.eastearthtrade.com
Fax Ordering: (530) 223-0944
International Ordering: (530) 233-2346
Contact Name: Michael Czehatowski, President
Catalog: Free. Frequency: Annual
Circulation: 50K. Sales: $500M
Products: Chinese herbs & herb products

CLIENTELE   (800) 327-4660
14101 NW 4th St. • Sunrise, FL 33325
E-Mail: info@clientele.org
Website: www.clientele.org
Fax Ordering: (954) 845-9505
International Ordering: (954) 845-9500
Contact Name: Patricia Riley, President
Catalog: Free. Frequency: Quarterly
Circulation: 10K. Sales: $10-20MM
Products: Exercise equipment & vitamins

CMC RESCUE, INC.   (800) 235-5741
P.O. Box 6870 • Santa Barbara, CA 93160   (800) 235-8951
Website: www.cmcrescue.com
E-Mail: info@cmcrescue.com
Fax Ordering: (805) 562-9870
International Ordering: (805) 562-9120
Catalog: Free. Frequency: Semiannual
Circulation: 100K. Sales: $3-5M
Products: Rescue equipment & supplies

COLLAGE VIDEO   (800) 819-7111
5390 Main St. NE • Minneapolis, MN 55421
E-Mail: collage@collagevideo.com
Website: www.collagevideo.com
Fax Ordering: (763) 571-5906
International Ordering: (763) 571-5840
Catalog: Free. Pages: 60. Frequency: Annual
Circulation: 150K. Sales: $5-10MM
Products: Exercise videos: DVDs & CDs

CONE INSTRUMENTS   (800) 321-6964
5201 Naiman Pkwy. • Solon, OH 44139
E-Mail: safety@coneinstruments.com
Website: www.coneinstruments.com
Fax Ordering: (800) 987-2663; (440) 248-9477
International Ordering: (440) 248-1035
Catalog: Free. Frequency: Semiannual
Circulation: 150K. Sales: $20-50MM
Products: Medical imaging systems products &
supplies: Ultrasound; Radiology; Nuclear Medicine

CONNEY SAFETY PROBLEM SOLVER   (888) 356-9100
P.O. Box 44190 • Madison, WI 53744
E-Mail: safety@conney.com
Website: www.conney.com
Fax Ordering: (800) 358-7947; 461-7583
International Ordering: (317) 290-8982
   Fax (317) 290-1086
Contact Name: Michael Stamn, President
Catalog: Free. Frequency: Semiannual
Circulation: 100K. Sales: $20-50MM
Products: Personal and industrial safety
products; training & compliance products;
first aid products

CONSUMER VITAMIN VALUES   (800) 777-2200
860 Grand Blvd. • Deer Park, NY 11729
Fax Ordering: (631) 586-2385
International Ordering: (631) 586-2266
Contact Name: Arthur Pollack, President
Catalog: Free. Frequency: Bimonthly
Circulation: 100K. Sales: $1-3MM
Products: Vitamin & mineral supplements

CREATIVE HEALTH PRODUCTS   (800) 742-4478
5148 Saddle Ridge Rd. • Plymouth, MI 48170
E-Mail: sales@chponline.com
Website: www.chponline.com
Fax Ordering: (734) 996-4650
International Ordering: (734) 996-5900
Contact Name: Marlene Donoghue, President
Catalog: $2. Frequency: Annual
Circulation: 50K. Sales: $1-3MM
Products: Fitness testing equipment

D&E PHARMACEUTICALS   (800) 221-1833
206 Macopin Rd. • Bloomingdale, NJ 07403
E-Mail: info@d-n-e.com
Website: www.d-n-e.com
Fax Ordering: (973) 838-0560
International Ordering: (973) 838-5254

Contact Name: Eric Organ, President
Catalog: Free. Frequency: Quarterly
Circulation: 1MM. Sales: $10-20MM
Products: Pharmaceutical products, health aids,
diet aids, energy vitamins, over-the-counter drugs,
sports/fitness aids; herbs, minerals, homeopathic
medicine

DABNEY HERBS (502) 893-5198
P.O. Box 22061 • Louisville, KY 40252
E-Mail: dabneyherb@win.net
Website: www.dabneyherbs.com
Contact Name: Diane Brown, Manager
Catalog: $2. Frequency: Annual
Circulation: 100K. Sales: $500K
Products: Herbs, perennials & wildflowers,
potpourri supplies & essential oils

DERMA-E BODYCARE PARTS (800) 933-9344
9751 Independence Ave.
Chatsworth, CA 91311
E-Mail: info@dermae.com
Website: www.dermae.com
Fax Ordering: (818) 718-6907
Catalog: Free. Frequency: Quarterly
Circulation: 100K. Sales: $5-10MM
Products: Facial & body moisturizers,
facial masks & cleansers; and other body
care products

DHARMACRAFTS (800) 794-9862
405 Waltham St. • Lexington, MA 02421
E-Mail: dharma@dharmacrafts.com
Website: www.dharmacrafts.com
Fax Ordering: (781) 862-8824
International Ordering: (781) 862-9211
Contact Name: Dyan Eagles, President
Catalog: Free. Frequency: 3x per year
Circulation: 250M. Sales: $1-3MM
Products: Buddhist meditation supplies

DISCOVER MAGNETICS (800) 497-9391
4901 E. 215th St. • Belton, MO 64012
E-Mail: sales@discovermagnetics.com
Website: www.discovermagnetics.com
Fax Ordering: (816) 618-7229
International Ordering: (816) 618-3499
Catalog: Free. Frequency: 10x per year
Circulation: 100M. Sales: $1-3MM
Products: Magnetic therapy products
for pain relief; magnetic jewelry

DOCTOR HOY'S NATURAL (800) 437-4698
BOTANICAL SKIN CARE
515 E. Carefree Hwy. 354
Phoenix, AZ 85085
E-Mail: doctor@doctorhoy.com
Website: www.dyna-doctorhoy.com
Fax Ordering: (623) 465-2002
International Ordering: (623) 465-2001
Contact Name: Bruce Houghey, President
Catalog: Free. Frequency: Semiannual
Circulation: 100K. Sales: $500K
Products: Handmade, natural lotions,
bodywashes, skincare, suncare, anti-aging,
and pain relief gel products

DR. LEONARD'S HEALTH CARE (800) 785-0880
P.O. Box 7821 • Edison, NJ 08818
E-Mail: info@drleonards-fitness.com
Website: www.drleonards.com
Fax Ordering: (732) 572-2118

International Ordering: (732) 225-0100
Customer Service: (800) 455-1918
Contact Name: Stephen Brotman, President
Catalog: Free. Frequency: Annual
Circulation: 100K. Sales: $500K - $1MM
Products: Health products; exercise &
nutrition, personal care, apparel, footwear;
home furnishings

DYNAMIC LIVING (888) 940-0605
95 W. Dudleytown Rd.
Bloomfield, CT 06002
E-Mail: info@dynamic-living.com
Website: www.dynamic-living.com
Fax Ordering: (866) 422-1150
International Ordering: (860) 683-4442
Catalog: Free. Frequency: Semiannual
Circulation: 100K. Sales: $5-10MM
Products: Specialty products designed for
people who need them to maintain
independence in their own homes.

EARTH SCIENCE (800) 222-6720
475 N. Sheridan St.
Corona, CA 91720
E-Mail: info@earthscienceinc.com
Website: www.thenewes.com
Fax Ordering: (909) 371-0509
International Ordering: (909) 371-7565
Contact Name: Kristine Schoenauer, President
Catalog: Product sheet. Frequency: Semiannual
Circulation: 100K. Sales: $10-20MM
Products: All-natural, environmentally sound
skin & hair care products; nutritional supplements

ECO-STORE (800) 556-9949
P.O. Box 181102
Casselberry, FL 32707
E-Mail: beth@eco-store.com
Website: www.eco-store.com
Fax Ordering: (407) 649-3148
International Ordering: (407) 426-9949
Catalog: Free. Frequency: 10x per year
Products: Environmentally safe ho
me/healthcare products

ERGONOMICS/OCCUPATIONAL (800) 225-2610
HEALTH & SAFETY
AliMed • 297 High St.
Dedham, MA 02026
E-Mail: info@alimed.com
Website: www.alimed.com
Fax Ordering: (800) 437-2966;(781) 329-8392
International Ordering: (781) 329-2900
Contact Name: Julian Cherubini, President
Catalog: Free. Frequency: Monthly
Circulation: 250K. Sales: $10-20MM
Products: Medical and ergonomic products &
accessories for the healthcare and business
professional

ERLANDER'S NATURAL PRODUCTS (800) 562-8873
Nature's Department Store
2279 Lake Ave. • Altadena, CA 91001
E-Mail: erlander@webtv.net
Fax Ordering: (626) 798-2663
International Ordering: (626) 797-7004
Contact Name: Stig Erlander, Manager
Catalog: Free. Frequency: Weekly.
Circulation: 50K. Sales: $250K
Products: All-natural, organic products,
including soaps, matresses, olive oil, wine, etc.

ESPECIALLY YOURS (800) 939-9447
P.O. Box 105 • South Easton, MA 02375
E-Mail: customerservice@especiallyyours.com
Website: www.especiallyyours.com
Fax Ordering: (508) 238-1965
Customer Service: (800) 748-6910
Catalog: Free. Frequency: Semiannual
Circulation: 200K. Sales: $5-10MM
Products: Wigs, hair pieces, falls & headbands,
apparel & accessories; especially for African
American women

FEATHER SPRING INTERNATIONAL (800) 628-4693
712 N. 34th St. • Seattle, WA 98103
E-Mail: info@featherspring.com
Website: www.featherspring.com
Fax Ordering: (206) 547-8589
International Ordering: (206) 545-8585
Contact Name: Peter Rothschild, President
Catalog: Free. Frequency: Semiannual
Circulation: 100K. Sales: $3-5MM
Products: Foot supports & supplies

FEELGOOD CATALOG (800) 997-6789
10311 W. Hampdon A108
Lakewood, CO 80227
E-Mail: info@feelgoodfast.com
Website: www.feelgoodfast.com
Fax Ordering: (800) 966-6387
International Ordering: (303) 762-0466
Contact Name: Jason Zinn, President
Catalog: Free. Frequency: Quarterly
Circulation: 100K. Sales: $3-5MM
Products: Health enhancement & pain
relief products

FILM TECHNOLOGIES INTERNATIONAL (800) 777-1770
2544 Terminal Dr. S.
St. Petersburg, FL 33712
E-Mail: info@filmtechnologies.com
Website: www.filmtechnologies.com
Fax Ordering: (727) 327-7132
International Ordering: (727) 327-2544
Contact Name: Donald O. Wheeler, President
Catalog: $15. Frequency: Annual
Circulation: 50K. Sales: $20-50MM
Products: Solar, safety & security window film

FITNESS FACTORY OUTLET (800) 383-9300
1900 S. Des Plaines Ave.
Forest Park, IL 60130
E-Mail: sales@fitnessfactory.com
Website: www.fitnessfactory.com
Fax Ordering: (708) 345-9981
International Ordering: (708) 427-3500
Catalog: Free. Frequency: Semiannual
Circulation: 100K. Sales: $10-20MM
Products: Fitness & exercise equipment

FITNESS QUEST (800) 321-9236
1400 Raff Rd. SW • Canton, OH 44750
E-Mail: info@fitnessquest.com
Website: www.fitnessquest.com
Fax Ordering: (330) 479-9213
International Ordering: (330) 478-0755
Contact Name: Robert Schnabel, President
Catalog: Free. Frequency: Annual
Circulation: 100K. Sales: $5-10MM
Products: Home fitness equipment

FITNESS SYSTEMS CATALOG (800) 967-1827
Fitness Systems Manufacturing Corp.
P.O. Box 2073 • Reading, PA 19608
E-Mail: vitaminout@aol.com
Website: www.fitness-systems.net
Fax Ordering: (800) 461-3979; (610) 678-9022
International Ordering: (610) 670-0135
Customer service: (800) 822-9995
Contact Name: David Hoffman, President
Catalog: Free. Frequency: Annual
Circulation: 10K. Sales: $500K
Products: Athletic/sports proteins, amino acids,
,vitamins & supplements at wholesale prices

FOOT SMART (800) 532-3303
P.O. Box 922908
Waycross, GA 30010
E-Mail: info@footsmart.com
Website: www.footsmart.com
Fax Ordering: (800) 841-3843
Customer Service: (866) 532-3303
Catalog: Free. Frequency: Annual
Circulation: 150K. Sales: $3-5MM
Products: Shoes & shoe aids & accessories

FRAGRENCENET.COM, INC. (800) 727-3867
104 Parkway Dr. South
Hauppauge, NY 11788
E-Mail: info@fragrencenet.com
Website: www.fragrencenet.com
Fax Ordering: (631) 582-8433
International Ordering: (631) 582-5204
Catalog: Online. Sales: $1-3MM
Products: Fine perfumes, colognes,
skin care & hair care products at discounts

FREEDA VITAMINS (800) 777-3737
36 E. 41st St. • New York, NY 10017
E-Mail: freedavits@aol.com
Website: www.freedavitamins.com
Fax Ordering: (212) 685-7297
International Ordering: (212) 685-4980
Contact Name: Philip Zimmerman, President
Catalog: Free. Frequency: Weekly
Circulation: 100M. Sales: $1-3MM
Products: Vitamin & mineral supplements

FULL OF LIFE (800) 558-6967
P.O. Box 25600 • Bradenton, FL 34206
E-Mail: custservfol@jsls.com
Website: www.fulloflife.com
Fax Ordering: (800) 551-4406
Catalog: Free. Frequency: Semiannual
Circulation: 100K. Sales: $1-3MM
Products: Mobility, Personal Care, Therapeutic
& Health Aids: allergy relief, diabetic care,
senior fitness, and sexuality

FULLER BRUSH CATALOG (800) 732-1115
One Fuller Way (800) 522-0499
Great Bend, KS 67530
E-Mail: info@fuller.com
Website: www.fuller.com
Fax Ordering: (620) 792-1906
International Ordering: (620) 792-1711
Contact Name: Norbert Schneider, President
Catalog: Free. Frequency: Quarterly
Circulation: 500K. Sales: $20-50MM
Products: Cleaning supplies & personal care
products

GAIA CLEAN EARTH PRODUCTS (800) 726-5496
P.O. Box 20007 • York, PA 17405
E-Mail: gaia@blazenet.net
Fax Ordering: (800) 726-5496
International Ordering: (717) 840-1638
Contact Name: Brian N. Hartman, President
Catalog: Free. Frequency: Weekly
Products: Environmentally-compatible
cleaning products

GALLS CATALOG (866) 290-3385
P.O. Box 54308 • Lexington, KY 40509 (800) 477-7766
E-Mail: help-desk@galls.com (800) 914-2557
Website: www.galls.com
Fax Ordering: (800) 944-2557; (859) 268-5954
International Ordering: (859) 266-7227;
Catalog: Free. Frequency: Semiannual
Circulation: 100K. Sales: $5-10MM
Products: Public safety equipment & apparel;
uniforms, badges, duty gear, fire/rescue gear,
footgear, flashlights & spotlights

GLOBAL OCCUPATIONAL SAFETY (800) 433-4848
Systemax Global
22 Harbor Dr. • Port Washington, NY 11050
E-Mail: info@systemaxpc.com
Website: www.systemaxpc.com
Fax Ordering: (800) 336-3818
International Ordering: (516) 625-8787
Contact Name: Richard Leeds, President
Catalog: Free. Frequency: Quarterly
Circulation: 2MM. Sales: $20-50MM
Products: Protective clothing & hazardous
material storage

GLOBAL SALES CORPORATION (800) 521-8006
P.O. Box 126 • New Hyde Park, NY 11040
Fax Ordering: (516) 352-3718
International Ordering: (516) 437-1917
Contact Name: Bill Morales, President
Catalog: Free. Frequency: 3x per year
Circulation: 300K. Sales: $1-3MM
Products: Health & beauty products

GOLD MEDAL HAIR PRODUCTS (516) 378-6900
1 Bennington Ave. • Freeport, NY 11520
Fax Ordering: (516) 378-0168
Contact Name: Phil Laban, President
Catalog: Free. Frequency: Bimonthly
Circulation: 300K. Sales: $5-10MM
Products: Black hair care products and wigs

GOLDEN AGE PRODUCTS CATALOG (954) 978-0597
3038 NW 25th Ave.
Pompano Beach, FL 33069
Fax Ordering: (954) 960-1357
Contact Name: Michael Stephens, President
Catalog: Free. Frequency: Monthly
Circulation: 100K. Sales: $1-3MM
Products: Health care products

GOLDEN RATIO WOODWORKS (800) 345-1129
P.O. Box 297 • Emigrant, MT 59027 (800) 735-8829
E-Mail: sales@goldenratio.com
Website: www.goldenratio.com
Fax Ordering: (406) 333-4769
International Ordering: (333-4193) 744-5999
Catalog: Free. Frequency: Semiannual
Circulation: 200K. Sales: $10-20MM
Products: Manufacturers of multi-use beauty,
spa & therapy tables; equipment & supplies for
sap, massage, holistic and alternative health.

GUIDE TO EXERCISE VIDEOS (800) 819-7111
Collage Video (800) 433-6769
5390 Main St. NE
Minneapolis, MN 55421
E-Mail: sales@collagevideo.com
Website: www.collagevideo.com
Fax Ordering: (763) 571-5906
International Ordering: (763) 571-5840
Contact Name: Jim Craft, President
Catalog: Free. Frequency: Annual
Circulation: 50K. Sales: $1-3MM
Products: Exercise videos

GUIDE TO THE PERFORMING ARTS (800) 523-0961
Stage Step
2000 Hamilton St. • Philadelphia, PA 19130
E-Mail: randy@stagestep.com
Website: www.stagestep.com
Fax Ordering: (800) 877-3342; (215) 564-4206
International Ordering: (215) 639-9000
Contact Name: Randy Swartz, President
Catalog: Free. Frequency: Annual
Circulation: 250K. Sales: $3-5MM
Products: Health & finess flooring for dance
studios, theatres, fitness and athletic facilities;
dance & aerobic flooring & maintenance products

HAIR FACTORY (800) 999-9328
271 North Ave. • New Rochelle, NY 10801
E-Mail: hairfactory@msn.com
Website: www.hairfactory.com
Fax Ordering: (914) 576-1462
International Ordering: (914) 576-1647
Contact Name: Ann Carroll, President
Catalog: Free. Frequency: Annual
Circulation: 100K. Sales: $1-3MM
Products: Suppliers of products & educational
material for the hair weaving industry

HAMMER STRENGTH (513) 221-2600
2245 Gilbert Ave. • Cincinnati, OH 45206
E-Mail: info@lifefitness.com
Website: www.lifefitness.com
Fax Ordering: (513) 221-8084
International Ordering: (425) 483-3313
Catalog: Free. Frequency: Annual
Circulation: 100K. Sales: $3-5MM
Products: Fitness/weightlifting machines,
equipment & products for the home & gyms

HARVEST HEALTH FOODS (616) 245-6268
28th & Cascade • Grand Rapids, MI 49507
E-Mail: info@harvesthealthfoods.com
Website: www.harvesthealthfoods.com
Fax Ordering: (616) 245-8034
Contact Name: Cathy Atsma, President
Catalog: Free. Frequency: Annual
Circulation: 50K. Sales: $1-3MM
Products: Vitamins, health foods,
herbs & spices

HEALTH CARE (800) 558-9595
Nasco • 901 Janesville Ave.
Ft. Atkinson, WI 53538
E-Mail: info@nascofa.com
Website: www.nascofa.com
Fax Ordering: (920) 563-8296
International Ordering: (920) 674-6000
Contact Name: Richard Ciurczak, President
Catalog: Free. Frequency: Annual
Circulation: 200K. Sales: $10-20MM
Products: Health supplies

HEALTHWATCHERS SYSTEM CATALOG   (800) 321-6917
1233 Montauk Hwy. • Oak Dale, NY 11769
Fax Ordering: (800) 948-8150
Contact Name: Arthur Rudolph, President
Catalog: Free. Frequency: Quarterly
Circulation: 500K. Sales: $5-10MM
Products: Vitamin & mineral supplements
at herbal products

HEALTHY LIGHTING CATALOG   (888) 544-4861
P.O. Box 2455 • Stamford, CT 06906
E-Mail: info@healthylight.com
Website: www.healthylight.com
Fax Ordering: (203) 921-2427
International Ordering: (203) 708-8937
Contact Names: Nicholas & Michelle Harmon
Catalog: Free. Frequency: Semiannual
Circulation: 25K. Sales: $1-3MM
Products: Natural spectrum incandescent bulbs,
natural daylight compact fluorescent and full
spectrum fluorescent tubes; bright light systems

HEALTHY LIVING   (800) 800-0100
Amerimark Direct
6864 Engle Rd. • Cleveland, OH 44130
E-Mail: info@amerimark.com
Website: www.amerimark.com
Fax Ordering: (440) 826-1267
International Ordering: (440) 826-1900
Contact Name: Gary Geisler, President
Catalog: Free. Frequency: Quarterly
Circulation: 10MM. Sales: $20-50MM
Products: Exercise & fitness products,
health remedies; general health products;
diet & weight loss products; health
improvement & personal care products

HEAR-MORE CATALOG   (800) 881-4327
42 Executive Blvd. • Farmingdale, NY 11735
E-Mail: sales@hearmore.com
Website: www.hearmore.com
Fax Ordering: (631) 752-0689
International Ordering: (631) 752-1145
Catalog: Free. Frequency: Quarterly
Circulation: 150K. Sales: $5-10M
Products: Products for the hearing impaired
& deaf; aids & appliances for assistive living

HEART ZONES COMPANY   (916) 481-7283
2636 Fulton Ave. • Sacramento, CA 95821
E-Mail: staff@heartzone.com
Website: www.heartzone.com
Fax Ordering: (916) 481-2213
Contact Name: Sally Edwards, President
Catalog: Free. Frequency: Quarterly
Circulation: 25K. Sales: $250M
Products: Books on a variety of fitness,
sports & health topics

HERB PRODUCTS COMPANY   (888) 339-4372
P.O. Box 898 • N. Hollywood, CA 91603
E-Mail: info@herbproducts.com
Website: www.herbproducts.com
Fax Ordering: (818) 508-6567
International Ordering: (818) 761-0351
Customer Service: (800) 877-3104
Contact Name: John W. Du Val, President
Catalog: Free. Frequency: Quarterly
Circulation: 100K. Sales: $3-5MM
Products: Herb products; botanicals, oils &
fragrences, extracts & tinctures, potpourri;
supplements & vitamins; personal care; books

HERBAL HEALER ACADEMY CATALOG   (870) 269-4177
HC 32 Box 97B
Mountain View, AR 72560
E-Mail: info@herbalhealer.com
Website: www.herbalhealer.com
Fax Ordering: (870) 269-5424
Catalog: Free. Frequency: Annual
Circulation: 10K. Sales: $500K
Products: Natural health care products

HERITAGE STORE   (800) 862-2923
P.O. Box 444 • Virginia Beach, VA 23458
E-Mail: heritage@caycecures.com
Website: www.caycecures.com
Fax Ordering: (757) 428-0100
International Ordering: (757) 428-3632
Contact Name: Tom Johnson, President
Catalog: Free. Frequency: 8x per year
Circulation: 300K. Sales: $10-20MM
Products: Edgar Cayce health products

MICHELLE HERSCHNER
HEALTH & BEAUTY AIDES   (800) 451-5773
Continental Quest Corp.
220 W. Carmel Dr. • Carmel, IN 46032
E-Mail: sales@continentalquest.com
Website: www.continentalquest.com
Fax Ordering: (317) 843-1674
International Ordering: (317) 843-2501
Contact Name: B. Paul Auer, President
Catalog: Free. Frequency: 5x per year
Circulation: 50K. Sales: $1-3MM
Products: Health & beauty aides;
over-the-counter pharmaceutical,
nutritional, & personal care products

HOBE LABORATORIES   (800) 528-4482
6479 S. Ash Ave. • Tempe, AZ 85283
E-Mail: hobelabs@aol.com
Website: www.hobelabs.com
Fax Ordering: (480) 413-2005
International Ordering: (480) 413-1950
Contact Name: Bill Robertson, President
Catalog: Free. Frequency: Semiannual
Circulation: 200K. Sales: $20-50MM
Products: Natural health & beauty products,
herbal teas and tropical analgesics

HOMEOPATHIC REFERENCE CATALOG   (800) 624-9659
Standard Homeopathic Company
P.O. Box 61067 • Los Angeles, CA 90061
E-Mail: info@hylands.com
Website: www.hylands.com
Fax Ordering: (310) 516-8579
International Ordering: (310) 768-0700
Contact Name: J.P. Borneman, President
Catalog: Free. Frequency: Annual
Circulation: 200K. Sales: $10-20MM
Products: Manufactures homeopathic
remedies & medicines

HOMEOPATHY-LUYTIES PHARMACEUTICAL   (800) 325-8080
P.O. Box 8080 • Richford, VT 05476   (800) 466-3672
E-Mail: info@1800homeopathy.com
Website: www.1800homeopathy.com
Fax Ordering: (877) 999-0090
Contact Name: Forrest Murphy, President
Catalog: Free. Frequency: Semiannual
Circulation: 200K. Sales: $5-10MM
Products: Manufactures homeopathic
medicines, natural medicines, health &
beauty aids, and vitamins

HUMAN KINETICS SPORTS
SPORTS & FITNESS CATALOG
(800) 747-4457
P.O. Box 5076 • Champaign, IL 61825
E-Mail: info@jkusa.com
Website: www.humankinetics.com
Fax Ordering: (217) 351-1549
International Ordering: (217) 351-5076
Catalog: Free. Frequency: Annual
Circulation: 100K. Sales: $1-3MM
Products: Instructional books on specific sports, coaching education & sports administration; fitness/training topics

INDEPENDENT LIVING AIDS
(800) 537-2118
200 Robbins Ln. • Jericho, NY 11753
E-Mail: info@independentliving.com
Website: www.independentliving.com
Fax Ordering: (516) 937-3906
Catalog: Free. Frequency: Annual
Circulation: 100K. Sales: $5-10MM
Products: Low vision aids: talking clocks & watches, canes & mobility aids, magnifiers, large print books, braille products, talking cooking products, smoke detectors,voice recognition software. Products for deaf or hard of hearing: amplified corded & cordless answering machines, assistive technology, wireless doorbells, hearing aid batteries & accessories,

INNER BALANCE
(800) 345-3371
(877) 989-6321
Gaiam • 360 Interlocken Blvd.
Broomfield, CO 80021
E-Mail: customerservice@gaiam.com
Website: www.gaiam.com
Fax Ordering: (800) 456-1139
Catalog: Free. Frequency: Annual
Circulation: 50K. Sales: $1-3MM
Products: Healthcare products for the home; natural solutions

INTERACTIVE THERAPEUTICS, INC.
(800) 253-5111
P.O. Box 1805 • Stowe, OH 44224
E-Mail: info@interactivetherapy.com
Website: www.interactivetherapy.com
Fax Ordering: (330) 923-3030
International Ordering: (330) 923-7500
Catalog: Free. Frequency: Annual
Circulation: 100K. Sales: $5-10MM
Products: Speech & hearing products for stroke survivors

INTERNATURAL HEALTH & WELLNESS
(800) 643-4221
P.O. Box 489 • Twin Lakes, WI 53181
E-Mail: internatural@internatural.com
Website: www.internatural.com
Fax Ordering: (262) 889-8591
International Ordering: (262) 889-8581
Contact Name: Santosh Krinsky, President
Catalog: Free. Frequency: Weekly
Circulation: 50K. Sales: $1-3MM
Products: Health & wellness products: vitamins & supplements, herbs and spices, personal care products; aromatherapy, biomagnetics, candles, clothing, jewelry, massage tools

INVITE HEALTH.COM
(800) 632-0572
Integrating vitamins into your life

JANICE CORPORATION
(800) 526-4237
198 U.S. Hwy. 46 • Budd Lake, NJ 07828
E-Mail: jswack@worldnet.att.net
Website: www.janices.com
Fax Ordering: (760) 931-5809
International Ordering: (760) 438-2511
Contact Name: Janice Swack, President
Catalog: Free. Frequency: Semiannual
Circulation: 200K. Sales: $3-5MM
Products: Products providing comfort & relief to persons suffering from allergies, sennsitivities, and dermatological problems, including bedding, clothing, soaps and grooming products.

JASON NATURAL COSMETICS
(877) 527-6601
8468 Warren Dr. • Culver City, CA 90232
E-Mail: jnp@jason-natural.com
Website: www.jason-natural.com
Fax Ordering: (310) 838-9274
Contact Name: Jeffrey Light, President
Catalog: Free. Frequency: Semiannual
Products: All natural cosmetics; skin, hair and body care products

JENASOL CATALOG
(800) 327-8485
580 Ansin Blvd. • Hallandale, FL 33309
E-Mail: sales@jenasolvitamins.com
Website: www.jenasolvitamins.com
Fax Ordering: (800) 920-5890; (954) 458-8887
International Ordering: (954) 458-5900
Contact Names: Maxine & Jack Fried
Catalog: Free. Frequency: Monthly
Circulation: 100K. Sales: $1-3MM
Products: Specialty vitamins

KETTLE CARE
(406) 862-9851
6950 Farms to Market Rd.
Whitefish, MT 59937
E-Mail: info@kettlecare.com
Website: www.kettlecare.com
Fax Ordering: (406) 862-9851
Contact Name: Lynn Wallingford, President
Catalog: $1. Frequency: Annual
Circulation: 25K. Sales: $500M
Products: Herbal body care products using organic herbs from Montana, aromatherapy oils

KEY WEST ALOE
(800) 445-2563
P.O. Box 1079 • Key West, FL 33041
E-Mail: kwaloe1@aol.com
Website: www.keywestaloe.com
Fax Ordering: (305) 294-0138
International Ordering: (305) 294-5592
Contact Name: Helen Cates, President
Catalog: Free. Frequency: 5x per year
Circulation: 150K. Sales: $1-3MM
Products: Skin care, suntan, bath & fragrance products

KSA JOJOBA
(818) 701-1534
19025 Parthenia St. • Northridge, CA 91324
E-Mail: jojoba99@hotmail.com
Website: www.jojoba-ksa.com
Fax Ordering: (818) 993-0194
International Ordering: (760) 438-2511
Contact Name: Kathie Aamodt, President
Catalog: Free. Frequency: Annual
Circulation: 25KM. Sales: $500K - $1MM
Products: Cosmetics, haircare products, toiletries, oils, skin care and pet skin care products; all from the Jojoba plant

KYTEC ATHLETIC SPEED EQUIPMENT   (800) 732-4883
8337 Penn Ave. S
Bloomington, MN 55431
E-Mail: order@kytec.us
Website: www.kytec.us
Fax Ordering: (952) 571-5906
International Ordering: (952) 571-5840
Contact Name: Jodi Michaelson, President
Catalog: Free. Frequency: Semiannual
Circulation: 50K. Sales: $500K
Products: Athletic speed equipment, parachutes,
reaction balls, speed & endurance equipment;
bunji and rehabilitation equipment

LATEST PRODUCTS CORP.   (516) 367-4700
36 Orchard Dr. • Woodbury, NY 11797
E-Mail: lpcorp@aol.com
Fax Ordering: (516) 367-4714
Contact Name: Steven Spaeth, President
Catalog: Free. Frequency: Quarterly
Circulation: 100K. Sales: $1-3MM
Products: Specialty items for nursing homes,
hospitals, government agencies

LEAK & SPILL   (800) 468-4647
New Pig
P.O. Box 304 • Tipton, PA 16684
E-Mail: sales@newpig.us
Website: www.newpig.us
Fax Ordering: (800) 621-7447
International Ordering: (952) 571-5840
Contact Name: Nino Vella, President
Catalog: Free. Frequency: Semiannual
Circulation: 50K. Sales: $500K
Products: Solutions for a clean & safe
workplace; absorbent mats

LONGEVITY NETWORK CATALOG   (702) 454-7000
15 Cactus Garden Dr.
Henderson, NV 89014
E-Mail: sales@prohealthinc.com
Website: www.prohealthinc.com
Fax Ordering: (702) 435-4786
Catalog: Free. Frequency: Annual
Circulation: 50K. Sales: $500K
Products: Healthy & fat free foods,
healthcare products

LUCKY HEART COSMETICS   (800) 283-1014
138 Huling Ave. • Memphis, TN 38103
E-Mail: info@luckyheart.com
Website: www.luckyheart.com
Fax Ordering: (901) 526-7660
International Ordering: (901) 526-7658
Contact Name: Gary Young, President
Catalog: Free. Frequency: Semiannual
Circulation: 100K. Sales: $3-5MM
Products: Cosmetics

LUXIS CATALOG   (800) 628-4693
Luxis International, Inc.
105 W. Lincoln Way
DeKalb, IL 60115
E-Mail: customerservice@luxis.com
Website: www.luxis.com
Fax Ordering: (800) 261-1164
Catalog: Free. Frequency: Semiannual
Circulation: 100K. Sales: $5-10MM
Products: Products for body pain ranging
from custom crafted foot orthopedics, to knee
supports, to soothing arthritis cremes & soaps.

MAIL ORDER CATALOG   (800) 695-2241
FOR HEALTHY EATING
The Mail Order Catalog, LLC
P.O. Box 180
Summertown, TN 38483
E-Mail: askus@healthy-eating.com
Website: www.healthy-eating.com
Fax Ordering: (931) 964-2291
International Ordering: (931) 964-2241
Contact Name: Cynthia Holzapfel, President
Catalog: Free. Frequency: 5x per year
Circulation: 250K. Sales: $500M
Products: Quick-cooking, vegetarian meat
substitutes, featuring textured soy proteins
and other vegetarian entree products; books

MAINE BALSAM FIR PRODUCTS   (800) 522-5726
P.O. Box 9 • West Paris, ME 04289
E-Mail: wendy@mainebalsam.com
Website: www.mainebalsam.com
Fax Ordering: (207) 674-5094
International Ordering: (207) 674-5073
Contact Name: Wendy J. Newmeyer, President
Catalog: Free. Frequency: Semiannual
Circulation: 25K. Sales: $500K
Products: Natural fragrant balsam fir filled
pillows, sachets, and other scented items

MAINE MOUNTAIN SOAP & CANDLE CO.   (800) 287-2141
P.O. Box 130 • Greenville, ME 04441
E-Mail: info@mainmountain.com
Website: www.mainemountain.com
Fax Ordering: (207) 695-2337
International Ordering: (207) 695-3926
Catalog: Free. Frequency: Annual
Circulation: 25K. Sales: $500K
Products: Scented candles, natural bath
products, herbal soaps, lotions, beeswax
candles, aromatherapy candles; bath &
body products

MAMA'S EARTH   (800) 620-7388
Environmental General Store
P.O. Box 786 • Housatonic, MA 01236
E-Mail: carolyn@mamasearth.com
Website: www.mamasearth.com
International Ordering: (413) 274-6226
Catalog: Free. Frequency: Semiannual
Circulation: 25K. Sales: $500K
Products: All-natural, handmade soaps,
candles, lotions and personal care products,
clothing made from organic cotton; earth-friendly
baby care products; kits for making toys

MEDCO SPORTS MEDICINE   (800) 556-3326
Medco Supply Company
500 Fillmore Ave.
Tonawanda, NY 14150
E-Mail: info@medcosupply.com
Website: www.medco-supply.com
Fax Ordering: (800) 222-1934
International Ordering: (716) 695-3244
Contact Name: Mark Ladoucceur, President
Catalog: Free. Frequency: 5x per year
Circulation: 500K. Sales: $5-10MM
Products: Medical, health & related safety
products; suppliers to athletic trainers, sports
medicine professions, & physical therapists;
school first-aid, occupational health

MEGACARE CATALOG (800) 803-8895
2602 N. Loma Ave.
So. El Monte, CA 91733
E-Mail: info@megacare.com
Website: www.megacare.com
Fax Ordering: (626) 279-5989
International Ordering: (626) 279-9886
Contact Name: Miau Huang, Marketing
Catalog: Free. Frequency: Quarterly
Circulation: 25K. Sales: $500M
Products: Dietary supplements, vitamins
& herbal products

MIRACLE OF ALOE (800) 966-2563
P.O. Box 5230
Pagosa Springs, CO 81147
E-Mail: customerservice@miracleofaloe.com
Website: www.miracleofaloe.com
Fax Ordering: (970) 264-6706
International Ordering: (970) 264-6709
Contact Name: Chris F. Clarke, Marketing
Catalog: Free. Frequency: Quarterly
Circulation: 1MM. Sales: $1-3MM
Products: Aloe Vera therapeutic & skincare
products

MOMS (MAIL ORDER MEDICAL SUPPLY) (800) 232-7443
25230 Ave. Standford
Valencia, CA 91355
E-Mail: info@momscatalog.com
Website: www.momscatalog.com
Fax Ordering: (800) 622-3429
Contact Name: Tim Baker, President
Catalog: Free. Frequency: Monthly
Circulation: 250K. Sales: $20-50MM
Products: Healthcare products & home
medical equipment & supplies

MOUNTAIN HIGH EQUIPMENT & SUPPLY CO. (800) 468-8185
516 12th Ave.
Salt Lake City, UT 84103
E-Mail: sales@mtn-high.com
Website: www.mtn-high.com
Fax Ordering: (801) 561-2846
Catalog: Free. Frequency: Annual
Circulation: 50K. Sales: $3-5MM
Products: Custom carry on & built in
oxygen systems

MOUNTAIN NATURALS FROM VERMONT (800) 992-8451
20 New England Dr.
Essex Junction, VT 05453
E-Mail: catalog@mountainnaturals.com
Website: www.mountainnaturals.com
Fax Ordering: (800) 878-0549
International Ordering: (541) 741-7341
Catalog: Free. Frequency: Annual
Circulation: 100K. Sales: $3-5MM
Products: Human & pet vitamins & supplements

MOUNTAIN ROSE HERBS CATALOG (800) 879-3337
P.O. Box 50220 • Eugene, OR 97405
E-Mail: customerservice@mountainroseherbs.com
Website: www.mountainroseherbs.com
Fax Ordering: (510) 217-4012
International Ordering: (541) 741-7341
Catalog: Free. Frequency: Annual
Circulation: 100M. Sales: $1-3MM
Products: Organic herbal products,
including spices & teas; natural body care
products, essential oils & bulk ingredients

NATIONAL ALLERGY SUPPLY (800) 522-1448
1620-D Satellite Blvd. • Duluth, GA 30097
E-Mail: info@natlallergy.com
Website: www.natlallergy.com
Fax Ordering: (770) 623-5568
International Ordering: (770) 623-3237
Contact Name: Steve Hill, Marketing
Catalog: Free. Frequency: Weekly
Circulation: 100K. Sales: $10-20MM
Products: Non-drug allergy, asthma &
sinus relief products

NATIONAL CLEARINGHOUSE FOR (800) 729-6686
ALCOHOL & DRUG INFORMATION
P.O. Box 2345 • Rockville, MD 20847
E-Mail: info@health.org
Website: www.health.org
Fax Ordering: (301) 468-6433
International Ordering: (301) 468-2600
Catalog: Free. Frequency: Annual
Circulation: 100K. Sales: $3-5MM
Products: Audiotapes, videos, pamphlets,
posters and resources providing information
about drugs & alcohol abuse

NATIONAL SAFETY EQUIPMENT OUTLET (800) 443-0300
Old Springfield Rd. • Charlestown, NH 03603
Fax Ordering: (603) 628-6912
Contact Name: Helen Archer, President
Catalog: Free. Frequency: Semiannual
Circulation: 250K. Sales: $1-3MM
Products: Warning flashers, safety signs,
strobe lights, flashlights & other safety equiment

NATIONWIDE CATALOG (800) 237-3759
P.O. Box 309 • Delmont, PA 15626
Fax Ordering: (724) 325-2223
International Ordering: (724) 325-3100
Contact Name: Eileen Cox, Marketing Manager
Catalog: Free. Frequency: Bimonthly
Circulation: 75K. Sales: $500K
Products: Diet aids, herbal remedies,
vitamin supplements

NATURAL HEALTHCARE CATALOG (801) 489-1500
Natures Way Products
10 Mountain Springs Pkwy.
Springville, UT 84663
E-Mail: info@naturesway.com
Website: www.naturesway.com
Fax Ordering: (801) 489-1700
Catalog: Free. Frequency: Annual
Circulation: 250K. Sales: $3-5MM
Products: Natural herbs, oils & extracts,
herbal formulas; phytomedicines, vitamins,
minerals & special formulas, homeopathics;
specialty & diet products

NATURAL NUTRITION NEWS (800) 526-4240
Great Life Laboratories
P.O. Box 837 • Westfield, NJ 07091
E-Mail: greatlife@aol.com
Website: www.greatlife.com
Fax Ordering: (908) 233-6060
International Ordering: (908) 233-4788
Contact Name: Dr. Arnold J. Susser, President
Catalog: Free. Frequency: Bimonthly
Circulation: 150K. Sales: $3-5MM
Products: Special vitamin supplement for
mulas; healthcare products related to aging, allergies,
backaches, memory & concentration, macular
degeneration & othe eye problems, PMS, menopause

NATURE'S SUNSHINE PRODUCTS   (800) 223-8225
P.O. Box 19005 • Provo, UT 84603
E-Mail: info@naturessunshine.com
Website: www.naturessunshine.com
Fax Ordering: (801) 342-4305
International Ordering: (801) 342-4300
Contact Name: Daniel P. Howells, President
Catalog: Free. Frequency: Semiannual
Circulation: 1MM. Sales: $50-100MM
Products: Herbs, vitamins, nutritional
supplements, natural personal care products

NEW LIFE SYSTEMS   (800) 852-3082
2853 Hedberg Dr. • Minnetonka, MN 55305
E-Mail: sales@newlifesystems.com
Website: www.newlifesystems.com
Fax Ordering: (888) 717-7701 (952) 546-1040
International Ordering: (952) 546-4100
Contact Name: Allan Share, President
Catalog: Free. Frequency: Annual
Circulation: 50K. Sales: $1-3MM
Products: Spa, slon & massage products
& equipment

NUTRITION EXPRESS   (800) 338-7979
P.O. Box 4076 • Torrance, CA 90510
E-Mail: sales@nutritionexpress.com
Website: www.nutritionexpress.com
Fax Ordering: (310) 784-8522
International Ordering: (310) 784-8500
Catalog: Free. Frequency: Annual
Circulation: 100K. Sales: $3-5MM
Products: Vitamins & sports nutritional
supplements at discounted prices

OLEDA & CO. CATALOG   (800) 731-4247
7700 Camp Bowie West
Fort Worth, TX 76116
E-Mail: oleda@oleda.com
Website: www.oleda.com
Fax Ordering: (817) 731-1149
International Ordering: (817) 731-1147
Contact Name: Oleda Baker, President
Catalog: Free. Frequency: Annual
Circulation: 100K. Sales: $3-5MM
Products: Anti-aging skin, hair & health & beauty
products; vitamins & supplements; bath & spa,
perfume, weight loss, pain relief products

OPTP HEALTH CARE CATALOG   (800) 367-7393
P.O. Box 47009 • Minneapolis, MN 55447   (888) 819-0121
E-Mail: customerservice@optp.com
Website: www.optp.com
Fax Ordering: (763) 553-9355
International Ordering: (763) 553-0452
Contact Name: Shari Schroeder, President
Catalog: Free. Frequency: Weekly
Circulation: 20K. Sales: $500K - $1MM
Products: Orthopedic physical therapy products

ORJENE NATURAL COSMETICS   (800) 886-7536
5-43 48 Ave. • Long Island City, NY 11101
E-Mail: info@orjenenaturalcosmetics.com
Website: www.orjene.com
Fax Ordering: (718) 784-3793
International Ordering: (718) 937-2666
Contact Name: Dennis Machicao, President
Catalog: Free. Frequency: Semiannual
Circulation: 250K. Sales: $20-50MM
Products: Natural beauty and personal
care products

OTC CATALOG   (800) 548-3546
N.V.E. Pharmaceuticals
33 Newton Sparta Rd.
Newton, NJ 07860
E-Mail: stacker2@ptd.net
Website: www.stacker2.com
Fax Ordering: (973) 383-8379
International Ordering: (973) 383-5444
Contact Name: Robert Occhifinto, President
Catalog: Free. Frequency: Quarterly
Circulation: 500K. Sales: $20-50MM
Products: Diet aids & energy products;
stimulants, sleep aids

PAIN & STRESS CENTER PRODUCTS   (800) 669-2256
5282 Medical Dr. • San Antonio, TX 78229
E-Mail: psctr@painstresscenter.com
Website: www.painstresscenter.com
Fax Ordering: (210) 614-4336
International Ordering: (210) 614-7246
Contact Name: Billie J. Sahley, President
Catalog: $4. Frequency: Annual
Circulation: 50K. Sales: $500K
Products: Products for pain, stress, annxiety,
hyperactivity/ADD, amino acids/nutrient formulas

PARKSIDE PUBLISHING CORPORATION   (800) 221-6364
205 W. Touhy Ave. • Park Ridge, IL 60068
Fax Ordering: (888) 590-4082
International Ordering: (847) 698-8500
Contact Name: Jerry Seibert, President
Catalog: Free. Frequency: Quarterly
Circulation: 100K. Sales: $500K - $1MM
Products: Books, videos & recordings on
alcohol addiction

THE PARTHENON COMPANY   (800) 453-8898
3311 West 2400 South
Salt Lake City, UT 84119
E-Mail: info@parthenoninc.com
Website: www.parthenoninc.com
Fax Ordering: (801) 972-4734
International Ordering: (801) 972-5184
Catalog: Free. Frequency: Semiannual
Circulation: 50K. Sales: $10-20MM
Products: Specialty discounter of ostomy
supplies; footcare products, urological supplies,
nutritional products; skin care products.

PEDIFIX FOOTCARE PRODUCTS   (800) 733-4349
310 Guinea Rd. • Brewster, NY 10509
E-Mail: sales@pedifix.com
Website: www.pedifix.com
Fax Ordering: (845) 277-2851
Contact Name: Christopher B. Case, President
Catalog: Free. Frequency: 3x per year
Circulation: 100K. Sales: $10-20MM
Products: Footcare products to help relieve pain,
improve comfort, and make feet more attractive

POWER SHACK FITNESS PRODUCTS   (800) 359-4792
291 Covenant Square Dr.
Biloxi, MS 39531
E-Mail: tom@powershack.com
Website: www.powershack.com
Fax Ordering: (805) 965-0042
International Ordering: (805) 564-3064
Contact Name: Tom Banisch, President
Catalog: Free. Frequency: Monthly
Circulation: 100K. Sales: $1-3MM
Products: Health & fitness products

PRIORITIES CATALOG   (800) 606-9455
70 Walnut St. • Wellesley, MA 02481
E-Mail: getrelief@priorities.com
Website: www.priorities.com
Fax Ordering: (207) 748-0046
International Ordering: (207) 748-3013
Contact Name: Deborah Parish, President
Catalog: Free. Frequency: Bimonthly
Circulation: 100K. Sales: $5-10MM
Products: Allergy & asthma relief products ·

PRO HEALTH   (800) 366-6056
2040 Alameda Padre Serra, Suite101
Santa Barbara, CA 93103
E-Mail: sales@prohealthinc.com
Website: www.prohealthinc.com
Fax Ordering: (805) 965-0042
International Ordering: (805) 564-3064 ·
Contact Name: Rich Carson, President
Catalog: Free. Frequency: Monthly
Circulation: 100K. Sales: $5-10MM
Products: Nutritional supplements

PRO-MED PRODUCTS   (800) 542-9297
6445 Powers Ferry Rd. #199
Atlanta, GA 30339
E-Mail: info@promedproducts.com
Website: www.promedproducts.com
Fax Ordering: (770) 951-2786
Catalog: Free. Frequency: Semiannual
Circulation: 150K. Sales: $5-10MM
Products: Products, equipment & supplies
for health care professionals

PURITANS PRIDE   (800) 645-1030
NBTY
P.O. Box 9001 • Oakdale, NY 11769
E-Mail: info@puritan.com
Website: www.puritan.com
Fax Ordering: (631) 471-5693
International Ordering: (631) 567-9500
Customer Service: (800) 645-9584
Contact Name: Harvey Kamil, President
Catalog: Free. Frequency: 6x per year
Circulation: 10MM. Sales: $20-50MM
Products: Discount health products, including
vitamins, minerals, herbs and cosmetics

PURITY PRODUCTS   (800) 718-2003
139 Haven Ave. • Port Washington, NY 11050   (800) 281-7781
E-Mail: sales@purityproducts.com
Website: www.purityproducts.com
Fax Ordering: (516) 767-1722
Customer Service: (888) 769-7873
Contact Name: Jahn Levin, President
Catalog: Free. Pages: 36. Frequency: Quarterly
Circulation: 250K. Sales: $5-10 MM
Products: Vitamins, specialty formulas

PYRAMID MEDIA   (800) 421-2304
P.O. Box 1048 • Santa Monica, CA 90406
E-Mail: info@pyramidmedia.com
Website: www.pyramidmedia.com
Fax Ordering: (310) 453-9083
International Ordering: (310) 828-7577
Contact Name: Denise Adams, Manager
Catalog: Free. Frequency: Semiannual
Circulation: 50K. Sales: $500K - $1MM
Products: Education, health, safety and
business films and videos

QUANTERRON   (952) 890-1940
11531 Rupp Dr. • Burnsville, MN 55337
Fax Ordering: (952) 890-0418
International Ordering: (541) 345-5556
Contact Name: Terry Noble, President
Catalog: Free. Frequency: Quarterly
Circulation: 100M. Sales: $20-50MM
Products: Pharmaceutical products

QUANTUM MEDICINE   (800) 448-1448
754 Washington St.
Eugene, OR 97401
E-Mail: sales@prohealthinc.com
Website: www.prohealthinc.com
Fax Ordering: (541) 345-9796
International Ordering: (541) 345-5556
Contact Name: David Shaw, President
Catalog: Free. Frequency: Semiannual
Circulation: 100M. Sales: $10-20MM
Products: Nutritional products & vitamins

REAL HEALTH LABORATORIES   (800) 565-6656
1185 Linda Vista Dr. • San Marcos, CA 92078
E-Mail: answers@realhealthlabs.com
Website: www.realhealthlabs.com
International Ordering: (619) 213-2200
Catalog: Online. Sales: $10-20MM
Products: Natural solutions to general health
concerns; nutritional products and vitamins

RELAX THE BACK   (800) 222-5728
17785 Center Court Dr. #250
Cerritos, CA 90703
E-Mail: customerservice@relaxtheback.com
Website: www.relaxtheback.com
Fax Ordering: (800) 218-1250
Contact Name: Dick Palfreyman, President
Catalog: Free. Frequency: Annual
Circulation: 100K. Sales: $10-20MM
Products: Fibromylagia treatment with
Ergonomic furniture; back supports, massage
chairs & products; exercise & therapy equipment;
mattresses & office chairs; recliners & sleep
accessories; books & videos

REVIVA LABS   (800) 257-7774
705 Hopkins Rd.
Haddonfield, NJ 08033
E-Mail: revivalabs@aol.com
Website: www.revivalabs.com
Fax Ordering: (856) 429-0767
International Ordering: (856) 428-3885
Contact Name: Stephen Strassler, President
Catalog: Free. Frequency: Annual
Circulation: 100K. Sales: $3-5MM
Products: Natural skin care products,
including cleansers, toners, moisturizers,
night creams, & beauty masks; aromatherapy
oils, acne and anti-aging products

REXALL SUNDOWN VITAMINS   (800) 738-8482
851 Broken Sound Pkwy NW
Boca Raton, FL 33487
Fax Ordering: (561) 995-6884
International Ordering: (561) 241-9400
Contact Name: Carl DeSantis, President
Catalog: Free. Frequency: Semiannual
Circulation: 500K. Sales: $5-10MM
Products: Nutritional supplements &
other related items

YVES ROCHER, INC. (888) 909-2887
P.O. Box 1701 • Champlain, NY 12919
E-Mail: customer_service@yvnet.com
Website: www.welcome2beauty.com
Fax Ordering: (800) 321-4909
Catalog: Free. Pages: 40. Frequency: Quarterly
Circulation: 200K. Sales: $5-10MM
Products: Beauty & cosmetics; skin care,
bath & body care, fragrance, makeup.

ROCK-N-RESCUE CATALOG (800) 346-7673
P.O. Box 213 • Valencia, PA 16059
E-Mail: info@rocknrescue.com
Website: www.rocknrescue.com
Fax Ordering: (724) 898-3139
International Ordering: (724) 898-2335
Contact Name: John Weinel, III, President
Catalog: Free. Frequency: Weekly
Circulation: 50K. Sales: $1-3MM
Products: Rescue equipment

SAFETY SHORTS (800) 458-2236
Safety Short Productions
950 Gemini, Suite 1
Houston, TX 77058
E-Mail: info@safetyshorts.com
Website: www.safetyshorts.com
Fax Ordering: (281) 956-1000
International Ordering: (281) 956-1028
Contact Name: J.L. Dunn, President
Catalog: Free. Frequency: Annual
Circulation: 50K. Sales: $1-3MM
Products: Safety, health & environmental
training products

SAMMONS PRESTON (800) 323-5547
4 Sammons Ct. • Bolingbrook, IL 60440
E-Mail: sp@sammonspreston.com
Website: www.sammonspreston.com
Fax Ordering: (800) 547-4333
International Ordering: (630) 226-1300
Contact Name: Edward Donnelly, President
Catalog: Free. Frequency: 3x per year
Circulation: 300M. Sales: $20-50MM
Products: Rehabilitation, fitness,
personal care, self-help products

SAN FRANCISCO HERB COMPANY (800) 227-4530
250 14th St. • San Francisco, CA 94103
E-Mail: customerservice@sfherb.com
Website: www.sfherb.com
Fax Ordering: (415) 861-4440
International Ordering: (415) 861-7174
Contact Name: Neil Hanscomb, President
Catalog: Free. Frequency: Semiannual
Circulation: 50K. Sales: $500K - $1MM
Products: Culinary herbs, spices & potpourri
ingredients, teas, extracts, essential oils

SELLSTROM MANUFACTURING CO. (800) 323-7402
One Sellstrom Dr. • Palatine, IL 60067
E-Mail: info@sellstrom.com
Website: www.sellstrom.com
Fax Ordering: (847) 358-8564
International Ordering: (847) 358-2000
Contact Name: David Peters, President
Catalog: Free. Frequency: Annual.
Circulation: 50K. Sales: $10-20MM
Products: Industrial products; safety products
for the home and workplace

SANDY'S INTIMATE APPAREL (800) 696-3547
1605 N. State Rd. 7 • Margate, FL 33063
E-Mail: sandysia@sandysintimateapparel.com
Website: www.sabdysboutique.com
Fax Ordering: (954) 978-9059
International Ordering: (954) 968-4410
Contact Name: F. Savino, President
Catalog: Free. Frequency: Annual
Circulation: 10K. Sales: $500K - $1MM
Products: Post mastectomy & specialty
products

SCHOOL HEALTH CORP. CATALOG (800) 323-1305
865 Muirfield Dr. • Hanover Park, IL 60133
E-Mail: info@schoolhealth.com
Website: www.schoolhealth.com
Fax Ordering: (800) 235-1305
Catalog: Free. Frequency: Semiannual
Circulation: 100K. Sales: $10-20MM
Products: Medicine & health supplies &
equipment/accessories for school nurse
facilities & athletic departments

SEARS HEALTH & WELLNESS CATALOG (800) 349-4358
Sears • 333 Beverly Rd.
Hoffman Estates, IL 60179
E-Mail: info@sears.com
Website: www.sears.com
Catalog: Free. Frequency: Semiannual
Circulation: 1MM. Sales: $50-100MM
Products: Healthcare aids & rehabilitation
supplies

SELF HEALING THROUGH (800) 528-2737
MIND BODY MEDICINE
Emmett Miller, MD
131 E. Placer St. • Auburn, CA 95603
E-Mail: drmiller@drmiller.com
Website: www.drmiller.com
Fax Ordering: (530) 478-0160
International Ordering: (530) 478-1807
Contact Name: Emmett Miller, MD, President
Catalog: Free. Frequency: Annual
Circulation:100K. Sales: $500M
Products: Self healing tapes, CD's, books
& training by Emmett Miller, MD

SKINSTORE.COM (888) 586-7546
11344 Coloma Rd., Suite 605
Gold River, CA 95670
E-Mail: sales@skinstore.com
Website: www.skinstore.com
Fax Ordering: (916) 475-1499
International Ordering: (916) 475-1464
Contact Name: Jim Steeb, President & CEO
Catalog: Free. Frequency: Monthly
Circulation: 300K. Pages: 24. Sales: $10-20MM
Products: The catalog contains hundreds of
skin care products and is arranged by brand
with useful beauty tips and regimen guides
throughout. Includes in-depth product description,
ingredient listings & articles written by renowned
physicians. The online store contains over
1,800 products.

SLEEP BUYERS CLUB (888) 236-7231
486 Totten Pond Rd. • Waltham, MA 02451
Website: www.sleepbuyersclub.com
E-Mail: info@sleepbuyersclub.com
Fax Ordering: (781) 890-3560

International Ordering: (781) 419-5500
Catalogs: Free. Frequency: Annual
Circulation: 100K. Sales: $3-5MM
Products: Sleep products & supplies

SOFT SURROUNDINGS (800) 749-7638
P.O. Box 4205 • Hazelwood, MO 63042
E-Mail: customerservice@softsurroundings.com
Website: www.softsurroundings.com
Customer Service: (800) 240-7076
Catalog: Free. Frequency: Quarterly
Circulation: 200K. Sales: $10-20MM
Products: Beauty products; bedding & bath
products; apparel & accessories

SPORTAID (800) 743-7203
78 Bay Creek Rd. • Loganville, GA 30052
E-Mail: info@sportaid.com
Website: www.sportaid.com
Fax Ordering: (770) 554-5944
International Ordering: (770) 554-5130
Contact Name: Stacy Green, Contact
Catalog: Free. Frequency: Semiannual
Circulation: 200K. Sales: $10-50MM
Products: Wheelchairs; wheelchair parts
& supplies

SPORTSMITH (888) 713-2880
5929 S. 118th E. Ave. • Tulsa, OK 74146
E-Mail: info@sportsmith.net
Website: www.sportsmith.com
Fax Ordering: (918) 307-0216
International Ordering: (918) 307-2446
Catalog: Free. Frequency: Semiannual
Circulation: 150K. Sales: $10-50MM
Products: Gym supplies & equipment;
fitness products

STANLEY HOME PRODUCTS (800) 628-9032
50 Payson Ave. • Easthampton, MA 01027
E-Mail: info@shponline.com
Website: www.shponline.com
Fax Ordering: (413) 527-5075
International Ordering: (413) 527-4001
Contact Name: Javier Paredes, President
Catalog: $1. Frequency: Quarterly
Circulation: 2MM. Sales: $20-50MM
Products: Personal care, wellness &
home care products

STRESS LESS (800) 555-3783
5790 Mountain Creek Dr. • Atlanta, GA 30328
E-Mail: customerservice@stressless.com
Website: www.stressless.com
Fax Ordering: (404) 303-0416
International Ordering: (404) 303-0002
Contact Name: Grey Moore, Marketing Manager
Catalog: Free. Frequency: Quarterly
Circulation: 100K. Sales: $1-3MM
Products: Products and equipment for stress
relief; stress education courses, books, videos,
and music

STRESS & WELLNESS RESOURCES (800) 247-6789
Whole Person Associates
210 W. Michigan St. • Duluth, MN 55802
E-Mail: books@wholeperson.com
Website: www.wholeperson.com
Fax Ordering: (218) 727-0505
International Ordering: (218) 727-0500
Contact Name: Carlene Sippola, President
Catalog: Free. Frequency: Monthly

Circulation: 300K. Sales: $500M to $1MM
Products: Publishes stress-management
and wellness-promotion training & self-care
resources

SUNBURST BIORGANICS (800) 645-8448
832 Merrick Rd. • Baldwin, NY 11510
E-Mail: sales@vitasaver.com
Website: www.vitasaver.com
Fax Ordering: (516) 623-2413
International Ordering: (516) 623-8478
Contact Name: Andrew Reminick, President
Catalog: Free. Frequency: Quarterly
Circulation: 500K. Sales: $1-3MM
Products: Vitamins, minerals, health & diet
aids at discounted prices

SUNCO TANNING BEDS (800) 382-8932
876 Holliston Mills Rd.
Church Hill, TN 37642
E-Mail: email@suncotanning.com
Website: www.suncotanning.com
Fax Ordering: (423) 357-9837
International Ordering: (423) 357-0680
Catalog: Free. Frequency: Annual
Circulation: 100K. Sales: $5-10MM
Products: Tanning beds, supplies & accessories

SUNFEATHER NATURAL SOAP CO. (315) 265-3648
1551 State Hwy. 72 • Potsdam, NY 13676
E-Mail: sandy@sunsoap.com
Website: www.sunsoap.com
Fax Ordering: (315) 265-2902
Contact Name: Sandy Maine, President
Catalog: $2. Frequency: Annual
Circulation: 25K. Sales: $1-3MM
Products: Soap and soap making supplies

SUNRISE LANE PRODUCTS (212) 243-4745
780 Greenwich St. • New York, NY 10014
Contact Name: Rossella Mocerino, President
Catalog: Free. Frequency: Annual.
Circulation: 50K. Sales: $300M
Products: Environmentally safe and cruelty-free
products for home and personal care

SUPPORT PLUS (800) 229-2910
Surgical Products Company
P.O. Box 500 • Medfield, MA 02052
E-Mail: edjanos@aol.com
Fax Ordering: (508) 359-0139
International Ordering: (508) 359-2910
Contact Name: Edward H. Janos, President
Catalog: Free. Frequency: 10x per year
Circulation: 2MM. Sales: $10-20MM
Products: Medical hosiery, comfort shoes
and aids

TANNING EQUIPMENT (800) 553-9590
ETS, Inc. (800) 228-6292
6270 Corporate Dr. (800) 449-3605
Indianapolis, IN 46278
E-Mail: info@etstan.com
Website: www.etstan.com
Fax Ordering: (800) 358-7947; 461-7583
International Ordering: (317) 290-8982
  Fax (317) 290-1086
Contact Name: Trevor Gary, President
Catalog: Free. Frequency: Semiannual
Circulation: 100K. Sales: $50-100MM
Products: Tanning equipment, lotions, apparel
& accessories; tanning beds & supplies

THERAPRO CATALOG (800) 257-5376
225 Arlington St. • Framingham, MA 01702
E-Mail: info@theraproducts.com
Website: www.theraproducts.com
Fax Ordering: (800) 268-6624; (508) 266-6110
International Ordering: (508) 872-9494
Contact Name: Karen Conrad &
  Paul Weihrauch, Owners
Catalog: Free. Frequency: Semiannual
Circulation: 200K. Sales: $5-10MM
Products: Occupational, speech & physical
therapy supplies for families, educators &
professionals.

TIAN MING CATALOG OF (888) 219-2221
NATURAL HEALTH PRODUCTS
Tian Ming Herb Company
P.O. Box 244 • Whitehall, PA 18052
E-Mail: info@tianmingco.com
Website: www.tianmingco.com
Fax Ordering: (610) 266-6110
Contact Name: David Molony, PhD, President
Catalog: Free. Frequency: Annual
Circulation: 50M. Sales: $500M
Products: Books, videos, audiotapes,
herbs supplements; herb tea formulas

TOM'S OF MAINE CATALOG (800) 367-8667
P.O. Box 710 • Kennebunk, ME 04043
E-Mail: info@tomsofmaine.com
Website: www.tomsofmaine.com
Fax Ordering: (207) 985-5656
Catalog: Free. Frequency: Semiannial
Circulation: 200K. Sales: $3-5MM
Products: Natural cosmetics; wellness
products; dental; other products that do
not contain artifical preservatives, flavors,
colors, sweeteners, animal ingredients

TOOLS FOR WELLNESS (800) 456-9887
8943-B Oso Ave. • Chatsworth, CA 91311
E-Mail: info@toolsforwellness.com
Website: www.toolsforwellness.com
Fax Ordering: (818) 407-0850
International Ordering: (818) 885-9090
Catalog: Free. Frequency: Semiannual
Circulation: 150K. Sales: $1-3MM
Products: Natural & alternative therapy products,
brain & mind healing products, and biofeedback
tools for helping to improve your health

TOTAL NUTRITION (800) 645-4446
75 Bi-County Blvd. • Farmingdale, NY 11735
Fax Ordering: (631) 694-9799
International Ordering: (631) 694-9777
Contact Name: Jay Silverman, President
Catalog: Free. Frequency: Bimonthly
Circulation: 100M. Sales: $5-10MM
Products: Vitamins & minerals

U.S. HEALTH CLUB (800) 431-2186
400 Warburton Ave.
Hastings-on-Hudson, NY 10706
E-Mail: team@ushc.net
Website: www.ushc.net
Fax Ordering: (914) 478-5017
International Ordering: (914) 478-2505
Customer Service: (888) 874-2462
Contact Name: Kenneth L. Okin, President
Catalog: Free. Frequency: Semiannual
Circulation: 100M. Sales: $1-3MM
Products: Vitamins and health aids

USEFUL GUIDE TO HERBAL HEALTH CARE (941) 643-6563
Health Center for Better Living
1414 Rosemary Lane • Naples, FL 34103
E-Mail: sales@hcbl.com
Website: www.hcbl.com
Fax Ordering: (941) 643-6335
International Ordering: (941) 643-6563
Catalog: Free. Frequency: Quarterly
Circulation: 10K. Sales: $500K - $1MM
Products: Variety of herbs in many forms
for health care uses

ELIZABETH VAN BUREN AROMATHERAPY (800) 710-7759
303 Potrero St. • Santa Cruz, CA 95060
E-Mail: sales@evb-aromatherapy.com
Website: www.evb-aromatherapy.com
Fax Ordering: (831) 425-8258
International Ordering: (831) 425-8218
Contact Name: Elizabeth Jones, President
Catalog: Free. Frequency: Semiannual
Circulation: 25K. Sales: $1-3MM
Products: Aromatherapy essential oils
and blends

VALLEY NATURALS.COM (866) 373-2175
1118 Pony Express Hwy.
Marysville, KS 66508
E-Mail: service@valleynaturals.com
Website: www.valleynaturals.com
Fax Ordering: (866) 373-2112
Catalog: Online. Sales: $5-10MM
Products: Discount priced vitamins &
nutritional supplements; natural beauty
& personal care products.

VEGETARIAN & HEALTH CATALOG (800) 695-2241
The Book Publishing Co.
P.O. Box 180
Summertown, TN 38483
E-Mail: askus@healthy-eating.com
Website: www.healthy-eating.com
Fax Ordering: (931) 964-2291
International Ordering: (931) 964-2241
Contact Names: Cynthia Holzapfel, President
Catalog: Free. Frequency: Semiannual
Circulation: 50K. Sales: $500K
Products: Quick-cooking meat substitutes
& soyfoods, vegetarian products & books

VITAL SIGNS (608) 735-4718
Country Technology
P.O. Box 87
Gays Mills, WI 54631
E-Mail: etech@mwt.net
Website: www.fitnessmart.com
Fax Ordering: (608) 735-4859
Contact Name: S. Peterson, President
Catalog: Free. Frequency: 8x per year
Circulation: 250M. Sales: $3-5MM
Products: Sports/fitness & rehabilitation
and conditioning equipment

VITAMIN FACTORY (800) 619-1199
P.O. Box 278 • Hillside, NJ 07205
E-Mail: sales@vitafac.com
Website: www.vitafac.com
Fax Ordering: (973) 923-9661
Contact Name: Seymour Flug, President
Catalog: Free. Frequency: Semiannual
Circulation: 100M. Sales: $500M to $1MM
Products: Vitamins, minerals, herbs, &
nutritional supplements

VITAMIN RESEARCH PRODUCTS (800) 877-2447
579 U.S. Hwy. 50 E • Carson City, NV 89701
E-Mail: mail@vrp.com
Website: www.vrp.com
Fax Ordering: (800) 877-3292; (775) 884-1331
International Ordering: (775) 884-1300
Contact Name: Robert Watson, President
Catalog: Free. Frequency: Semiannual
Circulation: 100K. Sales: $5-10MM
Products: Anti-aging nutritional supplements
by Ward Dean, MD

VITAMIN SHOPPE (800) 223-1216
4700 Westside Ave.
North Bergen, NJ 07047
E-Mail: sales@vitaminshoppe.com
Website: www.vitaminshoppe.com
Fax Ordering: (800) 852-7153; (201) 866-9513
International Ordering: (201) 866-7711
Contact Name: Jeff Howard, President
Catalog: Free. Frequency: Quarterly
Circulation: 100K. Sales: $5-10MM
Products: Vitamins & supplements;
herbal & homeopathic products; sports
nutrition products; beauty, health &
personal care products

VITAMIN TRADER (800) 334-9310
211 Montano Rd. NW
Albuquerque, NM 87107
E-Mail: vitrader@swcp.com
Website: www.vitamintrader.com
Fax Ordering: (505) 345-7146
International Ordering: (505) 344-6060
Contact Name: Bryan Flamm, President
Catalog: Free. Frequency: Semiannual
Circulation: 75K. Sales: $3-5MM
Products: Nutritional supplements

VITAMINS.COM (800) 221-1152
3233 47th Ave.
Long Island City, NY 11101
E-Mail: sales@vitamins.com
Website: www.vitamins.com
Fax Ordering: (718) 361-1437
International Ordering: (805) 564-3064
Contact Name: Karen Kaplan, Manager
Catalog: Free. Frequency: Semiannual
Circulation: 100K. Sales: $5-10MM
Products: Nutritional supplements &
self-treatment products

WATERWISE CATALOG (800) 874-9028
3608 Parkway Blvd.
Leesburg, FL 34748
E-Mail: info@waterwise.com
Website: www.waterwise.com
Fax Ordering: (866) 329-8123; (352) 787-8123
International Ordering: (352) 787-5008
Contact Name: Jack Barber, President
Catalog: Free. Pages: 36. Frequency: Weekly
Circulation: 100K. Sales: $5-10MM
Products: Drinking water purifiers, distillers,
and filterless air purifiers.

WELEDA (800) 289-1969
P.O. Box 249 • Congers, NY 10920
E-Mail: sales@weleda.com
Website: www.weleda.com
Fax Ordering: (800) 280-4899
International Ordering: (845) 268-8572
Catalog: Free. Frequency: Semiannual

Circulation: 100M. Sales: $5-10MM
Products: Natural personal care products

WESTERN NATURAL PRODUCTS (800) 926-7455
5242 Bolsa Ave.
Huntington Beach, CA 92649
E-Mail: placata@prodigy.net
Fax Ordering: (714) 897-5677
International Ordering: (714) 893-0017
Contact Name: Paul Lacata, President
Catalog: Free. Frequency: Annual
Circulation: 100K. Sales: $1-3MM
Products: Natural vitamins and food
supplements

WESTERN VITAMINS & HEALTH PRODUCTS (800) 777-9847
2525 Davie Rd. • Davie, FL 33317
Fax Ordering: (618) 529-4553
International Ordering: (954) 474-9088
Contact Name: Bob White, President
Catalog: $1. Frequency: Monthly
Circulation: 100M. Sales: $5-10MM
Products: Vitamins; diet, skin care &
specialty health products

WHAT'S NEW FOR HOME & AUTO (800) 525-8624
Progressive Energy Corporation
650 Corte Raquel • San Marcos, CA 92069
E-Mail: pkilleen@pec.win.net
Fax Ordering: (760) 727-0947
International Ordering: (760) 727-2906
Contact Name: Patrick Killeen, President
Catalog: Free. Frequency: 5x per year
Circulation: 150K. Sales: $5-10MM
Products: Auto accessories & home security

WHOLE LIFE PRODUCTS (800) 634-9057
Pacific Spirit Corporation
1334 Pacific Ave. • Forest Grove, OR 97116
E-Mail: sales@mystictrader.com
Website: www.mystictrader.com
Fax Ordering: (503) 357-1669
International Ordering: (503) 357-1566
Contact Name: Joseph Meyer, President
Catalog: $1. Frequency: Bimonthly
Circulation: 2.MM. Sales: $5-10MM
Products: Alternative health, holistic,
herbal products, massage tools and
yoga products; books, tapes, videos,
sound tools.

WILLIAMS DISTRIBUTORS (262) 597-9865
1801 S. Cardinal Lane
New Berlin, WI 53151
Contact Name: G.L. Williams, President
Catalog: Free. Frequency: 3x per year
Circulation: 100K. Sales: $500K
Products: All natural products; nutrition,
health, home care and personal care;
water purification systems

WILLNER CHEMISTS (800) 633-1106
100 Park Ave. • New York, NY 10017
E-Mail: custserv@willner.com
Website: www.willner.com
Fax Ordering: (212) 682-6192
International Ordering: (212) 682-2817
Contact Name: Len Goldstein, General Manager
Catalog: Free. Frequency: Semiannual
Credit Cards: All. Sales: $5-10MM
Products: Nutritional supplements

WILSON OPHTHALMIC   (800) 222-2020
P.O. Box 496 • Mustang, OK 73064
E-Mail: info@wilsonophthalmic.com
Website: www.wilsonophthalmic.com
Fax Ordering: (800) FAX-9133
International Ordering: (405) 376-9114
Catalog: Free. Frequency: Semiannual
Circulation: 50K. Sales: $1-3MM
Products: Vision products

WONDER LABORATORIES   (800) 992-1672
P.O. Box 820 • White House, TN 37188
E-Mail: wonder@wonderlabs.com
Website: www.wonderlabs.com
Fax Ordering: (877) 992-0820
International Ordering: (615) 672-4989
Contact Name: Harry Hester, President
Catalog: Free. Frequency: Annual
Circulation: 150M. Sales: $500M to $1MM
Products: Generic health care products,
including vitamins, herbs, homeopathic
and pharmacy items

THE WRIGHT STUFF   (877) 750-0376
135 Floyd G. Harrell Dr.
Grenada, MS 38901
E-Mail: info@thewright-stuff.com
Website: www.thewright-stuff.com
Fax Ordering: (662) 294-1445
International Ordering: (662) 294-1444
Contact Name: Amy Wright, President
Catalog: Free. Frequency: Annual
Circulation: 150M. Sales: $1-3MM
Products: Home health care products &
adaptive equipment for independence.
Arthritis & caregiver products; rehabilitation
products

WYSONG PRODUCTS   (800) 748-0188
FOR THINKING PEOPLE
Wysong Corporation
1880 N. Eastman Rd.
Midland, MI 48642
E-Mail: wysong@tm.net
Website: www.wysong.net
Fax Ordering: (989) 631-8801
International Ordering: (989) 631-0009
Contact Name: R.L. Wysong, President
Catalog: Free. Frequency: Monthly
Circulation: 100K. Sales: $5-10MM
Products: Natural health foods and
supplements for people and pets

XPEDITIMS IN TANNING   (800) 331-6678
MOST Products
326 Wikalamazoo Ave.
Kalamazoo, MI 49006
E-Mail: most@mostinc.com
Website: www.mostinc.com
Fax Ordering: (616) 381-1820
International Ordering: (616) 381-6678
Contact Name: David Thomasma, President
Catalog: Free. Frequency: Semiannual
Circulation: 100K. Sales: $1-3MM
Products: Tanning products, lotions,
oils, cream and body care

YATES & BIRD CATALOG   (800) 662-5021
300 N. Elizabeth St.
Chicago, IL 60607
E-Mail: sales@yates-motiold.com
Website: www.yates-motiold.com
Fax Ordering: (312) 226-2480
International Ordering: (312) 226-2473
Contact Name: Mona Zemsky, Manager
Catalog: Free. Frequency: Annual
Circulation: 100K. Sales: $500K - $1MM
Products: Dental products

YOUCAN TOOCAN   (888) 663-9396
2223 S. Monaco Pkwy.
Denver, CO 80222
E-Mail: sales@youcantoocan.com
Website: www.youcantoocan.com
International Ordering: (303) 759-9525
Contact Name: Martha Hansen, President
Catalog: Free. Frequency: Annual
Circulation: 100K. Sales: $500K - $1MM
Products: Home health products: mobility
products, cooking aids, exercise products,
low vision & hearing, bathroom safety,
incontinence products,

PAULA YOUNG   (800) 343-9695
P.O. Box 246 • South Easton, MA 02375
E-Mail: customerservice@paulayoung.com
Website: www.paulayoung.com
Customer Service: (800) 472-4017
Catalog: Free. Frequency: Semiannual
Circulation: 150K. Sales: $3-5MM
Products: Wigs, hair pieces, falls &
headbands, apparel & accessories

ZIA NATURAL SKINCARE   (800) 334-7546
1337 Evans Ave.
San Francisco, CA 94124
E-Mail: sales@zianatural.com
Website: www.zianatural.com
Fax Ordering: (415) 641-2437
International Ordering: (415) 642-8339
Contact Name: Dawn Gonzales, Manager
Catalog: Free. Frequency: Annual
Circulation: 100K. Sales: $1-3MM
Products: Natural cosmetics and skincare products

A2Z CORP. MODEL AIRPLANE CATALOG   (877) 754-7465
1530 W. Tufts Ave. Unit B
Englewood, CO 80110
E-Mail: info@a2zcorp.us
Website: www.a2zcorp.us
Fax Ordering: (619) 448-1833
International Ordering: (619) 448-1818
Catalog: $4. Frequency: Semiannual
Circulation: 50K. Sales: $500M to $1MM
Products: Peck-Polymers model airplane
kits & supplies

AIRCRAFT FREEBIE   (785) 625-6346
RANS • 4600 Hwy. 183 Alt.
Hays, KS 67601
E-mail: rans@rans.com
Website: www.rans.com
Fax Ordering: (785) 625-2795
Contact Names: Randy Schlitter, President
Catalog: Free. Frequency: Bimonthly
Circulation: 25K. Sales: $1-3MM
Products: Sport aircraft kits & aircraft parts

DAVID T. ALEXANDER COLLECTIBLES   (813) 968-1805
P.O. Box 273086 • Tampa, FL 33688
E-Mail: davidt@cultureandthrills.com
Website: www.cultureandthrills.com
Fax Ordering: (813) 264-6226
Contact Name: David Alexander, President
Catalog: Free. Frequency: 3x per year
Circulation: 25K. Sales: $500K
Products: Comic books from 1933 to 1990

ALLEN'S COLLECTOR WHOLESALER   (800) 848-3966
399 S. State St. • Westerville, OH 43081
E-Mail: info@allensinc.com
Website: www.allensinc.com
Fax Ordering: (614) 882-0662
International Ordering: (614) 882-3937
Catalog: Free. Frequency: Quarterly
Circulation: 25K. Sales: $500K
Products: Collectibles & gifts; coins, currency,
plates, figurines, jewelry, ornaments, supplies

AMERICAN COIN & STAMP BROKERAGE   (800) 682-2272
30 Merrick Ave. • Merrick, NY 11566
E-Mail: pricelist@acsb.com
Website: www.acsb.com
Fax Ordering: (516) 546-2315
International Ordering: (516) 546-2300
Contact Name: Richard Cincotta, President
Catalog: Free. Frequency: Monthly
Circulation: 200K. Sales: $500K - $1MM
Products: U.S. & foreign coins, stamps &
baseball cards

AMERICAN MARINE MODEL GALLERY   (978) 745-5777
P.O. Box 6102 • Gloucester, MA 01930
E-Mail: wall@shipmodel.com
Website: www.shipmodel.com
Fax Ordering: (978) 281-2166
International Ordering: (978) 281-1166
Contact Names: R. Michael Wall, President
Catalog: $10. Frequency: Annual
Circulation: 10K. Sales: $500K to $1MM
Products: Catalogs: Kites, flags, banners
& windsocks

ATLAS MODEL RAILROAD COMPANY   (800) 872-2521
378 Florence Ave. • Hillside, NJ 07205
E-Mail: dawn@atlasrr.com
Website: www.atlasmodelrailroad.com

Fax Ordering: (908) 851-2550
International Ordering: (908) 687-0880
Catalog: Free. Frequency: Annual
Circulation: 100K. Sales: $5-10MM
Products: Model trains & supplies

AUTHENTIC MODELS, INC.   (800) 888-1992
P.O. Box 21710 • Eugene, OR 97402
E-Mail: sales@authenticmodels.com
Website: www.authenticmodels.com
Fax Ordering: (541) 686-5111
International Ordering: (541) 686-4666
Catalog: Free. Frequency: Semiannual
Circulation: 100K. Sales: $5-10MM
Products: Nautical replicas

BARON/BARCLAY BRIDGE SUPPLY   (800) 274-2221
3600 Chamberlain Ln. • Louisville, KY 40241
E-Mail: baronbarclay@baronbarclay.com
Website: www.baronbarclay.com
Fax Ordering: (502) 426-2044
International Ordering: (502) 426-0410
Contact Name: Randall Baron, President
Catalog: Free. Frequency: Semiannual
Circulation: 200K. Sales: $1-3MM
Products: Bridge supplies & books

BEER & WINE HOBBY   (800) 523-5423
155 New Boston St. - Unit T
Woburn, MA 01801
E-Mail: shop@beer-wine.com
Website: www.beer-wine.com
Fax Ordering: (781) 933-1359
International Ordering: (781) 933-8818
Contact Name: Karin Baker, President
Catalog: Free. Frequency: Annual
Circulation: 50K. Sales: $250-500K
Products: Home beer & winemaking
supplies

BERYL'S CAKE DECORATING   (800) 488-2749
& PASTRY SUPPLIES
P.O. Box 1584 • N. Springfield, VA 22151
E-Mail: beryls@beryls.com
Website: www.beryls.com
Fax Ordering: (703) 750-3779
International Ordering: (703) 256-6951
Contact Name: Beryl Loveland, President
Catalog: $8. Pages: 350. Frequency: Weekly
Circulation: 5K. Sales: $250-500K
Products: Cutters, equipment, books &
videos on cake decorating

CAMPBELL TOOLS COMPANY   (800) 878-8562
125 N. Tecumseh Rd.
Springfield, OH 45504
E-Mail: campbell@campbelltools.com
Website: www.campbelltools.com
Fax Ordering: (937) 882-6648
International Ordering: (937) 882-6716
Contact Name: Leo Foster, President
Catalog: Free. Frequency: Annual
Circulation: 25K. Sales: $500K to $1MM
Products: Lathes, mills, metals, steam
engine kits, books, videos & precision
instruments for hobbyists & industrial use

CASTOLITE   (815) 338-4670
4915 Dean St. • Woodstock, IL 60098
E-Mail: castolite@foxvalley.net
Website: www.castolite.com
Fax Ordering: (815) 338-4661

Contact Names: John Kunzie, President
Catalog: $3. Frequency: 36x per year
Circulation: 50K. Sales: $500K to $1MM
Products: Liquid plastics & fiberglass; mold making and plastic casting supplies for making models, prototypes and clear castings for embedments

THE CELLAR HOMEBREW   (800) 342-1871
14320 Greenwood Ave. N.
Seattle, WA 98133
E-Mail: staff@cellar-homebrew.com
Website: www.cellar-homebrew.com
Fax Ordering: (206) 365-7677
International Ordering: (206) 365-7660
Contact Name: Joe Marleau, President
Catalog: Free. Frequency: Semiannual
Circulation: 25K. Sales: $500K to $1MM
Products: Brewing & winemaking supplies

COINS & STAMPS FOR COLLECTORS   (818) 997-6496
Bick International
P.O. Box 854 • Van Nuys, CA 91408
E-Mail: libick@sbcglobal.net
Website: www.bick.net
Fax Ordering: (818) 988-4337
Contact Name: Israel I. Bick, President
Catalog: Free; $2 Int'l. Frequency: Annual
Circulation: 25K. Sales: $500K to $1MM
Products: Sponsors coin, currency & stamp expos in California, Arizona & Nevada

COLE'S POWER MODELS   (409) 547-3400
P.O. Box 623 • Warren, TX 77664
E-Mail: info@colespowermodels.com
Website: www.colespowermodels.com
Fax Ordering: (409) 547-3444
Contact Names: Betty Cole, President
Catalog: Free. Frequency: Annual
Circulation: 25K. Sales: $250-500K
Products: Authentic steam engines & scale model castings; engine casting kits; books

THE COLLECTIBLE STAMPS GALLERY   (303) 261-2350
P.O. Box 1115 • Longmont, CO 80502
E-Mail: service@collectiblestampsgallery.com
Website: www.collectiblestampsgallery.com
Fax Ordering: (409) 547-3444
Contact Names: Betty Cole, President
Catalog: Free. Frequency: Annual
Circulation: 25K. Sales: $3-5MM
Products: Stamp collectibles

COLOSSEUM COIN EXCHANGE   (732) 264-1161
P.O. Box 21 • Hazlet, NJ 07730
E-Mail: cceinc@verizon.net
Website: www.colocoinex.com
Fax Ordering: (732) 264-6467
Catalog: Free. Frequency: Quarterly
Circulation: 25K. Sales: $250-500K
Products: Ancient & world numismatics, 18-20th century antiques

THE COMPLETE WINEMAKER   (707) 963-9681
955 Vintage Ave.
Saint Helena, CA 94574
E-Mail: info@tcw-web.com
Website: www.tcw-web.com
Fax Ordering: (707) 963-7739
Contact Name: Curtis Caviness, President
Catalog: Free. Frequency: Annual
Circulation: 10K. Sales: 500K - $1MM

Products: Winemaking supplies; bottling, conveyors, crush/destemmers, filters, fittings, hose & tubing, test & measure, labelers

CON-COR   (888) 255-7688
8101 E. Research Ct. • Tucson, AZ 85710   (888) 255-7826
E-Mail: concor@con-cor.com
Website: www.con-cor.com
Fax Ordering: (520) 721-8940
International Ordering: (520) 721-8939
Contact Names: James M. Conway, President
Catalog: Free. Frequency: Quarterly
Circulation: 150K. Sales: $3-5MM
Products: Model trains, buildings, dioramas &railroad memorabilia

CRAFT HOUSE CATALOG   (800) 628-1910
Chartpak, Inc.
One River Rd. • Leeds, MA 01053
E-Mail: info@crafthouse.net; info@chartpak.com
Website: www.crafthouse.net; www.chartpak.com
Fax Ordering: (413) 584-6781
Catalog: Free. Frequency: Semiannual
Circulation: 100K. Sales: $1-3MM
Products: Hobby & craft items for kids; Paint-by-Numbers, Pencil-by-Number; Sun Catcher product line; Kreative Kids products; Snap Art

CUSTOM AQUATIC   (800) 397-7238
P.O. Box 2588 • Carlsbad, CA 92008
E-Mail: info@customaquatic.com
Website: www.customaquatic.com
Fax Ordering: (877) 647-FISH; (760) 277-6760
International Ordering: (760) 277-6128
Customer Service: (760) 599-6838
Catalog: Free. Frequency: Semiannual
Circulation: 100K. Sales: $3-5MM
Products: Aquarium hobby setups

DISCOUNT PLASTIC MODELS   (800) 233-0872
Hobby Surplus
P.O. Box 2170 • New Britain, CT 06050
E-Mail: info@discountplasticmodels.com
Website: www.discountplasticmodels.com
Fax Ordering: (860) 225-5316
International Ordering: (860) 223-0600
Contact Names: Vincent Amato, President
Catalog: Free. Frequency: Semiannual
Circulation: 150K. Sales: $3-5MM
Products: Plastic model kits of all types; trains, plastic & wooden models, rockets, slotcars, radio control. big bang cannons

DISCOUNT TRAINS ONLINE   (877) 529-2834
Go Hobbies, Inc.
231 E. Alessandro Blvd., Suite A-299
Riverside, CA 92508
E-Mail: service@gohobbies.com
Website: www.discounttrainsonline.com
Fax Ordering: (215) 634-2122
Contact Names: Paul Bowman, Marketing
Catalog: Online. Sales: $5-10MM
Products: Model trains, cars, airplanes & toys

DUCKS, DUCKS & MORE DUCKS   (800) 782-6770
Brookman Stamp Co. /Michael Jaffe Stamps
P.O. Box 90 • Vancouver, WA 98666
E-Mail: mjaffe@brookmanstamps.com
Website: www.brookmanstamps.com
Fax Ordering: (360) 695-1616
International Ordering: (360) 695-1391

Contact Names: Michael Jaffe, President
Catalog: Free. Frequency: Bimonthly
Circulation: 100K. Sales: $1-3MM
Products: Federal & state duck stamps & prints

DUMAS PRODUCTS   (800) 458-2828
909 E. 17th St. • Tucson, AZ 85719
E-Mail: dumasinc@dumasproducts.com
Website: www.dumasproducts.com
Fax Ordering: (520) 620-1329
International Ordering: (520) 623-4900
Contact Names: Robert Brandon, President
Catalog: Free. Frequency: Monthly
Circulation: 25K. Sales: $3-5MM
Products: Model boats and kits

DUNCRAFT-BIRDFEEDING AT ITS BEST   (888) 879-5095
102 Fisherville Rd. • Concord, NH 03303
E-Mail: info@duncraft.com
Website: www.duncraft.com
International Ordering: (603) 224-3522
Contact Names: Shelby Dunn Kimball, Manager
Catalog: Free. Frequency: Quarterly
Circulation: 25K. Sales: $3-5MM
Products: Bird feeders, bird houses,
bird seeds & foods, bird baths; solar
products & accessories

EARL P.L. APFELBAUM, INC.   (800) 523-4648
261 Old York Rd. #831
Jenkintown, PA 19046
E-Mail: info@apfelbauminc.com
Website: www.apfelbauminc.com
Fax Ordering: (267) 763-0227
International Ordering: (267) 763-0216
Contact Names: Diane Apfelbaum, President
Catalog: Free. Frequency: Monthly
Circulation: 25K. Sales: $3-5MM
Products: Stamps for collectors

FLAX ART & DESIGN CATALOG   (415) 552-2355
1699 Market St.
San Francisco, CA 94103
E-Mail: sales@flaxart.com
Website: www.flaxart.com
Contact Name: Philip Flax, President
Catalog: Free. Frequency: Weekly
Circulation: 50K. Sales: $10-20MM
Products: Art supplies, crafts; hobby
kits; albums, journals, gifts

GARDENING WITH KIDS   (800) 538-7476
National Gardening Association
1100 Dorset St. • South Burlington, VT 05403
E-Mail: sarahp@kidsgardening.org
Website: www.kidsgardening.org
Fax Ordering: (802) 864-6889
Catalog: Free. Frequency: Semiannual
Circulation: 100K. Sales: $1-3MM
Products: Gardening tools for kids

HARD TO FIND COINS   (800) 645-3122
Littleton Coin Company
1309 Mt. Eustis Rd. • Littleton, NH 03561
E-Mail: info@littletoncoin.com
Website: www.littletoncoin.com
Fax Ordering: (603) 444-0121
International Ordering: (603) 444-0625
Contact Name: David Sundman, President
Catalog: Free. Frequency: Quarterly
Circulation: 250K. Sales: $10-20M
Products: Coins & stamps

HERITAGE AUCTION, INC.   (800) 872-6467
Heritage Capital Corporation
3500 Maple Ave. 35th Fl. • Dallas, TX 75219
E-Mail: info@ha.com
Website: www.ha.com
Fax Ordering: (214) 520-6968
International Ordering: (214) 528-3500
Contact Name: James Halperin, President
Catalog: Free. Frequency: Annual
Circulation: 25K. Sales: $1-3MM
Products: Coins & collectibles

HOBBY BUILDER'S SUPPLY   (800) 926-6464
Benamy International, Inc.
2388 Pleasantdale Rd. • Atlanta, GA 30340
E-Mail: info@miniatures.com
Website: www.miniatures.com
Fax Ordering: (770) 242-1497
International Ordering: (770) 242-1498
Customer Service: (800) 223-7171
Contact Names: Ernie Collier, President
Catalog: Free. Frequency: Annual
Circulation: 100K. Sales: $3-5MM
Products: Discount dollhouses; miniatures,
home accessories

HOBBY SURPLUS   (800) 233-0872
Connecticut Hobby Craft Distribution
P.O. Box 2170 • New Britain, CT 06050
E-Mail: info@hobbysurplus.com
Website: www.hobbysurplus.com
Fax Ordering: (860) 225-5316
International Ordering: (860) 223-0600
Contact Names: Vincent Amato, President
Catalog: Free. Frequency: Semiannual
Circulation: 150K. Sales: $3-5MM
Products: Model railroading and general
hobby supplies; trains of all scales, wooden
& plastic models, slot racing; train repair parts

INTERNATIONAL COINS & CURRENCY   (800) 451-4463
62 Ridge St. • Montpelier, VT 05602
E-Mail: info@iccoin.com
Website: www.iccoin.com
Fax Ordering: (800) 229-3239; (802) 229-4933
International Ordering: (802) 888-5683
Contact Name: Michael Boardman, President
Catalog: Free. Frequency: Monthly
Circulation: 100K. Sales: $3-5MM
Products: Coins & collectibles

INTERNATIONAL HOBBY SUPPLIES   (800) 638-2519
8839 Shirley Ave. • Northridge, CA 91324
E-Mail: inthobby@pacbell.com
Website: www.plasticmodels.com
Fax Ordering: (818) 886-2551
International Ordering: (818) 886-3113
Contact Name: Rick Watson, President
Catalog: Free. Frequency: Annual
Circulation: 25K. Sales: $3-5MM
Products: Hobby supplies

INTERNATIONAL WINE ACCESSORIES   (800) 527-4072
205 Concourse Blvd. • Santa Rosa, CA 95403
E-Mail: customerservice@iwawine.com
Website: www.iwawine.com
Contact Name: Robert S. Orenstein, President
Catalog: Free. Frequency: 14x per year
Circulation: 2MM. Sales: $20-50MM
Products: Wine accessories, wine cellars,
wine storage & racking systems; corkscrews
& wineglasses; wine books, videos & software

JAMESTOWN STAMP COMPANY   (888) 782-6776
341 E. 3rd St. • Jamestown, NY 14701
E-Mail: jkl@stamp-co.com
Websites: www.stamp-co.com;
   www.jamestownstamp.com
Fax Ordering: (716) 664-2211
International Ordering: (716) 488-0763
Contact Names: Sandra & Dan Kavanaugh, Owners
Catalog: Free. Frequency: Semiannual
Circulation: 50K. Sales: $1-3MM
Products: Worldwide stamps, coins,
banknotes, supplies

JKL COMPONENTS CORPORATION   (800) 421-7244
13343 Paxton St. • Pacoima, CA 91331
E-Mail: jkl@jkllamps.com
Website: www.jkllamps.com
Fax Ordering: (818) 897-3056
International Ordering: (818) 896-0019
Contact Name: Joe Velas, President
Catalog: Free. Frequency: Annual
Circulation: 100K. Sales: $20-50MM
Products: Miniature lighting products

KELLYCO METAL DETECTORS   (800) 327-9697
1085 Belle Ave. • Winter Springs, FL 32708   (888) 535-5926
E-Mail: kellycom@magicnet.net
Website: www.kellycodetectors.com
Fax Ordering: (407) 699-6796
International Ordering: (407) 699-8700
Contact Name: Stuart Auerbach, President
Catalog: Free. Frequency: 5x per year
Circulation: 1MM. Sales: $5-10MM
Products: Coin detectors, metal detectors,
treasure locators, security systems

KENMORE STAMP COMPANY   (800) 225-5059
119 West St. • Milford, NH 03055
E-Mail: info@kenmorestamp.com
Website: www.kenmorestamp.com
Fax Ordering: (603) 673-3222
International Ordering: (603) 673-1745
Contact Name: Henry Ellis Harris, Jr., President
Catalog: Free. Frequency: Semiannual
Circulation: 100K. Sales: $3-5MM
Products: U.S. & foreihn postal stamps

LITTLETON COIN COMPANY   (800) 645-3122
1309 Mt. Eustis Rd. • Littleton, NH 03561
E-Mail: info@littletoncoin.com
Website: www.littletoncoin.com
Fax Ordering: (603) 444-0121
International Ordering: (603) 444-5386
Customer Service: (800) 581-2646
Contact Name: David Sundman, President
Catalog: Free. Frequency: Periodic
Circulation: 100K. Sales: $3-5MM
Products: U.S. coins, paper money,
ancient coins, world coins, American
Silver Eagle; albums, folders, books
& collecting supplies

M.A. STORCK COMPANY   (800) 734-7271
651 Forest Ave. • Portland, ME 04101
E-Mail: info@mastorck.com
Website: www.mastorck.com
Fax Ordering: (207) 774-7272
International Ordering: (207) 774-7271
Contact Name: James G. Simmons, President
Catalog: Free. Frequency: Annual
Circulation: 50K. Sales: $1-3MM
Products: Coin & stamp collectibles

MAYER'S CIDER MILL, INC.   (800) 543-0043
699 Five Mile Line Rd.
Webster, NY 14580
E-Mail: info@mayerscidermill.com
Website: www.mayerscidermill.com
Fax Ordering: (585) 671-5269
International Ordering: (585) 671-1955
Contact Name: David N. Bower, Sr., President
Catalog: Free. Frequency: Annual
Circulation: 50K. Sales: $500K to $1MM
Products: Beermaking & winemaking kits;
recipes, instructions & supplies for making
everything from wine to cheese kits, beer to
mustard kits

MICRO-MARK   (800) 225-1066
340 Snyder Ave.
Berkeley Heights, NJ 07922
E-Mail: info@micromark.com
Website: www.micromark.com
Fax Ordering: (908) 665-9383
International Ordering: (908) 464-2984
Contact Name: Tom Piccirillo, President
Catalog: Free. Frequency: Monthly
Circulation: 100K. Sales: $3-5MM
Products: Model building tools & supplies

MINERALS UNLIMITED   (760) 375-5279
P.O. Box 877
Ridgecrest, CA 93556
E-Mail: wendy@mineralsunlimited.com
Website: www.mineralsunlimited.com
Fax Ordering: (760) 375-2300
Catalog: Free. Frequency: Annual
Circulation: 25K. Sales: $500K
Products: Suppliers of mineral speciments,
ultraviolet lamps, and rock samples to
collectors, teachers and researchers

MODELCARS.COM   (718) 267-7026
3801 23rd Ave. #407
Astoria, NY 11105
E-Mail: customerservice@modelcars.com
Website: www.modelcars.com
Fax Ordering: (718) 267-7029
Catalog: Online. Sales: $1-3MM
Products: Model cars, trucks & hobby
supplies

MODEL EXPO   (800) 222-3876
3850 N. 29th Ter. #103
Hollywood, FL 33020
E-Mail: info@modelexpo-online.com
Website: www.modelexpo-online.com
Fax Ordering: (800) 742-7171
International Ordering: (954) 925-5551
Catalog: Free. Frequency: Semiannual
Circulation: 150K. Sales: $5-10MM
Products: Ship models, hobby tools,
airplanes; model kits

MYSTIC U.S. STAMP CATALOG   (800) 433-7811
9700 Mill St. • Camden, NY 13316   (866) 660-7147
E-Mail: info@mysticstamp.com
Website: www.mysticstamp.com
Fax Ordering: (800) 385-4919; (315) 245-0036
International Ordering: (315) 245-2690
Contact Names: Donald Sundman, President
Catalog: Free. Pages: 140.
Frequency: Semiannual
Circulation: 200K. Sales: $5-10MM
Products: Postage stamps for collectors

NORTHEASTERN SCALE LUMBER, INC. (800) 343-2094
99 Cross St. • Methuen, MA 01844
E-Mail: info@northeastscalelumber.com
Website: www.northeastscalelumber.com
Fax Ordering: (978) 794-9104
International Ordering: (978) 688-6019
Catalog: Free. Frequency: Annual
Circulation: 50K. Sales: $3-5MM
Products: Hobby scale lumber products;
dollhouse building materials and general
model building materials

NORTHEASTERN SCALE MODELS, INC. (800) 840-0028
609 Entler Ave. #3 • Chico, CA 95928
E-Mail: info@northeastscalelumber.com
Website: www.nesm.com
Fax Ordering: (530) 896-0831
International Ordering: (530) 896-0801
Catalog: Free. Frequency: Annual
Circulation: 50K. Sales: $3-5MM
Products: Custom laser design model
railroad structure kits, miniature dollhouse
kits, dollhouse furniture kits

NORTHWEST SHORT LINE (406) 375-7555
P.O. Box 1349 • Hamilton, MT 59840
E-Mail: info@nwsl.com
Website: www.nwsl.com
Fax Ordering: (406) 375-7559
Contact Name: Dave & Lynda Rygmyr, Owners
Catalog: Free. Frequency: Annual
Circulation: 50K. Sales: $1-3MM
Products: Model railroad upgrade &
repair parts; model building tools, miniature
mechanisms; books & periodicals

PHANTOM FIREWORKS CATALOG (800) 777-1699
B.J. Alan Company
555 Martin Luther King, Jr. Blvd.
Youngstown, OH 44502
E-Mail: INFO@fireworks.com
Website: www.fireworks.com
Fax Ordering: (330) 746-4410
International Ordering: (330) 746-1064
Contact Names: Bruce J. Zoldan, President
Catalog: Free. Frequency: Annual
Circulation: 100M. Sales: $20-50MM
Products: Fireworks

QUALITY WINE & ALE SUPPLY (800) 321-2739
530 E. Lexington Ave. • Elkhart, IN 46516
E-Mail: info@homebrewit.com
Website: www.homebrewit.com
Fax Ordering: (574) 295-9932
International Ordering: (574) 295-9975
Contact Name: Sam Wammack, President
Catalog: Online. Sales: $3-5MM
Products: Wine & beer making supplies
for home brewers & vintners

RARE COIN & CURRENCY & COLLECTORS (770) 393-8000
SUPPLY CATALOGUES
Southern Coin Investments
P.O. Box 720714 • Atlanta, GA 30358
E-Mail: sales@southerncoin.com
Website: www.southerncoin.com
Fax Ordering: (770) 396-1734
Contact Name: William R. Hodges, President
Catalog: Free. Frequency: Semiannual
Circulation: 50K. Sales: $5-10MM
Products: Coins & collectibles;
special occasion coin holders

RARE COIN REVIEW (800) 458-4646
Bowers & Merena Auctions
18061 Fitch • Irvine, CA 92614
E-Mail: info@bowersandmerena.com
Website: www.bowersandmerena.com
Fax Ordering: (949) 253-4091
International Ordering: (949) 253-0916
Contact Name: Jim Fehr, Director of Sales
Catalog: Free. Frequency: Semiannual
Circulation: 100K. Sales: $10-20MM
Products: Coin collectibles

SAFE STAMP & COIN SUPPLIES (215) 357-9049
Safe Publications
P.O. Box 263 • Southampton, PA 18966
E-Mail: sales@safepub.com
Website: www.safepub.com
Fax Ordering: (215) 357-5202
Contact Name: Axel J. Braun, President
Catalog: Free. Frequency: Annual
Circulation: 75K. Pages: 48. Sales: $1-3MM
Products: Stamp & coin collecting supplies,
postcard albums, magnifiers and other
examining equipment; aids for vision i
mpaired people for hobby & industrial use;
aids for reading stamp & coin supplies

SCOTSMAN AUCTION CO. (800) 642-4305
COIN & CURRENCY
11262 Olive Blvd. • St. Louis, MO 63141
E-Mail: coininfo@scoins.com
Website: www.scoins.com
Fax Ordering: (314) 692-0410
International Ordering: (314) 692-2646
Contact Name: John J. Woodside, President
Catalog: Free. Frequency: Annual
Circulation: 50K. Sales: $3-5MM
Products: Coin & currency dealer

SHELDONS HOLDERS (408) 943-0220
2135 Oakland Rd. • San Jose, CA 95131
Fax Ordering: (408) 943-0904
Contact Name: Ronald Sheldon, President
Catalog: Free. Frequency: Annual
Circulation: 100K. Sales: $1-3MM
Products: Radio control parts &
accessories for models

SHILLCRAFT CATALOG (951) 674-4307
P.O. Box 325 • Bonsall, CA 92003
E-Mail: support@shillcraft.com
Website: www.shillcraft.com
Fax Ordering: (951) 674-4325
Contact Name: Joyce Wenberg, President
Catalog: $5. Frequency: Semiannual
Circulation: 25K. Sales: $3-5MM
Products: Latch hook kits & accessories;
pre-cut rug yarn; hundreds of new designs

ROBERT A. SIEGEL AUCTION GALLERIES (212) 753-6421
60 E. 55th St. • New York, NY 10022
E-Mail: stamps@siegelauctions.com
Website: www.siegelauctions.com
Fax Ordering: (212) 753-6429
Contact Names: Scott Trepel, President
Catalog: Free. Frequency: Annual
Circulation: 25K. Sales: $10-20MM
Products: Rare stamps

SIG MANUFACTURING CO., INC. (641) 623-5154
P.O. Box 520 • Montezuma, IA 50171
E-Mail: mail@sigmfg.com

Website: www.sigmfg.com
Fax Ordering: (641) 623-3922
Contact Name: Dave Arenat, President
Catalog: $3. Frequency: Annual
Circulation: 25K. Sales: $10-20MM
Products: Model kits for aircraft; electric
flight accessories; also cars, boats, radios,
engines, field & building equipment

STACK COIN COMPANY   (212) 582-2580
123 W. 57th St. • New York, NY 10019
E-Mail: sales@stacks.com
Website: www.stacks.com
Fax Ordering: (212) 245-5018
Contact Name: Lawrence Stack, President
Catalog: $10. Frequency: Quarterly
Circulation: 10K. Sales: $5-10MM
Products: Rare coins & coin collecting
supplies

STAMP & COIN COLLECTIBLES   (800) 782-6776
Falcon Stamp Company
P.O. Box 300 • Falconer, NY 14733
Fax Ordering: (716) 664-2211
International Ordering: (716) 488-0763
Contact Names: James Auria, President
Catalog: Free. Frequency: Semiannual
Circulation: 400K. Sales: $5-10MM
Products: Stamps, coins, postcards,
sportscards & related supplies

SUPERIOR GALLERIES   (800) 421-0754
Superior Galleries Beverly Hills
20011 Ventura Blvd.
Woodland Hills, CA 91364
E-Mail: info@sgbh.com
Website: www.sgbh.com
International Ordering: (818) 444-8699
Contact Name: Steve Deeds, President
Catalog: Free. Frequency: Semiannual
Circulation: 50K. Sales: $10-20MM
Products: Rare coins & stamps ;
precious metals

TED'S ENGINE HOUSE   (856) 662-0222
6307 Westfield Ave.
Pennsauken, NJ 08110
E-Mail: info@tedsenginehouse.com
Website: www.tedsenginehouse.com
Fax Ordering: (856) 662-1767
Contact Name: Ted E. Lohr, Owner
Catalog: Free. Frequency: Monthly
Circulation: 50K. Sales: $500K
Products: Brass engines, locomotives,
military models and railroad books

THAT PET PLACE   (888) 842-8738
237 Centerville Rd.
Lancaster, PA 17603
E-Mail: info@thatpetplace.com
Website: www.thatpetplace.com
Fax Ordering: (800) 786-3829; (717) 295-7210
International Ordering: (717) 299-5691
Contact Name: Bernard Leboowitz, President
Catalog: Free. Frequency: Quarterly
Circulation: 200K. Sales: $1-3MM
Products: Aquarium supplies, pond supplies
& pet suppliesSupplies for fish & reptiles

TNT FIREWORKS   (866) 868-3953
P.O. Box 1318 • Florence, AL 35630   (800) 456-2264
E-Mail: info@tntfireworks.com

Website: www.tntfireworks.com
Fax Ordering: (256) 760-0154
International Ordering: (256) 764-6131
Catalog: Free. Frequency: Semiannual
Circulation: 150K. Sales: $5-10MM
Products: Class C consumer fireworks

TOWER HOBBIES   (800) 637-4989
P.O. Box 9078 • Champaign, IL 61828   (800) 637-6050
E-Mail: info@towerhobbies.com
Website: www.towerhobbies.com
Fax Ordering: (800) 637-7303; (217) 358-6608
International Ordering: (217) 398-3636
Contact Name: Kevin Hisel, Marketing Manager
Catalog: $3. Frequency: Annual
Circulation: 25K. Sales: $3-5MM
Products: Radio controlled models

TREASURE BOOK CATALOG   (800) 345-8588
Research Unlimited
P.O. Box 219 • Oscoda,, MI 48750
E-Mail: treasure@research-unlimited.com
Website: www.research-unlimited.com
Fax Ordering: (989) 739-3562
International Ordering: (989) 739-3294
Contact Name: Jay Foss, President
Catalog: Free. Frequency: Annual
Circulation: 25K. Sales: $500K
Products: Lost treasure books, recovery
equipment, dowsing supplies, videos,
maps, CDs

FREDERICK J. TYSON   (239) 415-4543
16576 Wellington Lakes Cir.
Fort Myers, FL 33908
E-Mail: racetrack43@comcast.net
Website: www.replicasbytyson.com
Fax Ordering: (239) 415-4547
Contact Names: Frederick J. Tyson, President
Catalog: Free. Frequency: Annual
Circulation: 150K. Sales: $500K to $1MM
Products: Custom made replicas, models &
miniatures; general aviation, military;
large scale outdoor models

UNICOVER CORP.   (800) 443-4225
1 Unicover Center
Cheyenne, WY 82007
E-Mail: info@unicover.com
Website: www.unicover.com
Fax Ordering: (307) 771-3134
International Ordering: (307) 771-3000
Contact Name: James A. Helzer, President
Catalog: Free. Frequency: Weekly
Circulation: 1MM. Sales: $20-50MM
Products: Coins, stamps, art prints, &
first day covers; custom packaging

VANTAGE PRO WIRELESS   (800) 678-3669
WEATHER STATION
Davis Instruments
3465 Diablo Ave. • Hayward, CA 94545
E-Mail: sales@davisnet.com
Website: www.davisnet.com
Fax Ordering: (510) 670-0589
International Ordering: (510) 732-9229
Technical Support: (510) 732-7814
Contact Name: Jim Acquistapace, President
Catalog: Free. Frequency: Annual
Circulation: 150K. Sales: $3-5MM
Products: Professional weather stations
for individual/home use

VILLAGE COIN SHOP   (800) 782-9349
P.O. Box 207 • Plaistow, NH 03865
E-Mail: coins@villagecoin.com
Website: www.villagecoin.com
Fax Ordering: (603) 382-5682
International Ordering: (603) 382-5492
Contact Name: Domenic J. Mangano, President
Catalog: Free. Frequency: Annual
Circulation: 50K. Sales: $500K
Products: Coins, currency & supplies for collectors

WALTHERS TERMINAL HOBBY SHOP   (800) 877-7171
William K. Walthers Trains
P.O. Box 3039 • Milwaukee, WI 53201
E-Mail: info@walthers.com
Website: www.walthers.com
Fax Ordering: (414) 527-4423
International Ordering: (414) 527-0770
Customer Service: (800) 487-2467;
  (414) 461-1050
Contact Name: J.P. Walthers, President
Catalog: $20. Frequency: Annual
Circulation: 50M. Sales: $50-100MM
Products: Model railroad equipment;
reference manual/catalog of products
for model railroaders and hobbyists

HAROLD B. WEITZ & COMPANY   (800) 245-4807
6315 Forbes Ave. • Pittsburgh, PA 15217
E-Mail: info@thinkcoins.com
Website: www.thinkcoins.com
Fax Ordering: (412) 521-1750
International Ordering: (412) 521-1879
Contact Name: Harold Weitz, President
Catalog: Free. Frequency: 3x per year
Circulation: 25K. Sales: $500K to $1MM
Products: Coin collectibles

WILLIAM'S BREWING CO.   (800) 759-6025
2088 Burroughs Ave.
San Leandro, CA 94577
E-Mail: service@williamsbrewing.com
Website: www.williamsbrewing.com
Fax Ordering: (510) 895-2745
International Ordering: (510) 895-2739
Catalog: Free. Frequency: Quarterly
Circulation: 100K. Sales: $3-5MM
Products: Home brewing kits, winemaking
& coffee roasting supplies

WINE APPRECIATION GUILD STORE   (800) 242-9462
360 Swift Ave. Unit 30-40   (800) 231-9463
South San Francisco, CA 94080
E-Mail: info@wineappreciation.com
Website: www.wineappreciation.com
Fax Ordering: (650) 866-3513
International Ordering: (650) 866-3020
Contact Name: Donna Bottrell, President
Catalog: Free. Frequency: Semiannual
Circulation: 50K. Sales: $3-5MM
Products: Wine storage custom racking
& display fixtures; wine accessories,
including corkscrews, glassware, wine racks,
cellars, specialty items, gifts, and wine books

WINE PRODUCTS CATALOG   (800) 224-9463
Gusmer Enterprises, Inc.   (866) 213-1131
640 Airpark Rd., Suite D • Napa, CA 94558
E-Mail: info@thewinelab.com
Website: www.thewinelab.com
Fax Ordering: (707) 255-2019
International Ordering: (707) 224-7903
Contact Name: Leo Foster, President
Catalog: Online. Sales: $3-5MM
Products: Winemaking supplies

WOOD MODELER'S CATALOG   (800) 222-3876
Model Expo
3850 N. 29th Ter. #103
Hollywood, FL 33020
E-Mail: info@modelexpoinc.com
Website: www.modelexpoinc.com
Fax Ordering: (800) 742-7171
International Ordering: (954) 378-2608
Contact Name: Marc Mosko, President
Catalog: Free. Frequency: Bimonthly
Circulation: 200K. Sales: $3-5MM
Products: Hobby kits, specializing in

ACCURATE METAL WEATHER STRIP CO.   (800) 536-6043
725 S. Fulton Ave. • Mt. Vernon, NY 10550
E-Mail: info@accurateweatherstrip.com
Website: www.accurateweatherstrip.com
Fax Ordering: (914) 668-6062
International Ordering: (914) 668-6042
Contact Names: Fred Kammerer, President
Catalog: Free. Frequency: Annual
Circulation: 50K. Sales: $500K to $1MM
Products: Weather stripping

ADAMS ARCHITECTURAL MILLWORK CO   (888) 285-8120
950 Jackson St. • Dubuque, IA 52001
E-Mail: info@adamsarch.com
Website: www.adamsarch.com
Fax Ordering: (563) 557-8852
International Ordering: (563) 690-1358
Contact Names: Patricia J. Adams, President
Catalog: Free. Frequency: Annual
Circulation: 50K. Sales: $1-3MM
Products: Storm & screen windows

ALTERNATIVE ENERGY TECHNOLOGIES   (800) 874-2190
1057 N. Ellis Rd. #4
Jacksonville, FL 32254
E-Mail: info@aetsolar.com
Website: www.aetsolar.com
Fax Ordering: (904) 781-1911
International Ordering: (904) 781-8305
Contact Names: Rich Squires, President
Catalog: Free. Frequency: Semiannual
Circulation: 100K. Sales: $5-10MM
Products: Solar water heating & solar
electrical systems

AMERICAN CONCRETE INSTITUTE   (248) 848-3800
P.O. Box 9094 • Farmington Hills, MI 48333
Website: www.concrete.org
E-Mail: bkstore@concrete.org
Fax Ordering: (248) 848-3801
International Ordering: (248) 848-3800
Contact Names: William R. Tolley, Executive VP
Catalog: Free. Frequency: Annual
Circulation: 100K. Sales: $1-3MM
Products: Concrete building information
including books, journals, Institute's products
& services

DON ASLETT'S CLEANING CENTER   (800) 451-2402
311 South 5th Ave. • Pocatello, ID 83201
E-Mail: info@cleanreport.com
Website: www.cleanreport.com
Fax Ordering: (800) 451-2402; (208) 232-6286
International Ordering: (208) 478-4407
Contact Names: Don Aslett, President
Catalog: Free. Frequency: Quartely
Circulation: 100K. Sales: $1-3MM
Products: Professional cleaning products
for the home

BACKWOODS SOLAR ELECTRIC SYSTEMS   (208) 263-4290
1589 Rapid Lighting Creek Rd.
Sandpoint, ID 83864
E-Mail: info@backwoodssolar.com
Website: www.backwoodssolar.com
Fax Ordering: (208) 265-4788
Contact Names: Steve Willey, President
Catalog: $5. Pages: 185. Frequency: Annual
Circulation: 50K. Sales: $3-5MM
Products: Solar electric power systems for remote
homes where power lines are not available.

JIM BARNA LOG & TIMBER HOMES   (800) 962-4734
P.O. Box 4529 • Oneida, TN 37841
E-Mail: sales@jimbarna.com
Website: www.barnahomes.com
Fax Ordering: (423) 569-5903
International Ordering: (423) 569-8448
Contact Names: James Barna, Sr., President
Catalog: Free. Frequency: Annual
Circulation: 25K. Sales: $3-5MM
Products: Log home floor plans, materials
packages, and services

BERRIDGE MANUFACTURING CO.   (800) 231-8127
1720 Maury St. • Houston, TX 77026
E-Mail: info@berridge.com
Website: www.berridge.com
Fax Ordering: (713) 236-9422
International Ordering: (713) 223-4971
Contact Names: Jack Berridge, President
Catalog: Free. Frequency: Annual
Circulation: 25K. Sales: $10-20MM
Products: Metal roofing products

BLAINE WINDOW HARDWARE   (800) 678-1919
17319 Blaine Dr.
Hagerstown, MD 21740
E-Mail: info@blainewindow.com
Website: www.blainewindow.com
Fax Ordering: (888) 250-3960
International Ordering: (301) 797-6500
Contact Name: William Pasquerette, President
Catalog: Free. Frequency: Weekly
Circulation: 150K. Sales: $3-5MM
Products: Replacement hardware for
windows, doors, custom screens

BMI SUPPLY   (800) 836-0524
571 Queensbury Ave.
Queensbury, NY 12804
E-Mail: bminy@bmusupply.com
Website: www.bmisupply.com
Fax Ordering: (518) 793-6181
International Ordering: (518) 793-6706
Contact Names: Robert Barber, President
Catalog: Free. Frequency: Annual
Circulation: 50K. Sales: $3-5MM
Products: Entertainment industry building
supplier

CAMPBELLSVILLE INDUSTRIES   (800) 467-8135
P.O. Box 278 • Campbellsville, KY 42719
E-Mail: steeple@cvilleindustries.com
Website: www.cvilleindustries.com
Fax Ordering: (270) 465-6839
International Ordering: (270) 465-8135
Contact Names: Jerry Bennett, President
Catalog: Free. Frequency: Weekly
Circulation: 10K. Sales: $10-20MM
Products: Repro Victorian roof parts;
cupolas, steeples, clocks, railings

CAPE COD CUPOLA COMPANY   (508) 994-2119
78 State Rd.
N. Dartmouth, MA 02747
E-Mail: sales@capecodcupola.com
Website: www.capecodcupola.com
Fax Ordering: (508) 997-2511
Contact Names: John Bernier, Jr., President
Catalog: Online. Sales: $1-3MM
Products: Cupolas, weathervanes, finials,
lanterns, home accents

CHATSWORTH 1.800.COLUMNS CATALOG   (800) 486-2118
277 N. Front St. • Wilmington, NC 28401   (800) 265-8667
E-Mail: catalog@columns.com
Website: www.columns.com
Fax Ordering: (910) 763-3191
International Ordering: (910) 763-7600
Contact Names: Jeff Davis, President
Catalog: Free. Frequency: Monthly
Circulation: 50K. Sales: $3-5MM
Products: Columns, balustrades, pergolas, shutters

COMPTON PRODUCTS COMPANY   (800) 922-4445
1160 Mount Pleasant Rd.
Harrisville, RI 02830
E-Mail: comptonproducts@aol.com
Fax Ordering: (401) 769-7334
Contact Names: Armand Desnoyers, President
Catalog: Free. Frequency: Annual
Circulation: 50K. Sales: $1-3MM
Products: Products & supplies for mobile homes

CONSTRUCTION BOOK EXPRESS   (800) 253-0541
P.O. Box 5196 • Janesville, WI 53547
E-Mail: info@constructionbook.com
Website: www.constructionbook.com
Fax Ordering: (800) 647-7233; (608) 743-8037
International Ordering: (631) 743-8031
Contact Name: Scott Forde, President
Catalog: Free. Frequency: Annual
Circulation: 150K. Sales: $3-5MM
Products: Construction books, manuals, audio & videotapes, CD-ROMs & software covering building codes & contractor's guides

CONSTRUCTION REFERENCE   (800) 829-8123
Craftsman Book Company
6058 Corte Del Cedro • Carlsbad, CA 92009
E-Mail: info@craftsman-book.com
Website: www.craftsman-book.com
Fax Ordering: (760) 438-0398
International Ordering: (760) 438-7828
Contact Name: Gary Moselle, President
Catalog: Free. Frequency: Annual
Circulation: 150K. Sales: $3-5MM
Products: Professional construction books

COPPA WOODWORKING, INC.   (310) 548-4142
1231 Paraiso St. • San Pedro, CA 90731
E-Mail: info@coppawoodworking.com
Website: www.coppawoodworking.com
Fax Ordering: (310) 548-6740
Contact Names: Ciro Coppa, President
Catalog: Free. Frequency: Annual
Circulation: 25K. Sales: $1-3MM
Products: Wood screen doors & wood storm doors

DOHENY'S WATER WAREHOUSE   (800) 874-8289
Doheny Enterprises
6950 51 St. • Kenosha, WI 53144
E-Mail: info@waterwarehouse.com
Website: www.waterwarehouse.com
Fax Ordering: (262) 605-1075
International Ordering: (630) 952-8848
Contact Names: Michael Reeves, President
Catalog: Free. Frequency: Annual
Circulation: 100K. Sales: $10-20MM
Products: Swimming pool equipment & supplies

ELLIOTT'S HARDWARE   (214) 634-9900
4901 Maple Ave. • Dallas, TX 75235
E-Mail: info@elliottshardware.com
Website: www.elliottshardware.com
Fax Ordering: (214) 905-9601
Catalog: Free. Frequency: Annual
Circulation: 25K. Sales: $500K
Products: Restoration & renovation hardware

ENERGY SAVERS CATALOG   (603) 668-8186
Solar Components Corp.
121 Valley St.
Manchester, NH 03103
E-Mail: solarcomponents@yahoo.com
Website: www.solar-components.com
Fax Ordering: (603) 668-1783
Contact Names: Scott Keller, President
Catalog: Free. Frequency: Weekly
Circulation: 50K. Sales: $1-3MM
Products: Solar energy equipment & products; aquaculture products

ENERTIA BUILDING SYSTEMS   (919) 556-0177
P.O. Box 845 • Youngsville, NC 27596   (919) 556-2391
E-Mail: enertia@mindspring.com
Website: www.enertia.com
Contact Names: Michael Sykes, President
Catalog: $20. Frequency: Annual
Circulation: 5K. Sales: $3-5MM
Products: Solar/Geothermal-kit homes designed using new enertia technology

FASTFLOORS.COM   (800) 764-1212
Tonger Industries
5817 N. Andrews Way
Ft. Lauderdale, FL 33309
E-Mail: sales@fastfloors.com
Website: www.fastfloors.com
International Ordering: (954) 776-1998
Catalog: Online. Sales: $1-3MM
Products: Various floors & installation materials

FOUR SEASONS SUNROOMS   (800) 368-7732
Four Seasons Solar Products, LLC
5005 Veterans Memorial Hwy.
Holbrook, NY 11741
E-Mail: info@four-seasons-sunrooms.com
Website: www.four-seasons-sunrooms.com
Fax Ordering: (631) 563-4010
International Ordering: (631) 563-4000
Contact Names: Chris Esposito, President
Catalog: Free. Frequency: Monthly
Circulation: 150K. Sales: $20-50MM
Products: Manufacturers of wood, aluminum & vinyl sunrooms

GRANVILLE MANUFACTURING CO.   (800) 828-1005
Route 100 • Grannville, VT 05747
E-Mail: woodsiding@woodsiding.com
Website: www.woodsiding.com
Fax Ordering: (802) 767-3107
International Ordering: (802) 767-4747
Contact Names: Robert Fuller, President
Catalog: Free. Frequency: Semiannual
Circulation: 25K. Sales: $1-3MM
Products: Clapboards, wooden bowls & wooden kitchenware

GREATWOOD LOG HOMES (800) 707-0449
Wilderness Log & Timber Co.
P.O. Box 902 • Plymouth, WI 53073
E-Mail: info@wildernessloghomes.com
Website: www.wildernessloghomes.com
Fax Ordering: (920) 892-2414
International Ordering: (920) 893-8416
Contact Names: Jeff Servis, President
Catalog: Free. Frequency: Semiannual
Circulation: 25K. Sales: $10-20MM
Products: Clapboards, wooden bowls
& wooden kitchenware

HABITAT POST & BEAM CATALOG (800) 992-0121
21 Elm St. • South Deerfield, MA 01373
E-Mail: SALES@postandbeam.com
Website: www.postandbeam.com
Fax Ordering: (413) 665-4008
International Ordering: (413) 665-4006
Contact Names: Peter May, President
Catalog: Free. Frequency: Semiannual
Circulation: 25K. Sales: $1-3MM
Products: Timber frame & additions

HD SUPPLY MAINTENANCE SOLUTIONS (877) 694-4932
P.O. Box 509055 • San Diego, CA 92150
E-Mail: customercare@hdsupply.com
Website: www.hdsupplysolutions.com
Fax Ordering: (800) 859-8889
International Ordering: (808) 431-3000
Contact Names: Jonathan Neeley, President
Catalog: Free. Frequency: Semiannual
Circulation: 100K. Sales: $3-5MM
Products: Hand tools, hardware, lighting,
paints & power tools

HINGES & HANDLES CATALOG (800) 533-4782
100 Lincoln Way E. • Osceola, IN 46561
Fax Ordering: (574) 674-5767
International Ordering: (574) 674-8878
Contact Name: Tom Krueger, Manager
Catalog: Free. Frequency: Annual
Circulation: 100K. Sales: $3-5MM
Products: Decorative cabinet, door
& builders hardware

HISTORICAL REPLICATIONS, INC. (800) 426-5628
Authentic Historical Designs, LLC
3908 N. State St. • Jackson, MS 39206
E-Mail: cecilia@historicaldesigns.com
Website: www.historicaldesigns.com
Fax Ordering: (601) 981-8185
International Ordering: (601) 981-8743
Contact Names: Cecilia Reese Bullock, President
Catalogs: $25 ea. Frequency: Annual
Circulation: 25K. Sales: $3-5MM
Products: Six Catalogs: Victorians & Farmhouses;
Louisiana Collection; Colonial Heritage;
Classic Cottages; The Courtyard Collection;
The Masterpiece Collection. Blueprints & plans
for historical homes

HOME BUILDER BOOKSTORE CATALOG (800) 368-5242
National Association of Home Builders
1201 15th St., NW • Washington, DC 20005
E-Mail: info@nahb.com
Website: www.nahb.com
Fax Ordering: (202) 266-8400
International Ordering: (202) 266-8200
Contact Names: Charlotte McKenny, President
Catalog: Free. Frequency: 5x per year
Circulation: 100K. Sales: $500K to $1MM

Products: Professional books for the
residential builder, remodeler or developer

HORTON BRASSES, INC. CATALOG (800) 754-9127
49 Nooks Hill Rd. • Cromwell, CT 06416
E-Mail: contact@horton-brasses.com
Website: www.horton-brasses.com
Fax Ordering: (860) 635-6473
International Ordering: (860) 635-4400
Contact Name: Barbara Rockwell, President
Catalog: Free. Frequency: Annual
Circulation: 50K. Sales: $3-5MM
Products: Brass & wrought iron reproduction
hardware for furniture and cabinetry, handles,
knobs, hinges, latches & slides

IMPROVEMENTS (800) 642-2112
5568 West Chester Rd. (800) 634-9484
West Chester, OH 45069
E-Mail: custserv@improvementscatalog.com
Website: www.improvementscatalog.com
Fax Ordering: (800) 757-9997
Catalog: Free. Frequency: Semiannual
Circulation: 100K. Sales: $10-20MM
Products: Do-it-yourself home improvements;
items for home upkeep

KYOCERA SOLAR, INC. (800) 223-9580
7812 E. Acoma • Scottsdale, AZ 85260
E-Mail: info@kyocerasolar.com
Website: www.kyocerasolar.com
Fax Ordering: (800) 523-2329
International Ordering: (480) 948-8003
Contact Names: Doug Allday, President
Catalog: Free. Frequency: Annual
Circulation: 100K. Sales: $50-100MM
Products: Solar electric systems &
design guide

MAC THE ANTIQUE PLUMBER (800) 916-2284
6325 Elvas Ave. • Sacramento, CA 95819
E-Mail: sales@antiqueplumber.com
Website: www.antiqueplumber.com
Fax Ordering: (916) 454-4150
International Ordering: (916) 454-4507
Contact Names: Bryan C. McIntire, President
Catalog: $10. Pages: 200+. Frequency: Annual
Circulation: 25K. Sales: $5-10MM
Products: Antique plumbing, bath
accessories, lighting, hardware

MELTON CLASSICS (800) 963-3060
P.O. Box 465020
Lawrenceville, GA 30042
E-Mail: mclassics@aol.com
Website: www.meltonclassics.com
Fax Ordering: (770) 962-6988
International Ordering: (843) 448-7501
Contact Names: Randy Schlitter, President
Catalog: Free. Frequency: Annual
Circulation: 50K. Sales: $1-3MM
Products: Fine architectural millwork products;
columns, balustrades, mouldings, domes
manufactured from fiberglass, marble, cast
stone, wood, etc.

NATURAL SPACES DOMES (800) 733-7107
37955 Bridge Rd. • North Branch, MN 55056
E-Mail: nsd@naturalspacesdomes.com
Website: www.naturalspacesdomes.com
Fax Ordering: (651) 674-5005
International Ordering: (651) 674-4292

Catalog: $12. **Frequency:** Annual
Circulation: 10K. **Sales:** $10-50MM
Products: Information on the construction
of energy & resource efficient domes

THE NEW ENGLAND SLATE CO. (888) 637-5283
363 VT Rt. 30 S
Poultney, VT 05764
E-Mail: slate@neslate.com
Website: www.neslate.com
Fax Ordering: (802) 247-0089
International Ordering: (802) 287-2295
Contact Names: Charles Smid, President
Catalog: Free. **Frequency:** Annual
Circulation: 50K. **Sales:** $3-5MM
Products: Slate roofing, slate tools &
hardware; slate roof restoration

NEW ENGLAND SOLAR ELECTRIC (800) 914-4131
P.O. Box 435 • Worthington, MA 01098
E-Mail: spschulze@newenglandsolar.com
Website: www.newenglandsolar.com
Fax Ordering: (413) 238-0203
International Ordering: (413) 238-5974
Contact Names: Stephen Schulze, President
Catalog: Free. **Frequency:** Semiannual
Circulation: 25K. **Sales:** $500K - $1MM
Products: Solar electric kits, components,
gas appliances and wind mills

OAK LOG HOMES (800) 654-9253
Gastineau Log Homes
10423 Old Hwy. 54
New Bloomfield, MO 65063
E-Mail: sales@oakloghome.com
Website: www.oakloghome.com
Fax Ordering: (573) 896-5510
International Ordering: (573) 896-5122
Contact Names: Lynn Gastineau, President
Catalog: Free. **Frequency:** Semiannual
Circulation: 25K. **Sales:** $5-10MM
Products: Feature stories on 12 custom
log homes, with technical information,
photos, floor plans, price lists

ORIGINAL LOG CABIN HOMES (800) 562-2246
P.O. Drawer 1457
Rocky Mount, NC 27802
E-Mail: info@logcabinhomes.com
Website: www.logcabinhomes.com
Fax Ordering: (252) 454-1550
International Ordering: (252) 454-1500
Contact Names: Tom Vesce, President
Catalog: Free. **Frequency:** Annual
Circulation: 25K. **Sales:** $20-50MM
Products: Log cabin homes

PLANHOUSE HOME PLANS (800) 752-6468
Planhouse Publications, Inc.
20 E. Gate Dr., Suite A
Brandon, MS 39042
E-Mail: shelms@planhouse.com
Website: www.planhouse.com
Fax Ordering: (601) 932-4707
International Ordering: (601) 939-2828
Catalog: Free. **Frequency:** Annual
Circulation: 25K. **Sales:** $1-3MM
Products: Plans for the home owner
& home builder

REAL GOODS SOLAR, INC . (800) 762-7325
833 W. South Boulder Rd. (800) 442-1972
Louisville, CO 80027
E-Mail: sales@realgoods.com
Website: www.realgoods.com
Fax Ordering: (800) 508-2342
Customer Service: (800) 919-2400
Contact Names: John Schaeffer, President
Catalog: Free. **Frequency:** Semiannual
Circulation: 2MM. **Sales:** $20-50MM
Products: Wind & hydro powered systems;
solar hot water heaters, super efficient
refrigerators; books & videos

REVERE PRODUCTS (800) 321-1976
P.O. Box 35311 • Cleveland, OH 44135
E-Mail: sales@revereproducts.com
Website: www.revereproducts.com
Fax Ordering: (800) 966-0502; (216) 671-4598
International Ordering: (216) 671-2393
Contact Names: Jim Schattinger, President
Catalog: Free. **Frequency:** Monthly
Circulation: 1MM. **Sales:** $10-20MM
Products: Do-it-yourself maintenance products

SAN FRANCISCO VICTORIANA, INC. (415) 648-0313
2070 Newcombe Ave.
San Francisco, CA 94124
E-Mail: sales@sfvictoriana.com
Website: www.sfvictoriana.com
Fax Ordering: (415) 648-2812
Contact Names: Gary Root, President
Catalog: $5. **Frequency:** Annual
Circulation: 50K. **Sales:** $5-10MM
Products: Architectural ornament for
traditional Victorian style building
materials & accessories

SCOTT SIGN SYSTEMS, INC. (800) 237-9447
P.O. Box 1047 • Tallevast, FL 34270
E-Mail: mail@scottsigns.com
Website: www.scottsigns.com
Fax Ordering: (941) 351-1787
International Ordering: (941) 355-5171
Contact Names: Kathy Hannon, President
Catalog: Free. **Frequency:** Annual
Circulation: 25K. **Sales:** $1-3MM
Products: Sign systems

SHELDON DESIGNS (800) 572-5934
1330 Rt. 206 #103-326
Skillman, NJ 08558
E-Mail: service@sheldondesigns.com
Website: www.sheldondesigns.com
Fax Ordering: (609) 683-5976
International Ordering: (609) 683-4388
Catalog: Free. **Frequency:** Annual
Circulation: 25K. **Sales:** $500MKto $1MM
Products: Designs and plans for home
renovation projects, including house plans,
cabin plans, cottage plans, barn plans &
shed plans

SHELTER-KIT, INC. (603) 286-7611
22 Mill St. • Tilton, NH 03276
E-Mail: shelterkit@gmail.com
Website: www.shelter-kit.com
Fax Ordering: (603) 286-2839
Contact Names: Andy Prokosch, President
Catalog: $3. **Frequency:** Semiannual
Circulation: 10K. **Sales:** $500K to $1MM
Products: Owner-built house, barn, green home kits;

SIERRA SOLAR SYSTEMS   (888) 667-6527
563 C Idaho Maryland Rd.
Grass Valley, CA 95945
E-Mail: solarjon@sierrasolar.com
Website: www.sierrasolar.com
Fax Ordering: (530) 273-1760
International Ordering: (530) 273-6754
Contact Names: Jonathan Hill, President
Catalog: Free. Frequency: Semiannual
Circulation: 50K. Sales: $3-5MM
Products: Solar electric systems &
components

SUNBILT SOLAR PRODUCTS   (718) 297-6040
J. Sussman, Inc.
109 - 10 180th St. • Jamaica, NY 11433
E-Mail: info@sunbilt.com
Website: www.sunbilt.com
Fax Ordering: (718) 297-3090
Contact Names: Steve Sussman, President
Catalog: Online. Sales: $3-5MM
Products: Sunrooms, skylights & custom
windows, glass & metal bending

SUNPORCH STRUCTURES, INC.   (866) 919-9620
495 Post Rd. E. • Westport, CT 06880
E-Mail: info@sunporch.com
Website: www.sunporch.com
Fax Ordering: (203) 454-0020
International Ordering: (203) 454-0040
Contact Names: Dean Schwartz, President
Catalog: Free. Frequency: Semiannual
Circulation: 25K. Sales: $5-10MM
Products: SunPorch do-it-yourself sunroom
kits; patio enclosures & rooms

SUNWIZE SOLAR PRODUCT CATALOG   (800) 817-6527
1155 Flatbush Rd. • Kingston, NY 12401   **West Coast**
E-Mail: info@sunwize.com   (866) 476-9493
Website: www.sunwize.com
Catalog: Online. Sales: $1-3MM
Products: Solar power systems;
electric products; solar modules
& components

SURFACE PREPARATION   (800) 872-4933
& MAINTANENCE TOOLS
Hyde Manufacturing Co.
54 Eastford Rd. • Southbridge, MA 01550
E-Mail: info@hydetools.com
Website: www.hydetools.com
Fax Ordering: (508) 765-5250
International Ordering: (508) 764-4344
Catalog: Free. Frequency: Quarterly
Circulation: 50K. Sales: $500K to $1MM
Products: Paint & decorating tools, drywall &
plaster tools, tile & adhesive tools, guilder's
hand tools; wallcoverings & cement

TEXAS REFINERY CORPORATION   (800) 827-0711
P.O. Box 711 • Fort Worth, TX 76101
E-Mail: jhopkins@texasrefinery.com
Website: www.texasrefinery.com
Fax Ordering: (817) 332-2340
International Ordering: (817) 332-1161
Contact Names: Jerry Hopkins, President
Catalog: Free. Frequency: Annual
Circulation: 100K. Sales: $20-50MM
Products: Building maintenance products,
protective coating; lubricants

TIMBERLANE WOODCRAFTERS   (800) 250-2221
150 Domorah Dr.
Montogomeryville, PA 19454
E-Mail: info@timberlaneshutters.com
Website: www.timberlaneshutters.com
Fax Ordering: (215) 616-0753
International Ordering: (215) 616-0600
Contact Names: Rick Skidmore, President
Catalog: Free. Frequency: Annual
Circulation: 100K. Sales: $5-10MM
Products: Custom exterior wood shutters

TIMBERLINE GEODESICS   (800) 366-3466
2015 Blake St. • Berkeley, CA 94704
E-Mail: info@domehome.com
Website: www.domehome.com
Fax Ordering: (510) 849-3265
International Ordering: (510) 849-4481
Contact Names: Robert M. Singer, President
Catalog: Free. Frequency: Annual
Circulation: 15K. Sales: $3-5MM
Products: Designer & manufacturer of
geodesic dome kits used for housing &
commercial applications

TOTAL FLOOR SOLUTIONS   (800) 631-5380
Garon Products, Inc.
P.O. Box 1924 • Wall, NJ 07719
E-Mail: custserv@garonproducts.com
Website: www.garonproducts.com
Fax Ordering: (732) 223-2002
International Ordering: (732) 223-2500
Contact Names: Arthur Crowley, President
Catalog: Free. Frequency: Monthly
Circulation: 1MM. Sales: $10-20MM
Products: Floor coatings, antislip safety
coatings, concrete repair, tile floor finishes,
asphalt coatings & industrial floor cleaners

TOWN & COUNTRY CEDAR HOMES   (800) 968-3178
4772 S. U.S. Hwy. 131 S
Petoskey, MI 49770
E-Mail: town@cedarhomes.com
Website: www.cedarhomes.com
Fax Ordering: (231) 347-7255
International Ordering: (231) 347-4360
Contact Names: Steve Biggs, President
Catalog: Free. Frequency: Annual
Circulation: 25K. Sales: $10-20MM
Products: Log home building kits

TRELLIS STRUCTURES   (888) 285-4624
P.O. Box 408 • E. Templeton, MA 01438   (800) 649-6920
E-Mail: sales@trellisstructures.com
Website: www.trellisstructures.com
Fax Ordering: (978) 630-8725
International Ordering: (978) 630-8787
Contact Names: David Valcovic, President
Catalog: Free. Frequency: Annual
Circulation: 25K. Sales: $1-3MM
Products: Arbors, trellises, garden
furniture in western cedar

VERMONT CASTINGS   (802) 234-2300
Monessem Hearth Systems Co.
P.O. Box 501 • Bethel, VT 05032
E-Mail: sales@vermontcastings.com
Website: www.vermontcastings.com
Fax Ordering: (802) 234-2340
Contact Names: Dennis Dillon, President

Catalog: Free. Frequency: Semiannual
Circulation: 100K. Sales: $5-10MM
Products: Stoves & fireplaces

VERMONT LOG BUILDINGS   (800) 732-5564
Real Log Homes
P.O. Box 202 • Hartland, VT 05048
E-Mail: sales@realloghomes.com
Website: www.realloghomes.com
Fax Ordering: (802) 436-2128
International Ordering: (802) 436-2123
Contact Names: Todd Schweizer, President
Catalog: $10. Pages: 100. Frequency: Annual
Circulation: 10K. Sales: $10-20MM
Products: Energy conservation, alternate
energy, recycled products

WARD CEDAR LOG HOMES   (800) 341-1566
P.O. Box 72 • Houlton, ME 04730
E-Mail: info@wardloghomes.com
Website: www.wardloghomes.com
Fax Ordering: (207) 532-7806
International Ordering: (207) 532-6531
Contact Names: Jonathan French, President
Catalog: $10. Frequency: Annual
Circulation: 5K. Sales: $5-10MM
Products: Descriptions & drawings of
more than 30 models, eight cabins, and
ten detached garages, exterior photos
& floor plans; constructions details,
pricing, material lists

WHERE'S HOME FOR YOU?   (800) 767-7674
International Homes of Cedar, Inc.
P.O. Box 886 • Woodinville, WA 98072
E-Mail: ihc@ihoc.com
Website: www.cedarleader.com
Fax Ordering: (360) 668-5562
International Ordering: (360) 668-8511
Contact Names: Pete Geffa, President
Catalog: $15. Frequency: Semiannual
Circulation: 5K. Sales: $5-10MM
Products: Pre-cut engineered home building
material packages

WISCONSIN LOG & CEDAR HOMES   (800) 678-9107
Wisconsin Log Homes, Inc.
2390 Pamperin Rd. • Green Bay, WI 54307
E-Mail: info@wisconsinloghomes.com
Website: www.wisconsinloghomes.com
Fax Ordering: (920) 434-2140
International Ordering: (920) 434-3010
Contact Names: Dave Janczak, President
Catalog: $10. Frequency: Annual
Circulation: 10K. Sales: $20-50MM
Products: Manufacturer of custom log
& cedar home packages; includes log
home plans, price & materials lists

ADDED TOUCH   (888) 238-6824
P.O. Box 4 • Niagara Falls, NY 14304
E-Mail: added@addedtouch.com
Website: www.addedtouch.com
Fax Ordering: (905) 338-1486
International Ordering: (905) 338-7399
Catalog: Free. Frequency: Annual
Circulation: 100M. Sales: $3-5MM
Products: Practical items for the home
& garden

ALSTO'S   (800) 447-0048
Hanover, PA 17333-0093
E-Mail: custserv@alsto.com
Website: www.alsto.com
Fax Ordering: (800) 522-5786
Customer Service: (800) 621-8258
Catalog: Free. Frequency: Quarterly
Circulation: 150M. Sales: $5-10MM
Products: Outdoor furniture & accessories

AMERICAN BLIND & WALLPAPER FACTORY (800) 758-8040
909 N. Sheldon Rd. • Plymouth, MI 48170
E-Mail: info@decoratetoday.com
Website: www.decoratetoday.com
Fax Ordering: (800) 391-2293
Contact Name: Steven Katzman, President
Catalog: Free. Frequency: Annual
Circulation: 200M. Sales: $10-50MM
Products: Rugs, wall art, lighting, curtains,
home decor, shutters, paint

AMERICAN SITE FURNITURE   (800) 366-3080
Titan Manufacturers
P.O. Box 158 • Concord, MA 01742
E-Mail: dfmr@americantitan.com
Website: www.americantitan.com
Fax Ordering: (978) 369-4472
International Ordering: (978) 371-3080
Contact Name: Gregory J. Hill, President
Catalog: Free. Frequency: 30x per year
Circulation: 300M. Sales: $3-5MM
Products: Benches, planters, trash
receptacles

ANGLO-AMERICAN BRASS COMPANY   (408) 246-0203
P.O. Box 9486 • San Jose, CA 95157   (408) 246-9918
E-Mail: vhprs@earthlink.net
Website: www.vintagehardware.com
Fax Ordering: (408) 248-1308
Contact Name: Kenneth Kelly, President
Catalog: Free. Frequency: Annual
Circulation: 200M. Sales: $3-5MM
Products: Reproduction brass hardware;
antique lighting

ANTIQUE HARDWARE & HOME   (800) 422-9982
19 Buckingham Plantation Dr.
Bluffton, SC 29910
E-Mail: treasurea@hargray.com
Website: www.antiquehardware.com
Fax Ordering: (800) 961-2684; (843) 837-9790
International Ordering: (843) 837-9789
Contact Names: Ellen & Tim Judge
Catalog: Free. Frequency: Annual
Circulation: 150M. Sales: $1-3MM
Products: Antique-style home remodeling
products, decorative home accessories

ARTS & CRAFTS PERIOD TEXTILES   (510) 654-1645
5427 Telegraph Ave. • Oakland, CA 94609
E-Mail: acptextile@aol.com

Website: www.textilestudio.com
Fax Ordering: (510) 654-1256
Contact Name: Dianne Ayres
Catalog: $10. Frequency: Annual
Circulation: 10M. Sales: $500M to $1MM
Products: Pillows, table linens, curtains,
curtain hardware, bedspreads, embroidery kits

ASHLEY MANOR   (800) 582-1401
P.O. Box 477 • High Point, NC 27261
Fax Ordering: (336) 889-5532
International Ordering: (336) 882-8131
Catalog: $10. Frequency: Semiannual
Circulation: 10M. Sales: $5-10MM
Products: Fine furniture

ASI HOME   (800) 263-8608
36 Gumbletown Rd. • Paupack, PA 18451
E-Mail: sales@asihome.com
Website: www.asihome.com
Fax Ordering: (570) 844-0678
International Ordering: (570) 226-8549
Contact Name: Leo Soderman, President
Catalog: Free. Frequency: Semiannual
Circulation: 100M. Sales: $10-20MM
Products: Home products, including heating
& cooling, lighting & appliance control, home
security, home theater, telephones & intercoms,
outdoor & garage; tools, books, videos

BALLARD DESIGNS   (800) 367-2775
5568 West Chester Rd.
West Chester, OH 45069
E-Mail: info@ballarddesigns.com
Website: www.ballarddesigns.com
Fax Ordering: (800) 989-4510
  or (404) 352-1660
International Ordering: (404) 352-8486
Customer Service: (800) 367-2810
Contact Name: Stewart Tarkington, President
Catalog: Free. Frequency: Monthly
Circulation: 250K. Sales: $20-50M
Products: Home & office furnishings; beds &
bedding accessories; rugs, lighting, wall decor,
window treatments. Outlet centers in Atlanta
and Cincinnati areas.

BARCO PRODUCTS   (800) 338-2697
11 N. Batavia Ave. • Batavia, IL 60510
E-Mail: service@barcoproducts.com
Website: www.barcoproducts.com
Fax Ordering: (630) 879-8687
Catalog: Free. Pages: 32.
Frequency: Quarterly
Circulation: 250M. Sales: $10-20MM
Products: Commercial site furnishings;
commecial floor mattings: entrance mats,
personalized entrance mats, logo mats;
waste receptacles; educational rugs; bike
racks, wheel stops, safety barricades; parking
lot supplies; picnic tables, park benches

BARTLEY COLLECTION   (800) 787-2800
65 Engerman Ave. • Denton, MD 21629
E-Mail: customerservice@wbstore.com
Website: www.bartleycollection.com
Fax Ordering: (410) 479-4514
International Ordering: (410) 479-4480
Contact Name: Steve Hart, President
Catalog: Free. Frequency: Monthly
Circulation: 25M. Sales: $1-3MM
Products: Fine antique reproduction furniture kits

BEHR'S FURNITURE CATALOG   (516) 541-2347
1220 Hicksville Rd. •Seaford, NY 11783
E-Mail: customerservice@behrsfurniture.com
Website: www.behrsfurniture.com
Fax Ordering: (516) 541-2353
Catalog: Free. Frequency: 10x per year
Circulation: 100M. Sales: $3-5MM
Products: Furniture & accessories
for babies & children

BEREA COLLEGE   (800) 347-3892
STUDENT CRAFT INDUSTRIES
P.O. Box 2217 • Berea, KY 40404
E-Mail: info@bereacollegecrafts.com
Website: www.bereacollegecrafts.com
Fax Ordering: (859) 985-3900
International Ordering: (859) 986-9341
Contact Name: Steve Fain, Marketing
Catalog: $6. Frequency: Annual
Circulation: 20M. Sales: $1-3MM
Products: Handcrafted furniture

BIOFIRE, INC.   (801) 486-0266
3220 Melbourne
Salt Lake City, UT 84106
E-Mail: info@biofireinc.com
Website: www.biofire.com
Fax Ordering: (801) 486-8100
Catalog: $3. Frequency: Annual
Circulation: 100M. Sales: $1-3MM
Products: Stucco, tile stoves, and
combination fireplaces

BLACKWELDER'S CATALOG   (800) 438-0201
Blackwelder's Furniture Company
1950 S. University Dr. • Davie, FL 33324
E-Mail: tkb@blackwelders.com
Website: www.blackwelders.com
Fax Ordering: (859) 985-3900
International Ordering: (859) 986-9341
Contact Name: John N. Blackwelder, President
Catalog: $22.95. Frequency: Annual
Circulation: 10M. Sales: $3-5MM
Products: Fine furniture & accessories

BLAIR SHOPPE HOME PRODUCTS   (800) 458-2000
Blair Corporation
220 Hickory St.
Warren, PA 16366
E-Mail: blair@blair.com
Website: www.blair.com
Fax Ordering: (814) 726-6466
International Ordering: (814) 723-3600
Contact Name: Blair T. Smoulder, President
Catalog: Free. Frequency: 6x per year
Circulation: 15-20MM. Sales: $50-100MM
Products: Area rugs, bedding, bed & bath
accessories, window treatments, kitchen
utensils, appliances, flatware & cookware;
exercise equipment; furniture

BOMBAY COMPANY CATALOG   (800) 829-7789
P.O. Box 161009 • Fort Worth, TX 76161
E-Mail: customerservice@bombayco.com
Website: www.bombayco.com
Contact Name: Bob Jackson, President
Catalog: Free. Frequency: 8x per year
Circulation: 4MM. Sales: $20-50MM
Products: Furniture, accessories, lighting,
wall decor, bedding & textiles, gifts; 18th &
19th century antique reproduction furniture

BRITE START CATALOG   (800) 243-9232
S&S Worldwide
75 Mill St. • Colchester, CT 06415
E-Mail: info@snswide.com
Website: www.snswide.com
Fax Ordering: (860) 537-2866
International Ordering: (860) 537-3451
Contact Names: Adam & Hy Schwartz
Catalog: Free. Frequency: Weekly
Circulation: 500M. Sales: $20-50MM
Products: Housewares, appliances,
cookware, crafts, sporting goods, toys

BRUMBAUGH'S FURNITURE & RUG   (817) 624-4123
108 NE 28th St. • Fort Worth, TX 76106
E-Mail: sales@brumbaughs.com
Website: www.brumbaughs.com
Fax Ordering: (817) 624-8464
Catalog: Online only. Sales: $1-3MM
Products: Rugs & furniture inspired by
the spirit of the West

CAROLINA PATIO WAREHOUSE   (800) 672-8466
58 Largo Dr. • Stamford, CT 06907
E-Mail: sales@carolinapatio.com
Website: www.carolinapatio.com
Fax Ordering: (203) 975-7897
International Ordering: (203) 975-8559
Catalog: Free. Frequency: Semiannual
Circulation: 50M. Sales: $3-5MM
Products: Patio furniture & accessories

CARRUTH STUDIO CATALOG   (800) 225-1178
1178 Farnsworth Rd.
Waterville, OH 43566
E-Mail: info@carruthstudio.com
Website: www.carruthstudio.com
Fax Ordering: (419) 878-3261
International Ordering: (419) 878-3060
Contact Name: George Carruth, President
Catalog: $3. Frequency: 10x per year
Circulation: 50M. Sales: $500M
Products: Planters, plaques, all cast
from original designs

CHAIR COVERS & LINENS   (800) 260-1030
25914 John R • Madison Hts., MI 48071
E-Mail: info@chaircovers.net
Website: www.chaircovers.net
Fax Ordering: (248) 548-6390
International Ordering: (248) 548-5600
Catalog: Free. Frequency: Annual
Circulation: 10M. Sales: $1-3MM
Products: Chair covers & linens for
special occasions

CHAIRWORKS CATALOG   (800) 282-9406
14 Boyleston Hwy. • Horse Shoe, NC 28742
E-Mail: sales@chairworks.com
Website: www.chairworks.com
Fax Ordering: (770) 277-2578
International Ordering: (770) 277-2577
Contact Name: Debbie James, President
Catalog: $2. Frequency: Annual
Circulation: 50M. Sales: $5-10MM
Products: Handmade traditional furniture

W.A. CHARNSTROM CO.   (800) 328-2962
5391 12th Ave. E.
Shakopeeton, MN 55379
E-Mail: mail@charnstrom.com

Website: www.charnstrom.com
Fax Ordering: (952) 403-1113
International Ordering: (952) 403-0303
Contact Name: Greg Hedlund, President
Catalog: Free. Frequency: Annual
Circulation: 150M. Sales: $5-10MM
Products: Mailroom furniture

CHIASSO (877) 244-2776
1440 N. Dayton St. #307
Chicago, IL 60622
E-Mail: orders@chiasso.com
Website: www.chiasso.com
Fax Ordering: (877) 881-3327; (773) 342-5490
International Ordering: (773) 342-7900
Customer Service: (800) 654-3570
Contact Name: David Marshall, President
Catalog: Free. Frequency: 10x per year
Circulation: 5MM. Sales: $20-50MM
Products: Modern design gifts &
accessories for the home & office

CHILTON FURNITURE (888) 510-6300
410 Payne Rd.
Scarborough, ME 04074
E-Mail: chilton@gwi.net
Website: www.chiltons.com
Fax Ordering: (207) 865-9051
International Ordering: (207) 883-3366
Catalog: Free. Frequency: Semiannual
Circulation: 75M. Sales: $3-5MM
Products: Shaker style furniture

CIRCA 1820 (888) 887-1820
RR 1 Box 4040
Vassalboro, ME 04989
E-Mail: info@circa1820.com
Website: www.circa1820.com
Fax Ordering: (207) 877-9863
International Ordering: (207) 877-9863
Contact Name: William Devine, President
Catalog: $5. Frequency: Annual
Circulation: 50M. Sales: $1-3MM
Products: Furnishings & accessories for
the American Country Home 1790-1850

CLASSIC DESIGNS BY MATTHEW BURAK (800) 843-7405
P.O. Box 329 • St. Johnsbury, VT 05819
E-Mail: legs@tablelegs.com
Website: www.tablelegs.com
Fax Ordering: (802) 748-4350
International Ordering: (802) 748-9378
Contact Name: Matthew Burak, President
Catalog: Free. Frequency: Annual
Circulation: 150M. Sales: $3-5MM
Products: Turned & carved furniture parts
from solid wood, including table legs,
bed posts, bun feet; table base kits

CLEAN REPORT (800) 451-2402
210 Halliday • Pocatello, ID 83204
E-Mail: info@cleanreport.com
Website: www.cleanreport.com
Fax Ordering: (208) 232-6286
International Ordering: (208) 232-6212
Contact Name: Don Aslett, President
Catalog: Free. Frequency: Weekly
Circulation: 250M. Sales: $1-3MM
Products: Professional cleaning products
for the home

COHASSET COLONIALS (800) 288-2389
P.O. Box 548 • Ashburnham, MA 01430
E-Mail: cohasset@cohassetcolonials.com
Website: www.cohassetcolonials.com
Fax Ordering: (978) 827-3227
International Ordering: (978) 827-3001
Contact Name: Richard Dabrowski, President
Catalog: Free. Frequency: Semiannual
Circulation: 100M. Sales: $3-5MM
Products: Reproduction colonial furniture &
windsor chair kits; lighting & home accessories

COLONIAL WILLIAMSBURG (757) 229-1000
REPRODUCTIONS
P.O. Box 1776 • Williamsburg, VA 23187
E-Mail: catalog@cwf.org
Website: www.williamsburgmarketplace.com
Fax Ordering: (757) 565-8948
Contact Name: Frederick Nahm, President
Catalog: Free. Frequency: Annual
Circulation: 2MM. Sales: $3-5MM
Products: Reproduction home furnishings
& gift accessories

CONSUMER BROCHURE (570) 374-2711
Wood-Mode
1 Second St. • Kreamer, PA 17833
E-Mail: info@wood-mode.com
Website: www.wood-mode.com
Fax Ordering: (570) 374-2700
Catalog: Free. Pages: 132.
Frequency: Monthly
Circulation: 250M. Sales: $5-10MM
Products: Guide to dealers &
custom-built cabinetry

COUNTED CROSS-STITCH (800) 225-9848
Potpourri Collection
120 N. Meadows Rd. • Medfield, MA 02052
E-Mail: info@potpourrigifts.com
Website: www.potpourrigifts.com
Fax Ordering: (508) 359-8089
International Ordering: (508) 359-7702
Contact Name: Jack Rosenfeld, President
Catalog: Free. Frequency: Annual
Circulation: 10MM. Sales: $10-20MM
Products: Home furnishings, tableware,
gifts, needlecraft kits

COUNTRY CASUAL (800) 284-8325
9085 Comprint Ct.
Gaithersburg, MD 20877
E-Mail: sales@countrycasual.com
Website: www.countrycasual.com
Fax Ordering: (301) 926-9198
International Ordering: (301) 926-9195
Contact Name: Bobbie Goldstein, President
Catalog: Free. Frequency: Semiannual
Circulation: 100M. Sales: $3-5MM
Products: English style, solid teak garden
furniture including benches, chairs, tables,
swings, umbrellas & planters

COUNTRY CURTAINS (800) 456-0321
P.O. Box 955 • Stockbridge, MA 01262
E-Mail: dearjane@countrycurtains.com
Website: www.countrycurtains.com
Fax Ordering: (413) 243-1067
Customer Service: (800) 937-1237
Contact Name: Jane Fitzpatrick, President

Catalog: Free. Frequency: Semiannual
Circulation: 150M. Sales: $5-10MM
Products: Window treatment designs

COUNTRY HOUSE (800) 331-3602
805 E. Main St. • Salisbury, MD 21804
E-Mail: web@thecountryhouse.com
Website: www.thecountryhouse.com
Fax Ordering: (800) 721-6023
International Ordering: (410) 860-1987
Customer Service: (800) 596-4666
Contact Name: Mike Delano, President
Catalog: Free. Frequency: 5x per year
Circulation: 2MM. Sales: $10-20MM
Products: Americana, bath & laundry,
candles, collectibles, furniture & shelves,
kitchen & bath, beddings, wall decor,
wallpaper, garden, seasonal gifts, etc.

THE COUNTRY IRON FOUNDRY (800) 233-9945
65 Twelfth St. S. • Naples, FL 34102
E-Mail: info@firebacks.com
Website: www.firebacks.com
Fax Ordering: (239) 434-7207
International Ordering: (239) 434-2181
Contact Name: Wendy Stoughton, President
Catalog: Free. Frequency: Weekly
Circulation: 10M. Sales: $500M to $1MM
Products: Replicas of 18th century American
& French antique firebacks & stove plates for
fireplaces

COUNTRY TINWARE (800) 528-9382
Irvin's Country Tinware (800) 800-4846
RR 1 Box 73
Mt. Pleasant Mills, PA 17853
E-Mail: info@countrytinware.com
Website: www.countrytinware.com
Fax Ordering: (737) 539-2721
International Ordering: (737) 539-2366
Contact Name: Irvin Hoover, President
Catalog: Free. Frequency: Weekly
Circulation: 100M. Sales: $500M to $1MM
Products: Reproduction Early American
handcrafted lighting fixtures; home decor
& gifts, candle accessories, clocks, furniture

CRATE & BARREL CATALOG (800) 323-5461
P.O. Box 3210 • Naperville, IL 60566 Corporate (800) 717-1112
E-Mail: info@crateandbarrel.com
Website: www.crateandbarrel.com
Fax Ordering: (630) 527-1404, 527-1516
International Ordering: (847) 272-2888
Customer Service: (800) 237-5672
Catalog: Free. Frequency: Monthly
Circulation: 20MM. Sales: $100-200MM
Products: Home furnishings, outdoor
furniture, housewares

CRAZY CREEK PRODUCTS (800) 331-0304
P.O. Box 1050 • Red Lodge, MT 59068
E-Mail: chairs@crazycreek.com
Website: www.crazycreek.com
Fax Ordering: (406) 446-1411
International Ordering: (406) 446-3446
Contact Name: Rob Hart, President
Catalog: Free. Frequency: Annual
Circulation: 100M. Sales: $3-5MM
Products: Outdoor, lightweight, portable
chairs for sailing, camping, hiking, fishing,
hunting, lounging at the beach

CRYSTAL CLASSICS (800) 999-0655
6185-K Huntley Rd. • Columbus, OH 43229
E-Mail: info@crystalclassics.com
Website: www.crystalclassics.com
Fax Ordering: (614) 430-8727
International Ordering: (614) 430-8180
Catalog: Free. Frequency: Annual
Circulation: 100M. Sales: $3-5MM
Products: Fine crystal, especially glassware

CRYSTAL FARM CATALOG (970) 963-2350
18 Antelope Dr. • Redstone, CO 81623
E-Mail: crystalfarm@direcway.com
Website: www.crystalfarm.com
Fax Ordering: (970) 963-0709
Contact Name: Stephen C. Kent, President
Catalog: $25. Pages: 60. Frequency: Annual
Circulation: 10M. Sales: $1-3MM
Products: Antler chandeliers & furniture,
tables, armoires, beds, chairs, mirrors

DECORATIVE CRAFTS (800) 431-4455
P.O. Box 4308 • Greenwich, CT 06830
E-Mail: info@decorativecrafts.com
Website: www.decorativecrafts.com
Fax Ordering: (203) 531-1590
International Ordering: (203) 531-1500
Contact Name: Jeff Martin, President
Catalog: Free. Frequency: Quarterly
Circulation: 100MM. Sales: $10-20MM
Products: Imported decorative furniture
lamps & accessories

DAVIS & SMALL'S DECOR'S CATALOG (800) 849-5082
P.O. Box 2024 • Mt. Pleasant, SC 29465
E-Mail: info@davisandsmalldecor.com
Website: www.davisandsmalldecor.com
Fax Ordering: (800) 227-7398
International Ordering: (843) 881-8990
Contact Name: Thomas Davis, President
Catalog: Free. Frequency: Annual
Circulation: 250M. Sales: $5-10MM
Products: Wall decor, nostalgic recreations,
wooden signs framed & matted; vintage photos
& framed posters

DESIGN TOSCANO (800) 525-5141
1400 Morse Ave. • Elk Grove, IL 60007
E-Mail: customerservice@designtoscano.com
Website: www.designtoscano.com
Fax Ordering: (847) 255-7466
International Ordering: (847) 255-6799
Contact Names: Michael Stopka, President
Catalog: Free. Frequency: Annual
Circulation: 50K. Sales: $500K to $1MM
Products: Historical reproductions for home
& garden; garden & indoor statues; furniture,
decorative accessories; jewelry & gifts;
apparel; wall art & accents, garden statuary

DESIGN WITHIN REACH (800) 944-2233
225 Bush St., 20th Fl.
San Francisco, CA 94104
E-Mail: info@dwr.com
Website: www.dwr.com
Fax Ordering: (800) 846-0411;
(415) 676-6799
International Ordering: (415) 248-5397
Catalog: Free. Frequency: Semiannual
Circulation: 100M. Sales: $5-10MM
Products: Mid 20th century home furnishings

DIALOGICA   (212) 966-1934
59 Greene St. • New York, NY 10012 .
E-Mail: info@dialogica.com
Website: www.dialogica.com
Fax Ordering: (212) 966-2870
Contact Name: Monique Savarese, President
Catalog: Free. Frequency: Annual
Circulation: 100M. Sales: $3-5MM
Products: Furniture & home furnishings

DOMESTICATIONS   (800) 962-2211
Hanover Direct
P.O. Box 1568 • La Crosse, WI 54602
E-Mail: info@domestications.com
Website: www.domestications.com
Fax Ordering: (717) 630-4202
International Ordering: (717) 637-6000
Contact Name: Michael Ippolito, President
Catalog: Free. Frequency: 8x per year
Circulation: 10MM. Sales: $250-500MM
Products: Home furnishings & decorations;
home linens

DOOLINGS OF SANTA FE   (800) 835-0107
525 Airport Rd. • Santa Fe, NM 87505
Fax Ordering: (505) 471-1568
International Ordering: (505) 471-5956
Contact Name: Robert Dooling, President
Catalog: $5. Frequency: Annual
Circulation: 10MM. Sales: $1-3MM
Products: Southwestern furniture

EDUCATIONAL LUMBER   (800) 554-1722
P.O. Box 5373 • Asheville, NC 28803
Fax Ordering: (828) 255-8767
International Ordering: (828) 255-8765
Contact Name: Clark Bourne, President
Catalog: Free. Frequency: Annual
Circulation: 25M. Sales: $500M
Products: Furniture grade hardwoods &
softwoods for schools, homecraftsmen &
cabinmakers

ELLENBURG'S FURNITURE   (704) 873-2900
Ellenburg's Wicker & Casual Company
P.O. Box 5638 • Statesville, NC 28687
E-Mail: efurn@bellsouth.net
Website: www.ellenburgs.com
Fax Ordering: (704) 873-6002
Contact Name: Betty Ellenburg, President
Catalog: $7. Frequency: Annual
Circulation: 25M. Sales: $1-3MM
Products: Wicker, rattan & wood furniture

EVERYTHING NAUTICAL   (888) 211-4490
Wayzata, Inc.
1161 Wayzata Blvd. E. #20
Wayzata, MN 55391
E-Mail: everythingnautical@gmail.com
Website: www.everythingnautical.com
Fax Ordering: (952) 473-5801
International Ordering: (952) 473-9452
Contact Name: Elisha, President
Catalog: Free. Frequency: Annual
Circulation: 50M. Sales: $1-5MM
Products: Nautical decor & gifts

FACTORY DIRECT TABLE PAD CO.   (800) 428-4567
1501 W. Market St.
Indianapolis, IN 46222
E-Mail: info@tablepads.com

Website: www.tablepads.com
Fax Ordering: (317) 631-2584
International Ordering: (317) 631-2577
Contact Name: David Berger, President
Catalog: $1. Frequency: Annual
Circulation: 100M. Sales: $500M
Products: Custom made table pads

FLAGHOUSE FURNITURE EXPRESS   (800) 793-7900
46 W. Flaghouse Dr.
Hasbrouck Hts., NJ 07604
E-Mail: info@flaghouse.com
Website: www.flaghouse.com
Fax Ordering: (201) 288-7887
International Ordering: (201) 288-7600
Contact Name: George Carmel, President
Catalog: Free. Frequency: Bimonthly
Circulation: 2MM. Sales: $20-50MM
Products: Institutional, physical education,
recreation, rehabilitation & special education
furniture

FOREIGN TRADERS CATALOG   (866) 530-9080
202 Galisteo St. • Santa Fe, NM 87501
E-Mail: laura@foreigntraders.com
Website: www.foreigntraders.com
Fax Ordering: (505) 989-8917
International Ordering: (505) 983-6441
Contact Name: Alexander Tschursin, President
Catalog: $5. Frequency: Annual
Circulation: 25M. Sales: $500M to $1MM
Products: Handcrafted furniture & accessories

FRAN'S BASKET HOUSE   (973) 584-2230
295 Rt. 10 E • Succasunna, NJ 07876
E-Mail: sales@franswicker.com
Website: www.franswicker.com
Fax Ordering: (973) 584-7446
Contact Name: Fran Gruber President
Catalog: $1. Frequency: 3x per year
Circulation: 15M. Sales: $500M
Products: Wicker & rattan furniture &
accessories

FRONTGATE   (800) 626-6488
5566 West Chester Rd.   (888) 263-9850
West Chester, OH 45069
E-Mail: info@frontgate.com
Website: www.frontgate.com
Fax Ordering: (800) 436-2105; (513) 603-1492
International Ordering: (513) 603-1434
Customer Service: (800) 537-8484
Contact Name: Pete McAdams
Catalog: Free. Frequency: Quarterly
Circulation: 250M. Sales: $20-50MM
Products: Indoor furnishings; kitchen,
bed & bath, and home office accessories;
electronics and outdoor furniture ; holiday
& gifts

FULLER BRUSH CATALOG   (800) 732-1115
One Fuller Way • Great Bend, KS 67530   (800) 522-0499
E-Mail: info@fuller.com
Website: www.fuller.com
Fax Ordering: (620) 792-1906
International Ordering: (620) 792-1711
Contact Name: Norbert Schneider, President
Catalog: Free. Frequency: Quarterly
Circulation: 500M. Sales: $20-50MM
Products: Cleaning supplies & personal care
products

FURNITURE SAMPLER   (800) 323-8469
Triad Furniture Discounters
9654 N. Kings Hwy. • Myrtle Beach, SC 29577
Fax Ordering: (843) 499-5887
International Ordering: (843) 464-9646
Contact Name: John Clements, President
Catalog: Free. Frequency: Weekly
Circulation: 15M. Sales: $5-10MM
Products: Home & office furnishings

GARNET HILL   (800) 622-6216
231 Main St. • Franconia, NH 03580
E-Mail: customerservice@garnethill.com
Website: www.garnethill.com
Fax Ordering: (888) 842-9696
International Ordering: (603) 823-5545
Catalog: Free. Frequency: Bimonthly
Circulation: 25M. Sales: $1-3MM
Products: Natural fibers catalog for home &
fashion, including clothing, bedding, home
furnishings, etc.

GAVILLAN'S HANDSOME REWARDS   (951) 943-2011
Starcrest Products of California
3660 Brennan Ave. • Perris, CA 92599
Fax Ordering: (951) 943-2971
Contact Name: Tim Calandra, President
Catalog: Free. Frequency: Semiannual
Circulation: 2MM. Sales: $100-500MM
Products: Housewares

GAYLORD BROTHERS LIBRARY   (800) 634-6307
REFERENCE CATALOG
P.O. Box 4901 • Syracuse, NY 13221
E-Mail: customerservice@gaylord-inc.com
Website: www.gaylord-inc.com
Fax Ordering: (315) 457-0564
International Ordering: (315) 457—5070
Contact Name: Ronald Beckman, President
Catalog: Free. Frequency: Annual
Circulation: 250M. Sales: $1-3MM
Products: Library & archives furniture
& supplies

GRAND ERA REPRODUCTIONS   (800) 258-3822
KLH Marketing Corporation
925 N. Monroe St. • Lapeer, MI 48446
E-Mail: klhmkt@cardina.net
Website: www.grand-era.com
Fax Ordering: (714) 490-8269
International Ordering: (714) 999-0100
Contact Name: Lew Hunt, President
Catalog: $2. Frequency: Annual
Circulation: 100M. Sales: $500M
Products: Victorian doors & porch
decorations

GREEN DESIGN FURNITURE   (800) 853-4234
267 Commercial St. • Portland, ME 04101
E-Mail: info@greendesigns.com
Website: www.greendesigns.com
Fax Ordering: (207) 773-3320
International Ordering: (207) 775-4234
Catalog: Free. Frequency: Annual
Circulation: 25M. Sales: $1-3MM
Products: American classic wood furniture

GUMPS BY MAIL   (800) 284-8677
P.O. Box 489 • New Oxford, PA 17350   (800) 882-8055
E-Mail: info@gumps.com   (800) 766-7628
Website: www.gumps.com
Fax Ordering: (800) 945-9042

International Ordering: (717) 633-3317
TDD Ordering: (800) 617-2381
Customer Service: (800) 436-4311
Contact Name: Amy Berry, Manager
Catalog: Free. Pages: 48. Frequency: Quarterly
Circulation: 1MM. Sales: $10-20MM
Products: Furniture & rugs, bed & bath,
tabletop & entertaining, jewelry, collectibles,
gifts & holiday, corporate gifts, decorative &
garden

HEIRLOOM EUROPEAN TAPESTRIES   (800) 699-6836
14309 Hart Lane • Dobbins, CA 95935
E-Mail: heirloom@tapestries-inc.com
Website: www.tapestries-inc.com
Fax Ordering: (530) 692-2927
International Ordering: (530) 692-2022
Contact Name: James Waite, President
Catalog: Free. Frequency: Weekly
Circulation: 1MM. Sales: $5-10MM
Products: Museum reproductions loomed
in France, Belgium and Italy, plus aubasson
handwoven carpets & tapestry accessories

HEIRLOOM REPRODUCTIONS   (800) 288-1513
1834 W. 5th St. • Montgomery, AL 36106
E-Mail: victorianx@aol.com
Website: www.heirloomreproductions.com
Fax Ordering: (334) 263-3313
International Ordering: (334) 268-3511
Contact Name: Bush Gilchrist, Marketing
Catalog: $3. Frequency: Annual
Circulation: 15M. Sales: $100-250MM
Products: Victorian & French reproduction
furniture

HENKEL-HARRIS   (540) 667-4900
P.O. Box 2170 • Winchester, VA 22604
E-Mail: sales@henkelharris.com
Website: www.henkelharris.com
Fax Ordering: (540) 667-8261
Contact Name: William Henkel, President
Catalog: $20. Frequency: Annual
Circulation: 10M. Sales: $3-5MM
Products: Reproduction 18th century
furniture

HICKORY CHAIR COMPANY   (828) 328-1801
P.O. Box 2147 • Hickory, NC 28603
E-Mail: info@hickorychair.com

Website: www.hickorychair.com
Fax Ordering: (828) 328-8954
Contact Name: Jay Reardon, President
Catalog: $25. Pages: 176. Frequency: Quarterly
Circulation: 25M. Sales: $10-20MM
Products: Wood & upholstery furnishings

HOLDEVERYTHING CATALOG   (800) 421-2264
P.O. Box 379906 • Las Vegas, NV 89137
E-Mail: info@holdeverything.com
Website: www.holdeverything.com
Fax Ordering: (702) 363-2541
Customer Service: (800) 421-2285
Catalog: Free. Pages: 84. Frequency: Monthly
Circulation: 25MM. Sales: $10-50MM
Products: Home furnishings

HOME DECORATORS COLLECTION   (800) 445-6811
Knights, Ltd.   (877) 537-8539
2025 Concourse Dr. • St. Louis, MO 63146
E-Mail: info@homedecorators.com

Website: www.homedecorators.com
Fax Ordering: (314) 993-0502
International Ordering: (314) 993-1516
Contact Name: Gil Kemp, President
Catalog: Free. Frequency: Quarterly
Circulation: 2MM. Sales: $100-250MM
Products: Home & outdoor furnishings &
gifts: lighting, rugs, furniture, housewares,
bed & bath

MARTHA M. HOUSE FURNITURE   (800) 255-4195
1022 S. Decatur St. • Montgomery, AL 36104
E-Mail: sales@marthahouse.com
Website: www.marthahouse.com
Fax Ordering: (334) 262-2610
International Ordering: (334) 264-3558
Catalog: Free. Frequency: Quarterly
Circulation: 2MM. Sales: $100-250MM
Products: Furniture reproductions & accessories

HOWERTON ANTIQUE REPRODUCTIONS   (800) 443-4755
120 Buffalo Rd. • Clarksville, VA 23927
E-Mail: info@howertonfurniture.com
Website: www.howertonfurniture.com
Fax Ordering: (434) 374-2532
International Ordering: (434) 374-5715
Contact Name: Burton Sydnor, President
Catalog: $3. Frequency: Annual
Circulation: 100M. Sales: $500M to $1MM
Products: Antique reproductions furniture

HUNT COUNTRY FURNITURE   (845) 832-6601
RR 1 Box 208 • Wingdale, NY 12594
E-Mail: info@huntcountryfurniture.com
Website: www.huntcountryfurniture.com
Fax Ordering: (845) 832-3994
Contact Name: Jeffrey E. Gillette, President
Catalog: $2. Frequency: Annual
Circulation: 150M. Sales: $10-20MM
Products: Solid wood handcrafted furniture
including rockers, hutches, Windsor dining
room chairs, buffets, sideboard cupboards

HUNT GALLERIES   (800) 248-3876
P.O. Box 2324 • Hickory, NC 28603
E-Mail: info@huntgalleries.com
Website: www.huntgalleries.com
Fax Ordering: (828) 324-9921
International Ordering: (828) 324-9934
Contact Name: Robin Hunt-Hesner, President
Catalog: $10. Frequency: Annual
Circulation: 25M. Sales: $1-3MM
Products: Upholstered funiture

HUNTER FAN COMPANY   (888) 830-1326
11660 Central Pkwy.• Jacksonville, FL 32224
E-Mail: info@hunterfan.com
Website: www.hunterfan.com
Fax Ordering: (904) 642-4020
International Ordering: (904) 642-4340
Contact Name: Robert Beasley, President
Catalog: Free. Frequency: Weekly
Circulation: 250M. Sales: $20-50MM
Products: Antique reproduction ceiling
fans; air purifiers, humidifiers, thermostats

JACOBSEN ORIENTAL RUGS   (315) 422-7832
401 N. Salina St. • Syracuse, NY 13203
E-Mail: rugpeople@jacobsenrugs.com
Website: www.jacobsenrugs.com
Fax Ordering: (315) 422-6909
Contact Name: Bruce E. Kitney, President

Catalog: Free. Frequency: Annual
Circulation: 150M. Sales: $3-5MM
Products: Oriental rugs

LEVENGER COMPANY   (800) 544-0880
    (800) 667-8034
420 S. Congress Ave.
Delray Beach, FL 33445
E-Mail: orders@levenger.com
Website: www.levenger.com
Fax Ordering: (800) 544-6910
International Ordering: (561) 276-4141
Contact Name: Steven Leveen, President
Catalog: Free. Frequency: Semiannual
Circulation: 20MM. Sales: $50-100MM
Products: Kitchen collectibles & gifts; dishes
& crystal ; bookcases; halogen lighting

LINENSOURCE   (800) 434-9812
P.O. Box 31151 • Tampa, FL 33631
E-Mail: orders@linensource.com
Website: www.linensource.com
Fax Ordering: (813) 882-4605
Customer Service: (800) 466-8447
Catalog: Free. Frequency: Quarterly
Circulation: 200M. Sales: $5-10MM
Products: Sheets, bed ensembles, bedspreads,
basic bedding, bath, blankets, quilts; home decor

MAGNOLIA HALL   (866) 410-2755
8515 Haven Wood Trail • Roswell, GA 30076
E-Mail: orders@magnoliahall.com
Website: www.magnoliahall.com
Fax Ordering: (404) 351-2151
International Ordering: (404) 351-1910
Contact Name: David Rosinger, President
Catalog: $4. Frequency: Weekly
Circulation: 2MM. Sales: $500M to $1MM
Products: Victorian reproduction furniture
& accessories

MAILBOXES SALSBURY   (800) 725-7287
Salsbury Industries Mailboxes
1010 E. 62nd St. • Los Angeles, CA 90001
E-Mail: salsbury@mailboxes.com
Website: www.mailboxes.com
Fax Ordering: (800) 624-5299; (323) 846-6800
International Ordering: (323) 846-6700
Contact Name: Dennis Fraher, President
Catalog: Free. Frequency: Semiannual
Circulation: 100M. Sales: $5-10MM
Products: Commercial and residential
mailboxes; postal specialties

MAPLE GROVE RESTORATIONS   (860) 742-5432
P.O. Box 396 • Andover, CT 06232
E-Mail: info@maple-grove.com
Website: www.maple-grove.com
Fax Ordering: (860) 742-5393
Catalog: Free. Frequency: Monthly
Circulation: 250M. Sales: $500M to $1MM
Products: Interior raised panel shutters &
raised panel waals, wainscotting, mantels,
interior paneled doors, fireplace & entrance
way surrounds

MARION TRAVIS CATALOG   (704) 528-4424
P.O. Box 946 • Troutman, NC 28166
Fax Ordering: (704) 528-3526
Contact Name: Jason Warlick, Marketing
Catalog: Free. Frequency: 4x per year
Circulation: 10M. Sales: $500M
Products: Chairs, stools, tables, benches

MARYLAND CHINA COMPANY   (800) 638-3880
54 Main St. • Reisterstown, MD 21136
E-Mail: mdchina@worldnet.att.net
Website: www.marylandchina.com
Fax Ordering: (410) 833-1851
International Ordering: (410) 833-5559
Contact Name: Ed Weiner, President
Catalog: Free. Frequency: 24x per year
Circulation: 100M. Sales: $3-5MM
Minimum Order: $200
Products: China, porcelain & ceramic
giftware

McGUIRE CATALOG   (800) 662-4847
1201 Bryant St. • San Francisco, CA 94103
E-Mail: info@mcguirefurniture.com
Website: www.mcguirefurniture.com
Fax Ordering: (415) 864-8593
International Ordering: (415) 626-1414
Catalog: $20. Frequency: Annual
Circulation: 10M. Sales: $5-10MM
Products: Handcrafted & handfinished
furniture

MIKASA   (866) 645-2721
25 Enterprise Ave. N. • Secaucus, NJ 07094
E-Mail: info@mikasa.com
Website: www.mikasa.com
Fax Ordering: (201) 867-4480
International Ordering: (201) 867-3517
Contact Name: Peter Sienna, President
Catalog: Free. Frequency: Semiannual
Circulation: 1MM. Sales: $10-20MM
Products: Tableware, dinnerware, stemware
& barware, flatware & serveware, specialty
gifts & home decor

MILES KIMBALL OF OSHKOSH   (800) 255-4590
41 W. Eighth Ave. • Oshkosh, WI 54901
E-Mail: csr@mileskimball.com
Website: www.mileskimball.com
Fax Ordering: (920) 231-4804
International Ordering: (920) 231-3800
Contact Name: Doug Meyer, Marketing Manager
Catalog: Free. Frequency: 10x per year
Circulation: 50MM. Sales: $100-250MM
Products: Housewares, kitchen, home decor,
desktop & office, apparel, personal care, outdoor,
travel & auto, leisure, kids, holiday giftware

MODERN OFFICE   (800) 443-5117
9855 Hamilton Rd. • Eden Prairie, MN 55344
E-Mail: sales@modernofficefurniture.com
Website: www.modernofficefurniture.com
Fax Ordering: (952) 949-9816
International Ordering: (952) 941-2837
Catalog: Free. Frequency: Semiannual
Circulation: 100M. Pages: 100. Sales: $10-20MM
Products: Modern office furniture

MONROE COMPANY CATALOG   (800) 247-2488
316 N. Walnut St. • Colfax, IA 50054
Fax Ordering: (515) 674-3513
International Ordering: (515) 674-3511
Catalog: Free. Frequency: Annual
Circulation: 50M. Sales: $5-10MM
Products: Chair & table trucks & chairs
that are collapsable

THOS. MOSER CABINETMAKERS   (877) 708-1973
P.O. Box 1237 • Auburn, ME 04211
E-Mail: salesinfo@thosmoser.com

Website: www.thosmoser.com
Fax Ordering: (207) 784-6973
International Ordering: (207) 784-3332
Customer Service: (800) 708-9703
Contact Name: Thomas Moser, President
Catalog: $12. Frequency: Semiannual
Circulation: 100M. Sales: $10-20MM
Products: Handcrafted wood furniture

CLAIRE MURRAY   (800) 252-4733
P.O. Box 390 • Ascutney, VT 05030
E-Mail: orders@clairemurray.com
Website: www.clairemurray.com
Fax Ordering: (800) 544-6910
International Ordering: (561) 276-4141
Contact Name: Michael Blackman, President
Catalog: $5. Frequency: Semiannual
Circulation: 100M. Sales: $10-20MM
Products: Handhooked rugs

MURROW FURNITURE GALLERIES   (910) 799-4010
P.O. Box 4337 • Wilmington, NC 28406
E-Mail: orders@murrowfurniture.com
Website: www.murrowfurniture.com
Fax Ordering: (910) 791-2791
Contact Name: Linda Thorburn, President
Catalog: Free. Frequency: Annual
Circulation: 100M. Sales: $5-10MM
Products: Furniture

NAPASTYLE   (866) 776-6272
574 Gateway Dr. • Napa, CA 94558
E-Mail: customerservice@napastyle.com
Website: www.napastyle.com
Fax Ordering: (707) 252-1470
Customer Service: (866) 776-1600
Contact Name: Michael Chiarello, President
Furniture Specialist: (888) 865-7472
Catalog: Free. Pages: 80. Frequency: Quarterly
Circulation: 50M. Sales: $500M to $1MM
Products: Michael Chiarello's unique collection
of home furnishings, cooking tools & recipes

NATURAL HOME PRODUCTS CATALOG   (707) 824-0914
P.O. Box 1677 • Sebastopol, CA 95473
E-Mail: info@naturalhomeproducts.com
Website: www.naturalhomeproducts.com
Fax Ordering: (800) 329-9398
Contact Name: Susan B. Hendrickson, President
Catalog: Free. Frequency: Annual
Circulation: 25M. Sales: $1-3MM
Products: Natural home products including
floor covering and flooring; wool carpeting,
linoleum, rugs, natural paints, organic bedding
& sheets

OLD ADIRONDACK CATALOG   (800) 342-3373
7 Station Rd. • Willsboro, NY 12996
E-Mail: info@oldadirondack.com
Website: www.oldadirondack.com
Fax Ordering: (518) 963-7337
International Ordering: (518) 963-7184
Contact Name: Stephen Maselli, President
Catalog: Free. Frequency: Annual
Circulation: 100M. Sales: $1-3MM
Products: Cedar furniture

OUTDOORDECOR.COM   (800) 422-1526
Arthur Wilbur Co., Inc.
P.O. Box 3089 • Tuscaloosa, AL 35403
E-Mail: sales@outdoordecor.com
Website: www.outdoordecor.com

Fax Ordering: (205) 345-3788
International Ordering: (205) 345-1103
Catalog: Online. **Sales:** $5-10MM
Products: Patio furniture; home, garden &
outddor decorative merchandise such as
sundials, weathervanes, address plaques,
door mats, et al.

PIERRE DEUX   **(888) 743-7732**
40 Enterprise Ave. • Secaucus, NJ 07094
E-Mail: cservice@pierredeux.com
Website: www.pierredeux.com
Fax Ordering: (800) 769-8058; (610) 532-9001
International Ordering: (201) 809-2500
Catalog: Free. Frequency: Semiannual
Circulation: 50M. **Sales:** $5-10MM
Products: Fine French country furniture

PTI PYRAMID TECHNOLOGIES   **(888) 479-7264**
48 Elm St. • Meriden, CT 06450
E-Mail: sales@pti.com
Website: www.pyramidtechnologies.com
Fax Ordering: (203) 634-1696
International Ordering: (203) 238-0550
Contact Name: T. Jay Soboleski, President
Catalog: Free. Frequency: Monthly
Circulation: 25M. **Sales:** $5-10MM
Products: Decorative & commercial
clocks; lighting

PLEXI-CRAFT QUALITY PRODUCTS CORP.   **(800) 247-5394**
514 W. 24th St. • New York, NY 10011
E-Mail: info@plexi-craft.com
Website: www.plexi-craft.com
Fax Ordering: (212) 924-3508
International Ordering: (212) 924-3244
Contact Name: Shirley Rose, Marketing
Catalog: $2. Frequency: 7x per year
Circulation: 150M. **Sales:** $5-10MM
Products: Clear acrylic & custom furniture
& accessories in plexi-glass & lucite

PLOW & HEARTH   **(800) 627-1712**
Rt. 29 North • Madison, VA 22727
E-Mail: info@plowhearth.com
Website: www.plowhearth.com
Fax Ordering: (800) 843-2509
International Ordering: (540) 948-5412
Contact Name: Peter Rice, President
Catalog: Free. Frequency: Monthly
Circulation: 30MM. **Sales:** $20-50MM
Products: Products for country living;
home, garden, pets

POTTERY BARN   **(888) 779-5176**
Williams-Sonoma
100 7th Ave. • New York, NY 10001
E-Mail: customerservice@potterybarn.com
Website: www.potterybarn.com
Fax Ordering: (702) 363-2541
International Ordering: (702) 360-7002
Contact Name: Howard Lester, President
Catalog: Free. Frequency: Monthly
Circulation: 12MM. **Sales:** $20-50MM
Products: Household products; cookware
& utensils

PRIBA FURNITURE & INTERIORS   **(336) 855-9034**
210 Stage Coach Trail
Greensboro, NC 27415
E-Mail: orders@pribafurniture.com
Website: www.pribafurniture.com

Fax Ordering: (336) 855-1370
Contact Name: Priscilla Knox, President
Catalog: Free. Frequency: Annual
Circulation: 100M. **Sales:** $5-10MM
Products: Furniture & accessories

QUIMPER FAIENCE   **(800) 470-7339**
141 Water St. • Stonington, CT 06378
E-Mail: mail@quimperfaience.com
Website: www.quimperfaience.com
Fax Ordering: (860) 535-3509
International Ordering: (860) 535-1712
Contact Names: Paul & Sarah Janssens, President
Catalog: Free. Frequency: Semiannual
Circulation: 50M. **Sales:** $1-3MM
Products: Dinnerware, accessories &
decorative pottery handpainted in France
by Quimper artists

A.L. RANDALL   **(800) 257-2700**
P.O. Box 1482 • Lincolnshire, IL 60069
Fax Ordering: (847) 452-9217
International Ordering: (847) 634-4300
Contact Name: Dennis Stanek, President
Catalog: Free. Frequency: Annual
Circulation: 100M. **Sales:** $5-10MM
Products: Glassware, pottery & baskets

REPLACEMENTS, INC.   **(800) 737-5223**
P.O. Box 26029 • Greensboro, NC 27420
E-Mail: inquire@replacements.com
Website: www.replacements.com
Fax Ordering: (336) 697-3100
International Ordering: (336) 697-3000
Contact Name: Robert L. Page, President
Catalog: Free. Frequency: 3x per year
Circulation: 500M. **Sales:** $10-20MM
Products: China, crystal, and silver flatware

RESTORATION HARDWARE   **(800) 762-1005**
104 Challenger Dr. • Portland, TN 37148   **(800) 910-9845**
E-Mail: webcs@restorationhardware.com
Website: www.restorationhardware.com
Fax Ordering: (615) 325-1398
Customer Service: (800) 816-0901
Contact Name: Stephen Gordon
Catalog: Free. Frequency: Bimonthly
Circulation: 1MM. **Sales:** $20-50MM
Products: Furniture, lighting, cabinet
hardware, gardenware & unique gift items

ROOM & BOARD   **(800) 486-6554**
4600 Olson Memorial Hwy.
Minneapolis, MN 55422
E-Mail: info@roomandboard.com
Website: www.roomandboard.com
Fax Ordering: (763) 588-7971
International Ordering: (763) 588-7525
Contact Name: John Gabbert, President
Catalog: Free. Frequency: Semiannual
Circulation: 1MM. **Sales:** $50-100MM
Products: Home furnishings: sofas,
bookcases, chairs, tables

ROSS-SIMONS   **(800) 556-7376**
9 Ross Simons Dr. • Cranston, RI 02920   **(800) 835-0919**
E-Mail: customerservice@ross-simons.com
Website: www.ross-simons.com
Fax Ordering: (401) 463-8599
International Ordering: (401) 463-3100
Customer Service: (800) 835-1343
Contact Name: Darrell Ross, President

Catalog: Free. Frequency: Monthly
Circulation: 50MM. Sales: $100-250MM
Products: Home decor, tableware, jewelry,
gifts & collectibles, bridal & gift registry

RUGMAN.COM   (877) 784-6261
P.O. Box 2712 • Buffalo, NY 14240
E-Mail: sales@rugman.com
Website: www.rugman.com
International Ordering: (905) 471-7600
Catalog: Online. Sales: $5-10MM
Products: Area rugs, Persian rugs,
oriental rugs

RUGS EXPRESS.COM   (888) 727-7847
5610 Hollister Ave.
Santa Barbara, CA 93117
E-Mail: info@rugsexpress.com
Website: www.rugsexpress.com
Catalog: Online. Sales: 5-10MM
Products: Brand name rugs;
contemporary & traditional oriental rugs

RUGS USA   (800) 982-7210
106 E. Jericho Tpke.
Mineola, NY 11501
E-Mail: info@rugsusa.com
Website: www.rugsusa.com
Fax Ordering: (866) 681-8138
International Ordering: (516) 248-2220
Catalog: Free. Frequency: Semiannual
Circulation: 150M. Sales: $10-20MM
Products: Rugs, tapestries, slipcovers,
clocks, mirrors, lighting, art, auctions

SCULLY & SCULLY   (800) 223-3717
504 Park Ave. • New York, NY 10022
E-Mail: info@scullyandscully.com
Website: www.scullyandscully.com
Fax Ordering: (212) 486-1430
International Ordering: (212) 755-2590
Contact Name: Michael E. Scully, President
Catalog: Free. Frequency: Annual
Circulation: 50M. Sales: $1-5MM
Products: Home furnishings, accessories
& gifts for your home; designed & crafted items

SECRET COVE CATALOG   (800) 821-1946
76 George St.
St. Augustine, FL 32084
E-Mail: info@secretcove.com
Website: www.secretcove.com
Fax Ordering: (904) 829-8776
International Ordering: (904) 825-1946
Contact Name: James C. Keil, President
Catalog: Free. Frequency: 12x per year
Circulation: 150M. Sales: $3-5MM
Products: Decorative art for home,
office & garden

SHAKER WORKSHOPS   (800) 840-9121
P.O. Box 8001
Ashburnham, MA 01430
E-Mail: shaker@shakerworkshops.com
Website: www.shakerworkshops.com
Fax Ordering: (978) 827-9900
Contact Name: Richard C. Dabrowski, President
Catalog: Free. Frequency: 3x per year
Circulation: 150M. Sales: $5-10MM
Products: Reproductions of Shaker furniture
& accessories; gift items

SHIRLEY PEWTER SHOP   (800) 550-5356
P.O. Box 553
Williamsburg, VA 23187
E-Mail: info@shirleypewter.com
Website: www.shirleypewter.com
Fax Ordering: (757) 220-0452
International Ordering: (757) 229-5356
Contact Name: Bruce Robertson, President
Catalog: Free. Frequency: Annual
Circulation: 5M. Sales: $1-3MM
Products: Pewter products

SILVER QUEEN   (800) 262-3134
730 Indian Rocks Rd. N.
Belleair Bluffs, FL 33770
E-Mail: sales@silverqueen.com
Website: www.silverqueen.com
Fax Ordering: (757) 586-0822
International Ordering: (757) 581-6827
Contact Name: Greg Arbutine, President
Catalog: Free. Frequency: Semiannual
Circulation: 2MM. Sales: $5-10MM
Products: Silver flatware, china & crystal

SKY-MALL   (800) 759-6255
Sky Mall, Inc.
1520 E. Pima St. • Phoenix, AZ 85036
E-Mail: info@skymall.com
Website: www.skymall.com
Fax Ordering: (602) 254-6075
International Ordering: (602) 254-9777
Contact Name: Robert Worsley, President
Catalog: Free. Frequency: Quarterly
Circulation: 12MM. Sales: $20-50MM
Products: Household products; electronics; bed
& bath products; computer supplies; apliances,
telephones, automotive; audio, apparel

DAVID T. SMITH & COMPANY   (888) 353-9387
3600 Shawhan Rd. • Morrow, OH 45152
E-Mail: sales@davidtsmith.com
Website: www.davidtsmith.com
Fax Ordering: (513) 933-0467
International Ordering: (513) 932-2472
Contact Name: John Dell, President
Catalog: $5. Frequency: Annual
Circulation: 25M. Sales: $3-5MM
Products: Museum quality handcrafted
18th & 19th century furniture and pottery
reproductions.

SMITH+NOBLE   (800) 248-8888
P.O. Box 1838 • Corona, CA 92878
E-Mail: contactus@smithnoble.com
Website: www.smithandnoble.com
Fax Ordering: (800) 426-7780
Catalog: Free. Frequency: Semiannual
Circulation: 100M. Sales: $1-3MM
Products: Windoware, including shades,
blinds, fabrics, and hardware.

SOBOL HOUSE OF FURNISHINGS   (828) 669-8031
141 Richardson Blvd.
Black Mountain, NC 28711
E-Mail: info@sobolhouse.com
Website: www.sobolhouse.com
Fax Ordering: (828) 669-7969
Contact Name: John Sobol, President
Catalog: Free. Frequency: Annual
Circulation: 25M. Sales: $1-3MM
Products: Discount furniture

SOFT SURROUNDINGS   (800) 749-7638
P.O. Box 4205 • Hazelwood, MO 63042
E-Mail: info@softsurroundings.com
Website: www.softsurroundings.com
Fax Ordering: (314) 521-5780
Customer Service: (888) 414-7638
Catalog: Free. Frequency: Quarterly
Circulation: 100M. Sales: $3-5MM
Products: Women's fashions, accessories,
makeup, home furnishings, bed & bath, etc.

SOUTHERN HEIRLOOMS   (800) 255-4195
FROM MARTHA M. HOUSE
1022 S. Decatur St.
Montgomery, AL 36104
E-Mail: sales@marthahouse.com
Website: www.marthahouse.com
Fax Ordering: (212) 924-3508
International Ordering: (212) 924-3244
Contact Name: William House, President
Catalog: $3. Frequency: Annual
Circulation: 50M. Sales: $1-3MM
Products: Furniture & occasional furniture;
Victorian & French reproductions

SPACE - IKEA CATALOG   (610) 834-1520
400 Allenwood Rd.
Conshohocken, PA 19428
E-Mail: info@ikea.com
Website: www.ikea.com
Fax Ordering: (610) 834-0439
Contact Name: Anders Dahlvig, President
Catalog: Free. Frequency: Annual
Circulation: 10MM. Sales: $50-100MM
Products: Furniture & accessories;
housewares, gift items

C.G. SPARKS   (801) 595-6900
454 South 500 West
Salt Lake City, UT 84101
E-Mail: info@cgsparks.com
Website: www.cgsparks.com
Fax Ordering: (801) 519-6900
Catalog: Free. Frequency: Semiannual
Circulation: 100M. Sales: $5-10MM
Products: Indian furniture & antiques,
rustic furniture, handmade furniture

SPORTY'S CATALOGS   (800) 776-7897
Clermont Airport • Batavia, OH 45103
E-Mail: info@sportys-catalogs.com
Website: www.sportys-catalogs.com
Fax Ordering: (513) 735-9200
International Ordering: (513) 735-9000
Contact Name: Howard Law, Buyer
Catalogs: Preferred Living; Sporty's Tool Shop;
Outdoor Leisure; Wright Brothers Collection;
and Pilot Shop. All are Free. Frequency: Quarterly.
Circulation: 20MM. Sales: $20-50MM
Products: Home items; lawn care; tools/
maintenance; outdoor furniture; apparel/clothing

MARTHA STEWART LIVING   (800) 950-7130
20 W. 43 St. • New York, NY 10036
E-Mail: mail@marthastewart.com
Website: www.marthastewart.com
Fax Ordering: (212) 827-8289
International Ordering: (212) 522-7800
Contact Name: Martha Stewart, President
Catalog: Free. Frequency: Quarterly
Circulation: 2MM. Sales: $5-10MM
Products: Household products

STICKLEY CATALOG   (315) 682-5500
P.O. Box 480 • Manlius, NY 13104
E-Mail: orders@stickley.com
Website: www.stickley.com
Fax Ordering: (315) 682-6306
International Ordering: (561) 276-4141
Contact Name: Alfred Audi, President
Catalog: $10. Frequency: Annual
Circulation: 50M. Sales: $20-50MM
Products: Solid wood furniture

STITCHERY CATALOG   (800) 225-9848
Potpourri Collection   (800) 388-9662
120 N. Meadows Rd.
Medfield, MA 02052
E-Mail: customerservice@thestitchery.com
Website: www.thestitchery.com
Fax Ordering: (508) 359-8089
International Ordering: (508) 359-7702
Customer Service: (800) 688-8051
Contact Name: Suzanne Knowles, President
Catalog: Free. Frequency: Bimonthly
Circulation: 12MM. Sales: $10-20MM
Products: Home furnishings, tableware,
needlecraft kits, gifts

STURBRIDGE YANKEE WORKSHOP   (800) 343-1144
90 Blueberry Rd. • Portland, ME 04102   (800) 231-8060
E-Mail: info@sturbridgeyankee.com
Website: www.sturbridgeyankee.com
Fax Ordering: (207) 774-2561
International Ordering: (207) 774-9045
Contact Name: Thomas Binnie, President
Catalog: Free. Frequency: 5x per year
Circulation: 15MM. Sales: $20-50MM
Products: Country furnishings; household
textiles; furniture, rugs, lighting, wall decor,
kitchen, garden & hearth, decorative accents.

SURE FIT SLIPCOVERS BY MAIL   (800) 305-5857
Sure Fit, Inc.   (888) 754-7166
7339 Industrial Blvd.
Allentown, PA 18106
E-Mail: info@surefit.com
Website: www.surefit.com
Fax Ordering: (610) 336-8996
Contact Name: Bert Shlesky, President
Catalog: Free. Frequency: Weekly
Circulation: 6MM. Sales: $20-50MM
Products: Ready-made furniture & slipcovers

TEAK PATIO WAREHOUSE   (866) 535-6558
702 Jessie St. • San Fernando, CA 91340
E-Mail: sales@teakpatiowarehouse.com
Website: www.teakpatiowarehouse.com
Fax Ordering: (818) 898-3201
International Ordering: (818) 898-7767
Catalog: Free. Frequency: Quarterly
Circulation: 150K. Sales: $5-10MM
Products: Teakwood patio & garden furniture
& accessories; indoor teakwood furniture

TELESCOPE CASUAL FURNITURE   (518) 642-1100
85 Church St. • Granville, NY 12832
E-Mail: sales@telescopecasual.com
Website: www.telescopecasual.com
Fax Ordering: (518) 642-2536
Contact Name: Shelley Campbell, President
Catalog: Free. Frequency: Semiannual
Circulation: 15M. Sales: $20-50MM
Products: Summer & casual furniture

THIS END UP CATALOG   (800) 627-5161
This End Up Furniture Co.
1309 Exchange Ally • Richmond, VA 23219
E-Mail: sales@marthahouse.com
Website: www.marthahouse.com
Fax Ordering: (804) 783-2159
International Ordering: (434) 774-3024
Contact Name: Robert Kemeny, President
Catalog: Free. Frequency: 3x per year
Circulation: 2M. Sales: $50-100M
Products: Furniture & accessories for
the whole house

TIDEWATER WORKSHOP   (800) 666-8433
P.O. Box 456 • Egg Harbor City, NJ 08215
E-Mail: customers@tidewaterworkshop.com
Website: www.tidewaterworkshop.com
Fax Ordering: (609) 965-8212
International Ordering: (609) 965-4000
Customer Service: (609) 965-5127
Contact Name: Ron Schwarcz, President
Catalog: Free. Frequency: Annual
Circulation: 150K. Sales: $5-10M
Products: White Cedar outdoor furnishings

TOUCH OF CLASS CATALOG   (800) 457-7456
709 W. 12th St. • Huntingburg, IN 47542
E-Mail: sales@touchofclass.com
Website: www.touchofclass.com
Fax Ordering: (812) 683-5921
International Ordering: (812) 683-3707
Contact Name: Frederick Bell, President
Catalog: Free. Frequency: Monthly
Circulation: 5M. Sales: $50-100M
Products: Home decor including bedding,
bath, wall decor, lamps, home accents,
kids; patio furniture, garden accents, rugs,
outdoor art & plaques

TROSBY CATALOG   (800) 243-5141
95 Chastian Rd. • Kennesaw, GA 30144
E-Mail: sales@trosbyfurniture.com
Website: www.trosbyfurniture.com
Fax Ordering: (770) 795-9421
International Ordering: (770) 795-9420
Contact Name: Charlie Harper, President
Catalog: $12. Frequency: Annual
Circulation: 5M. Sales: $1-3MM
Products: Residential & commercial furniture

TWIN OAKS HAMMOCKS CATALOG   (800) 688-8946
138 Twin Oaks Rd. • Louisa, VA 23093
E-Mail: hammocks@twinoaks.org
Website: www.twinoakshammocks.com
Fax Ordering: (540) 894-4112
International Ordering: (540) 894-5125
Contact Name: Paxus Calta, Marketing
Catalog: Free. Frequency: Annual
Circulation: 15M. Sales: $1-3MM
Products: Hammocks & hanging chairs

UNITED FORCE PRODUCTS   (800) 741-1344
P.O. Box 3491 • Sumas, WA 98295
E-Mail: info@unitedforce.com
Website: www.unitedforce.com
Fax Ordering: (800) 742-8250
International Ordering: (402) 331-5511
Contact Name: Russ Hogan, President
Catalog: Free. Frequency: Weekly
Circulation: 25M. Sales: $500M to $1MM
Products: Antique reproductions, handcrafted
wooden signs

VERMONT INDUSTRIES   (800) 639-1715
RR 1 Box 301 • Cuttingsville, VT 05738
E-Mail: vtindus@together.com
Website: www.ironcreations.com
Fax Ordering: (802) 492-3500
International Ordering: (802) 492-3451
Contact Name: Phil Burns, President
Catalog: Online. Sales: $1-3MM
Products: Home furnishings; wrought iron
lighting & home accessories; garden accessories;
bathroom accessories, outdoor lighting

VERMONT OUTDOOR FURNITURE CO.   (800) 588-8834
9 Auburn St. • Barre, VT 05641
E-Mail: sales@vermontoutdoorfurniture.com
Website: www.vermontoutdoorfurniture.com
Fax Ordering: (802) 476-8834
Contact Name: Bruce Gratz, President
Catalog: $3. Frequency: Semiannual
Circulation: 25M. Sales: $5-10MM
Products: Classic cedar furniture for the
outdoors, including tables, chairs, benches,
porch swings, gliders

VICTOR STANLEY   (800) 368-2573
P.O. Drawer 330 • Dunkirk, MD 20754
E-Mail: sales@victorstanley.com
Website: www.victorstanley.com
Fax Ordering: (410) 257-7579
Contact Name: Stanley Skalka, President
Catalog: Free. Frequency: Annual
Circulation: 50M. Sales: $3-5MM
Products: Outdoor furniture & accessories

WALPOLE WOODWORKERS   (800) 343-6948
767 E St., Rt. 27 • Walpole, MA 02081
E-Mail: sales@walpolewoodworkers.com
Website: www.walpolewoodworkers.com
Fax Ordering: (508) 668-7301
International Ordering: (508) 668-2800
Contact Name: Lou Maglio, President
Catalog: $6. Frequency: Annual
Circulation: 100M. Sales: $20-50MM
Products: Furniture, fence & small buildings

WEDDING LINENS   (845) 426-3300
80 Red Schoolhouse Rd. #215
Spring Valley, NY 10977
E-Mail: orderinfo@weddinglinens.com
Website: www.weddinglinens.com
Fax Ordering: (845) 426-3365
Catalog: Free. Frequency: Annual
Circulation: 10M. Sales: $1-3MM
Products: Line of wedding specialty linen
available for rental

WHITECHAPEL LIMITED   (800) 468-5534
P.O. Box 11719 • Jackson, WY 83002
E-Mail: whitechapel@wyoming.com
Website: www.whitechapel-ltd.com
Fax Ordering: (307) 739-9458
International Ordering: (307) 739-9478
Contact Name: Robert Dunstan, President
Catalog: $5. Frequency: Annual
Circulation: 10M. Sales: $1-3MM
Products: Furniture maker; high quality
hardware

WHITEHALL PRODUCTS   (800) 728-5449
8786 Water St. • Montague, MI 49437
E-Mail: info@whitehallproducts.com
Website: www.whitehallproducts.com

Fax Ordering: (231) 893-1757
International Ordering: (231) 894-2688
Customer Service: (800) 728-2164
Contact Name: Brad Bruns, President
Catalog: Free. Frequency: Semiannual
Circulation: 250M. Sales: $10-20MM
Products: Hand cast aluminum home decorations

WICKER WAREHOUSE   (800) 989-4253
195 S. River St.
Hackensack, NJ 07601
E-Mail: sales@wickerwarehouse.com
Website: www.wickerwarehouse.com
Fax Ordering: (201) 342-1495
International Ordering: (201) 342-6709
Contact Name: Bob Ermillo, President
Catalog: Free. Frequency: Annual
Circulation: 50M. Sales: $1-3MM
Products: Wicker & rattan furniture & gifts

WILD WINGS COLLECTION   (800) 445-4833
S. Hwy. 61 • Lake City, MN 55041   (800) 248-7312
E-Mail: info@wildwings.com
Website: www.wildwings.com
Fax Ordering: (651) 345-2981
Contact Name: Mary Coyle, Buyer
Catalog: Free. Frequency: Monthly
Circulation: 5MM. Sales: $5-10MM
Products: Home furnishings, apparel, nature art prints, sculpture

WOODBURY PEWTERERS   (800) 648-2014
860 Main St. S. • Woodbury, CT 06793
E-Mail: pewter@snet.net
Website: www.woodburypewter.com
Fax Ordering: (800) 819-9492
International Ordering: (203) 263-2668
Contact Name: Paul Titcomb, President
Catalog: Free. Frequency: Semiannual
Circulation: 50M. Sales: $1-3MM
Products: Pewter gifts, collectibles, housewares and decorative accessories

WORTHINGTON ARCHITECTURAL DETAILS   (800) 872-1608
331 Love St. • Troy, AL 36081
E-Mail: worthingtonsales@usa.net
Website: www.worthingtononline.com
Fax Ordering: (334) 566-5390
International Ordering: (334) 566-4537
Contact Name: Amy Ingalls, President
Catalog: $3. Frequency: Annual
Circulation: 50M. Sales: $500M to $1MM
Products: Furniture & architectural columns, medallions, mantels, domes & moulding

YIELD HOUSE CATALOG   (800) 659-0206
71 Hobbs St. • Conway, NH 03818
Fax Ordering: (603) 447-1717
International Ordering: (603) 447-8500
Contact Name: Linda Como, Buyer
Catalog: Free. Frequency: Annual
Circulation: 50M. Sales: $1-3MM
Products: Solid wood Earl American furniture & accessories

ABC VACUUM WAREHOUSE (800) 285-8145
6720 Burnet Rd. • Austin, TX 78757
E-Mail: customerservice@abcvacuum.com
Website: www.abcvacuum.com
Fax Ordering: (512) 451-2352
International Ordering: (512) 459-7643
Contact Name: Ralph Baccus, President
Catalog: Free. Frequency: Annual
Circulation: 100K. Sales: $3-5MM
Products: Vacuum cleaners

ALBION ENTERPRISES CATALOG (800) 248-1475
5577 Skylane Blvd. 5A
Santa Rosa, CA 95403
E-Mail: albion@sonic.net
Website: www.albionjuicer.com
Fax Ordering: (707) 528-0608
International Ordering: (707) 528-1473
Contact Name: Ralph Baccus, President
Catalog: Free. Frequency: Annual
Circulation: 100K. Sales: $3-5MM
Products: Kitchen equipment related to
health food; juicers, blenders, ionizers,
pressure cookers, water filters, yogurt
makers; books

ATLANTA CUTLERY CORPORATION (800) 883-0300
2147 Gees Mill Rd. • Conyers, GA 30013 (800) 883-8838
E-Mail: custserv@atlantacutlery.com
Website: www.atlantacutlery.com
Fax Ordering: (770) 388-0246
International Ordering: (770) 922-7500
Contact Name: Pradeep Windlass, President
Catalog: Free. Frequency: Annual
Circulation: 150K. Sales: $5-10MM
Products: Cutlery, hunting & pocket knives,
military knives & swords, antique knives;
Early American bowie reproductions; blades
& materials for custom knifemaking

B&J PEERLESS FOOD (800) 255-3663
SERVICE EQUIPMENT (888) 621-6165
1616 Dielman Rd. • St. Louis, MO 63132
E-Mail: peerless@bjpeerless.com
Website: www.bjpeerless.com
Fax Ordering: (314) 731-7284
International Ordering: (314) 428-1247
Contact Name: Deb Davis, Contact
Catalog: Free. Frequency: Annual
Circulation: 100K. Sales: $5-10MM
Products: Wholesale restaurant supplies &
commercial kitchen equipment for foodservice
operations & professional quality kitchens at
home

BALL & BALL CATALOG (800) 257-3711
463 W. Lincoln Hwy. • Exton, PA 19341
E-Mail: info@ballandball-us.com
Website: www.ballandball-us.com
Fax Ordering: (610) 363-7639
International Ordering: (610) 363-7330
Contact Name: Bill Ball, President
Catalog: Free. Frequency: Semiannual
Circulation: 200K. Sales: $3-5MM
Products: Quality hardware reproductions
& restoration

BERYL'S CAKE DECORATING (800) 488-2749
& PASTRY SUPPLIES
P.O. Box 1584 • N. Springfield, VA 22151
E-Mail: beryls@beryls.com
Website: www.beryls.com

Fax Ordering: (703) 750-3779
International Ordering: (703) 256-6951
Contact Name: Beryl Loveland, President
Catalog: $8. Pages: 225. Frequency: Annual
Circulation: 5K. Sales: $500K
Products: Diamonds & fine jewelry

BRIDGE KITCHENWARE CORP. (973) 287-6163
563C Eagle Rock Ave. • Roseland, NJ 07068
E-Mail: customerservice@bridgekitchenware.com
Website: www.bridgekitchenware.com
Contact Name: Kathy & Steven Bridge, Owners
Catalog: $3. Frequency: Annual
Circulation: 25K. Sales: $3-5MM
Products: Imported kitchen equipment
& supplies

JEFF CAMPBELL'S (800) 717-2532
CLEAN TEAM CATALOG (800) 238-2996
206 N. Main St. • Jackson, CA 95642 TDD (888) 223-1136
E-Mail: inquire@thecleanteam.com
Website: www.thecleanteam.com
Fax Ordering: (209) 223-7994
International Ordering: (209) 223-5906
Contact Name: Jeff Campbell, President
Catalog: Free. Frequency: Quarterly
Circulation: 150K. Sales: $1-3MM
Products: Home maintenance products,
household cleaning products

BETTY CROCKER ENTERPRISES (800) 446-1898
P.O. Box 9452 • Minneapolis, MN 55440
E-Mail: info@bettycrocker.com
Website: www.bettycrocker.com
Fax Ordering: (763) 764-8330
International Ordering: (763) 764-8330
Contact Name: Bruce Atwater, President
Catalog: Free. Frequency: Semiannual
Circulation: 250K. Sales: $50-100MM
Products: Kitchen convenience items

BRYLANE HOME & KITCHEN CATALOGS (800) 528-5150
P.O. Box 4401 • Taunton, MA 02780 (800) 544-3793
E-Mail: bhcustserv@brylane.com
Website: www.brylanehome.com
Fax Ordering: (800) 528-5152
Customer Service: (800) 528-5156
Catalog: Free. Pages: 76. Frequency: Quarterly
Circulation: 200K. Sales: $20-50MM
Products: Bedding, windows, rugs, furniture,
towels; kitchenware; bathroom products

CENTRAL RESTAURANT PRODUCTS (800) 215-9293
7750 Georgetown Rd.
Indianapolis, IN 46268
E-Mail: sales@centralrestaurant.com
Website: www.centralrestaurant.com
Fax Ordering: (317) 634-5476
International Ordering: (317) 634-2550
Customer Service: (800) 882-8339
Contact Name: Richard Weinstein, President
Catalog: Free. Frequency: Annual
Circulation: 150K. Sales: $5-10MM
Products: Restaurant & kitchen equipment

CHEFS CATALOG (800) 884-2433
5070 Centennial Blvd. (800) 338-3232
Colorado Springs, CO 80919
E-Mail: sales@chefscatalog.com
Website: www.chefscatalog.com
Fax Ordering: (800) 967-2433
International Ordering: (719) 272-2700

Contact Name: Marshall Marcovitz, President
Catalog: Free. Frequency: Semiannual
Circulation: 3MM. Sales: $10-20MM
Products: Gourmet kitchenware

A COOK'S WARE   (800) 915-9788
211 37th St. Ext. • Beaver Falls, PA 15010
E-Mail: sales@cookswares.com
Website: www.cookswares.com
Fax Ordering: (724) 846-9562
International Ordering: (724) 846-9490
Contact Name: Bryon Bitar, President
Catalog: Free. Frequency: Annual
Circulation: 200K. Sales: $3-5MM
Products: Cookware & kitchen utensils

COOKING.COM   (800) 663-8810
4086 Del Rey Ave.
Marina Del Rey, CA 90292
E-Mail: info@cooking.com
Website: www.cooking.com
International Ordering: (310) 450-3270
Customer Service: (877) 999-2433
Catalog: Free. Frequency: Semiannual
Circulation: 150K. Sales: $50-100MM
Products: Housewares: bakeware, barware,
cooking tools, BBQ & patio, cutlery, small
appliances, tableware, cookbooks, furnishings

CRYSTAL CLASSICS   (800) 999-0655
6185-K Huntley Rd. • Columbus, OH 43229
E-Mail: info@crystalclassics.com
Website: www.crystalclassics.com
Fax Ordering: (614) 430-8727
International Ordering: (614) 430-8180
Catalog: Free. Frequency: Quarterly
Circulation: 150K. Sales: $3-5MM
Products: Fine crystal, especially glassware

CUISINE PARTS INTERNATIONAL   (800) 852-3150
P.O. Box 480239 • Fort Lauderdale, FL 33348
E-Mail: cservice1@cuisineparts.com
Website: www.cuisineparts.com
Fax Ordering: (954) 754-6904
International Ordering: (954) 785-6224
Catalog: Free. Frequency: Semiannual
Circulation: 100K. Sales: $5-10MM
Products: Tools & accessories for the kitchen

CUTCO CUTLERY CATALOG   (800) 633-8323
Vector Marketing Corp.   Canada (800) 361-8800
322 Houghton Ave. • Olean, NY 14760
E-Mail: service@cutco.com
Website: www.cutco.com
Fax Ordering: (716) 790-7173
International Ordering: (716) 790-7000
Customer Service: (800) 828-0448
Contact Name: James M. Stitt, President
Catalog: Free. Frequency: Semiannual
Circulation: 25K. Sales: $1-3MM
Products: Knives of all kinds, scissors

CUTLERY SHOPPE   (800) 231-1272
3956 E. Vantage Pointe Ln.
Meridian, ID 83642
E-Mail: orders@cutleryshoppe.com
Website: www.cutleryshoppe.com
Fax Ordering: (208) 884-4433
International Ordering: (208) 884-5250
Catalog: Free. Frequency: Semiannual
Circulation: 100K. Sales: $1-3MM
Products: Collectible & everyday knives

DEA BATHROOM MACHINERIES   (800) 255-4426
495 Main St. • Murphys, CA 95247
E-Mail: sales@deabath.com
Website: www.deabath.com
Fax Ordering: (209) 728-2320
International Ordering: (209) 728-2031
Contact Name: Thomas W. Scheller, President
Catalog: Free. Frequency: Annual
Circulation: 100K. Sales: $3-5MM
Minimum Order: $100 (International)
Products: Antique plumbing fixtures, parts
& decorator accessories; lighting & hardware

DECORATIVE HARDWARE STUDIO   (914) 238-5251
P.O. Box 627 • Chappaqua, NY 10514
E-Mail: decordhwr@aol.com
Website: www.decorative-hardware.com
Fax Ordering: (914) 238-4880
Contact Name: Ron Prezner, President
Catalog: Free. Frequency: Monthly
Circulation: 150K. Sales: $1-3MM
Products: Decorative hardware

EBA APPLIANCE WORLD CORP.   (866) 227-5322
2361 Nostrand Ave. • Brooklyn, NY 11210
E-Mail: sales@shopeba.com
Website: www.shopeba.com
Fax Ordering: (718) 253-6002
International Ordering: (718) 252-3400
Contact Name: Tom Tesoriero, President
Catalog: Free. Frequency: Annual
Circulation: 100K. Sales: $5-10MM
Products: Wholesale distributors of electronics,
bedding & appliances.

ECOLOGICAL ENGINEERING GROUP   (866) 432-6364
P.O. Box 415 • Weston, MA 01742
E-Mail: info@ecological-engineering.com
Website: www.ecological-engineering.com
Fax Ordering: (978) 369-2484
International Ordering: (978) 369-9440
Contact Name: David Delporto, President
Catalog: Free. Frequency: Annual
Circulation: 50K. Sales: $1-3MM
Products: Solar-equatics systems for irrigation
of plants & groundwater recharge; flushing toilets.

EUROPEAN KITCHEN BAZAAR   (800) 243-8540
P.O. Box 480239 • Fort Lauderdale, FL 33348   (888) 243-8540
E-Mail: cservice1@europeankitchenbazaar.com
Website: www.europeankitchenbazaar.com
Fax Ordering: (954) 754-6904
International Ordering: (954) 785-6224
Contact Name: Robert Johnson, President
Catalog: Free. Frequency: 3x per year
Circulation: 100K. Sales: $1-3MM
Products: Food processors, parts,
accessories & repairs

FOODCRAFTER'S SUPPLY CATALOG   (800) 776-0575
Kitchen Krafts, Inc.
P.O. Box 442 • Waukon, IA 52172
E-Mail: orders@kitchenkrafts.com
Website: www.kitchenkrafts.com
Fax Ordering: (563) 535-8001
International Ordering: (563) 535-8000
Customer Service: (800) 298-5389
Contact Name: Lynn Sorensen, President
Catalog: Free. Frequency: Annual
Circulation: 100K. Sales: $5-10MM
Products: Specialty cooking tools, supplies,
ingredients, books, videos, & packaging products

GLOBE EQUIPMENT CATALOG (800) 972-4972
Globe Equipment Co.
300 Dewey St. • Bridgeport, CT 06605
E-Mail: household@globeequipment.com
Website: www.globeequipment.com
Fax Ordering: (203) 366-7003
International Ordering: (203) 367-6611
Contact Name: Brian Ringelheim, President
Catalog: Free. Frequency: Annual
Circulation: 300K. Sales: $50-100MM
Products: Commercial restaurant equipment
& supplies; dishwasher racks, dispensers
& trays

GOLD MEDAL FUN FOOD (800) 888-3346
EQUIPMENT & SUPPLIES (800) 543-0862
Gold Medal Products Co.
10700 Medallion Dr.
Cincinnati, OH 45241
E-Mail: info@gmpopcorn.com
Website: www.gmpopcorn.com
Fax Ordering: (336) 852-5062
International Ordering: (336) 852-5996
Contact Name: John Evans, VP Sales
Catalog: Free. Frequency: Annual
Circulation: 150K. Sales: $10-50MM
Products: Concession equipment &
supplies for making popcorn; gourmet
popcorn; cotton candy, hot dogs,
candy apples, fried foods, et al.

GRANVILLE MANUFACTURING CO. (800) 828-1005
Route 100 • Grannville, VT 05747
E-Mail: woodsiding@woodsiding.com
Website: www.woodsiding.com
Fax Ordering: (802) 767-3107
International Ordering: (802) 767-4747
Contact Names: Robert Fuller, President
Catalog: Free. Frequency: Semiannual
Circulation: 50K. Sales: $3-5MM
Products: Wooden bowls & wooden
kitchenware

GRILL LOVERS CATALOG (866) 239-6777
Char-Broil Warranty
P.O. Box 1240 • Columbus, GA 31902
E-Mail: info@charbroil.com
Website: www.charbroil.com
Fax Ordering: (706) 565-2132
International Ordering: (706) 565-2100
Customer Service: (800) 241-7548
Contact Names: Connie Warner, VP/Director
Catalog: Free. Frequency: Bimonthly
Circulation: 2MM. Sales: $20-50MM
Products: BBQ's, grills, smokers & fryers;
outdoor fireplaces; accessories, recipes;
replacement parts

HARBOR FREIGHT TOOLS (800) 423-2567
3491 Mission Oaks Blvd.
Camarillo, CA 93012
E-Mail: info@harborfreight.com
Website: www.harborfreight.com
Fax Ordering: (800) 905-5220
International Ordering: (805) 388-3000
Customer Service: (800) 444-3353
Contact Name: Gerry Dammler, President
Catalog: Free. Frequency: Bimonthly
Circulation: 150K. Sales: $3-5MM
Products: Hand tools, hardware

HOME TRENDS CATALOG (800) 810-2340
P.O. Box 20403 • Rochester, NY 14602
E-Mail: customercare@gcidirect.com
Website: www.shophometrends.com
Fax Ordering: (585) 889-8686
International Ordering: (585) 254-6520
Customer Service: (888) 488-3088
Contact Name: Jane L. Glazer, President
Catalog: Free. Frequency: Quarterly
Circulation: 5MM. Sales: $20-50MM
Products: Home care products; household
cleaning supplies; bed & bath products;
windows, wall & ceilings; silver, crystal &
china; kitchen & home office; furniture care

HOUSE OF WEBSTER (800) 369-4641
P.O. Box 1988 • Rogers, AR 72757
E-Mail: info@houseofwebster.com
Website: www.houseofwebster.com
Fax Ordering: (479) 636-2974
International Ordering: (479) 636-4640
Contact Name: Dale Webster, President
Catalog: Free. Frequency: Semiannual
Circulation: 250K. Sales: $5-10MM
Products: Gourmet food items; business food
gift packages; cast iron electric appliances

KING ARTHUR FLOUR BAKER'S CATALOG (800) 827-6836
58 Billings Farm Rd. (800) 777-4434
White River Junction, VT 05001
E-Mail: customercare@kingarthurflour.com
Website: www.kingarthurflour.com
Fax Ordering: (800) 343-3002; (802) 649-3365
International Ordering: (802) 649-3361
Contact Name: Steve Voigt, President
Catalog: Free. Frequency: Monthly
Circulation: 2MM. Sales: $20-50MM
Products: Baking equipment, supplies &
ingredients

KORIN JAPANESE TRADING CORP. (800) 626-2172
57 Warren St. • New York, NY 10007
E-Mail: sales@korin.com
Website: www.korin.com
Fax Ordering: (212) 587-7027
International Ordering: (212) 587-7021
Contact Name: Saori Kawano, President
Catalog: Free. Frequency: Semiannual
Circulation: 50K. Sales: $20-50MM
Products: Japanese porcelain tableware &
chef knives; restaurant supplies, including
sushi bar equipment; books

LEHMAN'S CATALOG (888) 438-5346
P.O. Box 270 • Kidron, OH 44636 (877) 438-5346
E-Mail: getlehman@aol.com
Website: www.lehmans.com
Fax Ordering: (888) 780-4975; (330) 857-5785
International Ordering: (330) 857-5757
Contact Name: Galen Ervin, Marketing
Catalog: $3. Frequency: Semiannual
Circulation: 100K. Sales: $50-100MM
Products: Non-electric appliances; gas
refrigerators, wood stoves, lighting, kitchenware,
water pumps, water filters, oil lamps; health &
beauty products

LENOX COLLECTIONS (800) 225-1779
P.O. Box 2006 • Bristol, PA 19047 (800) 223-4311
E-Mail: info@lenoxcollections.com
Website: www.lenox.com

Fax Ordering: (215) 741-1799
International Ordering: (215) 750-6900
Contact Name: Martha A. Curren, President
Catalog: Free. Frequency: Semiannual
Circulation: 2MM. Sales: $20-50MM
Products: Kitchen collectibles & gifts;
dishes & crystal

LODGE CAST IRON COOKWARE   (423) 837-7181
Lodge Manufacturing Co.
P.O. Box 380 • South Pittsburg, TN 37380
E-Mail: info@lodgemfg.com
Website: www.lodgemfg.com
Fax Ordering: (423) 837-8279
Contact Name: Henry Lodge, President
Catalog: Free. Frequency: Semiannual
Circulation: 250K. Sales: $20-50MM
Products: Cast iron cookware & accessories;
bakeware, campware & grillware

MAC THE ANTIQUE PLUMBER, INC.   (800) 916-2284
6325 Elvas Ave. • Sacramento, CA 95819
E-Mail: info@antiqueplumber.com
Website: www.antiqueplumber.com
Fax Ordering: (916) 454-4150
International Ordering: (916) 454-4507
Contact Name: Bryan C. McIntire, President
Catalog: Free. Frequency: Quarterly
Circulation: 150K. Sales: $5-10MM
Products: Antique plumbing fixtures &
hardware, bath accessories, lighting

MID-AMERICA VACUUM CENTERS   (800) 649-7996
Lakewood Marketing Co.
6221 Northwest Hwy.
Crystal Lake, IL 60014
E-Mail: sales@vacuumstore.com
Website: www.vacuumstore.com
Catalog: Free. Frequency: Annual
Circulation: 100K. Sales: $5-10MM
Products: Vacuum cleaners; central vacuums;
vacuum parts & supplies; carpet cleaners &
shampoos

MOUNTAIN WOODS   (800) 835-0479
Web Pro, Inc.
28008 Harrison Pkwy.
Valencia, CA 91355
E-Mail: info@mountainwoods.com
Website: www.mountainwoods.com
Fax Ordering: (661) 775-0444
International Ordering: (661) 775-0333
Contact Name: Carl Haggar, President
Catalog: Free. Frequency: Annual
Circulation: 50K. Sales: $5-10MM
Products: Gourmet hand-crafted kitchen
accessories; cutting boards; bread &
cheese knives; wooden bowls; kitchen
organizers & unique gift.

ORECK CORPORATION   (800) 289-5888
1400 Salem Rd.   Canada (888) 676-7325
Cookeville, TN 38506
E-Mail: sales@oreck.com
Website: www.oreck.com
Customer Service: (800) 989-3535
Contact Name: David Oreck, President
Catalog: Free. Frequency: Annual
Circulation: 100K. Sales: $20-50MM
Products: Vacuum cleaners, appliances,
floor care products

PROFESSIONAL CUTLERY DIRECT   (800) 859-6994
Cooking Enthusiast   (800) 792-6650
242 Branford Rd. • N. Branford, CT 06471
E-Mail: custserv@cookingenthusiast.com
Website: www.cookingenthusiast.com
Fax Ordering: (800) 296-8039; (203) 871-1010
International Ordering: (203) 871-1000
Contact Name: Terri S. Albert, President
Catalog: Free. Frequency: Semiannual
Circulation: 150K. Sales: $10-50MM
Products: Kitchen cutlery, cookware &
cookbooks

PURE 'N NATURAL SYSTEMS   (800) 237-9199
P.O. Box 1137 • Streamwood, IL 60107
E-Mail: info@purennatural.com
Website: www.purennatural.com
Fax Ordering: (847) 470-1686
International Ordering: (847) 470-1653
Contact Name: Joseph A. Roy, Jr., President
Catalog: Free. Frequency: Annual
Circulation: 100K. Sales: $5-10MM
Products: Air & water purification systems

RENOVATOR'S SUPPLY, INC.   (800) 659-2211
Renovator's Old Mill
Millers Falls, MA 01349
E-Mail: reno@vaunet.com
Website: www.rensup.com
Fax Ordering: (413) 423-3800
International Ordering: (413) 423-3572
Customer Service: (413) 423-3402
Contact Name: Claude Jeanloz, President
Catalog: Free. Frequency: Quarterly
Circulation: 1MM. Sales: $20-50MM
Products: Reproduction antique hardware
& decorative home items; pedestal sinks,
bath fixtures & accessories, lighting,
cabinet & door hardware

ROSENTHAL USA   (201) 804-8000
355 Michele Pl. • Carlstadt, NJ 07072
Fax Ordering: (201) 804-9300
Contact Name: Georg Simon, President
Catalog: Free. Frequency: Quarterly
Circulation: 200K. Sales: $10-50MM
Products: Dinnerware, china flatware,
stemware, giftware & crystal

RUBBERMAID PRODUCTS CATALOG   (800) 362-1000
Consolidated Plastics Co.
8181 Darrow Rd. • Twinsburg, OH 44087
E-Mail: sales@consolidatedplastics.com
Website: www.consolidatedplastics.com
Fax Ordering: (800) 858-5001; (330) 425-3333
International Ordering: (330) 425-3900
Contact Name: Brent Harland, President
Catalog: Free. Frequency: Annual
Circulation: 100K. Sales: $20-50MM
Products: Rubbermaid products; bottles,
containers & bags; commercial matting &
carpeting

S&S WORLDWIDE   (800) 243-9232
75 Mill St. • Colchester, CT 06415   (800) 937-3482
E-Mail: cservice@ssww.com   (800) 288-9941
Website: www.snswwide.com
Fax Ordering: (800) 566-6678; (860) 537-2866
International Ordering: (860) 537-3451
Contact Name: Stephen Schwartz, President
Catalog: Free. Frequency: Monthly

Circulation: 250K. Sales: $20-50MM
Products: Housewares; cookware; arts & crafts; domestics; pool supplies; games & toys; sporting goods

NAT SCHWARTZ & COMPANY (800) 526-1440
524 Bloomfield Ave. • Verona, NJ 07044
E-Mail: info@natschwartz.com
Website: www.natschwartz.com
Fax Ordering: (973) 571-2165
Contact Name: Rose Schwartz, President
Catalog: Free. Frequency: Bimonthly
Circulation: 100K. Sales: $3-5MM
Products: Fine china, silverware & gifts for your home; bridal registry

SEARS CATALOGS (800) 948-8800
P.O. Box 40 • Hanover, PA 17331   (800) 349-4358
E-Mail: sales@sears.com
Website: www.sears.com
Fax Ordering: (800) 757-9997
International Ordering: (717) 633-3333
Catalog: Free. Frequency: Annual
Circulation: 10MM. Sales: $200-500MM
Products: Appliances, housewares, kitchen & bath

STARCREST OF CALIFORNIA (800) 551-2843
Starcrest Products of California   (800) 777-0327
19465 Brennan Ave. • Perris, CA 92599
E-Mail: mail@starcrest.com
Website: www.starcrest.com
Fax Ordering: (951) 943-5574; 940-1388
International Ordering: (951) 943-2011
Contact Name: Tim Calandra, President
Catalog: Free. Frequency: Weekly
Circulation: 25MM. Sales: $50-100MM
Products: Housewares

MARTHA STEWART LIVING (800) 950-0019
20 W. 43 St. • New York, NY 10036
E-Mail: customersupport@marthastewart.com
Website: www.marthastewart.com
Fax Ordering: (212) 827-8289
International Ordering: (212) 522-7800
Contact Name: Martha Stewart, President
Catalog: Free. Frequency: Quarterly
Circulation: 2MM. Sales: $10-50MM
Products: Household products

SUR LA TABLE (800) 243-0852
P.O. Box 840 • Brownsburg, IN 46112
E-Mail: customerservice@surlatable.com
Website: www.surlatable.com
Fax Ordering: (317) 858-5521
Customer Service: (866) 328-5412
Contact Name: Tim Hopkins, President
Catalog: Free. Frequency: Monthly
Circulation: 2MM. Sales: $10-20MM
Products: Bakeware, cookware, cutlery, kitchen & bar tools, heneral housewares for domestic & professional kitchens

TABLECRAFT PRODUCTS (800) 323-8321
801 Lakeside Dr. • Gurnee, IL 60031
E-Mail: sales@tablecraft.com
Website: www.tablecraft.com
Fax Ordering: (800) 323-8320
International Ordering: (847) 855-9000
Catalog: Free. Frequency: Annual
Circulation: 250K. Sales: $20-50MM
Products: Baskets, tabletop, condiments dispensers & racks & squeeze dispensers

VITA MIX CORPORATION (800) 848-2649
8615 Usher Rd. • Cleveland, OH 44138
E-Mail: household@vitamix.com
Website: www.vitamix.com
Fax Ordering: (440) 235-3726
International Ordering: (440) 235-4840
Contact Name: John Barnard, President
Catalog: Free. Frequency: Quarterly
Circulation: 250K. Sales: $10-20MM
Products: Mixing & blending machines, high performance Vita Mix 5000

VOICE OF THE MOUNTAINS (802) 362-4667
Vermont Country Store   (802) 776-5730
P.O. Box 1108
Manchester Center, VT 05255
E-Mail: sales@vermontcountrystore.com
Website: www.vermontcountrystore.com
Fax Ordering: (802) 362-8288
Contact Name: Lyman Orton, President
Catalog: Free. Frequency: 13x per year
Circulation: 10MM. Sales: $20-50MM
Products: Kitchen gadgets, rubber boots, work gloves, rugs

WILLIAMS-SONOMA FOR COOKS (800) 541-2233
3250 Van Ness Ave.   (877) 812-6235
San Francisco, CA 904109
E-Mail: info@williams-sonoma.com
Website: www.williams-sonoma.com
Fax Ordering: (702) 363-2541
International Ordering: (405) 717-6131
Contact Name: Howard Lester, President
Catalog: Free. Frequency: Monthly
Circulation: 5MM. Sales: $50-100MM
Products: Cooking & baking supplies, equipment & accessories

WILTON HOMEWARES (800) 772-7111
Wilton Brands, Inc.   (800) 794-5866
7511 Lemont Rd. • Darien, IL 60561
E-Mail: info@wilton.com
Website: www.wilton.com
Fax Ordering: (888) 824-9520; (630) 963-7196
International Ordering: (630) 985-6000
Contact Name: Vincent Naccarato, President
Catalog: $6. Frequency: Annual
Circulation: 100M. Sales: $50-100MM
Products: Homewares; cake decorating supplies

A&I SUPPLY (800) 260-2647
Central Tool & Equipment
900 S. Main St. • East Peoria, IL 61611
E-Mail: catalog@ai-supply.com
Website: www.ai-supply.com
Fax Ordering: (309) 698-0877
International Ordering: (309) 694-9100
Contact Name: Preston Windom, President
Catalog: Free. Frequency: 8x per year
Circulation: 200K. Sales: $5-10MM
Products: Woodworking, automotive &
industrial tools and supplies

ACCU TRAK TOOL CORPORATION (800) 433-4933
490 Stafford St.
Cherry Valley, MA 01611
E-Mail: roland@accu-trak.com
Website: www.accu-trak.com
Fax Ordering: (508) 892-1789
International Ordering: (508) 892-1787
Contact Name: Roland Mason, President
Catalog: Free. Frequency: Annual
Circulation: 50K. Sales: $3-5MM
Products: Knurling tools: dies & holders
for turning machines

AIR HANDLING SYSTEMS (800) 367-3828
5 Lunar Dr. • Woodbridge, CT 06525
E-Mail: sales@airhand.com
Website: www.airhand.com
Fax Ordering: (203) 389-8340
International Ordering: (203) 389-9595
Catalog: Free. Frequency: Annual
Circulation: 50K. Sales: $10-20M
Products: Industrial ventilation, pollution
control & dust & fume collection systems;
spiral pipe ductwork

AIR TOOLS, HAND TOOLS, (800) 521-7394
SHEET METAL TOOLS
U.S. Industrial Tool & Supply Co.
15101 Cleat St. • Plymouth, MI 48170
E-Mail: sales@ustool.com
Website: www.ustool.com
Fax Ordering: (734) 455-3256
International Ordering: (734) 455-3388
Catalog: Free. Frequency: 10x per year
Circulation: 50K. Sales: $5-10M
Products: Construction & hardware tools

ALBION INDUSTRIES (800) 835-8911
P.O. Box 411 • Albion, MI 49224
E-Mail: sales@albioninc.com
Website: www.albioninc.com
Fax Ordering: (517) 629-9501
International Ordering: (517) 629-9441
Contact Name: Scott Chanalis, President
Catalog: Free. Frequency: Annual
Circulation: 50M. Sales: $10-20MM
Products: Casters & wheels

AMERICAN SAW & MANUFACTURING CO. (800) 628-3030
P.O. Box 504
East Longmeadow, MA 01028
E-Mail: info@lenoxsaw.com
Website: www.lenoxsaw.com
Fax Ordering: (413) 525-2336
International Ordering: (413) 525-3961
Contact Name: Stephen A. Davis, President
Catalog: Free. Frequency: Annual
Circulation: 50K. Sales: $20-50MM
Products: Lenox saw blades & hand tools

BALLYMORE COMPANY (800) 762-8327
220 Garfield Ave.
West Chester, PA 19380
E-Mail: sales@ballymore.com
Website: www.ballymore.com
Fax Ordering: (610) 696-1217
International Ordering: (610) 696-3250
Contact Name: John Colgan, III, President
Catalog: Free. Frequency: Annual
Circulation: 50K. Sales: $5-10MM
Products: Rolling & safety ladders

BEALL TOOL COMPANY (800) 331-4718
541 Swans Rd. NE
Newark, OH 43055
E-Mail: jrbeall@bealltool.com
Website: www.bealltool.com
Fax Ordering: (740) 345-5880
International Ordering: (740) 345-5045
Contact Name: Judith Beall, President
Catalog: Free. Frequency: Annual
Circulation: 25K. Sales: $500K
Products: Buffing supplies & accessories
for putting threads on dowling

BERG'S PRECISION (800) 232-BERG
MECHANICAL COMPONENTS
W.M. Berg, Inc.
499 Ocean Ave.
East Rockaway, NY 11518
E-Mail: sales@wmberg.com
Website: www.wmberg.com
Fax Ordering: (800) 455-BERG; (516) 599-3274
International Ordering: (516) 599-5010
Contact Name: Richard Halen, President
Catalog: Free. Frequency: Annual
Circulation: 50M. Sales: $10-20MM
Products: Precision mechanical components;
gears, belts & sprockets

BLACKSTONE INDUSTRIES (203) 792-8622
16 Stony Hill Rd. • Bethel, CT 06801
E-Mail: sales@wmberg.com
Website: www.wmberg.com
Fax Ordering: (203) 790-9832
Contact Name: Willard Nelson, President
Catalog: Free. Frequency: Annual
Circulation: 25K. Sales: $10-20MM
Products: Unique saber saws

BLUE RIDGE MACHINERY & TOOLS (800) 872-6500
2905 Putnam Ave.
Hurricane, WV 25526
E-Mail: blueridgemachine@worldnet.att.net
Website: www.blueridgemachinery.com
Fax Ordering: (304) 562-5311
International Ordering: (304) 562-3538
Contact Name: Paul Stonestreet, President
Catalog: Free. Frequency: Annual
Circulation: 25K. Sales: $1-3MM
Products: Lathes, milling machines,
machine shop supplies

BONNEVILLE INDUSTRIAL SUPPLY CO. (800) 892-7534
45 S. 1500 W • Orem, UT 84058
Fax Ordering: (801) 224-1456
International Ordering: (801) 225-7770
Contact Name: Greg Lupus, President
Catalog: Free. Frequency: Annual
Circulation: 50K. Sales: $10-20MM
Products: Mechanical components;
gears, belts & sprockets

CAMPBELL TOOLS COMPANY (937) 322-8562
125 N. Tecumseh Rd.
Springfield, OH 45505
E-Mail: campbell@campbelltools.com
Website: www.campbelltools.com
Fax Ordering: (937) 322-8344
Contact Name: Leo Foster, President
Catalog: Free. Frequency: Annual
Circulation: 25K. Sales: $3-5MM
Products: Metalworking tools and machinery,
including lathes, steam engine kits, mills, metals,
precision instruments, books & videos

COASTAL TOOL & SUPPLY (877) 551-8665
510 New Park Ave.
West Hartford, CT 06110
E-Mail: sales@coastaltool.com
Website: www.coastaltool.com
Fax Ordering: (860) 233-6295
International Ordering: (860) 233-8205
Catalog: Free. Frequency: Semiannual
Circulation: 50K. Sales: $10-20MM
Products: Power tools & hand tools

DARNELL-ROSE PRODUCT CATALOG (800) 327-6355
P.O. Box 7009 • La Puente, CA 91744
E-Mail: drcatalog@casters.com
Website: www.darnell-rose.com
Fax Ordering: (626) 912-3765
International Ordering: (626) 912-1688
Contact Name: Bill Dye, President
Catalog: Free. Frequency: Annual
Circulation: 10K. Sales: $500 to $1MM
Products: Casters, wheels, bumpers, couplers

DAWG, INC. CATALOG (800) 935-3294
25 Lassy Ct. • Terryville, CT 06786
E-Mail: info@dawginc.com
Website: www.dawginc.com
Fax Ordering: (800) 545-7297; (860) 540-0611
International Ordering: (860) 540-0600
Contact Name: Vinod Gupta, CEO
Catalog: Free. Frequency: Quarterly
Circulation: 100K. Sales: $10-20MM
Products: Spill control products; industrial
oil absorbents; spill kits, absorbent mats,
material handling

DIAMOND MACHINING TECHNOLOGY (800) 666-4368
85 Hayes Memorial Dr.
Marlborough, MA 01752
E-Mail: dmtsharp@dmtsharp.com
Website: www.dmtsharp.com
Fax Ordering: (508) 485-3924
International Ordering: (508) 481-5944
Contact Name: Christine M. Miller, President
Catalog: Free. Frequency: 10x per year
Circulation: 50K. Sales: $5-10MM
Products: Hand-held diamond sharpeners

MARTIN J. DONNELLY ANTIQUE TOOLS (800) 869-0695
P.O. Box 281 • Bath, NY 14810
E-Mail: info@mjdtools.com
Website: www.mjdtools.com
Fax Ordering: (607) 566-2575
International Ordering: (607) 776-9322
Contact Name: Martin J. Donelly, President
Catalog: $24.95. Frequency: Annual
Circulation: 150K. Sales: $1-3MM
Products: Antique tools for collectors & users;
books about tools & trades

DOZIER EQUIPMENT INTERNATIONAL (800) 251-1234
770 S. 70th St. • Milwaukee, WI 53214
Fax Ordering: (800) 336-6608
International Ordering: (414) 443-0581
Contact Name: David Stark, President
Catalog: Free. Frequency: Semiannual
Circulation: 50K. Sales: $20-50MM
Products: Material handling products

EUGENE ERNST PRODUCTS COMPANY (732) 938-2641
116 Main St. • Farmingdale, NJ 07727
Fax Ordering: (888) 992-2843; (732) 938-9463
Contact Name: Roger Ernst, President
Catalog: Free. Frequency: Bimonthly
Circulation: 200K. Sales: $1-3MM
Products: Machinery

FINE TOOL JOURNAL (800) 248-8114
Antique & Collectible Tools, Inc.
27 Fickett Rd. • Pownal, ME 04069
E-Mail: finetooljournal@aol.com
Website: www.finetoolj.com
Fax Ordering: (207) 688-4831
International Ordering: (207) 688-4962
Contact Name: Clarence Blanchard, President
Catalog: $29. Frequency: Quarterly
Circulation: 10K. Sales: $1-3MM
Products: Features antique, obsolete &
modern tools for the user & collector

FLEXBAR MACHINE CORPORATION (800) 879-7575
250 Gibbs Rd. • Islandia, NY 11749
E-Mail: sales@flexbar.com
Website: www.flexbar.com
Fax Ordering: (631) 582-8487
International Ordering: (631) 582-8440
Contact Name: Jonathan Adler, President
Catalog: Free. Frequency: Annual
Circulation: 25K. Sales: $5-10MM
Products: Precision measurement
instruments, machine tool accessories,
machine safety guards, metrology inspection
apparatus, hardness testers, surface
roughness gages, and optical & video
inspection systems casting materials

FOLEY-BELSAW INSTITUTE CATALOG (800) 821-3452
6301 Equitable Rd. • Kansas City, MO 64120
E-Mail: foley@foley-belsaw.com
Website: www.foley-belsaw.com
Fax Ordering: (816) 483-5010
International Ordering: (816) 483-4200
Contact Name: George Doetzl, President
Catalog: Free. Frequency: 15x per year
Circulation: 25K. Sales: $20-50MM
Products: Home study correspondence
courses in locksmithing, saw & tool sharpening,
woodworking, A.C./refrigeration, home inspection,
computer repair, etc.

W.L. FULLER CATALOG (401) 467-2900
P.O. Box 8767 • Warwick, RI 02888
E-Mail: info@wlfuller.com
Website: www.wlfuller.com
Fax Ordering: (401) 467-2905
Contact Name: Warren L. Fuller, President
Catalog: Free. Pages: 128.
Frequency: Semiannual
Circulation: 100K. Sales: $5-10MM
Products: Countersinks, counterbores,
plug cutters, drills; woodworking tools

GLOBAL INDUSTRIAL EQUIPMENT   (800) 645-1232
Systemax Global • 22 Harbor Park Dr.
Port Washington, NY 11050
Fax Ordering: (800) 336-3818
International Ordering: (516) 625-8787
Contact Name: Richard Leeds, President
Catalog: Free. Frequency: Monthly
Circulation: 150K. Sales: $20-50MM
Products: Material handling products,
shelving & carts

W.W. GRAINGER, INC. CATALOG   (800) 487-3279
P.O. Box 3074 • Northbrook, IL 60065
E-Mail: sales@grainger.com
Website: www.grainger.com
Fax Ordering: (800) 722-3291
International Ordering: (847) 535-1000
Tech Service: (800) 323-0620
Customer Service: (888) 361-8649
Contact Name: Richard L. Keyser, President
Catalog: Free. Frequency: 3x per year
Circulation: 150K. Sales: $10-20MM
Products: Industrial & lawn equipment,
tools, motors & pumps

GRIFHOLD TOOLS   (800) 344-6445
Griffin Manufacturing Company
P.O. Box 308 • Webster, NY 14580
E-Mail: grifhold@aol.com
Website: www.grifhold.com
Fax Ordering: (716) 265-2621
International Ordering: (716) 265-1991
Contact Name: Gary Papia, President
Catalog: Free. Frequency: Annual
Circulation: 25K. Sales: $5-10MM
Products: Specialty, knives, blades,
knife kits, compasses, tools for fne art

GRIOT'S GARAGE CATALOG   (800) 345-5789
3500 20th St. E • Tacoma, WA 98424
E-Mail: info@griotsgarage.com
Website: www.griotsgarage.com
Fax Ordering: (952) 894-1020
International Ordering: (952) 894-9510
Contact Name: Don Kotula, President
Catalog: Free. Frequency: Quarterly
Circulation: 200K. Sales: $3-5MM
Products: Tools & products for every garage

GRIZZLY INDUSTRIAL CATALOG   (800) 523-4777
1812 Valencia St. • Bellingham, WA 98227
E-Mail: info@grizzlyindustrial.com
Website: www.grizzlyindustrial.com
Fax Ordering: (800) 438-5901
International Ordering: (570) 546-9663
Catalog: Free. Frequency: Annual
Circulation: 100K. Sales: $5-10MM
Products: Hand & power tools for
woodworking & metalworking

HARBOR FREIGHT TOOLS   (800) 423-2567
3491 Mission Oaks Blvd.
Camarillo, CA 93012
E-Mail: info@harborfreight.com
Website: www.harborfreight.com
Fax Ordering: (952) 894-1020
International Ordering: (952) 894-9510
Contact Name: Don Kotula, President
Catalog: Free. Frequency: Bimonthly
Circulation: 100K. Sales: $10-20MM
Products: Hand tools & hardware

HOLZ TOOL SUPPLY   (800) 233-4676
819 Broadway St.
Mt. Vernon, IL 62864
E-Mail: holztool@accessus.net
Fax Ordering: (618) 242-4679
International Ordering: (618) 242-4676
Catalog: $1. Frequency: Semiannual
Circulation: 50K. Sales: $1-3MM
Products: Professional quality tools

HUSQVARNA FOREST & GARDEN CO.   (800) 427-5962
9006 Perimeter Woods Dr. #J
Charlotte, NC 28216
Fax Ordering: (704) 597-8802
International Ordering: (704) 597-5000
Contact Name: David Zerfoss, President
Catalog: Free. Frequency: Annual
Circulation: 100K. Sales: $5-10MM
Products: Forest & garden equipment
& power saws

ILLUSTRATED FASTENER CATALOG   (800) 800-2658
Atlantic Fasteners
P.O. Box 1168
West Springfield, MA 01090
E-Mail: info@atlanticfasteners.com
Website: www.atlanticfasteners.com
Fax Ordering: (413) 785-5770
International Ordering: (413) 785-1687
Contact Name: Patrick O'Toole, President
Catalog: Free. Frequency: 10x per year
Circulation: 50K. Sales: $5-10MM
Products: Nuts, screws, washers, bolts
and other fasteners in stainless steel

IMPROVEMENTS CATALOG   (800) 642-2112
23297 Commerce Park
Beachwood, OH 44122
E-Mail: custserv@improvements.com
Website: www.improvements.com
Fax Ordering: (216) 831-4026
International Ordering: (216) 831-6191
Contact Name: Kenneth J. Ellingsen, President
Catalog: Free. Frequency: Monthly
Circulation: 25MM. Sales: $10-20MM
Products: Problem solvers for home,
yard & car

JENSEN TOOLS   (800) 426-1194
7815 S. 46th St.
Phoenix, AZ 85044
E-Mail: info@jensentools.com
Website: www.jensentools.com
Fax Ordering: (800) 366-9662;
  (602) 438-1690
International Ordering: (602) 453-3169
Contact Name: Kai Juel, President
Catalog: Free. Frequency: Semiannual
Circulation: 25K. Sales: $10-20MM
Products: Tool kits & test equipment for
electronics service industry

JOINER'S QUARTERLY   (207) 935-3720
Fox Maple Tools
P.O. Box 249 • Brownfield, ME 04010
Fax Ordering: (207) 935-4575
Contact Name: Steve Chappel, President
Catalog: $3.50. Frequency: Quarterly
Circulation: 50K. Sales: $3-5MM
Products: Products for timberframers
& builders

KASTAR CATALOG   (800) 645-1142
5501 21st St. • Racine, WI 53406
E-Mail: info@kastar.com
Website: www.kastar.com
Fax Ordering: (262) 554-7503
International Ordering: (262) 554-7500
Contact Name: Daniel Peterson, President
Catalog: Free. Frequency: Annual
Circulation: 100K. Sales: $210-20MM
Products: Specialty tools, sockets,
ratching box wrenches

KBC TOOLS & MACHINERY   (800) 521-5606
P.O. Box 8006 • Sterling Hts., MI 48311   (800) 521-1740
E-Mail: info@kbctools.com
Website: www.kbctools.com
Fax Ordering: (800) 322-4292; (810) 979-4292
International Ordering: (810) 264-6600
Contact Name: Karel Bass, President
Catalog: Free. Frequency: Annual
Circulation: 100K. Sales: $10-20MM
Products: Metal cutting tools & machinery

KC STORE FIXTURES   (800) 258-8710
7400 E. 12th St.
Kansas City, MO 64126
E-Mail: info@kc.store.fixtures.com
Website: www.kc.store.fixtures.com
Fax Ordering: (800) 868-2013
International Ordering: (816) 842-8866
Catalog: Free. Frequency: Semiannual
Circulation: 100K. Sales: $10-20MM
Products: Custom counters & showcases;
store fixtures; racks, shelving, displays

KETT TOOL COMPANY   (513) 271-0333
5055 Madison Rd.
Cincinnati, OH 45227
E-Mail: info@kett-tool.com
Website: www.kett-tool.com
Fax Ordering: (513) 271-5318
Contact Name: William A. Berlier, President
Catalog: Free. Frequency: Annual
Circulation: 50K. Sales: $5-10MM
Products: Specialty wood boring tools;
drilling & cutting tools for aircraft maintenance;
electric & pneumatic shears, saws & nibblers

KLINGSPOR'S SADNING CATALOG   (800) 228-0000
P.O. Box 3737 • Hickory, NC 28603
E-Mail: info@sandingcatalog.com
Website: www.sandingcatalog.com
Fax Ordering: (800) 872-2005
International Ordering: (828) 327-7263
Contact Name: Four Shee, President
Catalog: $2. Frequency: Annual
Circulation: 50K. Sales: $5-10MM
Products: Sanding & power tools

KOHLER GENERATORS   (800) 544-2444
444 Highland Dr. • Kohler, WI 53044
E-Mail: info@kohlergenerators.com
Website: www.kohlergenerators.com
Fax Ordering: (920) 457-1271
International Ordering: (920) 457-4441
Contact Name: R.R. Parnitke, President
Catalog: Free. Frequency: Annual
Circulation: 10K. Sales: $5-10MM
Products: Diesel & gasoline generators

KOMET OF AMERICA   (847) 923-8400
2050 Mitchell Blvd. • Schaumburg, IL 60193
E-Mail: info@komet.com
Website: www.komet.com
Fax Ordering: (800) 865-6638; (847) 923-8463
Contact Name: Rick Martin, President
Catalog: Free. Frequency: Annual
Circulation: 50K. Sales: $10-20MM
Products: Metal cutting tools

KREG TOOL COMPANY   (800) 447-8638
201 Campus Dr. • Huxley, IA 50124
E-Mail: kregtool@kregtool.com
Website: www.kregtool.com
Fax Ordering: (515) 597-2354
International Ordering: (515) 597-2234
Contact Name: Kreg Sommerfeld, President
Catalog: Free. Frequency: Annual
Circulation: 50K. Sales: $5-10MM
Products: Pocket hole tools

LBI CATALOG   (800) 231-6537
973 N. Road, Rt. 117 • Groton, CT 06340
E-Mail: info@kett-tool.com
Website: www.kett-tool.com
Fax Ordering: (513) 271-5318
International Ordering: (952) 894-9510
Contact Name: Peter J. Legnos, President
Catalog: Free. Frequency: Annual
Circulation: 50K. Sales: $5-10MM
Products: Fiberglass supplies, tools
& equipment

LIGNOMAT USA   (800) 227-2105
14345 NE Morris Ct.
Portland, OR 97230
E-Mail: info@lignomat.com
Website: www.lignomat.com
Fax Ordering: (503) 255-1430
Contact Name: Uli Heimerchinger, President
Catalog: Free. Frequency: Annual
Circulation: 50K. Sales: $1-3MM
Products: Handheld moisture meters,
wireless wood moisture measuring systems,
computer kiln controls, in-line moisture detectors

MSC INDUSTRIAL DIRECT CO., INC.   (800) 255-5067
75 Maxess Rd. • Melville, NY 11747
E-Mail: info@mscdirect.com
Website: www.mscdirect.com
Fax Ordering: (516) 812-1711
International Ordering: (516) 812-2000
Customer Service: (800) 645-7270
E-Commerce Customer Service: (800) 753-7970
Contact Names: Mitchell Jacobson, President
Catalog: Free. Frequency: Annual
Circulation: 250K. Sales: $100-500MM
Products: Industrial supplies & equipment

MACHINE SHOP SUPPLIES & BOOKS   (309) 342-7474
Cardinal Engineering, Inc.
2211 155th St. • Cameron, IL 61423
E-Mail: cardinaleng@grics.net
Website: www.cardinaleng.com
Fax Ordering: (309) 342-3182
Contact Name: Roland Friestad, President
Catalog: $2. Frequency: Semiannual
Circulation: 50K. Sales: $1-3MM
Products: Machine shop supplies & books;
steel, brass, aluminum and tool steel for
machine shops and home shop users

MAKITA USA CATALOG   (800) 462-5482
14930 Northam St. • La Mirada, CA 90638
E-Mail: info@makita.com
Website: www.makita.com
Fax Ordering: (714) 522-8133
International Ordering: (714) 522-8088
Contact Name: Paul Sukatsu, President
Catalog: Free. Frequency: Annual
Circulation: 100K. Sales: $50-100MM
Products: Electric & cordless power tools

MARSON CORPORATION   (800) 451-1760
44 Campanelli Pkwy. • Stoughton, MA 02072
E-Mail: marson@marsoncorp.com
Website: www.marsoncorp.com
Fax Ordering: (781) 302-3857
International Ordering: (781) 344-4464
Contact Name: Carl Annese, President
Catalog: Free. Frequency: Annual
Circulation: 50K. Sales: $20-50MM
Products: Rivets, inserts & setting tools

MATERIAL CONTROL PLUS   (800) 926-0376
Material Control, Inc.
338 E. Sullivan Rd. • Aurora, IL 60504
E-Mail: sales@materialcontrolplus.com
Website: www.materialcontrolplus.com
Fax Ordering: (630) 892-4931
International Ordering: (630) 892-4274
Contact Name: Clint Simpson, President
Catalog: Free. Frequency: Monthly
Circulation: 250K. Sales: $10-20MM
Products: Bin systems, industrial carts,
cans & trucks; rubbermaid products,
safety storage equipment

McFEELY'S SQUARE DRIVE SCREWS   (800) 443-7937
1620 Wythe Rd. • Lynchburg, VA 24501
E-Mail: tech@mcfeelys.com
Website: www.mcfeelys.com
Fax Ordering: (434) 847-7136
International Ordering: (434) 846-2729
Contact Name: James C. Ray, President
Catalog: Free. Frequency: 5x per year
Circulation: 1MM. Sales: $5-10MM
Products: Square drive screws; stainless
steel, silicon, bronze, brass, aluminum,
hardened steel

MEADOWS MILLS   (800) 626-2282
1352 W. D St. • No. Wilkesboro, NC 28659
E-Mail: info@meadowmills.com
Website: www.meadowmills.com
Fax Ordering: (336) 667-6501
International Ordering: (336) 838-2282
Contact Name: Robert Hege, III, President
Catalog: Free. Frequency: Semiannual
Circulation: 100K. Sales: $3-5MM
Products: Stoneburr, hammer & saw mills;
saw sharpeners; edgers, log turners, trim saws

MILL-ROSE COMPANY   (800) 321-3598
7995 Tyler Blvd. • Mentor, OH 44060   (800) 321-3533
E-Mail: sales@millrose.com
Website: www.millrose.com
Fax Ordering: (440) 271-5318
International Ordering: (440) 894-9510
Contact Name: Paul M. Miller, President
Catalog: Free. Frequency: Monthly
Circulation: 50K. Sales: $500K
Products: Twisted wire brushes
for the manufacturing sector

MR. G'S ENTERPRSIES   (817) 838-3501
5613 Elliott Reeder Rd.
Fort Worth, TX 76117
E-Mail: mrgs@earthlink.net
Website: www.mrgusa.com
Fax Ordering: (817) 831-0638
Contact Name: Glenn Garrison, President
Catalogs: $8.95, $12.95. CD available
Pages: 112, 230. Frequency: Semiannual
Circulation: 10K. Sales: $1-3MM
Products: Fasteners, screws, bolt kits,
nuts & clamps

MUTUAL HARDWARE CORPORATION   (718) 361-2480
545 49th Ave. • Long Island City, NY 11101
E-Mail: sales@mutualhardware.com
Website: www.mutualhardware.com
Fax Ordering: (718) 729-8296
Contact Name: Vince Mallardi, President
Catalog: Free. Frequency: Monthly
Circulation: 50K. Sales: $1-3MM
Products: Hardware, tools & equipment
for theaters

MY LITTLE SALESMAN, INC.   (800) 352-0642
2895 Chad Dr. • Eugene, OR 97408
E-Mail: sales@mlsinc.com
Website: www.mlsinc.com
Fax Ordering: (440) 271-5318
International Ordering: (440) 894-9510
Contact Name: Richard Pierce, President
Catalog: $18. Frequency: Monthly
Circulation: 200K. Sales: $20-50MM
Products: New & used heavy equipment
& machinery

NATIONAL SAFETY EQUIPMENT OUTLET   (800) 443-0300
Old Springfield Rd.
Charlestown, NH 03603
Fax Ordering: (603) 628-6912
Contact Name: Helen Archer, President
Catalog: Free. Frequency: Semiannual
Circulation: 250K. Sales: $1-3MM
Products: Warning flashers, safety signs,
strobe lights, flashlights & other safety
equiment

NORTHERN TOOL & EQUIPMENT CO.   (800) 221-0516
P.O. Box 1499 • Burnsville, MN 55337   (800) 556-7885
E-Mail: info@northerntool.com
Website: www.northerntool.com
Fax Ordering: (952) 894-1020, 882-6927
International Ordering: (952) 894-9510
Contact Name: Don Kotula, President
Catalog: Free. Frequency: Quarterly
Circulation: 500K. Sales: $10-20MM
Products: Handyman & professional tools
& hardware

NORTON ABRASIVES   (800) 825-7471
P.O. Box 15008 • Worcester, MA 01615
E-Mail: sales@norton.abrasives.com
Website: www.norton.abrasives.com
Fax Ordering: (508) 795-2420
International Ordering: (508) 795-5000
Customer Service: (800) 201-3654
Contact Name: Richard Kennedy, President
Catalog: Free. Frequency: Monthly
Circulation: 250K. Sales: $10-20MM
Products: Tools, abrasives, grinding wheels,
sharpening sticks & belts

NUTTY COMPANY (800) 468-8891
P.O. Box 473 • Derby, CT 06418
E-Mail: sales@nutty.com
Website: www.nutty.com
Fax Ordering: (203) 735-1097
International Ordering: (203) 734-1604
Contact Name: Tim Kanuch, President
Catalog: Free. Frequency: Annual
Circulation: 100M. Sales: $1-3MM
Products: Fasteners

ORLANDO PRODUCTS COMPANY (888) 214-3748
2639 Merchant Dr. • Baltimore, MD 21230 (866) 659-0099
E-Mail: info@orlandoproductsinc.com
Website: www.orlandoproductsinc.rtrk.com
Fax Ordering: (410) 525-2435
International Ordering: (443) 986-9709
Contact Name: Sam Orlando, President
Catalog: Free. Frequency: Semiannual
Circulation: 50K. Sales: $20-50MM
Products: Custom packaging & design;
foam packaging & inserts for sensitive
instruments, computers, electronics,
medical, appliances; custom cases,
boxes, crates

PARTS & SUPPLY CATALOG (800) 321-2704
V&V Appliance Parts
27 W. Myrtle Ave.
Youngstown, OH 44507
Fax Ordering: (440) 271-5318
International Ordering: (440) 894-9510
Catalog: $18. Frequency: Monthly
Circulation: 25K. Sales: $20-50MM
Products: New & used heavy equipment
& machinery

PICO ELECTRONICS, INC. (800) 431-1064
143 Sparks Ave. • Pelham, NY 10803
E-Mail: info@picoelectronics.com
Website: www.picoelectronics.com
Fax Ordering: (914) 738-8225
International Ordering: (914) 738-1400
Catalog: Free. Frequency: Semiannual
Circulation: 100K. Sales: $5-10MM
Products: Miniaturized suface mount
transformers & inductors; AC-DC power
supplies

PLANO MOLDING COMPANY (800) 874-6905
431 E. South St. • Plano, IL 60545
E-Mail: sales@planomolding.com
Website: www.planomolding.com
Fax Ordering: (630) 552-8989
International Ordering: (630) 552-3111
Contact Name: Peter Henning, President
Catalog: Free. Frequency: Annual
Circulation: 50K. Sales: $50-100MM
Products: Tool boxes, shelving

POBCO PLASTICS & HARDWOOD (800) 222-6376
99 Hope Ave. • Worcester, MA 01603
E-Mail: sales@pobcoplastics.com
Website: www.pobcoplastics.com
Fax Ordering: (508) 791-3247
International Ordering: (508) 791-6376
Contact Name: Stephen Johnson, President
Catalog: Free. Frequency: Monthly
Circulation: 25K. Sales: $5-10MM
Products: Conveyor components &
friction reducing components

PORTA-BRACE/K&H PRODUCTS (802) 442-8171
PortaBrace, Inc.
P.O. Box 220 • N. Bennington, VT 05257
E-Mail: info@portabrace.com
Website: www.portabrace.com
Fax Ordering: (802) 442-9118
Contact Name: Robert Howe, President
Catalog: Free. Frequency: Semiannual
Circulation: 50M. Sales: $3-5MM
Products: Tool kits; field cases for professional
video, audio & film production equipment

PUTNAM ROLLING LADDER COMPANY (212) 226-5147
32 Howard St. • New York, NY 10013
E-Mail: putnam1905@aol.com
Website: www.putnamrollingladder.com
Fax Ordering: (212) 941-1836
Contact Name: Warren Monsees, President
Catalog: Free. Frequency: Annual
Circulation: 100M. Sales: $3-5MM
Products: Step, straight & extension ladders

PYLAM PRODUCTS COMPANY (800) 645-6096
2175 E. Cedar St. • Tempe, AZ 85281
Fax Ordering: (330) 743-3221
International Ordering: (330) 743-5144
Catalog: Free. Frequency: Annual
Circulation: 100M. Sales: $5-10MM
Products: Appliance parts & testing equipment

RED DEVIL CATALOG (800) 423-3845
2400 Vauxhall Rd. • Union, NJ 07083
E-Mail: sales@reddevil.com
Website: www.reddevil.com
Fax Ordering: (908) 688-8872
International Ordering: (908) 688-6900
Contact Name: Don MacPherson, President
Catalog: Free. Frequency: Annual
Circulation: 25K. Sales: $20-50MM
Products: Hand tools, tile tools, paint
mixing & tinting equipment

REELCRAFT INDUSTRIES (800) 444-3134
One Reelcraft Center
Columbia City, IN 46725
E-Mail: sales@reelcraft.com
Website: www.reelcraft.com
Fax Ordering: (800) 444-4587; (260) 248-2605
International Ordering: (260) 248-8188
Contact Name: Sanford Penn, President
Catalog: Free. Frequency: Semiannual
Circulation: 50K. Sales: $10-20MM
Products: Spring retractable, manual
& motor driven hose reels

RIDGE CARBIDE TOOL COMPANY (800) 443-0992
595 New York Ave. • Lyndhurst, NJ 07071
E-Mail: rcttools@bellatlantic.com
Website: www.catalogcity.com
Fax Ordering: (888) 728-8665
International Ordering: (201) 438-8778
Contact Name: John Ferrie, President
Catalog: $3. Frequency: Annual
Circulation: 50K. Sales: $1-3MM
Products: Custom router bits, cutters, knives,
saw blades

ROYAL UNITED CORPORATION (800) 682-0097
7601 River Rd. • North Bergen, NJ 07047
Fax Ordering: (201) 869-6655
International Ordering: (201) 869-3900
Contact Name: Arthur S. Wenig, President

Catalog: Free. Frequency: Annual
Circulation: 100M. Sales: $20-50MM
Products: Hand tools

RUTLAND TOOL & SUPPLY CO. (800) 289-4787
2225 Workman Mill Rd.
Whittier, CA 90601
E-Mail: rutland@earthlink.net
Website: www.rutlandtool.com
Fax Ordering: (562) 566-5001
International Ordering: (562) 566-5050
Contact Name: Mike Grebeo, President
Catalog: Free. Frequency: 10x per year
Circulation: 3MM. Sales: $50-100MM
Products: Cutting tools, machine shop
supplies & safety supplies

S-T INDUSTRIES (800) 798-3531
301 Arnstrong Blvd. North (800) 326-2039
St. James, MN 56081
E-Mail: sales@stindustries.com
Website: www.stindustries.com
Fax Ordering: (507) 375-4503
International Ordering: (507) 375-3211
Contact Name: Margaret Smith, President
Catalog: Free. Frequency: Annual
Circulation: 50K. Sales: $10-20MM
Products: Precision measuring tools

SHINDALWA CATALOG (800) 521-7733
P.O. Box 2810 • Tualatin, OR 97062
Fax Ordering: (503) 692-6696
International Ordering: (503) 692-3070
Contact Name: Dave Dahlstrom, President
Catalog: Free. Frequency: Annual
Circulation: 50K. Sales: $5-10MM
Products: Outdoor power hand-held
equipment including chainsaws, grass
trimmers, lawn tools & water pumps

SMALL ENGINE PARTS, LOCKSMITHING (800) 821-3452
SHARPENING TOOLS
Foley Belsaw
6301 Equitable Rd. • Kansas City, MO 64120
E-Mail: sales@foleybelsaw.com
Website: www.foleybelsaw.com
Fax Ordering: (816) 483-5010
International Ordering: (816) 483-6400
Contact Name: George Doetzl, President
Catalogs: Free. Frequency: Quarterly
Circulation: 25KM. Sales: $20-50MM
Products: Small engine parts; sharpening tools,
high speed sawmills, woodworking & molding
equipment

SMITHY COMPANY CATALOG (800) 345-6342
P.O. Box 1517 • Ann Arbor, MI 48106
E-Mail: info@smithy.com
Website: www.smithy.com
Fax Ordering: (734) 913-6663
International Ordering: (734) 913-6700
Contact Name: Joe Christensen, President
Catalog: $3. Frequency: Semiannual
Circulation: 50K. Sales: $5-10MM
Products: Metalworking & woodworking
tools for the hobbyist & light industry

SOLUTIONS IN SAFETY (800) 548-0909
Airgas, Inc.
259 N. Radnor-Chester Rd. #100
Radnor, PA 19087
E-Mail: sales@airgas.com

Website: www.airgas.com
Fax Ordering: (610) 687-1052
International Ordering: (610) 687-5253
Contact Name: Peter McClauseland, President
Catalog: Free. Frequency: Annual
Circulation: 150K. Sales: $50-100MM
Products: Industrial & safety products; full line
of industrial tools

SPECIALIZED PRODUCTS COMPANY (800) 866-5353
1100 S. Kimball Ave.
Southlake, TX 76092
E-Mail: spc@specialized.net
Website: www.specialized.net
Fax Ordering: (817) 329-6195
International Ordering: (817) 424-3530
Contact Name: Peter Smith, President
Catalog: Free. Frequency: Semiannual
Circulation: 150K. Sales: $10-20MM
Products: Tool kits, test equipment, telecom
testers, field service diagnostic equipment
& tools

STACK-ON PRODUCTS COMPANY (800) 323-9601
1360 N. Old Rand Rd.
Wauconda, IL 60084
E-Mail: sales@stack-on.com
Website: www.stack-on.com
Fax Ordering: (847) 526-6599
International Ordering: (847) 526-1611
Contact Name: John Lynn, President
Catalog: Free. Frequency: Annual
Circulation: 25K. Sales: $50-100MM
Products: Plastic & steel roller cabinets,
chests, portable tool storage, drawer liners
& tool set with chest

L.S. STARRETT COMPANY (978) 249-3551
121 Crescent St. • Athol, MA 01331
E-Mail: general@starrett.com
Website: www.starrett.com
Fax Ordering: (978) 249-8495
Contact Name: Douglas Starrett, President
Catalog: Free. Frequency: Semiannual
Circulation: 50K. Sales: $5-10MM
Products: Precision measuring instruments;
precision tools & gages; construction tools

JOHN STORTZ & SON (888) 847-3456
210 Vine St. • Philadelphia, PA 19106
E-Mail: info@stortz.com
Website: www.stortz.com
Fax Ordering: (215) 627-6306
International Ordering: (215) 627-3855
Contact Name: John C. Stortz, President
Catalog: $5. Frequency: Annual
Circulation: 10K. Sales: $1-3MM
Products: Tools, hand tools

SUPERGRIT ABRASIVES, (800) 822-4003
SUPERTACK ADHSIVES
Red Hill Corporation
P.O. Box 4234 • Gettysburg, PA 17325
E-Mail: custserv@supergrit.com
Website: www.supergrit.com
Fax Ordering: (717) 337-0732
International Ordering: (717) 337-3038
Contact Name: Arturo Ottolenghi, President
Catalog: Free. Frequency: Annual
Circulation: 100K. Sales: $1-3MM
Products: Industrial quality abrasives &
adhesives

SURFACE PREPARATION (800) 872-4933
& MAINTENANCE TOOLS
54 Eastford Rd. • Southbridge, MA 01550
E-Mail: custrelations@hydetools.com
Website: www.hydetools.com
Fax Ordering: (508) 765-5250
International Ordering: (508) 764-4344
Contact Name: Ralph Lawrence, President
Catalog: Free. Frequency: Annual
Circulation: 50K. Sales: $20-50MM
Products: Hand tools & industrial hand knives

SYNTEX RUBBER CORPORATION (203) 367-8469
P.O. Box 4006 • Bridgeport, CT 06607
E-Mail: synrub@aol.com
Website: www.syntexrubber.com
Fax Ordering: (203) 367-6403
Contact Name: Edward Kirik, Jr., President
Catalog: Free. Frequency: Annual
Circulation: 25K. Sales: $5-10MM
Products: Rubber components for OEM
applications; custom molded & stamped
rubber products

TIME MOTION TOOLS (800) 779-8170
12778 Brookprinter Pl.
Poway, CA 92064
E-Mail: sales@timemotion.com
Website: www.timemotion.com
Fax Ordering: (800) 779-8171
International Ordering: (858) 679-0000
Contact Name: Ed Durfey, President
Catalog: Free. Frequency: Bimonthly
Circulation: 200K. Sales: $10-20MM
Products: Tools & voice data telecom
test equipment

TOOL CRIB OF THE NORTH (800) 884-9132
P.O. Box 14040
Grand Forks, ND 58208
Website: www.amazon.com
Fax Ordering: (701) 787-3600
International Ordering: (701) 746-6481
Catalog: Free. Frequency: Quarterly
Circulation: 200K. Sales: $10-20MM
Products: Tools & hardware

TORRINGTON BRUSHES (800) 262-7874
P.O. Box 56 • Torrington, CT 06790
Fax Ordering: (860) 489-1089
International Ordering: (860) 482-3517
Contact Name: John Fitzgerald, President
Catalog: Free. Frequency: Annual
Circulation: 100K. Sales: $1-3MM
Products: Bristle brushes, paint brushes,
mops & brooms

TP TOOLS & EQUIPMENT (800) 321-9260
Div. of Tip Plus Corp.
P.O. Box 649 • Canfield, OH 44406
E-Mail: info@tptools.com
Website: www.tptools.com
Fax Ordering: (330) 533-2876
International Ordering: (330) 533-3384
Catalog: Free. Frequency: Semiannual
Circulation: 100K. Pages: 156. Sales: $5-10MM
Products: Abrasive blasting, Air compressors,
Air line hookup, Air tools, auto body repair tools,
buffing & detailing toolspaint spray guns,
safety items, welding equipment

TRAVERS TOOL COMPANY (800) 221-0270
P.O. Box 1550 • Flushing, NY 11354
E-Mail: ideas@travers.com
Website: www.travers.com
Fax Ordering: (800) 722-0703;
    (718) 886-7895
International Ordering: (718) 886-7200
Contact Name: Barry Zolot, President
Catalog: Free. Frequency: Monthly
Circulation: 1MM. Sales: $20-50MM
Products: Metalworking tools & industrial
supplies

TRIMCO PRODUCTS CATALOG (800) 231-5809
1256 Brittmoore • Houston, TX 77043
E-Mail: sales@trimco.com
Website: www.trimco.com
Fax Ordering: (713) 465-1653
International Ordering: (713) 465-8368
Contact Name: Doug Sihvonen, Sales Director
Catalog: Free. Frequency: Annual
Circulation: 50K. Sales: $10-20MM
Products: Metal building component source;
manufacturers of metal building products,
including roof & wall components, doors
& windows, trim & flashing, tank stprage
& sealants

TRINCO DRY-BLAST (800) 587-4626
Trinity Tool Company
P.O. Box 98 • Fraser, MI 48026
E-Mail: sales@trinco.com
Website: www.trinco.com
Fax Ordering: (586) 296-5836
International Ordering: (586) 296-5900
Contact Name: Kathy Boyle, President
Catalog: Free. Frequency: Annual
Circulation: 50K. Sales: $3-5MM
Products: Sandblasting equipment,
abrasives, parts & service

VAUGHN & BUSHNELL (800) 435-6000
MANUFACTURING COMPANY
11414 Maple Ave. • Hebron, IL 60034
E-Mail: sales@vaughanmfg.com
Website: www.vaughanmfg.com
Fax Ordering: (815) 648-4300
International Ordering: (815) 648-2446
Contact Name: Howard Vaughan, President
Catalog: Free. Frequency: Bimonthly
Circulation: 250K. Sales: $10-20MM
Products: Bear saws

WD-40 COMPANY (888) 324-7596
P.O. Box 80607
San Diego, CA 92138
E-Mail: sales@wd40.com
Website: www.wd40.com
Fax Ordering: (619) 275-5823
International Ordering: (619) 275-1400
Contact Name: Garry O. Ridge, President
Catalog: Free. Frequency: Semiannual
Circulation: 250K. Sales: $10-20MM
Products: Multi purpose lubricant oil;
heavy duty hand cleaners

WESTERN SLING & SUPPLY COMPANY (800) 748-2651
5453 N. Peterson Rd. • Sedalia, CO 80135
Fax Ordering: (303) 688-5905
International Ordering: (303) 331-0396

Contact Name: Stan Truitt, President
Catalog: Free. **Frequency:** Annual
Circulation: 100K. **Sales:** $5-10MM
Products: Material handling tools & equipment

WHOLESALE TOOL CATALOG   (800) 521-3420
12155 Stephens Dr.
Warren, MI 48089
E-Mail: wtmich@aol.com
Website: www.wttool.com
Fax Ordering: (800) 521-3661; (586) 754-8652
International Ordering: (586) 754-9270
Contact Name: Mark A. Dowdy, President
Catalog: $3. **Frequency:** Annual
Circulation: 50K. **Sales:** $10-20MM
Products: Cutting tools, precision tools,
machinery, machine tool accessories,
hand tools, power tools

ZIP POWER PARTS CATALOG   (800) 824-8521
2008 E. 33rd St. • Erie, PA 16514
Fax Ordering: (800) 983-7278
International Ordering: (814) 898-1738
Contact Name: Bill Bethel, President
Catalog: Free. **Frequency:** Annual
Circulation: 50K. **Sales:** $500M to $1MM
Products: Parts for chain saws, lawnmowers,
snowmobiles

AGED WOODS (800) 233-9307
Yesteryear Floorworks Co.
2331 E. Market St. #6 • York, PA 17402
E-Mail: info@agedwoods.com
Website: www.agedwoods.com
Fax Ordering: (717) 840-1468
International Ordering: (717) 840-0330
Contact Name: Jeffrey Horn, President
Catalog: Free. Frequency: Annual
Circulation: 25K. Sales: $1-3MM
Products: Antique woodflooring; antique
heart pine & cypress; American hardwoods;
custom door & shutters, wall paneling &
molding, cabinet & door stock

ALBANY WOODWORKS (800) 551-1282
P.O. Box 729 • Albany, LA 70711
E-Mail: woods@i-55.com
Website: www.albanywoodworks.com
Fax Ordering: (225) 567-5150
International Ordering: (225) 567-1155
Contact Name: Richard Woods, President
Catalog: Free. Frequency: Annual
Circulation: 25K. Sales: $1-3MM
Products: Antique heart pine flooring

AMERICAN BLINDS, WALLPAPER & MORE (800) 575-8016
31478 Industrial Rd. #300 • Livonia, MI 48170 (800) 575-9019
E-Mail: info@americanblinds.com
Website: www.americanblinds.com
Fax Ordering: (800) 391-2293
International Ordering: (734) 266-3999
Contact Name: Joel Levine, President
Catalog: Free. Frequency: Annual
Circulation: 200K. Sales: $10-50MM
Products: Blinds & shades; wallpaper;
rugs, wall art, lighting, curtains, home
decor, shutters, paint

AMERICAN CUSTOM MILLWORK (888) 608-9663
ACMI, Inc.
3904 Newton Rd. • Albany, GA 31707
E-Mail: info@acmimillwork.com
Website: www.acmimillwork.com
Fax Ordering: (229) 888-9245
International Ordering: (229) 888-3303
Contact Name: Reed Mitchell, V.P.
Catalog: Free. Frequency: Annual
Circulation: 25K. Sales: $3-5MM
Products: Wood moulding, carvings
& custom millwork; interior decorating
materials

ANDERSON & McQUAID (800) 640-3250
170 Fawcett St. • Cambridge, MA 02138
E-Mail: sales@andersonmcquaid.com
Website: www.andersonmcquaid.com
Fax Ordering: (617) 876-8928
International Ordering: (617) 876-3250
Contact Name: Kevin McQuid, President
Catalog: Free. Frequency: Annual
Circulation: 50K. Sales: $3-5MM
Products: Domestic & exotic hardwood;
stock & custom mouldings

ARCHITECTURAL COMPONENTS, INC. (413) 367-9441
26 N. Leverett Rd. • Montague, MA 01351
E-Mail: kw@architecturalcomponentsinc.com
Website: www.architecturalcomponentsinc.com
Fax Ordering: (413) 367-9461
Contact Names: Chuck Bellinger, President
Catalog: Free. Frequency: Annual

Circulation: 50K. Sales: $3-5MM
Products: Architectural entryways;
reproduction and custom windows,
doors & architectural millwork

ARCHITECTURAL PANELING (212) 371-9632
979 Third Ave. • New York, NY 10022
E-Mail: apaneling@aol.com
Website: www.apaneling.com
Fax Ordering: (212) 759-0276
Contact Names: Anthony Lombards, President
Catalog: Free. Frequency: Annual
Circulation: 10K. Sales: $3-5MM
Products: Repro French & English paneling,
cabinets & ceilings; hand-carved wood mantels,
moldings & wood ornaments

ARCTIC SUPPLY GLASS OUTLET HOME (800) 428-9276
565 County Route T • Hammond, WI 54015
E-Mail: arctic@kissourglass.com
Website: www.kissourglass.com
Fax Ordering: (715) 639-2039
International Ordering: (715) 639-3762
Contact Names: Joseph Bacon, President
Catalog: Free. Frequency: Annual
Circulation: 50K. Sales: $3-5MM
Products: Sunrooms, greenhouses;
weather shields; windows & doors;
insulated tempered glass

B&W TILE COMPANY (310) 538-9579
14600 S. Western Ave.
Gardena, CA 90249
E-Mail: info@bwtile.com
Website: www.bwtile.com
Fax Ordering: (310) 538-2190
Contact Name: Joseph Logan, President
Catalog: Free. Frequency: Annual
Circulation: 10K. Sales: $5-10MM
Products: Manufacturer of porcelain
& ceramic tile

BEARDEN BROTHERS (800) 433-0074
CARPET & TEXTILES CORP.
1009 St. Charles St. • Dalton, GA 30720
E-Mail: info@abeardenbrothers.com
Website: www.beardenbrothers.com
Fax Ordering: (706) 277-1754
International Ordering: (706) 277-3265
Catalog: Free. Frequency: Annual
Circulation: 100K. Sales: $5-10MM
Products: Carpeting, rugs, padding,
hardwood & laminate flooring

BEDLAM ARCHITECTURAL METALWORKS (800) 233-5261
202 12th Ave. • Paterson, NJ 07026
E-Mail: sales@bedlam.biz
Website: www.bedlam.biz
Fax Ordering: (800) 233-5262; (973) 478-7900
International Ordering: (973) 546-5000
Contact Name: Dick Grabowsky, President
Catalog: Free. Frequency: Annual
Circulation: 25K. Sales: $3-5MM
Products: Solid brass tubing, ornaments,
caps, scrolls, railing posts & bed parts

BIOSHIELD PAINT (800) 621-2591
Echo Design Co.
3005 S. St. Francis #2A
Santa Fe, NM 87505
E-Mail: sales@bioshieldpaint.com
Website: www.bioshieldpaint.com

Fax Ordering: (505) 438-0199
International Ordering: (505) 438-3448
Contact Name: Rudolph Reitz, President
Catalog: Free. Frequency: Semiannual
Circulation: 100K. Sales: $3-5MM
Products: Non-toxic paints, stains & waxes;
solvent free wall paint; floor & furntiure
finishes; color wash brushes

BRADBURY & BRADBURY (707) 746-1900
ART WALLPAPERS
P.O. Box 155 • Benicia, CA 94510
E-Mail: info@bradbury.com
Website: www.bradbury.com
Fax Ordering: (707) 745-9417
Contact Name: Bruce Bradbury, President
Catalog: Free. Frequency: Annual
Circulation: 10K. Sales: $3-5MM
Products: Victorian wallpaper & wall art;
140 historic wallpaper patterns for the
recreation of historic interiors; arts &
crafts collection

BRUCE HARDWOOD FLOORS (800) 722-4647
Armstrong World Industries
P.O. Box 3001 • Lancaster, PA 17604
E-Mail: info@armstrong.com
Website: www.armstrong.com
International Ordering: (717) 397-0611
Catalog: Free. Frequency: Annual
Circulation: 100K. Sales: $50-100MM
Products: Hardwood & laminate flooring
designs; cabinets, acoustical ceilings

J.R. BURROWS & COMPANY (800) 347-1795
P.O. Box 522 • Rockland, MA 02370
E-Mail: merchant@burrows.com
Website: www.burrows.com
Fax Ordering: (781) 982-1636
International Ordering: (781) 982-1812
Contact Name: John Burrows, President
Catalog: Free. Frequency: Weekly
Circulation: 200K. Sales: $10-50MM
Products: Victorian arts & crafts; reproduction
wallpaper & carpet; movement lace curtains

CHELSEA DECORATIVE METAL CO. (713) 721-9200
8212 Braewick Dr. • Houston, TX 77074
E-Mail: info@thetinman.com
Website: www.thetinman.com
Fax Ordering: (713) 776-8661
Contact Name: Glenn Eldridge, President
Catalog: Free. Frequency: Annual
Circulation: 10K. Sales: $500K to $1MM
Products: Pressed tin for ceilings & walls,
Victorian to Art Deco

COPPER BEECH MILLWORK (800) 532-9110
Amherst Woodworking & Supply, Inc.
P.O. Box 718 • Northampton, MA 01061
E-Mail: sales@copperbeech.com
Website: www.copperbeech.com
Fax Ordering: (413) 582-0164
International Ordering: (413) 584-3003
Contact Name: David Short, President
Catalog: Free. Frequency: Annual
Circulation: 10K. Sales: $5-10MM
Products: Decking, doors, flooring,
mantels, wood moldings, stairws

COUNTRY CURTAINS (800) 876-6123
P.O. Box 955 • Stockbridge, MA 01262 (800) 937-1237
E-Mail: sales@countrycurtains.com
Website: www.countrycurtains.com
Fax Ordering: (413) 243-1067
International Ordering: (413) 243-1474
Contact Name: Robert Trask, President
Catalog: Free. Frequency: Semiannual
Circulation: 100K. Sales: $50-100MM
Products: Curtains, bedspreads, home
decorating accessories

CUMBERLAND WOODCRAFT CO. (800) 367-1884
P.O. Drawer 609 • Carlisle, PA 17013
E-Mail: sales@cumberlandwoodcraft.com
Website: www.cumberlandwoodcraft.com
Fax Ordering: (717) 243-6502
International Ordering: (717) 243-0063
Contact Name: Randolph Reese, President
Catalog: Free. Frequency: Annual
Circulation: 50K. Sales: $3-5MM
Products: Ceiling medallions; Repro
Victorian woodwork, period mantels &
millwork

DECORATORS SUPPLY CORP. CATALOGS (773) 847-6300
3610 S. Morgan St. • Chicago, IL 60609
E-Mail: sales@decoratorssupply.com
Website: www.decoratorssupply.com
Fax Ordering: (773) 847-6357
Contact Name: Elmer Grage, President
Catalog: $25 ea.. Frequency: Annual
Circulation: 10K. Sales: $10-20MM
Products: Manufacturers of ornamental
plaster & woodworking; furniture ornamentation;
over 14,000 designs

DESIGNS IN TILE (530) 926-2629
P.O. Box 358 • Mount Shasta, CA 96067
E-Mail: info@designsintile.com
Website: www.designsintile.com
Fax Ordering: (530) 926-6467
Contact Name: Selene Seltzer, President
Catalog: Free. Frequency: Monthly
Circulation: 100K. Sales: $5-10MM
Products: Custom historic ceramic tile
& murals

DOROTHY'S ORIGINALS, INC. (800) 367-6849
6721 Market St. • Wilmington, NC 28405 (888) 367-6844
E-Mail: curtains@dorothysoriginals.com
Website: www.dorothysoriginals.com
Fax Ordering: (877) 569-0729
International Ordering: (910) 791-0924
Contact Name: Dorothy C. Noe, Owner
Catalog: Free. Frequency: Annual
Circulation: 5K. Sales: $500MK to $1MM
Products: Decorator fabrics & custom
services

DRIWOOD MOULDING COMPANY (843) 669-2478
P.O. Box 1729 • Florence, SC 29503 (843) 662-0541
E-Mail: sales@driwood.com
Website: www.driwood.com
Fax Ordering: (843) 669-4874
Catalog: $8. Frequency: Annual
Circulation: 10K. Sales: $5-10MM
Products: Period ornamental mouldings
& architectural millwork

ELLIOTT'S HARDWARE (888) 653-8963
4901 Maple Ave. • Dallas, TX 75235
E-Mail: info@elliottshardware.com
Website: www.elliottshardware.com
Fax Ordering: (214) 905-9601
Catalog: Free. Frequency: Annual
Circulation: 10K. Sales: $1-3MM
Products: Restoration & renovation hardware, including antiquing solutions, appliques & trims, cabinet/door/furniture hardware, kitchen & window hardware

EXCALIBUR COLLECTION (718) 366-3444
Excalibur Bronze
309 Starr St. • Brooklyn, NY 11237
E-Mail: sales@excaliburbronze.com
Website: www.excaliburbronze.com
Fax Ordering: (718) 366-7927
Contact Name: William Gold, President
Catalog: $50. Frequency: Annual
Circulation: 2K. Sales: $1-3MM
Products: Bronze interior furnishings; sculptural reproductions; furniture & lighting; sculpture

FAUCET OUTLET (888) 381-8837
1 Coates Dr. • Goshen, NY 10924 (800) 444-5783
E-Mail: info@faucet.com
Website: www.faucet.com
Fax Ordering: (888) 278-6898;
  (845) 294-9626
Contact Name: Daniel Auer, President
Catalog: Free. Frequency: Semiannual
Circulation: 50K. Sales: $3-5MM
Products: Decorative faucets & plumbing fixtures at wholesale discounts

FELBER ORNAMENTAL PLASTERING CORP. (800) 392-6896
P.O. Box 57 • Norristown, PA 19404
E-Mail: jk@felber.net
Website: www.felber.net
Fax Ordering: (610) 275-6636
International Ordering: (610) 275-4713
Contact Name: James Kuryloski, President
Catalog: $3. Frequency: Annual
Circulation: 10K. Sales: $1-3MM
Products: Architectural ornaments & mouldings; glass reinforced gypsum shapes, ceiling medallions, cornices, domes, niches & brackets

FOCAL POINT LIGHTING (773) 247-9494
4141 S. Pulaski Rd. • Chicago, IL 60632
E-Mail: sales@focalpointlights.com
Website: www.focalpointlights.com
Fax Ordering: (773) 247-8484
Catalog: Free. Frequency: Semiannual
Circulation: 100K. Sales: $5-10MM
Products: Architectural lighting

FOX VALLEY SYSTEMS, INC. (800) 323-4770
640 Industrial Dr. • Cary, IL 60013 (800) 323-4700
E-Mail: info@foxpaint.com
Website: www.foxpaint.com
Fax Ordering: (847) 639-8190
International Ordering: (847) 639-5744
Contact Name: Paul Hoeft, President
Catalog: Free. Frequency: Annual
Circulation: 150K. Sales: $20-50MM
Products: Aerosol paints, stripping & marking equipment

FYPON (800) 955-5748
960 W. Barre Rd. • Archbold, OH 43502 (800) 446-3040
E-Mail: info@fypon.com
Website: www.fypon.com
Fax Ordering: (800) 446-9373; (419) 445-4440
International Ordering: (419) 445-0116
Contact Name: Thomas Smart, President
Catalog: Free. Frequency: Monthly
Circulation: 100K. Sales: $20-50MM
Products: Molded millwork

H.A. GUDEN CO., INC. (800) 344-6437
99 Raynor Ave. • Ronkonkoma, NY 11779
E-Mail: info@guden.com
Website: www.guden.com
Fax Ordering: (631) 737-2933
International Ordering: (631) 737-2900
Contact Name: Paul Guden, President
Catalog: Free. Frequency: Annual
Circulation: 25K. Sales: $5-10MM
Products: Industrial hardware; hinges, handles, dampers, gas springs

HOMESPUN FABRICS & DRAPERIES (888) 543-2998
P.O. Box 24255 • Ventura, CA 91359
E-Mail: sales@homespunfabrics.com
Website: www.homespunfabrics.com
Fax Ordering: (206) 338-2576
International Ordering: (805) 642-1152
Contact Name: DeAnna Decker, President
Catalog: Free. Frequency: Quarterly
Circulation: 20K. Sales: $3-5MM
Products: Textured fabric for seamless draperies, slipcovers, upholstery, bedspreads, tablecloths, walls; books & videos

HORTON BRASSES, INC. (800) 754-9127
49 Nooks Hill Rd. • Cromwell, CT 06416
E-Mail: contact@horton-brasses.com
Website: www.horton-brasses.com
Fax Ordering: (860) 635-6473
International Ordering: (860) 635-4400
Contact Name: Barbara Rockwell, President
Catalog: Free. Frequency: Annual
Circulation: 50K. Sales: $5-10MM
Products: Brass and wrought iron reproduction hardware for furniture and cabinetry, handles, knobs, latches, hinges & slides

HUNTER CEILING FANS (888) 830-1326
11660 Central Pkwy.
Jacksonville, FL 32224
E-Mail: info@hunterfan.com
Website: www.hunterfan.com
Fax Ordering: (904) 642-4020
International Ordering: (904) 642-4340
Contact Name: Robert Beasley, President
Catalog: Free. Frequency: Annual
Circulation: 50K. Sales: $25-50MM
Products: Ceiling fans, humidifiers, air purifiers, thermostats

THE IRON SHOP (800) 523-7427
P.O. Box 547 • Broomall, PA 19008
E-Mail: info@theironshop.com
Website: www.theironshop.com/pm
Fax Ordering: (610) 544-7297
International Ordering: (610) 544-7100
Catalog: Free. Frequency: Annual
Circulation: 50K. Sales: $5-10MM
Products: Spiral staircase kits

PHYLLIS KENNEDY HARDWARE   (800) 621-1245
10655 Andrade Dr. • Zionsville, IN 46077
E-Mail: philken@kennedyhardware.com
Website: www.kennedyhardware.com
Fax Ordering: (317) 873-8662
International Ordering: (317) 873-1316
Contact Name: Phyllis Kennedy, President
Catalog: $3. Frequency: Annual
Circulation: 10K. Sales: $1-3MM
Products: Antique furniture restoration
hardware and parts for Hoosier cabinets,
general furniture hardware; books

KENTUCKY WOOD FLOORS   (812) 923-8875
Koetter Woodworking, Inc.
533 Louis Smith Rd. • Borden, IN 47106
E-Mail: kwsales@koetterwoodworking.com
Website: www.koetterwoodworking.com
Fax Ordering: (812) 923-9048
Catalog: Free. Frequency: Annual
Circulation: 50K. Sales: $20-50MM
Products: Architectural millwork;
solid wood doors; wood flooring

KESTREL SHUTTERS & DOORS   (800) 494-4321
Kestrel Manufacturing
9 E. Race St. • Stowe, PA 19464
E-Mail: sales@diyshutters.com
Website: www.diyshutters.com
Fax Ordering: (610) 326-6779
International Ordering: (610) 326-6679
Contact Names: James W. Lapic, Buyer
Catalog: Free. Frequency: Annual
Circulation: 50K. Sales: $3-5MM
Products: Kestrel shutters, folding screens,
hardware and closet doors

KOFFLER SALES CO.   (800) 323-0951
100-A Oakwood Rd. • Lake Zurich, IL 60047   (888) 355-6287
E-Mail: customerservice@kofflersales.com
Website: www.kofflersales.com
Fax Ordering: (847) 438-1514
International Ordering: (847) 438-1152
Contact Names: Ron Star, President
Catalog: Free. Frequency: Semiannual
Circulation: 50K. Sales: $3-5MM
Products: Floor mats, matting, and
rubber stair treads

LAMP SHOP   (603) 224-1603
P.O. Box 3606 • Concord, NH 03302
E-Mail: info@lampshop.com
Website: www.lampshop.com
Fax Ordering: (603) 224-6677
International Ordering: (610) 224-1603
Contact Names: Scott O'Kenyon, President
Catalog: Free. Frequency: Monthly
Circulation: 25K. Sales: $3-5MM
Products: Lampshade making materials
& supplies

LOVELIA ENTERPRISES   (800) 843-8438
356 E. 41st St. • New York, NY 10017
E-Mail: sales@oldhousejournal.com
Website: www.oldhousejournal.com
Fax Ordering: (212) 697-8550
International Ordering: (212) 490-0930
Contact Name: Lovelia Albright, President
Catalog: Free. Frequency: Annual
Circulation: 10K. Sales: $500K
Products: Tapestries; restoration projects

MAD RIVER WOODWORKS   (707) 668-5671
P.O. Box 1067 • Blue Lake, CA 95525
E-Mail: info@madriverwoodworks.com
Website: www.madriverwoodworks.com
Fax Ordering: (707) 668-5673
Contact Names: Tim Thornton, President
Catalog: $3. Frequency: Annual
Circulation: 10K. Sales: $500K - $1MM
Products: Victorian millwork, custom
moldings, brackets, porch parts

MOUNTAIN LUMBER   (800) 445-2671
6812 Spring Hill Rd. • Ruckersville, VA 22968
E-Mail: sales@mountainlumber.com
Website: www.mountainlumber.com
Fax Ordering: (434) 985-4105
International Ordering: (434) 985-3646
Contact Names: Willie Drake, President
Catalog: Free. Frequency: Annual
Circulation: 10K. Sales: $3-5MM
Products: Historic Heart Pine and other
antique wood flooring

MYLEN STAIR KITS   (800) 431-2155
650 Washington St. • Peekskill, NY 10566
E-Mail: info@mylenstairs.com
Website: www.mylenstairs.com
Fax Ordering: (914) 439-9744
International Ordering: (914) 739-8486
Contact Names: Monroe Gelfand, President
Catalog: Free. Frequency: Annual
Circulation: 50K. Sales: $5-10MM
Products: Manufacturers of spiral stairs &
architectural stair systems

W.F. NORMAN CORPORATION   (800) 641-4038
P.O. Box 323 • Nevada, MO 64772
E-Mail: ceilings@wfnorman.com
Website: www.wfnorman.com
Fax Ordering: (417) 667-2708
International Ordering: (417) 667-5552
Contact Names: Annette Quitno, President
Catalog: Free. Frequency: Annual
Circulation: 50K. Sales: $3-5MM
Products: Decorative metal ceilings, roofs,
exterior siding & ornaments; wainscotting
& cornices

NOSTALGIC WAREHOUSE   (800) 522-7336
DOOR HARDWARE
4661 Monaco St. • Denver, CO 80216
E-Mail: nostalgicwarehouse@acmemfgco.com
Website: www.nostalgicwarehouse.com
Fax Ordering: (800) 322-7002
International Ordering: (303) 355-2344
Contact Names: Larry Broderick, President
Catalog: Free. Frequency: Annual
Circulation: 25K. Sales: $3-5MM
Products: Decorative door & cabinet hardware

PATTERNS OF THE PAST   (800) 798-7979
Amazon Drygoods
411 Brady St. • Davenport, IA 52801
E-Mail: info@amazondrygoods.com
Website: www.amazondrygoods.com
Fax Ordering: (563) 322-4003
International Ordering: (563) 322-6800
Contact Name: Janet Burgess, President
Catalog: $7. Frequency: Annual
Circulation: 25K. Sales: $3-5MM
Products: Specialty fabrics & patterns;
19th century inspired products

PEERLESS IMPORTED RUGS   (800) 621-6573
3033 N. Lincoln Ave. • Chicago, IL 60657
E-Mail: info@peerlessrugs.com
Website: www.peerlessrugs.com
Fax Ordering: (773) 525-4055
International Ordering: (773) 525-0296
Contact Name: Philip Liss, President
Catalog: Free. Frequency: Semiannual
Circulation: 50K. Sales: $5-10MM
Products: Rugs & tapestries

PRESTIGE CARPETS   (800) 887-6807
P.O. Box 516 • Dalton, GA 30722
E-Mail: sales@prestigecarpet.com
Website: www.prestigecarpet.com
Fax Ordering: (706) 217-2429
International Ordering: (706) 217-6640
Contact Name: Roy Johnson, Jr., President
Catalog: Free. Frequency: Weekly
Circulation: 25K. Sales: $3-5MM
Products: Carpet, vinyl, wood, laminates,
custom rugs & carpets

RARE EARTH HARDWOOD   (800) 968-0074
6778 E. Traverse Hwy.
Traverse City, MI 49684
E-Mail: info@rare-earth-hardwoods.com
Website: www.rare-earth-hardwoods.com
Fax Ordering: (800) 968-0094; (231) 946-6221
International Ordering: (231) 946-0043
Contact Names: Rick Paid, President
Catalog: Free. Frequency: Annual
Circulation: 50K. Sales: $10-20MM
Products: Hardwood flooring & decks;
wood moldings, stair treads, risers;
exotic veneer & lumber

THE REGGIO REGISTER COMPANY   (800) 880-3090
31 Jytek Rd. • Leominster, MA 01453
E-Mail: reggio@reggioregister.com
Website: www.reggioregister.com
Fax Ordering: (978) 772-5513
International Ordering: (978) 772-3493
Contact Names: Michael Reggio, President
Catalog: Free. Frequency: Quarterly
Circulation: 150K. Sales: $3-5MM
Products: Cast iron, brass, aluminum
and wood decorative grilles & registers

RESTORATION WORKS, INC.   (815) 937-0556
200 E. North St. • Bradley, IL 60915
E-Mail: mk@restoworks.com
Website: www.restoworks.com
Fax Ordering: (815) 937-4072
Contact Name: Gail Wallace, President
Catalog: Free. Frequency: Annual
Circulation: 25K. Sales: $5-10MM
Products: Restoration products; vwood
window restoration; intage tubs; decorative
plumbing fixtures & accessories; hardware
& architectural trims

S&S MILLS CARPET   (800) 241-4013
200 Howell Dr. • Dalton, GA 30721   (800) 363-5067
E-Mail: info@ssmills.com
Website: www.ssmills.com
Fax Ordering: (706) 277-3922
International Ordering: (610) 277-3677
Catalog: Free. Frequency: Annual
Circulation: 100K. Sales: $10-20MM
Products: Carpeting for home & office

SALTER INDUSTRIES   (800) 368-8280
105 G.P. Clement Dr. • Collegeville, PA 19426
E-Mail: general@salterspiralstair.com
Website: www.salterspiralstair.com
Fax Ordering: (610) 489-9286
International Ordering: (610) 489-5799
Contact Names: Barry Salter, President
Catalog: Free. Pages: 32. Frequency: Annual
Circulation: 50K. Sales: $10-20MM
Products: Spiral staircases

SHUTTERCRAFT, INC.   (203) 245-2608
282 Stepstone Hill Rd.
Guilford, CT 06437
E-Mail: all@shuttercraftinc.com
Website: www.shuttercraftinc.com
Fax Ordering: (203) 245-5969
Contact Names: Dwight M. Carlson, President
Catalog: Free. Frequency: Annual
Circulation: 25K. Sales: $3-5MM
Products: Interior & exterior wood shutters
and hardware

SILK TRADING COMPANY   (323) 954-9280
360 S. La Brea Ave.
Los Angeles, CA 90036
E-Mail: info@silktrading.com
Website: www.silktrading.com
Fax Ordering: (323) 954-8024
International Ordering: (323) 954-9280
Contact Name: Andrea & Warren Kay, Owners
Catalog: Free. Frequency: Quarterly
Circulation: 100K. Sales: $10-20MM
Products: Custom luxury draperies, fabrics,
paints, trimmings & accessories

SMITH & NOBLE WINDOWARE   (800) 248-8888
P.O. Box 1838 • Corona, CA 92878
E-Mail: help@smithandnoble.com
Website: www.smithandnoble.com
Fax Ordering: (800) 426-7780
Catalog: Free. Frequency: Annual
Circulation: 100K. Sales: $5-10MM
Products: Custom-made window blinds
and shades

SOMERSET DOOR & COLUMN CO.   (800) 242-7916
174 Sagamore St. • Somerset, PA 15501
E-Mail: info@doorandcolumn.com
Website: www.doorandcolumn.com
Fax Ordering: (814) 445-1980
International Ordering: (814) 445-9608
Contact Names: Dean Hottle, President
Catalog: Free. Frequency: Annual
Circulation: 75K. Sales: $3-5MM
Products: Architectural columns,
custom doors and other millwork items

STAIRWAYS, INC.   (800) 231-0793
4166 Pinemont Dr. • Houston, TX 77018
E-Mail: swinfo@stairwaysinc.com
Website: www.stairwaysinc.com
Fax Ordering: (713) 680-2571
International Ordering: (713) 680-3110
Contact Names: John Anderson, President
Catalog: Free. Frequency: 10x per year
Circulation: 100K. Sales: $5-10MM
Products: Manufactures spiral & straight
stairs in wood, metal, stainless steel, aluminum,
brass and wrought iron; parts & supplies for
repair and modification

STYLE UNLIMITED   (508) 224-7234
45 Leeward Way
Plymouth, MA 02360
E-Mail: info@yourstyleunlimited.com
Website: www.yourstyleunlimited.com
Fax Ordering: (508) 830-0313
Contact Name: Diane Corcoran, Owner
Catalog: Free. Frequency: Annual
Circulation: 25K. Sales: $500K - $1MM
Products: Curtains & accessories

TOTAL WOOD RESTORATION SYSTEM   (800) 827-3480
Wood Care Systems
P.O. Box 2160 • Kirkland, WA 98083
E-Mail: staff@ewoodcare.com
Website: www.ewoodcare.com
Fax Ordering: (425) 822-5800
International Ordering: (425) 827-6000
Contact Names: Jim Renfroe, President
Catalog: Free. Frequency: Annual
Circulation: 50K. Sales: $500K to $1MM
Products: Wood care & restoration products

JP WEAVER COMPANY   (818) 500-1740
941 Air Way • Glendale, CA 91201
E-Mail: info@jpweaver
Website: www.jpweaver.com
Fax Ordering: (818) 500-1798
Contact Name: Lenna Tyler-Kast, President
Catalog: Free. Frequency: Annual
Circulation: 50K. Sales: $10-20MM
Products: Segments, for walls, doors,
ceilings and fireplaces, that form European
design composites

WHITEHALL PRODUCTS, LLC   (800) 728-5449
8786 Water St. • Montague, MI 49437
E-Mail: sales@whitehallproducts.com
Website: www.whitehallproducts.com
Fax Ordering: (231) 894-6235
International Ordering: (231) 894-2688
Customer Service: (800) 728-2164
Contact Names: Brad Bruns, President
Catalog: Free. Frequency: Annual
Circulation: 50K. Sales: $1-3MM
Products: Handcast aluminum products
for your home and garden; mailboxes,
architectural plaques, bird feeders,
weathervanes

WINDOW TREATMENT CATALOG   (800) 798-7979
Amazon Drygoods
411 Brady St. • Davenport, IA 52801
E-Mail: info@amazondrygoods.com
Website: www.amazondrygoods.com
Fax Ordering: (563) 322-4003
International Ordering: (563) 322-6800
Contact Name: Janet Burgess, President
Catalog: $3. Frequency: Annual
Circulation: 50K. Sales: $5-10MM
Products: More than 50 full-sized
valence, drapery & shade patterns

WOODARD WEAVE   (800) 332-7847
Woodard & Greenstein American Antiques
506 E. 74th St. • New York, NY 10021
E-Mail: wgantiques@aol.com
Website: www.woodardweave.com
Fax Ordering: (212) 734-9665
International Ordering: (212) 988-2906
Contact Names: Thomas Woodard, President
Catalog: $7. Frequency: Monthly
Circulation: 10K. Sales: $5-10MM
Products: Rugs, carpets; antique American
rug carpets; reproduction of early American
flat woven rugs

WORLD OF WINDOW FASHIONS   (847) 251-7700
Perkowitz Window Fashions
135 Green Bay Rd. • Wilmette, IL 60091
E-Mail: jperkow181@aol.com
Website: www.perkowitzwindowfashion.com
Fax Ordering: (847) 853-1232
Contact Name: Richard Woods, President
Catalog: Online. Frequency: Annual
Circulation: 25K. Sales: $500K to $1MM
Products: Window coverings: shutters,
shades, blinds & draperies

YANKEE PRIDE   (800) 848-7610
29 Parkside Cir. • Braintree, MA 02184
E-Mail: customerservice@yankee-pride.com
Website: www.yankee-pride.com
Fax Ordering: (781) 848-6218
International Ordering: (781) 848-7610
Contact Names: Robert Packard, President
Catalog: $2. Pages: 72. Frequency: Weekly
Circulation: 10K. Sales: $500K to $1MM
Products: Braided rugs, wool hand-hooked
rugs; rag, woven & oriental style rugs

ACTIVA/INVICTA WATCHES   (800) 469-2824
Invicta Watch Group
3069 Taft St. • Hollywood, FL 33021
E-Mail: sales@invictawatch.com
Website: www.invictawatch.com
Fax Ordering: (954) 921-4222
International Ordering: (954) 921-2444
Contact Name: Eyal Lalo, President
Catalog: Free. Frequency: Bimonthly
Circulation: 500K. Sales: $3-5MM
Products: Watches

AKTEO WATCH COMPANY   (800) 360-2586
, Universal Watch Company
2 Fredericks St.
Framingham, MA 01702
E-Mail: info@akteo.com
Website: www.akteo.com
Fax Ordering: (508) 620-8756
International Ordering: (508) 620-8755
Contact Name: Rafael Cohen, Chairman
Catalog: Free. Frequency: Annual
Circulation: 100K. Sales: $1-3MM
Products: Akteo watches made in France

ALPHA SUPPLY   (800) 257-4211
P.O. Box 2133 • Bremerton, WA 98310
E-Mail: two@alpha-supply.com
Website: www.alpha-supply.com
Fax Ordering: (800) 257-4244; (360) 377-9235
International Ordering: (360) 373-3302
Contact Name: Tom Orme, President
Catalog: $5. Frequency: Quarterly
Circulation: 150K. Sales: $3-5MM
Products: Jewelry & lapidary tools &
supplies

AMULET   (800) 777-9940
P.O. Box 2089 • Sonoma, CA 95476
E-Mail: amulet@gemstones.com
Website: www.gemstones.com
Fax Ordering: (707) 939-1733
Catalog: Free. Frequency: Annual
Circulation: 100K. Sales: $1-3MM
Products: Diamonds, gemstones,
jewelry & gifts

JAMES AVERY CRAFTSMAN   (800) 283-1770
P.O. Box 291367 • Kerrville, TX 78029
E-Mail: inetcustomerservice@jamesavery.com
Website: www.jamesavery.com
Fax Ordering: (830) 895-4044
International Ordering: (830) 895-6800
Customer Service: (800) 283-0550
Contact Name: Chris Avery, President
Catalog: Free. Frequency: Quarterly
Circulation: 100K. Sales: $20-50MM
Products: Handcrafted silver & gold jewelry

BADALI JEWELRY, INC.   (800) 788-1888
320 W. 1550 N., Suite E
Layton, UT 84041
E-Mail: badalijewelry@badalijewelry.com
Website: www.badalijewelry.com
Fax Ordering: (801) 773-1804
International Ordering: (801) 773-1801
Contact Name: Paul J. Badali, President
Catalog: Free. Frequency: Annual
Circulation: 25K. Sales: $1-3MM
Products: Handcrafted & custom
designed jewelry

MAURICE BADLER JEWELRY   (800) 622-3537
578 Fifth Ave. • New York, NY 10036
E-Mail: info@badler.com
Website: www.badler.com
Fax Ordering: (212) 575-9205
International Ordering: (212) 575-9632
Contact Name: Jeffrey Badler, President
Catalog: Free. Frequency: Annual
Circulation: 25K. Sales: $1-3MM
Products: Fine jewelry

BALLY BEAD CO., INC.   (800) 543-0280
2304 Ridge Rd. • Rockwell, TX 75087
E-Mail: ballybead@sbcglobal.net
Website: www.ballybead.com
Fax Ordering: (972) 722-1979
International Ordering: (972) 771-4515
Catalog: Free. Frequency: 10x per year
Circulation: 25K. Sales: $1-3MM
Products: Jewelry & beads from around
the world

BOURGET BROS. JEWELERS   (800) 828-3024
BOURGET FLAGSTONE CO.
1636 11th St. • Santa Monica, CA 90404
E-Mail: info@bourgetbros.com
Website: www.bourgetbros.com
Fax Ordering: (800) 607-2201; (310) 450-2201
International Ordering: (310) 450-6556
Contact Name: Lawrence J. Bourget, President
Catalog: Free. Frequency: Bimonthly
Circulation: 250K. Sales: $3-5MM
Products: Jewelry tools & casting supplies;
natural stone products

BRAND NAME ONLY   (845) 352-1221
19 Valencia Dr.. • Monsey, NY 10952
E-Mail: info@brandnameonly.com
Website: www.brandnameonly.com
Catalog: Free. Frequency: Annual.
Circulation: Online. Sales: $10-50MM
Products: Items for satellite TV home theatre

J.H. BREAKELL & COMPANY   (800) 767-6411
132 Spring St. • Newport, RI 02840
E-Mail: sales@breakell.com
Website: www.breakell.com
Fax Ordering: (401) 849-6590
International Ordering: (401) 849-3522
Contact Name: Jim Breakell, President
Catalog: Free. Frequency: Bimonthly
Circulation: 25K. Sales: $1-3MM
Products: Fine jewelry designed by
James Breakell

BULGARI   (800) 285-4274
530 Fifth Ave. • New York, NY 10019
E-Mail: info@bulgari.com
Website: www.bulgari.com
Fax Ordering: (212) 541-8060
Catalog: Free. Frequency: Quarterly
Circulation: 50K. Sales: $3-5MM
Products: Fine jewelry & gifts

CAPETOWN DIAMOND CORPORATION   (800) 442-7866
270 E. Crossville Rd. • Roswell, GA 30075
E-Mail: sales@capetowndiamond.com
Website: www.capetowndiamond.com
Fax Ordering: (770) 645-0450
International Ordering: (770) 645-8555
Contact Name: Colon Cooper, President

Catalog: Free. Frequency: Annual
Circulation: 50K. Sales: $5-10MM
Products: Upscale watches & imported
jewelry

CARTIER CATALOG (800) 227-8437
653 Fifth Ave. • New York, NY 10022
E-Mail: eboutique.us@cartier.com
Website: www.cartier.com
Fax Ordering: (203) 925-6406
Catalog: Online. Sales: $100-200MM
Products: Watches, jewelry, leather goods,
stationery, gifts

A.G.A. CORREA & SON (800) 341-0788
P.O. Box 1, Edgecomb, ME 04556
E-Mail: sales@agacorrea.com
Website: www.agacorrea.com
Fax Ordering: (207) 882-9744
International Ordering: (207) 882-7873
Contact: Tony Correa, President
Catalog: Free. Frequency: Semiannual
Circulation: 100K. Sales: $1-3MM
Products: Men's & women's fine jewelry

COVINGTON ENGINEERING (877) 793-6636
P.O. Box 35 • Redlands, CA 92374
E-Mail: lapidary@discover.net
E-Mail: info@covington-engineering.com
Website: www.covington-engineering.com
Fax Ordering: (909) 793-7641
International Ordering: (909) 793-6636
Contact Name: Dorothy Covington, President
Catalog: Free. Frequency: Annual
Circulation: 50K. Sales: $5-10MM
Products: Lapidary machines & supplies;
glass equipment; rock cutting & polishing
equipment

CRAFTSTONES (760) 789-1620
P.O. Box 847 • Ramona, CA 92065
E-Mail: craftstones@craftstones.com
Website: www.craftstones.com
Fax Ordering: (760) 789-3432
Contact Name: Herbert Walters, President
Catalog: Free. Frequency: Annual
Circulation: 10K. Sales: $1-3MM
Products: Tumble-polished gems,
gemstone souvenirs, gifts, jewelry;
candles & soaps

CROWN GALLERIES (800) 544-8200
1706 Morrissey Dr. • Bloomington, IL 61704
E-Mail: customercare@crowngalleries.com
Website: www.crowngalleries.com
Fax Ordering: (309) 663-6691
International Ordering: (309) 663-9551
Contact Name: Richard Owen, President
Catalog: Free. Frequency: Semiannual
Circulation: 25K. Sales: $3-5MM
Products: Fine & costume jewelry;
lawn & garden items

DENATALE JEWELERS (800) 828-2930
170 Broadway, Suite 205
New York, NY 10038
E-Mail: info@denatale.com
Website: www.denatale.com
Fax Ordering: (212) 964-9597
International Ordering: (212) 349-2355
Contact Name: John DeNatale, President
Catalog: Free. Frequency: Annual

Circulation: 100K. Sales: $5-10MM
Products: Fine jewelry

DIAMOND ESSENCE (888) 807-4007
Meeshaa, Inc.
2401 Timber Oaks Rd. • Edison, NJ 08820
E-Mail: info@diamond-essence.com
Website: www.diamond-essence.com
Fax Ordering: (908) 462-3881
International Ordering: (908) 279-7986
Contact Name: Ranjit Singh, President
Catalog: Free. Frequency: Bimonthly
Circulation: 1MM. Sales: $10-20MM
Products: Men's & women's fine jewelry

DIAMOND PACIFIC (800) 253-2954
P.O. Box 1180 • Barstow, CA 92312
E-Mail: diamondpacific@aol.com
Website: www.diamondpacific.com
Fax Ordering: (760) 255-1077
International Ordering: (760) 255-1030
Contact Name: Bill Depue, President
Catalog: Free. Frequency: Quarterly
Circulation: 50K. Sales: $3-5MM
Products: Lapidary equipment, jewelers
tools & supplies

DISCOVERIES, INC. CARTOUCHE, LTD. (800) 283-4978
100 S. Early St. • Alexandria, VA 22304
E-Mail: sales@egyptianimports.com
Website: www.egyptianimports.com
Fax Ordering: (888) 283-4978
International Ordering: (703) 823-7904
Catalog: Free. Frequency: Annual
Circulation: 50K. Sales: $5-10MM
Products: Jewelry & gifts from the times
of the pharoahs

EASY LEAF PRODUCTS (800) 569-5323
NEI Group, LLC (Neuberg-Ebel Importers)
6001 Santa Monica Blvd.
Los Angeles, CA 90038
E-Mail: info@easyleaf.com
Website: www.easyleaf.com
Fax Ordering: (877) 386-1489; (323) 769-4840
International Ordering: (323) 769-4800
Contact Name: Larry Neuberg, President
Catalog: Free. Frequency: Annual
Circulation: 25K. Sales: $5-10MM
Products: Imitation & genuine gold leaf &
related supplies; gold leaf & metallic powders

EBERSOLE LAPIDARY SUPPLY (888) 323-7765
5830 W. Hendryx • Wichita, KS 67209
E-Mail: info@ebersolelapidary.com
E-Mail: president@ebersolelapidary.com
Fax Ordering: (309) 691-2632
International Ordering: (316) 722-8888
Contact Name: Delbert Ebersole, President
Catalog: Free. Frequency: Quarterly
Circulation: 25K. Sales: $3-5MM
Products: Lapidary & jewelry making
supplies & equipment

ELOXITE WHOLESALE (307) 322-3050
Eloxite Corporation
P.O. Box 729 • Wheatland, WY 82201
E-Mail: president@eloxite.com
Website: www.eloxite.com
Fax Ordering: (307) 322-3055
Contact Name: Pat Murphy, President
Catalog: Free. Frequency: Annual

Circulation: 50K. **Sales:** $3-5MM
Products: Lapidary supplies; wholesale jewelry parts, cut stones, beads and beading supplies, craft items

EXCLUSIVE SPORTS JEWELRY   (800) 533-3653
4517 Dean Dr. • Wilmington, NC 28405
E-Mail: customerservice@exclusivesportsjewelry.com
Website: www.exclusivesportsjewelry.com
International Ordering: (910) 799-9200
Catalog: Free. Frequency: Annual
Circulation: 25K. **Sales:** $1-3MM
Products: Sports related trophies & jewelry

MICHAEL C. FINA COMPANY   (800) 289-3462
5454 Fifth Ave. • New York, NY 10017
E-Mail: info@mcfina.com
Website: www.michaelcfina.com
Fax Ordering: (212) 557-3862
International Ordering: (212) 557-2500
Catalog: Free. Frequency: Annual
Circulation: 100K. **Sales:** $100-200MM
Products: Jewelry, tableware, giftware

ALAN FURMAN & COMPANY   (800) 654-7184
12250 Rockville Pike #270
Rockville, MD 20852
E-Mail: watches@alanfurman.com
Website: www.alanfurman.com
Fax Ordering: (301) 881-0810
Contact Name: Frank A. Griffin, President
Catalog: Free. Frequency: Semiannual
Circulation: 250K. **Sales:** $10-20MM
Products: Fine jewelry, watches & diamonds

GARDEN OF BEADIN'   (800) 232-3588
752 Redwood Dr. • Garberville, CA 95542
E-Mail: info@gardenofbeadin.com
Website: www.gardenofbeadin.com
Fax Ordering: (707) 923-9160
International Ordering: (707) 923-9120
Contact Name: Charlotte Silverstein, President
Catalog: Free. Frequency: Annual
Circulation: 50K. **Sales:** $3-5MM
Products: Beads and beading supplies

GEARY'S CATALOG   (800) 243-2797
Geary's of Beverly Hills
351 N. Beverly Dr.
Beverly Hills, CA 90210
E-Mail: sales@gearys.com
Website: www.gearys.com
Fax Ordering: (310) 858-7555
International Ordering: (310) 273-4741
Contact Name: Darrell S. Ross, President
Catalog: Free. Frequency: Bimonthly
Circulation: 2MM. **Sales:** $20-50MM
Products: Fine jewelry, tableware & giftware for the home

GILMAN'S CATALOG   (888) 529-1907
P.O. Box M • Hellertown, PA 18055
Fax Ordering: (610) 838-2961
International Ordering: (610) 838-8767
Contact Name: Robert Gilman, President
Catalog: Free. Frequency: Annual
Circulation: 50K. **Sales:** $3-5MM
Products: Jewelry, mineral, & lapidary tools, supplies & equipment for technicians & craftsmen

GRAVES LAPIDARY   (800) 327-9103
EQUIPMENT & SUPPLIES
Graves Company
1800 N. Andrews Ave.
Pompano Beach, FL 33069
E-Mail: sales@gravescompany.com
Website: www.gravescompany
Fax Ordering: (954) 960-0301
International Ordering: (954) 960-0300
Contact Names: Peter & Vicky Erdo, Owners
Catalog: Free. Frequency: Annual
Circulation: 50K. **Sales:** $5-10MM
Products: Lapidary & jeweler's tools & supplies; diamond abrasives; books & videos

HEAVEN & EARTH, LLC   (800) 942-9423
MINERALS, JEWELRY & GEMS
P.O. Box 249 • East Montpelier, VT 05651
E-Mail: heavenandearthmailorder@earthlink.net
Website: www.heavenandearthjewelry.com
Fax Ordering: (888) 400-6288; (802) 479-5923
International Ordering: (802) 476-4775
Contact Name: Kathy Warner, President
Catalog: Free. Frequency: Semiannual
Circulation: 100K. **Sales:** $5-10MM
Products: Fine jewelry, crystals & gems

HOUSE OF ONYX   (800) 844-3100
120 N. Main St. • Greenville, KY 42345
E-Mail: sales@houseofonyx.com
Website: www.houseofonyx.com
Fax Ordering: (270) 338-9605
International Ordering: (270) 338-2363
Contact Name: Shirley Rowe, President
Catalog: Free. Frequency: Monthly
Circulation: 250K. **Sales:** $10-50MM
Products: Jewelry, gemstones, carvings, minerals, gift items

INDIAN JEWELERS SUPPLY CO.   (800) 545-6540
601 E. Coal Ave. • Gallup, NM 87305
E-Mail: orders@ijsinc.com
Website: www.ijsinc.com
Fax Ordering: (888) 722-4172; (505) 722-4172
International Ordering: (505) 722-4451
Catalog: Free. Frequency: Annual
Circulation: 100K. **Sales:** $5-10MM
Products: Jewelry & jewelry parts, precious base metals, semi-precious stones, tools

INTERNATIONAL CRYSTAL CO.   (800) 343-6657
3008 34th St. • Lubbock, TX 79410
E-Mail: intcrysco@aol.com
Website: www.internationalcrystal.com
Fax Ordering: (806) 791-1502
Contact Name: Michael Leach, President
Catalog: Free. Frequency: Annual
Circulation: 50K. **Sales:** $1-3MM
Products: Sterling silver with semi-precious stones

JEEP COLLINS   (800) 343-9757
648 Post Oak Rd.
Fredericksburg, TX 78624
E-Mail: info@jeepcollins.com
Website: www.jeepcollins.com
Fax Ordering: (830) 997-0007
International Ordering: (830) 997-3135
Contact Name: Jeep Collins, President

Catalog: Free. Pages: 50.
Frequency: Semiannual
Circulation: 150K. Sales: $3-5MM
Products: Jewelry, bead jewelry,
religious symbols

JEWELRY CATALOG (877) 843-6468
The Franklin Mint
U.S. Rt. 1 • Franklin Center, PA 19091
E-Mail: info@franklinmint.com
Website: www.franklinmint.com
Fax Ordering: (610) 459-6880
International Ordering: (610) 459-6000
Contact Name: Adam Berger, President
Catalog: Free. Frequency: Annual
Circulation: 100K. Sales: $5-10MM
Products: Jewelry, furniture, sculpture

JEWELRY MAKERS SUPPLIES (800) 355-2137
Fire Mountain Gems & Beads
1 Fire Mountain Way
Grants Pass, OR 97526
E-Mail: info@firemountaingems.com
Website: www.firemountaingems.com
Fax Ordering: (800) 292-3473
International Ordering: (541) 592-2222
Customer Service: (800) 423-2319
Contact Name: Stuart Freedman, President
Catalog: Free. Frequency: Quarerly
Circulation: 250K. Sales: $10-20MM
Products: Jewelry making supplies, beads,
gemstones, mountings, tools, earrings

KASSOY TOOLS & SUPPLIES (800) 452-7769
FOR THE JEWELRY TRADE
101 Commercial St. #200
Plainview, NY 11803
E-Mail: sales@kassoy.com
Website: www.kassoy.com
Fax Ordering: (516) 942-0402
International Ordering: (516) 942-0560
Contact Name: Peter Gollon, President
Catalog: Free. Frequency: Annual
Circulation: 100K. Sales: $5-10MM
Products: Jeweler's tools, equipment
& supplies

KINGSLEY NORTH, INC. (800) 338-9280
P.O. Box 216 • Norway, MI 49870
E-Mail: sales@kingsleynorth.com
Website: www.kingsleynorth.com
Fax Ordering: (906) 563-7143
International Ordering: (906) 563-9228
Contact Name: Dan Paupore, President
Catalog: Free. Frequency: Quarterly
Circulation: 250K. Sales: $5-10MM
Products: Jewelry manufacturing tools,
equipment & supplies; gemology, findings,
beads

LAPCRAFT USA CATALOG (800) 432-4748
195 W. Olentangy St. • Powell, OH 43065
E-Mail: custservice@lapcraft.com
Website: www.lapcraft.com
Fax Ordering: (614) 764-1860
International Ordering: (614) 764-8993
Contact Name: Stephan Ussery, President
Catalog: Free. Frequency: Monthly
Circulation: 50K. Sales: $3-5MM
Products: Diamond & diamond & CBN
superabrasives; electroplated tools for l
apidary & glass

LIMOGES JEWELRY (800) 400-2854
1556 W. Carroll St. • Chicago, IL 60607
E-Mail: info@limogesjewelry.com
Website: www.limogesjewelry.com
International Ordering: (847) 375-1326
Catalog: Free. Frequency: Quarterly
Circulation: 150K. Sales: $3-5MM
Products: Personalized rings, pendants &
chains; bracelets, watches & accessories,
earrings.

LINDENWOLD FINE JEWELRY (800) 764-0008
& COSMETICS
Suarez International
7800 Whipple Ave. NW
North Canton, OH 44720
E-Mail: suarez@suarez.com
Website: www.suarez.com
Fax Ordering: (330) 497-6837
International Ordering: (330) 494-4282
Contact Name: Benjamin Suarez, President
Catalog: Free. Frequency: 8x per year
Circulation: 2MM. Sales: $50-100MM
Products: Fine & fashion jewelry; collectibles
& household items & cosmetics

LUX BOND & GREEN (800) 524-7336
46 LaSalle Rd. • W. Hartford, CT 06107
E-Mail: service@lbgreen.com
Website: www.lbgreen.com
Fax Ordering: (860) 521-8693
International Ordering: (860) 521-3015
Contact Name: Robert Green, President
Catalog: Free. Frequency: Annual
Circulation: 50K. Sales: $5-10MM
Products: Fine jewelry, diamonds & watches

MIDNIGHT VELVET (800) 398-3020
Seventh Ave.
1112 7th Ave. • Monroe, WI 53566
E-Mail: sales@midnightvelvet.com
Website: www.midnightvelvet.com
Fax Ordering: (800) 814-1650
International Ordering: (608) 324-7000
Customer Service: (800) 383-5283
Catalog: Free. Frequency: Semiannual
Circulation: 50K. Sales: $3-5MM
Products: Jewelry; home decor; health
& beauty products; clothing, shoes,
accessories & gifts

MUSEUM OF JEWELRY (MOJ) CATALOG (800) 835-2700
401 1st St. Suite 205 • Richmond, CA 94109
E-Mail: sales@capetowndiamond.com
Website: www.museumofjewelry.com
Fax Ordering: (510) 237-9971
Customer Service: (800) 258-0888
Contact Name: Sashi Singapuri, President
Catalog: Free. Frequency: Quarterly
Circulation: 2MM. Sales: $5-10MM
Products: Upscale watches & imported jewelry

NATURE'S JEWELRY (800) 333-3235
222 Mill Rd. • Chelmsford, MA 01824
E-Mail: sales@naturesjewelry.com
Website: www.naturesjewelry.com
Fax Ordering: (978) 256-0344
International Ordering: (978) 256-6019
Contact Names: Jonathan Fleischman, President
Catalog: Free. Frequency: Semiannual
Circulation: 200K. Sales: $10-20MM
Products: Jewelry, clothing & gifts with a wildlife motif

NEW YORK FINDINGS (888) 925-5745
72 Bowery • New York, NY 10013
E-Mail: newyorkfindings@aol.com
Website: www.newyorkfindings.com
Fax Ordering: (212) 925-5870
International Ordering: (212) 925-5745
Contact Name: Ebonizer King, President
Catalog: Free. Frequency: Monthly
Circulation: 50K. Sales: $10-50MM
Products: Precious metal jewelry, castings,
findings, settings to the trade

1928 JEWELRY COMPANY (800) 729-0042
3000 Empire Blvd. • Burbank, CA 91504
E-Mail: sales@1928.com
Website: www.1928.com
Fax Ordering: (818) 526-4558
International Ordering: (818) 841-1928
Contact Names: Melvyn Bernie, President
Catalog: Free. Frequency: Annual
Circulation: 100K. Sales: $25-50MM
Products: Fashion jewelry & accessory
items; children's jewelry, promotional items

NOVEL BOX COMPANY, LTD. (800) 965-9192
825 Lehigh Ave. • Union, NJ 07083
E-Mail: sales@novelbox.com
Website: www.novelbox.com
Fax Ordering: (908) 686-7774
International Ordering: (908) 686-7772
Catalog: Free. Frequency: Annual
Circulation: 150K. Sales: $5-10MM
Products: Jewelry boxes, displays,
packaging, supplies, etc.

OPEN CIRCLE/ANCIENT CIRCLES (800) 726-8032
190 North St. • Willits, CA 95490
E-Mail: orders@ancientcircles.com
Website: www.ancientcircles.com
Fax Ordering: (541) 488-7870
International Ordering: (541) 488-7880
Customer Service: (707) 459-2418
Contact Name: Ann Weller, President
Catalog: Free. Frequency: Annual
Circulation: 100K. Sales: $1-3MM
Products: Celtic & medieval jewelry,
tapestries, textiles & clothing, both
retail & wholesale

ORLEANS JEWELS (800) 433-6849
DeGrado, Inc.
P.O. Box 389 • Benton, MS 39039
E-Mail: info@orleansjewels.com
Website: www.orleansjewels.com
Fax Ordering: (662) 673-1277
International Ordering: (662) 673-1400
Contact Name: Joseph Degrado, President
Catalog: Free. Frequency: Quarterly
Circulation: 100K. Sales: $500K - 1MM
Products: Costume jewelry; cubic zirconia
jewelry

PALM BEACH INTERNATIONAL (888) 449-5262
JEWELRY COLLECTION (800) 581-6573
Seta Corporation (800) 497-7209
6400 E. Rogers Cir. • Boca Raton, FL 33499
E-Mail: info@palmbeachjewelry.com
Website: www.palmbeachjewelry.com
Fax Ordering: (561) 994-1710
International Ordering: (561) 994-2660
Contact Name: Joe Seta, President
Catalog: Free. Frequency: 10x per year

Circulation: 150K. Sales: $5-10MM
Products: Fine jewelry at discounted prices

PRIMA BEAD CATALOG (800) 366-2218
P.O. Box 2918 • Largo, FL 33779
E-Mail: customerservice@primabead.com
Website: www.primabead.com
Fax Ordering: (800) 366-6121
International Ordering: (727) 536-1492
Contact Name: Michael Cousin, President
Catalog: Free. Frequency: Semiannual
Circulation: 200K. Sales: $5-10MM
Products: Jewelry-making supplies &
accessories, including beads, and kits

QUALITY GEM DIAMONDS & JEWELRY (203) 748-4239
E-Mail: info@qualitygem.com
Website: www.qualitygem.com
Fax Ordering: (203) 748-4239
Contact Name: Dennis Janofsky, President
Catalog: Free. Frequency: Annual
Circulation: 50K. Sales: $1-3MM
Products: Diamonds & jewelry; custom
jewelryl silver beads & charms

REACTIVE METALS STUDIO (800) 876-3434
P.O. Box 890 • Clarkdale, AZ 86324
E-Mail: reactive@commspeed.net
Website: www.reactivemetals.com
Fax Ordering: (928) 634-6734
International Ordering: (928) 634-3434
Catalog: Free. Frequency: Annual
Circulation: 50K. Sales: $500M to1MM
Products: Reactive metals for jewelry
making

RIO GRANDE CATALOGS (800) 545-6566
7500 Bluewater Rd. NW
Albuquerque, NM 87121
E-Mail: info@tbg.riogrande.com
Website: www.riogrande.com
Fax Ordering: (800) 965-2329
International Ordering: (505) 839-3000
Contact Name: Hugh Bell, President
Catalog: Free. Frequency: Annual
Circulation: 250K. Sales: $20-50MM
Products: Jewelry tools, equipment &
supplies. The Gems & Findings & Display
& Packaging Catalog, $10; The Tools &
Equipment Catalog, $10; The Creative
Arts Catalog, $5; The Finished Jewelry
Collection Catalog, $5.

ROSS-SIMONS (800) 835-0919
9 Ross-Simons Dr. • Cranston, RI 02920 (800) 556-7376
E-Mail: info@ross-simons.com
Website: www.ross-simons.com
Fax Ordering: (800) 896-9191
Customer Service: (800) 835-1343
Contact Name: Darrell S. Ross, President
Catalog: Free. Frequency: Quarterly
Circulation: 200K. Sales: $20-50MM
Products: Fine jewelry, fashion jewelry,
estate jewelry, watches, diamond engagement
rings, wedding gifts, home decor gifts, procelain,
figurines, crystal; gifts & collectibles.

STAR STRUCK, LLC (800) 243-6144
P.O. Box 308 • Bethel, CT 06801
E-Mail: cs@starstruckllc.com
Website: www.starstruckllc.com
Fax Ordering: (800) 962-8345; (203) 778-6938

International Ordering: (203) 778-4925
Contact Name: Ken Karlan, President
Catalog: Free. Frequency: Semiannual
Circulation: 50K. Sales: $5-10MM
Products: Watch tools, parts, straps, batteries
& testers; bench tools; jeweler's tools & supplies;
diamond meters, filters, testers, scales & weights;
books, cleaners

SHIPWRECK BEADS   (800) 950-4232
8560 Commerce Pl. NE
Lacey, WA 98516
E-Mail: info@shipwreckbeads.com
Website: www.shipwreckbeads.com
Fax Ordering: (360) 754-2510
International Ordering: (360) 754-2323
Contact Name: Glenn Vincent, President
Catalog: Free. Frequency: Annual
Circulation: 100K. Sales: $5-10MM
Products: Beads; turquoise & amber beads;
findings & components; beading tools &
accessories; pendants & charms; stringing
materials; jeweler's tools, equipment &
supplies; books & videos

SIMPLY WHISPERS JEWELRY   (800) 451-5700
Roman Research, Inc.
800 Franklin St. • Hanson, MA 02341
E-Mail: custserv@romanresearch.com
Website: www.simplywhispers.com
Fax Ordering: (781) 447-0995
Contact Name: Dale Southworth, President
Catalog: Free. Frequency: Quarterly
Circulation: 200K. Sales: $5-10MM
Products: Hypoallergenic, nickel free
earrings for sensitive skin; ear-replaceable
earring accessories & spare jewelry parts

SOUTHWEST INDIAN FOUNDATION   (800) 504-2723
100 W. Coal Ave. • Gallup, NM 87301
E-Mail: swif@cia-g.com
Website: www.southwestindian.com
Fax Ordering: (505) 863-2760
International Ordering: (505) 863-4037
Customer Service: (877) 788-9962
Contact Name: William McCarthy, CEO
Catalog: Free. Frequency: Quarterly
Circulation: 200K. Sales: $3-5MM
Products: Southwest Indian jewelry,
fashion, art, crafts, books & media; gifts

STULLER, INC.   (800) 877-7777
P.O. Box 87777 • Lafayette, LA 70598
E-Mail: info@stuller.com
Website: www.stuller.com
Fax Ordering: (800) 444-4741; (337) 981-1655
International Ordering: (337) 262-7700
Technical Service: (877) 619-2174
Contact Name: Gary Fuller, Marketing
Catalog: Free. Frequency: Annual
Circulation: 150K. Sales: $50-100MM
Products: Jewelry, tools, supplies &
equipment

TEMPUS VITAE CATALOG   (570) 822-1900
Wilkes-Barre Blvd.
Wilkes-Barre, PA 18702
E-Mail: info@rogerdubuis.com
Website: www.rogerdubuis.com
Fax Ordering: (570) 822-4699
Contact Name: Margaret V. Pane, Marketing
Catalog: Free. Frequency: Annual
Circulation: 100K. Sales: $5-10MM
Products: Watches

TIFFANY & COMPANY   (800) 526-0649
727 Fifth Ave. • New York, NY 10022   (800) 843-3269
E-Mail: info@tiffany.com
Website: www.tiffany.com
Fax Ordering: (212) 605-4673
International Ordering: (212) 755-8000
Contact Name: Michael Powskay, President
Catalog: Free. Frequency: Quarterly
Circulation: 2MM. Sales: $100-500MM
Products: Jewelry, watches, giftware

TOURNEAU SALES CATALOGS   (800) 424-3113
500 Madison Ave. • New York, NY 10022   (800) 348-3332
E-Mail: info@tourneau.com
Website: www.tourneau.com
Fax Ordering: (212) 759-9511
International Ordering: (212) 758-6098
Customer Service: (800) 223-1288
Contact Name: Robert Wexler, President
Catalog: Free. Frequency: Annual
Circulation: 250K. Sales: $10-20MM
Products: Watches, fine jewelry, corporate gifts

WEDDING RING HOTLINE   (800) 985-7464
Bride & Grooms West
172 Route 9 North
Englishtown, NJ 07726
E-Mail: info@weddingringhotline.com
Website: www.weddingringhotline.com
Fax Ordering: (732) 972-0720
International Ordering: (732) 972-7777
Contact Name: Mitch Slachman, President
Catalog: Online. Sales: $5-10MM
Products: Wedding bands, diamonds &
engagement rings

THE WINDSOR COLLECTION CATALOG   (800) 800-0500
AmeriMark Direct   (877) 268-9594
6864 Engle Rd.
Cleveland, OH 44130
E-Mail: info@amerimark.com
Website: www.amerimark.com
Fax Ordering: (440) 826-1267
International Ordering: (440) 826-1900
Contact Name: Gary Geisler, President
Catalog: Free. Frequency: Annual
Circulation: 100K. Sales: $10-20MM
Products: Fashionable, fine & costume
jewelry & watches

AJP COPPERSMITH & CO.   (800) 545-1776
20 Industrial Pkwy. • Woburn, MA 01801
E-Mail: info@ajpcoppersmith.com
Website: ajpcoppersmith.com
Fax Ordering: (781) 245-1747
International Ordering: (781) 245-1216
Contact Name: Donald Webster, President
Catalog: $3. Frequency: Semiannual
Circulation: 200M. Sales: $1-3MM
Products: Handcrafted colonial lighting:
lanterns, chandeliers, ceiling fixtures,
scones; brass lighting, copper lights.

ALADDIN LAMP CATALOG   (800) 457-5267
Aladdin Mantle Lamp Co.
681 International Blvd.
Clarksville, TN 37040
E-Mail: info@aladdinlamps.com
Website: www.aladdinlamps.com
International Ordering: (931) 647-4949
Contact Name: Tony Batts, Manager
Catalog: Free. Frequency: Annual
Circulation: 50M. Sales: $1-3MM
Products: Kerosene mantle lamps

AMERICAN HOME SUPPLY   (408) 246-1962
P.O. Box 697 • Campbell, CA 95009
Fax Ordering: (408) 296-2450
International Ordering: (408) 246-1962
Contact Name: Marie Stevens, President
Catalog: Free. Frequency: Annual
Circulation: 500K. Sales: $1-5MM
Products: Reproduction lighting

AMERICAN LIGHT SOURCE   (800) 741—0571
215 Bobby Jones Expwy.
Martinez, GA 80900
E-Mail: service@americanlightsource.com
Website: www.americanlightsource.com
Fax Ordering: (706) 868-5083
Contact Name: Bill Mack, President
Catalog: $5. Frequency: Annual
Circulation: 25M. Sales: $3-5MM
Products: Light fixtures & ceiling fans;
pendants, sconces, outdoor lighting,
bath lighting, ceiling lights.

AMERICAN ULTRAVIOLET CO.   (800) 288-9288
212 S. Mt. Zion Rd. • Lebanon, IN 46052
E-Mail: mstines@auvco.com
Website: www.americanultraviolet.com
Fax Ordering: (765) 483-9525
International Ordering: (765) 483-9514
Contact Name: Meredith C. Stines, President
Catalog: Free. Frequency: Annual
Circulation: 25M. Sales: $5-10MM
Products: Ultraviolet lighting equipment
& replacement lamps

ARROYO CRAFTSMAN   (800) 400-2776
4509 Little John St.
Baldwin Park, CA 91706
E-Mail: framburg@framburg.com
Website: www.arroyo-craftsman.com
Fax Ordering: (888) 960-9521; (626) 960-9521
International Ordering: (626) 960-9411
Catalog: Free. Frequency: Annual
Circulation: 50K. Sales: 5-10MM
Products: Arts & crafts inspired lighting

ATLAS SPECIALTY LIGHTING   (800) 227-6745
1111 W. 22nd St. • Hialeah, FL 33010
E-Mail: sales@asltg.com
Website: www.asltg.com
Fax Ordering: (305) 888-2973
International Ordering: (305) 885-8941
Contact Name: A. Gordich, President
Catalog: Free. Frequency: Annual
Circulation: 50K. Sales: $10-20MM
Products: Specialty light bulbs & lamps

AUTHENTIC DESIGNS   (800) 844-9416
The Mill Rd. • West Rupert, VT 05776
E-Mail: adlights@sover.net
Website: www.authentic-designs.com
Fax Ordering: (802) 394-2422
International Ordering: (802) 394-7713
Contact Name: Daniel Krauss, President
Catalog: $3. Frequency: Annual
Circulation: 50K. Sales: $500K to $1MM
Products: Colonial & Early American lighting
fixtures; exterior lanterns, chandeliers, table
lamps, wall sconces

BELLACOR   (877) 723-5522
2425 Enterprise Dr., Suite 900   (800) 735-3377
Mendota Heights, MN 55120
E-Mail: customerservice@bellacor.com
Website: www.bellacor.com
Fax Ordering: (800) 760-6678; (651) 294-2595
International Ordering: (651) 294-2500
Customer Service: (877) 723-5522
Catalog: Online. Sales: $5-10MM
Products: Lighting fixtures, lamps, mirrors;
ceiling fans, track lighting, chandeliers; wall
sconces, bath fixtures, outdoor lighting;
furniture & home accessories

BEND A LITE CATALOG   (800) 235-2201
905 G St. • Hampton, VA 23661   (800) 236-3254
E-Mail: cs@bendalite.com
Website: www.bendalite.com
Fax Ordering: (877) 445-7298 (757) 244-4819
International Ordering: (757) 245-7675
Customer Service: (800) 729-7734
Catalog: Free. Frequency: Annual
Circulation: 100K. Sales: 1-5MM
Products: Signs & architectural lighting;
decorative lighting; disco lights & accessories;
neon signs

BRANDON INDUSTRIES CATALOG   (800) 247-1274
1601 N. Wilmeth Rd. • McKinney, TX 75069
E-Mail: info@brandonindustries.com
Website: www.brandonindustries.com
Fax Ordering: (972) 542-1015
International Ordering: (972) 542-3000
Contact Name: Bryan Hall, President
Catalog: $3. Frequency: Annual
Circulation: 100K. Sales: $10-20MM
Products: Cast aluminum outdoor lighting,
lamp posts, decorative mail boxes

BRASS LIGHT GALLERY   (800) 243-9595
P.O. Box 674 • Milwaukee, WI 53201
E-Mail: customerservice@brasslight.com
Website: www.brasslight.com
Fax Ordering: (800) 505-9404; (414) 271-7755
International Ordering: (414) 271-8300
Customer Service: (888) 212-4953

Contact Name: Steven Kaniewski, President
Catalog: $10. **Frequency:** Annual
Circulation: 5K. **Sales:** $1-3MM
Products: Brass mission & prairie style light fixtures & exterior lighting

BULB DIRECT   (800) 772-5267
1 Fishers Rd. • Pittsford, NY 14534
E-Mail: sales@bulbdirect.com
Website: www.bulbdirect.com
Fax Ordering: (800) 257-0760; (585) 385-4976
International Ordering: (585) 385-3540
Contact Name: Charles T. Graham, President
Catalog: Free. **Frequency:** Annual
Circulation: 25K. **Sales:** $1-3MM
Products: Light bulbs for your LCD,
Medical LED; LED MR16 lamps; LED lighting
& flashlights; compact flourescent needs.

BULBTRONICS   (800) 588-2852
45 Banfi Plaza • Farmingdale, NY 11735   (800) 624-2852
E-Mail: custserv@bulbtronics.com   (800) 654-8542
Website: www.bulbtronics.com
Fax Ordering: (631) 249-6066
International Ordering: (631) 249-2272
Customer Service: (800) 654--8542 x375
Contact Name: John Roberts, Marketing
Catalog: Online. **Sales:** $5-10MM
Products: Light bulbs; Lamps, LEDs, batteries
& lighting-related and electrical products

CLASSIC LAMP POSTS & LIGHTING   (310) 327-5401
Rotonics California Manufacturing, Inc.
17038 So. Figueroa St. • Gardena, CA 90248
E-Mail: corporate@rotonics.com
Website: www.rotonics.com
Fax Ordering: (310) 323-9567
Catalog: Free. **Frequency:** Semiannual
Circulation: 250K. **Sales:** $20-50MM
Products: Lamp posts, light globes, bollards,
sconces, mailboxes, clocks

COPPER HOUSE   (800) 281-9798
P.O. Box 1 • Epsom, NH 03234
E-Mail: sales@thecopperhouse.com
Website: www.thecopperhouse.com
Fax Ordering: (603) 736-4921
Contact Name: Bruce L. Coutu, President
Catalog: $4. **Frequency:** Semiannual
Circulation: 25K. **Sales:** $1-3MM
Products: Indoor & outdoor brass & copper
lighting; wall lamps; copper weathervanes;
arts & crafts

COUNTRY STORE OF GENEVA   (800) 232-1220
28 James St. • Geneva, IL 60134
E-Mail: customerservice@countrystoreofgeneva.com
Website: www.countrystoreofgeneva.com
Fax Ordering: (630) 232-6165
International Ordering: (630) 879-0098
Contact Name: David Dudley, President
Catalog: $3. **Frequency:** Semiannual
Circulation: 100K. **Sales:** $3-5MM
Products: Country decor & lighting, including
chandeliers, flush mount ceiling lights, table &
floor lamps, sconces & track lights, candles;
antiques & replicas; country style curtains

CRYSTAL FARM CATALOG   (970) 963-2350
18 Antelope Dr. • Redstone, CO 81623
E-Mail: crystalfarm@hughes.net
Website: www.crystalfarm.com

Fax Ordering: (970) 963-0709
Contact Name: Stephen C. Kent, President
Catalog: $25. **Frequency:** Annual
Circulation: 5K. **Sales:** $1-3MM
Products: Antler chandeliers & furniture

DAZOR MANUFACTURING CORP.   (800) 345-9103
2079 Congressional • St. Louis, MO 63146
E-Mail: info@dazor.com
Website: www.dazor.com
Fax Ordering: (314) 652-2069
International Ordering: (314) 652-2400
Contact Name: Mark Hogrebe, President
Catalog: Free. **Frequency:** Annual
Circulation: 50K. **Sales:** $5-10MM
Products: LED Task lighting; full spectrum
lighting; energy-efficient lighting; lamps;
electronic video magnifier; low vision &
reading lighting; free dazor video; accessories;
Spectrowave Diamond Grading Cabinet.

FOCAL POINT LIGHTING   (773) 247-9494
4141 S. Pulaski Rd. • Chicago, IL 60632
E-Mail: sales@focalpointlights.com
Website: www.focalpointlights.com
Fax Ordering: (773) 247-8484
Catalog: Free. **Frequency:** Semiannual
Circulation: 100K. **Sales:** $5-10MM
Products: Architectural lighting

FRAMBURG LIGHTING   (800) 796-5514
941 Cernan Dr. • Bellwood, IL 60104
E-Mail: sales@framburg.com
Website: www.framburg.com
Fax Ordering: (800) 423-0098; (708) 547-0064
International Ordering: (708) 547-5757
Catalog: Free. **Frequency:** Semiannual
Circulation: 250K. **Sales:** $5-10MM
Products: Handcrafted fixtures

HEARTH-GLO LIGHTING   (800) 777-3689
6 Fremont St. • Worcester, MA 01603
E-Mail: hwhg@comcast.net
Website: www.hearth-glo.com
Fax Ordering: (603) 279-7352
International Ordering: (603) 279-7352
Catalog: Free. **Frequency:** Annual
Circulation: 50M. **Sales:** $500M
Products: Handcrafted colonial lighting: wall
& post lanterns; hanging lanterns; wooden
lantern posts; wall sconces; chandeliers;
ceiling lights

HEATH SEDGWICK CO.   (888) 751-1158
P.O. Box 1305 • Stony Brook, NY 11790
E-Mail: info@heathsedgwick.com
Website: www.heathsedgwick.com
Fax Ordering: (631) 751-1114
International Ordering: (631) 751-1129
Contact Name: Rose Marie Byrne, President
Catalog: $4 (refundable). **Frequency:** Monthly
Circulation: 500M. **Sales:** $5-10MM
Products: Victorian floor & table lamps,
wall and hanging light fixtures, lamp shades,
upholstered and wicker furniture, table & window
lace, picture frames, brass wall sconces, brass
& crystal candelabras

HERITAGE LANTERNS   (800) 648-4449
25 Yarmouth Crossing Dr.
Yarmouth, ME 04009
E-Mail: finest@heritagelanterns.com

Website: www.heritagelanterns.com
Fax Ordering: (207) 846-9732
International Ordering: (207) 846-3911
Contact Name: Karla Gustaphson, President
Catalog: $6 (refundable). Frequency: Annual
Pages: 40. Circulation: 25K. Sales: $3-5MM
Products: Heritage lanterns reproductions

HOUSE OF TROY CATALOG   (800) 428-5367
902 Silver Ridge Rd.
Hyde Park, VT 05655
E-Mail: customerservice@houseoftroy.com
Website: www.houseoftroy.com
Fax Ordering: (888) 881-7952; (802) 888-2942
International Ordering: (802) 888-7984
Contact Name: Kent Mitchell, President
Catalog: Free. Frequency: Semiannual
Circulation: 250M. Sales: $5-10MM
Products: Handcrafted picture lights &
piano desk lamps

HUBBARDTON FORGE   (802) 468—3090
P.O. Box 827 • Castleton, VT 05735
E-Mail: info@vtforge.com
Website: www.vtforge.com
Fax Ordering: (802) 468-3284
Catalog: $3. Pages: 165. Frequency: Annual
Circulation: 40K. Sales: $1-3MM
Products: Hand-forged, Vermont-made w
rought-iron lighting & accessories

IDAHO WOOD LIGHTING   (800) 635-1100
P.O. Box 488 • Sandpoint, ID 83864
E-Mail: idahowood@imbris.net
Website: www.idahowood.com
Fax Ordering: (208) 263-3102
International Ordering: (208) 263-9521
Contact Name: Leon Lewis, President
Catalog: Free. Frequency: Annual
Circulation: 50K. Sales: $1-3MM
Products: Landscape lighting designs
in cedar & oak; ceiling, hanging fixtures
& chandeliers; bath & wood accessories

INTERLIGHT   (800) 743-0005
International Lighting Corp.
7939 New Jersey Ave.
Hammond, IN 46323
E-Mail: mail@interlight.biz
Website: www.interlight.biz
Fax Ordering: (219) 989-1022
International Ordering: (219) 989-0060
Catalog: Free. Frequency: Annual
Circulation: 100K. Sales: $20-50MM
Products: Specialty bulbs: projection bulbs,
replacement projection bulbs, LCD bulbs &
lamps; replacement DLP bulbs & lamps

IRVIN'S COUNTRY TINWARE   (800) 800-4846
115 Cedar Lane
Mt. Pleasant Mills, PA 17853
E-Mail: service@irvins.com
Website: www.irvins.com
Fax Ordering: (570) 539-2721
International Ordering: (570) 539-8200
Contact Name: Irvin Hoover, President
Catalog: Free. Frequency: Quarterly
Circulation: 100K. Sales: $1-3MM
Products: Reproduction Early American
handcrafted lighting fixtures; home decor
& gifts, candle accessories, clocks, furniture

KING'S CHANDELIER   (336) 623-6188
P.O. Box 667 • Eden, NC 27289
E-Mail: crystal@chandelier.com
Website: www.chandelier.com
Fax Ordering: (336) 627-9935
Contact Name: Nancy Talbert, Marketing
Catalog: $5. Frequency: Weekly
Circulation: 10K. Sales: $20-50MM
Products: European crystal chandeliers &
lighting fixtures & Victorian gaslight reproductions;
replacment parts; sconces & candelabras

BRIGHT STAR LIGHTING PRODUCTS   (800) 631-3814
Koehler-Bright Star, Inc.
380 Stewart Rd. • Wilkes-Barre, PA 18706
E-Mail: sales@kbs-inc.net
Website: www.flashlight.com
Fax Ordering: (570) 825-1984
International Ordering: (570) 825-1900
Contact Name: Matt Malcolm, Vice President
Catalog: Free. Frequency: Annual
Circulation: 50K. Sales: $20-50MM
Products: Industrial lighting; industrial
rechargeable flashlights, lanterns, batteries;
high intensity spotlights; extension lights

LCD LIGHTING   (800) 245-4458
37 Robinson Blvd. • Orange, CT 06477
E-Mail: ukret@lcdl.com
Website: www.lcdl.com
Fax Ordering: (203) 795-2874
International Ordering: (203) 795-1520
Contact Name: Christian Sauska, President
Catalog: Free. Frequency: Annual
Circulation: 100M. Sales: $10-20MM
Products: Designer & manufacturer of specialty
fluorescent lighting; lamps & liquid crystal lighting
devices; commercial, military & private avionics
backlighting

LAMPLIGHT FARMS, INC.   (888) 473-1088
            (800) 645-5267
W.C. Bradley Co.
W140 N4900 N. Lilly Rd.
Menomonee, WI 53051
E-Mail: sales@lamplight.com
Website: www.lamplight.com
Fax Ordering: (262) 781-6774
International Ordering: (262) 781-9590
Contact Name: J. Michael Tendick, President
Catalog: Free. Frequency: Semiannual
Circulation: 250K. Sales: $20-50MM
Products: Home decor; outdoor lighting,
lamps, candles, accessories, oil

LAMPS PLUS   (800) 782-1967
20250 Plummer St.
Chatsworth, CA 91311
E-Mail: pr@lampsplus.com
Website: www.lampsplus.com
Catalog: Free. Frequency: Annual
Circulation: 100M. Sales: $5-10MM
Products: Lamps & lighting fixtures;
ceiling lights, wall lights, outdoor lights,
ceiling fans.

LIGHTING BY HAMMERWORKS   (800) 777-3689
6 Fremont St. • Worcester, MA 01603
E-Mail: hwhg@comcast.net
Website: www.hammerworks.com
Fax Ordering: (603) 279-7352
International Ordering: (508) 755-3434

Contact Name: Mark Rocheford, President
Catalog: Free. Frequency: Semiannual
Circulation: 50K. Sales: $3-5MM
Products: Handmade colonial lighting;
primitive chandeliers, lanterns, arts & crafts

LITTLITE, LLC   (810) 231-9373
P.O. Box 430 • Hamburg, MI 48139
E-Mail: sales@littlite.com
Website: www.littlite.com
Fax Ordering: (810) 231-1631
Contact Name: Donn Deniston, Manager
Catalog: Free. Frequency: Annual
Circulation: 150K. Sales: $5-10MM
Products: Gooseneck lamps & accessories

NRG RESEARCH   (800) 753-0357
P.O. Box 390 • Merlin, OR 97532
E-Mail: sales@nrgresearch.com
Website: www.nrgresearch.com
Fax Ordering: (541) 471-6251
International Ordering: (541) 479-9433
Catalog: Free. Frequency: Annual
Circulation: 100K. Sales: $5-10MM
Products: Professional lighting; power
& audio - microphones & stands

NEWSTAMP LIGHTING CORP.   (508) 238-7071
227 Bay Rd., P.O. Box 189
North Easton, MA 02356
E-Mail: info@newstamplighting.com
Website: www.newstamplighting.com
Fax Ordering: (508) 230-8312
Contact Name: Robert Zeitsiff, President
Catalog: $3. Pages: 28. Frequency: Annual
Circulation: 10K. Sales: $3-5MM
Products: Copper & brass lighting fixtures

O'RYAN INDUSTRIES   (800) 426-4311
P.O. Box 1736 • Vancouver, WA 98668
E-Mail: info@oryanindustries.com
Website: www.oryanindustries.com
Fax Ordering: (360) 892-6742
International Ordering: (360) 892-0447
Contact Name: Benson Perry, Manager
Catalog: Free. Frequency: Annual
Circulation: 50K. Sales: $3-5MM
Products: Lighting & power supplies for
pools, spas & whirlpool baths; dental composit
curing lights; fiberoptic light sources for the
dental & medical industries

ORIGINAL CAST LIGHTING   (314) 863-1895
11902 Lackland Rd. • St. Louis, MO 63146
E-Mail: tlux@ocl.com
Website: www.ocl.com
Fax Ordering: (314) 863-3278
Contact Name: Neal Shapiro, President
Catalog: Free. Frequency: Annual
Circulation: 50K. Sales: $3-5MM
Products: Architectural lighting fixtures:
pendants, sconces, outdoor, ceiling, pedestal.

PERIOD LIGHTING FIXTURES   (800) 828-6990
167 River Rd. • Clarksburg, MA 01247
E-Mail: sales@periodlighting.com
Website: www.periodlighting.com
Fax Ordering: (413) 664-0312
International Ordering: (413) 664-7141
Contact Name: Edward Scofield, President
Catalog: $5. Frequency: Annual
Circulation: 50K. Sales: $5-10MM

Products: Handmade reproduction
period-style American lighting fixtures;
chandeliers, sconces, lanterns

REJUVENATION LAMP & FIXTURE CO.   (888) 401-1900
Rejuvenation, Inc.
2550 NW Nicolai St. • Portland, OR 97210
E-Mail: info@rejuvenation.com
Website: www.rejuvenation.com
Fax Ordering: (800) 526-7329
Contact Name: Mary Roberts, President
Catalog: Free. Frequency: Annual
Circulation: 200K. Sales: $10-20MM
Products: Authentic period lighting &
restoration hardware including chandeliers,
sconces, porch lights and lamps in Victorian
& Neoclassic styles

SMARTLIVING CATALOG   (800) 527-4448
EFI Utility Division
40 Washington St. #2000
Westborough, MA 01581
E-Mail: custserv@efi.org
Website: www.efi.org/smartliving
Fax Ordering: (508) 655-3811
International Ordering: (860) 665-5000
Catalog: Free. Frequency: Semiannual
Circulation: 250M. Sales: $20-50MM
Products: UFI customers only. Lighting &
energy-efficient products for a comfortable,
safe home. Includes lamps, light fixtures,
wall sconces, outdoor lighting.

SPEER COLLECTIBLES   (800) 241-7515
5315 S. Cobb Dr. • Atlanta, GA 30080
E-Mail: customerservice@speercollectibles.com
Website: www.speercollectibles.com
International Ordering: (404) 794-4000
Catalog: $15. Frequency: 10x per year
Circulation: 100M. Sales: $3-5MM
Products: Light fixtures & collectibles;
home furnishings & accessories

THE STONE HOUSE   (800) 923-2260
28 E. Market St. • Middleburg, PA 17842
E-Mail: sjm@stonehouse-lighting.com
Website: www.stonehouse-lighting.com
Fax Ordering: (570) 837-1475
Contact Name: Tim Smith, President
Catalog: $4. Frequency: Annual
Circulation: 150M. Sales: $1-3MM
Products: Colonial Period lighting fixtures,
handmade lighting fixtures

STREAMLIGHT   (800) 523-7488
30 Eagleville Rd. • Eagleville, PA 19403
E-Mail: cs@streamlight.com
Website: www.streamlight.com
Fax Ordering: (800) 220-7007; (610) 631-0712
International Ordering: (610) 631-0600
Contact Name: C. Bradford Penney, President
Catalog: Free. Frequency: Annual
Circulation: 200M. Sales: $10-20MM
Products: Line of standard & rechargeable
battery flashlights, lanterns & accessories

TASK & FUNCTIONAL LIGHTING   (800) 544-4877
Superior Lamp & Electrical Supply
934 Broadway • New York, NY 10010
Fax Ordering: (212) 529-3307
International Ordering: (212) 677-9191
Contact Name: David Brooks, President

Catalog: Free. Frequency: Annual
Circulation: 50M. **Sales:** $5-10MM
Products: Task & functional lighting

TASK LIGHTING CORP.   (800) 445-6404
910 E. 25th St. • Kearney, NE 68847
E-Mail: sales@tasklighting.com
Website: www.tasklighting.com
Fax Ordering: (308) 234-9401
International Ordering: (308) 236-6707
Contact Name: Kenneth Anderson, President
Catalog: Free. Frequency: Semiannual
Circulation: 20M. **Sales:** $1-3MM
Products: Incandescent lighting

TEREX LIGHT CORP.   (800) 433-3026
P.O. Box 3147 • Rock Hill, SC 29732
E-Mail: sales@terexlight.com
Website: www.terexlight.com
Fax Ordering: (803) 366-1101
International Ordering: (803) 324-3011
Contact Name: Jackie Reardon, Manager
Catalog: Free. Frequency: Annual
Circulation: 150K. **Sales:** $20-50MM
Products: Lighting systems, compaction,
traffic control

TIN BIN CATALOG   (717) 569-6210
20 Valley Rd. • Neffsville, PA 17601
E-Mail: sales@thetinbin.com
Website: www.thetinbin.com
Fax Ordering: (717) 569-7641
Contact Name: Susan Prentiss, President
Catalog: $2.50. Frequency: Semiannual
Circulation: 10K. **Sales:** $1-3MM
Products: 18th century lighting; outdoor
lighting, lamp shades, antique fixtures

TRIARCH INTERNATIONAL, INC.   (800) 874-2724
1190 NW 159th Dr.
Maimi Gardens, FL 33169
E-Mail: info@triarchindustries.com
Website: www.triarchindustries.com
Fax Ordering: (305) 620-6166
Catalog: Free. Frequency: Annual
Circulation: 100K. **Sales:** $10-20MM
Products: Lighting products

VERILUX - LIFE IN A BETTER LIGHT   (800) 454-4408
340 Mad River Park
Waitsfield, VT 05673
E-Mail: info@verilux.com
Website: www.verilux.com
Fax Ordering: (802) 496-3105
Customer Service: (800) 786-6850
Catalog: Free. Frequency: Annual
Circulation: 100K. **Sales:** $5-10MM
Products: Full spectrum lighting & light
therapy products: floor & desk lamps; light
therapy lamps; compact flourescent bulbs

VERMONT INDUSTRIES   (800) 639-1715
Rt. 103 Box 301
Cuttingsville, VT 05738
E-Mail: vtindus@together.com
Website: www.vermontindustries.com
Fax Ordering: (802) 492-3500
International Ordering: (802) 492-3451
Contact Name: Phil Burns, President
Catalog: Online. **Sales:** $500M to 1MM
Products: Wrought iron lighting & home
accessories

VICTORIAN LIGHTING WORKS   (800) 822-1898
251 S. Pennsylvania Ave.
Centre Hall, PA 16828
E-Mail: vlworks@aol.com
Website: www.vlworks.com
Fax Ordering: (814) 364-2920
International Ordering: (814) 364-9577
Contact Name: Byrant Musser, President
Catalog: $5. Frequency: Annual
Circulation: 10M. **Sales:** $1-3MM
Products: Period lighting fixtures:
chandeliers, wall sconces & pendants

AW ENTERPRISES (800) 334-4884
6543 S. Laramie Ave.
Bedford Park, IL 60638
E-Mail: sales@caseguys.net
Website: www.awenterprises.com
Fax Ordering: (708) 458-9023
International Ordering: (708) 458-8989
Contact Name: Edward Otrusina, President
Catalog: Free. Frequency: Annual
Circulation: 150K. Sales: $3-5MM
Products: Carrying cases for two-way radios,
scanners & pagers, cell phones, guitar &
musical instruments

ALTENBURG PIANO HOUSE (800) 526-6979
1150 E. Jersey St. • Elizabeth, NJ 07207
E-Mail: altenburgpiano@optonline.net
Website: www.altenburgpiano.com
Fax Ordering: (908) 527-9210
International Ordering: (908) 351-2000
Contact Name: O. Altenburg, President
Catalog: Free. Frequency: Annual
Circulation: 150K. Sales: $3-5MM
Products: Pianos & organs

AMERICAN PIE MUSIC (818) 706-2194
P.O. Box 1590
Agoura Hills, CA 91376-1590
E-Mail: questions@ample.com
Website: www.ample.com
Fax Ordering: (818) 707-3729
International Ordering: (818) 706-2194
Contact Names: Wayne Volat, President
Catalog: Online. Sales: $500K
Products: CDs & 45s original recordings
by the original artists

ARHOOLIE RECORDS (888) 274-6654
10341 San Pablo Ave.
El Cerrito, CA 94530
E-Mail: info@arhoolie.com
Website: www.arhoolie.com
Fax Ordering: (510) 525-1204
International Ordering: (510) 525-7471
Contact Names: C. Strachwitz, President
Catalog: Free. Frequency: Annual
Circulation: 25M. Sales: $3-5MM
Products: Records and CDs of Blues,
Jazz, Country, World Music, Cajun,
Tex-Mex, Zydeco and other regional styles.

SAM ASH CATALOG (800) 800-4654
Sam Ash Music Stores (800) 472-6274
7726 Cheri Court Blvd. • Tampa, FL 33634
E-Mail: help@samash.com
Website: www.samash.com
Fax Ordering: (800) 818-9050; (813) 881-1896
International Ordering: (813) 889-3874
Contact Name: Elliott Rubinson, President
Catalog: Free. Frequency: Quarterly
Circulation: 1MM. Sales: $50-100MM
Products: Keyboards, drums, percussion,
guitars, amps, electronic percussion,
compute music & audio equipment

AUDIO-TECHNICA U.S., INC. (330) 686-2600
1221 Commerce Dr. • Stowe, OH 44224
E-Mail: sales@atus.com
Website: www.audio-technica.com
Fax Ordering: (800) 329-8628; (330) 686-0719
Contact Name: Phil Cajka, President
Catalog: Free. Frequency: Annual

Circulation: 150K. Sales: $10-20MM
Products: Guitar microphones, headphones,
wireless systems

BERKSHIRE RECORD OUTLET, INC. (800) 992-1200
461 Pleasant St. • Lee, MA 01238
E-Mail: broinc@@berkshirerecordoutlet.com
Website: www.berkshirerecordoutlet.com
Fax Ordering: (413) 243-4340
International Ordering: (413) 243-4080
Contact Names: Joe Eckstein, President
Catalog: $2. Frequency: Monthly
Circulation: 75K. Sales: $1-3MM
Products: Deleted & overstocked classical
records, cassettes & CDs plus remaindered
books on music videos.

BEVERLY RARE RECORDS (773) 779-0066
11612 S. Western Ave. • Chicago, IL 60643
E-Mail: info@beverlyrecords.com
Website: www.beverlyrecords.com
Fax Ordering: (773) 779-2434
Contact name: Jack Dreznes, President
Catalog: Free. Frequency: Semiannual.
Circulation: 50K. Sales: $500K to 1MM
Products: Long-playing old records, 45's,
cassettes, CDs, and karaoke tapes

CANYON RECORDS (800) 268-1141
3131 W. Claredon Ave. • Phoenix, AZ 85017
E-Mail: rdoyle@canyonrecords.com
Website: www.canyonrecords.com
Fax Ordering: (602) 279-9233
Catalog: Free. Frequency: Semiannual
Circulation: 100K. Sales: $5-10MM
Products: Native American music,
including R. Carlos Nakai, Ed Lee Natay,

CARVIN GUITARS (800) 854-2235
12340 World Trade Dr.
San Diego, CA 92128
E-Mail: info@carvin.com
Website: www.carvin.com
Fax Ordering: (858) 487-8160
International Ordering: (858) 487-8700
Contact Name: Carson Kiesel, President
Catalog: Free. Frequency: Quarterly
Circulation: 200K. Sales: $20-50MM
Products: Guitars, amplifiers & recording
equipment

CASTIGLIONE ACCORDIONS (800) 325-1832
13300 E. 11 Mile Rd. • Warren, MI 48089
E-Mail: johncast@bignet.net
Website: www.castiglioneaccordions.com
Fax Ordering: (586) 755-6339
International Ordering: (586) 755-6050
Contact Name: John Castiglione, President
Catalog: Free. Frequency: Annual
Circulation: 50K. Sales: $3-5MM
Products: New & used accordions &
concertinas

CHARLES DOUBLE REED CO. CATALOG (800) 733-3847
2988 White Mountain Hwy.
North Conway, NH 03860
E-Mail: info@charlesmusic.com
Website: www.charlesmusic.com
Fax Ordering: (603) 356-9891
International Ordering: (603) 356-9890
Contact Name: Brian Charles, President
Catalog: Free. Frequency: Annual

Circulation: 50K. **Sales:** $1-3MM
Products: Professional services for oboe
& bassoon players; reeds, cane, instruments,
tools & accessories

CLARUS MUSIC, LTD. (614) 224-4257
Stanton's Sheet Music
330 South 4th St. • Columbus. OH 43215
E-Mail: clarus@stantons.com
Website: www.clarusmusic.com
Fax Ordering: (914) 669-1182
Contact Name: Sarah Fass, President
Catalog: Free. Frequency: Annual
Circulation: 25K. **Sales:** $500K to 1MM
Products: Records, cassettes, filmstrips,
musical plays, & posters for young people
K-12

COLLECTORS' CHOICE MUSIC (800) 993-6344
P.O. Box 838 • Itasca, IL 60143
E-Mail: mcatalog@ccmusic.com
Website: www.ccmusic.com
Fax Ordering: (630) 775-3355
Contact Name: Herb Laney, President
Catalog: Free. Frequency: Annual
Circulation: 25K. **Sales:** $10-20MM
Products: Over 2,000 hard-to-find CD's &
cassettes including folk, blues, rock, pop,
big band, country, jazz and comedy.

CONKLIN GUITARS & BASSES (417) 886-3525
P.O. Box 1394 • Springfield, MO 65801
E-Mail: conklin@conklinguitars.com
Website: www.conklinguitars.com
Fax Ordering: (417) 886-2934
Contact Name: O. Altenburg, President
Catalog: Free. Frequency: Annual
Circulation: 100K. **Sales:** $5-10MM
Products: Pianos & organs; groove tools

CRYSTAL RECORDS, INC. (360) 834-7022
28818 NE Hancock Rd. • Camas, WA 98607
E-Mail: info@@crystalrecords.com
Website: www.crystalrecords.com
Fax Ordering: (360) 834-9680
Contact Name: Peter Christ, President
Catalogs: Free. Frequency: Aannual
Circulation: 50K. **Sales:** $1-3MM
Products: Classical music CDs, specializing
in instrumental solo and ensemble

DAEDALUS BOOKS & MUSIC (800) 395-2665
P.O. Box 6000 • Columbia, MD 21045
E-Mail: custserv@daedalusbooks.com
Website: www.daedalusbooks.com
Fax Ordering: (800) 866-5578; (410) 309-2707
International Ordering: (410) 309-2705
Customer Service: (800) 944-8879
Catalog: Free. Frequency: Quarterly
Circulation: 1MM. **Sales:** $5-10MM
Products: Music on sale. Overstock
cassettes & CDs

DAVIDSONS MUSIC (913) 262-4982
6727 Metcalf Ave.
Shawnee Mission, KS 66204
E-Mail: madonna@everestkc.net
Website: www.davidsonsmusic.com
Fax Ordering: (913) 722-2980
Contact Name: David Woods, President
Catalog: Free. Frequency: Quarterly

Circulation: 50K. **Sales:** $250-500K
Products: Self-instruction music courses

DEERING BANJO COMPANY (800) 845-7791
3733 Kenora Dr.
Spring Valley, CA 91977
E-Mail: info@deeringbanjos.com
Website: www.deeringbanjos.com
Fax Ordering: (619) 464-0833
International Ordering: (619) 464-8252
Catalog: Free. Frequency: Annual
Circulation: 50K. **Sales:** $500K - $1MM
Products: Banjos & banjo related accessories

DISC MAKERS CATALOGS (800) 468-9353
7905 N. Rt. 130 • Pennsauken, NJ 08110   (866) 707-0012
E-Mail: info@discmakers.com
Website: www.discmakers.com
Fax Ordering: (856) 661-3458
International Ordering: (856) 663-9030
Catalog: Free. Frequency: Annual
Circulation: 100K. **Sales:** $5-10MM
Products: Music CDs, film DVDs, business
DVDs & CD-ROMs, duplicators, short-run discs,
blank discs & supplies, templates.,

DISCOUNT REED COMPANY (800) 428-5993
P.O. Box 181 • Valencia, CA 91355
E-Mail: ken@discountreed.com
Website: www.discountreed.com
Fax Ordering: (661) 294-9762
International Ordering: (661) 294-9437
Catalog: Free. Frequency: Annual
Circulation: 100K. **Sales:** $500K - $1MM
Products: Musical supplies for clarinet &
saxaphone reeds

DULCIMER SHOPPE (877) 269-4422
P.O. Box 1230 • Mountain View, AR 72560
E-Mail: info@mcspaddendulcimers.com
Website: www.mcspaddendulcimers.com
Fax Ordering: (870) 269-5283
International Ordering: (870) 269-4313
Contact Names: Jim & Betty Woods
Catalog: Free. Frequency: Monthly
Circulation: 100K. **Sales:** $500K - $1MM
Products: Dulcimer instruments & kits

EARTHBEAT! (800) 346-4445
MUSIC FOR A WHOLE PLANET
P.O. Box 1460 • Redway, CA 95560
E-Mail: eb@earthbeatrecords.com
Website: www.earthbeatrecords.com
Fax Ordering: (707) 923-3241
International Ordering: (707) 923-3991
Contact Name: Sharon Sherman, President
Catalog: Free. Frequency: Annual
Circulation: 25K. **Sales:** $500K - $1MM
Products: Multicultural CDs & cassettes

ELDERLY INSTRUMENTS (888) 473-5810
P.O. Box 14210 • Lansing, MI 48901
E-Mail: web@elderly.com
Website: www.elderly.com
Fax Ordering: (517) 372-5155
International Ordering: (517) 372-7890
Contact Name: Stan Werbin, President
Catalog: Free. Frequency: Quarterly
Circulation: 250K. **Sales:** $5-10MM
Products: Electric & acoustic guitars &
other instruments; accessories, strings,
CDs, books & videos

THE FEST FOR BEATLES FANS   (866) THE-FEST
Mark Lapidos Productions, Ltd.
P.O. Box 436 • Westwood, NJ 07675
E-Mail: mark@thefest.com
Website: www.thefest.com
Fax Ordering: (201) 666-8687
International Ordering: (201) 666-5450
Contact Name: Mark Lapidos, President
Catalog: Free. Frequency: Quarterly
Circulation: 500K. Sales: $5-10MM
Products: The Beatles Mail Order Store with
more than 1,000 licensed Beatles items, CDs,
videos, books, clothes

FRIENDSHIP HOUSE MUSIC CATALOG   (800) 791-9876
29355 Ranney Pkwy. • Westlake, OH 44145
E-Mail: info@friendshiphouse.com
Website: www.friendshiphouse.com
Fax Ordering: (440) 871-0858
International Ordering: (440) 871-8040
Contact Name: Mike Bennett, President
Catalog: Free. Frequency: Semiannual
Circulation: 50K. Sales: $1-3MM
Products: Musical gifts, awards &
teaching aids

GAMBLE MUSIC CO.   (800) 621-4290
1313 W. Randolph St. #305
Chicago, IL 60607
E-Mail: custserv@gamblemusic.com
Website: www.gamblemusic.com
Fax Ordering: (800) 421-3153; (312) 421-7979
International Ordering: (312) 427-6652
Contact Name: Joan Avila, VP
Catalog: Free. Frequency: Semiannual
Circulation: 50K. Sales: $1-3MM
Products: Musical instruments, gifts
& accessories

GREEN LINNET RECORDS   (615) 320-7672
916 19th Ave. So. • Nashville, TN 37212
E-Mail: info@compassrecords.com
Website: www.greenlinnet.com
Fax Ordering: (615) 320-7378
Contact Name: Alison Brown & Garry West, Owners
Catalog: Free. Frequency: Semiannual
Circulation: 150K. Sales: $5-10MM
Products: Celtic, folk & world music

HARVARD SQUARE RECORDS   (877) 465-7669
P.O. Box 2525 • Round Rock, TX 78680
E-Mail: lpnow@yahoo.com
Website: www.lpnow.com
Fax Ordering: (617) 547-2838
International Ordering: (617) 868-3385
Contact Name: Barry D. Mayer, President
Catalog: Free. Frequency: Semiannual
Circulation: 100K. Sales: $1-3MM
Products: Rare out-of-print LPs & cassettes

HOMESPUN TAPES, LTD.   (800) 338-2737
MUSIC INSTRUCTION
P.O. Box 340 • Woodstock, NY 12498
E-Mail: info@homespuntapes.com
Website: www.homespuntapes.com
Fax Ordering: (845) 246-5282
International Ordering: (845) 246-2550
Contact Name: Happy & Jane Traum, Co-owners
Catalog: Free. Frequency: Monthly
Circulation: 200K. Sales: $500K to 1MM
Product: Instructional CDs, audio & video cassette
lessons in a wide variety of musical instruments & styles

HUBBARD HARPSICHORDS   (508) 877-1735
KIT CATALOGS
31 Union Ave. • Sudbury, MA 01776
E-Mail: hubharp@aol.com
Website: www.hubharp.com
Fax Ordering: (508) 877-1736
Contact Name: Diane Hubbard, President
Catalog: Free. Frequency: Quarterly
Circulation: 25K. Sales: $500K
Products: Harpsichords & accessories

INDIAN HOUSE CATALOG   (800) 748-0522
P.O. Box 472 • Taos, NM 87571
E-Mail: music@indianhouse.com
Website: www.indianhouse.com
Fax Ordering: (505) 776-2804
International Ordering: (505) 776-2953
Contact Name: Tony Isaacs, President
Catalog: Free. Frequency: Annual
Circulation: 50K. Sales: $1-3MM
Products: Traditional Native American
music; cassettes & CD's

INNER PEACE MUSIC   (800) 909-0707
P.O. Box 2644 • San Anselmo, CA 94979   (888) 765-9697
E-Mail: info@innerpeacemusic.com
Website: www.innerpeacemusic.com
Fax Ordering: (541) 488-7870
International Ordering: (541) 488-9424
Contact Name: Steven Halpern, President
Catalog: Free. Frequency: Semiannual
Circulation: 50K. Sales: $500K - $1MM
Products: Healing music; CDs & cassettes
to relax and meditate

THE INSTRUMENT WORKSHOP   (800) 442-6038
P.O. Box 1060 • Ashland, OR 97520
E-Mail: shop77@fortepiano.com
Website: www.fortepiano.com
Fax Ordering: (541) 488-5846
International Ordering: (541) 552-0989
Contact Name: Lutz Bungart, President
Catalog: $2.50. Frequency: Semiannual
Circulation: 25K. Sales: $500K - $1MM
Products: Parts, plans & supplies for owners
& makers of early keyboard instruments;
repairs & restors historical keyboard instruments

INTERNATIONAL VIOLIN COMPANY, LTD.   (800) 542-3538
1421 Clarkview Rd. #118
Baltimore, MD 21209
E-Mail: sales@internationalviolin.com
Website: www.internationalviolin.com
Fax Ordering: (410) 832-2528
International Ordering: (410) 832-2525
Contact Name: Lori Kirr, President
Catalog: Free. Frequency: Annual
Circulation: 25K. Sales: $1-3MM
Products: String bowed instruments, bows,
accessories, tonewood, cases, strings,
luthier tools at wholesale prices

INTERSTATE MUSIC   (800) 982-2263
Cascio Music Co.
13819 W. National Ave.
New Berlin, WI 53151
E-Mail: customerservice@interstatemusic.com
Website: www.interstatemusic.com
Fax Ordering: (800) 529-0382; (262) 786-6840
International Ordering: (262) 789-7600
Contact Name: Mike Cascio, President
Catalog: Free. Frequency: Quarterly

Circulation: 50K. **Sales:** $3-5MM
Products: Instruments, electronics
& accessories

KEYBOARDS TODAY (800) 266-2159
P.O. Box 5127 • Huntington Beach, CA 92615 (800) 492-9999
E-Mail: info@keyboardstoday.com
Website: www.keyboardstoday.com
Fax Ordering: (800) 711-5470; (949) 631-5695
International Ordering: (949) 548-6784
Contact Name: Steve Seltzer, President
Catalog: Free. Frequency: Semiannual
Circulation: 100K. **Sales:** $5-10MM
Products: Casio, Technics & Yamaha music
keyboard accessories, software, music books,
and printed manuals

KIMBO EDUCATIONAL (800) 631-2187
P.O. Box 477 • Long Branch, NJ 07740
E-Mail: info@kimboed.com
Website: www.kimboed.com
Fax Ordering: (732) 870-3340
International Ordering: (732) 229-4949
Contact Name: Gertrude Kimble, President
Catalog: Free. Frequency: Semiannual
Circulation: 250K. **Sales:** $3-5MM
Products: Music & instruments for children

LARK IN THE MORNING (877) 964-5569
P.O. Box 799 • Fort Bragg, CA 95437
E-Mail: info@larkinam.com
Website: www.larkinam.com
Fax Ordering: (707) 964-1979
International Ordering: (707) 964-5569
Contact Names: Debora & Bill Taylor, Owners
Catalog: Free. Frequency: Annual
Circulation: 50K. **Sales:** $3-5MM
Products: Hard-to-find musical instruments;
books, DVDs, music & accessories

LATIN PERCUSSION (800) 526-2668
KMC Music
160 Belmont Ave. • Garfield, NJ 07026
E-Mail: info@lpmusic.com
Website: www.lpmusic.com
Fax Ordering: (973) 772-3568
International Ordering: (973) 478-6903
Contact Name: Ken Valentine, President
Catalog: Free. Frequency: Annual
Circulation: 100K. **Sales:** $5-10MM
Products: Percussion musical instruments

VICTOR LITZ MUSIC CENTER (800) 828-5518
306 E. Diamond Ave.
Gaithersburg, MD 20877
E-Mail: info@victorlitz.com
Website: www.victorlitz.com
Fax Ordering: (301) 977-9220
International Ordering: (301) 948-7478
Contact Name: Creston E. Stewart, President
Catalog: Free. Frequency: 5x per year
Circulation: 100K. **Sales:** $1-3MM
Products: Musical instruments & equipment

LYONS MUSIC PRODUCTS (800) 292-4955
P.O. Box 1003 • Elkhart, IN 46515
E-Mail: customer-service@4lyons.com
Website: www.4lyons.com
Fax Ordering: (574) 251-3545
International Ordering: (574) 288-1359
Contact Name: Greg Spretnjak, President
Catalog: Free. Frequency: Semiannual

Circulation: 75K. **Sales:** $1-3MM
Products: Educational music products

MANDOLIN BROTHERS, LTD. (718) 981-8585
629 Forest Ave. • Staten Island, NY 10310
E-Mail: mandolin@mandoweb.com
Website: www.mandoweb.com
Fax Ordering: (718) 816-4416
Contact Name: Stanley M. Jay, President
Catalog: Free. Frequency: Annual
Circulation: 75K. **Sales:** $1-3MM
Products: Guitars, banjos, mandolins,
ukeleles, acoustic bass guitars; new &
vintage American fretted instruments;
acoustic amplioflers, accessories &
instructional books & video tapes

MARTIN GUITAR CATALOG (800) 633-2060
C.F. Martin & Co., Inc.
P.O. Box 329 • Nazareth, PA 18064
E-Mail: info@martinguitar.com
Website: www.martinguitar.com
Fax Ordering: (610) 759-5757
International Ordering: (610) 759-2837
Contact Name: C.F. Martin, President
Catalog: Free. Frequency: Semiannual
Circulation: 100K. **Sales:** $5-10MM
Products: Guitar kits, parts & accessories

MIDNIGHT RECORDS (212) 675-2768
P.O. Box 390, Old Chelsea Sta.
New York, NY 10011
E-Mail: midnightrecords@attglobal.net
Website: www.midnightrecords.com
Fax Ordering: (212) 741-7230
Contact Name: J.B. Martignon, President
Catalog: Free. Frequency: Annual
Circulation: 25K. **Sales:** $500K to 1MM
Products: Rare LPs and CDs of rock'n'roll
from the 1950s to the 1990s

MOSAIC RECORDS (203) 327-7111
35 Melrose Pl. • Stamford, CT 06902
E-Mail: info@mosaicrecords.com
Website: www.mosaicrecords.com
Fax Ordering: (203) 323-3526
Contact Name: Charlie Lourie, President
Catalog: Free. Frequency: Quarterly
Circulation: 200K. **Sales:** $3-5MM
Products: Limited edition jazz collections,
CDs and LPs

THE MUSIC BARN (800) 984-0047
P.O. Box 1083 • Niagara Falls, NY 14304
E-Mail: order@countrymusictreasures.com
Website: www.countrymusictreasures.com
Fax Ordering: (905) 513-6918
Catalog: Free. Pages: 40. Frequency: Semiannual
Circulation: 100K. **Sales:** $1-3MM
Products: Country music; polkas/waltzes;
fiddle music; gospel/religious music; bluegrass
music; popular & instrumental music CDs, DVDs,
box sets, books & cassettes.

MUSIC BOOKS PLUS (800) 265-8481
4600 Witmer Industrial estates #6
Niagara Falls, NY 14305
E-Mail: order@nor.com
Website: www.musicbooksplus.com
Fax Ordering: (888) 665-1307; (716) 297-0975
International Ordering: (905) 641-0552
Contact Name: Linda Beretta

Catalog: Free. Frequency: Annual
Circulation: 100K. **Sales:** $3-5MM
Products: Books, videos, audiocassettes,
DVDs, CD-ROMs & software

MUSIC DISPATCH ELECTRONIC   (800) 637-2852
KEYBOARD & ORGAN CATALOG
P.O. Box 13920 • Milwaukee, WI 53213
E-Mail: info@musicdispatch.com
Website: www.musicdispatch.com
Fax Ordering: (414) 774-3259
Customer Service: (800) 321-3408
Catalog: Free. Frequency: Annual
Circulation: 100K. **Sales:** $1-3MM
Products: Sheet music, songbooks,
music instruction, videos

MUSIC FOR LITTLE PEOPLE   (877) 286-4701
P.O. Box 1460 • Redway, CA 95560   (800) 409-2457
E-Mail: customerservice@mflp.com
Website: www.musicforlittlepeople.com
Fax Ordering: (707) 923-3241
International Ordering: (707) 923-3991
Contact Name: Sharon Sherman, President
Catalog: Free. Frequency: Annual
Circulation: 125K. **Sales:** $1-3MM
Products: Children's music, toys, gifts
& DVDs

MUSIC IN MOTION   (800) 445-0649
1601 E. Plano Pkwy. • Plano, TX 75074
E-Mail: info@musicmotion.com
Website: www.musicmotion.com
Fax Ordering: (972) 943-8906
International Ordering: (972) 943-8744
Contact Name: Mary Ann Stewart, President
Catalog: Free. Frequency: Annual
Circulation: 50K. **Sales:** $1-3MM
Products: Music education & gifts; instruments
& equipment; books & Audio; software, stationery,
teaching aids; videos

MUSIC MINUS ONE   (800) 669-7464
MMO Music Group, Inc.
50 Executive Blvd. • Elmsford, NY 10523
E-Mail: customerservice@musicminusone.com
Website: www.musicminusone.com
Fax Ordering: (914) 592-3116
International Ordering: (914) 592-1188
Contact Name: Irv Kratka, President
Catalog: Free. Frequency: Semiannual
Circulation: 200K. **Sales:** $3-5MM
Products: Karaoke/sing along tapes &
CDs; classical play-along CDs

MUSIC TREASURES COMPANY   (800) 666-7565
P.O. Box 9138 • Richmond, VA 23227   (800) 798-8613
E-Mail: musict@musictreasures.com
Website: www.musictreasures.com
Fax Ordering: (888) 687-4282; (440) 871-0858
International Ordering: (804) 730-8800
Contact Name: Daniel T. Tuszynski, Jr., President
Catalog: Free. Frequency: Semiannual
Circulation: 250K. **Sales:** $3-5MM
Products: Music & dance educational
resources: apparel, learning tools; music
awards, books, candy, games & toys; posters

THE MUSIC TREE   (408) 779-4312
17470 Monterey St. • Morgan Hill, CA 95037
E-Mail: sales@themusictree.com
Website: www.themusictree.com

Contact Name: Eleanor Ross, President
Catalog: Free. Frequency: Annual
Circulation: 25K. **Sales:** $1-3MM
Products: Instrumental music on
cassettes and CDs

MUSIC VIDEO DISTRIBUTORS   (800) 888-0486
P.O. Box 280 • Oaks, PA 19456
E-Mail: sales@musicvideodistributors.com
Website: www.musicvideodistributors.com
Fax Ordering: (610) 650-9102
International Ordering: (610) 650-8200
Catalog: Free. Frequency: Annual
Circulation: 25K. **Sales:** $1-3MM
Products: Music videos, DVDs, VHS,
laserdiscs; t-shirts

MUSIC BY EMAIL   (772) 286-5549
Music By Mail
P.O. Box 368 • Palm City, FL 34991
E-Mail: email@gate.net
Website: www.musicbymail.com
Fax Ordering: (718) 921-2380
Catalog: Online. **Sales:** $500K to $1MM
Products: CDs & DVDs

MUSIC OF THE AMERICAN INDIAN   (800) 895-4859
Drumbeat Indian Arts, Inc.
4143 N. 16th St. • Phoenix, AZ 85016
E-Mail: info@drumbeatindianarts.com
Website: www.drumbeatindianarts.com
Fax Ordering: (602) 265-2402
International Ordering: (602) 266-4823
Contact Name: Bob Nuss, President
Catalog: Free. Frequency: Annual
Circulation: 100K. **Sales:** $5-10MM
Products: Offers about 2,000 titles of
contemporary American Indian prerecorded
cassettes, CDs and videocassettes, as well
as the Native American cedar flute and old
tribal songs.

MUSICAL HERITAGE SOCIETY   (800) 777-6105
1710 Hwy. 35 • Oakhurst, NJ 07755
E-Mail: memberservices@musicalheritage.org
Website: www.musicalheritage.com
Fax Ordering: (732) 517-0438
International Ordering: (732) 531-7003
Contact Name: Jeffrey Nissim, President
Catalog: Free. Frequency: Annual
Circulation: 50K. **Sales:** $3-5MM
Products: CDs and DVDs

MUSICAL INSTRUMENTS   (888) 549-4108
Freeport Music • Farmingville, NY 11743
E-Mail: sales@freeportmusic.com
Website: www.musicalinstruments.com
Fax Ordering: (631) 696-4337
International Ordering: (631) 5549-4108
Contact Name: Lon T. Palmer, President
Catalog: Free. Frequency: Semiannual
Circulation: 100K. **Sales:** $500K - $1MM
Products: Musical instruments & accessories;
rare and hard-to-find instruments

MUSICIAN'S FRIEND   (866) 498-7882
Guitar Center, Inc.
P.O. Box 720 • Riverton, UT 84065
P.O. Box 4400 • Medford, OR 97501
E-Mail: info@guitarcenter.com
Website: www.guitarcenter.com
Fax Ordering: (866) 498-7874; (818) 735-8811

International Ordering: (818) 735-8800
Contact Name: Larry Thomas, President
Catalog: Free. Frequency: Annual
Circulation: 100K. Sales: $3-5MM
Products: Guitars, bass, keyboards; amps
& effects; stage & studio gear; books & videos

MUSICIAN'S WORKSHOP, INC. (800) 543-6125
319 Merrimon Ave. • Asheville, NC 28801
E-Mail: mail@musiciansworkshop.com
Website: www.musiciansworkshop.com
Fax Ordering: (828) 251-9323
International Ordering: (828) 252-1249
Contact Name: Frank & Becky Dosier, Owners
Catalog: Free. Frequency: Monthly
Circulation: 100K. Sales: $5-10MM
Products: Music instruction videos, DVD's,
CD's, cassettes, books, accessories,
electronics & instruments

MUSICMAKERS KITS (800) 432-5487
P.O. Box 2117 • Stillwater, MN 55082
E-Mail: info@harpkit.com
Website: www.harpkit.com
Fax Ordering: (651) 439-9130
International Ordering: (651) 439-9120
Contact Name: Jerry Brown, President
Catalog: $5. Frequency: Semiannual
Circulation: 25K. Sales: $3-5MM
Products: Musical instruments, kits & plans
& supplies for making harps, guitars,
dulcimers, banjos, mandolins, string bass

NATIONAL EDUCATIONAL MUSIC CO. (800) 526-4593
P.O. Box 1130 • Mountainside, NJ 07092
E-Mail: info@nemc.com
Website: www.nemc.com
Fax Ordering: (908) 789-3025
International Ordering: (908) 232-6700
Contact Name: Ray Benedetto, President
Catalog: Free. Frequency: 5x per year
Circulation: 50K. Sales: $1-3MM
Products: Band & orchestra instruments
& accessories

OMEGA SOUND STAR TRACKS (800) 336-0637
1112 Garrison Ave.
Fort Smith, AR 72901
E-Mail: info@omegasound.com
Website: www.omegasound.com
Fax Ordering: (501) 782-4795
International Ordering: (501) 782-1332
Contact Name: Randy McFarland, President
Catalog: Free. Frequency: Semiannual
Circulation: 25K. Sales: $1-3MM
Products: Performance tracks for singers;
music for individuals competing in pageants
& talent competitions offering tracks with no
background vocals & edited time lengths

OPERA FANATIC'S CATALOG (800) 347-5056
Bel Canto Society, Inc.
85 Fuurniture Dr. • Milford, CT 06460
E-Mail: info@belcantosociety.org
Website: www.belcantosociety.org
Fax Ordering: (212) 877-2792
International Ordering: (212) 877-5813
Catalog: Free. Frequency: Semiannual
Circulation: 25K. Sales: $500K - $1MM
Products: Opera videos, CDs, and DVDs;
posters, magazines & books

PAIA ELECTRONICS (405) 340-6300
3200 Teakwood Lane
Edmond, OK 73013
E-Mail: sales@paia.com
Website: www.paia.com
Fax Ordering: (405) 340-6378
Contact Name: John Simonton, President
Catalog: Free. Frequency: Semiannual
Circulation: 150K. Sales: $500K to $1MM
Products: Musical supplies & accessories

PATTI MUSIC COMPANY (800) 777-2884
521 Rising Star Rd. • Brooks, GA 30205
E-Mail: info@pattimusic.com
Website: www.pattimusic.com
Fax Ordering: (770) 716-8204
Contact Name: A.J. Schwegel, President
Catalog: Free. Frequency: Annual
Circulation: 200K. Sales: $3-5MM
Products: Stringed instruments
replacement parts & tools

PLAY PIANO WAY (541) 664-7052
P.O. Box 700 • Medford, OR 97501
E-Mail: duane@playpiano.com
Website: www.playpiano.com
Fax Ordering: (541) 664-7052
Contact Name: Duane Shinn, President
Catalog: Free. Frequency: Monthly
Circulation: 150K. Sales: $250-500K
Products: Piano courses on video &
cassette

POCKET SONGS (800) 669-7464
MMO Music Group, Inc.
50 Executive Blvd.
Elmsford, NY 10523
E-Mail: info@pocketsongs.com
Website: www.pocketsongs.com
Fax Ordering: (914) 592-3116
International Ordering: (914) 592-1188
Contact Name: Irv Kracka, President
Catalog: Free. Frequency: Annual
Circulation: 10K. Sales: $500K
Products: Karaoke, sing-along cassettes
and CDs

POWER MUSIC, INC. (800) 777-2328
P.O. Box 3030
Salt Lake City, UT 84110
E-Mail: sales@powermusic.com
Website: www.powermusic.com
Fax Ordering: (800) 773-2937 or (801) 328-8885
International Ordering: (801) 328-8884
Contact Name: Richard Petty, CEO & President
Catalog: Free. Frequency: Annual
Circulation: 25K. Sales: $5-10MM
Products: Music for meditation; aerobic
workout music; music for cheerleading

PRECISION DRUM COMPANY (888) 512-3786
2012 Rte. 44
Pleasant Valley, NY 12569
E-Mail: info@precisiondrum.com
Website: www.precisiondrum.com
Fax Ordering: (845) 635-8442
International Ordering: (845) 635-9820
Contact Name: George Folchi, President
Catalog: Free. Frequency: Annual
Circulation: 10K. Sales: $500K - $1MM
Products: Percussion instruments

QCCS PRODUCTIONS, INC.   **(541) 345-0212**
1350 Chambers St. • Eugene, OR 07402
E-Mail: support@pbtmlive.com
Website: www.pbtmlive.com
Fax Ordering: (541) 345-8117
Contact Name: Mike Brewer, President
Catalog: Free. Frequency: Annual
Circulation: 10K. Sales: $500K to $1MM
Products: Royalty-free pro background theme
music delivered in MP-3 format at only $20
per full long play theme and $15 for 60 second
version, and $12 for 30 second version.

QUALITON IMPORTS LTD.   **(718) 937-8515**
24-02 40th Ave.
Long Island City, NY 11101
E-Mail: qualiton@qualiton.com
Website: www.qualiton.com
Fax Ordering: (718) 729-3239
Contact Name: Otto Quittner, President
Catalog: Free. Frequency: Annual
Circulation: 100K. Sales: $5-10MM
Products: Rare music in all genres
on LPs and CDs

RECORDS BY MAIL   **(503) 232-1735**
Craig Moerer
2541 NW 30th Ave. • Portland, OR 97210
E-Mail: cmoerer@recordsbymail.com
Website: www.recordsbymail.com
Fax Ordering: (503) 232-1746
Contact Name: Craig Moerer, President
Catalog: Free. Frequency: Annual
Circulation: 25K. Sales: $500K - $1MM
Products: Out-of-print recordings of jazz,
popular vocals, popular instrumentals &
Latin LOs

RECORDS INTERNATIONAL   **(888) 804-5513**
4601 E. Camino Rosa • Tucson, AZ 85718
E-Mail: sales@recordsinternational.com
Website: www.recordsinternational.com
Fax Ordering: (877) 527-7129; (520) 299-5845
International Ordering: (520) 299-5801
Contact Name: Jeff Joneikis, President
Catalog: Free. Frequency: Monthly
Circulation: 25K. Sales: $10-50MM
Products: Imported classical records & CDs

REDISCOVER MUSIC CATALOG   **(800) 232-7328**
705 S. Washington St.
Naperville, IL 60540
E-Mail: amy@folkera.com
Website: www.rediscovermusic.com
Fax Ordering: (630) 305-0782
International Ordering: (630) 305-0770
Customer Service: (888) 232-7328
Contact Name: Allan Shaw, President
Catalog: Free. Frequency: Bimonthly
Circulation: 100K. Sales: $1-3MM
Products: CDs...primarily of 1960s folk acts

PAUL REED SMITH GUITARS   **(410) 643-9970**
380 Log Canoe Cir.
Stevensville, MD 21666
E-Mail: info@prsguitars.com
Website: www.prsguitars.com
Fax Ordering: (410) 643-9980
Contact Name: Paul Reed Smith, President
Catalog: Free. Frequency: Semiannual
Circulation: 10K. Sales: $3-5MM
Products: Guitars; fashion

REGO IRISH RECORDS   **(800) 854-3746**
P.O. Box 1515 • Green Island, NY 12183   **(800) 458-7346**
E-Mail: support@regoirishrecords.com
Website: www.regorecords.com
Fax Ordering: (516) 354-7768
International Ordering: (518) 266-0765
Contact Name: Patrick Noonan, President
Catalog: Free. Frequency: Semiannual
Circulation: 150K. Sales: $1-3MM
Products: Irish music; CDs, cassettes,
vinyl, video, DVDs, books

RESOURCE GUIDE & CATALOG OF   **(800) 634-6044**
CD's, RECORDS & TAPES BY WOMEN
Ladyslipper Music
P.O. Box 3124 • Durham, NC 27715
E-Mail: info@ladyslipper.org
Website: www.ladyslipper.org
Fax Ordering: (919) 383-3525
International Ordering: (919) 383-8773
Catalog: Free. Frequency: Semiannual
Circulation: 100K. Sales: $1-3MM
Products: Over 1,500 recordings by women;
female musicians, writers, performers &
composers

RHYTHM BAND INSTRUMENTS   **(800) 424-4724**
P.O. Box 126 • Fort Worth, TX 76101
E-Mail: sales@rhythmband.com
Website: www.rhythmband.com
Fax Ordering: (800) 784-9401; (817) 332-5654
International Ordering: (817) 335-2561
Contact Name: Bob Bergin, President
Catalog: Free. Frequency: Annual
Circulation: 50K. Sales: $3-5MM
Products: Musical instruments for
preschool & elementary school

ROUNDER RECORDS GROUP   **(800) 768-6337**
One Rounder Way
Burlington, MA 01803
E-Mail: info@rounder.com
Website: www.rounder.com
Fax Ordering: (617) 491-1970
International Ordering: (617) 354-0700
Contact Name: John Virant, President
Catalog: Free. Frequency: Semiannual
Circulation: 150K. Sales: $3-5MM
Products: 3,000 titles, including blues,
jazz, bluegrass, folk, cajun/zydeco, world,
and children;s music.

SISU HOME ENTERTAINMENT   **(800) 223-7478**
Kol Ami, Inc.
340 W. 39th St., 6th Fl.
New York, NY 10018
E-Mail: sisu@sisuent.com
Website: www.sisuent.com
Fax Ordering: (888) 221-7478; (212) 947-8388
International Ordering: (212) 947-7888
Contact Name: Haim Scheininger, President
Catalog: Free. Frequency: Monthly
Circulation: 100K. Sales: $500K to 1MM
Products: Jewish and Israeli music, videos,
DVDs, books, and CD-ROMs

SCORPIO MUSIC DISCOUNT MUSIC   **(609) 890-6000**
Princeton Record Exchange, Inc.   **(609) 921-0881**
20 S. Tulane St. • Princeton, NJ 08542
E-Mail: info@prex.com; scorpiomus@aol.com
Website: www.prex.com
Fax Ordering: (609) 890-0247

Contact Name: Steven Parelman, President
Catalog: Free. Frequency: Bimonthly
Circulation: 100K. Sales: $10-20MM
Products: Blues, folk, jazz, rock, soul,
dance, country records & cassettes

SHAR PRODUCTS COMPANY (800) 248-7427
P.O. Box 1411 • Ann Arbor, MI 48106
E-Mail: sharserv@sharmusic.com
Website: www.sharmusic.com
Fax Ordering: (734) 665-0829
International Ordering: (734) 665-3978
Customer Service: (800) 793-4334
Contact Name: C. Avsharian, President
Catalog: Free. Frequency: Bimonthly
Circulation: 250K. Sales: $20-50MM
Products: Stringed instruments,
accessories & sheet music

SOARING SPIRIT (800) 421-6603
Valley of the Sun Publishing
P.O. Box 38 • Malibu, CA 90265
E-Mail: soaringspirits@aol.com
Website: www.dicksutphen.com
Fax Ordering: (818) 706-3606
International Ordering: (818) 706-0963
Contact Name: Richard Sutphen, President
Catalog: Free. Frequency: Quarterly
Circulation: 75K. Sales: $1-3MM
Products: New Age CDs, books & videos;
self-help audios, videos and books

SOUNDTRACK.NET (301) 524-3578
P.O. Box 10808 • Silver Spring, MD 20914
E-Mail: info@soundtrack.net
Website: www.soundtrack.net
Fax Ordering: (301) 879-4741
Contact Name: David A. Koran, Exec. Producer
Catalog: Free. Frequency: Quarterly
Circulation: 25K. Sales: $500K - $1MM
Products: Soundtrack CDs & DVDs

STEWART-McDONALD'S (800) 848-2273
GUITAR SHOP & SUPPLY
P.O. Box 900 • Athens, OH 45701
E-Mail: info@stewmac.com
Website: www.stewmac.com
Fax Ordering: (740) 583-7922
International Ordering: (740) 592-3021
Contact Name: Creston E. Stewart, President
Catalog: Free. Frequency: Quarterly
Circulation: 200K. Sales: $5-10MM
Products: Stringed instruments replacement
parts & tools; guitars & supplies; books, plans,
videos, software

TEXAS MUSIC & VIDEO ONLINE CATALOG (512) 474-2500
Waterloo Records & Video
600A N. Lamar Blvd. • Austin, TX 78703
E-Mail: info@waterloorecords.com
Website: www.waterloorecords.com
Fax Ordering: (512) 474-2522
Catalog: Online. Sales: $3-5MM
Products: Records, CDs, tapes & videos
& DVDs in all genres

WEINER MUSIC PRODUCTS (800) 622-2675
168 Jericho Tpke. • Mineola, NY 11501
E-Mail: sharon@weinermusic.com
Website: www.weinermusic.com
Fax Ordering: (516) 294-4289
International Ordering: (516) 747-5004

Contact Name: Frederic H. Weiner, President
Catalog: Free. Frequency: Quarterly
Circulation: 100K. Sales: $3-5MM
Products: Woodwind instruments &
accessories

WEINKRANTZ MUSICAL SUPPLY CO. (800) 736-8742
351 Hayes St. • San Francisco, CA 94102
Fax Ordering: (415) 399-1705
International Ordering: (415) 581-0303
Catalog: Free. Frequency: Annual
Circulation: 100K. Sales: $1-3MM
Products: Stringed instruments, parts
& supplies

WERSI MUSIC CENTER (800) 233-3865
241 W. Roseville Rd. • Lancaster, PA 17601
E-Mail: info@wersimusic.com
Website: www.wersimusic.com
Fax Ordering: (717) 392-3324
International Ordering: (717) 299-4327
Contact Name: Ralph Conti, President
Catalog: Free. Frequency: Annual
Circulation: 50K. Sales: $500M to $1MM
Products: Electronic organs, pianos & keyboards

WESTHEIMER CORP. GROOVE TOOLS (847) 498-9850
3451 W. Commercial Ave. (847) 498-6491
Northbrook, IL 60062
E-Mail: sales@westheimercorp.com
Website: www.westheimercorp.com
Fax Ordering: (847) 498-5370
Contact Name: O. Altenburg, President
Catalog: Free. Frequency: Annual
Circulation: 100K. Sales: $5-10MM
Products: Manufacture, import & export of fine
musical instruments; electric & acoustice guitars
& basses; procussion& groove tools for guitars,
basses, pianos & organs

WILLIS MUSIC COMPANY (800) 354-9799
P.O. Box 548 • Florence, KY 41042
E-Mail: orderdpt@willismusic.com
Website: www.willismusic.com
Fax Ordering: (859) 283-1784
International Ordering: (859) 283-2050
Contact Name: Kevin Cranley, President
Catalog: Free. Frequency: Annual
Circulation: 150K. Sales: $3-5MM
Products: 13,000+ titles of sheet music

WOODWIND & BRASSWIND (800) 348-5003
4004 Technology Dr. • South Bend, IN 46628 (800) 288-2334
E-Mail: woodwind@wwbw.com
Website: www.wwbw.com
Fax Ordering: (574) 251-3501
International Ordering: (574) 251-3500
Contact Name: Bruce Morrow, Marketing
Catalog: Free. Frequency: Bimonthly
Circulation: 25K. Sales: $5-10MM
Products: Musical instruments & related
accessories

WORLD'S RAREST RECORDS (800) 955-1326
P.O. Box 1727 • Grants Pass, OR 97528
E-Mail: teftellr@cdsnet.net
Website: www.tefteller.com
Fax Ordering: (541) 476-3523
International Ordering: (541) 476-1326
Contact Name: John Tefteller, President
Catalog: Free. Frequency: 5x per year
Circulation: 5K. Sales: $100-500K

Products: Rare 45's and 78's from the
1930's to the early 1960's, including blues,
rhythm and blues and rock and roll.

WORLDS RECORDS   (800) 742-6663
P.O. Box 1922 • Novato, CA 94947
E-Mail: info@worldsrecords.com
Website: www.worldsrecords.com
Fax Ordering: (415) 898-6348
International Ordering: (415) 898-1609
Catalog: Free. **Frequency:** Semiannual
Circulation: 100K. **Sales:** $1-3MM
Products: Audiotapes & CDs of famous
world reknown artists

WYNNCO ENTERPRISES   (864) 878-6469
P.O. Box 39 • Pickens, SC 29671
E-Mail: wynnco@wynnco.com
Website: www.wynnco.com
Fax Ordering: (864) 878-6267
Contact Name: Jack J. Wynn, III, President
Catalog: $1. **Frequency:** Semiannual
Circulation: 10K. **Sales:** $100-500M

A.R.E. PRESS CATALOG (800) 723-1112
215 67th St. • Virginia Beach, VA 23451 (800) 333-4499
E-Mail: are@edgarcayce.org
Website: www.edgarcayce.org
Fax Ordering: (757) 491-0689
International Ordering: (757) 428-3588
Contact Name: Melinda Ball, Manager
Catalog: Free. Frequency: Monthly
Circulation: 150K. Sales: $5-10MM
Products: Educational videos, software,
CD-ROMs, books and posters; Edgar Cayce
& related books & tapes for personal
transformation & spiritual development

AMBER LOTUS PUBLISHING (800) 326-2375
5018 N.E. 22nd Ave.
Portland, OR 97211
E-Mail: info@amberlotus.com
Website: www.amberlotus.com
Fax Ordering: (503) 284-6417
International Ordering: (503) 284-6400
Contact Name: Lawson Day, President
Catalog: Free. Frequency: Annual
Circulation: 50K. Sales: $500K to $1MM
Products: New age calendars, books,
journals, cards & giftwrap

ARTSCROLL CATALOG (800) 637-6724
Mesorah Publications, Ltd.
222 44th St. • Brooklyn, NY 11232
E-Mail: orders@artscroll.com
Website: www.artscroll.com
Fax Ordering: (718) 680-1875
International Ordering: (718) 921-9000
Contact Name: Meir Zlotowitz, President
Catalog: Free. Frequency: Annual
Circulation: 50K. Sales: $3-5MM
Products: Jewish books

AUROMERE AYUVEDIC PRODUCTS (800) 735-4691
Auromere Books
2621 W. Hwy. 12 • Lodi, CA 95242
E-Mail: info@auromere.com
Website: www.auromere.com
Fax Ordering: (209) 339-3715
International Ordering: (209) 339-3710
Contact Name: Dakshina Vanzetti, President
Catalog: Free. Frequency: Annual
Circulation: 10K. Sales: $500K
Products: Spiritual books from India

AURORA PRESS CATALOG (505) 989-9804
P.O. Box 573 • Santa Fe, NM 87504
E-Mail: info@aurorapress.com
Website: www.aurorapress.com
Fax Ordering: (505) 982-8321
Catalog: Free. Frequency: Annual
Circulation: 100K. Sales: $250-500K
Products: Alternative health, astrology
& metaphysics

BEACON HILL PRESS CATALOG (800) 877-0700
P.O. Box 419527
Kansas City, MO 64109
E-Mail: info@bhillkc.com
Website: www.bhillkc.com
Fax Ordering: (816) 753-4071
International Ordering: (816) 931-1900
Catalog: Free. Frequency: 10x per year
Circulation: 150K. Sales: $3-5MM
Products: Christian books

BIBLICA (800) 524-1588
1820 Jet Steam Dr.
Colorado Springs, CO 80921
E-Mail: info@biblica.com
Website: www.biblica.com
Fax Ordering: (719) 488-0870
International Ordering: (719) 488-9200
Contact Name: Paul Moede, Marketing
Catalog: Free. Frequency: Semiannual
Circulation: 150K. Sales: $10-20MM
Products: Bibles, new testaments &
scripture-related materials

BIBLICAL ARCHAEOLOGY (800) 221-4644
SOCIETY BOOKS
4710 41st St., NW
Washington, DC 20016
E-Mail: info@bib-arch.org
Website: www.bib-arch.org
Fax Ordering: (202) 364-2636
International Ordering: (202) 364-3300
Contact Name: Hershel Shanks, President
Catalog: Free. Frequency: Annual
Circulation: 50K. Sales: $500K to $1MM
Products: Books, videos & slide sets on the
archaeology of the lands of the Bible

BRIDGE BUILDING IMAGES (800) 325-6263
P.O. Box 1048 • Burlington, VT 05402
E-Mail: bbi@bridgebuilding.com
Website: www.bridgebuilding.com
Fax Ordering: (802) 865-2434
International Ordering: (802) 864-8346
Contact Name: William J. Flynn, President
Catalog: Free. Frequency: Quarterly
Circulation: 100K. Sales: $500K
Products: Religious cards & gifts; prayer
& holy cards, calendars, prints, plaques &
magnets; Native American spiritual cards

CELESTIAL PRODUCTS (800) 235-3783
P.O. Box 801 • Middleburg, VA 20118
E-Mail: info@celestialproducts.com
Website: www.celestialproducts.com
Fax Ordering: (540) 338-4042
International Ordering: (978) 338-4040
Catalog: Free. Frequency: Semiannually
Circulation: 200K. Sales: $5-10MM
Products: Publishes & distributes popular
reference materials, calendars, charts,
notecards & gifts designed to stimulate
understanding of our universe. Moon &
astronomy calendars, lunar phase charts.

CHRISTIAN BOOK DISTRIBUTORS (800) 247-4784
140 Summit St. • Peabody, MA 01960
E-Mail: info@christianbook.com
Website: www.christianbook.com
Fax Ordering: (978) 977-5010
International Ordering: (978) 977-5000
Contact Name: S. Hendrickson, President
Catalog: Free. Frequency: Bimonthly
Circulation: 250K. Sales: $5-10MM
Products: Christian books, videos,
software, gifts

GATEWAY BOOKS & TAPES (800) 869-0658
P.O. Box 370 • Nevada City, CA 95959
E-Mail: orders@gatewaybooksandtapes.com
Website: www.gatewaybooksandtapes.com
Fax Ordering: (530) 272-0184

International Ordering: (530) 271-2239
Contact Name: Nancy Christie, President
Catalog: Free. Frequency: Annual
Circulation: 10K. Sales: $500K
Products: Books, videos, CDs & audiotapes
ontransformational psychology, death & dying,
shamanism, judaica, mysticism, spiritual practice

GOSPEL ADVOCATE BOOKSTORE   (800) 251-8446
1006 Elm Hill Pike • Nashville, TN 37210
E-Mail: service@gospeladvocate.com
Website: www.gospeladvocate.com
Fax Ordering: (615) 254-7411
International Ordering: (615) 254-8781
Contact Name: Kerry Anderson, President
Catalog: Free. Frequency: Annual
Circulation: 100K. Sales: $3-5MM
Products: Religious books; bibles,
bible software; church supplies

HAMILTON NEW AGE/OCCULT SUPPLIES   (805) 529-5900
P.O. Box 1258 • Moorpark, CA 93020
E-Mail: info@hamiltonnewage.com
Website: www.hamiltonnewage.com
Fax Ordering: (805) 529-2934
Contact Name: Carol Hamilton, President
Catalog: $3. Frequency: Monthly
Circulation: 25K. Sales: $500K
Products: Occult/New Age supplies;
books, divination tools, crystal balls,
ouija boards, pendulum boards, tarot cards,
scrying mirrors; videos, cassettes; oils,
incense, candles, jewelry, herbs, etc.

HOHM PRESS CATALOG   (800) 381-2700
P.O. Box 2501 • Prescott, AZ 86302
E-Mail: hppublisher@cableone.net
Website: www.hohmpress.com
Fax Ordering: (928) 717-1779
International Ordering: (928) 778-9189
Contact Name: Dasya Zuccarello, President
Catalog: Free. Frequency: Annual
Circulation: 50K. Sales: $500K
Products: Books on natural health,
transpersonal psychology, women's issues,
religious studies

INDIO PRODUCTS CATALOG   (800) 944-1414
2750 S. Alameda St. • Vernon, CA 90058
E-Mail: sales@indioproducts.com
Website: www.indioproducts.com
Fax Ordering: (323) 750453-3348
International Ordering: (323) 234-3089
Contact Name: Martin Mayer, President
Catalog: Free. Frequency: Annual
Circulation: 50K. Sales: $5-10MM
Products: Spiritual new age supplies
& seven day candles

INNER TRADITIONS   (800) 246-8648
Bear & Company Publishing
P.O. Box 388 • Rochester, VT 05767
E-Mail: customerservice@innertraditions.com
Website: www.innertraditions.com
Fax Ordering: (802) 989-3726
International Ordering: (802) 767-3174
Contact Name: Ehud C. Sperling, President
Catalog: Free. Frequency: Semiannual
Circulation: 50K. Sales: $5-10MM
Products: New Age & philosophy books

INSIGHTS CATALOG   (800) 423-7087
Hampton Roads Publishing Co.
Dist. by Red Wheel/Weiser
65 Parker St. #7 • Newburyport, MA 01950
E-Mail: info@hamptonroadspub.com
Website: www.hamptonroadspub.com
Fax Ordering: (978) 465-0243
International Ordering: (978) 465-0504
Catalog: Free. Frequency: Semiannual
Circulation: 100K. Sales: $1-3MM
Products: Shamanism, past life experiences,
UFOs, out-of-body experiences, spiruatlity &
metaphysics, health

INSPIRATIONS   (800) 348-6483
Oriental Trading Co.
P.O. Box 2308 • Omaha, NE 68103
E-Mail: info@oriental.com
Website: www.oriental.com
Fax Ordering: (800) 327-8904; (402) 596-2364
International Ordering: (402) 331-6800
Contact Name: Terry Watanabe-Gerdes, President
Catalog: Free. Frequency: Semiannual
Circulation: 2MM. Sales: $10-20MM
Products: Religious home decor, gifts &
novelties

JEWISH LIGHTS PUBLISHING   (800) 962-4544
P.O. Box 237 • Woodstock, VT 05091
E-Mail: sales@jewishlights.com
Website: www.jewishlights.com
Fax Ordering: (802) 457-4004
International Ordering: (802) 457-4000
Contact Name: Stuart M. Matlins, President
Catalog: Free. Frequency: Semiannual
Circulation: 50K. Sales: $500K to $1MM
Products: Books on spirituality, philosophy,
theology, healing/recovery, life cycle,
children's issues

JUDAICA BOOK GUIDE   (718) 456-8611
Jonathan David Publishers, Inc.
68-22 Eliot Ave. • Flushing, NY 11379
E-Mail: customerservice@jdbooks.com
Website: www.jdbooks.com
Fax Ordering: (718) 894-2818
Contact Name: Alfred Kolatch, President
Catalog: Free. Frequency: Semiannual
Circulation: 150K. Sales: $500K to $1MM
Products: Books on Judaica

MYSTIC TRADER CATALOG   (800) 634-9057
Pacific Spirit
1334 Pacific Ave.
Forest Grove, OR 97116
E-Mail: csrservice@mystictrader.com
Website: www.mystictrader.com
Fax Ordering: (503) 357-1669
International Ordering: (503) 357-1566
Catalog: Free. Frequency: Quarterly
Circulation: 25K. Sales: $500K
Products: Spiritual books, art, jewelry
& other items

NEW WORLDS OF MIND & SPIRIT   (800) 843-6666
Llewellyn Worldwide
2143 Wooddale Dr. • Woodbury, MN 55125
E-Mail: customerservice@llewellyn.com
Website: www.llewellyn.com
Fax Ordering: (651) 291-1908

International Ordering: (651) 291-1970
Contact Name: Carl Weschcke, President
Catalog: Free. Frequency: Quarterly
Circulation: 250K. Sales: $20-50MM
Products: Books on astrology, tarot decks,
new age, healing, spirituality & fiction

PRINTERY HOUSE CONCEPTION ABBEY (800) 889-0105
P.O. Box 112 • Conception, MO 64433
E-Mail: custserv@printeryhouse.org
Website: www.printeryhouse.org
Fax Ordering: (888) 556-8262
Contact Name: Gerald Nelson, President
Catalog: Free. Frequency: Quarterly
Circulation: 1MM. Sales: $3-5MM
Products: Religious greeting cards,
stationery & gifts

PYRAMID COLLECTION (800) 333-4220
P.O. Box 3333 • Chelmsford, MA 01824
E-Mail: info@pyramidcollection.com
Website: www.pyramidcollection.com
Fax Ordering: (800) 866-3235; (978) 256-2492
Contact Names: Phil Vander Ploeg, President
Catalog: Free. Pages: 60. Frequency: Quarterly
Circulation: 200K. Sales: $3-5MM
Products: Mind/body/spirit-renewing products
and gift ideas. Includes crystals & faceted
gemstones, angel and faerie ornaments &
collectibles; scented candles & aroma-
therapeutic essences & incense; historical
& theme-drsigned dresses & casual apparel;
indoor/outdoor sculptures.

RED WHEEL / WEISER, LLC (800) 423-7087
65 Parker St. #7 • Newburyport, MA 01950
E-Mail: info@redwheelweiser.com
Website: www.redwheelweiser.com
Fax Ordering: (978) 465-0243
International Ordering: (978) 465-0504
Contact Name: Michael Kerber, President
Catalog: Free. Frequency: Annual
Circulation: 250K. Sales: $5-10MM
Products: Books on New Age, astrology,
oriental philosophy, tarot, self-development,
western mystery & Kabbalahi

RESOURCE PUBLICATIONS (408) 286-8505
160 E. Virginia St. • San Jose, CA 95112
E-Mail: info@rpinet.com
Website: www.rpinet.com
Fax Ordering: (408) 287-8748
Contact Name: William Burns, President
Catalog: Free. Frequency: Quarterly
Circulation: 150K. Sales: $1-3MM
Products: Religious books, software
& educational books

SISU HOME ENTERTAINMENT CATALOG (800) 223-7478
Kol Ami, Inc.
340 W. 39th St. • New York, NY 10018
E-Mail: sisu@sisuent.com
Website: www.sisuent.com
Fax Ordering: (888) 221-7478; (212) 947-8388
International Ordering: (212) 947-7888
Contact Name: Haim Scheininger, President
Catalog: Free. Frequency: Quarterly
Circulation: 25K. Sales: $500K to $1MM
Products: Jewish & Israeli music, videos,
books, CD-ROMs

SOARING SPIRIT CATALOG (800) 421-6603
Valley of the Sun Publishing
P.O. Box 38 • Malibu, CA 90265
E-Mail: soaringspirit@aol.com
Website: www.dicksutphen.com
Fax Ordering: (818) 706-3606
International Ordering: (818) 706-0963
Contact Name: Richard Sutphen, President
Catalog: Free. Frequency: Quarterly
Circulation: 75K. Sales: $1-3MM
Products: New Age CDs; self-help
books, audiotapes & videos

SPIRITUAL BOOKS CATALOG (617) 742-2110
Beacon Press
25 Beacon St. • Boston, MA 02108
E-Mail: konell@beacon.org
Website: www.beacon.org
Fax Ordering: (617) 723-3097
Contact Name: Tom Magness, President
Catalog: Free. Frequency: Semiannual
Circulation: 150K. Sales: $500K
Products: Books about spirituality from
over 100 publishers covering numerous
religious traditions

TRADITIONAL BUDDHIST BOOKS (800) 873-4276
Dharma Publishing
2910 San Pablo Ave.
Berkeley, CA 94702
E-Mail: info@dharmapublishing.com
Website: www.dharmapublishing.com
Fax Ordering: (510) 548-2230
International Ordering: (510) 548-5407
Catalog: Free. Frequency: Annual
Circulation: 50K. Sales: $500K
Products: Buddhist/Tibetan books

WAYFARER PUBLISHING CATALOG (800) 888-9119
P.O. Box 39938 • Los Angeles, CA 90039
E-Mail: taichi@tai-chi.com
Website: www.tai-chi.com
Fax Ordering: (323) 665-1627
International Ordering: (323) 665-7773
Contact Name: Marvin Smalheiser, President
Catalog: Free. Pages: 48. Frequency: Semiannual
Circulation: 150K. Sales: $500K
Products: Videos, books, CDs, cassettes &
other products about Taichi & related martial
arts & health practices

WHITFORD PRESS & DONNING (610) 593-1777
Schiffer Publishing
4880 Lower Valley Rd.
Atglen, PA 19310
E-Mail: info@schifferbookscom
Website: www.schifferbooks.com
Fax Ordering: (610) 593-2002
Contact Name: Peter B. Schiffer, President
Catalog: Free. Frequency: Semiannual
Circulation: 100K. Sales: $1-3MM
Products: Metaphysical, ghost, astrological,
health & cooking books

WHOLE LIFE PRODUCTS (800) 634-9057
Pacific Spirit Corporation
1334 Pacific Ave.
Forest Grove, OR 97116
E-Mail: csrservice@mystictrader.com
Website: www.mystictrader.com

Fax Ordering: (503) 357-1669
International Ordering: (503) 357-1566
Contact Name: Joseph Meyer, Buyer
Catalog: Free. Frequency: Bimonthly
Circulation: 250K. Sales: $3-5MM
Products: New Age books, videos, jewelry,
spiritual items; alternative health, holistic,
herbal products, massage tools & yoga
products

WOODLAND PUBLISHING   (800) 777-2665
515 South 700 East, Suite 2D
Salt Lake City, UT 84102
E-Mail: info@woodlandpublishing.com
Website: www.woodlandpublishing.com
Fax Ordering: (801) 334-1913
International Ordering: (801) 277-3243
Contact Name: Trent Tenney, President
Catalog: Free. Frequency: Semiannual
Circulation: 50K. Sales: $3-5MM
Products: Natural health titles covering
herbs, nutrition & dietary supplements

A-WALL BUILDING SYSTEMS   **(800) 345-4400**
Component Systems, Inc.
2245 West 114 St. • Cleveland, OH 44102
E-Mail: gsa@a-wall.com
Website: www.a-wall.com
Fax Ordering: (888) 432-9274
International Ordering: (216) 252-9292
Contact Name: Nancy Hamilton, Manager
Catalog: Free. Frequency: Annual
Circulation: 100K. Sales: $1-3MM
Products: Modular in-plant buildings
& partitions

ACRO OFFICE PRODUCTS   **(800) 423-9717**
2821 W. 59th St. • Chicago, IL 60629   **(800) 266-5583**
E-Mail: ken@acroonline.com
Website: www.acroonline.com
Fax Ordering: (773) 925-4511
International Ordering: (773) 925-4206
Contact Name: Kenneth Henderson, President
Catalog: Free. Frequency: Monthly
Circulation: 50K. Sales: $3-5MM
Products: Office & computer supplies;
furniture, machines

AGIO DESIGNS   **(800) 688-2446**
21195 NW Evergreen Pkwy.
Hillsboro, OR 97124
E-Mail: info@agiodesigns.com
Website: www.agiodesigns.com
Fax Ordering: (503) 629-8545
International Ordering: (503) 439-6633
Contact Name: Bert Good, President
Catalog: Free. Frequency: Semiannual
Circulation: 150K. Sales: $3-5MM
Products: Compact mobile workstations for
computer users; desks, chairs & accessories

ADAPTO STORAGE PRODUCTS   **(800) 923-2786**
225 Main St. • Tatamy, PA 18085
E-Mail: info@adapto.com
Website: www.adapto.com
Fax Ordering: (888) 859-2121 ; (305) 327-0745
International Ordering: (305) 887-9563
Contact Name: Joseph Carignan, Marketing
Catalog: Free. Frequency: Annual
Circulation: 200K. Sales: $10-20MM
Products: Office shelving & storage equipment

ADIRONDACK DIRECT   **(800) 221-2444**
Adirondack Wholesale Sale Furniture Co.
3040 48th Ave. • Long Island City, NY 11101
E-Mail: info@adirondackdirect.com
Website: www.adirondackdirect.com
Fax Ordering: (800) 477-1330
International Ordering: (718) 204-4500
Customer Service: (800) 243-4392
Contact Name: Arnold Siegel, President
Catalog: Free. Frequency: Quarterly
Circulation: 200K. Sales: $50-100MM
Products: Wholesale furniture for churches,
schools, offices, institutional & government
offices

AMERICAN MAP   **(800) 432-6277**
Langenscheidt Publishing Group
15 Tyger River Dr. • Duncan, SC 29334
E-Mail: customerservice@americanmap.com
Website: www.americanmap.com
Fax Ordering: (888) 773-7979; (864) 486-8289
International Ordering: (864) 486-0214
Customer Service: (800) 432-6277

Contact Name: Stuart Dolgins, President
Catalog: Free. Frequency: Annual
Circulation: 100K. Sales: $10-20MM
Products: Commercial maps, travel guides,
language learning products, & dictionaries.

AMERICAN THERMOPLASTIC CO.   **(800) 456-6602**
106 Gamma Dr. • Pittsburgh, PA 15238   **(800) 245-6600**
E-Mail: atc@binders.com
Website: www.binders.com
Fax Ordering: (412) 967-9990
International Ordering: (412) 967-0900
Contact Name: Steven Silberman, President
Catalog: Free. Frequency: Annual
Circulation: 250K. Sales: $10-20MM
Products: Custom-imprinted binders &
related loose-leaf products

AMERISTAMP - SIGN*A*RAMA   **(800) 223-3086**
1300 N. Royal Ave. • Evansville, IN 47715
E-Mail: websales@signsoveramerica.com
Website: www.signsoveramerica.com
Fax Ordering: (812) 477-7898
International Ordering: (812) 477-7763
Catalog: $2.50. Frequency: Annual
Circulation: 10K. Sales: $5-10MM
Products: Outdoor & indoor signs & banners,
electronic signs, rubber stamps & seals, ink
pads & ink; promotional products; flags; wall
murals; vehicle & tradeshow graphics;
corporate apparel

ASSOCIATED BAG COMPANY   **(800) 926-6100**
400 W. Boden St. • Milwaukee, WI 53207
E-Mail: customerservice@associatedbag.com
Website: www.associatedbag.com
Fax Ordering: (800) 926-4610; (414) 769-6530
International Ordering: (800) 945-3800; (414) 769-1000
Contact Name: Herbert Rubenstein, President
Catalog: Free. Frequency: Annual
Circulation: 250K. Sales: $5-10MM
Products: Packaging & shipping supplies;
office supplies; floor matting

ATD-AMERICAN COMPANY   **(866) 283-9327**
135 Greenwood Ave.
Wyncote, PA 19095
E-Mail: orders@atd.com
Website: www.atdamerican.com
Fax Ordering: (800) 283-7363; (215) 576-1827
International Ordering: (215) 576-1380
Contact Name: Jerome Zaslow, President
Catalog: Free. Frequency: Semiannual
Circulation: 500K. Sales: $50-100MM
Products: Catalogs for Business Furniture,
School Furniture, Religious Furniture; Outdoor
Furniture; Office Accessories

ATLAS PEN & PENCIL CORP.   **(866) 866-4030**
12121 Scripps Summit Dr.
San Diego, CA 92131
E-Mail: dealer@atlaspencil.com
Website: www.atlaspencil.com
Fax Ordering: (866) 866-4034
Catalog: Online. Sales: $5-10MM
Products: Pens & pencils; accessories

BAGS PLUS   **(815) 344-6700**
300 N. State St., Suite 2327
Chicago, IL 60654
E-Mail: mail@bagsplus.com
Website: www.bagsplus.com

Fax Ordering: (815) 344-6702
Contact Name: Fred Cwynar, President
Catalog: Free. Frequency: Annual
Circulation: 150K. Sales: $5-10MM
Products: Printed gift basket bags,
shopping bags, t-shirt bags, zipclose bags,
zip handle bags, twist ties & hang bags,
cellophane bags; tissue paper.

BEAVERITE PRODUCTS   (800) 424-6337
128 Main St. • Beaver Falls, NY 13305
E-Mail: sales@beaverite.com
Website: www.beaveritepkg.com
Fax Ordering: (315) 346-1575
International Ordering: (315) 346-6011
Contact Name: Alvin Gesford, President
Catalog: Online. Sales: $5-10M
Products: Packaging & presentation
solutions; binders, report cases & portfolios

BINDERTEK   (800) 456-3453
P.O. Box 2120 • Amherst, MA 01004
E-Mail: sales@bindertek.com
Website: www.bindertek.com
Fax Ordering: (800) 765-3299; (413) 253-7868
International Ordering: (413) 256-3200
Catalog: Free. Frequency: Annual
Circulation: 200K. Sales: $5-10M
Products: Binders, index tabs, rolling cases
& briefcases, organizing accessories, storage
systems

BLUMBERG EXCELSIOR   (800) LAW-MART
62 White St. • New York, NY 10013   (800) 529-6278
E-Mail: weborders@blum.com
Website: www.blumberg.com
Fax Ordering: (800) 561-9018; (212) 431-5111
International Ordering: (212) 431-5000
Customer Service: (800) 221-2972
Contact Name: Robert Blumberg, President
Catalog: Free. Frequency: 3x per year
Circulation: 500K. Sales: $5-10M
Products: Products & services for the
legal profession; engraved thermographed
& printed stationery; corporate kits & supplies;
online legal forms; patent & trademark folders;
will envelopes & paper; legal supplies; holiday
& Christmas cards; legal & attorney software;
printing services.

BROWNCOR INTERNATIONAL   (800) 327-2278
530 W. Ooklahoma Ave.
Milwaukee, WI 53207
E-Mail: info@browncor.com
Website: www.browncor.com
Fax Ordering: (800) 343-9228
International Ordering: (414) 271-2250
Contact Name: David Stark, President
Catalog: Free. Frequency: Monthly
Circulation: 400K. Sales: $20-50M
Products: Office & packaging supplies

C&H DISTRIBUTORS   (888) 316-2223
770 S. 70th St. • Milwaukee, WI 53214
E-Mail: customerservice@chdist.com
Website: www.chdist.com
Fax Ordering: (800) 336-1331
International Ordering: (414) 443-1700
Customer Service: (800) 443-6142
Contact Name: David Stark, President
Catalog: Free. Frequency: Semiannual
Circulation:300K. Sales: $10-20MM

Products: Material handling equipment;
Industrial storage, shelving & shop furniture

CHISWICK PACKAGING PRODUCTS   (800) 335-4471
Chiswick Trading   (800) 225-8708
3 Union Ave. • Sudbury, MA 01776
E-Mail: info@chiswick.com
Website: www.chiswick.com
Fax Ordering: (800) 638-9899
International Ordering: (978) 443-9592
Contact Name: Ted Pasquarello, President
Catalog: Free. Frequency: 4x per year
Circulation: 10K. Sales: $1-3MM
Products: Packaging products & office
supplies

CLEAR VINYL: PHOTO   (800) 223-1357
& OFFICE PRODUCTS
Bardes Products
5245 W. Clinton Ave. • Milwaukee, WI 53223
E-Mail: sales@bardes.com
Website: www.bardes.com
Fax Ordering: (414) 354-1921
International Ordering: (414) 354-9000
Contact Name: Mary Strupp, Marketing
Catalog: Free. Frequency: Annual
Circulation: 20K. Sales: $1-3M
Products: Vinyl products for storage,
displays, promotions & protection

COMBO PRINT CALENDARS   (800) 822-8445
380 E. Bonita Ave. • Pomona, CA 91767
E-Mail: calendar@comboprint.com
Website: www.comboprint.com
Fax Ordering: (909) 593-8206
International Ordering: (909) 593-7777
Contact Name: Anny Chang, President
Catalog: Free. Frequency: Annual
Circulation: 150K. Sales: $1-3MM
Products: Customized calendars, stock
calendars

COOK RECEIPT BOOK MANUFACTURING   (800) 842-0444
278 E. Main St. #2005 • Dothan, AL 36301
E-Mail: cookmfg@ala.net
Fax Ordering: (334) 793-7283
International Ordering: (334) 671-1116
Contact Name: Russell Cook, President
Catalog: Free. Frequency: Annual
Circulation: 100M. Sales: $500M to $1MM
Products: Various types of receipt books

COPI-PAK   (800) 690-5300
468 Acorn Ln. • Downington, PA 19335
E-Mail: dirtcheap@copi-pak.com
Website: www.copi-pak.com
Fax Ordering: (610) 873-2600
Catalog: Free. Frequency: Bimonthly
Circulation: 100K. Sales: $1-3MM
Products: Shipping & packaging products;
janitorial & material handling supplies

CORNELL / ROBBINS COMPANY   (888) 251-1297
162 Van Dyke St. • Brooklyn, NY 11231   (888) 251-1551
Fax Ordering: (845) 255-2155
International Ordering: (845) 255-2177
Contact Name: Mark Robbins, President
Catalog: Free. Frequency: Quarterly
Circulation: 2MM. Sales: $5-10MM
Minimum Order: $50
Products: Mailroom, shipping &
warehouse supplies

DALLAS MIDWEST (800) 527-2417
4100 Alpha Rd. • Dallas, TX 75244
Fax Ordering: (972) 866-9433
International Ordering: (305) 887-9563
Contact Name: George Mosher, President
Catalog: Free. Frequency: 11x per year
Circulation: 200K. Sales: $5-10MM
Products: Office & Institutional furniture

DATA CONTROL (800) 325-5648
277 David Pkwy. • Ontario, NY 14519
Website: www.datacontrolinc.com
E-Mail: datacontrol@frontiernet.net
Fax Ordering: (800) 524-3702; (315) 524-3606
International Ordering: (315) 524-0027
Contact Name: Lori Ferguson, President
Catalog: Free. Frequency: 4x per year
Circulation: 100K. Sales: $5-10MM
Products: Magnetic scheduling boards;
cork bulletin boards; magnetic markerboards
& accessories

DAY RUNNER (800) 232-9786
2750 Moore Ave. • Fullerton, CA 92833
E-Mail: info@dayrunner.com
Website: www.dayrunner.com
Fax Ordering: (714) 441-4840
International Ordering: (714) 680-3500
Contact Name: K. Muller, President
Catalog: Free. Frequency: Annual
Circulation: 100K. Sales: $1-3MM
Products: Organizer books, calendars
& refills

DAY-TIMERS, INC. (800) 752-6281
One Willow Lane (800) 805-2615
East Texas, PA 18046
E-Mail: info@daytimer.com
Website: www.daytimer.com
Fax Ordering: (800) 452-7398; (610) 398-5520
International Ordering: (610) 398-1151
Contact Name: Dave Clark, President
Catalog: Free. Frequency: Semiannual
Circulation: 2MM. Sales: $20-50MM
Products: Organizer books, calendars & refills

DEMCO (800) 356-1200
P.O. Box 7488 • Madison, WI 53707
E-Mail: info@demco.com
Website: www.demco.com
Fax Ordering: (608) 241-1799
International Ordering: (608) 241-1201
Contact Name: Ed Muir, President
Catalog: Free. Frequency: Annual
Circulation: 200K. Sales: $50-100MM
Products: Office, school & library supplies
& furniture

DILLEY MANUFACTURING COMPANY (800) 247-5087
215 E. 3rd St. • Des Moines, IA 50309
E-Mail: info@dilleymfg.com
Website: www.dilleymfg.com
Fax Ordering: (515) 288-4210
International Ordering: (515) 288-7289
Contact Name: David Dilley, President
Catalog: Free. Frequency: Annual
Circulation: 200K. Sales: $5-10MM
Products: Binders, dividers & emblems

DO-IT-YOURSELF LAMINATION (800) 243-4565
USI • 98 Fort Path Rd.
Madison, CT 06443
Fax Ordering: (203) 245-7337
International Ordering: (203) 245-8586
Catalog: Free. Frequency: Monthly
Circulation: 250K. Sales: $5-10MM
Products: Lamination equipment & supplies;
binding equipment & supplies; overhead
projectors

EMCO INSTOCK FURNITURE CATALOG (800) 925-3626
Emco Sales & Service
5601 W. Side Ave. • N. Bergen, NJ 07047
E-Mail: info@emcosales.com
Website: www.emcosales.com
Fax Ordering: (201) 295-3800
International Ordering: (201) 295-9200
Catalog: Free. Frequency: Annual
Circulation: 100K. Sales: $5-10MM
Products: Office supplies, machines &
furniture

EMPIRE IMPORTS (800) 544-4744
P.O. Box 2728 • Amherst, MA 01004
E-Mail: custserv@empireimports.com
Website: www.empireimports.com
Fax Ordering: (800) 835-5140; (413) 256-4645
International Ordering: (413) 256-4917
Contact Name: Andy Beall, President
Catalog: Free. Frequency: 4x per year
Circulation: 1.5MM. Sales: $10-20MM
Products: Importers of European office
supplies

FACTORY DIRECT FURNITURE (800) 972-6570
121 E. Mason St. • Milwaukee, WI 53203
E-Mail: sales@officefurniture.com
Website: www.officefurniture.com
Fax Ordering: (800) 696-8142
International Ordering: (414) 289-9770
Contact Name: Steve Twining, President
Catalog: Free. Frequency: Semiannual
Circulation: 10K. Sales: $500M to $1MM
Products: Office & computer furniture;
desks, chairs, files, panels

FAHRNEY'S PENS (800) 624-7367
8329 Old Marlboro Pike, Suite 813
Upper Marlboro, MD 20772
E-Mail: custserv@fahrneyspens.com
Website: www.fahrneyspens.com
Fax Ordering: (301) 736-2926
International Ordering: (301) 568-6550
Customer Service: (800) 336-4775
Contact Name: Jon Sullivan, President
Catalog: Free. Frequency: 5x per year
Circulation: 250K. Sales: $1-3MM
Products: Writing instruments & desk
accessories; watches, watch cases & jewelry

FAX CITY (800) 426-6499
2711 Pinedale Rd. #B
Greensboro, NC 27408
International Ordering: (336) 288-2454
Contact Name: Mickie Adams, President
Catalog: Free. Frequency: Bimonthly
Circulation: 100K. Sales: $1-3MM
Products: Fax machines & supplies

FIDELITY OFFICE SUPPLIES (800) 328-3034
Fidelity Products Company
5601 International Pkwy.
Minneapolis, MN 55440
Fax Ordering: (800) 842-2725; (763) 536-6584

Contact Name: Rick Black, President
Catalog: Free. Frequency: 6x per year
Circulation: 4MM. Sales: $5-10MM
Products: General office & graphic supplies

FILOFAX ORGANIZER CATALOG (800) 345-6798
372 Danbury Rd. • Wilton, CT 06897
E-Mail: info@filofax.com
Website: www.filofax.com
Fax Ordering: (860) 563-2222
International Ordering: (860) 563-2200
Contact Name: Andy Roth, President
Catalog: Free. Frequency: Annual
Circulation: 150K. Sales: $3-5MM
Products: Leather organizer books,
calendars & filers

FORBES PRODUCT CORPORATION (800) 836-7237
45 High Tech Dr. • Rush, NY 14543
E-Mail: info@forbesproducts.com
Website: www.forbesproducts.com
Fax Ordering: (585) 334-6180
International Ordering: (585) 334-4800
Contact Name: Patrick Oliveto, President
Catalog: Free. Frequency: Annual
Circulation: 250K. Sales: $3-5MM
Products: Custom information packaging
products, including pocket & desk calendars,
ring binders; insurance & financial products;
portfolios, etc.

FORDHAM EQUIPMENT COMPANY (800) 249-5922
3308 Edison Ave. • Bronx,. NY 10469
E-Mail: alrobbi@attglobal.net
Fax Ordering: (718) 379-7312
International Ordering: (718) 379-7300
Contact Name: Al Robbins, President
Catalog: Free. Frequency: Semiannual
Circulation: 100K. Sales: $1-3MM
Products: Library supplies, furnishings,
shelving

FOUNTAIN PEN HOSPITAL (800) 253-7367
10 Warren St. • New York, NY 10007
E-Mail: info@fountainpenhospital.com
Website: www.fountainpenhospital.com
Fax Ordering: (212) 227-5916
International Ordering: (212) 964-0580
Contact Name: Terry Wiederlight, President
Catalog: Free. Frequency: Monthly
Circulation: 500K. Sales: $5-10MM
Products: Writing instruments, pens & pencils

FRANK EASTERN COMPANY (800) 221-4914
599 Broadway • New York, NY 10012
Fax Ordering: (212) 219-0722
International Ordering: (212) 219-0007
Contact Name: Stan Frank, President
Catalog: Free. Frequency: Semiannual
Circulation: 200K. Sales: $10-20MM
Products: Office & computer furniture

FREUND CONTAINER, INC. (800) 363-9822
11535 S. Central Ave. • Alsip, IL 60803
E-Mail: customerservice@freundcan.com
Website: www.freundcan.com
Fax Ordering: (800) 423-7545; (708) 272-7001
Contact Name: Kenneth Freund, President
Catalog: Free. Frequency: 4x per year
Circulation: 1MM. Sales: $20-50MM
Products: Hardware & office supplies;
hard-to-find containers

THE GALLERY COLLECTION (201) 641-0070
Prudent Publishing Company
65 Challenger Rd. • Ridgefield Park, NJ 07660
E-Mail: info@gallerycollection.com
Website: www.gallerycollection.com
Fax Ordering: (800) 772-1144
Contact Name: Alan Solow, President
Catalog: Free. Frequency: Annual
Circulation: 150K. Sales: $5-10MM
Products: Greeting cards, calendars &
diaries with custom imprint

GERALD FRIED DISPLAY COMPANY (800) 828-7701
550 Fillmore Ave. • Tonawanda, NY 14150
E-Mail: sales@gfried.com
Website: www.gfried.com
Fax Ordering: (716) 692-5458
International Ordering: (716) 692-2705
Contact Name: Gerald Fried, President
Catalog: Free. Frequency: Annual
Circulation: 250K. Sales: $3-5MM
Products: Packaging products &
office supplies

FURNITURE SAMPLER (800) 323-8469
Triad Furniture Discounters
9654 N. Kings Hwy.
Myrtle Beach, SC 29577
Fax Ordering: (843) 499-5887
International Ordering: (843) 464-9646
Contact Name: John Clements, President
Catalog: $12. Frequency: Weekly
Circulation: 10K. Sales: $5-10MM
Products: Home & office furniture

FURNITURE FOR TEACHING (800) 328-1061
& TECHNOLOGY
Smith System
P.O. Box 860415 • Plano, TX 75086
E-Mail: sales@planostar.com
Website: www.planostar.com
Fax Ordering: (972) 424-4388
International Ordering: (972) 424-6591
Contact Name: Charles Risdall, President
Catalog: Free. Frequency: Annual
Circulation: 150K. Sales: $10-20MM
Products: Technology furniture; ergonomically
sound and functional; modular design with
optional accessories

GBC OFFICE PRODUCTS (800) 541-0094
General Binding Corporation
5700 Old Orchard Rd. • Skokie, IL 60077
E-Mail: contactus@gbc.com
Website: www.gbc.com
Fax Ordering: (847) 965-0912
International Ordering: (847) 965-0600
Contact Name: Govi Reddy, President
Catalog: Free. Frequency: Semiannual
Circulation: 250K. Sales: $20-50MM
Products: Binding products

GLOBAL INDUSTRIAL EQUIPMENT (888) 978-7759
Global Direct Mail Corp. (800) 645-1232
22 Harbor Park Dr.
Port Washington, NY 11050
E-Mail: service@globalindustrial.com
Website: www.globalindustrial.com
Fax Ordering: (888) 381-2868
International Ordering: (516) 625-3663
Customer Service: (800) 645-2986
Catalog: Free. Frequency: Quarterly

irculation: 4MM. Sales: $50-100MM
Products: Office & computer furniture;
mailroom, shipping & warehouse supplies

G HIGH GAIN LABELS (800) 648-0541
020 California St. • Omaha, NE 68102
Fax Ordering: (402) 228-1912
International Ordering: (402) 344-2564
Contact Name: Don Meyer, President
Catalog: Free. Frequency: 3x per year
Circulation: 500K. Sales: $5-10MM
Products: Labels

IDEA ART (800) 433-2278
434 Atrium Way • Nashville, TN 37214
E-Mail: info@ideaart.com
Website: www.ideaart.com
Fax Ordering: (800) 435-2278; (615) 889-6731
International Ordering: (615) 889-4989
Contact Name: Bud Chamberlain, President
Catalog: Free. Frequency: Semiannual
Circulation: 2MM. Sales: $1-3MM
Products: Design paper for desktop publishing

INTERNATIONAL PEN SHOP (800) 772-7367
Arthur Brown & Brothers
2 W. 46th St. • New York, NY 10036
E-Mail: penshop@artbrown.com
Website: www.artbrown.com
Fax Ordering: (212) 575-5825
International Ordering: (212) 575-5555
Contact Name: David Brown, President
Catalog: Free. Frequency: 4x per year
Circulation: 1MM. Sales: $5-10MM
Products: Writing instruments, desk sets

INTERSTATE LABEL COMPANY (800) 969-5261
1715 E. Main St. • Freeland, WA 98249
E-Mail: customerservice@label.com
Website: www.label.com
Fax Ordering: (408) 531-0442
International Ordering: (408) 531-1440
Catalog: Free. Frequency: Semiannual
Circulation: 1MM. Sales: $10-20MM
Products: Media storage, labeling kits,
software, CD-R labels

IROQUOIS PRODUCTS (800) 453-3355
2220 W. 56th St. • Chicago, IL 60636
E-Mail: sales@iroquoisproducts.com
Website: www.iroquoisproducts.com
Fax Ordering: (800) 453-3344;
   (773) 436-4908
International Ordering: (773) 436-4900
Contact Name: Alan Gordon, President
Catalog: Free. Frequency: Annual
Circulation: 1MM. Sales: $10-20MM
Products: Packaging & shipping supplies,
including labels, boxes, tape & wipers

JACKSON MARKING PRODUCTS (800) 782-6722
9105 N. Rainbow Ln.
Mt. Vernon, IL 62864
E-Mail: jmpco@rubber-stamp.com
Website: www.rubber-stamp.com
Fax Ordering: (800) 782-6732
International Ordering: (618) 242-1334
Contact Name: Coy E. Jackson, President
Catalog: Free. Frequency: 4x per year
Circulation: 200M. Sales: $1-3MM
Products: Made-to-order rubber stamps

JACOBS GARDNER SUPPLY COMPANY (800) 638-0983
6911 Laurel Bowie Rd. • Bowie, MD 20715
Fax Ordering: (301) 805-0941
International Ordering: (301) 779-3700
Contact Name: Gary Luiza, President
Catalog: Free. Frequency: Annual
Circulation: 250K. Sales: $3-5MM
Products: Office furniture & supplies

KENBERMA EMPLOYEE ID/BADGES (800) 343-5978
Kenberma Products
5 Suosso Lane • Plymouth, MA 02360
E-Mail: info@chiswick.com
Website: www.chiswick.com
Fax Ordering: (508) 746-9284
International Ordering: (508) 747-4100
Contact Name: Al Swartz, President
Catalog: Free. Frequency: Monthly
Circulation: 500K. Sales: $100-500MM
Products: Employee name badges &
motivational products, buttons, ribbons,
patches & ID jewelry

KOLE INDUSTRIES (800) 327-6085
P.O. Box 520152 • Miami, FL 33152
Fax Ordering: (305) 638-5821
International Ordering: (305) 633-2556
Contact Name: Arthur Kaplan, President
Catalog: Free. Frequency: Bimonthly
Circulation: 500K. Sales: $10-20MM
Products: Corregated products for storage,
shipping & mailing

KRAFTBILT ACCOUNTING CATALOG (800) 331-7290
P.O. Box 800 • Tulsa, OK 74101
E-Mail: info@kraftbilt.com
Website: www.kraftbilt.com
Fax Ordering: (918) 627-7138
International Ordering: (978) 443-9592
Contact Name: Debbie Rule, President
Catalog: Free. Frequency: Annual
Circulation: 1MM. Sales: $5-10MM
Products: Accounting & business forms,
envelopes & office supplies

LLT BAR CODE & LABEL (800) 882-4050
4560 Darrow Rd. • Stow, OH 44685
E-Mail: sales@lltproducts.com
Website: www.lltproducts.com
Fax Ordering: (800) 395-4721
International Ordering: (330) 896-3573
Catalog: Free. Frequency: 4x per year
Circulation: 1MM. Sales: $10-20MM
Products: Bar code systems, thermal
printing supplies, laser & impact supplies,
point-of-sale systems

LANGLEY (800) 225-4499
2 Sycamore Ave. • Medford, MA 02155
Fax Ordering: (781) 343-4291
International Ordering: (781) 395-8010
Contact Name: Melvin Stairman, President
Catalog: Free. Frequency: Annual
Circulation: 200K. Sales: $10-20MM
Products: Office equipment

LESLIE COMPANY CATALOG (800) 255-6210
P.O. Box 610 • Olathe, KS 66051
E-Mail: info@leslieco.com
Website: www.leslieco.com
Fax Ordering: (913) 764-4962

International Ordering: (913) 764-6660
Contact Name: Jerald Byrd, President
Catalog: Free. Frequency: Annual
Circulation: 50K. Sales: $5-10MM
Products: Custom presentation products,
looseleaf binders, pocket folders, index tabs,
covers, book printing, document holders,
specialty items

MAGNA VISUAL, INC.   (800) 843-3399
9400 Watson Rd. • St. Louis, MO 63126
E-Mail: magna@magnavisual.com
Website: www.magnavisual.com
Fax Ordering: (314) 843-0000
International Ordering: (314) 843-9000
Contact Name: William Cady, President
Catalog: Free. Frequency: Annual
Circulation: 100K. Sales: $5-10MM
Products: Magnetic visual communication
systems; magnetic custom planning board kits

MARKLINE BUSINESS PRODUCTS   (800) 343-8572
HDK Sales Company
411 Waverly Oaks Rd.
Waltham, MA 02154
E-Mail: hkline@msn.com
Fax Ordering: (781) 899-1833
International Ordering: (781) 899-0222
Contact Name: Herbert Kline, President
Catalog: Free. Frequency: 3x per year
Circulation: 250K. Sales: $5-10MM
Products: Office & computer equipment
& supplies

BETTY MILLS COMPANY   (877) 238-8964
60 E. 3rd Ave. • San Mateo, CA 94401
Fax Ordering: (509) 757-8012
International Ordering: (650) 344-8228
Catalog: Free. Frequency: Annual
Circulation: 100K. Sales: $10-20MM
Products: Cleaning & maintenance
products & general supplies

NCR DIRECT   (800) 543-8130
9095 Washington Church Rd.
Miamisburg, OH 45342
E-Mail: info@ncr.com
Website: www.ncr.com
Fax Ordering: (937) 439-8572
International Ordering: (937) 439-8200
Contact Name: Dan Enneking, President
Catalog: Free. Frequency: Semiannual
Circulation: 500K. Sales: $20-50MM
Products: Cash registers, security systems

NATIONAL BUSINESS FURNITURE   (800) 558-1010
P.O. Box 514052 • Milwaukee, WI 53203
E-Mail: sales@nationalbusinessfurniture.com
Website: www.nationalbusinessfurniture.com
Fax Ordering: (800) 329-9349
International Ordering: (414) 276-8511
Customer Service: (800) 626-6060
Contact Name: George Mosher, President
Catalog: Free. Frequency: Weekly
Circulation: 12MM. Sales: $50-100MM
Products: Business furniture & accessories

NEW GEN SYSTEMS CORP.   (800) 888-1689
3545 Cadillac Ave. • Costa Mesa, CA 92626
E-Mail: sales@newgen.com
Website: www.newgen.com
Fax Ordering: (714) 641-2800

International Ordering: (714) 641-8600
Contact Name: Al Dubrow, President
Catalog: Free. Frequency: Semiannual
Circulation: 50K. Sales: $5-10MM
Products: Postscript laser printers

NORTH WESTERN OFFICE SUPPLIERS   (800) 432-0095
800 Main St. • Hays, KS 67601
Fax Ordering: (785) 625-7326
International Ordering: (785) 625-7323
Contact Name: Jim Keller, President
Catalog: Free. Frequency: Annual
Circulation: 150K. Sales: $5-10MM
Products: Office supplies

NSC INTERNATIONAL   (800) 643-1520
7090 Central Ave. • Hot Springs, AR 71903
E-Mail: info@binding.com
Website: www.binding.com
Fax Ordering: (800) 960-2727
International Ordering: (501) 525-0133
Contact Name: Bud West, President
Catalog: Free. Frequency: Semiannual
Circulation: 50M. Sales: $100-500MM
Products: Laminating & binding products
for presentation professionals

OFFICE ACCESS   (800) 348-1564
P.O. Box 620 • Hartland, WI 53029
E-Mail: sales@office-access.com
Website: www.office-access.com
Fax Ordering: (262) 367-1362
International Ordering: (262) 367-1240
Contact Name: Leigh Ann Miller, Marketing
Catalog: Free. Frequency: Quarterly
Circulation: 150K. Sales: $1-3MM
Products: Printing, copier & fax supplies;
office equipment & supplies; computers

OFFICE DEPOT   (800) 923-4624
Military Trail • Boca Raton, FL 33487   (800) 463-3768
E-Mail: sales@officedepot.com
Website: www.officedepot.com
Fax Ordering: (800) 685-5010; (561) 438-4400
International Ordering: (561) 438-4800
Contact Name: David Fuente, President
Catalog: Free. Frequency: Monthly
Circulation: 2MM. Sales: $25-50MM
Products: Office supplies and furniture;
printers, copiers and supplies; scanners,
fax machines, etc.

OFFICE - ELECTRONICS CATALOG   (800) 332-3536
National Wholesale Company
26 Parkridge Rd. • Haverhill, MA 01835
Fax Ordering: (978) 556-0801
International Ordering: (978) 556-0800
Contact Name: James Polino, President
Catalog: Free. Frequency: Annual
Circulation: 25K. Sales: $5-10MM
Products: Office supplies, electronic equipment

OFFICE SUPPLY/STORAGE PRODUCTS   (800) 243-3774
Durham Manufacturing Co.
201 Main St. • Durham, CT 06422
Fax Ordering: (860) 349-3160
International Ordering: (860) 537-3488
Contact Name: Richard Patterson, President
Catalog: Free. Frequency: Semiannual
Circulation: 50K. Sales: $20-50MM
Products: Steel storage bins/cabinets/
drawers with scoop compartment boxes

OFFICEMAX CATALOG (877) 633-4236
263 Shuman Blvd. • Naperville, IL 60563
E-Mail: sales@officemax.com
Website: www.officemax.com
Fax Ordering: (800) 995-9644; (216) 491-4040
International Ordering: (630) 438-7800
Customer Service: (877) 4-THE-MAX
Contact Name: John Martin, President
Catalog: Free. Pages: 76. Frequency: Quarterly
Circulation: 4MM. Sales: $100-500MM
Products: Office supplies & equipment

ORGANIZERS, PLANNERS (800) 631-2233
& SCHEDULING SYSTEMS
Abbott Office Systems
P.O. Box 688 • Farmingdale, NJ 07727
Fax Ordering: (732) 938-4419
International Ordering: (732) 938-6000
Contact Name: C.W. Nelson, President
Catalog: Free. Frequency: 3X per year
Circulation: 250K. Sales: $5-10MM
Products: Products to organize your
business or home office

PAPER DIRECT CATALOG (800) 272-7377
P.O. Box 2970 • Colorado Springs, CO 80901
Fax Ordering: (800) 443-2973
Contact Name: Ted Struhl, President
Catalog: Free. Frequency: 5x per year
Circulation: 200K. Sales: $5-10MM
Products: Paper for laser printers, copiers,
and desktop publishing needs

PAPER SHOWCASE (800) 287-8163
Thayer Publishing
P.O. Box 8465 • Mankato, MN 56002
E-Mail: info@papershowcase.com
Website: www.papershowcase.com
Fax Ordering: (800) 842-3371
International Ordering: (507) 388-5256
Catalog: Free. Frequency: Annual
Circulation: 150K. Sales: $10-20MM
Products: Preprinted laser paper designs

PAPERBOARD SPECIALIST (800) 872-6670
Mailers Co.
575 Benett Rd. • Elk Grove, IL 60007
E-Mail: info@mailersco.com
Website: www.mailersco.com
Fax Ordering: (847) 734-1958
International Ordering: (847) 734-9000
Contact Name: Patrick Pulver, President
Catalog: Free. Frequency: Annual
Circulation: 100M. Sales: $20-50MM
Products: Mailing packages & storage cartons

B.A. PARGH COMPANY (800) 227-1000
P.O. Box 24510 • Nashville, TN 37202
E-Mail: dealer@atlaspencil.com
Website: www.atlaspencil.com
Fax Ordering: (800) 247-4329
International Ordering: (615) 254-2500
Contact Name: Bernard Pargh, President
Catalog: Free. Frequency: Semiannual
Circulation: 500K. Sales: $20-50MM
Products: Office supplies & equipment;
computer supplies

PENNY WISE OFFICE PRODUCTS (800) 942-3311
6911 Laurel Bowie Rd. • Bowie, MD 20715
E-Mail: sales@penny-wise.com
Website: www.penny-wise.com

Fax Ordering: (301) 622-4411
International Ordering: (301) 805-7733
Contact Name: Gary Luiza, President
Catalog: Free. Frequency: 3x per year
Circulation: 1MM. Sales: $5-10MM
Products: Office equipment, products
& supplies

PERSONAL STAMP EXCHANGE (800) 845-2312
Stamp Diego
2650 Jamacha Rd. • El Cajon, CA 92019
E-Mail: stampdiego@aol.com
Website: www.stampdiego.com
International Ordering: (619) 670-4782
Contact Name: Jenny Griffiths, President
Catalog: $12. Frequency: Annual
Circulation: 10K. Sales: $1-3MM
Products: Rubber stamps & accessories

PHOTO MATERIALS CATALOG (800) 225-5644
Martin Yale Industries, Inc.
251 Wedcor Ave. • Wabash, IN 46992
E-Mail: sales@martinyale.com
Website: www.martinyale.com
Fax Ordering: (800) 654-8339; (260) 563-4575
International Ordering: (260) 563-0641
Contact Name: Bill Reed, President
Catalog: Free. Frequency: Annual
Circulation: 100K. Sales: $5-10MM
Products: Office equipment

PHYSICAL EDUCATION & RECREATION (800) 793-7900
FlagHouse • 601 FlagHouse Dr.
Hasbrouck Hts., NJ 07604
E-Mail: sales@flaghouse.com
Website: www.flaghouse.com
Fax Ordering: (800) 793-7922; (201) 288-7887
International Ordering: (201) 288-7600
Contact Name: George. Frequency: Bimonthly
Circulation: 2MM. Sales: $20-50MM
Products: Institutional & office furniture

PRECISION DATA PRODUCTS (800) 968-2468
P.O. Box 8367 • Grand Rapids, MI 49518 (800) 968-0888
E-Mail: sales@precision.com
Website: www.precision.com
Fax Ordering: (616) 698-9047
International Ordering: (616) 698-2242
Contact Name: Kevin Andrea, Marketing
Catalog: Free. Frequency: Quarterly
Circulation: 25K. Sales: $500M to $1MM
Products: Printer ribbons & cartridges for
computers printers; hardware

QUILL CORPORATION (800) 789-1331
100 Schelter Rd. • Lincolnshire, IL 60069
E-Mail: sales@officefurniture.com
Website: www.officefurniture.com
Fax Ordering: (800) 789-8955
International Ordering: (847) 634-6690
Contact Name: Jack Miller, President
Catalog: Free. Frequency: Semiannual
Circulation: 2MM. Sales: $100-500MM
Products: Office equipment, machines,
furniture & supplies

RAND MATERIAL HANDLING EQUIPMENT (800) 366-2300
515 Narragansett Park Dr. • Pawtucket, RI 02861
E-Mail: sales@randmh.com
Website: www.randmh.com
Fax Ordering: (401) 724-5960
International Ordering: (401) 751-7657

Contact Name: James Fitzgerald, Sr., President
Catalog: Free. Frequency: Monthly
Circulation: 7MM. Sales: $100-200MM
Products: Packaging equipment & materials
handling equipment

REAL ESTATE GRAPHICS (800) 328-0594
7644 W. 78th St. • Minneapolis, MN 55439
E-Mail: reg@realestategraphics.com
Website: www.realestategraphics.com
Fax Ordering: (800) 621-1636
Contact Name: Dennis Herkel, President
Catalog: Free. Frequency: Annual
Circulation: 100K. Sales: $1-3MM
Products: Real estate office products

RELIABLE OFFICE SUPPLIES (800) 735-4000
P.O. Box 1502 • Ottawa, IL 61350 (800) 328-3034
E-Mail: sales@reliable.com (800) 326-7555
Website: www.reliable.com
Fax Ordering: (800) 326-3233; (800) 842-2725
International Ordering: (630) 773-5000
Customer Service: (800) 359-5000
Catalog: Free. Frequency: Annual
Circulation: 3MM. Sales: $20-50MM
Products: Office supplies & equipment

REPEAT-O-TYPE MFG. CORP. (800) 288-3330
665 State Hwy. 23 • Wayne, NJ 07470
E-Mail: info@repeatotype.com
Website: www.repeatotype.com
Fax Ordering: (973) 694-7287
International Ordering: (973) 696-3330
Contact Name: Whitney Keen, President
Catalog: $1. Frequency: Semiannual
Circulation: 100K. Sales: $5-10MM
Products: Ink jet printing & digital
duplicating supplies

RIBCO PRODUCTS (800) 323-7420
5120 Belmont Rd. • DownersGrove, IL 60515
Fax Ordering: (630) 963-8103
International Ordering: (630) 963-9540
Catalog: Free. Frequency: Annual
Circulation: 150K. Sales: $10-20MM
Products: Office products, including fax
& register paper, cash register & bank rolls,
teletype paper, diskettes, ribbons, tapes

RUSH RECEIPT BOOK COMPANY (800) 654-4237
457 Houston St. • Mobile, AL 36606
E-Mail: rush@superiorptg.com
Website: www.rushreceiptbook.com
Fax Ordering: (251) 476-1286
International Ordering: (251) 471-4059
Contact Name: Donald Webb, President
Catalog: Free. Frequency: Annual
Circulation: 100K. Sales: $3-5MM
Products: Custom receipt books &
wire special binding

S.P. RICHARDS COMPANY (770) 436-6881
P.O. Box 1266 • Smyrna, GA 30081
E-Mail: sales@sprichards.com
Website: www.sprichards.com
Fax Ordering: (770) 801-5619
Catalog: Free. Frequency: Annual
Circulation: 2MM. Sales: $20-50MM
Products: Office products, including office
furniture, computer supplies, general office
supplies, school supplies. business equipment,
warehouse & safety items

SCOTT SIGN SYSTEMS, INC. (800) 237-9447
P.O. Box 1047 • Tallevast, FL 34270
E-Mail: mail@scottsigns.com
Website: www.scottsigns.com
Fax Ordering: (941) 351-1787
International Ordering: (941) 355-5171
Contact Name: Kathy Hannon, President
Catalog: Free. Frequency: Annual
Circulation: 100K. Sales: $3-5MM
Products: Architectural sign systems,
ADGlo illuminated signs; letters, logos,
graphics

STANDARD REGISTER (800) 435-5555
P.O. Box 1167 • Dayton, OH 45401 (800) 926-7806
E-Mail: supplies@standardregister.com (800) 755-6405
Website: www.standardregister.com
Fax Ordering: (800) 443-4877; (847) 756-3219
International Ordering: (937) 221-1000
Contact Name: Peter Redeng, President
Catalog: Free. Frequency: 9x per year
Circulation: 10MM. Sales: $100-500MM
Products: Office & computer equipment,
supplies & furniture

STAPLES DIRECT (800) 333-3330
P.O. Box 9256 • Framingham, MA 01701 (800) STAPLES
E-Mail: sales@staples.com
Website: www.staples.com
Fax Ordering: (800) 333-3199
Contact Name: Jack Bingleman
Catalog: Free. Frequency: Monthly
Circulation: 5MM. Sales: $100-500MM
Products: Office equipment & supplies;
furniture, business machines, computers
& accessories

STORE SMART EXPRESS (800) 424-1011
Visual Horizons
180 Metro Park • Rochester, NY 14623
E-Mail: info@storesmart.com
Website: www.storesmart.com
Fax Ordering: (800) 424-5411; (585) 424-5313
International Ordering: (585) 424-5300
Contact Name: Stanley Feingold, President
Catalog: Free. Frequency: Weekly
Circulation: 250K. Sales: $10-50MM
Products: Media storage products;
computer diskettes & CD-ROMs;
laminating equipment; flip charts, binders
& page protectors; plaques & awards

SUNRISE BUSINESS PRODUCTS (800) 222-7367
99 Mark Tree Rd. • Centereach, NY 11729
E-Mail: sales@sun-rise.com
Website: www.sun-rise.com
Fax Ordering: (631) 698-0837
International Ordering: (631) 698-0700
Contact Name: Warren Selinger, President
Catalog: Free. Frequency: Annual
Circulation: 150K. Sales: $5-10MM
Products: Business & commercial products,
office supplies, promotional products

TAMARACK PACKAGING LTD. (800) 836-6980
P.O. Box 693 • Meaville, PA 16335
E-Mail: sales@tamarackpackaging.com
Website: www.tamarackpackaging.com
Fax Ordering: (814) 333-8975
International Ordering: (814) 724-2860
Contact Name: Robert Stamp, President
Catalog: Free. Frequency: Weekly

Circulation: 100M. Sales: $500M to $1MM
Products: Vinyl products; looseleaf binders

TIE OFFICE-MATES (800) 238-3957
P.O. Box 306 • Sussex, WI 53089
E-Mail: info@tieofficemates.com
Website: www.tieofficemates.com
Fax Ordering: (262) 246-4828
International Ordering: (262) 246-8538
Contact Name: Tom Touchett, President
Catalog: Free. Frequency: Quarterly
Circulation: 50K. Sales: $3-5MM
Products: Office supplies, vinyl products

TURNKEY WHOLESALE BUYERS GUIDE (800) 828-7540
Turnkey Material Handling
500 Fillmore Ave. • Tonawanda, NY 14150
E-Mail: sales@office furniture.com
Website: www.officefurniture.com
Fax Ordering: (800) 246-5250
International Ordering: (716) 743-8400
Contact Name: John Greenberger, President
Catalog: Free. Frequency: Semiannual
Circulation: 250K. Sales: $10-20MM
Products: Office & institutional products

20TH CENTURY OFFICE SUPPLIES (800) 227-7010
2821 Merrick Rd. • Bellmore, NY 11710
E-Mail: info@20thcenturysupplies.com
Website: www.20thcenturysupplies.com
Fax Ordering: (718) 392-7214
International Ordering: (212) 422-0040
Catalog: Free. Frequency: Semiannual
Circulation: 100K. Sales: $3-5MM
Products: Office supplies; audio visual
equipment

U.S. BOX CORPORATION (800) 221-0999
1296 McCarter Hwy. • Newark, NJ 07104
E-Mail: sales@usbox.com
Website: www.usbox.com
Fax Ordering: (973) 481-2002
International Ordering: (973) 481-2000
Contact Name: Irwin Kossoff, President
Catalog: Free. Frequency: Quarterly
Circulation: 400K. Sales: $5-10MM
Products: Boxes, bags & packaging
material for gifts, jewelry, baskets, crafts
& shipping; custom & printed available

ULINE SHIPPING SUPPLIES (800) 295-5510
2200 S. Lakeside Dr.
Waukegan, IL 60085
E-Mail: info@uline.com
Website: www.uline.com
Fax Ordering: (800) 295-5571
Customer Service: (888) 952-6937
Contact Name: Elizabeth Ulhlein, President
Catalog: Free. Pages: 384.
Frequency: Semiannual
Circulation: 250K. Sales: $20-50MM
Products: Shipping supplies

USI, INC. CATALOG (800) 243-4565
98 Fort Path Rd. • Madison, CT 06443
E-Mail: sales@usi-laminate.com
Website: www.usi-laminate.com
Fax Ordering: (203) 245-7337
Technical Support: (800) 752-9131
Catalog: Free. Frequency: Semiannual
Circulation: 150K. Sales: $5-10MM
Products: Laminators, pouch kits,
mounting materials, binding machines
& covers, transparency films & projectors,
cutters & trimmers

VIKING OFFICE PRODUCTS (800) 421-1222
950 W. 190th St. • Torrance, CA 90502 (800) 711-4242
E-Mail: support@vikingop.com
Website: www.vikingop.com
Fax Ordering: (800) 762-7329;
  (310) 327-2376
International Ordering: (310) 225-4500
Contact Name: Bruce Nelson, President
Catalog: Free. Frequency: Monthly
Circulation: 5MM. Sales: $50-100MM
Products: Office products & supplies

VULCAN INFORMATION PACKAGING (800) 633-4526
P.O. Box 29 • Vincent, AL 35178
E-Mail: sales@vulcan-online.com
Website: www.vulcan-online.com
Fax Ordering: (800) 344-8939
International Ordering: (847) 634-6690
Contact Name: Walter B. Evans, Jr., President
Catalog: Free. Frequency: 3x per year
Circulation: 250K. Sales: $5-10MM
Products: Looseleaf binders

THE WRITE STUFF (800) 642-8885
Atlas Penn & Pencil Corporation
Dealer Division • Hollywood, FL 33022
E-Mail: dealer@atlaspencil.com
Website: www.atlaspencil.com
Fax Ordering: (800) 342-8889
International Ordering: (954) 922-6160
Contact Name: Harold Schneider, President
Catalog: Free. Frequency: Annual
Circulation: 500K. Sales: $10-20MM
Products: Office supplies & advertising
specialties

XEROX OFFICE SUPPLIES (800) 822-2200
Rt. 303 & Bradley Rd.
Blauvelt, NY 10913
E-Mail: info@xerox.com
Website: www.xerox.com
Fax Ordering: (800) 338-7020
International Ordering: (845) 365-5350
Catalog: Free. Frequency: Quarterly
Circulation: 400K. Sales: $50-100MM
Products: Xerox supplies

ASTRONOMICS / CHRISTOPHERS, LTD. (800) 422-7876
680 S.W. 24th Ave. • Norman, OK 73069 (800) 356-6603
E-Mail: questions@astronomics.com
Website: www.birdbino.com
Fax Ordering: (405) 447-3337
International Ordering: (405) 364-0858
Contact Name: Fred Bieler, President
Catalog: Free. Frequency: Quarterly
Circulation: 50K. Sales: $10-20MM
Products: Telescopes, binoculars &
spotting scopes

BROCK MAGISCOPE (800) 780-9111
Brock Optical, Inc.
1959 Barber Rd. • Sarasota, FL 34240
E-Mail: info@magiscope.com
Website: www.magiscope.com
Fax Ordering: (941) 378-9046
International Ordering: (941) 342-7727
Contact Name: Dennis Brock, President
Catalog: Free. Frequency: Semiannual
Circulation: 100K. Sales: $5-10MM
Products: Microscopes for use indoors
& outdoors

DEBBY BURKE OPTICAL (800) 789-6322
7 Overlook Lane
Plainview, NY 11803
E-Mail: help@debspecs.com
Website: www.debspecs.com
Fax Ordering: (516) 932-5628
International Ordering: (516) 935-4584
Contact Name: Debby Burke, President
Catalog: Free. Frequency: Weekly
Circulation: 50K. Sales: $3-5MM
Products: Reading glaasses, eyeglasses
& eyeglass accessories; designer reading
glasses; sun & computer glasses; low
vision aids.

BUSHNELL CORPORATION (800) 423-3537
9200 Cody • Overland Park, KS 66214 (800) 221-9035
E-Mail: rgitlan@bushnell.com
Website: www.bushnell.com
Fax Ordering: (913) 752-3550
International Ordering: (913) 752-3400
Contact Name: James F. Huntington, President
Catalog: Free. Frequency: Annual
Circulation: 100K. Sales: $20-50MM
Products: Binoculars, telescopes &
rifle scopes, laser rangefinders, digital
compasses

CONTACT LENS REPLACEMENT CENTER (800) 779-2654
P.O. Box 615
Wheatley Hts., NY 11798
E-Mail: info@clrc.com
Website: www.clrc.com
Fax Ordering: (631) 643-4009
International Ordering: (631) 491-7763
Contact Name: Neil Lazinsky, President
Catalog: Free. Frequency: Quarterly
Circulation: 50K. Sales: $5-10MM
Products: Replacement contact lenses;
sunglasses

DEUTSCHE OPTIK (800) 225-9407
321 S. Main St.
Yerington, NV 89447
E-Mail: info@deutscheoptik.com
Website: www.deutscheoptik.com
Fax Ordering: (775) 463-1582

Contact Name: Mike Rivkin, President
Catalog: Free. Frequency: Semiannual
Circulation: 200K. Sales: $20-50MM
Products: High-end commercial & military
binoculars, scopes, compasses, nautical
antiques, and militaria

EAGLE OPTICS (800) 289-1132
2120 W. Greenview Dr.
Middleton, WI 53562
E-Mail: information@eagleoptics.com
Website: www.eagleoptics.com
Fax Ordering: (608) 836-4416
Catalog: Free. Frequency: Annual
Circulation: 100K. Sales: $5-10MM
Products: Binoculars, spotting scopes;
optic supplies; diogital cameras;
outdoor gear

EDMUND OPTICS, INC. (800) 363-1992
101 E. Gloucester Pike
Barrington, NJ 08007
E-Mail: sales@edmundoptics.com
Website: www.edmundoptics.com
Fax Ordering: (856) 573-6295
International Ordering: (856) 573-6250
Contact Name: Gwynne Edmund, President
Catalog: Free. Frequency: Semiannual
Circulation: 1MM. Sales: $20-50MM
Products: Optics line of products; 2,000 brand
new optical, imaging & mechanical components;
science & optical equipment, OEM optics, lasers
& lenses

LENS EXPRESS (800) 266-8228
350 SW 12th Ave.
Deerfield Beach, FL 33442
E-Mail: INFO@contacts.com
Website: www.1800contacts.com/lensexpress
Fax Ordering: (954) 480-9446
International Ordering: (954) 421-5800
Contact Name: Mike Lorelli, President
Catalog: Free. Frequency: Monthly
Circulation: 2MM. Sales: $10-20MM
Products: Contact lenses, eyeglasses,
sunglasses

MAGEYES, INC. (800) 210-6662
P.O. Box 293010
Kerrville, TX 78029
E-Mail: sales@mageyes.com
Website: www.mageyes.com
Fax Ordering: (830) 896-6064
International Ordering: (830) 896-6060
Contact Name: Mary Frances Sherlock, President
Catalog: Free. Frequency: Quarterly
Circulation: 100K. Sales: $3-5MM
Products: Head mounted, hands-free
magnifiers

MEADE TELESCOPE CATALOG (800) 626-3233
Meade Instruments Corporation
27 Hubble • Irvine, CA 92618
E-Mail: info@meade.com
Website: www.meade.com
Fax Ordering: (949) 451-1460
International Ordering: (949) 451-1450
Contact Name: Steven G. Murdock, President
Catalog: $3. Frequency: Semiannual
Circulation: 50K. Sales: $5-10MM
Products: Telescopes, binoculars, spotting
scopes, microscopes

NATIONAL CAMERA EXCHANGE   (800) 624-8107
National Camera Exchange & Video
9300 Olson Memorial Hwy.
Golden Valley, MN 55427
E-Mail: sales@natcam.com
Website: www.natcam.com
Fax Ordering: (763) 546-7043
International Ordering: (763) 546-6831
Contact Name: Jon Liss, President
Catalog: Free. Frequency: Monthly
Circulation: 150K. Sales: $10-20MM
Products: Photographic equipment;
digital cameras, camcorders, SLR lenses,
binoculars & cameras; printers & scanners,
bags & cases, photo accessories, tripods,
flashes, used equipment, spotting scopes
& accessories

OPTECH   (800) 848-6624
19 Lupine Rd. • Andover, MA 01810
E-Mail: optech@erols.com
Website: www.optechlightbulbs.com
Fax Ordering: (978) 475-6370
International Ordering: (978) 475-4831
Contact Names: Gary Keleshian, President
Catalog: Free. Frequency: Annual
Circulation: 25K. Sales: $1-3MM
Products: Projection lamps for photography

ORION TELESCOPES & BINOCULARS   (800) 447-1001
89 Hangar Way
Watsonville, CA 95076
E-Mail: sales@telescope.com
Website: www.orionbinoculars.com
Fax Ordering: (831) 763-7024
International Ordering: (831) 763-7000
Customer Service: (800) 676-1343
Catalog: Free. Frequency: Semiannual
Circulation: 250K. Sales: $10-20MM
Products: Telescopes & binoculars

PARKS OPTICAL   (805) 522-6722
750 E. Easy St.
Simi Valley, CA 93065
E-Mail: parksoptical@parksoptical.com
Website: www.parksoptical.com
Fax Ordering: (805) 522-0033
Contact Name: Maurice Sweiss, President
Catalog: Free. Frequency: Annual
Circulation: 25K. Sales: $5-10MM
Products: Astronomical products,
including telescopes, reflectors, binoculars,
spotting scopes, microscopes

PRISM OPTICAL, INC.   (800) 637-4104
P.O. Box 680030
North Miami, FL 33168
E-Mail: rgitlan@prismoptical.com
Website: www.prismoptical.com
Fax Ordering: (800) 617-5367; (305) 754-7352
International Ordering: (305) 754-5894
Contact Name: Ron Gitlan, President
Catalog: Free. Frequency: Quarterly
Circulation: 100K. Sales: $5-10MM
Products: Eyeglasses, eyewear accessories,
contact lenses & sunglasses

RAMSEY OUTDOOR   (800) 699-5874
P.O. Box 1689 • Paramus, NJ 07652
E-Mail: customerservice@ramseyoutdoor.com
Website: www.ramseyoutdoor.com
Fax Ordering: (201) 261-2742
International Ordering: (201) 261-5000
Contact Name: Stuart Levine, President
Catalog: Free. Frequency: Semiannual
Circulation: 1MM. Sales: $10-20MM
Products: Eyeglasses & sunglasses

SEILER INSTRUMENTS & MFG. CO.   (800) 489-2282
3433 Tree Court Industrial Blvd.
St. Louis, MO 63122
E-Mail: sales@seilerinst.com
Website: www.seilerinst.com
Fax Ordering: (314) 968-2637
International Ordering: (314) 968-2282
Contact Name: Eric Seiler, President
Catalog: Free. Frequency: Semiannual
Circulation: 100K. Sales: $20-50MM
Products: Microscopes & telescopes

SUNGLASS HUT INTERNATIONAL   (800) 786-4527
Luxottica Group   (800) SUNGLAS
255 Alhambra Cir. • Coral Gables, FL 33134
E-Mail: sunglasshut@luxoticaretail.com
Website: www.sunglasshut.com
Fax Ordering: (800) 786-4327; (678) 432-4070
International Ordering: (770) 305-7400
Catalog: Free. Frequency: Quarterly
Circulation: 150K. Sales: $20-50MM
Products: Sunglasses, watches

AMERICA'S PET DOOR STORE   (800) 826-2871
Patio Pacific
1931 N. Gaffey St.
San Pedro, CA 90731
E-Mail: petdoors@juno.com
Website: www.petdoors.com
Fax Ordering: (310) 547-3715
International Ordering: (310) 547-5586
Contact Name: Alan Lethers, President
Catalog: Free. Frequency: Quarterly
Circulation: 20K. Sales: $1-3MM
Products: Pet doors, all major brands &
installation types, with installer referrals
in most areas

AMERICAN HEALTH SERVICE   (800) 422-4733
VETERINARY DISTRIBUTOR CATALOG
13822 W. Boulton Blvd.
Mettawa, IL 60045
E-Mail: bill@americanhealthservice.com
Website: www.americanhealthservice.com
Fax Ordering: (847) 680-4440
International Ordering: (847) 680-3050
Contact Name: William Lapietra, President
Catalog: Free. Frequency: Quarterly
Circulation: 150K. Sales: $1-3MM
Products: Name brand and first quality
medical/surgical supplies

AMERICAN INDIAN HORSE REGISTRY   (512) 398-6642
9028 State Park Rd. • Lockhart, TX 78644
E-Mail: info@indianhorse.com
Website: www.indianhorse.com
Catalog: Free. Frequency: Quarterly
Circulation: 25K. Sales: $100K
Products: Art, books, gifts pertaining
to the American Indian horse.

AMERICAN LIVESTOCK SUPPLY - HORSE   (800) 356-0700
& GENERAL LIVESTOCK CATALOGS
613 Atlas Ave. • Madison, WI 53714
Website: www.americanlivestock.com
E-Mail: mary.bohne@americanlivestock.com
Fax Ordering: (800) 309-8947
Contact Name: Mary Bohne
Catalogs: Free. Frequency: Annual
Circulation: 100K. Sales: $1-3MM
Products: Horses supplies & equipment;
livestock products & supplies

ANIMAL MEDIC CATALOG   (800) 767-5611
P.O. Box 575 • Manchester, PA 17345
E-Mail: info@animalmedic.com
Website: www.animalmedic.com
Fax Ordering: (717) 266-2594
International Ordering: (717) 266-5611
Contact Name: Larry Gladfelter, President
Catalog: Free. Frequency: Semiannual
Circulation: 50K. Sales: $1-3MM
Products: Animal health, pet, farm &
home supplies

ANIMAL VETERINARY PRODUCTS   (800) 962-1211
500 Kehoe Blvd. • Carol Stream, IL 60188
Fax Ordering: (309) 344-3265
International Ordering: (630) 792-8151
Contact Name: Bob Davison, President
Catalog: Free. Frequency: Quarterly
Circulation: 300K. Sales: $1-3MM
Products: Pet health care & veterinary
supplies

BAR-F PRODUCTS CATALOG   (800) 372-8899
1955 Airport Blvd.
Red Bluff, CA 96080
E-Mail: info@horseboots.com
Website: www.horseboots.com
Fax Ordering: (530) 529-5011
International Ordering: (530) 529-0524
Catalog: Free. Frequency: Semiannual
Circulation: 100K. Sales: $500K to $1MM
Products: Equine protective boots &
products for the horse & rider

BEST CARE PET CATALOG   (800) 367-4444
KHR Ltd. - Omaha Vaccine Company
3030 L St. • Omaha, NE 68107
E-Mail: info@omahavaccine.com
Website: www.omahavaccine.com
Fax Ordering: (800) 242-9447; (402) 731-9829
International Ordering: (402) 731-9600
Contact Name: Scott Remington, President
Catalog: Free. Frequency: Annual
Circulation: 1.5MM. Sales: $10-20MM
Products: Kennel & pet supplies for all
animals

BUSH HERPETOLOGICAL SUPPLY   (800) 451-6178
Twin Rivers Industrial Park
Neodesha, KS 66757
E-Mail: info@bushherp.com
Website: www.bushherp.com
Fax Ordering: (620) 325-3098
International Ordering: (620) 325-2250
Contact Name: Ted Peitz, President
Catalog: Free. Frequency: Annual
Circulation: 20K. Sales: $500M
Products: Cages, snake handling
equipment & supplies

CARE-A-LOT PET SUPPLY   (800) 343-7680
1617 Diamond Springs Rd.
Virginia Beach, VA 23455
E-Mail: customerservice@carealotpets.com
Website: www.carealotpets.com
Fax Ordering: (757) 460-6327
International Ordering: (757) 460-9771
Catalog: Free. Frequency: Quarterly
Circulation: 150K. Sales: $1-3MM
Products: Dog & cat supplies

CAT BARN CATALOG   (888) 659-8585
P.O. Box 239
Mountlake Terrace, WA 98043
E-Mail: katnmouzer@sprynet.com
Website: www.catbarn.com
Fax Ordering: (425) 672-7455
International Ordering: (425) 672-9578
Catalog: Free. Frequency: Annual
Circulation: 100K. Sales: $500K
Products: Cat houses & supplies

CAT CLAWS CATALOG   (800) 783-0977
1004 W. Broadway St.
Morrilton, AR 72110
E-Mail: info@catclaws.com
Website: www.catclaws.com
Fax Ordering: (501) 354-4843
International Ordering: (501) 354-5015
Contact Name: William Seliskar, President
Catalog: Free. Frequency: Monthly
Circulation: 2.5MM. Sales: $3-5MM
Products: Unique cat products

CHERRYBROOK DOG & CAT SUPPLIES (800) 524-0820
Cherrybrook, Inc.
Box 15 Route 57 • Broadway, NJ 08808
E-Mail: custserv@cherrybrook.com
Website: www.cherrybrook.com
Fax Ordering: (908) 689-7988
International Ordering: (908) 689-7979
Contact Name: Wayne Ferguson, President
Catalog: Free. Frequency: Semiannual
Circulation: 1MM. Sales: $5-10MM
Products: Dog & cat supplies for kennels,
shows, pet grooming & vet hospitals

COLLAR CLINIC CATALOG (800) 430-2010
1517 Northern Star Dr.
Traverse City, MI 49686
E-Mail: info@collarclinic.com
Website: www.collarclinic.com
Fax Ordering: (231) 947-6566
Catalog: Free. Frequency: Annual
Circulation: 50K. Sales: $500K
Products: Electronic dog training equipment

COUNTRY MANUFACTURING CATALOG (800) 335-1880
P.O. Box 104 • Fredericktown, OH 43019
E-Mail: info@countrymfg.com
Website: www.countrymfg.com
Fax Ordering: (740) 694-5088
International Ordering: (740) 694-9926
Contact Name: Joe Chattin, President
Catalog: Free. Frequency: Monthly
Circulation: 50K. Sales: $1-3MM
Products: Horse barn equipment

DIRECT PET SUPERSTORE (800) 360-4838
Division of Valley Vet Supply
P.O. Box 504 • Marysville, KS 66508
E-Mail: service@valleyvet.com
Website: www.valleyvet.com
Fax Ordering: (800) 446-5597
International Ordering: (785) 562-5106
Contact Name: Arnold Nagely, President
Catalog: Free. Pages: 80. Frequency: Quarterly
Circulation: 100K. Sales: $5-10MM
Products: Pet products & supplies

DOCTORS FOSTER & SMITH CATALOG (800) 826-7206
P.O. Box 100 • Rhinelander, WI 54501
E-Mail: info@drsfostersmith.com
Website: www.drsfostersmith.com
Fax Ordering: (800) 776-8872; (715) 369-2821
International Ordering: (715) 369-3305
Contact Name: Martin Smith, President
Catalog: Free. Frequency: 8x per year
Circulation: 1MM. Sales: $50-100MM
Products: Pet health care products

DOGTREAT WAREHOUSE (888) 364-2439
51 Roberts Rd. • New City, NY 10956
E-Mail: info@dogtreatwarehouse.com
Website: www.dogtreatwarehouse.com
Catalog: Online. Sales: $3-5MM
Products: Natural dog treats & toys

DOGWISE CATALOG (800) 776-2665
701 Poplar Ave. • Wenatchee, WA 98801
E-Mail: mail@dogwise.com
Website: www.dogwise.com
Fax Ordering: (509) 662-7233
International Ordering: (509) 663-9115
Contact Name: Lawrence A. Woodward, President
Catalog: Free. Frequency: Semiannual

Circulation: 200K. Sales: $1-3MM
Products: Dog books & videos on training,
breeding, showing, grooming & veterinary care

DROLL YANKEES CATALOG (800) 352-9164
27 Mill Rd. • Foster, RI 02825
E-Mail: info@drollyankees.com
Website: www.drollyankees.com
Fax Ordering: (401) 647-7620
International Ordering: (401) 647-3324
Contact Name: Betsy Colwell, President
Catalog: Free. Frequency: Annual
Circulation: 35K. Sales: $500K to $1MM
Products: Bird feeders & accessories

DUNCRAFT - LIVING WITH NATURE (800) 593-5656
102 Fisherville Rd. • Concord, NH 03303
E-Mail: info@duncraft.com
Website: www.duncraft.com
Fax Ordering: (603) 226-3735
International Ordering: (603) 224-0200
Contact Name: John Ela, President
Catalog: Free. Frequency: Monthly
Circulation: 3MM. Sales: $5-10MM
Products: Bird feeders, specialty seeds,
birdhouses, baths & accessories to attract
wild birds

EASYCARE, INC. (800) 447-8836
2300 E. Vistoso Commerce Loop Rd.
Tucson, AZ 85755
E-Mail: info@easycareinc.com
Website: www.easycareinc.com
Fax Ordering: (520) 297-9600
International Ordering: (520) 297-1900
Catalog: Free. Frequency: Annual
Circulation: 100K. Sales: $1-3MM
Products: Horse care products; hoof care
accessories; EasyCare apparel

ETHICAL PRODUCTS CATALOG (800) 223-7768
216 1st Ave. W • Newark, NJ 07107
E-Mail: info@ethicalpet.com
Website: www.ethicalpet.com
Fax Ordering: (973) 484-4830
International Ordering: (973) 484-1000
Contact Name: Jonathan Zelinger, President
Catalog: Free. Frequency: Annual
Circulation: 250K. Sales: $10-50MM
Products: Wholesale pet supplies

FINNEY WORLD CLASS (800) 543-4921
PET PRODUCTS
147 Circle Freeway Dr.
Cincinnati, OH 45246
Fax Ordering: (513) 874-7269
International Ordering: (513) 874-5383
Catalog: Free. Frequency: Quarterly
Circulation: 100K. Sales: $500K
Products: Pet foods, products & supplies

GEORGE CATALOG (877) 322-3232
55 Dorman Ave.
San Francisco, CA 94124
E-Mail: info@georgesf.com
Website: www.georgesf.com
Fax Ordering: (415) 642-1534
International Ordering: (415) 642-0684
Contact Name: Bobby Wise, President
Catalog: Free. Frequency: Annual
Circulation: 25K. Sales: $1-3MM
Products: Dog & cat pet supplies

GLOBAL PIGEON SUPPLIES (800) 562-2295
2301 Rowland Ave.
Savannah, GA 31404
E-Mail: gpswo@aol.com
Website: www.globalpigeon.com
Fax Ordering: (912) 356-1691
International Ordering: (912) 356-1320
Contact Name: Bert Oostlander, President
Catalog: Free. Frequency: Annual
Circulation: 25K. Sales: $3-5MM
Products: Supplies for racing pigeon hobby,
including lofts & medication

GREAT COMPANIONS (800) 829-2138
P.O. Box 200 • Orange City, IA 51041
E-Mail: custserv@greatcompanions.com
Website: www.greatcompanions.com
Fax Ordering: (800) 734-4750
International Ordering: (912) 356-1320
Catalog: Free. Frequency: Semiannual
Circulation: 50K. Sales: $3-5MM
Products: Bird cages & accessories;
bird food, treats, toys, grooming &
cleaning products

HEARTLAND VETERINARY (800) 934-9398
SUPPLY & PHARMACY
401 W. 33rd St. • Hastings, NE 68901
E-Mail: info@heartlandvetsupply.com
Website: www.heartlandvetsupply.com
Fax Ordering: (888) 424-0484
Catalog: Free. Frequency: Semiannual
Circulation: 100K. Sales: $5-10MM
Products: Veterinary supplies; pet products
& supplies

HORST COMPANY CATALOG (800) 221-4724
937 A St. • Greeley, CO 80631
E-Mail: horst@horstcompany.com
Website: www.horstcompany.com
Fax Ordering: (970) 353-7774
International Ordering: (970) 353-7724
Contact Name: Dan Horst, President
Catalog: Free. Frequency: Semiannual
Circulation: 10K. Sales: $500K to $1MM
Products: Customized animal enclosures:
kennels, cages & accessories

IN THE COMPANY OF DOGS (800) 544-4595
P.O. Box 3330 • Chelmsford, MA 01824
E-Mail: info@inthecompanyofdogs.com
Website: www.inthecompanyofdogs.com
Fax Ordering: (800) 952-5638
International Ordering: (978) 256-2492
Customer Service: (800) 544-4595
Contact Name: Kathy & Ted Royce
Catalog: Free. Pages: 52. Frequency: Quarterly
Circulation: 150M. Sales: $1-3MM
Products: Gifts and gear for dogs &
their owners

J-B WHOLESALE PET SUPPLIES (800) 526-0388
5 Raritan Rd. • Oakland, NJ 07436
E-Mail: info@jbpet.com
Website: www.jbpet.com
Fax Ordering: (201) 405-1706
International Ordering: (201) 405-1111
Contact Name: Bill Scolnik, President
Catalog: Free. Frequency: 10x per year
Minimum Order: $25.
Circulation: 100K. Sales: $5-10MM
Products: Vet, kennel & pet supplies

JEFFERS CATALOG (800) 533-3377
P.O. Box 100 • Dothan, AL 36302
E-Mail: info@jefferspet.com
Website: www.jefferspet.com
Fax Ordering: (334) 793-5179
International Ordering: (334) 793-6257
Contact Names: Dr. Keith Jeffers, President
Catalog: Free. Frequency: Quarterly
Circulation: 100K. Sales: $10-20MM
Products: Vet & livestock supplies

KENNEL-AIRE CATALOG (800) 346-0134
3580 Holly Lane N • Plymouth, MN 55447
Fax Ordering: (763) 519-0522
International Ordering: (763) 519-0521
Contact Name: Mike Pouers, President
Catalog: Free. Frequency: Annual
Circulation: 25K. Sales: $1-3MM
Products: Dog cages, kennels & supplies

KV VET SUPPLY / KV HEALTHLINKS (800) 423-8211
3190 N Rd. • David City, NE 68632 (877) 345-3848
E-Mail: sales@kvsupply.com
Website: www.kvsupply.com
Fax Ordering: (800) 269-0093; (402) 367-6214
International Sales: (402) 367-6047
Contact Names: Dr. Raymond Metzner, President
Catalog: Free. Frequency: Semiannual
Circulation: 100K. Sales: $10-20MM
Products: Dog, cat & horse supplies

LAFEBER COMPANY CATALOG (800) 842-6445
24981 N 1400 E Rd.
Cornell, IL 61319
E-Mail: info@lafeber.com
Website: www.lafeber.com
Fax Ordering: (815) 358-2352
International Ordering: (815) 358-2301
Contact Name: Jim Buscher, Marketing
Catalog: Free. Frequency: Annual
Circulation: 25K. Sales: $500M
Products: Pet bird food & treats

LAZY HILL FARM DESIGNS (800) 369-3566
P.O. Box 235 • Colerain, NC 27924
E-Mail: gardendesigns@lazyhill.com
Website: www.lazyhill.com
Fax Ordering: (252) 356-2040
International Ordering: (252) 356-2828
Contact Name: Betty Baker, President
Catalog: Free. Frequency: Weekly
Circulation: 50K. Sales: $500M to $1MM
Products: Bird houses, feeders & garden
furniture

LEATHER BROTHERS CATALOG (800) 442-5522
1314 Nabbolz Ave. • Conway, AR 72033
E-Mail: info@leatherbrothers.com
Website: www.leatherbrothers.com
Fax Ordering: (501) 730-0324
International Ordering: (501) 329-9471
Contact Name: Louis Schrekenhofer, President
Catalog: Free. Frequency: Annual
Circulation: 150K. Sales: $5-10MM
Products: Wholesale pet supplies

MAIL ORDER PET SHOP CATALOG (800) 326-6677
250 W. Executive Dr. • Edgewood, NY 11717
E-Mail: info@mopetshop.com
Website: www.mopetshop.com
Fax Ordering: (800) 877-3834
International Ordering: (631) 595-1782

Contact Name: Philip A. Steiner, President
Catalog: Free. Frequency: Annual
Circulation: 750M. Sales: $5-10MM
Products: Discount products for dogs,
cats, aquariums, birds & reptiles

MASON COMPANY CATALOG   (800) 543-5567
260 Depot St. • Leesburg, OH 45135
E-Mail: info@masonco.com
Website: www.masonco.com
Fax Ordering: (937) 780-6336
International Ordering: (937) 780-2321
Contact Name: Bruce Rowe, President
Catalog: Free. Frequency: Annual
Circulation: 50K. Sales: $3-5MM
Products: Modular dog cages & kennels

MASTER ANIMAL CARE CATALOG   (800) 346-0749
Humboldt Industries
1 Maplewood Dr. • Hazleton, PA 18201
E-Mail: info@masteranimalcare.com
Website: www.masteranimalcare.com
Fax Ordering: (570) 384-2500
International Ordering: (570) 384-5555
Contact Name: Judith Patterson, President
Catalog: Free. Frequency: 11x per year
Circulation: 3MM. Sales: $20-50MM
Products: Wholesale distributor of dog
& cat pet supplies & gifts

MERION MAIL ORDER COPANY   (800) 333-8247
P.O. Box 11 • Jenkintown, PA 19046
E-Mail: katz1233@aol.com
Fax Ordering: (215) 885-6281
International Ordering: (973) 484-1000
Contact Name: Linda R. Katz, President
Catalog: Free. Frequency: Bimonthly
Circulation: 50K. Sales: $500K
Products: Pet supplies

NEW ENGLAND SERUM COMPANY   (800) 637-3786
P.O. Box 128 • Topsfield, MA 01983
E-Mail: info@neserum.com
Website: www.neserum.com
Fax Ordering: (978) 887-8499
International Ordering: (978) 887-2368
Contact Name: Andy Katz, President
Catalog: Free. Frequency: Monthly
Circulation: 150K. Sales: $20-50MM
Products: Pet care products & equipment
for petcare professionals

PET DOORS USA   (800) 749-9609
4523 30th St. West
Bradenton, FL 34207
E-Mail: support@dogdoors.com;
  support@catdoors.com
Website: www.dogdoors.com; catdoors.com
Fax Ordering: (800) 283-8045; (941) 758-0274
International Ordering: (941) 758-1951
Contact Name: Joseph Ambrose, President
Catalog: Free. Frequency: Annual
Circulation: 100K. Sales: $3-5MM
Products: Plexidor pet doors for dogs & cats

PET SUPPLIES DELIVERED CATALOG   (800) 367-4444
FIRST PLACE EQUINE CATALOG
Omaha Vaccine Co. - CSR Co., Inc.
11143 Mockingbird Dr. • Omaha, NE 68137
E-Mail: customerservice@omahavaccine.com
Website: www.omahavaccine.com
Fax Ordering: (800) 242-9447

Catalog: Free. Frequency: Semiannual
Circulation: 150K. Sales: $10-25MM
Products: Dog, cat & horse supplies;
bird/ferret supplies; Rx products;

PET SUPPLIERS 4 LESS   (877) 813-7387
P.O. Box 214 • Fairbury, NE 68352
E-Mail: sales@petsupplies4less.com
Website: www.petsupplies4less.com
Fax Ordering: (866) 787-1185
Catalog: Free. Frequency: Semiannual
Circulation: 100K. Sales: $10-50M
Products: Pet care products; videos

PETCARE RX   (800) 844-1427
52 Merton Ave. • Lynbrook, NY 11563
E-Mail: sales@petcarerx.com
Website: www.petcarerx.com
Fax Ordering: (888) 295-5216
Catalog: Online. Sales: $3-5M
Products: Pet pharmacy & supplies.
Veterinarians can fax prescriptions

PETMARKET.COM   (800) 782-0627
KVS Corp.
P.O. Box 523 • Laurel, DE 19956
E-Mail: info@petmarket.com
Website: www.petmarket.com
Fax Ordering: (302) 875-1310
International Ordering: (302) 875-7111
Contact Name: Meryl Kretschmann, President
Catalog: Free. Frequency: Annual
Circulation: 150K. Sales: $3-5MM
Products: Discounted dog & cat supplies,
including grooming & kennel supplies

PETSMART DIRECT CATALOG   (888) 839-9638
P.O. Box 910 • Brockport, NY 14420   (800) 872-3773
E-Mail: cs@petsmart.com   (800) 548-4786
Website: www.petsmart.com
Fax Ordering: (716) 637-8244
International Ordering: (716) 637-7508
Contact Name: Robert F. Moran, President
Catalog: Free. Frequency: Monthly
Circulation: 7MM. Sales: $100-500MM
Products: Pet products & supplies for
profesionals & consumers; vet, kennel &
groomer supplies; animal-oriented gifts

PETSOLUTIONS   (800) 737-3868
802 N. Orchard Lane
Beavercreek, OH 45434
E-Mail: petinfo@petsolutions.com
Website: www.800.com
Fax Ordering: (866) 257-8774
Catalog: Free. Frequency: Semiannual
Circulation: 100K. Sales: $1-3MM
Products: Pet supplies for dogs, cats,
birds, fish & reptiles.

RAE'S HARNESS SHOP CATALOG   (800) 770-1177
401 W. International Airport
Anchorage, AK 99518
E-Mail: info@raesharness.com
Website: www.raesharness.com
Fax Ordering: (907) 563-2581
International Ordering: (907) 563-3411
Contact Name: Patricia Rae, President
Catalog: $5. Frequency: Semiannual
Circulation: 25K. Sales: $1-3MM
Products: Working dog & sled dog equipment

SAFEGUARD PRODUCTS CATALOG   (800) 433-1819
P.O. Box 8 • New Holland, PA 17557
E-Mail: info@safeguardproducts.com
Website: www.safeguardproducts.com
Fax Ordering: (717) 355-2505
International Ordering: (717) 354-4586
Contact Names: Willis Kurtz, President
Catalog: Free. Frequency: Semiannual
Circulation: 100K. Sales: $5-10MM
Products: Pet homes

SCOTT'S DOG SUPPLY CATALOG   (800) 966-3647
9252 Crawfordsville Rd.
Indianapolis, IN 46234
E-Mail: info@scottsdog.com
Website: www.scottsdog.com
Fax Ordering: (317) 293-9852
International Ordering: (317) 293-9850
Contact Name: C.J. Murphy, President
Catalog: Free. Frequency: Annual
Circulation: 75K. Sales: $500K to $1MM
Products: Dog supplies, hunting equipment

SHAMPOO-CHEZ CATALOG   (800) 727-7387
56 Chandon • Laguna Niguel, CA 92677
E-Mail: info@shampoochez.com
Website: www.shampoochez.com
Fax Ordering: (949) 495-9330
International Ordering: (949) 495-8554
Contact Name: Jonathan Rivers, President
Catalog: Free. Frequency: Annual
Circulation: 300K. Sales: $500K
Products: Natural pet products

SPORTING DOG SPECIALTIES CATALOG   (800) 972-3773
R.C. Steele
1989 Transit Way • Brockport, NY 14420
E-Mail: info@rcsteele.com
Website: www.rcsteele.com
Fax Ordering: (716) 637-7625
International Ordering: (716) 352-9160
Contact Name: Tony Leonardi, President
Catalog: Free. Frequency: 5x per year
Circulation: 50K. Sales: $1-3MM
Products: Breeding & showing pet supplies

SWELLAND'S CAGE & SUPPLY CATALOG   (800) 662-2089
1414 Barnett Rd. • Ramona, CA 92065
216 1st Ave. W • Newark, NJ 07107
E-Mail: swelland@adnc.com
Website: www.swellands.com
Fax Ordering: (760) 789-2994
International Ordering: (760) 789-3572
Contact Name: Dave Swelland, President
Catalog: Free. Frequency: Annual
Circulation: 150K. Sales: $500K - $1MM
Products: Bird cages & supplies

THAT FISH PLACE   (877) 255-7387
237 Centerville Rd. • Lancaster, PA 17603
Fax Ordering: (717) 295-7210
International Ordering: (717) 299-5691
Contact Name: Bernard Leboowitz, President
Catalog: Free. Frequency: Quarterly
Circulation: 200K. Sales: $1-3MM
Products: Supplies for fish & reptiles

TRAINERS CHOICE CATALOG   (800) 678-7535
231 Morrison Rd. • Columbus, OH 43213
E-Mail: info@k9stuff.com
Website: www.k9stuff.com
Fax Ordering: (614) 759-4718
International Ordering: (614) 864-0336
Contact Name: Donna Mueller, President
Catalog: $2. Frequency: Annual
Circulation: 150M. Sales: $500K - $1MM
Products: Dog training supplies & equipment

UPCO WHOLESALE PET SUPPLIES   (800) 444-8651
P.O. Box 969 • St. Joseph, MO 64502   (800) 254-8726
E-Mail: sales@upco.com
Website: www.upco.com
Fax Ordering: (816) 233-9696
International Ordering: (816) 233-8800
Contact Name: Frank Evans, President
Catalog: Free. Pages: 210. Frequency: Annual
Circulation: 250K. Sales: $10-20MM
Products: Wholesale pet supplies; products
for pet owners, veterinarians & stores

VALLEY VET SUPPLY -   (800) 468-0059
P.O. Box 504 • Marysville, KS 66508   (800) 356-1005
E-Mail: service@valleyvet.com
Website: www.valleyvet.com
Fax Ordering: (800) 446-5597
International Ordering: (785) 562-5106
Contact Name: Arnold Nagely, President
Catalog: Free. Pages: 96. Frequency: Quarterly
Circulation: 100K. Sales: $10-20MM
Products: Veterinarian equipment & supplies;
Fram & Ranch & Equine Editions

VET MED DIRECT   (877) 483-8633
414 G St. • Fairbury, NE 68352
E-Mail: kim@vetmeddirect.com
Website: www.vetmeddirect.com
Fax Ordering: (866) 787-1185
International Ordering: (402) 729-5354
Catalog: Free. Frequency: Semiannual
Circulation: 150K. Sales: $5-10MM
Products: Veterinary quality pet supplies

VET-VAX CATALOG   (800) 369-8297
P.O. Box 400 • Tonganoxie, KS 66086
E-Mail: orders@vetvax.com
Website: www.vetvax.com
Fax Ordering: (620) 325-3098
International Ordering: (620) 325-2250
Contact Name: Bud Moomau, President
Catalog: Free. Frequency: Semiannual
Circulation: 50K. Sales: $5-10MM
Products: Vaccines, medications,
supplements & grooming supplies for pets
& livestock; pet toys & training equipment

ABC PHOTO & IMAGING SERVICES (703) 369-1906
9016 Prince William St.
Manassas, VA 20110
E-Mail: info@imageabc.com
Website: www.imageabc.com
Fax Ordering: (703) 631-8064
International Ordering: (703) 369-1906
Contact Names: Wes Billstone, President
Catalog: Free. Frequency: Monthly
Circulation: 25K. Sales: $1-3MM
Products: Digital imaging, film processing,
wedding & portrait printing, displays & exhibits

ADORAMA CAMERA (800) 223-2500
42 W. 18th St. • New York, NY 10011
E-Mail: info@adorama.com
Website: www.adorama.com
Fax Ordering: (212) 463-7223 ; 741-9087
International Ordering: (800) 815-0702
Customer Service: (800) 221-5743
   Fax (212) 645-4533
Contact Names: M. Mendlewitz, President
Catalog: Free. Frequency: Quarterly
Circulation: 25K. Sales: $5-10MM
Products: Cameras & lenses; cell phones
& accessories;albums, storage & frames;
batteries & chargers; film & darkroom;
binoculars & scopes; underwater cameras

ALBUMS, INC. (800) 827-0363
                 (800) 662-1000
15900 Foltz Pkwy.
Strongsville, OH 44149
E-Mail: customercare@albumsinc.com
Website: www.albumsinc.com
Fax Ordering: (800) 662-3102
International Ordering: (216) 781-6000
Contact Names: Michele Cardello, President
Catalog: Free. Frequency: Annual
Circulation: 150K. Sales: $10-20MM
Products: Photographic albums

B&H PHOTO VIDEO (800) 606-6969
420 9th Ave. • New York, NY 10001
E-Mail: info@bhphotovideo.com
Website: www.bhphotovideo.com
Fax Ordering: (866) 521-7375; (212) 502-9426
International Ordering: (212) 239-7765
Customer Service: (800) 221-5743
Contact Names: Sam Goldstein, President
Catalog: Free. Frequency: Annual
Circulation: 100K. Sales: $5-10MM
Products: Photography & imaging equipment,
video & pro-audio equipment & supplies

BERGER BROTHERS (800) 542-8811
DIGITAL PHOTOGRAPHY & VIDEO
209 Broadway • Amityville, NY 11701
E-Mail: info@berger-bros.com
Website: www.berger-bros.com
Fax Ordering: (631) 264-1007
International Ordering: (631) 264-4160
Contact Names: Brad Berger, President
Catalog: Free. Frequency: Semiannual
Circulation: 250K. Sales: $5-10MM
Products: Photographic equipment &
accessories

CAMERA WORLD CATALOG (800) 226-3721
P.O. Box 19705 • Irvine, CA 92623
E-Mail: info@cameraworld.com
Website: www.cameraworld.com
Fax Ordering: (877) 333-9957

International Ordering: (503) 207-8000
Contact Names: Curtis Scheel, President
Catalog: Free. Frequency: Annual
Circulation: 100K. Sales: $10-50MM
Products: Cameras, photography equipment,
supplies & accessories

VERONICA CASS, INC. (800) 472-9336
7506 New Jersey Ave. • Hudson, FL 34667
Fax Ordering: (727) 727-3567
International Ordering: (727) 863-2738
Contact Names: Veronica Cass, President
Catalog: Free. Frequency: Annual
Circulation: 100K. Sales: $3-5MM
Products: Photographic retouching supplies;
archival storage materials for storage of
photographs, negatives & slides

CENTURY PHOTO PRODUCTS CATALOG (800) 767-0777
P.O. Box 2100
Santa Fe Springs, CA 90670
E-Mail: info@centuryphoto.com
Website: www.centuryphoto.com
Fax Ordering: (800) 786-7939
Contact Names: Bill Martin, President
Catalog: Free. Frequency: Quarterly
Circulation: 1MM. Sales: $5-10MM
Products: Photo products, including albums,
scrapbooks & accessories

CPM/DELTA 1 DARKROOM (800) 627-0252
CPM • 10830 Sanden Dr.
Dallas, TX 75238
E-Mail: teresa@cpmdelta1.com
Website: www.cpmdelta1.com
Fax Ordering: (214) 503-1557
International Ordering: (214) 349-6886
Contact Names: Teresa Dingus, Manager
Catalog: Free. Frequency: Annual
Circulation: 25K. Sales: $500K to $1MM
Products: Studio & darkroom equipment
& accessories

CREATIVE VIDEO PRODUCTS (800) 339-8158
P.O. Box 7032 • Endicott, NY 13761
E-Mail: info@creativevideopro.com
Website: www.creativevideopro.com
Fax Ordering: (607) 754-0476
International Ordering: (607) 754-6767
Catalog: Free. Frequency: Annual
Circulation: 25K. Sales: $500K to $1MM
Products: Photo albums & photo mounts,
specializing in videocassette albums;

ELKHART CASES (800) 582-0319
P.O. Box 1414 • Elkhart, IN 46515
E-Mail: elkcases@aol.com
Contact Names: Dale D. Fahlbeck, President
Catalog: Free. Frequency: Annual
Circulation: 10K. Sales: $500M to $1MM
Products: Custom carrying cases for
instruments, camcorders & cameras

EXPOSURES (800) 222-4947
Miles Kimball
P.O. Box 3615 • Oshkosh, WI 54903
E-Mail: csr@exposuresonline.com
Website: www.exposuresonline.com
Fax Ordering: (800) 699-6993; (920) 231-6942
International Ordering: (920) 231-3800
Customer Service: (800) 572-5750
Contact Names: Randy Bourne, President

Catalog: Free. Frequency: 11x per year
Circulation: 100K. Sales: $3-5MM
Products: Picture frames, photo albums,
photo-related gifts, photo storage systems

FOCUS CAMERA (800) 221-0828
4523 13th Ave. • Brooklyn, NY 11219
E-Mail: info@focuscamera.com
Website: www.focuscamera.com
Fax Ordering: (800) 863-6287;
   (718) 437-8895
International Ordering: (718) 437-8810
Customer Service: (888) 901-4438;
   (718) 437-8899
Catalog: Free. Frequency: Quarterly
Circulation: 100K. Sales: $5-10MM
Products: Cameras, video, telescopes &
binoculars; home electronics; appliances;
housewares; watches; luggage.

FOTOSEARCH/PUBLISHING PERFECTION (800) 827-7495
Publiteck, Inc. (800) 827-3920
21155 Watertown Rd.
Waukesha, WI 53186
E-Mail: purchaseimages@fotosearch.com
E-Mail: ct59@pubperfect.com
Website: www.pubperfect.com
Website: www.fotosearch.com
Fax Ordering: (262) 717-0745
International Ordering: (262) 717-0740/0600
Catalog: Free. Pages: 72. Frequency: Annual
Circulation: 250K. Sales: $20-50MM
Products: Stock photography, rights-managed
photos, stock illustration, clip art graphics maps,
stock footage video clips, stock music audio
clips; graphic design software

FRANK'S HIGHLAND PARK CAMERA (323) 255-5151
5715 N. Figueroa St.
Los Angeles, CA 90042
E-Mail: info@frankscamera.com
Website: www.frankscamera.com
Fax Ordering: (323) 255-1036
International Ordering: (323) 255-0123
Contact Name: Frank Vacek, President
Catalog: $3. Frequency: Semiannual
Circulation: 50K. Sales: $1-3MM
Products: Cameras, photographic equipment
& accessories; filters & adapter rings

FREESTYLE PHOTOGRAPHIC SUPPLIES (800) 292-6137
5124 Sunset Blvd. • Hollywood, CA 90027
E-Mail: info@freestylephoto.biz
Website: www.freestylephoto.biz
Fax Ordering: (800) 616-3686
International Ordering: (323) 660-3460
Catalog: Free. Frequency: Semiannual
Circulation: 100K. Sales: $3-5MM
Products: Cameras, photographic
supplies & accessories

IKELITE UNDERWATER SYSTEMS (317) 923-4523
50 West 33rd St. • Indianapolis, IN 46208
E-Mail: ikelite@ikelite.com
Website: www.ikelite.com
Fax Ordering: (317) 924-7988
Contact Names: O.H. Brigham, President
Catalog: Free. Frequency: Annual
Circulation: 15K. Sales: $5-10MM
Products: Underwater camera housings
& accessories

INTERNATIONAL CENTER OF PHOTOGRAPHY (800) 688-8171
1133 Ave. of the Americas
New York, NY 10036
E-Mail: info@icp.org or store@icp.org
Website: www.icp.org
Fax Ordering: (212) 857-0090
International Ordering: (212) 857-0002
Catalog: Free. Frequency: Annual
Circulation: 50K. Sales: $1-3MM
Products: Photography books &
related gifts

KEH CAMERA BROKERS (800) 342-5534
4900 Highlands Pkwy. SE • Smyna, GA 30082
E-Mail: sales@keh.com
Website: www.keh.com
Fax Ordering: (770) 333-4242
International Ordering: (770) 333-4220
Contact Names: King Grant, Jr., President
Catalog: Free. Frequency: Annual
Circulation: 50K. Sales: $3-5MM
Products: Used cameras, photographic products

KODAK PROFESSIONAL (800) 242-2424
PHOTOGRAPHIC CATALOG
343 State St. • Rochester, NY 14650
E-Mail: info@kodak.com
Website: www.kodak.com
Fax Ordering: (716) 724-0663
International Ordering: (716) 724-4000
Contact Names: Daniel Carp, President
Catalog: Free. Frequency: Annual
Circulation: 25K. Sales: $20-50MM
Products: Photographic products; papers,
chemicals, films & publications

LIGHT-IMPRESSIONS (800) 828-6216
P.O. Box 2100 • Santa Fe Springs, CA 90670
E-Mail: info@limpressionsdirect.com
Website: www.lightimpressionsdirect.com
Fax Ordering: (800) 828-5539
Catalog: Free. Frequency: Quarterly
Circulation: 25K. Sales: $5-10MM
Products: Archival & presentation supplies;
storage materials for storage of photographs,
negatives & slides; photography supplies

THE MILLER GROUP (800) 325-3350
1112 Westmark Dr. • St. Louis, MO 63131
E-Mail: info@themillergroup.com
Website: www.themillergroup.com
Fax Ordering: (314) 822-6504
International Ordering: (314) 822-8090
Contact Names: Kathy Webster, President
Catalog: Free. Frequency: Annual
Circulation: 25K. Sales: $1-3MM
Products: Systems for displaying charts,
photos, frame art, molding, etc.

MODERNAGE CUSTOM (212) 997-1800
DIGITAL IMAGING LABS
1150 Sixth Ave. • New York, NY 10036
E-Mail: info@modernage.com
Website: www.modernage.com
Fax Ordering: (212) 869-4796
Contact Names: Rick Troiano, President
Catalog: Free. Frequency: Annual
Circulation: 15K. Sales: $3-5MM
Products: Full-service custom lab
specializing in single roll development,
duratrans, duraflex or C-prints to any size

NATIONAL CAMERA EXCHANGE (888) 873-1979
National Camera Exchange & Video
9300 Olson Hwy. • Golden Valley, MN 55427
E-Mail: sales@natcam.com
Website: www.natcam.com
Fax Ordering: (763) 546-7043
International Ordering: (763) 591-5175
Contact Name: Jon Liss, President
Catalog: Free. Frequency: 36x per year
Circulation: 150K. Sales: $5-10MM
Products: Binoculars & cameras;
spotting scopes & accessories

NEGAFILE SYSTEMS (800) 523-5874
Electron Microscopy Sciences
P.O. Box 550 • Hatfield, PA 18925
E-Mail: sgkcck@aol.com
Website: www.negafile.com
Fax Ordering: (215) 412-8450
International Ordering: (215) 412-8400
Contact Names: Peter Goodman, President
Catalog: Free. Frequency: Annual
Circulation: 25K. Sales: $1-3MM
Products: Photographic print & slide files;
storage products

NIKON USA (800) 247-3464
1300 Walt Whitman Rd. • Melville, NY 11747
E-Mail: sales@nikonusa.com
Website: www.nikonusa.com
Fax Ordering: (800) 645-6687
International Ordering: (631) 547-4200
Catalog: Free. Frequency: Semiannual
Circulation: 250K. Sales: $50-100MM
Products: Digital camers, camcorders,
scanners, binoculars/scopes, microscopes,
instruments, surveying

NORMAN CAMERA & VIDEO (800) 900-6676
3602 S. Westnedge Ave.
Kalamazoo, MI 49008
E-Mail: sales@normancamera.com
Website: www.normancamera.com
Fax Ordering: (616) 343-6410
International Ordering: (616) 3443-0460
Contact Names: Mert Norman, President
Catalog: Free. Frequency: Annual
Circulation: 50K. Sales: $5-10MM
Products: Photo equipment, camera
accessories, videos

OPTECH USA (800) 848-6624
304 Andrea Dr. • Belgrade, MT
Fax Ordering: (406) 388-2063
International Ordering: (406) 388-1377
Contact Names: Gary Keleshian, President
Catalog: Free. Frequency: Annual
Circulation: 25K. Sales: $3-5MM
Products: Projection lamps for photography;
straps & harnesses; lens/Optics; tripod
accessories; digital accessories; general
accessories; rain covers

PHOTO THERM- (609) 396-1456
TEMPERATURE CONTROLS
110 Sewell Ave. • Trenton, NJ 08610
E-Mail: serve@phototherm.com
Website: www.phototherm.com
Fax Ordering: (609) 396-9395
Contact Names: Roman Kuzyk, President
Catalog: Free. Frequency: Semiannual
Circulation: 25K. Sales: $3-5MM

Products: Portable automatic film processors,
temperature controls, plasma thawing units,
dryers for slides & negatives

PHOTOGRAPHER'S CATALOG (800) 225-8638
Calumet Photographic
890 Supreme Dr. • Bensenville, IL 60106
E-Mail: custserv@calumetphoto.com
Website: www.calumetphoto.com
Fax Ordering: (800) 577-3686
International Ordering: (630) 860-7447
Customer Service: (800) 453-2550
Contact Names: Peter Beasotti President
Catalog: Free. Frequency: Annual
Circulation: 100K. Sales: $10-20MM
Products: Photographic accessories;
high quality imaging products

PHOTOGRAPHERS FORMULARY (800) 922-5255
P.O. Box 950 • Condon, MT 59826
E-Mail: formulary@blackfoot.net
Website: www.photoformulary.com
Fax Ordering: (406) 754-2896
International Ordering: (406) 754-2891
Contact Names: Lynn Wilson, President
Catalog: Free. Frequency: Annual
Circulation: 25K. Sales: $3-5MM
Products: Photograde chemicals,
alternative processes, toners, holography,
and intensifiers

PIERCE COMPANY (800) 338-9801
3307 Snelling Ave. S • Minneapolis, MN 55406
E-Mail: sales@thepierceco.com
Website: www.thepierceco.com
Fax Ordering: (612) 721-7279
International Ordering: (612) 721-7254
Contact Names: Robert Day, President
Catalog: Free. Frequency: Annual
Circulation: 25K. Sales: $3-5MM
Products: Photo supplies & accessories

PITTSBURGH CAMERA EXCHANGE (412) 422-6372
529 E. Ohio St. • Pittsburgh, PA 15212
E-Mail: spiratone@juno.com
Website: www.spiratone.com
Fax Ordering: (412) 321-4209
International Ordering: (412) 321-4200
Contact Names: David Porco, President
Catalog: Free. Frequency: Annual
Circulation: 150K. Sales: $5-10MM
Products: Photographic supplies;
enlargement equipment & supplies

PORTER'S CAMERA STORE (800) 553-2001
P.O. Box 628 • Cedar Falls, IA 50613
E-Mail: pcsgeneralmail@porters.com
Website: www.porters.com
Fax Ordering: (319) 277-5254
International Ordering: (319) 266-0303
Contact Names: Jeff Schmitt, President
Catalog: Free. Frequency: Monthly
Circulation: 250K. Sales: $5-10MM
Products: Digital cameras & imaging;
photographic equipment & supplies

REGAL/ARKAY CORP. (800) 695-2055
2769 S. 34th St. • Milwaukee, WI 53215
E-Mail: regalarkay@aol.com
Fax Ordering: (414) 645-9515
International Ordering: (414) 645-2050
Contact Names: Tony Milnar, President

Catalog: Free. Frequency: Annual
Circulation: 25K. Sales: $3-5MM
Products: Photographic darkroom
equipment

RITZ CAMERA   (877) 690-0099
6711 Ritz Way • Beltsville, MD 20705
P.O. Boix 19705 • Irvine, CA 92623
E-Mail: customerservice@ritzcamera.com
Website: www.ritzcamera.com
Fax Ordering: (877) 552-2244; (301) 419-2995
International Ordering: (301) 419-0000
Customer Service: (877) 999-7489
Contact Names: David Ritz, President
Catalog: Free. Frequency: Quarterly
Circulation: 100K. Sales: $10-20MM
Products: Photographic equipment
& accessories

RIZZOLI/UNIVERSE   (800) 733-3000
INTERNATIONAL PUBLICATIONS
300 Park Ave. So., 3rd FL.
New York, NY 10010
E-Mail: sales@rizzoliusa.com
Website: www.rizzoliusa.com
Fax Ordering: (212) 387-3535
International Ordering: (212) 387-3400
Contact Names: William Gworkin,, Marketing
Catalog: FREE. Frequency: Annual
Circulation: 50K. Sales: $5-10MM
Products: Books on art, architecture
& photography

ROCKLAND COLLOID CORP.   (845) 359-5559
P.O. Box 376 • Piermont, NY 10968
E-Mail: info@rockaloid.com
Website: www.rockaloid.com
Fax Ordering: (866) 737-0174; (845) 365-6663
Contact Names: Robert Cone, President
Catalog: Free. Frequency: Weekly
Circulation: 50K. Sales: $1-3MM
Products: Photographic chemcials

L.L. RUE CATALOG   (908) 362-6616
Leonard Rue Enterprises
138 Millbrook Rd. • Blairstown, NJ 07825
E-Mail: rue@rue.com
Website: www.rue.com
Fax Ordering: (908) 362-5808
International Ordering: (908) 362-6616
Contact Name: Leonard Rue, III, President
Catalog: Free. Frequency: Semiannual
Circulation: 100K. Sales: $3-5MM
Products: Photographic equipment,
books, videos

SAMY'S CAMERA CATALOG   (800) 321-4726
475 S. Fairfax Ave. • Los Angeles, CA 90036   (866) 726-9463
E-Mail: industrial@samys.com
Website: www.samys.com
Fax Ordering: (323) 937-2919; 692-0750
International Ordering: (323) 938-2420
Contact Names: Samy Kamienowicz, President
Catalog: Free. Frequency: Semiannual
Circulation: 100K. Sales: $5-10MM
Products: Cameras, lenses & accessories;
lighting, digital imaging, darkroom equipment
& supplies; printers, scanners & supplies;
binoculars & scopes; video & film

SIGMA CORPORATION OF AMERICA   (800) 896-6858
15 Fleetwood Ct. • Ronkonkoma, NY 11779
E-Mail: info@sigmaphoto.com
Website: www.sigmaphoto.com
Fax Ordering: (631) 585-1895 or 585-7661
International Ordering: (631) 585-1144
Contact Names: Yoshio Yamaki, President
Catalog: Free. Frequency: Semiannual
Circulation: 100K. Sales: $20-50MM
Products: Fully automatic Sigma Digital
& 35mm autofocus SLR cameras

SKOLNICK PHOTO FRAMES, INC.   (800) 972-5286
29245 Dequindre Rd. • Madison Hts., MI 48071
E-Mail: info@skolnicks.com
Website: www.skolnicks.com
Fax Ordering: (248) 547-2449
International Ordering: (248) 547-0347
Contact Names: David B. Sandler, President
Catalog: Free. Frequency: Annual
Circulation: 50K. Sales: $1-3MM
Products: Photo albums & frames; folios,
photomounts & photo supplies

TAMRAC, INC.   (800) 662-0717
9240 Jordan Ave. • Chatsworth, CA 91311
E-Mail: mailboxY@tamrac.com
Website: www.tamrac.com
Fax Ordering: (818) 407-9501
International Ordering: (818) 407-9500
Contact Names: Jesselyn Cyr, President
Catalog: Free. Frequency: Annual
Circulation: 100K. Sales: $20-50MM
Products: Camera bags; photo backpacks
& accessories

THE TIFFEN COMPANY, LLC   (800) 645-2522
90 Oser Ave. • Hauppauge, NY 11788
E-Mail: techsupport@tiffen.com
Website: www.tiffen.com
Fax Ordering: (631) 273-2557
International Ordering: (631) 273-2500
Contact Names: Steven Tiffen, President
Catalog: Free. Frequency: Annual
Circulation: 100K. Sales: $20-50MM
Products: Tiffen digital camera lenses;
photographic filters & lens accessories;
tripods & steadicams; photo & imaging books

ULTIMA CASES   (727) 490-0449
2101 28th St. N. • St. Petersburg, FL 33713
E-Mail: customerservice@ultimacases.com
Website: www.ultimacases.com
Fax Ordering: (727) 490-0450
International Ordering: (727) 490-0449
Contact Names: Tom Messmer, President
Catalog: Free. Frequency: Annual
Circulation: 50K. Sales: $10-20MM
Products: Carrying cases for cameras,
videos, computers

VINTEN   (888) 284-6836
Camera Dynamics, Inc. The Vitec Group
709 Executive Blvd. • Valley Cottage, NY 10989
E-Mail: info-cd-usa@vitecgroup.com
Website: www.vinten.com
Fax Ordering: (845) 268-0113
International Ordering: (845) 268-0100
Contact Names: Joanne Snider, President
Catalog: Free. Frequency: Weekly
Circulation: 10K. Sales: $10-50MM
Products: Television camera support equipment

ALARM & SIGNAL SYSTEMS   (800) 237-6387
AES Corporation
285 Newbury St. • Peabody, MA 01960
E-Mail: sales@aes-intellinet.com
Website: www.aes-intellinet.com
Fax Ordering: (978) 535-7313
International Ordering: (978) 535-7310
Contact Names: Thomas Kenty, Manager
Catalog: Free. Frequency: Semiannual
Circulation: 50K. Sales: $10-20MM
Products: Residential & commercial security
alarm systems; wireless communication products

BRIGADE • QUARTERMASTERS   (800) 338-4327
P.O. Box 100001 • Kennesaw, GA 30156
E-Mail: info@brigadeqm.com
Website: www.brigadeqm.com
Fax Ordering: (800) 892-2999; (770) 426-7726
International Ordering: (770) 428-1234
Customer Service: (800) 228-7344
Catalog: Free. Frequency: Semiannual
Circulation: 150K. Sales: $5-10MM
Products: Tactical shorts & pants; gun
holsters, shoulder systems, cleaning systems,
slings, scopes; goggles, tactical gloves &
handcuffs, assault packs, backpacks, boots,
knives, flashlights, etc.

CSI/SPECO CATALOG   (800) 645-5516
200 New Hwy. • Amityville, NY 11701
E-Mail: info@csi-speco.com
Website: www.csi-speco.com
Fax Ordering: (631) 957-9142 or 957-3880
International Ordering: (631) 957-8700
Contact Name: L.W. Keller, President
Catalog: Free. Frequency: Annual
Circulation: 200K. Sales: $10-20MM
Products: Residential & commercial audio
& video security products specializing in
CCTV cameras, video monitors, in-wall
speakers

HOME AUTOMATION SYSTEMS   (800) 762-7846
Smarthome, Inc.
16542 Millikan Ave. • Irvine, CA 92606
E-Mail: custsvc@smarthome.com
Website: www.smarthome.com
Fax Ordering: (800) 242-7329 (949) 221-9240
International Ordering: (949) 221-9200
Contact Names: David Tan, President
Catalog: Free. Frequency: Annual
Circulation: 100K. Sales: $5-10MM
Products: Home security, automation,
wireless systems

HOME CONTROLS, INC.   (800) 266-8765
8525 Redwood Creek Ln.
San Diego, CA 92126
E-Mail: service@homecontrols.com
Website: www.homecontrols.com
Fax Ordering: (858) 693-8892
International Ordering: (858) 693-8887
Catalog: Free. Frequency: Annual
Circulation: 50K. Sales: $5-10MM
Products: Home automation products,
from security to phones

MARKET INTELLIGENCE & FORECASTING   (800) 451-4975
Forecast International
22 Commerce Rd. • Newtown, CT 06470
E-Mail: consulting@forecast1.com
Website: www.forecastinternational.com

Fax Ordering: (203) 426-0223
International Ordering: (203) 426-0800
Catalog: Free. Pages: 36. Frequency: Annual
Circulation: 50K. Sales: $20-50MM
Products: Aerospace, defense, electronics
& power systems

MOUNTAIN WEST ALARM SUPPLY CO.   (800) 528-6169
5116 E. Charter Oak Rd.
Scottsdale, AZ 85254
E-Mail: mountainwest@earthlink.net
Fax Ordering: (602) 996-5077
International Ordering: (602) 971-1200
Contact Name: Faye Dunbar
Catalog: Free. Frequency: Annual
Circulation: 150K. Sales: $5-10MM
Products: Consumer electronics, security
systems & products; fire systems

NATIONAL MARKER COMPANY   (800) 453-2727
100 Providence Pike
Slatersville, RI 02876
E-Mail: sales@nationalmarker.com
Website: www.nationalmarker.com
Fax Ordering: (800) 338-0309;
    (401) 762-1010
International Ordering: (401) 762-9700
Contact Names: Peter Bonner, President
Catalog: Free. Frequency: Annual
Circulation: 100K. Sales: $5-10MM
Products: Fire & safety identification
products & warning systems

QUARTERMASTER LAWPRO   (800) 444-8643
Quartermaster Uniform Company
P.O. Box 4147 • Cerritos, CA 90703
E-Mail: info@qmuniforms.com
Website: www.qmuniforms.com
Fax Ordering: (562) 304-7335
International Ordering: (562) 304-7300
Contact Name: Jennifer Miller, President
Catalog: Free. Frequency: Annual
Circulation: 1MM. Sales: $5-10MM
Products: Public safety, security &
military uniforms & equipment

ROBERTS EMT CATALOG   (800) 729-1482
Roberts Company
180 Franklin St.
Framingham, MA 01702
E-Mail: info@emtcatalog.com
Website: www.emtcatalog.com
Fax Ordering: (508) 879-3735
International Ordering: (508) 875-8877
Contact Names: Joseph Gross, President
Catalog: $3. Frequency: Quarterly
Circulation: 1MM. Sales: $5-10MM
Products: Police service equipment & supplies,
gifts, novelties, awards, badges, nametags

SANDPIPER TECHNOLOGIES   (209) 239-7460
535 W. Yosemite Ave.
Manteca, CA 95337
E-Mail: sales@sandpipertech.com
Website: www.sandpipertech.com
Fax Ordering: (209) 239-1571
International Ordering: (209) 239-7460
Contact Name: John Christensen, CEO
Catalog: Free Frequency: Annual
Circulation: 100K. Sales: $5-10MM
Products: Video cameras & surveillance
systems

SECURITY CAMERAS DIRECT   (800) 316-6027
1 Security Cameras Direct Way   (877) 316-6027
Luling, TX 78648
E-Mail: sales@scdlink.com
Website: www.scdlink.com
Fax Ordering: (830) 875-9010
Catalog: Free. Frequency: Annual
Circulation: 100K. Sales: $10-20MM
Products: Security cameras, monitors,
recorders, accessories, systems. In both
English & Spanish

SPY OUTLET   (716) 695-8660
2468 Niagara Falls Blvd.
Tonawanda, NY 14150
E-Mail: sales@spyoutlet.com
Website: www.spyoutlet.com
Fax Ordering: (716) 695-7380
Contact Names: Robert J. Crowley, President
Catalog: Free. Frequency: Semiannual
Circulation: 50K. Sales: $5-10MM
Products: Wholesale source for spy
cameras, bug detectors, surveillance &
security equipment; phone tap detectors,
vehicle tracking

ABBEON CAL, INC. PLASTIC WORKING (800) 922-0977
123 Gray Ave. • Santa Barbara, CA 93101
E-Mail: abbeoncal@abbeon.com
Website: www.abbeon1.com
Fax Ordering: (805) 966-7659
International Ordering: (805) 966-0810
Contact Name: A.J. Wertheim, President
Catalog: Free. Frequency: Semiannual
Circulation: 100K. Sales: $5-10MM
Products: Industrial instruments &
products; tools for working plastics

ACTION MINING SERVICES, INC. (800) 624-1511
37482 Ruben Lane • Sandy, OR 97055
E-Mail: contact_us@actionmining.com
Website: www.actionmining.com
Fax Ordering: (800) 711-7807; (503) 826-1340
International Ordering: (503) 826-9330
Contact Names: Nancy Glenn, Manager
Catalog: Free. Frequency: Annual
Circulation: 100K. Sales: $5-10MM
Products: Mining & laboratory equipment;
Micron Mill Wave Tables

ADVANCE SCIENTIFIC & CHEMICAL, INC. (800) 524-2436
2345 SW 34th St.
Fort Lauderdale, FL 33312
E-Mail: sales@advance-scientific.com
Website: www.advance-scientific.com
Fax Ordering: (954) 327-0903
International Ordering: (954) 327-0900
Catalog: $5. Frequency: Semiannual
Circulation: 100K. Sales: $5-10MM
Products: Laboratory chemicals & supplies;
lab glassware & instruments, microscopes
& supplies

ALL WEATHER, INC. (800) 824-5873
1165 National Dr.
Sacramento, CA 95834
E-Mail: info@allweatherinc.com
Website: www.allweatherinc.com
Fax Ordering: (916) 928-1165
International Ordering: (916) 928-1000
Contact Name: Don Soenen, President
Catalog: Free. Frequency: Annual
Circulation: 25K. Sales: $5-10MM
Products: Meteological equipment &
tactical weather measurement systems;
aviation weather systems; air traffic
control displays

AMBION CATALOG (800) 888-8804
Applied Biosystems
2130 Woodward St. • Austin, TX 78744
E-Mail: custom@ambion.com
Website: www.ambion.com
Fax Ordering: (512) 651-0190
International Ordering: (512) 651-0200
Contact Name: Bruce Leander, President
Catalog: Free. Frequency: Annual
Circulation: 50K. Sales: $10-20MM
Products: Products & technical information for
researchers whose work involves RNA analysis

AMERICAN GEOLOGICAL INSTITUTE (703) 379-2480
4220 King St. • Alexandria, VA 22302
Website: www.agiweb.org/pubs/catalog.html
E-Mail: jr@agiweb.org
Fax Ordering: (703) 379-7563
Contact Name: John P. Rasanen, Manager
Catalog: Online as PDF. Sales: $3-5MM

Products: Geologic posters, glossary
of geology, data pages, environmental
awareness series, books & magazines.

AMERICAN SCIENCE & SURPLUS (888) 724-7587
P.O. Box 1030 • Skokie, IL 60076
E-Mail: info@sciplus.com
Website: www.sciplus.com
Fax Ordering: (800) 934-0722
International Ordering: (847) 647-0011
Contact Name: Phillip Cable, President
Catalog: Free. Frequency: Monthly
Circulation: 1MM. Sales: $5-10MM
Products: Science tools and toys; surplus
equipment, military and electronic parts,
optics, lab and educational supplies,
magnets, motors, kits, books.

AMERICAN SLIDE CHART/PERRYGRAF (800) 323-4433
25W550 Geneva Rd.
Carol Stream, IL 60188
E-Mail: info2@americanperrygraf.com
Website: www.americanslidechart.com
Fax Ordering: (630) 665-3491
International Ordering: (630) 665-3333
Contact Name: James Johnson, President
Catalog: Free. Frequency: Annual
Circulation: 150K. Sales: $10-20MM
Products: Slide charts, wheel charts,
pop-ups

ANALYTICAL SCIENTIFIC, LTD. (800) 364-4848
11049 Bandera Rd.
San Antonio, TX 78250
E-Mail: info@analyticalsci.com
Website: www.analyticalsci.com
Fax Ordering: (210) 520-3344
International Ordering: (210) 684-7373
Contact Name: James Aldrich, Manager
Catalog: Free. Frequency: Semiannual
Circulation: 150K. Sales: $10-25MM
Products: Lab equipment and supplies;
science kits, telescopes, microscopes,
binoculars, biology & geology products;
books, videos, posters, toys.

ARBOR SCIENTIFIC (800) 367-6695
P.O. Box 2750 • Ann Arbor, MI 48106
E-Mail: peter@arborsci.com
Website: www.arborsci.com
Fax Ordering: (866) 477-9373; (734) 477-9373
International Ordering: (734) 477-9370
Contact Name: C. Peter Rea, President
Catalog: Free. Frequency: Semiannual
Circulation: 100K. Sales: $10-20MM
Products: Arbor labs and labware; physical
science demonstration products; elementary
science supplies; promotional items

ARROW ENGINEERING CO. (800) 724-8665
260 Pennsylvania Ave.
Hillside, NJ 07205
E-Mail: sales@arroweng.com
Website: www.arroweng.com
Fax Ordering: (908) 353-8362
International Ordering: (908) 353-5229
Contact Name: Lou Spitzer, President
Catalog: Free. Frequency: Annual
Circulation: 25K. Sales: $500K - $1MM
Products: Explosion-proof and electric overhead
stirrers and accessories; laboratory supplies,

ASTRONOMICAL SOCIETY
OF THE PACIFIC   (800) 335-2624
390 Ashton Ave. • San Francisco, CA 94112
E-Mail: service@astrosociety.org
Website: www.astrosociety.org
Fax Ordering: (415) 337-5205
International Ordering: (415) 337-1100
Contact Name: James Manning, Director
Catalog: Free. Frequency: Quarterly
Circulation: 200K. Sales: $1-3MM
Products: Astronomy posters, CD-ROMs,
books, videotapes, observing aids, slides,
educational materials & globes

ASTRONOMY RESOURCE MANUAL   (410) 366-1222
MMI Corporation
P.O. Box 19907 • Baltimore, MD 21211
E-Mail: mail@mmicorporation.com
Website: www.mmicorporation.com
Fax Ordering: (410) 366-6311
Contact Name: R.C. Levy, President
Catalog: Free. Frequency: Annual
Circulation: 25K. Sales: $1-3MM
Products: Astronomy materials for
educators, including slides, laserdiscs,
videos, CD-ROMs, globes, portable &
permanent planetariums, earth science
models, telescopes & teaching manuals.

BEL-ART PRODUCTS   (800) 423-5278
6 Industrial Rd. • Pequannock, NJ 07440
E-Mail: feedback@belart.com
Website: www.belart.com
Fax Ordering: (800) 545-9796; (973) 694-7199
International Ordering: (973) 694-0500
Contact Name: Steve Levine, Manager
Catalog: Free. Frequency: Semiannual
Circulation: 100K. Sales: $10-20MM
Products: Scienceware brand laboratory devices

BIODEX MEDICAL SYSTEMS   (800) 224-6339
20 Ramsey Rd. • Shirley, NY 11967
E-Mail: info@biodex.com
Website: www.biodex.com
Fax Ordering: (631) 924-8355
International Ordering: (631) 924-9000
Contact Names: James Reiss, President
Catalog: Free. Frequency: Quarterly
Circulation: 50K. Sales: $10-20MM
Products: Physical medicine & rehabiliation
products; nuclear medicine supplies &
accessories; medical imaging tables &
accessories

BRINKMANN INSTRUMENTS CO.   (800) 645-3050
P.O. Box 1019 • Westbury, NY 11590
E-Mail: info@brinkmann.com
Website: www.brinkmann.com
Fax Ordering: (516) 334-7506
International Ordering: (516) 334-7500
Contact Name: Martin Farb, President
Catalog: Free. Frequency: Semiannual
Circulation: 300K. Sales: $50-100MM
Products: Scientific instruments &
apparatus for educational laboratories

BUNTING MAGNETICS COMPANY   (800) 835-2526
P.O. Box 468 • Newton, KS 67114
E-Mail: bmc@buntingmagnetics.com
Website: www.buntingmagnetics.com
Fax Ordering: (316) 283-4975
International Ordering: (316) 284-2020

Contact Names: Bob Bunting, President
Catalog: Free. Frequency: Annual
Circulation: 50K. Sales: $20-50MM
Products: Magnets & magnetic equipment;
metal detection equipment

CAROLINA BIOLOGICAL SUPPLY CO.   (800) 334-5551
2700 York Rd. • Burlington, NC 27215   Canada (877) 933-7833
E-Mail: carolina@carolina.com
Website: www.carolina.com
Fax Ordering: (800) 222-7112;
   (336) 584-3399; Canada (519) 737-7901
International Ordering: (336) 584-0381
Contact Names: Larry Gross, President
Catalog: Free. Frequency: Annual
Circulation: 50K. Sales: $20-50MM
Products: Instructional materials & services
for teaching in biology, biotechnology, chemistry,
health, physics & mathematics

CHEM SCIENTIFIC   (888) 527-5827
1250 Washington St. • Norwood, MA 02062
E-Mail: info@chemscientific.com
Website: www.chemscientific.com
Fax Ordering: (781) 440-0088
International Ordering: (781) 440-0900
Contact Name: Richard Coombs, Manager
Catalog: Free. Frequency: Annual
Circulation: 100K. Sales: $1-3MM
Products: Education and scientific materials
& supplies

CHEMSW   (800) 536-0404
420 F Executive Ct. North
Fairfield, CA 94534
E-Mail: info@chemsw.com
Website: www.chemsw.com
Fax Ordering: (707) 864-2815
International Ordering: (707) 864-0845
Contact Names: Brian Stafford, President
Catalog: Free. Frequency: Annual
Circulation: 50K. Sales: $1-3MM
Products: Windows-based chemistry &
laboratory software

CIRCUIT SPECIALISTS, INC.   (800) 528-1417
220 S. Country Dr. • Mesa, AZ 85210
E-Mail: health@cir.com
Website: www.web-tronics.com
Fax Ordering: (480) 464-5824
International Ordering: (480) 464-2485
Contact Name: Wayne Thorpe, President
Catalog: Free. Frequency: Annual
Circulation: 100K. Sales: $10-50M
Products: Industrial computers, test
equipment, accessories, components
& applications; educational fiber optics
& lasers; educational electronic lab kitting
service for schools; electronic kits &
developmental projects

COLE-PARMER INSTRUMENT CO.   (800) 323-4340
625 E. Bunker Ct. • Vernon Hills, IL 60061   (888) 358-4717
E-Mail: info@coleparmer.com
Website: www.coleparmer.com
Fax Ordering: (847) 247-2929
International Ordering: (847) 549-7600
Contact Names: John Palmer, President
Catalog: Free. Frequency: Annual
Circulation: 100K. Sales: $20-50M
Products: Instruments for measurement
& control, laboratory equipment & supplies

CRYSTAL PRODUCTIONS (800) 255-8629
P.O. Box 2159 • Glenview, IL 60025
E-Mail: custserv@crystalproductions.com
Website: www.crystalproductions.com
Fax Ordering: (800) 657-8149
International Ordering: (847) 657-8144
Catalog: Free. Frequency: Semiannual
Circulation: 50K. Sales: $10-20MM
Products: Art education resource materials for elementary, secondary, and college levels. Includes posters and prints, multimedia packs, books, CD-ROMs, videodiscs, and games.

CUDA PRODUCTS (877) 677-2832
Sunoptic Technologies
6018 Bowdendale Ave.
Jacksonville, FL 32216
E-Mail: sales@sunopticssurgical.com
Website: www.sunopticssurgical.com
Fax Ordering: (904) 733-4832
International Ordering: (904) 737-7611
Contact Names: Doug Tillett, Manager
Catalog: Free. Frequency: Annual
Circulation: 50K. Sales: $10-20MM
Products: Fiberoptic cables; high intensity light sources; video cameras

DELTA BIOLOGICALS (800) 821-2502
P.O. Box 26666 • Tucson, AZ 85726
E-Mail: sales@deltbio.com
Website: www.deltabio.com
Fax Ordering: (520) 745-7888
International Ordering: (520) 790-7737
Contact Name: Dave Watson, President
Catalog: Free. Frequency: Annual
Circulation: 100K. Sales: $5-10MM
Products: Biological formalin-free specimens, supplies, laboratory tables, multimedia

DELTA EDUCATION (800) 442-5444
80 Northwest Blvd. • Nashua, NH 03061 (800) 258-1302
E-Mail: webadmin@delta-education.com
Website: www.delta-education.com
Fax Ordering: (800) 282-9560; (603) 886-4632
International Ordering: (603) 579-3454
Customer Service: (800) 258-1302
Contact Name: Stefan Kohler, President
Catalog: Free. Frequency: Semiannual
Circulation: 150K. Sales: $20-50MM
Products: K-12 hands-on science & math manipulatives, from batteries & tangrams to complete modular classroom kits

DENOYER-GEPPERT SCIENCE CO. (800) 621-1014
P.O. Box 1727 • Skokie, IL 60076
E-Mail: sales@denoyer.com
Website: www.denoyer.com
Fax Ordering: (866) 531-1221
Contact Name: Richard Gilbert, President
Catalog: Free. Frequency: Annual
Circulation: 150K. Sales: $5-10MM
Products: Human anatomy models, skulls & skeletons, hospital dolls, patient simulators, CPR manikins, classroom videos & software, wall charts and posters.

DYNALAB CORPORATION (800) 828-6595
350 Commerce Dr. • Rochester, NY 14623
E-Mail: labinfo@dyna-labware.com
Website: www.dynalabcorp.com
Fax Ordering: (585) 334-0241
Contact Name: Martin Davies, President

Catalog: Free. Frequency: Annual
Circulation: 200K. Sales: $5-10MM
Products: Plasticware, glassware & equipment for the laboratory

EDVOTEK (800) 338-6835
The Biotechnology Education Co.
P.O. Box 341232 • Bethesda, MD 20827
E-Mail: edvotek@aol.com
Website: www.edvotek.com
Fax Ordering: (301) 340-0582
International Ordering: (301) 251-6605
Catalog: Free. Frequency: Annual.
Circulation: 50K. Sales: $10-20MM
Products: Biotechnology/scientific education equipment, kits and systems

ENGINEERED SYSTEMS & DESIGNS (302) 456-0446
119 A Sandy Dr. • Newark, DE 19713
E-Mail: esd@esdinc.com
Website: www.esdinc.com
Fax Ordering: (302) 456-0441
Contact Names: Robert Spring, President
Catalog: Free. Frequency: 3x per year
Circulation: 25K. Sales: $1-3MM
Products: Scientific instruments

EUREKA CARTOGRAPHY (510) 845-6277
2809 Telegraph Ave. Suite 206
Berkeley, CA 94705
E-Mail: mapmaker@maps-eureka.com
Website: www.maps-eureka.com
Fax Ordering: (510) 845-1474
Contact Name: Judith Timmel, President
Catalog: Free. Frequency: Weekly
Circulation: 25K. Sales: $1-3MM
Products: Custom maps & globes

ED FAGAN, INC. (800) 782-9657
10537 Humboldt St.
Los Alamitos, CA 90720
E-Mail: sales@edfagan.com
Website: www.edfagan.com
Fax Ordering: (562) 598-7122
International Ordering: (562) 431-2568
Contact Name: Ed Fagan, President
Catalog: Free. Frequency: Annual
Circulation: 75K. Sales: $5-10MM
Products: Special purpose alloys

FISHER SCIENCE EDUCATION (800) 955-1177
Fisher Scientific International, Inc.
4500 Turnberry • Hanover Park, IL 60133
E-Mail: info@fisheredu.com
Website: www.fisheredu.com
Fax Ordering: (800) 955-0740
Customer Service: (800) 766-7000
Contact Name: Josh Leichtung, Manager
Catalog: Free. Frequency: Annual
Circulation: 150K. Sales: $3-5MM
Products: Science supplies for teachers; scientific, clinical, educational, & occupational health and safety products.

FORESTRY SUPPLIERS, INC. (800) 647-5368
303 Commerce Park Dr. (800) 647-6450
Jackson, MS 38213
E-Mail: info@forestry-suppliers.com
Website: www.forestry-suppliers.com
Fax Ordering: (800) 543-4203
International Ordering: (601) 354-3565
Customer Service: (800) 752-8460

Catalog: Free. Pages: 650. Frequency: Annual
Circulation: 50K. Sales: $10-20MM
Products: Environmental science research &
education programs. Test kits for field experiments

FOTODYNE, INC. (800) 362-4657
950 Walnut Ridge Dr. • Hartland, WI 53029 (800) 362-3686
E-Mail: info@fotodyne.com
Website: www.fotodyne.com
Fax Ordering: (800) 362-3642 (orders);
  (262) 369-7017
International Ordering: (262) 369-7000
Contact Name: Brian Walsh, Manager
Catalog: Free. Frequency: Annual
Circulation: 100K. Sales: $5-10MM
Products: Molecular biology research
information; molecular biology equipment
& supplies for the classroom; teaching aids
and educational services.

FREY SCIENTIFIC (888) 225-3739
100 Paragon Pkwy. • Mansfield, OH 44903
E-Mail: catalog@freyscientific.com
Website: www.freyscientific.com
Fax Ordering: (877) 256-3739; (419) 589-1413
International Ordering: (419) 589-1900
Contact Name: Dave McKeon, Manager
Catalogs: Free. Frequency: Annual
Circulation: 50K. Sales: $10-50MM
Products: Science classroom furniture,
equipment and supplies, including labs,
chemicals, teaching aids; lab planning
services available.

HEMCO CORPORATION (800) 779-4362
111 Powell Rd.
Independence, MO 64056
E-Mail: info@hemcocorp.com
Website: www.hemcocorp.com
Fax Ordering: (816) 796-3333
International Ordering: (816) 796-2900
Contact Name: Ron Hill, President
Catalog: Free. Frequency: Annual
Circulation: 50K. Sales: $5-10MM
Products: Laboratory equipment: fume hoods,
furniture, and clean labs; safety enclosures,
modular rooms

HARVARD APPARATUS (800) 272-2775
84 October Hill Rd. • Holliston, MA 01746
E-Mail: bioscience@harvardapparatus.com
Website: www.harvardapparatus.com
Fax Ordering: (508) 429-5732
International Ordering: (508) 893-8999
Contact Name: David Green, President
Catalog: Free. Pages: 300. Frequency: Annual
Circulation: 100K. Sales: $5-10MM
Products: Scientific instruments;
bioscience/bioresearch products

HAWKHILL SCIENCE (800) 422-4295
125 E. Gilman St. • Madison, WI 53703
E-Mail: customerservice@hawkhill.com
Website: www.hawkhill.com
Fax Ordering: (608) 251-3924
International Ordering: (608) 251-3934
Contact Name: Bill Stonebarger, President
Catalog: Free. Frequency: Semiannual
Circulation: 50K. Sales: $3-5MM
Products: Videos, CD-ROMs and DVDs to
help the teacher in secondary & college
classes teach science & civic literacy

HUMBOLDT MANUFACTURING CO. (800) 544-7220
7300 W. Agatite Ave. • Norridge, IL 60706
E-Mail: hmc@humboldtmfg.com
Website: www.humboldtmfg.com
Fax Ordering: (708) 456-0137
International Ordering: (708) 456-6300
Contact Name: Dennis Burgess, President
Catalog: Free. Frequency: Annual
Circulation: 100K. Sales: $5-10MM
Products: Testing equipment for asphalt,
concrete, soil & aggregate; general lab
equipment

INDUSTRIAL LAB & PLASTICS (800) 362-1000
Consolidated Plastics Company
8181 Darrow Rd. • Twinsburg, OH 44087
E-Mail: info@consolidatedplastics.com
Website: www.consolidatedplastics.com
Fax Ordering: (330) 425-3333
International Ordering: (330) 425-3900
Catalogs: Free. Frequency: 3x per year
Products: Laboratory plastics, including
containers, bottles, lab supplies, tanks,
tube fittings; Rubbermaid commercial
products; bags, packaging & shipping
supplies; commercial mats and matting.

INTELITOOL (800) 955-7621
Phipps & Bird
P.O. Box 7475 • Richmond, VA 23221
E-Mail: information@intelitool.com
Website: www.intelitool.com
Fax Ordering: (804) 254-2955
International Ordering: (816) 358-4787
Contact Name: Steven Schacht, President
Catalog: Free. Frequency: Annual
Circulation: 100K. Sales: $1-3MM
Products: Software & equipment for
physiology education

KEN-A-VISION MANUFACTURING CO. (800) 627-1953
5615 Raytown Rd. • Kansas City, MO 64133 (800) 501-7366
E-Mail: info@ken-a-vision.com
Website: www.ken-a-vision.com
Fax Ordering: (816)) 358-5072
International Ordering: (816) 353-4787
Contact Name: Steven Dunn, Marketing Mgr.
Catalog: Free. Frequency: Annual
Circulation: 100K. Sales: $5-10MM
Products: Video Flex (flexible cameras),
microscopes, microprojectors, video imaging
products and accessories, including
battery-packs, powers supplies, cables

KEWAUNEE CORPORATION (704) 873-7202
P.O. Box 1842 • Statesville, NC 28687
E-Mail: marketing@kewaunee.com
Website: www.kewaunee.com
Fax Ordering: (704) 873-5160
Contact Name: Eli Manchester, Jr., President
Catalog: Free. Frequency: Annual
Circulation: 50K. Sales: $5-10MM
Products: Science laboratory furniture,
modular systems, fume hoods & accessories

KIEFER SUPPLIES (800) 596-5967
Adolph Kiefer & Associates
1700 Kiefer Dr. • Zion, IL 60099
E-Mail: info@kilgoreinternational.com
Website: www.kilgoreinternational.com
Fax Ordering: (847) 746-8885
International Ordering: (847) 746-1667

Contact Name: Adolph Kiefer, President
Catalog: Free. Frequency: Annual
Circulation: 100K. Sales: $3-5MM
Products: Pool, swim supplies &
chemicals

KILGORE INTERNATIONAL, INC.   (800) 892-9999
36 W. Pearl St. • Coldwater, MI 49036
E-Mail: Info@kilgoreinternational.com
Website: www.kilgoreinternational.com
Fax Ordering: (517) 278-2956
International Ordering: (517) 279-9000
Contact Name: Craig Kilgore, President
Catalog: Free. Frequency: Annual
Circulation: 150K. Sales: $5-10MM
Products: Plastic, anatomical & dental
study models

KOBOLD INSTRUMENTS   (800) 998-1020
1801 Parkway View Dr.
Pittsburgh, PA 15205
E-Mail: kobold@koboldusa.com
Website: www.koboldusa.com
Fax Ordering: (412) 788-4890
International Ordering: (412) 788-2830
Contact Name: K.J. Kobold, President
Catalog: Free. Frequency: Annual
Circulation: 150K. Sales: $10-50MM
Products: Flow meters, switches & flow
indicators; level, pressure & temperature
switches & transmitters

KONTES CHEMISTRY &   (888) 546-2531
LIFE SCIENCES PRODUCTS   (800) 223-7150
1022 Spruce St. • Vineland, NJ 08360
E-Mail: cs@kimkon.com
Website: www.kontes.com
Fax Ordering: (856) 692-3242; 794-9762
International Ordering: (856) 692-8500
Customer Service: (856) 692-3600
Contact Name: Dave McLuckey, President
Catalog: Free. Frequency: Annual
Circulation: 150K. Sales: $5-10MM
Products: Dental study models; plastic,
anatomical & dental models

THE LAB MART   (800) 684-1234
J & H Berge, Inc.
P.O. Box 310
So. Plainfield, NJ 07080
E-Mail: Info@labmartexpress.com
Website: www.labmartexpress.com
Fax Ordering: (908) 561-3002
International Ordering: (908) 561-1234
Contact Name: Steven Krupp, President
Catalog: Free. Frequency: Quarterly
Circulation: 200K. Sales: $5-10MM
Products: Scientific laboratory equipment,
instruments, furniture, supplies & reagent
chemicals; plasticware and glassware.

LAB SAFETY SUPPLY, INC.   (800) 356-0783
P.O. Box 1368
Janesville, WI 53547
E-Mail: Info@labsafety.com
Website: www.labsafety.com
Fax Ordering: (800) 543-9910; (608) 754-1806
International Ordering: (608) 754-7160
Catalog: Free. Frequency: Annual
Circulation: 100K. Sales: $3-5MM
Products: Safety and industrial supplies

LAB SHARK   (800) 227-9997
Midwest Scientific
280 Vance Rd. • St. Louis, MO 63088
E-Mail: custserv@midsci.com
Website: www.midsci.com
Fax Ordering: (800) 610-4488; (636) 225-9998
International Ordering: (636) 225-9997
Tech Support: (877) 227-9911
Contact Name: Larry Degenhart, President
Catalog: Free. Frequency: Annual
Circulation: 250K. Sales: $5-10MM
Products: Laboratory supplies & equipment
for biotechnology

LAFAYETTE INSTRUMENT CO.   (800) 428-7545
P.O. Box 5729 • Lafayette, IN 47904
E-Mail: lic@lafayetteinstrument.com
Website: www.lafayetteinstrument.com
Fax Ordering: (765) 423-4111
International Ordering: (765) 423-1505
Contact Name: Roger McClellan, President
Catalog: Free. Frequency: Annual
Circulation: 100K. Sales: $5-10MM
Products: Student lab recording systems &
accessories; polygraph software & instruments;
products for life sciences, animal sciences,
evaluation and assessment, sports, & soil
impact testing.

THE MAGNET SOURCE   (800) 525-3536
Master Magnetics, Inc.
607 S. Gilbert St. • Castle Rock, CO 80104
E-Mail: magnet@magnetsource.com
Website: www.magnetsource.com
Fax Ordering: (303) 688-5303
International Ordering: (303) 688-3966
Catalog: Free. Frequency: Annual
Circulation: 50K. Sales: $5-10MM
Products: Magnets, magnetic devices
for the hardware, industrial, craft and hobby,
toy and educational markets

McNAB, INC.   (914) 699-1616
20 N. Macquesten Pkwy.
Mt. Vernon, NY 10550
E-Mail: info@themcnab.com
Website: www.themcnab.com
Fax Ordering: (914) 699-1671
Contact Name: John Byrnes, President
Catalog: Free. Frequency: Annual
Circulation: 50K. Sales: $5-10MM
Products: Quality control instrumentation

MEDICAL PLASTICS LABORATORY   (800) 433-5539
P.O. Box 38 • Gatesville, TX 76528
E-Mail: kbullington@mpltx.com
Website: www.medicalplastics.com
Fax Ordering: (254) 865-8011
International Ordering: (254) 865-7221
Contact Name: Ken Bullington
Catalog: Free. Frequency: Annual
Circulation: 150K. Sales: $5-10MM
Products: Anatomical reproductions,
skeletons, patient simulators & models
for healthcare education.

METEOROLOGIC INSTRUMENTS, INC.   (800) 667-8400
Educational Laser Department
90 Coles Rd. • Blackwood, NJ 08012
E-Mail: info@metrologic.com
Website: www.metrologic.com

Fax Ordering: (856) 228-1879; 537-6474
International Ordering: (856) 228-8100
Contact Name: Thomas Mills, President
Catalog: Free. Frequency: 10x per year
Circulation: 50K. Sales: $5-10MM
Products: Educational lasers, kits, labs,
manuals, accessories and parts

METTLER-TOLEDO, INC. (800) 638-8537
1900 Polaris Pkwy.
Columbus, OH 43240
E-Mail: tellmemore@mt.com
Website: www.mt.com
Fax Ordering: (614) 438-4525
Contact Name: Robert Spoemy, President
Catalog: Free. Frequency: Annual
Products: Precision lab equipment

MICRO-OPTICS (800) 776-1771
6823 Fresh Meadow Ln.
Flushing, NY 11365
E-Mail: info@micro-opticsmicroscopes.com
Website: www.micro-optics.biz
Fax Ordering: (718) 461-2904
International Ordering: (718) 961-8833
Contact Name: Philip Weissman, President
Catalog: Free. Frequency: Quarterly
Circulation: 50K. Sales: $5-10MM
Products: Video imaging systems & equipment
for education; auto leaders; microscopes;
binoculars; lab equipment and supplies

MINERS CATALOG (800) 824-7452
P.O. Box 1301 • Riggins, ID 83549
E-Mail: sales@minerox.com
Website: www.minerox.com
Fax Ordering: (208) 628-3749
International Ordering: (208) 628-3247
Contact Name: Mary E. Carter, President
Catalog: $2. Frequency: Monthly
Circulation: 50K. Sales: $5-10MM
Products: Geological supplies, equipment
& books

MISONIX, INC. (800) 694-9612
1938 New Hwy. • Farmingdale, NY 11735
E-Mail: sales@misonix.com
Website: www.misonix.com
Fax Ordering: (631) 694-9412
International Ordering: (631) 694-9555
Contact Name: Michael McManus, President
Catalog: Free. Frequency: Weekly
Circulation: 50K Sales: $10-50MM
Products: Ultrasonic medical devices &
other equipment; forensic laboratory products;
ductless fume hoods.

NADA SCIENTIFIC, LTD. (800) 799-6232
P.O. Box 2040 • Champlain, NY 12919
E-Mail: support@nadasci.com
Website: www.nadasci.com
Fax Ordering: (518) 297-3524
International Ordering: (518) 297-3208
Contact Name: Ahmed Dassi, President
Catalog: Free. Frequency: Annual
Circulation: 50K. Sales: $5-10MM
Products: Science equipment & supplies
in physical science, biology, chemistry,
science kits; automotive structural models
& science related gifts.

NEBRASKA SCIENTIFIC (800) 228-7117
Div. of Cyrgus Co., Inc.
3823 Leavenworth St. • Omaha, NE 68105
E-Mail: staff@nebraskascientific.com
Website: nebraskascientific.com
Fax Ordering: (402) 346-2216
Contact Name: Howard Epstein, President
Catalog: Free. Pages: 176. Frequency: Semiannual
Circulation: 100K. Sales: $5-10MM
Products: Educational science supplies;
biological specimens & supplies

NURNBERG SCIENTIFIC DISTRIBUTORS (800) 826-3470
6310 SW Virginia Ave. • Portland, OR 97201 (877) 668-2467
E-Mail: sales@scientificdistributors.com
Website: www.nurnberg.com
Fax Ordering: (503) 246-0360
International Ordering: (503) 246-8297
Contact Name: Dan Jauchius, President
Catalog: Free. Frequency: Annual
Circulation: 150M. Sales: $5-10MM
Products: Teaching microscopes;
laboratory equipment & supplies

OHAUS CORPORATION (800) 672-7722
P.O. Box 2033 • Pine Brook, NJ 07058
E-Mail: maria.bormann@ohaus.com
Website: www.ohaus.com
Fax Ordering: (800) 642-8765; (973) 944-7177
International Ordering: (973) 377-9000
Contact Name: Maria Bormann, Sales Manager
Catalog: Free. Frequency: Annual
Circulation: 250K. Sales: $20-50MM
Products: Electronic and mechanical scales
& balances for the laboratory, education,
industrial andspecialty markets

PASCO SCIENTIFIC CO. (800) 772-8700
10101 Foothills Blvd. • Roseville, CA 95747
E-Mail: sales@pasco.com
Website: www.pasco.com
Fax Ordering: (916) 786-7565
International Ordering: (916) 786-3800
Contact Name: Paul Stokstad, President
Catalog: Free. Frequency: Annual
Circulation: 200K. Sales: $20-50MM
Products: Products for science educators;
teaching supplies

PARCO SCIENTIFIC CO. (800) 247-2726
P.O. Box 189 • Vienna, OH 44473
E-Mail: info@parcoscientific.com
Website: www.parcoscientific.com
Fax Ordering: (330) 394-2403
International Ordering: (330) 394-1100
Contact Name: Brian Martorana, President
Catalog: Free. Frequency: Annual. Sales: $5-10MM
Circulation: 50K. Sales: $5-10MM
Products: Compound & stereo microscopes
for the educational & medical markets.

PERKINELMER LIFE/ANALYTICAL SCIENCES (800) 762-4000
710 Bridgeport Ave. • Shelton, CT 06484
E-Mail: customercare@perkinelmer.com
Website: www.las.perkinelmer.com
Fax Ordering: (203) 944-4904
International Ordering: (203) 925-4600
Contact Name: Thomas Mills, President
Catalog: Free. Frequency: 10x per year
Circulation: 50K. Sales: $50-100MM
Products: Supplies & accessories for
analytical instruments

PITSCO SCIENCE EDUCATION (800) 835-0686
P.O. Box 1708 • Pittsburg, KS 66762
E-Mail: info@pitsco.com
Website: www.shop-pitsco.com
Fax Ordering: (800) 533-8104; (620) 231-0000
International Ordering: (620) 231-1339
Contact Name: Harvey R. Dean, President
Catalog: Free. Frequency: Semiannual
Circulation: 200M. Sales: $50-100MM
Products: Technology/science educational materials; teaching supplies

PRECISION WEATHER INSTRUMENTS CO. (800) 678-3669
Davis Instruments Corp.
3465 Diablo Ave. • Hayward, CA 94545
E-Mail: sales@davisnet.com
Website: www.davisnet.com
Fax Ordering: (510) 670-0589
International Ordering: (510) 732-9229
Technical Support: (510) 732-7814
Contact Name: Susan Foxall, Manager
Catalog: Free. Frequency: Annual
Circulation: 150K. Sales: $10-20MM
Products: Professional weather monitoring stations for use in homes, schools, industry, and agriculture

PREMIER PRODUCTS (800) 323-2799
P.O. Box 944 • Columbus, NE 68602
E-Mail: customerservice@weatherhorizons.com
Website: www.weatherhorizons.com
Fax Ordering: (402) 564-3703
International Ordering: (402) 564-4909
Contact Name: Rodney Behlen, President
Catalog: Free. Frequency: Annual
Circulation: 200K. Sales: $20-50MM
Products: Weather stations; temperature systems; weather instruments for home & business; radio controlled clocks & watches.

PROMEGA BIOSCIENCES (800) 356-9526
2800 Woods Hollow Rd. • Madison, WI 53711
E-Mail: custserv@promega.com
Website: www.promega.com
Fax Ordering: (800) 356-1970; (608) 277-2516
International Ordering: (608) 274-4330
Contact Name: William Linton, President
Catalog: Free. Frequency: Annual
Circulation: 50M. Sales: $10-20MM
Products: Integrated products to help researchers explore gene, protein & cellular interactions

SCIENTIFIC SALES (800) 788-5666
P.O. Box 6725 • Lawrenceville, NJ 08648
E-Mail: sales@scientificsales.com
Website: www.scientificsales.com
Fax Ordering: (609) 844-0466
International Ordering: (609) 844-0055
Contact Names: Thomas Tesauro, President
Catalog: Free. Frequency: Annual
Circulation: 100K. Sales: $5-10MM
Products: Vantage Pro Weather Station; Wireless Weather Station; consumer & industrial weather instruments & equipment; meteorological balloons

SCIENTIFIC SYSTEMS (800) 221-1705
Information Unlimited
P.O. Box 716 • Amherst, NH 03031
E-Mail: wako2@wavewizard.com

Website: www.amazing1.com
Fax Ordering: (603) 672-5406
International Ordering: (603) 673-4730
Contact Name: Robert Iannini, President
Catalog: $3. Frequency: Annual
Circulation: 100M. Sales: $1-5MM
Products: Lasers, phasers, hypnosis/mind control, home & personal security, night vision equipment; high voltage devices.

SCIENTIFICS CATALOG (800) 728-6999
Edmund Optics, Inc. (800) 363-1992
101 E. Gloucester Pike
Barrington, NJ 08007
E-Mail: sales@edmundoptics.com
Website: www.edmundoptics.com
Fax Ordering: (800) 828-3299; (856) 573-6295
International Ordering: (856) 573-6250 x6005
Contact Name: Gwynne Edmund, President
Catalog: Free. Frequency: Semiannual
Circulation: 2MM. Sales: $10-20MM
Products: Science & optical equipment, OEM optics, lasers & lenses

SKC CATALOG (724) 941-9701
863 Valley View Rd. • Eighty Four, PA 15330
E-Mail: skcinc@skcinc.com
Website: www.skcinc.com
Fax Ordering: (724) 941-1369
International Ordering: (724) 941-9701
Catalog: Free. Frequency: Semiannual
Circulation: 150K. Sales: $10-20MM
Products: Air sampling products for the industrial hygiene, safety, occupational health, environmental, & indoor air quality professional

SKULLDUGGERY, INC. (800) 336-7745
624 South B St. • Tustin, CA 92780
E-Mail: fossil@skullduggery.com
Website: www.skullduggery.com
Fax Ordering: (714) 832-1215
International Ordering: (714) 832-8488
Contact Name: Stephen Koehl, President
Catalog: Free. Frequency: Semiannual
Circulation: 100M. Sales: $1MM
Products: Fossil replicas, skulls & science education kits

SKULLS UNLIMITED INTERNATIONAL, INC. (800) 659-7585
10313 South Sunnylane
Oklahoma City, OK 73160
E-Mail: info@skullsunlimited.com
Website: www.skullsunlimited.com
Fax Ordering: (405) 794-6985
International Ordering: (405) 794-6985
Contact Name: Michelle Hayer, Manager
Catalog: Free. Frequency: Annual
Circulation: 150K. Sales: $1-3M
Products: Osteological specimens; over 350 varieties of human & animal skulls

SKY & TELESCOPE CATALOG (800) 253-0245
Sky Publishing Corporation
49 Bay State Rd. • Cambridge, MA 02138
E-Mail: info@skyandtelescope.com
Website: www.skyandtelescope.com
Fax Ordering: (617) 864-6117
International Ordering: (617) 864-7360
Catalog: Free. Frequency: Semiannual
Circulation: 150K. Sales: $5-10MM
Products: Astronomy supplies including books, star atlases, software, posters

SPEX CERTIPREP   (800) 522-7739
203 Norcross Ave. • Metuchen, NJ 08840
E-Mail: crmsales@spexcsp.com
Website: www.spexcsp.com
Fax Ordering: (732) 603-9647
International Ordering: (732) 549-7144
Contact Name: Ralph Obenauf, President
Catalogs: Free. Frequency: Annual
Circulation: 25M. Sales: $5-10MM
Products: Sample prep products &
certified reference materials; grinders,
mixers, auto extractors

STANO COMPONENTS   (888) 782-6639
P.O. Box STANO • Silver City, NV 89428
E-Mail: nv@night-vision.com
Website: www.night-vision.com
Fax Ordering: (775) 246-5211
International Ordering: (775) 246-5281/3
Contact Name: Allan Glanze, President
Catalogs: $8. Frequency: Annual
Circulation: 10K. Sales: $5-10MM
Products: Night vision, radar & seismic intrusion

START INTERNATIONAL   (800) 259-1986
4270 Airborn Dr. • Addison, TX 75001
E-Mail: info@startinternational.com
Website: www.startinternational.com
Fax Ordering: (972) 248-1991
International Ordering: (972) 248-1999
Contact Name: Daniel Sternberg, President
Catalog: Free. Frequency: Annual.
Circulation: 25K. Sales: $5-10MM
Products: Optical inspection devices,
magnifiers, tape & label dispensers

STRONGBOX   (310) 305-8288
P.O. Box 2726 • Culver City, CA 90231
E-Mail: rackchassis@aol.com
Website: www.rackmountchassis.com
Fax Ordering: (310) 305-1905
Contact Name: L. Martinek, President
Catalog: Free. Frequency: Annual
Circulation: 75K. Sales: $3-5MM
Products: Heavy-duty rack-mounted
enclosures for electronics

TEMPO GLOVE MANUFACTURING   (800) 558-8520
3820 W. Wisconsin Ave.
Milwaukee, WI 53208
E-Mail: info@tempoglove.com
Website: www.tempoglove.com
Fax Ordering: (414) 344-4084
International Ordering: (414) 344-1100
Contact Name: Michael Mandlman, President
Catalogs: Free. Frequency: Annual
Circulation: 50K. Sales: $5-10MM
Products: Protective hand gloves for
firefighting, industrial & outdoor uses

TESSERACT   (914) 478-2594
P.O. Box 151
Hastings-on-Hudson, NY 10706
E-Mail: mail@etesseract.com
Website: www.etesseract.com
Fax Ordering: (203) 393-2457
Contact Name: David & Yola Coffeen, Owners
Catalog: $8 per copy; $30 per year.
Frequency: Quarterly
Circulation: 25M. Sales: $5-10M
Product: Scientific & medical instruments

THERMO FISHER SCIENTIFIC   (800) 553-0039
P.O. Box 797 • Dubuque, IA 52004
E-Mail: mkt@thermo.com
Website: www.thermo.com
Fax Ordering: (563) 589-0516
International Ordering: (563) 556-2241
Contact Names: Joe Lyons, President
Catalog: Free. Frequency: Annual
Circulation: 100K. Sales: $20-50MM
Products: Laboratory & industrial equipment;
analytical instruments; software; LIMS;
air & water purification systems; radiation
measurement instruments.

UNIVERSE COLLECTION   (203) 393-3395
Bethany Sciences
P.O. Box 3726 • New Haven, CT 06525
E-Mail: bethanysci@aol.com
Website: www.universecollection.com
Fax Ordering: (203) 393-2457
Contact Name: Ronald Farrell, President
Catalog: $2. Frequency: Semiannual
Circulation: 25K. Sales: $500K - $1MM
Product: Meteorite specimens; posters,
art & prints; slide sets; tektites; space jewelry;
books

WHEATON SCIENCE PRODUCTS   (800) 225-1437
1501 N. 10th St. • Millville, NJ 08332
E-Mail: sales@wheatonsci.com
Website: www.wheatonsci.com
Fax Ordering: (856) 825-1368
International Ordering: (856) 825-1100
Contact Name: Stephen Drozdow, President
Catalogs: Free. Frequency: Annual
Circulation: 100M. Sales: $3-5MM
Products: Products for pharmaceutical &
life-sciences research and pilot-scale laboratories;
general analytical laboratories; and glass shops
converting technical glass tubing into laboratory
apparatus.

WILDLIFE SUPPLY CO.   (800) 799-8301
86475 Gene Lasserre Blvd.
Yulee, FL 32097
E-Mail: goto@wildco.com
Website: www.wildco.com
Fax Ordering: (800) 799-8115; (904) 225-2228
International Ordering: (904) 225-9889
Contact Name: Nancy Bell, President
Catalog: Free. Frequency: Semiannual
Circulation: 100K. Sales: $3-5MM
Products: Aquatic sampling kits for students,
volunteers & professionals

WIND & WEATHER   (877) 255-3700
P.O. Box 5000 • Madison, VA 22727
E-Mail: customerservice@windandweather.com
Website: www.windandweather.com
Fax Ordering: (800) 843-2509; (707) 964-1278
Customer Service: (800) 922-9463
International Ordering: (707) 961-2931
Contact Name: D. Snyder, President
Catalog: Free. Frequency: Monthly
Circulation: 2MM. Sales: $10-50MM
Products: Weather instruments, weathervanes,
sundials, home & garden art & ornaments

AUDITIONS   (800) 462-7739
Massey's • 128 W. River St.   (800) 280-0846
Chippewa Falls, WI 54729
E-Mail: sales@emasseys.com
Website: www.auditionsshoes.com
Fax Ordering: (800) 446-2329
Contact Name: John Kuehl, Marketing
Catalogs: Free. Frequency: 16x per year
Circulation: 15MM. Sales: $20-50MM
Products: Women's footwear: athletic,
casual, dress, outdoor, slippers

AUSSIE SLIPPERS   (800) 950-7668
Aussie Imports of Oregon
28 SW First Ave. #103 • Portland, OR 97204
E-Mail: aussco@earthlink.net
Website: www.aussieslippers.com
Fax Ordering: (503) 693-8469
International Ordering: (503) 693-8441
Contact Name: Gary A. LaHaie, Production
Catalogs: Free. Frequency: Annual
Circulation: 100K. Sales: $500K to $1MM
Products: Australian sheepskin slippers
& boots

BABYSHOE.COM   (800) 543-8566
306 Hebron St.
Hendersonville, NC 28739
E-Mail: info@babyshoe.com
Website: www.babyshoe.com
Fax Ordering: (828) 697-5815
International Ordering: (828) 697-5811
Contact Name: Michael Schwartz, President
Catalog: Free. Frequency: Annual
Circulation: 100K. Sales: $5-10MM
Products: Personalized baby gifts;
name/date baby shoes & blankets

BELGIAN SHOES   (212) 755-7372
110 E. 55th St. • New York, NY 10022
E-Mail: info@belgianshoes.com
Website: www.belgianshoes.com
Fax Ordering: (212) 755-7627
Catalogs: $5. Frequency: Annual
Circulation: 100K. Sales: $5-10MM
Products: Shoes

ARTHUR BEREN FINE FOOTWEAR   (800) 886-9797
Salvatore Ferragaino
474 Bryant St. • San Francisco, CA 94107
E-Mail: sales@berenshoes.com
Website: www.berenshoes.com
Fax Ordering: (415) 371-0162
International Ordering: (415) 362-0142
Contact Name: Arthur Beren, President
Catalogs: Free. Frequency: Annual
Circulation: 50K. Sales: $3-5MM
Products: Variety of shoes for men
& women

BIRKENSTOCK EXPRESS   (800) 451-1459
Footwise
301 SW Madison Ave. • Corvallis, OR 97333
E-Mail: mailorder@birkenstockexpress.com
Website: www.birkenstockexpress.com
Fax Ordering: (541) 752-6313
International Ordering: (541) 754-5021
Contact Name: Peter Wendel, President
Catalogs: Free. Frequency: Semiannual
Circulation: 100K. Sales: $3-5MM
Products: Men's & women's shoes

CINDERLLA OF BOSTON   (800) 274-3338
6452-A Industry Way
Westminister, CA 92683
Fax Ordering: (714) 899-2024
International Ordering: (714) 899-2020
Contact Name: Cliff Thygesen, President
Catalogs: Free. Frequency: Quarterly
Circulation: 100K. Sales: $5-10MM
Products: Fashionable shoes for women

COMFORT CORNER   (800) 735-4994
P.O. Box 649 • Nashua, NH 03061
E-Mail: info@comfortcorner.com
Website: www.comfortcorner.com
Fax Ordering: (603) 880-3884
Contact Name: Robert Morrison, President
Catalogs: Free. Frequency: Quarterly
Circulation: 5MM. Sales: $10-20MM
Products: Women's shoes in hard-to-find
sizes and widths; footcare products; apparel
& accessories, handbags, intimate apparel,
sleepwear, hosiery & socks

DANNER BOOTS & SHOES   (800) 345-0430
18550 NE Riverside Pkwy.
Portland, OR 97230
E-Mail: info@danner.com
Website: www.danner.com
Fax Ordering: (503) 251-1119
International Ordering: (503) 251-1100
Contact Name: Joe Schneider, President
Catalogs: Free. Frequency: Semiannual
Circulation: 500K. Sales: $20-50MM
Products: Hunting, hiking, outdoor boots;
work, military, police, fishing boots; accessories

FOOT LOCKER   (800) 991-6815
P.O. Box 8066 • Wausau, WI 54402
E-Mail: customer_service@footlocker.com
Website: www.footlocker.com
Catalogs: Free. Frequency: Semiannual
Circulation: 500K. Sales: $50-100MM
Products: Basketball & running shoes
for men, women & kids

GIORDANO'S SHOES   (212) 688-7195
1150 Second Ave. • New York, NY 10021
E-Mail: info@petiteshoes.com
Website: www.petiteshoes.com
Fax Ordering: (212) 688-7199
Catalogs: $4. Frequency: Quarterly
Circulation: 50K. Sales: $1-3MM
Products: Petite designer shoes,
sizes 4-6 medium only

AUSTIN HALL BOOT COMPANY   (915) 771-6113
230 Chelsea St. • El Paso, TX 79005
E-Mail: austinhallboot@aol.com
Website: www.austinhallboot.com
Fax Ordering: (915) 771-6347
Contact Name: Diana Farmer, President
Catalogs: $1. Frequency: Annual
Circulation: 50K. Sales: $5-10MM
Products: Over 50 styles of genuine
hand-made leather boots

HARRYS SHOES   (866) 442-7797
2299 Broadway • New York, NY 10024
E-Mail: sales@harrys-shoes.com
Website: www.harrys-shoes.com
Catalogs: Free. Frequency: Semiannual

Circulation: 50M. Sales: $3-5MM
Products: Brand name comfort footwar
for men, women and children.

HITCHCOCK SHOES (800) 992-9433
225 Beal St. • Hingham, MA 02043
E-Mail: hitchcock@wideshoes.com
Website: www.wideshoes.com
Fax Ordering: (781) 749-3576
International Ordering: (781) 749-3260
Catalogs: Free. Frequency: 8x per year
Circulation: 100K. Sales: $5-10MM
Products: Men's wide width shoes

JOHNSTON & MURPHY (800) 424-2854
Box 1090 Genesco Park
Nashville, TN 37202
E-Mail: sales@johnstonmurphy.com
Website: www.johnstonmurphy.com
Fax Ordering: (800) 654-2371;
   (615) 367-7483
International Ordering: (615) 367-7168
Contact Name: Hal Pennington, President
Catalogs: Free. Pages: 52.
Frequency: Quarterly
Circulation: 200K. Sales: $10-20MM
Products: Men's footwear, apparel &
accessories

JUST JUSTIN (800) 292-2668
1505 Wycliff Ave. • Dallas, TX 75207
E-Mail: info@bootsforless.com
Website: www.bootsforless.com
Fax Ordering: (214) 631-2747
International Ordering: (214) 630-2858
Contact Name: Jimmy Vells, President
Catalogs: Free. Frequency: Semiannual
Circulation: 100K. Sales: $500M to $1MM
Products: Cowboy boots & belts.

KNAPP SHOES (800) 869-9955
Robinson Plaza Three, Suite 400
Pittsburgh, PA 15205
E-Mail: info@knappshoes.com
Website: www.knappshoes.com
Fax Ordering: (800) 276-1074
Contact Name: Bill Mills, President
Catalogs: Free. Frequency: Semiannual
Circulation: 200K. Sales: $20-50MM
Products: Safety boots & shoes for people
in the workplace; uniform shoes.

LADY FOOT LOCKER (800) 877-5239
P.O. Box 8066 • Wausau, WI 54402
E-Mail: customer_service@ladyfootlocker.com
Website: www.ladyfootlocker.com
Catalogs: Free. Frequency: Annual
Circulation: 250K. Sales: $20-50MM
Products: Ladies footwear

LITTLE'S BOOTS (210) 923-2221
110 Division Ave.
San Antonio, TX 78214
E-Mail: smlboots@satx.rr.com
Website: www.davelittleboots.com
Fax Ordering: (210) 923-6818
Contact Name: Sharon Little, President
Catalogs: $25. Frequency: Annual
Circulation: 15K. Sales: $5-10MM
Products: Custom made boots & belts
made from crocodile, alligator,
lizzard, ostrich & kangaroo skin.

MARYLAND SQUARE (800) 678-9138
1350 Williams St. • Chippewa Falls, WI 54729 (800) 274-7196
E-Mail: sales@marylandsquare.com (800) 727-3895
Website: www.marylandsquare.com
Fax Ordering: (800) 446-2329; (715) 720-4247
International Ordering: (715) 723-5501
Contact Name: Jan Keel, Contact
Catalogs: Free. Pages: 56.
Frequency: Quarterly
Circulation: 5MM. Sales: $20-50MM
Products: Women's footwear & accessories

B.A. MASON SHOE MANUFACTURING CO. (800) 422-1000
1251 1st Ave. • Chippewa Falls, WI 54729
E-Mail: sales@bamason.com
Website: www.bamason.com
Fax Ordering: (800) 446-2329
International Ordering: (715) 723-1871
Customer Service: (800) 893-8508
Contact Name: John Lubs, President
Catalogs: Free. Frequency: 10x per year
Circulation: 5MM. Sales: $50-100MM
Products: Men's & women's dress, work
& casual footwear

NIKE USA FOOTWEAR (800) 344-6453
1 Bowerman Dr. • Beaverton, OR 97005
E-Mail: sales@nike.com
Website: www.nike.com
Fax Ordering: (503) 684-9553
International Ordering: (503) 671-6453
Contact Name: Phillip H. Knight, President
Catalogs: Free. Frequency: 4x per year
Circulation: 15MM. Sales: $20-50MM
Products: Athletic shoes for men, women
& children

ONLINESHOES.COM (800) 786-3141
4702 Harbour Pointe Blvd. SW, #201
Mukilteo, WA 98275
E-Mail: info@onlineshoes.com
Website: www.onlineshoes.com
Fax Ordering: (206) 436-5198
International Ordering: (206) 812-7800
Contact Name: Dan Gerler, President
Catalogs: Free. Frequency: Semiannual
Circulation: 150K. Sales: $5-10MM
Products: Footwear for men, women & kids
in more than 33,000 trend-setting stylesand
over 200 premium brands; also bags, athletic
apparel & accessories.

RICHLEE SHOE COMPANY (800) 343-3810
P.O. Box 3566 • Frederick, MD 21705
E-Mail: sales@elevatorshoes.com
Website: www.elevatorshoes.com
Fax Ordering: (301) 663-1066
International Ordering: (301) 663-5111
Contact Name: Robert Martin, President
Catalogs: Free. Frequency: 10x per year
Circulation: 150K. Sales: $3-5MM
Products: Men's elevator shoes

ROAD RUNNER SPORTS (800) 551-5558
5549 Copley Dr. • San Diego, CA 92111
E-Mail: sales@roadrunnersports.com
Website: www.roadrunnersports.com
Fax Ordering: (800) 453-5443; (858) 636-7650
International Ordering: (858) 671-6453
Customer Service: (800) 636-3560
Contact Name: Jeff Rohling, Marketing
Catalogs: Free. Frequency: 8x per year

Circulation: 10MM. Sales: $50-100MM
Products: Running shoes & products

W.C. RUSSELL MOCCASIN COMPANY (920) 361-2252
P.O. Box 309 • Berlin, WI 54923
E-Mail: russell@russellmoccasin.com
Website: www.russellmoccasin.com
Fax Ordering: (920) 361-3274
Contact Name: Ralph Fabricius, President
Catalogs: Free. Pages: 30. Frequency: Annual
Circulation: 25K. Sales: $20-50MM
Products: Handmade moccasin shoes & boots

SCHNEE'S BOOTS & SHOES (800) 922-1562
6597 Falcon Ln. • Bozeman, MT 59718 (888) 922-1510
E-Mail: boots@schnees.com
Website: www.schnees.com
Fax Ordering: (406) 587-7789
Contact Name: Steve Schnee, President
Catalogs: Free. Frequency: Semiannual
Circulation: 350K. Sales: $1-3MM
Products: Outdoor footwear & clothing;
hiking, hunting & pac boots & gear

SEBAGO CATALOG (800) 377-8474
P.O. Box 3000 • Westbrook, ME 04098
E-Mail: consumer@sebago.com
Website: www.sebago.com
Fax Ordering: (207) 854-2856
International Ordering: (207) 854-8474
Contact Name: Dan Marshall, President
Catalogs: Free. Frequency: Semiannual
Circulation: 10K. Sales: $20-50MM
Products: Handcrafted shoes & casual
footwear for men, women & children

SELBY FIFTH AVENUE (800) 346-3348
417 Fifth Ave. • New York, NY 10016
Fax Ordering: (212) 328-1029
International Ordering: (212) 725-0110
Catalogs: Free. Frequency: Annual
Circulation: 50K. Sales: $5-10MM
Products: Women's shoes

SEXY SHOES (800) 716-8617
Leslie Shoe Company, Inc.
P.O. Box 48 • Rogers City, MI 49779
E-Mail: info@sexyshoes.com
Website: www.sexyshoes.com
Fax Ordering: (989) 734-4337
International Ordering: (989) 734-4030
Contact Name: Jim Kloosterman, President
Catalogs: $3. Frequency: Semiannual
Circulation: 50K. Sales: $5-10MM
Products: Women's high heel dress shoes

SHIMANO AMERICA CORPORATION (800) 353-3817
1 Shimano Dr. • Irvine, CA 92718
Fax Ordering: (949) 951-7519
International Ordering: (949) 470-4291
Catalog: Free. Frequency: Semiannual
Circulation: 50K. Sales: $10-20MM
Products: Footwear

THE SHOE CATALOG (800) 798-7979
Amazon Dry Goods
411 Brady St. • Davenport, IA 52801
E-Mail: info@amazondrygoods.com
Website: www.amazondrygoods.com
Fax Ordering: (563) 322-4003
International Ordering: (563) 322-6800
Contact Name: J. Burgess, President

Catalog: $5. Frequency: Annual
Circulation: 100K. Sales: $10-50MM
Products: Footwear needs for the
ntertainment industry; historic reproduction
shoes from all periods

SHOE EXPRESS CATALOG (800) 874-0469
P.O. Box 61537 • Lafayette, LA 70596
E-Mail: orders@shoexpress.com
Website: www.shoexpress.com
Fax Ordering: (337) 235-5359
International Ordering: (337) 235-5191
Catalogs: Free. Frequency: Semiannual
Circulation: 200K. Sales: $5-10MM
Products: Women's shoes, sizes 11-15;
dress & casual shoes, boots & sandals

TEVA, SPORTS SANDAL (800) 367-8382
P.O. Box 968 • Flagstaff, AZ 86002
E-Mail: customerservice@tevasandals.com
Website: www.teva.com
Fax Ordering: (928) 779-6004
International Ordering: (928 779-5938
Contact Name: Mark Thatcher, President
Catalogs: Free. Frequency: Semiannual
Circulation: 200K. Sales: $3-5MM
Products: Sandals, sandal boots & sports
sandals

WEHMEIER'S BELT SHOP (888) 525-2758
719 Toulouse St. • New Orleans, LA 70130
E-Mail: sales@wehmeiers.com
Website: www.wehmeiers.com
Fax Ordering: (504) 525-4438
International Ordering: (504) 525-2758
Catalogs: Free. Frequency: Annual
Circulation: 50K. Sales: $3-5MM
Products: Alligator shoes, belts, boots,
handbags, attaches, wallets

WHITE'S OUTDOOR CATALOG (800) 541-3786
4002 East Ferry • Spokane, WA 99202
E-Mail: whites@whitesoutdoor.com
Website: www.whitesboots.com
Fax Ordering: (800) 676-2668
International Ordering: (509) 535-2422
Contact Name: Skip March, President
Catalogs: Free. Frequency: 4x per year
Circulation: 5MM. Sales: $10-20MM
Products: Boots, fishing equipment,
outdoor clothing & accessories

WISSOTA TRADER (800) 833-6421
1313 1st Ave. • Chippewa Falls, WI 54729 (800) 281-4063
E-Mail: sales@wissotatrader.com
Website: www.wissotatrader.com
Fax Ordering: (715) 723-2169
International Ordering: (715) 723-6496
Contact Name: John Kuehl, Marketing
Catalogs: Free. Frequency: 10x per year
Circulation: 5MM. Sales: $10-20MM
Products: Men's & women's dress, casual,
outdoor, athletic footwear; shoecare & accessories

E.T.WRIGHT (800) 944-4816
Chippewa Falls, WI 54729
E-Mail: sales@etwright.com
Website: www.etwright.com
Catalogs: Free. Frequency: Quarterly
Circulation: 1MM. Sales: $10-20MM
Products: Handcrafted men's leather footwear
including, athletic, casual, outdoor & slippers.

ADVANTAGE TENNIS SUPPLY　　(800) 476-5432
Femco Corporation
235 Arcadia St. • Richmond, VA 23225
E-Mail: info@advantagetennissupply.com
Website: www.advantagetennissupply.com
Fax Ordering: (804) 276-0557
International Ordering: (804) 276-0011
Contact Name: Frank McDavid, President
Catalog: Free. Frequency: Annual
Circulation: 50K. Sales: $500M
Products: Tennis court equipment

AKERS SKI CATALOG　　(207) 392-4582
P.O. Box 280 • Andover, ME 04216
E-Mail: sales@akers-ski.com
Website: www.akers-ski.com
Fax Ordering: (207) 392-1225
Contact Name: Leon Akers, President
Catalog: Free. Frequency: Annual
Circulation: 25K. Sales: $500M to $1MM
Products: Ski equipment

ALDEN ROWING SHELLS　　(800) 477-1507
P.O. Box 368 • Eliot, ME 03903
E-Mail: rowalden@aol.com
Website: www.rowalden.com
Fax Ordering: (207) 439-0762
International Ordering: (207) 439-1507
Contact Name: Edward Jarvis, President
Catalog: Free. Frequency: Annual
Circulation: 25M. Sales: $1-3MM
Products: Rowing shells, rowing art &
rowing accessories

AMERICA'S FOREMOST SPORTING BOOKS　　(800) 899-7810
Wolfe Publishing Company
6471 Airpark • Prescott, AZ 86301
E-Mail: info@riflemagazine.com
Website: www.riflemagazine.com
Fax Ordering: (928) 778-5124
International Ordering: (928) 445-7810
Contact Name: Mark Harris, President
Catalog: Free. Frequency: Semiannual
Circulation: 25K. Sales: $1-3MM
Products: Western, hunting, wildlife,
military & reloading books

AMERICAN CYCLE EXPRESS　　(800) 231-5979
223 Main St. • Binghamton, NY 13905
E-Mail: sales@americancycle.com
Website: www.americancycle.com
Fax Ordering: (607) 729-8930
International Ordering: (607) 777-1223
Contact Name: Jalal Zuwiyya, President
Catalog: Free. Frequency: Semiannual
Circulation: 100K. Sales: $500M to $1MM
Products: Bicycles & accessories

AMERICAN FENCERS SUPPLY　　(415) 863-7911
1180 Folsom St.
San Francisco, CA 94103
E-Mail: amfence@amfence.com
Website: www.amfence.com
Fax Ordering: (415) 431-4931
Contact Name: Matthew Porter, President
Catalog: Free. Frequency: Annual
Circulation: 50M. Sales: $500M to $1MM
Products: Fencing supplies, apparel &
equipment

AMERICAN SPORTS NETWORK　　(626) 292-2222
P.O. Box 6100 • Rosemead, CA 91770
E-Mail: info@fitnessamerica.com
Website: www.fitnessamerica.com
Fax Ordering: (626) 292-2221
Contact Name: Louis Zwick, President
Catalog: Free. Frequency: Bimonthly
Circulation: 25K. Sales: $5-10MM
Products: Sport, fitness, health &
bodybuilding videos

ANY MOUNTAIN CATALOG　　(888) 311-2001
71 Tamel Vista • Cortemadera, CA 94225
E-Mail: info@anymountaingear.com
Website: www.anymountaingear.com
Fax Ordering: (408) 255-9466
International Ordering: (408) 255-6162
Contact Name: Mark Valentine, President
Catalog: Free. Frequency: Annual
Circulation: 100K. Sales: $5-10MM
Products: Ski apparel for men & women

ARTISTIC VIDEO CATALOG　　(888) 982-4244
87 Tyler Ave. • Sound Beach, NY 11789
E-Mail: bobklein@villagenet.com
Website: www.artisticvideos.com
Fax Ordering: (631) 744-5993
International Ordering: (631) 744-5999
Contact Name: Bob Kein, President
Catalog: Free. Frequency: Annual
Circulation: 25M. Sales: $500M
Products: Martial arts, fitness & environmental
videos; alternative healing instructional videos

ASIAN WORLD OF MARTIAL ARTS　　(800) 345-2962
11601 Caroline Rd.
Philadelphia, PA 19154
E-Mail: info@awma.com
Website: www.awma.com
Fax Ordering: (800) 922-2962
International Ordering: (215) 969-3500
Contact Name: George Ciukurescu, President
Catalog: $3. Frequency: Annual
Circulation: 50K. Sales: $500M to $1MM
Products: Martial arts equipment

ASSOCIATED TENNIS SUPPLIERS　　(800) 866-7071
ATS Sports • 200 Waterfront Dr.
Pittsburgh, PA 15222
E-Mail: tennis@atssports.com
Website: www.atssports.com
Fax Ordering: (412) 323-1320
International Ordering: (412) 323-9612
Contact Name: Harry Ferrari, President
Catalog: Free. Frequency: Annual
Circulation: 250K. Sales: $10-20MM
Products: Tennis equipment, supplies
& accessories

ATHLETA　　(888) 322-5515
1622 Corporate Cr.
Petaluma, CA 94954
E-Mail: sales@athleta.com
Website: www.athleta.com
Fax Ordering: (888) 806-4499
Catalog: Free. Pages: 52. Frequency: Quarterly
Circulation: 250M. Sales: $5-10MM
Products: Women's athletic, workout,
fitness apparel

ATLANTIC FITNESS PRODUCTS   (800) 445-1855
P.O. Box 300 • Linthicum, MD 21090
E-Mail: atlantic@atlantic-fitness.com
Website: www.atlantic-fitness.com
Fax Ordering: (410) 859-3907
International Ordering: (410) 859-3538
Contact Name: Faye Miller, President
Catalog: Free. Frequency: Semiannual
Circulation: 100M. Sales: $3-5MM
Products: Equipment for weightlifting
and fitness

ATS SPORTS   (800) 866-7071
200 Waterfront Dr. • Pittsburgh, PA 15222
E-Mail: tennis@corp.atssports.com
Website: www.atssports.com
Fax Ordering: (412) 323-1320
Catalog: Free. Frequency: Annual
Circulation: 200M. Sales: $5-10MM
Products: Tennis strings, accessories,
apparel & gear, bags, balls, ball machines,
court equipment

AUSTAD'S GOLF   (800) 444-1234
2801 E. 10th St. • Sioux Falls, SD 57103
E-Mail: customerservice@austads.com
Website: www.austads.com
Fax Ordering: (800) 332-2320; (605) 332-3373
International Ordering: (605) 336-3135
Contact Name: Dave Austad, President
Catalog: Free. Frequency: Monthly
Circulation: 100K. Sales: $3-5MM
Products: Golf equipment, golf clubs,
gifts for golfers

AUSTIN SPORTSGEAR CATALOG   (800) 999-7543
209 E. Washington Ave.
Jackson, MI 49201
E-Mail: tennis@atssports.com
Website: www.atssports.com
Fax Ordering: (517) 784-1735
International Ordering: (517) 784-1120
Contact Name: Dale Lehman, President
Catalog: Free. Frequency: Annual
Circulation: 50K. Sales: $1-3MM
Products: Specialized in compression
shorts & padded shorts for sports that
need protective gear

BACHARACH CATALOG   (800) 726-2468
Bacharach Rasin Sporting Goods
802 Gleneagles Ct. • Baltimore, MD 21286
E-Mail: bachrasin@aol.com
Website: www.bacharach.com
Fax Ordering: (410) 321-0720
International Ordering: (410) 825-6747
Contact Name: Christopher Hutchins, President
Catalog: Free. Frequency: Annual
Circulation: 50K. Sales: $3-5MM
Products: Lacrosse equipment & uniforms

BACK IN THE SADDLE   (800) 865-2478
570 Turner Dr. • Durango, CO 81303
E-Mail: info@backinthesaddle.com
Website: www.backinthesaddle.com
Fax Ordering: (800) 333-3810
Catalog: Free. Frequency: Annual
Circulation: 50K. Sales: $1-3MM
Products: Western gear, home furnishings
& clothing for those who love horses &
all things western.

BASEBALL DIRECT   (888) 244-8837
P.O. Box 7563
Charlottesville, VA 22906
E-Mail: baseball@cstone.net
Website: www.baseballdirect.com
Fax Ordering: (434) 974-4986
Customer Service: (800) 558-6273
Catalog: Free. Frequency: Annual
Circulation: 100K. Sales: $1-3MM
Products: Baseball videos, books, CDs,
DVDs, audiotapes, calendars & collectible

BASEBALL EXPRESS   (800) 937-4824
   (800) 882-1166
P.O. Box 792310 • San Antonio, TX 78279
E-Mail: baseball@baseballexpress.com
Website: www.baseballexpress.com;
  www.softball.com
Fax Ordering: (800) 460-9986
Catalog: Free. Pages: 90.
Frequency: Semiannual
Circulation: 300K. Sales: $10-20MM
Products: Baseball apparel & accessories
including balls, bats, caps, gloves, shoes,
sunglasses; videos & books; pitching machines;
training accessories; sports medicine

BELSON OUTDOORS   (800) 323-5664
111 N. River Rd. • N. Aurora, IL 60542
E-Mail: sales@belson.com
Website: www.belson.com
Fax Ordering: (630) 395-1220
International Ordering: (630) 256-4100
Catalog: Free. Frequency: Annual
Circulation: 1MM. Sales: $10-25MM
Products: Equipment for recreational
facilities; sports equipment, bike racks,
campstoves, universal access equipment;
picnic tables

BERRY SCUBA COMPANY   (800) 621-6019
6674 N. NW Hwy. • Chicago, IL 60631
Fax Ordering: (773) 775-1815
International Ordering: (773) 763-1626
Contact Name: Bob Croll, President
Catalog: Free. Frequency: Semiannual
Circulation: 25K. Sales: $500K - $1MM
Products: Scuba equipment

BEVAL SADDLERY   (800) 524-0136
10 Lackawanna Ave.
Gladstone, NJ 07934
E-Mail: sales@beval.com
Website: www.beval.com
Fax Ordering: (908) 234-1952
International Ordering: (908) 234-2828
Catalog: Free. Frequency: Annual
Circulation: 100K. Sales: $3-5MM
Products: Horseback riding equipment
& apparel; sporting clothes; books & gifts

BIKE BASEBALL/SOFTBALL & FOOTBALL   (800) 251-9230
BIKE Athletic Company
P.O. Box 666 • Knoxville, TN 37901
E-Mail: info@bikeathletic.com
Website: www.bikeathletic.com
Fax Ordering: (865) 549-7988
International Ordering: (865) 546-4703
Catalog: Free. Frequency: Semiannual
Circulation: 200M. Sales: $5-10MM
Products: Baseball, softball & football
uniforms & protective equipment

BIKE NASHBAR   (800) 627-4227
6103 State Rt. 446
Canfield, OH 44406
E-Mail: custserv@nashbar.com
Website: www.nashbar.com
Fax Ordering: (877) 778-9456
Contact Name: Steve Piragis, Marketing
Catalog: Free. Frequency: Semiannual
Circulation: 100K. Sales: $3-5MM
Products: Bicycles, biking apparel &
accessories

BLACK KNIGHT USA   (800) 535-3300
5355 Sierra Rd. • San Jose, CA 95132
E-Mail: racquets@blacknight.cc
Website: www.bksquash.com
Fax Ordering: (408) 923-7794
International Ordering: (408) 923-7777
Contact Name: Bob Morgan, President
Catalog: Free. Frequency: Semiannual
Circulation: 10K. Sales: $500K
Products: Squash & badminton rackets
& accessories

BRANFORD BIKE   (800) 272-6367
202 Main St. • Branford, CT 06405
E-Mail: info@branfordbike.com
Website: www.branfordbike.com
Fax Ordering: (203) 483-0703
International Ordering: (203) 488-0482
Contact Name: Tim Brockett, President
Catalog: Free. Frequency: Quarterly
Circulation: 100K. Sales: $1-3MM
Products: Biking apparel, parts &
accessories

BRAWN INTERNATIONAL MALE   (800) 419-1114
Brawn of California   (800) 293-9333
741 "F" St. • San Diego, CA 92101
E-Mail: info@internationalmale.com
Website: www.internationalmale.com
International Ordering: (619) 544-9900
Contact Name: Don Wilson, President
Catalog: $2. Frequency: Quarterly
Circulation:100K. Sales: $10-20MM
Products: Workout & fitness apparel

BRISTOL ATHLETIC   (800) 336-8775
P.O. Box 158 • Bristol, TN 37621
E-Mail: mailbox@bristolproducts.com
Website: www.bristolproducts.com
Fax Ordering: (423) 968-2084
International Ordering: (423) 968-4140
Catalog: Free. Frequency: 10x per year
Circulation: 250K. Sales: $10-20MM
Products: Sports apparel; athletic socks;
cheerleading outfits

BROWNELL SPORTS PRODUCTS   (860) 873-8625
Brownell & Company
429 E. Haddam Moodus Rd.
Moodus, CT 06469
E-Mail: brownell@brownellco.com
Website: www.brownellco.com
Fax Ordering: (860) 873-1944
Contact Name: Anthony Ferraz, President
Catalog: Free. Frequency: Annual
Circulation: 100K. Sales: $5-10MM
Products: Tennis & archery equipment,
supplies & accessories; aviation & cargo
nets; fishing twines & netting

BSN SPORTS - COLLEGIATE PACIFIC   (800) 527-7510
P.O. Box 7726 • Dallas, TX 75209
E-Mail: sales@bsncp.com
Website: www.bsncp.com
Fax Ordering: (800) 899-0149
Catalog: Free. Pages: 340.
Frequency: Quarterly
Circulation: 250K. Sales: $5-10MM
Products: Sporting goods

CALIFORNIA CHEAP SKATES   (800) 477-9283
2701 McMillan Ave.
San Luis Obispo, CA 93401
Fax Ordering: (805) 546-0330
International Ordering: (805) 541-00504
Catalog: Free. Frequency: Annual
Circulation: 100K. Sales: $10-20MM
Products: Skateboard & snowboard
related products

CANNON SPORTS   (800) 223-0064
P.O. Box 11179 • Burbank, CA 91510
E-Mail: csi@cannonsports.com
Website: www.cannonsports.com
Fax Ordering: (800) 388-1993; (818) 771-5233
International Ordering: (818) 771-5201
Contact Name: Jon Warner, Marketing
Catalog: Free. Frequency: Semiannual
Circulation: 500K. Sales: $10-20MM
Products: Sporting goods including aerobics,
archery, baseball, softball, basketball, apparel

CAPEZIO CATALOG   (800) 533-1887
1650 Broadway • New York, NY 10019
Fax Ordering: (212) 262-1747
International Ordering: (212) 586-5140
Contact Name: Gayle Miller, President
Catalog: $1. Frequency: Annual
Circulation: 100K. Sales: $1-3MM
Products: Complete line of dance &
exercise wear

CARRON NET COMPANY   (800) 558-7768
P.O. Box 177 • Two Rivers, WI 54241
E-Mail: info@carronnet.com
Website: www.carronnet.com
Fax Ordering: (920) 793-2122
International Ordering: (920) 793-2217
Contact Name: William E. Kiel, Sr., President
Catalog: Free. Frequency: Annual
Circulation: 50K. Sales: $5-10MM
Products: Full line of nets & accessories or
a variety of sports, including tennis, soccer,
volleyball & golf

CARUSHKA BODYWEAR   (800) 247-5113
7716 Kester Ave. • Van Nuys, CA 91405
Fax Ordering: (818) 988-8419
International Ordering: (818) 904-0574
Contact Name: Carushka Jarecka, President
Catalog: $5. Frequency: Monthly
Circulation: 5K. Sales: $5-10MM
Products: Women's exercise clothing &
sportswear

CATALOG FROM GOLF HOUSE   (908) 234-2300
U.S. Golf Association
Golf House • Far Hills, NJ 07931
E-Mail: usga@usga.org
Website: www.usga.org
Fax Ordering: (908) 234-9687
Catalog: Free. Frequency: Semiannual

Circulation: 1MM. Sales: $10-20MM
Products: Golf related accessories

CCS CATALOG　　　　(800) 477-9283
P.O. Box 6144 • Westerville, OH 43086
E-Mail: cs@ccsmerch.com
Website: www.ccs.com
Fax Ordering: (800) 317-8105
Customer Service: (800) 875-1800
Catalog: Free. Pages: 90. Frequency: 3x per year
Circulation: 100K. Sales: $1-3MM
Products: Skateboarding & snowboarding
equipment & supplies

CENTURY MARTIAL ARTS　　　　(800) 626-2787
Century, Inc.
1000 Century Blvd. • Midwest City, OK 73110
E-Mail: sales@centuryfitness.com
Website: www.centuryfitness.com
Fax Ordering: (800) 400-5485; (405) 732-3751
International Ordering: (405) 732-2226
Contact Name: Gary Hestilow, President
Catalog: $2. Frequency: Annual
Circulation: 50K. Sales: $5-10MM
Products: Martial arts supplies

CHAMISA RIDGE CATALOG　　　　(800) 743-3188
P.O. Box 23294 • Santa Fe, NM 87502
E-Mail: info@chamisaridge.com
Website: www.chamisaridge.com
Fax Ordering: (505) 438-8205
International Ordering: (505) 989-7280
Contact Name: Katrina Prull, President
Catalog: Free. Frequency: 5x per year
Circulation: 50K. Sales: $500M to $1MM
Products: Hilton herbs for horses, dogs,
people, cats, birds; also books, audios,
videos & accessories for horseback riders

CHAMPIONS ON FILM　　　　(800) 521-2832
School-Tech
P.O. Box 1941 • Ann Arbor, MI 48108
E-Mail: info@school-tech.com
Website: www.school-tech.com
Fax Ordering: (800) 654-4321
International Ordering: (734) 761-5173
Contact Name: D.N. Canham, Marketing
Catalog: Free. Frequency: Semiannual
Circulation: 500K. Sales: $500M to $1MM
Products: Instructional sports videos

CHAPARRAL MOTORSPORTS　　　　(800) 841-2960
555 South "H" St. • San Bernardino, CA 92410
E-Mail: info@chaparralmotorsports.com
Website: www.chaparral-racing.com
Fax Ordering: (800) 841-4261; (909) 884-3183
International Ordering: (909) 889-2761
Catalog: Free. Frequency: Semiannual
Circulation: 300M. Sales: $3-5MM
Products: Motorcycle parts & accessories

CHO-PAT, INC.　　　　(800) 221-1601
SPORT MEDICAL DEVICES
P.O. Box 293 • Hainesport, NJ 08036
E-Mail: sales@cho-pat.com
Website: www.cho-pat.com
Fax Ordering: (609) 261-7593
International Ordering: (609) 261-1336
Contact Name: George Ganvry, President
Catalog: Free. Frequency: Semiannual
Circulation: 25K. Sales: $1-3MM
Products: Sports medicine products

CLIENTELE　　　　(800) 327-4660
14101 NW 4th St. • Sunrise, FL 33325
E-Mail: info@clientele.org
Website: www.clientele.org
Fax Ordering: (954) 845-9505
International Ordering: (954) 845-9500
Contact Name: Patricia Riley, President
Catalog: Free. Frequency: Quarterly
Circulation: 25K. Sales: $10-20MM
Products: Exercise equipment & vitamins

COBRA GOLF　　　　(800) 223-3537
1818 Aston Ave. • Carlsbad, CA 92008
E-Mail: sales@cobragolf.com
Website: www.cobragolf.com
Fax Ordering: (760) 929-0370
International Ordering: (760) 929-0377
Contact Name: Steve Pelesik, President
Catalog: Free. Frequency: Semiannual
Circulation: 150K. Sales: $10-20MM
Products: King Cobra golf products

COLLAGE VIDEO　　　　(800) 819-7111
5390 Main St. NE • Minneapolis, MN 55421
E-Mail: collage@collagevideo.com
Website: www.collagevideo.com
Fax Ordering: (763) 571-5906
International Ordering: (763) 571-5840
Catalog: Free. Pages: 60. Frequency: Annual
Circulation: 150K. Sales: $5-10MM
Products: Exercise videos: DVDs & CDs

COMPETITIVE EDGE GOLF　　　　(800) 433-4465
Genesis Direct
100 Plaza Dr. • Secaucus, NJ 07094
Fax Ordering: (201) 867-7081
International Ordering: (201) 912-0926
Contact Name: David Sable, Marketing
Catalog: Free. Frequency: Semiannual
Circulation: 250K. Sales: $10-20MM
Products: Golf accessories

COUNTRYSPORT CATALOG　　　　(800) 367-4114
23 Broad St. • Selma, AL 36701
E-Mail: info@countrysport.com
Website: www.countrysport.com
Fax Ordering: (334) 872-6443
International Ordering: (334) 872-6400
Contact Name: Robert J. Hunter, President
Catalog: Free. Frequency: Semiannual
Circulation: 250K. Sales: $500K
Products: Books & art for the sportsman

COURT PRODUCTS, INC.　　　　(800) 323-9388
3935 Grove Ave. • Gurnee, IL 60031
E-Mail: info@courtproducts.com
Website: www.courtproducts.com.com
Fax Ordering: (847) 662-9055
International Ordering: (847) 662-9000
Catalog: Free. Frequency: Annual
Circulation: 100K. Sales: $1-3MM
Products: Sports equipment, apparel &
accessories

CRASH PADS　　　　(800) 964-5993
2625 SE 39th Loop
Hillsboro, OR 97123
E-Mail: crashpads@aol.com
Website: www.crash-pads.com
Fax Ordering: (503) 648-1319
International Ordering: (503) 681-0587
Contact Name: Sheila Lehner, President

Catalog: Free. Frequency: Monthly
Circulation: 10K. Sales: $500K - $1MM
Products: Body pads for all sports

CROWN AWARDS　(800) 227-1557
9 Skyline Dr. • Hawthorne, NY 10532
E-Mail: info@crowntrophy.com
Website: www.crownawards.com
Fax Ordering: (914) 347-7008
International Ordering: (914) 347-7700
Contact Name: Elyse Weisenfeld, President
Catalog: Free. Frequency: Semiannual
Circulation: 100K. Sales: $3-5MM
Products: Trophies, medals, pins, patches,
ribbons, plaques

CSG COMPONENT GOLF SUPPLIES　(800) 597-5241
116 E. Nora • Spokane, WA 99207
E-Mail: sales@csggolf.com
Website: www.csggolf.com
Fax Ordering: (509) 232-0474
Catalog: Free. Frequency: Annual
Circulation: 100K. Sales: $10-20MM
Products: Golf supplies & accessories

CYCLOSOURCE　(800) 755-2453
Adventure Cycling Association
P.O. Box 8308 • Missoula, MT 59807
E-Mail: info@adventurecycling.org
Website: www.adventurecycling.org
Fax Ordering: (406) 721-8754
International Ordering: (406) 721-1776
Contact Name: Teri Maloughney, Director
Catalog: Free. Frequency: Semiannual
Circulation: 100M. Sales: $1-3MM
Products: Bicycling touring maps & books

DARTON ARCHERY　(989) 728-4231
3540 Darton Rd. • Hale, MI 48739
E-Mail: sales@dartonarchery.com
Website: www.dartonarchery.com
Fax Ordering: (989) 728-2410
Tech Support: (989) 728-9511
Contact Name: R.F. Darlington, President
Catalog: Free. Frequency: Annual
Circulation: 25K. Sales: $3-5MM
Products: Archery equipment & supplies

DIAMOND TOUR GOLF　(800) 826-5340
203 E. Lincoln • Dekalb, IL 60115
E-Mail: sales@diamondtour.com
Website: www.diamondtour.com
Fax Ordering: (815) 787-3720
International Ordering: (815) 787-2649
Catalog: Free. Frequency: Annual
Circulation: 100K. Sales: $5-10MM
Products: Golf supplies & accessories

DIVERS DIRECT　(800) 348-3872
1020 NW 6th St.
Deerfield Beach, FL 33442
E-Mail: ksenecal@diversdirect.com
Website: www.diversdirect.com
Fax Ordering: (954) 429-8572
International Ordering: (954) 429-0116
Contact Name: Kevin Senecal, President
Catalog: Free. Frequency: Annual
Circulation: 50K. Sales: $10-20MM
Products: Scuba diving equipment &
accessories

DRAGON INTERNATIONAL　(800) 535-7573
12310 Hwy. 99 • Everett, WA 98204
Fax Ordering: (425) 514-0197
Contact Name: Poku Chan, President
Catalog: $2. Frequency: Annual
Circulation: 50K. Sales: $500K
Products: Martial arts apparel

DYNACRAFT GOLF PRODUCTS　(800) 321-4833
P.O. Box 4550 • Newark, OH 43055
E-Mail: support@dynacraftgolf.com
Website: www.dynacraftgolf.com
Fax Ordering: (800) 424-0394
International Ordering: (740) 344-1191
Customer Service: (800) 423-2968
Tech Support: (800) 942-5872
Catalog: Free. Frequency: Annual
Circulation: 100K. Sales: $10-20MM
Products: Golf clubs, components, tools
& supplies; accessories

EASTBAY　(800) 826-2205
111 S. First Ave. • Wausau, WI 54401
E-Mail: sales@eastbay.com
Website: www.eastbay.com
International Ordering: (715) 261-9588
Catalog: Free. Frequency: Annual
Circulation: 100K. Sales: $20-50MM
Products: Athletic footwear, apparel &
sports equipment

EBBETS FIELD FLANNEL PRESENTS　(866) 900-4411
Stall & Dean
P.O. Box 4858 • Seattle, WA 98104
E-Mail: sales@stallanddean.com
Website: www.stallanddean.com
Fax Ordering: (206) 342-4411
Catalog: Free. Frequency: Annual
Circulation:100K. Sales: $1-3MM
Products: Authentic golden age baseball
apparel

ELITE SPORTSWEAR, LP　(800) 345-4087
P.O. Box 16400 • Reading, PA 19612
E-Mail: custumerservice@gkelite.com
Website: www.gk-elitesportswear.com
Fax Ordering: (610) 921-0208
International Ordering: (610) 921-1469
Contact Name: Sallie Weaver, President
Catalog: Free. Frequency: Quarterly
Circulation: 2MM. Sales: $50-100MM
Products: GK gymnastics apparel, warmup
suits, skating wear; cheerleader briefs;
special order team apparel

EUROSPORT, SOCCER TRADERS　(800) 950-1994
Sports Endeavors
431 U.S. Highway 70A East
Hillsborough, NC 27278
E-Mail: custserv@sportsendeavors.com
Website: www.soccer.com
Fax Ordering: (800) 204-1198; (919) 644-6808
International Ordering: (919) 644-6800
Contact Name: Michael F. Moylan, President
Catalog: Free. Frequency: Monthly
Circulation: 1MM. Sales: $10-20MM
Products: Soccer gear & accessories

FARNAM EQUIPMENT COMPANY　(800) 267-5211
P.O. Box 34820 • Phoenix, AZ 85067
E-Mail: info@farnam.com
Website: www.farnam.com

Fax Ordering: (800) 456-0212
International Ordering: (602) 285-1660
Contact Name: Charles Duff, President
Catalog: Free. Frequency: Annual
Circulation: 150K. Sales: $1-3MM
Products: Golf clubs & supplies

FITNESS FACTORY OUTLET (800) 383-9300
1900 S. Des Plaines Ave.
Forest Park, IL 60130
E-Mail: sales@fitnessfactory.com
Website: www.fitnessfactory.com
Fax Ordering: (708) 345-9981
International Ordering: (708) 427-3500
Catalog: Free. Frequency: Semiannual
Circulation: 100K. Sales: $10-20MM
Products: Fitness & exercise equipment

FITNESS QUEST (800) 321-9236
1400 Raff Rd. SW • Canton, OH 44750
E-Mail: info@fitnessquest.com
Website: www.fitnessquest.com
Fax Ordering: (330) 479-9213
International Ordering: (330) 478-0755
Contact Name: Robert Schnabel, President
Catalog: Free. Frequency: Annual
Circulation: 100K. Sales: $5-10MM
Products: Home fitness equipment

FITNESS STUFF CATALOG (877) 937-8833
4141 D3 State St.
Santa Barbara, CA 93110
E-Mail: info@fitness-stuff.com
Website: www.fitness-stuff.com
Fax Ordering: (805) 884-0724
Contact Name: Carol Woody, President
Catalog: Free. Frequency: Quarterly
Circulation: 50K. Sales: $500M
Products: Exercise wear, sportswear
& exercise equipment

FITNESS SYSTEMS CATALOG (800) 967-1827
Fitness Systems Manufacturing Corp.
P.O. Box 2073 • Reading, PA 19608
E-Mail: vitaminout@aol.com
Website: www.fitness-systems.net
Fax Ordering: (800) 461-3979; (610) 678-9022
International Ordering: (610) 670-0135
Customer service: (800) 822-9995
Contact Name: David Hoffman, President
Catalog: Free. Frequency: Annual
Circulation: 10K. Sales: $500K
Products: Athletic/sports proteins,
amino acids, vitamins & supplements
at wholesale prices

FLAGHOUSE PHYSICAL (800) 793-7900
EDUCATION & RECREATION
601 Flaghouse Dr. • Hasbrouck Hts., NJ 07604
E-Mail: sales@flaghouse.com
Website: www.flaghouse.com
Fax Ordering: (800) 793-7922
International Ordering: (201) 288-7600
Contact Name: George Carmel, President
Catalog: Free. Frequency: Annual
Circulation: 150K. Sales: $20-50MM
Products: Children's sporting goods;
physical education & recreation

FOOTBALL AMERICA (877) 697-7678
1051 East Nakoma • San Antonio, TX 78216
E-Mail: info@footballamerica.com

Website: www.footballamerica.com
Fax Ordering: (800) 322-1763
Catalog: Free. Pages: 104. Frequency: Annual
Circulation: 150K. Sales: $20-50MM
Products: Football equipment & accessories;
uniform supplier

FORT - THE SPORTING LIFE (800) 467-8429
American Rugby Outfitters
1510 Midway Ct. • Elk Grove, IL 60007
E-Mail: info@americanrugby.com
Website: www.americanrugby.com
Fax Ordering: (847) 981-1244
International Ordering: (847) 981-1242
Catalog: Free. Frequency: Semiannual
Circulation: 500K. Sales: $10-20MM
Products: Rugby apparel, jerseys &
warm-up suits; specialty apparel

GATOR CATALOG (800) 325-3729
Gator Sports
3789 South 300 West, Bldg. C
Salt Lake City, UT 84115
E-Mail: gatorsports@juno.com
Website: www.gatorsportsinc.com
Fax Ordering: (801) 264-8412
International Ordering: (801) 325-3729
Contact Name: Kent R. Jones, President
Catalog: Free. Frequency: Annual
Circulation: 100K. Sales: $1-3MM
Products: Bicycling gear & accessories

GEAR DIRECT CATALOG (888) 411-GEAR
2907 55th St. • Boulder, CO 80301
E-Mail: info@geardirect.com
Website: www.geardirect.com
Fax Ordering: (303) 369-3714
International Ordering: (303) 440-8434
Catalog: Free. Frequency: Quarterly
Circulation: 50K. Sales: $1-3MM
Products: Skiwear, skis, bikes,
snowboards, apparel, accessories

GIANT BICYCLE CATALOG (800) 874-4268
737 W. Artesia Blvd.
Compton, CA 90220
E-Mail: sales@flaghouse.com
Website: www.flaghouse.com
Fax Ordering: (800) 793-7922
International Ordering: (201) 288-7600
Contact Name: George Carmel, President
Catalog: Free. Frequency: Annual
Circulation: 150K. Sales: $20-50MM
Products: Bicycles, bicycling gear
& accessories

GOAL SPORTING GOODS (800) 334-4625
P.O. Box 243 • Essex, CT 06426
E-Mail: sales@goalsports.com
Website: www.goalsports.com
Fax Ordering: (860) 767-9121
International Ordering: (860) 767-9112
Contact Name: Morton Reich, President
Catalog: Free. Frequency: Quarterly
Circulation: 100K. Sales: $5-10MM
Products: Goals, gymnasium equipment,
nets & mats, bleachers, soccer equipment,
referee gear

GOLF AROUND THE WORLD (800) 824-4279
1396 N. Killian Dr. • Lake Park, FL 33403
E-Mail: info@golfaroundtheworld.com

Website: www.golfaroundtheworld.com
Fax Ordering: (561) 848-0870
International Ordering: (561) 848-8896
Contact Name: Dane Wiren, President
Catalog: Free. Frequency: Annual
Circulation: 50K. Sales: $1-3MM
Products: Golf training products

GOLF MOLE　　(800) 342-5059
299 Big Run Rd. • Lexington, KY 40503
E-Mail: info@golfmole.com
Website: www.golfmole.com
Fax Ordering: (859) 278-4418
International Ordering: (859) 277-0005
Catalog: Free. Frequency: Semiannual
Circulation: 100M. Sales: $1-3MM
Products: Golf club components, pendulum
puttersa, heads, shafts, accessories; custom
built products

GOLF SUPPLY AMERICA　　(800) GSA-5559
1820 6th Ave. SE • Decatur, AL 35601
E-Mail: golf@golfsupply.com
Website: www.golfsupply.com
Fax Ordering: (256) 355-9909
International Ordering: (256) 355-8888
Catalog: Free. Frequency: Annual
Circulation: 50M. Sales: $5-10MM
Products: Wholesale golf compenent
distributor

GOLFPAC GOLF TOURS　　(888) 848-8941
Golfpac • P.O. Box 162366
Atamonte Springs, FL 32716
E-Mail: info@golfpactravel.com
Website: www.golfpactravel.com
Fax Ordering: (407) 260-8989
International Ordering: (407) 260-2288
Catalog: Free. Frequency: Annual
Circulation: 100M. Sales: $3-5MM
Products: Golf trip packages for business

GOLFSMITH STORE CATALOG　　(800) 396-0099
11000 NIH 35 • Austin, TX 78753
E-Mail: info@golfsmith.com
Website: www.golfsmith.com
Fax Ordering: (512) 837-1245
International Ordering: (512) 837-8810
Contact Name: Frank Paul, President
Catalog: Free. Frequency: 14x per year
Circulation: 25MM. Sales: $50-100MM
Products: Golfing equipment, apparel &
accessorieS

GOPHER SPORT EQUIPMENT　　(800) 533-0446
P.O. Box 998 • Owatonna, MN 55060
E-Mail: info@gophersport.com
Website: www.gophersport.com
Fax Ordering: (800) 451-4855; (507) 451-4755
International Ordering: (507) 451-7470
Contact Name: Dan Gorman, President
Catalog: Free. Frequency: Semiannual
Circulation: 400M. Sales: $10-20MM
Products: Physical education, recreation
& athletic & fitness products

GREAT ATLANTIC LACROSSE CO.　　(800) 955-3876
Sports Endeavors
431 U.S. Highway 70E
Hillsborough, NC 27278
E-Mail: custserv@sportsendeavors.com
Website: www.lacrosse.com

Fax Ordering: (800) 204-1198; (919) 644-6808
International Ordering: (919) 644-6800
Contact Name: Char Watson, President
Catalog: Free. Frequency: Annual
Circulation: 50K. Sales: $3-5MM
Products: Lacrosse gear & accessories

GREAT SKATE HOCKEY SUPPLY CO.　　(800) 828-7496
3395 Sheridan Dr. • Amherst, NY 14226
E-Mail: info@greatskate.com
Website: www.greatskate.com
Fax Ordering: (716) 838-5123
International Ordering: (716) 838-5100
Contact Name: Tom Farkas, President
Catalog: Free. Frequency: Semiannual
Circulation: 50K. Sales: $1-3MM
Products: Hockey equipment

HAMMER STRENGTH　　(800) 328-9714
Life Fitness
5100 N. River Rd.
Schiller Park, IL 60175
E-Mail: homeproductservice@lifefitness.com
Website: www.lifefitness.com
Fax Ordering: (847) 288-3765
Catalog: Free. Frequency: Annual
Circulation: 100K. Sales: $3-5MM
Products: Fitness/weightlifting machines,
equipment & products for the home & gyms

RICHARD HARRIS CLASSICS　　(800) 427-5657
872 N. Highway Cir. • Dayton, MN 55108
E-Mail: info@harriscollection.com
Website: www.harriscollection.com
Fax Ordering: (651) 688-8733
International Ordering: (763) 971-0781
Contact Name: Dick Harris, President
Catalog: Free. Frequency: Annual
Circulation: 50M. Sales: $1-3MM
Products: Traditional golf apparel &
merchandise

HERITAGE GOLF COMPANY　　(800) 342-5059
299 Big Run Rd. • Lexington, KY 40503
E-Mail: info@heritagegolfco.com
Website: www.heritagegolfco.com
Fax Ordering: (859) 278-4418
International Ordering: (859) 277-0005
Contact Name: Steve Lewis, President
Catalog: Free. Frequency: Annual
Circulation: 50M. Sales: $1-3MM
Products: Golf clubs & supplies

HIGHLANDER GOLF & CLOTHING　　(800) 334-2230
Highlander Company
1072 Jacoby Rd. • Copley, OH 44321
E-Mail: highlogo@aol.com
Website: www.highlanderlogo.com
Fax Ordering: (866) 666-4525
International Ordering: (330) 666-7390
Contact Name: Thomas E. Dieghan, President
Catalog: Free. Frequency: 5x per year
Circulation: 50M. Sales: $1-3MM
Products: Men's clothing; golf clothing

HOLABIRD SPORTS　　(410) 687-6400
9220 Pulaski Hwy. • Baltimore, MD 21220
E-Mail: holabird@holabirdsports.com
Website: www.holabirdsports.com
Fax Ordering: (410) 687-7311
Catalog: Free. Frequency: Monthly
Circulation: 350M. Sales: $10-20MM

Products: All racquet sport equipment;
apparel & athletic footwear

THE HOUSE (800) 409-7669
300 S. Owasso Blvd.
St. Paul, MN 55117
E-Mail: info@the-house.com
Website: www.the-house.com
Fax Ordering: (651) 482-1353
International Ordering: (651) 482-9995
Customer Service: (800) 247-2763
Contact Name: Steve Poindexter, President
Catalog: Free. Frequency: Semiannual
Circulation: 200M. Sales: $5-10MM
Products: Windsurfing, snowboarding,
inline skating & kayaking equipment

HUMAN KINETICS SPORTS (800) 747-4457
SPORTS & FITNESS CATALOG
P.O. Box 5076 • Champaign, IL 61825
E-Mail: info@humankinetics.com
Website: www.humankinetics.com
Fax Ordering: (217) 351-1549
International Ordering: (217) 351-5076
Catalog: Free. Frequency: Annual
Circulation: 100M. Sales: $1-3MM
Products: Instructional books on specific sports,
coaching education & sports administration;
fitness/training topics

IN THE SWIM (800) 288-7946
320 Industrial Dr.
West Chicago, IL 60185
E-Mail: hq@intheswim.com
Website: www.intheswim.com
Fax Ordering: (800) 766-5329;
  (800) 448-7329
International Ordering: (630) 876-0040
  Fax (630) 876-1091
Customer Service: (800) 374-1500
Catalog: Free. Frequency: Semiannual
Circulation: 50K. Sales: $5-10MM
Products: Pool supplies & equipment;
spa supplies

INTERNATIONAL TAEKWONDO ASSN. (810) 232-6482
P.O. Box 281 • Grand Blanc, MI 48439
E-Mail: customerservice@itatkd.com
Website: www.itatkd.com
Fax Ordering: (810) 235-8594
Contact Name: James S. Benko, President
Catalog: $3. Frequency: Quarterly
Circulation: 25K. Sales: $500M
Products: Taekwondo martial arts videos,
audios, books & supplies

JAZZERTOGS CATALOG (800) 348-4748
1050 Joshua Way • Vista, CA 92083
E-Mail: jazzine@jazzercise.com
Website: www.jazzercise.com
Fax Ordering: (760) 602-7180
International Ordering: (760) 598-3837
Contact Name: Judi Sheppard Missett, President
Catalog: Free. Frequency: 10x per year
Circulation: 1MM. Sales: $3-5MM
Products: Aerobic, dance-fitness apparel;
accessories & fitness products

JUGS COMPANY CATALOG (800) 547-6843
P.O. Box 3126 • Tualatin, OR 97062
E-Mail: sales@jugsbaseball.com
Website: www.jugsbaseball.com

Fax Ordering: (503) 691-1100
International Ordering: (503) 692-1635
Contact Name: John K. Paulson, President
Catalog: Free. Frequency: 10x per year
Circulation: 50M. Sales: $3-5MM
Products: Ball throwing machines

JUMPKING TRAMPOLINES (800) 220-9343
901 W. Miller Rd. • Garland, TX 75041
E-Mail: info@jumpking.com
Website: www.jumpking.com
Fax Ordering: (972) 290-7306
International Ordering: (972) 290-7300
Customer Service: (800) 322-2211
Catalog: Free. Frequency: Annual
Circulation: 100M. Sales: $10-20MM
Products: Trampolines, parts & accessories

KART WORLD (440) 357-5569
KW Marketing
1488 Mentor Ave. • Painesville, OH 44077
E-Mail: help@kwmarketing.com
Website: www.kartworld.com
Fax Ordering: (440) 357-1903
Contact Name: Robert N. Loomis, President
Catalog: $4. Frequency: Annual
Circulation: 75M. Sales: $3-5MM
Products: Racing karts, all-terrain kits,
minibikes, trailer kits & scooters at
discount prices

KAST-A-WAY SWIMWEAR (800) 543-2763
9356 Cincinnati Columbus Rd.
Cincinnati, OH 45241
E-Mail: sales@kastawayswimwear.com
Website: www.kastawayswimwear.com
Fax Ordering: (513) 777-1062
International Ordering: (513) 777-7967
Contact Name: Patti Kast, President
Catalog: Free. Frequency: Semiannual
Circulation: 175K. Sales: $5-10MM
Products: Competition swimwear & accessories,
aquatic fitness videos, training equipment & books

KEMP'S HOCKEY SUPPLY CO. (800) 223-8571
580 New Loudon Rd. • Latham, NY 12110
E-Mail: info@kempshockey.com
Website: www.kempshockey.com
Fax Ordering: (518) 785-1820
International Ordering: (518) 785-5297
Contact Name: Jerry Kemp, President
Catalog: Free. Frequency: Annual
Circulation: 50K. Sales: $1-3MM
Products: Hockey & lacrosse equipment

KESTREL BICYCLES (831) 464-9079
5300 Soquel Ave., Suite 101
Santa Cruz, CA 95062
E-Mail: info@kestrel-usa.com
Website: www.kestrel-usa.com
Fax Ordering: (831) 464-9069
Brochure: Free. Frequency: Annual
Circulation: 100K. Sales: $3-5MM
Products: Road & mountain bikes & accessories

ADOLPH KIEFER & ASSOCIATES (800) 323-4071
1700 Kiefer Dr. • Zion, IL 60099
E-Mail: catalog@kiefer.com
Website: www.kiefer.com
Fax Ordering: (847) 746-8888
International Ordering: (847) 872-8866
Contact Name: Louis Cohen, President

Catalog: Free. Frequency: 8x per year
Circulation: 1MM. Sales: $10-20MM
Products: Swimming supplies & training
equipment

KING LOUIE SPORTS CATALOG (816) 765-5212
13500 15th St.
Grandview, MO 64030
E-Mail: sales@kinglouie.com
Website: www.kinglouie.com
Fax Ordering: (816) 777-1062
Contact Name: Robert Palan, President
Catalog: Free. Frequency: Annual
Circulation: 200K. Sales: $10-20MM
Products: Bowling shirts, sweaters,
activewear & hats

KOALA MEN'S SWIMWEAR (800) 238-2941
P.O. Box 5519
Sherman Oaks, CA 91413
E-Mail: sales@koalaswim.com
Website: www.koalaswim.com
Fax Ordering: (818) 780-5170
International Ordering: (818) 727-7620
Contact Name: Michael D. Young, President
Catalog: $2. Frequency: 3x per year
Circulation: 1MM. Sales: $3-5MM
Products: Swimwear for men

KRYPTONITE CORPORATION (800) 729-5625
320 Turnpike St. • Canton, MA 02021
E-Mail: sales@flaghouse.com
Website: www.flaghouse.com
Fax Ordering: (781) 821-4777
International Ordering: (781) 828-6655
Contact Name: Peter Zane, President
Catalog: Free. Frequency: Annual
Circulation: 150K. Sales: $5-10MM
Products: Bicycle & car locks

KYTEC ATHLETIC SPEED EQUIPMENT (800) 732-4883
8337 Penn Ave. S.
Bloomington, MN 55431
E-Mail: order@kytec.us
Website: www.kytec.us
Fax Ordering: (952) 884-3424
International Ordering: (952) 884-3424
Contact Name: Jodi Michaelson, President
Catalog: Free. Frequency: Semiannual
Circulation: 50K. Sales: $500M to $1MM
Products: Athletic speed equipment,
parachutes, bunji, fitness, rehabilitation
equipment, apparel videos & books

LACROSSE INTERNATIONAL (800) 333-5229
15 Green St. • Downington, PA 19335
Fax Ordering: (610) 873-7550
International Ordering: (610) 873-1450
Contact Name: Deborah Stevens, President
Catalog: Free. Frequency: Annual
Circulation: 50K. Sales: $1-3MM
Products: Lacrosse equipment

LEAGUE DIRECT (800) 774-6972
P.O. Box 7726 • Dallas, TX 75209
E-Mail: leaguedirectfeed@sportssupplygroup.com
Website: www.ssgecom.com
Fax Ordering: (800) 866-5760
Catalog: Free. Frequency: Semiannual
Circulation: 150K. Sales: $5-10MM
Products: Sports teams products

LEFTIES ONLY-GOLF SPECIALTY SHOP (800) 533-8437
1972 Williston Rd. • So. Burlington, VT 05403
E-Mail: leftiesonlygolf@msn.com
Website: www.leftiesonlygolf.com
Fax Ordering: (802) 864-7701
International Ordering: (802) 862-1114
Contact Name: Walt Tripovich, President
Catalog: Free. Frequency: 5x per year
Circulation: 100K. Sales: $1-3MM
Products: Windsurfing, snowboarding,
inline skating & kayaking equipment

LONE PEAK DESIGNS (800) 777-7679
3474 S 2300 E • Salt Lake City, UT 84109
E-Mail: lppacks@aol.com
Fax Ordering: (801) 272-5240
International Ordering: (801) 272-5217
Contact Name: Scott Sterrett, President
Catalog: Free. Frequency: Annual
Circulation: 150K. Sales: $5-10MM
Products: Bicycling bags & accessories

LOOSE SCREWS/ (541) 488-4800
BICYCLE SMALL PARTS
12225 Hwy. 66 • Ashland, OR 97520
E-Mail: inquiry@thethirdhand.com
Website: www.thethirdhand.com
Fax Ordering: (541) 482-0080
Catalog: Free. Frequency: Annual
Circulation: 50K. Sales: $1-3MM
Products: Small parts to fix bicycles

LYMAN PRODUCTS CORPORATION (800) 225-9626
475 Smith St. • Middletown, CT 06457
E-Mail: sales@lymanproducts.com
Website: www.lymanproducts.com
Fax Ordering: (860) 632-1699
International Ordering: (860) 632-2020
Contact Name: J. Mace Thompson, President
Catalog: $2. Frequency: Annual
Circulation: 50K. Sales: $10-20MM
Products: Sporting goods; jewelry & lapidary
equipment

RALPH MALTBY'S GOLFWORKS (800) 848-8358
The Golfworks
4820 Jacksontown Rd. • Newark, OH 43055
E-Mail: golfworks@golfworks.com
Website: www.golfworks.com
Fax Ordering: (800) 800-3290
International Ordering: (740) 328-4193
Contact Name: Kevin Davis
Catalog: Free. Frequency: Quarterly
Circulation: 1MM. Sales: $20-50MM
Products: Golf equipment & supplies

MANNY'S BASEBALL LAND (800) 232-5939
Genesis Direct
100 Plaza Dr. • Secaucus, NJ 07094
Fax Ordering: (201) 847-8626
International Ordering: (201) 947-8181
Catalog: Free. Frequency: Semiannual
Circulation: 250K. Sales: $10-20MM
Products: Official catalog of Major League
Baseball

MARK'S ATHLETIC SOLES (800) 666-6222
7395 SW 45th St. • Miami, FL 33155
E-Mail: sales@saveyoursole.com
Website: www.saveyoursole.com
Fax Ordering: (305) 665-8989

International Ordering: (305) 665-8601
Contact Name: Pat McCabe, President
Catalog: $2. Frequency: Semiannual
Circulation: 200K. Sales: $500M
Products: Sports apparel & equipment

MASKA USA   (800) 232-9226
CCM, Maska USA, Inc.
P.O. Box 381 • Bradford, VT 05033
E-Mail: info@ccmsports.com
Website: www.ccmsports.com
Fax Ordering: (800) 232-9226
International Ordering: (802) 222-4751
Contact Name: Gerald Wasserman, President
Catalog: Free. Frequency: Annual
Circulation: 50K. Sales: $20-50MM
Products: Hockey equipment & apparel

MEMPHIS NET & TWINE   (901) 458-2656
COMPANY-SPORTS
2481 Matthews Ave. • Memphis, TN 38108
E-Mail: mcmnet@memphisnet.com
Website: www.memphisnet.com
Fax Ordering: (901) 458-1601
Contact Name: Albert Carrthers, President
Catalog: Free. Frequency: Semiannual
Circulation: 250K. Sales: $3-5MM
Products: Baseball cages & backstops

MF ATHLETIC   (888) 556-7464
P.O. Box 8090 • Cranston, RI 02921
E-Mail: mfathletic@mfathletic.com
Website: www.mfathletic.com
Fax Ordering: (800) 682-6950; (401) 942-7645
International Ordering: (401) 942-9363
Catalog: Free. Frequency: Semiannual
Circulation: 100K. Sales: $5-10MM
Products: Track & field equipment & supplies

MARKERS, INC.   (866) 617-6275
33490 Pin Oak Pkwy.
Avon Lake, OH 44012
E-Mail: sales@markersinc.com
Website: www.markersinc.com
Fax Ordering: (440) 933-7839
Catalog: Free. Frequency: Semiannual
Circulation: 150K. Sales: $5-10MM
Products: Golf course supplies & equipment;
athletic field supplies & equipment

MINNESOTA FATS'   (212) 366-6981
ALL FUN & GAMES
160 W. 26th St. • New York, NY 10001
E-Mail: marne@mnfats.com
Website: www.mnfats.com
Fax Ordering: (212) 206-6491
Contact Name: Paul Giegerich, Marketing
Catalog: Free. Frequency: Annual
Circulation: 10M. Sales: $1-3MM
Products: Everything for your game room:
pool tables, cues & billiard accessories;
bars & barstools; foosball, air hockey,
darts, casino supplies

MORLEY ATHLETIC SUPPLY   (800) 811-1931
P.O. Box 557 • Amsterdam, NY 12010
E-Mail: sales@morleyathletic.com
Website: www.morleyathletic.com
Fax Ordering: (518) 843-6248
International Ordering: (518) 842-9191
Contact Name: K. Richard Morley, Jr., President
Catalog: Free. Frequency: Annual

Circulation: 50K. Sales: $5-10MM
Products: Athletic & physical education
supplies

MOUNTAIN BIKE SPECIALISTS   (800) 255-8377
949 Main Ave. • Durango, CO 81301
Fax Ordering: (970) 385-7445
International Ordering: (970) 247-4066
Contact Name: Ed Zink, President
Catalog: Free. Frequency: Annual
Circulation: 25K. Sales: $1-3MM
Products: Mountain bikes & accessories

MOUNTAIN GEAR   (800) 829-2009
E.6021 Mansfield
Spokane Valley, WA 99212
E-Mail: info@mgear.com
Website: www.mountaingear.com
Fax Ordering: (509) 325-3030
International Ordering: (509) 340-1165
Catalog: Free. Frequency: Semiannual
Circulation: 100K. Sales: $10-20MM
Products: Mountain climbing gear, apparel
& footwear

MURRAY WIND & WATER SPORTS   (800) 788-8964
Murray Sports Center
6389 Rose Lane • Carpenteria, CA 93013
Fax Ordering: (805) 684-8966
Contact Name: Steve Murray, President
Catalog: $2. Frequency: Semiannual
Circulation: 50K. Sales: $1-3MM
Products: Sailing, windsurfing & kite surf
accessories & surf, boards & accessories
by Terra Sports

NDL PRODUCTS   (800) 979-4343
4031 NE 12th Ter.
Oakland Park, FL 33334
Fax Ordering: (954) 568-6906
International Ordering: (954) 566-0040
Contact Name: Deborah Barnes, President
Catalog: Free. Frequency: Annual
Circulation: 25K. Sales: $1-3MM
Products: Boxing & fitness equipment

NEVCO SCOREBOARD   (800) 851-4040
301 E. Harris Ave.   Canada (800) 461-8550
Greenville, IL 62246
E-Mail: nevo@nevcoscoreboard.com
Website: www.nevcoscoreboard.com
Fax Ordering: (618) 664-0398
International Ordering: (618) 664-0360
Contact Name: Mary Gayle Nevinger, President
Catalog: Free. Frequency: Weekly
Circulation: 100K. Sales: $1-3MM
Products: Scoreboards

OBERMEYER CATALOG   (800) 525-4203
115 ABC • Aspen, CO 81611
E-Mail: info@obermeyer.com
Website: www.obermeyer.com
Fax Ordering: (970) 925-9203
International Ordering: (970) 925-5060
Contact Name: Klaus Obermeyer, President
Catalog: Free. Frequency: Annual
Circulation: 250K. Sales: $20-50MM
Products: Ski outerwear

OCEAN HOCKEY SUPPLY COMPANY   (800) 631-2159
197 Chambersbridge Rd. • Brick, NJ 08723
Fax Ordering: (732) 477-1167

International Ordering: (732) 477-4411
Catalog: Free. Frequency: Annual
Circulation: 50K. Sales: $3-5MM
Products: Hockey equipment

O'NEAL/USA AZONIC CATALOG   (818) 998-1049
9600 Topanga Canyon Blvd.
Chatsworth, CA 91311
E-Mail: atlantic@atlantic-fitness.com
Website: www.atlantic-fitness.com
Fax Ordering: (818) 882-0435
Contact Name: Rich Walsh, Manager
Catalog: $2. Frequency: Annual
Circulation: 25K. Sales: $3-5MM
Products: Dirt bikes, mountain bikes;
biking apparel & accessories

PACIFIC SPORTS WAREHOUSE   (800) 835-1055
10746 Kenney St. • Santee, CA 92071
E-Mail: sales@pacificsports.com
Website: www.pacificsports.com
Fax Ordering: (619) 596-2140
International Ordering: (619) 596-2135
Contact Name: Jeff Lehrer, President
Catalog: Free. Frequency: 3x per year
Circulation: 150K. Sales: $1-3MM
Products: Racquetball equipment, supplies
& accessories

PACIFIC WATERSPORTS   (800) 231-6481
ACCESSORIES CORPORATION
P.O. Box 30801 • Santa Barbara, CA 93130
E-Mail: ronwest@west.net
Fax Ordering: (805) 963-1502
International Ordering: (805) 963-1502
Contact Name: Ron Westerman, President
Catalog: $2. Frequency: Semiannual
Circulation: 25K. Sales: $10-20MM
Products: Sport watches, sun block,
sunglasses, beach & water accessories

PANTHER PRODUCTIONS   (800) 332-4442
P.O. Box 73610
San Clemente, CA 92673
E-Mail: info@panthervideo.com
Website: www.panthervideo.com
Fax Ordering: (949) 492-7533
International Ordering: (949) 498-7765
Contact Name: Joseph Jennings, President
Catalog: Free. Frequency: Annual
Circulation: 50K. Sales: $500K - $1MM
Products: Martial arts training videos

PATAGONIA CATALOG   (800) 336-9090
Patagonia, Inc.   (800) 638-6464
P.O. Box 32050 • Reno, NV 89523
E-Mail: sales@patagonia.com
Website: www.patagonia.com
Fax Ordering: (800) 543-5522; (775) 747-6159
International Ordering: (775) 747-1992
Contact Name: Yvon Chounard, President
Catalog: Free. Frequency: Bimonthly
Circulation: 1MM. Sales: $100-250MM
Products: Outdoor, sportsman's apparel
for men & women

BEN PEARSON ARCHERY   (870) 534-6411
734 Industrial Park Dr.
Brewton, AR 36426
E-Mail: sales@benpearson.com
Website: www.benpearson.com
Fax Ordering: (870) 534-3177

Contact Name: Jim L. Taylor, President
Catalog: Free. Frequency: Annual
Circulation: 100K. Sales: $5-10MM
Products: Archery products

PERFORMANCE BICYCLE   (800) 727-2453
Performance Products
P.O. Box 2741 • Chapel Hill, NC 27515
Fax Ordering: (800) 727-3291
International Ordering: (919) 933-9113
Contact Name: Bob Martin, President
Catalog: Free. Frequency: Quarterly
Circulation: 2MM. Sales: $50-100MM
Products: Cycling apparel, equipment
& accessories

POWER MUSIC   (800) 777-2328
435 W. 400 S., 2nd Fl.
Salt Lake City, UT 84101
E-Mail: sales@powermusic.com
Website: www.powermusic.com
Fax Ordering: (800) 773-2937;
   (801) 328-8885
International Ordering: (801) 328-8884
Contact Name: Richard Petty, Manager
Catalog: Free. Frequency: Annual
Circulation: 100K. Sales: $5-10MM
Products: Workout fitness music; music for
meditation; aerobic workout music; music for
cheerleading

PRICE POINT BICYCLE   (800) 774-2376
Price Point Mail Order Ltd.
1442 W. 135th St. • Gardena, CA 90249
E-Mail: sales@pricepoint.com
Website: www.pricepoint.com
Fax Ordering: (800) 888-3294; (310) 769-6189
International Ordering: (310) 323-3473
Catalog: Free. Frequency: Annual
Circulation: 150K. Sales: $5-10MM
Products: Bicycles; bicycling apparel,
parts, frames

RACELINE DIRECT   (800) 454-8929
435 Main St. • Johnson City, NY 13790
E-Mail: info@racelinedirect.com
Website: www.racelinedirect.com
Fax Ordering: (607) 644-1551
Catalog: Free. Frequency: Annual
Circulation: 150K. Sales: $5-10MM
Products: NASCAR apparel including caps,
outerwear, shirts, sweatshirts, pants; gifts &
collectibles

RAINBO SPORT SHOPS   (800) 752-8370
4836 N. Clark St. • Chicago, IL 60640
Fax Ordering: (773) 275-5506
International Ordering: (773) 275-5500
Contact Name: Cale Carvell, President
Catalog: Free. Frequency: Quarterly
Circulation: 100M. Sales: $3-5MM
Products: Ice figure skating & speed skating
supplies, including skates, books, videos,
jewelry, training aids

RANS RECUMBENTS   (785) 625-6346
4600 Hwy. 183 Alt. • Hays, KS 67601
E-Mail: bikes@rans.com
Website: www.rans.com
Fax Ordering: (785) 625-2795
Contact Name: Randy Schlitter, President
Catalog: Free. Frequency: Annual

Circulation: 100M. **Sales: $5-10MM**
Products: Recumbent bicycles & tandem
hybrid bikes

RAWLINGS SPORTING GOODS (800) 729-5464
P.O. Box 22000 • St. Louis, MO 63126
E-Mail: info@rawlings.com
Website: www.rawlings.com
Fax Ordering: (636) 349-3580
International Ordering: (636) 349-3500
Contact Name: Howard Keene, President
Catalog: Free. Frequency: Semiannual
Circulation: 100K. **Sales: $10-20MM**
Products: Sports equipment & apparel
for baseball, hockey, basketball & football

REI CATALOG (800) 426-4840
REI, Inc. • Sumner, WA 98352
E-Mail: info@rei.com
Website: www.rei.com
Fax Ordering: (253) 891-2523
International Ordering: (253) 891-2523
Contact Name: Dennis Madsen, President
Catalog: Free. Frequency: Quarterly
Circulation: 3MM. **Sales: $20-50MM**
Products: Recreational equipment;
outdoor gear & clothing

REGENTS SPORTS CORPORATION (631) 234-2800
45 Ranick Rd. • Hauppauge, NY 11788
Fax Ordering: (631) 234-2948
Contact Name: Irv Lawner, President
Catalog: Free. Frequency: Annual
Circulation: 100K. **Sales: $5-10MM**
Products: Team sporting goods

RELIABLE RACING WINTER SPORTS (800) 223-4448
643 Upper Glen St.
Queensbury, NY 12804
E-Mail: comments@reliableracing.com
Website: www.reliableracing.com
Fax Ordering: (518) 793-6491
International Ordering: (518) 793-5677
Contact Name: Tom Jacobs, President
Catalog: Free. Frequency: Quarterly
Circulation: 250K. **Sales: $20-50MM**
Products: Ski racing equipment & apparel;
snowshoes

RINGSIDE CATALOG (877) 426-9464
9650 Dice Lane • Lenexa, KS 66215
E-Mail: davel@ringside.com
Website: www.ringside.com
Fax Ordering: (913) 888-2198
International Ordering: (913) 888-1719
Contact Name: John Brown, President
Catalog: Free. Frequency: Quarterly
Circulation: 100K. **Sales: $5-10MM**
Products: Boxing & martial arts equipment

ROAD RUNNER SPORTS (800) 551-5558
5549 Copley Dr. • San Diego, CA 92111
E-Mail: info@roadrunnersports.com
Website: www.roadrunnersports.com
Fax Ordering: (800) 453-5443; (858) 636-7650
Customer Service: (800) 636-3560
Contact Name: Jeff Rohling, Marketing
Catalog: Free. Frequency: 8x per year
Circulation: 8MM. **Sales: $50-100MM**
Products: Technical running products

ROBBINS TABLE TENNIS SPECIALTIES (800) 741-0333
38462 James Dr. • Clinton Twp., MI 48036
E-Mail: danspec@comcast.net
Website: www.robbinstabletennis.com
Fax Ordering: (586) 468-8760
International Ordering: (586) 468-8735
Contact Name: Katherine Robbins, President
Catalog: Free. Frequency: Quarterly
Circulation: 100K. **Sales: $500K - $1MM**
Products: Table tennis equipment; video

RUGBY & SOCCER SUPPLY (800) 336-3446
2744A Gallows Rd. • Merrifield, VA 22116 (800) 872-7842
E-Mail: info@rugbystore.com
Website: www.rugbystore.com
Fax Ordering: (703) 280-4543
International Ordering: (703) 280-5540
Contact Name: Matt Godek, President
Catalog: $2. Frequency: Annual
Circulation: 50K. **Sales: $3-5MM**
Products: Rugby & soccer gear &
accessories

SAMUELS TENNISPORT (800) 543-1153
7796 Montgomery Rd.
Cincinnati, OH 45236
E-Mail: tennisport@aol.com
Website: www.samuelstennissport.com
Fax Ordering: (513) 791-4036
International Ordering: (513) 791-4636
Contact Name: John Samuels, President
Catalog: Free. Frequency: Quarterly
Circulation: 25K. **Sales: $1-3MM**
Products: Tennis & racquet sports equipment

SAN SUN CATALOG (800) 241-6670
Daystone International Corporation
1856 Corporate Dr. • Norcross, GA 30093
E-Mail: nevo@nevcoscoreboard.com
Website: www.nevcoscoreboard.com
Fax Ordering: (770) 279-0309
International Ordering: (770) 279-0209
Contact Name: Day Shent Tong, President
Catalog: Free. Frequency: Annual
Circulation: 50K. **Sales: $3-5MM**
Products: Baseball & golf caps, tote bags
& umbrellas

GEORGE SANTELLI (201) 871-3105
465 S. Dean St. • Englewood, NJ 07631
E-Mail: gsantelli@aol.com
Website: www.santelli.com
Fax Ordering: (201) 871-8718
Contact Name: Carolyn Chesney, President
Catalog: Free. Frequency: Annual
Circulation: 100K. **Sales: $1-3MM**
Products: Fencing equipment; videos

SAUNDERS ARCHERY (800) 228-1408
P.O. Box 476 • Columbus, NE 68602
Fax Ordering: (402) 564-3260
International Ordering: (402) 564-7176
Contact Name: Eugene Saunders, President
Catalog: Free. Frequency: Annual
Circulation: 125K. **Sales: $3-5MM**
Products: Archery products

SAUNIER-WILHELM COMPANY (800) 284-5751
114 Gallery Dr. • McMurry, PA 15317
E-Mail: j.saunier@mindspring.com
Website: www.swcbilliards.com

Fax Ordering: (724) 969-4354
International Ordering: (724) 969-4350
Contact Name: Kevin Kautz, President
Catalog: Free. Frequency: Weekly
Circulation: 50K. Sales: $10-20MM
Products: Bowling & billiard supplies &
equipment

SKI LIMITED ENTERPRISES　　　　　(800) 477-4040
7825 South Ave. • Youngstown, OH 44512
E-Mail: vic@skilimited.com
Website: www.skilimited.com
Fax Ordering: (330) 758-8271
International Ordering: (330) 758-5214
Contact Name: Victor Daprile, President
Catalog: Free. Frequency: Weekly
Circulation: 2MM. Sales: $10-20MM
Products: Watersports equipment,
supplies & accessories

SKI & SNOWBOARD TOOLS　　　　　(800) 299-9904
Tognar toolworks
P.O. Box 212 • Mount Shasta, CA 96067
E-Mail: tools@tognar.com
Website: www.tognar.com
Fax Ordering: (800) 926-9904
International Ordering: (530) 926-2600
Contact Name: jack Moore, President
Catalog: Free. Frequency: Annual
Circulation: 25K. Sales: $500M
Products: Ski & snowboard tuning tools

SOFTBALL EQUIPMENT CATALOG　　　(800) 325-7238
Osborne Innovative Products
2221 2nd St. • Enumclaw, WA 98022
E-Mail: info@swingaway.com
Website: www.swingaway.com
Fax Ordering: (360) 825-0163
International Ordering: (360) 825-4299
Catalog: Free. Frequency: Annual
Circulation: 100K. Sales: $3-5MM
Products: Softball team equipment

SOFTBALL SALES　　　　　　　　　(800) 882-1166
E-Mail: info@softball.com
Website: www.softball.com
Catalog: Free. Frequency: Annual
Circulation: 100K. Sales: $3-5MM
Products: Softball equipment & apparel

SOFTBALL SUPPLY CATALOG　　　　(724) 225-1060
Pony Baseball
P.O. Box 225 • Washington, PA 15301
E-Mail: info@pony.odg.com
Website: www.pony.odg.com
Fax Ordering: (724) 225-9852
Catalog: Free. Frequency: Annual
Circulation: 100K. Sales: $5-10MM
Products: Scoreboards

SOFTRIDE CATALOG　　　　　　　　(800) 557-6387
P.O. Box 9709 • Bellingham, WA 98227
E-Mail: sales@softride.com
Website: www.softride.com
Fax Ordering: (360) 647-1884
International Ordering: (360) 647-7420
Contact Name: Anthony Varvaro, President
Catalog: Free. Frequency: Annual
Circulation: 50K. Sales: $1-3MM
Products: Bikes & bicycle suspension systems

SPORT FENCING CATALOG　　　　　(336) 835-7774
Triplette Competition Arms
331 Standard St. • Elkin, NC 28621
E-Mail: sales@triplette.com
Website: www.triplette.com
Fax Ordering: (336) 835-4099
Contact Name: Walter triplette, President
Catalog: Free. Frequency: Annual
Circulation: 100K. Sales: $1-3MM
Products: Fencing supplies

SPORTHILL CATALOG　　　　　　　(800) 622-8444
725 McKinley St. • Eugene, OR 97402
E-Mail: info@sporthill.com
Website: www.sporthill.com
Fax Ordering: (541) 343-7261
International Ordering: (541) 345-9623
Catalog: Free. Frequency: Annual
Circulation: 100K. Sales: $5-10MM
Products: Running, skiing & adventure
apparel

SPORTING LOOK CATALOG　　　　　(800) 750-8960
3251 SW 13th Dr.
Deerfield Beach, FL 33442
E-Mail: sales@sportinglook.com
Website: www.sportinglook.com
Fax Ordering: (954) 421-1157
International Ordering: (954) 570-5385
Contact Name: Harris Pollock, President
Catalog: $2. Frequency: Semiannual
Circulation: 250K. Sales: $5-10MM
Products: Tennis apparel, headbands
& wristbands

SPORTS ASYLUM　　　　　　　　　(800) 929-2159
9018 Balboa Blvd. #575A
Northridge, CA 91325
E-Mail: info@hockeybooks.com
Website: www.hockeybooks.com
Fax Ordering: (818) 893-4763
International Ordering: (818) 893-9970
Catalog: Free. Frequency: Annual
Circulation: 50K. Sales: $500MM
Products: Hockey books & videos

SPORTSMITH　　　　　　　　　　(888) 713-2880
5925 S. 188th E. Ave.
Tulsa, OK 74146
E-Mail: info@sportsmith.net
Website: www.sportsmith.net
Fax Ordering: (918) 307-0216
International Ordering: (918) 307-2446
Catalog: Free. Frequency: Semiannual
Circulation: 200K. Sales: $10-20MM
Products: Fitness & strength products;
fitness equipment parts; gym supplies

STAR STRUCK/PRO-TEAM　　　　　(877) 843-4263
8 F J Clark Cir. • Bethel, CT 06801
E-Mail: webmaster@starstruck.com
Website: www.starstruck.com
Fax Ordering: (800) 962-8345;
　(203) 778-6938
International Ordering: (203) 778-4925
Contact Name: Ken Karlan, President
Catalog: $2. Frequency: Annual
Circulation: 500K. Sales: $5-10MM
Products: Authentic apparel; baseball gifts
from major league teams

STATE LINE TACK CATALOG   (888) 839-9638
Petsmart Direct
P.O. Box 910 • Brockport, NY 14420
E-Mail: cs@petsmart.com
Website: www.petsmart.com
Fax Ordering: (716) 637-8244
International Ordering: (716) 637-7508
Contact Name: Samuel Parker, Chairman
Catalog: Free. Frequency: Annual
Circulation: 150K. Sales: $20-50MM
Products: Stable gear, harnesses

TABLE TENNIS TECHNOLOGY   (800) 611-7712
Butterfly Table Tennis Center
P.O. Box 157 • Wilson, NC 27890
E-Mail: info@butterflyonline.com
Website: www.butterflyonline.com
Fax Ordering: (252) 291-8203
International Ordering: (252) 291-4770
Contact Name: Bowie Martin, Jr., President
Catalog: Free. Frequency: Annual
Circulation: 100K. Sales: $3-5MM
Products: Tennis equipment, supplies
& accessories

10-S TENNIS SUPPLY   (800) 247-3907
1820 7th Ave. N • Lake Worth, FL 33461
E-Mail: sales@10-s.com
Website: www.10-s.com
Fax Ordering: (561) 547-3371
International Ordering: (561) 547-1772
Contact Name: David Buerkle, President
Catalog: Free. Frequency: Annual
Circulation: 100K. Sales: $3-5MM
Products: Tennis court supplies & accessories

TERRY PRECISION CYCLING   (800) 289-8379
1657 E. Park Rd. • Macedon, NY 14502
E-Mail: talktours@terrybicycles.com
Website: www.terrybicycles.com
Fax Ordering: (315) 986-2104
International Ordering: (315) 986-2103
Contact Name: Gregory Terry, President
Catalog: Free. Frequency: 10x per year
Circulation: 1MM. Sales: $5-10MM
Products: Bicycling apparel & accessories

TIFFIN ATHELTIC MATS   (800) 843-3467
P.O. Box 823 • Elkton, MD 21922
E-Mail: tiffin@tiffinmats.com
Website: www.tiffinmats.com
Fax Ordering: (410) 398-7397
International Ordering: (410) 398-0900
Contact Name: Dan Tiffin, President
Catalog: Free. Frequency: Semiannual
Circulation: 100M. Sales: $1-3MM
Products: Athletic mats; gymnastics equipment

TITLE NINE SPORTS   (800) 342-4448
6201 Doyle St. • Emeryville, CA 94608   (800) 609-0092
E-Mail: thefolks@title9sports.com
Website: www.title9sports.com
Fax Ordering: (510) 655-9191
Contact Name: Missy Park, President
Catalog: Free. Frequency: 8x per year
Circulation: 100M. Sales: $1-3MM
Products: Sportswear & acessories for women

TOLEDO PHYSICAL EDUCATION   (800) 225-7749
5101 Advantage Dr. • Toledo, OH 43612
E-Mail: toledope@glasscity.com
Website: www.tpesonline.com

Fax Ordering: (800) 489-6256
International Ordering: (419) 726-8122
Contact Name: Thomas McNutt, President
Catalog: Free. Frequency: Annual
Circulation: 150K. Sales: $5-10MM
Products: Sporting goods & athletic
equipment

TREK BICYCLE CORPORATION   (920) 478-2191
801 E. Madison St.
Waterloo, WI 53594
E-Mail: info@trekbikes.com
Website: www.trekbikes.com
Fax Ordering: (920) 478-3589
Contact Name: John Burke, President
Catalog: Free. Frequency: Annual
Circulation: 250K. Sales: $20-50MM
Products: Bikes

TSI SOCCER CATALOG   (800) 842-6679
4324 S. Alston Ave.
Durham, NC 27713
E-Mail: custserv@tsisoccer.com
Website: www.tsisoccer.com
Fax Ordering: (919) 484-0126
International Ordering: (919) 484-0818
Contact Name: John Pinto, President
Catalog: Free. Frequency: Monthly
Circulation: 2MM. Sales: $20-50MM
Products: Soccer apparel, footwear &
equipment

ULMAN SPORTS INTERNATIONAL   (800) 237-8425
7 W. Aylesbury Rd. • Timonium, MD 21093
Fax Ordering: (410) 560-5858
Contact Name: J. Ulman, President
Catalog: Free. Frequency: Annual
Circulation: 50K. Sales: $3-5MM
Products: Lacrosse equipment, supplies
& imprinted gifts

ULTIMATE DIRECTION   (800) 426-7229
1488 N. Salem Rd. • Rexburg, ID 83440
Fax Ordering: (208) 356-0114
International Ordering: (208) 356-0385
Contact Name: Bryce Thatcher, President
Catalog: Free. Frequency: Annual
Circulation: 100K. Sales: $20-50MM
Products: Hydration systems for cyclists

ULTIMATE SYSTEMS, LTD.   (800) 777-6387
4335 Santa Fe Dr. • Kingman, AZ 86401
E-Mail: info@homecourt.com
Website: www.homecourt.com
Fax Ordering: (613) 629-7211
International Ordering: (613) 629-7456
Contact Name: Keith Stettner, President
Catalog: Free. Frequency: Annual
Circulation: 15M. Sales: $500M
Products: Volleyball systems

VITAL SIGNS   (608) 735-4718
Country Technology
P.O. Box 87 • Gays Mills, WI 54631
E-Mail: ctech@mwt.net
Website: www.fitnessmart.com
Fax Ordering: (608) 735-4859
Contact Name: S. Peterson, President
Catalog: Free. Frequency: 8x per year
Circulation: 250M. Sales: $3-5MM
Products: Sports/fitness, rehabilitation
& conditioning equipment

VOLLEYBALL ONE SALES COMPANY   (800) 950-8844
15392 Assembly Lane
Huntington Beach, CA 92649
E-Mail: info@volleyballone.com
Website: www.volleyballone.com
Fax Ordering: (800) 642-8614
International Ordering: (714) 898-4432
Contact Name: Lucy Keller, President
Catalog: Free. Frequency: Annual
Circulation: 250M. Sales: $3-5MM
Products: Volleyball equipment, supplies
& accessories

WAFER WAREHOUSE   (800) 574-7665
Doney Enterprises
6950 51st St. • Kenosha, WI 53144
E-Mail: info@waferwarehouse.com
Website: www.waferwarehouse.com
Fax Ordering: (262) 605-1065
Catalog: $2. Frequency: Annual
Circulation: 50M. Sales: $1-3MM
Products: Swimming pool supplies

EDWIN WATTS GOLF   (800) 874-0146
20 Hill Ave.
Fort Walton Beach, FL 32548
E-Mail: sales@edwinwatts.com
Website: www.edwinwatts.com
Fax Ordering: (850) 244-5217
International Ordering: (850) 244-2066
Contact Name: Edwin Watts, President
Catalog: Free. Pages: 88.
  Frequency: Quarterly
Circulation: 250M. Sales: $20-50MM
Products: Golf equipment, apparel &
accessories from well known brands

WILDWASSER SPORT USA, INC.   (303) 444-2336
P.O. Box 4617 • Boulder, CO 80306
E-Mail: info@wildnet.com
Website: www.wildwasser.net.com
Fax Ordering: (303) 444-2375
Catalog: Free. Pages: 50.
Frequency: Semiannual
Circulation: 50M. Sales: $3-5MM
Products: Kayaks & accessories

WRESTLER'S EXPRESS   (800) 759-TEAM
Teamworks
P.O. Box 35040 • Chicago, IL 60707
E-Mail: sales@wrestlersexpress.com
Website: www.wrestlersexpress.com
Fax Ordering: (708) 456-9690
International Ordering: (708) 456-6664
Catalog: Free. Frequency: Annual
Circulation: 100M. Sales: $10-20MM
Products: Wrestling equipment, bags
& accessories

WRESTLING ONE SALES COMPANY   (800) 950-7744
Leisure One • 15392 Assembly Ln.
Huntington Beach, CA 92649
E-Mail: info@wrestlingone.com
Website: www.wrestlingone.com
Fax Ordering: (800) 642-8614
International Ordering: (714) 898-4432
Contact Name: Lucy Keller, President
Catalog: Free. Frequency: Annual
Circulation: 500M. Sales: $3-5MM
Products: Interscholastic & olympic
wrestling equipment & supplies

YMAA CATALOG OF PRODUCTS   (800) 669-8892
YMAA Publication Center
4354 Washington St.
Roslindale, MA 02131
E-Mail: ymaa@aol.com
Website: www.ymaa.com
Fax Ordering: (617) 323-7417
International Ordering: (617) 323-7215
Contact Name: Jwing-Ming Yang, President
Catalog: Free. Frequency: Annual
Circulation: 25M. Sales: $500M
Products: Books, videos & music on
martial arts, fitness & Asian culture

YOGA ZONE CATALOG   (800) 264-9642
138 5th Ave. • New York, NY 10011
E-Mail: info@yogazone.com
Website: www.yogazone.com
Fax Ordering: (540) 345-6546
Catalog: Free. Frequency: Semiannual
Circulation: 100M. Sales: $1-3MM
Products: Yoga accessories; mats & props,
clothing, videos & DVDs, books & gifts

AMERICAN STATIONERY COMPANY (800) 822-2577
AMERICAN WEDDING ALBUM (800) 428-0379
100 N. Park Ave. • Peru, IN 46970
E-Mail: custserv@americanstationery.com
E-Mail: custserv@theamericanwedding.com
Website: www.americanstationery.com
Website: www.theamericanwedding.com
Fax Ordering: (800) 253-9054; (800) 864-8673
International Ordering: (765) 473-4438
Contact Name: Don Bakehorn, President
Catalog: Free. Frequency: Semiannual
Circulation: 500K. Sales: $20-50MM
Products: Stationery & cards; wedding invitations

AMSTERDAM BUSINESS FORMS (800) 833-6231
Amsterdam Printing & Litho Corp. (800) 203-9917
166 Wallins Corners Rd.
Amsterdam, NY 12010
E-Mail: info@amsterdamprinting.com
Website: www.amsterdamprinting.com
Fax Ordering: (518) 843-5204
Contact Name: Robert Singer, President
Catalog: Free. Frequency: Quarterly
Circulation: 500K. Sales: $20-50MM
Products: Personalized business forms,
mailing labels, envelopes, business cards,
check writing systems, personnel forms,
advertising specialties

ANN'S BRIDAL BARGAINS (800) 821-7011
P.O. Box 188 • Sunman, IN 47041
E-Mail: service@annsbridalbargains.com
Website: www.annsbridalbargains.com
Fax Ordering: (800) 626-3670
International Ordering: (812) 654-2548
Customer Service: (800) 821-7011
Catalog: Free. Frequency: Semiannual
Circulation: 100K. Sales: $1-3MM
Products: Wedding stationery & supplies

ARTISTIC CHECKS (800) 243-2577
P.O. Box 1000 • Mabelvale, AR 72103 (800) 224-7621
E-Mail: service@artisticchecks.com
Website: www.artisticchecks.com
Fax Ordering: (410) 676-8269
International Ordering: (607) 733-9010
Contact Name: Stuart Komer, President
Catalog: Free. Frequency: Semiannual
Circulation: 1MM. Sales: $20-50MM
Products: Business & personal checks &
accessories; address labels, personal cards;
business cards; stationery

CELEBRATE THE SEASON (800) 735-0274
P.O. Box 100 • Lumberton, NJ 08048
E-Mail: service@celebrateseason.com
Website: www.celebrateseason.com
Fax Ordering: (800) 228-4795
Catalog: Free. Frequency: Quarterly
Circulation: 500K. Sales: $5-10MM
Products: Premium greeting cards

CHECK CRAFTERS (888) 404-5245
P.O. Box 100 • Edgewood, MD 21040
E-Mail: contact@checkcrafters.com
Website: www.checkcrafters.com
Fax Ordering: (410) 676-8269
Catalog: Free. Frequency: Semiannual
Circulation: 500K. Sales: $5-10MM
Products: Personalized computer &
personal checks & accessories

CHECKS IN THE MAIL (877) 367-2486
2435 Goodwin Lane (800) 733-4443
New Braunfels, TX 78135
E-Mail: service@citm.com
Website: www.citm.com
Fax Ordering: (800) 800-0005
Catalog: Free. Pages: 20, Frequency: Annual
Circulation: 500K. Sales: $10-20MM
Products: Business essentials: business
checks; personal & business products

CURRENT CATALOG (800) 525-7170
Order Processing (800) 848-2848
Colorado Springs, CO 80941
E-Mail: info@currentinc.com
Website: www.currentcatalog.com
Fax Ordering: (800) 993-3232; (791) 531-2122
International Ordering: (719) 593-5990
Customer Service: (877) 665-4458
Contact Name: Harold Haverty, President
Catalog: Free. Frequency: Monthly
Circulation: 1MM. Sales: $50-75MM
Products: Personal stationery & labels,
framed prints, giftwrap, ribbons, cards & gifts

DAY TIMERS, INC. (800) 752-6281
1 Willow Lane • East Texas, PA 18046 (800) 225-5005
E-Mail: info@daytimer.com
Website: www.daytimer.com
Fax Ordering: (800) 452-7398; (610) 398-5520
International Ordering: (610) 398-1151
Customer Service: (800) 805-2615
Technical Support: (800) 457-5702
Contact Name: Dave Clark, President
Catalog: Free. Frequency: Semiannual
Circulation: 1MM. Sales: $20-50MM
Products: Stationery, business forms &
desk accessories

DELUXE BUSINESS (800) 328-0304
CHECKS & SOLUTIONS (800) 342-5274
P.O. Box 1186 • Lancaster, CA 93534
E-Mail: info@deluxeforms.com
Website: www.deluxeforms.com
Fax Ordering: (800) 336-1112
International Ordering: (719) 528-8411
Contact Name: Gene Bidon, President
Catalog: Free. Frequency: Annual
Circulation: 200K. Sales: $20-50MM
Products: Checks & forms for businesses;
software compatible business forms, tags,
labels, stationery and business cards

THE DRAWING BOARD (800) 527-9530
10 E. Ninth St. • Waynesboro, PA 17268 (800) 272-4182
E-Mail: sales@drawingboard.com (800) 443-8847
Website: www.drawingboard.com
Fax Ordering: (800) 253-1838
International Ordering: (860) 379-1590
Contact Name: Lee Bracken, President
Catalog: Free. Frequency: Quarterly
Circulation: 2MM. Sales: $20-50MM
Products: Personalized forms, labels,
stationery, promotional products, all-
occasion & holiday greeting cards

FLAX ART CATALOGS (415) 552-2355
Flax Art & Design, Inc.
1699 Market St. • San Francisco, CA 94103
E-Mail: askus@flaxart.com
Website: www.flaxart.com

Contact Name: Philip Flax, President
Catalog: Free. Frequency: Quarterly
Circulation: 100K. Sales: $10-20MM
Products: Specialty papers & stationery;
writing instruments; desk accessories; gifts;
wrapping paper, tissue & lace, ribbons & cords

HOLIDAY CARDS FOR BUSINESS (800) 611-1599
National Wildlife Federation (800) 822-9919
11100 Wildlife Center Dr.
Reston, VA 20190
E-Mail: info@nwf.org
Website: www.nwf.org
Contact Name: Mark Van Putten, President
Catalog: Free. Frequency: Bimonthly
Circulation: 10MM. Sales: $20-50MM
Products: Christmas cards, calendars,
apparel and gifts with a wildlife theme

HOUSE MOUSE DESIGNS (800) 242-6423
P.O. Box 48 • Williston, VT 05495
E-Mail: sales@house-mouse.com
Website: www.house-mouse.com
Fax Ordering: (802) 660-8340
International Ordering: (802) 864-0314
Contact Name: Barry Percy, President
Catalog: $4. Frequency: Quarterly
Circulation: 25K. Sales: $1-3MM
Products: Mouse designs on stationery;
rubber stamps

HRDIRECT (800) 346-1231
P.O. Box 452049 • Sunrise, FL 33345
E-Mail: sales@hrdirect.com
Website: www.hrdirect.com
Fax Ordering: (800) 350-7760
Catalog: Free. Frequency: Quarterly
Circulation: 150K. Sales: $10-20MM
Products: Human resource products;
greeting cards

INVITATIONS BY DAWN (800) 364-6972
1 Stationery Pl. • Rexburg, ID 83440 (800) 332-3296
E-Mail: contact@invitationsbydawn.com
Website: www.invitationsbydawn.com
Fax Ordering: (800) 231-1279
Customer Service: (800) 361-1974
Catalog: Free. Frequency: Semiannual
Circulation: 200K. Sales: $3-5MM
Products: Wedding invitations

JEAN M WEDDING ESSENTIALS (800) 766-8595
P.O. Box 330 • Sugar City, ID 83448
E-Mail: guestservices@myjeanm.com
Website: www.myjeanm.com
Fax Ordering: (800) 826-2712
Catalog: Free. Frequency: Semiannual
Circulation: 150K. Sales: $3-5MM
Products: Wedding invitations & accessories

KOGLE CARDS-CORDIAL GREETINGS (800) 333-5575
Thayer Publishing (800) 523-9080
P.O. Box 8465 • Mankato, MN 56002
E-Mail: customerservice@koglecards.com
Website: www.koglecards.com
Fax Ordering: (800) 842-9371
Contact Name: Dave Humbert, President
Catalog: Free. Frequency: Annual
Circulation: 200K. Sales: $5-10MM
Products: Personalized holiday greeting
cards & calendars; mailing plans for all
businesses

LANDMARK COLLECTION (800) 854-0390
6253 W. 74th St., Box 2001
Bedford Park, IL 60499-2001
E-Mail: sales@landmarkcollection.com
Website: www.landmarkcollection.com
Fax Ordering: (800) 325-8262
International Ordering: (559) 651-2011
Customer Service: (800) 321-0986
Contact Name: Mike Johnson, President
Catalog: Free. Pages: 28. Frequency: Annual
Circulation: 150K. Sales: $5-10MM
Products: Personalized holiday cards &
calendars

McBEE CATALOG (800) 878-9443
P.O. Box 1186 • Lancaster, CA 93584 (800) 662-2331
E-Mail: mcbeecustomersvc@mcbeeinc.com
Website: www.mcbeeinc.com
Fax Ordering: (800) 213-1042
Contact Name: John Paukstis, President
Catalog: Free. Frequency: Semiannual
Circulation: 150K. Sales: $10-50MM
Products: Business checks, computer checks,
forms, folders, labels, stationery, office furniture

MERRIMADE, INC. (888) 720-8302
P.O. Box 207 • Peru, IN 46970 (800) 344-4256
E-Mail: custserv@merrimade.com
Website: www.merrimade.com
Fax Ordering: (800) 883-6515; (765) 472-8510
Contact Name: Mike Bakehorn, Marketing
Catalog: Free. Frequency: Semiannual
Circulation: 1MM. Sales: $10-20MM
Products: Personalized stationery & gifts

NEBS COMPUTER FORMS (800) 888-6327
Deluxe Co. New England Business Service (800) 225-9540
500 Main St. • Groton, MA 01470
E-Mail: customerservice@nebs.com
Website: www.nebs.com
Fax Ordering: (800) 234-4324 ; (866) 449-3794
International Ordering: (978) 448-6111
Contact Name: Robert J. Murray, President
Catalog: Free. Frequency: Annual
Circulation: 2MM. Sales: $50-100MM
Products: Business checks, forms, labels &
envelopes; standard & custom computer forms

NATIONAL WILDLIFE FEDERATION (800) 545-9099
HOLIDAY CARDS FOR BUSINESS
P.O. Box 9500 • Winchester, VA 22604-9500
E-Mail: sales@cardshop.nwf.org
Website: www.cardshop.nwf.org
Fax Ordering: (540) 5398
Contact Name: Larry J. Scweiger, President
Catalog: Free. Frequency: Annual
Circulation: 200K. Sales: $5-10MM
Products: Holiday stationery & greeting cards
for businesses

POSTY CARDS (800) 554-5018
1600 Olive St.
Kansas City, MO 64127
E-Mail: info@postycards.com
Website: www.postycards.com
Fax Ordering: (888) 577-3800; (816) 483-8135
International Ordering: (816) 231-2323
Contact Name: Lance H. Jessee, President
Catalog: Free. Frequency: Semiannual
Circulation: 150K. Sales: $3-5MM
Products: Greeting cards & calendars for
business use

PRECIOUS COLLECTION (800) 553-9080
P.O. Box 222 • Quency, PA 17247
E-Mail: sales@preciouscollection.com
Website: www.preciouscollection.com
Fax Ordering: (800) 647-6488
Customer Service: (800) 537-5222
Catalog: Free. Frequency: Annual
Circulation: 100K. Sales: $1-3MM
Products: Wedding invitations &
accessories

PRINTERY CATALOG DIRECT (800) 326-1965
800 Snow Hill Rd. • Salisbury, MD 21804
E-Mail: custsvc@printerymd.com
Website: www.printerymd.com
Fax Ordering: (410) 749-0747
International Ordering: (410) 749-2776
Contact Name: Timothy Ragan, President
Catalog: Free. Frequency: Semiannual
Circulation: 100M. Sales: $5-10MM
Products: Office supplies, forms, business
cards & stationery

PRINTERY HOUSE CONCEPTION ABBEY (800) 889-0105
P.O. Box 112 • Conception, MO 64433
E-Mail: custserv@printeryhouse.org
Website: www.printeryhouse.org
Fax Ordering: (888) 556-8262
Contact Name: Gerald Nelson, President
Catalog: Free. Frequency: Quarterly
Circulation: 1MM. Sales: $3-5MM
Products: Religious greeting cards,
stationery & gifts

RAPID FORMS CATALOG (800) 257-8354
301 Grove Rd. • Thorofare, NJ 08086
E-Mail: info@rapidforms.com
Website: www.rapidforms.com
Fax Ordering: (800) 451-8113
International Ordering: (856) 384-1144
Customer Service: (800) 257-5287
Contact Name: Richard Reilly, President
Catalog: Free. Frequency: Annual
Circulation: 2MM. Sales: $50-100MM
Products: Software compatible business
forms, checks, tags, envelopes, labels,
stationery and business cards

REXCRAFT CATALOG (800) 635-4653
1 Stationery Plaza • Rexburg, ID 83441 (800) 635-3898
E-Mail: sales@rexcraft.com
Website: www.rexcraft.com
Fax Ordering: (800) 826-2712
International Ordering: (208) 359-1000
Contact Name: Norm Doering, President
Catalog: Free. Frequency: Annual
Circulation: 150K. Sales: $5-10MM
Products: Wedding invitations & accessories

SPECIALTY LOOSE LEAF, INC. (800) 848-8020
1 Cabot St. • Holyoke, MA 01040 (800) 227-3623
E-Mail: sales@specialtylooseleaf.com
Website: www.specialtylooseleaf.com
Fax Ordering: (413) 534-4069
International Ordering: (413) 493-7801
Contact Name: Bruce Pratt, President
Catalog: Free. Frequency: Annual
Circulation: 25K. Sales: $5-10MM
Products: Specialty binder products

STRATFORD HALL CATALOG (800) 628-9028
P.O. Box 2001 • Bedford Park, IL 60499
E-Mail: sales@stratfordhall.com
Website: www.stratfordhall.com
Fax Ordering: (800) 325-8262
Customer Service: (800) 446-4415
Catalog: Free. Frequency: Annual
Circulation: 100K. Sales: $1-3MM
Products: Personalized holiday &
greeting cards

SUNSHINE BUSINESS CLASS (800) 873-7681
P.O. Box 8465 • Mankato, MN 56002
E-Mail: cs@sunshinebusinessclass.com
Website: www.sunshinebusinessclass.com
Fax Ordering: (800) 232-3633; (413) 525-5598
International Ordering: (413) 525-5599
Catalog: Free. Pages: 20. Frequency: Annual
Circulation: 50K. Sales: $1-3MM
Products: Personalized holiday calendars
& cards

TRUMBLE GREETINGS (800) 525-0656
Leanin' Tree
P.O. Box 9800 • Boulder, CO 80301
E-Mail: info@leanintree.com
Website: www.leanintree.com
Fax Ordering: (800) 777-4770; (303) 530-5124
International Ordering: (303) 530-7768
Contact Name: Thomas Trumble, President
Catalog: Free. Frequency: Quarterly
Circulation: 250K. Sales: $5-10MM
Products: Holiday greeting cards,
stationery & gifts

UNICEF BUSINESS COLLECTION (800) 227-3738
125 Maiden Ln. • New York, NY 10038 (800) 367-5437
E-Mail: cards@unicefusa.org (800) 486-4233
Website: www.unicefusa.org
Customer Service: (800) 577-3738
Catalog: Free. Pages: 16. Frequency: Annual
Circulation: 1MM. Sales: $10-20MM
Products: Greeting cards, stationery & gifts

VINTAGE IMAGES (800) 882-2737
Brian Smolens
P.O. Box 4435 • Silver Spring, MD 20914
E-Mail: brian@vintageimages.com
Website: www.vintageimages.com
Fax Ordering: (253) 679-6522
International Ordering: (301) 879-6522
Contact Name: Brian Smolens, President
Catalog: Free. Frequency: Annual
Circulation: 100K. Sales: $500MK
Products: Custom designed business post
cards, greeting cards, stock photography,
CD-ROM collections; original photos and
reproductions

VISIBLE COMPUTER SUPPLY CORP. (800) 323-0628
R.R. Donnelley (800) 262-4460
1750 Wallace Ave. • St. Charles, IL 60174 (877) 526-3894
E-Mail: info@visibletax.com
Website: www.visibletax.com
Fax Ordering: (800) 233-2016
International Ordering: (630) 377-2586
Contact Name: Bob Cronin, President
Catalog: Free. Frequency: Semiannual
Circulation: 250K. Sales: $10-20MM
Products: Computer tax forms

ALL BRANDS.COM (800) 289-5648
20415 Highland Rd. • Baton Rouge, LA 70817 (800) 739-7374
E-Mail: sales@allbrands.com
Website: www.allbrands.com
Fax Ordering: (800) 866-1261; (225) 923-1261
International Ordering: (225) 923-1285
Customer Service: (866) 255-2726
Contact Name: Annette Douthat, President
Catalog: Online. Sales: $10-20MM
Products: Sewing & knitting machines,
accessories & needles; embroidery
machines, supplies, software; irons &
steamers; vacuum cleaners; dress forms
& blocking cloth; videos, CDs & books

ALTER YEARS FOR THE COSTUMER (626) 569-9919
P.O. Box 98 • Rosemead, CA 91770
E-Mail: alteryears@earthlink.net
Website: www.alteryears.com
Fax Ordering: (626) 569-9909
Catalog: $6. Frequency: Annual
Circulation: 25K. Sales: $500K - $1MM
Products: Historical, ethnic, dance &
specialty patterns; costume books, supplies
& underpinnings.

ANNIE'S ATTIC CRAFT CATALOGS (800) 582-6643
1 Annie Lane • Big Sandy, TX 75755 (800) 282-6643
E-Mail: customer_service@anniesattic.com
Website: www.anniesattic.com
Fax Ordering: (800) 882-6643
International Ordering: (903) 636-4303
Contact Name: John Robinson, President
Catalog: Free. Frequency: Quarterly
Circulation: 500K. Sales: $20-50MM
Products: Patterns & supplies for needlecrafts

BARTLETTYARNS (207) 683-2251
20 Water St. • Harmony, ME 04942
E-Mail: sales@bartlettyarns.com
Website: www.bartlettyarns.com
Fax Ordering: (207) 683-2261
Contact Name: Russell B. Pierce, President
Catalog: Online. Sales: $1-3MM
Products: Wool knitting yarns, patterns &
knitting accessories

BUCKAROO BOBBINS (928) 636-1885
P.O. Box 1168 • Chino Valley, AZ 86323
E-Mail: buckaroobobbins@gmail.com
Website: www.buckaroobobbins.com
Fax Ordering: (928) 636-8134
Contact Name: Roger & Geneva Eads, Owners
Catalog: $2. Frequency: Annual
Circulation: 10K. Sales: $500K
Products: Sewing patterns for men,
women and children's Western clothing;
cowboy accessories, corsets, buttons,
trimmings & sewing notions; books, CDs, gifts

CARODAN FARM WOOL SHOP (800) 985-7083
P.O. Box 807
Chincoteague Island, VA 23336
E-Mail: carodan@direcway.com
Website: www.carodanfarm.com
Fax Ordering: (434) 985-7083
Contact Name: Caroline Hershey, President
Catalog: Free. Frequency: Semiannual
Circulation: 100K. Sales: $500K
Products: Yarns, supplies and handcrafted
gifts, knitting accessories, needles & crochet
hooks, pewter buttons & pins, & wool clothing

CENTRAL SHIPPEE-THE FELT PEOPLE (800) 631-8968
46 Star Lake Rd. • Bloomingdale, NJ 07403
E-Mail: felt@webspan.net
Website: www.centralshippee.com
Fax Ordering: (973) 838-8273
International Ordering: (973) 838-1100
Contact Name: Eric Hubner, President
Catalog: Free. Frequency: Annual
Circulation: 100K. Sales: $5-10MM
Products: Colored felt, decorative fabrics,
fixtures, tablecloths, screenprinting

CLOTHCRAFTERS (800) 876-2009
Hygiene Fabrics & Filters, Inc.
P.O. Box 1005 • Sheboygan, WI 53081
E-Mail: sales@hyfab.com
Website: www.clothcrafters.com
Fax Ordering: (920) 457-2558
International Ordering: (920) 457-7493
Contact Name: John F. Wilson, President
Catalog: Free. Frequency: Annual
Circulation: 50K. Sales: $500K
Products: Home textiles; products made
from 100% cotton suitable for dyeing,
printing or silkscreen techniques

COTTON CLOUDS (800) 322-7888
5176 S. 14th Ave. • Safford, AZ 85546
E-Mail: info@cottonclouds.com
Website: www.cottonclouds.com
Fax Ordering: (928) 428-6630
International Ordering: (928) 428-7000
Contact Name: Irene Schmoller, President
Catalog: $2.50; free with order of $35+
Frequency: Annual.
Circulation: 25K. Sales: $3-5MM
Products: Yarns, patterns, kits for weaving
crochet, knitting & spinning, spinning wheels,
knitting machines and kits; books & videos

DANA MARIE DESIGN CO. (888) 455-5143
P.O. Box 534 • Kamiah, ID 83536
E-Mail: info@danamarie.com
Website: www.danamarie.com
Fax Ordering: (360) 653-0932
International Ordering: (360) 653-0901
Contact Name: Dana Bontrager, President
Catalog: Free. Frequency: Annual
Circulation: 10K. Sales: $1-3MM
Products: Artistic garment patterns,
multisize from XS to 5XL, sewing notions

EDINBURGH IMPORTS (800) 334-6274
2808 Oregon Ct. Unit L-6
Torrance, CA 90503
E-Mail: info@edinburghimports.com
Website: www.edinburghimports.com
Fax Ordering: (310) 320-8154
International Ordering: (310) 320-8151
Contact Names: Elke & Ronald Block, Owners
Catalog: Free. Frequency: Annual
Circulation: 25K. Sales: $3-5MM
Products: Fabrics and tools to make, sew,
cut and joint teddy bears; teddy bear supplies,
over 1,000 mohair fabrics & 300 patterns & kits

EXOTIC SILKS (800) 845-7455
1959 Leghorn St.
Mountain View, CA 94043
Mail: silks@exoticsilks.com
Website: www.exoticsilks.com
Fax Ordering: (650) 965-0712

International Ordering: (650) 965-7760
Contact Name: Deanne Shute, President
Catalog: Free. Frequency: Semiannual
Circulation: 50M. Sales: $10-20MM
Products: Silk and cotton fabrics

FABRIC MART CATALOG (800) 242-3695
3911 Penn Ave. • Sinking Spring, PA 19608
E-Mail: orders@fabricmartfabrics.com
Website: www.fabricmartfabrics.com
Fax Ordering: (610) 670-7130
International Ordering: (610) 678-1330
Contact Name: Robert Richin, President
Catalog: $1. Frequency: Quarterly
Circulation: 50K. Sales: $3-5MM
Products: fabrics for the home sewer &
dressmaker at wholesale prices

FABRICS FOR HOME (800) 845-8723
& FABRICS FOR QUILTERS
Hancock's of Paducah
3841 Hinkleville Rd. • Paducah, KY 42001
E-Mail: customerservice@hancocks-paducah.com
Website: www.hancocks-paducah.com
Fax Ordering: (270) 442-3152
International Ordering: (270) 443-4410
Contact Name: W.R. Hancock, President
Catalog: Free. Frequency: Quarterly
Circulation: 1MM. Sales: $10-20MM
Products: Decorator fabrics, pillow forms,
upholstery & drapery fabrics, custom bedding
& furniture, and a line of quilting fabrics, tools
& supplies

FASHION FABRICS CLUB (800) 468-0602
10490 Baur Blvd., St. Louis, MO 63132
E-Mail: sales@fashionfabricsclub.com
Website: www.fashionfabricsclub.com
Fax Ordering: (314) 993-5802
International Ordering: (314) 993-4919
Contact Name: Thomas Samson, President
Catalog: Free. Frequency: Annual
Circulation: 50K. Sales: $1-3MM
Products: Dress fabrics

FIBER ARTS SUPPLIES CATALOG (800) 542-5227
Dharma Trading Co.
P.O. Box 150916 • San Rafael, CA 94915
E-Mail: catalog@dharmatrading.com
Website: www.dharmatrading.com
Fax Ordering: (415) 456-8747
International Ordering: (415) 456-7657
Contact Name: Isaac Goff, President
Catalog: Free. Frequency: Semiannual
Circulation: 100K. Sales: $3-5MM
Products: Textile crafts supplies &
clothing blanks to artists, craftspersons
& 'industry; dye and fabric paints, fabrics
for dyeing

GENERAL BAILEY HOMESTEAD FARM (877) 471-9665
340 Spier Falls Rd.
Greenfield Center, NY 12833
E-Mail: kathy-gbhf@msn.com
Website: www.generalbaileyfarm.com
Fax Ordering: (518) 893-0778
International Ordering: (518) 893-2015
Contact Name: Kathy Bourgeois, President
Catalog: Free. Frequency: Annual
Circulation: 25K. Sales: $1-3MM
Products: Wool products; supplies for
spinning, weaving, knitting, rug making,

fiber dying and felting; books;
pattern and button inventories

HALCYON YARN (800) 341-0282
12 School St. • Bath, ME 04530
E-Mail: service@halcyonyarn.com
Website: www.halcyonyarn.com
Fax Ordering: (207) 442-0633
International Ordering: (207) 442-7909
Contact Name: Halcyon Blake, President
Catalog: Free. Frequency: Monthly
Circulation: 50K. Sales: $500K - $1MM
Products: Yarns, fibers, equipment & supplies
for knitting, weaving, spinning, crochet, felting,
rug hooking, and other fiber crafts; books

HARRISVILLE DESIGNS- (800) 338-9415
YARN & LOOM CATALOG
P.O. Box 806 • Harrisville, NH 03450
E-Mail: info@harrisville.com
Website: www.harrisville.com
Fax Ordering: (603) 827-3335
International Ordering: (603) 827-3333
Contact Name: John Colony, III, President
Catalog: Free. Frequency: Semiannual
Circulation: 100K. Sales: $1-3MM
Products: Yarn & looms

HOMESPUN FABRICS & DRAPERIES (888) 543-2998
P.O. Box 24255 • Ventura, CA 93002
E-Mail: sales@homespunfabrics.com
Website: www.homespunfabrics.com
Fax Ordering: (206) 338-2576
International Ordering: (805) 642-1152
Contact Name: DeAnna Decker, President
Catalog: Free. Frequency: Quarterly
Circulation: 10K. Sales: $500K
Products: 10 foot wide, 100% cotton, washable,
textured fabric for seamless draperies, slipcovers,
upholstery, bedspreads, tablecloths; custom-
made or do-it-yourself

J.R. BURROWS CO. CATALOG (800) 347-1795
P.O. Box 522 • Rockland, MA 02370
E-Mail: merchant@burrows.com
Website: www.burrows.com
Fax Ordering: (781) 982-1636
International Ordering: (781) 982-1812
Contact Name: John Burrows, Founder
Catalog: Free. Frequency: Semiannual
Circulation: 100K. Sales: $10-20MM
Products: Historical design; lace curtains,
studio art wallpaper; carpet, rugs & runners;

MACOMBER LOOMS AND ME (207) 363-2808
P.O. Box 186 • York, ME 03909
Contact Name: Sarah Haskell, President
Catalog: Free. Pages: 16. Frequency: Annual
Circulation: 50K. Sales: $500K to $1MM
Products: Macomber Shop Looms;
Ad-A-Harness Looms; Ad-A-Cad/Cam Systems

MANNING'S (800) 223-7166
Manning's Handweaving School & Supply
P.O. Box 687 • East Berlin, PA 17316
E-Mail: info@the-mannings.com.com
Website: www.the-mannings.com
Fax Ordering: (717) 624-1425
International Ordering: (717) 624-2223
Contact Name: Carol J. Woolcock, President
Catalog: Free. Frequency: Annual
Circulation: 50K. Sales: $500K

Products: Tools, supplies and equipment for knitters, weavers, and spinners; fiber & dye; yarn

MARR HAVEN WOOL FARM   (800) 653-8810
772 39th St. • Allegan, MI 49010
E-Mail: mhyarnles@marrhaven.com
Website: www.marrhaven.com
Fax Ordering: (269) 686-0341
International Ordering: (269) 673-8800
Contact Name: Barbara Marr, President
Catalog: Free. Frequency: Monthly
Circulation: 25K. Sales: $500K to $1MM
Products: 100% Merino Rambouillet fine wool yarns for knitting, crochet and weaving; fiber art supplies for felt making, spinning or locker hooking; handmade soaps, wool wax creme and wool wash; knit supplies; jewelry & buttons.

McCALL PATTERN CO.   (800) 255-2762
120 Broadway, 34th Fl • New York, NY 10271
E-Mail: info@mccallpattern.com
Website: www.mccallpattern.com
Fax Ordering: (212) 465-6814
International Ordering: (212) 465-6800
Contact Names: Donna Pincus, Marketing
Catalog: Free. Frequency: Bimonthly
Circulation: 50K. Sales: $500K to $1MM
Products: Textiles and patterns

MERIDIAN SPECIALTY YARN GROUP   (828) 874-2151
312 Colombo St. SW • Valdese, NC 28690
E-Mail: customerservice@msyg.com
Website: www.mdyg.com
Fax Ordering: (828) 874-2151
Catalog: Free. Frequency: Quarterly
Circulation: 100K. Sales: $10-50MM
Products: Specialty yarns

MURIELLE ROY & COMPANY   (203) 729-0480
67 Platts Mill Rd. • Naugatuck, CT 06770
E-Mail: murielleroy@snet.net
Website: www.murielleroy.net
Fax Ordering: (203) 720-2101
Catalog: Online only. Sales: $500K
Products: Fabrics & trims for performers

NANCY'S NOTIONS   (800) 833-0690
P.O. Box 683 • Beaver Dam, WI 53916
E-Mail: sales@nancysnotions.com
Website: www.nancysnotions.com
Fax Ordering: (800) 255-8119; (920) 887-2133
International Ordering: (920) 887-0391
Customer Service: (800) 245-5116
Technical Support: (800) 595-6878
Contact Names: Nancy Zieman, President
Catalog: Free. Pages: 96. Frequency: Quarterly
Circulation: 100K. Sales: $3-5MM
Products: Sewing, quilting & machine embroidery collection & supplies

OHIO HEMPERY CATALOG   (800) 289-4367
P.O. Box 18 • Guysville, OH 45736
E-Mail: sales@cannabisculture.com
Website: www.cannabisculture.com
Contact Name: D. Daniels, Fulfillment
Catalog: Free. Frequency: Annual
Circulation: 25K. Sales: $500K
Products: Hemp products, including, twine & rope, clothing & accessories; fiber materials, fabric, oils, seeds, books

OUTDOOR WILDERNESS FABRICS   (800) 693-7467
16415 N. Midland Blvd. • Nampa, ID 83687
E-Mail: owfinc@owfinc.com
Website: www.owfinc.com
Fax Ordering: (800) 333-6930
International Ordering: (208) 466-1602
Contact Names: Ray Levis, President
Catalog: Free. Frequency: Semiannual
Circulation: 50K. Sales: $500K to $1MM
Products: Outdoor fabrics

AMAZON DRYGOODS PATTERN CATALOG   (800) 798-7979
411 Brady St. • Davenport, IA 52801
E-Mail: info@amazondrygoods.com
Website: www.amazondrygoods.com
Fax Ordering: (563) 322-4003
International Ordering: (563) 322-6800
Contact Name: J. Burgess, President
Catalogs: $7. Frequency: Annual
Circulation: 50K. Sales: $1-3MM
Products: Historic, ethnic, and hard-to-find clothing patterns for men, women, children & dolls; historic reproductions of sewing patterns

PATTERNWORKS   (800) 438-5464
P.O. Box 1618 • Center Harbor, NH 03226   (800) 723-9210
E-Mail: customerservice@patternworks.com
Website: www.patternworks.com
Fax Ordering: (603) 253-8346
International Ordering: (603) 253-8731
Contact Names: Linda & Marvin Skolnik
Catalog: Free. Frequency: Monthly
Circulation: 100K. Sales: $1-3MM
Products: Knitting and yarn supplies

PERSONAL THREADS BOUTIQUE   (800) 306-7733
8600 Cass St. • Omaha, NE 68114
E-Mail: sales@personalthreads.com
Website: www.personalthreads.com
Fax Ordering: (402) 391-0039
International Ordering: (402) 391-7733
Contact Name: Carolyn Lewis, President
Catalog: Free. Frequency: Semiannual
Circulation: 25K. Sales: $500K to $1MM
Products: Fine yarns, hand-panted needlepoints, knitting & needlecraft supplies

PLYMOUTH YARN COMPANY   (800) 523-8932
500 Lafayette St. • Bristol, PA 19007
E-Mail: pyc@plymouthyarn.com
Website: www.plymouthyarn.com
Fax Ordering: (215) 788-2269
International Ordering: (215) 788-0459
Contact Name: Richard W. Power, Jr., President
Catalog: Free. Frequency: Semiannual
Circulation: 50K. Sales: $3-5MM
Products: Variety of natural fiber & synthetic yarns; needlepoint & knitting yarns; knitting accessories; books

PRO CHEMICAL & DYE   (800) 228-9393
P.O. Box 14 • Somerset, MA 02726
E-Mail: prochemical@worldnet.net
Website: www.prochemical.com
Fax Ordering: (508) 676-3980
International Ordering: (508) 676-3838
Contact Name: Adelle Wiener, President
Catalog: Free. Frequency: Annual
Circulation: 150K. Sales: $1-3MM
Products: Dyes and pigments for fiber coloration

R & M YARMS
(800) 343-9276
P.O. Box 190 • Georgetown, TN 37336
E-Mail: info@rmyarns.com
Website: www.rmyarns.com
Fax Ordering: (423) 961-0691
Contact Name: Phyllis Narus, President
Catalog: Free. Frequency: Semiannual
Circulation: 50K. Sales: $3-5MM
Products: Yarns for knitting, crochet,
weaving & other crafts; hand-made M'Bears;
magazines & books

RICHARD THE THREAD
(800) 473-4997
10405 Washington Blvd.
Los Angeles, CA 90232
E-Mail: info@richardthethread.com
Website: www.richardthethread.com
Fax Ordering: (310) 836-4996
International Ordering: (310) 837-4997
Contact Name: Herb Braha, President
Catalog: Free. Frequency: Semiannual
Circulation: 50M. Sales: $1-3MM
Minimum Order: $35.
Products: Specialty sewing & costume
supplies

ROSE BRAND
(800) 223-1624
CA (800) 360-5056
4 Emerson Lane • Secaucus, NJ 07094
E-Mail: info@rosebrand.com
Website: www.rosebrand.com
Fax Ordering: (201) 809-1851
International Ordering: (201) 809-1730
Contact Name: George Jacobson, President
Catalog: Free. Frequency: Semiannual
Circulation: 150K. Sales: $5-10MM
Products: Fabrics production supplies,
including custom draperies for theaters,
churches, schools, events, etc.

TRIDENT INDUSTRIAL PRODUCTS CORP.
(800) 327-1830
5401 NW 102nd Ave., Suite 101
Sunrise, FL 33321
E-Mail: tridnt8555@aol.com
Website: www.tridentfabrics.com
Fax Ordering: (954) 726-3713
International Ordering: (954) 726-0270
Catalog: Free. Frequency: Annual
Circulation: 50K. Sales: $5-10MM
Products: Recreational, industrial &
marine fabrics; converters & distributors
of cotton, nylon, polyester, and acrylic

WEAVING SOUTHWEST CATALOG
(800) 765-1272
216 B Pueblo Norte • Taos, NM 87571
E-Mail: weaving@weavingsouthwest.com
Website: www.weavingsouthwest.com
Fax Ordering: (575) 758-5839
International Ordering: (575) 758-0433
Contact Name: Rachel Brown, President
Catalog: Free. Frequency: Quarterly
Circulation: 10K. Sales: $1-3MM
Products: Weaving & spinning equipment
& supplies

WEBS VALLEY YARNS
(800) 367-9327
75 Service Center Rd.
Northampton, MA 01060
E-Mail: info@yarn.com
Website: www.yarn.com
Fax Ordering: (413) 584-1603
Catalog: Free. Pages: 32
Frequency: Annual
Circulation: 50K. Sales: $5-10MM
Products: Knitting, weaving, spinning,
&crocheting yarns and supplies

WOODLAND WOOLWORKS CATALOGS
(800) 547-3725
S. Maple • Carlton, OR 97148
E-Mail: info@woolworks.com
Website: www.woolworks.com
Fax Ordering: (503) 662-3641
Contact Name: Melda Montgomery, President
Catalog: $4. Frequency: Annual
Circulation: 25K. Sales: $3-5MM
Products: Catalogs: Knitting, spinning &
weaving yarns, kits, crochet hooks, spinning
fibers, dyes, tolls & accessories; kits, books,
videos

WOOL GATHERING
(800) 968-5648
Schoolhouse Press
6899 Cary Bluff • Pittsville, WI 54466
E-Mail: info@schoolhousepress.com
Website: www.schoolhousepress.com
Fax Ordering: (715) 884-2829
International Ordering: (715) 884-2799
Contact Name: Meg Swansen, President
Catalog: $3. Frequency: Semiannual
Circulation: 25K. Sales: $5-10MM
Products: Wool, needles, buttons, knitting t
ools; books, instructional videos

WOOLERY
(800) 441-9665
239 W. Main St. • Frankfort, KY 40601
E-Mail: info@woolery.com
Website: www.woolery.com
Fax Ordering: (502) 352-9802
International Ordering: (502) 352-9800
Contact Name: Tim Horchler, President
Catalog: $4. Frequency: Semiannual
Circulation: 50K. Sales: $3-5MM
Products: Wool, angora, silk handknitting
yarns, knitting, crochet poatterns; spinning
wheels, looms; gift baskets; weaving supplies,
books, videos

ALIMED　　　　　　　　　　　　　　(800) 225-2610
297 High St. • Dedham, MA 02026
E-Mail: info@alimed.com
Website: www.alimed.com
Fax Ordering: (800) 437-2966; (781) 329-8392
International Ordering: (781) 329-2900
Customer Service E-Mail: cust_serv@alimed.com
Contact Name: Julian Cherubini, President
Catalog: Free. Frequency: Quarterly
Circulation: 100K. Sales: $5-10M
Products: Operating room products; medical surplies
& ergonomic products for healthcare, business & home,
including clinic/hospital supplies & equipment, diagnostic
imaging, durable medical equipment, home medical products,
industrial, healthcare & office ergonomics, orthopedics,
rehabilitation products, speech products, adult autism,
& wound management.

BECK-LEE CARDIOLOGY CATALOG　　　(800) 235-2852
P.O. Box 528 • Stratford, CT 06615
E-Mail: info@becklee.com
Website: www.becklee.com
Fax Ordering: (800) 525-4568
Catalog: Free. Frequency: Semiannual
Circulation: 100K. Sales: $10-20M
Products: Medical supplies; cardiology & echo products

BRUCE MEDICAL SUPPLY　　　　　　(800) 225-8446
411 Waverly Oaks Rd. • Waltham, MA 02154
E-Mail: sales@brucemedi.com
Website: www.brucemedical.com
Fax Ordering: (781) 894-9519
International Ordering: (781) 894-6262
Contact Name: Richard Najarian, President
Catalog: Free. Frequency: Quarterly
Circulation: 150K. Sales: $10-20M
Products: Three specialty medical supply catalogs:
Home Health Care & Convalescent Care; Larynectomy,
Speech Aids & Pre-Thickened Foods; Ostomy,
Incontinence & Skin Care/Wound Care.

DENTAL EQUIMENT BUYERS GUIDE　　(866) 815-7606
Dental Planet
707 N. Scott • Wichita Falls, TX 76306
E-Mail: sales@buydentalequipment.com
Website: www.buydentalequipment.com
Fax Ordering: (940) 767-6383
International Ordering: (940) 766-5209
Catalog: Free. Frequency: Semiannual
Circulation: 100K. Sales: $10-20M
Products: Dental equipment & supplies

DENTAL SUPPLY CATALOGS　　　　　(800) 372-4346
Henry Schein Dental
135 Duryea Rd. • Melville, NY 11747
E-Mail: susan.vassallo@henryschein.com
Website: www.henryschein.com
International Ordering: (631) 843-5500
Contact Name: James P. Breslawski, President
Catalog: Free. Frequency: Semiannual
Circulation: 100K. Sales: $10-20M
Products: Dental equipment & supplies

GALLS　　　　　　　　　　　　　　(800) 477-7766
P.O. Box 54308 • Lexington, KY 40555　　(800) 876-4242
E-Mail: help-desk@galls.com
Website: www.galls.com
Fax Ordering: (800) 944-2557
Customer Service: (800) 854-2706
Catalog: Free. Frequency: Semiannual
Circulation: 100K. Sales: $10-20M
Products: Emergency medical equipment & supplies

GIFTS FOR MEDICAL PROFESSIONALS　(888) 968-4696
969 Edgewater Blvd., Suite 980
Foster City, CA 94404
E-Mail: sales@e-corporategifts.com
Website: www.e-corporategifts.com
Fax Ordering: (650) 342-6062
Catalog: Free. Frequency: Seminnual
Circulation: 150K. Sales: $5-10M
Products: Gifts and collectibles to celebrate the
medical profession, including office decor, desk
accessories, jewelry, clothing, etc.

HDIS HEALTH CARE　　　　　　　　(800) 269-4663
9385 Dielman Ind. Dr.
Olivette, MO 63132
E-Mail: custcare@hdis.com
Website: www.hdis.com
Catalog: Free. Frequency: Semiannual
Circulation: 200K. Sales: $10-20MM
Products: Medical supplies for diabetes,
pain relief, vision & hearing, blood pressure
monitors, incontinence, catheters, mobility
products & personal care items.

HOPKINS MEDICAL PRODUCTS　　　　(800) 835-1995
5 Greenwood Pl. • Baltimore, MD 21208
E-Mail: customerservice@hopkinsmedical.net
Website: www.hopkinsmedicalproducts.com
Fax Ordering: (410) 484-4036
International Ordering: (410) 484-2036
Contact Name: Phillip Kenney, President
Catalog: Free. Pages: 36. Frequency: Annual
Circulation: 100K. Sales: $3-5M
Products: Medical supplies & equipment;
books & videos

JAMES MEDICAL SUPPLIES　　　　　(888) 848-4077
7821 Coldwater Rd. • Fort Wayne, IN 46825
E-Mail: sales@jamesmedical.com
Website: www.jamesmedical.com
Fax Ordering: (260) 423-6741
International Ordering: (260) 423-9571
Contact Name: Doug James, President
Catalog: Free. Frequency: Annual
Circulation: 100K. Sales: $3-5M
Products: Home care equipment

KILGORE INTERNATIONAL, INC.　　(800) 892-9999
36 W. Pearl St. • Coldwater, MI 49036
E-Mail: info@kilgoreinternational.com
Website: www.kilgoreinternational.com
Fax Ordering: (517) 278-2956
International Ordering: (517) 279-9123
Contact Name: Craig W. Kilgore, President
Catalog: Free. Frequency: Annual
Circulation: 150M. Sales: $1-3MM
Products: Dental & medical products used
in the training of health professionals, case
presentations & in-office staff training.

LAWYER'S DIARY & MANUAL　　　　(800) 444-4041
Skinder-Strauss Associates
P.O. Box 1027 • Summit, NJ 07902
E-Mail: mail@lawdiary.com
Website: www.lawdiary.com
Fax Ordering: (973) 642-4280; 242-1905
International Ordering: (973) 642-1440
Contact Name: Edward C. Denne, President
Catalog: Free. Frequency: Semiannual
Circulation: 500K. Sales: $10-20MM
Products: Directories, calendars & planners
for lawyers

MATRIX MEDICAL (800) 845-3550
1936 Cedar Lake Pkwy.
Minneapolis, MN 55416
E-Mail: sales@matrxmedical.com
Website: www.matrxmedical.com
Fax Ordering: (612) 377-5454
International Ordering: (612) 377-5252
Catalog: Free. Frequency: Semiannual
Circulation: 150K. Sales: $10-20M
Products: Professional medical equipment
& supplies

MEDCO SPORTS MEDICINE (800) 556-3326
500 Fillmore Ave. • Tonawanda, NY 14150
E-Mail: customersupport@medcosupply.com
Website: www.medco-athletics.com
Fax Ordering: (800) 222-1934
International Ordering: (716) 695-3244
Contact Name: Don Laux, Director
Catalog: Free. Frequency: Quarterly
Circulation: 500K. Sales: $10-20M
Products: Medical, health and related safety
products; suppliers to athletic trainers, sports medicine
professions, and physical therapists; school first-aid,
occupational health

MEDICAL ARTS PRESS (800) 328-2179
P.O. Box 43200 • Minneapolis, MN 55443
E-Mail: info@medicalartspress.com
Website: www.medicalartspress.com
Fax Ordering: (800) 328-0023
International Ordering: (763) 493-7300
Contact Name: Steven M. Wexler, President
Catalog: Free. Frequency: 4x per year
Circulation: 500M. Sales: $10-20MM
Products: Office supplies, medical ID tags,
filing systems

MEDICAL SPECIALTIES DISTRIBUTORS (800) 967-6400
800 Technology Center Dr.
Stoughton, MA 02072
E-Mail: customerservice@msdistributors.com
Website: www.msdistributors.com
Fax Ordering: (781) 344-7244
Contact Name: John Sills, President
Catalog: Free. Frequency: Semiannual
Circulation: 1M. Sales: $50-100M
Products: Medical equipment & supplies;
healthcare products

MOMS - Mail Order Medical Supply (800) 232-7443
24700 Ave. Rockefeller • Valencia, CA 91355
E-Mail: moms@axistive.com
Website: www.axistive.com/moms
Fax Ordering: (888) 874-4347
Catalog: Free. Frequency: Quartery
Circulation: 150K. Sales: $20-50MM
Products: Healthcare products & home
medical equipment & supplies

MOORE MEDICAL LL32 (800) 234-1464
P.O. Box 4066 • Farmington, CT 06050
E-Mail: e-support@mooremedical.com
Website: www.mooremedical.com
Fax Ordering: (800) 944-6667; (860) 223-2382
International Ordering: (860) 826-3600
Contact Name: Linda Autore, President
Catalog: Free. Frequency: Semiannual
Circulation: 250K Sales: $10-50MM
Products: Medical products & home medical
equipment & supplies

NURSES STATION (800) 227-1927
47 Industrial Park Rd. • Centerbrook, CT 06409
E-Mail: customerservice@nursesstationcatalog.com
Website: www.nursesstationcatalog.com
Fax Ordering: (860) 767-4381
International Ordering: (860) 767-4200
Customer Service: (800) 234-1024
Catalog: Free. Frequency: Quarterly
Circulation: 250K Sales: $10-20M
Products: Gifts for the nursing profession;
clothing & supplies for nurses

PRO-MED PRODUCTS (800) 542-9297
360 Veterans Pkwy. #115
Bollingbrook, IL 60440
E-Mail: info@promedexpress.com
Website: www.promedexpress.com
Fax Ordering: (888) 674-4380
International Ordering: (630) 771-7400
Catalog: Free. Frequency: Semiannual
Circulation: 150K Sales: $3-5MM
Products: Products, equipment & supplies for
health care professionals

PROSUPPLY COMPANY (877) 652-0031
12600 SW 1st St. • Beaverton, OR 97005
E-Mail: sales@prosupplyco.com
Website: www.prosupplyco.com
Contact Name: Kevin Stirtz, Customer Service
Catalog: Free. Frequency: Quarterly
Circulation: 100K Sales: $5-10M
Products: Medical imaging supplies & equipment

REDDING MEDICAL, INC. (800) 733-2796
152 Westminster Rd.
Reisterstown, MD 21136
E-Mail: info@reddingmedical.com
Website: www.reddingmedical.com
Fax Ordering: (410) 526-9759
International Ordering: (410) 526-9755
Contact Name: David Shipe, President
Catalog: Free. Frequency: Monthly
Circulation: 100M. Sales: $500M
Products: Medical instruments, equipment
& supplies

SMARTPRACTICE CATALOG (800) 522-0800
SmartHealth, Inc.
3400 E. McDowell Rd. • Phoenix, AZ 85008
E-Mail: info@smartpractice.com
Website: www.smartpractice.com
Fax Ordering: (800) 522-8329
International Ordering: (602) 225-0595
Customer Service: (800) 522-0800
Contact Name: Bruce Muller, Marketing
Catalog: Free. Frequency: Semiannual
Circulation: 250M. Sales: $10-20MM
Products: Dental products & services; veterinary
products & services; eye care products & services;
chiropractic products & services; medical products
& services

UA SCRUBS UNIFORM ADVANTAGE (800) 283-8708
150 S. Pine Island Rd. #300
Plantation, FL 33324
E-Mail: info@uniformadvantage.com
Website: www.uniformadvantage.com
Fax Ordering: (954) 626-2112
Catalog: Free. Frequency: Semiannual
Circulation: 150K Sales: $10-20MM
Products: Medical scrubs, shoes & accessories

ALCONE CO., INC.   (800) 466-7446
5-45 49th Ave. • Long Island City, NY 11101
E-Mail: info@alconeco.com
Website: www.alconeco.com
Fax Ordering: (718) 729-8296
International Ordering: (718) 361-8373
Catalog: Free. **Frequency:** Annual
Circulation: 75K. **Sales:** $3-5M
Products: Theatrical supplies & equipment;
makeup, salon & technical supplies. Make-Up
Catalog; Salon Catalog; Technical Catalog

ALL ABOUT DANCE   (800) 775-0578
180 Welles St. • Forty Fort, PA 18704
E-Mail: info@allaboutdance.com
Website: www.allaboutdance.com
Fax Ordering: (570) 300-2200
International Ordering: (570) 718-1166
Catalog: Free. **Frequency:** Semiannual
Circulation: 100K. **Sales:** $3-5MM
Products: Discount dancewear, dance shoes,
accessories & gifts; supplies

ART STONE DANCEWEAR   (800) 522-8897
1795 Express Dr. N.
P.O. Box 2505 • Smithtown, NY 11787
E-Mail: customerservice@artstonecostumes.com
Website: www.artstonecostume.com
Fax Ordering: (631) 582-9541
International Ordering: (631) 582-9500
Catalog: Free. **Frequency:** Quarterly
Circulation: 200K. **Sales:** $3-5MM
Products: Dancewear; Costumes on Demand; Statler Music

BACKDROP OUTLET   (800) 466-1755
3540 Seagate Way • Oceanside, CA 92056
E-Mail: cs@backdropoutlet.com
Website: www.backdropoutlet.com
Fax Ordering: (760) 547-2899
International Ordering: (760) 547-2900
Contact Name: Karen Gupta, President
Catalog: Free. **Frequency:** Annual
Circulation: 50K. **Sales:** $3-5M
Products: Full line of backgrounds, props,
sets, studio stands & studio props

BAUM'S DANCEWEAR, INC.   (800) 832-6246
106 S. 11th St. • Philadelphia, PA 19107
E-Mail: info@baumsdancewear.com
Website: www.baumsdancewear.com
Fax Ordering: (215) 592-4194
International Ordering: (215) 923-2244
Contact Name: Peter Cohen, President
Catalog: Free. **Frequency:** Quarterly
Circulation: 200K. **Sales:** $10-20M
Products: Dance & theatrical products; costumes

BUTTERFLY VIDEO/FLUTTERBY DVD   (800) 433-2623
P.O. Box 184 • Antrim, NH 03440
E-Mail: contactsherry@butterflyvideo.com
Website: www.butterflyvideo.com
Fax Ordering: (603) 588-3205
International Ordering: (603) 588-2105
Contact Name: Sherry Smythe-Green, President
Catalog: Free. **Frequency:** Annual
Circulation: 50K. **Sales:** $500K
Products: Ballroom dancing lesson videos & DVDs

COLLECTOR'S ARMOURY, LTD.   (877) 276-6879
P.O. Box 2948 • McDonough, GA 30253
E-Mail: sales@collectorsarmoury.com
Website: www.collectorsarmoury.com

Fax Ordering: (678) 593-2670
International Ordering: (678) 593-2660
Catalog: Free. **Frequency:** Annual
Circulation: 100K. **Sales:** $3-5M
Products: Theatrical props; original source
for replica guns & military collectibles

DANCE BOOKS & VIDEO CATALOG   (800) 220-7149
Princeton Book Company
614 Route 130 • Hightstown, NJ 08520
E-Mail: pbc@dancehorizons.com
Website: www.dancehorizons.com
Fax Ordering: (609) 426-1344
International Ordering: (609) 426-0602
Contact Name: Charles W. Woodford, President
Catalog: Free. **Frequency:** Semiannual
Circulation: 100K. **Sales:** $500K
Products: Dance books & videos

DANCE EQUIPMENT INTERNATIONAL   (800) 626-9258
2103 Lincoln Ave., Suite C • San Jose, CA 95125
E-Mail: info@danceequipmentintl.com
Website: www.danceequipmentintl.com
Fax Ordering: (408) 265-7290
International Ordering: (408) 267-1446
Contact Name: Joseph Reinke, President
Catalog: Free. **Frequency:** Quarterly
Circulation: 200K. **Sales:** $20-50MM
Products: Dance equipment

DANCE SHOP   (800) 223-2623
2485 Forest Park Blvd. • Fort Worth, TX 76110
E-Mail: thedanceshop@22dance.com
Website: www.22dance.com
Fax Ordering: (817) 923-4262
International Ordering: (817) 923-0017
Contact Name: Tina Phillips, President
Catalog: Free. **Frequency:** Semiannual
Circulation: 200K. **Sales:** $5-10M
Products: Dance & ballet wear

DANCE VISION   (800) 851-2813
8933 W. Sahara Ave. • Las Vegas, NV 89117
E-Mail: info@dancevision.com
Website: www.dancevision.com
Fax Ordering: (702) 256-4227
International Ordering: (702) 256-3830
Contact Name: Wayne Eng, President
Catalog: Free. **Frequency:** Annual
Circulation: 100K. **Sales:** $500K-1M
Products: Catalog of over 500 instruction videos on a
variety of ballroom/danceSport. CD's, fashion, jewelry.

DANCEWEAR SOLUTIONS   (866) 542-6500
6750 Manchester Ave. • St. Louis, MO 63139
E-Mail: info@dancewearsolutions.com
Website: www.dancewearsolutions.com
Fax Ordering: (800) 777-8270
Catalog: Free. **Frequency:** Semiannual
Circulation: 100K. **Sales:** $3-50MM
Products: Dancewear, dance shoes & accessories;
from jazz to ballet shoes, tap shoes to gymnastic leotards

DISCOUNT DANCE SUPPLY   (800) 328-7107
5065 E. Hunter Ave. • Anaheim, CA 92807   (800) 470-1664
E-Mail: info@discountdance.com
Website: www.discountdance.com
Fax Ordering: (714) 970-9075
International Ordering: (714) 970-6075
Catalog: Free. **Pages:** 125. **Frequency:** Semiannual
Circulation: 100K. **Sales:** $3-5M
Products: Dance supplies at discount prices

GUIDE TO THE PERFORMING ARTS (800) 523-0961
StageStep, Inc.
4701 Bath St. #46 • Philadelphia, PA 19137
E-Mail: stagestep@stagestep.com
Website: www.stagestep.com
Fax Ordering: (215) 564-4206
International Ordering: (215) 636-9000
Contact Name: Randy Swartz, President
Catalog: Free. Frequency: Annual
Circulation: 250K. Sales: $3-5M
Products: Dance, movie, theater, books, vieos,
CDs; dance & aerobic flooring & maintenance products

JUST FOR KIX/DANCE ETC. (800) 762-3347
P.O. Box 724 • Brainerd, MN 56401
E-Mail: info@justforkix.com
Website: www.justforkix.com
Fax Ordering: (218) 829-7618
International Ordering: (218) 829-3722
Contact Name: Stephen Clough, President
Catalog: Free. Frequency: Semiannual
Circulation: 200K. Sales: $3-5MM
Products: Unique dance gifts & active wear

KULTER PERFORMING (800) 573-3782
ARTS VIDEOCASSETTES
Kultur International Films
195 Hwy. 36 • West Long Branch, NJ 07764
E-Mail: sales@kultur.com
Website: www.kultur.com
Fax Ordering: (732) 229-0066
International Ordering: (732) 229-2343
Contact Name: Dennis M. Hedlund, Chairman
Catalog: Free. Frequency: Semiannual
Circulation: 150K. Sales: $1-3M
Products: Performing arts, visual arts,
history & literature videos

LOCHLIN'S COSTUME SUPERCENTER (888) 575-5575
45 Fernwood • Edison, NJ 08837
Website: www.costumesupercenter.com
Fax Ordering: (732) 862-1107
International Ordering: (513) 531-5800
Catalog: Online. Frequency: Annual
Sales: $5-10M
Products: Costumes for home & theatre

MAHER STUDIOS (800) 250-5125
P.O. Box 420 • Littleton, CO 80160
E-Mail: info@maherstudios.blogspot.com
Website: www.maherstudios.blogspot.com
Fax Ordering: (303) 470-9752
International Ordering: (303) 798-6830
Contact Name: Clinton Detweiler, President
Catalog: Free. Frequency: Annual
Circulation: 10K. Sales: $500K
Products: Ventriloquist supplies & instruction books

NORCOSTCO-NORTHWESTERN COSTUME (800) 220-6920
825 Rhode Island Ave. S. • Minneapolis, MN 55426
E-Mail: costumesmn@norcostco.com
Website: www.norcostco.com
Fax Ordering: (763) 525-8676
International Ordering: (763) 544-0601
Contact Name: Roger Deters, President
Catalog: Free. Frequency: Annual
Circulation: 100K. Sales: $5-10MM
Products: Theatrical costumes, lighting & stage equipment

PNTA STAGE & STUDIO SUPPLIES (800) 622-7850
2414 SW Andover St. • Seattle, WA 98106
E-Mail: sales@pnta.com

Website: www.pnta.com
Fax Ordering: (206) 267-1789
International Ordering: (206) 622-7850
Contact Name: Malcolm Perkins, Jr., President
Catalog: Free. Frequency: Annual
Circulation: 50K. Sales: $5-10M
Products: Stage & studio supplies

PACKAGE PUBLICITY SERVICE (212) 255-2872
255 W. 88th St. Apt. 3E • New York, NY 10024
Fax Ordering: (212) 799-7564
Contact Name: Avivah Simon, President
Catalog: Free. Frequency: Annual
Circulation: 25K. Sales: $500K
Products: Pressbooks, presskits, and related promotional
materials for standard plays & materials for publicists

PLAYERS PRESS CATALOG (818) 789-4980
P.O. Box 1132 • Studio City, CA 91614
Fax Ordering: (818) 990-2477
Contact Names: William-Alan Landes, President
Catalog: Free. Frequency: Annual
Circulation: 100K. Sales: $1-3M
Products: Books on the performing arts & play scripts

ROSE BRAND   EAST (800) 223-1624
4 Emerson Lane • Secaucus, NJ 07094
E-Mail: info@rosebrand.com
Website: www.rosebrand.com
Fax Ordering: (201) 809-1851
International Ordering: (201) 809-1730
Contact Name: George Jacobson, President
Catalog: Free. Frequency: Annual
Circulation: 150K. Sales: $5-10M
Products: Fabrics & custom draperies for theaters,
churches, schools, events & entertainment venues

SLD LIGHTING (800) 245-6630
318 W. 47th St. • New York, NY 10036
E-Mail: sales@sldlighting.com
Website: www.sldlighting.com
Fax Ordering: (212) 956-6537
International Ordering: (212) 245-4155
Catalog: Free. Frequency: Annual
Circulation: 100K. Sales: $5-10M
Products: Entertainment lighting, special effects,
theatrical & pro sound equipment

STAGING CONCEPTS (800) 337-5339
7008 Northland Dr., #150
Minneapolis, MN 55428
E-Mail: info@stagingconcepts.com
Website: www.stagingconcepts.com
Fax Ordering: (763) 533-2096
International Ordering: (763) 533-2094
Catalog: Free. Frequency: Annual
Circulation: 50K. Sales: $3-5M
Products: Modular, lightweight, portable stage
platforms, seating risers & accessories

WESTERN STAGE PROPS (800) 858-5568
3945 W. Reno Ave. Suite F
Las Vegas, NV 89118
E-Mail: wsprops@aol.com
Website: www.westernstageprops.com
Fax Ordering: (702) 873-0216
International Ordering: (702) 873-1100
Catalog: Free. Frequency: Annual
Circulation: 50K. Sales: $1-3M
Products: Stage props

CORONA CIGAR COMPANY   (888) 702-4427
7792 W. Sand Lake Rd. • Orlando, FL 32819
E-Mail: info@coronacigar.com
Website: www.coronacigar.com
Fax Ordering: (407) 248-1211
International Ordering: (407) 522-0006
Contact Name: Jeff Borysiewicz, President
Catalog: Free. Frequency: Quarterly
Circulation: 1M. Sales: $50-100M
Products: Cigars, humidors & accessories

FAMOUS SMOKE SHOP CIGAR CATALOG   (800) 564-2486
90 Mort Dr. • Easton, PA 18040
E-Mail: cigars@famous-smoke.com
Website: www.famous-smoke.com
Fax Ordering: (610) 559-7170
International Ordering: (610) 559-8800
Contact Name: Arthur Zaretsky, President
Catalog: Free. Frequency: Semiannual
Circulation: 50K. Sales: $10-20M
Products: Cigars, humidors & cigar
accessories

GEORGETOWN TOBACCO   (800) 345-1459
3144 M St., NW • Washington, DC 20007
E-Mail: info@gttobacco.com
Website: www.gttobacco.com
International Ordering: (202) 338-5100
Contact Name: Walter Gorski
Catalog: Free. Frequency: Quarterly
Circulation: 50K. Sales: $3-5M
Products: Tobacco, cigars, pipes,
smoking accessories

HOLTS TOBACCONIST   (800) 523-1641
Holts Cigar Company
12270 Townsend Rd. • Philadelphia, PA 19154
E-Mail: info@holts.com
Website: www.holts.com
Fax Ordering: (215) 676-9085
International Ordering: (215) 676-8778
Contact Name: Mike Pitkow, Marketing
Catalog: Free. Frequency: Quarterly
Circulation: 100K. Sales: $10-20M
Products: Tobacco products, premium
cigars & accessories

HOUSE OF OXFORD DISTRIBUTORS   (800) 831-8893
WHOLESALE CIGAR & TOBACCO
65 Clyde Rd. • Somerset, NJ 08873
E-Mail: info@houseofoxford.com
Website: www.houseofoxford.com
Fax Ordering: (877) FAX-HOXX or (732) 568-0340
International Ordering: (732) 568-0300
Contact Name: Mark Goldman, President
Catalog: Free. Frequency: Semiannual
Circulation: 150K. Sales: $10-20M
Products: Premium cigars, tobaccos &
accessories

IWAN RIES & COMPANY   (800) 621-1457
19 S. Wabash Ave. • Chicago, IL 60603
E-Mail: ron@iwanries.com
Website: www.iwanries.com
Fax Ordering: (312) 372-1416
International Ordering: (312) 372-1306
Contact Name: Charles Levi, President
Catalog: Free. Frequency: Annual
Circulation: 100K. Sales: $3-5MM
Products: Pipes, tobacco, cigars & smoker's
accessories

JR CIGARS   (800) 572-4427
2589 Eric Lane • Burlington, NC 27215
E-Mail: webmaster@jrcigars.com
Website: www.jrcigars.com
Fax Ordering: (800) 457-3299; (973) 884-9556
International Ordering: (973) 884-9555
Customer Service: (888) 574-3576
Contact Name: Paul Gunther, President
Catalog: Free. Frequency: Quarterly
Circulation: 300K. Sales: $50-100M
Products: Large selection of cigars at
discount prices; tobacco

KIRSTEN PIPE COMPANY   (206) 783-0700
1900 W. Nickerson St. #112
Seattle, WA 98119
E-Mail: stacy@kirstenpipe.com
Website: www.kirstenpipe.com
Fax Ordering: (206) 286-8891
Contact Name: Helen Kirsten, President
Catalog: Free. Frequency: Annual
Circulation: 100K. Sales: $1-3MM
Products: Pipes, cigars, lighters & accessories

LUIS MARTINEZ GALLERY
OF FINE CIGARS   (800) 822-4427
1604 E. Columbus Dr. • Tampa, FL 33605
E-Mail: info@luismartinez.com
Website: www.luismartinez.com
Fax Ordering: (813) 248-4175
International Ordering: (813) 248-2124
Contact Name: Eric Newman, President
Catalog: Free. Frequency: Quarterly
Circulation: 150K. Sales: $5-10M
Products: Tobacco products & supplies

SANTA FE NATURAL TOBACCO CO.   (800) 332-5595
P.O. Box 25140 • Santa Fe, NM 87507
E-Mail: feedback@sfntc.com
Website: www.sfntc.com
Fax Ordering: (800) 655-8265
International Ordering: (505) 982-4257
Contact Name: Robin Summers, President
Catalog: Free. Frequency: Semiannual
Circulation: 100K Sales: $5-10M
Products: Natural, 100% additive-free
natural tobacco

NAT SHERMAN CATALOG   (800) MY-CIGAR
12 E. 42nd St. • New York, NY 10017
E-Mail: info@natsherman.com
Website: www.natsherman.com
Fax Ordering: (201) 735-9099
Contact Name: Joel Sherman, President
Catalog: Free. Frequency: Seiannual
Circulation: 200K. Sales: $5-10M
Products: Pipes, cigars, cigarettes, tobacco,
lighters

THOMPSON CIGAR COMPANY   (800) 237-2559
P.O. Box 30303 • Tampa, FL 33630   (800) 216-7107
E-Mail: info@thompsoncigar.com
Website: www.thompsoncigar.com
Fax Ordering: (813) 882-4605
International Ordering: (813) 884-6344
Contact Name: Robert Franzblau, President
Catalog: Free. Frequency: Monthly
Circulation: 250K. Sales: $50-100M
Products: Cigars, pipes & accessories

TOBACCO TRADERS   **(877) 244-2701**
3604 N.W. 7th St. • Miami, FL 33125
E-Mail: sales@tobaccotraders.com
Website: www.tobaccotraders.com
Fax Ordering: (305) 573-0226
International Ordering: (305) 573-0222
Catalog: Free. Frequency: Semiannual
Circulation: 150K. Sales: $5-10M
Products: Cigars, tobacco products

AL'S FARM TOYS   (507) 226-8611
Northgate Shopping Center
1208 7th St. N.W. • Rochester, MN 55901
E-Mail: alsfarmtoys@yahoo.com
Website: www.alsfarmtoys.com
Contact Name: Alan Batzel, President
Catalog: Free. Frequency: Annual
Circulation: 50K.Sales: $1-3M
Products: Farm machinery & equipment toys

AMC SALES, INC.   (800) 262-0332
3241 Winpark Dr. • Minneapolis, MN 55427
E-Mail: prizes@amcsalesinc.com
Website: www.amcsalesinc.com
Fax Ordering: (763) 545-0480
International Ordering: (763) 545-0700
Catalog: Free. Frequency: Semiannual
Circulation: 150K Sales: $5-10M
Products: Toys, gifts, imprinted party supplies

AMERICA'S HOBBY CENTER   (800) 242-1931
8300 Tonnelle Ave. • North Bergen, NJ 07047
E-Mail: sales@ahc1931.com
Website: www.ahc1931.com
Fax Ordering: (201) 662-1450
International Ordering: (201) 662-0777
Contact Name: Jeffrey Murphy, Marketing Mgr.
Catalog: Free. Frequency: Annual
Circulation: 100K Sales: $500K - $1M
Products: Games & accessories; remote control cars,
airplanes, boats; radios & accessories; model rocketry
& display kits

AMERICAN FOLK TOYS   (877) 365-5869
Mountain Craft Shop Co.
RR 1 Box 122 • Proctor, WV 26055
E-Mail: info@folktoys.com
Website: www.folktoys.com
Fax Ordering: (304) 455-1740
International Ordering: (304) 455-3570
Contact Name: Ellie Conlon, President
Catalog: Free. Frequency: Annual
Circulation: 10K. Sales: $500K - $1M
Products: Folk toys, games, puzzles,
dolls, curios & books

AMERICAN GIRL CATALOG   (800) 360-1861
Pleasant Company
P.O. Box 620497• Middleton, WI 53562
E-Mail: sales@americangirl.com
Website: www.americangirl.com
Fax Ordering: (608) 836-0761
International Ordering: (608) 831-5210
Customer Service: (800) 845-0005 (order catalog)
Contact Name: Ellen Brothers, President
Catalog: Free. Frequency: Quarterly
Circulation: 200K. Sales: $20-50M
Products: Girls-children's dolls, gifts, clothing &
accessories, books, furniture, bath & body products

AMERICAN PLAYGROUND CORP.   (800) 541-1602
505 E. 31st St. • Anderson, IN 46016
E-Mail: info@american-playground.net
Website: www.american-playground.com
Fax Ordering: (765) 649-7162
International Ordering: (765) 642-0288
Contact Name: Phillip Abookire, President
Catalog: Free. Frequency: Annual
Circulation: 50K. Sales: $1-3M
Products: Playground & recreational equipment

AMERICAN SCIENCE & SURPLUS   (888) 724-7587
P.O. Box 1030 • Skokie, IL 60076
E-Mail: info@sciplus.com
Website: www.sciplus.com
Fax Ordering: (800) 934-0722
International Ordering: (847) 647-0011
Contact Names: Phillip Cable, President
Catalog: Free. Frequency: Monthly
Circulation: 1 M. Sales: $20-50M
Products: Science tools & toys; surplus equipment,
military & electronic parts, optics, lab & educational
supplies, magnets, motors, kits & books; lab supplies
& equipment

ANNALEE CATALOG   (800) 433-6557
Annalee Mobility Dolls
71 NH Route 104 • Meredith, NH 03253
E-Mail: customerservice@annalee.com
Website: www.annalee.com
Fax Ordering: (603) 279-6659
International Ordering: (603) 279-3333
Contact Name: Chuck Thorndike, President
Catalogs: Online. Sales: $3-5M
Products: Felt dolls

ARCHIE MCPHEE & CO.   (425) 349-3009
10915 47th Ave. W • Mukilteo, WA 98275
E-Mail: mcphee@mcphee.com
Website: www.mcphee.com
Fax Ordering: (425) 349-5188
International Ordering: (425) 349-3009
Catalog: Free. Frequency: Semiannul
Circulation: 150K. Sales: $5-10M
Products: Toys, gifts & novelties

ARISTOPLAY CATALOG   (800) 433-GAME
Talicor Corp.
8122 Main St. • Dexter, MI 48130
E-Mail: orders@aristoplay.com
Website: www.aristoplay.com
Fax Ordering: (269) 685-6789
International Ordering: (269) 685-2345
Contact Name: Michael Seagram, President
Catalog: Free. Frequency: Annual
Circulation: 100K. Sales: $3-5M
Products: Intellectual, learning board games

ATLAS MODEL RAILROAD CO.   (908) 687-0880
378 Florence Ave. • Hillside, NJ 07205
E-Mail: ahgames@atlasrr.com
Website: www.atlasrr.com
Catalog: $2. Frequency: Semiannual
Circulation: 25K. Sales: $3-5M
Products: Model railroads

BARON BARCLAY BRIDGE SUPPLIES   (800) 274-2221
3600 Chamberlain Ln. #206
Louisville, KY 40241
E-Mail: baronbarclay@baronbarclay.com
Website: www.baronbarclay.com
Fax Ordering: (502) 426-2044
International Ordering: (502) 426-0410
Contact Name: Randy Baron, President
Catalog: Free. Pages: 64.
Frequency: Semiannual
Circulation: 150K. Sales: $5-10M
Products: Bridge playing cards, computer programs,
tables & chairs, teaching materials, electronic games,
books, supplies & gifts

BEST OF CARDS CATALOG   (800) 544-2637
U.S. Games System
179 Ludlow St. • Stamford, CT 06902
E-Mail: usgames@aol.com
Website: www.usgamesinc.com
Fax Ordering: (203) 353-8431
International Ordering: (203) 353-8400
Contact Name: Yvette Romero, Marketing
Catalog: $2. Frequency: Annual
Circulation: 100K. Sales: $3-5M
Products: Tarot decks & books; delux playing cards;
motivational decks of cards; self-improvement decks
of cards

BIRTHDAY EXPRESS   (800) 424-7843
Celebrate Express-Buy Seasons, Inc.
5915 S. Moorland Rd. • New Berlin, WI 53151
E-Mail: info@birthdayexpress.com
Website: www.birthdayexpress.com
International Ordering: (262) 901-2000
Customer Service: (800) 247-8432
Catalog: Free. Frequency: Annual
Circulation: 250K. Sales: $5-10M
Products: Birthday & Christmas activities,
partyware & favors

BITS & PIECES CATALOG   (866) 503-6395
P.O. Box 4150 • Lawrenceburg, IN 47025
E-Mail: customerservice@bitsandpieces.com
Website: www.bitsandpieces.com
Fax Ordering: (513) 354-1290
Customer Service: (866) 503-6395
Catalog: Free. Frequency: Semiannual
Circulation: 250K. Sales: $10-20MM
Products: Puzzles, gifts, and kids games

BOTTELSEN DART COMPANY   (800) 537-2164
945 W. McCoy Lane
Santa Maria, CA 93455
E-Mail: info@bottelsendarts.com
Website: www.bottelsendarts.com
Fax Ordering: (805) 922-5961
International Ordering: (805) 922-4519
Contact Name: Jan Jewell, President
Catalog: Free. Frequency: Annual
Circulation: 150K. Sales: $10-20M
Products: Darts

BRIDGE STREET TOYS   (781) 237-5005
82 Ox Bow Rd. • Weston, MA 02493
E-Mail: questions@bridgestreettoys.com
Website: www.bridgestreettoys.com
Fax Ordering: (781) 237-5445
International Ordering: (781) 237-5005
Catalog: Free. Pages: 16. Frequency: Annual
Circulation: 100K. Sales: $5-10M
Products: Girder & panel building sets

BUDWEISER GENUINE COLLECTION   (800) 742-5283
20 Constitution Blvd. South
Shelton, CT 06484
E-Mail: info@budshop.com
Website: www.budshop.com
Catalog: Free. Frequency: Semiannual
Circulation: 100K. Sales: $5-10MM
Products: Budwesier racing team merchandise
& collectibles; hats, steins & gifts with Aheuser
Busch logo

CARNIVAL CATALOG   (800) 448-7830
    (800) 832-0224
U.S. Toy Company
13201 Arrington Rd.
Grandview, MO 64030
E-Mail: ustoy@ustoyco.com
Website: www.ustoy.com
Fax Ordering: (816) 761-9295
International Ordering: (816) 761-5900
Customer Service: (800) 255-6124
Contact Name: Jonathan & Seth Freiden, Owners
Catalog: Free. Frequency: Semiannual
Circulation: 2M. Sales: $50-100M
Products: Toys, games, books & records
for children

CEDAR WORKS OF MAINE   (800) 462-3327
P.O. Box 990 • Rockport, ME 04856
E-Mail: info@cedarworks.com
Website: www.cedarworks.com
Fax Ordering: (207) 596-7900
International Ordering: (207) 596-1010
Contact Name: Barrett Brown, President
Catalog: Free. Frequency: Annual
Circulation: 100K. Sales: $5-10M
Products: Children's wooden playsets &
accessories

CHILDCRAFT EDUCATION CORP.   (800) 631-5652
School Specialty
P.O. Box 1579 • Appleton, WI 54912
E-Mail: customercare@schoolspecialty.com
Website: www.childcraft.com
Fax Ordering: (419) 589-1600; (888) 388-6344
International Ordering: (419) 589-1600
Customer Service: (888) 388-3224
Catalog: Free. Frequency: Semiannual
Circulation: 250K. Sales: $20-50M
Products: Quality toys designed to
entertain & educate

CHILDLIFE CATALOG   (800) 966-3752
Woodplay - Escalade Sports, Inc.
817 Maxwell Ave. • Evansville, IN 47711
E-Mail: sales@childlife.com
Website: www.childlife.com
Catalog: Free. Frequency: Semiannual
Circulation: 150K. Sales: $10-20M
Products: Backyard play equipment: swing sets,
slides, treehouses, jungle gyms, sandboxes

CHILDSWORK/CHILDSPLAY   (800) 962-1141
303 Crossways Park Dr.
Woodbury, NY 11797
E-Mail: info@childswork.com
Website: www.childswork.com
Fax Ordering: (800) 262-1886
International Ordering: (516) 349-5520
Contact Name: Lawrence Shapiro, President
Catalog: Free. Frequency: Quarterly
Circulation: 100K. Sales: $15-10M
Products: Books, games & playtime
activities for childhood development

COMPLETE STRATEGIST   (800) 225-4344
11 E. 33rd St. • New York, NY 10016
E-Mail: complstat@aol.com
Website: www.thecompletestrategist.com
Fax Ordering: (212) 685-2123
International Ordering: (212) 685-3880

Contact Name: Danny Kilbert, President
Catalog: Free. Frequency: Annual
Circulation: 150K. Sales: $10-50M
Products: Board games; family & party games;
card games; military role playing games &
accessories/hobby/toys

CONSTRUCTIVE PLAYTHINGS   (800) 832-0572
U.S. Toy Company   (800) 448-1412
13201 Arrington Rd.
Grandview, MO 64030
E-Mail: ustoy@ustoy.com
Website: www.constructiveplaythings.com
Fax Ordering: (816) 761-9295
International Ordering: (816) 761-5900
Customer Service: (800) 448-1412
Contact Name: Jonathan & Seth Freiden
Catalog: Free. Frequency: Bimonthly
Circulation: 1M. Sales: $50-100M
Products: Toys, games, books & records
for children

CREATIVE PLAYTHINGS   (800) 247-9464
33 Loring Dr. • Framingham, MA 01707
E-Mail: info@creativeplaythings.com
Website: www.creativeplaythings.com
Fax Ordering: (508) 872-3120
Customer Service: (800) 598-4997
Contact Name: Keith Ente, Marketing
Catalog: Free. Frequency: Annual
Circulation: 100K. Sales: $20-50M
Products: Wooden swing sets, creative
playthings for children

CREATIVE TEACHING PRESS   (800) 287-8879
P.O. Box 2723, Huntington Beach, CA 92647
Website: www.creativeteaching.com
Fax Ordering: (714) 895-6547
International Ordering: (714) 895-5047
Contact Name: Richard Weiride, President
Catalog: Free. Frequency: Weekly
Circulation: 50K. Sales: $5-10M
Products: Over 200 non-electronic educational
games for grades K-12 covering math, language,
arts, science, geography & bible-based activities

DELTA FORCE CATALOG   (800) 852-4445
Delta Press Ltd.
215 S. Washington Ave.
El Dorado, AR 71730
E-Mail: info@deltapress.com
Website: www.deltapress.com
Fax Ordering: (870) 862-9671
International Ordering: (870) 862-3811
Contact Name: Billy Blann, President
Catalog: Free. Frequency: Semiannual
Circulation: 100K. Sales: $3-5M
Products: Gun accessories

DMI SPORTS   (800) 423-3220
375 Commerce Dr.
Ft. Washington, PA 19034
E-Mail: dartmart@aol.com
Website: www.dmisports.com
Fax Ordering: (215) 283-9573
International Ordering: (215) 283-0153
Contact Name: Gary Giegerich, President
Catalog: Free. Frequency: 3x per year
Circulation: 50K. Sales: $10-20MM
Products: Electronic & steel tip darts, boards
& accessories, billiard & table tennis

DOUGLAS CUDDLE TOYS   (800) 992-9002
Douglas Company
P.O. Box D • Keene, NH 03431
E-Mail: usa@douglascuddletoys.com
Website: www.douglascuddletoy.com
Fax Ordering: (603) 352-1248
International Ordering: (603) 352-3414
Contact Name: Scott Clarke, President
Catalog: Free. Frequency: Semiannual
Circulation: 200K. Sales: $5-10M
Products: Distinctive stuffed animals;
promotional toys

ELMS JIGSAW PUZZLES   (800) 353-3567
P.O. Box 537 • Harrison, ME 04040
E-Mail: info@elmspuzzles.com
Website: www.elmspuzzles.com
Fax Ordering: (207) 583-6534
International Ordering: (207) 583-6262
Contact Name: Elizabeth Stuart, Owner
Catalog: Free. Frequency: Annual
Circulation: 100K. Sales: $1-5M
Products: Handcut, personalized wooden
jigsaw puzzles

EDUCATIONAL INSIGHTS   (888) 800-7893
380 N. Fairway Dr. • Vernon Hills, IL 60061
E-Mail: cs@educationalinsights.com
Website: www.educationalinsights.com
Fax Ordering: (888) 892-8731
International Ordering: (847) 968-3722
Customer Service: (800) 995-4436
Contact Name: Jim Whitney, President
Catalog: Free. Frequency: Semiannual
Circulation: 150K. Sales: $10-20M
Products: Educational toys & games

ENTERTAINMENT EARTH   (800) 370-2320
61 Moreland Rd. • Simi Valley, CA 93065
E-Mail: cs@entertainmentearth.com
Website: www.entertainmentearth.com
Fax Ordering: (818) 255-0091
International Ordering: (818) 255-0095
Catalog: Free. Frequency: Semiannual
Circulation: 100K. Sales: $5-10M
Products: Action figures, toys & collectibles

FAO SCHWARZ CATALOG   (800) 426-8697
767 Fifth Ave. • New York, NY 10153
E-Mail: faonewyork@fao.net
Website: www.fao.com
Fax Ordering: (212) 644-2485
International Ordering: (212) 644-9400
Customer Service: (800) 876-7867
Contact Name: Bud Johnson, President
Catalog: Free. Frequency: Annual
Circulation: 350K. Sales: $50-100MM
Products: Unusual toys, games & stuffed
animals

FISHER-PRICE CATALOG   (800) 747-8697
636 Girard Ave. • East Aurora, NY 14052
E-Mail: info@fisher-price.com
Website: www.fisher-price.com
Fax Ordering: (716) 687-3636
International Ordering: (716) 687-3000
Contact Name: Byron Davis, President
Catalog: Free. Frequency: Semiannual
Circulation: 5M. Sales: $100-500M
Products: Toys, layette items

HIGHLIGHTS FOR CHILDREN (800) 603-0349
P.O. Box 269 • Columbus, OH 43216
E-Mail: info@highlights.com
Website: www.highlights.com
Fax Ordering: (614) 487-2700
International Ordering: (614) 486-0631
Customer Service: (800) 255-9517
Contact Names: Kent S. Johnson, CEO
Catalog: Free. Frequency: Quarterly
Circulation: 2M. Sales: $10-20M
Products: Children's books, toys, games,
puzzles, and activity kits

HORIZON DARTS (800) 542-3278
2415 S. 50th St. • Kansas City, KS 66106
E-Mail: darts@horiizondarts.com
Website: www.horizondarts.com
Fax Ordering: (913) 236-8829
International Ordering: (913) 236-9111
Contact Name: Dan Trost, President
Catalog: Free. Frequency: Annual
Circulation: 100K. Sales: $3-5M
Products: Darts & dart supplies

IMAGINE THE CHALLENGE (888) 777-1641
5401 Wayne Rd. • Battle Creek, MI 49037
E-Mail: customercare@imagetoys.com
Website: www.imaginetoys.com
Fax Ordering: (734) 941-8304
Catalog: Free. Frequency: Annual
Circulation: 150K. Sales: $10-20M
Products: Toys for children up to 12 years of age,
including arts & crafts toys, music & dance toys,
learning toys, games & puzzles, ride on toys,
pretend toys, infant & toddler toys, active toys, etc.

INTO THE WIND KITES (800) 541-0314
1408 Pearl St. • Boulder, CO 80302
E-Mail: kites@intothewind.com
Website: www.intothewind.com
Fax Ordering: (303) 449-7315
International Ordering: (303) 449-5356
Contact Names: George Emmons, President
Catalog: Free. Frequency: Annual
Circulation: 100K. Sales: $3-5M
Products: Kites

KAPLAN EARLY LEARNING CO. (800) 334-2014
1310 Lewisville Clemmons Rd.
Lewisville, NC 27023
E-Mail: info@kaplanco.com
Website: www.kaplanco.com
Fax Ordering: (800) 452-7526; (336) 712-3200
International Ordering: (336) 766-7374
Contact Names: Lee French, President
Catalog: Free. Frequency: Monthly
Circulation: 250K. Sales: $10-50M
Products: Educational toys

GOKART WORLD (440) 357-5569
KW Marketing
1488 Mentor Ave. • Painesville, OH 44077
E-Mail: info@kartworld.com
Website: www.kartworld.com
Fax Ordering: (440) 357-1903
Contact Names: Robert N. Loomis, President
Catalog: Free. Frequency: Annual
Circulation: 100K. Sales: $3-5M
Products: Fun karts, racing karts, all-terrain karts,
minibikes, engines, kits, parts, trailer kits & scooters

KLIG'S KITES (800) 333-5944
811 Seaboard St.
Myrtle Beach, SC 29577
E-Mail: info@kligs.com
Website: www.kligs.com
Fax Ordering: (843) 448-7370
International Ordering: (843) 448-7501
Contact Names: Richard Kligman, President
Catalog: Free. Frequency: Annual
Circulation: 50K. Sales: $1-3M
Products: Kites, flags, banners, windsocks,
novelties, toys

KOMPAN CATALOG (800) 426-9788
930 Broadway • Tacoma, WA 98402
E-Mail: contact@kompan.com
Website: www.kompan.us
Fax Ordering: (866) 943-6254
International Ordering: (607) 644-1203
Contact Names: Sue Kohlman, Marketing
Catalog: Free. Frequency: Annual
Circulation: 150K. Sales: $5-10
Products: Commercial playground equipment
& site amenities

LANE'S GIFTS & COLLECTIBLES (800) 421-8697
720 Realtor Ave. • Texarkana, AR 71854
E-Mail: sales@lanescollectibles.com
Website: www.lanescollectibles.com
Fax Ordering: (870) 773-2126
International Ordering: (870) 773-2123
Catalog: Free. Frequency: Annual
Circulation: 100K. Sales: $3-5M
Products: Toys & gifts

LEARNING MATERIALS WORKSHOP (800) 693-7164
274 N. Winooski Ave. • Burlington, VT 05401
E-Mail: info@learningmaterialswork.com
Website: www.learningmaterialswork.com
Fax Ordering: (802) 862-0794
International Ordering: (802) 862-8399
Contact Names: Karen Hewitt, President
Catalog: Free. Frequency: Annual
Circulation: 50K. Sales: $500K
Products: Educational toys

HANK LEE'S MAGIC FACTORY (800) 874-7400
P.O. Box 789 • Medford, MA 02155
E-Mail: magicfact@aol.com
Website: www.magicfact.com
Fax Ordering: (781) 395-2034
International Ordering: (781) 391-8749
Contact Names: Harry Levy, President
Catalog: Free. Frequency: Quarterly
Circulation: 150K. Sales: $1-3M
Products: Magic supplies

LILLIPUT (800) 846-8697
Lilliput Motor Company
P.O. Box 447 • Yerrington, NV 89447
E-Mail: lilliput@tele-net.net
Website: www.lilliputmotorcompany.com
Fax Ordering: (775) 463-1582
International Ordering: (775) 463-5181
Contact Name: Justus Bauschinger, President
Catalog: $3. Frequency: Monthly
Circulation: 10K. Sales: $3-5MM
Products: Toys and collectibles; dolls, toy cars,
games & puzzles, timepieces

MACKINAW KITE COMPANY   (866) 428-2335
106 Washington St.
Grand Haven, MI 49417
E-Mail: info@mackinawkiteco.com
Website: www.mackite.com
Fax Ordering: (616) 846-0106
International Ordering: (616) 846-7501
Catalog: Free. Frequency: Annual
Circulation: 100K. Sales: $3-5M
Products: Kites, toys, games puzzles;
kitesurf gear; kiteboarding

MAGIC CABIN, INC.   (888) 623-3655
7021 Wolftown-Hood Rd. • Madison, VA 22727
E-Mail: info@magiccabin.com
Website: www.magiccabin.com
Fax Ordering: (540) 846-0106
International Ordering: (540) 948-7347
Contact Names: Sara McDonald, President
Catalog: Free. Frequency: Semiannual
Circulation: 150K. Sales: $3-5M
Products: Children's toys & games, doll play,
arts & crafts, books, household items

MARY MEYER TOYS   (800) 451-4387
P.O. Box 275 • Townsend, VT 05353
E-Mail: info@marymeyer.com
Website: www.marymeyer.com
Fax Ordering: (802) 365-4233
International Ordering: (802) 365-7793
Contact Names: Kevin Meyer, President
Catalog: Free. Frequency: Bimonthly
Circulation: 150K. Sales: $3-5M
Products: Stuffed toy animals

MEADOW VIEW IMPORTS   (800) 249-9090
81 Kingstown Rd.
P.O. Box 407 • Wyoming, RI 02898
E-Mail: TOYS@meadowviewimports.com
Website: www.meadowviewimports.com
Fax Ordering: (401) 539-7199
International Ordering: (401) 539-9090
Contact Names: James Mathews, Production Mgr.
Catalog: Free. Frequency: Annual
Circulation: 100K. Sales: $1-3M
Products: Wooden toys & figures, handcrafted
& handpainted, imported from Germany

MUELLER RECREATIONAL PRODUCTS   (800) 627-8888
4825 S. 16th St. • Lincoln, NE 68512
E-Mail: info@muellers.com
Website: www.muellers.com
Fax Ordering: (402) 423-5964
International Ordering: (402) 423-8888
Contact Names: Kelly Neill, Production Manager
Catalog: Free. Frequency: Annual
Circulation: 150K. Sales: $5-10M
Products: Billiard & dart supplies, cues, darts,
table tennis, table hockey, shuffleboard equipment
& accessories; books, videos

NATURE CARD & GIFT CATALOG   (800) 756-3752
National Wildlife Federation
1 Stationery Pl. • Rexburg, ID 83441
E-Mail: info@shopnwf.org
Website: www.shopnwf.org
Fax Ordering: (800) 525-5562
Contact Name: Mark Van Patten, President
Catalog: Free. Frequency: Quarterly
Circulation: 2M. Sales: $10-20M
Products: Nature-related and educational gifts,
including holiday cards, calendars, clothing & toys

NORTH STAR TOYS   (800) 737-0112
HC81 Box 617 • Questa, NM 87556
E-Mail: northstartoys@gmail.com
Website: www.northstartoys.com
International Ordering: (575) 586-0112
Catalog: Free. Frequency: Quarterly
Circulation: 100K. Sales: $1-3M
Products: Wooden puzzles & toys

ONE STEP AHEAD   (800) 274-8440
LEAPS & BOUNDS   (800) 477-2189
P.O. Box 517 • Lake Bluff, IL 60044
E-Mail: customerservice@onestepahead.com
Website: www.onestepahead.com
Fax Ordering: (847) 615-7236
Customer Service: (800) 950-5120
Contact Names: Karen Scott, President
Catalog: Free. Frequency: Quarterly
Circulation: 250K. Sales: $20-50M
Products: Kids' & newborns' products: platime,
toys, outdoor fun, bedroom, bath, kitchen, safety,
travel, clothing, books

PARAGON GIFTS, INC.   (866) 752-3714
The Paragon
P.O. Box 4068 • Lawrenceburg, IN 47025
E-Mail: customerservice@theparagon.com
Website: www.theparagon.com
Fax Ordering: (513) 354-1294
Contact Names: Coy Clement, President
Catalog: Free. Frequency: Annual
Circulation: 5M. Sales: $20-50MM
Products: Unusual gifts & toys

POLKA-DOTS TOYS & GIFTS   (888) 564-4313
5227 Willing St. • Milton, FL 32570
E-Mail: cservice@mypolkadots.com
Website: www.mypolkadots.com
Fax Ordering: (850) 626-3568
International Ordering: (850) 564-4313
Catalog: Free. Frequency: Semiannual
Circulation: 100K. Sales: $1-3M
Products: Children's early learning toys
& games; dolls & plush; furniture for kids;
kid's bedding & lighting; wall art & special gifts

POOL TOY STORE CATALOG   (800) 996-9934
S&S Construction & Pools
41 Oxford-State Rd.
Middletown, OH 45044
E-Mail: sales@thepooltoystore.com
Website: www.thepooltoystore.com
Fax Ordering: (513) 424-2388
International Ordering: (513) 424-8057
Contact Names: Cathy Shepherd, Marketing
Catalog: Free. Frequency: Annual
Circulation: 25M. Sales: $20-50MM
Products: Swimming pool toys, floats
& loungers, games

SCIENTIFICS DIRECT   (800) 728-6999
Edmund Scientific   (800) 818-4955
60 Pearce Ave. • Tonawanda, NY 14150
E-Mail: scientifics@edsci.com
Website: www.scientificsonline.com
Fax Ordering: (800) 828-3299
International Ordering: (856) 547-3488
Contact Names: Gwynne Edmund, President
Catalog: Free. Frequency: Semiannual
Circulation: 2M. Sales: $20-50M
Products: Science gadgets, instruments & toys
for the student, teacher & inventor

SENSATIONAL BEGINNINGS (800) 444-2147
987 Stewart Rd. • Monroe, MI 48162
E-Mail: sens.beg@internet.mci.com
Website: www.sensationalbeginnings.com
Fax Ordering: (734) 242-8278
International Ordering: (734) 242-2147
Contact Names: Debra Shah, President
Catalog: Free. Frequency: Monthly
Circulation: 100K. Sales: $3-5MM
Products: Children's toys, games, costumes, strollers & carriers

SHERMAN SPECIALTY COMPANY (800) 645-6513
300 Jericho Quadrangle #240
Jericho, NY 11520
E-Mail: info@shermanspecialty.com
Website: www.shermanspecialty.com
Fax Ordering: (800) 853-8697; (516) 861-1034
International Ordering: (516) 861-6420
Contact Names: Stuart Krosser, President
Catalog: Free. Frequency: Monthly
Circulation: 2M. Sales: $10-20M
Products: Premium toys, novelties, party items & apparel

STORYTELLING CATALOG (800) 284-8784
August House Publishers, Inc.
3500 Piedmont Rd. NE #310
Atlanta, GA 30305
E-Mail: ahinfo@augusthouse.com
Website: www.augusthouse.com
Fax Ordering: (404) 442-4435
International Ordering: (404) 442-4420
Contact Name: Ted Parkhurst, President
Catalog: Free. Frequency: Annual
Circulation: 50K. Sales: $1-3M
Products: Books, spoken word CDs & audiocassettes

SUPER POWER SUPPLIES (800) 255-3700
Nintendo • P.O. Box 957
Redmond, WA 98073
E-Mail: nintendo@noa.nintendo.com
Website: www.nintendo.com
Fax Ordering: (425) 882-3585
International Ordering: (425) 882-2040
Contact Names: Minoru Arakawa, President
Catalog: Free. Frequency: 5x per year
Circulation: 2M. Sales: $20-50M
Products: Nintendo novelty gifts

3000TOYS.COM (417) 659-8697
4521 Reinmiller Rd. • Joplin, MO 64804
E-Mail: service@3000toys.com
Website: www.3000toys.com
Fax Ordering: (417) 659-9446
Contact Name: Katharine Stratton
Catalog: Online. Sales: $3-5MM
Products: Action figures, automotive, aviation, dolls for girls, military, remote control, ships & boats, trucks, trains & accessories.

TOM'S TOYS CATALOG (413) 528-3330
297 Main St. • Great Barrington, MA 01230
E-Mail: info@tomtoys.com
Website: www.tomtoys.com
Fax Ordering: (413) 528-3331
Catalog: Free. Frequency: Annual
Circulation: 50K. Sales: $1-3MM
Products: Specialty toys

THE TOY SOLDIER CO. CATALOG (888) 825-8697
100 Riverside Dr.
New York, NY 10024
E-Mail: info@toysoldier.com
Website: www.toysoldierco.com
Fax Ordering: (201) 792-2626
International Ordering: (201) 792-6665
Contact Names: James Delson, President
Catalog: $6. Frequency: Monthly
Circulation: 100K. Sales: $1-3M
Products: Plastic & lead toy soldiers

TOY VILLAGE CATALOG (517) 323-1143
3105 W. Saginaw St.
Lansing, MI 48917
E-Mail: info@toyvillage.com
Website: www.toyvillage.com
Fax Ordering: (517) 323-6287
Contact Names: Betty Gilson, President
Catalog: Free. Frequency: Annual
Circulation: 25K. Sales: $500K-$1M
Products: Dolls, toys

TOY WORKS CATALOG (800) 237-9566
101 Fiddler's Elbow Rd.
Middle Falls, NY 12848
E-Mail: orders@fiddlersebow.com
Website: www.fiddlerselbow.com
Fax Ordering: (518) 692-9186
International Ordering: (518) 692-9665
Contact Names: John Gunther, President
Catalog: Free. Frequency: Annual
Circulation: 100K. Sales: $3-5M
Products: Wholesale handprinted toys & gifts, licensed images

TOYS & JOYS CATALOG (360) 354-3448
P.O. Box 628 • Lynden, WA 98264
E-Mail: info@toysandjoys.com
Website: www.toysandjoys.com
Fax Ordering: (360) 354-3924
Contact Names: Phil Vander Ploeg, President
Catalog: $1. Frequency: Annual
Circulation: 50K. Sales: $500K - $1M
Products: Wooden toys, parts & patterns

TOYS R US CATALOG (800) 869-7787
One Geoffrey Way • Wayne, NJ 07470
E-Mail: contactus@toysrus.com
Website: www.toysrus.com
International Ordering: (973) 617-3500
Catalog: Free. Frequency: Quarterly
Circulation: 1M. Sales: $100-200M
Products: Baby, toddler & children products, toys and games

TOYS TO GROW ON CATALOG (800) 987-4454
2695 E. Dominguez St.
Carson, CA 90801
E-Mail: toyinfo@toystogrowon.com
Website: www.toystogrowon.com
Fax Ordering: (800) 537-5403; (310) 537-1741
International Ordering: (310) 537-8600
Customer Service: (800) 874-4242
Contact Names: Michael Kaplan, President
Catalog: Free. Frequency: Annual
Circulation: 1M. Sales: $20-50M
Products: Educational toys, arts & crafts supplies, hobby kits

TOYSMITH CATALOG   (800) 356-0474
3101 W. Valley Hwy E.
Sumner, WA 98390
E-Mail: info@toysmith.com
Website: www.toysmith.com
Fax Ordering: (800) 435-0703; (253) 863-0896
International Ordering: (253) 863-0886
Catalog: Free. Frequency: Annual
Circulation: 100K. Sales: $1-3M
Products: Toys & gifts

TRAINER'S WAREHOUSE   (800) 299-3770
89 Washington Ave.
Natick, MA 01760
E-Mail: info@trainerswarehouse.com
Website: www.trainerswarehouse.com
Fax Ordering: (508) 651-2674
Contact Names: Mike Doctoroff, Founder/CEO
Catalog: Free. Frequency: Semiannual
Circulation: 100K. Sales: $1-3MM
Products: Tools, tips and toys for training

U.S. CHESS FEDERATION   (800) 388-5464
USCF SALES CATALOG
1021 Production Court #100
Madison, AL 35758
E-Mail: info@chesscafe.com
Website: www.uscfsales.com
Fax Ordering: (877) 403-5464
International Ordering: (931) 787-1234
Contact Names: Hanon W. Russell & Dan Holland
Catalog: Free. Pages: 64. Frequency: Annual
Circulation: 250K. Sales: $5-10MM
Products: Chess boards & sets; computer
software, videos, books

VERMONT TEDDY BEAR CATALOG   (800) 282-3131
6655 Shelburne Rd. • Shelburne, VT 05482   (800) 829-BEAR
E-Mail: info@vermontteddybear.com
Website: www.vermontteddybear.com
Fax Ordering: (802) 985-1382
International Ordering: (802) 985-3001
Customer Service: (800) 988-8277
Contact Names: Elizabeth Robert, President
Catalog: Free. Frequency: 3x per year
Circulation: 2MM. Sales: $10-20MM
Products: Teddy bears

VIDEO TECHNOLOGIES CATALOG   (800) 521-2010
V Tech Electronics
1155 W. Dundee #130
Arlington Hts., IL 60004
E-Mail: vtechkids@vtechkids.com
Website: www.vtkids.com
Fax Ordering: (847) 400-3601
International Ordering: (847) 400-3600
Contact Names: Rick Schneider, President
Catalog: Free. Frequency: Annual
Circulation: 200K. Sales: $10-20MM
Products: Electronic toys & learning aids
for children

WOODPLAY CATALOG   (800) 982-1822
817 Maxwell Ave. • Evansville, IN 47711
E-Mail: sales@woodplay.com
Website: www.woodplay.com
Fax Ordering: (919) 875-4264
International Ordering: (919) 875-4499
Customer Service: (800) 966-3752
Contact Names: Jim Sally, President
Catalog: Free. Frequency: Weekly
Circulation: 50K. Sales: $3-5M
Products: Wooden swings, seesaws
& tree houses

YESTERYEAR TOYS & BOOKS   (800) 481-1353
P.O. Box 537 • Alexandria Bay, NY 13607
E-Mail: info@yesteryeartoys.com
Website: www.yesteryeartoys.com
Fax Ordering: (800) 305-5138; (613) 475-3748
Customer Service: (613) 475-1771
Catalog: $6.95. Frequency: Annual
Circulation: 25K. Sales: $3-5M
Products: Model steam engines, accessories
& parts; available in kits or assembled

YOUNG EXPLORERS CATALOG   (800) 239-7577
P.O. Box 3338 • Chelmsford, MA 01824
E-Mail: sales@youngexplorers.com
Website: www.youngexplorers.com
Fax Ordering: (800) 866-32355
International Ordering: (877) 756-5058
Contact Name: Paul Whittle, President
Catalog: Free. Frequency: Semiannual
Circulation: 100K. Sales: $3-5M
Products: Educational toys

ADVENTURE CARAVANS   (800) 872-7897
125 Promise Lane • Livingston, TX 77351
E-Mail: trackstoadventures@worldnet.att.net
Website: www.adventurecaravans.com
Fax Ordering: (800) 761-9821; (936) 327-3663
International Ordering: (936) 327-3428
Contact Name: Ron Kohn, President
Catalog: Free. Frequency: Monthly
Circulation: 150K. Sales: $5-10M
Products: Guided RV tours & rallies

ADVENTURE TRAVEL PREVIEW   (800) 227-8747
Adventure Center
1311 63rd St. • Emeryville, CA 94608
E-Mail: cc@adventurecenter.com
Website: www.adventurecenter.com
Fax Ordering: (510) 654-4200
International Ordering: (510) 654-1879
Contact Names: Dallyce Macas, President
Catalog: Free. Frequency: Annual
Circulation: 100K. Sales: $5-10M
Products: Affordable adventures worldwide:
safaries, expeditions, etc.

ADVENTUROUS TRAVELER BOOKSTORE   (800) 282-3963
702 H St., NW • Washington, DC 20001
E-Mail: books@attbook.com
Website: www.gyford.com
Fax Ordering: (800) 677-1821
Contact Name: Spencer Newman, President
Catalog: Free. Frequency: Bimonthly
Circulation: 100K. Sales: $3-5MM
Products: Books, videos & maps for the
adventurous traveler

ALASKA PREMIER CHARTERS   (800) 770-2628
P.O. Box 2300 • Sitka, AK 99835
E-Mail: info@wildstrawberrylodge.com
Website: www.wildstrawberrylodge.com
Fax Ordering: (907) 747-3646
International Ordering: (907) 747-3232
Contact Names: Theresa Weiser, President
Catalog: Free. Frequency: Annual
Circulation: 50K. Sales: $500K-$1M
Products: Saltwater sportfishing &
lodging packages

ARTA RIVER TRIPS   (800) 323-2782
24000 Casa Loma Rd.
Groveland, CA 95321
E-Mail: arta@arta.org
Website: www.arta.org
Fax Ordering: (209) 962-4819
International Ordering: (209) 962-7873
Contact Names: Steve Welch, President
Catalog: Free. Frequency: Annual
Circulation: 25K. Sales: $500K
Products: Whitewater rafting trips

ASIA TRANSPACIFIC JOURNEYS   (800) 642-2742
2995 Center Green Ct. • Boulder, CO 80301
E-Mail: travel@asiatranspacific.com
Website: www.asiatranspacific.com
Fax Ordering: (303) 443-7078
International Ordering: (303) 443-6789
Contact Names: Marilyn D. Staff, President
Catalog: Free. Frequency: Annual
Circulation: 50K. Sales: $5-10MM
Products: Special journeys to Southeast Asia & Nepal

JACK ATCHESON & SONS CATALOG   (406) 782-2382
3210 Ottawa St. • Butte, MT 59701]
E-Mail: office@atcheson@com
Website: www.atcheson.com
Fax Ordering: (406) 723-3318
Contact Name: Jack Atcheson, President
Catalog: Free. Frequency: Annual
Circulation: 25K. Sales: $500K
Products: Hunting & fishing trips

BACKROADS-BICYCLING VACATIONS   (800) 462-2848
801 Cedar St. • Berkeley, CA 94710
E-Mail: goactive@backroads.com
Website: www.backroads.com
Fax Ordering: (510) 527-1444
International Ordering: (510) 527-1555
Contact Names: Tom Hale, President
Catalog: Free. Frequency: Quarterly
Circulation: 150K. Sales: $3-5M
Products: Bicycle tours & vacation spots

BEST RAFTING VACATIONS IN THE WEST   (866) 904-1160
Western River Expeditions
7258 Racquet Club Dr.
Salt Lake City, UT 84121
E-Mail: info@westernriver.com
Website: www.westernriver.com
Fax Ordering: (801) 942-8514
International Ordering: (801) 942-6669
Contact Names: Tom Hale, President
Catalog: Free. Frequency: Quarterly
Circulation: 100K. Sales: $1-3M
Products: Bicycle tours & vacation spots

COMPLETE TRAVELER   (212) 685-9007
ANTIQUARIAN BOOKSTORE
199 Madison Ave. • New York, NY 10016
E-Mail: info@ctrarebooks.com
Website: www.ctrarebooks.com
Fax Ordering: (212) 481-3253
Contact Name: Harriet Greenberg, President
Catalog: $1. Frequency: Annual
Circulation: 25K. Sales: $500K
Products: Travel guides, books, maps
& accessories

COOPERSMITH'S ONE-OF-A-KIND TOURS   (415) 669-1914
P.O. Box 900 • Inverness, CA 94937
E-Mail: paul@coopersmiths.com
Website: www.coopersmiths.com
International Ordering: (415) 669-1914
Contact Names: Paul Coopersmith, President
Catalog: Free. Pages: 24. Frequency: Quarterly
Circulation: 25K. Sales: $500K
Products: Garden tours to Europe &
New Zealand

COUNTRY WALKERS   (800) 464-9255
P.O. Box 180 • Waterbury, VT 05676
E-Mail: info@countrywalkers.com
Website: www.countrywalkers.com
Fax Ordering: (802) 244-5661
International Ordering: (802) 244-1387
Contact Names: Robert Maymard, President
Catalog: Free. Frequency: Annual
Circulation: 100K. Sales: $1-3M
Products: Walking vacations in Europe, Africa,
North & South America & in the South Pacific

DANU ENTERPRISES   (888) 476-0543
P.O. Box 156 • Capitola, CA 95010
E-Mail: danu@earthlink.net
Website: www.danutours.com
Fax Ordering: (831) 476-0543
International Ordering: (831) 476-0543
Catalog: Free. Frequency: Monthly
Circulation: 10K. Sales: $500K to $1MM
Products: Specializes in travel to Bali, Greece,
India, Laos, Vietnam, Cambodia, Ukraine
& Indonesia

EARTHWATCH   (800) 776-0188
Earthwatch Institute
114 Western Ave. • Boston, MA 02134
E-Mail: info@earthwatch.org
Website: www.earthwatch.org
Fax Ordering: (978) 461-2332
International Ordering: (978) 461-0081
Contact Name: Roger Bergen, President
Catalog: $5. Frequency: Annual
Circulation: 25K. Sales: $5-10M
Products: Worldwide research expeditions

ECHO RIVER TRIPS   (800) 652-3246
116 Oak St., Suite 1
Hood River, OR 97031
E-Mail: info@echotrips.com
Website: www.echotrips.com
International Ordering: (541) 386-2271
Contact Name: Joe Daly, VP
Catalog: Free. Frequency: Annual
Circulation: 20M. Sales: $1-3MM
Products: Wilderness river touring trips

ECOTOURS EXPEDITIONS, INC.   (800) 688-1822
P.O. Box 128 • Jamestown, RI 02835
E-Mail: info@naturetours.com
Website: www.naturetours.com
Fax Ordering: (401) 423-9630
International Ordering: (401) 423-3377
Catalog: Free. Frequency: Annual
Circulation: 50K. Sales: $500M to $1M
Products: Nature trips to Central &
South America

EDELWEISS BIKE TRAVEL   (800) 582-2263
Tri Community & Edelweiss Bike Travel   (800) 507-4459
P.O. Box 1974 • Wrightwood, CA 92397
E-Mail: edelweiss@trict.com
Website: www.edelweissbike.com
Fax Ordering: (760) 249-3857
International Ordering: (760) 249-5825
Catalog: Free. Frequency: Annual
Circulation: 25K. Sales: $500M to $1M
Products: Motorcycle touring

GLOBE PEQUOT PRESS CATALOG   (888) 249-7586
P.O. Box 480 • Guilford, CT 06437
E-Mail: info@globepequot.com
Website: www.globepequot.com
Fax Ordering: (800) 820-2329
International Ordering: (860) 395-0440
Customer Service: (888) 249-7586
Contact Name: Linda Kennedy, President
Catalog: Free. Frequency: Semiannual
Circulation: 250K. Sales: $5-10M
Products: Travel, outdoor/recreation,
language books

GO AHEAD TOURS   (800) 590-1170 (US)
One Education St. • Cambridge, MA 02141   (800) 203-5051
(CAN) E-Mail: info@goaheadtours.com
Website: www.goaheadtours.com
Fax Ordering: (617) 619-1901
Customer Service: (800) 597-0350
Contact Name: Andrew Thick, President
Catalog: Free. Frequency: Monthly
Circulation: 10K. Sales: $500K - $1MM
Products: Nature & outdoor expeditions

GRAND CANYON FIELD INSTITUTE   (800) 858-2808
P.O. Box 399 • Grand Canyon, AZ 86023   (866) 471-4435
E-Mail: gcfi@grandcanyon.org
Website: www.grandcanyon.org
Fax Ordering: (928) 638-2484
International Ordering: (928) 638-2485
Contact Name: Robert W. Koons, President
Catalog: Free. Frequency: Annual
Circulation: 25K. Sales: $1-3M
Products: Grand Canyon outdoor adventures

HOLLAND AMERICA LINE CRUISES   (800) 626-9900
P.O. Box 34985 • Seattle, WA 98124   (877) 425-2228
E-Mail: reservations@hollandamerica.com
Website: www.hollandamerica.com
Fax Ordering: (206) 281-7110
International Ordering: (206) 281-3535
Customer Service: (877) 932-4259
Catalogs: Free. Frequency: Annual
Circulation: 50K. Sales: $10-20M
Products: Worldwide cruises;
Canadian Rockies & Alaskan tours

INTERNATIONAL EXPEDITIONS   (800) 633-4734
One Environs Park • Helena, AL 35080   (800) 234-9620
E-Mail: nature@ietravel.com
Website: www.ietravel.com
Fax Ordering: (205) 428-1714
International Ordering: (205) 428-1700
Contact Name: Ralph Hammelbacher, President
Catalogs: Free. Frequency: Annual
Circulation: 50K. Sales: $1-3M
Product: Nature Travel

JOURNEYS INTERNATIONAL   (800) 255-8735
107 April Dr., Suite 3
Ann Arbor, MI 48103
E-Mail: info@journeys.travel
Website: www.journeys.travel
Fax Ordering: (734) 665-2945
International Ordering: (734) 665-4407
Contact Name: Pat Ballard, Marketing
Catalog: Free. Frequency: Annual
Circulation: 25K. Sales: $500K - $1MM
Products: Nature & outdoor expeditions

LADATCO TOURS   (800) 327-6162
3006 Aviation Ave.
Coconut Grove, FL 33133
E-Mail: tailor@ladatco.com
Website: www.ladatco.com
Fax Ordering: (305) 285-0504
International Ordering: (305) 854-8422
Contact Name: Michelle Shelburne, President
Catalog: Free. Frequency: Annual
Circulation: 25K. Sales: $1-3M
Products: Tour wholesaler to Latin America

LEISURE LIVING — (800) 441-7789 / (800) 356-3025
574 Main St. • Tonawanda, NY 14213
E-Mail: support@poolsupplies.com
Website: www.poolsupplies.com
Fax Ordering: (800) 460-6830; (716) 773-8020
International Ordering: (716) 773-7665
Catalog: Free. Frequency: Semiannual
Circulation: 100K. Sales: $10-20M
Products: Pools, pool supplies & accessories

MOUNTAIN TRAVEL-SOBEK — (888) 687-6235 / (888) 831-7526
1266 66th St. #4 • Emeryville, CA 94608
E-Mail: info@mtsobek.com
Website: www.mtsobek.com
Fax Ordering: (510) 525-7710
International Ordering: (510) 527-8105
Contact Name: Mark Campbell, Marketing
Catalog: Free. Frequency: Annual
Circulation: 50K. Sales: $1-3M
Products: Outdoor adventures around the world

OCEANIC SOCIETY EXPEDITIONS — (800) 326-7491
P.O. Box 437 • Ross, CA 94957
E-Mail: info@oceanic-society.org
Website: www.oceanic-society.org
Fax Ordering: (415) 474-3395
International Ordering: (415) 256-9604
Contact Name: Birgit Winning, President
Catalog: Free. Frequency: Annual
Circulation: 25K. Sales: $1-3M
Products: Nature expeditions, whales & snorkeling

OFFICIAL CALIFORNIA STATE GUIDE — (800) 862-2543 / (877) 225-4367
California Tourism
P.O. Box 1499 • Sacramento, CA 95812
E-Mail: web@visitcalifornia.com
Website: www.visitcalifornia.com
International Ordering: (916) 444-4429
Catalog: Free. Frequency: Annual
Circulation: 100K. Sales: N/A
Products: California tours & sites

PERILLO TOURS — (800) 431-1515
577 Chestnut Ridge Rd.
Woodcliff Lake, NJ 07675
E-Mail: agents@perillotours.com
Website: www.perillotours.com
Fax Ordering: (201) 307-1808
Contact Name: Steve Perillo, President
Catalog: Free. Frequency: Annual
Circulation: 200K. Sales: $10-20M
Products: Cruises & vacations to Italy & Hawaii

PRINCESS TOURS — (800) 774-6237
24305 Town Center Dr.
Santa Clarita, CA 91355
E-Mail: customerrelations@princess.com
Website: www.princess.com
Contact Name: Charlie Ball, President
Catalog: Free. Frequency: Annual
Circulation: 250K. Sales: $20-50M
Products: Cruises & tours

RIVER ODYSSEYS WEST — (800) 451-6034
P.O. Box 579 • Coeur D'Alene, ID 83816
E-Mail: info@rowadventures.com
Website: www.rowadventures.com
Fax Ordering: (208) 667-6506
International Ordering: (208) 765-0841
Contact Name: Peter Grubb, President
Catalog: Free. Frequency: Annual
Circulation: 50K. Sales: $1-3MM
Products: Whitewater rafting, canoeing & hiking adventures in Idaho, Montana & Oregon. Specializes in family rafting trips for ages 5+.

SOUTH AMERICAN EXPLORERS CLUB — (800) 274-0568
126 Indian Creek Rd. • Ithaca, NY 14850
E-Mail: explorer@saexplores.org
Website: www.samexplorers.org
Fax Ordering: (607) 277-6122
International Ordering: (607) 277-0488
Contact Name: Don Montague, President
Catalog: Free. Frequency: Quarterly
Circulation: 50K. Sales: $500K - $1M
Products: South American guides, calendars, videos, etc.

SPA-FINDER WELLNESS — (800) 255-7727
SpaFinder, Inc.
257 Park Ave. So., 10th Fl.
New York, NY 10010
E-Mail: info@spafinders.com
Website: www.spafinders.com
Fax Ordering: (212) 924-7240
International Ordering: (212) 924-6800
Contact Name: Frank Van Putton, President
Catalog: Free. Frequency: Annual
Circulation: 100K. Sales: $1-3MM
Products: Spas, fitness resorts & new age retreats

4&5* SOUTH AMERICA TOURS — (800) 747-4540
110 Prefontaine Pl. #506
Seattle, WA 98104
E-Mail: info@southamerica.travel
Website: www.southamerica.travel
Fax Ordering: (206) 456-6707
International Ordering: (206) 260-1218
Catalog: Free. Frequency: Monthly
Circulation: 150K. Sales: $3-5M
Products: Inn-to-inn delux bicycling vacation tours

VBT BICYCLING & WALKING VACATIONS — (800) 245-3868
614 Monkton Rd, • Bristol, VT 05443
E-Mail: vbtinfo@vbt.com
Website: www.vbt.com
Fax Ordering: (802) 453-4806
International Ordering: (802) 453-4811
Contact Name: Gregg Martson, President
Catalog: Free. Frequency: 8x per year
Circulation: 200K. Sales: $5-10M
Products: Inn-to-inn delux bicycling vacation tours

VACATION DISCOUNTERS — (888) 626-0521 / (888) 655-6141
15 Crow Canyon Ct. #200
San Ramon, CA 94583
E-Mail: info@vacation-discounters.com
Website: www.vacation-discounters.com
Fax Ordering: (925) 831-8348
Catalog: Free. Frequency: Annual
Circulation: 100K. Sales: $5-10M
Products: Discount vacations

VACATIONS TO GO — (800) 338-4962
5851 San Felipe #500
Houston, TX 77057
E-Mail: contact@vacationstogo.com

Website: www.vacationstogo.com
Fax Ordering: (713) 974-0445
International Ordering: (713) 974-2121
Contact Name: Alan Fox, President
Catalog: Free. Frequency: Annual
Circulation: 100K. Sales: $10-30M
Products: Discounts on airfares, tourist
attractions, cruises, etc.

VILLAS & APARTMENTS ABROAD   (800) 433-3020
183 Madison Ave., #1111
New York, NY 10016
E-Mail: villas@vaanyc.com
Website: www.vaanyc.com
Fax Ordering: (212) 213-8252
International Ordering: (212) 213-6435
Contact Name: Sylvia Delvaille Jones, President
Catalog: Free. Frequency: Annual
Circulation: 25K. Sales: $500K
Products: Lodging information

WILDERNESS TRAVEL   (800) 368-2794
1102 Ninth St. • Berkeley, CA 94710
E-Mail: info@wildernesstravel.com
Website: www.wildernesstravel.com
Fax Ordering: (510) 558-2489
International Ordering: (510) 558-2488
Contact Name: Bill Abbott, President
Catalog: Free. Frequency: Weekly
Circulation: 75K. Sales: $500K to $1M
Products: Adventure travel to extraordinary,
cultural, hiking & wildlife adventures to over 50
countries with small groups

TRAVEL ITEMS & LUGGAGE

ABBEY PRESS   (800) 962-4760
One Hill Dr. • St. Meinrad, IN 47577   (800) 621-1588
E-Mail: customerservice@abbeypress.com
Website: www.abbeypress.com
Fax Ordering: (812) 357-8353
International Ordering: (812) 357-6611
Contact Name: Gerald Wilhite, President
Catalog: Free. Frequency: Monthly
Circulation: 250K. Sales: $10-20M
Products: Luggage, wallets, business cases,
pens, travel items

ACE LUGGAGE & GIFTS   (800) 342-5223
2122 Ave. U • Brooklyn, NY 11229
E-Mail: sales@aceluggage.com
Website: www.aceluggage.com
Fax Ordering: (718) 891-3878
International Ordering: (718) 891-9713
Contact Name: Andy Lubell, Buyer
Catalog: Free10 Frequency: Annual
Circulation: 50K. Sales: $5-10M
Products: Luggage, wallets, business
cases, pens, travel items

AIRLINE INTERNATIONAL   (800) 592-1234
LUGGAGE & GIFTS
8701 Montana Ave. • El Paso, TX 79925
E-Mail: orders@airlineintl.com
Website: www.airlineintl.com
Fax Ordering: (800) 742-8250
International Ordering: (915) 778-1234
Contact Name: Jerry Kallman, President
Catalog: Free. Frequency: Semiannual
Circulation: 100K. Sales: $5-10M

Products: Luggage, handbags, business
cases, writing instruments, gifts

BUGATTI, INC   (800) 284-2887
100 Condor St. • Boston, MA 02128
E-Mail: sales@bugatti.com
Website: www.bugatti.com
Fax Ordering: (617) 567-5541
International Ordering: (617) 567-7600
Contact Name: T. Scheller, President
Catalog: Free. Frequency: Annual
Circulation: 100K. Sales: $5-10M
Products: Leather accessories; luggage,
bags, portfolios, planners, wallets, business
cases, gifts

CREWGEAR   (800) 848-2739
2101 28th St. N.
St. Petersburg, FL 33713
E-Mail: service@crewgear.com
Website: www.crewgear.com
Fax Ordering: (800) FAX-JETS
Contact Names: Tom Hale, President
Catalog: $2. Frequency: 3x per year
Circulation: 100K. Sales: $5-10M
Products: Luggage & travel accessories

DOONEY & BOURKE   (800) 347-5000
P.O. Box 841 • Norwalk, CT 06856
E-Mail: cultserv@dooney.com
Website: www.dooney.com
Fax Ordering: (800) 326-1496; (203) 838-7754
International Ordering: (203) 853-7515
Contact Name: Peter Dooney, Buyer
Catalog: Free. Frequency: Semiannual
Circulation: 150K. Sales: $10-20M
Products: Briefcases, leather handbags,
belts and gifts

EAGLE CREEK TRAVEL GEAR   (800) 874-9925
5935 Darwin Ct. • Carlsbad, CA 92008
E-Mail: customerservice@eaglecreek.com
Website: www.eaglecreek.com
Fax Ordering: (800) 874-1038
International Ordering: (323) 325-98709
Catalog: Free. Frequency: Annual
Circulation: 100K. Sales: $10-20MM
Products: Travel gear

FIBER BILT CASES   (800) 847-4176
Case Designs Corp.
333 School Lane • Telford, PA 18969
E-Mail: sales@casedesigncorp.com
Website: www.casedesigncorp.com
Fax Ordering: (215) 703-0139
International Ordering: (215) 703-0130
Contact Name: Alan Ernst, President
Catalog: Free. Frequency: Annual
Circulation: 100K. Sales: $10-30MM
Products: Fiberbilt and softech cases
for equipment

J.W. HULME CO.   (800) 442-8212
678 W. Seventh St. • St. Paul, MN 55102
E-Mail: sales@jwhulmeco.com
Website: www.jwhulmeco.com
Fax Ordering: (651) 228-1181
International Ordering: (651) 222-7359
Catalog: Free. Frequency: Annual
Circulation: 150K. Sales: $10-20M
Products: Leather bags, luggage, briefcases,
leather totes, duffle bags, and other leather goods

MAGELLAN'S INTERNATIONAL (800) 962-4943
110 W. Sola St. • Santa Barbara, CA 93101
E-Mail: sales@magellans.com
Website: www.magellans.com
Fax Ordering: (800) 962-4940; (805) 568-5404
International Ordering: (805) 568-5408
Customer Service: (888) 962-5631
Contact Name: John McManus, President
Catalog: Free. Frequency: Bimonthly
Circulation: 20M. Sales: $20-50MM
Products: Travel accessories, luggage, clothing

TRAVEL SMITH (800) 950-1600
OUTFITTING GUIDE & CATALOG (800) 770-3387
60 Leveroni Ct. • West Chester, OH 45069
E-Mail: service@travelsmith.com
Website: www.travelsmith.com
Fax Ordering: (800) 950-1656
International Ordering: (513) 645-4310
Contact Name: Lisa Barnes, VP
Catalog: Free. Frequency: Quarterly
Circulation: 100K. Sales: $5-10M
Products: Men's & women's outdoor,
waterproof explorer shirts, jackets, shoes
& slickers; travel gear & accessories

ADAMS WOOD PRODUCTS   (423) 587-2942
P.O. Box 728 • Morristown, TN 37814
E-Mail: adamswood@lcs.net
Website: www.adamswoodproducts.com
Fax Ordering: (423) 586-2188
Contact Name: Larry Swinson, President
Catalog: Free. Frequency: Semiannual
Circulation: 100K. Sales: $5-10M
Products: Wood cabinet & furniture
components

ADVANCED MACHINERY   (800) 220-4264
P.O. Box 430 • New Castle, DE 19720   (800) 727-6553
E-Mail: jean@advmachinery.com
Website: www.advmachinery.com
Fax Ordering: (866) 686-1615
International Ordering: (302) 322-2226
Contact Name: W. Derke, President
Catalog: Free. Frequency: Semiannual
Circulation: 200K. Sales: $5-10M
Products: Specialty woodworking tools,
machinery & supplies

AMERICAN FURNITURE DESIGN CO.   (760) 743-6923
P.O. Box 300100 • Escondido, CA 92030
E-Mail: americanfurniture@cox.net
Website: www.americanfurnituredsgn.com
Fax Ordering: (760) 743-0707
Contact Name: Brian Murphy, President
Catalog: Free. Frequency: Semiannual
Circulation: 100K. Sales: $1-3M
Products: Woodworking designs & plans;
tools & hardware

ARMOR CRAFTS PRODUCTS   (800) 292-8296
P.O. Box 576 • Monterey, TN 38574
E-Mail: amorecrafts@armorplans.com
Website: www.armorplans.com
International Ordering: (931) 839-7065
Contact Name: John Capotosto, President
Catalog: Free. Frequency: Annual
Circulation: 100K. Sales: $1-3M
Products: Woodworking craft supplies
& plans

BAILEY'S CATALOG   (800) 322-4539
P.O. Box 550 • Laytonville, CA 95454
E-Mail: baileys@baileysonline.com
Website: www.baileysonline.com
Fax Ordering: (707) 984-8115
International Ordering: (707) 684-8995
Catalog: Free. Frequency: Annual
Circulation: 100K. Sales: $5-10M
Products: Outdoor power equipment,
chainsaws, logging & woodman supplies,
generators, water pumps, trimmers & tillers

BENNY'S WOODWORKS   (800) 255-1335
P.O. Box 269 • Bell Buckle, TN 37020
E-Mail: info@bennyswoodworks.com
Website: www.bennyswoodworks.com
Fax Ordering: (931) 437-2189
International Ordering: (931) 437-2188
Contact Name: Benny Pulley, President
Catalog: Free. Frequency: Annual
Circulation: 75K. Sales: $3-5M
Products: Woodworking supplies &
hardware

BLUE RIDGE MACHINERY & TOOLS   (800) 872-6500
P.O. Box 536 • Hurricane, WV 25526

E-Mail: catalog@blueridgemachinery.com
Website: www.blueridgemachinery.com
Fax Ordering: (304) 562-5311
International Ordering: (304) 562-3538
Contact Names: Paul & Linda Stonestreet, Owners
Catalog: Free. Frequency: Annual
Circulation: 50K. Sales: $3-5M
Products: Machine shop supplies, lathes,
milling machines

BRIDGE CITY TOOL WORKS   (800) 253-3332
2545 SW Spring Garden St.
Portland, OR 97219
E-Mail: sales@bridgecitytools.com
Website: www.bridgecitytools.com
Fax Ordering: (503) 287-1085
International Ordering: (503) 282-6997
Contact Name: John Economaki, President
Catalog: $2. Frequency: 5x per year
Circulation: 100K. Sales: $3-5M
Products: Precision layout woodworking
hand tools

CAMBIUM BOOKS   (800) 468-5865
57 Stoney Hill Rd. • Bethel, CT 06801
E-Mail: sales@cambiumbooks.com
Website: www.cambiumbooks.com
Contact Name: John Kelsey, President
Catalog: Free. Frequency: Quarterly
Circulation: 25K. Sales: $250-500K
Products: Woodworking books on furniture
plans & woodworking

CARTER PRODUCTS COMPANY   (888) 622-7837
2871 Northridge Dr. NW
Grand Rapids, MI 49554
E-Mail: sales@carterproducts.com
Website: www.carterproducts.com
Fax Ordering: (616) 647-3387
International Ordering: (616) 647-3380
Contact Name: Peter M. Perez, President
Catalog: Free. Frequency: Semiannual
Circulation: 25K. Sales: $3-5M
Products: Woodworking machinery supplies
and band saw guides

CASEY'S WOOD PRODUCTS, INC.   (800) 452-2739
P.O. Box 365 • Woolwich, ME 04579
E-Mail: caseys@caseyswood.com
Website: www.caseyswood.com
Fax Ordering: (207) 882-6554
International Ordering: (207) 865-3244
Contact Name: Eric Johnson, President
Catalog: Free. Frequency: Annual
Circulation: 50K. Sales: $500K to $1M
Products: Woodturnings & woodcrafts
tools & supplies

CATALOG OF FINE   (800) 537-7820
WOODWORKING TOOLS
The Japan Woodworker
1731 Clement Ave. • Alameda, CA 94501
E-Mail: support@japanwoodworker.com
Website: www.japanwoodworker.com
Fax Ordering: (510) 521-1864
International Ordering: (510) 521-1810
Contact Name: Fred Damsen, President
Catalog: Free. Frequency: Quarterly
Circulation: 100K. Sales: $3-5M
Products: Japanese woodworking tools,
gardening tools and cutlery

CHERRY TREE TOYS   (800) 848-4363
12446 W. State Road 81 • Beloit, WI 53511
E-Mail: sales@cherrytreetoys.com
Website: www.cherrytreetoys.com
Fax Ordering: (888) 848-4388; (608) 879-9042
International Ordering: (608) 879-2479
Contact Name: Matt Simon, Buyer
Catalog: Free. Frequency: Semiannual
Circulation: 500K. Sales: $5-10M
Products: Woodcrafting supplies & plans;
woodworking patterns, clock movements &
parts, scroll saw blades & patterns, wood parts,
hardware & craft supplies; kits

CID WOODWORKING   (717) 517-9428
P.O. Box 146 • Lampeter, PA 17537
E-Mail: admin@cidwoodworking.com
Website: www.cidwoodworking.com
Catalog: $2. Frequency: Annual
Circulation: 50K. Sales: $5-10M
Products: 500+ woodworking plans;
furniture kits

COASTAL TOOL & SUPPLY   (877) 551-8665
510 New Park Ave.
West Hartford, CT 06110
E-Mail: sales@coastaltool.com
Website: www.coastaltool.com
Fax Ordering: (860) 233-6295
International Ordering: (860) 233-8213
Catalog: Free. Frequency: Semiannual
Circulation: 150K. Sales: $10-20M
Products: Power tools and hand tools

CONSTANTINES WOOD CENTER   (800) 443-9667
1040 E. Oakland Park Blvd.
Ft. Lauderdale, FL 33334
E-Mail: info@constantines.com
Website: www.constantines.com
Fax Ordering: (954) 565-8149
International Ordering: (954) 561-1716
Contact Name: Glenn Dorcherty, President
Catalog: Free. Frequency: Annual
Circulation: 100K. Sales: $5-10M
Products: Woodworking/veneering supplies;
hardwoods, tools, furniture kits, hardware,
cane; books, videos & DVDs

COPPA WOODWORKING, INC.   (310) 548-4142
1231 Paraiso St. • San Pedro, CA 90731
E-Mail: info@coppawoodworking.com
Website: www.coppawoodworking.com
Fax Ordering: (310) 548-6740
Contact Names: Ciro Coppa, President
Catalog: Free. Frequency: Annual
Circulation: 50K. Sales: $$1-3M
Products: Wood screen & storm doors;
Adirondack furniture

EAGLE AMERICA   (800) 872-2511
2381 Philmont Ave. #107
Huntingdon Valley, PA 19006
E-Mail: info@eagleamerica.com
Website: www.eagleamerica.com
Fax Ordering: (800) 872-9471; (440) 286-3920
International Ordering: (440) 286-7429
Customer Service: (877) 953-4636
Contact Names: Dan Walter, President
Catalog: Free. Frequency: Quarterly
Circulation: 100K. Sales: $5-10M
Products: Woodworking tools, supplies &
accessories; router bits; books & videos

EMPEROR CLOCK, LLC   (800) 642-0011
P.O. Box 960 • Amherst, VA 24521
E-Mail: service@emperorclock.com
Website: www.emperorclock.com
Fax Ordering: (434) 946-1420
Contact Name: Gerd Hermle, President
Catalog: Free. Frequency: Annual
Circulation: 100K. Sales: $5-10M
Products: Clock & furniture kits

FACTORYNEW.COM/EX-FACTORY.COM   (800) 879-3002
1805 Sardis Rd. North
Charlotte, NC 28270
E-Mail: jody@factorynew.com
Website: www.factorynew.com; exfactory.com
Fax Ordering: (707) 841-1200
International Ordering: (704) 841-2001
Contact Name: Sharon Chisholm
Catalog: Free. Frequency: Annual
Circulation: 200K. Sales: $10-50M
Products: New & used woodworking machinery
& complete plants; woodworking tools; &
equipment; Whirlwind & CTD saws & sanders

FROG TOOL CO. LTD.   (815) 288-3811
2169 IL Rt. 26 • Dixon, IL 61021
E-Mail: info@frogwoodtools.com
Website: www.frogwoodtools.com
Fax Ordering: (815) 288-3919
Contact Name: Richard Watkins, III, President
Catalog: Free. Frequency: Annual
Circulation: 100K. Sales: $3-5M
Products: Hand woodworking tools;
furniture plans; books & finishing materials

W.L. FULLER, INC.   (401) 467-2900
P.O. Box 8767 • Warwick, RI 02888
E-Mail: info@wlfuller.com
Website: www.wlfuller.com
Fax Ordering: (401) 467-2905
Contact Names: Warren L. Fuller, President
Catalog: Free. Pages: 152
Frequency: Semiannual
Circulation: 250K. Sales: $10-20M
Products: Woodworking tools & supplies

GARRETT WADE COMPANY   (800) 221-2942
5389 E. Provident Dr.
Cincinnati, OH 45246
E-Mail: mail@garrettwade.com
Website: www.garrettwade.com
Catalog: Free. Frequency: Quarterly
Circulation: 200K. Sales: $5-10M
Products: Woodworking, gardening and
outdoor tools, supplies and accessories

GRIZZLY INDUSTRIAL, INC.   (800) 523-4777
P.O. Box 3110 • Bellingham, WA 98227
E-Mail: csr@grizzly.com
Website: www.grizzly.com
Fax Ordering: (800) 438-5901; (360) 671-8375
International Ordering: (360) 647-0801
Tech Support: (570) 546-9663
Catalog: Free. Frequency: Annual
Circulation: 100K. Sales: $5-10M
Products: Woodworking & metalworking
tools & supplies

HAMMER USA CATALOG   (800) 700-0071
Felder-Group USA   (800) 572-0061
3006 Beacon Blvd.
West Sacramento, CA 95691

E-Mail: sales@felderusa.com
Website: www.felderusa.com
Fax Ordering: (916) 375-3194
Contact Name: Wolfgang Geiger, President
Catalog: Free. Frequency: Annual
Circulation: 50K. Sales: $10-50M
Products: Woodworking machinery; tooling,
accessories & workshop equipment

HARTVILLE TOOL CATALOG   (800) 345-2396
13163 Market Ave. N
Hartville, OH 44632
E-Mail: sales@hartvilletool.com
Website: www.hartvilletool.com
Fax Ordering: (330) 877-4682
International Ordering: (330) 877-4685
Contact Name: Blaine Miller, President
Catalog: Free. Frequency: Quarterly
Circulation: 250K. Sales: $3-5M
Products: Woodworking tools & supplies

HAWK WOODWORKING TOOLS   (620) 562-3557
Bushton Manufacturing, LLC
P.O. Box 1217 • Bushton, KS 67427
E-Mail: customerservice@hawkwoodworkingtools.com
Website: www.hawkwoodworkingtools.com
Catalog: Free. Frequency: Annual
Circulation: 50K. Sales: $3-5M
Products: Woodworking tools and accessories

HOT TOOLS   (800) 777-6309
M.M. Newman Corp.
P.O. Box 615 • Marblehead, MA 01945
E-Mail: sales@mmnewman.com
Website: www.mmnewman.com
Fax Ordering: (781) 631-8887
International Ordering: (781) 631-7100
Contact Name: Charles Loutrel, President
Catalog: Free. Frequency: Monthly
Circulation: 200K. Sales: $5-10M
Products: Wood burning tools & supplies;
heat shrink tubing; industrial heavy wall tubing

HUMMUL FLIER   (800) 762-0235
Christian J. Hummul Co.
P.O. Box 522 • Nescopeck, PA 18635
E-Mail: mail@hummul.com
Website: www.hummul.com
Fax Ordering: (570) 752-0938
International Ordering: (570) 752-0936
Contact Name: Ray & Mary Zajac, President
Catalog: Free. Frequency: Annual
Circulation: 25K. Sales: $1-3M
Products: Woodcarving & woodburning supplies;
1,500+ bird & animal patterns, books, videos;
power & hand carving tools

HUT PRODUCTS   (800) 547-5461
4502 State Rd. J • Fulton, MO 65251
E-Mail: hutpfw@aol.com
Website: www.hutproducts.com
Fax Ordering: (800) 684-9371; (781) 631-8887
International Ordering: (781) 639-1000
Contact Name: Thomas C. Hutchinson, President
Catalog: Free. Frequency: Semiannual
Circulation: 50K. Sales: $1-3M
Products: Woodturning supplies, lathes,
woodfinishes & tools

INTARSIA TIMES   (800) 316-9010
Roberts Studio
2620 Heather Rd. • Seymour, TN 37865
E-Mail: jerry@intarsia.com
Website: www.intarsia.com
Fax Ordering: (865) 428-7870
International Ordering: (865) 428-8875
Contact Name: Jerry Booher, President
Catalog: Free. Frequency: Semiannual
Circulation: 100K. Sales: $500K to $1M
Products: Intarsia patterns, scroll saw pattern
books, scroll saw blades, Intarsia woodworking
how-to books and videos

JAMESTOWN DISTRIBUTORS   (800) 497-0010
17 Peckham Dr. • Bristol, RI 02809
E-Mail: info@jamestowndistributors.com
Website: www.jamestowndistributors.com
Fax Ordering: (800) 423-0542; (401) 254-5829
International Ordering: (401) 253-3840
Catalog: Free. Frequency: Semiannual
Circulation: 100K. Sales: $5-10M
Products: Boat building & woodworking
supplies; building & marine supplies

JAPAN WOODWORKER CATALOG   (800) 537-7820
1731 Clement Ave. • Alameda, CA 94501
E-Mail: support@thejapanwoodworker.com
Website: www.japanwoodworker.com
Fax Ordering: (510) 521-1864
International Ordering: (510) 521-1810
Contact Name: Fred Damsen, President
Catalog: Free. Frequency: Monthly
Circulation: 250K. Sales: $5-10MM
Products: Japanese woodworking,
garden tools, and cutlery

JESADA RAZOR TOOLS   (813) 875-5400
Razor Tools • 310 Mears Blvd.
Oldsmar, FL 34677
E-Mail: jesadatools@razorwoodworks.com
Website: www.razorwoodworks.com
Fax Ordering: (800) 870-7702; (813) 875-5430
Contact Name: Gerald Denich, President
Catalog: Free. Frequency: Monthly
Circulation: 200K. Sales: $10-20M
Products: Router bits & accessories, sawblades,
woodworking accessories, planner knives,
shaper cutters

KLINGSPOR'S WOODWORKING SHOP   (800) 228-0000
P.O. Box 3737 • Hickory, NC 28603
E-Mail: info@woodworkingshop.com
Website: www.woodworkingshop.com
Fax Ordering: (800) 872-2005
International Ordering: (828) 327-7263
Catalog: Free. Frequency: Semiannual
Circulation: 100K. Sales: $3-5M
Products: Woodworking tools and supplies

LRH ENTERPRISES   (800) 423-2544
9250 Independence Ave.
Chatsworth, CA 91311
E-Mail: sales@lrhent.com
Website: www.llrhent.com
Fax Ordering: (818) 909-7602
International Ordering: (818) 782-0226
Contact Name: Ralph Hubert, President
Catalog: $3. Frequency: Annual
Circulation: 50K. Sales: $5-10M
Products: Cutting tools for woodworking;
shaper cutters, router bits

LEE VALLEY WOODWORKING CATALOG (800) 871-8158
GARDEN & HARDWARE CATALOGS Canada (800) 267-8767
Lee Valley Tools Ltd.
P.O. Box 1780 • Ogdensburg, NY 13669
E-Mail: customerservice@leevalley.com
Website: www.leevalley.com
Fax Ordering: (800) 513-7885 (U.S.)
  (800) 668-1807 (Canada) (613) 596-6030
International Ordering: (613) 596-0350
Contact Name: Leonard Lee, President
Catalog: Free. Frequency: Monthly
Circulation: 250K. **Sales**: $20-50M
Products: Woodworking, gardening &
hardware tools & accessories

MLCS - ROUTER BITS & WOODWORKING (800) 533-9298
PRODUCTS CATALOG
P.O. Box 165 • Huntingdon Valley, PA 19006
E-Mail: sawdust@mlcswoodworking.com
Website: www.mlcswoodworking.com
Fax Ordering: (215) 938-5070
International Ordering: (215) 938-5067
Contact Name: Merle Levy, President
Catalog: Free. Frequency: Bimonthly
Circulation: 100K. Sales: $5-10M
Products: Woodworking machines; router bits,
tools, supplies and hobby center; instructional video

MANNY'S WOODWORKERS PLACE (800) 243-0713
881 NANDINO BLVD. #9 • Lexington, KY 40511
E-Mail: purchasing@mannyswoodworkersplace.com
Website: www.mannyswoodworkersplace.com
Fax Ordering: (859) 255-5444
International Ordering: (859) 255-5444
Catalog: Free. Frequency: Annual
Circulation: 50K. Sales: $500K - $1M
Products: Woodworking books & videos;
woodturning, carving, carpentry, furniture
making, toy making

MOLDING PATTERN KNIVES GUIDE (800) 468-4449
WOODWORKING MACHINERY &
ACCESSORIES CATALOG
The Belsaw Company
2156 Zanker Rd. • San Jose, CA 95131
E-Mail: belsaw@belsaw.com
Website: www.belsaw.com
Fax Ordering: (408) 453-5515; 441-1222
Contact Name: Jim Delzer, President
Catalog: Free. Pages: 64.
Frequency: Semiannual
Circulation: 50K. Sales: $3-5M
Products: Planer/molder accessories &
woodworking equipment

MOON'S SAW & TOOL CATALOG (800) 447-7371
Moon's Saw Shop Supplies
1620 Premier Row • Orlando, FL 32809
E-Mail: moonsorlando@aol.com
Website: www.moonssawandtool.com
Fax Ordering: (407) 857-8748
International Ordering: (407) 857-8727
Contact Name: Jesse Moon, President
Catalog: Free. Frequency: Quarterly
Circulation: 50K. Sales: $1-3M
Products: Sawblades, woodworking
clamps & tools

MOUNTAIN WOODCARVERS (800) 292-6788
WOODBURNERS CATALOG
390 W. Riverside Dr. • Estes Park, CO 80517
E-Mail: info@mountainwoodcarvers.com

Website: www.mountainwoodcarvers.com
Fax Ordering: (970) 586-5500
International Ordering: (970) 586-8678
Catalog: Free. Frequency: Semiannual
Circulation: 100K. Sales: $5-10M
Products: Hand carving tools from Europe
and the U.S.; woodcarving kits; power tools
& accessories; power sharpening; roughouts
& blanks; woodburners; books & videos

OSBORNE WOOD PRODUCTS (800) 849-8876
4618 GA Hwy. 123 N • Toccoa, GA 30577
E-Mail: info@osbornewood.com
Website: www.osbornewood.com
Fax Ordering: (888) 777-4304; (706) 886-8526
International Ordering: (706) 886-1065
Customer Service: (800) 746-3233
Contact Name: Leon Osborne, President
Catalog: Free. Frequency: Monthly
Circulation: 50K. Sales: $5-10M
Products: Wood turnings, table legs,
bed posts, hardware

PACKARD WOODWORKS (800) 683-8876
646 N. Trade St. • Tryon, NC 28782
E-Mail: packard@alltel.net
Website: www.packardwoodworks.com
Fax Ordering: (828) 859-5551
International Ordering: (828) 859-6762
Contact Name: Bradford Packard, President
Catalog: Free. Frequency: Semiannual
Circulation: 100K. Sales: $3-5M
Products: Woodturning tools & supplies;
boks & videos

PENN STATE INDUSTRIES (800) 377-7297
9900 Global Rd. • Philadelphia, PA 19115
E-Mail: psind@pennstateind.com
Website: www.pennstateind.com
Fax Ordering: (215) 676-7603
International Ordering: (215) 676-7606
Tech Support: (800) 656-4767
Contact Names: Marvin & Ed Levy
Catalog: Free. Frequency: Quarterly
Circulation: 250K. Sales: $5-10M
Products: Woodworking products; tools
specializing in dust collection, mini lathes,
lathe projects and supplies.

POPULAR WOODWORKING BOOKS (800) 888-6880
F&W Publications, Inc.
4700 E. Galbraith Rd.
Cincinnati, OH 45236
E-Mail: info@popularwoodworking.com
Website: www.popularwoodworking.com
Fax Ordering: (513) 531-7107
International Ordering: (513) 531-2690
Contact Names: Steve Shanesy, Publisher
Catalog: Free. Frequency: Semiannual
Circulation: 100K. Sales: $1-3M
Products: How-to books on woodworking
and home repair

ROCKLER WOODWORKING & HARDWARE (800) 403-9736
4365 Willow Dr. • Medina, MN 55340 (800) 279-4441
E-Mail: info@rockler.com
Website: www.rockler.com
Fax Ordering: (800) 865-1229; (763) 478-8393
International Ordering: (763) 478-8200
Technical Services: (800) 260-9663
Contact Names: Ann Rockler Jackson, President
Catalog: Free. Pages: 156. Frequency: Semiannual

Circulation: 300K. **Sales:** $25-50M
Products: Woodworking supplies & equipment;
hardware, kits, tools, lumber+

SCHIFFER ARTS & CRAFTS CATALOG   (610) 593-1777
WHILAFORD PRESS CATALOG
Schiffer Publishing Ltd.
4880 Lower Valley Rd. • Atglen, PA 19310
E-Mail: info@schifferbooks.com
Website: www.schifferbooks.com
Fax Ordering: (610) 593-2002
Contact Names: Peter B. Schiffer, President
Catalog: Free. **Frequency:** Semiannual
Circulation: 200K. **Sales:** $3-5M
Products: How-to books for woodworkers,
crafts, antiques, collectibles, art & design

SHAKER WORKSHOPS   (800) 840-9121
P.O. Box 8001 • Ashburnham, MA 01430
E-Mail: shaker9973@shakerworkshops.com
Website: www.shakerworkshops.com
Fax Ordering: (978) 827-6554
International Ordering: (978) 827-9900
Contact Names: Dan Walter, President
Catalog: Free. **Frequency:** Semiannual
Circulation: 100K. **Sales:** $3-5M
Products: Reproductions of Shaker furniture
and accessories, boxes and gift items

THE SHOP SOLUTIONS CATALOG   (800) 624—2027
HTC Products, Inc.
P.O. Box 839 • Fair Haven, MI 48023
Website: www.amazon.com/htc
Fax Ordering: (586) 716-8266
International Ordering: (586) 725-2701
Contact Names: Tim Hewitt, President
Catalog: Free. **Frequency:** 6x per year
Circulation: 250K. **Sales:** $3-5M
Products: Woodworking suppots and
workshop accessories

SHOPSMITH TOOL CATALOG   (800) 543-7586
Shopsmith, Inc.
6530 Poe Ave. • Dayton, OH 45414
E-Mail: info@pricecutter.com
Website: www.shopsmith.com
Fax Ordering: (800) 722-3965; (937) 890-5197
International Ordering: (937) 898-6070
Customer Service: (800) 762-7555
Contact Names: John R. Folkerth, President
Catalogs: Free. **Frequency:** Semiannual
Circulation: 500K. **Sales:** $10-20M
Products: Woodworking equipment and supplies
for home craftsmen; accessories; replacement
parts

SMITH WOODWORKS & DESIGN, INC.   (908) 832-2723
427 Co. Rd. 513 • Califon, NJ 07830
E-Mail: getknobs@niceknobs.com
Website: www.niceknobs.com
Fax Ordering: (908) 832-6994
Contact Name: Todd Smith, President
Catalog: Free. **Frequency:** Annual
Circulation: 50K. **Sales:** $1-3M
Products: Furniture & cabinet hardware;
wood knobs & pulls

SMITHY COMPANY CATALOG   (800) 345-6342
P.O. Box 1517 • Ann Arbor, MI 48106   (800) 476-4849
E-Mail: info@smithy.com
Website: www.smithy.com

Fax Ordering: (800) 431-8892; (734) 913-6663
International Ordering: (734) 913-6700
Contact Name: Joe Christensen, President
Catalog: Free. **Frequency:** Semiannual
Circulation: 200K. **Sales:** $5-10M
Products: Metalworking & woodworking
tools for the hobbyist & light industry

TOOLS ON SALE   (800) 328-0457
Seven Corners Ace Hardware
216 7th St. • St. Paul, MN 55102
E-Mail: info@7corners.com
Website: www.7corners.com
Fax Ordering: (651) 224-8263
International Ordering: (651) 224-4859
Catalog: Free. **Frequency:** Bimonthly
Circulation: 300K. **Sales:** $10-20M
Products: Electric power tools for the
woodworking industry

Van Dyke's RESTORERS   (800) 787-3355
Van Dyke's Supply Co.
1801 Van Dyke Dr. • Woonsocket, SD 57301
E-Mail: restoration@cabelas.com
Website: www.vandykes.com
Fax Ordering: (605) 996-3669
International Ordering: (605) 996-2840
Contact Names: L.J. Van Dyke, President
Catalog: Free. **Frequency:** Annual
Circulation: 250K. **Sales:** $10-20M
Products: Veneering tools and adhesives,
mouldings, fiber and leather replacement seats,
upholstery tools; gifts & accessories; books
& videos

WARREN TOOL CUTLERY   (845) 876-3444
P.O. Box 289 • Rhinebeck, NY 12572
E-Mail: info@warrencutlery.com
Website: www.warrencutlery.com
Fax Ordering: (845) 876-5664
Contact Names: James Zitz, President
Catalog: Free. **Frequency:** Annual
Circulation: 25K. **Sales:** $500K to $1M
Products: Wood carving tools & accessories;
woodworking machines; industrial blades;
kitchen tools

WILKE MACHINERY COMPANY   (800) 235-2100
C.H. Wilke, Inc.
801 N. Duke St. • York, PA 17404
E-Mail: info@chwilke.com
Website: www.chwilke.com
Fax Ordering: (717) 764-3778
International Ordering: (717) 764-5000
Contact Names: Curtis Wilke, President
Catalog: Free. **Frequency:** Semiannual
Circulation: 50K. **Sales:** $3-5M
Products: Bridgewood woodworking
machinery

THE WINFIELD COLLECTION   (800) 946-3435
8350 Silver Lake Rd. • Linden, MI 48451
E-Mail: cserv@thewinfieldcollection.com
Website: www.thewinfieldcollection.com
Fax Ordering: (810) 735-2481
International Ordering: (810) 735-2480
Contact Names: Mike Easler, President
Catalog: $3. **Frequency:** Quarterly
Circulation: 50K. **Sales:** $5-10M
Products: Wood patterns, supplies &
unique items

WOOD CARVER'S SUPPLY, INC. (800) 284-6229
P.O. Box 7500 • Englewood, FL 34295
E-Mail: info@woodcarverssupply.com
Website: www.woodcarverssupply.com
Fax Ordering: (941) 698-0329
International Ordering: (941) 698-0123
Contact Names: Timothy Effrem, Fulfillment
Catalog: Free. Pages: 73. Frequency: Annual
Circulation: 100K. Sales: $3-5M
Products: Hand & power carving tools; wood
& wood plates; wood burners; knives; mallets;
kits; books, videos, DVDs

WOOD MODELER'S CATALOG (800) 222-3876
Model Expo
3850 N. 29th Ter. #103 • Hollywood, FL 33020
E-Mail: sales@modelexpo-online.com
Website: www.modelexpo-online.com
Fax Ordering: (800) 742-7171
International Ordering: (954) 378-2608
Contact Name: Marc Mosko, President
Catalog: Online. Sales: $5-10M
Products: Hobby kits; specializing in ship
models, plastic kits; hand & power tools,
knives & cutters; materials for building; books

WOODCRAFT (800) 542-9115
Woodcraft Supply LLC (800) 225-1153
P.O. Box 1686 • Parkersburg, WV 26102
E-Mail: custserv@woodcraft.com
Website: www.woodcraft.com
Fax Ordering: (304) 428-8211
Customer Service: (800) 535-4482
Technical Support: (800) 535-4486
Contact Names: Bryan Katchur, President
Catalog: Free. Frequency: Quarterly
Circulation: 500K. Sales: $50-100M
Products: Woodworking tools & supplies;
plans & books

WOODCRAFTPLANS.COM (800) 296-6256
P.O. Box 1686 • Parkersburg, WV 26102
E-Mail: ernie@woodcraftplans.com
Website: www.woodcraftplans.com
Fax Ordering: (304) 428-8271
Catalog: $3. Frequency: Annual
Circulation: 25K. Sales: $5-10M
Products: Plans for making furniture;
woodworking, gardening and outdoor tools,
supplies and accessories

WOODMASTER TOOLS, INC. (800) 821-6651
1431 N. Topping Ave.
Kansas City, MO 64120
E-Mail: sales@woodmastertools.com
Website: www.woodmastertools.com
Fax Ordering: (816) 483-7203
International Ordering: (816) 483-0078
Contact Name: Sam Ababir, Marketing
Catalog: Free. Frequency: Semiannual
Circulation: 200K. Sales: $5-10M
Products: Tools, planers, molders, sanders, etc.

WOODTURNERS CATALOG (800) 551-8876
Craft Supplies USA
1287 E. 1120 S. • Provo, UT 84606
E-Mail: sales@woodturnerscatalog.com
Website: www.woodturnerscatalog.com
Fax Ordering: (801) 377-7742
International Ordering: (801) 373-0917
Tech Support: (800) 398-2743
Contact Name: Dale Nish, President
Catalog: Free. Frequency: Annual
Circulation: 500K. Sales: $10-50M
Products: Woodturning tools & supplies

WOODWORKER'S SUPPLY (800) 645-9292
Woodworkers Supply, Inc.
1108 N. Glenn Rd. • Casper, WY 82601
E-Mail: info@woodworker.com
Website: www.woodworker.com
Fax Ordering: (800) 853-9663; (307) 237-5272
International Ordering: (307) 237-5354
Customer Service: (800) 231-2748
Contact Names: John Wirth, Jr., President
Catalog: Free. Frequency: Semiannual
Circulation: 500K. Sales: $20-50M
Products: Woodworking machinery,
supplies & tools

WOODWRITE, LTD. CATALOG (866) 641-8064
979 York St. • Hanover, PA 17331
E-Mail: info@woodwriteltd.com
Website: www.woodwriteltd.com
Fax Ordering: (717) 646-0104
International Ordering: (717) 646-0102
Contact Name: F.J. Beste, President
Catalog: Free. Frequency: Annual
Circulation: 25K. Sales: $1-3M
Products: Lathes, lathe accessories,
wood turning supplies, pen kits

CASCADE OUTFITTERS CATALOG, 49	(800) 223-7238
CASEY'S WOOD PRODUCTS, 407	(800) 452-2739
CASTIGLIONE ACCORDION, 320	(800) 325-1832
CASTOLITE, 263	(815) 338-4670
CASUAL LIVING, 231	(800) 843-1881
CASWELL-MASSEY CATALOGUE, 248	(800) 326-0500
CAT BARN CATALOG, 344	(888) 659-8585
CAT CLAWS CATALOG, 344	(800) 783-0977
CATALOG FROM GOLF HOUSE, 368	(908) 234-2300
CATALOG OF BENEFICIALS, 207	(800) 248-2847
CATALOG OF FINE WOODWORKING TOOLS, 408	(800) 537-7820
CATALOG OF USED COMPACT DISCS, 158	(810) 695-3515
CATALOG SALES COMPANIES, 90	(800) 367-2374
CATHERINE'S CHOCOLATE SHOP, 174	(800) 345-2462
CATTLE KATE CATALOG, 90	(800) 332-5283
CAVIARTERIA, 186	(800) 422-8427
CAVINESS WOODWORKING, INC., 49	(800) 626-5195
CCC OF AMERICA, 158	(800) 935-2222
CCI SOLUTIONS, 144	(800) 426-8664
CCS CATALOG, 369	(800) 477-9283
CD WAREHOUSE, 159	(800) 641-9394
CDW CATALOG, 109	(800) 781-4CDW
CEDAR WORKS OF MAINE, 395	(800) 462-3327
CEF INDUSTRIES, 144	(800) 888-6419
CELEBRATE THE SEASON, 381	(800) 735-0274
CELESTAIRE CATALOG, 49	(800) 727-9785
CELESTIAL PRODUCTS CATALOG, 231, 329	(800) 235-3783
CELLAR HOMEBREW, 264	(800) 342-1871
CENTER ENTERPRISES, 132	(800) 542-2214
CENTERLINE ALFA PRODUCTS, 29	(888) 750-2532
CENTRAL RESTAURANT PRODUCTS, 289	(800) 215-9293
CENTRAL SHIPPEE-FELT PEOPLE, 384	(800) 631-8968
CENTURY BUSINESS SOLUTIONS, 69	(800) 767-0777
CENTURY MARTIAL ARTS, 369	(800) 626-2787
CENTURY PHOTO PRODUCTS, 349	(800) 767-0777
CERAMIC SUPPLY OF NY & NJ, 14	(800) 723-7264
CGS AVIATION INFORMATION PACK, 41	(251) 957-4295
CHADWICK'S OF BOSTON, 90	(800) 525-6650
CHAIR COVERS & LINENS, 277	(800) 260-1030
CHAIRWORKS CATALOG, 277	(800) 282-9406
CHAMBERS CATALOG, 44	(800) 334-9790
CHAMBLEE'S ROSE NURSERY, 207	(800) 256-7673
CHAMISA RIDGE CATALOG, 369	(800) 743-3188
CHAMPAGNE FORMALS, 91	(888) 245-5538
CHAMPIONS ON FILM, 369	(800) 521-2832
CHAMPLAIN VALLEY APIARIES, 188	(800) 841-7334
CHAMPS SOFTWARE, 109	(352) 795-2362
CHANNING L. BETE COMPANY, 56	(800) 477-4776
CHAPARRAL MOTORSPORTS, 369	(800) 841-2960
CHAPIN COMPANY, 91	(866) 888-8682
CHARLES DOUBLE REED CO. CATALOG, 320	(800) 733-3847
CHARLESTON TEA PLANTATION, 182	(800) 443-5987
CHARLEY'S GREENHOUSE SUPPLY, 207	(800) 322-4707
CHATSWORTH 1.800.COLUMNS CATALOG, 271	(800) 486-2118
CHECKS IN THE MAIL, 70, 381	(800) 733-4443
CHEESE BOX, 180	(800) 345-6105
CHEF REVIVIAL USA, 91	(800) 352-2433
CHEF'S CATALOG, 289	(800) 884-2433
CHEFWEAR CATALOG, 91	(800) 568-2433
CHELSEA DECORATIVE METAL CO., 304	(713) 721-9200
CHEM SCIENTIFIC, 356	(888) 527-5827
CHEMART COMPANY, 144	(800) 521-5001
CHEMSW, 109, 356	(800) 536-0404
CHENG & TSUI COMPANY, 132	(800) 554-1963
CHERRY LANE MUSIC CATALOG, 56	(212) 561-3000
CHERRY TREE TOYS, 408	(800) 848-4363
CHERRYBROOK DOG & CAT SUPPLIES, 345	(800) 524-0820
CHERYL & CO. GOURMET FOODS & GIFTS, 174	(800) 367-2714
CHEVROLET OFFICIAL LICENSED PRODUCTS, 4	(858) 558-2500
CHEVS OF THE 40s , 30	(800) 999-CHEV
CHEVY DUTY PICKUP PARTS CATALOG, 30	(800) 741-1678
CHEVYMALL CATALOG, 231	(858) 558-2550
CHIASSO CATALOG, 231, 278	(877) 244-2776
CHICK'S HARNESS & SUPPLY CATALOG, 76	(800) 444-2441
CHIEF AIRCRAFT CATALOG, 41	(800) 447-3408
CHILDCRAFT EDUCATION CORP., 395	(800) 631-5652
CHILDLIFE CATALOG, 395	(800) 462-4445
CHILDSWORK/CHILDSPLAY, 396	(800) 962-1141
CHILDWORKS/CHILDSPLAY CATALOG, 82	(800) 962-1141
CHILE SHOP, 171	(505) 983-6080
CHILTON FURNITURE, 278	(888) 510-6300
CHIME TIME CATALOG, 396	(800) 784-5717
CHINA BOOKS & PERIODICALS, 56	(800) 818-2017
CHINABERRY & ISABELLA CATALOG, 57	(800) 776-2242
CHINESE HERBS CATALOG, 248	(800) 258-6878
CHIPS BOOKS CATALOG, 57	(979) 263-5685
CHISWICK PACKAGING PRODUCTS, 334	(800) 335-4471
CHO-PAT, INC. SPORT MEDICAL DEVICES, 369	(800) 221-1601
CHOCK CATALOG, 82, 91	(800) 222-0020
CHOCOLATE INN, 174	(516) 887-4445
CHOICE BRANDS EQUESTRIAN, 76	(800) 214-4295
CHOICE OF VERMONT, 184	(800) 444-6261
CHRISTIAN BOOK DISTRIBUTORS, 329	(800) 247-4784
CHUKAR CHERRY CO., 174, 190	(800) 624-9544
CID WOODWORKING, 408	(717) 517-9428
CINDERLLA OF BOSTON, 363	(800) 274-3338
CINEMA CITY CATALOG, 4	(231) 739-8303
CIRCA 1820, 278	(888) 887-1820
CIRCUIT SPECIALISTS, 356	(800) 528-1417
CLAIRE MURRAY, 283	(800) 252-4733
CLAMBAKES-TO-GO, 186	(877) 792-7771
CLARK'S CORVAIR PARTS, 30	(888) 267-8247
CLARK'S REGISTER, 91	(877) 243-9060
CLARKCRAFT BOAT KITS & PLANS, 49	(716) 873-2640
CLARUS MUSIC, LTD., 321	(614) 224-4257
CLASSES IN MEDIA ARTS, 159	(800) 262-8862
CLASSIC AIRBOATERS CATALOG, 49	(800) 247-2628
CLASSIC DESIGNS BY MATTHEW BURAK, 278	(800) 843-7405
CLASSIC LAMP POSTS & LIGHTING, 316	(310) 327-5401
CLASSIC MOTORBOOKS, 30, 57	(800) 826-6600
CLASSIC MUSTANG CATALOG, 30	(800) 243-2742
CLASSIC MUSTANG PARTS OF OKLAHOMA, 30	(800) 706-8801
CLASSIC THUNDERBIRD ILLUSTRATED, 30	(800) 374-0914
CLASSIC TOY SOLDIERS, 231	(970) 225-9782
CLEAN REPORT, 278	(800) 451-2402
CLEAR VINYL: PHOTO & OFFICE PRODUCTS, 334	(800) 223-1357
CLEARBROOK FARMS, 188	(800) 222-9966
CLEVELAND MUSEUM OF ART, 231	(216) 707-2333
CLEVER GEAR, 396	(800) 311-0733
CLIENTELE, 248, 369	(800) 327-4660
CLOCKPARTS	(888) 827-2387
CLOSE UP PUBLISHING CATALOG, 57	(800) 765-3131
CLOSING THE GAP, 127	(507) 248-3294
CLOTHCRAFTERS, 384	(800) 876-2009
CLOTHES THAT WORK, 91	(800) 543-2040
CLOTILDE, 14	(800) 772-2891
CLOUD 9 SOARING CENTER CATALOG, 76	(801) 576-6460
CLUB MAC, 109	(800) 217-9153
CLUBS OF AMERICA, 192	(800) 258-2872
CLYDE ROBIN SEED COMPANY, 207	(800) 647-6475
CMC RESCUE EQUIPMENT, 76, 248	(800) 235-5741
COACH LEATHERWARE, 91	(888) 262-6224
COASTAL TOOL & SUPPLY, 295, 408	(877) 551-8665
COBBLESTONE PUBLISHING, 57	(800) 821-0115
COBRA GOLF, 369	(800) 223-3537
COBRA KAYAKS CATALOG, 49	(310) 327-9216
COCA COLA COLLECTORS CATALOG, 4, 231	(800) 438-2653
COHASSET COLONIALS, 278	(800) 288-2389

E

F

K

O

Q